AF126900

Analytical and Computational Methods in Differential Equations, Special Functions, Transmutations and Integral Transforms

Analytical and Computational Methods in Differential Equations, Special Functions, Transmutations and Integral Transforms

Editor

Sergei Sitnik

MDPI

Basel • Beijing • Wuhan • Barcelona • Belgrade • Novi Sad • Cluj • Manchester

Editor
Sergei Sitnik
Belgorod State National Research University
Belgorod
Russia

Editorial Office
MDPI
St. Alban-Anlage 66
4052 Basel, Switzerland

This is a reprint of articles from the Special Issue published online in the open access journal *Mathematics* (ISSN 2227-7390) (available at: https://www.mdpi.com/si/mathematics/analytical_and_computational_methods_in_differential_equations).

For citation purposes, cite each article independently as indicated on the article page online and as indicated below:

Lastname, A.A.; Lastname, B.B. Article Title. *Journal Name* **Year**, *Volume Number*, Page Range.

ISBN 978-3-0365-8626-7 (Hbk)
ISBN 978-3-0365-8627-4 (PDF)
doi.org/10.3390/books978-3-0365-8627-4

© 2023 by the authors. Articles in this book are Open Access and distributed under the Creative Commons Attribution (CC BY) license. The book as a whole is distributed by MDPI under the terms and conditions of the Creative Commons Attribution-NonCommercial-NoDerivs (CC BY-NC-ND) license.

Contents

About the Editor

Sergei Sitnik

Sergel Sitnik graduated from Voronezh State University (Russia), where his scientific advisers were Prof. Ivan Aleksandrovich Kipriyanov and Valerii Vyacheslavovich Katrachov. After receiving a Ph.D. at Voronezh State University in 1987, he worked in Voronezh Polytechnical University, Vladivostok Institute of Automation and Control Processes of the Far Eastern Branch of the Soviet/Russian Academy of sciences, Voronezh State University, Voronezh Militia Institute of the Russian Ministry of Foreign Affairs. From 2017, he has been a Professor of the Department of Applied Mathematics and Computer Modelling, Belgorod State National Research University.

mathematics

MDPI

Editorial

Editorial for the Special Issue "Analytical and Computational Methods in Differential Equations, Special Functions, Transmutations and Integral Transforms"

Sergei Sitnik

Department of Applied Mathematics and Computer Modeling, Institute of Engineering and Digital Technologies, Belgorod State National Research University (BelGU), Pobedy Street, 85, 308015 Belgorod, Russia; mathsms@yandex.ru

MSC: 35A22; 26A33; 33C20

This editorial text is a short introductory guide to the book edition of the Special Issue "Analytical and Computational Methods in Differential Equations, Special Functions, Transmutations and Integral Transforms", which was published in the MDPI journal Mathematics in the years 2022–2023.

This Special Issue includes research and survey papers that cover a wide range of topics in Classical, Computational and Applied Mathematics. High-quality papers on the next wide range of topics from different fields of Mathematics are included:

- Differential equations, especially concerning singular solutions and coefficients;
- Transmutation theory with all kinds of applications;
- Integral transforms;
- Special functions;
- Differential-difference equations;
- Classical and advanced inequalities, convex functions;
- Special-type polynomials;
- q-trigonometric and hypergeometric functions and q-differential equations;
- The Gauss hypergeometric functions, Fox–Wright generalized hypergeometric functions;
- Mathieu-type and extended hypergeometric series;
- Inverse Sturm–Liouville problems;
- The general fractional integrals and derivatives;
- Nonlinear equations with KPZ-type nonlinearities;
- Higher order differential equations;
- Cellular automaton and Markov Chains;
- Stochastic equations and systems;
- Numerical methods for all above mentioned problems.

As a whole, the Special Issue consists of 24 papers on the above-mentioned topics. Among its authors are the following well–known researchers in different fields of mathematics: Prof. Hari M. Srivastava (University of Victoria, Victoria, Canada), Prof. Dr. Tibor K. Pogány (Faculty of Maritime Studies, University of Rijeka, Croatia), Prof. Vasily Tarasov (Lomonosov Moscow State University, Russia), Dr. Natalia P. Bondarenko (Saratov State University, Saratov, Russia), Prof. Yuri Luchko (Berlin University of Applied Sciences and Technology, Berlin, Germany), Prof. Andrey Muravnik (the Director of S.M. Nikol'skii mathematical institute, Peoples Friendship University of Russia, Moscow, Russia), Prof. Vladimir Vasilyev (Belgorod State National Research University, Belgorod, Russia), Prof. Sergei M. Sitnik (Belgorod State National Research University, Belgorod, Russia), Prof. Vladimir Fedorov (Chelyabinsk State University, Chelyabinsk, Russia), Prof. Vladislav V. Kravchenko (Cinvestav, Unidad Querétaro, Querétaro, Mexico), Dr. Dmitrii Karp (Holon

Citation: Sitnik, S. Editorial for the Special Issue "Analytical and Computational Methods in Differential Equations, Special Functions, Transmutations and Integral Transforms". *Mathematics* **2023**, *11*, 3402. https://doi.org/10.3390/math11153402

Received: 20 July 2023
Revised: 1 August 2023
Accepted: 2 August 2023
Published: 4 August 2023

Copyright: © 2023 by the author. Licensee MDPI, Basel, Switzerland. This article is an open access article distributed under the terms and conditions of the Creative Commons Attribution (CC BY) license (https://creativecommons.org/licenses/by/4.0/).

Institute of Technology, Holon, Israel), Dr. Alexander Dyachenko (Keldysh Institute of Applied Mathematics, Moscow, Russia) and others.

Below, the papers of the Special Issue with corresponding brief annotations are listed as per their publication order.

In the paper [1], the author investigates the half-space Dirichlet problem with summable boundary-value functions for an elliptic equation with an arbitrary number of potentials undergoing translations in arbitrary directions. In the classical case of partial differential equations, the half-space Dirichlet problem for elliptic equations attracts great interest from researchers due to the following phenomenon: the solutions acquire qualitative properties specific for nonstationary (more exactly, parabolic) equations. In this paper, such a phenomenon is studied for nonlocal generalizations of elliptic differential equations, more exactly, for elliptic differential-difference equations with nonlocal potentials arising in various applications not covered by the classical theory. A Poisson-like kernel is found such that its convolution with the boundary-value function satisfies the investigated problem, proves that the constructed solution is infinitely smooth outside the boundary hyperplane, and proves its uniform power-like decay as the timelike independent variable tends to infinity.

In the paper [2], the authors define q-cosine and q-sine Apostol-type Frobenius–Euler polynomials and derive interesting relations and also obtain new properties by making use of power series expansions of q-trigonometric functions, properties of q-exponential functions, and q-analogues of the binomial theorem. By using the Mathematica program, the computational formulae and graphical representation for the aforementioned polynomials are obtained. By making use of a partial derivative operator, some interesting finite combinatorial sums are derived. Finally, some special cases for these results are considered.

In the paper [3], some infinite sums are calculated containing the digamma function in closed form. These sums are related either to the incomplete beta function or to the Bessel functions. The calculations yield interesting new results as by-products, such as parameter differentiation formulas for the beta incomplete function, reduction formulas for hypergeometric functions, or a definite integral, which does not seem to be tabulated in the most common literature. As an application of certain sums involving the digamma function, in the paper are calculated some reduction formulas for the parameter differentiation of the Mittag–Leffler function and the Wright function.

In the paper [4], integral form expressions are obtained for the Mathieu-type series and for their associated alternating versions, the terms of which contain an extended Gauss hypergeometric function. Contiguous recurrence relations are found for the Mathieu-type series with respect to two parameters, and finally, particular cases and related bounding inequalities are established.

In the paper [5], an extension of the general fractional calculus (GFC) is proposed as a generalization of the Riesz fractional calculus, which was suggested by Marsel Riesz in 1949. The proposed Riesz form of GFC can be considered as an extension GFC from the positive real line and the Laplace convolution to the m-dimensional Euclidean space and the Fourier convolution. To formulate the general fractional calculus in the Riesz form, the Luchko approach to construction of the GFC, which was suggested by Yuri Luchko in 2021, is used. The general fractional integrals and derivatives are defined as convolution-type operators. In these definitions the Fourier convolution on m-dimensional Euclidean space is used instead of the Laplace convolution on positive semi-axis. Some properties of these general fractional operators are described. The general fractional analogs of first and second fundamental theorems of fractional calculus are proved. The fractional calculus of the Riesz potential and the fractional Laplacian of the Riesz form are special cases of proposed general fractional calculus of the Riesz form.

In the paper [6], the authors study for the first time the inverse Sturm–Liouville problem with polynomials of the spectral parameter in the first boundary condition and with entire analytic functions in the second one. For the investigation of this new inverse problem, an approach is developed based on the construction of a special vector functional sequence in a suitable Hilbert space. The uniqueness of recovering the potential and the polynomials of the boundary condition from a part of the spectrum is proved. Furthermore, the main results are applied to the Hochstadt–Lieberman-type problems with polynomial dependence on the spectral parameter not only in the boundary conditions, but also in discontinuity (transmission) conditions inside the interval. Novel uniqueness theorems are proved, which generalize and improve the previous results in this direction. Note that all the spectral problems in this paper are investigated in the general non-self-adjoint form, and used methods does not require the simplicity of the spectrum. Moreover, the method under consideration is constructive and can be developed in the future for numerical solution and for the study of solvability and stability of inverse spectral problems.

In the paper [7], the general fractional integrals and derivatives considered so far in the Fractional Calculus literature have been defined for functions on the real positive semi-axis. The main contribution of this paper is in introducing the general fractional integrals and derivatives of the functions on a finite interval. As in the case of the Riemann–Liouville fractional integrals and derivatives on a finite interval, the authors define both the left- and right-sided operators and investigate their interconnections. The main results presented in the paper are the first and the second fundamental theorems of Fractional Calculus formulated for the general fractional integrals and derivatives of the functions on a finite interval as well as the formulas for integration by parts that involve the general fractional integrals and derivatives.

The paper [8] presents, for quasilinear partial differential and integrodifferential equations and inequalities containing nonlinearities of the Kardar—Parisi—Zhang type, various (old and recent) results on qualitative properties of solutions (such as the stabilization of solutions, blow-up phenomena, long-time decay of solutions, and others). Descriptive examples demonstrating the Bitsadze approach (the technique of monotone maps) applied in this research area are provided.

In the paper [9], the method of transmutation operators is used to construct an exact solution of the Goursat problem for a fourth-order hyperbolic equation with a singular Bessel operator. It is emphasized that in many other papers and monographs the fractional Erdélyi–Kober operators are used as integral operators, but our approach used them as transmutation operators with additional new properties and important applications. Specifically, it extends its properties and applications to singular differential equations, especially with Bessel-type operators. Using this operator, the problem under consideration is reduced to a similar problem without the Bessel operator. The resulting auxiliary problem is solved by the Riemann method. On this basis, an exact solution of the original problem is constructed and analyzed.

In the paper [10], the authors constructs highly accurate and efficient time integration methods for the solution of transient problems. The motion equations of transient problems can be described by the first-order ordinary differential equations, in which the right-hand side is decomposed into two parts, a linear part and a nonlinear part. In the proposed methods of different orders, the responses of the linear part at the previous step are transferred by the generalized Padé approximations, and the nonlinear part's responses of the previous step are approximated by the Gauss–Legendre quadrature together with the explicit Runge–Kutta method, where the explicit Runge–Kutta method is used to calculate function values at quadrature points. For reducing computations and rounding errors, the 2 m algorithm and the method of storing an incremental matrix are employed in the calculation of the generalized Padé approximations. The proposed methods can achieve higher-order accuracy, unconditional stability, flexible dissipation, and zero-order overshoots. For linear transient problems, the accuracy of the proposed methods can reach 10–16 (computer precision), and they enjoy advantages both in accuracy and efficiency compared with some well-known explicit Runge–Kutta methods, linear multi-step methods, and composite methods in solving nonlinear problems.

In the paper [11], the one-parameter two-dimensional cellular automaton with the Margolus neighborhood is analyzed based on considering the projection of the stochastic movements of a single particle. Introducing the auxiliary random variable associated with the direction of the movement, the problem under consideration is reduced to the study of a two-dimensional Markov chain. The master equation for the probability distribution is derived and solved exactly using the probability-generating function method. The probability distribution is expressed analytically in terms of Jacobi polynomials. The moments of the obtained solution allowed to derive the exact analytical formula for the parametric dependence of the diffusion coefficient in the two-dimensional cellular automaton with the Margolus neighborhood. Analytic results of the paper agree with earlier empirical results of other authors and refine them. The results are of interest for the modeling of two-dimensional diffusion using cellular automata especially for the multicomponent problem.

In the paper [12], the Cauchy problem is studied in a strip for a two-dimensional hyperbolic equation containing the sum of a differential operator and a shift operator acting on a spatial variable that varies over the real axis. An operating scheme is used to construct the solutions of the equation. The solution of the problem is obtained in the form of a convolution of the function found using the operating scheme and the function from the initial conditions of the problem. It is proved that classical solutions of the considered initial problem exist if the real part of the symbol of the differential-difference operator in the equation is positive.

In the paper [13], the unique solvability for the Cauchy problem in a class of degenerate multi-term linear equations with Gerasimov–Caputo derivatives in a Banach space is investigated. To this aim, is used the condition of sectoriality for the pair of operators at the oldest derivatives from the equation and the general conditions of the other operators' coordination with invariant subspaces, which exist due to the sectoriality. An abstract result is applied to the research of unique solvability issues for the systems of the dynamics and of the thermoconvection for some viscoelastic media.

In the paper [14], the purpose is to organize various types of higher order q-differential equations that are connected to q-sigmoid polynomials and obtain certain properties regarding their solutions. Using the properties of q-sigmoid polynomials, it is shown that the symmetric properties of q-differential equations of higher order. Moreover, special properties for the approximate roots of q-sigmoid polynomials that are solutions of higher order q-differential equations are derived.

In the paper [15], the authors consider the Sturm–Liouville equation on a finite interval with a real-valued integrable potential and propose a method for solving the following general inverse problem. They recover the potential from a given set of the output boundary values of a solution satisfying some known initial conditions for a set of values of the spectral parameter. Special cases of this problem include the recovery of the potential from the Weyl function, the inverse two-spectra Sturm–Liouville problem, as well as the recovery of the potential from the output boundary values of a plane wave that interacted with the potential. The method is based on the special Neumann series of Bessel function representations for solutions of Sturm–Liouville equations. With their aid, the problem is reduced to the classical inverse Sturm–Liouville problem of recovering the potential from two spectra, which is solved again with the help of the same representations. The overall approach leads to an efficient numerical algorithm for solving the inverse problem. Its numerical efficiency is illustrated by several examples.

In the paper [16], given real parameters a, b, c and integer shifts n_1, n_2, m, the authors consider the ratio of the Gauss hypergeometric functions. A formula is derived for two-sided limits of this ratio in terms of real hypergeometric polynomial P, beta density and the absolute value of the Gauss hypergeometric function. This allows the construction of explicit integral representations for the ratio of the Gauss hypergeometric functions when the asymptotic behavior at unity is mild and the denominator does not vanish. The results are illustrated with a large number of examples.

In the paper [17], the authors consider a nonlinear system of three connected delay differential neoclassical growth models along with stochastic effect and additive white noise, which is influenced by stochastic perturbation. The conditions are derived for positive equilibria, stability and positive solutions of the stochastic system. It is observed that when a constant delay reaches a certain threshold for the steady state, the asymptotic stability is lost, and the Hopf bifurcation occurs. In the case of the finite domain, the three connected, delayed systems will not collapse to infinity but will be bounded ultimately. A Legendre spectral collocation method is used for the numerical simulations. Moreover, a comparison of a stochastic delayed system with a deterministic delayed system is also provided. Some numerical test problems are presented to illustrate the effectiveness of the theoretical results. Numerical results further illustrate the obtained stability regions and behavior of stable and unstable solutions of the proposed system.

In the paper [18] are established new generalizations of the Hermite–Hadamard-type inequalities. These inequalities are formulated in terms of modules of certain powers of proper functions. Generalizations for convex functions are also considered. As applications, some new inequalities for the digamma function in terms of the trigamma function and some inequalities involving special means of real numbers are given. The results also include estimates via arithmetic, geometric and logarithmic means. The examples are derived in order to demonstrate that some of our results in this paper are more exact than the existing ones and some improve several known results available in the literature. The constants in the derived inequalities are calculated; some of these constants are sharp. As a visual example, graphs of some technically important functions are included in the text.

In the paper [19], several new functional bounds and uniform bounds (with respect to the variable) are established for the lower incomplete generalized Fox–Wright functions by means of the representation formulae for the McKay I_ν Bessel probability distribution's cumulative distribution function. New cumulative distribution functions are generated and expressed in terms of lower incomplete Fox–Wright functions and/or generalized hypergeometric functions, whilst in the closing part of the article, related bounding inequalities are obtained for them.

In the paper [20], the author considers fully degenerate Daehee numbers and polynomials by using a degenerate logarithm function. We investigate some properties of these numbers and polynomials. We also introduce higher-order multiple fully degenerate Daehee polynomials and numbers, which can be represented in terms of Riemann integrals on the interval $(0,1)$. Finally, some connected summation formulas are derived.

In the paper [21], exceptional orthogonal X1-polynomials of symmetric and nonsymmetric types are considered as eigenfunctions of a Sturm–Liouville problem. By defining a generic second-order differential equation, a unified classification of all these polynomials is presented, and ten particular cases of them are introduced and analyzed.

In the paper [22], the authors present a numerical approach to solving singularly perturbed semilinear convection-diffusion problems. The nonlinear part of the problem is linearized via the quasilinearization technique. A fitted operator by finite difference method is designed and operated to solve the sequence of linear singularly perturbed problems that emerges from the quasilinearization process. A rigorous analysis to attest to the convergence of the proposed procedure is performed. The method is first-order uniformly convergent. Some numerical evaluations are implemented on model examples to confirm the proposed theoretical results and to show the efficiency of the method.

In the paper [23], Cesáro means are investigated for the weighted orthogonal polynomial expansions on spheres with weights being invariant under a general finite reflection group on $\mathbb{R}^d$. The theorems in the paper extend previous results only for specific reflection groups and weight functions on the unit sphere. The upper estimates of the Cesáro kernels and Cesáro means are obtained and used to prove the convergence of the (C,δ) Cesáro means in the weighted L^p space for δ above the corresponding index. Similar results are also established for the corresponding estimates on the unit ball and the simplex.

In the paper [24], the authors study a general family of basic (or q-) polynomials with double q-binomial coefficients as well as some homogeneous q-operators in order to construct several q-difference equations involving seven variables. We derive the Rogers type and the extended Rogers type formulas as well as the Srivastava–Agarwal-type bilinear generating functions for the general q-polynomials, which generalize the generating functions for the Cigler polynomials. We also derive a class of mixed generating functions by means of the aforementioned q-difference equations. The various results, which we have derived in this paper, are new and sufficiently general in character. Moreover, the generating functions presented here are potentially applicable not only in the study of the general q-polynomials, which they have generated, but indeed also in finding solutions of the associated q-difference equations. Finally, we remark that it will be a rather trivial and inconsequential exercise to produce the so-called (p, q)-variations of the q-results, which we have investigated here, because the additional forced-in parameter p is obviously redundant.

Note that for a deeper understanding of background and problems that are basic for this Special Issue "Analytical and Computational Methods in Differential Equations, Special Functions, Transmutations and Integral Transforms", the following classical and relatively new monographs [25–40] are highly recommended.

The articles presented in this Special Issue provide insights into fields related to "Analytical and Computational Methods in Differential Equations, Special Functions, Transmutations and Integral Transforms", including pure mathematics and application developments. We wish that readers can benefit from the insights of these papers and contribute to these rapidly growing areas. We also hope that this Special Issue sheds light on major development areas of analytical and computational methods in differential equations, special functions, transmutations, integral transforms and attracts the attention of the scientific community to pursue further investigations leading to the rapid implementation of these fruitful topics and techniques.

Acknowledgments: We would like to express our appreciation to all the authors for their informative contributions and to the reviewers.

Conflicts of Interest: The authors declare no conflict of interest.

References

1. Muravnik, A.B. Differential-Difference Elliptic Equations with Nonlocal Potentials in Half-Spaces. *Mathematics* **2023**, *11*, 2698. [CrossRef]
2. Rao, Y.; Khan, W.A.; Araci, S.; Ryoo, C.S. Explicit Properties of Apostol-Type Frobenius–Euler Polynomials Involving q-Trigonometric Functions with Applications in Computer Modeling. *Mathematics* **2023**, *11*, 2386. [CrossRef]
3. González-Santander, J.L.; Sánchez Lasheras, F. Sums Involving the Digamma Function Connected to the Incomplete Beta Function and the Bessel functions. *Mathematics* **2023**, *11*, 1937. [CrossRef]
4. Parmar, R.K.; Pogány, T.K.; Saravanan, S. On Mathieu-Type Series with (p, ν)—Extended Hypergeometric Terms: Integral Representations and Upper Bounds. *Mathematics* **2023**, *11*, 1710. [CrossRef]
5. Tarasov, V.E. General Fractional Calculus in Multi-Dimensional Space: Riesz Form. *Mathematics* **2023**, *11*, 1651. [CrossRef]
6. Bondarenko, N.P.; Chitorkin, E.E. Inverse Sturm–Liouville Problem with Spectral Parameter in the Boundary Conditions. *Mathematics* **2023**, *11*, 1138. [CrossRef]
7. Al-Refai, M.; Luchko, Y. The General Fractional Integrals and Derivatives on a Finite Interval. *Mathematics* **2023**, *11*, 1031. [CrossRef]
8. Muravnik, A.B. Qualitative Properties of Solutions of Equations and Inequalities with KPZ-Type Nonlinearities. *Mathematics* **2023**, *11*, 990. [CrossRef]
9. Sitnik, S.M.; Karimov, S.T. Solution of the Goursat Problem for a Fourth-Order Hyperbolic Equation with Singular Coefficients by the Method of Transmutation Operators. *Mathematics* **2023**, *11*, 951. [CrossRef]
10. Ji, Y.; Xing, Y. Highly Accurate and Efficient Time Integration Methods with Unconditional Stability and Flexible Numerical Dissipation. *Mathematics* **2023**, *11*, 593. [CrossRef]
11. Kulagin, A.E.; Shapovalov, A.V. Analytical Description of the Diffusion in a Cellular Automaton with the Margolus Neighbourhood in Terms of the Two-Dimensional Markov Chain. *Mathematics* **2023**, *11*, 584. [CrossRef]
12. Vasilyev, V.; Zaitseva, N. Initial Problem for Two-Dimensional Hyperbolic Equation with a Nonlocal Term. *Mathematics* **2023**, *11*, 130. [CrossRef]
13. Fedorov, V.E.; Boyko, K.V. Degenerate Multi-Term Equations with Gerasimov–Caputo Derivatives in the Sectorial Case. *Mathematics* **2022**, *10*, 4699. [CrossRef]
14. Ryoo, C.-S.; Kang, J.-Y. Several Types of q-Differential Equations of Higher Order and Properties of Their Solutions. *Mathematics* **2022**, *10*, 4469. [CrossRef]
15. Kravchenko, V.V.; Khmelnytskaya, K.V.; Çetinkaya, F.A. Recovery of Inhomogeneity from Output Boundary Data. *Mathematics* **2022**, *10*, 4349. [CrossRef]

16. Dyachenko, A.; Karp, D. Integral Representations of Ratios of the Gauss Hypergeometric Functions with Parameters Shifted by Integers. *Mathematics* **2022**, *10*, 3903. [CrossRef]
17. Ali, I.; Khan, S.U. Asymptotic Behavior of Three Connected Stochastic Delay Neoclassical Growth Systems Using Spectral Technique. *Mathematics* **2022**, *10*, 3639. [CrossRef]
18. Srivastava, H.M.; Mehrez, S.; Sitnik, S.M. Hermite-Hadamard-Type Integral Inequalities for Convex Functions and Their Applications. *Mathematics* **2022**, *10*, 3127. [CrossRef]
19. Pogány, T.K. Bounds for Incomplete Confluent Fox–Wright Generalized Hypergeometric Functions. *Mathematics* **2022**, *10*, 3106. [CrossRef]
20. Albosaily, S.; Khan, W.A.; Araci, S.; Iqbal, A. Fully Degenerating of Daehee Numbers and Polynomials. *Mathematics* **2022**, *10*, 2528. [CrossRef]
21. Masjed-Jamei, M.; Moalemi, Z.; Saad, N. On All Symmetric and Nonsymmetric Exceptional Orthogonal X1-Polynomials Generated by a Specific Sturm–Liouville Problem. *Mathematics* **2022**, *10*, 2464. [CrossRef]
22. Munyakazi, J.B.; Kehinde, O.O. A New Parameter-Uniform Discretization of Semilinear Singularly Perturbed Problems. *Mathematics* **2022**, *10*, 2254. [CrossRef]
23. Feng, H.; Ge, Y. Cesáro Means of Weighted Orthogonal Expansions on Regular Domains. *Mathematics* **2022**, *10*, 2108. [CrossRef]
24. Cao, J.; Srivastava, H.M.; Zhou, H.-L.; Arjika, S. Generalized q-Difference Equations for q-Hypergeometric Polynomials with Double q-Binomial Coefficients. *Mathematics* **2022**, *10*, 556. [CrossRef]
25. Bateman, G.; Erdéyi, A. *Higher Transcendental Functions*; Nauka: Moscow, Russia, 1953; Volume 1–3.
26. Carroll, R.; Showalter, R.E. *Singular and Degenerate Cauchy Problems*; Academic Press: New York, NY, USA, 1976.
27. Kipriyanov, I. *Singular Elliptic Boundary Value Problems*; Nauka-Fizmatlit: Moscow, Russia, 1997.
28. Shishkina, E.; Sitnik, S. *Singular and Fractional Differential Equations with Applications to Mathematical Physics*; Mathematics in Science and Engineering; Academic Press: Cambridge, MA, USA, 2020.
29. Carroll, R. *Transmutation and Operator Differential Equations*; North Holland: Amsterdam, The Netherlands, 1979.
30. Carroll, R. *Transmutation, Scattering Theory and Special Functions*; North Holland: Amsterdam, The Netherlands, 1982.
31. Carroll, R. *Transmutation Theory and Applications*; North Holland: Amsterdam, The Netherlands, 1986.
32. Katrakhov, V.V.; Sitnik, S.M. Method of Transmutation Operators and Boundary Value Problems for Singular Elliptic Equations. *Mod. Math.* **2018**, *64*, 211–426. (In Russian); English Translation: arXiv:2210.02246. 2022; Fundamental Directions: Moscow, Russia, 2018.
33. Sitnik, S.M.; Shishkina, E.L. *The Transmutation Operators Method for Differential Equations with Bessel Operators*; Fizmatlit: Moscow, Russia, 2019.
34. Kravchenko, V.V.; Sitnik, S.M. (Eds.) *Transmutation Operators and Applications*; Trends in Mathematics; Birkhauser Cham, Springer Nature Switzerland AG: Basel, Switzerland, 2020; Volume XVII, 686p.
35. Gorenflo, R.; Kilbas, A.A.; Mainardi, F.; Rogosin, S. *The Classical Mittag-Leffler Function*; Springer: Berlin/Heidelberg, Germany, 2020.
36. Andrews, G.E.; Askey, R.; Roy, R. *Special Functions*; Cambridge University Press: Cambridge, UK, 1999.
37. Hardy, G.H.; Littlewood, J.E.; Pólya, G. *Inequalities*; Cambridge University Press: Cambridge/London, UK; New York, NY, USA, 1952.
38. Samko, S.G.; Kilbas, A.A.; Marichev, O.I. *Fractional Integrals and Derivatives. Theory and Applications*; Gordon and Breach Science Publishers: Philadelphia, PA, USA, 1993.
39. Urinov, A.; Sitnik, S.; Shishkina, E.; Karimov, S. *Fractional Integrals and Derivatives (Generalizations and Applications)*; Fargona Publishing: Fergana, Uzbekistan, 2020.
40. Urinov, A.; Karimov, S. *Erdélyi—Kober Operators and Their Applications to Partial Differential Equations. Monograph*; Fargona: Fergana, Uzbekistan, 2021.

Disclaimer/Publisher's Note: The statements, opinions and data contained in all publications are solely those of the individual author(s) and contributor(s) and not of MDPI and/or the editor(s). MDPI and/or the editor(s) disclaim responsibility for any injury to people or property resulting from any ideas, methods, instructions or products referred to in the content.

mathematics

MDPI

Article

Generalized q-Difference Equations for q-Hypergeometric Polynomials with Double q-Binomial Coefficients

Jian Cao [1], Hari M. Srivastava [2,3,4,5,*], Hong-Li Zhou [1] and Sama Arjika [6,7]

1 School of Mathematics, Hangzhou Normal University, Hangzhou 311121, China; 21caojian@hznu.edu.cn (J.C.); 2019111008035@stu.hznu.edu.cn (H.-L.Z.)
2 Department of Mathematics and Statistics, University of Victoria, Victoria, BC V8W 3R4, Canada
3 Department of Medical Research, China Medical University Hospital, China Medical University, Taichung 40402, Taiwan
4 Department of Mathematics and Informatics, Azerbaijan University, 71 Jeyhun Hajibeyli Street, Baku AZ1007, Azerbaijan
5 Section of Mathematics, International Telematic University Uninettuno, I-00186 Rome, Italy
6 Department of Mathematics and Informatics, University of Agadez, Agadez P.O. Box 199, Niger; rjksama2008@gmail.com
7 International Chair of Mathematical Physics and Applications (ICMPA-UNESCO Chair), University of Abomey-Calavi, P.O. Box 072, Cotonou 50, Benin
* Correspondence: harimsri@math.uvic.ca

Abstract: In this paper, we apply a general family of basic (or q-) polynomials with double q-binomial coefficients as well as some homogeneous q-operators in order to construct several q-difference equations involving seven variables. We derive the Rogers type and the extended Rogers type formulas as well as the Srivastava-Agarwal-type bilinear generating functions for the general q-polynomials, which generalize the generating functions for the Cigler polynomials. We also derive a class of mixed generating functions by means of the aforementioned q-difference equations. The various results, which we have derived in this paper, are new and sufficiently general in character. Moreover, the generating functions presented here are potentially applicable not only in the study of the general q-polynomials, which they have generated, but indeed also in finding solutions of the associated q-difference equations. Finally, we remark that it will be a rather trivial and inconsequential exercise to produce the so-called (p,q)-variations of the q-results, which we have investigated here, because the additional forced-in parameter p is obviously redundant.

Keywords: homogeneous q-difference operator; double q-binomial coefficients; q-difference equations; q-hypergeometric polynomials; generating functions

MSC: Primary 05A30; 33D15; 33D45; Secondary 05A40; 11B65

Citation: Cao, J.; Srivastava, H.M.; Zhou, H.-L.; Arjika, S. Generalized q-Difference Equations for q-Hypergeometric Polynomials with Double q-Binomial Coefficients. *Mathematics* **2022**, *10*, 556. https://doi.org/10.3390/math10040556

Academic Editor: Sergei M. Sitnik

Received: 2 January 2022
Accepted: 8 February 2022
Published: 11 February 2022

Publisher's Note: MDPI stays neutral with regard to jurisdictional claims in published maps and institutional affiliations.

Copyright: © 2022 by the authors. Licensee MDPI, Basel, Switzerland. This article is an open access article distributed under the terms and conditions of the Creative Commons Attribution (CC BY) license (https://creativecommons.org/licenses/by/4.0/).

1. Introduction

In this paper, we adopt the notation and terminology for the basic (or q-) hypergeometric series as in [1,2]. Throughout this paper, we assume that q is a fixed nonzero real or complex number and $|q| < 1$. The q-shifted factorial and its compact factorial forms are defined for any real or complex parameter a, a_1, a_2, $\cdots$, a_r, respectively, as follows [1,2]:

$$(a;q)_0 := 1, \quad (a;q)_n := \prod_{k=0}^{n-1}(1-aq^k) \qquad \text{and} \qquad (a;q)_\infty := \prod_{k=0}^{\infty}(1-aq^k), \tag{1}$$

and

$$(a_1,a_2,\cdots,a_r;q)_m = (a_1;q)_m(a_2;q)_m\cdots(a_r;q)_m$$
$$\big(m \in \mathbb{N}_0 := \{0,1,2\cdots\} = \mathbb{N}\cup\{0\}\big).$$

We will also frequently use the following relation:

$$(aq^{-n};q)_n = \left(\frac{q}{a};q\right)_n (-a)^n \, q^{-n-\binom{n}{2}}. \tag{2}$$

The generalized q-binomial coefficients are defined as follows (see [1]):

$$\begin{bmatrix} \alpha \\ k \end{bmatrix}_q = \frac{(q^{-\alpha};q)_k}{(q;q)_k} \, (-1)^k \, q^{\alpha k-\binom{k}{2}} \tag{3}$$

and

$$\begin{bmatrix} \alpha \\ k \end{bmatrix}_{-q} = \frac{(-q^{-\alpha};q)_k}{(-q;q)_k} \, q^{\alpha k-\binom{k}{2}} \qquad (\alpha \in \mathbb{C}), \tag{4}$$

so that

$$\binom{\alpha}{k} = \lim_{q\to 1-}\left\{\begin{bmatrix} \alpha \\ k \end{bmatrix}_q\right\} \qquad (\alpha \in \mathbb{C})$$

for the familiar binomial coefficient.

The basic (or q-) hypergeometric function ${}_r\Phi_s$ in the variable z is defined by (see, for details, Slater ([3], Chap. 3) and Srivastava and Karlsson ([4], p. 347, Eq. (272)); see also [5]):

$${}_r\Phi_s\left[\begin{matrix} a_1, a_2, \cdots, a_r; \\ \\ b_1, b_2, \cdots, b_s; \end{matrix} \; q; z\right] = \sum_{n=0}^{\infty} \left[(-1)^n q^{\binom{n}{2}}\right]^{1+s-r} \frac{(a_1, a_2, \cdots, a_r; q)_n}{(b_1, b_2, \cdots, b_s; q)_n} \frac{z^n}{(q;q)_n}$$

when $r > s+1$. In particular, for $r = s+1$, we have:

$${}_{r+1}\Phi_r\left[\begin{matrix} a_1, a_2, \cdots, a_{r+1}; \\ \\ b_1, b_2, \cdots, b_r; \end{matrix} \; q; z\right] = \sum_{n=0}^{\infty} \frac{(a_1, a_2, \cdots, a_{r+1}; q)_n}{(b_1, b_2, \cdots, b_r; q)_n} \frac{z^n}{(q;q)_n}.$$

We remark in passing that, in the recently-published survey-cum-expository review articles (see [6,7]), the so-called (p,q)-calculus was exposed to be a rather trivial and inconsequential variation of the classical q-calculus, the additional forced-in parameter p being redundant or superfluous (see, for details, ([6], p. 340) and ([7], pp. 1511–1512)).

Chen et al. [8] introduced the homogeneous q-difference operator D_{xy} as follows:

$$D_{xy}\{f(x,y)\} := \frac{f(x, q^{-1}y) - f(qx, y)}{x - q^{-1}y}, \tag{5}$$

which turns out to be suitable for dealing with the Cauchy polynomials. On the other hand, Wang and Cao [9] presented the following two extensions of Cigler's polynomials:

$$C_n^{(\alpha-n)}(x,y,b) = \sum_{k=0}^{n} (-1)^k \, q^{\binom{k}{2}} \begin{bmatrix} \alpha \\ k \end{bmatrix}_q b^k \, \frac{(q;q)_n}{(q;q)_{n-k}} \, p_{n-k}(x,y) \tag{6}$$

and

$$\mathcal{D}_n^{(\alpha-n)}(x,y,b) = \sum_{k=0}^{n} q^{\binom{k}{2}} \begin{bmatrix} \alpha \\ k \end{bmatrix}_q b^k \, \frac{(q;q)_n}{(q;q)_{n-k}} \left[(-1)^{n+k} q^{-\binom{n}{2}} \, p_{n-k}(y,x)\right], \tag{7}$$

where

$$p_n(x,y) := (x-y)(x-qy)\cdots(x-q^{n-1}y) = \left(\frac{y}{x};q\right)_n x^n$$

are the Cauchy polynomials.

Recently, Jia et al. [10] have introduced the following polynomials:

$$L_{\tilde{m},\tilde{n}}(\alpha, x, z, a) = \sum_{k=0}^{n} \begin{bmatrix} n \\ k \end{bmatrix}_q \begin{bmatrix} \alpha \\ k \end{bmatrix}_{-q} q^{\tau(\tilde{m},\tilde{n})+\binom{k}{2}} \, (a;q)_k \, z^k \, x^{n-k} \tag{8}$$

with

$$\tau(\tilde{m},\tilde{n}) = \tilde{m}\binom{k}{2} - \tilde{n}\binom{k+1}{2}, \tag{9}$$

where $\tilde{m}$ and $\tilde{n}$ are real numbers. More recently, Cao et al. [11] introduced an extension of the above q-polynomials as follows:

$$\tilde{L}_n^{(\tilde{r},\tilde{s})}(\alpha,x,y,z,a,b,c) = \sum_{k=0}^{n} \begin{bmatrix} n \\ k \end{bmatrix}_q \begin{bmatrix} \alpha \\ k \end{bmatrix}_{-q} q^{\tau(\tilde{r},\tilde{s})+\binom{k}{2}} (a;q)_k \, p_{n-k}(x,y) z^k \tag{10}$$

and gave the following result.

Proposition 1 (see [11]). *Let $f(\alpha,x,y,a,z,\tilde{r},\tilde{s})$ be a seven-variable analytic function in a neighborhood of*

$$(\alpha,x,y,a,z,\tilde{r},\tilde{s}) = (0,0,0,0,0,0,0) \in \mathbb{C}^7.$$

Then $f(\alpha,x,y,a,z,\tilde{r},\tilde{s})$ can be expanded in terms of $\tilde{L}_n^{(\tilde{r},\tilde{s})}(\alpha,x,y,a,z,\tilde{r},\tilde{s})$ if and only if f satisfies the following q-difference equation:

$$\begin{aligned}
&(x - q^{-1}y)\Big\{f(\alpha,x,y,a,z,\tilde{r},\tilde{s}) - f(\alpha,x,y,a,q^2z,\tilde{r},\tilde{s})\Big\} \\
&= q^{\alpha-\tilde{r}}z\Big\{f(\alpha,x,q^{-1}y,a,zq^{\tilde{r}-\tilde{s}},\tilde{r},\tilde{s}) - f(\alpha,qx,y,a,zq^{\tilde{r}-\tilde{s}},\tilde{r},\tilde{s})\Big\} \\
&\quad + q^{-\tilde{r}-1}(1-aq^{\alpha})z\Big\{f(\alpha,x,yq^{-1},a,zq^{1+\tilde{r}-\tilde{s}},\tilde{r},\tilde{s}) - f(\alpha,qx,y,a,zq^{1+\tilde{r}-\tilde{s}},\tilde{r},\tilde{s})\Big\} \\
&\quad - azq^{-\tilde{r}-2}\Big\{f(\alpha,x,yq^{-1},a,zq^{2+\tilde{r}-\tilde{s}},\tilde{r},\tilde{s}) - f(\alpha,qx,y,a,zq^{2+\tilde{r}-\tilde{s}},\tilde{r},\tilde{s})\Big\}.
\end{aligned} \tag{11}$$

Our present investigation is motivated essentially by the earlier works by Jia et al. [10] and by Cao et al. [11]. Our aim here is to introduce and study the following further extension of the above-mentioned q-polynomials:

$$\tilde{L}_n^{(\tilde{r},\tilde{s})}(\alpha,x,y,z,a,b,c) = \sum_{k=0}^{n} \begin{bmatrix} n \\ k \end{bmatrix}_q \begin{bmatrix} \alpha \\ k \end{bmatrix}_{-q} q^{\tau(\tilde{r},\tilde{s})+\binom{k}{2}} \frac{(a,b;q)_k}{(c;q)_k} \, p_{n-k}(x,y) z^k, \tag{12}$$

where $\tau(\tilde{r},\tilde{s})$ is defined as in (9).

Zhou and Luo [12] obtained some new generating functions for the q-Hahn polynomials and their proofs are based upon the homogeneous q-difference operator. Saad and Abdlhusein [13] utilized the Cauchy operator in proving some identities involving the homogeneous Rogers-Szegö polynomials. However, we found it to be difficult to continue to calculate and generalize the above-mentioned authors' results for general q-polynomials with more parameters (see, for example, [10,12–15]).

It is natural to ask whether some general q-hypergeometric polynomials exist, which are solutions of certain generalized q-difference equations. The novelty of this paper is to search and find these generalized q-difference equations that are satisfied by some of the general q-hypergeometric polynomials, which we have investigated in this paper. The methods and techniques, which we have presented and used here, have produced potentially useful generalizations of the above-mentioned results (see, for details, [10,12–15]). Derivations of various known or new particular cases of our results are indicated in Remark 1.

Remark 1. *The general q-polynomials $\tilde{L}_n^{(\tilde{r},\tilde{s})}(\alpha,x,y,z,a,b,c)$ defined in (12) provide a generalized and unified form of the Hahn polynomials and the Al-Salam-Carlitz polynomials. Some of these special cases of the general q-polynomials $\tilde{L}_n^{(\tilde{r},\tilde{s})}(\alpha,x,y,z,a,b,c)$ are being listed below.*

1. *Upon setting $y = 0$ and $b = c = 0$, the general q-polynomials $\tilde{L}_n^{(\tilde{r},\tilde{s})}(\alpha,x,y,z,a,b,c)$ defined in (12) would reduce to (8) (see [10])*

$$\tilde{L}_n^{(\tilde{r},\tilde{s})}(\alpha,x,0,z,a,b,c) = L_{\tilde{r},\tilde{s}}(\alpha,x,z,a). \tag{13}$$

2. *If we put*
$$(\alpha, \tilde{r}, \tilde{s}, x, y, z, a) = (\infty, 0, 0, y, x, -z, -q, 0, 0),$$
the general q-polynomials $\tilde{L}_n^{(\tilde{r},\tilde{s})}(\alpha, x, y, z, a, b, c)$ *reduce to the trivariate q-polynomials* $F_n(x, y, z; q)$ *(see [16]):*
$$\tilde{L}_n^{(0,0)}(\infty, y, x, -z, -q) = (-1)^n q^{\binom{n}{2}} F_n(x, y, z; q). \tag{14}$$
3. *Upon setting*
$$\alpha = n \in \mathbb{Z} \qquad \text{and} \qquad (\tilde{r}, \tilde{s}, a, b, c, x, y, z) = (0, -1, -yq, 0, 0, 1, 0, x),$$
the general q-polynomials $\tilde{L}_n^{(\tilde{r},\tilde{s})}(\alpha, x, y, z, a, b, c)$ *reduce to the polynomials* $\rho_e(n, y, x, q)$ *(see [10]):*
$$\tilde{L}_n^{(0,-1)}(n, 1, 0, x, -qy) = \rho_e(n, y, x, q). \tag{15}$$
4. *If we set*
$$(\alpha, \tilde{r}, \tilde{s}, y, a, b, c) = (\infty, -1, 0, 0, -q, 0, 0),$$
the general q-polynomials $\tilde{L}_n^{(\tilde{r},\tilde{s})}(\alpha, x, y, z, a, b, c)$ *reduce to the homogeneous Rogers-Szegö polynomials* $h_n(x, y|q)$ *(see [17]):*
$$\tilde{L}_n^{(-1,0)}(\infty, x, y, 1, -q) = h_n(x, y|q). \tag{16}$$
5. *By choosing*
$$(\alpha, \tilde{r}, \tilde{s}, a, b, c, x, y) = (\infty, -1, 0, -q, 0, 0, xq^{-n}, 0),$$
the q-polynomials $\tilde{L}_n^{(\tilde{r},\tilde{s})}(\alpha, x, y, z, a, b, c)$ *reduce to the Rogers-Szegö polynomials* $g_n(z, x|q)$ *(see [17]):*
$$\tilde{L}_n^{(-1,0)}(\infty, xq^{-n}, 0, z, -q) = g_n(z, x|q). \tag{17}$$

The rest of this paper is organized as follows. In Section 2, we establish the main results for the q-difference equations involving seven variables for the general q-polynomials. In Section 3, we obtain the generating function of the general q-polynomials by the method of q-difference equations. In Section 4, we derive the Rogers-type formula for the general q-polynomials by using the q-difference equations. In Section 5, we present a mixed generating function for the general q-polynomials by means of the q-difference equations. We also consider the Srivastava-Agarwal-type bilinear generating functions for the general q-polynomials in Section 5 itself. In Section 6, we derive a transformation identity involving a Hecke-type series for the general q-polynomials. Finally, in Section 7, we present several remarks and observations that are based upon the results and findings in this paper.

2. Fundamental Theorem

In this section, we first state and prove the following fundamental theorem.

Theorem 1. *Let* $f(\alpha, x, y, a, b, c, z, \tilde{r}, \tilde{s})$ *be a nine-variable analytic function in a neighborhood of:*
$$(\alpha, x, y, a, b, c, z, \tilde{r}, \tilde{s}) = (0, 0, 0, 0, 0, 0, 0, 0, 0) \in \mathbb{C}^9.$$

Then $f(\alpha, x, y, a, b, c, z, \tilde{r}, \tilde{s})$ *can be expanded in terms of* $\tilde{L}_n^{(\tilde{r},\tilde{s})}(\alpha, x, y, z, a, b, c)$ *if and only if the function f satisfies the following q-difference equation:*

$$
\begin{aligned}
&(x-q^{-1}y)\Big\{[f(\alpha,x,y,a,b,c,z,\tilde{r},\tilde{s})-f(\alpha,x,y,a,b,c,q^2z,\tilde{r},\tilde{s})]\\
&\quad-cq^{-1}[f(\alpha,x,y,a,b,c,qz,\tilde{r},\tilde{s})-f(\alpha,x,y,a,q^3z,\tilde{r},\tilde{s})]\Big\}\\
&=q^{\alpha-\tilde{r}}z\Big\{f(\alpha,x,q^{-1}y,a,b,c,zq^{\tilde{r}-\tilde{s}},\tilde{r},\tilde{s})-f(\alpha,qx,y,a,b,c,zq^{\tilde{r}-\tilde{s}},\tilde{r},\tilde{s})\Big\}\\
&\quad+q^{-\tilde{r}-1}(1-aq^{\alpha}-bq^{\alpha})z\Big\{f(\alpha,x,yq^{-1},a,b,c,zq^{1+\tilde{r}-\tilde{s}},\tilde{r},\tilde{s})-f(\alpha,qx,y,a,b,c,zq^{1+\tilde{r}-\tilde{s}},\tilde{r},\tilde{s})\Big\}\\
&\quad-(a+b-abq^{\alpha})zq^{-\tilde{r}-2}\Big\{f(\alpha,x,yq^{-1},a,b,c,zq^{2+\tilde{r}-\tilde{s}},\tilde{r},\tilde{s})-f(\alpha,qx,y,a,b,c,zq^{2+\tilde{r}-\tilde{s}},\tilde{r},\tilde{s})\Big\}\\
&\quad-abzq^{-\tilde{r}-3}\Big\{f(\alpha,x,yq^{-1},a,b,c,zq^{3+\tilde{r}-\tilde{s}},\tilde{r},\tilde{s})-f(\alpha,qx,y,a,b,c,zq^{3+\tilde{r}-\tilde{s}},\tilde{r},\tilde{s})\Big\}.
\end{aligned}
\tag{18}
$$

Remark 2. *For $b=c=0$ in Theorem 1, we can deduce Equation (11). Furthermore, if we set $y=0$ and $b=c=0$ in Theorem 1, we are led to the concluding remarks of Jia et al. [10].*

Lemma 1 (Hartogs's theorem). *If a complex-valued function is holomorphic (analytic) in each variable separately in an open domain $\mathbb{D}\in\mathbb{C}^n$, then it is holomorphic (analytic) in $\mathbb{D}$*

In order to prove Theorem 1, we need the following fundamental property of functions of several complex variables (see, for example [18–20]; see also [21]).

Lemma 2 (see ([18], Proposition 1)). *If $f(x_1,x_2,\cdots,x_k)$ is analytic at the origin $(0,0,\cdots,0)\in\mathbb{C}^k$, then the function $f(x_1,x_2,\cdots,x_k)$ can be expanded in an absolutely convergent power series given by*

$$
f(x_1,x_2,\cdots,x_k)=\sum_{n_1,n_2,\cdots,n_k=0}^{\infty}\Omega_{n_1,n_2,\cdots,n_k}\,x_1^{n_1}\,x_2^{n_2}\cdots x_k^{n_k}.
$$

Proof of Theorem 1. In light of Hartogs theorem and the theory of functions of several complex variables, we assume that

$$
f(\alpha,x,y,a,b,c,z,\tilde{r},\tilde{s})=\sum_{k=0}^{\infty}A_k(\alpha,x,y,a,b,c,\tilde{r},\tilde{s})\,z^k. \tag{19}
$$

Firstly, by substituting from (19) into (18), we get:

$$
\begin{aligned}
&(x-q^{-1}y)\sum_{k=0}^{\infty}(1-q^{2k})(1-cq^{k-1})A_k(\alpha,x,y,a,b,c,\tilde{r},\tilde{s})\,z^k\\
&=\sum_{k=0}^{\infty}\Big\{q^{\alpha+\tilde{r}(k-1)-\tilde{s}k}+q^{(\tilde{r}+1)(k-1)-\tilde{s}k}(1-bq^{\alpha}-aq^{\alpha})\\
&\qquad-q^{(\tilde{r}+2)(k-1)-\tilde{s}k}(b+a-abq^{\alpha})+abq^{(\tilde{r}+3)(k-1)-\tilde{s}k}\Big\}\\
&\qquad\cdot\Big\{A_k(\alpha,x,q^{-1}y,a,b,c,\tilde{r},\tilde{s})-A_k(\alpha,qx,y,a,b,c,\tilde{r},\tilde{s})\Big\}\,z^{k+1},
\end{aligned}
\tag{20}
$$

which readily yields

$$
\begin{aligned}
&(x-q^{-1}y)\sum_{k=0}^{\infty}(1-q^{2k})(1-cq^{k-1})A_k(\alpha,x,y,a,b,c,\tilde{r},\tilde{s})\,z^k\\
&=\sum_{k=0}^{\infty}q^{\tilde{r}(k-1)-\tilde{s}k}\Big\{q^{\alpha}+q^{k-1}(1-bq^{\alpha}-aq^{\alpha})-q^{2k-2}(b+a-abq^{\alpha})+abq^{3k-3}\Big\}\\
&\qquad\cdot\Big\{A_k(\alpha,x,q^{-1}y,a,b,c,\tilde{r},\tilde{s})-A_k(\alpha,qx,y,a,b,c,\tilde{r},\tilde{s})\Big\}\,z^{k+1}.
\end{aligned}
\tag{21}
$$

Upon equating the coefficients of z^k $(k \in \mathbb{N})$ on both sides of the Equation (21), we see that

$$\begin{aligned}(x - q^{-1}y)(1-q^k)(1+q^k)(1-cq^{k-1})A_k(\alpha, x, y, a, b, c, \tilde{r}, \tilde{s}) \\ = q^{\tilde{r}(k-1)-\tilde{s}k}(q^\alpha + q^{k-1})(1-aq^{k-1})(1-bq^{k-1}) \\ \cdot \Big\{A_{k-1}(\alpha, x, q^{-1}y, a, b, c, \tilde{r}, \tilde{s}) - A_{k-1}(\alpha, qx, y, a, b, c, \tilde{r}, \tilde{s})\Big\}\end{aligned} \tag{22}$$

or, equivalently, that

$$\begin{aligned}A_k(\alpha, x, y, a, b, c, \tilde{r}, \tilde{s}) &= q^{\tilde{r}(k-1)-\tilde{s}k}\frac{(q^\alpha + q^{k-1})(1-aq^{k-1})(1-bq^{k-1})}{(1-q^k)(1+q^k)(1-cq^{k-1})} \\ &\quad \cdot \frac{A_{k-1}(\alpha, x, q^{-1}y, a, b, c, \tilde{r}, \tilde{s}) - A_{k-1}(\alpha, qx, y, a, b, c, \tilde{r}, \tilde{s})}{x - q^{-1}y} \\ &= q^{\alpha+\tilde{r}(k-1)-\tilde{s}k}\,\frac{(1+q^{-\alpha+k-1})(1-aq^{k-1})(1-bq^{k-1})}{(1-q^k)(1+q^k)(1-cq^{k-1})} \\ &\quad \cdot D_{xy}\{A_{k-1}(\alpha, x, y, a, b, c, \tilde{r}, \tilde{s})\}.\end{aligned}$$

By iterating this process, we find that

$$A_k(\alpha, x, y, a, b, c, \tilde{r}, \tilde{s}) = q^{k\alpha+\tilde{r}\binom{k}{2}-\tilde{s}\binom{k+1}{2}}\,\frac{(-q^{-\alpha}, a, b; q)_k}{(q^2, c; q^2)_k} \cdot D^k_{xy}\{A_0(\alpha, x, y, a, b, c, \tilde{r}, \tilde{s})\},$$

which, upon letting

$$f(\alpha, x, y, a, b, c, 0, \tilde{r}, \tilde{s}) = A_0(\alpha, x, y, a, b, c, \tilde{r}, \tilde{s}) = \sum_{n=0}^{\infty} \mu_n p_n(x, y),$$

yields

$$\begin{aligned}A_k(\alpha, x, y, a, b, c, \tilde{r}, \tilde{s}) \quad &= q^{k\alpha+\tilde{r}\binom{k}{2}-\tilde{s}\binom{k+1}{2}}\,\frac{(-q^{-\alpha}, a, b; q)_k}{(q^2, c; q^2)_k} \\ \cdot \textstyle\sum_{n=0}^{\infty}\ \mu_n\ \frac{(q;q)_n}{(q;q)_{n-k}}\ p_{n-k}(x, y).\end{aligned} \tag{23}$$

We thus obtain

$$\begin{aligned}f(\alpha, x, y, z, a, b, c, \tilde{r}, \tilde{s}) &= \sum_{k=0}^{\infty} q^{k\alpha+\tilde{r}\binom{k}{2}-\tilde{s}\binom{k+1}{2}}\,\frac{(-q^{-\alpha}, a, b; q)_k}{(q^2, c; q^2)_k} \\ &\quad \cdot \sum_{n=0}^{\infty} \mu_n\ \frac{(q;q)_n}{(q;q)_{n-k}}\ p_{n-k}(x, y)z^k \\ &= \sum_{n=0}^{\infty} \mu_n \sum_{k=0}^{n} \begin{bmatrix} n \\ k \end{bmatrix}_q \begin{bmatrix} \alpha \\ k \end{bmatrix}_{-q} q^{\tau(\tilde{r},\tilde{s})+\binom{k}{2}}\,\frac{(a, b; q)_k}{(c; q)_k} p_{n-k}(x, y)\ z^k \\ &= \sum_{n=0}^{\infty}\ \mu_n\ \tilde{L}_n^{(\tilde{r},\tilde{s})}(\alpha, x, y, z, a, b, c).\end{aligned}$$

Secondly, if $f(\alpha, x, y, a, b, c, z, \tilde{r}, \tilde{s})$ can be expanded in terms of $\tilde{L}_n^{(\tilde{r},\tilde{s})}(\alpha, x, y, z, a, b, c)$, we can verify that the function $f(\alpha, x, y, a, b, c, z, \tilde{r}, \tilde{s})$ satisfies Equation (18). The proof of Theorem 1 is now complete. □

3. Generating Functions of the General q-Polynomials

In this section, we first give a generating function of the general q-polynomials by the method of q-difference equations as the application of our main results.

Theorem 2. *The following assertion holds true:*

$$\begin{aligned}&\sum_{n=0}^{\infty} \tilde{L}_n^{(\tilde{r},\tilde{s})}(\alpha,x,y,z,a,b,c)\,\frac{t^n}{(q;q)_n}\\ &=\frac{(yt;q)_\infty}{(xt;q)_\infty}\sum_{k=0}^{\infty}\frac{(-q^{-\alpha},a,b;q)_k}{(q^2,c;q^2)_k}q^{k\alpha+\tilde{r}\binom{k}{2}-\tilde{s}\binom{k+1}{2}}(zt)^k \qquad (|xt|<1).\end{aligned} \tag{24}$$

As a special case of Theorem 2, if we take $\tilde{r}=\tilde{s}=0$, we are led to Corollary 1 below.

Corollary 1. *For* $\max\{|xt|,|ztq^\alpha|\}<1$, *it is asserted that*

$$\sum_{n=0}^{\infty}\tilde{L}_n^{(0,0)}(\alpha,x,y,z,a,b,c)\,\frac{t^n}{(q;q)_n}=\frac{(yt;q)_\infty}{(xt;q)_\infty}\,{}_3\Phi_2\left[\begin{matrix}-q^{-\alpha},a,b;\\ \\ -q,c;\end{matrix}\;q;ztq^\alpha\right]. \tag{25}$$

Proof of Theorem 2. Denoting by $f(\alpha,x,y,a,,b,c,z,\tilde{r},\tilde{s})$ the right-hand side of the Equation (24), we can rewrite equivalently as follows:

$$\begin{aligned}f(\alpha,x,y,a,b,c,z,\tilde{r},\tilde{s})&=\sum_{k=0}^{\infty}\frac{(-q^{-\alpha},a,b;q)_k}{(q^2,c;q^2)_k}\,q^{k\alpha+\tilde{r}\binom{k}{2}-\tilde{s}\binom{k+1}{2}}\,z^k\cdot\frac{t^k\,(yt;q)_\infty}{(xt;q)_\infty}\\ &=\sum_{k=0}^{\infty}\frac{(-q^{-\alpha},a,b;q)_k}{(q^2,c;q^2)_k}q^{k\alpha+\tilde{r}\binom{k}{2}-\tilde{s}\binom{k+1}{2}}\,z^k\,D_{xy}^k\left\{\frac{(yt;q)_\infty}{(xt;q)_\infty}\right\}.\end{aligned} \tag{26}$$

Now, letting:

$$f(\alpha,x,y,a,b,c,z,\tilde{r},\tilde{s})=\sum_{k=0}^{\infty}A_k(\alpha,x,y,a,b,c,\tilde{r},\tilde{s})\,z^k$$

and

$$A_k(\alpha,x,y,a,b,c,\tilde{r},\tilde{s})=q^{k\alpha+\tilde{r}\binom{k}{2}-\tilde{s}\binom{k+1}{2}}\,\frac{(-q^{-\alpha},a,b;q)_k}{(q^2,c;q^2)_k}\,D_{xy}^k\left\{\frac{(yt;q)_\infty}{(xt;q)_\infty}\right\}, \tag{27}$$

we obtain:

$$A_0(\alpha,x,y,a,b,c,\tilde{r},\tilde{s})=\frac{(yt;q)_\infty}{(xt;q)_\infty} \tag{28}$$

and

$$f(\alpha,x,y,a,b,c,0,\tilde{r},\tilde{s})=A_0(\alpha,x,y,a,\tilde{r},\tilde{s}).$$

Thus, upon substituting from (28) into (27), we find that

$$\begin{aligned}A_k(\alpha,x,y,a,b,c,\tilde{r},\tilde{s})=&\;q^{k\alpha+\tilde{r}\binom{k}{2}-\tilde{s}\binom{k+1}{2}}\,\frac{(-q^{-\alpha},a,b;q)_k}{(q^2,c;q^2)_k}\\ &\cdot D_{xy}^k\{A_0(\alpha,x,y,a,b,c,\tilde{r},\tilde{s})\}.\end{aligned} \tag{29}$$

It is easily observed that $f(\alpha,x,y,a,,b,c,z,\tilde{r},\tilde{s})$ is a nine-variable analytic function in a neighborhood of

$$(\alpha,x,y,a,b,c,z,\tilde{r},\tilde{s})=(0,0,0,0,0,0,0,0,0)\in\mathbb{C}^9.$$

Hence, $f(\alpha,x,y,a,b,c,z,\tilde{r},\tilde{s})$ can be expanded in terms of $\tilde{L}_n^{(\tilde{r},\tilde{s})}(\alpha,x,y,z,a,b,c)$ as follows:

$$f(\alpha,x,y,a,b,c,z,\tilde{r},\tilde{s})=\sum_{n=0}^{\infty}\mu_n\cdot\tilde{L}_n^{(\tilde{r},\tilde{s})}(\alpha,x,y,z,a,b,c). \tag{30}$$

Setting $z=0$ and using the following relation:

$$\tilde{L}_n^{(\tilde{r},\tilde{s})}(\alpha,x,y,0,a,b,c)=p_n(x,y)$$

in the resulting equation, we get:

$$f(\alpha,x,y,a,b,c,0,\tilde{r},\tilde{s}) = \frac{(yt;q)_\infty}{(xt;q)_\infty} = \sum_{n=0}^{\infty} \mu_n \cdot p_n(x,y). \tag{31}$$

Finally, upon comparing the coefficients of $p_n(x,y)$, we find that

$$\mu_n = \frac{t^n}{(q;q)_n}.$$

Substituting the above equation into Equation (30), we deduce that $f(\alpha,x,y,a,b,c,z,\tilde{r},\tilde{s})$ equals the left-hand side of Equation (24). This evidently completes the proof of Theorem 2. □

Remark 3. *Setting $y = 0$ and $b = c = 0$ in (24), we get the following concluding remark in the earlier work [10]:*

$$\sum_{n=0}^{\infty} L_{\tilde{r},\tilde{s}}(\alpha,x,z,a)\, \frac{t^n}{(q;q)_n} = \frac{1}{(xt;q)_\infty} \sum_{k=0}^{\infty} \frac{(-q^{-\alpha},a;q)_k}{(q^2;q^2)_k} q^{k\alpha+\tilde{r}\binom{k}{2}-\tilde{s}\binom{k+1}{2}}\, (zt)^k \qquad (|xt|<1). \tag{32}$$

In Equation (24), we let $\alpha \to \infty$ and set $\tilde{r} = \tilde{s} = 0$, $a = -q$, and $b = c = 0$. Then, upon interchanging x and y, and replacing z by $-z$, we get the following corollary.

Corollary 2 ([16], Theorem 2.6). *For $|yt| < 1$, it is asserted that*

$$\sum_{n=0}^{\infty} F_n(x,y,z;q) \frac{(-1)^n\, q^{\binom{n}{2}}\, t^n}{(q;q)_n} = \frac{(xt,zt;q)_\infty}{(yt;q)_\infty}. \tag{33}$$

4. Rogers Type and Extended Rogers Type Formulas for the General q-Polynomials

In this section, we apply the main results to state and prove the Rogers type and the extended Rogers-type formulas for the general q-polynomials by using the q-difference equations, so that we can derive the Rogers formula for the trivariate q-polynomials.

We first recall that Chen and Liu [22] studied the q-exponential operator as follows (see [17]):

$$T(bD_a) = \sum_{n=0}^{\infty} \frac{(bD_a)^n}{(q;q)_n}, \tag{34}$$

where the usual q-differential operator, or the q-derivative, is defined by

$$D_a f(a) = \frac{f(a) - f(qa)}{a}. \tag{35}$$

The following q-Leibniz rule for the q-derivative operator D_a is a variation of the q-binomial theorem (see [23]):

$$D_a^n\{f(a)g(a)\} = \sum_{k=0}^{n} q^{k(k-n)} \begin{bmatrix} n \\ k \end{bmatrix}_q \cdot D_a^k\{f(a)\} D_a^{n-k}\left\{g(aq^k)\right\}, \tag{36}$$

where D_a^0 is understood as the identity operator.

The following important property of the q-derivative operator D_a is easily derivable.

Lemma 3. *For* $|a\omega| < 1$, *the following result holds true:*

$$D_a^n\left\{\frac{(as;q)_\infty}{(a\omega;q)_\infty}\right\} = \omega^n \frac{(s/\omega;q)_n}{(as;q)_n}\frac{(as;q)_\infty}{(a\omega;q)_\infty}. \tag{37}$$

Lemma 4. *For* $k \in \mathbb{N}_0$ *and* $|x\omega| < 1$, *it is asserted that*

$$\begin{aligned} T(tD_\omega)&\left\{\frac{(y\omega;q)_\infty}{(x\omega;q)_\infty}\omega^k\right\} \\ &= \frac{(y\omega;q)_\infty}{(x\omega;q)_\infty}\omega^k \sum_{j=0}^{k} \frac{(-1)^j\, q^{kj-\binom{j}{2}}(q^{-k}, x\omega;q)_j\,(t/\omega)^j}{(y\omega,q;q)_j} \\ &\quad \cdot {}_2\Phi_1\left[\begin{matrix} y/x, 0; \\ y\omega q^j; \end{matrix}\; q; xt\right]. \end{aligned} \tag{38}$$

We now turn to the generalized Rogers-Szegö polynomials which are defined by (see [24,25]):

$$r_n(x,y) = \sum_{k=0}^{n} \begin{bmatrix} n \\ k \end{bmatrix}_q x^k\, y^{n-k}, \tag{39}$$

where (see [25]):

$$r_n(x,y) = T(xD_y)\{y^n\}. \tag{40}$$

We are now in a position to state and prove the following Rogers-type formula for the general q-polynomials by using the q-difference equations.

Theorem 3. *For* $\max\{|x\omega|, |xt|\} < 1$, *the following Rogers-type formula holds true:*

$$\begin{aligned} \sum_{n=0}^{\infty}\sum_{m=0}^{\infty} &\tilde{L}_{n+m}^{(\tilde{r},\tilde{s})}(\alpha,x,y,z,a,b,c)\,\frac{t^n}{(q;q)_n}\frac{\omega^m}{(q;q)_m} \\ &= \frac{(y\omega;q)_\infty}{(x\omega;q)_\infty}\sum_{k=0}^{\infty}\sum_{j=0}^{k} q^{k\alpha+\tilde{r}\binom{k}{2}-\tilde{s}\binom{k+1}{2}}\,\frac{(-q^{-\alpha},a,b;q)_k(\omega z)^k}{(-q,c;q)_k(q;q)_{k-j}} \\ &\quad \cdot \frac{(x\omega;q)_j(t/\omega)^j}{(y\omega,q;q)_j}\,{}_2\Phi_1\left[\begin{matrix} y/x, 0; \\ y\omega q^j; \end{matrix}\; q; xt\right]. \end{aligned} \tag{41}$$

Remark 4. *As a special case of Theorem 3, we let* $\alpha \to \infty$ *and set* $\tilde{r} = \tilde{s} = 0$, $a = -q$, *and* $b = c = 0$ *(41). Then, upon interchanging* x *and* y, *and replacing* z *by* $-z$, *we get the following corollary.*

Corollary 3 (see [16], Theorem 3.1)**.** *It is asserted that*

$$\begin{aligned} \sum_{n=0}^{\infty}\sum_{m=0}^{\infty} &F_{n+m}(x,y,z;q)(-1)^{n+m}\, q^{\binom{n+m}{2}}\,\frac{t^n}{(q;q)_n}\frac{\omega^m}{(q;q)_m} \\ &= \frac{(x\omega,z\omega;q)_\infty}{(y\omega;q)_\infty}\sum_{j=0}^{\infty}\frac{(-1)^j\, q^{\binom{j}{2}}(y\omega;q)_j(zt)^j}{(x\omega,z\omega,q;q)_j} \\ &\quad \cdot {}_2\Phi_1\left[\begin{matrix} x/y, 0; \\ x\omega q^j; \end{matrix}\; q; yt\right] \qquad (|\omega y| < 1). \end{aligned} \tag{42}$$

Proof of Theorem 3. Denoting the right-hand side of the Equation (24) by $f(\alpha, x, y, a, b, c, z, \tilde{r}, \tilde{s})$, it can be written equivalently as follows:

$$\begin{aligned}
&f(\alpha, x, y, a, b, c, z, \tilde{r}, \tilde{s})\\
&= \frac{(y\omega;q)_\infty}{(x\omega;q)_\infty} \sum_{k=0}^{\infty}\sum_{j=0}^{\infty} q^{k\alpha+\tilde{r}\binom{k}{2}-\tilde{s}\binom{k+1}{2}} \frac{(-q^{-\alpha},a,b;q)_k(\omega z)^k}{(-q,c;q)_k(q;q)_{k-j}} \frac{(x\omega;q)_j\,(t/\omega)^j}{(y\omega,q;q)_j}\\
&\quad \cdot {}_2\Phi_1\left[\begin{matrix} y/x, 0; \\ & q; xt \\ y\omega q^j; \end{matrix}\right]\\
&= \sum_{k=0}^{\infty} q^{k\alpha+\tilde{r}\binom{k}{2}-\tilde{s}\binom{k+1}{2}} \frac{(-q^{-\alpha},a,b;q)_k z^k}{(q^2,c;q^2)_k} \sum_{j=0}^{k} \frac{(y\omega q^j;q)_\infty (q;q)_k\, \omega^{k-j}\, t^j}{(x\omega q^j;q)_\infty (q;q)_j (q;q)_{k-j}}\\
&\quad \cdot {}_2\Phi_1\left[\begin{matrix} y/x, 0; \\ & q; xt \\ y\omega q^j; \end{matrix}\right]\\
&= \sum_{k=0}^{\infty} \frac{(-q^{-\alpha},a,b;q)_k}{(q^2,c;q^2)_k} q^{k\alpha+\tilde{r}\binom{k}{2}-\tilde{s}\binom{k+1}{2}} z^k T(tD_\omega)\left\{\frac{(y\omega;q)_\infty}{(x\omega;q)_\infty}\,\omega^k\right\}\\
&= T(tD_\omega)\left\{\frac{(y\omega;q)_\infty}{(x\omega;q)_\infty}\sum_{k=0}^{\infty}\frac{(-q^{-\alpha},a,b;q)_k}{(q^2,c;q^2)_k} q^{k\alpha+\tilde{r}\binom{k}{2}-\tilde{s}\binom{k+1}{2}} (\omega z)^k\right\} \quad \text{(by using (24))}\\
&= T(tD_\omega)\left\{\sum_{m=0}^{\infty} \tilde{L}_m^{(\tilde{r},\tilde{s})}(\alpha,x,y,z,a,b,c)\,\frac{\omega^m}{(q;q)_m}\right\}\\
&= \sum_{m=0}^{\infty} \tilde{L}_m^{(\tilde{r},\tilde{s})}(\alpha,x,y,z,a,b,c)\,\frac{1}{(q;q)_m} T(tD_\omega)\{\omega^m\} \quad \text{(by (40))}\\
&= \sum_{m=0}^{\infty} \tilde{L}_m^{(\tilde{r},\tilde{s})}(\alpha,x,y,z,a,b,c)\,\frac{r_m(t,\omega)}{(q;q)_m}\\
&= \sum_{m=0}^{\infty} \tilde{L}_m^{(\tilde{r},\tilde{s})}(\alpha,x,y,z,a,b,c)\,\frac{1}{(q;q)_m}\sum_{n=0}^{m}\begin{bmatrix} m \\ n \end{bmatrix}_q t^n\,\omega^{m-n}\\
&= \sum_{n=0}^{\infty}\sum_{m=n}^{\infty} \tilde{L}_m^{(\tilde{r},\tilde{s})}(\alpha,x,y,z,a,b,c)\,\frac{t^n}{(q;q)_n}\,\frac{\omega^{m-n}}{(q;q)_{m-n}}.
\end{aligned}$$

It is easily seen that $f(\alpha, x, y, a, , b, c, z, \tilde{r}, \tilde{s})$ is a nine-variable analytic function in a neighborhood of:

$$(\alpha, x, y, a, b, c, z, \tilde{r}, \tilde{s}) = (0,0,0,0,0,0,0,0,0) \in \mathbb{C}^9.$$

Hence, $f(\alpha, x, y, a, b, c, z, \tilde{r}, \tilde{s})$ can be expanded in terms of $\tilde{L}_n^{(\tilde{r},\tilde{s})}(\alpha,x,y,z,a,b,c)$ by Theorem 1 as follows:

$$f(\alpha, x, y, a, b, c, z, \tilde{r}, \tilde{s}) = \sum_{m,n=0}^{\infty} \mu_{m,n} \cdot \tilde{L}_m^{(\tilde{r},\tilde{s})}(\alpha,x,y,z,a,b,c). \tag{43}$$

Letting $z = 0$ in Equation (43), we obtain:

$$
\begin{aligned}
f(\alpha, x, y, a, b, c, 0, \tilde{r}, \tilde{s}) &= \frac{(y\omega;q)_\infty}{(x\omega;q)_\infty} {}_2\Phi_1\left[\begin{matrix} x/y, 0; \\ & q; yt \\ y\omega; \end{matrix}\right] \\
&= \sum_{n=0}^{\infty} \frac{p_n(x,y)t^n}{(q;q)_n} \sum_{m=0}^{\infty} \frac{p_m(x, yq^n)\omega^m}{(q;q)_m} \\
&= \sum_{m,n=0}^{\infty} \mu_{m,n} \cdot p_m(x,y).
\end{aligned} \tag{44}
$$

Comparing the coefficients of $p_m(x,y)$, we deduce that

$$\mu_{m,n} = \frac{t^n \omega^{m-n}}{(q;q)_n (q;q)_{m-n}}.$$

Substituting the above equation into Equation (43), we find that $f(\alpha, x, y, a, b, c, z, \tilde{r}, \tilde{s})$ is equal to the left-hand side of Equation (41). This completes the proof of Theorem 3. □

5. Mixed Generating Functions for the General q-Polynomials

The Hahn polynomials [26,27] (or the Al-Salam-Carlitz polynomials [28,29]) are defined as follows:

$$\phi_n^{(\sigma)}(x|q) = \sum_{k=0}^{n} \begin{bmatrix} n \\ n \end{bmatrix}_q (\sigma;q)_k \, x^k. \tag{45}$$

In the year 1989, Srivastava and Agarwal [30] utilized the method of transformation theory in order to establish the following result. More recently, Cao [29] used the decomposition technique of exponential operators to give an alternative proof. For more information about the Srivastava-Agarwal-type generating functions and other related results, the reader is referred to the works [13,26–31].

Lemma 5 (see [30], Eq. (3.20)). *It is asserted that*

$$\sum_{n=0}^{\infty} \phi_n^{(\sigma)}(x|q)(\lambda;q)_n \frac{t^n}{(q;q)_n} = \frac{(\lambda t;q)_\infty}{(t;q)_\infty} {}_2\Phi_1\left[\begin{matrix} \lambda, \sigma; \\ & q; xt \\ \lambda t; \end{matrix}\right] \tag{46}$$

$$\left(\max\{|t|, |xt|\} < 1\right).$$

In Theorem 4 below, we apply the main results to state and prove a mixed generating function for the general q-polynomials by making use of the q-difference equations.

Theorem 4. *For $|ut| < 1$, the following result holds true:*

$$
\begin{aligned}
&\sum_{n=0}^{\infty} \phi_n^{(\sigma)}(x|q) \tilde{L}_n^{(\tilde{r},\tilde{s})}(\alpha, u, v, z, a, b, c) \frac{t^n}{(q;q)_n} \\
&= \frac{(vt;q)_\infty}{(ut;q)_\infty} \sum_{m=0}^{\infty} \sum_{k=0}^{\infty} \sum_{j=0}^{m} \frac{(\sigma;q)_m \, x^m}{(q;q)_m} \frac{(q^{-m}, ut;q)_j q^j}{(vt,q;q)_j} \\
&\quad \cdot \frac{(-q^{-\alpha};q)_k (a,b;q)_k \, (tzq^j)^k}{(q^2, c;q^2)_k} q^{k\alpha + \tilde{r}\binom{k}{2} - \tilde{s}\binom{k+1}{2}}.
\end{aligned} \tag{47}
$$

In our proof of Theorem 4, the following q-Chu-Vandermonde formula will be needed.

Lemma 6 (q-Chu-Vandermonde sum [1], Eq. (II.6)). *The following q-summation holds true:*

$$ {}_2\Phi_1\left[\begin{matrix} q^{-n}, a; \\ \\ c; \end{matrix} \; q; q\right] = \frac{(c/a;q)_n}{(c;q)_n}\, a^n. \tag{48} $$

Remark 5. *If we let $\alpha \to \infty$, set $a = -q$ and $b = c = 0$, and $\tilde{r} = \tilde{s} = 0$, interchange u and v, and replace z by $-z$, in Theorem 4, we are led to the following corollary.*

Corollary 4 (Mixed Generating Function for the Trivariate q-Polynomials $F_n(x,y,z;q)$). *The following mixed generating function holds true:*

$$ \sum_{n=0}^{\infty} \phi_n^{(\sigma)}(x|q) F_n(u,v,z;q)\, \frac{(-1)^n\, q^{\binom{n}{2}}\, t^n}{(q;q)_n} $$
$$ = \frac{(\sigma x, ut, zt;q)_\infty}{(vt, x;q)_\infty}\, {}_4\Phi_3\left[\begin{matrix} \sigma, vt, 0, 0; \\ \\ ut, zt, q/x; \end{matrix} \; q; q\right]. \tag{49} $$

Proof of Theorem 4. Equation (47) can be written equivalently as follows:

$$ \sum_{n=0}^{\infty} \phi_n^{(\sigma)}(x|q) \tilde{L}_n^{(\tilde{r},\tilde{s})}(\alpha,u,v,z,a,b,c)\, \frac{t^n}{(q;q)_n} $$
$$ = \sum_{m=0}^{\infty} \frac{(\sigma;q)_m\, x^m}{(q;q)_m} \sum_{j=0}^{m} \frac{(q^{-m};q)_j\, q^j}{(q;q)_j} \sum_{k=0}^{\infty} q^{k\alpha+\tilde{r}\binom{k}{2}-\tilde{s}\binom{k+1}{2}} \tag{50} $$
$$ \cdot \frac{(-q^{-\alpha};q)_k (a,b;q)_k\, z^k}{(q^2,c;q^2)_k}\, D_{uv}^k \left\{ \frac{(vtq^j;q)_\infty}{(utq^j;q)_\infty} \right\}. $$

Now, if we use $g(\alpha,u,v,a,b,c,z,\tilde{r},\tilde{s})$ to denote the right-hand side of (50), it is easy to see that $g(\alpha,u,v,a,,b,c,z,\tilde{r},\tilde{s})$ satisfies (18). Thus, upon letting

$$ g(\alpha,u,v,a,b,c,z,\tilde{r},\tilde{s}) = \sum_{k=0}^{\infty} B_k(\alpha,x,y,a,b,c,\tilde{r},\tilde{s}) z^k $$

and

$$ B_k(\alpha,u,v,a,b,c,\tilde{r},\tilde{s}) $$
$$ = q^{k\alpha+\tilde{r}\binom{k}{2}-\tilde{s}\binom{k+1}{2}}\, \frac{(-q^{-\alpha};q)_k (a,b;q)_k}{(q^2;c,q^2)_k} $$
$$ \cdot D_{uv}^k \left\{ \sum_{m=0}^{\infty} \frac{(\sigma;q)_m\, x^m}{(q;q)_m} \sum_{j=0}^{m} \frac{(q^{-m};q)_j q^j}{(q;q)_j}\, \frac{(vtq^j;q)_\infty}{(utq^j;q)_\infty} \right\}, \tag{51} $$

we obtain

$$\begin{aligned}
&B_0(\alpha,u,v,a,b,c,\tilde{r},\tilde{s})\\
&=\frac{(vt;q)_\infty}{(ut;q)_\infty}\sum_{m=0}^{\infty}\frac{(\sigma;q)_m\,x^m}{(q;q)_m}\sum_{j=0}^{m}\frac{(q^{-m},ut;q)_j q^j}{(vt,q;q)_j}\\
&=\frac{(vt;q)_\infty}{(ut;q)_\infty}\sum_{m=0}^{\infty}\frac{(\sigma;q)_m\,x^m}{(q;q)_m}{}_2\Phi_1\left[\begin{matrix}q^{-m},ut;\\ \\ vt;\end{matrix}\;q;q\right]\quad(\text{by (48)})\\
&=\frac{(vt;q)_\infty}{(ut;q)_\infty}\sum_{m=0}^{\infty}\frac{(\sigma;q)_m\,x^m}{(q;q)_m}\frac{(v/u;q)_m(ut)^m}{(vt;q)_m}\\
&=\frac{(vt;q)_\infty}{(ut;q)_\infty}\,{}_2\Phi_1\left[\begin{matrix}v/u,\sigma;\\ \\ vt;\end{matrix}\;q;uxt\right]\\
&=\sum_{n=0}^{\infty}\phi_n^{(\sigma)}(x|q)\,\frac{p_n(u,v)\,t^n}{(q;q)_n}
\end{aligned}\tag{52}$$

and

$$g(\alpha,u,v,a,b,c,0,\tilde{r},\tilde{s})=B_0(\alpha,u,v,a,b,c,\tilde{r},\tilde{s}).$$

Upon substituting from Equation (52) into Equation (51), we get:

$$\begin{aligned}
B_k(\alpha,u,v,a,b,c,\tilde{r},\tilde{s})=q^{k\alpha+\tilde{r}\binom{k}{2}-\tilde{s}\binom{k+1}{2}}\,\frac{(-q^{-\alpha},a,b;q)_k}{(q^2,c;q^2)_k}\\
D_{uv}^k\{B_0(\alpha,u,v,a,b,c,\tilde{r},\tilde{s})\}.
\end{aligned}\tag{53}$$

In light of the above identities, $g(\alpha,u,v,a,,b,c,z,\tilde{r},\tilde{s})$ satisfies Equation (18), so we have:

$$g(\alpha,u,v,a,b,c,z,\tilde{r},\tilde{s})=\sum_{n=0}^{\infty}\mu_n\cdot\tilde{L}_n^{(\tilde{r},\tilde{s})}(\alpha,u,v,z,a,b,c).\tag{54}$$

Furthermore, we deduce that

$$\begin{aligned}
&g(\alpha,u,v,a,b,c,z,\tilde{r},\tilde{s})\\
&=\sum_{k=0}^{n}\frac{(-q^{-\alpha},a,b;q)_k}{(q^2,c;q^2)_k}\,q^{k\alpha+\tilde{r}\binom{k}{2}-\tilde{s}\binom{k+1}{2}}\,z^k\,D_{uv}^k\left\{\sum_{n=0}^{\infty}\phi_n^{(\sigma)}(x|q)\,\frac{p_n(u,v)\,t^n}{(q;q)_n}\right\}\\
&=\sum_{n=0}^{\infty}\sum_{k=0}^{n}\frac{(-q^{-\alpha},a,b;q)_k}{(q^2,c;q^2)_k}\,q^{k\alpha+\tilde{r}\binom{k}{2}-\tilde{s}\binom{k+1}{2}}\,z^k\,\phi_n^{(\sigma)}(x|q)\,\frac{p_{n-k}(u,v)\,t^n}{(q;q)_{n-k}}\\
&=\sum_{n=0}^{\infty}\phi_n^{(\sigma)}(x|q)\,\frac{t^n}{(q;q)_n}\sum_{k=0}^{n}\begin{bmatrix}n\\k\end{bmatrix}_q\begin{bmatrix}\alpha\\k\end{bmatrix}_{-q}q^{\tau(\tilde{r},\tilde{s})+\binom{k}{2}}\,\frac{(a,b;q)_k}{(c;q)_k}p_{n-k}(u,v)\,z^k\\
&=\sum_{n=0}^{\infty}\phi_n^{(\sigma)}(x|q)\,\tilde{L}_n^{(\tilde{r},\tilde{s})}(\alpha,u,v,z,a,b,c)\,\frac{t^n}{(q;q)_n}.
\end{aligned}\tag{55}$$

By comparing the coefficients of $\tilde{L}_n^{(\tilde{r},\tilde{s})}(\alpha,u,v,z,a,b,c)$ on both sides of Equations (54) and (55), we obtain:

$$\mu_n=\phi_n^{(\sigma)}(x|q)\frac{t^n}{(q;q)_n}.\tag{56}$$

The proof of Theorem 4 is thus completed. □

6. A Transformation Identity Involving Hecke-Type Series for the General q-Polynomials

Jia and Zheng [32] proved a general expansion formula involving the Askey-Wilson polynomials by applying the Bailey transform and the Bressoud inversion.

Proposition 2 (see [32], Proposition 2.3). *The following series identity holds true for suitably-bounded sequences* $\{\beta_n\}_{n\in\mathbb{N}_n}$ *and* $\{\delta_n\}_{n\in\mathbb{N}_n}$*:*

$$\sum_{n=0}^{\infty}\beta_n\,\delta_n=\sum_{n=0}^{\infty}\frac{(1-aq^{2n})(a,a/b;q)_n(b/a)^n}{(1-a)(bq,q;q)_n}\sum_{k=0}^{n}\frac{(1-bq^{2k})(aq^n,q^{-n};q)_k\,q^k}{(1-b)(bq^{n+1},bq^{1-n}/a;q)_k}\,\beta_k \cdot\sum_{r=0}^{\infty}\frac{(b/a;q)_r(b;q)_{r+2n}}{(q;q)_r(aq;q)_{r+2n}}\,\delta_{r+n}. \tag{57}$$

In this section, we give an application of the above series identity (57).

Theorem 5. *For* $\max\{|aq|,|aq/\alpha\beta|\}<1$*, the following transformation identity holds true:*

$$\sum_{n=0}^{\infty}\begin{bmatrix}N\\n\end{bmatrix}_q\begin{bmatrix}\tilde{\alpha}\\n\end{bmatrix}_{-q}\frac{(\tilde{a},\tilde{b},\alpha,\beta;q)_n}{(\tilde{c};q)_n}\,q^{\tau(\tilde{r},\tilde{s})+\binom{n}{2}}\left(\frac{aq}{\alpha\beta}\right)^n P_{N-n}(x,y)\,z^n$$
$$=\frac{(aq/\alpha,aq/\beta;q)_\infty}{(aq,aq/\alpha\beta;q)_\infty}\sum_{n=0}^{\infty}\frac{(1-aq^{2n})(\alpha,\beta,a;q)_n}{(1-a)(aq/\alpha,aq/\beta,q;q)_n}\left(\frac{aq}{\alpha\beta}\right)^n \cdot\sum_{k=0}^{n}\begin{bmatrix}N\\k\end{bmatrix}_q\begin{bmatrix}\tilde{\alpha}\\k\end{bmatrix}_{-q}\frac{(aq^n,q^{-n},\tilde{a},\tilde{b};q)_k}{(\tilde{c};q)_k}\,q^{\tau(\tilde{r},\tilde{s})+\binom{k}{2}}\,P_{N-k}(x,y)\,z^k. \tag{58}$$

In our proof of Theorem 5, the following q-Gauss sum will be needed.

Lemma 7 (q-Gauss sum [1], Eq. (II.8)). *The following q-summation formula holds true:*

$${}_2\Phi_1\left[\begin{matrix}a,b;\\ c;\end{matrix}\;q;\frac{c}{ab}\right]=\frac{(c/a,c/b;q)_\infty}{(c,c/ab;q)_\infty}\qquad\left(\left|\frac{c}{ab}\right|<1\right). \tag{59}$$

Proof of Theorem 5. Upon setting $b=0$,

$$\beta_n=\begin{bmatrix}N\\n\end{bmatrix}_q\begin{bmatrix}\tilde{\alpha}\\n\end{bmatrix}_{-q}\frac{(\tilde{a},\tilde{b};q)_n}{(\tilde{c};q)_n}\,q^{\tau(\tilde{r},\tilde{s})+\binom{n}{2}}\,P_{N-n}(x,y)\,z^n$$

and

$$\delta_n=(\alpha,\beta;q)_n\left(\frac{aq}{\alpha\beta}\right)^n$$

in (57), we obtain

$$\sum_{n=0}^{\infty} \begin{bmatrix} N \\ n \end{bmatrix}_q \begin{bmatrix} \tilde{\alpha} \\ n \end{bmatrix}_{-q} \frac{(\tilde{a},\tilde{b},\alpha,\beta;q)_n}{(\tilde{c};q)_n} q^{\tau(\tilde{r},\tilde{s})+\binom{n}{2}} \left(\frac{aq}{\alpha\beta}\right)^n P_{N-n}(x,y)\, z^n$$
$$= \sum_{n=0}^{\infty} \frac{(1-aq^{2n})(\alpha,\beta,a;q)_n(aq/\alpha\beta)^n}{(1-a)(q;q)_n(aq;q)_{2n}} \sum_{k=0}^{n} \begin{bmatrix} N \\ k \end{bmatrix}_q \begin{bmatrix} \tilde{\alpha} \\ k \end{bmatrix}_{-q} \frac{(aq^n,q^{-n},\tilde{a},\tilde{b};q)_k}{(\tilde{c};q)_k}$$
$$\cdot q^{\tau(\tilde{r},\tilde{s})+\binom{k}{2}} P_{N-k}(x,y)\, z^k \sum_{r=0}^{\infty} \frac{(\alpha q^n,\beta q^n;q)_r}{(aq^{1+2n},q;q)_r} \left(\frac{aq}{\alpha\beta}\right)^r$$
$$= \sum_{n=0}^{\infty} \frac{(1-aq^{2n})(\alpha,\beta,a;q)_n}{(1-a)(q;q)_n(aq;q)_{2n}} \left(\frac{aq}{\alpha\beta}\right)^n \sum_{k=0}^{n} \begin{bmatrix} N \\ k \end{bmatrix}_q \begin{bmatrix} \tilde{\alpha} \\ k \end{bmatrix}_{-q} \frac{(aq^n,q^{-n},\tilde{a},\tilde{b};q)_k}{(\tilde{c};q)_k}$$
$$\cdot q^{\tau(\tilde{r},\tilde{s})+\binom{k}{2}} P_{N-k}(x,y)\, z^k \,{}_2\Phi_1\left[\begin{matrix} \alpha q^n,\beta q^n; \\ aq^{1+2n}; \end{matrix}\ q;\frac{aq}{\alpha\beta}\right]. \tag{60}$$

Thus, by applying the q-Gauss sum (48) in the right-hand side of the above equation, we find that

$$\sum_{n=0}^{\infty} \begin{bmatrix} N \\ n \end{bmatrix}_q \begin{bmatrix} \tilde{\alpha} \\ n \end{bmatrix}_{-q} \frac{(\tilde{a},\tilde{b},\alpha,\beta;q)_n}{(\tilde{c};q)_n} q^{\tau(\tilde{r},\tilde{s})+\binom{n}{2}} \left(\frac{aq}{\alpha\beta}\right)^n P_{N-n}(x,y)\, z^n$$
$$= \frac{(aq/\alpha,aq/\beta;q)_\infty}{(aq,aq/\alpha\beta;q)_\infty} \sum_{n=0}^{\infty} \frac{(1-aq^{2n})(\alpha,\beta,a;q)_n}{(1-a)(aq/\alpha,aq/\beta,q;q)_n} \left(\frac{aq}{\alpha\beta}\right)^n$$
$$\cdot \sum_{k=0}^{n} \begin{bmatrix} N \\ k \end{bmatrix}_q \begin{bmatrix} \tilde{\alpha} \\ k \end{bmatrix}_{-q} \frac{(aq^n,q^{-n},\tilde{a},\tilde{b};q)_k}{(\tilde{c};q)_k} q^{\tau(\tilde{r},\tilde{s})+\binom{k}{2}} P_{N-k}(x,y)\, z^k,$$

which completes the proof of the result asserted by Theorem 5. □

Remark 6. *In Theorem 5, we set $z = q$ and let $N, \tilde{\alpha}, \alpha, \beta \to \infty$. Then, upon putting $\tilde{r} = 0, \tilde{s} = 1$, $y = 0, x = 1$, and $\tilde{b} = 0$ in Theorem 5, we can deduce the following result:*

$$\sum_{n=0}^{\infty} \frac{(\tilde{a};q)_n}{(\tilde{c},-q,q;q)_n} a^n$$
$$= \frac{1}{(aq;q)_\infty} \sum_{n=0}^{\infty} \frac{q^{n^2}(1-aq^{2n})(a;q)_n\, a^n}{(1-a)(q;q)_n} \sum_{k=0}^{n} \frac{(aq^n,q^{-n},\tilde{a};q)_k}{(\tilde{c},-q,q;q)_k} q^k$$
$$= \frac{1}{(aq;q)_\infty} \sum_{n=0}^{\infty} \frac{q^{n^2}(1-aq^{2n})(a;q)_n\, a^n}{(1-a)(q;q)_n} \,{}_3\Phi_2\left[\begin{matrix} q^{-n},aq^n,\tilde{a}; \\ \tilde{c},-q; \end{matrix}\ q;q\right]. \tag{61}$$

7. Further Remarks and Observations

In our present investigation, we have made use of a general family of basic (or q-) polynomials, together with double q-binomial coefficients, as well as some homogeneous q-operators with a view to constructing several q-difference equations involving seven variables. We have derived the Rogers and the extended Rogers-type formulas as well as the Srivastava-Agarwal type bilinear generating functions for the q-polynomials considered in this paper, which generalize the generating functions for the Cigler polynomials. We have also derived a class of mixed generating functions by means of the above-mentioned q-difference equations.

In addition to the remarks and observations concerning the novelty and generality of the q-hypergeometric polynomials and their associated q-difference equations, which we have investigated in the preceding sections, by appropriately using the list of special cases presented in Remark 1, the various results which we have derived in this paper for the general q-polynomials $\tilde{L}_n^{(\tilde{r},\tilde{s})}(\alpha,x,y,z,a,b,c)$ defined in (12) would apply to derive the corresponding results for each of the q-polynomials listed in Remark 1. Indeed, as it is widely recognized, studies involving q-generating functions can lead naturally to interesting and useful properties of the q-polynomial sequences which they generate. Moreover, as pointed out in the monograph by Srivastava and Karlsson ([4], pp. 350–351), the widely- and extensively-investigated families of q-series and q-polynomials have been demonstrated to be useful in a wide variety of fields such as, for example, number theory and partition theory, Lie theory, quantum mechanics and particle physics, non-linear electric circuit theory, combinatorial analysis, and so on. Our results for a significantly wide class of q-polynomials are potentially useful in some of these fields. With a view to motivating the interested readers toward the theory and widespread applications of various families of q-series, q-polynomials, as well as q-difference and q-derivative operators, we have chosen here to include references (see, for example, [33–45]) to various related developments in recent years.

We remark in conclusion that, in the recently-published survey-cum-expository review articles by Srivastava (see [6,7]), the so-called (p,q)-calculus was exposed to be a rather trivial and inconsequential variation of the classical q-calculus, the additional forced-in parameter p being redundant or superfluous (see, for details, ([6], p. 340) and ([7], pp. 1511–1512)). This remarkable demonstration by Srivastava (see [6,7]) will surely apply to any attempt to produce the rather straightforward (p,q)-variations of the results that we have presented herein.

Author Contributions: Conceptualization, S.A.; funding acquisition, H.-L.Z.; investigation, J.C., H.M.S. and H.-L.Z.; methodology, J.C. and S.A.; supervision, H.M.S.; writing—original draft, J.C., H.-L.Z. and S.A.; writing—review and editing, H.M.S. All authors have read and agreed to the published version of the manuscript.

Funding: This work was supported by the Natural Science Foundation of the Zhejiang Province of the People's Republic of China under Grant No. LY21A010019.

Institutional Review Board Statement: Not applicable.

Informed Consent Statement: Not applicable.

Data Availability Statement: Not applicable.

Conflicts of Interest: The authors declare that they have no conflict of interest.

References

1. Gasper, G.; Rahman, M. *Basic Hypergeometric Series (with a Foreword by Richard Askey)*, 2nd ed.; Encyclopedia of Mathematics and Its Applications; Cambridge University Press: Cambridge, MA, USA; London, UK; New York, NY, USA, 2004; Volume 96.
2. Koekock, R.; Swarttouw, R.F. *The Askey-Scheme of Hypergeometric Orthogonal Polynomials and Its q-Analogue*; Report No. 98-17; Delft University of Technology: Delft, The Netherlands, 1998.
3. Slater, L.J. *Generalized Hypergeometric Functions*; Cambridge University Press: Cambridge, MA, USA; London, UK; New York, NY, USA, 1966.
4. Srivastava, H.M.; Karlsson, P.W. *Multiple Gaussian Hypergeometric Series*; Halsted Press (Ellis Horwood Limited, Chichester); John Wiley and Sons: New York, NY, USA; Chichester, UK; Brisbane, Australia; Toronto, ON, Canada, 1985.
5. Andrews, G.E. Applications of basic hypergeometric series. *SIAM Rev.* **1974**, *16*, 441–484. [CrossRef]
6. Srivastava, H.M. Operators of basic (or q-) calculus and fractional q-calculus and their applications in geometric function theory of complex analysis. *Iran. J. Sci. Technol. Trans. A Sci.* **2020**, *44*, 327–344. [CrossRef]
7. Srivastava, H.M. Some parametric and argument variations of the operators of fractional calculus and related special functions and integral transformations. *J. Nonlinear Convex Anal.* **2021**, *22*, 1501–1520.
8. Chen, W.Y.C.; Fu, A.M.; Zhang, B. The homogeneous q-difference operator. *Adv. Appl. Math.* **2003**, *31*, 659–668. [CrossRef]
9. Wang, X.-F.; Cao, J. q-Difference equations for the generalized Cigler's polynomials. *J. Differ. Equ. Appl.* **2018**, *24*, 479–502. [CrossRef]
10. Jia, Z.; Khan, B.; Hu, Q.; Niu, D.-W. Applications of generalized q-difference equations for general q-polynomials. *Symmetry* **2021**, *13*, 1222. [CrossRef]
11. Cao, J.; Arjika, S.; Hounkonnou, M.N. Generalized q-difference equations for general q-polynomials with double q-binomial coefficients. *J. Differ. Equ. Appl.* 2021, *Preprint*.
12. Zhou, Y.; Luo, Q.-M. Some new generating functions for q-Hahn polynomials. *J. Appl. Math.* **2014**, *2014*, 419365. [CrossRef]
13. Saad, H.L.; Abdlhusein, M.A. New application of the Cauchy operator on the homogeneous Rogers-Szegö polynomials. *Ramanujan J.* **2021**, *56*, 347–367. [CrossRef]
14. Liu, Z.-G. Two q-difference equations and q-operator identities. *J. Differ. Equ. Appl.* **2010**, *16*, 1293–1307. [CrossRef]

15. Liu, Z.-G.; Zeng, J. Two expansion formulas involving the Rogers-Szegö polynomials with applications. *Internat. J. Number Theory* **2015**, *11*, 507–525. [CrossRef]
16. Abdlhusein, M.A. Two operator representations for the trivariate q-polynomials and Hahn polynomials. *Ramanujan J.* **2016**, *40*, 491–509. [CrossRef]
17. Saad, H.L.; Sukhi, A.A. The q-exponential operator. *Appl. Math. Sci.* **2013**, *7*, 6369–6380. [CrossRef]
18. Malgrange, B. *Lectures on the Theory of Functions of Several Complex Variables*; Springer: Berlin/Heidelberg, Germany; New York, NY, USA, 1984.
19. Taylor, J.L. *Several Complex Variables with Connections to Algebraic Geometry and Lie Groups*; Graduate Studies in Mathematics; American Mathematical Society: Providence, RI, USA, 2002; Volume 46.
20. Gunning, R.C. *Introduction to Holomorphic Functions of Several Variables. I: Function Theory*; Chapman and Hall/CRC: Boca Raton, FL, USA, 1990.
21. Range, R.M. Complex analysis: A brief tour into higher dimensions. *Amer. Math. Monthly* **2003**, *110*, 89–108. [CrossRef]
22. Chen, W.Y.C.; Liu, Z.-G. Parameter augmenting for basic hypergeometric series. II. *J. Combin. Theory Ser. A* **1997**, *80*, 175–195. [CrossRef]
23. Roman, S. More on the umbral calculus, with emphasis on the q-umbral calculus. *J. Math. Anal. Appl.* **1985**, *107*, 222–254. [CrossRef]
24. Cigler, J. *Elementare q-Identitäten*; Publication de L'institute de Recherche Mathématique Avancée: Strasbourg, France, 1982; pp. 23–57.
25. Saad, H.L.; Abdlhusein, M.A. The q-exponential operator and generalized Rogers-Szegö polynomials. *J. Adv. Math.* **2014**, *8*, 1440–1455.
26. Hahn, W. Über Orthogonalpolynome, die q-Differenzengleichungen genügen. *Math. Nachr.* **1949**, *2*, 4–34. [CrossRef]
27. Hahn, W. Beiträge zur Theorie der Heineschen Reihen. Die 24 Integrale der hypergeometrischen q-Differenzengleichung. Das q-Analogon der Laplace-Transformation. *Math. Nachr.* **1949**, *2*, 340–379. [CrossRef]
28. Al-Salam, W.A.; Carlitz, L. Some orthogonal q-polynomials. *Math. Nachr.* **1965**, *30*, 47–61. [CrossRef]
29. Cao, J. Generalizations of certain Carlitz's trilinear and Srivastava-Agarwal type generating functions. *J. Math. Anal. Appl.* **2012**, *396*, 351–362. [CrossRef]
30. Srivastava, H.M.; Agarwal, A.K. Generating functions for a class of q-polynomials. *Ann. Mat. Pura Appl. (Ser. 4)* **1989**, *154*, 99–109. [CrossRef]
31. Jia, Z. Homogeneous q-difference equations and generating functions for the generalized $2D$-Hermite polynomials. *Taiwan. J. Math.* **2021**, *25*, 45–63. [CrossRef]
32. Jia, Z.; Zeng, J. Expansions in Askey-Wilson polynomials via Bailey transform. *J. Math. Anal. Appl.* **2017**, *452*, 1082–1100. [CrossRef]
33. Atakishiyev, M.K.; Atakishiyev, N.M.; Klimyk, A.U. Big q-Laguerre and q-Meixner polynomials and representations of the quantum algebra $U_q(su(1,1))$. *J. Phys. A Math. Gen.* **2003**, *36*, 10335–10347. [CrossRef]
34. Srivastava, H.M.; Khan, B.; Khan, N.; Hussain, A.; Khan, N.; Tahir, M. Applications of certain basic (or q-) derivatives to subclasses of multivalent Janowski type q-starlike functions involving conic domains. *J. Nonlinear Var. Anal.* **2021**, *5*, 531–547.
35. Atakishiyeva, M.K.; Atakishiyev, N.M. q-Laguerre and Wall polynomials are related by the Fourier-Gauss transform. *J. Phys. A Math. Gen.* **1997**, *30*, L429–L432. [CrossRef]
36. Cao, J. q-Difference equations for generalized homogeneous q-operators and certain generating functions. *J. Differ. Equ. Appl.* **2014**, *20*, 837–851. [CrossRef]
37. Cao, J.; Niu, D.-W. A note on q-difference equations for the Cigler's polynomials. *J. Differ. Equ. Appl.* **2016**, *22*, 1880–1892. [CrossRef]
38. Cigler, J. Operator methods for q identities. II: q-Laguerre polynomials. *Monatsh. Math.* **1981**, *91*, 105–117. [CrossRef]
39. Srivastava, H.M.; Tahir, M.; Khan, B.; Darus, M.; Khan, N.; Ahmad, Q.Z. Certain subclasses of meromorphically q-starlike functions associated with the q-derivative operators. *Ukrain. Math. J.* **2021**, *73*, 1260–1273. [CrossRef]
40. Chung, W.-S. q-Laguerre polynomial realization of $gl_q(N)$-covariant oscillator algebra. *Internat. J. Theoret. Phys.* **1998**, *37*, 2975–2978. [CrossRef]
41. Coulembier, K.; Sommen, F. q-Deformed harmonic and Clifford analysis and the q-Hermite and Laguerre polynomials. *J. Phys. A Math. Theoret.* **2010**, *43*, 115202. [CrossRef]
42. Liu, Z.-G. On the q-partial differential equations and q-series. In *The Legacy of Srinivasa Ramanujan*; Ramanujan Mathematical Society Lecture Note Series; Ramanujan Mathematical Society: Mysore, India, 2013; Volume 20, pp. 213–250.
43. Micu, C.; Papp, E. Applying q-Laguerre polynomials to the derivation of q-deformed energies of oscillator and coulomb systems. *Romanian Rep. Phys.* **2005**, *57*, 25–34.
44. Srivastava, H.M.; Cao, J.; Arjika, S. A note on generalized q-difference equations and their applications involving q-hypergeometric functions. *Symmetry* **2020**, *12*, 1816. [CrossRef]
45. Saad, H.L.; Sukhi, A.A. Another homogeneous q-difference operator. *Appl. Math. Comput.* **2010**, **215**, 4332–4339. [CrossRef]

mathematics

Article

Cesàro Means of Weighted Orthogonal Expansions on Regular Domains

Han Feng † and Yan Ge *,†

Department of Mathematics, City University of Hong Kong, Hong Kong, China; hanfeng@cityu.edu.hk
* Correspondence: yange3@cityu.edu.hk
† These authors contributed equally to this work.

Abstract: In this paper, we investigate Cesàro means for the weighted orthogonal polynomial expansions on spheres with weights being invariant under a general finite reflection group on $\mathbb{R}^d$. Our theorems extend previous results only for specific reflection groups. Precisely, we consider the weight function $h_\kappa(x) := \prod_{v\in R+} |\langle x, v\rangle|^{\kappa_v}$, $x \in \mathbb{R}^d$ on the unit sphere; the upper estimates of the Cesàro kernels and Cesàro means are obtained and used to prove the convergence of the Cesàro (C, δ) means in the weighted L^p space for δ above the corresponding index. We also establish similar results for the corresponding estimates on the unit ball and the simplex.

Keywords: spherical h-harmonics; Cesàro means; Christoffel functions

MSC: 33C50; 33C52; 42B08; 42C10

Citation: Feng, H.; Ge, Y. Cesàro Means of Weighted Orthogonal Expansions on Regular Domains. *Mathematics* **2022**, *10*, 2108. https://doi.org/10.3390/math10122108

Academic Editor: Sitnik Sergey

Received: 24 May 2022
Accepted: 15 June 2022
Published: 17 June 2022

Publisher's Note: MDPI stays neutral with regard to jurisdictional claims in published maps and institutional affiliations.

Copyright: © 2022 by the authors. Licensee MDPI, Basel, Switzerland. This article is an open access article distributed under the terms and conditions of the Creative Commons Attribution (CC BY) license (https://creativecommons.org/licenses/by/4.0/).

1. Introduction

Cesàro summation (also known as the Cesàro mean) is a collection of methods for the infinite summation of a series of numbers or functions. It was stated by E. Cesàro [1] in 1890 and ever since has been extensively studied in mathematical analysis. In the orthogonal expansion theory, generally for $N \in \mathbb{N}$ and $\delta \geq -1$, a Cesàro operator for a function f with a series of orthogonal projections $\{\mathrm{proj}_j f\}_{j=0}^{\infty}$ is defined as

$$S_N^\delta(f) := \frac{1}{A_N^\delta} \sum_{j=0}^{N} A_{N-j}^\delta \mathrm{proj}_j f,$$

where $A_N^\delta := \frac{\Gamma(N+\delta+1)}{\Gamma(\delta+1)\Gamma(N+1)}$ and Γ is the Gamma function. It coincides with the partial sum for $\delta = 0$ and the Fejèr sum for $\delta = 1$.

Classical results about the Cesàro operator were established for Fourier expansion of periodic functions [2]. In order to recover a periodic function f from its Fourier coefficients, it would be more convenient to use the Cesàro mean method than taking the limit of the partial sums of its Fourier series since this approach does not always work well. As straight extension but far beyond trivial, these classical results have been developed for spherical harmonic expansions on unit spheres. In the 1980s, C.D. Sogge [3,4] proved the boundedness and convergence of Cesàro operators. Furthermore, the critical index of δ for convergence was obtained under certain restrictions. The approach of Sogge is based on some delicate global estimates of the orthogonal projection operators, which, however, significantly relied on the translation invariance of the Lebesgue measure on the sphere. In recent decades, the theory of spherical h-harmonics was developed and attracted much attention. This theory was initially studied by Dunkl in [5–7] and has been applied in physics (see, for instance, [8,9] (pp. 360–370)). The weight functions in Dunkl theory are invariant under a finite reflection group G on $\mathbb{R}^d$. Specifically, for the case of group $G = \mathbb{Z}_2^d$ and $G = S_3$ (see [10,11]), Dai and Xu obtained a pointwise estimate for Cesàro kernel and proved the convergence of Cesàro means. Their analysis relied on an explicit "closed" integral representation of Cesàro kernels. It should be pointed out that the explicit integral representation, which is only known for several special groups $G = \mathbb{Z}_2^d$ and S_3, is essential in the works of [10–15].

In this paper, our goal is to extend the previous results about the convergence of Cesàro means for the weighted orthogonal polynomials expansions (WOPEs) with general finite reflection groups and to give a condition for the convergence of the Cesàro means with respect to the weights. To overcome the difficulty of the results of the integral representation, we shall apply the weighted Christoffel function to establish a delicate pointwise estimate of Cesàro kernels.

The paper is organized as follows: in Section 2, we describe some necessary notations and preliminary results on Jacobi polynomials. We also discuss the Dunkl operators in detail and the theory of spherical h-harmonics, which was developed by Dunkl ([5,6]). An important tool for our proofs of the main theorems is the weighted Christoffel function on the sphere. We will present some sharp asymptotic estimates of the weighted Christoffel functions. In Sections 3 and 4, we shall state and prove our main theorems. We apply the weighted Christoffel function to establish a highly localized pointwise estimate of a Cesàro kernel in spherical h-harmonic expansions. This pointwise kernel estimate plays a crucial role in proving an integral estimate and a convergence result. Finally, Section 5 is devoted to results on the unit ball $\mathbb{B}^d$ and the simplex $\mathbb{T}^d$: necessary notations and results on WOPEs on $\mathbb{B}^d$ and $\mathbb{T}^d$ are described briefly in this section, while we establish similar results on the ball and simplex.

Throughout this paper, $\|\cdot\|$ denotes the Euclidean norm in $\mathbb{R}^d$. We denote by c a generic constant that may depend on fixed parameters such as κ and d, whose value may change from line to line. Furthermore, we write $A \sim B$ if there exists a constant $c > 0$ such that $A \geq cB$ and $B \geq cA$.

2. Preliminaries

In this section, we describe the material necessary for the spherical h-harmonic analysis of the sphere.

2.1. Dunkl Theory and Spherical h-Harmonic Expansions

Let $G \subset O(d)$ be a finite reflection group on $\mathbb{R}^d$. Let v be a nonzero vector in $\mathbb{R}^d$. The reflection σ_v along v is defined by

$$\sigma_v x = x - \frac{2\langle x, v\rangle}{\|v\|^2} v, \quad x \in \mathbb{R}^d,$$

that is the reflection with respect to the hyperplane perpendicular to v. Let R be the root system of G, normalized so that $\langle x, v\rangle = 2$ for all $v \in R$, and fix a positive subsystem R_+ of R. It is known that (see, for instance, [16]) the set of reflections in G coincides with the set $\{\sigma v : v \in R_+\}$, which also generates the group G. Let $\kappa : R \to [0, \infty), v \to \kappa_v = \kappa(v)$ be a nonnegative multiplicity function on R (i.e., a nonnegative G-invariant function on R). Define weight function,

$$h_\kappa(x) := \prod_{v \in R+} |\langle x, v\rangle|^{\kappa_v}, \quad x \in \mathbb{R}^d, \tag{1}$$

as a homogeneous function of degree $\gamma_\kappa = \sum_{v \in R_+} \kappa_v$ and invariant under G.

The sphere $\mathbb{S}^{d-1} := \{x \in \mathbb{R}^d : \|x\| = 1\}$ is a metric space equipped with the geodesic metric $\rho(x, y) := \arccos\langle x, y\rangle$, $x, y \in \mathbb{S}^{d-1}$ and the usual rotation-invariant surface Lebesgue measure $d\sigma(x)$. We denote by $B_r(x)$ the spherical cap $\{y \in \mathbb{S}^{d-1} : \rho(x, y) < r\}$ centered at $x \in \mathbb{S}^{d-1}$ and having radius $r > 0$. Given a positive constant c and a spherical cap $B = B_r(x) \subset \mathbb{S}^{d-1}$, we use the notation cB to denote the spherical cap $B_{cr}(x)$ with the same center as that of B but c times the radius of B. The weight function we shall consider on the sphere $\mathbb{S}^{d-1}$ is $h_\kappa^2(x)$, which can also be written as $h_\kappa^2(x) := \prod_{v\in R} |\langle x, v\rangle|^{2\kappa_v}$. Given a measurable set $E \subset \mathbb{S}^{d-1}$, we write $\text{meas}_\kappa(E) := \omega_d^\kappa \int_E h_\kappa^2(x)\, d\sigma(x)$, where

$$\omega_d^\kappa := \Big(\int_{\mathbb{S}^{d-1}} h_\kappa^2(x)\, d\sigma(x)\Big)^{-1}. \tag{2}$$

It is easily seen that for $0 < r \le \pi$, (see [17]),

$$\text{meas}_\kappa(B_r(x)) \sim r^{d-1} \prod_{v\in R_+}^{d} (|\langle x, v\rangle| + r)^{2\kappa_v}, \ \ x \in \mathbb{S}^{d-1}, \tag{3}$$

where the constants of equivalence depend only on d and κ. This in particular implies that meas_κ is a doubling measure on $\mathbb{S}^{d-1}$ satisfying that for any $x \in \mathbb{S}^{d-1}$ and $r \in (0,\pi)$,

$$\text{meas}_\kappa(B_{2^m r}(x)) \le C 2^{m s_\kappa} \text{meas}_\kappa(B_r(x)), \ \ m = 1, 2, \ldots,$$

where $C > 0$ is a constant depending only on κ and d, and s_κ is the smallest positive number s for which

$$\text{sup}_B \text{sup}_{m\in\mathbb{N}} \frac{\text{meas}_\kappa(2^m B)}{2^{ms}\text{meas}_\kappa(B)} \le C < \infty,$$

with the first supremum being taken over all spherical caps $B \subset \mathbb{S}^{d-1}$ with radius $\le 2^{-m}$.

Given $0 < p \le \infty$, we denote by $L^p(h_\kappa^2) \equiv L^p(h_\kappa^2; \mathbb{S}^{d-1})$ the Lebesgue L^p-space defined with respect to the measure $h_\kappa^2(x)d\sigma(x)$ on $\mathbb{S}^{d-1}$, and $\|\cdot\|_{\kappa,p}$ the L^p-norm of the space $L^p(h_\kappa^2; \mathbb{S}^{d-1})$. Denote Π_n^d be the space of all spherical polynomials of degree at most n on the sphere $\mathbb{S}^{d-1}$. Set $\Pi_{-1}^d = \{0\}$, and let $\mathcal{H}_n^d(h_\kappa^2)$ denote the orthogonal complement of the space Π_{n-1}^d in the Hilbert space $\Pi_n^d \subset L^2(h_\kappa^2)$ (relative to the norm of $L^2(h_\kappa^2)$). Then the $\mathcal{H}_n^d(h_\kappa^2)$, $n = 0, 1, \cdots$ are mutually orthogonal, finite-dimensional linear subspaces of $L^2(h_\kappa^2)$. Denote by $P_n(h_\kappa^2)$ the reproducing kernel of the space $\mathcal{H}_n^d(h_\kappa^2)$; that is,

$$P_n(h_\kappa^2; x, y) := \sum_{j=1}^{a_n^d} Y_{n,j}^\kappa(x)\overline{Y_{n,j}^\kappa(y)}, \ \ x, y \in \mathbb{S}^{d-1},$$

where $a_n^d = \dim \mathcal{H}_n^d(h_\kappa^2)$ and $\{Y_{n,j}^\kappa : \ j = 1, 2, \cdots, a_n^d\}$ is an orthonormal basis of the space $\mathcal{H}_n^d(h_\kappa^2) \subset L^2(h_\kappa^2)$. Then the standard Hilbert space theory shows that each $f \in L^2(h_\kappa^2)$ can be represented as an orthogonal series converging in the norm of $L^2(h_\kappa^2)$:

$$f = \sum_{n=0}^{\infty} \text{proj}_n(h_\kappa^2; f), \tag{4}$$

where $\text{proj}_n(h_\kappa^2) : L^2(h_\kappa^2; \mathbb{S}^{d-1}) \mapsto \mathcal{H}_n^d(h_\kappa^2)$ is the orthogonal projection operator, which can be expressed as an integral operator,

$$\text{proj}_n(h_\kappa^2; f, x) = \omega_d^\kappa \int_{\mathbb{S}^{d-1}} f(y) P_n(h_\kappa^2; x, y) h_\kappa^2(y) d\sigma(y), \ \ x \in \mathbb{S}^{d-1}. \tag{5}$$

Clearly, in the case of $h_\kappa(x) \equiv 1$, the orthogonal expansion in (4) coincides with the ordinary spherical harmonic expansion on $\mathbb{S}^{d-1}$.

Let $\Pi^d := \Pi(\mathbb{R}^d)$ be the linear space of algebraic polynomials on $\mathbb{R}^d$, and $\mathbb{P}_n^d$ be the space of homogeneous polynomials of degree n on $\mathbb{R}^d$. One of the most important results in the Dunkl theory states that, associated with a reflection group G and multiplicity κ, there exists a unique linear operator $V_\kappa : \Pi^d \to \Pi^d$ called the Dunkl intertwining operator, such that:

$$V_\kappa(\mathbb{P}_n^d) = \mathbb{P}_n^d, \ \ V_\kappa(1) = 1.$$

The intertwining operator V_κ commutes with the G-action; that is, $g^{-1} \circ V_\kappa \circ g = V_\kappa$ for all $g \in G$. Here and throughout, we use the notation $g \circ f(x) := f(gx)$ for $g \in G$, $f \in C(\mathbb{S}^{d-1})$, and $x \in \mathbb{S}^{d-1}$. An explicit "closed" form for the intertwining operator is known so far only in the case of $G = \mathbb{Z}_2^d$ (see [6,18]) and the case of $G = S_3$ (see [11,19]). At the moment, little information is known about the intertwining operator for general finite reflection groups other than $\mathbb{Z}_2^d$ and S_3, except the following important result of Rösler (see [8]).

Proposition 1 ([8] (Theorem 1.2 and Corollary 5.3)). *For every $x \in \mathbb{R}^d$ there exists a unique probability measure μ_x^κ on the Borel σ-algebra of $\mathbb{R}^d$ such that:*

$$V_\kappa P(x) = \int_{\mathbb{R}^d} P(\xi) d\mu_x^\kappa(\xi), \quad P \in \Pi_n^d.$$

Furthermore, the representing measures μ_x^κ are compactly supported in the convex hull $\widehat{G}_x := co\{gx : g \in G\}$ of the orbit of x under G, and satisfy:

$$\mu_{rx}^\kappa(E) = \mu_x^\kappa(r^{-1}E), \ \ and \ \ \mu_{gx}^\kappa(E) = \mu_x^\kappa(g^{-1}E)$$

for all $r > 0, g \in G$ and each Borel subset E of $\mathbb{R}^d$.

In the theory of spherical h-harmonics, a crucial fact is that the reproducing kernel $P_n(h_\kappa^2; x, y)$ can be expressed in terms of the intertwining operator V_κ as (see [18] (Theorems 3.1 and 3.2)):

$$P_n(h_\kappa^2; x, y) = \frac{n + \lambda_\kappa}{\lambda_\kappa} V_\kappa \left[C_n^{\lambda_\kappa}(\langle x, \cdot \rangle) \right](y), \quad x, y \in \mathbb{S}^{d-1} \tag{6}$$

with $\lambda_\kappa := \frac{d-2}{2} + \sum_{v \in R_+} \kappa_v$. By means of (5) and (6), the projection $\operatorname{proj}_n(h_\kappa^2; f)$ can be extended to all $f \in L^1(h_\kappa^2; \mathbb{S}^{d-1})$.

2.2. Jacobi Polynomials

We denote by $P_n^{(\alpha,\beta)}$ the usual Jacobi polynomial of degree n with indices α and β. According to [20] (4.21.2), we have:

$$P_n^{(\alpha,\beta)}(x) = \frac{1}{n!} \sum_{v=0}^{n} \binom{n}{v} (n + \alpha + \beta + 1) \cdots (n + \alpha + \beta + v) \times$$
$$\times (\alpha + v + 1) \cdots (\alpha + n) \left(\frac{x-1}{2} \right)^v,$$

where $x \in [-1, 1]$, $n = 0, 1, \ldots$, and the general coefficient,

$$\binom{n}{v} (n + \alpha + \beta + 1) \cdots (n + \alpha + \beta + v)(\alpha + v + 1) \cdots (\alpha + n),$$

has to be replaced by $(\alpha + 1)(\alpha + 2) \cdots (\alpha + n)$ for $v = 0$, and by $(n + \alpha + \beta + 1)(n + \alpha + \beta + 2) \cdots (2n + \alpha + \beta)$ for $v = n$. They are mutually orthogonal with respect to the weight function $\omega_{\alpha,\beta}(x) = (1-x)^\alpha (1+x)^\beta$ on $[-1, 1]$. In the case when $\alpha, \beta > -1$, we have the following well known estimate on the Jacobi polynomials [20] ((7.32.5) and (4.1.3)):

Lemma 1. *For an arbitrary real number α and $t \in [0, 1]$,*

$$|P_n^{(\alpha,\beta)}(t)| \le cn^{-1/2}(1 - t + n^{-2})^{-(\alpha+1/2)/2}. \tag{7}$$

The estimate on $[-1, 0]$ follows from the fact that $P_n^{(\alpha,\beta)}(t) = (-1)^n P_n^{(\beta,\alpha)}(-t)$.

Next, we denote by C_n^λ the usual Gegenbauer polynomial of degree n with parameter $\lambda > -\frac{1}{2}$. As is well known, for $\alpha > -1$:

$$C_n^{\alpha+\frac{1}{2}}(x) = \frac{\Gamma(\alpha+1)}{\Gamma(2\alpha+1)}\frac{\Gamma(n+2\alpha+1)}{\Gamma(n+\alpha+1)}P_n^{(\alpha,\alpha)}(x).$$

2.3. Doubling Weights on the Sphere

Given a weight function w on $\mathbb{S}^{d-1}$, we write $w(E) := \int_E w(x)d\sigma(x)$ for $E \subset \mathbb{S}^{d-1}$. A weight function ω on $\mathbb{S}^{d-1}$ is called a doubling weight if there exists a constant $L > 0$ such that

$$w(2B) \le Lw(B), \text{ for all spherical caps } B \subset \mathbb{S}^{d-1},$$

where the least constant L is called the doubling constant of w. The following lemma collects some useful properties on doubling weights [21]:

Proposition 2. *Let w be a doubling weight on $\mathbb{S}^{d-1}$ with the doubling constant L. Then the following statements hold:*

1. *There exists a positive number s such that:*

$$w(2^m B) \le C2^{ms}w(B),\ \forall m \in \mathbb{N},\ \forall \text{ spherical caps } B \subset \mathbb{S}^{d-1}, \tag{8}$$

where the constant C is independent of m and B.

2. *For $0 < r < t$, and $x \in \mathbb{S}^{d-1}$,*

$$w(B_t(x)) \le C\left(\frac{t}{r}\right)^s w(B_r(x)), \tag{9}$$

where s is a positive number satisfying (8).

3. *For $0 < r < \pi$, and $x, y \in \mathbb{S}^{d-1}$,*

$$w(B_r(x)) \le C(1 + r^{-1}\rho(x,y))^s w(B_r(y)), \tag{10}$$

where s is a positive number satisfying (8).

As we stated for Equations (2) and (3), the weight function

$$h_\kappa(x) := \prod_{\nu\in R_+} |\langle x,\nu\rangle|^{\kappa_v}$$

satisfies the doubling condition. Indeed, a slight modification of the proof in [22] (5.3) shows that for $r \in (0,\pi)$ and $x \in \mathbb{S}^{d-1}$,

$$\int_{B_r(x)} h_\kappa^2(x)d\sigma(x) \sim r^{d-1} \prod_{\nu\in R_+} (|\langle x,\nu\rangle| + r)^{2\kappa_\nu}.$$

Thus, for a spherical cap $B := B_\theta(x)$ with $x \in \mathbb{S}^{d-1}$ and $\theta \in (0,\pi)$,

$$\text{meas}_\kappa(B) \sim \theta^{d-1} \prod_{\nu\in R_+} (|\langle x,\nu\rangle| + \theta)^{\kappa_\nu}, \tag{11}$$

which, in particular, implies that h_κ^2 is a doubling weight on $\mathbb{S}^{d-1}$.

2.4. Weighted Christoffel Functions

The main tool in our study is the weighted Christoffel function defined for a weight function w on $\mathbb{S}^{d-1}$ by

$$\lambda_n(w,x) := \inf_{P_n(x)=1} \int_{\mathbb{S}^{d-1}} |P_n(x)|^2 w(x) d\sigma(x), \ n = 0,1,2,\ldots,$$

where the infimum is taken over all spherical polynomials of degree n on $\mathbb{S}^{d-1}$ that take the value 1 at the point $x \in \mathbb{S}^{d-1}$. The connection between weighted Christoffel functions and weighted orthogonal polynomial expansions can be seen in the following lemma.

Lemma 2. *Let $P_{n,1}, \cdots, P_{n,a_n}$ be an orthonormal basis of the space Π_n^d with respect to the inner product $\langle f, g \rangle_w := \int_{\mathbb{S}^{d-1}} f(x)g(x)w(x)d\sigma(x)$. Then,*

$$\lambda_n(w,x) = \left(\sum_{j=1}^{a_n} |P_{n,j}(x)|^2 \right)^{-1}, \ x \in \mathbb{S}^{d-1}.$$

Lemma 3. *If w is a doubling weight on $\mathbb{S}^{d-1}$, then for $x \in \mathbb{S}^{d-1}$ and $n \in \mathbb{N}$,*

$$\lambda_n(w,x) \sim \int_{B_{n^{-1}}(x)} w(y) d\sigma(y),$$

where the constant of equivalence is independent of x and n.

We will then deduce the following lemma and proposition, which generalize the results of [23] (Lemma 3.5 and Theorem 3.1).

Lemma 4. *For each positive integer n, there exists a non-negative algebraic polynomial of degree n of the form:*

$$P_n(t) = \sum_{j=0}^{n} c_{n,j} \frac{j+\lambda_\kappa}{\lambda_\kappa} C_j^{\lambda_\kappa}(t), \quad t \in [-1,1], \tag{12}$$

which satisfies that:

$$P_n(\cos\theta) \sim n^\beta (1+n\theta)^{-\alpha}, \quad \theta \in (0,\pi), \tag{13}$$

and

$$\sup_j |c_{n,j}| = \begin{cases} n^{\beta-2\lambda_\kappa-1} & \text{if } \alpha > 2\lambda_\kappa + 1 \\ n^{\beta-2\lambda_\kappa-1}\log n & \text{if } \alpha = 2\lambda_\kappa + 1 \\ n^{\beta-\alpha} & \text{if } \alpha < 2\lambda_\kappa + 1. \end{cases} \tag{14}$$

Proof. We first prove (13). By Lemma 4.6 of [22], we can set $f(x) = n^\beta(1+nd(x,e))^{-\alpha}$ where $e \in \mathbb{S}^{d-1}$ be a fixed point, and prove that such f satisfies [22] (Lemma 4.6, (4.10)). That is, there exists α', such that:

$$(1+nd(x,e))^{-\alpha}(1+nd(y,e))^{\alpha} \le (1+nd(x,y))^{\alpha'}.$$

In fact, if $d(x,e) = d(y,e)$, then

$$\text{LHS} = (1+nd(x,e))^{-\alpha}(1+nd(y,e))^{\alpha} = 1 \le (1+nd(x,e))^{\alpha'}$$

for some $\alpha' \ge 0$. If $d(x,e) > d(y,e)$, we have

$$\text{LHS} = (1+nd(x,e))^{-\alpha}(1+nd(y,e))^{\alpha} \le (1+nd(x,e))^{-\alpha}(1+nd(x,e))^{\alpha} = 1 \le (1+nd(x,e))^{\alpha'}$$

for some $\alpha' \geq 0$. Lastly, if $d(x,e) < d(y,e)$, we have

$$\text{LHS} = \left(\frac{1+nd(y,e)}{1+nd(x,e)}\right)^{\alpha} = \left(\frac{1+nd(x,e)+nd(y,e)-nd(x,e)}{1+nd(x,e)}\right)^{\alpha}$$
$$\leq \left(1+\frac{nd(x,y)}{1+nd(x,e)}\right)^{\alpha} \leq (1+nd(x,y))^{\alpha'}$$

for some $\alpha' \geq 0$. Then, by Lemma 4.6 of [22] and setting $p=1, \theta = d(x,e)$, we can confirm there exists a non-negative algebraic polynomial $g = P_n(\cos\theta)$ such that $P_n(\cos\theta) \sim n^{\beta}(1+n\theta)^{-\alpha}$. Let the ultraspherical polynomial expansion of P_n be given by (12). It remains to show (14). We apply the same argument in [23] (Lemma 3.5). Recall that

$$\|C_j^{\lambda_\kappa}\|_{2,\lambda_\kappa}^2 = \frac{c}{j+\lambda_\kappa} C_j^{\lambda_\kappa}(1) = \frac{c'}{j+\lambda_\kappa}\frac{\Gamma(2\lambda_\kappa + j)}{\Gamma(j+1)} \sim j^{2\lambda_\kappa - 2},$$

and

$$\max_{\theta\in[0,\pi]} |C_j^{\lambda_\kappa}(\cos\theta)| = |C_j^{\lambda_\kappa}(1)| \sim j^{2\lambda_\kappa - 1},$$

here $\|\cdot\|_{2,\lambda_\kappa}$ denotes the L^2-norm computed with respect to the measure $(1-t^2)^{\lambda_\kappa - \frac{1}{2}}$ on $[-1,1]$. By orthogonality of the ultraspherical polynomials, we have:

$$j^{2\lambda_\kappa-1}|c_{n,j}| \sim |c_{n,j}|\frac{j+\lambda_\kappa}{\lambda_\kappa}\|C_j^{\lambda_\kappa}\|_{2,\lambda_\kappa}^2 = c\left|\int_0^{\pi} P_n(\cos\theta) C_j^{\lambda_\kappa}(\cos\theta)(\sin\theta)^{2\lambda_\kappa} d\theta\right|$$
$$\leq c n^{\beta} j^{2\lambda_\kappa - 1}\int_0^{\pi}(1+n\theta)^{-\alpha}(\sin\theta)^{2\lambda_\kappa} d\theta.$$

By the known fact that:

$$\int_0^{\pi}(1+n\theta)^{-a}\theta^b d\theta \sim \begin{cases} n^{-a} & \text{if } a < b+1 \\ n^{-b-1} & \text{if } a > b+1 \\ n^{-a}\log n & \text{if } a = b+1, \end{cases}$$

we then have

$$\sup_j |c_{n,j}| = \begin{cases} n^{\beta - 2\lambda_\kappa - 1} & \text{if } \alpha > 2\lambda_\kappa + 1 \\ n^{\beta-2\lambda_\kappa-1}\log n & \text{if } \alpha = 2\lambda_\kappa + 1 \\ n^{\beta-\alpha} & \text{if } \alpha < 2\lambda_\kappa + 1. \end{cases} \tag{15}$$

□

Proposition 3. *Let $\Phi_n, n = 1, 2, \cdots$, be a sequence of continuous functions on $[-1,1]$ satisfying that:*

$$|\Phi_n(\cos\theta)| \leq c n^{\beta}(1+n\theta)^{-\alpha}. \tag{16}$$

Then we have for any $x, y \in \mathbb{S}^{d-1}$,

$$V_\kappa[\Phi_n(\langle y,\cdot\rangle)](x) \leq c\begin{cases} n^{\beta-2\lambda_\kappa-1}\frac{(1+n\tilde{\rho}(x,y))^{-\alpha+\tau+\frac{s_\kappa}{2}}}{meas_\kappa(B_{n^{-1}}(x))} & \text{if } \alpha > 2\lambda_\kappa+1, \\ n^{\beta-2\lambda_\kappa-1}(\log n)\cdot\frac{(1+n\tilde{\rho}(x,y))^{\frac{s_\kappa}{2}}}{meas_\kappa(B_{n^{-1}}(x))} & \text{if } \alpha = 2\lambda_\kappa+1 \\ n^{\beta-\alpha}\frac{(1+n\tilde{\rho}(x,y))^{s_\kappa/2}}{meas_\kappa(B_{n^{-1}}(x))} & \text{if } \alpha < 2\lambda_\kappa+1, \end{cases}$$

where τ is a positive number satisfying $2\lambda_\kappa + 1 < \tau \leq \alpha$, and $\tilde{\rho}(x,y) = \min_{g\in G}\rho(gx,y)$ for $x, y \in \mathbb{S}^{d-1}$.

Proof. This is the analogue of [23] (Theorem 3.1). Using Proposition 1, we have

$$V_\kappa[\Phi_n(\langle y,\cdot\rangle)](x)=\int_{\widehat{G}_x}\Phi_n(\langle y,z\rangle)d\mu_x(z),$$

where $\widehat{G}_x$ denotes the convex hull of the orbit $G_x:=\{gx:g\in G\}$ of x under the group G. Since the group G has finite order, it follows that every element $z\in\widehat{G}_x$ can be written in the form $z=\sum_{g\in G}t_{g,z}gx$ for some $t_{g,z}\in[0,1]$ satisfying $\sum_{g\in G}t_{g,z}=1$. This implies that

$$\langle z,y\rangle=\sum_{g\in G}t_{g,z}\langle gx,y\rangle\le\max_{g\in G}\langle gx,y\rangle,\quad\forall z\in\widehat{G}_x,$$

and

$$\rho(z,y)\ge\min_{g\in G}\rho(gx,y)=:\widetilde{\rho}(x,y),\quad\forall z\in\widehat{G}_x.$$

Thus, using (16), we deduce that:

$$V_\kappa[\Phi_n(\langle y,\cdot\rangle)](x)\le V_\kappa\Big[n^\beta(1+n\rho(\cdot,y))^{-\alpha})\Big](x)=\int_{\widehat{G}_x}n^\beta(1+n\rho(z,y))^{-\alpha}d\mu_x(z).\qquad(17)$$

(i) If $\alpha>2\lambda_\kappa+1$, we have

$$\int_{\widehat{G}_x}n^\beta(1+n\rho(z,y))^{-\alpha}d\mu_x(z)\le(1+n\widetilde{\rho}(x,y))^{-\alpha+\tau}n^{\beta-2\lambda_\kappa-1}\int_{\widehat{G}_x}n^{2\lambda_\kappa+1}(1+n\rho(z,y))^{-\tau}d\mu_x(z).$$

Since $\tau>2\lambda_\kappa+1$, we can use the Lemma 4 and follow the same argument as in the proof of [23] (Theorem 3.1, (3.12)) to get

$$\int_{\widehat{G}_x}n^{2\lambda_\kappa+1}(1+n\rho(z,y))^{-\tau}d\mu_x(z)\le c\frac{(1+n\widetilde{\rho}(x,y))^{s_\kappa/2}}{\mathrm{meas}_\kappa(B_{n^{-1}}(x))},$$

and thus

$$V_\kappa[\Phi_n(\langle y,\cdot\rangle)](x)\le n^{\beta-2\lambda_\kappa-1}\frac{(1+n\widetilde{\rho}(x,y))^{-\alpha+\tau+\frac{s_\kappa}{2}}}{\mathrm{meas}_\kappa(B_{n^{-1}}(x))};$$

(ii) If $\alpha<2\lambda_\kappa+1$, we use the linearity of V_κ, Lemma 4, and the fact that

$$V_\kappa[\frac{\lambda_\kappa+j}{\lambda_\kappa}C_j^\lambda(\langle\cdot,y\rangle)](x)=\sum_{k=1}^{a_j}p_{j,k}(x)p_{j,k}(y),\quad x,y\in\mathbb{S}^{d-1},$$

where $\{p_{j,k}\}_{k=1}^{a_j}$ be an orthonormal basis of the space $\mathcal{H}_j^d(h_\kappa^2)$, to get:

$$\begin{aligned}\int_{\widehat{G}_x}n^\beta(1+n\rho(z,y))^{-\alpha}d\mu_x(z)&=\int_{\widehat{G}_x}P_n(\langle y,z\rangle)d\mu_x(z)=V_\kappa\left[\sum_{j=0}^n c_{n,j}\frac{j+\lambda_\kappa}{\lambda_\kappa}C_j^{\lambda_\kappa}(\langle y,\cdot\rangle)\right](x)\\&=\sum_{j=0}^n c_{n,j}\frac{j+\lambda_\kappa}{\lambda_\kappa}V_\kappa\Big[C_j^{\lambda_\kappa}(\langle y,\cdot\rangle)\Big](x)=\sum_{j=0}^n\sum_{k=1}^{a_j}c_{n,j}p_{j,k}(x)p_{j,k}(y).\end{aligned}$$

Then by (17), Lemma 4, and Hölder's inequality, we have:

$$\begin{aligned} V_\kappa[\Phi_n(\langle y,\cdot\rangle)](x) &\le cn^{\beta-\alpha}\sum_{j=0}^{n}\sum_{k=1}^{a_j}|p_{j,k}(x)p_{j,k}(y)| \\ &\le cn^{\beta-\alpha}\left(\sum_{j=0}^{n}\sum_{k=1}^{a_j}p_{j,k}(x)^2\right)^{1/2}\left(\sum_{j=0}^{n}\sum_{k=1}^{a_j}p_{j,k}(y)^2\right)^{1/2} \\ &\le cn^{\beta-\alpha}\left(\int_{B_{n^{-1}}(x)}h_\kappa^2(z)d\sigma(z)\right)^{-\frac{1}{2}}\left(\int_{B_{n^{-1}}(y)}h_\kappa^2(z)d\sigma(z)\right)^{-\frac{1}{2}} \\ &\le cn^{\beta-\alpha}\frac{(1+n\widetilde{\rho}(x,y))^{s_\kappa/2}}{\mathrm{meas}_\kappa(B_{n^{-1}}(x))}, \end{aligned}$$

where the last second inequality is followed by Lemmas 2 and 3. The last inequality followed by the fact the weight h_κ^2 is invariant under the group G, and by using (10), we have

$$\int_{B_{n^{-1}}(x)}h_\kappa^2(z)d\sigma(z)=\int_{B_{n^{-1}}(g_0x)}h_\kappa^2(z)d\sigma(z)\le c\big(1+n\rho(g_0x,y)\big)^{s_\kappa}\int_{B_{n^{-1}}(y)}h_\kappa^2(z)d\sigma(z),$$

where $g_0\in G$ is such that $\rho(g_0x,y)=\widetilde{\rho}(x,y)=\min_{g\in G}\rho(gx,y)$ for $x,y\in\mathbb{S}^{d-1}$;

(iii) If $\alpha=2\lambda_\kappa+1$, following the same idea as (ii), and using the Lemma 4, we have:

$$\begin{aligned} &\int_{\widehat{G}_x}n^\beta(1+n\rho(z,y))^{-\alpha}d\mu_x(z) \\ &\quad=\int_{\widehat{G}_x}P_n(\langle y,z\rangle)d\mu_x(z)=V_\kappa\Big[\sum_{j=0}^{n}c_{n,j}\frac{j+\lambda_\kappa}{\lambda_\kappa}C_j^{\lambda_\kappa}(\langle y,\cdot\rangle)\Big](x) \\ &\quad=\sum_{j=0}^{n}c_{n,j}\frac{j+\lambda_\kappa}{\lambda_\kappa}V_\kappa\big[C_j^{\lambda_\kappa}(\langle y,\cdot\rangle)\big](x) \\ &\quad\le cn^{\beta-2\lambda_\kappa-1}(\log n)\sum_{j=0}^{n}\sum_{k=1}^{a_j}|p_{j,k}(x)p_{j,k}(y)| \\ &\quad\le cn^{\beta-2\lambda_\kappa-1}(\log n)\left(\sum_{j=0}^{n}\sum_{k=1}^{a_j}p_{j,k}(x)^2\right)^{1/2}\left(\sum_{j=0}^{n}\sum_{k=1}^{a_j}p_{j,k}(y)^2\right)^{1/2} \\ &\quad\le cn^{\beta-2\lambda_\kappa-1}(\log n)\left(\int_{B_{n^{-1}}(x)}h_\kappa^2(z)d\sigma(z)\right)^{-\frac{1}{2}}\left(\int_{B_{n^{-1}}(y)}h_\kappa^2(z)d\sigma(z)\right)^{-\frac{1}{2}} \\ &\quad\le cn^{\beta-2\lambda_\kappa-1}(\log n)\frac{(1+n\widetilde{\rho}(x,y))^{s_\kappa/2}}{\mathrm{meas}_\kappa(B_{n^{-1}}(x))}. \end{aligned}$$

□

3. Main Results

We define the n-th Cesàro mean of order $\delta>0$ of the WOPE (4) of f by:

$$S_n^\delta(h_\kappa^2;f,x):=\frac{1}{A_n^\delta}\sum_{j=0}^{n}A_{n-j}^\delta\mathrm{proj}_j(h_\kappa^2;f,x),\ \ x\in\mathbb{S}^{d-1},$$

where $A_j^\delta=\frac{\Gamma(j+\delta+1)}{\Gamma(j+1)\Gamma(\delta+1)}$ for $j=0,1,\cdots$. According to (5), the Cesàro (C,δ) operators $S_n^\delta(h_\kappa^2)$ can be represented as:

$$S_n^\delta(h_\kappa^2;f,x)=\omega_d^\kappa\int_{\mathbb{S}^{d-1}}f(y)K_n^\delta(h_\kappa^2;x,y)h_\kappa^2(y)\,d\sigma(y),\ \ x\in\mathbb{S}^{d-1},$$

where

$$K_n^\delta(h_\kappa^2; x, y) = \sum_{j=0}^{n} \frac{A_{n-j}^\delta}{A_n^\delta} P_j(h_\kappa^2; x, y), \quad x, y \in \mathbb{S}^{d-1}.$$

The main point-wise estimate of the Cesàro kernel is as follows:

Theorem 1. *For $\delta > 0$ and $\ell \geq \tau > 2\lambda_\kappa + 1$, we have:*

$$\begin{aligned}|K_n^\delta(h_\kappa^2; x, y)| \leq & c_\kappa \cdot \Bigg[n^{-1} \sum_{j=1}^{n} (1+j)^{d-1} \cdot \frac{\prod_{v \in R_+} (|\langle x, v\rangle| + |\langle g_0 y, v\rangle| + \tilde{\rho}(x, y) + j^{-1})^{-2\kappa_v}}{(1 + j\tilde{\rho}(x, y))^{\lambda_\kappa + \ell - \tau - \frac{3}{2}s_\kappa + d - 1}} \\ & + \sum_{i=2}^{\lfloor \log_2 n \rfloor + 2} 2^{-i - i\delta + i\ell} \frac{n^{d-1}(1 + n\tilde{\rho}(x, y))^{-\ell + \tau + \frac{3}{2}s_\kappa - d + 1}}{\prod_{v \in R_+} (|\langle x, v\rangle| + |\langle g_0 y, v\rangle| + \tilde{\rho}(x, y) + n^{-1})^{2\kappa_v}} \\ & + \frac{n^{d-\delta-1}(1 + n\tilde{\rho}(x, y))^{\frac{3}{2}s_\kappa - d + 1}}{\prod_{v \in R_+} (|\langle x, v\rangle| + |\langle g_0 y, v\rangle| + n^{-1} + \tilde{\rho}(x, y))^{2\kappa_v}} \Bigg],\end{aligned}$$

where $g_0 \in G$ is such that $\rho(g_0 x, y) = \tilde{\rho}(x, y) = \min_{g \in G} \rho(gx, y)$ for $x, y \in \mathbb{S}^{d-1}$.

Our second main result can be stated as follows:

Theorem 2. *Let $\delta > 0$ and $\tau > 2\lambda_\kappa + 1$. Then*

$$\int_{\mathbb{S}^{d-1}} |K_n^\delta(h_\kappa^2; x, y)| h_\kappa^2(y) d\sigma(y) \leq \begin{cases} 1 & \text{if } \delta > \frac{3}{2}s_\kappa + \tau - 1 \\ \log n & \text{if } \delta = \frac{3}{2}s_\kappa + \tau - 1 \\ n^{-\delta + \frac{3}{2}s_\kappa - \tau + 1} & \text{if } \delta < \frac{3}{2}s_\kappa + \tau - 1\,. \end{cases}$$

As a consequence of the main kernel estimate, we can immediately obtain the following convergence result:

Corollary 1. *Let $\tau > 2\lambda_\kappa + 1$ and $\sigma_\kappa := \frac{3}{2}s_\kappa + \tau - 1$. Then if $\delta > \sigma_\kappa$, $S_n^\delta(h_\kappa^2; f)$ converges in $L^p(h_\kappa^2; \mathbb{S}^{d-1})$ for all $1 \leq p \leq \infty$.*

In Section 5, we will also establish similar results for WOPEs on unit ball $\mathbb{B}^d$ and the simplex $\mathbb{T}^d$, with weights being given by:

$$W_{\kappa,\mu}^B(x) := h_\kappa^2(x) \left(1 - \|x\|^2\right)^{\mu - 1/2}, \quad \mu \geq 0, x \in \mathbb{B}^d,$$

and

$$W_{\kappa,\mu}^T(x) := \frac{h_\kappa^2(\sqrt{x_1}, \cdots, \sqrt{x_d})}{\sqrt{x_1 \cdots x_d}} (1 - |x|)^{\mu - 1/2}, \quad \mu \geq 0, x \in \mathbb{T}^d,$$

respectively.

4. Proofs of Main Theorems

In this section, we will give the proofs of Theorems 1 and 2. Our main references are [12,14,23].

4.1. Proof of Theorem 1

Let $\varphi_0 \in C^\infty[0, \infty)$ be such that $\chi_{[0,1]} \leq \varphi_0 \leq \chi_{[0,2]}$, where χ_E denotes the characteristic function of the interval E, and let $\varphi(t) := \varphi_0(t) - \varphi_0(2t)$. Clearly, φ is a C^∞-function supported in $(\frac{1}{2}, 2)$ and satisfying $\sum_{i=0}^{\infty} \varphi(2^i t) = \varphi_0(t)$ for all $t > 0$. Thus, let $t = \frac{n-j}{n}$, we have $\sum_{i=0}^{\lfloor \log_2 n \rfloor + 2} \varphi\left(\frac{2^i(n-j)}{n}\right) = 1$ for $0 \leq j \leq n - 1$.

We decompose the Cesàro kernel as follows:

$$\begin{aligned}K_n^\delta(h_\kappa^2;x,y) &= \sum_{j=0}^{n}\frac{A_{n-j}^\delta}{A_n^\delta}\frac{\lambda_\kappa+j}{\lambda_\kappa}V_\kappa\Big[C_j^{\lambda_\kappa}(\langle x,\cdot\rangle)\Big](y)\\ &= \sum_{i=0}^{\lfloor\log_2 n\rfloor+2}\sum_{j=0}^{n}\varphi\Big(\frac{2^i(n-j)}{n}\Big)\frac{A_{n-j}^\delta}{A_n^\delta}\frac{\lambda_\kappa+j}{\lambda_\kappa}V_\kappa\Big[C_j^{\lambda_\kappa}(\langle x,\cdot\rangle)\Big](y)\\ &\quad+\frac{1}{A_n^\delta}\frac{\lambda_\kappa+n}{\lambda_\kappa}V_\kappa\Big[C_n^{\lambda_\kappa}(\langle x,\cdot\rangle)\Big](y) \qquad (18)\\ &= \sum_{i=0}^{\lfloor\log_2 n\rfloor+2}V_\kappa\big[\Psi_{\varphi_i}(\langle x,\cdot\rangle)\big](y)+\frac{1}{A_n^\delta}\frac{\lambda_\kappa+n}{\lambda_\kappa}V_\kappa\Big[C_n^{\lambda_\kappa}(\langle x,\cdot\rangle)\Big](y), \qquad (19)\end{aligned}$$

where

$$\Psi_{\varphi_i}(\cos\theta)=\sum_{j=0}^{n}\varphi_i(\frac{j}{2^i})\frac{\lambda_\kappa+j}{\lambda_\kappa}C_j^{\lambda_\kappa}(\cos\theta),\ \text{ and }\ \varphi_i(t)=\varphi\Big(\frac{2^i(n-2^it)}{n}\Big)\frac{A_{n-2^it}^\delta}{A_n^\delta}.$$

To show the Theorem 1, we will consider three parts to estimate Equation (18):
Part 1: When $2\le i\le\lfloor\log_2 n\rfloor+2$;
Part 2: When $i=0,1$;
Part 3: The last term, i.e., the reproducing kernel.

We follow the proof of Lemma 3.3 of [24] (pp. 413–414). We shall use the following formula for Jacobi polynomials (see [20] (4.5.3)):

$$\begin{aligned}&\sum_{n=0}^{k}\frac{(2n+\alpha+\beta+j+1)\Gamma(n+\alpha+\beta+j+1)}{\Gamma(n+\beta+1)}P_n^{(\alpha+j,\beta)}(t) \qquad (20)\\ &\quad=\frac{\Gamma(k+\alpha+\beta+j+2)}{\Gamma(k+\beta+1)}P_k^{(\alpha+j+1,\beta)}(t),\end{aligned}$$

where $j=0,1,\cdots$.

Define a sequence of functions $\{a_{n,v,\ell}(\cdot)\}_{\ell=0}^\infty$ recursively by:

$$\begin{aligned}a_{n,i,0}(j)&=2(j+\lambda_\kappa)\varphi_i(\frac{j}{2^i})=2(j+\lambda_\kappa)\varphi\Big(\frac{2^i(n-j)}{n}\Big)\frac{A_{n-j}^\delta}{A_n^\delta},\\ a_{n,i,\ell+1}(j)&=\frac{a_{n,i,\ell}(j)}{2j+2\lambda_\kappa+\ell}-\frac{a_{n,i,\ell}(j+1)}{2j+2\lambda_\kappa+\ell+2}\qquad \ell\ge 0.\end{aligned}$$

Using (20) and summation by parts finite times, we have for any integer $\ell\ge 0$,

$$\Psi_{\varphi_i}(t)=\sum_{j=0}^{n}\varphi_i(\frac{j}{2^i})\frac{\lambda_\kappa+j}{\lambda_\kappa}C_j^{\lambda_\kappa}(t)=c_\kappa\sum_{j=0}^{\infty}a_{n,i,\ell}(j)\frac{\Gamma(j+2\lambda_\kappa+\ell)}{\Gamma(j+\lambda_\kappa+\frac12)}P_j^{(\lambda_\kappa+\ell-\frac12,\lambda_\kappa-\frac12)}(t), \qquad (21)$$

where $\lambda_\kappa=\frac{d-2}{2}+\sum_{v\in R_+}\kappa_v$.

Part 1: When $2\le i\le\lfloor\log_2 n\rfloor+2$

Note that $a_{n,i,\ell}(j)=0$ if $j+\ell\le(1-\frac{1}{2^{i-1}})n$ or $j\ge(1-\frac{1}{2^{i+1}})n$, so that the sum is over $j\sim n$. Furthermore, it follows from the definition, and Leibniz rule that

$$\Big|\Delta^\ell\Big(\varphi_i(\frac{j}{2^i})\Big)\Big|\le c2^{-i\delta}\Big(\frac{2^i}{n}\Big)^\ell,\qquad \forall\ell\in\mathbb{N},\ 0\le j\le n,$$

and

$$\left|\triangle^s a_{n,i,\ell}(j)\right| \leq c2^{-i\delta}n^{-\ell+1}\left(\frac{2^i}{n}\right)^{s+\ell}, \qquad s,\ell = 0,1,\cdots. \tag{22}$$

Consequently, using (21) and (22) with $s = 0$, and the following well-known estimates on Jacobi polynomials [20] (7.32.6) for $k \geq 1$ and $\alpha, \beta > -\frac{1}{2}$,

$$P_k^{(\alpha,\beta)}(\cos\theta) \leq C_{\alpha,\beta}\begin{cases}\min\{k^\alpha, k^{-\frac{1}{2}}\theta^{-\alpha-\frac{1}{2}}\} & \text{if } 0 \leq \theta \leq \frac{\pi}{2}\\ \min\{k^\beta, k^{-\frac{1}{2}}(\pi-\theta)^{-\beta-\frac{1}{2}}\} & \text{if } \frac{\pi}{2} \leq \theta \leq \pi,\end{cases}$$

we obtain for $\theta \in [0, n^{-1}]$, and $\ell \geq 1$,

$$\begin{aligned}|\Psi_{\varphi_i}(\cos\theta)| &= |c_\kappa\sum_{j=0}^{n} a_{n,i,\ell}(j)\frac{\Gamma(j+2\lambda_\kappa+\ell)}{\Gamma(j+\lambda_\kappa+\frac{1}{2})}P_j^{(\lambda_\kappa+\ell-\frac{1}{2},\lambda_\kappa-\frac{1}{2})}(\cos\theta)|\\ &\leq c_\kappa \sum_{\substack{j\sim n\\ n-j\sim\frac{n}{2^i}}} 2^{-i\delta}n^{-\ell+1}\left(\frac{2^i}{n}\right)^{\ell}\cdot(j+\lambda_\kappa+\frac{1}{2})^{\lambda_\kappa+\ell-\frac{1}{2}}\cdot j^{\lambda_\kappa+\ell-\frac{1}{2}}\\ &\leq c_\kappa\cdot 2^{-i-i\delta+i\ell}\cdot n^{2\lambda_\kappa+1}.\end{aligned}$$

For $\theta \in [n^{-1}, \frac{\pi}{2}]$ and $\ell \geq 1$,

$$\begin{aligned}|\Psi_{\varphi_i}(\cos\theta)| &= |c_\kappa\sum_{j=0}^{n} a_{n,i,\ell}(j)\frac{\Gamma(j+2\lambda_\kappa+\ell)}{\Gamma(j+\lambda_\kappa+\frac{1}{2})}P_j^{(\lambda_\kappa+\ell-\frac{1}{2},\lambda_\kappa-\frac{1}{2})}(\cos\theta)|\\ &\leq c_\kappa \sum_{\substack{j\sim n\\ n-j\sim\frac{n}{2^i}}} 2^{-i\delta}n^{-\ell+1}\left(\frac{2^i}{n}\right)^{\ell}\cdot(j+\lambda_\kappa+\frac{1}{2})^{\lambda_\kappa+\ell-\frac{1}{2}}\cdot j^{-\frac{1}{2}}\theta^{-(\lambda_\kappa+\ell)}\\ &\leq c_\kappa\cdot 2^{-i-i\delta+i\ell}\cdot n^{2\lambda_\kappa+1}(n\theta)^{-(\lambda_\kappa+\ell)}.\end{aligned}$$

For $\theta \in [\frac{\pi}{2}, \pi]$ and $\ell \geq 1$,

$$\begin{aligned}|\Psi_{\varphi_i}(\cos\theta)| &= c_\kappa\sum_{j=0}^{\infty} a_{n,i,\ell}(j)\frac{\Gamma(j+2\lambda_\kappa+\ell)}{\Gamma(j+\lambda_\kappa+\frac{1}{2})}P_j^{(\lambda_\kappa+\ell-\frac{1}{2},\lambda_\kappa-\frac{1}{2})}(\cos\theta)\\ &\leq c_\kappa \sum_{\substack{j\sim n\\ n-j\sim\frac{n}{2^i}}} |a_{n,i,\ell}(j)|\cdot(j+\lambda_\kappa+\frac{1}{2})^{\lambda_\kappa+\ell-\frac{1}{2}}\cdot j^{\lambda_\kappa-\frac{1}{2}}\\ &\sim c_\kappa\cdot n^{-\ell+2\lambda_\kappa+1}\cdot 2^{-i-i\delta+i\ell}\\ &\sim c_\kappa\cdot 2^{-i-i\delta+i\ell}\cdot n^{2\lambda_\kappa+1}(n\theta)^{-\ell}.\end{aligned}$$

So, when $2 \leq i \leq \lfloor\log_2 n\rfloor + 2$, we have

$$|\Psi_{\varphi_i}(\cos\theta)| \leq c_\kappa\cdot 2^{-i-i\delta+i\ell}\cdot n^{2\lambda_\kappa+1}\min\{1,(n\theta)^{-\ell}\} \sim c_\kappa\cdot 2^{-i-i\delta+i\ell}\cdot n^{2\lambda_\kappa+1}(1+n\theta)^{-\ell}.$$

Then applying the Proposition 3, we can get for $\ell \geq \tau > 2\lambda_\kappa + 1$,

$$V_\kappa\left[\Psi_{\varphi_i}(\langle x,\cdot\rangle)\right](y) \leq c_\kappa\cdot 2^{-i-i\delta+i\ell}\frac{(1+n\widetilde{\rho}(x,y))^{-\ell+\tau+s_\kappa/2}}{\text{meas}_\kappa(B_{n^{-1}}(x))}.$$

Following along the same arguments as in [23] (Theorem 3.1, p. 569), we let $m \in \mathbb{N}$ be such that $2^m n^{-1} \sim n^{-1} + \widetilde{\rho}(x,y)$ and use the fact (9) to obtain

$$\text{meas}_\kappa(B_{n^{-1}+\widetilde{\rho}(x,y)}(x)) \leq c2^{ms_\kappa}\text{meas}_\kappa(B_{n^{-1}}(x)) \leq c(1+n\widetilde{\rho}(x,y))^{s_\kappa}\text{meas}_\kappa(B_{n^{-1}}(x)), \tag{23}$$

and by the equivalent,

$$\widetilde{\rho}(x,y)+n^{-1}+|\langle x,\nu\rangle|\sim|\langle x,\nu\rangle|+|\langle g_0y,\nu\rangle|+\widetilde{\rho}(x,y)+n^{-1}, \tag{24}$$

we then have

$$V_\kappa\big[\Psi_{\varphi_i}(\langle x,\cdot\rangle)\big](y)\le c_\kappa\cdot 2^{-i-i\delta+i\ell}\frac{n^{d-1}(1+n\widetilde{\rho}(x,y))^{-\ell+\tau+\frac{3}{2}s_\kappa-d+1}}{\prod_{\nu\in R_+}(|\langle x,\nu\rangle|+|\langle g_0y,\nu\rangle|+\widetilde{\rho}(x,y)+n^{-1})^{2\kappa_\nu}}. \tag{25}$$

Thus,

$$\sum_{i=2}^{\lfloor\log_2 n\rfloor+2}V_\kappa\big[\Psi_{\varphi_v}(\langle x,\cdot\rangle)\big](y)\le c_\kappa\sum_{i=2}^{\lfloor\log_2 n\rfloor+2}2^{-i-i\delta+i\ell}\frac{n^{d-1}(1+n\widetilde{\rho}(x,y))^{-\ell+\tau+\frac{3}{2}s_\kappa-d+1}}{\prod_{\nu\in R_+}(|\langle x,\nu\rangle|+|\langle g_0y,\nu\rangle|+\widetilde{\rho}(x,y)+n^{-1})^{2\kappa_\nu}}. \tag{26}$$

Part 2: When $i=0,1$

Next, we deal with the cases of $i=0,1$.

The proof is very similar to that of Part 1. The difference here comes from the fact that the coefficients $\varphi_i(\frac{j}{2^i})$ for $i=0,1$ are supported in $0\le j\le\frac{3}{4}n$ rather than $\frac{n}{2}\le j\le n$. Indeed, for the case of $i=0,1$, we have to replace the estimates (22) by:

$$\left|\triangle^k a_{n,i,\ell}(j)\right|\le\begin{cases}cn^{-k-1}, & \text{if } \ell=1,\\ cn^{-1}(j+1)^{-k-2\ell+2}, & \text{if } \ell\ge 2.\end{cases} \tag{27}$$

Using (21), we obtain that for $i=0,1$ and any $\ell\ge 2$,

$$V_\kappa\big[\Psi_{\varphi_i}(\langle x,\cdot\rangle)\big](y)=c_\kappa\sum_{j=0}^{\frac{3}{4}n}a_{n,i,\ell}(j)\frac{\Gamma(j+2\lambda_\kappa+\ell)}{\Gamma(j+\lambda_\kappa+\frac{1}{2})}V_\kappa\left[P_j^{(\lambda_\kappa+\ell-\frac{1}{2},\lambda_\kappa-\frac{1}{2})}(\langle x,\cdot\rangle)\right](y). \tag{28}$$

By using Equation (7) with $t=\cos\theta$, $\alpha=\lambda_\kappa+\ell-\frac{1}{2}$, and $\beta=\lambda_\kappa-\frac{1}{2}$, we have

$$|P_n^{(\lambda_\kappa+\ell-\frac{1}{2},\lambda_\kappa-\frac{1}{2})}(\cos\theta)|\le cn^{\lambda_\kappa+\ell-\frac{1}{2}}(1+n\theta)^{-(\lambda_\kappa+\ell)}. \tag{29}$$

Then, to estimate $V_\kappa\left[P_j^{(\lambda_\kappa+\ell-\frac{1}{2},\lambda_\kappa-\frac{1}{2})}(\langle x,\cdot\rangle)\right](y)$ on the right-hand side of (28), by (29) and Proposition 3, we have for $\ell\ge\tau>2\lambda_\kappa+1$,

$$V_\kappa\left[P_j^{(\lambda_\kappa+\ell-\frac{1}{2},\lambda_\kappa-\frac{1}{2})}(\langle x,\cdot\rangle)\right](y)\le j^{\lambda_\kappa+\ell-\frac{1}{2}-2\lambda_\kappa-1}\frac{(1+j\widetilde{\rho}(x,y))^{-(\lambda_\kappa+\ell)+\tau+s_\kappa/2}}{\operatorname{meas}_\kappa(B_{j^{-1}}(x))}.$$

We then use a similar argument of the proof in (25) to obtain that:

$$\begin{aligned}V_\kappa\left[P_j^{(\lambda_\kappa+\ell-\frac{1}{2},\lambda_\kappa-\frac{1}{2})}(\langle x,\cdot\rangle)\right](y)&\le j^{\ell-\lambda_\kappa-\frac{3}{2}}\frac{j^{d-1}(1+j\widetilde{\rho}(x,y))^{-(\lambda_\kappa+\ell)+\tau+\frac{3}{2}s_\kappa-d+1}}{\prod_{\nu\in R_+}(|\langle x,\nu\rangle|+\widetilde{\rho}(x,y)+j^{-1})^{2\kappa_\nu}}\\ &\sim j^{\ell-\lambda_\kappa-\frac{3}{2}}\frac{j^{d-1}(1+j\widetilde{\rho}(x,y))^{-(\lambda_\kappa+\ell)+\tau+\frac{3}{2}s_\kappa-d+1}}{\prod_{\nu\in R_+}(|\langle x,\nu\rangle|+|\langle g_0y,\nu\rangle|+\widetilde{\rho}(x,y)+j^{-1})^{2\kappa_\nu}}.\end{aligned} \tag{30}$$

Consequently, using (27), (28) and (30) , we conclude that for $i=0,1$, and a large ℓ,

$$V_\kappa\left[\Psi_{\varphi_i}(\langle x,\cdot\rangle)\right](y) = c_\kappa \sum_{j=0}^{\frac{3}{4}n} a_{n,i,\ell}(j)\frac{\Gamma(j+2\lambda_\kappa+\ell)}{\Gamma(j+\lambda_\kappa+\frac{1}{2})} V_\kappa\left[P_j^{(\lambda_\kappa+\ell-\frac{1}{2},\lambda_\kappa-\frac{1}{2})}(\langle x,\cdot\rangle)\right](y)$$
$$\leq c_\kappa n^{-1}\sum_{j=1}^{n}(1+j)^{-2\ell+2}\cdot j^{\lambda_\kappa+\ell-\frac{1}{2}}\cdot j^{-\lambda_\kappa+\ell-\frac{3}{2}}\cdot j^{d-1}\frac{\prod_{\nu\in R_+}(|\langle x,\nu\rangle|+|\langle g_0 y,\nu\rangle|+\widetilde{\rho}(x,y)+j^{-1})^{-2\kappa_\nu}}{(1+j\widetilde{\rho}(x,y))^{\lambda_\kappa+\ell-\tau-\frac{3}{2}s_\kappa+d-1}}$$
$$\leq c_\kappa n^{-1}\sum_{j=1}^{n}(1+j)^{d-1}\cdot\frac{\prod_{\nu\in R_+}(|\langle x,\nu\rangle|+|\langle g_0 y,\nu\rangle|+\widetilde{\rho}(x,y)+j^{-1})^{-2\kappa_\nu}}{(1+j\widetilde{\rho}(x,y))^{\lambda_\kappa+\ell-\tau-\frac{3}{2}s_\kappa+d-1}}. \tag{31}$$

Part 3: The last term(reproducing kernel)
Finally, we consider the last term of (18):

$$\frac{1}{A_n^\delta}\frac{\lambda_\kappa+n}{\lambda_\kappa}V_\kappa\left[C_n^{\lambda_\kappa}(\langle x,\cdot\rangle)\right](y),$$

that is, the reproducing kernel $\frac{1}{A_n^\delta}\cdot P_n(h_\kappa^2;x,y)$. Similarly, let $p_{j,1},\ldots,p_{j,a_j}$ be an orthonormal basis of the space $\mathcal{H}_j^d(h_\kappa^2)$ with respect to the inner product of $L^2(h_\kappa^2;\mathbb{S}^{d-1})$. Then, we have

$$\sum_{k=1}^{a_j} p_{j,k}(x)p_{j,k}(y) = \frac{\lambda_\kappa+j}{\lambda_\kappa}V_\kappa\left[C_j^\lambda(\langle\cdot,y\rangle)\right](x),\quad x,y\in\mathbb{S}^{d-1}.$$

Thus,

$$P_n(h_\kappa^2;x,y) = \frac{\lambda_\kappa+n}{\lambda_\kappa}V_\kappa\left[C_n^\lambda(\langle\cdot,y\rangle)\right](x) = \sum_{k=1}^{a_n}p_{n,k}(x)p_{n,k}(y) \leq (\sum_{m=0}^{n-1}\sum_{k=1}^{a_m}+\sum_{k=1}^{a_n})p_{n,k}(x)p_{n,k}(y)$$
$$=\sum_{m=0}^{n}\sum_{k=1}^{a_m}p_{n,k}(x)p_{n,k}(y).$$

By the Hölder's inequality, Lemmas 2 and 3, (11) and (23), and the equivalent (24), we have:

$$|P_n(h_\kappa^2;x,y)| \leq \sum_{m=0}^{n}\sum_{k=1}^{a_m}|p_{n,k}(x)p_{n,k}(y)| \leq \left(\sum_{m=0}^{n}\sum_{k=1}^{a_m}|p_{n,k}(x)|^2\right)^{\frac{1}{2}}\left(\sum_{m=0}^{n}\sum_{k=1}^{a_m}|p_{n,k}(y)|^2\right)^{\frac{1}{2}}$$
$$\leq c\left(\int_{B_{n^{-1}}(x)}h_\kappa^2(z)d\sigma(z)\right)^{-\frac{1}{2}}\left(\int_{B_{n^{-1}}(y)}h_\kappa^2(z)d\sigma(z)\right)^{-\frac{1}{2}}$$
$$\leq c(1+n\widetilde{\rho}(x,y))^{s_\kappa/2}\left(\int_{B_{n^{-1}}(x)}h_\kappa^2(z)d\sigma(z)\right)^{-1}$$
$$\leq \frac{(1+n\widetilde{\rho}(x,y))^{s_\kappa/2}}{(1+n\widetilde{\rho}(x,y))^{-s_\kappa}\mathrm{meas}_\kappa(B_{n^{-1}+\widetilde{\rho}(x,y)}(x))} = \frac{(1+n\widetilde{\rho}(x,y))^{\frac{3}{2}s_\kappa}}{\mathrm{meas}_\kappa(B_{n^{-1}+\widetilde{\rho}(x,y)}(x))}$$
$$\sim \frac{(1+n\widetilde{\rho}(x,y))^{\frac{3}{2}s_\kappa}}{(n^{-1}+\widetilde{\rho}(x,y))^{d-1}\prod_{\nu\in R_+}(|\langle x,\nu\rangle|+n^{-1}+\widetilde{\rho}(x,y))^{2\kappa_\nu}}$$
$$= \frac{n^{d-1}(1+n\widetilde{\rho}(x,y))^{\frac{3}{2}s_\kappa-d+1}}{\prod_{\nu\in R_+}(|\langle x,\nu\rangle|+n^{-1}+\widetilde{\rho}(x,y))^{2\kappa_\nu}}$$
$$\sim \frac{n^{d-1}(1+n\widetilde{\rho}(x,y))^{\frac{3}{2}s_\kappa-d+1}}{\prod_{\nu\in R_+}(|\langle x,\nu\rangle|+|\langle g_0 y,\nu\rangle|+n^{-1}+\widetilde{\rho}(x,y))^{2\kappa_\nu}}.$$

So,

$$\frac{1}{A_n^\delta}|P_n(h_\kappa^2;x,y)| \le c\frac{n^{d-\delta-1}(1+n\widetilde{\rho}(x,y))^{\frac{3}{2}s_\kappa-d+1}}{\prod_{\nu\in R_+}(|\langle x,\nu\rangle|+|\langle g_0y,\nu\rangle|+n^{-1}+\widetilde{\rho}(x,y))^{2\kappa_\nu}}. \tag{32}$$

Finally, to estimate the Cesàro kernel, by using the (26), (31) and (32), we have:

$$\begin{aligned}|K_n^\delta(h_\kappa^2;x,y)| =&\left|\left(\sum_{i=0,1}+\sum_{i=2}^{\lfloor\log_2 n\rfloor+2}\right)V_\kappa[\Psi_{\varphi_i}(\langle x,\cdot\rangle)](y)+\frac{1}{A_n^\delta}\frac{\lambda_\kappa+n}{\lambda_\kappa}V_\kappa\left[C_n^{\lambda_\kappa}(\langle x,\cdot\rangle)\right](y)\right|\\ \le& c_\kappa\cdot\left[n^{-1}\sum_{j=1}^{n}(1+j)^{d-1}\cdot\frac{\prod_{\nu\in R_+}(|\langle x,\nu\rangle|+|\langle g_0y,\nu\rangle|+\widetilde{\rho}(x,y)+j^{-1})^{-2\kappa_\nu}}{(1+j\widetilde{\rho}(x,y))^{\lambda_\kappa+\ell-\tau-\frac{3}{2}s_\kappa+d-1}}\right.\\ &+\sum_{i=2}^{\lfloor\log_2 n\rfloor+2}2^{-i-i\delta+i\ell}\frac{n^{d-1}(1+n\widetilde{\rho}(x,y))^{-\ell+\tau+\frac{3}{2}s_\kappa-d+1}}{\prod_{\nu\in R_+}(|\langle x,\nu\rangle|+|\langle g_0y,\nu\rangle|+\widetilde{\rho}(x,y)+n^{-1})^{2\kappa_\nu}}\\ &\left.+\frac{n^{d-\delta-1}(1+n\widetilde{\rho}(x,y))^{\frac{3}{2}s_\kappa-d+1}}{\prod_{\nu\in R_+}(|\langle x,\nu\rangle|+|\langle g_0y,\nu\rangle|+n^{-1}+\widetilde{\rho}(x,y))^{2\kappa_\nu}}\right].\end{aligned}$$

4.2. *Proof of Theorem 2*

To show this Theorem, we will estimate $|K_n^\delta(h_\kappa^2;x,y)|h_\kappa^2(y)$, where $h_\kappa(y):=\prod_{\nu\in R_+}|\langle y,\nu\rangle|^{\kappa_\nu}$, and then give the upper estimate of the integral $\int_{\mathbb{S}^{d-1}}|K_n^\delta(h_\kappa^2;x,y)|h_\kappa^2(y)d\sigma(y)$. By Theorem 1 we proved,

$$\begin{aligned}&|K_n^\delta(h_\kappa^2;x,y)|h_\kappa^2(y)\\ &\le c_\kappa\cdot\left[n^{-1}\sum_{j=1}^{n}(1+j)^{d-1}\cdot\frac{\prod_{\nu\in R_+}(|\langle x,\nu\rangle|+|\langle g_0y,\nu\rangle|+\widetilde{\rho}(x,y)+j^{-1})^{-2\kappa_\nu}}{(1+j\widetilde{\rho}(x,y))^{\lambda_\kappa+\ell-\tau-\frac{3}{2}s_\kappa+d-1}}\prod_{\nu\in R_+}|\langle y,\nu\rangle|^{2\kappa_\nu}\right.\\ &+\sum_{i=2}^{\lfloor\log_2 n\rfloor+2}2^{-i-i\delta+i\ell}\frac{n^{d-1}(1+n\widetilde{\rho}(x,y))^{-\ell+\tau+\frac{3}{2}s_\kappa-d+1}}{\prod_{\nu\in R_+}(|\langle x,\nu\rangle|+|\langle g_0y,\nu\rangle|+\widetilde{\rho}(x,y)+n^{-1})^{2\kappa_\nu}}\prod_{\nu\in R_+}|\langle y,\nu\rangle|^{2\kappa_\nu}\\ &\left.+\frac{n^{d-\delta-1}(1+n\widetilde{\rho}(x,y))^{\frac{3}{2}s_\kappa-d+1}}{\prod_{\nu\in R_+}(|\langle x,\nu\rangle|+|\langle g_0y,\nu\rangle|+n^{-1}+\widetilde{\rho}(x,y))^{2\kappa_\nu}}\prod_{\nu\in R_+}|\langle y,\nu\rangle|^{2\kappa_\nu}\right]\\ &=:c_\kappa\cdot[A_1+A_2+A_3].\end{aligned} \tag{33}$$

Let

$$\begin{aligned}I_\nu:=&\left(|\langle x,\nu\rangle|+|\langle g_0y,\nu\rangle|+\widetilde{\rho}(x,y)+n^{-1}\right)^{-2\kappa_\nu}|\langle y,\nu\rangle|^{2\kappa_\nu}\\ =&\left(|\langle x,\nu\rangle|+|\langle g_0y,\nu\rangle|+\widetilde{\rho}(x,y)+n^{-1}\right)^{-2\kappa_\nu}|\langle g_0y,\nu\rangle|^{2\kappa_\nu},\end{aligned}$$

where the second equality is followed by the G-invariant of the weight. Thus, we have

$$\prod_{\nu\in R+}I_\nu\le\text{Const}. \tag{34}$$

Hence, by (34) and a straightforward calculation, we have:

$$\begin{aligned}
A_1 := & \, n^{-1}\sum_{j=1}^{n}(1+j)^{d-1}\cdot\frac{\prod_{\nu\in R_+}(|\langle x,\nu\rangle|+|\langle g_0y,\nu\rangle|+\widetilde{\rho}(x,y)+j^{-1})^{-2\kappa_\nu}}{(1+j\widetilde{\rho}(x,y))^{\lambda_\kappa+\ell-\tau-\frac{3}{2}s_\kappa+d-1}}\prod_{\nu\in R_+}|\langle y,\nu\rangle|^{2\kappa_\nu} \\
& \le c_\kappa n^{-1}\sum_{j=1}^{n}j^{d-1}\cdot\frac{1}{(1+j\widetilde{\rho}(x,y))^{\lambda_\kappa+\ell-\tau-\frac{3}{2}s_\kappa+d-1}} \\
& \le c'_\kappa n^{-1}\left(\widetilde{\rho}(x,y)+n^{-1}\right)^{-d} \\
& = c_\kappa\frac{n^{d-1}}{(1+n\widetilde{\rho}(x,y))^{d}}.
\end{aligned} \tag{35}$$

For A_2, we will consider two cases below to give the estimate:
(1) If $0\le\widetilde{\rho}(x,y)\le n^{-1}$, then by (34),

$$\begin{aligned}
A_2 = & \sum_{i=2}^{\lfloor\log_2 n\rfloor+2}2^{-i-i\delta+i\ell}\frac{n^{d-1}(1+n\widetilde{\rho}(x,y))^{-\ell+\tau+\frac{3}{2}s_\kappa-d+1}}{\prod_{\nu\in R_+}(|\langle x,\nu\rangle|+|\langle g_0y,\nu\rangle|+\widetilde{\rho}(x,y)+n^{-1})^{2\kappa_\nu}}\prod_{\nu\in R_+}|\langle y,\nu\rangle|^{2\kappa_\nu} \\
& \le cn^{d-1}\frac{1}{(1+n\widetilde{\rho}(x,y))^{\ell-\tau-\frac{3}{2}s_\kappa+d-1}}\sum_{i=2}^{\lfloor\log_2 n\rfloor+2}2^{-i-i\delta+i\ell} \\
& \le c_{\ell,\kappa,d}\cdot n^{d-1}\frac{1}{(1+n\widetilde{\rho}(x,y))^{\delta-\tau-\frac{3}{2}s_\kappa+d-1}}\sum_{i=2}^{\lfloor\log_2 n\rfloor+2}2^{-i}\quad[\text{by setting }\ell=\delta] \\
& \le c_{\ell,\kappa,d}\cdot n^{d-1} \\
& \sim c'_{\ell,\kappa,d}\cdot n^{d-1}\frac{1}{(1+n\widetilde{\rho}(x,y))^{\delta+\frac{d}{2}}};
\end{aligned}$$

(2) If $\widetilde{\rho}(x,y)\ge n^{-1}$, then we break the sum by $A_2=\sum_{i=2}^{\lfloor\log_2 n\rfloor+2}=\sum_{2^i\le n\widetilde{\rho}}+\sum_{2^i>n\widetilde{\rho}}$. For large enough ℓ and δ, we apply (34) to obtain:

$$\begin{aligned}
& \sum_{2^i\le n\widetilde{\rho}}2^{-i-i\delta+i\ell}\frac{n^{d-1}(1+n\widetilde{\rho}(x,y))^{-\ell+\tau+\frac{3}{2}s_\kappa-d+1}}{\prod_{\nu\in R_+}(|\langle x,\nu\rangle|+|\langle g_0y,\nu\rangle|+\widetilde{\rho}(x,y)+n^{-1})^{2\kappa_\nu}}\prod_{\nu\in R_+}|\langle y,\nu\rangle|^{2\kappa_\nu} \\
& \le cn^{d-1}(n\widetilde{\rho}(x,y))^{-\ell+\tau+\frac{3}{2}s_\kappa-d+1}\sum_{2^i\le n\widetilde{\rho}}2^{i(\ell-\delta-1)} \\
& \le cn^{d-1}(n\widetilde{\rho}(x,y))^{-\ell+\tau+\frac{3}{2}s_\kappa-d+1}(n\widetilde{\rho}(x,y))^{(\ell-\delta-1)}\quad[\text{if }\ell>\delta+1] \\
& \le cn^{d-1}\frac{1}{(1+n\widetilde{\rho}(x,y))^{\delta+d-\tau-\frac{3}{2}s_\kappa}},
\end{aligned}$$

and

$$\begin{aligned}
& \sum_{2^i>n\widetilde{\rho}}2^{-i-i\delta+i\ell}\frac{n^{d-1}(1+n\widetilde{\rho}(x,y))^{-\ell+\tau+\frac{3}{2}s_\kappa-d+1}}{\prod_{\nu\in R_+}(|\langle x,\nu\rangle|+|\langle g_0y,\nu\rangle|+\widetilde{\rho}(x,y)+n^{-1})^{2\kappa_\nu}}\prod_{\nu\in R_+}|\langle y,\nu\rangle|^{2\kappa_\nu} \\
& \le cn^{d-1}(n\widetilde{\rho}(x,y))^{-\ell+\tau+\frac{3}{2}s_\kappa-d+1}\sum_{2^i>n\widetilde{\rho}}2^{i(\ell-\delta-1)} \\
& \le cn^{d-1}(n\widetilde{\rho}(x,y))^{-\delta+\tau+\frac{3}{2}s_\kappa-d+1}(n\widetilde{\rho}(x,y))^{-1}\quad[\text{by setting }\ell=\delta] \\
& \le cn^{d-1}\frac{1}{(1+n\widetilde{\rho}(x,y))^{\delta+d-\tau-\frac{3}{2}s_\kappa}}.
\end{aligned}$$

So,

$$A_2\le c_\kappa n^{d-1}\frac{1}{(1+n\widetilde{\rho}(x,y))^{\delta+d-\tau-\frac{3}{2}s_\kappa}}. \tag{36}$$

Lastly, for A_3, by using (34), we have:

$$\begin{aligned} A_3 &= \frac{n^{d-\delta-1}(1+n\widetilde{\rho}(x,y))^{\frac{3}{2}s_\kappa-d+1}}{\prod_{v\in R_+}(|\langle x,v\rangle|+|\langle g_0y,v\rangle|+n^{-1}+\widetilde{\rho}(x,y))^{2\kappa_v}}\prod_{v\in R_+}|\langle y,v\rangle|^{2\kappa_v} \\ &\le cn^{d-\delta-1}\frac{1}{(1+n\widetilde{\rho}(x,y))^{d-\frac{3}{2}s_\kappa-1}} \\ &= cn^{d-1}(n^{-1}+\widetilde{\rho}(x,y))^{\delta}\frac{1}{(1+n\widetilde{\rho}(x,y))^{\delta+d-\frac{3}{2}s_\kappa-1}} \\ &\le cn^{d-1}\frac{1}{(1+n\widetilde{\rho}(x,y))^{\delta+d-\frac{3}{2}s_\kappa-1}}. \end{aligned} \tag{37}$$

Therefore, by (35)–(37), we have:

$$\begin{aligned} |K_n^\delta(h_\kappa^2;x,y)|h_\kappa^2(y) &\le c_\kappa[A_1+A_2+A_3] \\ &\le c_\kappa n^{d-1}(1+n\widetilde{\rho}(x,y))^{-\beta(\delta)}, \end{aligned}$$

where

$$\beta(\delta):=\min\{d,\delta+d-\tau-\frac{3}{2}s_\kappa,\delta-\frac{3}{2}s_\kappa+d-1\}=\min\{d,\delta+d-\tau-\frac{3}{2}s_\kappa\}.$$

Thus, we can get:

$$\begin{aligned} \int_{\mathbb{S}^{d-1}}|K_n^\delta(h_\kappa^2;x,y)|h_\kappa^2(y)d\sigma(y) &\le cn^{d-1}\int_0^{\frac{\pi}{2}}(1+n\theta)^{-\beta(\delta)}(\sin\theta)^{d-2}d\theta \\ &\sim \begin{cases} 1 & \text{if } \delta>\frac{3}{2}s_\kappa+\tau-1 \\ \log n & \text{if } \delta=\frac{3}{2}s_\kappa+\tau-1 \\ n^{-\delta+\frac{3}{2}s_\kappa-\tau+1} & \text{if } \delta<\frac{3}{2}s_\kappa+\tau-1\,. \end{cases} \end{aligned}$$

5. Weighted Orthogonal Polynomial Expansions (WOPEs) on the Ball and the Simplex

In this section, we shall describe briefly some necessary notations and results for WOPEs on the unit ball $\mathbb{B}^d$ and the simplex $\mathbb{T}^d$. Unless otherwise stated, most of the results described in this section can be found in the paper [25] and the books [9,21].

5.1. WOPEs in Several Variables

Let Ω denote a compact domain in $\mathbb{R}^d$ endowed with the usual Lebesgue measure dx. Given a weight function W on Ω, we denote by $L^p(W;\Omega)$ the usual L^p-space defined with respect to the measure Wdx on Ω, and $\mathcal{V}_n^d(W)$ the space of orthogonal polynomials of degree n with respect to the weight function W on Ω. Thus, if we denote by Π_n^d the space of all algebraic polynomials in d variables of total degree at most n, then $\mathcal{V}_n^d(W)$ is the orthogonal complement of Π_{n-1}^d in the space Π_n^d with respect to the inner product of $L^2(W;\Omega)$, where it is agreed that $\Pi_{-1}^d=\{0\}$.

Since Ω is compact, each function $f\in L^2(W;\Omega)$ has a weighted orthogonal polynomial expansion on Ω, $f=\sum_{n=0}^\infty \mathrm{proj}_n(W;f)$, converging in the norm of $L^2(W;\Omega)$, where $\mathrm{proj}_n(W;f)$ denotes the orthogonal projection of f onto the space $\mathcal{V}_n^d(W)$. Let $P_n(W;\cdot,\cdot)$ denote the reproducing kernel of the space $\mathcal{V}_n^d(W)$; that is,

$$P_n(W;x,y)=\sum_{j=1}^{a_n^d}\varphi_{n,j}(x)\overline{\varphi_{n,j}(y)},\quad x,y\in\Omega$$

for an orthonormal basis $\left\{\varphi_{n,j} : 1 \leq j \leq a_n^d := \dim \mathcal{V}_n^d(W)\right\}$ of the space $\mathcal{V}_n^d(W)$. The orthogonal projection operator $\operatorname{proj}_n(W) : L^2(W;\Omega) \mapsto \mathcal{V}_n^d(W)$ can be expressed as an integral operator,

$$\operatorname{proj}_n(W; f, x) = \int_\Omega f(y) P_n(W; x, y) W(y) dy, \quad x \in \Omega,$$

which also extends the definition of $\operatorname{proj}_n(W; f)$ to all $f \in L^1(W; \Omega)$ since the kernel $P_n(W; x, y)$ is a polynomial in both x and y.

Let $S_n^\delta(W; f), n = 0, 1, \cdots$, denote the Cesàro (C, δ)-means of the WOPEs of $f \in L^1(W; \Omega)$. Each $S_n^\delta(W; f)$ can be expressed as an integral against a kernel, $K_n^\delta(W; x, y)$, called the Cesàro (C, δ)-kernel,

$$S_n^\delta(W; f, x) := \int_\Omega f(y) K_n^\delta(W; x, y) W(y) dy, \quad x \in \Omega$$

where

$$K_n^\delta(W; x, y) := \frac{1}{A_n^\delta} \sum_{j=0}^n A_{n-j}^\delta P_j(W; x, y), \quad x, y \in \Omega.$$

5.2. WOPEs on the Unit Ball $\mathbb{B}^d$

Recall that G is a finite reflection group on $\mathbb{R}^d$ with a root system $R \subset \mathbb{R}^d$; $\kappa : R \to [0, \infty)$ is a nonnegative multiplicity function on R; the weight functions h_κ on $\mathbb{S}^{d-1}$ and $W_{\kappa,\mu}^B$ on $\mathbb{B}^d$ are given by

$$h_\kappa(x) := \prod_{\nu \in R_+} |\langle x, \nu \rangle|^{\kappa_\nu}$$

and

$$W_{\kappa,\mu}^B(x) := h_\kappa^2(x)(1 - \|x\|^2)^{\mu - \frac{1}{2}}, \quad \mu \geq 0, x \in \mathbb{B}^d, \tag{38}$$

respectively. For $1 \leq p \leq \infty$, we denote by $L^p(W_{\kappa,\mu}^B; \mathbb{B}^d)$ the L^p-space defined with respect to the measure $W_{\kappa,\mu}^B(x)dx$ on $\mathbb{B}^d$, and $\|\cdot\|_{L^p(W_{\kappa,\mu}^B)}$ the norm of $L^p(W_{\kappa,\mu}^B; \mathbb{B}^d)$. Let $\widetilde{G}$ be the finite reflection group on $\mathbb{R}^{d+1}$ associated with the root system,

$$\widetilde{R} := \left\{\widetilde{\nu} = (\nu, 0) \in \mathbb{R}^{d+1} : \nu \in R\right\} \cup \{\pm e_{d+1}\},$$

and define $\widetilde{\kappa} : \widetilde{R} \to [0, \infty)$ by $\widetilde{\kappa}(\widetilde{\nu}) = \kappa(\nu)$ for $\nu \in R$ and $\widetilde{\kappa}(\pm e_{d+1}) = \mu$. Clearly, $\widetilde{\kappa}$ is a $\widetilde{G}$-invariant nonnegative multiplicity function on $\widetilde{R}$. Let $h_{\widetilde{\kappa}}$ be the $\widetilde{G}$-invariant weight function on $\mathbb{R}^{d+1}$ associated with the root system $\widetilde{R}$ and the multiplicity function $\widetilde{\kappa}$ as defined in (1); that is,

$$h_{\widetilde{\kappa}}(x, x_{d+1}) = |x_{d+1}|^\mu \prod_{\nu \in R_+} |\langle x, \nu \rangle|^{\kappa_\nu}, \quad x \in \mathbb{R}^d, x_{d+1} \in \mathbb{R}.$$

The weight $h_{\widetilde{\kappa}}$ on $\mathbb{S}^d$ is related to the weight function $W_{\kappa,\mu}^B$ on $\mathbb{B}^d$ by

$$h_{\widetilde{\kappa}}^2\left(x, \sqrt{1 - \|x\|^2}\right) = W_{\kappa,\mu}^B(x)\sqrt{1 - \|x\|^2}, \quad x \in \mathbb{B}^d.$$

Furthermore, a change of variables $y = \phi(x)$ with:

$$\phi : \mathbb{B}^d \to \mathbb{S}^d, \quad x \in \mathbb{B}^d \mapsto \left(x, \sqrt{1 - \|x\|^2}\right) \in \mathbb{S}^d$$

shows that

$$\int_{\mathbb{S}^d} f(y)h_{\tilde{\kappa}}^2(y)d\sigma(y)$$
$$= \int_{\mathbb{B}^d} \left[f\left(x, \sqrt{1-\|x\|^2}\right) + f\left(x, -\sqrt{1-\|x\|^2}\right) \right] W_{\kappa,\mu}^B(x)dx. \quad (39)$$

Given a function $f : \mathbb{B}^d \to \mathbb{R}$, define $\widetilde{f} : \mathbb{S}^d \to \mathbb{R}$ by:

$$\widetilde{f}(x, x_{d+1}) = f(x), \quad x \in \mathbb{B}^d, \quad (x, x_{d+1}) \in \mathbb{S}^d.$$

Clearly, $\widetilde{f} \circ \phi = f$, and by (39), the mapping $f \to \widetilde{f}$ is an isometry from $L^p(W_{\kappa,\mu}^B; \mathbb{B}^d)$ to $L^p(\mathbb{S}^{d-1}; h_{\tilde{\kappa}/2}^2)$. More importantly, the orthogonal structure on the weighted ball $\mathbb{B}^d$ is preserved under the mapping $\phi : \mathbb{B}^d \to \mathbb{S}^d$. To be precise, let $\nu_n^d(W_{\kappa,\mu}^B)$ denote the space of weighted orthogonal polynomials of degree n with respect to the measure $W_{\kappa,\mu}^B(x)dx$ on $\mathbb{B}^d$, and let $\text{proj}_n(W_{\kappa,\mu}^B; f)$ denote the orthogonal projection of f onto the space $\nu_n^d(W_{\kappa,\mu}^B)$. Then a function f on $\mathbb{B}^d$ belongs to the space $\nu_n^d(W_{\kappa,\mu}^B)$ if and only if $\widetilde{f} \in \mathcal{H}_n^{d+1}(h_{\tilde{\kappa}}^2)$ and, moreover (see [9,25,26]),

$$\text{proj}_n(W_{\kappa,\mu}^B; f, x) = \text{proj}_n(W_{\kappa,\mu}^B; \widetilde{f} \circ \phi, x) = \text{proj}_n(h_{\tilde{\kappa}}^2; \widetilde{f}, \phi(x)), \quad x \in \mathbb{B}^d.$$

This relation allows us to deduce results on the convergence of orthogonal expansions with respect to $W_{\kappa,\mu}^B$ on $\mathbb{B}^d$ from those of h-harmonic expansions on $\mathbb{S}^d$.

5.3. Results on the Ball

For $x \in \mathbb{B}^d$, we set $x_{d+1} := \sqrt{1-\|x\|^2}$. Let $\rho_B : \mathbb{B}^d \times \mathbb{B}^d \to [0, \pi]$ denote the metric on $\mathbb{B}^d$ given by:

$$\rho_B(x, y) = \arccos(x \cdot y + x_{d+1}y_{d+1}), \quad x, y \in \mathbb{B}^d.$$

For $x \in \mathbb{B}^d$ and $\theta > 0$, define:

$$B^B(x, \theta) := \left\{ y \in \mathbb{B}^d : \quad \rho_B(x, y) \le \theta \right\}.$$

We write:

$$\text{meas}_{\tilde{\kappa}}^B(E) := \int_E W_{\kappa,\mu}^B(x)dx, \quad E \subset \mathbb{B}^d,$$

where $W_{\kappa,\mu}^B$ is the weight function on $\mathbb{B}^d$ given in (38). It is easily seen that $\text{meas}_{\tilde{\kappa}}^B$ is a doubling measure on $\mathbb{B}^d$, satisfying that for any $x \in \mathbb{B}^d$ and $\theta \in (0, \pi]$,

$$\text{meas}_{\tilde{\kappa}}^B\left(B^B\left(x, 2^j\theta\right)\right) \le C2^{js_{\tilde{\kappa}}} \text{meas}_{\tilde{\kappa}}^B\left(B^B(x, \theta)\right), \quad j = 1, 2, \cdots, \quad (40)$$

where $C > 0$ is a constant depending only on $\tilde{\kappa}$ and d, and $s_{\tilde{\kappa}}$ is the optimal constant for which (40) holds. Recall that $P(W_{\kappa,\mu}^B; x, y)$ denotes the reproducing kernel of the space $\mathcal{V}_n^d(W_{\kappa,\mu}^B)$ of orthogonal polynomials of degree n with respect to the weight $W_{\kappa,\mu}^B$ on $\mathbb{B}^d$, $S_n^\delta(W_{\kappa,\mu}^B; f)$ denotes the n-th Cesàro mean of order $\delta \ge 0$ of the WOPE of f with respect to the weight function $W_{\kappa,\mu}^B$ on $\mathbb{B}^d$, and $K_n^\delta(W_{\kappa,\mu}^B; x, y)$ is the Cesàro kernel of the operator $S_n^\delta(W_{\kappa,\mu}^B)$. The point-wise estimate of the Cesàro kernel $K_n^\delta(W_{\kappa,\mu}^B; x, y)$ is as follows:

Theorem 3. *For $\delta > 0$ and $\ell \geq \tau > 2\lambda_{\tilde{\kappa}} + 1$, we have:*

$$
\begin{aligned}
|K_n^\delta(W_{\kappa,\mu}^B; x, y)| \leq & c_{\tilde{\kappa}} \cdot \Bigg[n^{-1} \sum_{j=1}^{n} (1+j)^d \cdot \frac{\prod_{v \in \tilde{R}_+} (|\langle x, v\rangle| + |\langle g_0 y, v\rangle| + \tilde{\rho}_B(x,y) + j^{-1})^{-2\tilde{\kappa}_v}}{(1 + j\tilde{\rho}_B(x,y))^{\lambda_{\tilde{\kappa}} + \ell - \tau - \frac{3}{2}s_{\tilde{\kappa}} + d}} \\
& + \sum_{i=2}^{\lfloor \log_2 n \rfloor + 2} 2^{-i - i\delta + i\ell} \frac{n^d (1 + n\tilde{\rho}_B(x,y))^{-\ell + \tau + \frac{3}{2}s_{\tilde{\kappa}} - d}}{\prod_{v \in \tilde{R}_+} (|\langle x, v\rangle| + |\langle g_0 y, v\rangle| + \tilde{\rho}_B(x,y) + n^{-1})^{2\tilde{\kappa}_v}} \\
& + \frac{n^{d-\delta} (1 + n\tilde{\rho}_B(x,y))^{\frac{3}{2}s_{\tilde{\kappa}} - d}}{\prod_{v \in \tilde{R}_+} (|\langle x, v\rangle| + |\langle g_0 y, v\rangle| + n^{-1} + \tilde{\rho}_B(x,y))^{2\tilde{\kappa}_v}} \Bigg],
\end{aligned}
$$

where $g_0 \in G$ is such that $\rho_B(g_0 x, y) = \tilde{\rho}_B(x,y) = \min_{g \in G} \rho_B(gx, y)$ for $x, y \in \mathbb{B}^d$.

Our next result can be stated as follows:

Theorem 4. *Let $\delta > 0$, $\tau > 2\lambda_{\tilde{\kappa}} + 1$,*

$$
\int_{\mathbb{B}^d} |K_n^\delta(W_{\kappa,\mu}^B; x, y)| W_{\kappa,\mu}^B(y) d\sigma(y) \leq \begin{cases} 1 & \text{if } \delta > \frac{3}{2}s_{\tilde{\kappa}} + \tau - 1 \\ \log n & \text{if } \delta = \frac{3}{2}s_{\tilde{\kappa}} + \tau - 1 \\ n^{-\delta + \frac{3}{2}s_{\tilde{\kappa}} - \tau + 1} & \text{if } \delta < \frac{3}{2}s_{\tilde{\kappa}} + \tau - 1\,. \end{cases}
$$

As a consequence of the kernel estimate, we can prove the following:

Corollary 2. *Let $\tau > 2\lambda_{\tilde{\kappa}} + 1$ and $\sigma_{\tilde{\kappa}} := \frac{3}{2}s_{\tilde{\kappa}} + \tau - 1$. Then if $\delta > \sigma_{\tilde{\kappa}}$, $S_n^\delta(W_{\kappa,\mu}^B; f)$ converges in $L^p(W_{\kappa,\mu}^B; \mathbb{B}^d)$ for all $1 \leq p \leq \infty$.*

These results can be deduced directly from the corresponding results on the sphere $\mathbb{S}^d$. Since the proofs are almost identical to those in [10,14], we skip the details here.

5.4. WOPEs on the Simplex $\mathbb{T}^d$

In this subsection, we will deduce similar results on the simplex $\mathbb{T}^d$ from the already proven results on the ball $\mathbb{B}^d$. Our argument is based on the connections between WOPEs on $\mathbb{B}^d$ and WOPEs on $\mathbb{T}^d$, as observed by Y. Xu, see [21,26].

The weight function $W_{\kappa,\mu}^T$ we consider on the simplex $\mathbb{T}^d$ is given by:

$$
W_{\kappa,\mu}^T(x) := \frac{h_\kappa^2(\sqrt{x_1}, \cdots, \sqrt{x_d})}{\sqrt{x_1 \cdots x_d}} (1 - |x|)^{\mu - \frac{1}{2}}, \quad \mu \geq 0, x \in \mathbb{T}^d. \tag{41}
$$

It is related to the weight $W_{\kappa,\mu}^B$ on $\mathbb{B}^d$ through the mapping,

$$
\psi : (x_1, \ldots, x_d) \in \mathbb{B}^d \mapsto \left(x_1^2, \ldots, x_d^2\right) \in \mathbb{T}^d, \tag{42}
$$

by

$$
W_{\kappa,\mu}^T(\psi(x)) = \frac{W_{\kappa,\mu}^B(x)}{|x_1 \cdots x_d|}, \quad x \in \mathbb{B}^d.
$$

Furthermore, a change of variables shows that:

$$
\int_{\mathbb{B}^d} g(\psi(x)) W_{\kappa,\mu}^B(x) dx = \int_{\mathbb{T}^d} g(x) W_{\kappa,\mu}^T(x) dx. \tag{43}
$$

For $1 \le p \le \infty$, we denote by $L^p\left(W^T_{\kappa,\mu};\mathbb{T}^d\right)$ the L^p-space defined with respect to the measure $W^T_{\kappa,\mu}(x)dx$ on $\mathbb{T}^d$, and by $\|\cdot\|_{L^p(W^T_{\kappa,\mu})}$ the norm of $L^p\left(W^T_{\kappa,\mu};\mathbb{T}^d\right)$. Note that (43) particularly implies that the mapping,

$$L^p\left(W^T_{\kappa,\mu};\mathbb{T}^d\right) \to L^p\left(W^B_{\kappa,\mu};\mathbb{B}^d\right), \quad f \mapsto f \circ \psi,$$

is an isometry.

Let $\mathcal{V}^d_n\left(W^T_{\kappa,\mu}\right)$ denote the space of weighted orthogonal polynomials of degree n with respect to the weight $W^T_{\kappa,\mu}$ on $\mathbb{T}^d$. The orthogonal structure is preserved under the mapping (42) in the sense that $R \in \mathcal{V}^d_n\left(W^T_{\kappa,\mu}\right)$ if and only if $R \circ \psi \in \mathcal{V}^d_{2n}\left(W^B_{\kappa,\mu}\right)$. Furthermore, the orthogonal projection, $\mathrm{proj}_n\left(W^T_{\kappa,\mu}; f\right)$, of f onto $\mathcal{V}^d_n\left(W^T_{\kappa,\mu}\right)$ can be expressed in terms of the orthogonal projection of $f \circ \psi$ onto $\mathcal{V}^d_{2n}\left(W^B_{\kappa,\mu}\right)$ as follows (see [9,13]):

$$\mathrm{proj}_n\left(W^T_{\kappa,\mu}; f, \psi(x)\right) = \mathrm{proj}_{2n}\left(W^B_{\kappa,\mu}; f \circ \psi, x\right), \quad x \in \mathbb{B}^d.$$

5.5. Results on the Simplex

For $x = (x_1, \cdots, x_d) \in \mathbb{T}^d$, let $|x| = x_1 + x_2 + \cdots + x_d$ and $x_{d+1} := 1 - |x|$. Let $\rho_T : \mathbb{T}^d \times \mathbb{T}^d \to [0, \pi]$ be the metric on $\mathbb{T}^d$ given by:

$$\rho_T(x,y) = \arccos\left(\sum_{j=1}^{d+1} \sqrt{x_j y_j}\right), \quad x, y \in \mathbb{T}^d.$$

For $x \in \mathbb{B}^d$ and $\theta > 0$, define:

$$B^T(x,\theta) := \left\{y \in \mathbb{T}^d : \quad \rho_T(x,y) \le \theta\right\}.$$

We write:

$$\mathrm{meas}^T_{\tilde{\kappa}}(E) := \int_E W^T_{\kappa,\mu}(x)dx, \quad E \subset \mathbb{T}^d,$$

where $W^T_{\kappa,\mu}$ is the weight function on $\mathbb{T}^d$ given in (41). It is easily seen that $\mathrm{meas}^T_{\tilde{\kappa}}$ is a doubling measure on $\mathbb{T}^d$ satisfying that for any $x \in \mathbb{T}^d$ and $\theta \in (0, \pi]$,

$$\mathrm{meas}^T_{\tilde{\kappa}}\left(B^T\left(x, 2^j\theta\right)\right) \le C 2^{js_{\tilde{\kappa}}}\, \mathrm{meas}^T_{\tilde{\kappa}}\left(B^T(x,\theta)\right), \quad j = 1, 2, \cdots, \tag{44}$$

where $C > 0$ is a constant depending only on $\tilde{\kappa}$ and d, and $s_{\tilde{\kappa}}$ is the optimal constant for which (44) holds. Recall that $P\left(W^T_{\kappa,\mu}, x, y\right)$ denotes the reproducing kernel of the space $\mathcal{V}^d_n(W^T_\kappa)$ of orthogonal polynomials of degree n with respect to the weight W^T_κ on $\mathbb{T}^d$; $S^\delta_n\left(W^T_{\kappa,\mu}; f\right)$ denotes the n-th Cesàro mean of the WOPE of f with respect to the weight function W^T_κ on $\mathbb{T}^d$, and $K^\delta_n\left(W^T_{\kappa,\mu}; x, y\right)$ is the Cesàro kernel of the operator $S^\delta_n\left(W^T_{\kappa,\mu}\right)$.

The point-wise estimate of the Cesàro kernel $K^\delta_n(W^T_{\kappa,\mu}; x, y)$ is as follows:

Theorem 5. *For $\delta > 0$ and $\ell \ge \tau > 2\lambda_{\tilde{\kappa}} + 1$, we have:*

$$
\begin{aligned}
|K_n^\delta(W_{\kappa,\mu}^T;x,y)| \le & c_{\tilde{\kappa}} \cdot \Bigg[n^{-1} \sum_{j=1}^{n} (1+j)^d \cdot \frac{\prod_{v\in\tilde{R}_+}(|\langle x,v\rangle| + |\langle g_0 y,v\rangle| + \tilde{\rho}_T(x,y) + j^{-1})^{-2\tilde{\kappa}_v}}{(1+j\tilde{\rho}_T(x,y))^{\lambda_{\tilde{\kappa}}+\ell-\tau-\frac{3}{2}s_{\tilde{\kappa}}+d}} \\
& + \sum_{i=2}^{\lfloor \log_2 n\rfloor+2} 2^{-i-i\delta+i\ell} \frac{n^d(1+n\tilde{\rho}_T(x,y))^{-\ell+\tau+\frac{3}{2}s_{\tilde{\kappa}}-d}}{\prod_{v\in\tilde{R}_+}(|\langle x,v\rangle| + |\langle g_0 y,v\rangle| + \tilde{\rho}_T(x,y) + n^{-1})^{2\tilde{\kappa}_v}} \\
& + \frac{n^{d-\delta}(1+n\tilde{\rho}_T(x,y))^{\frac{3}{2}s_{\tilde{\kappa}}-d}}{\prod_{v\in\tilde{R}_+}(|\langle x,v\rangle| + |\langle g_0 y,v\rangle| + n^{-1} + \tilde{\rho}_T(x,y))^{2\tilde{\kappa}_v}} \Bigg],
\end{aligned}
$$

where $g_0 \in G$ *is such that* $\rho_T(g_0 x,y) = \tilde{\rho}_T(x,y) = \min_{g\in G}\rho_T(gx,y)$ *for* $x,y \in \mathbb{T}^d$.

Our next result can be stated as follows:

Theorem 6. *Let* $\delta > 0$, $\tau > 2\lambda_{\tilde{\kappa}} + 1$,

$$
\int_{\mathbb{T}^d} |K_n^\delta(W_{\kappa,\mu}^T;x,y)| W_{\kappa,\mu}^T(y)\,d\sigma(y) \le \begin{cases} 1 & \text{if } \delta > \frac{3}{2}s_{\tilde{\kappa}} + \tau - 1 \\ \log n & \text{if } \delta = \frac{3}{2}s_{\tilde{\kappa}} + \tau - 1 \\ n^{-\delta+\frac{3}{2}s_{\tilde{\kappa}}-\tau+1} & \text{if } \delta < \frac{3}{2}s_{\tilde{\kappa}} + \tau - 1\,. \end{cases}
$$

As a consequence of the kernel estimate, we can prove the following:

Corollary 3. *Let* $\tau > 2\lambda_{\tilde{\kappa}} + 1$ *and* $\sigma_{\tilde{\kappa}} := \frac{3}{2}s_{\tilde{\kappa}} + \tau - 1$. *Then, if* $\delta > \sigma_{\tilde{\kappa}}$, $S_n^\delta(W_{\kappa,\mu}^T;f)$ *converges in* $L^p(W_{\kappa,\mu}^T;\mathbb{T}^d)$ *for all* $1 \le p \le \infty$.

These results can be deduced directly from the corresponding results on the sphere $\mathbb{B}^d$. Since the proofs are almost identical to those in [10,14], we skip the details here.

Author Contributions: Formal analysis, H.F. and Y.G.; Funding acquisition, H.F.; Methodology, H.F.; Project administration, H.F.; Supervision, H.F.; Validation, Y.G.; Writing—original draft, Y.G.; Writing—review & editing, Y.G. All authors have read and agreed to the published version of the manuscript.

Funding: The authors are supported partially by the Research Grants Council of Hong Kong [Project # CityU 21207019, C1013-21GF], and by the City University of Hong Kong [Project # CityU 7200608].

Institutional Review Board Statement: Not applicable.

Informed Consent Statement: Not applicable.

Acknowledgments: The authors are grateful to Feng Dai, and Yuan Xu for helpful discussions. They also express their deep gratitude to anonymous referees for giving many helpful comments and constructive suggestions that led to an improved presentation of this paper.

Conflicts of Interest: The authors declare no conflict of interest.

References

1. Cesàro, E. Sur la multiplication des séries. *Bull. Sci. Math.* **1890**, *14*, 114–120.
2. Dai, F.; Wang, K.Y. A Survey of Polynomial Approximation on the Sphere. *Int. J. Wavelets Multiresolut. Inf. Process.* **2019**, *7*, 749–771 . [CrossRef]
3. Sogge, C.D. Oscillatory integrals and spherical harmonics. *Duke Math. J.* **1986**, *53*, 43–65. [CrossRef]
4. Sogge, C.D. On the convergence of Riesz means on compact manifolds. *Ann. Math.* **1987**, *126*, 439–447. [CrossRef]
5. Dunkl, C.F. Differential-difference operators associated to reflection groups. *Trans. Am. Math. Soc.* **1989**, *311*, 167–183. [CrossRef]
6. Dunkl, C.F. Integral kernels with reflection group invariance. *Can. J. Math.* **1991**, *43*, 1213–1227. [CrossRef]
7. Dunkl, C.F. Reflection groups and orthogonal polynomials on the sphere. *Math. Z.* **1988**, *197*, 33–60. [CrossRef]
8. Rösler, M. Positivity of Dunkl's intertwining operator. *Duke Math. J.* **1999**, *98*, 445–463. [CrossRef]
9. Dunkl, C.F.; Xu, Y. *Orthogonal Polynomials of Several Variables*; Encyclopedia of Mathematics and Its Applications; Cambridge University Press: Cambridge, UK, 2014.

10. Dai, F.; Xu, Y. Cesàro means of orthogonal expansions in several variables. *Const. Approx.* **2009**, *29*, 129–155. [CrossRef]
11. Xu, Y. Intertwining operator associated to symmetric groups and summability on the unit sphere. *J. Approx. Theory* **2021**, *272*, 105649. [CrossRef]
12. Dai, F.; Xu, Y. Boundedness of projection operators and Cesàro means in weighted L^p space on the unit sphere. *Trans. Am. Math. Soc.* **2009**, *361*, 3189–3221. [CrossRef]
13. Dai, F.; Wang, S.; Ye, W.R. Maximal estimates for the Cesàro means of weighted orthogonal polynomial expansions on the unit sphere. *J. Funct. Anal.* **2013**, *265*, 2357–2387. [CrossRef]
14. Dai, F.; Ge, Y. Sharp estimates of the Cesàro kernels for weighted orthogonal polynomial expansions in several variables. *J. Funct. Anal.* **2021**, *280*, 108865. [CrossRef]
15. Li, Z.-K.; Xu, Y. Summability of orthogonal expansions of several variables. *J. Approx. Theory* **2003**, *122*, 267–333. [CrossRef]
16. Rösler, M. Dunkl operators: Theory and applications. In *Orthogonal Polynomials and Special Functions, Leuven*; Springer: Berlin, Germany, 2003; pp. 93–135.
17. Berens, H.; Schmid, H.J.; Xu, Y. Bernstein-Durrmeyer polynomials on a simplex. *J. Approx. Theory* **1992**, *68*, 247–261. [CrossRef]
18. Xu, Y. Integration of the intertwining operator for *h*-harmonic polynomials associated to reflection groups. *Proc. Am. Math. Soc.* **1997**, *125*, 2963–2973. [CrossRef]
19. Dunkl, C.F. Intertwining operator associated to the group S_3. *Trans. Am. Math. Soc.* **1995**, *347*, 3347–3374.
20. Szegö, G. *Orthogonal Polynomials*; American Mathematical Society: Providence, RI, USA, 1975; Volume XXIII.
21. Dai, F.; Xu, Y. *Approximation Theory and Harmonic Analysis on Spheres and Balls*; Springer Monographs in Mathematics; Springer: New York, NY, USA, 2013.
22. Dai, F. Multivariate polynomial inequalities with respect to doubling weights and A_∞ weights. *J. Funct. Anal.* **2006**, *235*, 137–170. [CrossRef]
23. Dai, F.; Feng, H. Riesz transforms and fractional integration for orthogonal expansions on spheres, balls and simplices. *Adv. Math.* **2016**, *301*, 549–614. [CrossRef]
24. Brown, G.; Dai, F. Approximation of smooth functions on compact two-point homogeneous spaces. *J. Funct. Anal.* **2005**, *220*, 401–423. [CrossRef]
25. Xu, Y. Orthogonal polynomials and summability in Fourier orthogonal series on spheres and on balls. In *Mathematical Proceedings of the Cambridge Philosophical Society*; Cambridge University Press: Cambridge, UK, 2001; Volume 31, pp. 139–155.
26. Xu, Y. Orthogonal polynomials and cubature formulae on balls, simplices, and spheres. *J. Comput. Appl. Math.* **2001**, *127*, 349–368. [CrossRef]

mathematics

MDPI

Article

A New Parameter-Uniform Discretization of Semilinear Singularly Perturbed Problems

Justin B. Munyakazi * and Olawale O. Kehinde

Department of Mathematics and Applied Mathematics, University of the Western Cape, Private Bag X17, Bellville 7535, South Africa; 4059639@myuwc.ac.za
* Correspondence: jmunyakazi@uwc.ac.za

Abstract: In this paper, we present a numerical approach to solving singularly perturbed semilinear convection-diffusion problems. The nonlinear part of the problem is linearized via the quasilinearization technique. We then design and implement a fitted operator finite difference method to solve the sequence of linear singularly perturbed problems that emerges from the quasilinearization process. We carry out a rigorous analysis to attest to the convergence of the proposed procedure and notice that the method is first-order uniformly convergent. Some numerical evaluations are implemented on model examples to confirm the proposed theoretical results and to show the efficiency of the method.

Keywords: singularly perturbed problems; semilinear differential equation; quasilinearization; boundary layer; fitted operator finite difference method; uniform convergence

MSC: 65L10; 65L11; 65L12

Citation: Munyakazi, J.B.; Kehinde, O.O. A New Parameter-Uniform Discretization of Semilinear Singularly Perturbed Problems. *Mathematics* **2022**, *10*, 2254. https://doi.org/10.3390/math10132254

Academic Editor: Sitnik Sergey

Received: 29 April 2022
Accepted: 9 June 2022
Published: 27 June 2022

Publisher's Note: MDPI stays neutral with regard to jurisdictional claims in published maps and institutional affiliations.

Copyright: © 2022 by the authors. Licensee MDPI, Basel, Switzerland. This article is an open access article distributed under the terms and conditions of the Creative Commons Attribution (CC BY) license (https://creativecommons.org/licenses/by/4.0/).

1. Introduction

Differential problems in which a small parameter, often referred to as a perturbation parameter, multiply the highest derivatives are called singularly perturbed differential problems. These problems arise in different fields of study such as fluid dynamics, magnetohydrodynamics, aerodynamics, oceanography, quantum mechanics, plasma dynamics, chemical reactions, and liquid crystal modeling [1–3]. As an example, the heat and mass transport phenomena [4] are described by singularly perturbed differential equations in which the diffusion coefficient is regarded as a perturbation parameter.

Classical numerical methods have often failed to solve singularly perturbed problems. This is because one or more boundaries or interior layers may arise as the perturbation parameter approaches zero, thereby give undesirable results. To overcome this problem, constructed numerical methods such as finite difference methods, in the form of fitted mesh and fitted operator finite difference methods, finite element methods, and spline methods are adopted. These methods are used on layer-adapted meshes such as the Shishkin mesh, which is easy to construct, the Bakhvalov mesh, which gives superior accuracy, the Bakhvalov–Shishkin mesh, and the Vulanovic–Shishkin mesh (see [5–10]). In this paper, we consider the singularly perturbed semilinear convection-diffusion problems

$$\varepsilon y''(x) + a(x)y'(x) + f(x, y(x)) = 0, \quad x \in \Omega := (0,1), \tag{1}$$

subject to the following boundary conditions:

$$y(0) = A, \qquad y(1) = B, \tag{2}$$

where ε is the perturbation parameter such that $0 < \varepsilon << 1$, A and B are given constants, and the functions $a(x)$ and $f(x, y(x))$ are sufficiently smooth in the intervals Ω and $C^2\ (\Omega \times R)$, respectively, satisfying

$$a(x) \geq \alpha > 0, \qquad \forall\, x \in \Omega, \tag{3}$$

where α is a positive constant.

We obtain the reduced problem of Equation (1) by setting ε to zero, given as

$$a(x)y'(x) + f(x, y(x)) = 0. \tag{4}$$

Under these conditions, Equations (1) and (2) and the reduced problem in Equation (4) have a unique solution. This unique solution to Equations (1) and (2) exhibits a boundary layer at the origin of the interval Ω as the perturbation parameter ε approaches zero (i.e., at $x = 0$) (see [11–14]).

Not much work has been conducted on convection-diffusion semilinear singularly perturbed problems related to Equation (1). Cimen and Amiraliyev [15] constructed an exponential finite difference scheme, which flourishes by the method of integral identities to solve a singularly perturbed semilinear delay differential equation. They obtained a first-order uniform convergence in the discrete maximum norm. Niijima and Stynes [16,17] separately solved a singularly perturbed boundary value problem of the form in Equation (1). They adopted the use of finite difference schemes, and each obtained an almost first-order uniform accuracy in a discrete L_1 norm. Cakir and Arslan [18] used a fitted mesh finite difference scheme constructed on a Shishkin mesh to solve a singularly perturbed semilinear problem with integral boundary conditions. Their proposed scheme was found to be first-order uniformly convergent in the discrete maximum norm. Cakir and Amiraliyev [19] constructed a uniform finite difference scheme on a Shishkin-type mesh to solve a singularly perturbed semilinear convection-diffusion three-point boundary value problem. This method was shown to be first-order uniform convergent in the discrete maximum norm. Igor and Pack [20] solved a singularly perturbed semilinear convection-diffusion problem with discontinuous data using a difference scheme on local Green's functions. The authors achieved a first-order uniform convergent scheme on arbitrary meshes.

Linß [21] constructed a fitted mesh finite difference scheme on a Shishkin mesh to solve singularly perturbed convection-diffusion with a boundary layer of attractive turning points. He achieved an almost first-order convergence. Shishkin and Shishkina [22] examined a Dirichlet problem on a vertical strip for a singularly perturbed semilinear convection-diffusion problem. The authors used an iterative monotone difference scheme to solve the problem and obtained a first-order uniform convergent results. They then improved the order of convergence to second-order uniform (and improved the accuracy) using a Richardson scheme. Linß and Vulanović [23] solved a semilinear convection-diffusion problem with attractive boundary turning points by constructing a fitted mesh finite difference method on a Shishkin mesh type. This method was established to be of first-order uniform convergence.

More recently, further works were completed on semilinear singularly perturbed scalar boundary value problems [24], scalar parabolic problems [25], or on systems of such problems [26–29]. Again, the methods adopted in these works are essentially the fitted finite difference methods based on Shishkin meshes.

Based on the literature, we observed that authors have mostly exploited the fitted mesh finite difference schemes as well as some other methods to solve singularly perturbed semilinear convection-diffusion problems. However, none of them, to the best of our knowledge, have proposed a numerical method in the framework of nonstandard finite difference (NSFD) methods to solve such problems.

In this paper, we propose an NSFD scheme to solve singularly perturbed semilinear convection-diffusion problems. This scheme falls under the category of fitted operator finite difference methods (FOFDMs), as they are known in previously published works such as [30–32]. We transform the semilinear problem into a sequence of linear equations via the quasilinearization technique. We then construct a fitted operator finite difference scheme on the transformed problem. We show that the proposed method is ε-uniform convergent to the first order. Unlike its fitted mesh counterpart, not only do the fitted operator finite difference methods provide a simpler platform for analysis owing to their use of a uniform mesh, but their error bounds are not adversely affected by a logarithmic factor, as pointed out in [33].

The rest of this paper is structured as follows. In Section 2, we transform the semilinear problem into a system of linear singularly perturbed problems by the quasilinearization technique. In Section 3, we analyze some properties of the system of linear problems. In Section 4, we construct a fitted operator finite difference scheme, which is analyzed in Section 5. In Section 6, we present numerical examples to demonstrate the ε-uniformity of the proposed method. Finally, we present the conclusion in Section 7.

2. Quasilinearization

We use the quasilinearization technique to transform the semilinear singularly perturbed convection-diffusion problem into a sequence of linear equations. We choose a reliable initial approximation for the function $y(x)$ in $f(x,y(x))$, and by a Taylor series, we expand $f(x,y(x))$ around the chosen initial approximation and obtain

$$f(x,y^{(k+1)}(x)) = f(x,y^{(k)}(x)) + (y^{(k+1)}(x) - y^{(k)}(x))\left(\frac{\partial f^{(k)}}{\partial y}\right)_{(x,y^{(0)})} + \dots \quad (5)$$

By putting Equation (5) into Equations (1) and (2), we have

$$\varepsilon y''^{(k+1)}(x) + a(x)y'^{(k+1)}(x) + \left(\frac{\partial f^{(k)}}{\partial y}\right)y^{(k+1)} = -f(x,y^{(k)}(x)) + \left(\frac{\partial f^{(k)}}{\partial y}\right)y^{(k)}(x), \quad (6)$$

$$y^{(k+1)}(0) = A, \qquad y^{(k+1)}(1) = B, \quad (7)$$

for the iteration index $k = 0,1,2\dots$.

Notice that Equation (6) is linear in $y^{(k+1)}$. Therefore, we solve the sequence of linear Equations (6) and (7) in place of the semilinear problem in Equations (1) and (2) by the fitted operator finite difference method that will be introduced in Section 4.

For the solution of the semilinear boundary value problem, we require that

$$\max_{k\to\infty} y^{(k)}(x) = y^*(x), \quad (8)$$

where $y^*(x)$ is the solution of the semilinear problem. Numerically, we require that

$$|y^{(k+1)}(x) - y^{(k)}(x)| < \lambda, \quad (9)$$

where λ is a small tolerance chosen by us. Then, $y^{(k+1)}$ is the approximate solution of the semilinear problem.

3. Some Properties of the Linear Problem

We rewrite Equations (6) and (7) as

$$\varepsilon u''(x) + a(x)u'(x) + b(x)u(x) = F(x), \quad (10)$$

where

$$b(x) = \frac{\partial f^{(k)}}{\partial y}, \qquad F(x) = -f(x,y^{(k)}(x)) + \frac{\partial f^{(k)}}{\partial y}y^{(k)}(x),$$

and $y^{(k+1)}(x) = u(x)$ such that

$$u(0) = A, \qquad u(1) = B. \quad (11)$$

We present some important properties for the solution of Equations (10) and (11) which will be useful in the subsequent section for the analysis of relevant numerical solutions. Without a loss of generality, we assume that f is a decreasing function of y:

Lemma 1. *Continuous minimum principle: Assume that $v(x)$ is a sufficiently smooth function which satisfies $v(0) \geq 0$ and $v(1) \geq 0$. Then, $\mathcal{L}v(x) \leq 0,\ \forall x \in \Omega$ implies that $v(x) \geq 0, \forall x \in \bar{\Omega}$.*

Proof. Let v be a value such that $v(x^*) = \min_{x \in \Omega} v(x)$, and assume that $v(x^*) < 0$. Clearly, $x^* \notin \{0,1\}$, and therefore $v'(x^*) = 0$ and $v''(x^*) \geq 0$. Moreover, there is

$$\mathcal{L}v(x^*) = \varepsilon v''(x^*) + a(x^*)v'(x^*) + b(x^*)v(x^*) \geq 0,$$

which is a contradiction. It follows that $v(x^*) \geq 0$, and thus $v(x) \geq 0,\ \forall\ x \in \Omega$. □

Lemma 2. *Uniform stability estimate: Let u(x) be the solution of Equations (10) and (11). Then, we have*

$$||u(x)|| \leq \alpha^{-1}||F|| + \max(|A|,|B|), \quad \forall\ x \in \Omega. \tag{12}$$

Proof. We construct two barrier functions $\Psi^{\pm}$ defined by

$$\Psi^{\pm}(x) = \alpha^{-1}||F|| + \max(|A|,|B|) \pm u(x).$$

Then, it can be said that

$$\begin{aligned}
\Psi^{\pm}(0) &= \alpha^{-1}||F|| + \max(|A|,|B|) \pm u(0) \\
&= \alpha^{-1}||F|| + \max(|A|,|B|) \pm A \\
&\geq 0; \\
\Psi^{\pm}(1) &= \alpha^{-1}||F||| + \max(|A|,|B|) \pm u(1) \\
&= \alpha^{-1}||F|| + \max(|A|,|B|) \pm B \\
&\geq 0.
\end{aligned}$$

It follows that

$$\begin{aligned}
\mathcal{L}\Psi^{\pm}(x) &= \varepsilon(\Psi^{\pm}(x))'' + a(x)(\Psi^{\pm}(x))' + b(x)\Psi^{\pm}(x) \\
&= b(x)[\alpha^{-1}||F|| + \max(|A|,|B|) \pm \mathcal{L}u(x)] \\
&= b(x)[\alpha^{-1}||F|| + \max(|A|,|B|) \pm f(x)] \\
&\geq b(x)[\alpha^{-1}||F|| + \max(|A|,|B|)] \\
&\geq 0, \quad \text{since} \quad ||F|| \geq F(x).
\end{aligned}$$

Through Lemma 1, we obtain $\Psi^{\pm}(x) \geq 0,\ \forall\, x \in \Omega$. □

Lemma 3. *By letting u(x) be the solution of Equations (10) and (11) and $a(x), b(x)$, and $F(x)$ be smooth functions, then*

$$|v^{(i)}(x)| \leq C(1 + \varepsilon^{-i}e^{-\alpha x/\varepsilon}), \qquad i = 1, \ldots 4,\ \ x \in (0,1), \tag{13}$$

where α and C are positive constants independent of ε.

The proof can be seen in [7].

4. Construction of the FOFDM

In this section, we design a fitted operator finite different scheme base on the Mickens rules [34,35]. We denote the approximations of u_j at the grid point x_j by the unknown U_j. We partitioned the domain $\Omega := [0,1]$ into N subintervals of a length h such that

$$x_o = 0, \quad x_j = x_o + jh, \quad j = 1(1)N-1, \quad h_j = x_j - x_{j-1}, \quad x_N = 1.$$

We denote the set of these mesh points by Ω^N. We then discretized Equations (10) and (11) as

$$\varepsilon\delta^2 U_j + a_j D^+ U_j + b_j U_j = F_j, \qquad j = 1, \ldots N-1, \tag{14}$$

with the boundary condition

$$U_0 = A, \qquad U_N = B, \tag{15}$$

where

$$D^+ U_j = \frac{U_{j+1} - U_j}{h}, \quad \delta^2 U_j = \frac{U_{j+1} - 2U_j + U_{j-1}}{\phi_j^2},$$

and ϕ_j^2 is the denominator function given by

$$\phi_j^2 = \frac{\varepsilon h}{a_j}\left(\exp\left(\frac{a_j h}{\varepsilon}\right) - 1\right). \tag{16}$$

The difference equations consist of $N-1$ equations for $N+1$ unknowns $U_0, U_1, \ldots, U_N$, where U_0 and U_N are given boundary conditions. We write Equations (14) and (15) in matrix form as

$$AU = G$$

where $U = [U_1, U_2, \ldots, U_{N-1}]^T$ and A is a tridiagonal matrix whose entries are of the form

$$A_{ij} = r_j^-, \; i = j+1, \; j = 1, \ldots, N-2, \tag{17}$$

$$A_{ij} = r_j^c, \; i = j, \; j = 1, \ldots, N-1, \tag{18}$$

$$A_{ij} = r_j^+, \; i = j-1, \; j = 2, \ldots, N-1, \tag{19}$$

where

$$r_j^- = \frac{\varepsilon}{\phi_j^2}, \qquad r_j^c = -\frac{2\varepsilon}{\phi_j^2} - \frac{a_j}{h} + b_j, \qquad r_j^+ = \frac{\varepsilon}{\phi_j^2} + \frac{a_j}{h},$$

and G is obtained as

$$G_1 = F_1 - (r_1^-)U_0, \tag{20}$$

$$G_j = F_j, \qquad j = 2, \ldots, N-2, \tag{21}$$

$$G_{N-1} = F_{N-1} - (r_{N-1}^+)U_N. \tag{22}$$

Thus, the unknown $U_1, U_2, \ldots U_{N-1}$ is solved. The following lemma are relevant in the convergence analysis of this method:

Lemma 4. *Discrete minimum principle: Let η_j be a discrete function defined on Ω^N and satisfying $\eta_o \geq 0$, $\eta_N \geq 0$. Then, $\mathcal{L}^N \eta_j \leq 0$, $\forall\, 1 \leq j \leq N-1$ implies $\eta_j \geq 0$, $\forall\, 0 \leq j \leq N$.*

Proof. Let k be a value such that $\eta_k = \min_{x \in \Omega^N} \eta_j$, and assume $\eta_k < 0$. Clearly, $k \neq 0$, $k \neq N$, $\eta_{k+1} - \eta_k \geq 0$, and $\eta_k - \eta_{k-1} \leq 0$. It follows that

$$\mathcal{L}^N \eta_j = \frac{\varepsilon}{\phi_k^2}(\eta_{k+1} - 2\eta_k + \eta_{k-1}) + \frac{a_k}{h}(\eta_{k+1} - \eta_k) + b_k \eta_k \tag{23}$$

$$= \frac{\varepsilon}{\phi_k^2}[(\eta_{k+1} - \eta_k) - (\eta_k - \eta_{k-1})] + \frac{a_k}{h}(\eta_{k+1} - \eta_k) + b_k \eta_k \geq 0 \tag{24}$$

Thus, $\mathcal{L}^N \eta_j \leq 0$, $1 \leq k \leq N-1$, which is a contradiction. Hence, $\eta_j \geq 0$, $\forall\, x \in \Omega$. □

Lemma 5. *Uniform stability estimate: If μ_i is in any mesh function such that $\mu_o = \mu_N = 0$, then*

$$|\mu_i| \leq \frac{1}{\alpha} \max_{1\leq j\leq N-1} |\mathcal{L}^N \mu_j|, \qquad 0 \leq i \leq N. \tag{25}$$

Proof. Put $Z_i = \frac{1}{\alpha} \max_{1\leq j\leq N-1} |\mathcal{L}^N \mu_i|$ for $1 \leq i \leq N-1$. Introduce two mesh functions $\psi^{\pm}$ defined by

$$\psi_i^{\pm} = Zx_i \pm \mu_i$$

Clearly, $\psi_o^{\pm} = 0$, $\psi_N^{\pm} = 0$ and $\forall\ 1 \leq i \leq N-1$:

$$\mathcal{L}^N \psi_i^{\pm} = Za_i + \mathcal{L}^N \mu_i \leq 0.$$

Since $a_i > \alpha$, Lemma 4 implies that $\psi_i^{\pm} \geq 0, \quad \forall \quad 0 \leq i \leq N$, and this completes the proof. □

5. Convergence Analysis

In this section, we analyze the convergence property of the proposed method described in the previous section. The truncation error at the grid point x_i is

$$\mathcal{L}^h(u-U)_i = (\mathcal{L} - \mathcal{L}^h)u_i \tag{26}$$

$$= \varepsilon u_i'' + a_i u_i' - \frac{\varepsilon}{\phi_i^2}(u_{i+1} - 2u_i + u_{i-1}) - \frac{a_i}{h}(u_{i+1} - u_i). \tag{27}$$

By taking the Taylor series expansion of u_{i+1} and u_{i-1} and the truncated Taylor series expansion of $\phi_i^{-2} = \dfrac{1}{h^2} + \dfrac{a_i}{2\varepsilon h} - \dfrac{a_i^2}{12\varepsilon^2}$, we obtain

$$\begin{aligned}
\mathcal{L}^h(u-U)_i &= \varepsilon u_i'' - \left(h^2 u_i'' + \frac{h^4}{12} u_i^{iv}(\xi_i)\right) \times \left(\frac{\varepsilon}{h^2} + \frac{a_i}{2h} - \frac{a_i^2}{12\varepsilon}\right) - a_i\left(\frac{h}{2}u_i''\right) \\
&= \varepsilon u_i'' - \left(h^2 u_i'' + \frac{h^4}{12} u_i^{iv}(\xi_i)\right) \times \left(\frac{\varepsilon}{h^2} + \frac{1}{2}\left(\frac{a_{i+1} - a_i}{h}\right) - \frac{a_i^2}{12\varepsilon}\right) - a_i\left(\frac{h}{2}u_i''\right) \\
&= -\frac{a_i h u''}{2} + \left(\frac{\varepsilon u^{iv}}{12}(\xi_i) - \frac{a_i^2 u''}{12\varepsilon} + \frac{a_{i(x)} u''}{2}\right) h^2 + \left(\frac{a_{i(x)} u^{iv}}{24}(\xi_i) - \frac{a_i^2 u^{iv}}{144\varepsilon}(\xi_i)\right) h^4,
\end{aligned}$$

where $\xi_i \in (x_{i-1}, x_{i+1})$. By applying the boundary of the solution and its derivative (see Lemma 3) along with Lemma 5.2 in [36], we obtain

$$\mathcal{L}^h(u-U)_i \leq -\frac{a_i h}{2} + \left(\frac{\varepsilon}{12} - \frac{a_i^2}{12\varepsilon} + \frac{a_{i(x)}}{2}\right) h^2 + \left(\frac{a_{i(x)}}{24} - \frac{a_i^2}{144\varepsilon}\right) h^4.$$

From the relation $h > h^2 > h^4$, we have

$$|\mathcal{L}^h(u-U)_i| \leq Ch.$$

By applying the uniform stability estimate (Lemma 5), we obtain

$$\max_{0\leq j\leq N} |(u-U)_i| \leq Ch. \tag{28}$$

Theorem 1. *Let $u(x)$ be the solution of Equations (10) and (11) and $U(x)$ be the numerical approximation of Equations (14) and (15). If $a(x), b(x)$ and $F(x)$ are sufficiently smooth functions, then the truncation error is given by*

$$\max_{0\leq j\leq N} |(u-U)_j| \leq Ch, \tag{29}$$

where C is a constant independent of ε and h. This establishes that the numerical method developed is first-order uniformly convergent.

6. Numerical Results

In this section, we consider four test examples of singularly perturbed semilinear convection-diffusion problems to confirm our theoretical findings and to illustrate the performance of the proposed method in practice. We compute the maximum error and the rate of convergence and display the results in tables for different values of N and ε. Because the exact solution of Example 3 does not behave well for ε values close to 1, we chose $N = 2^i$ and $\varepsilon = 10^{-j}$ for $i \geq 4$ and $j \geq 2$. In the case where the exact solution is known, the point-wise maximum error is given by

$$E_{N,\varepsilon} = \max_{0 \leq j \leq N} |u_j - U_j|, \tag{30}$$

where U is the approximate solution and u is the exact solution. In cases where the exact solution is unknown, we compute the maximum point-wise error using the double mesh principle [37]:

$$E_{N,\varepsilon} = \max_{0 \leq j \leq N} |U_j^{\varepsilon,N} - U_{2j}^{\varepsilon,2N}|, \tag{31}$$

where U_N and U_{2N} are the numerical solutions computed on the meshes Ω^N and Ω^{2N}, respectively.

The rates of convergence are computed using the formula

$$R_{N,\varepsilon} = \log_2(E_{N_k}/E_{2N_k}), \tag{32}$$

In the iteration process, the initial guess is $U_N^{(0)} = (A, 0, 0, \ldots, 0, B)$, and the stopping criterion is

$$\max_k |U^{(k+1)} - U^{(k)}| \leq 10^{-10}, \qquad k = 1, 2, \ldots \tag{33}$$

Example 1. *Consider the following singularly perturbed semilinear problem [38]:*

$$\varepsilon u'' + 2u' + \exp(u) = 0, \qquad x \in [0,1],$$

$$u(0) = 0, \qquad u(1) = -\frac{\ln 2}{\exp(2/\varepsilon)}.$$

The exact solution is

$$u(x) = \ln\left(\frac{2}{1+x}\right) - \exp\left(\frac{-2x}{\varepsilon}\right)\ln 2.$$

In this case, the exact value is known, the maximum error, and the rate of convergence are obtained with the formula described in Equations (30) and (32).

The quasilinearization process equations are

$$\varepsilon u''^{(k+1)}(x) + 2u'^{(k+1)}(x) + \exp(u^{(k)}(x))u^{(k+1)}(x) = \exp(u^{(k)}(x))(u^{(k)}(x) - 1), \tag{34}$$

$$u^{(k)}(0) = 0, \qquad u^{(k)}(1) = 0.$$

Example 2. *Consider the following singularly perturbed semilinear problem [39]:*

$$\varepsilon u'' + u' + u^2 = 0, \qquad x \in [0,1],$$

$$u(0) = 0, \quad u(1) = 1/2.$$

In this case, the exact value is unknown, and mthe aximum error and rate of convergence are obtained with the formula describe in Equations (31) and (32). The quasilinearization process equations are

$$\varepsilon u''^{(k+1)}(x) + u'^{(k+1)}(x) + 2u^{(k)}(x)u^{(k+1)}(x) = (u^{(k)}(x))^2, \tag{35}$$

$$u^{(k)}(0) = 0, \qquad u^{(k)}(1) = 1/2.$$

Example 3. *Consider the following singularly perturbed semilinear problem [40]:*

$$\varepsilon u'' + (2x+1)u' + u^2 = 0, \qquad x \in [0,1],$$

$$u(0) = 1, \quad u(1) = 1.$$

The exact value is unknown, and the maximum error and rate of convergence are obtained with the formula described in Equations (31) and (32). The quasilinearization process equations are

$$\varepsilon u''^{(k+1)}(x) + (2x+1)u'^{(k+1)}(x) + 2u^{(k)}(x)u^{(k+1)}(x) = (u^{(k)}(x))^2, \tag{36}$$

$$u^{(k)}(0) = 1, \qquad u^{(k)}(1) = 1.$$

Example 4. *Consider the following singularly perturbed semilinear problem [41]:*

$$\varepsilon u'' + u' = u\exp(u), \qquad x \in [0,1],$$

$$u(0) = 1, \qquad u(1) = 0.$$

The exact value is unknown, and the maximum error and rate of convergence are also obtained with the formula described in Equations (31) and (32). The quasilinear process equations are

$$\varepsilon u''^{(k+1)}(x) + u'^{(k+1)}(x) + \exp(u^{(k)}(x))(u^k(x)+1)(x)u^{(k+1)}(x) = (u^{(k)}(x))\exp(u^{(k)}(x)), \tag{37}$$

$$u^{(k)}(0) = 1, \qquad u^{(k)}(1) = 0.$$

In each of the four examples, the solution has a boundary layer at the left side of the interval Ω. Tables 1–4 present the point-wise maximum error E_N and the rate of convergence R_N for different values of ε and N. The results shown in the tables reveal that the proposed method is of first-order uniform convergence, as projected by the theoretical analysis. Figure 1 provides the plots of the exact and numerical solutions of Example 1 for $\varepsilon = 10^{-2}$ and $N = 512$, intuitively showing that this numerical solution is a "good" approximation of the exact solution. In Figure 2, for the fixed number of subintervals $N = 256$, we plot the numerical solution for Example 1 for different values of ε, showing that the impact of ε on the numerical solution disappears as ε approaches 0, thus confirming the ε-uniform aspect of the proposed method. These conclusions were arrived at when observing the tabulated results. When ε is small, the nodal maximum errors and the rate of convergence remain unaffected by the change in value of this parameter.

Table 1. Results for Example 1: maximum errors and convergence rates for FOFDM.

ε	$N=16$	$N=32$	$N=64$	$N=128$	$N=256$	$N=512$	$N=1024$
10^{-2}	1.60×10^{-2}	9.36×10^{-3}	5.37×10^{-3}	3.82×10^{-3}	3.37×10^{-3}	3.25×10^{-3}	3.22×10^{-3}
	0.77	0.80	0.49	0.18	0.05	0.01	
10^{-3}	1.60×10^{-2}	9.33×10^{-3}	5.03×10^{-3}	2.61×10^{-3}	1.33×10^{-3}	6.95×10^{-4}	4.45×10^{-4}
	0.78	0.89	0.95	0.97	0.94	0.64	
10^{-4}	1.60×10^{-2}	9.33×10^{-3}	5.03×10^{-3}	2.61×10^{-3}	1.33×10^{-3}	6.71×10^{-4}	3.37×10^{-4}
	0.78	0.89	0.95	0.97	0.99	0.99	
10^{-4}	1.60×10^{-2}	9.33×10^{-3}	5.03×10^{-3}	2.61×10^{-3}	1.33×10^{-3}	6.71×10^{-4}	3.37×10^{-4}
$\vdots$	$\vdots$	$\vdots$	$\vdots$	$\vdots$	$\vdots$	$\vdots$	$\vdots$
10^{-20}	1.60×10^{-2}	9.33×10^{-3}	5.03×10^{-3}	2.61×10^{-3}	1.33×10^{-3}	6.71×10^{-4}	3.37×10^{-4}
	0.78	0.89	0.95	0.97	0.99	0.99	
E_N	1.60×10^{-2}	9.33×10^{-3}	5.03×10^{-3}	2.61×10^{-3}	1.33×10^{-3}	6.71×10^{-4}	3.37×10^{-4}
R_N	0.78	0.89	0.95	0.97	0.99	0.99	

Table 2. Results for Example 2: maximum errors and convergence rate for FOFDM.

ε	$N=16$	$N=32$	$N=64$	$N=128$	$N=256$	$N=512$	$N=1024$
10^{-2}	4.03×10^{-2}	1.85×10^{-2}	5.58×10^{-3}	1.10×10^{-3}	1.71×10^{-4}	3.52×10^{-5}	7.68×10^{-6}
	1.13	1.72	2.35	2.68	2.28	2.20	
10^{-3}	4.01×10^{-2}	2.03×10^{-2}	1.02×10^{-2}	5.12×10^{-3}	2.48×10^{-3}	8.71×10^{-4}	1.93×10^{-4}
	0.98	0.99	0.99	1.05	1.51	2.18	
10^{-4}	4.01×10^{-2}	2.03×10^{-2}	1.02×10^{-2}	5.10×10^{-3}	2.55×10^{-3}	1.28×10^{-3}	6.39×10^{-4}
	0.98	0.99	1.00	1.00	1.00	1.00	
10^{-5}	4.01×10^{-2}	2.03×10^{-2}	1.02×10^{-2}	5.10×10^{-3}	2.55×10^{-3}	1.28×10^{-3}	6.38×10^{-4}
	0.98	0.99	1.00	1.00	1.00	1.00	
$\vdots$	$\vdots$	$\vdots$	$\vdots$	$\vdots$	$\vdots$	$\vdots$	$\vdots$
10^{-20}	4.01×10^{-2}	2.03×10^{-2}	1.02×10^{-2}	5.10×10^{-3}	2.55×10^{-3}	1.28×10^{-3}	6.38×10^{-4}
	0.98	0.99	1.00	1.00	1.00	1.00	
E_N	4.01×10^{-2}	2.03×10^{-2}	1.02×10^{-2}	5.10×10^{-3}	2.55×10^{-3}	1.28×10^{-3}	6.38×10^{-4}
R_N	0.98	0.99	1.00	1.00	1.00	1.00	

Table 3. Results for Example 3: maximum errors and convergence rate for FOFDM.

ε	$N=16$	$N=32$	$N=64$	$N=128$	$N=256$	$N=512$	$N=1024$
10^{-2}	2.39×10^{-2}	1.16×10^{-2}	6.45×10^{-2}	1.24×10^{-1}	1.14×10^{-1}	7.52×10^{-2}	4.29×10^{-2}
	1.04	−2.47	−0.95	0.13	0.60	0.81	
10^{-3}	2.38×10^{-2}	1.11×10^{-2}	5.38×10^{-3}	2.65×10^{-3}	1.33×10^{-3}	3.29×10^{-2}	1.09×10^{-1}
	1.10	1.05	1.02	0.99	−4.62	−1.72	
10^{-4}	2.38×10^{-2}	1.11×10^{-2}	5.38×10^{-3}	2.65×10^{-3}	1.31×10^{-3}	6.54×10^{-4}	3.26×10^{-4}
	1.10	1.05	1.02	1.01	1.01	1.00	
10^{-5}	2.38×10^{-2}	1.11×10^{-2}	5.38×10^{-3}	2.65×10^{-3}	1.31×10^{-3}	6.54×10^{-4}	3.26×10^{-4}
	1.10	1.05	1.02	1.01	1.01	1.00	
$\vdots$	$\vdots$	$\vdots$	$\vdots$	$\vdots$	$\vdots$	$\vdots$	$\vdots$
10^{-20}	2.38×10^{-2}	1.11×10^{-2}	5.38×10^{-3}	2.65×10^{-3}	1.31×10^{-3}	6.54×10^{-4}	3.26×10^{-4}
	1.10	1.05	1.02	1.01	1.01	1.00	
E_N	2.38×10^{-2}	1.11×10^{-2}	5.38×10^{-3}	2.65×10^{-3}	1.31×10^{-3}	6.54×10^{-4}	3.26×10^{-4}
R_N	1.10	1.05	1.02	1.01	1.01	1.00	

Table 4. Results for Example 4: maximum errors and convergence rates for FOFDM.

ε	$N=16$	$N=32$	$N=64$	$N=128$	$N=256$	$N=512$	$N=1024$
10^{-2}	2.36×10^{-1} 1.51	7.94×10^{-2} 1.96	2.04×10^{-2} 2.47	3.67×10^{-3} 2.00	9.17×10^{-4} 1.47	3.31×10^{-4} 1.21	1.43×10^{-4}
10^{-3}	2.43×10^{-1} 1.28	9.97×10^{-2} 1.12	4.58×10^{-2} 1.08	2.17×10^{-2} 1.20	9.48×10^{-3} 1.63	3.05×10^{-3} 2.25	6.41×10^{-4}
10^{-4}	2.43×10^{-1} 1.28	9.97×10^{-2} 1.12	4.58×10^{-2} 1.06	2.20×10^{-2} 1.03	1.08×10^{-2} 1.01	5.36×10^{-3} 1.01	2.65×10^{-3}
10^{-5}	2.43×10^{-1} 1.28	9.97×10^{-2} 1.12	4.58×10^{-2} 1.06	2.20×10^{-2} 1.03	1.08×10^{-2} 1.01	5.36×10^{-3} 1.01	2.67×10^{-3}
$\vdots$	$\vdots$	$\vdots$	$\vdots$	$\vdots$	$\vdots$	$\vdots$	$\vdots$
10^{-20}	2.43×10^{-1} 1.28	9.97×10^{-2} 1.12	4.58×10^{-2} 1.06	2.20×10^{-2} 1.03	1.08×10^{-2} 1.01	5.36×10^{-3} 1.01	2.67×10^{-3}
E_N	2.43×10^{-1}	9.97×10^{-2}	4.58×10^{-2}	2.20×10^{-2}	1.08×10^{-2}	5.36×10^{-3}	2.67×10^{-3}
R_N	1.28	1.12	1.06	1.03	1.01	1.01	

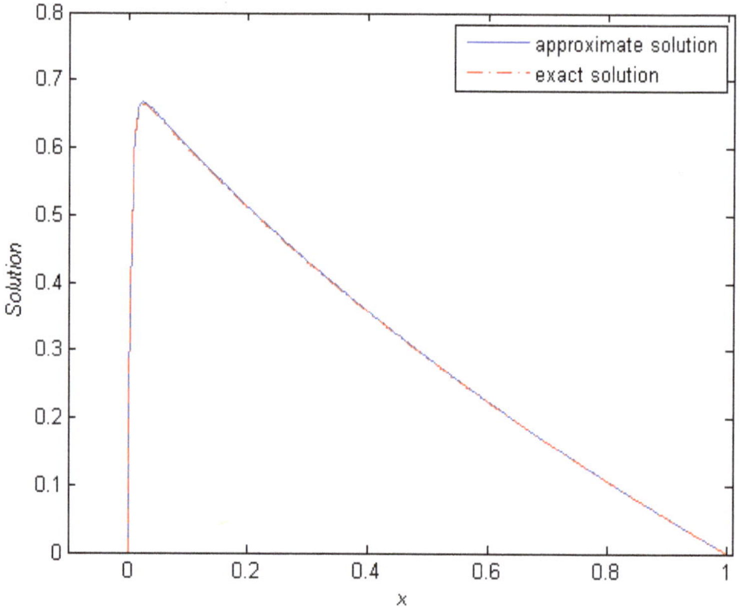

Figure 1. Comparison of the exact and approximate solutions of Example 1 for $\varepsilon=10^{-2}$ and $N=512$.

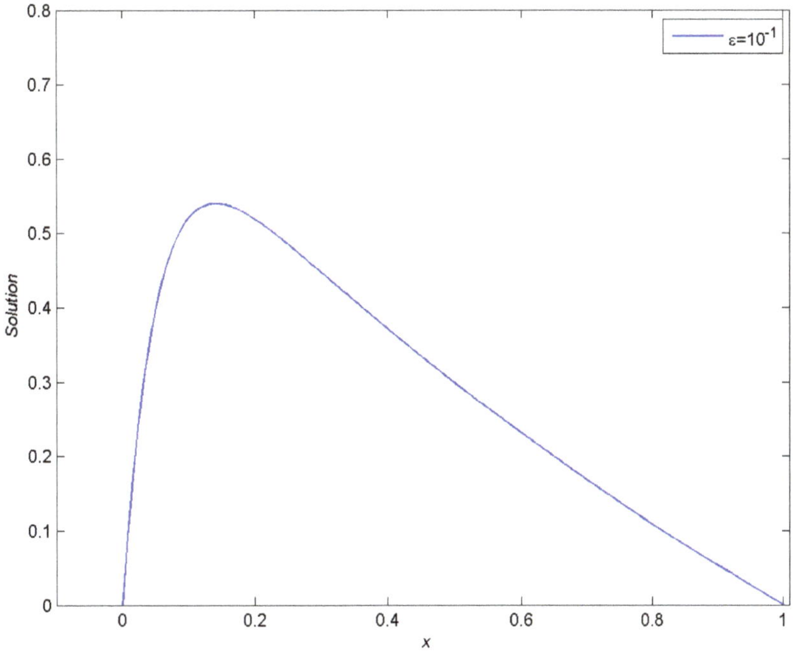

(a)

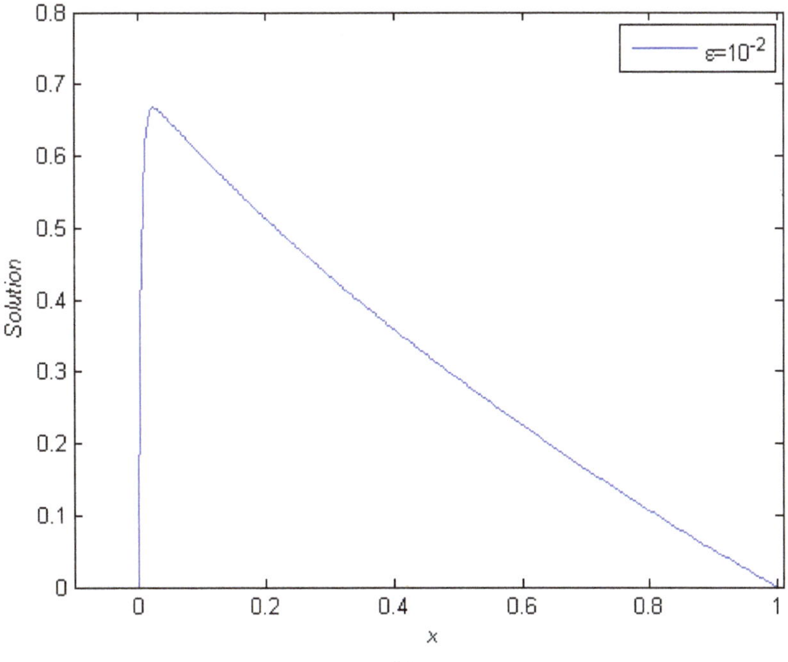

(b)

Figure 2. *Cont.*

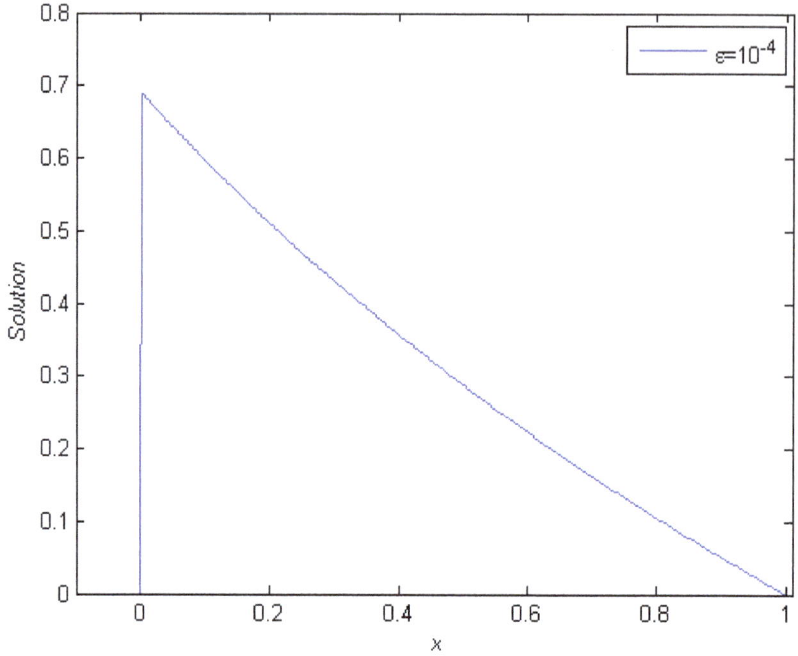

(**c**)

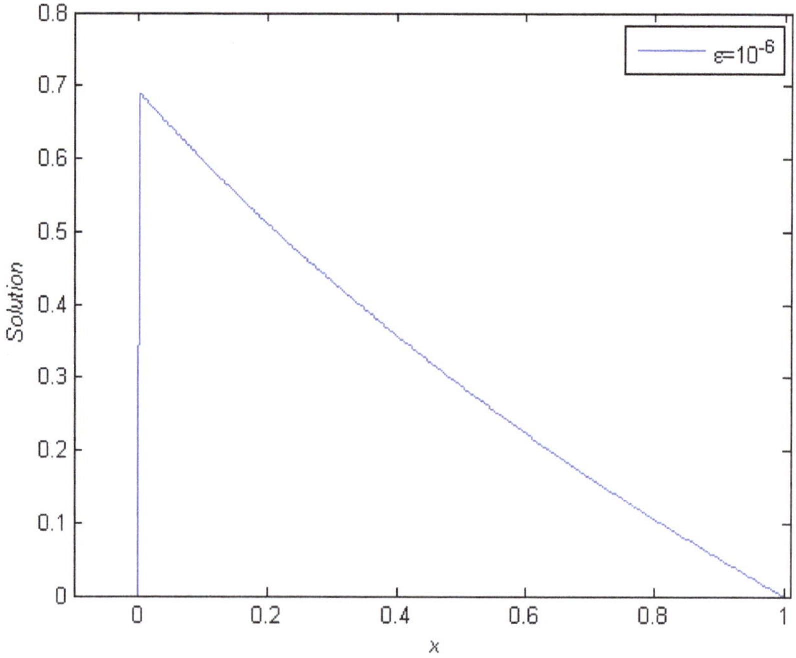

(**d**)

Figure 2. Plots of the approximate solution of Example 1 for (**a**) $\varepsilon = 10^{-1}$, (**b**) $\varepsilon = 10^{-2}$, (**c**) $\varepsilon = 10^{-4}$, and (**d**) $\varepsilon = 10^{-6}$ with $N = 256$.

7. Conclusions

We designed a fitted operator finite difference method for the numerical solution of a singularly perturbed semilinear convection-diffusion problem. The semilinear problem is transformed into a system of linear problems via the quasilinearization technique. The analysis and the numerical illustration conform to an agreement of a first-order ε-uniform convergence rate independent of the perturbation parameter. We present the maximum error and rate of convergence for different values of ε and N in tables. This work presents an alternative to numerical approaches for this class of problems. This is, to the best of our knowledge, the first time that singularly perturbed semilinear convection-diffusion two-point boundary value problems are solved using fitted operator finite difference methods.

The few previous works on singularly perturbed semilinear problems considered majorly fitted mesh methods based on Shishkin meshes. Although uniformly convergent, these methods suffer the drawback of presenting error bounds that depend on a logarithmic factor. This factor contributes to lowering both the accuracy and the rate of convergence. A further advantage of fitted operator finite difference methods is the simplicity of their analysis due to their use of uniform meshes.

Author Contributions: Conceptualization, J.B.M.; Methodology, J.B.M. and O.O.K.; Supervision, J.B.M.; Visualization, O.O.K.; Writing—original draft, O.O.K.; Writing—review & editing, J.B.M. All authors have read and agreed to the published version of the manuscript.

Funding: This research received no external funding.

Institutional Review Board Statement: Not applicable.

Informed Consent Statement: Not applicable.

Data Availability Statement: Not applicable.

Conflicts of Interest: The authors declare no conflict of interest. The funders had no role in the design of the study; in the collection, analyses, or interpretation of data; in the writing of the manuscript, or in the decision to publish the results.

References

1. Carusotto, I.; Ciuti, C. Quantum fluids of light. *Rev. Mod. Phys.* **2013**, *85*, 299. [CrossRef]
2. Malchow, A.K.; Azhand, A.; Knoll, P.; Engel, H.; Steinbock, O. From nonlinear reaction-diffusion processes to permanent microscale structures. Chaos. *Interdiscip. J. Nonlinear Sci.* **2019**, *29*, 53–129.
3. Shyy, W.; Udaykumar, H.S.; Rao, M.M. *Computational Fluid Dynamics with Moving Boundaries*; CRC Press: Boca Raton, FL, USA, 1995.
4. Nagy, A.; Saleh, M.; Omle, I.; Kareem, H.; Kovács, E. New Stable, Explicit, Shifted-Hopscotch Algorithms for the Heat Equation. *Math. Comput. Appl.* **2021**, *26*, 61. [CrossRef]
5. Farrell, P.; Hegarty, A.; Miller, J.M.; O'Riordan, E.; Shishkin, G.I. *Robust Computational Techniques for Boundary Layers*; CRC Press: Boca Raton, FL, USA, 2000.
6. Linß, T. Layer-adapted meshes for convection-diffusion problems. *Comput. Methods Appl. Mech. Eng.* **2003**, *192*, 1061–1105. [CrossRef]
7. Miller, J.J.; O'riordan, E.; Shishkin, G.I. *Fitted Numerical Methods for Singular Perturbation Problems: Error Estimates in the Maximum Norm for Linear Problems in One and Two Dimensions*; World Scientific: Singapore, 1996.
8. O'Malley, R.E. *Historical Developments in Singular Perturbations*; Springer International Publishing: Cham, Switzerland, 2014.
9. Roos, H.G.; Stynes, M.; Tobiska, L.; Kellogg, R.B. Numerical methods for singularly perturbed differential equations. *SIAM Rev.* **1997**, *39*, 535.
10. Roos, H.G.; Stynes, M.; Tobiska, L. *Robust Numerical Methods for Singularly Perturbed Differential Equations: Convection-Diffusion-Reaction and Flow Problems*; Springer Science & Business Media: Cham, Switzerland, 2008; p. 24.
11. Gracia, J.L.; O'Riordan, E. A defect-correction parameter-uniform numerical method for ia singularly perturbed convection-diffusion problem in one dimension. *Numer. Algorithms* **2006**, *41*, 359–385. [CrossRef]
12. Kopteva, N.; O'Riordan, E. Shishkin meshes in the numerical solution of singularly perturbed differential equations. *Int. J. Numer. Anal. Modeling* **2010**, *7*, 393–415.
13. Mo, J.Q. Quasilinear singularly perturbed problem with boundary perturbation. *J. Zhejiang Univ.-Sci. A* **2004**, *5*, 1144–1147. [CrossRef]
14. Vulanovic, R.; Teofanov, L. On the quasilinear boundary-layer problem and its numerical solution. *J. Comput. Appl. Math.* **2014**, *268*, 56–67. [CrossRef]

15. Cimen, E.; Amiraliyev, G.M. A uniform convergent method for singularly perturbed nonlinear differential-difference equation. *J. Inform. Math. Sci.* **2017**, *9*, 191–199.
16. Niijima, K. A uniformly convergent difference scheme for a semilinear singular perturbation problem. *Numer. Math.* **1984**, *43*, 175–198. [CrossRef]
17. Stynes, M. An adaptive uniformly convergent numerical method for a semilinear singular perturbation problem. *SIAM J. Numer. Anal.* **1989**, *26*, 442–455. [CrossRef]
18. Cakir, M.; Arslan, D. Finite difference method for nonlocal singularly perturbed problem. *Int. J. Mod. Res. Eng. Technol.* **2016**, *1*, 25–39.
19. Cakir, M.; Amiraliyev, G.M. Numerical solution of a singularly perturbed three-point boundary value problem. *Int. J. Comput. Math.* **2007**, *84*, 1465–1481. [CrossRef]
20. Boglaev, I.; Pack, S. A uniformly convergent method on arbitrary meshes for a semilinear convection-diffusion problem with discontinuous data. *Int. J. Numer. Anal. Model* **2008**, *5*, 24–39.
21. Linß, T. Robustness of an upwind finite difference scheme for semilinear convection-diffusion problems with boundary turning points. *J. Comput. Math.* **2003**, *21*, 401–410.
22. Shishkin, G.I.; Shishkina, L.P. A higher order richardson scheme for a singularly perturbed semilinear elliptic convection-diffusion equation. *Comput. Math. Math. Phys.* **2010**, *50*, 437–456. [CrossRef]
23. Linss, T.; Vulanović, R. Uniform methods for semilinear problems with attractive boundary turning points. *PAMM Proc. Appl. Math. Mech.* **2002**, *1*, 518–519. [CrossRef]
24. Yamac, K.; Erdogan, F. A Numerical scheme for semilinear singularly perturbed reaction-diffusion problems. *Appl. Math. Nonlinear Sci.* **2020**, *5*, 405–412. [CrossRef]
25. Kabeto, M.J.; Duressa, G.F. Robust numerical method for singularly perturbed semilinear parabolic differential difference equations. *Math. Comput. Simul.* **2021**, *188*, 537–547. [CrossRef]
26. Clavero, C.; Jorge, J.C. An efficient and uniformly convergent scheme for one-dimensional parabolic singularly perturbed semilinear systems of reaction-diffusion type. *Numer. Algorithms* **2020**, *85*, 1005–1027. [CrossRef]
27. Kumar, S.; Rao, S.C.S. A robust domain decomposition algorithm for singularly perturbed semilinear systems. *Int. J. Comput. Math.* **2017**, *94*, 1108–1122. [CrossRef]
28. Mariappan, M.; Tamilselvan, A. Higher order numerical method for a semilinear system of singularly perturbed differential equations. *Math. Commun.* **2021**, *26*, 41–52.
29. Rao, S.C.S.; Chaturvedi, A.K. Analysis of an almost fourth-order parameter-uniformly convergent numerical method for singularly perturbed semilinear reaction-diffusion system with non-smooth source term. *Appl. Math. Comput.* **2022**, *421*, 126944.
30. Munyakazi, J.B. A robust finite difference method for two-parameter parabolic convection-diffusion problems. *Appl. Math. Inf. Sci.* **2015**, *9*, 2877–2883.
31. Munyakazi, J.B. A uniformly convergent nonstandard finite difference scheme for a system of convection-diffusion equations. *Comput. Appl. Math.* **2015**, *34*, 1153–1165. [CrossRef]
32. Patidar, K.C. High order fitted operator numerical method for self-adjoint singular perturbation problems. *Appl. Math. Comput.* **2005**, *171*, 547–566. [CrossRef]
33. Munyakazi, J.B.; Patidar, K.C. A fitted numerical method for singularly perturbed parabolic reaction-diffusion problems. *Comput. Appl. Math.* **2013**, *32*, 509–519. [CrossRef]
34. Mickens, R.E. *Nonstandard Finite Difference Models of Differential Equations*; World Scientific: Singapore, 1994.
35. Micken, R.E. *Applications of Nonstandard Finite Difference Schemes*; World Scientific: Singapore, 2000.
36. Kadalbajoo, M.K.; Patidar, K.C. ε-uniformly convergent fitted mesh finite difference methods for general singular perturbation problems. *Appl. Math. Comput.* **2006**, *179*, 248–266. [CrossRef]
37. Doolan, E.P.; Miller, J.J.; Schilders, W.H.A. *Uniform Numerical Methods for Problems with Initial and Boundary Layers*; Boole Press: Dublin, Ireland, 1980.
38. Bender, C.M.; Orszag, S.A. *Advanced Mathematical Methods for Scientists and Engineers I: Asymptotic Methods and Perturbation Theory*; Springer Science and Business Media: Berlin/Heidelberg, Germany, 2013.
39. Cash, J.R.; Wright, M.H. A deferred correction method for nonlinear two-point boundary value problems: Implementation and numerical evaluation. *SIAM J. Sci. Stat. Comput.* **1991**, *12*, 971–989. [CrossRef]
40. Kadalbajoo, M.K.; Patidar, K.C. Numerical solution of singularly perturbed non-linear two point boundary value problems by spline in compression. *Int. J. Comput. Math.* **2002**, *79*, 271–288. [CrossRef]
41. Tikhovskaya, S.V.; Zadorin, A.I. A two-grid method with Richardson extrapolation for a semilinear convection-diffusion problem. *AIP Conf. Proc.* **2015**, *1684*, 090007.

mathematics MDPI

Article

On All Symmetric and Nonsymmetric Exceptional Orthogonal X_1-Polynomials Generated by a Specific Sturm–Liouville Problem

Mohammad Masjed-Jamei [1,†], Zahra Moalemi [1,†] and Nasser Saad [2,*]

1 Department of Mathematics, K. N. Toosi University of Technology, Tehran P.O. Box 16315-1618, Iran; mmjamei@kntu.ac.ir (M.M.-J.); zmoalemi@mail.kntu.ac.ir (Z.M.)
2 School of Mathematical and Computational Sciences, University of Prince Edward Island, Charlottetown, PE C1A 4P3, Canada
* Correspondence: nsaad@upei.ca
† These authors contributed equally to this work.

Abstract: Exceptional orthogonal X_1-polynomials of symmetric and nonsymmetric types can be considered as eigenfunctions of a Sturm–Liouville problem. In this paper, by defining a generic second-order differential equation, a unified classification of all these polynomials is presented, and 10 particular cases of it are then introduced and analyzed.

Keywords: Sturm–Liouville problems; exceptional orthogonal X_1-polynomials; Pearson distributions family; generalized Jacobi, Laguerre and Hermite differential equations

MSC: 34B24; 34L10; 33C45; 33C47

Citation: Masjed-Jamei, M.; Moalemi, Z.; Saad, N. On All Symmetric and Nonsymmetric Exceptional Orthogonal X_1-Polynomials Generated by a Specific Sturm–Liouville Problem. *Mathematics* **2022**, *10*, 2464. https://doi.org/10.3390/math10142464

Academic Editor: Sitnik Sergey

Received: 11 June 2022
Accepted: 12 July 2022
Published: 15 July 2022

Publisher's Note: MDPI stays neutral with regard to jurisdictional claims in published maps and institutional affiliations.

Copyright: © 2022 by the authors. Licensee MDPI, Basel, Switzerland. This article is an open access article distributed under the terms and conditions of the Creative Commons Attribution (CC BY) license (https://creativecommons.org/licenses/by/4.0/).

1. Introduction

Classical orthogonal polynomials can be considered eigenfunctions of a Sturm–Liouville problem [1–3] of the form

$$\frac{d}{dx}\left(k(x)\frac{dy}{dx}\right) - (\lambda\rho(x) + q(x))y = 0, \tag{1}$$

on an open interval, say (a,b), with the boundary conditions

$$\begin{aligned} \alpha_1 y(a) + \beta_1 y'(a) = 0, \\ \alpha_2 y(b) + \beta_2 y'(b) = 0, \end{aligned} \tag{2}$$

in which α_1, α_2 and β_1, β_2 are given constants and the functions $k(x) > 0$, $q(x)$ and $\rho(x) > 0$ in (1) are assumed to be continuous for $x \in [a,b]$. The boundary value problem (1) and (2) is called singular [4] if one of the points a and b is singular, i.e., $k(a) = 0$ or $k(b) = 0$. Sturm–Liouville problems appear in various branches of physics, engineering and biology and are usually studied in three different continuous, discrete and q-discrete spaces; see, for example, [5].

Let $y_n(x)$ and $y_m(x)$ be two solutions of Equation (1). Following the Sturm–Liouville theory [4,6], they are orthogonal with respect to the positive weight function $\rho(x)$ on (a,b) under the given conditions (2), i.e.,

$$\int_a^b \rho(x)y_n(x)y_m(x)\,dx = \left(\int_a^b \rho(x)y_n^2(x)\,dx\right)\delta_{n,m}, \tag{3}$$

where

$$\delta_{n,m} = \begin{cases} 0 & (n \neq m), \\ 1 & (n = m). \end{cases}$$

Many special functions in theoretical and mathematical physics are solutions of a regular or singular Sturm–Liouville problem, satisfying the orthogonality condition (3) [4,7].

There are totally six sequences of real polynomials [5] that are orthogonal with respect to the Pearson distributions family

$$W\left(\begin{array}{c} d^*,\ e^* \\ a,\ b,\ c \end{array} \middle| \, x \right) = \exp\left(\int \frac{d^* x + e^*}{ax^2 + bx + c} dx \right) \qquad (a, b, c, d^*, e^* \in \mathbb{R}). \tag{4}$$

Three of them (i.e., Jacobi, Laguerre and Hermite polynomials [3]) are infinitely orthogonal with respect to three special cases of the positive function (4) (i.e., beta, gamma and normal distributions [8]) and three other ones are finitely orthogonal limited to some parametric constraints with respect to F-Fisher, inverse gamma and generalized T-student distributions [8]. Table 1 shows the main properties of these six sequences.

Table 1. Characteristics of six sequences of classical orthogonal polynomials.

Polynomial Notation	Distribution	Weight Function	Kind Interval Parameters Constraint
$P_n^{(\alpha,\beta)}(x)$	Beta	$W\left(\begin{array}{c} -\alpha-\beta,\ -\alpha+\beta \\ -1,\ 0,\ 1 \end{array} \middle| \, x \right) = (1-x)^{\alpha}(1+x)^{\beta}$	Infinite $[-1, 1]$ $\forall n, \alpha > -1, \beta > -1$
$L_n^{(\alpha)}(x)$	Gamma	$W\left(\begin{array}{c} -1,\ \alpha \\ 0,\ 1,\ 0 \end{array} \middle| \, x \right) = x^{\alpha} \exp(-x)$	Infinite $[0, \infty)$ $\forall n, \alpha > -1$
$H_n(x)$	Normal	$W\left(\begin{array}{c} -2,\ 0 \\ 0,\ 0,\ 1 \end{array} \middle| \, x \right) = \exp(-x^2)$	Infinite $(-\infty, \infty)$ —
$M_n^{(p,q)}(x)$	Fisher F	$W\left(\begin{array}{c} -p,\ q \\ 1,\ 1,\ 0 \end{array} \middle| \, x \right) = x^{q}(x+1)^{-(p+q)}$	Finite $[0, \infty)$ $\max n < (p-1)/2$ $q > -1$
$N_n^{(p)}(x)$	Inverse Gamma	$W\left(\begin{array}{c} -p,\ 1 \\ 1,\ 0,\ 0 \end{array} \middle| \, x \right) = x^{-p} \exp(-1/x)$	Finite $[0, \infty)$ $\max n < (p-1)/2$
$J_n^{(p,q)}(x)$	Generalized T	$W\left(\begin{array}{c} -2p,\ q \\ 1,\ 0,\ 1 \end{array} \middle| \, x \right) = (1+x^2)^{-p} \exp(q \arctan x)$	Finite $(-\infty, \infty)$ $\max n < p - 1/2$

It was shown by S. Bochner [7,9] that if an infinite sequence of polynomials $\{P_n\}_{n=0}^{\infty}$ satisfies a second-order eigenvalue equation of the form

$$\sigma(x)P_n''(x) + \tau(x)P_n'(x) + r(x)P_n(x) = \lambda_n P_n(x) \qquad n = 0, 1, 2, \ldots,$$

then $\sigma(x)$, $\tau(x)$ and $r(x)$ must be polynomials of degree 2, 1 and 0, respectively. Moreover, if the sequence $\{P_n\}_{n=0}^{\infty}$ is an orthogonal set, then it has to be one of the classical Jacobi, Laguerre or Hermite polynomials, which satisfy a second order differential equation of the form [9–11]

$$\sigma(x)y_n''(x) + \tau(x)y_n'(x) - \lambda_n y_n(x) = 0, \tag{5}$$

where

$$\sigma(x) = ax^2 + bx + c \quad \text{and} \quad \tau(x) = dx + e,$$

and

$$\lambda_n = n\big(d + (n-1)a\big),$$

is the eigenvalue depending on $n = 0, 1, 2, \ldots$. However, there are three other sequences of hypergeometric polynomials that are solutions of Equation (5) but finitely orthogonal [12].

It is the presumption in the theory of special functions that any orthogonal polynomial system starts with a polynomial of degree 0. Nevertheless, from the Sturm–Liouville theory point of view, such a restriction is not necessary, and that point gives birth to the so-called 'exceptional orthogonal polynomials'. In this sense, two families of exceptional orthogonal polynomials were recently introduced in [13,14] as solutions of a second-order eigenvalue equation of the form

$$\Big(k_2(x-b)^2 + k_1(x-b) + k_0\Big)y_n''(x) + \frac{ax - ab - 1}{x-b}\Big(k_1(x-b) + 2k_0\Big)y_n'(x) \\ - \Big(\frac{a}{x-b}\big(k_1(x-b) + 2k_0\big) + \lambda_n\Big)y_n(x) = 0,$$

for $n \geq 1$, where

$$\lambda_n = (n-1)(nk_2 + ak_1),$$

and $k_0 \neq 0, k_1, k_2$ are real constants. It was also shown in [13] that if a self-adjoint second-order operator has a polynomial eigenfunctions of type $\{P_i(x)\}_{i=1}^{\infty}$, then it can be X_1-Jacobi polynomials $\hat{P}_n^{(\alpha,\beta)}(x)$ with the weight function

$$\hat{W}_{\alpha,\beta}(x) = \Big(x - \frac{\beta+\alpha}{\beta-\alpha}\Big)^{-2}(1-x)^{\alpha}(1+x)^{\beta} \qquad \text{for} \quad x \in (-1,1), \tag{6}$$

where $\alpha, \beta > -1$, $\alpha \neq \beta$, $\operatorname{sgn}\alpha = \operatorname{sgn}\beta$, and/or X_1-Laguerre polynomials $\hat{L}_n^{(\alpha)}(x)$ with the weight function

$$\hat{W}_{\alpha}(x) = \big(x+\alpha\big)^{-2}x^{\alpha}e^{-x} \qquad \text{for} \quad x \in (0,\infty) \quad \text{and} \quad \alpha > 0. \tag{7}$$

Exceptional orthogonal polynomials were recently of interest due to their important applications in exactly solvable potentials and supersymmetry, Dirac operators minimally coupled to external fields and entropy measures in quantum information theory [15,16].

This paper is organized as follows. In the next section, we consider six sequences of orthogonal X_1-polynomials as particular solutions of a generic differential equation in the form

$$(x-r)\Big(a_2x^2 + a_1x + a_0\Big)y_n''(x) + \Big(b_2x^2 + b_1x + b_0\Big)y_n'(x) \\ - \big(\lambda_n(x-r) + c_0^*\big)y_n(x) = 0, \quad n \geq 1, \tag{8}$$

where r is a real parameter such that $a_2r^2 + a_1r + a_0 \neq 0$ and the roots of $b_2x^2 + b_1x + b_0$ are supposed to be real, see Section 3 for more details. Both infinite and finite types of nonsymmetric exceptional orthogonal X_1-polynomials can be extracted from Equation (8). Although some infinite polynomial sequences were investigated in [17] for particular values of r, the finite cases of nonsymmetric exceptional X_1-polynomials orthogonal on infinite intervals are introduced in this paper for the first time. A key point in this sense is that the weight functions corresponding to these six sequences are exactly a multiplication of the Pearson distributions family introduced in Table 1. Hence, in Section 2, we first have a review on six classical orthogonal polynomials in order to present a unified classification for nonsymmetric exceptional orthogonal X_1-polynomials in Section 3. In Section 4, we study a series of solutions of the generic Equation (8) in order to find some of its polynomial-type solutions. In Section 5, six extended differential equations, as particular cases of the main Equation (8), are introduced, and it is shown that their polynomial solutions are X_1-orthogonal. Finally in Section 6, we apply the generic Equation (8) once again to establish a symmetric Sturm–Liouville equation of the form

$$A(x)\,y_n''(x) + B(x)\,y_n'(x) + \Big(\lambda_n\,C(x) + D(x) + \frac{1-(-1)^n}{2}E(x)\Big)\,y_n(x) = 0,$$

and then to introduce four main classes of symmetric orthogonal X_1-polynomials.

2. Classical Orthogonal Polynomials: A Brief Review

It is shown in [5] that the monic polynomial solution of Equation (5) can be represented as

$$y_n(x) = \bar{P}_n\left(\begin{matrix} d,\ e \\ a,\ b,\ c \end{matrix}\,\middle|\, x\right) = \sum_{k=0}^{n}\binom{n}{k} G_k^{(n)}(a,b,c,d,e)\,x^k, \tag{9}$$

where

$$G_k^{(n)} = \left(\frac{2a}{b+\sqrt{b^2-4ac}}\right)^{k-n} {}_2F_1\left(\begin{matrix} k-n,\ \frac{2ae-bd}{2a\sqrt{b^2-4ac}}+1-\frac{d}{2a}-n \\ -\frac{d}{a}+2-2n \end{matrix}\,\middle|\, \frac{2\sqrt{b^2-4ac}}{b+\sqrt{b^2-4ac}}\right),$$

and

$${}_2F_1\left(\begin{matrix} a,\ b \\ c \end{matrix}\,\middle|\, x\right) = \sum_{k=0}^{\infty}\frac{(a)_k(b)_k}{(c)_k}\frac{x^k}{k!},$$

denotes the Gauss hypergeometric function for $(a)_k = a(a+1)\dots(a+k-1)$.

The general Formula (9) is a suitable tool to compute the coefficients of x^k for any fixed degree k and arbitrary a, so that after simplifying it, we obtain

$$\begin{aligned}
\bar{P}_n\left(\begin{matrix} d,\ e \\ a,\ b,\ c \end{matrix}\,\middle|\, x\right) &= x^n + \binom{n}{1}\frac{e+(n-1)b}{d+2(n-1)a}x^{n-1} \\
&+ \binom{n}{2}\frac{(e+(n-1)b)(e+(n-2)b)+c(d+2(n-1)a)}{(d+2(n-1)a)(d+(2n-3)a)}x^{n-2} + \dots \\
&+ \binom{n}{n}\left(\frac{b+\sqrt{b^2-4ac}}{2a}\right)^n {}_2F_1\left(\begin{matrix} -n,\ 1-n-\frac{bd-2ae}{2a\sqrt{b^2-4ac}}-\frac{d}{2a} \\ 2(1-n)-\frac{d}{a} \end{matrix}\,\middle|\, \frac{2\sqrt{b^2-4ac}}{b+\sqrt{b^2-4ac}}\right).
\end{aligned}$$

Moreover, by referring to the Nikiforov and Uvarov approach [6] and considering Equation (5) as a self-adjoint form, the Rodrigues representation of the monic polynomials is derived as

$$\begin{aligned}
\bar{P}_n\left(\begin{matrix} d,\ e \\ a,\ b,\ c \end{matrix}\,\middle|\, x\right) &= \frac{1}{\left(\prod_{k=1}^{n} d+(n+k-2)a\right) W\left(\begin{matrix} d,\ e \\ a,\ b,\ c \end{matrix}\,\middle|\, x\right)} \\
&\times \frac{d^n\left((ax^2+bx+c)^n W\left(\begin{matrix} d,\ e \\ a,\ b,\ c \end{matrix}\,\middle|\, x\right)\right)}{dx^n},
\end{aligned} \tag{10}$$

where

$$W\left(\begin{matrix} d,\ e \\ a,\ b,\ c \end{matrix}\,\middle|\, x\right) = \exp\left(\int\frac{(d-2a)x+e-b}{ax^2+bx+c}dx\right).$$

Using the Formula (9) or (10), we can also obtain a generic three term recurrence equation as [5]

$$\bar{P}_{n+1}(x) = \left(x + \frac{2n(n+1)ab + (d-2a)(e+2nb)}{(d+2na)(d+(2n-2)a)}\right)\bar{P}_n(x)$$
$$+ n(d+(n-2)a)\frac{\left(c(d+(2n-2)a)^2 - nb^2(d+(n-2)a) + (e-b)(a(e+b)-bd)\right)}{(d+(2n-3)a)(d+(2n-2)a)^2(d+(2n-1)a)}\bar{P}_{n-1}(x),$$

in which $\bar{P}_n(x)$ denotes the monic polynomials of (9) with the initial values

$$\bar{P}_0(x) = 1 \text{ and } \bar{P}_1(x) = x + \frac{e}{d}.$$

Finally, the norm square value of the monic polynomials (9) can be calculated as follows: Let $[L, U]$ be a predetermined orthogonality interval which consists of the zeros of $\sigma(x) = ax^2 + bx + c$ or $\pm\infty$. By noting the Rodrigues representation (10), we have

$$\|\bar{P}_n\|^2 = \int_L^U \bar{P}_n^2\left(\begin{matrix} d, & e \\ a, & b, & c \end{matrix} \middle| x\right) W\left(\begin{matrix} d, & e \\ a, & b, & c \end{matrix} \middle| x\right) dx$$
$$= \frac{1}{\prod_{k=1}^{n} d+(n+k-2)a} \int_L^U \bar{P}_n\left(\begin{matrix} d, & e \\ a, & b, & c \end{matrix} \middle| x\right) \frac{d^n}{dx^n}\left((ax^2+bx+c)^n W\left(\begin{matrix} d, & e \\ a, & b, & c \end{matrix} \middle| x\right)\right) dx. \quad (11)$$

Hence, integrating by parts from the right hand side of (11) eventually yields

$$\|\bar{P}_n\|^2 = \frac{n!\,(-1)^n}{\prod_{k=1}^{n} d+(n+k-2)a} \int_L^U (ax^2+bx+c)^n \left(\exp \int \frac{(d-2a)x+e-b}{ax^2+bx+c} dx\right) dx.$$

Although the Jacobi polynomials

$$\bar{P}_n^{(\alpha,\beta)}(x) = \bar{P}_n\left(\begin{matrix} -\alpha-\beta-2, & \beta-\alpha \\ -1, & 0, & 1 \end{matrix} \middle| x\right),$$

Laguerre polynomials

$$\bar{L}_n^{(\alpha)}(x) = \bar{P}_n\left(\begin{matrix} -1, & \alpha+1 \\ 0, & 1, & 0 \end{matrix} \middle| x\right),$$

and Hermite polynomials

$$\bar{H}_n(x) = \bar{P}_n\left(\begin{matrix} -2, & 0 \\ 0, & 0, & 1 \end{matrix} \middle| x\right),$$

are three polynomial solutions of Equation (5), there are three other sequences of hypergeometric polynomials that are finitely orthogonal with respect to the generalized T, inverse Gamma and F distributions [12] and are solutions of Equation (5). The first finite sequence, i.e.,

$$\bar{M}_n^{(p,q)}(x) = \bar{P}_n\left(\begin{matrix} 2-p, & 1+q \\ 1, & 1, & 0 \end{matrix} \middle| x\right),$$

satisfies the differential equation

$$(x^2+x)y_n''(x) + ((2-p)x+q+1)y_n'(x) - n(n+1-p)y_n(x) = 0,$$

and is finitely orthogonal with respect to the weight function

$$W_1(x;p,q) = x^q(1+x)^{-(p+q)},$$

on $[0,\infty)$ if and only if [12]

$$p > 2\{\max n\} + 1 \quad \text{and} \quad q > -1.$$

The second finite sequence, i.e.,

$$\bar{N}_n^{(p)}(x) = \bar{P}_n\left(\begin{array}{c} 2-p,\ 1 \\ 1,\ 0,\ 0 \end{array}\middle|\, x\right),$$

satisfies the differential equation

$$x^2 y_n''(x) + ((2-p)x+1)y_n'(x) - n(n+1-p)y_n(x) = 0,$$

and is finitely orthogonal with respect to the weight function [12]

$$W_2(x;p) = x^{-p}e^{-\frac{1}{x}},$$

on $(0,\infty)$ for $n = 0,1,2,\ldots,N < \frac{p-1}{2}$. The third finite sequence, which is finitely orthogonal with respect to the generalized T-student distribution weight function

$$W_3(x;p,q) = \left(1+x^2\right)^{-p}\exp(q\arctan x),$$

is defined on $(-\infty,\infty)$ as

$$\bar{J}_n^{(p,q)}(x) = \bar{P}_n\left(\begin{array}{c} 2-2p,\ q \\ 1,\ 0,\ 1 \end{array}\middle|\, x\right),$$

satisfying the equation

$$(1+x^2)\,y_n''(x) + (2(1-p)x+q)\,y_n'(x) - n(n+1-2p)\,y_n(x) = 0,$$

and the orthogonality property holds if

$$n = 0,1,2,\ldots,N < p - \frac{1}{2} \text{ and } q \in \mathbb{R}.$$

3. A Unified Classification of Nonsymmetric Exceptional Orthogonal X_1-Polynomials

Using identity, which is valid for every real A, B, C, x, r

$$Ax^2 + Bx + C = A(x-r)^2 + (2Ar+B)(x-r) + Ar^2 + Br + C,$$

another form of Equation (8) is as

$$\begin{aligned}(x-r)\Big(a_2(x-r)^2 + (2a_2r+a_1)(x-r) + a_2r^2 + a_1r + a_0\Big)y_n''(x)&\\ + \Big(b_2(x-r)^2 + (2b_2r+b_1)(x-r) + b_2r^2 + b_1r + b_0\Big)\,y_n'(x)&\\ - \Big(\lambda_n(x-r) + c_0^*\Big)\,y_n(x) = 0, \qquad n \geq 1.& \quad (12)\end{aligned}$$

We choose λ_n in (12) so that the relative eigenfunction y_n is a polynomial of degree n. Hence, we first consider a subspace of the whole space of polynomials of degree at most n as

$$\Pi_{n,r,v} = \operatorname{span}\Big\{(x-r-v), (x-r)^2, \ldots, (x-r)^n\Big\},$$

in which v is a real constant. By substituting $y_1(x) = x - r - v$ and $y_n(x) = (x-r)^n$ for $n \geq 2$ into (12), we respectively obtain

$$(b_2-\lambda_1)(x-r)^2 + (2\,b_2\,r + b_1 - c_0^* + v\,\lambda_1)(x-r) + b_2\,r^2 + b_1\,r + b_0 + v\,c_0^* = 0, \quad (13)$$

and

$$n(n-1)\Big(a_2(x-r)^2+(2a_2r+a_1)(x-r)+a_2r^2+a_1r+a_0\Big)(x-r)^{n-1}$$
$$+n\Big(b_2(x-r)^2+(2b_2r+b_1)(x-r)+b_2r^2+b_1r+b_0\Big)(x-r)^{n-1}$$
$$-\Big(\lambda_n(x-r)+c_0^*\Big)(x-r)^n=0 \qquad n\geq 2.$$

Therefore,

$$\lambda_n=n\big((n-1)a_2+b_2\big) \qquad \text{for} \qquad n\geq 1,$$

and, using Equation (13) with $n=1$,

$$\begin{cases} 2b_2r+b_1-c_0^*+\nu b_2=0, \\ b_2r^2+b_1r+b_0+\nu c_0^*=0. \end{cases} \tag{14}$$

Solving the system (14) gives

$$\nu=\frac{-b_1\pm\sqrt{b_1^2-4b_0b_2}}{2b_2}-r=\begin{cases} r_1-r, \\ r_2-r, \end{cases}$$

where r_1, r_2 are roots of $b_2x^2+b_1x+b_0$, and

$$c_0^*=c_0^*\Big\{r;b_2,b_1,b_0\Big\}=\frac{1}{2}\Big(2b_2r+b_1\mp\sqrt{b_1{}^2-4b_0b_2}\Big)=\begin{cases} b_2(r-r_2), \\ b_2(r-r_1). \end{cases}$$

Corollary 1. *If we take $b_2x^2+b_1x+b_0=b_2(x-r_1)(x-r_2)$ for $b_2\neq 0$ and*

$$\Pi_{n,r,\nu}=span\{e_k(x)\}_{k=1}^n,$$

then
(i) $e_1(x)=x-r_1$ and $\{e_k(x)\}_{k=2}^\infty=\{(x-r)^k\}_{k=2}^\infty$ lead to $c_0^*=b_2(r-r_2)$.

(ii) $e_1(x)=x-r_2$ and $\{e_k(x)\}_{k=2}^\infty=\{(x-r)^k\}_{k=2}^\infty$ lead to $c_0^*=b_2(r-r_1)$.

Also note that for $b_2=0$, we respectively have $c_0^*=b_1$ and $\nu=-r-\frac{b_0}{b_1}$.

We can now show that the polynomial solutions of Equation (12) in $\Pi_{n,r,\nu}$ are orthogonal on an interval, say $[L,U]$, with respect to a weight function in the form

$$\rho(x)=(x-r)\omega(x),$$

where $\omega(x)$ satisfies the equation

$$\frac{\omega'(x)}{\omega(x)}=\frac{(b_2-3a_2)x^2+(b_1-2a_1+2a_2r)x+b_0-a_0+a_1r}{(x-r)(a_2x^2+a_1x+a_0)}. \tag{15}$$

To prove the orthogonality, we first consider the self-adjoint form of Equation (12) as

$$\Big(\omega(x)(x-r)(a_2x^2+a_1x+a_0)y_n'\Big)'=\omega(x)\Big(\lambda_n(x-r)+c_0^*\Big)y_n(x), \tag{16}$$

and for the index m as

$$\Big(\omega(x)(x-r)(a_2x^2+a_1x+a_0)y_m'\Big)'=\omega(x)\Big(\lambda_m(x-r)+c_0^*\Big)y_m(x). \tag{17}$$

Multiplying by $y_m(x)$ and $y_n(x)$ in relations (16) and (17) respectively, subtracting them and then integrating from both sides yields

$$\Big[\omega(x)(x-r)\big(a_2x^2+a_1x+a_0\big)\big(y_n'(x)y_m(x)-y_m'(x)y_n(x)\big)\Big]_L^U \\ =(\lambda_n-\lambda_m)\int_L^U(x-r)\omega(x)y_n(x)y_m(x)\,dx. \quad (18)$$

Now if the following conditions

$$\omega(L)(L-r)\big(a_2L^2+a_1L+a_0\big)=0,$$
$$\omega(U)(U-r)\big(a_2U^2+a_1U+a_0\big)=0,$$

hold, the left hand side of (18) is equal to zero and therefore

$$\int_L^U(x-r)\omega(x)y_n(x)y_m(x)\,dx=0 \qquad m\neq n,$$

which approves the orthogonality of polynomial sequence $\{y_n(x)\}_{n=1}^{\infty}$ with respect to the weight function $\rho(x)=(x-r)\omega(x)$.

On the other hand, the explicit solution of Equation (15) is as

$$\omega(x)=\exp\left(\int\frac{(b_2-3a_2)x^2+(b_1-2a_1+2a_2r)x+b_0-a_0+a_1r}{(x-r)\big(a_2x^2+a_1x+a_0\big)}dx\right). \quad (19)$$

The key point in this relation is that $\omega(x)$ is exactly a multiplication of the Pearson distribution given in (4), because if the integrand function of (19) is written as a sum of two fractions with linear and quadratic denominators in the form

$$\frac{(b_2-3a_2)x^2+(b_1-2a_1+2a_2r)x+b_0-a_0+a_1r}{(x-r)(a_2x^2+a_1x+a_0)}=\frac{\frac{b_2r^2+b_1r+b_0}{a_2r^2+a_1r+a_0}-1}{x-r} \\ +\frac{\Big(b_2-a_2\big(2+\frac{b_2r^2+b_1r+b_0}{a_2r^2+a_1r+a_0}\big)\Big)x+b_1+b_2r-\big(\frac{b_2r^2+b_1r+b_0}{a_2r^2+a_1r+a_0}\big)(a_1+a_2r)-a_1}{a_2x^2+a_1x+a_0},$$

then we obtain

$$\omega(x)=(x-r)^{\frac{b_2r^2+b_1r+b_0}{a_2r^2+a_1r+a_0}-1} \\ \times\exp\left(\int\frac{\Big(b_2-a_2\big(2+\frac{b_2r^2+b_1r+b_0}{a_2r^2+a_1r+a_0}\big)\Big)x+b_1+b_2r-\big(\frac{b_2r^2+b_1r+b_0}{a_2r^2+a_1r+a_0}\big)(a_1+a_2r)-a_1}{a_2x^2+a_1x+a_0}dx\right) \\ =(x-r)^{\frac{b_2r^2+b_1r+b_0}{a_2r^2+a_1r+a_0}-1} \\ \times W\left(\begin{matrix}b_2-a_2\big(2+\frac{b_2r^2+b_1r+b_0}{a_2r^2+a_1r+a_0}\big),\ b_1+b_2r-\big(\frac{b_2r^2+b_1r+b_0}{a_2r^2+a_1r+a_0}\big)(a_1+a_2r)-a_1\\ a_2,\ a_1,\ a_0\end{matrix}\ \middle|\ x\right),$$

and accordingly,

$$\rho(x)=(x-r)^{\frac{b_2r^2+b_1r+b_0}{a_2r^2+a_1r+a_0}} \\ \times W\left(\begin{matrix}b_2-a_2\big(2+\frac{b_2r^2+b_1r+b_0}{a_2r^2+a_1r+a_0}\big),\ b_1+b_2r-\big(\frac{b_2r^2+b_1r+b_0}{a_2r^2+a_1r+a_0}\big)(a_1+a_2r)-a_1\\ a_2,\ a_1,\ a_0\end{matrix}\ \middle|\ x\right). \quad (20)$$

Corollary 2. *The polynomial solutions of the generic equation*

$$(x-r)\left(a_2x^2+a_1x+a_0\right)y_n''(x)+\left(b_2x^2+b_1x+b_0\right)y_n'(x)$$
$$-\Big(n\big(b_2+(n-1)a_2\big)(x-r)+c_0^*(r;b_2,b_1,b_0)\Big)y_n(x)=0, \quad (21)$$

where $(-1)^{\frac{b_2r^2+b_1r+b_0}{a_2r^2+a_1r+a_0}}=1$ *and* $n\geq 1$ *are nonsymmetric exceptional* X_1*-polynomials orthogonal with respect to the weight function* (20).

Now let us assume that the polynomial solution of Equation (21) is symbolically indicated as

$$y_n(x)=Q_{n,r}\left(\begin{array}{c|c} b_2,b_1,b_0 & \\ & x \\ a_2,a_1,a_0 & \end{array}\right). \quad (22)$$

By referring to the Pearson distributions family (4), an inverse process can also be considered as follows.

Suppose that a simplified case of the weight function (20) is given as

$$\rho(x)=(x-r)^{\theta}\,W\left(\begin{array}{c|c} d^*,\ e^* & \\ & x \\ a\ ,\ b\ ,\ c & \end{array}\right), \quad (23)$$

in which $(-1)^{\theta}=1$. Then, by noting Equation (21), the unknown polynomials $p_2(x)$ and $q_2(x)$ of degree 2 in the differential equation

$$(x-r)p_2(x)y_n''(x)+q_2(x)y_n'(x)-\left(\lambda_n(x-r)+c_0^*\right)y_n=0, \quad (24)$$

can be directly derived by computing the logarithmic derivative of the function

$$\frac{\rho(x)}{x-r}=(x-r)^{\theta-1}W\left(\begin{array}{c|c} d^*,\ e^* & \\ & x \\ a\ ,\ b\ ,\ c & \end{array}\right)=(x-r)^{\theta-1}W(x),$$

as

$$\frac{\left((x-r)^{\theta-1}W(x)\right)'}{(x-r)^{\theta-1}W(x)}=\frac{\theta-1}{x-r}+\frac{W'(x)}{W(x)}=\frac{\theta-1}{x-r}+\frac{d^*x+e^*}{ax^2+bx+c}$$
$$=\frac{\left(d^*+(\theta-1)a\right)x^2+\left(e^*-rd^*+(\theta-1)b\right)x-re^*+(\theta-1)c}{(x-r)(ax^2+bx+c)},$$

and then equating the result with

$$\frac{q_2(x)-\left((x-r)p_2(x)\right)'}{(x-r)p_2(x)},$$

so that we finally obtain

$$p_2(x)=ax^2+bx+c, \quad (25)$$

and

$$q_2(x)=\left(d^*+(\theta+2)a\right)x^2+\left(e^*-r(d^*+2a)+(\theta+1)b\right)x+\theta c-r(e^*+b), \quad (26)$$

provided that the roots of q_2 are real. Relations (25) and (26) show that the polynomial solution of Equation (24) with $\lambda_n = n\big((n+1+\theta)a + d^*\big)$ can be written in terms of the symbol (22) as

$$y_n(x) = Q_{n,r}\left(\begin{array}{c} d^* + (\theta+2)a,\ e^* - r(d^*+2a) + (\theta+1)b,\ \theta c - r(e^*+b) \\ a,\ b,\ c \end{array} \middle| \, x \right).$$

Additionally, according to the Corollary 1, c_0^* in (24) directly depends on the roots of $q_2(x)$ in (26) and is therefore computed as

$$c_0^* = 2\theta(ar^2+br+c)\big(d^*+(\theta+2)a\big)\Big(e^*+rd^*+(\theta+1)(2ra+b) \mp \sqrt{\big(e^*-r(d^*+2a)+(\theta+1)b\big)^2 - 4\big(d^*+(\theta+2)a\big)\big(\theta c - r(e^*+b)\big)}\Big)^{-1}.$$

As we observed, $\rho(x)$ was indeed the product of $(x-r)^\theta$ for

$$\theta = \frac{b_2r^2+b_1r+b_0}{a_2r^2+a_1r+a_0},$$

and a special case of the Pearson distributions family. This means that we can classify the nonsymmetric exceptional orthogonal X_1-polynomials into six main sequences.

Corollary 3. *By referring to Table 1 and relation (23), there are, in total, six sequences of nonsymmetric orthogonal X_1-polynomials as follows:*

1. *Infinite X_1-Jacobi polynomials orthogonal with respect to the weight function*

$$\rho_1(x) = (x-r)^\theta(1-x)^\alpha(1+x)^\beta, \qquad (-1 \le x \le 1).$$

2. *Infinite X_1-Laguerre polynomials orthogonal with respect to the weight function*

$$\rho_2(x) = (x-r)^\theta x^\alpha \exp(-x), \qquad (0 \le x < \infty).$$

3. *Infinite X_1-Hermite polynomials orthogonal with respect to the weight function*

$$\rho_3(x) = (x-r)^\theta \exp\left(-x^2\right), \qquad (-\infty < x < \infty).$$

4. *Finite X_1-polynomials orthogonal with respect to the weight function*

$$\rho_4(x) = (x-r)^\theta x^q (x+1)^{-(p+q)}, \qquad (0 \le x < \infty).$$

5. *Finite X_1-polynomials orthogonal with respect to the weight function*

$$\rho_5(x) = (x-r)^\theta x^{-p} \exp\left(-\frac{1}{x}\right), \qquad (0 \le x < \infty).$$

6. *Finite X_1-polynomials orthogonal with respect to the weight function*

$$\rho_6(x) = (x-r)^\theta \left(1+x^2\right)^{-p} \exp(q \arctan x), \qquad (-\infty < x < \infty).$$

In all six above-mentioned cases, $r \in \mathbb{R}$ and θ is a real parameter such that $(-1)^\theta = 1$.

Remark 1. *For $\theta = -2$ in the first and second kind of the above corollary, the weight functions represented in (6) and (7) are retrieved when $r = (\beta+\alpha)/(\beta-\alpha)$ and $r = -\alpha$, respectively.*

4. On the Series Solutions of Equation (12)

Let us reconsider Equation (12) in the form

$$y_n''(x) + \frac{b_2x^2 + b_1x + b_0}{(x-r)(a_2x^2 + a_1x + a_0)} y_n'(x) - \frac{\lambda_n(x-r) + c_0^*}{(x-r)(a_2x^2 + a_1x + a_0)} y_n(x) = 0. \quad (27)$$

The indicial equation corresponding to (27) is

$$t^2 + \left(\frac{b_2r^2 + b_1r + b_0}{a_2r^2 + a_1r + a_0} - 1\right)t = 0.$$

Hence, using the Frobenius method, we can obtain the series solutions of Equation (12) when

$$t_1 = 1 - \frac{b_2r^2 + b_1r + b_0}{a_2r^2 + a_1r + a_0} = 1 - \theta,$$

for different values of θ.

If $\theta \notin \mathbb{Z}$, the two basic solutions of Equation (27) are, respectively, in the forms

$$y_{n,1}(x) = \sum_{k=0}^{\infty} C_k(x-r)^k, \quad C_0 \neq 0,$$

and

$$y_{n,2}(x) = (x-r)^{1-\theta} \sum_{k=0}^{\infty} d_k(x-r)^k, \quad d_0 \neq 0.$$

If $\theta \in \mathbb{Z}$, three cases can occur for the basis solutions:

(i) If $\theta = 1$, then

$$\begin{cases} y_{n,1}(x) = \sum\limits_{k=0}^{\infty} C_k(x-r)^k, \quad C_0 \neq 0, \\ y_{n,2}(x) = y_{n,1}(x) \ln|x-r| + \sum\limits_{k=1}^{\infty} d_k(x-r)^k. \end{cases}$$

(ii) If $\theta < 1$, then,

$$\begin{cases} y_{n,1}(x) = (x-r)^{1-\theta} \sum\limits_{k=0}^{\infty} C_k(x-r)^k, \quad C_0 \neq 0, \\ y_{n,2}(x) = w y_{n,1}(x) \ln|x-r| + \sum\limits_{k=0}^{\infty} d_k(x-r)^k, \quad d_0 \neq 0, \quad w \in \mathbb{R}. \end{cases}$$

(iii) Finally, if $\theta > 1$, then

$$\begin{cases} y_{n,1}(x) = \sum\limits_{k=0}^{\infty} C_k(x-r)^k, \quad C_0 \neq 0, \\ y_{n,2}(x) = w y_{n,1}(x) \ln|x-r| + |x-r|^{1-\theta} \sum\limits_{k=0}^{\infty} d_k(x-r)^k, \quad d_0 \neq 0, \quad w \in \mathbb{R}. \end{cases}$$

In either case, there is at least one series solution, that it may assume the form

$$y_n(x) = \sum_{k=0}^{\infty} C_k(x-r)^{k-\theta+1}, \qquad (\theta \in \mathbb{Z},\ \theta < 1). \quad (28)$$

Substituting

$$y_n'(x) = \sum_{k=0}^{\infty}(k-\theta+1)C_k(x-r)^{k-\theta},$$
$$y_n''(x) = \sum_{k=0}^{\infty}(k-\theta+1)(k-\theta)C_k(x-r)^{k-\theta-1},$$

in Equation (12) eventually leads to the three-term recurrence relation

$$\begin{aligned}&((k-\theta)\,(a_2(k-\theta-1)+b_2)-\lambda_n)C_{k-1}\\&\quad+((k-\theta+1)((2a_2r+a_1)(k-\theta)+(2b_2r+b_1))-c_0^*)C_k\\&\quad+(k-\theta+2)\Big((a_2r^2+a_1r+a_0)(k-\theta+1)+(b_2r^2+b_1r+b_0)\Big)C_{k+1}=0.\end{aligned} \quad (29)$$

Note that, in a similar way, for $\theta \in \mathbb{Z}$ and $\theta \geq 1$, or $\theta \notin \mathbb{Z}$ the assumption

$$y_n(x) = \sum_{k=0}^{\infty} C_k(x-r)^k,$$

eventually leads to the same as recurrence relation (29) for $\theta = 1$.

Some Polynomial Solutions of Equation (21)

According to Corollary 1, the coefficients of the polynomial $B(x) = b_2x^2 + b_1x + b_0$ in (21) have a significant role in determining the value c_0^* in the system (14). In this section, we investigate six special cases of $B(x)$ based on its roots and the real value r, leading to particular cases of Equation (21). First, suppose that $b_2 \neq 0$ and r is a root of $B(x)$. So $b_2r^2 + b_1r + b_0 = 0$, and relations (14) reduce to

$$\begin{cases} 2b_2r + b_1 - c_0^* + \nu b_2 = 0, \\ \nu c_0^* = 0. \end{cases} \quad (30)$$

The equation $\nu\, c_0^* = 0$ in (30) gives three different cases as follows:

- **Case 1.** $\nu = 0$ and $c_0^* = 2b_2r + b_1 = B'(r) \neq 0$,
- **Case 2.** $c_0^* = 0$ and $\nu = -\dfrac{2b_2r + b_1}{b_2} = -\dfrac{B'(r)}{b_2} \neq 0$,
- **Case 3.** $c_0^* = 0$ and $\nu = 0$, leading to $B'(r) = 2b_2r + b_1 = 0$ which means that r is a multiple root of $B(x)$.

  Second, suppose that $b_2 = 0$ and $b_1 \neq 0$. So, relations (14) reduce to

$$\begin{cases} c_0^* = b_1, \\ \nu c_0^* = -(b_1r + b_0). \end{cases}$$

  Now, if r is a root of $B(x)$, we have $\nu c_0^* = 0$ leading to
- **Case 4.** $c_0^* = b_1 \neq 0$ and $\nu = 0$, which is indeed a particular case of the first Case 1 for $b_2 = 0$.

  Otherwise, we obtain
- **Case 5.** $c_0^* = b_1 \neq 0$ and $\nu = -\dfrac{b_1r + b_0}{c_0^*} = -\dfrac{B(r)}{b_1} \neq 0$.

Finally, suppose that $b_2 = b_1 = 0$. In this case, relations (14) reduce to

$$\begin{cases} c_0^* = 0, \\ b_0 + \nu c_0^* = 0, \end{cases}$$

which yield $b_0 = 0$ leading to $B(x) \equiv 0$. Therefore, the last case can be considered

- **Case 6.** $c_0^* = 0$ and ν is arbitrary.

Now we consider each of these six cases:

For Case 1. Under the conditions stated in Case 1, the differential Equation (21) reads with $b_0 = -b_1 r - b_2 r^2$, as

$$(a_2x^2 + a_1x + a_0)y_n''(x) + (b_2x + b_2r + b_1)y_n'(x) - \left(n\big(b_2 + (n-1)a_2\big) + \frac{2b_2r + b_1}{x - r}\right)y_n(x) = 0, \quad (31)$$

for $n \geq 1$, whose solutions belong to the space

$$\Pi_{n,r,0} = \text{span}\left\{(x-r), (x-r)^2, \ldots, (x-r)^n\right\}. \quad (32)$$

Relation (32) shows that the solution of Equation (31) can be considered as follows:

$$y_n(x) = (x-r)A_{n-1}(x-r) = (x-r)\sum_{k=0}^{n-1} d_k(x-r)^k. \quad (33)$$

Hence, replacing

$$\begin{cases} y_n' = A_{n-1}(x-r) + (x-r)A_{n-1}'(x-r), \\ y_n'' = 2A_{n-1}'(x-r) + (x-r)A_{n-1}''(x-r) \end{cases}$$

in (31) yields

$$(x-r)^2(a_2x^2 + a_1x + a_0)A_{n-1}'' + \Big(2(x-r)\big(a_2(x-r)^2 + (2a_2r + a_1)(x-r) + a_2r^2 + a_1r + a_0\big) + (x-r)^2(b_2x + b_2r + b_1)\Big)A_{n-1}' - (n-1)(b_2 + na_2)(x-r)^2A_{n-1} = 0. \quad (34)$$

Now, if in (34), we assume that $a_2r^2 + a_1r + a_0 = 0$, which is equivalent to

$$a_0 = -r(a_2r + a_1),$$

then Equation (34) is simplified as

$$\big(a_2x^2 + a_1x - r(a_2r + a_1)\big)A_{n-1}'' + \Big((2a_2 + b_2)x + (2a_2 + b_2)r + 2a_1 + b_1\Big)A_{n-1}' - (n-1)(b_2 + na_2)A_{n-1} = 0. \quad (35)$$

By comparing Equation (35) and Equation (5) and referring to the polynomial solution (9) and also relation (33), we can finally conclude that the polynomial solution of Equation (31) for $a_0 = -r(a_2r + a_1)$ is as

$$y_n(x) = (x-r)P_{n-1}\left(\begin{matrix} 2a_2 + b_2, & (2a_2 + b_2)r + 2a_1 + b_1 \\ a_2, \quad a_1, & -r(a_2r + a_1) \end{matrix} \middle| x - r\right).$$

In other words, we have

$$\bar{Q}_{n,r}\left(\begin{array}{c} b_2,\ b_1,\ -r(b_2r+b_1) \\ a_2, a_1, -r(a_2r+a_1) \end{array}\middle|\, x\right)$$
$$= (x-r)\bar{P}_{n-1}\left(\begin{array}{c} 2a_2+b_2,\ (2a_2+b_2)r+2a_1+b_1 \\ a_2,\ a_1,\ -r(a_2r+a_1) \end{array}\middle|\, x-r\right).$$

For cases 2, 3 and 6: The differential Equation (21) respectively reads as

$$\begin{aligned}(a_2x^2+a_1x+a_0)y_n''(x)+(b_2x+b_2r+b_1)y_n'(x)-n\big(b_2+(n-1)a_2\big)y_n(x)&=0,\\ (a_2x^2+a_1x+a_0)y_n''(x)+b_2(x-r)y_n'(x)-n\big(b_2+(n-1)a_2\big)y_n(x)&=0,\\ (a_2x^2+a_1x+a_0)y_n''(x)-n(n-1)a_2\,y_n(x)&=0,\end{aligned}$$

which are all particular cases of the well-known Equation (5). **Finally, for the Case 5,** The differential Equation (21) reduces to

$$(a_2x^2+a_1x+a_0)y_n''(x)+\left(b_1+\frac{b_1r+b_0}{x-r}\right)y_n'(x)-\left(n(n-1)a_2+\frac{b_1}{x-r}\right)y_n(x)=0, \quad (36)$$

with the polynomial solution space

$$\Pi_{n,r,v}=\operatorname{span}\left\{(x+\frac{b_0}{b_1}),(x-r)^2,\ldots,(x-r)^n\right\}.$$

5. On the Differential Equations of Six Nonsymmetric Exceptional Orthogonal X_1-Polynomials

Noting the Corollary 3, in this section, we consider six special cases of the main Equation (21) and study their orthogonal polynomial solutions. For finite cases, we also determine some necessary conditions in order to satisfy the orthogonality relations.

5.1. On the Differential Equation of Exceptional X_1-Jacobi Polynomials

As a generalization of the Jacobi differential equation for $\theta=0$, consider the following equation

$$\begin{aligned}&(x-r)(1-x^2)y_n''(x)+\Big(-(\alpha+\beta+\theta+2)x^2+(\beta-\alpha+r(\alpha+\beta+2))x+\theta-r(\beta-\alpha)\Big)y_n'(x)\\ &\qquad+\Big(n(n+\alpha+\beta+\theta+1)(x-r)-c_0^{(P)}\Big)y_n(x)=0 \qquad n\geq 1, \quad (37)\end{aligned}$$

where r,θ,α,β are real parameters such that $\alpha,\beta>-1$, $(-1)^\theta=1$ and

$$\begin{aligned}c_0^{(P)}&=2\theta(1-r^2)(\alpha+\beta+\theta+2)\Big((\alpha+\beta+2\theta+2)r+\alpha-\beta\\ &\qquad\pm\sqrt{\big((\alpha+\beta+2)r+\beta-\alpha\big)^2+4(\alpha+\beta+\theta+2)(\theta-r(\beta-\alpha))}\Big)^{-1}.\end{aligned}$$

According to Section 3, the polynomial solution of Equation (37), i.e.,

$$y_n(x)=P_{n,r,\theta}^{(\alpha,\beta)}(x)=Q_{n,r}\left(\begin{array}{c}-(\alpha+\beta+\theta+2),\ \beta-\alpha+r(\alpha+\beta+2),\ \theta-r(\beta-\alpha)\\ -1,\ 0,\ 1\end{array}\middle|\, x\right),$$

is orthogonal with respect to the weight function

$$\rho_1(x;r,\alpha,\beta,\theta)=(x-r)^\theta\, W\left(\begin{array}{c}-\alpha-\beta,\ \beta-\alpha\\ -1,\ 0,\ 1\end{array}\middle|\, x\right)=(x-r)^\theta(1-x)^\alpha(1+x)^\beta,$$

on $[-1,1]$. Additionally, for $\theta=0$, $r=-1$ or $r=1$ in (37), $c_0^{(P)}=0$ and the weight function $\rho_1(x;r,\alpha,\beta,\theta)$ will be a special case of the beta distribution. In fact, in each of these circumstances, Equation (37) is simplified as

$$(1-x^2)\,y_n''(x)+\big(-(\alpha+\beta+2)x+\beta-\alpha\big)\,y_n'(x)+n(n+\alpha+\beta+1)\,y_n(x)=0,$$

for $\theta=0$ and

$$(1-x^2)\,y_n''(x)+\big(-(\alpha+\beta+\theta+2)x+\beta+\theta-\alpha\big)\,y_n'(x)+n(n+\alpha+\beta+\theta+1)\,y_n(x)=0,$$

for $r=-1$ and

$$(1-x^2)\,y_n''(x)+\big(-(\alpha+\beta+\theta+2)x+\beta-\theta-\alpha\big)\,y_n'(x)+n(n+\alpha+\beta+\theta+1)\,y_n(x)=0,$$

for $r=1$ with the following Jacobi-type polynomial solutions

$$\begin{aligned}P_{n,r,0}^{(\alpha,\beta)}(x)&=P_n^{(\alpha,\beta)}(x),\\P_{n,-1,\theta}^{(\alpha,\beta)}(x)&=P_n^{(\alpha,\beta+\theta)}(x),\\P_{n,1,\theta}^{(\alpha,\beta)}(x)&=P_n^{(\alpha+\theta,\beta)}(x).\end{aligned}$$

5.2. On the Differential Equation of Exceptional X_1-Laguerre Polynomials

As a generalization of Laguerre differential equation for $\theta=0$, consider the following equation

$$\begin{aligned}x(x-r)y_n''(x)&+\Big(-x^2+(\alpha+r+\theta+1)x-r(\alpha+1)\Big)y_n'(x)\\&+\big(n(x-r)-c_0^{(L)}\big)y_n(x)=0\qquad n\geq 1,\end{aligned}\tag{38}$$

where r,θ,α are real parameters such that $\alpha>-1$, $(-1)^\theta=1$ and

$$c_0^{(L)}=2r\theta\Big(r-\alpha-\theta-1\pm\sqrt{(r+\theta)^2+(\alpha+1)(\alpha+1+2\theta-2r)}\Big)^{-1}.$$

According to the Section 3, the polynomial solution of Equation (38), i.e.,

$$y_n(x)=L_{n,r,\theta}^{(\alpha)}(x)=Q_{n,r}\left(\begin{array}{c}-1,\ \alpha+r+\theta+1,\ -r(\alpha+1)\\0,\ 1,\ 0\end{array}\middle|\,x\right),$$

is orthogonal with respect to the weight function

$$\rho_2(x;r,\alpha,\theta)=(x-r)^\theta\,W\left(\begin{array}{c}-1,\ \alpha\\0,\ 1,\ 0\end{array}\middle|\,x\right)=(x-r)^\theta x^\alpha e^{-x},$$

on $[0,\infty)$. Also, for $\theta=0$ or $r=0$ in (38), $c_0^{(L)}=0$ and the weight function $\rho_2(x;r,\alpha,\theta)$ will be a special case of Gamma distribution. In fact, in each of these circumstances Equation (38) is simplified as

$$x\,y_n''(x)+(-x+\alpha+1)\,y_n'(x)+n\,y_n(x)=0,$$

for $\theta=0$ and

$$x\,y_n''(x)+(-x+\alpha+\theta+1)\,y_n'(x)+n\,y_n(x)=0,$$

for $r=0$ with the following Laguerre-type polynomial solutions

$$L_{n,r,0}^{(\alpha)}(x)=L_n^{(\alpha)}(x),$$

and

$$L_{n,0,\theta}^{(\alpha)}(x) = L_n^{(\alpha+\theta)}(x).$$

5.3. *On the Differential Equation of Exceptional X_1-Hermite Polynomials*

As a generalization of Hermite differential equation for $\theta = 0$, consider the equation

$$(x-r)y_n''(x) + (-2x^2 + 2rx + \theta)y_n'(x) + \Big(2n(x-r) - \frac{2\theta}{r \pm \sqrt{r^2+2\theta}}\Big)y_n(x) = 0, \quad n \geq 1, \tag{39}$$

where r, θ are real parameters and $(-1)^\theta = 1$. The polynomial solution of Equation (39), i.e.,

$$y_n(x) = H_{n,r,\theta}(x) = Q_{n,r}\left(\begin{array}{c} -2,\ 2r,\ \theta \\ 0,\ 0,\ 1 \end{array} \middle| \, x\right),$$

is orthogonal with respect to the weight function

$$\rho_3(x; r,\theta) = (x-r)^\theta\, W\left(\begin{array}{c} -2,\ 0 \\ 0,\ 0,\ 1 \end{array} \middle| \, x\right) = (x-r)^\theta e^{-x^2},$$

on $(-\infty, \infty)$ and for $\theta = 0$, the solution of Equation (39) is the same as classical Hermite polynomials.

5.4. *The First Finite Sequence of Exceptional Orthogonal X_1-Polynomials*

Consider the differential equation

$$x(x-r)(x+1)y_n''(x) + \Big((\theta+2-p)x^2 + (q+\theta+1+r(p-2))x - r(q+1)\Big)y_n'(x) - \Big(n(n+1+\theta-p)(x-r) + c_0^{(M)}\Big)y_n(x) = 0 \qquad n \geq 1, \tag{40}$$

where r, θ are real parameters, $(-1)^\theta = 1$ and

$$c_0^{(M)} = \frac{2\theta r(r+1)(p-\theta-2)}{rp - q - (\theta+1)(2r+1) \pm \Big((q+\theta+1+r(p-2))^2 + 4r(q+1)(\theta+2-p)\Big)^{\frac{1}{2}}}.$$

Here we show that the polynomial solution of Equation (40), i.e.,

$$y_n(x) = M_{n,r,\theta}^{(p,q)}(x) = Q_{n,r}\left(\begin{array}{c} \theta+2-p,\ q+\theta+1+r(p-2),\ -r(q+1) \\ 1,\ 1,\ 0 \end{array} \middle| \, x\right),$$

is finitely orthogonal with respect to the weight function

$$\rho_4(x; r,p,q,\theta) = (x-r)^\theta\, W\left(\begin{array}{c} -p,\ q \\ 1,\ 1,\ 0 \end{array} \middle| \, x\right) = (x-r)^\theta x^q (x+1)^{-(p+q)},$$

on $[0, \infty)$ if and only if

$$p > 2\{\max n\} + \theta + 1 \qquad \text{and} \qquad q > -1.$$

In other words, if the self-adjoint form of Equation (40) is written as

$$\left((x-r)^{\theta}x^{q+1}(x+1)^{1-(p+q)}y_n'(x)\right)' \\ = (x-r)^{\theta-1}x^{q}(x+1)^{-(p+q)}\left(n(n+1+\theta-p)(x-r)+c_0^{(M)}\right)y_n(x), \quad (41)$$

and for the index m as

$$\left((x-r)^{\theta}x^{q+1}(x+1)^{1-(p+q)}y_m'(x)\right)' \\ = (x-r)^{\theta-1}x^{q}(x+1)^{-(p+q)}\left(m(m+1+\theta-p)(x-r)+c_0^{(M)}\right)y_m(x), \quad (42)$$

then multiplying (41) and (42) by $y_m(x)$ and $y_n(x)$, respectively and subtracting them and finally integrating the resulting equation on the interval $[0,\infty)$ gives

$$\left[(x-r)^{\theta}x^{q+1}(x+1)^{1-(p+q)}\left(y_n'(x)y_m(x)-y_m'(x)y_n(x)\right)\right]_0^{\infty} \\ = \left(n(n+1+\theta-p)-m(m+1+\theta-p)\right)\int_0^{\infty}(x-r)^{\theta}x^{q}(x+1)^{-(p+q)}y_n(x)y_m(x)\,dx. \quad (43)$$

Now, since

$$\max\deg\,\{y_n'(x)y_m(x)-y_m'(x)y_n(x)\}=m+n-1,$$

if

$$q>-1 \quad \text{and} \quad p>2N+\theta+1 \quad \text{for} \quad N=\max\{m,n\},$$

the left hand side of (43) tends to zero and for $m,n\geq 1$, we obtain

$$\int_0^{\infty}\frac{(x-r)^{\theta}x^{q}}{(x+1)^{p+q}}\,M_{n,r,\theta}^{(p,q)}(x)\,M_{m,r,\theta}^{(p,q)}(x)\,dx=0 \\ \Leftrightarrow \; m\neq n,\; N=\max\{m,n\}<\frac{p-1-\theta}{2},\; q>-1 \text{ and } (-1)^{\theta}=1.$$

Note that for $\theta=0$, $r=-1$ or $r=0$, $\rho_4(x;r,p,q,\theta)$ reduces to a special case of the F-Fisher distribution. Indeed, in each of these circumstances, $c_0^{(M)}=0$ and Equation (40) reads as

$$x(x+1)y_n''(x)+((2-p)x+q+1)y_n'(x)-n(n+1-p)y_n(x)=0,$$

for $\theta=0$ and

$$x(x+1)y_n''(x)+((\theta+2-p)x+q+1)y_n'(x)-n(n+1+\theta-p)y_n(x)=0,$$

for $r=-1$ and

$$x(x+1)y_n''(x)+((\theta+2-p)x+q+\theta+1)y_n'(x)-n(n+1+\theta-p)y_n(x)=0,$$

for $r=0$ with the following polynomial solutions

$$M_{n,r,0}^{(p,q)}(x)=M_n^{(p,q)}(x),$$

$$M_{n,-1,\theta}^{(p,q)}(x)=M_n^{(p-\theta,q)}(x),$$

and

$$M_{n,0,\theta}^{(p,q)}(x)=M_n^{(p-\theta,q+\theta)}(x).$$

5.5. The Second Finite Sequence of Exceptional Orthogonal X_1-Polynomials

Consider the equation

$$(x-r)x^2y_n''(x)+\Big((\theta+2-p)x^2+(1+r(p-2))x-r\Big)y_n'(x) \\ -\Big(n(n+1+\theta-p)(x-r)+c_0^{(N)}\Big)y_n(x)=0 \qquad n\geq 1, \quad (44)$$

where r,θ are real parameters, $(-1)^\theta=1$ and

$$c_0^{(N)}=\frac{2\theta r^2(p-\theta-2)}{r(p-2(\theta+1))-1\pm\Big((1+r(p-2))^2+4r(\theta+2-p)\Big)^{\frac{1}{2}}}.$$

It can be shown that the polynomial solution of Equation (44), i.e.

$$y_n(x)=N_{n,r,\theta}^{(p)}(x)=Q_{n,r}\left(\begin{array}{c}\theta+2-p,\ 1+r(p-2),\ -r\\ 1,\ 0,\ 0\end{array}\,\middle|\, x\right),$$

is finitely orthogonal with respect to the weight function

$$\rho_5(x;r,p,\theta)=(x-r)^\theta\, W\left(\begin{array}{c}-p,\ 1\\ 1,\ 0,\ 0\end{array}\,\middle|\, x\right)=(x-r)^\theta x^{-p}e^{-\frac{1}{x}},$$

on $[0,\infty)$ if and only if

$$p>2\{\max n\}+\theta+1,$$

because if the self-adjoint form of Equation (44) is written as

$$\Big((x-r)^\theta x^{-p+2}e^{-\frac{1}{x}}y_n'(x)\Big)'=(x-r)^{\theta-1}x^{-p}e^{-\frac{1}{x}}\Big(n(n+1+\theta-p)(x-r)+c_0^{(N)}\Big)y_n(x), \quad (45)$$

and for the index m as

$$\Big((x-r)^\theta x^{-p+2}e^{-\frac{1}{x}}y_m'(x)\Big)'=(x-r)^{\theta-1}x^{-p}e^{-\frac{1}{x}}\Big(m(m+1+\theta-p)(x-r)+c_0^{(N)}\Big)y_m(x), \quad (46)$$

then multiplying (45) and (46) by $y_m(x)$ and $y_n(x)$, respectively and subtracting them and finally integrating the resulting equation over $[0,\infty)$ gives

$$\Big[(x-r)^\theta x^{-p+2}e^{-\frac{1}{x}}\big(y_n'(x)y_m(x)-y_m'(x)y_n(x)\big)\Big]_0^\infty \\ =\big(n(n+1+\theta-p)-m(m+1+\theta-p)\big)\int_0^\infty (x-r)^\theta x^{-p}e^{-\frac{1}{x}}y_n(x)y_m(x)\,dx. \quad (47)$$

Now, if

$$p>2N+\theta+1 \quad \text{for} \quad N=\max\{m,n\},$$

the left-hand side of (47) tends to zero and for $m,n\geq 1$ we obtain

$$\int_0^\infty (x-r)^\theta x^{-p}e^{-\frac{1}{x}}\,N_{n,r,\theta}^{(p)}(x)\,N_{m,r,\theta}^{(p)}(x)\,dx=0 \\ \Leftrightarrow\ m\neq n,\ N=\max\{m,n\}<\frac{p-\theta-1}{2}\ \text{and}\ (-1)^\theta=1.$$

Note that for $\theta=0$ or $r=0$, $\rho_5(x;r,p,\theta)$ reduces to a special case of inverse Gamma distribution and in each of these circumstances $c_0^{(N)}=0$ so that Equation (44) changes to

$$x^2y_n''(x)+((2-p)x+1)y_n'(x)-n(n+1-p)y_n(x)=0,$$

for $\theta = 0$ and

$$x^2 y_n''(x) + ((\theta + 2 - p)x + 1)y_n'(x) - n(n + 1 + \theta - p)y_n(x) = 0,$$

for $r = 0$ with the following polynomial solutions

$$N_{n,r,0}^{(p)}(x) = N_n^{(p)}(x),$$

and

$$N_{n,0,\theta}^{(p)}(x) = N_n^{(p-\theta)}(x).$$

5.6. The Third Finite Sequence of Exceptional Orthogonal X_1-Polynomials

Consider the differential equation

$$(x - r)(1 + x^2)y_n''(x) + \Big((\theta + 2 - 2p)x^2 + (q + 2r(p - 1))x + \theta - rq\Big)y_n'(x) \\ - \Big(n(n + 1 + \theta - 2p)(x - r) + c_0^{(J)}\Big)y_n(x) = 0 \qquad n \geq 1, \quad (48)$$

where r, θ are real parameters, $(-1)^{\theta} = 1$ and

$$c_0^{(J)} = \frac{2\theta(r^2 + 1)(2p - \theta - 2)}{2r(p - \theta - 1) - q \pm \Big((q + 2r(p - 1))^2 - 4(\theta + 2 - 2p)(\theta - rq)\Big)^{\frac{1}{2}}}.$$

The polynomial solution of Equation (48), i.e.,

$$J_{n,r,\theta}^{(p,q)}(x) = Q_{n,r}\left(\begin{array}{c} \theta + 2 - 2p,\ q + 2r(p - 1),\ \theta - rq \\ 1,\ 0,\ 1 \end{array} \middle| \, x \right),$$

is finitely orthogonal with respect to the weight function

$$\rho_6(x; r, p, q, \theta) = (x - r)^{\theta}\, W\left(\begin{array}{c} -2p,\ q \\ 1,\ 0,\ 1 \end{array} \middle| \, x \right) = (x - r)^{\theta}(1 + x^2)^{-p} \exp(q \arctan x),$$

on $(-\infty, \infty)$ if and only if

$$p > \{\max n\} + \frac{\theta + 1}{2},$$

because if the self-adjoint form of Equation (48) is written as

$$\Big((x - r)^{\theta}\big(1 + x^2\big)^{1-p} \exp(q \arctan x) y_n'(x)\Big)' \\ = (x - r)^{\theta - 1}\big(1 + x^2\big)^{-p} \exp(q \arctan x)\Big(n(n + 1 + \theta - 2p)(x - r) + c_0^{(J)}\Big)y_n(x), \quad (49)$$

and for the index m as

$$\Big((x - r)^{\theta}\big(1 + x^2\big)^{1-p} \exp(q \arctan x) y_m'(x)\Big)' \\ = (x - r)^{\theta - 1}\big(1 + x^2\big)^{-p} \exp(q \arctan x)\Big(m(m + 1 + \theta - 2p)(x - r) + c_0^{(J)}\Big)y_m(x), \quad (50)$$

then multiplying (49) and (50) by $y_m(x)$ and $y_n(x)$, respectively and subtracting them and finally integrating from both sides on $(-\infty, \infty)$ gives

$$\begin{aligned}
&\left[(x-r)^{\theta}\left(1+x^2\right)^{1-p}\exp(q\arctan x)\left(y_n'(x)y_m(x)-y_m'(x)\,y_n(x)\right)\right]_{-\infty}^{\infty}\\
&\qquad=\left(n(n+1+\theta-2p)-m(m+1+\theta-2p)\right)\\
&\qquad\times\int_{-\infty}^{\infty}(x-r)^{\theta}\left(1+x^2\right)^{-p}\exp(q\arctan x)\,J_{n,r,\theta}^{(p,q)}(x)J_{m,r,\theta}^{(p,q)}(x)\,dx. \qquad (51)
\end{aligned}$$

Now, if

$$p > N + \frac{\theta+1}{2} \qquad \text{for} \qquad N = \max\{m,n\},$$

the left-hand side of (51) tends to zero and for $m, n \geq 1$ we have

$$\begin{aligned}
&\int_{-\infty}^{\infty}(x-r)^{\theta}(1+x^2)^{-p}\exp(q\arctan x)\,J_{n,r,\theta}^{(p,q)}(x)J_{m,r,\theta}^{(p,q)}(x)\,dx = 0\\
&\qquad\Leftrightarrow\quad m\neq n\,,\ N=\max\{m,n\}<p-\frac{\theta+1}{2}\ \text{and}\ (-1)^{\theta}=1.
\end{aligned}$$

For $\theta = 0$, $\rho_6(x; r, p, q, \theta)$ reduces to the generalized T-Student distribution and Equation (48) reads as

$$(1+x^2)y_n''(x) + (2(1-p)x+q)y_n'(x) - n(n+1-2p)y_n(x) = 0,$$

with the polynomial solution

$$J_{n,r,0}^{(p,q)}(x) = J_n^{(p,q)}(x).$$

6. A Unified Classification for Symmetric Exceptional Orthogonal X_1-Polynomials

Fortunately, most of special functions in theoretical and mathematical physics which are the solutions of Sturm–Liouville problems have the symmetry property, namely

$$\Phi_n(x) = (-1)^n \Phi_n(-x).$$

These functions have usually interesting applications in physics and engineering; see e.g., [4,6] for more details. Hence, if they can be extended when their orthogonality property is preserved, new applications should naturally appear. The following theorem shows this matter.

Theorem 1 ([18])**.** *Let $\Phi_n(x) = (-1)^n\Phi_n(-x)$ be a sequence of independent symmetric functions that satisfy the differential equation*

$$A(x)\,\Phi_n''(x) + B(x)\,\Phi_n'(x) + \left(\lambda_n\,C(x) + D(x) + \frac{1-(-1)^n}{2}E(x)\right)\Phi_n(x) = 0, \qquad (52)$$

where $A(x)$, $B(x)$, $C(x)$, $D(x)$ and $E(x)$ are real functions and $\{\lambda_n\}$ is a sequence of constants. If $A(x)$, $(C(x) > 0)$, $D(x)$ and $E(x)$ are even functions and $B(x)$ is odd, then

$$\int_{-v}^{v} W^*(x)\,\Phi_n(x)\,\Phi_m(x)\,dx = \left(\int_{-v}^{v} W^*(x)\,\Phi_n^2(x)\,dx\right)\delta_{n,m},$$

where $W^*(x)$ denotes the corresponding weight function as

$$W^*(x) = C(x)\exp\left(\int \frac{B(x)-A'(x)}{A(x)}\,dx\right) = \frac{C(x)}{A(x)}\exp\left(\int \frac{B(x)}{A(x)}\,dx\right). \qquad (53)$$

Of course, the weight function defined in (53) *must be positive and even on* $[-v, v]$ *and* $x = v$ *must be a root of the function*

$$A(x)K(x) = A(x)\exp\Big(\int \frac{B(x) - A'(x)}{A(x)}\,dx\Big) = \exp\Big(\int \frac{B(x)}{A(x)}\,dx\Big),$$

i.e., $A(v)\,K(v) = 0$. *Notice since* $K(x) = \dfrac{W^*(x)}{C(x)}$ *is an even function, the relation* $A(-v)\,K(-v) = 0$ *follows automatically.*

Based on the above theorem, many symmetric orthogonal functions were recently generalized; see, for example, [19]. In this section, by applying Theorem 1 and the polynomial sequence (22), we establish a class of symmetric orthogonal X_1-polynomials and introduce four special cases of it in the sequel.

For this purpose, let us reconsider the differential Equation (21) for $a_0 = 0$ as

$$(x-r)x(a_2x + a_1)y_n''(x) + (b_2x^2 + b_1x + b_0)y_n'(x) \\ - \Big(n\big(b_2 + (n-1)a_2\big)(x-r) + c_0^*\Big)y_n(x) = 0, \tag{54}$$

in which

$$c_0^* = c_0^*\Big\{r; b_2, b_1, b_0\Big\} = b_2 r + \frac{b_1 \mp \sqrt{b_1^2 - 4b_0b_2}}{2}. \tag{55}$$

To obtain a symmetric differential equation of type (52), we first substitute

$$\Phi_{2n}(x) = Q_{n,r}\left(\begin{array}{c} b_2, b_1, b_0 \\ a_2, a_1, 0 \end{array}\middle|\, x^2\right),$$

into Equation (54) to obtain

$$x^2(a_2x^2 + a_1)(x^2 - r)\Phi_{2n}''(x) + x\Big((2b_2 - a_2)x^4 + (2b_1 - a_1 + ra_2)x^2 + 2b_0 + ra_1\Big)\Phi_{2n}'(x) \\ - 4x^2\Big(n(b_2 + (n-1)a_2)(x^2 - r) + c_0^*\Big\{r; b_2, b_1, b_0\Big\}\Big)\Phi_{2n}(x) = 0. \tag{56}$$

In a similar manner, for

$$\Phi_{2n+1}(x) = x\,Q_{n,r}\left(\begin{array}{c} b_2^*, b_1^*, b_0^* \\ a_2^*, a_1^*, 0 \end{array}\middle|\, x^2\right),$$

we obtain

$$x^2(a_2^*x^2 + a_1^*)(x^2 - r)\Phi_{2n+1}''(x) \\ + x\Big((2b_2^* - 3a_2^*)x^4 + (2b_1^* - 3a_1^* + 3ra_2^*)x^2 + 2b_0^* + 3ra_1^*\Big)\Phi_{2n+1}'(x) \\ + \Big((3a_2^* - 2b_2^*)x^4 + (3a_1^* - 3ra_2^* - 2b_1^*)x^2 - 2b_0^* - 3ra_1^* - 4x^2\big(n(b_2^* + (n-1)a_2^*)(x^2 - r) \\ + c_0^*\Big\{r; b_2^*, b_1^*, b_0^*\Big\}\big)\Big)\Phi_{2n+1}(x) = 0. \tag{57}$$

Now, if for simplicity we assume that

$$a_2^* = a_2, \quad a_1^* = a_1,$$

and

$$b_2^* = b_2 + a_2, \quad b_1^* = b_1 + a_1 - ra_2, \quad b_0^* = b_0 - ra_1,$$

the differential Equation (57) changes to

$$\begin{aligned}&x^2(a_2x^2+a_1)(x^2-r)\Phi''_{2n+1}(x)+x\Big((2b_2-a_2)x^4+(2b_1-a_1+ra_2)x^2+2b_0+ra_1\Big)\Phi'_{2n+1}(x)\\&\quad+\Big((a_2-2b_2)x^4+(a_1-ra_2-2b_1)x^2-2b_0-ra_1\\&\quad-4x^2\big(n(b_2+na_2)(x^2-r)+c_0^*\big\{r;b_2+a_2,b_1+a_1-ra_2,b_0-ra_1\big\}\big)\Big)\Phi_{2n+1}(x)=0,\end{aligned}\tag{58}$$

with the polynomial solution

$$\Phi_{2n+1}(x)=x\,Q_{n,r}\left(\begin{array}{c}b_2+a_2,\ b_1+a_1-ra_2,\ b_0-ra_1\\a_2,\ a_1,\ 0\end{array}\middle|\ x^2\right).$$

Therefore, by defining the symbol

$$\sigma_n=\frac{1-(-1)^n}{2},$$

and combining both equations (56) and (58) in a unique form, we finally obtain

$$\begin{aligned}&x^2(a_2x^2+a_1)(x^2-r)\Phi''_n(x)+x\Big((2b_2-a_2)x^4+(2b_1-a_1+ra_2)x^2+2b_0+ra_1\Big)\Phi'_n(x)\\&\qquad+\Big(\big((a_2-2b_2)x^4+(a_1-ra_2-2b_1\\&\quad-4c_0^*\big\{r;b_2+a_2,b_1+a_1-ra_2,b_0-ra_1\big\}+4c_0^*\big\{r;b_2,b_1,b_0\big\})x^2-2b_0-ra_1\big)\sigma_n\\&\quad-4x^2\big((n-\sigma_n)(2b_2+(n+\sigma_n-2)a_2)\big)(x^2-r)+c_0^*\big\{r;b_2,b_1,b_0\big\}\big)\Big)\Phi_n(x)=0,\end{aligned}\tag{59}$$

with the symmetric polynomial solution

$$\Phi_n(x)=x^{\sigma_n}Q_{[\frac{n}{2}],r}\left(\begin{array}{c}b_2+\sigma_na_2,\ b_1+\sigma_n(a_1-ra_2),\ b_0-\sigma_nra_1\\a_2,\ a_1,\ 0\end{array}\middle|\ x^2\right).$$

Once again, if for simplicity we set

$$2b_2-a_2=p_2,\qquad 2b_1-a_1+ra_2=p_1\qquad\text{and}\qquad 2b_0+ra_1=p_0,$$

then Equation (59) is finally simplified as

$$\begin{aligned}&x^2(a_2x^2+a_1)(x^2-r)\Phi''_n(x)+x(p_2x^4+p_1x^2+p_0)\Phi'_n(x)\\&\quad-\Big(\big(p_2x^4+(p_1+4c_0^*\{r;\frac{p_2+3a_2}{2},\frac{p_1+3a_1-3ra_2}{2},\frac{p_0-3ra_1}{2}\}\\&\qquad-4c_0^*\{r;\frac{p_2+a_2}{2},\frac{p_1+a_1-ra_2}{2},\frac{p_0-ra_1}{2}\})x^2+p_0\big)\sigma_n\\&\qquad+4x^2\big((n-\sigma_n)(p_2+(n+\sigma_n-1)a_2)(x^2-r)\\&\qquad+c_0^*\{r;\frac{a_2+p_2}{2},\frac{a_1+p_1-ra_2}{2},\frac{p_0-ra_1}{2}\}\big)\Big)\Phi_n(x)=0.\end{aligned}\tag{60}$$

Note in (60) that

$$\begin{aligned}&c_0^*\Big\{r;\frac{p_2+3a_2}{2},\frac{p_1+3a_1-3ra_2}{2},\frac{p_0-3ra_1}{2}\Big\}\\&\quad=\frac{1}{4}\Big(3a_1+p_1+3ra_2+2rp_2\mp\big((3a_1+p_1-3ra_2)^2-4(p_0-3ra_1)(3a_2+p_2)\big)^{\frac{1}{2}}\Big),\end{aligned}$$

and

$$c_0^*\left\{r; \frac{p_2+a_2}{2}, \frac{p_1+a_1-ra_2}{2}, \frac{p_0-ra_1}{2}\right\}$$

$$= \frac{1}{4}\left(a_1+p_1+ra_2+2rp_2 \mp \left((a_1+p_1-ra_2)^2-4(p_0-ra_1)(a_2+p_2)\right)^{\frac{1}{2}}\right),$$

are directly computed by referring to (55).

Corollary 4. *If in Theorem 1 we take*

$$\begin{aligned}
A(x) &= x^2(a_2x^2+a_1)(x^2-r),\\
B(x) &= x(p_2x^4+p_1x^2+p_0),\\
C(x) &= x^2(x^2-r),\\
D(x) &= -4x^2c_0^*\left\{r; \frac{p_2+a_2}{2}, \frac{p_1+a_1-ra_2}{2}, \frac{p_0-ra_1}{2}\right\},\\
E(x) &= -p_2x^4\Big(p_1+4c_0^*\left\{r; \frac{p_2+3a_2}{2}, \frac{p_1+3a_1-3ra_2}{2}, \frac{p_0-3ra_1}{2}\right\}\\
&\quad -4c_0^*\left\{r; \frac{p_2+a_2}{2}, \frac{p_1+a_1-ra_2}{2}, \frac{p_0-ra_1}{2}\right\}\Big)x^2-p_0\\
&= -p_2x^4-\Big(p_1+2a_1+2ra_2 \pm \left((a_1+p_1-ra_2)^2-4(p_0-ra_1)(a_2+p_2)\right)^{\frac{1}{2}}\\
&\qquad \mp \left((3a_1+p_1-3ra_2)^2-4(p_0-3ra_1)(3a_2+p_2)\right)^{\frac{1}{2}}\Big)x^2-p_0,
\end{aligned}$$

and

$$\lambda_n = -4(n-\sigma_n)(p_2+(n+\sigma_n-1)a_2),$$

then its symmetric polynomial solution, i.e.,

$$\Phi_n(x) = x^{\sigma_n}Q_{[\frac{n}{2}],r}\left(\begin{array}{c} \frac{p_2+a_2}{2}+a_2\sigma_n,\ \frac{p_1+a_1-ra_2}{2}+(a_1-ra_2)\sigma_n,\ \frac{p_0-ra_1}{2}-ra_1\sigma_n \\ a_2,\ a_1,\ 0 \end{array}\middle|\, x^2\right),$$
$$n \geq 1, \tag{61}$$

is orthogonal with respect to the weight function

$$\rho^*(x) = \frac{1}{a_2x^2+a_1}\exp\left(\int \frac{p_2x^4+p_1x^2+p_0}{x(a_2x^2+a_1)(x^2-r)}\,dx\right),$$

which can be simplified as

$$\rho^*(x) = (x^2-r)^{\mu}\exp\left(\int \frac{(p_2-2a_2(\mu+1))x^2-\frac{p_0}{r}}{x(a_2x^2+a_1)}\,dx\right), \tag{62}$$

for

$$\mu = \frac{p_2r^2+p_1r+p_0}{2r(a_1+ra_2)}.$$

Remark 2. *If in (62) we take $\mu = 0$, which is equivalent to $p_0 = -r(p_2r+p_1)$, then we will reach a symmetric class of orthogonal polynomials. In other words, let $p, q, r, s \in \mathbb{R}$ and consider the differential equation*

$$x^2(px^2+q)\,\Phi_n''(x)+x(rx^2+s)\,\Phi_n'(x)-\left(n(r+(n-1)p)x^2+\frac{1-(-1)^n}{2}s\right)\Phi_n(x)=0,$$

whose polynomial solution can be directly represented as [19]

$$\Phi_n(x) = S_n\left(\begin{array}{cc} r, & s \\ p, & q \end{array} \middle| x\right) = \sum_{k=0}^{[\frac{n}{2}]} \binom{[\frac{n}{2}]}{k} \left(\prod_{i=0}^{[\frac{n}{2}]-(k+1)} \frac{\left(2i + (-1)^{n+1} + 2\left[\frac{n}{2}\right]\right)p + r}{\left(2i + (-1)^{n+1} + 2\right)q + s} \right) x^{n-2k}.$$

Additionally, the weight function corresponding to these polynomials is as [19]

$$W^*\left(\begin{array}{cc} r, & s \\ p, & q \end{array} \middle| x\right) = \exp\left(\int \frac{(r-2p)x^2 + s}{x(px^2+q)}\, dx\right).$$

Now, replacing $\mu = 0$ in (62) gives

$$\rho^*(x) = W^*\left(\begin{array}{cc} p_2, & p_2 r + p_1 \\ a_2, & a_1 \end{array} \middle| x\right).$$

Therefore, the symmetric polynomial (61) can be directly represented for $p_0 = -r(p_2 r + p_1)$ as follows

$$x^{\sigma_n} Q_{[\frac{n}{2}],r}\left(\begin{array}{c} \frac{p_2+a_2}{2} + a_2\sigma_n,\ \frac{p_1+a_1-ra_2}{2} + (a_1 - ra_2)\sigma_n,\ -\frac{r}{2}(rp_2 + p_1 + (1+2\sigma_n)a_1) \\ a_2,\ a_1,\ 0 \end{array} \middle| x^2\right)$$

$$= S_n\left(\begin{array}{cc} p_2, & p_2 r + p_1 \\ a_2, & a_1 \end{array} \middle| x\right).$$

There are four sequences of symmetric exceptional orthogonal X_1-polynomials as follows.

6.1. First Symmetric Class

Assume in Corollary 4 that

$$(a_2, a_1, p_2, p_1, p_0) = (-1, 1, -2(a+b+\mu+1), 2(a + (a+b+1)r - \mu), -2ra),$$

with the symmetric polynomial solution

$$\Phi_n(x) = \phi^{(a,b)}_{n,r,\mu}(x) =$$

$$x^{\sigma_n} Q_{[\frac{n}{2}],r}\left(\begin{array}{c} -(a+b+\mu+\frac{3}{2}+\sigma_n),\ (a+b+1)r + a + \mu + (1+r)(\frac{1}{2}+\sigma_n),\ -r(a+\frac{1}{2}+\sigma_n) \\ -1,\ 1,\ 0 \end{array} \middle| x^2\right),$$

$$n \geq 1. \quad (63)$$

According to Theorem 1, the symmetric polynomials (63) are orthogonal with respect to the weight function

$$\rho_1^*(x) = (x^2 - r)^{\mu}\, x^{2a}(1-x^2)^b,$$

on $[-1,1]$ if $(-1)^{\mu} = (-1)^{2a} = 1$, $b > -1$ and $a > -(\frac{1}{2}+\mu)$, (or $a > -\frac{1}{2}$) if $\mu < 0$, (or $\mu \geq 0$).

By noting remark 2, there are three particular cases of the symmetric polynomial $\phi^{(a,b)}_{n,r,\mu}(x)$ for $\mu = 0, r = 0$ and $r = 1$.

If $\mu = 0$, then we have

$$\phi^{(a,b)}_{n,r,0}(x) = S_n\left(\begin{array}{cc} -2(a+b+1), & 2a \\ -1, & 1 \end{array} \middle| x\right).$$

If $r = 0$, then

$$\phi_{n,0,\mu}^{(a,b)}(x) = S_n\left(\begin{array}{cc} -2(a+b+\mu+1), & 2(a+\mu) \\ -1, & 1 \end{array} \middle| x\right),$$

and, finally for $r = 1$, the corresponding symmetric polynomial is given by

$$\phi_{n,1,\mu}^{(a,b)}(x) = S_n\left(\begin{array}{cc} -2(a+b+\mu+1), & 2a \\ -1, & 1 \end{array} \middle| x\right).$$

6.2. Second Symmetric Class

Assume in Corollary 4 that

$$(a_2, a_1, p_2, p_1, p_0) = (0, 1, -2, 2(\mu+a+r), -2ra),$$

with the symmetric polynomial solution

$$\begin{aligned} \Phi_n(x) &= \Phi_{n,r,\mu}^{(a)}(x) \\ &= x^{\sigma_n} Q_{[\frac{n}{2}],r}\left(\begin{array}{c} -1,\ \mu+a+r+\frac{1}{2}+\sigma_n,\ -r(a+\frac{1}{2}+\sigma_n) \\ 0,\ 1,\ 0 \end{array} \middle| x^2\right), \quad n \geq 1. \end{aligned} \tag{64}$$

According to Theorem 1, the symmetric polynomials (64) are orthogonal with respect to the weight function

$$\rho_2^*(x) = (x^2 - r)^{\mu}\, x^{2a} e^{-x^2},$$

on $(-\infty, \infty)$ if $(-1)^{\mu} = (-1)^{2a} = 1$ and $a > -(\frac{1}{2}+\mu)$, (or $a > -\frac{1}{2}$) if $\mu < 0$, (or $\mu \geq 0$).

By noting remark 2, there are two particular cases of the symmetric polynomial $\Phi_{n,r,\mu}^{(a)}(x)$ for $\mu = 0$ and $r = 0$.

If $\mu = 0$, then we have

$$\Phi_{n,r,0}^{(a)}(x) = S_n\left(\begin{array}{cc} -2, & 2a \\ 0, & 1 \end{array} \middle| x\right).$$

and for $r = 0$, the corresponding symmetric polynomial is given by

$$\Phi_{n,0,\mu}^{(a)}(x) = S_n\left(\begin{array}{cc} -2, & 2(a+\mu) \\ 0, & 1 \end{array} \middle| x\right).$$

6.3. Third Symmetric Class

Assume in Corollary 4 that

$$(a_2, a_1, p_2, p_1, p_0) = \Big(1, 1, 2(\mu-a-b+1), 2\big(\mu-a+r(a+b-1)\big), 2ra\Big),$$

with the symmetric polynomial solution

$$\Phi_n(x) = \varphi_{n,r,\mu}^{(a,b)}(x) = x^{\sigma_n} Q_{[\frac{n}{2}],r}\left(\begin{array}{c} \mu-a-b+\frac{3}{2}+\sigma_n,\ \mu-a+r(a+b-1)+(1-r)(\frac{1}{2}+\sigma_n),\ r(a-\frac{1}{2}-\sigma_n) \\ 1,\ 1,\ 0 \end{array} \middle| x^2\right),$$
$$n \geq 1. \tag{65}$$

As three particular cases for $\mu = 0, r = 0$ and $r = -1$, we respectively have

$$\varphi_{n,r,0}^{(a,b)}(x) = S_n\left(\begin{array}{cc} -2a-2b+2, & -2a \\ 1, & 1 \end{array}\middle| x\right),$$

$$\varphi_{n,0,\mu}^{(a,b)}(x) = S_n\left(\begin{array}{cc} -2(a-\mu)-2b+2, & -2(a-\mu) \\ 1, & 1 \end{array}\middle| x\right),$$

and

$$\varphi_{n,-1,\mu}^{(a,b)}(x) = S_n\left(\begin{array}{cc} -2a-2b+4, & -2a \\ 1, & 1 \end{array}\middle| x\right).$$

According to Theorem 1, the symmetric polynomials (65), $\left\{\varphi_{n,r,\mu}^{(a,b)}\right\}_{n=1}^{N}$, are finitely orthogonal with respect to the weight function

$$\rho_3^*(x) = (x^2-r)^{\mu}\, x^{-2a}\left(1+x^2\right)^{-b},$$

on $(-\infty, \infty)$ if

$$(-1)^{2a} = (-1)^{\mu} = 1,$$
$$b > 0,\ a < \frac{1}{2}+\mu, (\text{or } a < \frac{1}{2}) \text{ if } \mu < 0, (\text{or } \mu \geq 0), \text{and } N \leq a+b-\mu-\frac{1}{2}.$$

To observe that why the limitation on N is $a+b-\mu-\frac{1}{2}$, first consider the differential equation

$$\begin{aligned} & x^2(x^2+1)(x^2-r)\Phi_n''(x) + 2x((\mu-a-b+1)x^4 + (\mu-a+r(a+b-1))x^2 + ra)\Phi_n'(x) \\ & -2\Big(((\mu-a-b+1)x^4 + (\mu-a+r(a+b-1)+2d(r;a,b,\mu))x^2 + ra)\sigma_n \\ & + 2x^2(n(n+\mu-a-b+\frac{1}{2}+\sigma_n)(x^2-r) \\ & + c_0^*\Big\{r; -a-b+\mu+\frac{3}{2}, -a+\mu+\frac{1}{2}+(a+b-\frac{3}{2})r, (a-\frac{1}{2})r\Big\}\Big)\Phi_n(x) = 0, \end{aligned} \tag{66}$$

in which $c_0^*\{.\}$ and $d(r;a,b,\mu)$ are, respectively, computed as

$$\begin{aligned} & c_0^*\Big\{r; -a-b+\mu+\frac{3}{2}, -a+\mu+\frac{1}{2}+(a+b-\frac{3}{2})r, (a-\frac{1}{2})r\Big\} \\ & = \frac{1}{2}\Big(\mu-a-2r(a+b-\mu-\frac{3}{2})+r(a+b-\frac{3}{2})+\frac{1}{2} \\ & \mp((\mu-a+r(a+b-\frac{3}{2})+\frac{1}{2})^2+4r(a-\frac{1}{2})(a+b-\mu-\frac{3}{2}))^{\frac{1}{2}}\Big), \end{aligned}$$

and

$$\begin{aligned} d(r;a,b,\mu) &= c_0^*\Big\{r; -a-b+\mu+\frac{5}{2}, -a+\mu+\frac{3}{2}+(a+b-\frac{5}{2})r, (a-\frac{3}{2})r\Big\} \\ & - c_0^*\Big\{r; -a-b+\mu+\frac{3}{2}, -a+\mu+\frac{1}{2}+(a+b-\frac{3}{2})r, (a-\frac{1}{2})r\Big\} \\ & = \frac{1}{2}\Big(r+1 \pm ((\mu-a+r(a+b-\frac{3}{2})+\frac{1}{2})^2+4r(a-\frac{1}{2})(a+b-\mu-\frac{3}{2}))^{\frac{1}{2}} \\ & \mp((\mu-a+r(a+b-\frac{5}{2})+\frac{3}{2})^2+4r(a-\frac{3}{2})(a+b-\mu-\frac{5}{2}))^{\frac{1}{2}}\Big). \end{aligned}$$

Then write the self-adjoint form of Equation (66) as

$$\begin{aligned}
&\Big((x^2-r)^{\mu}x^{-2a}(x^2+1)^{-b+1}\Phi_n'(x)\Big)' \\
&= 2(x^2-r)^{\mu-1}x^{-2a-2}(x^2+1)^{-b} \\
&\times\Big(\big((\mu-a-b+1)x^4+(\mu-a+r(a+b-1)+2d(r;a,b,\mu))x^2+ra\big)\sigma_n \\
&+2x^2\big(n(n+\mu-a-b+\tfrac{1}{2}+\sigma_n\big)(x^2-r) \\
&+c_0^*\Big\{r;-a-b+\mu+\frac{3}{2},-a+\mu+\frac{1}{2}+(a+b-\frac{3}{2})r,(a-\frac{1}{2})r\Big\}\Big)\Phi_n(x),
\end{aligned}\tag{67}$$

and for the index m as

$$\begin{aligned}
&\Big((x^2-r)^{\mu}x^{-2a}(x^2+1)^{-b+1}\Phi_m'(x)\Big)' = 2(x^2-r)^{\mu-1}x^{-2a-2}(x^2+1)^{-b} \\
&\times\Big(\big((\mu-a-b+1)x^4+(\mu-a+r(a+b-1)+2d(r;a,b,\mu))x^2+ra\big)\sigma_m \\
&+2x^2\big(m(m+\mu-a-b+\tfrac{1}{2}+\sigma_m\big)(x^2-r) \\
&+c_0^*\Big\{r;-a-b+\mu+\frac{3}{2},-a+\mu+\frac{1}{2}+(a+b-\frac{3}{2})r,(a-\frac{1}{2})r\Big\}\Big)\Phi_m(x).
\end{aligned}\tag{68}$$

Multiplying by $\Phi_m(x)$ and $\Phi_n(x)$ in relations (67) and (68) respectively and subtracting them and finally integrating from both sides on $(-\infty,\infty)$ gives

$$\begin{aligned}
&\Big[(x^2-r)^{\mu}x^{-2a}(x^2+1)^{-b+1}\big(\Phi_n'(x)\Phi_m(x)-\Phi_m'(x)\Phi_n(x)\big)\Big]_{-\infty}^{\infty} \\
&\quad= 4\Big((m-n)\big(2(\mu-a-b)+n+m-1\big)-2(\sigma_m-\sigma_n)(\mu-a-b+1)\Big) \\
&\qquad\times\int_{-\infty}^{\infty}(x^2-r)^{\mu}\,x^{-2a}\big(1+x^2\big)^{-b}\,\Phi_n(x)\Phi_m(x)\,dx.
\end{aligned}\tag{69}$$

Now, since

$$\max\deg\,\{\Phi_n'(x)\Phi_m(x)-\Phi_m'(x)\Phi_n(x)\}=m+n-1,$$

if

$$N\le a+b-\mu-\frac{1}{2}\quad\text{for}\quad N=\max\{m,n\},$$

the left hand side of (69) tends to zero and for $m,n\ge 1$, we obtain

$$\int_{-\infty}^{\infty}(x^2-r)^{\mu}\,x^{-2a}\big(1+x^2\big)^{-b}\,\varphi_{n,r,\mu}^{(a,b)}(x)\,\varphi_{m,r,\mu}^{(a,b)}(x)\,dx=0,\qquad(m\ne n).$$

6.4. *Fourth Symmetric Class*

Assume in Corollary 4 that

$$(a_2,a_1,p_2,p_1,p_0)=\Big(1,0,2(\mu-a+1),2\big(r(a-1)+1\big),-2r\Big),$$

with the symmetric polynomial solution

$$\begin{aligned}
\Phi_n(x)&=\Phi_{n,r,\mu}^{(a)}(x) \\
&=x^{\sigma_n}Q_{[\frac{n}{2}],r}\left(\begin{array}{c}\mu-a+\frac{3}{2}+\sigma_n,\ r(a-\frac{3}{2}-\sigma_n)+1,\ -r\\ 1,\ 0,\ 0\end{array}\,\middle|\,x^2\right),\quad n\ge 1.
\end{aligned}\tag{70}$$

As two particular cases for $\mu = 0$ and $r = 0$, we respectively have

$$\Phi^{(a)}_{n,r,0}(x) = S_n\left(\begin{array}{cc} -2a+2, & 2 \\ 1, & 0 \end{array} \middle| \, x \right),$$

and

$$\Phi^{(a)}_{n,0,\mu}(x) = S_n\left(\begin{array}{cc} -2(a-\mu)+2, & 2 \\ 1, & 0 \end{array} \middle| \, x \right).$$

According to Theorem 1, the symmetric polynomials (70), $\left\{\Phi^{(a)}_{n,r,\mu}\right\}_{n=1}^{N}$, are finitely orthogonal with respect to the weight function

$$\rho_4^*(x) = (x^2-r)^{\mu}\, x^{-2a} e^{-\frac{1}{x^2}},$$

on $(-\infty,\infty)$ if $(-1)^{\mu} = (-1)^{2a} = 1$ and $N \le a-\mu-\frac{1}{2}$. To observe that why the limitation on N is $a-\mu-\frac{1}{2}$, first consider the differential equation

$$\begin{aligned} x^4(x^2-r)\Phi_n''(x) + 2x((\mu-a+1)x^4 + (r(a-1)+1)x^2 - r)\Phi_n'(x) \\ -2\Big(((\mu-a+1)x^4 + (r(a-1)+1+2d(r;a,\mu))x^2 - r)\sigma_n \\ +2x^2(n(n+\mu-a+\frac{1}{2}+\sigma_n)(x^2-r) + c_0^*\Big\{r;-a+\mu+\frac{3}{2},1+(a-\frac{3}{2})r,-r\Big\})\Big)\Phi_n(x) = 0, \end{aligned} \tag{71}$$

in which $c_0^*\{.\}$ and $d(r;a,\mu)$ are respectively computed as

$$\begin{aligned} &c_0^*\Big\{r;-a+\mu+\frac{3}{2},1+(a-\frac{3}{2})r,-r\Big\} \\ &\quad = \frac{1}{2}\Big(2r(\mu-a+\frac{3}{2}) + r(a-\frac{3}{2}) + 1 \mp ((r(a-\frac{3}{2})+1)^2 + 4r(\mu-a+\frac{3}{2}))^{\frac{1}{2}}\Big), \end{aligned}$$

and

$$\begin{aligned} d(r;a,\mu) &= c_0^*\Big\{r;-a+\mu+\frac{5}{2},1+(a-\frac{5}{2})r,-r\Big\} - c_0^*\Big\{r;-a+\mu+\frac{3}{2},1+(a-\frac{3}{2})r,-r\Big\} \\ &= \frac{1}{2}\Big(r \pm ((r(a-\frac{3}{2})+1)^2 + 4r(\mu-a+\frac{3}{2}))^{\frac{1}{2}} \mp ((r(a-\frac{5}{2})+1)^2 + 4r(\mu-a+\frac{5}{2}))^{\frac{1}{2}}\Big). \end{aligned}$$

Then write the self-adjoint form of Equation (71) as

$$\begin{aligned} &\Big((x^2-r)^{\mu} x^{-2a+2} e^{-\frac{1}{x^2}} \Phi_n'(x)\Big)' \\ &\quad = 2e^{-\frac{1}{x^2}}(x^2-r)^{\mu-1} x^{-2a-2}\Big(((\mu-a+1)x^4 + (r(a-1)+1+2d(r;a,\mu))x^2 - r)\sigma_n \\ &\quad +2x^2(n(n+\mu-a+\frac{1}{2}+\sigma_n)(x^2-r) + c_0^*\Big\{r;-a+\mu+\frac{3}{2},1+(a-\frac{3}{2})r,-r\Big\})\Big)\Phi_n(x), \end{aligned} \tag{72}$$

and for the index m as

$$\begin{aligned} &\Big((x^2-r)^{\mu} x^{-2a+2} e^{-\frac{1}{x^2}} \Phi_m'(x)\Big)' \\ &\quad = 2e^{-\frac{1}{x^2}}(x^2-r)^{\mu-1} x^{-2a-2}\Big(((\mu-a+1)x^4 + (r(a-1)+1+2d(r;a,\mu))x^2 - r)\sigma_m \\ &\quad +2x^2(m(m+\mu-a+\frac{1}{2}+\sigma_m)(x^2-r) + c_0^*\Big\{r;-a+\mu+\frac{3}{2},1+(a-\frac{3}{2})r,-r\Big\})\Big)\Phi_m(x). \end{aligned} \tag{73}$$

Multiplying by $\Phi_m(x)$ and $\Phi_n(x)$ in relations (72) and (73) respectively and subtracting them and finally integrating from both sides on $(-\infty,\infty)$ gives

$$\begin{aligned}&\left[(x^2-r)^{\mu}x^{-2a+2}e^{-\frac{1}{x^2}}\left(\Phi_n'(x)\Phi_m(x)-\Phi_m'(x)\Phi_n(x)\right)\right]_{-\infty}^{\infty}\\&=4\Big((m-n)(2\mu-2a+n+m+1)-2(\sigma_m-\sigma_n)(2\mu-2a+1)\Big)\\&\times\int_{-\infty}^{\infty}(x^2-r)^{\mu}\,x^{-2a}e^{-\frac{1}{x^2}}\,\Phi_n(x)\Phi_m(x)\,dx.\end{aligned}\tag{74}$$

Now, again since

$$\max\deg\,\{\Phi_n'(x)\Phi_m(x)-\Phi_m'(x)\Phi_n(x)\}=m+n-1,$$

if

$$N\le a-\mu-\frac{1}{2}\quad\text{for}\quad N=\max\{m,n\},$$

the left-hand side of (74) tends to zero and for $m,n\ge 1$, we obtain

$$\int_{-\infty}^{\infty}(x^2-r)^{\mu}\,x^{-2a}e^{-\frac{1}{x^2}}\,\Phi_{n,r,\mu}^{(a)}(x)\,\Phi_{m,r,\mu}^{(a)}(x)\,dx=0,\qquad(m\neq n).$$

Corollary 5. *There are, in total, four sequences of symmetric orthogonal X_1-polynomials as follows:*

1. *Infinite X_1 symmetric polynomials orthogonal with respect to the weight function*

$$\rho_1^*(x)=(x^2-r)^{\mu}x^{2a}(1-x^2)^b,\qquad(-1\le x\le 1).$$

2. *Infinite X_1 symmetric polynomials orthogonal with respect to the weight function*

$$\rho_2^*(x)=(x^2-r)^{\mu}x^{2a}e^{-x^2},\qquad(-\infty<x<\infty).$$

3. *Finite X_1 symmetric polynomials orthogonal with respect to the weight function*

$$\rho_3^*(x)=(x^2-r)^{\mu}x^{-2a}(1+x^2)^{-b},\qquad(-\infty<x<\infty).$$

4. *Finite X_1 symmetric polynomials orthogonal with respect to the weight function*

$$\rho_4^*(x)=(x^2-r)^{\mu}x^{-2a}e^{-\frac{1}{x^2}},\qquad(-\infty<x<\infty).$$

In all four above-mentioned cases, $r\in\mathbb{R}$ and μ is a real parameter such that $(-1)^{\mu}=1$.

7. Conclusions

In this paper, a unified classification of all exceptional orthogonal X_1-polynomials of symmetric and nonsymmetric types is established as a solution of generic second-order differential equations. Ten extended differential equations are introduced, and it is shown that they have polynomial solutions; six of them are X_1-orthogonal and four of them are X_1-symmetric orthogonal. When it comes to the classification nonsymmetric types, the key point is that the weight functions corresponding to the six sequences are exactly a multiplication of Pearson distributions family. Moreover, the finite cases of nonsymmetric exceptional X_1-polynomials orthogonal on infinite intervals and the class of symmetric orthogonal X_1-polynomials are introduced in this paper for the first time. More interesting properties of these polynomials and their applications in theoretical and computational [20] mathematical physics can be investigated in future research.

Author Contributions: Investigation, M.M.-J. and Z.M.; validation, M.M.-J., Z.M. and N.S.; conceptualization, M.M.-J. and Z.M.; methodology, M.M.-J., Z.M. and N.S.; formal analysis, M.M.-J., Z.M. and N.S.; funding acquisition, N.S.; writing—review and editing, M.M.-J., Z.M. and N.S.; writing—original draft preparation, M.M.-J. and Z.M. The authors contributed equally to the work. All authors have read and agreed to the published version of the manuscript.

Funding: The work of the first author has been supported by the Alexander von Humboldt Foundation under the grant number: Ref 3.4—IRN—1128637—GF-E. Partial financial support of this work, under Grant No. GP249507 from the Natural Sciences and Engineering Research Council of Canada is gratefully acknowledged by the second author.

Data Availability Statement: Data sharing is not applicable to this article as no new data were created or analyzed in this study.

Acknowledgments: The work of the first author has been supported by the *Alexander von Humboldt Foundation* under the grant number: Ref 3.4—IRN—1128637—GF-E. Partial financial support of this work under Grant Nos. GP249507 from the Natural Sciences and Engineering Research Council of Canada is gratefully acknowledged (NS).

Conflicts of Interest: The authors declare no conflict of interest.

References

1. Ismail, M.; Ismail, M.E.; van Assche, W. *Classical and Quantum Orthogonal Polynomials in One Variable*; Cambridge University Press, Cambridge, UK, 2005.
2. Koekoek, R.; Lesky, P.A.; Swarttouw, R.F. *Hypergeometric Orthogonal Polynomials and Their q-Analogues*; Springer Monographs in Mathematics; Springer: Berlin, Germany, 2010.
3. Nikiforov, A.F.; Suslov, S.K.; Uvarov, V.B. *Classical Orthogonal Polynomials of a Discrete Variable*; Springer Series in Computational Physics; Springer: Berlin, Germany, 1991.
4. Arfken, G. *Mathematical Methods for Physicists*; Academic Press: Cambridge, MA, USA, 1985.
5. Masjed-Jamei, M. *Special Functions and Generalized Sturm-Liouville Problems*; Springer Nature, Birkhäuser: Basel, Switzerland, 2020.
6. Nikiforov, A.F.; Uvarov, V.B. *Special Functions of Mathematical Physics*; Birkhäuser: Basel, Switzerland; Boston, MA, USA, 1988.
7. Chihara, T.S. *An Introduction to Orthogonal Polynomials*; Gordon and Breach Science Publishers: New York, NY, USA, 1978.
8. Johnson, N.L.; Kotz, S.; Balakrishnan, N. *Continuous Univariate Distributions*, 2nd ed.; John Wiley & Sons Inc.: Hoboken, NJ, USA, 1994.
9. Bochner, S. Über Sturm-Liouvillesche Polynomsysteme. *Math. Z.* **1929**, *29*, 730–736. [CrossRef]
10. Al-Salam, W. Characterization theorems for orthogonal polynomial. In *Orthogonal Polynomials: Theory and Practice*; NATO ASI Series; Kluwer Academic: Dordrecht, The Netherlands, 1990; Volume 294, pp. 1–24.
11. Andrews, G.E.; Askey, R.; Roy, R. *Special Functions. Encyclopedia of Mathematics and Its Applications 71*; Cambridge University Press: Cambridge, UK, 1999.
12. Masjed-Jamei, M. Three finite classes of hypergeometric orthogonal polynomials and their application in functions approximation. *Integral Transforms Spec. Funct.* **2002**, *13*, 169–191. [CrossRef]
13. Gómez-Ullate, D.; Kamran, N.; Milson, R. An extended class of orthogonal polynomials defined by a Sturm-Liouville problem. *J. Math. Anal. Appl.* **2009**, *359*, 352–367. [CrossRef]
14. Gómez-Ullate, D.; Kamran, N.; Milson, R. An extension of Bochner's problem: Exceptional invariant subspaces. *J. Approx. Theory* **2010**, *162*, 987–1006. [CrossRef]
15. Dutta, D.; Roy, P. Darboux transformation, exceptional orthogonal polynomials and information theoretic measures of uncertainty. In *Algebraic Aspects of Darboux Transformations, Quantum Integrable Systems and Supersymmetric Quantum Mechanics*; Volume 563 of Contemporary Mathematics; American Mathematical Society: Providence, RI, USA, 2012; pp. 33–49.
16. Ho, C.-L. Dirac(-Pauli), Fokker-Planck equations and exceptional Laguerre polynomials. *Ann. Phys.* **2011**, *326*, 797–807. [CrossRef]
17. García-Ferrero, M.; Gómez-Ullate, D.; Milson, R. A Bochner type characterization theorem for exceptional orthogonal polynomials. *J. Math. Anal. Appl.* **2019**, *472*, 584–626. [CrossRef]
18. Masjed-Jamei, M. A generalization of classical symmetric orthogonal functions using a symmetric generalization of Sturm-Liouville problems. *Integral Transforms Spec. Funct.* **2007**, *18*, 871–883. [CrossRef]
19. Masjed-Jamei, M. A basic class of symmetric orthogonal polynomials using the extended Sturm-Liouville theorem for symmetric functions. *J. Math. Anal. Appl.* **2007**, *325*, 753–775. [CrossRef]
20. Qiao, L.; Xu, D. A fast ADI orthogonal spline collocation method with graded meshes for the two-dimensional fractional integro-differential equation. *Adv. Comput. Math.* **2021**, *47*, 64. [CrossRef]

mathematics

Article

Fully Degenerating of Daehee Numbers and Polynomials

Sahar Albosaily [1], Waseem Ahmad Khan [2], Serkan Araci [3] and Azhar Iqbal [2,*]

[1] Department of Mathematics, College of Science, University of Ha'il, Ha'il 2440, Saudi Arabia; s.albosaily@uoh.edu.sa
[2] Department of Mathematics and Natural Sciences, Prince Mohammad Bin Fahd University, P.O. Box 1664, Al Khobar 31952, Saudi Arabia; wkhan1@pmu.edu.sa
[3] Department of Basic Sciences, Faculty of Engineering, Hasan Kalyoncu University, Gaziantep TR-27410, Turkey; serkan.araci@hku.edu.tr
* Correspondence: aiqbal@pmu.edu.sa

Abstract: In this paper, we consider fully degenerate Daehee numbers and polynomials by using degenerate logarithm function. We investigate some properties of these numbers and polynomials. We also introduce higher-order multiple fully degenerate Daehee polynomials and numbers which can be represented in terms of Riemann integrals on the interval $[0, 1]$. Finally, we derive their summation formulae.

Keywords: degenerate Daehee polynomials; multiple degenerate Daehee numbers; higher-order degenerate Daehee polynomials

MSC: 11B83; 11B73; 05A19

Citation: Albosaily, S.; Khan, W.A.; Araci, S.; Iqbal, A. Fully Degenerating of Daehee Numbers and Polynomials. *Mathematics* **2022**, *10*, 2528. https://doi.org/10.3390/math10142528

Academic Editor: Sitnik Sergey

Received: 4 June 2022
Accepted: 15 July 2022
Published: 20 July 2022

Publisher's Note: MDPI stays neutral with regard to jurisdictional claims in published maps and institutional affiliations.

Copyright: © 2022 by the authors. Licensee MDPI, Basel, Switzerland. This article is an open access article distributed under the terms and conditions of the Creative Commons Attribution (CC BY) license (https://creativecommons.org/licenses/by/4.0/).

1. Introduction

The generalizations of special polynomials have been one of the most emerging research fields in mathematical analysis and extensively investigated in order to find interesting identities and relations. Applications of the generalized special polynomials arise in problems of number theory, combinatorics, mathematical physics and other subareas of pure and applied mathematics provide motivation for introducing a new class of generalized polynomials. For example, some special polynomials occur in probability as the Edgeworth series; in combinatorics, they arise in the umbral calculus as an example of an Appell sequence which plays an important role in various problems connected with functional equations, interpolation problems, approximation theory, summation methods; in numerical analysis, they play a role in Gaussian quadrature; and in physics, they appear in quantum mechanical and optical beam transport problems. (see [1] for detail).

Recently, many mathematicians as the systematic study of degenerate versions of some special polynomials and numbers (see Kim-Kim [2–4], Kim et al. [5], Khan et al. [6–8], and Sharma et al. [9]) have been established due to Carlitz's degenerate version of Bernoulli polynomials given by (see [10,11])

$$\sum_{\ell=0}^{\infty} \beta_{\ell,\lambda}(\zeta)\frac{\omega^{\ell}}{\ell!} = \frac{\omega}{(1+\lambda\omega)^{\frac{1}{\lambda}}-1}(1+\lambda\omega)^{\frac{\zeta}{\lambda}}, \quad (\lambda \in \mathbb{R}-\{0\}), \tag{1}$$

and the degenerate Bernoulli polynomials of higher order are also given by

$$\left(\frac{\omega}{(1+\lambda\omega)^{\frac{1}{\lambda}}-1}\right)^{r}(1+\lambda\omega)^{\frac{\zeta}{\lambda}} = \sum_{\ell=0}^{\infty} \beta_{l,\lambda}^{(r)}(\zeta), \tag{2}$$

with the case

$$\lim_{\lambda\to 0} \beta_{j,\lambda}^{(r)}(\zeta) = B_{j}^{(r)}(\zeta) \quad (j \geq 0), \tag{3}$$

where $B_j^{(r)}(\zeta)$ are the Bernoulli polynomials of higher order.

For any $\lambda \in \mathbb{R}-\{0\}$, degenerate version of the exponential function $e_\lambda^\zeta(\omega)$ is defined as (see [2,3,6–8,10,11])

$$e_\lambda^\zeta(\omega) := (1+\lambda\omega)^{\frac{\zeta}{\lambda}} = \sum_{\ell=0}^{\infty}(\zeta)_{\ell,\lambda}\frac{\omega^\ell}{\ell!}, \tag{4}$$

where $(\zeta)_{0,\lambda} = 1$ and $(\zeta)_{\ell,\lambda} = \zeta(\zeta-\lambda)\cdots(\zeta-(\ell-1)\lambda)$ for $\ell \geq 1$, (see [2–7,10,12]). It is obvious that $\lim_{\lambda\to 0} e_\lambda^\zeta(\omega) = e^{\zeta\omega}$. Additionally, we note that $e_\lambda^1(\omega) := e_\lambda(\omega)$.

The generating functions of the degenerating Stirling numbers of the first and second kinds are defined by

$$\frac{1}{k!}(\log_\lambda(1+\omega))^k = \sum_{j=k}^{\infty} S_{1,\lambda}(j,k)\frac{\omega^j}{j!} \text{ and } \frac{1}{k!}(e_\lambda(\omega)-1)^k = \sum_{j=k}^{\infty} S_{2,\lambda}(j,k)\frac{\omega^j}{j!} \tag{5}$$

where

$$\log_\lambda(1+\omega) = \frac{(1+\omega)^\lambda - 1}{\lambda}, \tag{6}$$

which is the inverse of degenerate exponential function (see [4,6]).

Roman [13] defined the Bernoulli polynomials of the second kind given by means of the following generating function:

$$\frac{\omega}{\log(1+\omega)}(1+\omega)^\zeta = \sum_{\ell=0}^{\infty} b_\ell(\zeta)\frac{\omega^\ell}{\ell!}. \tag{7}$$

From (3) and (7), we note that, see [8,14].

$$b_\ell(\zeta) = B_\ell^{(\ell)}(\zeta+1), \quad (\ell \geq 0),$$

It is well known from [2] that

$$\left(\frac{\omega}{\log_\lambda(1+\omega)}\right)^k (1+\omega)^{\zeta-1} = \sum_{\ell=0}^{\infty} B_{\ell,\lambda}^{(\ell-k+1)}(\zeta)\frac{\omega^\ell}{\ell!}, \quad (k \in \mathbb{Z}). \tag{8}$$

where $B_{\ell,\lambda}^{(\alpha)}(\zeta)$ are called λ-analogue of Bernoulli polynomials of higher order given via the following generating function:

$$\left(\frac{\omega}{\lambda e^\omega - 1}\right)^\alpha e^{\zeta\omega} = \sum_{j=0}^{\infty} B_{j,\lambda}^{(\alpha)}(\zeta)\frac{\omega^j}{j!}.$$

In [2], the degenerate Bernoulli polynomials of the second kind are defined by

$$\frac{\omega}{\log_\lambda(1+\omega)}(1+\omega)^\zeta = \sum_{\ell=0}^{\infty} b_{\ell,\lambda}(\zeta)\frac{\omega^\ell}{\ell!}. \tag{9}$$

Note that

$$\lim_{\lambda\to 0} b_{\ell,\lambda}(\zeta) = b_\ell(\zeta), \quad (\ell \geq 0).$$

The Daehee polynomials are known as, (see [7–9]).

$$\frac{\log(1+\omega)}{\omega}(1+\omega)^\zeta = \sum_{j=0}^{\infty} D_j(\zeta)\frac{\omega^j}{j!}, \tag{10}$$

In the case when $\zeta = 0$, $D_j = D_j(0)$ are called the Daehee numbers. The Equation (10) will be our main focus to proceed its fully degenerate version with their identities and properties with Section 2. In Section 3, we consider multiple fully degenerate Daehee polynomials of higher order which can be represented in terms of Riemann integrals on the interval $[0,1]$. We derive their identities and properties among some other polynomials which will be mentioned in the next sections.

2. Fully Degenerating Daehee Numbers and Polynomials

Recall from Equation (6) that

$$\begin{aligned}\log_\lambda(1+\omega) &= \frac{(1+\omega)^\lambda - 1}{\lambda} \\ &= \sum_{j=1}^{\infty} \lambda^{j-1}(1)_{j,1/\lambda}\frac{\omega^j}{j!},\end{aligned} \tag{11}$$

where

$$(1)_{j,1/\lambda} = (1-\frac{1}{\lambda})(1-\frac{2}{\lambda})\cdots(1-(j-1)\frac{1}{\lambda}).$$

In the case λ approaches to 0, we see that the Equation (11) turns out to be classical one as follows:

$$\lim_{\lambda\to 0}\log_\lambda(1+\omega) = \sum_{j=1}^{\infty}(-1)^{j-1}\frac{\omega^j}{j!} = \log(1+\omega).$$

Note that $e_\lambda(\log_\lambda(\omega)) = \log_\lambda(e_\lambda(\omega)) = \omega$. By making use of Equation (11), Kim et al. [5] introduced the new type of degenerate Daehee polynomials as follows:

$$\sum_{\ell=0}^{\infty} D_{\ell,\lambda}(\zeta)\frac{\omega^\ell}{\ell!} = \frac{\log_\lambda(1+\omega)}{\omega}(1+\omega)^\zeta \tag{12}$$

$$= \frac{\log(1+\omega)}{\omega}\int_0^1 (1+\omega)^{\lambda\eta+\zeta}d\eta. \tag{13}$$

At the value $\zeta = 0$, $D_{j,\lambda} = D_{j,\lambda}(0)$ are called the degenerate Daehee numbers. Motivated by (12) and (13), we give the following definition.

Definition 1. *Let $\lambda \in \mathbb{R}-\{0\}$. The fully degenerating Daehee polynomials are defined by means of the following generating function:*

$$\sum_{j=0}^{\infty}\tilde{d}_{j,\lambda}(\zeta)\frac{\omega^j}{j!} = \frac{\log_\lambda(1+\omega)}{\omega}e^{\zeta\log_\lambda(1+\omega)}. \tag{14}$$

Then, from (13), we see that

$$\sum_{j=0}^{\infty}\tilde{d}_{j,\lambda}(\zeta)\frac{\omega^j}{j!} = \frac{\log(1+\omega)}{\omega}\int_0^1 (1+\omega)^{\lambda\eta}d\eta\; e^{\zeta\log_\lambda(1+\omega)}. \tag{15}$$

Note that, $\lim_{\lambda\to 0}\tilde{d}_{j,\lambda}(\zeta) = \tilde{d}_j(\zeta)$, $(j \geq 0)$. We note that $\zeta = 0, \tilde{d}_{j,\lambda} := \tilde{d}_{j,\lambda}(0)$ are called the new type of fully degenerate Daehee numbers. The following identity will be useful for proving next theorem already known in [2]:

$$e^{\zeta\log_\lambda(1+\omega)} = \sum_{\ell=0}^{\infty}\left\{\sum_{k=0}^{\ell} S_{1,\lambda}(\ell,k)\zeta^\ell\right\}\frac{\omega^\ell}{\ell!}. \tag{16}$$

Theorem 1. *Let $j \geq 0$, the following identity holds true:*

$$\tilde{d}_{j,\lambda}(\zeta) = \sum_{r=0}^{j}\sum_{k=0}^{r}\binom{j}{r}\tilde{d}_{j-r,\lambda}S_{1,\lambda}(r,k)\zeta^{r}.$$

Proof. It is proved by using (11) that

$$\begin{aligned}
\sum_{j=0}^{\infty}\tilde{d}_{j,\lambda}(\zeta)\frac{\omega^{j}}{j!} &= \frac{\log_{\lambda}(1+\omega)}{\omega}e^{\zeta\log_{\lambda}(1+\omega)} \\
&= \sum_{l=0}^{\infty}\tilde{d}_{l,\lambda}\frac{\omega^{l}}{l!}\sum_{r=0}^{\infty}\zeta^{r}\frac{(\log_{\lambda}(1+\omega))^{r}}{r!} \\
&= \sum_{l=0}^{\infty}\tilde{d}_{l,\lambda}\frac{\omega^{l}}{l!}\sum_{r=0}^{\infty}\sum_{k=0}^{r}S_{1,\lambda}(r,k)\zeta^{r}\frac{\omega^{r}}{r!} \\
&= \sum_{j=0}^{\infty}\left(\sum_{r=0}^{j}\sum_{k=0}^{r}\binom{j}{r}\tilde{d}_{j-r,\lambda}S_{1,\lambda}(r,k)\zeta^{r}\right)\frac{\omega^{j}}{j!}.
\end{aligned}$$

By comparing the coefficients of $\frac{\omega^{j}}{j!}$ on the above, we get the proof of this theorem. □

Theorem 2. *For $j \geq 0$, we have*

$$\tilde{d}_{j,\lambda}(\zeta) = \sum_{i=0}^{j}\frac{1}{j-i+1}\sum_{r=1}^{j-i+1}\sum_{k=0}^{i}\binom{j}{i}\lambda^{r-1}S_{1}(j-i+1,r)\zeta^{k}S_{1,\lambda}(i,k). \tag{17}$$

Proof. By using (11), we get

$$\begin{aligned}
\sum_{j=0}^{\infty}\tilde{d}_{j,\lambda}(\zeta)\frac{\omega^{j}}{j!} &= \frac{\log(1+\omega)}{\omega}\int_{0}^{1}(1+\omega)^{\lambda\eta}d\eta e^{\zeta\log_{\lambda}(1+\omega)} \\
&= \frac{\log(1+\omega)}{\omega}\sum_{r=0}^{\infty}\lambda^{r}\frac{(\log(1+\omega))^{r}}{(r+1)!}\sum_{k=0}^{\infty}\zeta^{k}\frac{(\log_{\lambda}(1+\omega))^{k}}{k!} \\
&= \frac{1}{\omega}\left(\sum_{r=1}^{\infty}\lambda^{r-1}\frac{(\log(1+\omega))^{r}}{r!}\right)\left(\sum_{k=0}^{\infty}\zeta^{k}\frac{(\log_{\lambda}(1+\omega))^{k}}{k!}\right) \\
&= \frac{1}{\omega}\left(\sum_{j=1}^{\infty}\sum_{r=1}^{j}\lambda^{r-1}S_{1}(j,r)\frac{\omega^{j}}{j!}\right)\left(\sum_{i=0}^{\infty}\sum_{k=0}^{i}\zeta^{k}S_{1,\lambda}(i,k)\frac{\omega^{i}}{i!}\right) \\
&= \left(\sum_{j=0}^{\infty}\frac{1}{j+1}\sum_{r=1}^{j+1}\lambda^{r-1}S_{1}(j+1,r)\frac{\omega^{j}}{j!}\right)\left(\sum_{i=0}^{\infty}\sum_{k=0}^{i}\zeta^{k}S_{1,\lambda}(i,k)\frac{\omega^{i}}{i!}\right) \\
&= \sum_{j=0}^{\infty}\left(\frac{1}{j-i+1}\sum_{i=0}^{j}\sum_{r=1}^{j-i+1}\sum_{k=0}^{i}\binom{j}{i}\lambda^{r-1}S_{1}(j-i+1,r)\zeta^{k}S_{1,\lambda}(i,k)\right)\frac{\omega^{j}}{j!}
\end{aligned}$$

Thus, we get the result. □

From (1), we note that

$$\left(\sum_{j=0}^{\infty}\beta_{j,\lambda}\frac{\omega^{j}}{j!}\right)\left(\sum_{r=0}^{\infty}\zeta^{r}\frac{\omega^{r}}{r!}\right) = \frac{\omega}{e_{\lambda}(\omega)-1}e^{\zeta\omega} = \sum_{j=0}^{\infty}\left(\sum_{r=0}^{j}\binom{j}{r}\beta_{j-r,\lambda}\zeta^{r}\right)\frac{\omega^{j}}{j!} \tag{18}$$

Theorem 3. *For $j \geq 0$, we have*

$$\tilde{d}_{j,\lambda}(\zeta) = \sum_{i=0}^{j} \sum_{r=0}^{i} \binom{i}{r} \beta_{i-r,\lambda} \zeta^r S_{1,\lambda}(j,i). \tag{19}$$

Proof. By replacing ω by $\log_\lambda(1+\omega)$ in (18), we get

$$\begin{aligned} \frac{\log_\lambda(1+\omega)}{\omega} e^{x \log_\lambda(1+\omega)} &= \sum_{i=0}^{\infty} \sum_{r=0}^{i} \binom{i}{r} \beta_{i-r,\lambda} \zeta^r \frac{(\log_\lambda(1+\omega))^i}{i!} \\ &= \sum_{i=0}^{\infty} \sum_{r=0}^{i} \binom{i}{r} \beta_{i-r,\lambda} \zeta^r \sum_{j=i}^{\infty} S_{1,\lambda}(j,i) \frac{\omega^j}{j!} \\ &= \sum_{j=0}^{\infty} \left(\sum_{i=0}^{j} \sum_{r=0}^{i} \binom{i}{r} \beta_{i-r,\lambda} \zeta^r S_{1,\lambda}(j,i) \right) \frac{\omega^j}{j!}. \end{aligned} \tag{20}$$

On the other hand,

$$\frac{\log_\lambda(1+\omega)}{\omega} e^{\zeta \log_\lambda(1+\omega)} = \sum_{r=0}^{\infty} \tilde{d}_{j,\lambda}(\zeta) \frac{\omega^j}{j!}. \tag{21}$$

Therefore, by (20) and (21), we obtain the required result. □

Theorem 4. *For $j \geq 0$, we have*

$$\beta_{j,\lambda} = \sum_{r=0}^{j} \tilde{d}_{r,\lambda}(\zeta) S_{2,\lambda}(j,r).$$

Proof. By replacing ω by $e_\lambda(\omega) - 1$ in (11), we get

$$\begin{aligned} \frac{\omega}{e_\lambda(\omega)-1} e^{\zeta\omega} &= \sum_{r=0}^{\infty} \tilde{d}_{r,\lambda}(\zeta) \frac{(e_\lambda(\omega)-1)^r}{r!} \\ &= \sum_{j=0}^{\infty} \left(\sum_{r=0}^{j} \tilde{d}_{r,\lambda}(\zeta) S_{2,\lambda}(j,r) \right) \frac{\omega^j}{j!}. \end{aligned} \tag{22}$$

By using (18) and (22), we conclude the proof. □

Theorem 5. *For $j \geq 0$, we have*

$$\sum_{r=0}^{j} \binom{j}{r} b_{j-r} \tilde{d}_{r,\lambda}(\zeta) = \sum_{i=0}^{j} \binom{j}{i} \sum_{r=0}^{j-i} \sum_{k=0}^{i} \frac{\lambda^r}{r+1} \zeta^k S_{j-i,r} S_{1,\lambda}(i,k).$$

Proof. By using (11), we note that

$$\begin{aligned} \int_0^1 (1+\omega)^{\lambda\eta} d\eta \, e^{\zeta \log_\lambda(1+\omega)} &= \frac{\omega}{\log(1+\omega)} \frac{\log_\lambda(1+\omega)}{\omega} e^{\zeta \log_\lambda(1+\omega)} \\ &= \left(\sum_{j=0}^{\infty} b_j \frac{\omega^j}{j!} \right) \left(\sum_{r=0}^{\infty} \tilde{d}_{r,\lambda}(\zeta) \frac{\omega^r}{r!} \right) \\ &= \sum_{j=0}^{\infty} \left(\sum_{r=0}^{j} \binom{j}{r} b_{j-r} \tilde{d}_{r,\lambda}(\zeta) \right) \frac{\omega^j}{j!}. \end{aligned} \tag{23}$$

On the other hand, we have

$$\int_0^1 (1+\omega)^{\lambda\eta} d\eta \, e^{\zeta \log_\lambda(1+\omega)} = \sum_{r=0}^{\infty} \frac{\lambda^r(\log(1+\omega))^r}{(r+1)!} \sum_{k=0}^{\infty} \zeta^k \frac{(\log_\lambda(1+\omega))^k}{k!}$$

$$= \sum_{r=0}^{\infty} \frac{\lambda^r}{r+1} \sum_{j=r}^{\infty} S_1(j,r) \frac{\omega^j}{j!} \sum_{k=0}^{\infty} \zeta^k \sum_{i=k}^{\infty} S_{1,\lambda}(i,k) \frac{\omega^i}{i!}$$

$$= \sum_{j=0}^{\infty} \frac{\lambda^r}{r+1} \sum_{r=0}^{j} S_1(j,r) \frac{\omega^j}{j!} \sum_{i=0}^{\infty} \zeta^k \sum_{k=0}^{i} S_{1,\lambda}(i,k) \frac{\omega^i}{i!}$$

$$= \sum_{j=0}^{\infty} \left(\sum_{i=0}^{j} \binom{j}{i} \sum_{r=0}^{j-i} \sum_{k=0}^{i} \frac{\lambda^r}{r+1} \sigma^k S_{j-i,r} S_{1,\lambda}(i,k) \right) \frac{\omega^j}{j!}. \tag{24}$$

Thus, by (23) and (24), we arrive at the required the proof. □

3. New Type of Higher-Order Fully Degenerating Daehee Numbers and Polynomials

Let us define the new type of fully degenerate Daehee polynomials of order r ($\in \mathbb{N}$) by the following multiple Riemann integral on the interval $\underbrace{[0,1] \times [0,1] \times \cdots \times [0,1]}_{\text{k-times}}$:

$$\left(\frac{\log(1+\omega)}{\omega}\right)^r \int_0^1 \cdots \int_0^1 (1+\omega)^{\lambda(\zeta_1+\cdots+\zeta_r)} d\zeta_1 \cdots d\zeta_r \, e^{\zeta \log_\lambda(1+\omega)} \tag{25}$$

$$= \left(\frac{\log_\lambda(1+\omega)}{\omega}\right)^r e^{\zeta \log_\lambda(1+\omega)} = \sum_{j=0}^{\infty} \tilde{d}_{j,\lambda}^{(r)}(\zeta) \frac{\omega^j}{j!}$$

In the case when $\zeta = 0, \tilde{d}_{j,\lambda}^{(r)} = \tilde{d}_{j,\lambda}^{(r)}(0)$ are called the new type of fully degenerate Daehee numbers of the order r.

Theorem 6. *For $j \geq 0$, we have*

$$\tilde{d}_{j,\lambda}^{(r)}(\zeta) = \sum_{k=0}^{j} \binom{j}{k} \sum_{i=0}^{k} \tilde{d}_{j-k,\lambda}^{(r)} \zeta^i S_{1,\lambda}(k,i).$$

Proof. From (25), we note that

$$\left(\frac{\log_\lambda(1+\omega)}{\omega}\right)^r e^{\zeta \log_\lambda(1+\omega)}$$

$$= \sum_{j=0}^{\infty} \tilde{d}_{j,\lambda}^{(r)} \frac{\omega^j}{j!} \sum_{i=0}^{\infty} \frac{1}{i!} \zeta^i (\log_\lambda(1+\omega))^i = \sum_{j=0}^{\infty} \tilde{d}_{j,\lambda}^{(r)} \frac{\omega^j}{j!} \sum_{i=0}^{\infty} \zeta^i \sum_{k=i}^{\infty} S_{1,\lambda}(k,i) \frac{\omega^k}{k!}$$

$$= \sum_{j=0}^{\infty} \tilde{d}_{j,\lambda}^{(r)} \frac{\omega^j}{j!} \sum_{k=0}^{\infty} \zeta^i \sum_{i=0}^{k} S_{1,\lambda}(k,i) \frac{\omega^k}{k!}$$

$$= \sum_{j=0}^{\infty} \left(\sum_{k=0}^{j} \binom{j}{k} \sum_{i=0}^{k} \zeta^i S_{1,\lambda}(k,i) \tilde{d}_{j-k,\lambda}^{(r)} S_{1,\lambda}(j,i) \right) \frac{\omega^j}{j!}.$$

Thus, by comparing the coefficients of $\frac{\omega^j}{j!}$ on the above, we obtain the result. □

Theorem 7. *For $n \geq 0$, we have*

$$\tilde{d}_{j,\lambda}^{(r)}(\zeta) = \sum_{i=0}^{j} \sum_{k=0}^{j-i} \binom{j}{i} \frac{S_{1,\lambda}(i+r,r)}{\binom{i+r}{i}} \zeta^k S_{1,\lambda}(j-i,k).$$

Proof. Using (25), we have

$$\sum_{j=0}^{\infty} \tilde{d}_{j,\lambda}^{(r)}(\zeta) \frac{\omega^j}{j!} = \frac{r!}{\omega^r} \frac{1}{r!} (\log_\lambda(1+\omega))^r e^{\zeta \log_\lambda(1+\omega)}$$

$$= \frac{r!}{\omega^r} \left(\sum_{i=r}^{\infty} S_{1,\lambda}(i,r) \frac{\omega^i}{i!} \right) \left(\sum_{k=0}^{\infty} \zeta^k \frac{(\log_\lambda(1+\omega))^k}{k!} \right)$$

$$= \left(\sum_{i=0}^{\infty} \frac{S_{1,\lambda}(i+r,r)}{\binom{i+r}{i}} \frac{\omega^i}{i!} \right) \left(\sum_{j=0}^{\infty} \sum_{k=0}^{j} \zeta^k S_{1,\lambda}(j,k) \frac{\omega^j}{j!} \right)$$

$$= \sum_{j=0}^{\infty} \left(\sum_{i=0}^{j} \sum_{k=0}^{j-i} \binom{j}{i} \frac{S_{1,\lambda}(i+r,r)}{\binom{i+r}{i}} \zeta^k S_{1,\lambda}(j-i,k) \right) \frac{\omega^j}{j!}.$$

Therefore, by comparing the coefficients of $\frac{\omega^j}{j!}$ on the above, we arrive at the desired result. □

Theorem 8. *For $j \geq 0$, we have*

$$\sum_{i=0}^{j} \binom{j}{i} \beta_{j-i,\lambda} \zeta^i = \sum_{\ell=0}^{j} \tilde{d}_{\ell,\lambda}^{(r)}(\zeta) S_{2,\lambda}(j,\ell).$$

Proof. By replacing ω by $e_\lambda(\omega)-1$ in (25), we get

$$\sum_{i=0}^{\infty} \tilde{d}_{i,\lambda}^{(r)}(\zeta) \frac{(e_\lambda(\omega)-1)^i}{i!} = \left(\frac{\omega}{e_\lambda(\omega)-1} \right)^r e^{\zeta\omega}$$

$$= \sum_{j=0}^{\infty} \beta_{j,\lambda} \frac{\omega^j}{j!} \sum_{i=0}^{\infty} \zeta^i \frac{\omega^i}{i!}$$

$$= \sum_{j=0}^{\infty} \left(\sum_{i=0}^{j} \binom{j}{i} \beta_{j-i,\lambda} \zeta^i \right) \frac{\omega^j}{j!}. \tag{26}$$

On the other hand, we have

$$\sum_{i=0}^{\infty} \tilde{d}_{i,\lambda}^{(r)}(\zeta) \frac{[e_\lambda(\omega)-1]^i}{i!} = \sum_{i=0}^{\infty} \tilde{d}_{i,\lambda}^{(r)}(\zeta) \sum_{j=i}^{\infty} S_{2,\lambda}(j,i) \frac{\omega^j}{j!}$$

$$= \sum_{j=0}^{\infty} \left(\sum_{\ell=0}^{j} \tilde{d}_{\ell,\lambda}^{(r)}(\zeta) S_{2,\lambda}(j,\ell) \right) \frac{\omega^j}{j!}. \tag{27}$$

By (26) and (27), we complete the proof. □

From (2), we get

$$\left(\frac{\omega}{e_\lambda(\omega)-1} \right)^r e^{\zeta\omega} = \sum_{j=0}^{\infty} \left(\sum_{i=0}^{j} \binom{j}{i} \beta_{j-i,\lambda} \zeta^i \right) \frac{\omega^j}{j!} \tag{28}$$

Theorem 9. *For $j \geq 0$, we have*

$$\tilde{d}_{j,\lambda}^{(r)}(\zeta) = \sum_{p=0}^{j}\sum_{q=0}^{p}\binom{p}{q}\beta_{p-q,\lambda}\zeta^q S_{1,\lambda}(j,p).$$

Proof. By changing t to $\log_\lambda(1+t)$ in (28), we get

$$\begin{aligned}\left(\frac{\log_\lambda(1+\omega)}{\omega}\right)^r e^{\zeta\log_\lambda(1+\omega)} &= \sum_{p=0}^{\infty}\sum_{q=0}^{p}\binom{p}{q}\beta_{p-q,\lambda}\zeta^q\frac{[\log_\lambda(1+\omega)]^p}{p!} \\ &= \sum_{p=0}^{\infty}\sum_{q=0}^{p}\binom{p}{q}\beta_{p-q,\lambda}\zeta^q\sum_{j=p}^{\infty}S_{1,\lambda}(j,p)\frac{\omega^j}{j!} \\ &= \sum_{j=0}^{\infty}\left(\sum_{p=0}^{j}\sum_{q=0}^{p}\binom{p}{q}\beta_{p-q,\lambda}\zeta^q S_{1,\lambda}(j,p)\right)\frac{\omega^j}{j!}. \end{aligned} \tag{29}$$

In view of (25) and (29), we get the result. □

Theorem 10. *For $j \geq 0$, we have*

$$\begin{aligned}&\sum_{k=0}^{j}\binom{j}{k}B_k^{(k-r+1)}\tilde{d}_{j-k,\lambda}^{(r)}(\zeta) \\ &= \sum_{i=0}^{j}\binom{j}{i}\sum_{p=0}^{i}\lambda^p\sum_{q_1+\cdots+q_r=p}\binom{p}{q_1,\cdots,q_r}\frac{1}{(q_1+1)\cdots(q_r+1)}S_1(i,p) \\ &\quad\times\sum_{k=0}^{j-i}\zeta^k S_{1,\lambda}(j-i,k).\end{aligned}$$

Proof. From (25), we see that

$$\begin{aligned}&\int_0^1\cdots\int_0^1(1+\omega)^{\lambda(\zeta_1+\cdots+\zeta_r)}d\zeta_1\cdots d\zeta_r e^{\zeta\log_\lambda(1+\omega)} \\ &= \left(\frac{\omega}{\log(1+\omega)}\right)^r\left(\frac{\log_\lambda(1+\omega)}{\omega}\right)^r e^{\zeta\log_\lambda(1+\omega)} = \sum_{k=0}^{\infty}B_k^{(k-r+1)}\frac{\omega^k}{k!}\sum_{j=0}^{\infty}\tilde{d}_{j,\lambda}^{(r)}(\zeta)\frac{\omega^j}{j!} \\ &= \sum_{j=0}^{\infty}\left(\sum_{k=0}^{j}\binom{j}{k}B_k^{(k-r+1)}\tilde{d}_{j-k,\lambda}^{(r)}(\zeta)\right)\frac{\omega^j}{j!}.\end{aligned} \tag{30}$$

On the other hand, we have

$$\begin{aligned}&\int_0^1\cdots\int_0^1(1+\omega)^{\lambda(\zeta_1+\cdots+\zeta_r)}d\zeta_1\cdots d\zeta_r e^{\zeta\log_\lambda(1+\omega)} \\ &= \sum_{p=0}^{\infty}\lambda^p\frac{(\log(1+\omega))}{p!}\int_0^1\cdots\int_0^1(\zeta_1+\cdots+\zeta_r)^p d\zeta_1\cdots d\zeta_r\sum_{k=0}^{\infty}\zeta^k\frac{(\log_\lambda(1+\omega))^k}{k!} \\ &= \sum_{p=0}^{\infty}\lambda^p\sum_{q_1+\cdots+q_r=p}\binom{p}{q_1,\cdots,q_r}\frac{1}{(q_1+1)\cdots(q_r+1)}\frac{(\log(1+\omega))^p}{p!} \\ &\quad\times\sum_{k=0}^{\infty}\zeta^k\frac{[\log_\lambda(1+\omega)]^k}{k!}\end{aligned}$$

$$= \sum_{p=0}^{\infty} \lambda^p \sum_{q_1+\cdots+q_r=p} \binom{p}{q_1,\cdots,q_r} \frac{1}{(q_1+1)\cdots(q_r+1)} \sum_{i=p}^{\infty} S_1(i,p)\frac{\omega^i}{i!}$$
$$\times \sum_{j=0}^{\infty}\sum_{k=0}^{j} \zeta^k S_{1,\lambda}(j,k)\frac{\omega^j}{j!}$$
$$= \sum_{i=0}^{\infty}\sum_{p=0}^{i} \lambda^p \sum_{q_1+\cdots+q_r=p} \binom{p}{q_1,\cdots,q_r} \frac{1}{(q_1+1)\cdots(q_r+1)} \sum_{p=0}^{i} S_1(i,p)\frac{\zeta^i}{i!}$$
$$\times \sum_{j=0}^{\infty}\sum_{k=0}^{j} \zeta^k S_{1,\lambda}(j,k)\frac{\omega^j}{j!}$$
$$= \sum_{j=0}^{\infty}\sum_{i=0}^{j} \binom{j}{i} \sum_{p=0}^{i} \lambda^p \sum_{q_1+\cdots+q_r=p} \binom{p}{q_1,\cdots,q_r} \frac{1}{(q_1+1)\cdots(q_r+1)} S_1(i,p)$$
$$\times \sum_{k=0}^{j-i} \zeta^k S_{1,\lambda}(j-i,k)\frac{\omega^j}{j!}. \tag{31}$$

Therefore, by (30) and (31), we get the result. □

Theorem 11. *The following relationship holds true*

$$\sum_{p=0}^{j}\sum_{k=0}^{j-p} \binom{j}{p} S_{1,\lambda}(q,k)\zeta^k \int_0^1 (\lambda(\zeta_1+\cdots+\zeta_r))_p d\zeta_1\cdots d\zeta_r$$
$$= \sum_{k=0}^{j} \binom{j}{k} B_k^{(k-r+1)} \tilde{d}_{j-k,\lambda}^{(r)}(\zeta).$$

Proof. From (25), we see that

$$\int_0^1 \cdots \int_0^1 (1+\omega)^{\lambda(\zeta_1+\cdots+\zeta_r)} d\zeta_1\cdots d\zeta_r e^{\zeta\log_\lambda(1+\omega)}$$

$$= \left(\frac{\omega}{\log(1+\omega)}\right)^r \left(\frac{\log_\lambda(1+\omega)}{\omega}\right)^r e^{\zeta\log_\lambda(1+\omega)} = \sum_{k=0}^{\infty} B_k^{(k-r+1)}\frac{\omega^k}{k!} \sum_{j=0}^{\infty} \tilde{d}_{j,\lambda}^{(r)}(\zeta)\frac{\omega^j}{j!}$$
$$= \sum_{j=0}^{\infty}\left(\sum_{k=0}^{j}\binom{j}{k} B_k^{(k-r+1)} \tilde{d}_{j-k,\lambda}^{(r)}(\zeta)\right)\frac{\omega^j}{j!}. \tag{32}$$

On the other hand, we have

$$\int_0^1 \cdots \int_0^1 (1+\omega)^{\lambda(\zeta_1+\cdots+\zeta_r)} d\zeta_1\cdots d\zeta_r e^{\zeta\log_\lambda(1+\omega)}$$
$$= \sum_{p=0}^{\infty} \int_0^1 \cdots \int_0^1 (\lambda(\zeta_1+\cdots+\zeta_r))_p d\zeta_1\cdots d\zeta_r \frac{\omega^p}{p!} \sum_{q=0}^{\infty}\sum_{k=0}^{q} S_{1,\lambda}(q,k)\zeta^k\frac{\omega^q}{q!}$$
$$= \sum_{j=0}^{\infty}\sum_{p=0}^{j}\sum_{k=0}^{j-p} \binom{j}{p} S_{1,\lambda}(q,k)\zeta^k \int_0^1 (\lambda(\zeta_1+\cdots+\zeta_r))_p d\zeta_1\cdots d\zeta_r\frac{\omega^j}{j!}. \tag{33}$$

Thus, by (32) and (33), we complete the proof. □

Theorem 12. *For $j \geq 0$, we have*

$$\tilde{d}_{j,\lambda}^{(r)}(\zeta)=\sum_{k=0}^{j}\binom{j}{k}\sum_{p=0}^{j-k}\sum_{q_1+\cdots+q_r=k}\binom{k}{q_1,\cdots,q_r}\tilde{d}_{q_1,\lambda}^{(r)}\cdots\tilde{d}_{q_r,\lambda}^{(r)}\zeta^p S_{1,\lambda}(j-k,p).$$

Proof. From (25), we note that

$$\sum_{j=0}^{\infty}\tilde{d}_{j,\lambda}^{(r)}(\zeta)\frac{\omega^j}{j!}=\left(\frac{\log_\lambda(1+\omega)}{\omega}\right)^r e^{\zeta\log_\lambda(1+\omega)}$$

$$=\underbrace{\left(\frac{\log_\lambda(1+\omega)}{\omega}\right)\times\cdots\times\left(\frac{\log_\lambda(1+\omega)}{\omega}\right)}_{\text{r-times}}e^{\zeta\log_\lambda(1+\omega)}$$

$$=\left(\sum_{k=0}^{\infty}\sum_{q_1+\cdots+q_r=k}\binom{k}{q_1,\cdots,q_r}\tilde{d}_{q_1,\lambda}^{(r)}\cdots\tilde{d}_{q_r,\lambda}^{(r)}\frac{\omega^k}{k!}\right)$$

$$\times\left(\sum_{j=0}^{\infty}\sum_{p=0}^{j}\zeta^p S_{1,\lambda}(j,p)\frac{\omega^j}{j!}\right)$$

$$=\sum_{j=0}^{\infty}\left(\sum_{k=0}^{j}\binom{j}{k}\sum_{p=0}^{j-k}\sum_{q_1+\cdots+q_r=k}\binom{k}{q_1,\cdots,q_r}\tilde{d}_{q_1,\lambda}^{(r)}\cdots\tilde{d}_{q_r,\lambda}^{(r)}\zeta^p S_{1,\lambda}(j-k,p)\right)\frac{\omega^j}{j!}. \quad (34)$$

In view of (34), we complete the proof. □

Theorem 13. *For $n \geq 0$, we have*

$$\tilde{d}_{j,\lambda}^{(r)}(\zeta)=\sum_{i=0}^{j}\binom{j}{i}\sum_{p=0}^{i}\lambda^p\sum_{q_1+\cdots+q_r=p}\frac{\binom{i}{q_1,\cdots,q_r}}{(q_1+1)\cdots(q_r+1)}S_1(i+r,p+r)\frac{\binom{p+r}{r}}{\binom{i+r}{r}}$$

$$\times\sum_{k=0}^{j-i}\zeta^k S_{1,\lambda}(j-i,k).$$

Proof. By (25), we note that

$$\sum_{j=0}^{\infty}\tilde{d}_{j,\lambda}^{(r)}(\zeta)\frac{\omega^j}{j!}=\left(\frac{\log(1+\omega)}{\omega}\right)^r\int_0^1\cdots\int_0^1(1+\omega)^{\lambda(\zeta_1+\cdots+\zeta_r)}d\zeta_1\cdots d\zeta_r e^{\zeta\log_\lambda(1+\omega)}$$

$$=\left(\frac{\log(1+\omega)}{\omega}\right)^r\sum_{p=0}^{\infty}\lambda^p\frac{(\log(1+\omega))}{p!}\int_0^1\cdots\int_0^1(\zeta_1+\cdots+\zeta_r)^p d\zeta_1\cdots d\zeta_r\sum_{k=0}^{\infty}\zeta^k\frac{[\log_\lambda(1+\omega)]^k}{k!}$$

$$=\frac{1}{\omega^r}\sum_{p=0}^{\infty}\lambda^p\sum_{q_1+\cdots+q_r=p}\binom{p}{q_1,\cdots,q_r}\frac{1}{(q_1+1)\cdots(q_r+1)}\frac{(\log(1+\omega))^{p+r}}{m!}$$

$$\times\sum_{k=0}^{\infty}\zeta^k\frac{[\log_\lambda(1+\omega)]^k}{k!}$$

$$=\frac{1}{\omega^r}\sum_{p=0}^{\infty}\lambda^p\sum_{q_1+\cdots+q_r=p}\binom{p}{q_1,\cdots,q_r}\frac{1}{(q_1+1)\cdots(q_r+1)}\frac{(p+r)!}{p!}\sum_{i=p+r}^{\infty}S_1(i,p+r)\frac{\omega^i}{i!}$$

$$\times\sum_{j=0}^{\infty}\sum_{k=0}^{j}\zeta^k S_{1,\lambda}(j,k)\frac{\omega^j}{j!}$$

$$=\sum_{p=0}^{\infty}\sum_{q_1+\cdots+q_r=p}\binom{p}{q_1,\cdots,q_r}\frac{1}{(q_1+1)\cdots(q_r+1)}\frac{(p+r)!}{m!}\sum_{i=p}^{\infty}S_1(i+r,p+r)\frac{\omega^i}{(i+r)!}$$
$$\times\sum_{j=0}^{\infty}\sum_{k=0}^{j}\zeta^k S_{1,\lambda}(j,k)\frac{\omega^j}{j!}$$
$$=\sum_{i=0}^{\infty}\sum_{p=0}^{i}\lambda^p\sum_{q_1+\cdots+q_r=p}\frac{\binom{i}{q_1,\cdots,q_r}}{(q_1+1)\cdots(q_r+1)}S_1(i+r,p+r)\frac{\binom{p+r}{r}}{\binom{i+r}{r}}\frac{\omega^i}{i!}$$
$$\times\sum_{j=0}^{\infty}\sum_{k=0}^{j}\zeta^k S_{1,\lambda}(j,k)\frac{\omega^j}{j!}$$
$$=\sum_{j=0}^{\infty}\sum_{i=0}^{j}\binom{j}{i}\sum_{p=0}^{i}\lambda^p\sum_{q_1+\cdots+q_r=p}\frac{\binom{i}{q_1,\cdots,q_r}}{(q_1+1)\cdots(q_r+1)}S_1(i+r,p+r)\frac{\binom{p+r}{r}}{\binom{i+r}{r}}$$
$$\times\sum_{k=0}^{j-i}\zeta^k S_{1,\lambda}(j-i,k)\frac{\omega^j}{j!}. \tag{35}$$

Thus we get what we want. □

Theorem 14. *For $j \geq 0$, we have*

$$\tilde{d}_{j,\lambda}^{(-r)}(\zeta)=\sum_{i=0}^{j}\sum_{k=0}^{i}\binom{j}{i}d_{j-i,\lambda}^{(r)}\zeta^k S_{1,\lambda}(i,k).$$

Proof. From 25, we note that

$$\sum_{j=0}^{\infty}\tilde{d}_{j,\lambda}^{(-r)}(\zeta)\frac{\omega^j}{j!}=\left(\frac{\log_\lambda(1+\omega)}{\omega}\right)^r e^{\zeta\log_\lambda(1+\omega)}$$
$$=\left(\sum_{j=0}^{\infty}d_{j,\lambda}^{(r)}\frac{\omega^j}{j!}\right)\left(\sum_{i=0}^{\infty}\sum_{k=0}^{i}\zeta^k S_{1,\lambda}(i,k)\frac{\omega^i}{i!}\right)$$
$$=\sum_{j=0}^{\infty}\left(\sum_{i=0}^{j}\sum_{k=0}^{i}\binom{j}{i}d_{j-i,\lambda}^{(r)}\zeta^k S_{1,\lambda}(i,k)\right)\frac{\omega^j}{j!}. \tag{36}$$

Therefore, by (25) and (36), we complete the proof. □

Theorem 15. *For $r,k \in \mathbb{N}$, with $r > k$, we have*

$$\tilde{d}_{j,\lambda}^{(r)}(\zeta)=\sum_{i=0}^{j}\binom{j}{i}\tilde{d}_{i,\lambda}^{(r-k)}\tilde{d}_{j-i,\lambda}^{(k)}(\zeta),(j\geq 0).$$

Proof. Since

$$\sum_{j=0}^{\infty}\tilde{d}_{j,\lambda}^{(r)}(\zeta)\frac{\omega^j}{j!}=\left(\frac{\log_\lambda(1+\omega)}{\omega}\right)^r e^{\zeta\log_\lambda(1+\omega)},$$

we have

$$=\left(\frac{\log_\lambda(1+\omega)}{\omega}\right)^{r-k}\left(\frac{\log_\lambda(1+\omega)}{\omega}\right)^k e^{\zeta\log_\lambda(1+\omega)}$$
$$=\left(\sum_{i=0}^{\infty}\tilde{d}_{i,\lambda}^{(r-k)}\frac{\omega^i}{i!}\right)\left(\sum_{p=0}^{\infty}\tilde{d}_{m,\lambda}^{(k)}(x)\frac{\omega^p}{p!}\right)$$

$$= \sum_{j=0}^{\infty}\left(\sum_{i=0}^{j}\binom{j}{i}\tilde{d}_{i,\lambda}^{(r-k)}\tilde{d}_{j-i,\lambda}^{(k)}(\zeta)\right)\frac{\omega^j}{j!}. \tag{37}$$

Therefore, by (25) and (37), we obtain the result. □

Theorem 16. *For $j \geq 0$, we have*

$$\tilde{d}_{j,\lambda}^{(r)}(\zeta+\eta) = \sum_{k=0}^{j}\sum_{p=0}^{k}\binom{j}{k}\tilde{d}_{j-k,\lambda}^{(r)}(\zeta)S_{1,\lambda}(k,p)\eta^p.$$

Proof. Now, we observe that

$$\sum_{j=0}^{\infty}\tilde{d}_{j,\lambda}^{(r)}(\zeta+\eta)\frac{\omega^j}{j!} = \left(\frac{\log_\lambda(1+\omega)}{\omega}\right)^r e^{(\zeta+\eta)\log_\lambda(1+\omega)}$$

$$= \left(\sum_{j=0}^{\infty}\tilde{d}_{j,\lambda}^{(r)}(\zeta)\frac{\omega^j}{j!}\right)\left(\sum_{k=0}^{\infty}\left(\sum_{p=0}^{k}S_{1,\lambda}(k,p)\eta^p\right)\frac{t^k}{k!}\right)$$

$$= \sum_{j=0}^{\infty}\left(\sum_{k=0}^{j}\sum_{p=0}^{k}\binom{j}{k}\tilde{d}_{j-k,\lambda}^{(r)}(\zeta)S_{1,\lambda}(k,p)\eta^p\right)\frac{\omega^j}{j!}.$$

Equating the coefficients of $\frac{\omega^j}{j!}$ on both sides of the above, we get the result. □

4. Conclusions and Observation

Motivated by [2], we have defined fully degenerating Daehee polynomials, which turn out to be classical ones in the special cases, as follows:

$$\sum_{j=0}^{\infty}\tilde{d}_{j,\lambda}(\zeta)\frac{\omega^j}{j!} = \frac{\log(1+\omega)}{\omega}\int_0^1(1+\omega)^{\lambda\eta}d\eta\; e^{\zeta\log_\lambda(1+\omega)}.$$

By making use of this generating function, we derived some new explicit expressions and identities. Later, we have considered multiple point of view this generating function as follows:

$$\sum_{j=0}^{\infty}\tilde{d}_{j,\lambda}^{(r)}(\zeta)\frac{\omega^j}{j!} = \left(\frac{\log(1+\omega)}{\omega}\right)^r\int_0^1\cdots\int_0^1(1+\omega)^{\lambda(\zeta_1+\cdots+\zeta_r)}d\zeta_1\cdots d\zeta_r\; e^{\zeta\log_\lambda(1+\omega)}$$

$$= \left(\frac{\log_\lambda(1+\omega)}{\omega}\right)^r e^{\zeta\log_\lambda(1+\omega)},$$

by virtue of which we obtained some new identities, equalities and properties. Seemingly, the new generalizations, methods and applications for special polynomials involve some known special polynomials, such as Bernoulli polynomials, Euler polynomials, Genocchi polynomials, Frobenius–Euler polynomials, Daehee polynomials, and Changee polynomials, and these will be continued because they have interesting relations in mathematical physics and statistics.

Author Contributions: Conceptualization, S.A. (Sahar Albosaily), W.A.K., S.A. (Serkan Araci) and A.I.; Formal analysis, S.A. (Sahar Albosaily), W.A.K., S.A. (Serkan Araci) and A.I.; Investigation, S.A. (Sahar Albosaily), W.A.K., S.A. (Serkan Araci) and A.I.; Methodology, W.A.K.; Validation, S.A. (Sahar Albosaily) and W.A.K.; Writing—original draft, W.A.K.; Writing—review & editing, S.A. (Sahar Albosaily), S.A. (Serkan Araci) and A.I. All authors have read and agreed to the published version of the manuscript.

Funding: This research received no external funding.

Institutional Review Board Statement: Not applicable.

Informed Consent Statement: Not applicable.

Data Availability Statement: Not applicable.

Conflicts of Interest: The authors declare no conflict of interest.

References

1. Sharma, S.K.; Khan, W.A.; Araci, S.; Ahmed, S.S. New construction of type 2 degenerate central Fubini polynomials with their certain properties. *Adv. Differ Equ.* **2020**, *587*, 1–11. [CrossRef]
2. Jang, L.C.; Kim, D.S.; Kim, T.; Lee, H. p-Adic integral on $\mathbb{Z}_p$ associated with degenerate Bernoulli polynomials of the second kind. *Adv. Diff. Equ.* **2020**, *278*, 1–20.
3. Kim, T. On degenerate Cauchy numbers and polynomials. *Proc. Jangjeon Math. Soc.* **2015**, *18*, 307–312.
4. Kim, T. A note on degenerate Stirling numbers of the second kind. *Proc. Jangjeon Math. Soc.* **2017**, *20*, 319–331.
5. Kim, T.; Kim, D.S.; Kim, H.-Y.; Kwon, J. Some results on degenerate Daehee and Bernoulli numbers and polynomials. *Adv. Diff. Equ.* **2020**, *311*, 1–13. [CrossRef]
6. Khan, W.A.; Ahmad, M. Partially degenerate poly-Bernoulli polynomials associated with Hermite polynomials. *Adv. Stud. Contemp. Math.* **2018**, *28*, 487–496.
7. Khan, W.A.; Nisar, K.S.; Acikgoz, M.; Duran, U. Multifarious implicit summation formulae of Hermite-based poly-Daehee polynomials. *Appl. Math. Inf. Sci.* **2018**, *12*, 305–310. [CrossRef]
8. Khan, W.A. A note on q-analogue of degenerate Catalan numbers associated with p-adic Integral on $\mathbb{Z}_p$. *Symmetry* **2022**, *14*, 1119. [CrossRef]
9. Sharma, S.K.; Khan, W.A.; Araci, S.; Ahmed, S.S. New type of degenerate Daehee polynomials of the second kind. *Adv. Differ. Equ.* **2020**, *428*, 1–14. [CrossRef]
10. Catlitz, L. Degenerate Stirling, Bernoulli and Eulerian numbers. *Util. Math.* **1979**, *15*, 51–88.
11. Catlitz, L. A degenerate Staudt-Clausen theorem. *Arch. Math.* **1967**, *7*, 28–33. [CrossRef]
12. Kim, D.S.; Kim, T. A note on new type of degenerate Bernoulli numbers. *Russ. J. Math. Phys.* **2020**, *27*, 227–235. [CrossRef]
13. Roman, S. The umbral calculus. In *Pure and Applied Mathematics, 111*; Academic Press, Inc.: New York, NY, USA, 1984; p. x+193, ISBN 0-12-594380-6.
14. Alam, N.; Khan, W.A.; Ryoo, C.S. A note on Bell-based Apostol-type Frobenius-Euler polynomials of complex variable with its certain applications. *Mathematics* **2022**, *10*, 2109. [CrossRef]

mathematics

MDPI

Article

Bounds for Incomplete Confluent Fox–Wright Generalized Hypergeometric Functions

Tibor K. Pogány [1,2]

1 Institute of Applied Mathematics, John von Neumann Faculty of Informatics, Óbuda University, Bécsi út 96/b, 1034 Budapest, Hungary; pogany.tibor@nik.uni-obuda.hu
2 Faculty of Maritime Studies, University of Rijeka, Studentska 2, 51000 Rijeka, Croatia; tibor.poganj@uniri.hr

Abstract: We establish several new functional bounds and uniform bounds (with respect to the variable) for the lower incomplete generalized Fox–Wright functions by means of the representation formulae for the McKay I_ν Bessel probability distribution's cumulative distribution function. New cumulative distribution functions are generated and expressed in terms of lower incomplete Fox–Wright functions and/or generalized hypergeometric functions, whilst in the closing part of the article, related bounding inequalities are obtained for them.

Keywords: modified Bessel functions of the first kind; McKay's I_ν Bessel distribution; lower incomplete Fox–Wright functions; cumulative distribution function; functional bounding inequality

MSC: 26D15; 33C20; 33C47; 33E20; 60E05

Citation: Pogány, T.K. Bounds for Incomplete Confluent Fox–Wright Generalized Hypergeometric Functions. *Mathematics* **2022**, *10*, 3106. https://doi.org/10.3390/math10173106

Academic Editor: Sitnik Sergey

Received: 13 August 2022
Accepted: 25 August 2022
Published: 29 August 2022

Publisher's Note: MDPI stays neutral with regard to jurisdictional claims in published maps and institutional affiliations.

Copyright: © 2022 by the author. Licensee MDPI, Basel, Switzerland. This article is an open access article distributed under the terms and conditions of the Creative Commons Attribution (CC BY) license (https://creativecommons.org/licenses/by/4.0/).

1. Introduction and Motivation

The incomplete special functions having integral expressions with nonnegative integrands are obviously bounded above with their complete variants, when the incomplete variants integration domain is contained in the complete variant's integration domain, provided the considered integrals converge, as it happens, for instance, in the case of lower and upper incomplete gamma functions (p. 174, Equations (8).2.1-2, [1])

$$\gamma(p,x) = \int_0^x t^{p-1}\,\mathrm{e}^{-t}\,\mathrm{d}t, \qquad \Gamma(p,x) = \int_x^\infty t^{p-1}\,\mathrm{e}^{-t}\,\mathrm{d}t, \qquad x, \Re(p) > 0, \tag{1}$$

respectively, whose sum gives the Euler function of the second kind called also (complete) gamma function (p. 136, Equation (5).2.1, [1]):

$$\gamma(p,x) + \Gamma(p,x) = \Gamma(p) = \int_0^\infty t^{p-1}\,\mathrm{e}^{-t}\,\mathrm{d}t, \qquad \Re(p) > 0. \tag{2}$$

The straightforward consequence of these relations is

$$\max\big(\gamma(x,p), \Gamma(p,x)\big) \le \Gamma(p).$$

However, the question of the existence of more precise upper and/or lower bounds for the incomplete versions of special functions is frequent in applications.

In this note, we derive upper bounds for a set of special functions coming from the hypergeometric family of functions, the class of lower incomplete confluent Fox–Wright generalized hypergeometric functions, which nowadays have numerous appearances in the mathematical literature, see, e.g., [2–5] and the relevant titles therein.

We start with the definition of the incomplete Fox–Wright function. The Fox–Wright generalized hypergeometric function consisting of p numerator parameter couples (a_1, A_1),

$\cdots, (a_p, A_p)$ and q denominator parameter pairs $(b_1, B_1), \cdots, (b_q, B_q)$, possesses the series form (pp. 286–287, [6])

$$ {}_p\Psi_q\left[\begin{array}{c} (a_1, A_1), \cdots, (a_p, A_p) \\ (b_1, B_1), \cdots, (b_q, B_q) \end{array} \Big| z\right] = {}_p\Psi_q\left[\begin{array}{c} (\mathbf{a}_p, \mathbf{A}_p) \\ (\mathbf{b}_q, \mathbf{B}_q) \end{array} \Big| z\right] = \sum_{n\geq 0} \frac{\prod_{j=1}^{p} \Gamma(a_j + nA_j)}{\prod_{j=1}^{q} \Gamma(b_j + nB_j)} \frac{z^n}{n!}, \tag{3} $$

where A_j, $B_k \geq 0, j = 1, \ldots, p, k = 1, \ldots, q$. The series (3) converges for all $z \in \mathbb{C}$ when

$$ \Delta := 1 + \sum_{j=1}^{q} B_j - \sum_{k=1}^{p} A_k > 0. $$

When $\Delta = 0$, the series in (3) converges for $|z| < \nabla$ and $|z| = \nabla$ under the condition $\Re(\mu) > 1/2$, where

$$ \nabla := \left(\prod_{i=1}^{p} A_i^{-A_i}\right)\left(\prod_{j=1}^{q} B_j^{B_j}\right), \qquad \mu = \sum_{j=1}^{q} b_j - \sum_{i=1}^{p} a_i + \frac{p-q}{2}. $$

Taking $A_1 = \cdots = A_p = B_1 = \cdots = B_q = 1$ in (3), the Fox–Wright function reduces to the generalized hypergeometric function ${}_pF_q$, up to the multiplicative constant in the following way:

$$ {}_pF_q\left[\begin{array}{c} \mathbf{a}_p \\ \mathbf{b}_q \end{array} \Big| z\right] = \frac{\Gamma(b_1)\cdots\Gamma(b_q)}{\Gamma(a_1)\cdots\Gamma(a_p)} \, {}_p\Psi_q\left[\begin{array}{c} (\mathbf{a}_p, \mathbf{1}) \\ (\mathbf{b}_q, \mathbf{1}) \end{array} \Big| z\right]. \tag{4} $$

Now, we denote by ${}_p\Psi_q^{(\gamma)}[\cdot]$ the lower incomplete Fox–Wright function by replacing *one* gamma function out of p in the product in the numerator of (3) with a lower incomplete gamma function $\gamma(\mu + \cdot\, M, x)$, in which the new parameters μ, M, x take place. So, by this change, the defining power series (3) becomes (p. 196, Equation (6), [4]) (also see (p. 982, [5]))

$$ {}_p\Psi_q^{(\gamma)}\left[\begin{array}{c} (\mu, M, x), (\mathbf{a}_{p-1}, \mathbf{A}_{p-1}) \\ (\mathbf{b}_q, \mathbf{B}_q) \end{array} \Big| z\right] = \sum_{n\geq 0} \frac{\gamma(\mu + nM, x) \prod_{j=1}^{p-1} \Gamma(a_j + nA_j)}{\prod_{j=1}^{q} \Gamma(b_j + nB_j)} \frac{z^n}{n!}. \tag{5} $$

The parameters $M, A_j, B_k > 0$ should satisfy the constraint

$$ \Delta^{(\gamma)} = 1 + \sum_{j=1}^{q} B_j - M - \sum_{j=1}^{p-1} A_j \geq 0, $$

while the other convergence conditions remain the same as the ones for the complete Fox–Wright (3), which we have for $x = \infty$ in (5). We point out that the upper incomplete Fox–Wright generalized hypergeometric function ${}_p\Psi_q^{(\Gamma)}$ is presented with associated comments in Section 5 under A.

The probability distributions involving Bessel functions were pioneered by McKay [7] considering two classes of continuous distributions involving modified Bessel functions of the first and second kinds I_ν and K_ν, which we call today Bessel function distributions. However, we observe here McNolty's version [8] of McKay's I_ν Bessel distribution. The random variable (rv) X defined on a probability space $(\Omega, \mathscr{A}, \mathsf{P})$ behaves according to

McNolty's variant of McKay's distribution when the probability distribution function (pdf) is of the form (p. 496, Equation (13), [8])

$$f_I(x;a,b;\nu) = \frac{\sqrt{\pi}(b^2-a^2)^{\nu+1/2}}{(2a)^\nu \Gamma\left(\nu+\frac{1}{2}\right)} \mathrm{e}^{-bx} x^\nu I_\nu(ax), \qquad x \geq 0, \tag{6}$$

defined for all $\nu > -1/2$ and $b > a > 0$. The related cumulative distribution function (cdf) reads

$$F_I(x;a,b;\nu) = \frac{\sqrt{\pi}(b^2-a^2)^{\nu+1/2}}{(2a)^\nu \Gamma\left(\nu+\frac{1}{2}\right)} \int_0^x \mathrm{e}^{-bt} t^\nu I_\nu(at)\,\mathrm{d}t, \qquad x \geq 0, \tag{7}$$

where the power series form of the modified Bessel function of the first kind is (p. 13, [9])

$$I_\nu(x) = \sum_{n\geq 0} \frac{1}{\Gamma(\nu+n+1)\,n!}\left(\frac{x}{2}\right)^{2n+\nu}.$$

We write this correspondence as $X \sim \mathrm{McKayI}(a,b,\nu)$. We consider McNolty's pdf (6) and cdf (7) in our calculations.

New expressions for cdf of rv $X \sim \mathrm{McKayI}(a,b,\nu)$ were given recently in [2]. In turn, these results imply several by-products. For instance, we can deduce several functional and uniform bounds for the incomplete generalized Fox–Wright functions and other hypergeometric-type functions which are the building blocks of cdfs; we discuss these elsewhere. We derive the bounds by simple methods applying certain known and less known properties of cdfs.

2. The First Set of Results

Here, we report on a uniform and a functional bound for the incomplete confluent Fox–Wright function ${}_1\Psi_1^{(\gamma)}$ and for the generalized hypergeometric function ${}_1F_2[\cdot]$, consult (4).

Theorem 1. *For all $b > a > 0$ and $\nu > -1/2$, we have*

$${}_1\Psi_1^{(\gamma)}\left[\begin{matrix}(2\nu+1,2,bx)\\(\nu+1,1)\end{matrix}\,\middle|\,\frac{a^2}{4b^2}\right] \leq \frac{4^\nu\left(\frac{1}{2}\right)_\nu b^{2\nu+1}}{(b^2-a^2)^{\nu+\frac{1}{2}}}.$$

Moreover, for $\nu \geq 0$ and $a \geq 1$, the following holds:

$${}_1\Psi_1^{(\gamma)}\left[\begin{matrix}(2\nu+1,2,bx)\\(\nu+1,1)\end{matrix}\,\middle|\,\frac{a^2}{4b^2}\right] \leq \frac{b^{2\nu}x^{2\nu}(1-\mathrm{e}^{-bx})}{(2\nu+1)\,\Gamma(\nu+1)}\,{}_1F_2\left[\begin{matrix}\nu+\frac{1}{2}\\ \nu+1,\,\nu+\frac{3}{2}\end{matrix}\,\middle|\,\frac{a^2x^2}{4}\right]. \tag{8}$$

Proof. According to the result of Theorem 1 in [2], for the rv $X \sim \mathrm{McKayI}(a,b,\nu)$, the related cdf reads

$$F_I(x;a,b;\nu) = \frac{\sqrt{\pi}(b^2-a^2)^{\nu+1/2}}{2^{2\nu}\,b^{2\nu+1}\Gamma\left(\nu+\frac{1}{2}\right)}\,{}_1\Psi_1^{(\gamma)}\left[\begin{matrix}(2\nu+1,2,bx)\\(\nu+1,1)\end{matrix}\,\middle|\,\frac{a^2}{4b^2}\right], \qquad x \geq 0. \tag{9}$$

From $F_I(x;a,b;\nu) \leq 1$, the assertion of the theorem immediately follows. As to the functional upper bound (8), we apply the estimate (Equation 8.10.2, [1])

$$\gamma(a,t) \leq \frac{t^{a-1}}{a}\left(1-\mathrm{e}^{-t}\right), \qquad a \geq 1,\, t > 0. \tag{10}$$

This bound, taken in (9) for $a = 2\nu + 1 + 2n$ and $t = bx$, increases the sum and implies

$$\begin{aligned} {}_1\Psi_1^{(\gamma)}\left[\begin{array}{c} (2\nu+1,2,bx) \\ (\nu+1,1) \end{array} \middle| \frac{a^2}{4b^2} \right] &\le \sum_{n\ge 0} \frac{(bx)^{2(\nu+n)}\left(1-\mathrm{e}^{-bx}\right)}{4^n(2\nu+1+2n)\Gamma(\nu+1+n)\,n!}\left(\frac{a^2}{b^2}\right)^n \\ &= \frac{(bx)^{2\nu}(1-\mathrm{e}^{-bx})}{2\Gamma(\nu+1)} \sum_{n\ge 0} \frac{\Gamma(\nu+\frac12+n)\,(ax)^{2n}}{4^n\,(\nu+1)_n\,\Gamma(\nu+\frac32+n)\,n!} \\ &= \frac{(bx)^{2\nu}(1-\mathrm{e}^{-bx})}{(2\nu+1)\Gamma(\nu+1)} \sum_{n\ge 0} \frac{(\nu+\frac12)_n\left(\frac{ax}{2}\right)^{2n}}{(\nu+1)_n(\nu+\frac32)_n\,n!}, \end{aligned}$$

which is equivalent to the stated inequality (8). Finally, the constraint $1 \le a = 2\nu+1+2n$ in (10), which holds for all $n \in \mathbb{N}_0$, shows that $\nu \ge 0$ is indeed the parameter range. The proof is complete. □

In the next part of this section, we establish a bilateral functional bound upon the lower incomplete confluent Fox–Wright function. In turn, the upper bound contains the same incomplete confluent Fox–Wright function whose argument is reciprocal.

Theorem 2. *Let $b > a > 0$ and $2\nu + 1 > 0$. Then, for all $x \ge 1$, the two-sided functional inequality holds:*

$$ {}_1\Psi_1^{(\gamma)}\left[\frac{b}{x}\right] \le {}_1\Psi_1^{(\gamma)}[bx] \le {}_1\Psi_1^{(\gamma)}\left[\frac{b}{x}\right] + \frac{2\Gamma(2\nu)\,b^{2\nu+1}}{\Gamma(\nu)\,(b^2-a^2)^{\nu+\frac12}}, \tag{11}$$

where

$$ {}_1\Psi_1^{(\gamma)}[z] := {}_1\Psi_1^{(\gamma)}\left[\begin{array}{c} (2\nu+1,2,z) \\ (\nu+1,1) \end{array} \middle| \frac{a^2}{4b^2} \right].$$

Proof. Let $X \sim F(x)$ be a continuous nonnegative random variable with $F(0) = 0$. Consider the rv $\max\left(X, X^{-1}\right)$. For the related cdf, the following holds:

$$\mathsf{P}\left\{\max\left(X, X^{-1}\right) < x\right\} = \mathsf{P}\left\{x^{-1} < X < x\right\} = F(x) - F(x^{-1}),$$

which implies that (p. 45, 2.1.8, [10])

$$G(x) = \begin{cases} F(x) - F(x^{-1}), & x \ge 1 \\ 0, & x < 1 \end{cases}$$

is also a cdf. Replacing the general rv with $X \sim \mathrm{McKayI}(a, b, \nu)$ and keeping our standard parameter space $b > a > 0$, $2\nu + 1 > 0$, we obtain that

$$0 \le G_I(x) = F_I(x; a, b; \nu) - F_I(x^{-1}; a, b; \nu) \le 1, \qquad x \ge 1. \tag{12}$$

Hence,

$$ {}_1\Psi_1^{(\gamma)}[bx] - {}_1\Psi_1^{(\gamma)}\left[\frac{b}{x}\right] \ge 0,$$

which implies the left-hand-side inequality in (11). Next, from $G_I(x) \le 1$, we conclude

$$\begin{aligned} {}_1\Psi_1^{(\gamma)}[bx] &\le {}_1\Psi_1^{(\gamma)}\left[\frac{b}{x}\right] + \frac{2^{2\nu}b^{2\nu+1}\Gamma(\nu+\frac12)}{\sqrt{\pi}\,(b^2-a^2)^{\nu+\frac12}} \\ &= {}_1\Psi_1^{(\gamma)}\left[\frac{b}{x}\right] + \frac{2^{2\nu}b^{2\nu+1}\Gamma(\nu+\frac12)\Gamma(\nu+1)}{\sqrt{\pi}\,\Gamma(\nu+1)\,(b^2-a^2)^{\nu+\frac12}} \end{aligned}$$

$$= {}_1\Psi_1^{(\gamma)}\left[\frac{b}{x}\right] + \frac{b^{2\nu+1}\Gamma(2\nu+1)}{\Gamma(\nu+1)\,(b^2-a^2)^{\nu+\frac{1}{2}}} \tag{13}$$

$$= {}_1\Psi_1^{(\gamma)}\left[\frac{b}{x}\right] + \frac{2\,b^{2\nu+1}\Gamma(2\nu)}{\Gamma(\nu)(b^2-a^2)^{\nu+\frac{1}{2}}}, \tag{14}$$

where (13) is obtained by the Legendre duplication formula for the gamma function (Equation 5.5.5, [1])

$$\Gamma(2\nu) = \frac{2^{2\nu-1}}{\sqrt{\pi}}\,\Gamma(\nu)\,\Gamma(\nu+\tfrac{1}{2}), \qquad -2\nu \notin \mathbb{N}_0\,.$$

This explains at the same time that the quotient of gamma functions is well defined for the nonpositive values of $\nu \in (-\frac{1}{2}, 0]$ in (14). The rest is obvious. □

3. The Second Set of Results

The rv $X \sim \mathrm{McKayI}(a,b,\nu)$ possesses a counterpart result to the representation Formula (9) for the related cdf, also in terms of the lower incomplete confluent Fox–Wright generalized hypergeometric function ${}_1\Psi_1^{(\gamma)}$, the exponential function and the modified Bessel function of the first kind I_ν.

We establish bounding inequalities and monotonicity results applying the simple properties of the cdfs used in the previous section. Therefore, according to Theorem 1 of [2], we have

$$F_I(x;a,b;\nu) = \frac{\sqrt{\pi}(b^2-a^2)^{\nu+1/2}}{2^{2\nu-1}\,b^{2\nu+1}\Gamma\left(\nu+\frac{1}{2}\right)}\left\{{}_1\Psi_1^{(\gamma)}\left[\begin{array}{c}(2\nu,2,bx)\\(\nu,1)\end{array}\,\middle|\,\frac{a^2}{4b^2}\right] - \frac{2^{\nu-1}b^{2\nu}\,x^\nu}{a^\nu}\,\mathrm{e}^{-bx}I_\nu(ax)\right\}. \tag{15}$$

for all $x \geq 0$.

Theorem 3. *For all $b > a > 0$, $\nu > -1/2$ and for all $x \geq 0$, it holds true that*

$$\frac{1}{2}\left(\frac{2b^2x}{a}\right)^\nu \mathrm{e}^{-bx}I_\nu(ax) \leq {}_1\Psi_1^{(\gamma)}\left[\begin{array}{c}(2\nu,2,bx)\\(\nu,1)\end{array}\,\middle|\,\frac{a^2}{4b^2}\right]$$
$$\leq \frac{1}{2}\left(\frac{2b^2x}{a}\right)^\nu \mathrm{e}^{-bx}I_\nu(ax) + \frac{2^{2\nu-1}b^{2\nu+1}\,(\frac{1}{2})_\nu}{(b^2-a^2)^{\nu+\frac{1}{2}}}.$$

Moreover, when $x \geq 1$, we have the bilateral functional inequality

$$H(x) \leq {}_1\Psi_1^{(\gamma)}[bx] - {}_1\Psi_1^{(\gamma)}\left[\frac{b}{x}\right] \leq H(x) + \frac{\Gamma(2\nu)\,b^{2\nu+1}}{\Gamma(\nu)\,(b^2-a^2)^{\nu+\frac{1}{2}}}, \tag{16}$$

where

$$H(x) := \frac{1}{2}\left(\frac{2b^2}{a}\right)^\nu\left\{x^\nu\mathrm{e}^{-bx}\,I_\nu(ax) - x^{-\nu}\mathrm{e}^{-\frac{b}{x}}I_\nu\left(\frac{a}{x}\right)\right\},$$

and ${}_1\Psi_1^{(\gamma)}[z]$ denotes the same function as in Theorem 2.

Proof. Applying $0 \leq F_I(x;a,b;\nu) \leq 1$ to the representation Formula (15), the first statement of theorem immediately follows.

As to the bilateral inequality (16), we take into account the same property, now for the cdf $G_I(x)$, defined in (12). After some routine calculations, following the steps of the proof of Theorem 2, we arrive at the assertion (16). □

4. The Third Set of Results

Let us treat $F_I(x; a, b; \nu)$ by virtue of the property which holds for any continuous baseline cdf $F(x)$ and states that (p. 45, Equation (2).1.7, [10])

$$F_1(x) = \frac{1}{h}\int_x^{x+h} F(t)\,\mathrm{d}t\,, \qquad h > 0\,,$$

is also a cdf. Consequently, we can consider the newly generated cdf

$$F_{I,1}^{(1)}(x; h) = \frac{1}{h}\int_x^{x+h} F_I(t; a, b; \nu)\,\mathrm{d}t\,, \qquad h > 0\,. \tag{17}$$

The main result in this part of the article is the special function representation formula for the generated cdf $F_{I,1}(x; h)$.

Theorem 4. *Let the* rv $X \sim \mathrm{McKayI}(a, b, \nu)$, *and the* cdf $F_{I,1}^{(1)}(x; h)$ *defined by* (17) *be. Then, for all* $b > a > 0, \nu > -\frac{1}{2}$ *and* $x, h \geq 0$ *we have*

$$\begin{aligned} F_{I,1}^{(1)}(x; h) = \frac{C_\nu}{h}\Bigg\{ &(x+h)\, {}_2\Psi_2^{(\gamma)}\left[\begin{matrix} (2\nu+2, 2, b(x+h)),\ (\nu+\frac{1}{2}, 1) \\ (\nu+1, 1),\ (\nu+\frac{3}{2}, 1) \end{matrix} \,\Bigg|\, \frac{a^2}{4b^2} \right] \\ &- \frac{2}{b}\, {}_1\Psi_1^{(\gamma)}\left[\begin{matrix} (2\nu+2, 2, b(x+h)) \\ (\nu+1, 1) \end{matrix} \,\Bigg|\, \frac{a^2}{4b^2} \right] \\ &+ \frac{2[b(x+h)]^{2\nu+2}\mathrm{e}^{-b(x+h)}}{b\,(2\nu+1)\Gamma(\nu+1)}\, {}_1F_2\left[\begin{matrix} \nu+\frac{1}{2} \\ \nu+1,\ \nu+\frac{3}{2} \end{matrix} \,\Bigg|\, \frac{a^2}{4}(x+h)^2 \right] \\ &- x\, {}_2\Psi_2^{(\gamma)}\left[\begin{matrix} (2\nu+2, 2, bx),\ (\nu+\frac{1}{2}, 1) \\ (\nu+1, 1),\ (\nu+\frac{3}{2}, 1) \end{matrix} \,\Bigg|\, \frac{a^2}{4b^2} \right] \\ &+ \frac{2}{b}\, {}_1\Psi_1^{(\gamma)}\left[\begin{matrix} (2\nu+2, 2, bx) \\ (\nu+1, 1) \end{matrix} \,\Bigg|\, \frac{a^2}{4b^2} \right] \\ &- \frac{2(bx)^{2\nu+2}\mathrm{e}^{-bx}}{b\,(2\nu+1)\Gamma(\nu+1)}\, {}_1F_2\left[\begin{matrix} \nu+\frac{1}{2} \\ \nu+1,\ \nu+\frac{3}{2} \end{matrix} \,\Bigg|\, \frac{a^2}{4}x^2 \right] \Bigg\}, \end{aligned}$$

where

$$C_\nu = \frac{\sqrt{\pi}\,(b^2 - a^2)^{\nu+\frac{1}{2}}}{4^\nu b^{2\nu+1}\,\Gamma(\nu+\frac{1}{2})}\,.$$

Proof. Because the baseline cdf $F_I(x; a, b; \nu)$ contains the incomplete confluent Fox–Wright term ${}_1\Psi_1^{(\gamma)}$, which is built by $\gamma(\cdot, bx)$, we should know the integral of this function, see (5). As (Equation 8.5.1, [1])

$$\gamma(\alpha, z) = \frac{z^\alpha}{\alpha}\, {}_1F_1\left[\begin{matrix} \alpha \\ \alpha+1 \end{matrix} \,\Big|\, -z \right], \qquad -\alpha \notin \mathbb{N}_0\,,$$

we conclude

$$\int_0^x \gamma(\alpha, z)\,\mathrm{d}z = \frac{1}{\alpha}\sum_{k\geq 0}\frac{(-1)^k\,(\alpha)_k}{(\alpha+1)_k\,k!}\frac{x^{\alpha+k+1}}{\alpha+k+1} = \frac{x^{\alpha+1}}{\alpha(\alpha+1)}\sum_{k\geq 0}\frac{(\alpha)_k\,(-x)^k}{(\alpha+2)_k\,k!} = \frac{x^{\alpha+1}}{\alpha(\alpha+1)}\, {}_1F_1\left[\begin{matrix} \alpha \\ \alpha+2 \end{matrix} \,\Big|\, -x \right],$$

that is

$$\int_0^x \gamma(\alpha, z)\,\mathrm{d}z = \frac{x-\alpha}{\alpha}\,\gamma(\alpha+1, x) + \frac{1}{\alpha}\,x^{\alpha+1}\,\mathrm{e}^{-x}\,. \tag{18}$$

The final formula follows by (p. 583, Equation (7).11.3.2, [11]).

By virtue of relations (9), (17) and (18), we infer:

$$F_{I,1}^{(1)}(x;h) = \frac{(b^2-a^2)^{\nu+\frac{1}{2}}}{b^{2\nu+2}\,\Gamma(2\nu+1)\,h} \sum_{n\geq 0} \frac{a^{2n} \int\limits_{bx}^{b(x+h)} \gamma(2\nu+1+2n,t)\,\mathrm{d}t}{(2b)^{2n}\,(\nu+1)_n\,n!}$$

$$= \frac{(b^2-a^2)^{\nu+\frac{1}{2}}}{b^{2\nu+2}\,\Gamma(2\nu+1)\,h} \sum_{n\geq 0} \frac{(a^2/b^2)^n}{4^n\,(\nu+1)_n\,n!} \left\{ \left(\frac{b(x+h)}{2\nu+1+2n} - 1\right) \right.$$

$$\cdot\, \gamma(2\nu+2+2n, b(x+h)) + \frac{(b(x+h))^{2\nu+2+2n}}{2\nu+1+2n}\,\mathrm{e}^{-b(x+h)}$$

$$\left. - \left(\frac{bx}{2\nu+1+2n} - 1\right)\gamma(2\nu+2+2n, bx) - \frac{(bx)^{2\nu+2+2n}}{2\nu+1+2n}\,\mathrm{e}^{-bx} \right\}$$

$$=: I_1(x+h) - I_2(x+h) + I_3(x+h) - I_1(x) + I_2(x) - I_3(x)\,.$$

This linear combination of six series we separate and sum up. Thus, not changing the order of the outcoming series the first (fourth) series can be expressed in terms of the lower incomplete Fox–Wright function ${}_2\Psi_2^{(\gamma)}$. Indeed, comparing with (5), this results in

$$I_1(t) = \frac{\left(1-\frac{a^2}{b^2}\right)^{\nu+\frac{1}{2}} t}{\Gamma(2\nu+1)\,h} \sum_{n\geq 0} \frac{1}{(\nu+1)_n\,n!}\,\frac{\gamma(2\nu+2+2n, b\,t)}{2\nu+1+2n} \left(\frac{a^2}{4b^2}\right)^n$$

$$= \frac{\left(1-\frac{a^2}{b^2}\right)^{\nu+\frac{1}{2}} \Gamma(\nu+1)\,t}{2\,\Gamma(2\nu+1)\,h} \sum_{n\geq 0} \frac{\gamma(2\nu+2+2n, b\,t)\,\Gamma(\nu+\frac{1}{2}+n)}{\Gamma(\nu+1+n)\,\Gamma(\nu+\frac{3}{2}+n)\,n!} \left(\frac{a^2}{4b^2}\right)^n$$

$$= \frac{\left(1-\frac{a^2}{b^2}\right)^{\nu+\frac{1}{2}} \Gamma(\nu+1)\,t}{2\,\Gamma(2\nu+1)\,h}\; {}_2\Psi_2^{(\gamma)}\left[\begin{matrix} (2\nu+2, 2, b\,t),\ (\nu+\frac{1}{2}, 1) \\ (\nu+1, 1),\ (\nu+\frac{3}{2}, 1) \end{matrix} \,\middle|\, \frac{a^2}{4b^2} \right],$$

where $t \in \{x+h, x\}$. Now, with the lower incomplete confluent Fox–Wright function ${}_1\Psi_1^{(\gamma)}$ we get

$$I_2(t) = \frac{(b^2-a^2)^{\nu+\frac{1}{2}}}{b^{2\nu+2}\Gamma(2\nu+1)\,h} \sum_{n\geq 0} \frac{\gamma(2\nu+2+2n, b\,t)}{(\nu+1)_n\,n!} \left(\frac{a^2}{4b^2}\right)^n$$

$$= \frac{\left(1-\frac{a^2}{b^2}\right)^{\nu+\frac{1}{2}} \Gamma(\nu+1)}{\Gamma(2\nu+1)\,bh} \sum_{n\geq 0} \frac{\gamma(2\nu+2+2n, b\,t)}{\Gamma(\nu+1+n)\,n!} \left(\frac{a^2}{4b^2}\right)^n$$

$$= \frac{\left(1-\frac{a^2}{b^2}\right)^{\nu+\frac{1}{2}} \Gamma(\nu+1)}{\Gamma(2\nu+1)\,bh}\; {}_1\Psi_1^{(\gamma)}\left[\begin{matrix} (2\nu+2, 2, b\,t) \\ (\nu+1, 1) \end{matrix} \,\middle|\, \frac{a^2}{4b^2} \right],$$

where $t \in \{x+h, x\}$ covers two integrals as well.

Finally, the third (sixth) series becomes

$$I_3(t) = \frac{(b^2-a^2)^{\nu+\frac{1}{2}}\, t^{2\nu+2} \mathrm{e}^{-bt}}{\Gamma(2\nu+2)\,h}\; {}_1F_2\left[\begin{matrix} \nu+\frac{1}{2} \\ \nu+1,\ \nu+\frac{3}{2} \end{matrix} \,\middle|\, \frac{a^2}{4} t^2 \right], \qquad t \in \{x+h, x\}\,.$$

Collecting these integrals, the expression for $F_{I,1}(x;h)$ is confirmed. □

Remark 1. The constant C_ν, whose form we owe to McNolty's pdf (6) and which appears for the first time in the proof of **Theorem 1** (9), is introduced in **Theorem 4**. This constant remains unchanged throughout, in all further results to the end of the exposition.

The same questions occur for the cdf which is reported as (p. 45, 2.1.7, [10])

$$F_2(x) = \frac{1}{2h}\int_{x-h}^{x+h} F(t)\,dt, \qquad h > 0,$$

when we take the baseline cdf $F_I(x; a, b; \nu)$. This gives

$$F_{I,1}^{(2)}(x; h) = \frac{1}{2h}\int_{x-h}^{x+h} F_I(t; a, b; \nu)\,dt. \tag{19}$$

As a consequence of Theorem 4, we deduce the following specified result.

Corollary 1. *Let the rv* $X \sim \text{McKayI}(a, b, \nu)$, *and the cdf* $F_{I,1}^{(2)}(x; h)$ *defined by* (19) *be. Then, for all* $b > a > 0, \nu > -\frac{1}{2}$ *and* $x \geq 0; h > 0$ *the following holds true:*

$$F_{I,1}^{(2)}(x;h) = \frac{C_\nu}{h}\left\{\frac{x+h}{2}\,{}_2\Psi_2^{(\gamma)}\left[\begin{array}{c}(2\nu+2,2,b(x+h)),(\nu+\tfrac{1}{2},1)\\(\nu+1,1),(\nu+\tfrac{3}{2},1)\end{array}\bigg|\frac{a^2}{4b^2}\right]\right.$$
$$-\frac{1}{b}\,{}_1\Psi_1^{(\gamma)}\left[\begin{array}{c}(2\nu+2,2,b(x+h))\\(\nu+1,1)\end{array}\bigg|\frac{a^2}{4b^2}\right]$$
$$+\frac{[b(x+h)]^{2\nu+2}e^{-b(x+h)}}{b\,(2\nu+1)\Gamma(\nu+1)}\,{}_1F_2\left[\begin{array}{c}\nu+\tfrac{1}{2}\\\nu+1,\nu+\tfrac{3}{2}\end{array}\bigg|\frac{a^2}{4}(x+h)^2\right]$$
$$-\frac{x-h}{2}\,{}_2\Psi_2^{(\gamma)}\left[\begin{array}{c}(2\nu+2,2,b(x-h)),(\nu+\tfrac{1}{2},1)\\(\nu+1,1),(\nu+\tfrac{3}{2},1)\end{array}\bigg|\frac{a^2}{4b^2}\right]$$
$$+\frac{1}{b}\,{}_1\Psi_1^{(\gamma)}\left[\begin{array}{c}(2\nu+2,2,b(x-h))\\(\nu+1,1)\end{array}\bigg|\frac{a^2}{4b^2}\right]$$
$$\left.-\frac{(b(x-h))^{2\nu+2}e^{-b(x-h)}}{b\,(2\nu+1)\Gamma(\nu+1)}\,{}_1F_2\left[\begin{array}{c}\nu+\tfrac{1}{2}\\\nu+1,\nu+\tfrac{3}{2}\end{array}\bigg|\frac{a^2}{4}(x-h)^2\right]\right\}.$$

Remark 2. *The first kind of two-sided inequalities which we can obtain are the straightforward consequences of* $0 \leq F_{I,1}^{(j)}(x;h) \leq 1$; $j = 1, 2$ *for the same parameter space* $b > a > 0; 2\nu + 1 > 0$, $h > 0$ *as in* **Theorem 4** *and* **Corollary 4.1**, *respectively.*

On the other hand, generating with the baseline cdfs $F_{I,1}^{(j)}(x;h)$—mimicking (12)—another associated cdfs $G_{I,1}^{(j)}(x;h); j = 1, 2$, a new set of bilateral inequalities follow for $\text{supp}(G_{I,1}^{(j)}) = [1, \infty); j = 1, 2$ for positive $h > 0$. These results can also be understood as a kind of monotonicity with respect to the argument x since the cdfs are monotone nondecreasing per definitionem.

Finally, we introduce a generalization of (17). Let $r \in \mathbb{N}$. We are looking for the cdf $F_{I,r}^{(1)}(x;h)$, which we build by r-tuple successive application of the integral operator $F_{I,r}^{(1)}$ to the baseline cdf F_I defined by (17). This gives

$$F_{I,r}^{(1)} = \underbrace{F_{I,1}^{(1)} \circ \cdots \circ F_{I,1}^{(1)}}_{r}(F_I), \tag{20}$$

where under $u \circ v$, we mean the composition of functions u, v. Obviously, $F_{I,r}^{(1)}(x;h)$ is a cdf as well.

Theorem 5. *For all $b > a > 0$; $2\nu + 1 > 0$; $r \in \mathbb{N}$ and $x \geq 0$, $h > 0$, we have*

$$F_{I,r}^{(1)}(x;h) = \frac{C_\nu}{r!}\left(\frac{x}{h}\right)^r \sum_{k=0}^{r} \binom{r}{k} \frac{(-1)^{k+1}}{(b\,x)^k} \Big\{ {}_1\Psi_1^{(\gamma)}\Big[\begin{matrix} (2\nu+1+k, 2, bx) \\ (\nu+1,1) \end{matrix} \Big| \frac{a^2}{4b^2} \Big] - \left(1+\frac{h}{x}\right)^{r-k} {}_1\Psi_1^{(\gamma)}\Big[\begin{matrix} (2\nu+1+k, 2, b(x+h)) \\ (\nu+1,1) \end{matrix} \Big| \frac{a^2}{4b^2} \Big] \Big\}.$$

Proof. Introducing the shorthand $\mathbf{dx}^{r-1} := \mathrm{d}x_1\,\mathrm{d}x_2 \cdots \mathrm{d}_{x_{r-1}}$, we rewrite the operator $F_{I,r}^{(1)}$ in (20), as the r-tuple integral

$$F_{I,r}^{(1)}(x;h) = \frac{C_\nu}{h^r} \sum_{n\geq 0} \frac{1}{\Gamma(\nu+1+n)\,n!}\left(\frac{a^2}{4b^2}\right)^n \int_{\prod_{j=1}^{r-1}[x_j, x_j+h]\times[x,x+h]} \gamma(2\nu+1+2n, bt)\,\mathrm{d}t\,\mathbf{dx}^{r-1}.$$

The use of the special form of the formula ((p. 23, Equation **1.2.1.1**), [12]) for $\min(\alpha,\beta) > 0$, $\lambda \geq 0$, implies

$$\int_0^x x^\lambda \gamma(\alpha, \beta x)\,\mathrm{d}x = \frac{x^{\lambda+1}}{\lambda+1}\gamma(\alpha,\beta x) - \frac{\gamma(\lambda+1+\alpha, \beta x)}{(\lambda+1)\,\beta^{\lambda+1}},$$

which provides the expression

$$I(\alpha,\beta;x) = \int_{\prod_{j=1}^{r-1}[0,x_j]\times[0,x]} \gamma(\alpha,\beta t)\,\mathrm{d}t\,\mathbf{dx}^{r-1} = \frac{x^r}{r!}\sum_{k=0}^{r}\binom{r}{k}\frac{(-1)^k}{(\beta x)^k}\gamma(\alpha+k,\beta x). \quad (21)$$

Indeed, the first few iterations read

$$\int_0^x \gamma(\alpha,\beta t)\,\mathrm{d}t = x\,\gamma(\alpha,\beta x) - \frac{1}{\beta}\gamma(\alpha+1,\beta x),$$

$$\int_0^x\int_0^{x_1} \gamma(\alpha,\beta t)\,\mathrm{d}t\,\mathrm{d}x_1 = \frac{1}{2!}\Big[x^2\,\gamma(\alpha,\beta x) - \frac{2}{\beta}\,x\,\gamma(\alpha+1,\beta x) + \frac{1}{\beta^2}\gamma(\alpha+2,\beta x)\Big],$$

$$\int_0^x\int_0^{x_2}\int_0^{x_1} \gamma(\alpha,\beta t)\,\mathrm{d}t\,\mathrm{d}x_1\,\mathrm{d}x_2 = \frac{1}{3!}\Big[x^3\,\gamma(\alpha,\beta x) - \frac{3}{\beta}\,x^2\,\gamma(\alpha+1,\beta x) + \frac{3}{\beta^2}\,x\,\gamma(\alpha+2,\beta x) - \frac{1}{\beta^3}\gamma(\alpha+3,\beta x)\Big], \quad \cdots$$

accordingly, we obtain (21) by induction. Consequently,

$$\begin{aligned} F_{I,r}^{(1)}(x;h) &= \frac{C_\nu}{h^r}\sum_{n\geq 0}\frac{1}{\Gamma(\nu+1+n)\,n!}\left(\frac{a^2}{4b^2}\right)^n \cdot \big[I(2\nu+1+2n, b; x+h) - I(2\nu+1+2n, b; x)\big] \\ &= \frac{C_\nu\,x^r}{r!\,h^r}\sum_{k=0}^{r}\binom{r}{k}\frac{(-1)^{k+1}}{(b\,x)^k}\Big\{\sum_{n\geq 0}\frac{\gamma(2\nu+1+k+2n, bx)}{\Gamma(\nu+1+n)\,n!}\left(\frac{a^2}{4b^2}\right)^n \\ &\quad - \left(1+\frac{h}{x}\right)^{r-k}\sum_{n\geq 0}\frac{\gamma(2\nu+1+k+2n, b(x+h))}{\Gamma(\nu+1+n)\,n!}\left(\frac{a^2}{4b^2}\right)^n\Big\} \\ &= \frac{C_\nu}{r!}\left(\frac{x}{h}\right)^r\sum_{k=0}^{r}\binom{r}{k}\frac{(-1)^{k+1}}{(b\,x)^k}\Big\{{}_1\Psi_1^{(\gamma)}\Big[\begin{matrix}(2\nu+1+k,2,bx)\\(\nu+1,1)\end{matrix}\Big|\frac{a^2}{4b^2}\Big] \\ &\quad - \left(1+\frac{h}{x}\right)^{r-k}{}_1\Psi_1^{(\gamma)}\Big[\begin{matrix}(2\nu+1+k,2,b(x+h))\\(\nu+1,1)\end{matrix}\Big|\frac{a^2}{4b^2}\Big]\Big\}. \end{aligned}$$

In turn, this provides the statement of the theorem. □

Corollary 2. *Let the situation be the same as in* Theorem 5. *Denote*

$$\mathscr{A}_r\big({}_1\Psi_1^{(\gamma)};t\big) := \sum_{k=0}^{r} \frac{(-r)_k}{b^k k!}\, t^{r-k}\; {}_1\Psi_1^{(\gamma)}\left[\begin{matrix}(2\nu+1+k,2,bt)\\(\nu+1,1)\end{matrix}\,\middle|\,\frac{a^2}{4b^2}\right].$$

Then, for all $x>0$, we have

$$\mathscr{A}_r\big({}_1\Psi_1^{(\gamma)};x\big) \le \mathscr{A}_r\big({}_1\Psi_1^{(\gamma)};x+h\big) \le \mathscr{A}_r\big({}_1\Psi_1^{(\gamma)};x\big) + C_\nu\, r!\, h^r\,.$$

Proof. The statement follows, since $F_{I,r}^{(1)}(x;h)$ is a cdf having a unit interval codomain for the $\mathrm{supp}\big(F_{I,r}^{(1)}\big)=\mathbb{R}_+$ and any positive h. □

5. Concluding Remarks

A. Inserting the lower and upper incomplete gamma functions (1) from relation (2) into (5) we deduce the upper incomplete Fox–Wright function's power series definition:

$${}_p\Psi_q^{(\Gamma)}\left[\begin{matrix}(\mu,M,x),(\mathbf{a}_{p-1},\mathbf{A}_{p-1})\\(\mathbf{b}_q,\mathbf{B}_q)\end{matrix}\,\middle|\,z\right] = \sum_{n\ge 0} \frac{\Gamma(\mu+nM,x)\prod\limits_{j=1}^{p-1}\Gamma(a_j+nA_j)}{\prod\limits_{j=1}^{q}\Gamma(b_j+nB_j)}\,\frac{z^n}{n!}\,.$$

Consequently, it follows that

$$\begin{aligned}{}_p\Psi_q^{(\gamma)}\left[\begin{matrix}(\mu,M,x),(\mathbf{a}_{p-1},\mathbf{A}_{p-1})\\(\mathbf{b}_q,\mathbf{B}_q)\end{matrix}\,\middle|\,z\right] &+ {}_p\Psi_q^{(\Gamma)}\left[\begin{matrix}(\mu,M,x),(\mathbf{a}_{p-1},\mathbf{A}_{p-1})\\(\mathbf{b}_q,\mathbf{B}_q)\end{matrix}\,\middle|\,z\right]\\ &= {}_p\Psi_q\left[\begin{matrix}(\mu,M),(\mathbf{a}_{p-1},\mathbf{A}_{p-1})\\(\mathbf{b}_q,\mathbf{B}_q)\end{matrix}\,\middle|\,z\right],\end{aligned}$$

consult (pp. 196–197 , Equations (6)–(7), [4]). Obviously, the parameter space remains unchanged. The reduction to the confluent function, which builds (9), results in

$${}_1\Psi_1^{(\gamma)}\left[\begin{matrix}(2\nu+1,2,bx)\\(\nu+1,1)\end{matrix}\,\middle|\,\frac{a^2}{4b^2}\right] + {}_1\Psi_1^{(\Gamma)}\left[\begin{matrix}(2\nu+1,2,bx)\\(\nu+1,1)\end{matrix}\,\middle|\,\frac{a^2}{4b^2}\right] = {}_1\Psi_1\left[\begin{matrix}(2\nu+1,2,bx)\\(\nu+1,1)\end{matrix}\,\middle|\,\frac{a^2}{4b^2}\right].$$

Now, let $X\sim\mathrm{McKayI}(a,b,\nu)$, where $b>a>0$, $2\nu+1>0$. The associated reliability (or survival) function and the hazard function, which also characterize the probability distributions, are

$$R_I(x;a,b;\nu) = 1 - F_I(x;a,b;\nu)\,, \qquad h_I(x;a,b;\nu) = \frac{f_I(x;a,b,\nu)}{R_I(x;a,b;\nu)}\,.$$

Hence, in conjunction with the pdf (6) and cdf (9), we perform for all $x\ge 0$ the following formulae

$$\begin{aligned} R_I(x;a,b;\nu) &= \frac{\sqrt{\pi}\,(b^2-a^2)^{\nu+\frac12}}{2^{2\nu}b^{2\nu+1}(\nu+\frac12)}\;{}_1\Psi_1^{(\Gamma)}\left[\begin{matrix}(2\nu+1,2,bx)\\(\nu+1,1)\end{matrix}\,\middle|\,\frac{a^2}{4b^2}\right],\\ h_I(x;a,b;\nu) &= \left(\frac{2b^2}{a}\right)^{\nu} \frac{\mathrm{e}^{-bx}\,I_0(ax)}{{}_1\Psi_1^{(\Gamma)}\left[\begin{matrix}(2\nu+1,2,bx)\\(\nu+1,1)\end{matrix}\,\middle|\,\frac{a^2}{4b^2}\right]}\,.\end{aligned}$$

These expressions show that in fact, no novel quality can be achieved by applying the upper incomplete gamma and upper Fox–Wright functions instead of the lower ones. In turn, the obtained inequality bounds become reversed, bearing in mind the reliability function terminology. The problem of how to achieve these bounds, we leave to the interested reader.

B. The probabilistic research methodology is in fact unique with respect to the confluent Fox–Wright function ${}_1\Psi_1^{(\gamma)}$, since McNolty's pdf (6) and cdf (9) are expressible by this special case of (5). On the other hand, this strategy of considerations can lead to other useful bounds for special functions appearing in the formulae of the pdf and cdf for "classical" and/or newly introduced random variables.

C. New research directions can be formulated for other special functions which participate in representing either the rv $X \sim \mathrm{McKayI}(a, b, \nu)$, or its counterpart variable with the so-called $\mathrm{McKayK}(a, b, \nu)$ distribution, see [2,7,8]. However, these goals will be addressed and presented in future work.

Funding: No external funding support.

Institutional Review Board Statement: Not applicable.

Informed Consent Statement: Not applicable.

Acknowledgments: The author is immensely grateful to Dragana Jankov Maširević for valuable suggestions and comments which she provided during this research. Furthermore, the author owes sincerest thanks to all three unknown referees for constructive remarks, insightful questions and their crucial help with improving the article.

Conflicts of Interest: The author declares no conflict of interest.

References

1. Olver, F.W.J.; Lozier, D.W.; Boisvert, R.F.; Clark, C.W. (Eds.) *NIST Handbook of Mathematical Functions*; NIST and Cambridge University Press: Cambridge, UK, 2010.
2. Górska, K.; Horzela, A.; Jankov Maširević, D.; Pogány, T.K. Observations on the McKay I_ν Bessel distribution. *J. Math. Anal. Appl.* **2022**, *516*, 126481. [CrossRef]
3. Jankov Maširević, D.; Pogány, T.K. On new formulae for cumulative distribution function for McKay Bessel distribution. *Comm. Stat. Theory Methods* **2021**, *50*, 143–160. [CrossRef]
4. Srivastava, H.M.; Pogány, T.K. Inequalities for a unified family of Voigt functions in several variables. *Russ. J. Math. Phys.* **2007**, *14*, 194–200. [CrossRef]
5. Mehrez, K.; Pogány, T.K. Integrals of ratios of Fox-Wright and incomplete Fox-Wright functions with applications. *J. Math. Inequal.* **2021**, *15*, 981–1001. [CrossRef]
6. Wright, E.M. The asymptotic expansion of the generalized hypergeometric function. *J. London Math. Soc.* **1935**, *10*, 286–293. [CrossRef]
7. McKay, A.T. A Bessel function distribution. *Biometrika* **1932**, *24*, 39–44. [CrossRef]
8. McNolty, F. Some probability density functions and their characteristic functions. *Math. Comp.* **1973**, *27*, 495–504. [CrossRef]
9. Baricz, Á.; Jankov Maširević, D.; Pogány, T.K. *Series of Bessel and Kummer-Type Functions*; Lecture Notes in Mathematics 2207; Springer: Cham, Switzerland, 2017.
10. Bognár, K.; Mogyoródi, J.; Prékopa, A.; Rényi, A.; Szász, D. *Exercises in Probability Theory*, 4th ed.; Typotex Kiadó: Budapest, Hungary, 2001. (In Hungarian)
11. Prudnikov, A.P.; Brychkov, Y.A.; Marichev, O.I. *More Special Functions*; Integrals and series; Gordon and Breach Science Publishers: New York, NY, USA, 1990; Volume 3.
12. Prudnikov, A.P.; Brychkov, Y.A.; Marichev, O.I. *Special Functions*; Integrals and series; Gordon and Breach Science Publishers: New York, NY, USA, 1986; Volume 2.

mathematics MDPI

Article

Hermite-Hadamard-Type Integral Inequalities for Convex Functions and Their Applications

Hari M. Srivastava [1,2,3,4,*], Sana Mehrez [5] and Sergei M. Sitnik [6]

1 Department of Mathematics and Statistics, University of Victoria, Victoria, BC V8W 3R4, Canada
2 Department of Medical Research, China Medical University Hospital, China Medical University, Taichung 40402, Taiwan
3 Department of Mathematics and Informatics, Azerbaijan University, 71 Jeyhun Hajibeyli Street, Baku AZ1007, Azerbaijan
4 Section of Mathematics, International Telematic University Uninettuno, I-00186 Rome, Italy
5 Department of Mathematics, Faculty of Sciences of Sfax, University of Sfax, Sfax 3029, Tunisia
6 Applied Mathematics and Computer Modeling, Belgorod State National Research University (BelGU), 85 Pobedy Street, 308015 Belgorod, Russia
* Correspondence: harimsri@math.uvic.ca

Abstract: In this paper, we establish new generalizations of the Hermite-Hadamard-type inequalities. These inequalities are formulated in terms of modules of certain powers of proper functions. Generalizations for convex functions are also considered. As applications, some new inequalities for the digamma function in terms of the trigamma function and some inequalities involving special means of real numbers are given. The results also include estimates via arithmetic, geometric and logarithmic means. The examples are derived in order to demonstrate that some of our results in this paper are more exact than the existing ones and some improve several known results available in the literature. The constants in the derived inequalities are calculated; some of these constants are sharp. As a visual example, graphs of some technically important functions are included in the text.

Keywords: Hermite-Hadamard inequality; digamma function; trigamma function; absolutely continuous mapping; convex function; arithmetic mean; geometric mean; logarithmic mean

MSC: 26D07; 26D10; 26D15; 26A33; 33B10

Citation: Srivastava, H.M.; Mehrez, S.; Sitnik, S.M. Hermite-Hadamard-Type Integral Inequalities for Convex Functions and Their Applications. *Mathematics* **2022**, *10*, 3127. https://doi.org/10.3390/math10173127

Academic Editor: Janusz Brzdęk

Received: 11 July 2022
Accepted: 27 August 2022
Published: 31 August 2022

Publisher's Note: MDPI stays neutral with regard to jurisdictional claims in published maps and institutional affiliations.

Copyright: © 2022 by the authors. Licensee MDPI, Basel, Switzerland. This article is an open access article distributed under the terms and conditions of the Creative Commons Attribution (CC BY) license (https://creativecommons.org/licenses/by/4.0/).

1. Introduction

The Hermite-Hadamard-type inequalities are very important in many topics of mathematics and its applications, and its original version is defined in the following way [1,2]:

$$h\left(\frac{a+b}{2}\right) \leqq \frac{1}{b-a}\int_a^b h(x)\,dx \leqq \frac{h(a)+h(b)}{2}, \tag{1}$$

where a convex function h is defined on the interval $I \subseteq \mathbb{R} \to \mathbb{R}$ for real numbers $a, b \in I \ (a < b)$.

The Hermite-Hadamard-type inequalities (1) are an important instrument in abstract and applied mathematical fields, such as mathematical analysis, function theory, optimization, control theory, the theory of special means and different variants of entropy problems, interpolations and approximations, numerical methods including numerical integration, information theory, probability and statistics. The results of this article may be applied to integral inequalities for fractional interval-valued functions and the corresponding differential equations and optimization problems. Integral inequalities of the Hermite-Hadamard type are also important in the transmutation theory for estimating different kinds of kernels for transmutational operators (see [3]). Thus, obviously, the results of this paper are matched with the topic of this Special Issue, "Analytical and Computational Methods in Differential Equations, Special Functions, Transmutations and Integral Transforms".

A considerable amount of work on these types of inequalities are known and recently, new proofs, generalizations, refinements, computer and numerical applications and illustrations were developed. As a result, many authors have focused on the Hermite-Hadamard-type inequalities for various classes of convex functions and mappings (see, for instance, [1,2,4–23]; see also the references cited therein).

From among very recent important papers, let us mention [20] in its connections with inclusion theory, and fuzzy sets are studied with the use of an interval analysis. Namely, different kinds of convexity and non-convexity conditions lead to interesting classes of inequalities, including problems with inclusions. For studying fuzzy order relations, an idea of logarithmic convexity is vital and fruitful. In this way, various discrete forms of Hermite-Hadamard and Jensen and Schur inequalities are studied for fuzzy interval-valued functions based upon considerations for logarithmic convex settings. It leads to new ideas and novel approaches in fuzzy optimization problems and interval-valued functions and the corresponding mathematical modeling. Moreover, the connected notion of interval-valued preinvex functions is also exploited; as an example, in [21], it is applied to the Riemann–Liouville fractional integrals in fractional calculus.

Dragomir and Agarwal [7], among other important results, proved the following inequality connected with the right-hand side of the inequality (1):

Theorem 1. *If h is a differentiable function on an interval $[a,b]$, and $|h'|$ is a convex function on $[a,b]$, then the following inequality holds true:*

$$\left|\frac{h(a)+h(b)}{2}-\frac{1}{b-a}\int_a^b h(x)\,dx\right| \leqq \frac{b-a}{8}\Big(|h'(a)|+|h'(b)|\Big). \tag{2}$$

Kirmaci [12] proved the following result connected with the left part of the inequality (1).

Theorem 2. *Under assumptions of the above Theorem A, the following holds true:*

$$\left|h\left(\frac{a+b}{2}\right)-\frac{1}{b-a}\int_a^b h(x)\,dx\right| \leqq \frac{b-a}{8}\Big(|h'(a)|+|h'(b)|\Big). \tag{3}$$

Other interesting results in this direction were proved in [23], with several refinements and extensions of the Hermite–Hadamard and Jensen inequalities in n variables.

In this paper, we establish some new Hermite-Hadamard-type inequalities for a class of functions with convex derivatives under some conditions. As consequences of our results, new inequalities involving the digamma and trigamma functions are obtained and some inequalities involving special means of real numbers are given. The analytical and numerical computation shows that the obtained results are better than the corresponding similar inequalities in (2) and (3).

2. New Hermite-Hadamard-Type Inequalities for Convex Functions

The notion of convexity is very important and basic in mathematics. For results on convex functions, we may mention references [1,2,24–27].

The following lemma is very useful to obtain the results of this paper. Its proof is based on an integration by parts. We, therefore, omit the details involved.

Lemma 1. *Let h be an absolutely continuous function on an interval $[a,b]$ and let its derivative $h' \in L_1[a,b]$. Then the following result holds true:*

$$\frac{1}{3}\left[h(a)+h\left(\frac{a+b}{2}\right)+h(b)\right]-\frac{1}{b-a}\int_a^b h(x)\,dx$$
$$=(b-a)\left[\int_0^{\frac{1}{2}}\left(x-\frac{1}{3}\right)h'(a+x(b-a))\,dx\right.$$
$$\left.+\int_{\frac{1}{2}}^1 (x-\frac{2}{3})h'(a+x(b-a))\,dx\right]. \tag{4}$$

Theorem 3. *Let h be an absolutely continuous function on an interval $[a,b]$ and let its derivative $h' \in L_1[a,b]$. Suppose also that $|h'|^q$ is convex on $[a,b]$ for some $q \geqq 1$. Then the following result holds true:*

$$\left|\frac{1}{3}\left[h(a)+h\left(\frac{a+b}{2}\right)+h(b)\right]-\frac{1}{b-a}\int_a^b h(x)\,dx\right| \leqq (b-a)\left(\frac{5}{72}\right)^{1-\frac{1}{q}}$$
$$\cdot\left\{\left(\frac{111|h'(a)|^q}{1944}+\frac{|h'(b)|^q}{81}\right)^{\frac{1}{q}}+\left(\frac{|h'(a)|^q}{81}+\frac{111|h'(b)|^q}{1944}\right)^{\frac{1}{q}}\right\}. \tag{5}$$

Proof. From Lemma 1, we have

$$\left|\frac{1}{3}\left[h(a)+h\left(\frac{a+b}{2}\right)+h(b)\right]-\frac{1}{b-a}\int_a^b h(x)\,dx\right|$$
$$=(b-a)\left|\int_0^{\frac{1}{2}}\left(x-\frac{1}{3}\right)h'(a+x(b-a))\,dx\right.$$
$$\left.+\int_{\frac{1}{2}}^1\left(x-\frac{2}{3}\right)h'(a+x(b-a))\,dx\right|$$
$$\leqq (b-a)\left\{\int_0^{\frac{1}{2}}\left|x-\frac{1}{3}\right||h'(a+x(b-a))|\,dx\right.$$
$$\left.+\int_{\frac{1}{2}}^1\left|x-\frac{2}{3}\right||h'(a+x(b-a))|\,dx\right\}. \tag{6}$$

Firstly, we assume that $q=1$, and by using the fact that the function $|h'|$ is convex on $[a,b]$, we derive the following inequality:

$$\int_0^{\frac{1}{2}}\left|x-\frac{1}{3}\right||h'(a+x(b-a))|\,dx+\int_{\frac{1}{2}}^1\left|x-\frac{2}{3}\right||h'(a+x(b-a))|\,dx$$
$$\leqq \int_0^{\frac{1}{2}}\left|x-\frac{1}{3}\right|[(1-x)|h'(a)|+x|h'(b)|]\,dx$$
$$+\int_{\frac{1}{2}}^1\left|x-\frac{2}{3}\right|((1-x)|h'(a)|+x|h'(b)|)\,dx$$
$$\leqq |h'(a)|\left(\int_0^{\frac{1}{2}}(1-x)\left|x-\frac{1}{3}\right|+\int_{\frac{1}{2}}^1(1-x)\left|x-\frac{2}{3}\right|\,dx\right)$$
$$+|h'(b)|\left(\int_0^{\frac{1}{2}}x\left|x-\frac{1}{3}\right|+\int_{\frac{1}{2}}^1 x\left|x-\frac{2}{3}\right|\,dx\right)$$
$$=\frac{5(|h'(a)|+|h'(b)|)}{72}. \tag{7}$$

Therefore, the desired inequality asserted by Theorem 3 in the case $q=1$ holds true.

Now, we suppose that $q > 1$. Further, we will use the Hölder integral inequality in the classical settings for $L_p - L_q$ functions; About this inequality, see, e.g., the monograph [2]. Thus, from the Hölder integral inequality (with $p = \frac{q}{q-1}$), we obtain

$$\begin{aligned}
&\int_0^{\frac{1}{2}} \left| x - \frac{1}{3} \right| |h'(a + x(b-a))| \, dx \\
&= \int_0^{\frac{1}{2}} \left| x - \frac{1}{3} \right|^{1-\frac{1}{q}} \left(\left| x - \frac{1}{3} \right|^{\frac{1}{q}} |h'(a + x(b-a))| \right) dx \\
&\leqq \left(\int_0^{\frac{1}{2}} \left| x - \frac{1}{3} \right| dx \right)^{1-\frac{1}{q}} \left(\int_0^{\frac{1}{2}} \left| x - \frac{1}{3} \right| |h'(a + x(b-a))|^q \, dx \right)^{\frac{1}{q}} \\
&\leqq \left(\frac{5}{72} \right)^{1-\frac{1}{q}} \left(|h'(a)|^q \int_0^{\frac{1}{2}} (1-x) \left| x - \frac{1}{3} \right| dx + |h'(b)|^q \int_0^{\frac{1}{2}} x \left| x - \frac{1}{3} \right| dx \right)^{\frac{1}{q}} \\
&\leqq \left(\frac{5}{72} \right)^{1-\frac{1}{q}} \left(\frac{111|h'(a)|^q}{1944} + \frac{|h'(b)|^q}{81} \right)^{\frac{1}{q}}. \qquad (8)
\end{aligned}$$

In the same way, we find that

$$\int_{\frac{1}{2}}^1 \left| x - \frac{2}{3} \right| |h'(a + x(b-a))| \, dx \leqq \left(\frac{5}{72} \right)^{1-\frac{1}{q}} \left(\frac{|h'(a)|^q}{81} + \frac{111|h'(b)|^q}{1944} \right)^{\frac{1}{q}}. \qquad (9)$$

Keeping (6), (8) and (9) in mind, we obtain the result (5) asserted by Theorem 3. □

Theorem 4. *Let h be an absolutely continuous function on an interval $[a, b]$ and let its derivative $h' \in L_1[a, b]$. Suppose also that $|h'|^q$ is convex on $[a, b]$ for some $q > 1$. Then the following result holds true:*

$$\begin{aligned}
&\left| \frac{1}{3} \left[h(a) + h\left(\frac{a+b}{2} \right) + h(b) \right] - \frac{1}{b-a} \int_a^b h(x) \, dx \right| \\
&\leqq \frac{b-a}{12} \left(\frac{1 + 2^{p+1}}{3(p+1)} \right)^{\frac{1}{p}} \left[|h'(a)|^q + |h'(b)|^q \right]^{\frac{1}{q}} \qquad (10)
\end{aligned}$$

with

$$\frac{1}{p} + \frac{1}{q} = 1.$$

Proof. As the function $|h'|^q$ is convex on $[a, b]$, we have

$$\int_0^{\frac{1}{2}} |h'(a + x(b-a))|^q \, dx \leqq \frac{3|h'(a)|^q + |h'(b)|^q}{8},$$

and

$$\int_{\frac{1}{2}}^1 |h'(a + x(b-a))|^q \, dx \leqq \frac{|h'(a)|^q + 3|h'(b)|^q}{8}.$$

Straightforward calculation yields

$$\int_0^{\frac{1}{2}} |x - \frac{1}{3}|^p \, dx = \int_{\frac{1}{2}}^1 |x - \frac{2}{3}|^p \, dx = \frac{1 + 2^{p+1}}{6^{p+1}(p+1)}. \qquad (11)$$

Thus, by applying the Hölder integral inequality, we obtain

$$\begin{aligned}
&\int_0^{\frac{1}{2}} \left| x - \frac{1}{3} \right| \cdot \left| h'(a + x(b-a)) \right| dx \\
&\leqq \left(\int_0^{\frac{1}{2}} \left| x - \frac{1}{3} \right|^p dx \right)^{\frac{1}{p}} \left(\int_0^{\frac{1}{2}} \left| h'(a + x(b-a)) \right|^q dx \right)^{\frac{1}{q}} \\
&\leqq \left(\frac{1 + 2^{p+1}}{6^{p+1}(p+1)} \right)^{\frac{1}{p}} \left(\frac{3|h'(a)|^q + |h'(b)|^q}{8} \right)^{\frac{1}{q}},
\end{aligned} \tag{12}$$

and

$$\begin{aligned}
&\int_{\frac{1}{2}}^{1} \left| x - \frac{2}{3} \right| \cdot \left| h'(a + x(b-a)) \right| dx \\
&\leqq \left(\int_{\frac{1}{2}}^{1} \left| x - \frac{2}{3} \right|^p dx \right)^{\frac{1}{p}} \left(\int_0^{\frac{1}{2}} \left| h'(a + x(b-a)) \right|^q dx \right)^{\frac{1}{q}} \\
&\leqq \left(\frac{1 + 2^{p+1}}{6^{p+1}(p+1)} \right)^{\frac{1}{p}} \left(\frac{|h'(a)|^q + 3|h'(b)|^q}{8} \right)^{\frac{1}{q}}.
\end{aligned} \tag{13}$$

Finally, upon combining (6), (12) and (13) and making some elementary simplifications, the asserted result (10) follows. □

Next, for the sake of brevity, we define

$$\Xi(a,b) := \frac{1}{3}\left[h(a) + h(b) + h\big(A(a,b)\big)\right] - \frac{1}{b-a}\int_a^b h(x)\,dx \neq 0$$

and

$$A(a,b) := \frac{a+b}{2}.$$

As usual, we denote by $A(a,b)$ an arithmetic mean of two non-negative numbers a and b.

Theorem 5. *Under the conditions of Theorem 3, the following Hermite-Hadamard-type inequality holds true:*

$$\begin{aligned}
\left| h\left(\frac{a+b}{2} \right) - \frac{1}{b-a} \int_a^b h(x)\,dx \right| &\leqq (b-a)|\rho_1(a,b)| \left(\frac{5}{72} \right)^{1-\frac{1}{q}} \\
&\cdot \left\{ \left(\frac{111|h'(a)|^q}{1944} + \frac{|h'(b)|^q}{81} \right)^{\frac{1}{q}} + \left(\frac{|h'(a)|^q}{81} + \frac{111|h'(b)|^q}{1944} \right)^{\frac{1}{q}} \right\},
\end{aligned} \tag{14}$$

where

$$\rho_1(a,b) := 1 - 2\frac{A\big(h(a), h(b)\big) - h\big(A(a,b)\big)}{3\,\Xi(a,b)}.$$

Furthermore, the next result is true:

$$\left| h\left(\frac{a+b}{2} \right) - \frac{1}{b-a} \int_a^b h(x)\,dx \right| \leqq \frac{5(b-a)|\rho_1(a,b)|}{72} \Big[|h'(a)| + |h'(b)| \Big]. \tag{15}$$

Proof. With the aid of the Formula (4), we obtain

$$\begin{aligned}
&\left|h\left(\frac{a+b}{2}\right)-\frac{1}{b-a}\int_a^b h(x)\,dx\right| \\
&= (b-a)\left|\int_0^{\frac{1}{2}}(x-\frac{1}{3})h'(a+x(b-a))\,dx+\int_{\frac{1}{2}}^1(x-\frac{2}{3})h'(a+x(b-a))\,dx\right. \\
&\quad \left.-\frac{2}{3}\left(\frac{A(h(a),h(b))-h(A(a,b))}{(b-a)}\right)\right| \\
&= (b-a)\left|\int_0^{\frac{1}{2}}(x-\frac{1}{3})h'(a+x(b-a))\,dx+\int_{\frac{1}{2}}^1(x-\frac{2}{3})h'(a+x(b-a))\,dx\right| \\
&\quad \cdot\left|1-\frac{2}{3}\left(\frac{A(h(a),h(b))-h(A(a,b))}{\Xi(a,b)}\right)\right|. \qquad (16)
\end{aligned}$$

Obviously, by repeating the same calculations as in the proof of Theorem 3 with the help of (16), we achieve the required result (14).

Finally, taking $q=1$ in (14) leads to the inequality (15). This completes the proof of Theorem 5. □

Remark 1. *We note that, if $|\rho_1| < \frac{9}{5}$, then the inequality (15) is better than the inequality (3). It means that the absolute positive constant at the right-hand side of the inequality (15) is smaller, and so better, than the right-hand side of the inequality (3). Consequently, under the above condition $|\rho_1| < \frac{9}{5}$, the inequality (15) is more exact than the inequality (3).*

Now, we present some examples to illustrate cases that the right-hand side of inequality (15) is better than the right-hand side of inequality (3).

- Let us consider the function $h(x)=e^x$ and $[a,b]=[t,t+1],\ t\in\mathbb{R}$. Then, we have

$$\rho_1=\frac{3+3\sqrt{e}-3e}{4+\sqrt{e}-2e}\approx -0.98362.$$

  Consequently, the inequality (15) is better than the inequality (3). It means that the positive constant on the right-hand side of the inequality (15) is smaller (better!) than the positive constant on the right-hand side of the inequality (3).
- Let us take $h(x)=\psi(x)$, where

$$\psi(x):=\frac{\Gamma'(x)}{\Gamma(x)}$$

  is the digamma function and $[a,b]=[t,t+2]\ \ (t>0)$. It is known that the trigamma function $\psi'(x)$ is convex on $(0,\infty)$. Hence, by using the following identity:

$$\psi(t+1)=\psi(t)+\frac{1}{t}, \qquad (17)$$

  we have

$$A(h(t),h(t+2))-h(A(t,t+2))=-\frac{1}{2t(t+1)}$$

  and

$$\Xi(t,t+2)=\psi(t)+\frac{2}{3t}+\frac{1}{3(t+1)}-\frac{1}{2}\log(t^2+t).$$

  Therefore, we get

$$\rho_1(t,t+2)=1+\frac{2}{6t(t+1)\psi(t)-3t(t+1)\log\left(t(t+1)\right)+6t+4}.$$

Hence, we obtain

$$F(t) := |\rho_1(t, t+2|| < \frac{9}{5}$$

for all $t > 0$ (see Figure 1 which verifies our claim). Consequently, for this case, the right-hand side of the inequality (15) is better than the right-hand side of the inequality (3).

- Next, we let $h(x) = \psi(x)$ and $[a, b] = [t, t+1]$ $(t > 0)$. Hence, for this case, we have

$$A(h(t), h(t+1)) - h(A(t, t+1)) = \psi(t) - \psi\left(t + \frac{1}{2}\right) + \frac{1}{2t},$$

and

$$\Xi(t, t+1) = \frac{2}{3}\psi(t) + \frac{1}{3}\psi\left(t + \frac{1}{2}\right) - \log t + \frac{1}{3t}.$$

Hence, we obtain

$$\rho_1(t, t+1) = \frac{3t\psi(t+1/2) - 3t\log t}{2t\psi(t) + t\psi(t+1/2) - 3t\log t + 1}.$$

By Figure 1, we see that

$$G(t) := |\rho_1(t, t+1)| < \frac{9}{5},$$

which implies that (15) improves (3).

Theorem 6. *Under the conditions of Theorem 4, it is asserted that*

$$\left| h\left(\frac{a+b}{2}\right) - \frac{1}{b-a}\int_a^b h(x)\,dx \right| \leqq \frac{(b-a)|\rho_1(a,b)|}{12}\left(\frac{1+2^{p+1}}{3(p+1)}\right)^{\frac{1}{p}} \left[|h'(a)|^q + |h'(b)|^q\right]^{\frac{1}{q}} \tag{18}$$

for

$$\frac{1}{p} + \frac{1}{q} = 1.$$

In particular, the following inequality holds true:

$$\left| h\left(\frac{a+b}{2}\right) - \frac{1}{b-a}\int_a^b h(x)\,dx \right| \leqq \frac{(b-a)|\rho_1(a,b)|}{12}\left[|h'(a)|^2 + |h'(b)|^2\right]^{\frac{1}{2}}. \tag{19}$$

Proof. By using the same consequent steps as in Theorem 4 with the help of the Formula (16), we obtain the inequality (18) asserted by Theorem 6. We choose to omit the details involved. □

Remark 2. *Under the conditions of Theorem 6, we see that the left-hand side of the inequality (19) is better than the inequality (3) if $|\rho_1(a,b)| < \frac{3}{2}$. It means that the absolute positive constant on the right-hand side of the inequality (19) is smaller, and so better, than the right-hand side of the inequality (3). Consequently, under the above condition $|\rho_1(a,b)| < \frac{3}{2}$, the inequality (19) is more exact than the inequality (3).*

We note that the examples used in Remark 1 also verify conditions $|\rho_1(a,b)| < \frac{3}{2}$, and it is illustrated by Figure 1 (see below).

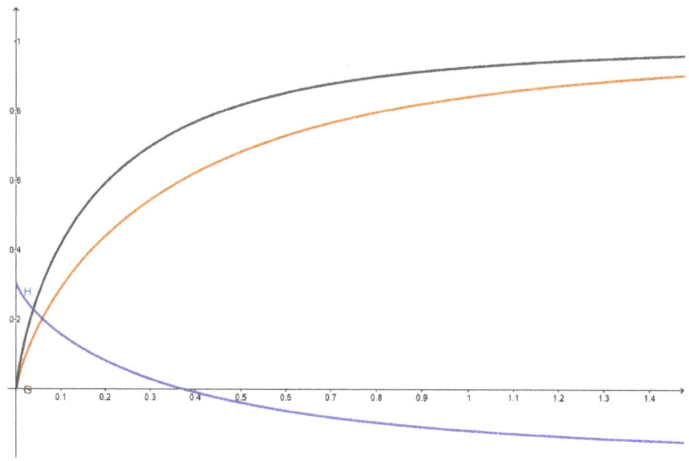

Figure 1. Graphs of the functions F and G (from Remark 1) and H (from Remark 3).

Theorem 7. *Under the assumptions of Theorem 3, the following inequality holds true:*

$$\left|\frac{h(a)+h(b)}{2} - \frac{1}{b-a}\int_a^b h(x)\,dx\right| \leqq |\rho_2(a,b)|(b-a)\left(\frac{5}{72}\right)^{1-\frac{1}{q}} \cdot\left\{\left(\frac{111|h'(a)|^q}{1944} + \frac{|h'(b)|^q}{81}\right)^{\frac{1}{q}} + \left(\frac{|h'(a)|^q}{81} + \frac{111|h'(b)|^q}{1944}\right)^{\frac{1}{q}}\right\}, \quad (20)$$

where

$$\rho_2(a,b) =: 1 - \frac{h\big(A(a,b)\big) - A\big(h(a),h(b)\big)}{3\,\Xi(a,b)}.$$

Proof. From Lemma 1, we have

$$\begin{aligned}
&\left|\frac{h(a)+h(b)}{2} - \frac{1}{b-a}\int_a^b h(x)\,dx\right| \\
&= (b-a)\left|\int_0^{\frac{1}{2}}\left(x-\frac{1}{3}\right)h'(a+x(b-a))\,dx + \int_{\frac{1}{2}}^1\left(x-\frac{2}{3}\right)h'(a+x(b-a))\,dx - \frac{h\big(A(a,b)\big) - A\big(h(a),h(b)\big)}{3(b-a)}\right| \\
&= (b-a)\left|\int_0^{\frac{1}{2}}\left(x-\frac{1}{3}\right)h'(a+x(b-a))\,dx + \int_{\frac{1}{2}}^1\left(x-\frac{2}{3}\right)h'(a+x(b-a))\,dx\right| \cdot\left|1 - \frac{h\big(A(a,b)\big) - A\big(h(a),h(b)\big)}{3\,\Xi(a,b)}\right|. \quad (21)
\end{aligned}$$

By repeating the same steps as in the proof of Theorem 3 together with the above relation, we derive the assertion of Theorem 7. Exactly, these steps consist of using integral representation with the derivative h' via the arithmetic means (21) and following obvious integral estimates instead of (6), and after that, using the Hölder integral inequality [2] for the cases $q = 1$ and $q > 1$ one by one. □

Remark 3. *If we take $q = 1$ in Theorem 7, we obtain*

$$\left|\frac{h(a)+h(b)}{2} - \frac{1}{b-a}\int_a^b h(x)\,dx\right| \leqq \frac{5|\rho_2(a,b)|(b-a)}{72}\Big(|h'(a)| + |h'(b)|\Big). \tag{22}$$

We note that the obtained midpoint inequality (22) is better than the inequality (2) if $|\rho_2| < \frac{9}{5}$. It means that the absolute positive constant at the right-hand side of the inequality (22) is smaller, and so better, than the right-hand side of the inequality (2); so, under the above condition $|\rho_2| < \frac{9}{5}$, the inequality (22) is more exact than the inequality (2).

In order to support this observation, we consider the following example: set $h(x) = \psi(x)$ and $[a,b] = [t,t+2]$ $t > 0$. In this case, we have

$$h\big(A(t,t+2)\big) - A\big(h(t),h(t+2)\big) = \frac{1}{2t(t+1)}$$

and

$$\rho_2(t,t+2) = 1 - \frac{1}{6t(t+1)\psi(t) - 3t(t+1)\log\big(t(t+1)\big) + 6t + 4}.$$

We set

$$H(t) = \frac{9}{5} - \left|1 - \frac{1}{6t(t+1)\psi(t) - 3t(t+1)\log\big(t(t+1)\big) + 6t + 4}\right|.$$

Figure 1 illustrates that the right-hand side of the inequality (22) is sharper than the right-hand side of the inequality (2) on the interval $[t, t+2]$, where $t \in (0, 0.367217)$.

Theorem 8. *With the assumptions of Theorem 4, the following inequality holds true:*

$$\left|\frac{h(a)+h(b)}{2} - \frac{1}{b-a}\int_a^b h(x)\,dx\right| \leqq \frac{(b-a)|\rho_2(a,b)|}{12}\left(\frac{1+2^{p+1}}{3(p+1)}\right)^{\frac{1}{p}} \big[|h'(a)|^q + |h'(b)|^q\big]^{\frac{1}{q}} \tag{23}$$

with

$$\frac{1}{p} + \frac{1}{q} = 1.$$

Proof. We just repeat the same calculations as in the proof of Theorem 4 using (21). □

On setting $p = q = 2$ in (23), we obtain the following consequence.

Corollary 1. *With the conditions of Theorem 4, it is asserted that*

$$\left|\frac{h(a)+h(b)}{2} - \frac{1}{b-a}\int_a^b h(x)\,dx\right| \leqq \frac{(b-a)|\rho_2(a,b)|}{12}\sqrt{|h'(a)|^2 + |h'(b)|^2}. \tag{24}$$

Remark 4. *We note that the left-hand side of the inequality (24) is better than the left-hand side of the inequality (2) if $|\rho_2| < \frac{3}{2}$. It means that the absolute positive constant on the right-hand side of the inequality (24) is smaller, and so better, than the right-hand side of the inequality (2). Consequently, under the above condition $|\rho_2| < \frac{3}{2}$, the inequality (24) is sharper than the inequality (2).*

3. Applications

3.1. Some New Inequalities for the Digamma Function in Terms of the Trigamma Function

Our aim in this section is to establish new inequalities involving the digamma and trigamma functions.

Proposition 1. *For $t > 0$, the next inequality holds true:*

$$\left|\psi(t) - \log\left(\sqrt{t(t+1)}\right) + \frac{3t+2}{3t(t+1)}\right| \leqq \frac{5}{72}\left(2\psi'(t) - \frac{2t^2+2t+1}{t^2(t+1)^2}\right). \tag{25}$$

Proof. Upon setting $h(x) = \psi(x)$ and $[a,b] = [t, t+2]$ in Theorem 3 ($q = 1$) and using (17), we obtain

$$\left|3\psi(t) + \frac{2}{t} + \frac{1}{t+1} - \frac{3}{2}\log\left(t(t+1)\right)\right| \leqq \frac{5}{24}\left(|\psi'(t+2)| + |\psi'(t)|\right). \tag{26}$$

Again, by using (17), we have

$$\psi'(t+2) = \psi'(t) - \frac{1}{t^2} - \frac{1}{(t+1)^2}.$$

In view of the above relations and straightforward calculation, we derive the desired inequality (25) asserted by Proposition 1. □

Proposition 2. *For any $t > 0$, the following inequality holds true:*

$$\left|2\psi(t) + \psi\left(t + \frac{1}{2}\right) - 3\log t + \frac{1}{t}\right| \leqq \frac{5}{24}\left(2\psi'(t) + \frac{1}{t}\right). \tag{27}$$

Proof. We set $h(x) = \psi(x)$ and $[a,b] = [t, t+1]$, $t > 0$ in Theorem 3. The details involved are derived by a straightforward calculation. □

3.2. Applications of Hermite-Hadamard-Type Inequalities to Linear Combinations of Some Special Means

The study of different kinds of means is fulfilled in (for example) [2,25,28–30]. It is one of the most important notions in mathematical analysis and its applications.

With the aid of some results in Section 3, our aim in this section is to derive some new inequalities involving combinations of special means and its powers.

As usual, for arbitrary positive real numbers a and b, we define the following items.

1. The arithmetic and geometric means given by

$$A(x,y) = \frac{x+y}{2} \quad \text{and} \quad G(x,y) = \sqrt{ab}.$$

2. The logarithmic mean given by

$$L(a,b) = \frac{b-a}{\log b - \log a} \qquad (a \neq b).$$

3. The generalized logarithmic mean given by

$$L_n(a,b) = \left(\frac{b^{p+1} - a^{p+1}}{(p+1)(b-a)}\right)^{\frac{1}{p}} \qquad (p \in \mathbb{R} \setminus \{-1, 0\};\ a \neq b).$$

In fact, the logarithmic mean and a generalized logarithmic mean are special cases of the means introduced by Tibor Radó. Tibor Radó also established several important inequalities for them (see, for details, [2]).

Proposition 3. *Let $r \in (0,1]$ and $a, b \in \mathbb{R}$ such that $0 < a < b$. Then the following inequality holds true:*

$$\left|\frac{2}{3}A(a^r, b^r) + \frac{1}{3}A^r(a,b) - L_r^r(a,b)\right| \leqq r(b-a)\left(\frac{5}{72}\right)^{1-\frac{1}{q}} \cdot \left\{\left(\frac{111a^{q(r-1)}}{1944} + \frac{b^{q(r-1)}}{81}\right)^{\frac{1}{q}} + \left(\frac{a^{q(r-1)}}{81} + \frac{111b^{q(r-1)}}{1944}\right)^{\frac{1}{q}}\right\} \tag{28}$$

for all $q \geqq 1$.

Proof. Proposition 3 follows from Theorem 3 upon setting $q = 1$ and

$$h(x) = x^r \qquad (r \in (0,1]).$$

□

Proposition 4. *Under the assumptions of Proposition 3, the following inequalities hold true:*

$$\left|\frac{2}{3}A(a^r, b^r) + \frac{1}{3}A^r(a,b) - L_r^r(a,b)\right| \leqq \frac{r(b-a)}{6}\left(\frac{1+2^{p+1}}{6(p+1)}\right)^{\frac{1}{p}} A^{\frac{1}{q}}\left(a^{q(r-1)}, b^{q(r-1)}\right), \tag{29}$$

where

$$\frac{1}{p} + \frac{1}{q} = 1 \qquad (p > 1).$$

Proof. Proposition 4 follows from Theorem 4 by putting $h(x) = x^r \quad (\alpha \in (0,1])$. □

If we set

$$h(x) = \frac{1}{x^r} \qquad (r \in (0,1])$$

in Theorem 3, we deduce the following inequality.

Proposition 5. *With the conditions of Proposition 3, the following result holds true:*

$$\left|\frac{2}{3}A(a^{-r}, b^{-r}) + \frac{1}{3}A^{-r}(a,b) - L_{-r}^{-r}(a,b)\right| \leqq r(b-a)\left(\frac{5}{72}\right)^{1-\frac{1}{q}} \cdot \left\{\left(\frac{111\, a^{-q(r+1)}}{1944} + \frac{b^{-q(r+1)}}{81}\right)^{\frac{1}{q}} + \left(\frac{a^{-q(r+1)}}{81} + \frac{111\, b^{-q(r+1)}}{1944}\right)^{\frac{1}{q}}\right\} \tag{30}$$

for all $q \geqq 1$.

Remark 5. *If we set $r = 1$ in (30), we obtain*

$$\left|\frac{2}{3}A(a^{-1}, b^{-1}) + \frac{1}{3}A^{-1}(a,b) - L_{-1}^{-1}(a,b)\right| \leqq (b-a)\left(\frac{5}{72}\right)^{1-\frac{1}{q}} \left\{\left(\frac{111\, a^{-2q}}{1944} + \frac{b^{-2q}}{81}\right)^{\frac{1}{q}} + \left(\frac{a^{-2q}}{81} + \frac{111\, b^{-2q}}{1944}\right)^{\frac{1}{q}}\right\}, \tag{31}$$

where $q \geqq 1$.

Upon setting

$$f(t) = \frac{1}{t^r} \qquad (r \in (0,1])$$

in Theorem 4, we get the following inequality.

Proposition 6. *With the assumptions of Proposition 3, the following inequality is valid:*

$$\left|\frac{2}{3}A(a^{-r},b^{-r})+\frac{1}{3}A^{-r}(a,b)-L_{-r}^{-r}(a,b)\right|$$
$$\leqq\frac{r(b-a)}{6}\left(\frac{1+2^{p+1}}{6(p+1)}\right)^{\frac{1}{p}}A\left(a^{-q(r+1)},a^{-q(r+1)}\right) \tag{32}$$

with

$$\frac{1}{p}+\frac{1}{q}=1\qquad\left(\min\{p,q\}>1\right).$$

In particular, we obtain

$$\left|\frac{2}{3}A(a^{-1},b^{-1})+\frac{1}{3}A^{-1}(a,b)-L_{-1}^{-1}(a,b)\right|$$
$$\leqq\frac{b-a}{6}\left(\frac{1+2^{p+1}}{6(p+1)}\right)^{\frac{1}{p}}A\left(a^{-2q},a^{-2q}\right), \tag{33}$$

where

$$\frac{1}{p}+\frac{1}{q}=1\qquad\left(\min\{p,q\}>1\right).$$

4. Conclusions

In this paper, we have establishd new Hermite-Hadamard-type inequalities for a class of functions with some convexity conditions on their derivatives. As consequences of some of our main results, we have obtained some new inequalities for the digamma function in terms of the trigamma function. Some applications to special means of real numbers are also given. The analytical and numerical computation show that some of the obtained results are better than the the corresponding known results.

Author Contributions: Conceptualization, S.M. and S.M.S.; methodology, H.M.S., S.M. and S.M.S.; software, S.M.; validation, H.M.S. and S.M.S.; formal analysis, S.M. and S.M.S.; investigation, S.M. and S.M.S.; resources, S.M.S.; data curation, S.M.; writing—original draft preparation, S.M. and S.M.S.; writing—review and editing, H.M.S. and S.M.S.; visualization, S.M.; supervision, S.M.S.; project administration, S.M.S.; funding acquisition, S.M.S. All authors have read and agreed to the published version of the manuscript.

Funding: This research received no external funding.

Institutional Review Board Statement: Not applicable.

Informed Consent Statement: Not applicable.

Data Availability Statement: This article has no associated data.

Conflicts of Interest: The author declares that they have no conflict of interest.

References

1. Dragomir, S.S.; Pearce, C.E.M. *Selected Topics on Hermite–Hadamard Inequalities and Applications*; RGMIA Monograph Series; Victoria University of Technology: Melbourne, Australia, 2003. Available online: https://ssrn.com/abstract=3158351 (accessed on 5 July 2022).
2. Mitrinović, D.S.; Pečarić, J.; Fink, A. *Classical and New Inequalities in Analysis*; (Eastern European Series on Mathematics and Its Applications); Kluwer Academic Publishers: Dordrecht, The Netherlands, 1993; Volume 61.
3. Shishkina, E.; Sitnik, S. M. *Transmutations, Singular and Fractional Differential Equations with Applications to Mathematical Physics*; (Series on Mathematics in Science and Engineering); Academic Press: Cambridge, MA, USA, 2020.
4. Alomari, M.; Darus, M.; Dragomir, S.S. New inequalities of Hermite–Hadamard type for functions whose second derivates absolute values are quasi-convex. *RGMIA Res. Rep. Collect.* **2009**, *12*, 1–5.

5. Azpeitia, A.G. Convex functions and the Hadamard inequality. *Rev. Colomb. Mat.* **1994**, *28*, 7–12.
6. Bakula, M.K.; Pečarić, J.E. Note on some Hadamard-type inequalities. *J. Inequal. Pure Appl. Math.* **2004**, *5*, 74.
7. Dragomir, S.S.; Agarwal, R.P. Two inequalities for differentiable mappings and applications to special means of real numbers and to trapezoidal formula. *Appl. Math. Lett.* **1998**, *11*, 91–95. [CrossRef]
8. Dragomir, S.S. On some new inequalities of Hermite-Hadamard type for *m*-convex functions. *Tamkang J. Math.* **2002**, *33*, 45–56. [CrossRef]
9. Dragomir, S.S. Two mappings in connection to Hadamard's inequalities. *J. Math. Anal. Appl.* **1992**, *167*, 49–56. [CrossRef]
10. Erden, S.; Sarikaya, M.Z. New Hermite-hadamard type inequalities for twice differentiable convex mappings via green function and applications. *Moroccan J. Pure Appl. Anal.* **2016**, *2*, 107–117. [CrossRef]
11. Kavurmaci, H.; Avci, M.; Özdemir, M.E. New inequalities of hermite-hadamard type for convex functions with applications. *J. Inequal. Appl.* **2011**, *2011*, 86. [CrossRef]
12. Kirmaci, U.S. Inequalities for differentiable mappings and applications to special means of real numbers to midpoint formula. *Appl. Math. Comput.* **2004**, *147*, 137–146. [CrossRef]
13. Kirmaci, U.S.; Bakula, M.K.; Özdemir, M.E.; Pečarić, J.E. Hadamard-tpye inequalities for *s*-convex functions. *Appl. Math. Comput.* **2007**, *193*, 26–35. [CrossRef]
14. Pearce, C.E.M.; Pečarić, J.E. Inequalities for differentiable mappings with application to special means and quadrature formula. *Appl. Math. Lett.* **2000**, *13*, 51–55. [CrossRef]
15. Özdemir, M.E.; Avci, M.; Set, E. On some inequalities of Hermite-Hadamard type via *m*-convexity. *Appl. Math. Lett.* **2010**, *23*, 1065–1070. [CrossRef]
16. Sarikaya, M.Z.; Set, E.; Özdemir, M.E. On some new inequalities of hadamard-type involving *h*-convex functions. *Acta Math. Univ. Comenian. (N.S.)* **2010**, *79*, 265–272.
17. Sarikaya, M.Z.; Kiris, M.E. Some new inequalities of Hermite-Hadamard type for *s*-convex functions. *Miskolc Math. Notes* **2015**, *16*, 491–501. [CrossRef]
18. Set, E.; Özdemir, M.E.; Dragomir, S.S. On the Hermite-Hadamard inequality and other integral inequalities involving two functions. *J. Inequal. Appl.* **2010**, *9*, 148102. [CrossRef]
19. Set, E.; Özdemir, M.E.; Dragomir, S.S. On Hadamard-type inequalities involving several kinds of convexity. *J. Inequal. Appl.* **2010**, *12*, 286845. [CrossRef]
20. Khan, M.B.; Srivastava, H.M.; Mohammed, P.O.; Nonlaopon, K.; Hamed, Y.S. Some new Jensen, Schur and Hermite-Hadamard inequalities for log convex fuzzy interval-valued functions. *AIMS Math.* **2022**, *7*, 4338–4358. [CrossRef]
21. Srivastava, H.M.; Sahoo, S.K.; Mohammed, P.O.; Baleanu, D.; Kodamasingh, B. Hermite-Hadamard type inequalities for interval-valued preinvex functions via fractional integral operators. *Internat. J. Comput. Intel. Syst.* **2022**, *15*, 8. [CrossRef]
22. Khan, M.B.; Srivastava, H.M.; Mohammed, P.O.; Macías-Diaz, J.E.; Hamed, Y.S. Some new versions of integral inequalities for log-preinvex fuzzy-interval-valued functions through fuzzy order relation. *Alex. Eng. J.* **2022**, *61*, 7089–7101. [CrossRef]
23. Srivastava, H.M.; Zhang, Z.-H.; Wu, Y.-D. Some further refinements and extensions of the Hermite-Hadamard and Jensen inequalities in several variables. *Math. Comput. Model.* **2011**, *54*, 2709–2717. [CrossRef]
24. Pečarić, J.E.; Proschan, F.; Tong, Y.L. *Convex Functions, Partial Orderings, and Statistical Applications*; Academic Press Incorporated: Cambridge, MA, USA, 1992.
25. Hardy, G.H.; Littlewood, J.E.; Pólya, G. *Inequalities*; Cambridge University Press: Cambridge/London, UK; New York, NY, USA, 1952.
26. Karp, D.; Sitnik, S.M. Log-convexity and log-concavity of hypergeometric-like functions. *J. Math. Anal. Appl.* **2010**, *364*, 384–394. [CrossRef]
27. Niculescu, C.; Persson, L.E. *Convex Functions and Their Applications: A Contemporary Approach*; Springer: Berlin/Heidelberg, Germany; New York, NY, USA, 2006.
28. Bullen, P.S.; Mitrinović, D.S.; Vasić, P.M. *Means and Their Inequalities*; D. Reidel Publishing Company: Dordrecht, The Netherlands, 1988.
29. Bullen, P.S. *Handbook of Means and Their Inequalities*; (Kluwer Series on Mathematics and Its Applications); Kluwer Academic Publishers: Dordrecht, The Netherlands, 2003; Volume 560.
30. Bullen, P.S. *Dictionary of Inequalities*; (Pitman Monographs and Surveys in Pure and Applied Mathematics); CRC Press: Boca Raton, FL, USA, 1998; Volume 97.

mathematics

MDPI

Article

Asymptotic Behavior of Three Connected Stochastic Delay Neoclassical Growth Systems Using Spectral Technique

Ishtiaq Ali [1,*] and Sami Ullah Khan [2]

[1] Department of Mathematics and Statistics, College of Science, King Faisal University, P.O. Box 400, Al-Ahsa 31982, Saudi Arabia
[2] Department of Mathematics, City University of Science and Information Technology, Peshawar 2500, KP, Pakistan; samiullah.khan@cusit.edu.pk
* Correspondence: iamirzada@kfu.edu.sa

Abstract: In this study, we consider a nonlinear system of three connected delay differential neoclassical growth models along with stochastic effect and additive white noise, which is influenced by stochastic perturbation. We derived the conditions for positive equilibria, stability and positive solutions of the stochastic system. It is observed that when a constant delay reaches a certain threshold for the steady state, the asymptotic stability is lost, and the Hopf bifurcation occurs. In the case of the finite domain, the three connected, delayed systems will not collapse to infinity but will be bounded ultimately. A Legendre spectral collocation method is used for the numerical simulations. Moreover, a comparison of a stochastic delayed system with a deterministic delayed system is also provided. Some numerical test problems are presented to illustrate the effectiveness of the theoretical results. Numerical results further illustrate the obtained stability regions and behavior of stable and unstable solutions of the proposed system.

Keywords: three connected neoclassical growth models; stochastic delay system; stability analysis; Itô formula; spectral method

MSC: 34K50; 37H30; 65M70

Citation: Ali, I.; Khan, S.U. Asymptotic Behavior of Three Connected Stochastic Delay Neoclassical Growth Systems Using Spectral Technique. *Mathematics* **2022**, *10*, 3639. https://doi.org/10.3390/math10193639

Academic Editor: Sitnik Sergey

Received: 7 September 2022
Accepted: 29 September 2022
Published: 5 October 2022

Publisher's Note: MDPI stays neutral with regard to jurisdictional claims in published maps and institutional affiliations.

Copyright: © 2022 by the authors. Licensee MDPI, Basel, Switzerland. This article is an open access article distributed under the terms and conditions of the Creative Commons Attribution (CC BY) license (https://creativecommons.org/licenses/by/4.0/).

1. Introduction

In mathematical economics, the examination of the stochastic delay differential neoclassical growth model (NGM) plays a key role. In general, this model is constructed with two very simple assumptions; one is capital and full-time labor hiring, while the other is the immediate adjustment in the market, which helps in the long-run behavior of the economy [1–3]. The main advantage of these models is that they are well-behaved and are usually asymptotically stable for the steady state, but in reality, these growth path models constantly exhibit fluctuations. For this reason, the neoclassical model could be a good alternative to show how such persistent behavior can emerge when nonlinearities and a production delay are present. Since the neoclassical growth model is always affected by environmental noises, the stochastic models are more suitable in the real world [4–7].

In economics, the most frequently discussed issue is to test the economic growth models. Many researchers have investigated these models for various population data and complex behaviors. Day studied a neoclassical growth model with time delay and noticed that despite its simple structure, the resulting dynamic system shows the emergence of erratic fluctuations in the capital accumulation process when the production function is unimodal and the delay in production is explicitly considered [8,9]. However, his models were totally occupying discrete time and a mound-shaped function that described the negative effect of subsequent pollution from increasing fundamentals. It was identified by numerical approaches that such models could achieve periodic and even chaotic behavior. Following the pioneering work of Day, Matsumoto and Szidarovszky, an economics-based model for understanding the complex dynamics of economics was created [10–12]. In earlier work in this field, most of the researchers only considered discrete time scales [13–15]. For the detection of chaos, the three period condition, introduced by Li and Yorke, has many applications in nonlinear differential equations of the first-order, followed by the work of Rosser, which offers many applications [16,17]. Very little work has been performed that is committed to the case of continuous time scales due to the fact that there is no preferred criterion to detect chaos and the system has three dimensions.

In this article, we will examine an extension of the NGM to the early works of Swan and Solow [18,19]. The new NGM is constructed with three connected assumptions; one is the permanent labor employment, the second is the continual adjustment in the market output and the third one is the instantaneous growth of the products. Thus, it is very convenient to describe the long-term behavior of the economy due to the well-operating production function. We provide a detailed stability analysis of the steady state in the continuous time structure with time delays. We further investigate the equilibrium points of a system of three connected NGMs, positive equilibria and conditions for stability with stochastic-type effects that are directly proportional to the obtained equilibrium from deviation of the system state. For the numerical simulations, we use spectral methods based on Legendre polynomials [20–27].

The remaining structure of the article is: In Section 2, the mathematical model is formulated with time delays, followed by the description of the method in Section 3. Some preliminary results are given in Section 4. A stability analysis is presented in Section 5. For the confirmation of theoretical results, some numerical tests are performed in Section 6, and Section 7 concludes the article.

2. Model Description

To study the three connected NGMs and discuss the stability of the zero equilibrium under stochastic effects, the stochastic three connected NGMs have the following form:

$$\begin{cases} dx_1(t) = \big[-\alpha_1 x_1(t) + \beta_1 x_2(t) + \gamma_1 x_3(t) + \delta_1 x_1^{\nu_1}(t-\tau_1)e^{-\rho_1 x_1(t-\tau_1)}\big]dt + \sigma_1 x_1(t)dB_1(t) \\ dx_2(t) = \big[-\alpha_2 x_2(t) + \beta_2 x_3(t) + \gamma_2 x_1(t) + \delta_2 x_2^{\nu_2}(t-\tau_2)e^{-\rho_2 x_2(t-\tau_2)}\big]dt + \sigma_2 x_2(t)dB_2(t) \\ dx_3(t) = \big[-\alpha_3 x_3(t) + \beta_3 x_1(t) + \gamma_3 x_2(t) + \delta_3 x_3^{\nu_3}(t-\tau_3)e^{-\rho_3 x_3(t-\tau_3)}\big]dt + \sigma_3 x_3(t)dB_3(t), \end{cases} \tag{1}$$

with initial values:

$$x_i(s) = \varrho_i(s); \quad s \in [-\tau, 0]; \quad \varrho \in C([-\tau, 0], \mathbb{R}_+); \quad i = 1, 2, 3. \tag{2}$$

x is the capital per labor, where $\mathbb{R}_+ = (0, +\infty)$, and $\alpha_i, (i = 1, 2, 3)$ are each positive. Moreover, β_i and γ_i are the coupling coefficients, where all the remaining parameters δ_i, ν_i, ρ_i and $\tau = \max\{\tau_1, \tau_2, \tau_3\}$, are greater than zero. $\beta_i(t)(i = 1, 2, 3)$ are independent white noises and $\sigma_i^2(i = 1, 2, 3)$ denote noises intensities. For brief details of the above parameters backdrop, we refer the readers to [28]. The neoclassical growth differential system with a delay and with variable coefficients is investigated in [29–31]. Shaikhet studies the two connected NGMs with stochastic perturbation and investigates the stability of equilibrium [32]. Some research work related to the stochastic delay system, stochastic fractional delay system, stochastic complex network with delay and stochastic highly nonlinear coupled system with delays can be found in [33–37]. In the literature, to the best of our knowledge, no one has considered the three connected stochastic systems. The main motivation of this work is to consider the three connected NGMs and to apply a high-order numerical scheme based on Legendre polynomials along with theoretical justifications.

3. Description of the Method

This section incorporated the spectral method (SM) for solving the stochastic neoclassical growth model given by Equation (1). In the present method, we used Legendre Gauss quadrature along with the weight function. For the SM, we consider the Legendre Gauss Lobatto points $\{t_j\}_{j=0}^{N}$.

Our aim in this study is to develop an approximate solution to Equation (1). We apply the integral of Equation (1) from $[0, t]$, then:

$$\begin{aligned}
x_1(t) &= x_1(0) + \int_0^t \Big(- \alpha_1 x_1(s) + \beta_1 x_2(s) + \gamma_1 x_3(s) + \delta_1 x_1^{\nu_1}(s - \tau_1) e^{-\rho_1 x_1(s-\tau_1)} \Big) ds \\
&+ \int_0^t \sigma_1 x_1(s) dB(s), \\
x_2(t) &= x_2(0) + \int_0^t \Big(- \alpha_2 x_2(s) + \beta_2 x_3(s) + \gamma_2 x_1(s) + \delta_2 x_2^{\nu_2}(s - \tau_2) e^{-\rho_2 x_2(s-\tau_2)} \Big) ds \\
&+ \int_0^t \sigma_2 x_2(s) dB(s), \\
x_3(t) &= x_3(0) + \int_0^t \Big(- \alpha_3 x_3(s) + \beta_3 x_1(s) + \gamma_3 x_2(s) + \delta_3 x_3^{\nu_3}(s - \tau_3) e^{-\rho_3 x_3(s-\tau_3)} \Big) ds \\
&+ \int_0^t \sigma_3 x_3(s) dB(s), \qquad (3)
\end{aligned}$$

where $x_1(0), x_2(0)$ and $x_3(0)$ are the initial values for the functions $x_1(t), x_2(t)$ and $x_3(t)$, respectively. Taking linear transformation $s = \frac{t}{2}(1+\theta) = \eta$(say) to analyze the SM over standard interval $[-1, 1]$ in Equation (3):

$$\begin{aligned}
x_1(t) &= x_1(0) + \frac{t}{2} \int_{-1}^1 \Big(- \alpha_1 x_1(\eta) + \beta_1 x_2(\eta) + \gamma_1 x_3(\eta) + \delta_1 x_1^{\nu_1}(\eta - \tau_1) e^{-\rho_1 x_1(\eta-\tau_1)} \Big) d\theta \\
&+ \frac{t}{2} \int_{-1}^1 \sigma_1 x_1(\eta) dB(\theta), \\
x_2(t) &= x_2(0) + \frac{t}{2} \int_{-1}^1 \Big(- \alpha_2 x_2(\eta) + \beta_2 x_3(\eta) + \gamma_2 x_1(\eta) + \delta_2 x_2^{\nu_2}(\eta - \tau_2) e^{-\rho_2 x_2(\eta-\tau_2)} \Big) d\theta \\
&+ \frac{t}{2} \int_{-1}^1 \sigma_2 x_2(\eta) dB(\theta), \\
x_3(t) &= x_3(0) + \frac{t}{2} \int_{-1}^1 \Big(- \alpha_3 x_3(\eta) + \beta_3 x_1(\eta) + \gamma_3 x_2(\eta) + \delta_3 x_3^{\nu_3}(\eta - \tau_3) e^{-\rho_3 x_3(\eta-\tau_3)} \Big) d\theta \\
&+ \frac{t}{2} \int_{-1}^1 \sigma_3 x_3(\eta) dB(\theta), \qquad (4)
\end{aligned}$$

The spectral equations (semi-discretised) form of Equation (4) is given by

$$\begin{aligned}
x_1(t) &= x_1(0) + \frac{t}{2} \sum_{k=0}^N \Big(- \alpha_1 x_1(\eta) + \beta_1 x_2(\eta) + \gamma_1 x_3(\eta) + \delta_1 x_1^{\nu_1}(\eta - \tau_1) e^{-\rho_1 x_1(\eta-\tau_1)} \Big) \omega_k \\
&+ \frac{t}{2} \sum_{k=0}^N \sigma_1 x_1(\eta) \omega_k^*, \\
x_2(t) &= x_2(0) + \frac{t}{2} \sum_{k=0}^N \Big(- \alpha_2 x_2(\eta) + \beta_2 x_3(\eta) + \gamma_2 x_1(\eta) + \delta_2 x_2^{\nu_2}(\eta - \tau_2) e^{-\rho_2 x_2(\eta-\tau_2)} \Big) \omega_k \\
&+ \frac{t}{2} \sum_{k=0}^N \sigma_2 x_2(\eta) \omega_k^*, \\
x_3(t) &= x_3(0) + \frac{t}{2} \sum_{k=0}^N \Big(- \alpha_3 x_3(\eta) + \beta_3 x_1(\eta) + \gamma_3 x_2(\eta) + \delta_3 x_3^{\nu_3}(\eta - \tau_3) e^{-\rho_3 x_3(\eta-\tau_3)} \Big) \omega_k \\
&+ \frac{t}{2} \sum_{k=0}^N \sigma_3 x_3(\eta) \omega_k^*, \qquad (5)
\end{aligned}$$

where the Legendre–Gauss quadrature with weights are

$$\omega_k = \frac{2}{[L'_{N+1}(s_k)]^2(1-s_k^2)}, \qquad 0 \le k \le N.$$

Similarly, $\omega_k^* = \sqrt{\omega_k} \times randn(1,N)$ is the stochastic weight function.

To find the numerical solution for the proposed system, we used the Legendre polynomials of the following form:

$$x_1(t) = \sum_{n=0}^{N} a_n P_n(t), \quad x_2(t) = \sum_{n=0}^{N} b_n P_n(t), \quad x_3(t) = \sum_{n=0}^{N} c_n P_n(t) \tag{6}$$

In the above equation, a_n, b_n, c_n are the Legendre coefficients for the classes x_1, x_2, x_3, respectively, where $P_n(t)$ are the Legendre polynomials. Incorporating Equation (6) into Equation (5), we get the following algebraic system

$$\begin{aligned}
\sum_{n=0}^{N} a_n P_n(t) &= \sum_{n=0}^{N} a_n P_n(0) + \frac{t}{2}\sum_{k=0}^{N}\Big(-\alpha_1 \sum_{n=0}^{N} a_n P_n(\eta) + \beta_1 \sum_{n=0}^{N} b_n P_n(\eta) + \gamma_1 \sum_{n=0}^{N} c_n P_n(\eta) \\
&\quad + \delta_1 \sum_{n=0}^{N} a_n^{\nu_1} P_n^{\nu_1}(\eta-\tau_1) e^{-\rho_1 \sum_{n=0}^{N} a_n P_n(\eta-\tau_1)}\Big)\omega_k + \frac{t}{2}\sum_{k=0}^{N}\sigma_1 \sum_{n=0}^{N} a_n P_n(\eta)\omega_k^*, \\
\sum_{n=0}^{N} b_n P_n(t) &= \sum_{n=0}^{N} b_n P_n(0) + \frac{t}{2}\sum_{k=0}^{N}\Big(-\alpha_2 \sum_{n=0}^{N} b_n P_n(\eta) + \beta_2 \sum_{n=0}^{N} c_n P_n(\eta) + \gamma_2 \sum_{n=0}^{N} a_n P_n(\eta) \\
&\quad + \delta_2 \sum_{n=0}^{N} b_n^{\nu_2} P_n^{\nu_2}(\eta-\tau_2) e^{-\rho_2 \sum_{n=0}^{N} b_n P_n(\eta-\tau_2)}\Big)\omega_k + \frac{t}{2}\sum_{k=0}^{N}\sigma_2 \sum_{n=0}^{N} b_n P_n(\eta)\omega_k^*, \\
\sum_{n=0}^{N} c_n P_n(t) &= \sum_{n=0}^{N} c_n P_n(0) + \frac{t}{2}\sum_{k=0}^{N}\Big(-\alpha_3 \sum_{n=0}^{N} c_n P_n(\eta) + \beta_3 \sum_{n=0}^{N} a_n P_n(t)(\eta) + \gamma_3 \sum_{n=0}^{N} b_n P_n(\eta) \\
&\quad + \delta_3 \sum_{n=0}^{N} c_n^{\nu_3} P_n^{\nu_3}(\eta-\tau_3) e^{-\rho_3 \sum_{n=0}^{N} c_n P_n(\eta-\tau_3)}\Big)\omega_k + \frac{t}{2}\sum_{k=0}^{N}\sigma_3 \sum_{n=0}^{N} c_n P_n(\eta)\omega_k^*.
\end{aligned} \tag{7}$$

Thus there is $3N+3$ unknowns in the system given in Equation (7) with $3N$ nonlinear algebraic equations. After incorporating the initial conditions, we get

$$\sum_{n=0}^{N} a_n P_n(0) = \sum_{n=0}^{N} (\varrho_1)_n, \quad \sum_{n=0}^{N} b_n P_n(0) = \sum_{n=0}^{N} (\varrho_2)_n \quad \sum_{n=0}^{N} c_n P_n(0) = \sum_{n=0}^{N} (\varrho_3)_n. \tag{8}$$

Now, using Equation (7) along with Equation (8) results in $3N+3$ nonlinear equations having $3N+3$ unknowns. We obtain the numerical solution to the proposed stochastic system given in Equation (1) by incorporating the values of these unknowns into Equation (6).

4. Preliminary Results

In the current section, we recommend a few fundamental lemmas and definitions, which might be useful for showing the continuation of the unique global positive solution of Equation (1).

Definition 1. *The proposed system in Equation (1) is bounded in the mean if for each positive $M > 0$ free from the initial conditions of Equation (2) as*

$$\limsup_{t\to\infty} \mathbb{E}|x(t)| \le M \tag{9}$$

Lemma 1. *Let $\nu, \rho > 0$, and $f(x) = x^\nu e^{-\rho x}$, then $f(x) \le (\frac{\nu}{\rho e})^\nu$ for $x \in \mathbb{R}_+$.*

Proof. The proof is simple and is left for the reader. □

Lemma 2. *If* $a_i \in \mathbb{R}, b_i, c_i \in \mathbb{R}_+, (i = 1,2,3)$, *then* $\frac{a_1x^2+(b_1+c_1)x+a_2y^2+(b_2+c_2)y+a_3z^2+(b_3+c_3)z}{1+x^2+y^2+z^2}$ $\leq D(a_1, a_2, a_3, b_1, b_2, b_3, c_1, c_2, c_3)$ *where* $D(a_1, a_2, a_3, b_1, b_2, b_3, c_1, c_2, c_3) =$

$$\begin{cases} \left(a_1 + \sqrt{a_1^2 + b_1^2 + c_1^2} + a_2 + \sqrt{a_2^2 + b_2^2 + c_2^2} + a_3 + \sqrt{a_3^2 + b_3^2 + c_3^2}\right)/2, & a_1, a_2, a_3 \geq 0, \\ -(b_1^2 + c_1^2)/4a_1 - (b_2^2 + c_2^2)/4a_2 - (b_3^2 + c_3^2)/4a_3, & a_1, a_2, a_3 < 0, \\ \left(a_1 + \sqrt{a_1^2 + b_1^2 + c_1^2}\right)/2 - (b_2^2 + c_2^2)/4a_2 - (b_3^2 + c_3^2)/4a_3, & a_1 \geq 0; a_2, a_3 < 0, \\ \left(a_2 + \sqrt{a_2^2 + b_2^2 + c_2^2} + a_3 + \sqrt{a_3^2 + b_3^2 + c_3^2}\right)/2 - (b_1^2 + c_1^2)/4a_1, & a_1 < 0; a_2, a_3 \geq 0. \end{cases}$$

Proof. By using Lemma 1.2 of [38] for the two connected neoclassical models, we can obtain the result easily for three connected neoclassicals, so we discard the proof. □

Lemma 3. *For any given initial conditions of Equation (2), there exists a unique global positive solution* $x(t) = (x_1(t), x_2(t), x_3(t))$ *of Equation (1) in a closed interval* $[-\tau, +\infty]$, *and each* $x_i(t), (i = 1,2,3)$ *will be a positive with unit probability.*

Proof. It is simple to see that for $t \in [0, \tau]$, then the proposed system given in Equation (1) along with the initial conditions of Equation (2) reduces to the linear stochastic system, now by using Theorem 3.3.1 of [39], provided that there is a unique stable solution $x(t)$ in the interval $[0, \tau]$: if solution $x(t)$ is in the interval $[0, \tau]$ once it is known, then we can easily proceed such arguments in the intervals $[\tau, 2\tau]$, $[2\tau, 3\tau]$... Therefore, we will obtain the solution of the max interval $[-\tau, \mu_e]$, where μ_e denotes the explosion time. Now, to prove $\mu_e = \infty$, we assume that $m_0 \geq 1$, is a sufficiently large number, such as:

$$\frac{1}{m_0} < \min_{\tau \leq t \leq 0} \varrho_i(t) \leq \max_{\tau \leq t \leq 0} \varrho_i(t) < m_0.$$

Therefore, for each integer $m \geq m_0$, the stopping time is defined by:

$$\mu_m = \inf\left\{t \in [0, \mu_e) : x_i(t) \in (\frac{1}{m}, m), \qquad i = 1,2,3\right\},$$

where we assume that ϕ is the empty set with the usual convention $\inf \phi = +\infty$. Obviously, μ_m is consistently increasing as $m \to \infty$. We set $\mu_\infty = \lim_{m\to\infty} \mu_m$, where $\mu_\infty \leq \mu_e$. If $\mu_\infty = \infty$ can be proven, then $\mu_e = \infty$ where $x_i(t) \in \mathbb{R}_+ \;\; i = 1,2,3$ as $t \geq 0$. For this we need to prove that $\mu_\infty = \infty$. To do this, we must define C^2-function $V : \mathbb{R}_+ \times \mathbb{R}_+ \times \mathbb{R}_+ \to \mathbb{R}_+$ by $V(x_1, x_2, x_3) = \sum_{i=1}^{3}(x_i - 1 - \ln x_i)$. For $t \in [0, \mu_m \wedge T)$ to show this, we use the Itô formula:

$$\begin{aligned} dV(x_1(t), x_2(t), x_3(t)) &= LV(x_1(t), x_2(t), x_3(t), x_1(t-\tau_1), x_2(t-\tau_2), x_3(t-\tau_3))dt \\ &+ \sum_{i=1}^{3} \sigma_i(x_i(t) - 1)dB_i(t), \end{aligned} \tag{10}$$

where $m \geq m_0, T > 0$ is arbitrary, and the operator's LV is defined by

$$\begin{aligned} &LV(x_1(t), x_2(t), x_3(t), x_1(t-\tau_1), x_2(t-\tau_2), x_3(t-\tau_3)) \\ &= \sum_{i=1}^{3}\left(\alpha_i + \frac{\sigma_i^2}{2} + \delta_i x_i^{\nu_i}(t-\tau_i)e^{-\rho x_i(t-\tau_i)} - \frac{\delta_i x_i^{\nu_i}(t-\tau_i)e^{-\rho x_i(t-\tau_i)}}{x_i(t)}\right) \\ &- (\alpha_1 - (\beta_3 + \gamma_2))x_1(t) - (\alpha_2 - (\beta_1 + \gamma_3))x_2(t) - (\alpha_3 - (\beta_2 + \gamma_1))x_3(t) \\ &- \frac{(\beta_1 + \gamma_3)x_2^2(t) + (\beta_2 + \gamma_1)x_3^2(t) + (\beta_3 + \gamma_2)x_1^2(t)}{x_1(t)x_2(t)x_3(t)}. \end{aligned} \tag{11}$$

We use the inequality $y \leq 3(y-1-\ln y)+3$ for all $y \in \mathbb{R}_+$, along with Lemma 1, then we can find Equation (11):

$$\begin{aligned}
&LV\big(x_1(t), x_2(t), x_3(t), x_1(t-\tau_1), x_2(t-\tau_2), x_3(t-\tau_3)\big) \\
&\leq \sum_{i=1}^{3}\left(\alpha_i + \frac{\sigma_i^2}{2} + \delta_i\left(\frac{v_i}{\rho_i e}\right)^{v_i}\right) + 6\max\Big\{|\alpha_1-(\gamma_2+\beta_3)|, |\alpha_2-(\beta_1+\gamma_3)|, |\alpha_3-(\gamma_1+\beta_2)|\Big\} \\
&+ 3\max\Big\{|\alpha_1-(\gamma_2+\beta_3)|, |\alpha_2-(\beta_1+\gamma_3)|, |\alpha_3-(\gamma_1+\beta_2)|\Big\}V\big(x_1(t), x_2(t), x_3(t)\big) \\
&= 3\max\Big\{|\alpha_1-(\gamma_2+\beta_3)|, |\alpha_2-(\beta_1+\gamma_3)|, |\alpha_3-(\gamma_1+\beta_2)|\Big\}V\big(x_1(t), x_2(t), x_3(t)\big) + L,
\end{aligned} \tag{12}$$

where $L = \sum_{i=1}^{3}\left(\alpha_i + \frac{\sigma_i^2}{2} + \delta_i\left(\frac{v_i}{\rho_i e}\right)^{v_i}\right) + 6\max\Big\{|\alpha_1-(\gamma_2+\beta_3)|, |\alpha_2-(\beta_1+\gamma_3)|, |\alpha_3-(\gamma_1+\beta_2)|\Big\}$.

We assume that each $m \geq m_0$ applies integrals on both sides of Equation (10) from 0 to $\mu_m \wedge T$, then

$$\begin{aligned}
&\mathbb{E}V\big(x_1(\mu_m \wedge T), x_2(\mu_m \wedge T), x_3(\mu_m \wedge T)\big) \\
&\leq L_1 + 3\max\Big\{|\alpha_1-(\gamma_2+\beta_3)|, |\alpha_2-(\beta_1+\gamma_3)|, |\alpha_3-(\gamma_1+\beta_2)|\Big\} \\
&\times \mathbb{E}\int_0^{\mu_m \wedge T} V\big(x_1(t), x_2(t), x_3(t)\big)dt \\
&\leq L_1 + 3\max\Big\{|\alpha_1-(\gamma_2+\beta_3)|, |\alpha_2-(\beta_1+\gamma_3)|, |\alpha_3-(\gamma_1+\beta_2)|\Big\} \\
&\times \int_0^{T} \mathbb{E}V\big(x_1(\mu_m \wedge t), x_2(\mu_m \wedge t), x_3(\mu_m \wedge t)\big)dt,
\end{aligned} \tag{13}$$

where $L_1 := V\big(x_1(0), x_2(0), x_3(0)\big) + LT$. Using the Gronwall inequality, we obtain from Equation (13) that

$$\begin{aligned}
&\mathbb{E}V\big(x_1(\mu_m \wedge T), x_2(\mu_m \wedge T), x_3(\mu_m \wedge t)\big) \\
&\leq L_1 e^{3T\max\{|\alpha_1-(\beta_3+\gamma_2)|, |\alpha_2-(\beta_1+\gamma_3)|, |\alpha_3-(\beta_2+\gamma_1)|\}}.
\end{aligned} \tag{14}$$

Since for each $\eta \in \{\mu_m \wedge T\}$ there certainly exists one of $x_1(\mu_m, \eta)$ or $x_2(\mu_m, \eta)$ or $x_3(\mu_m, \eta)$, which are equal to m or $1/m$, therefore, $V\big(x_1(\mu_m \wedge T), x_2(\mu_m \wedge T), x_3(\mu_m \wedge t)\big) \geq (m-1-\ln m) \wedge (\frac{1}{m} + \ln m - 1)$. Then it follows from Equation (14) that

$$\begin{aligned}
&L_1 e^{3T\max\{|\alpha_1-(\gamma_2+\beta_3)|, |\alpha_2-(\beta_1+\gamma_3)|, |\alpha_3-(\gamma_1+\beta_2)|\}} \\
&\geq \mathbb{E}V\big(x_1(\mu_m \wedge T), x_2(\mu_m \wedge T), x_3(\mu_m \wedge t)\big) \\
&\geq \mathbb{E}\Big[I_{\mu_m \leq T}(\eta)V\big(x_1(\mu_m \wedge T), x_2(\mu_m \wedge T), x_3(\mu_m \wedge t)\big)\Big] \\
&\geq P\{\mu_m \leq T\}(m - \ln m - 1) \wedge (\frac{1}{m} + \ln m - 1),
\end{aligned}$$

here, $I_{\mu_m \leq T}$ should be the indicator function of $\{\mu_m \leq T\}$. Since $m \to \infty$, there exists $\lim_{m \to \infty} P\{\mu_m \leq T\} = 0$; therefore, $P\{\mu_\infty \leq T\} = 0$. Since T is an arbitrary positive, we must have $P\{\mu_\infty < \infty\} = 0$. Therefore, $P\{\mu_\infty = \infty\} = 1$ is the required result. □

Remark 1. *It is essential to the inspection whether or not the solution of Equation (1), along with initial values of Equation (2), will not collapse to infinity in a finite time (global existence). Indeed, we cannot obtain the global existence of the proposed solution only from the explicit expression of the given system. Although Lemma 3 is fundamental to the study of the global existence of the positive solution for the proposed system of Equation (1). It is worth declaring that by using Lemma 3, we can show the proposed stochastic delay Equation (1) in the sense that we have a positive solution that will not collapse to infinity in finite time.*

5. Main Results

In the present section, we discuss the important properties of the proposed system given in Equation (1), which are the criteria for the alternate boundedness in the mean.

Theorem 1. *If $(\alpha_1 > \beta_3 + \gamma_2)$, $(\alpha_2 > \beta_1 + \gamma_3)$ and $(\alpha_3 > \beta_2 + \gamma_1)$, then the global solution $x(t) = (x_1(t), x_2(t), x_3(t))$ of Equation (1) with the initial values Equation (2) of $t \geq 0$ are positive almost surely and satisfy:*

$$\limsup_{t\to\infty} \mathbb{E}|x(t)| \leq \frac{\delta}{\alpha} \tag{15}$$

and

$$\limsup_{t\to\infty} \frac{1}{t}\int_0^t \mathbb{E}(x_1^p(t) + x_2^p(t) + x_3^p(t))ds \leq Q_1 + Q_2 + Q_3, \tag{16}$$

*where $\alpha = \min\{\alpha_1 - (\beta_3 + \gamma_2), \alpha_2 - (\beta_1 + \gamma_3), \alpha_3 - (\beta_2 + \gamma_1)\}$, $\delta = \sum_{i=1}^{3} \delta_i \left(\frac{v_i}{\rho_i e}\right)^{v_i}$, and $p \geq 1$ such that $A_1 := \alpha_1 - (\beta_3 + \gamma_2) - \frac{p-1}{2}\sigma_1^2 + \frac{p-1}{p}(\beta_3 + \gamma_2 - (\beta_1 + \gamma_1)) > 0$,
$A_2 := \alpha_2 - (\beta_1 + \gamma_3) - \frac{p-1}{2}\sigma_2^2 + \frac{p-1}{p}(\beta_1 + \gamma_3 - (\beta_2 + \gamma_2)) > 0$ and
$A_3 := \alpha_3 - (\beta_2 + \gamma_1) - \frac{p-1}{2}\sigma_3^2 + \frac{p-1}{p}(\beta_2 + \gamma_1 - (\beta_3 + \gamma_3)) > 0$,
$Q_i = \max_{y\geq 0}\{-pA_i y^p + p\delta_i(\frac{v_i}{\rho_i e})^{v_i} y^{p-1}\}, i = 1, 2, 3$. Namely, Equation (1) is ultimately bounded in the mean.*

Proof. In the highlights of Lemma 3, we can easily see that $x(t) > 0$ for $t \geq 1$ almost surely. Moreover, by using Lemma 1, we get:

$$d(x_1(t) + x_2(t) + x_3(t)) \leq [-\alpha(x_1(t) + x_2(t) + x_3(t)) + \delta]dt + \sum_{i=1}^{3} \sigma_i x_i(t) dB_i(t), \tag{17}$$

Now, applying Itô formula, Equation (17) takes the form:

$$d[e^{\alpha t}(x_1(t) + x_2(t) + x_3(t))] \leq \delta e^{\alpha t} dt + \sum_{i=1}^{3} \sigma_i e^{\alpha t} x_i(t) dB_i(t), \tag{18}$$

now integrating Equation (18) from $0, t$, we get:

$$e^{\alpha t}\mathbb{E}(x_1(t) + x_2(t) + x_3(t)) \leq x_1(0) + x_2(0) + x_3(0) + \frac{\delta}{\alpha}(e^{\alpha t} - 1),$$

$$\Rightarrow \limsup_{t\to\infty} \mathbb{E}(x_1(t) + x_2(t) + x_3(t)) \leq \frac{\delta}{\alpha},$$

In view of Lemma 1, Young's inequality and the Itô formula follow from Equation (1), such that:

$$
\begin{aligned}
d(x_1^p(t)+x_2^p(t)+x_3^p(t)) &= p\Big\{-\Big(\alpha_1-\frac{p-1}{2}\sigma_1^2\Big)x_1^p(t)-\Big(\alpha_2-\frac{p-1}{2}\sigma_2^2\Big)x_2^p(t)\\
&-\Big(\alpha_3-\frac{p-1}{2}\sigma_3^2\Big)x_3^p(t)+(\beta_3+\gamma_2)x_1^{p-1}(t)x_2(t)x_3(t)\\
&+(\beta_1+\gamma_3)x_2^{p-1}(t)x_1(t)x_3(t)+(\beta_2+\gamma_1)x_3^{p-1}(t)x_2(t)x_1(t)\\
&+\sum_{i=1}^{3}\delta_i x_i^{p-1}(t)x_i^{\nu_i}(t-\tau_i)e^{-\rho_i x_i(t-\tau_i}\Big\}dt+\sum_{i=1}^{3}p\sigma_i x_i^p(t)dB_i(t)\\
&\le p\Big\{-\Big(\alpha_1-(\beta_3+\gamma_2)-\frac{p-1}{2}\sigma_1^2\\
&+\frac{p-1}{p}(\beta_3+\gamma_2-(\beta_1+\gamma_1))\Big)x_1^p(t)\\
&-\Big(\alpha_2-(\beta_1+\gamma_3)-\frac{p-1}{2}\sigma_2^2+\frac{p-1}{p}(\beta_1+\gamma_3-(\beta_2+\gamma_2))\Big)x_2^p(t)\\
&-\Big(\alpha_3-(\beta_2+\gamma_1)-\frac{p-1}{2}\sigma_3^2+\frac{p-1}{p}(\beta_2+\gamma_1-(\beta_3+\gamma_3))\Big)x_3^p(t)\\
&+\sum_{i=1}^{3}\delta_i\Big(\frac{\nu_i}{\rho_i e}\Big)^{\nu_i}x_i^{p-1}(t)\Big\}dt+\sum_{i=1}^{3}p\sigma_i x_i^p(t)dB_i(t)\\
&=\sum_{i=1}^{3}\Big\{-pA_i x_i^p(t)+p\delta_i\Big(\frac{\nu_i}{\rho_i e}\Big)^{\nu_i}x_i^{p-1}(t)\Big\}dt+\sum_{i=1}^{3}p\sigma_i x_i^p(t)dB_i(t)\\
&\le\sum_{i=1}^{3}Q_i dt+\sum_{i=1}^{3}p\sigma_i x_i^p(t)dB_i(t),
\end{aligned}
$$

which suggests

$$\lim_{t\to\infty}\sup\frac{1}{t}\int_0^t\mathbb{E}\{x_1^p(t)+x_2^p(t)+x_3^p(t)\}ds\le Q_1+Q_2+Q_3. \tag{19}$$

□

To define the asymptotic estimation for the solution of almost surely, Mao [39] defines the assumptions: $\lim_{t\to\infty}\sup\frac{1}{t}\ln|x(t)|$, known as the sample Lyapunov exponent. Therefore, we will next estimate the Lyapunov exponent of Equation (1) along with with the initial conditions of Equation (2).

Theorem 2. *The sample Lyapunov exponent of the $x(t)=(x_1(t),x_2(t),x_3(t))$ solution of Equation (1) with initial the conditions of Equation (2) satisfies:*

$$\lim_{t\to\infty}\sup\frac{\ln x(t)}{t}\le\frac{G}{3} \tag{20}$$

where $G=D\Big\{-3\alpha_1+\beta_1+\beta_2+\beta_3+\sigma_1^2,-3\alpha_2+\beta_1+\beta_2+\beta_3+\sigma_2^2,-3\alpha_3+\beta_1+\beta_2+\beta_3+\sigma_3^2,-3\alpha_1+\gamma_1+\gamma_2+\gamma_3+\sigma_1^2,-3\alpha_2+\gamma_1+\gamma_2+\gamma_3+\sigma_2^2,-3\alpha_3+\gamma_1+\gamma_2+\gamma_3+\sigma_3^2,3\delta_1\big(\frac{\nu_1}{\rho_1 e}\big)^{\nu_1},3\delta_2\big(\frac{\nu_2}{\rho_2 e}\big)^{\nu_2},3\delta_3\big(\frac{\nu_3}{\rho_3 e}\big)^{\nu_3}\Big\}.$

Proof. Using the Young inequality, Itô formula and Lemma 1 along with Lemma 2, then from Equation (1) we get:

$$
\begin{aligned}
&\ln\left(1+x_1^2(t)+x_2^2(t)+x_3^2(t)\right)\\
&\quad=\ln\left(1+x_1^2(0)+x_2^2(0)+x_3^2(0)\right)+\int_0^t \frac{1}{1+x_1^2(s)+x_2^2(s)+x_3^2(s)}\\
&\quad\times\Big[(-3\alpha_1+\sigma_1^2)x_1^2(s)+(-3\alpha_2+\sigma_2^2)x_2^2(s)+(-3\alpha_3+\sigma_3^2)x_3^2(s)\\
&\quad+3(\beta_1+\beta_2+\beta_3+\gamma_1+\gamma_2+\gamma_3)x_1(s)x_2(s)x_3(s)\\
&\quad+\sum_{i=1}^{3}3\delta_i x_i(s)x_i^{\nu_i}(s-\tau_i)e^{-\rho_i x_i(s-\tau)}\Big]ds\\
&\quad+\sum_{i=1}^{3}\left[M_i(t)-\int_0^t \frac{3\sigma_i^2x_i^4(s)}{\left(1+x_1^2(s)+x_2^2(s)+x_3^2(s)\right)^2}ds\right]\\
&\quad\le\ln\left(1+x_1^2(0)+x_2^2(0)+x_3^2(0)\right)+\int_0^t \frac{1}{1+x_1^2(s)+x_2^2(s)+x_3^2(s)}\\
&\quad\times\Big[(-3\alpha_1+\beta_1+\gamma_1+\beta_2+\gamma_2+\beta_3+\gamma_3+\sigma_1^2)x_1^2(s)\\
&\quad+(-3\alpha_2+\beta_1+\gamma_1+\beta_2+\gamma_2+\beta_3+\gamma_3+\sigma_2^2)x_2^2(s)\\
&\quad+(-3\alpha_3+\beta_1+\gamma_1+\beta_2+\gamma_2+\beta_3+\gamma_3+\sigma_3^2)x_3^2(s)\\
&\quad+\sum_{i=1}^{3}3\delta_i\left(\frac{\nu_i}{\rho_i e}\right)^{\nu_i}x_i(s)\Big]ds+\sum_{i=1}^{3}\left[M_i(t)-\int_0^t \frac{3\sigma_i^2x_i^4(s)}{\left(1+x_1^2(s)+x_2^2(s)+x_3^2(s)\right)^2}ds\right]\\
&\quad\le\ln\left(1+x_1^2(0)+x_2^2(0)+x_3^2(0)\right)+\int_0^t G\,ds\\
&\quad+\sum_{i=1}^{3}\left[M_i(t)-\int_0^t \frac{3\sigma_i^2x_i^4(s)}{\left(1+x_1^2(s)+x_2^2(s)+x_3^2(s)\right)^2}ds\right]
\end{aligned}
\tag{21}
$$

$M_i(t)=\int_0^t \frac{3\sigma_i x_i^2(s)}{1+x_1^2(s)+x_2^2(s)+x_3^2(s)}dB_i(s), i=1,2,3$. Now, for each positive n, applications of the exponential martingale inequality [39] yield to:

$$
p\left\{\sup_{0\le t\le n}\left[M_i(t)-\int_0^t \frac{3\sigma_i^2x_i^4(s)}{\left(1+x_1^2(s)+x_2^2(s)+x_3^2(s)\right)^2}ds\right]>3\ln n\right\}\le\frac{1}{n^2}, i=1,2,3.
$$

By applying the lemma of Borel-Cantelli, for certainly all $\omega\in\Lambda$ there are $n_i=n_i(\omega)\ge 1$ (i = 1, 2, 3) random integers such as:

$$
\sup_{0\le t\le n}\left[M_i(t)-\int_0^t \frac{3\sigma_i^2x_i^4(s)}{\left(1+x_1^2(s)+x_2^2(s)+x_3^2(s)\right)^2}ds\right]\le 3\ln n,\quad n\ge n_i.
$$

Therefore,

$$
M_i(t)\le\int_0^t \frac{3\sigma_i^2x_i^4(s)}{\left(1+x_1^2(s)+x_2^2(s)+x_3^2(s)\right)^2}ds+3\ln n, (i=1,2,3). \tag{22}
$$

Then using Equation (21), together with Equation (22), implies

$$
\ln\left(1+\sum_{i=1}^{3}x_i^2(t)\right)\le Gt+4\ln n+\ln\left(1+\sum_{i=1}^{3}x_i^2(0)\right),
$$

However, each $0 \le t \le n, n \ge n_1 \vee n_2 \vee n_3$. Hence for each $\omega \in \Lambda$, if $n \ge n_1 \vee n_2 \vee n_3$, $n-1 \le t \le n$, certainly we have:

$$\frac{\ln\left(1+x_1^2(t)+x_2^2(t)+x_3^2(t)\right)}{t} \le \frac{\left[Gt+4\ln n+\ln\left(1+x_1^2(0)+x_2^2(0)+x_3^2(0)\right)\right]}{n-1}.$$

When n tends to infinity, then we get:

$$\begin{aligned}\limsup_{n\to\infty}\frac{\ln x_i(t)}{t} &\le \limsup_{n\to\infty}\frac{\ln\left(1+x_1^2(t)+x_2^2(t)+x_3^2(t)\right)}{3t}\\ &\le \limsup_{n\to\infty}\frac{\left[Gn+\frac{4\ln n}{n-1}+\ln\left(1+x_1^2(0)+x_2^2(0)+x_3^2(0)\right)\right]}{3(n-1)}\\ &= \frac{G}{3}, i=1,2,3. \end{aligned} \quad (23)$$

□

Remark 2. *For the existence of a positive solution, the conditions are not necessary from Lemma 3. Therefore, in this article, we have generalized the main results [29,32,40].*

6. Results and Discussion

In the present section, we provide some test examples along with numerical simulations to confirm the theoretical justifications.

Consider the stochastic delay differential NGM system given in Equation (1), with the parameter values given by $\alpha_1 = 1.32, \alpha_2 = 1.9, \alpha_3 = 1.9, \beta_1 = 1, \beta_2 = 1, \beta_3 = 0.5, \gamma_1 = 1, \gamma_2 = 0.8, \gamma_3 = 0.6, \delta_1 = 3, \delta_2 = 2, \delta_3 = 2, \nu_i = 2, \tau_i = \rho_i = 1 (i = 1,2,3)$, with initial values $\varrho_1 = \varrho_2 = \varrho_3 = 1$. From Theorem 2 with Lemma 3 , it follows that the proposed three connected stochastic delay neoclassical growth systems, along with the initial conditions given in Equation (2), have a unique global positive solution, as shown in Figure 1. It also satisfies the sample Lyapunov exponent for the proposed parameter values $\lim_{n\to\infty}\sup\frac{1}{t}\ln x_i(t) \le 24/e^2, (i = 1,2,3)$. Although we choose $p = 1.5$ then we have each $A_1 := \alpha_1 - (\beta_3+\gamma_2) - \frac{p-1}{2}\sigma_1^2 + \frac{p-1}{p}(\beta_3+\gamma_2-(\beta_1+\gamma_1)) > 0$,
$A_2 := \alpha_2 - (\beta_1+\gamma_3) - \frac{p-1}{2}\sigma_2^2 + \frac{p-1}{p}(\beta_1+\gamma_3-(\beta_2+\gamma_2)) > 0$ and
$A_3 := \alpha_3 - (\beta_2+\gamma_1) - \frac{p-1}{2}\sigma_3^2 + \frac{p-1}{p}(\beta_2+\gamma_1-(\beta_3+\gamma_3)) > 0$, $Q_i = \max_{y\ge 0}\{-pA_iy^p + p\delta_i\left(\frac{\nu_i}{\rho_i e}\right)^{\nu_i} y^{p-1}\}, i = 1,2,3$. Namely, Equation (1) is ultimately bounded in the mean by Theorem 1, as shown in Figure 1. Similarly, for the same parameter values given in Figure 1, we draw the comparison of the deterministic (to take in Equation (1) $\sigma_i = 0, i = 1,2,3$) with the stochastic one in Figure 2. We can clearly see that both solutions are in very good agreement. In Figure 3, we use the parameter values $\alpha_1 = 1.26, \alpha_2 = 1.8, \alpha_3 = 1.6, \beta_1 = 1, \beta_2 = 0.8, \beta_3 = 0.5, \gamma_1 = 1, \gamma_2 = 0.8, \gamma_3 = 0.7, \delta_1 = 3, \delta_2 = 2, \delta_3 = 2, \nu_i = 2, \tau_i = \rho_i = 1, \sigma_i = 1, (i = 1,2,3)$. For the above parameter values, the proposed stochastic delay NGM system has an unstable positive solution, clearly seen in Figure 3. Again, using the same parameter values as given in Figure 3 above, we draw the comparisons of both the stochastic system with the deterministic one in Figure 4. Using the parameter values $\alpha_1 = 1.3, \alpha_2 = 1.9, \alpha_3 = 1.9, \beta_1 = 1, \beta_2 = 1, \beta_3 = 0.5, \gamma_1 = 1, \gamma_2 = 0.8, \gamma_3 = 0.6, \delta_1 = 5, \delta_2 = 5, \delta_3 = 4, \nu_i = 0.7, \tau_i = \rho_i = 1, \sigma_i = 1, (i = 1,2,3)$. From the above parameter values, the system given in Equation (1) satisfies the sample Lyapunov exponent and each $A_i, i = 1,2,3$ is greater then zero, along with $Q_i = \max_{y\ge 0}\{-pA_iy^p + p\delta_i\left(\frac{\nu_i}{\rho_i e}\right)^{\nu_i} y^{p-1}\}, i = 1,2,3$. Therefore, from Theorem 1 and Theorem 2, the models are exponentially mean square stable and merge to zero, as shown in Figure 5. Similarly, for the same parameter values as given in Figure 6 above, we draw the comparison of the deterministic with the stochastic one.

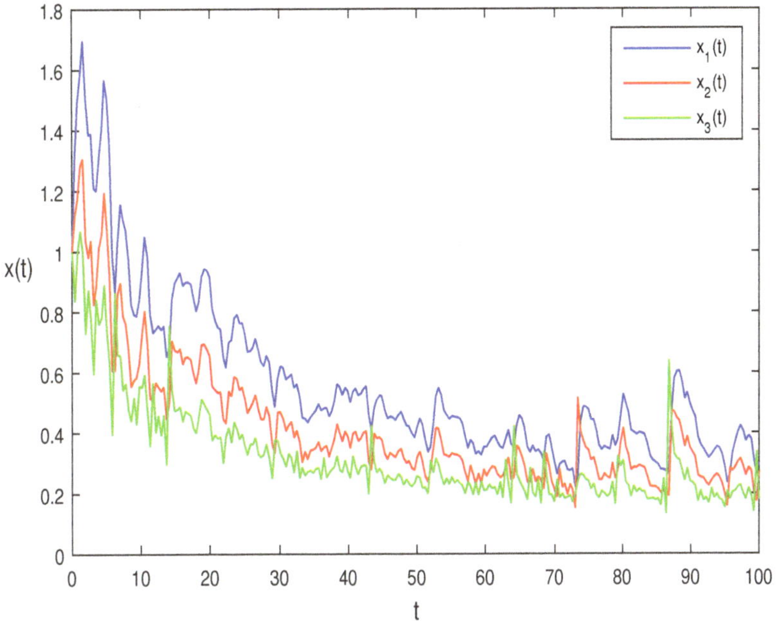

Figure 1. Solution for each class of stochastic delay NGM systems from Equation (1).

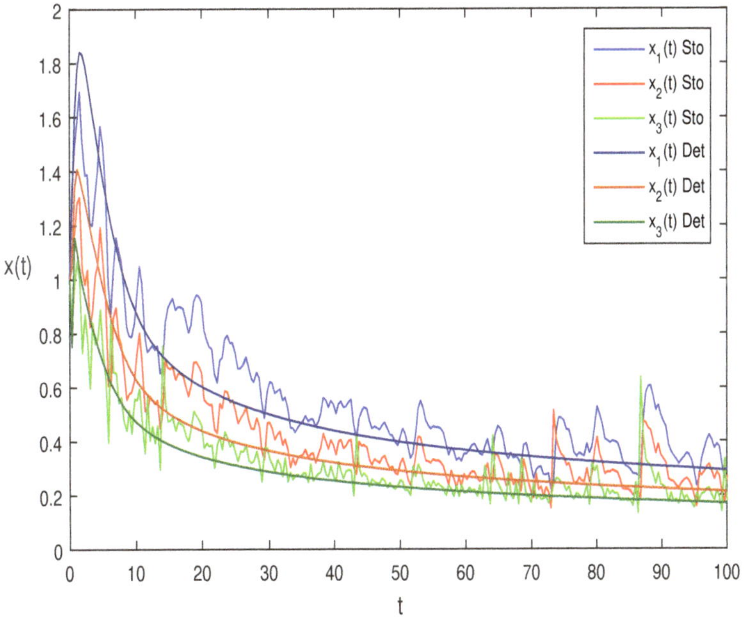

Figure 2. Comparisons of the solutions for each class of stochastic delay NGM systems from Equation (1) with the deterministic model $(\sigma_i = 0), i = 1, 2, 3$.

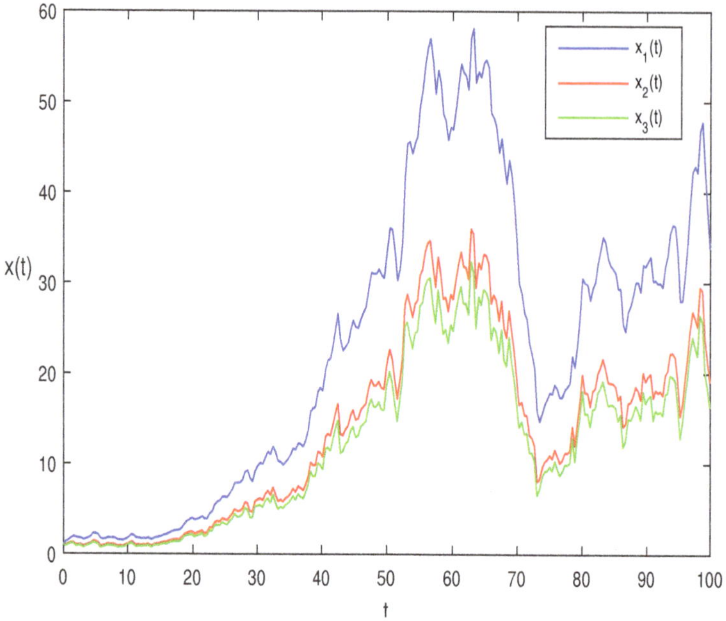

Figure 3. Solution for each class of stochastic delay NGM systems from Equation (1), with $\tau_i = \rho_i = 1$ (i = 1, 2, 3).

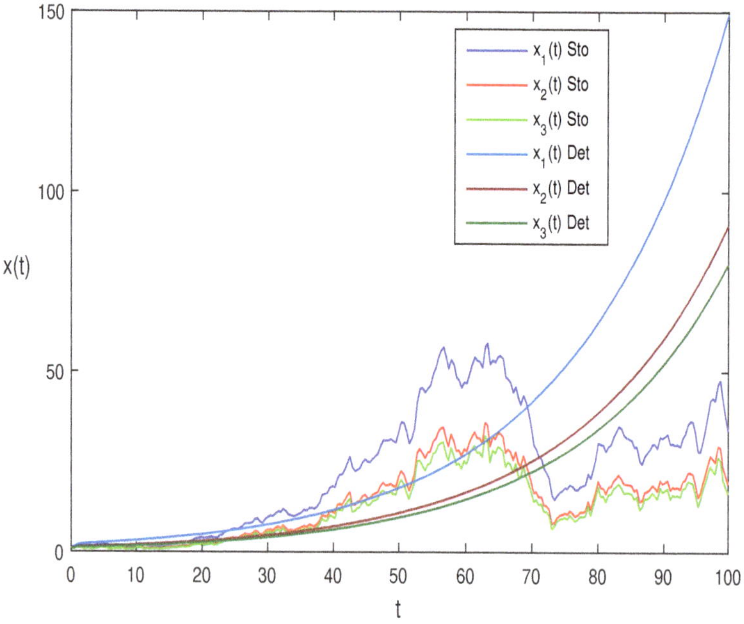

Figure 4. Comparisons of the unstable positive solutions for each class of stochastic delay NGM systems from Equation (1) with the deterministic model, $\sigma_i = 1, (i = 1, 2, 3)$.

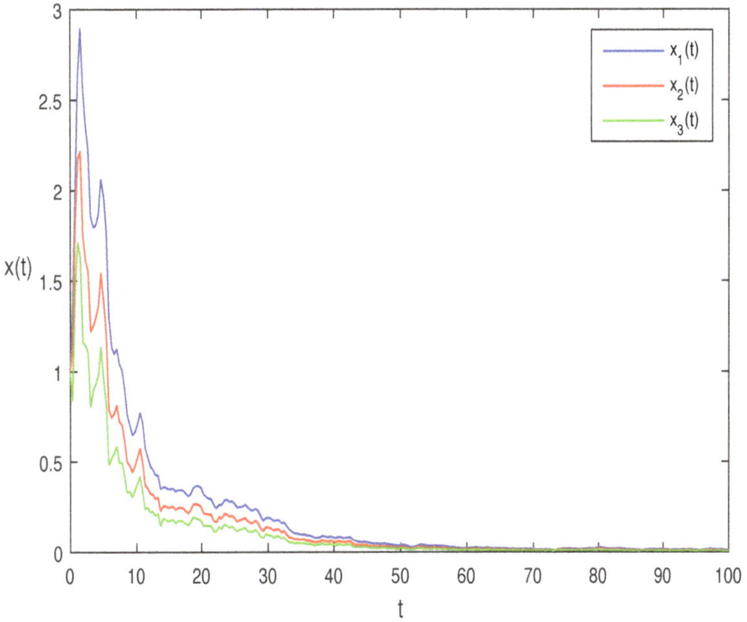

Figure 5. Mean square stable solution for each class of stochastic delay NGM systems from Equation (1).

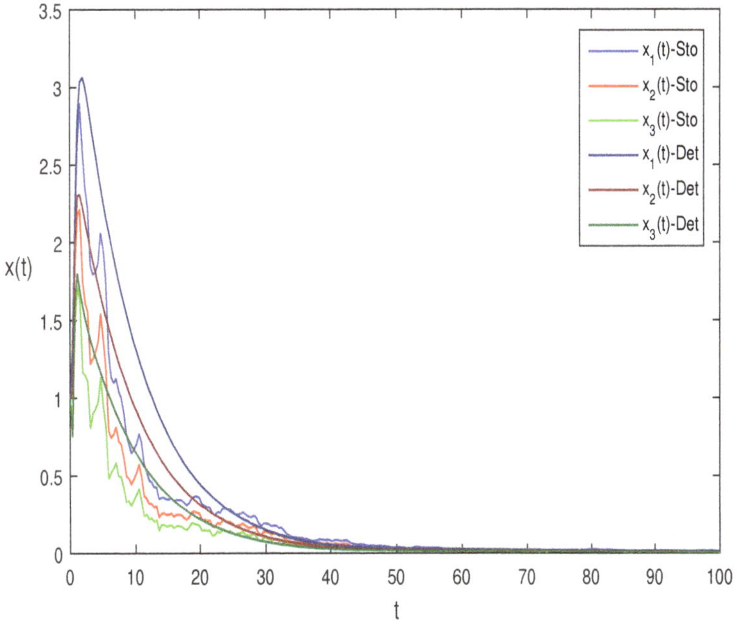

Figure 6. Comparisons of the stable solutions for each class of stochastic delay NGM systems from Equation (1) with the deterministic model, $\sigma_i = 1, (i = 1, 2, 3)$.

7. Conclusions

In this article, we consider a novel approach for three connected delay differential NGMs under stochastic perturbations. It is observed that the nonlinearity and delay can be sources of continuous time chaos. Constant delay can generate complex dynamics involving chaos via period-doubling bifurcation. Stability conditions for positive and zero equilibria of the proposed model are obtained. For numerical simulations, we convert the proposed system to a nonlinear system using a polynomial with Legendre-Gauss quadrature and respective weight functions. We consider both deterministic and stochastic models. It is shown that the proposed stochastic delay NGM system given in Equation (1), along with initial conditions given in Equation (2), has a global positive solution that is conclusively bounded. The numerical results confirm the theoretical justifications.

Author Contributions: Funding acquisition, I.A.; Methodology, S.U.K.; Software, S.U.K.; Supervision, I.A.; Validation, I.A.; Writing—original draft, S.U.K.; Writing—review and editing, I.A. All authors have read and agreed to the published version of the manuscript.

Funding: This work was financially supported by the Deanship of Scientific Research, Vice Presidency for Graduate Studies and Scientific Research, King Faisal University, Saudi Arabia [Project No. GRANT796].

Data Availability Statement: Not applicable.

Acknowledgments: This work was financially supported by the Deanship of Scientific Research, Vice Presidency for Graduate Studies and Scientific Research, King Faisal University, Saudi Arabia [Project No. GRANT796].

Conflicts of Interest: The authors declare no conflict of interest.

References

1. Chen, W.; Wang, W. Global exponential stability for a delay differential neoclassical growth model. *Adv. Differ. Equ.* **2014**, *2014*, 325. [CrossRef]
2. Matsumoto, A.; Szidarovszky, F. Delay differential neoclassical growth model. *J. Econ. Behav. Organ.* **2011**, *78*, 272–289. [CrossRef]
3. Shaikhet, L. Stability of equilibriums of stochastically perturbed delay differential neoclassical growth model. *Discret. Contin. Dyn. Syst.-B* **2017**, *22*, 1565–1573. [CrossRef]
4. Berezansky, L.; Braverman, E.; Idels, L. Nicholson's blowflies differential equations revisited: Main results and open problems. *Appl. Math. Model.* **2010**, *34*, 1405–1417. [CrossRef]
5. Bradul, N.; Shaikhet, L. Stability of the positive point of equilibrium of Nicholson's blowflies equation with stochastic perturbations: Numerical analysis. *Discret. Dyn. Nat. Soc.* **2007**, *2007*, 092959. [CrossRef]
6. Li, J.; Zhang, B.; Li, Y. Dependence of stability of Nicholson's blowflies equation with maturation stage on parameters. *J. Appl. Anal. Comput.* **2017**, *7*, 670–680.
7. Shaikhet, L. Stability of equilibrium states of a nonlinear delay differential equation with stochastic perturbations. *Int. J. Robust Nonlinear Control* **2017**, *27*, 915–924. [CrossRef]
8. Day, R. The emergence of chaos from classical economic growth. *Q. J. Econ.* **1983**, *98*, 203–213. [CrossRef]
9. Day, R. Irregular growth cycles. *Am. Econ. Rev.* **1982**, *72*, 406–414.
10. Bacar, N.; Khaladi, M. On the basic reproduction number in a random environment. *J. Math. Biol.* **2013**, *67*, 1729–1739. [CrossRef]
11. Bacar, N.; Ed-Darraz, A. On linear birth-and-death processes in a random environment. *J. Math. Biol.* **2014**, *69*, 7390. [CrossRef] [PubMed]
12. Matsumoto, A.; Szidarovszky, F. Asymptotic Behavior of a Delay Differential Neoclassical Growth Model. *Sustainability* **2013**, *5*, 440–455. [CrossRef]
13. Day, R. *Complex Economic Dynamics: An Introduction to Dynamical Systems and Market Mechanism*; MIT Press: Cambridge, MA, USA, 1994.
14. Puu, T. *Attractions, Bifurcations and Chaos: Nonlinear Phenomena in Economics*, 2nd ed.; Springer: Berlin/Heidelberg, Germany; New York, NY, USA, 2003.
15. Bischi, G.-I.; Chiarella, C.; Kopel, M.; Szidarovszky, F. *Nonlinear Oligopolies*; Springer: Berlin/Heidelberg, Germany, 2010.
16. Hunt, B.R.; Kennedy, J.A.; Li, T.Y.; Nusse, H.E. (Eds.) *The Theory of Chaotic Attractors*; Springer Science and Business Media: New York, NY, USA, 2013.
17. Rosser, J.B. *Complexity in Economics: The International Library of Critical Writings in Economics*; Edward Elgar Publishing: Aldergate, UK, 2004; 174.
18. Swan, T.W. Economic growth and capital accumulation. *Econ. Rec.* **1956**, *32*, 334–361. [CrossRef]
19. Solow, R.M. A contribution to the theory of economic growth. *Q. J. Econ.* **1956**, *70*, 65–94. [CrossRef]
20. Gul, N.; Khan, S.U.; Ali, I.; Khan, F.U. Transmission dynamic of stochastic hepatitis C model by spectral collocation method. *Comput. Methods Biomech. Biomed. Eng.* **2022**, *25*, 578–592. [CrossRef]

21. Ali, A.; Khan, S.U.; Ali, I.; Khan, F.U. On dynamics of stochastic avian influenza model with asymptomatic carrier using spectral method. *Math. Methods Appl. Sci.* **2022**, *45*, 8230–8246. [CrossRef]
22. Khan, S.U.; Ali, I. Application of Legendre spectral-collocation method to delay differential and stochastic delay differential equation. *AIP Adv.* **2018**, *8*, 035301. [CrossRef]
23. Khan, S.U.; Ali, M.; Ali, I. A spectral collocation method for stochastic Volterra integro-differential equations and its error analysis. *J. Adv. Differ. Equ.* **2019**, *1*, 161. [CrossRef]
24. Khan, S.U.; Ali, I. Numerical analysis of stochastic SIR model by Legendre spectral collocation method. *Adv. Mech. Eng.* **2019**, *11*, 1687814019862918. [CrossRef]
25. Ali, I.; Khan, S.U. Analysis of stochastic delayed SIRS model with exponential birth and saturated incidence rate. *Chaos Solitons Fractals* **2020**, *138*, 110008. [CrossRef]
26. Khan, S.U.; Ali, I. Convergence and error analysis of a spectral collocation method for solving system of nonlinear Fredholm integral equations of second kind. *Comput. Appl. Math.* **2019**, *38*, 125. [CrossRef]
27. Khan, S.U.; Ali, I. Applications of Legendre spectral collocation method for solving system of time delay differential equations. *Adv. Mech. Eng.* **2020**, *12*, 1687814020922113. [CrossRef]
28. Wang, W.; Chen, W. Stochastic delay differential neoclassical growth system. *Stoch. Model.* **2021**, *37*, 415–425. [CrossRef]
29. Keeling, M.J.; Rohani, P. *Modeling Infectious Diseases in Human and Animals*; Princeton University Press: Princeton, NJ, USA, 2008.
30. Long, Z.; Wang, W. Positive pseudo almost periodic solutions for a delayed differential neoclassical growth model. *J. Differ. Equ. Appl.* **2016**, *22*, 1893–1905. [CrossRef]
31. Duan, L.; Huang, C. Existence and global attractivity of almost periodic solutions for a delayed differential neoclassical growth model. *Math. Methods Appl. Sci.* **2017**, *40*, 814–822. [CrossRef]
32. Shaikhet, L. Stability of the Zero and Positive Equilibria of Two Connected Neoclassical Growth Models under Stochastic Perturbations. *Commun. Nonlinear Sci. Numer. Simul.* **2019**, *68*, 86–93 [CrossRef]
33. Ali, I.; Khan, S.U. Threshold of Stochastic SIRS Epidemic Model from Infectious to Susceptible Class with Saturated Incidence Rate Using Spectral Method. *Symmetry* **2022**, *14*, 1838. [CrossRef]
34. Liu, Y.; Li, Y.-M.; Wang, J.-L. Intermittent Control to Stabilization of Stochastic Highly Non-Linear Coupled Systems With Multiple Time Delays. *IEEE Trans. Neural Netw. Learn. Syst.* **2021**, 1–13. [CrossRef]
35. Guo, Y.; Li, Y. Bipartite leader-following synchronization of fractional-order delayed multilayer signed networks by adaptive and impulsive controllers. *Appl. Math. Comput.* **2022**, *430*, 127243. [CrossRef]
36. Liu, Y.; Yang Z.; Zhou, H. Periodic self-triggered intermittent control with impulse for synchronization of hybrid delayed multi-links systems. *IEEE Trans. Netw. Sci. Eng.* **2022**, 1–13. [CrossRef]
37. Zhai, Y.; Wang, P.; Su, H. Stabilization of stochastic complex networks with delays based on completely aperiodically intermittent control. *Nonlinear Anal. Hybrid Syst.* **2021**, *42*, 101074. [CrossRef]
38. Zhu, Y.; Wang, K.; Ren, Y.; Zhuang, Y. Stochastic Nicholson's blowflies delay differential equation with regime switching. *Appl. Math. Lett.* **2019**, *94*, 187–195. [CrossRef]
39. Mao, X.R. *Stochastic Differential Equations and Their Applications*; Horwood Publ. House: Chichester, UK, 1997.
40. Yang, G. Dynamical behaviors on a delay differential neoclassical growth model with patch structure. *Math. Methods Appl. Sci.* **2018**, *41*, 3856–3867. [CrossRef]

mathematics

Article

Integral Representations of Ratios of the Gauss Hypergeometric Functions with Parameters Shifted by Integers

Alexander Dyachenko [1] and Dmitrii Karp [2,3,*]

1 Keldysh Institute of Applied Mathematics, 125047 Moscow, Russia
2 Department of Mathematics, Holon Institute of Technology, Holon 5810201, Israel
3 School of Economics and Management and Far Eastern Center for Research and Education in Mathematics, Far Eastern Federal University, 690922 Vladivostok, Russia
* Correspondence: dmitrika@hit.ac.il

Abstract: Given real parameters a, b, c and integer shifts n_1, n_2, m, we consider the ratio $R(z) = {}_2F_1(a+n_1, b+n_2; c+m; z)/{}_2F_1(a,b;c;z)$ of the Gauss hypergeometric functions. We find a formula for $\operatorname{Im} R(x \pm i0)$ with $x > 1$ in terms of real hypergeometric polynomial P, beta density and the absolute value of the Gauss hypergeometric function. This allows us to construct explicit integral representations for R when the asymptotic behaviour at unity is mild and the denominator does not vanish. The results are illustrated with a large number of examples.

Keywords: gauss hypergeometric function; gauss continued fraction; integral representation

MSC: 33C05; 30E20

Citation: Dyachenko, A.; Karp, D. Integral Representations of Ratios of the Gauss Hypergeometric Functions with Parameters Shifted by Integers. *Mathematics* **2022**, *10*, 3903. https://doi.org/10.3390/math10203903

Academic Editor: Sitnik Sergey

Received: 17 September 2022
Accepted: 17 October 2022
Published: 20 October 2022

Publisher's Note: MDPI stays neutral with regard to jurisdictional claims in published maps and institutional affiliations.

Copyright: © 2022 by the authors. Licensee MDPI, Basel, Switzerland. This article is an open access article distributed under the terms and conditions of the Creative Commons Attribution (CC BY) license (https://creativecommons.org/licenses/by/4.0/).

1. Introduction

The Gauss hypergeometric functions ([1], [2] (Chapter II), [3] (Chapter 15))

$$ {}_2F_1(a,b;c;z) = {}_2F_1\left(\begin{matrix} a,b \\ c \end{matrix}\,\middle|\, z\right) = \sum_{n=0}^{\infty} \frac{(a)_n (b)_n}{(c)_n n!} z^n \tag{1} $$

and ${}_2F_1(a+n_1, b+n_2; c+m; z)$ are called contiguous in a wide sense if $n_1, n_2, m \in \mathbb{Z}$; see [4]. Any three functions of this type satisfy a linear relation with coefficients rational in a, b, c, z. If $n_1, n_2, m \in \{-1, 0, 1\}$, then the coefficients of this relation are linear in z, and the functions are called contiguous in a narrow sense. Such a contiguous relation was used by Euler to derive a continued fraction (much later termed T-fraction) for the ratio ${}_2F_1(a, b+1; c+1; z)/{}_2F_1(a,b;c;z)$. Gauss described all three-term relations among the functions contiguous in the narrow sense and found another continued fraction for the above ratio, which has the following form [1] (p. 134) (see also [5] (Formula (89.9)) or [6] (p. 123)):

$$ G(z) = \frac{F(a,b+1;c+1;z)}{F(a,b;c;z)} = \cfrac{\alpha_0}{1 - \cfrac{\alpha_1 z}{1 - \cfrac{\alpha_2 z}{1 - \cdots}}}, \tag{2} $$

where $\alpha_0 = 1$, and for $n \geq 0$,

$$ \alpha_{2n+1} = \frac{(a+n)(c-b+n)}{(c+2n)(c+2n+1)}, \quad \alpha_{2n+2} = \frac{(b+n+1)(c-a+n+1)}{(c+2n+1)(c+2n+2)}. \tag{3} $$

Clearly, we have $\lim_{n\to\infty} \alpha_n = 1/4$, while $\sup_n |\alpha_n| =: \gamma/4 \geq 1/4$. So, if $\alpha_n > 0$, $n = 1, 2, \ldots$, then it follows from [7] that there exists a unique positive measure $d\mu(s)$

on $[0,\gamma]$ whose support is dense in $[0,1]$ and has at most finitely many points in $(1,\gamma]$, such that

$$G(z) = \int_{[0,\gamma]} \frac{d\mu(s)}{1-sz}. \tag{4}$$

(The fact that $d\mu(s)$ has at most finitely many atoms in this interval directly follows from the fact that ${}_2F_1(a,b;c;z)$ has finitely many zeros in $[0,1)$. The latter is given by Theorem 4, a corollary of [8].) In general, on sending γ to infinity in (4) so that the integration is over $[0,+\infty)$, and letting $d\mu(s)$ run over all positive measures $d\mu(s)$ such that $\int_0^\infty (1-s)^{-1}d\mu(s) < \infty$, we obtain the collection of functions called the Stieltjes class $\mathcal{S}$. For functions asymptotically behaving as $\sum_{k=0}^{\infty} s_k z^k$ at the origin, the class $\mathcal{S}$ is characterized by a continued fraction $\alpha_0/(1-\alpha_1 z/(1-\cdots))$ with $\alpha_j \geq 0$ for all j, see [7] or, for example, [9] (p. 6). Such functions arise often in different areas, ranging from analysis and operator theory to combinatorics and probability.

The tighter collection of functions obtained by taking $\gamma = 1$ in (4) and letting $d\mu(s)$ run over all positive measures, making the integral convergent, is known as the Markov class $\mathcal{M}$. The same class can be described as the collection of generating functions of the Hausdorff moment sequences; see [5] (Chapter XIV). Certainly, if $\gamma < \infty$, we can re-scale the integration variable to make γ equal 1.

Theorem 69.2 from [5] asserts that one may take $\gamma = 1$ in (4) if $\alpha_n = (1-g_{n-1})g_n$ for all $n \geq 1$ with some numbers $g_n \in [0,1]$ (the cases where g_n for some n is 0, or 1 corresponds to rational $G(z)$). It is immediate to see that the condition $\alpha_n > 0$ is satisfied for the Gauss continued fraction for all n when $-1 < b < c$ and $0 < a < c+1$. The more restrictive condition $g_n \in [0,1]$ holds true if $0 \leq a \leq c+1$, $0 \leq b \leq c$; see [10] (Proof of Theorem 1.1) for details. Surprisingly enough, the representing measure $d\mu$ in (4) for the Gauss continued fraction was only computed in 1982 by Vitold Belevitch [11]. Around the same time, Jet Wimp [12] constructed explicit formulae for the odd convergence of the continued fraction (2) in terms of hypergeometric polynomials.

The main protagonist of this paper is the following generalization of the Gauss ratio (2)

$$R_{n_1,n_2,m}(z) = \frac{{}_2F_1(a+n_1,b+n_2;c+m;z)}{{}_2F_1(a,b;c;z)}, \tag{5}$$

where $n_1, n_2, m \in \mathbb{Z}$ are arbitrary. This ratio was studied in our recent preprint [13]. The ideas presented in this preprint were developed further in [14]. The present work constitutes a corrected, streamlined and elaborated version of a part of [13]. The main objectives are to furnish a complete derivation of the integral representation of $R_{n_1,n_2,m}(z)$, including all detailed proofs omitted in [14], and to illustrate its structure with numerous examples. As a by-product, each example contains sufficient conditions for $R_{n_1,n_2,m} \in \mathcal{M}$ in terms of the parameters a, b, c.

The ratios of the Gauss hypergeometric functions are a recurring theme in the literature. An important particular case of this ratio is the logarithmic derivative of the Gauss hypergeometric function. Its Stieltjes transform representation can be used to study the infinite divisibility of certain ratios of beta-distributed beta variables in a way similar to the investigation of the ratios of the gamma random variables in [15]. Furthermore, integral representations of the ratios of the Gauss hypergeometric functions are useful when determining whether they belong to certain important functional classes. For example, the authors of [16] applied such a representation to verify that $R_{0,1,0}(z)$ can be written as (4), and hence a certain pair of hypergeometric weights forms the so-called Nikishin system—an important property in the realm of multiple orthogonal polynomials.

Concerning further applications, observe that the membership of $R_{n_1,n_2,m}$ in the Markov class $\mathcal{M}$, conditions for which we give in each of the examples of Section 3, has a number of important implications. These include the normality of all Padé approximants and uniform convergence to $R_{n_1,n_2,m}(z)$ of the para-diagonal Padé approximants on all compact subsets of $\mathbb{C}\setminus[1,\infty)$; two sided bounds on the real line in terms of Padé approximants;

the univalence of $R_{n_1,n_2,m}(z)$ and $zR_{n_1,n_2,m}(z)$ in $\mathrm{Re}(z) < 1$ and its various consequences; and the starlikeness of $zR_{n_1,n_2,m}(z)$ in the disk $|z| < r^*$ with $r^* = \sqrt{13\sqrt{13} - 46} \approx 0.934$. Details regarding these claims and further references can be found in [17,18].

There are many intriguing open questions related to our work. For example, the case when the shifts are no longer an integer is also of interest for applications, but requires additional tools. For the Jacobi polynomials, certain relevant results are presented in [19]. For the non-polynomial case, there are only very fragmentary results of this type, such as [20] (Lemma 4.5).

Another compelling problem is to extend the results of this paper to the ratios of the generalized hypergeometric functions ${}_pF_q$ which, for certain integer shifts, have explicitly known branched continued fractions generalizing the Gauss continued fraction (2); see [9] (Sections 13–14). Similar problems may be posed, mutatis mutandis, for the basic hypergeometric functions, cf. [9] (Section 15). The basic analogue of the Gauss continued fraction is considered in detail in [21,22].

This paper is organized as follows. Section 2.1 deals with the asymptotic behavior of $R_{n_1,n_2,m}(z)$ near the point $z = 1$ and at infinity. In Section 2.2, we derive a formula for the values of $\mathrm{Im}(R_{n_1,n_2,m}(x \pm i0))$ for $x > 1$ using a recent duality identity for the Gauss hypergeometric function. Section 2.3 is at the heart of our work: it contains the integral representation for $R_{n_1,n_2,m}(z)$. The basic ingredients are Theorem 4, which is a corollary of Runckel's theorem from [8] and Lemma 4 connecting $\mathrm{Im}(R_{n_1,n_2,m}(x \pm i0))$ with a Cauchy-type integral. The largest section of this paper—Section 3—illustrates our study with 15 different examples. In the last section, we show how our results may help to calculate "generalized beta integrals", as well as obtaining integral representations of such functions as $z/\mathrm{Log}(1+z)$.

2. Main Results

2.1. Asymptotic Behavior

In this section, we will record the behavior of $R_{n_1,n_2,m}(z)$ in the neighborhood of the singular points $z = 1$ and $z = \infty$. It will be convenient to use the following notation: if a is a real number, then

$$(a)_- := \min(a,0) \quad \text{and} \quad (a)_+ := \max(a,0).$$

Denote also $\mathbb{N} := \{1,2,\dots\}$ and $\mathbb{N}_0 := \mathbb{N} \cup \{0\} = \{0,1,\dots\}$. We will use the standard symbols $\phi_1(z) = o(\phi(z))$ and $\phi_2(z) = O(\phi(z))$ as $z \to A$ to denote the functions satisfying the relations

$$\lim_{z \to A} \frac{\phi_1(z)}{\phi(z)} = 0 \quad \text{and} \quad |\phi_2(z)| \le C|\phi(z)| \text{ for } z \text{ near } A,$$

respectively (C is a positive constant independent of z). The goal of this section is the following theorem, which is a slightly corrected version of [14] (Lemma 1) presented there without proof.

Theorem 1. *Let $a,b,c \in \mathbb{R}$ and $c, c+m \notin -\mathbb{N}_0$. Then there exist four constants $\varepsilon_1, \varepsilon_\infty \in \{-1,0,1\}$ and $L_1, L_\infty \neq 0$ independent of z such that*

$$R_{n_1,n_2,m}(z) = L_1\,(1-z)^{\eta(a+n_1,b+n_2,c+m)-\eta(a,b,c)}\,[\log(1-z)]^{\varepsilon_1}(1+o(1)) \quad \text{as } z \to 1; \tag{6}$$

$$R_{n_1,n_2,m}(-z) = L_\infty\,z^{\zeta(a+n_1,b+n_2,c+m)-\zeta(a,b,c)}\,[\log(z)]^{\varepsilon_\infty}(1+o(1)) \quad \text{as } z \to \infty, \tag{7}$$

where

$$\eta(a,b,c) = \begin{cases} (c-a-b)_+, & \text{if } -a, b-c \in \mathbb{N}_0 \text{ or } -b, a-c \in \mathbb{N}_0; \\ 0, & \text{if } -a \in \mathbb{N}_0 \text{ and/or } -b \in \mathbb{N}_0 \text{ while } a-c, b-c \notin \mathbb{N}_0; \\ c-a-b, & \text{if } -a, -b \notin \mathbb{N}_0, \text{ while } a-c \in \mathbb{N}_0 \text{ and/or } b-c \in \mathbb{N}_0; \\ (c-a-b)_-, & \text{otherwise} \end{cases} \tag{8}$$

and

$$\zeta(a,b,c) = \begin{cases} -a, & \text{if } A(b,a,c)=0 \\ -b, & \text{if } A(a,b,c)=0 \\ -\min(a,b), & \text{otherwise} \end{cases} \quad \text{where } A(x_1,x_2,x_3) = \frac{\Gamma(x_3)\Gamma(x_2-x_1)}{\Gamma(x_2)\Gamma(x_3-x_1)}. \tag{9}$$

Remark 1. *The function $A(x_1, x_2, x_3)$ is defined by continuity if some of the arguments of the gamma functions become non-positive integers. Details can be found in this section below Formula (12).*

The above theorem is a corollary of three lemmas giving a more precise description of the behavior of $R_{n_1,n_2,m}(z)$ in the neighborhood of the singular points $z = 1$ and $z = \infty$. We will furnish a detailed proofs of these lemmas below. Before formulating the first lemma, note that the condition

$$\{a, a+n_1, b, b+n_2, c-a, c+m-a-n_1, c-b, c+m-b-n_2\} \cap -\mathbb{N}_0 = \emptyset \tag{10}$$

is equivalent to the claim that neither ${}_2F_1(a+n_1, b+n_2; c+m; z)$ nor ${}_2F_1(a,b;c;z)$ reduce to a polynomial or polynomial multiple of a power of $(1-z)$—the cases we will refer to as degenerate. Note that Formulae (6) and (7) also hold for such degenerate cases.

Our first lemma deals with the singular point $z = 1$.

Lemma 1. *Suppose that $-c, -c-m \notin \mathbb{N}_0$ and condition (10) hold true for some $a, b, c \in \mathbb{R}$ and $n_1, n_2, m \in \mathbb{Z}$. Denote $\rho = c-a-b$, $q = m-n_1-n_2$ and write $\delta_{x,y}$ for the Kronecker delta. Then*

$$R_{n_1,n_2,m}(z) = M\frac{(1-z)^{(\rho+q)_-}[1-\delta_{\rho+q,0}+\delta_{\rho+q,0}\log(1-z)]}{(1-z)^{(\rho)_-}[1-\delta_{\rho,0}+\delta_{\rho,0}\log(1-z)]}(1+o(1)) \tag{11}$$

as $z \to 1$ with some constant $M \neq 0$ independent of z. If (10) is violated, Formula (11) should be modified as follows:

- *(a) If $-a \in \mathbb{N}_0$ ($-b \in \mathbb{N}_0$), then the denominator should be replaced by 1, except when $-a \geq \rho \in \mathbb{N}$ ($-b \geq \rho \in \mathbb{N}$) in which case it should be replaced by $(1-z)^\rho$.*
- *(b) If $-a-n_1 \in \mathbb{N}_0$ ($-b-n_2 \in \mathbb{N}_0$), then the numerator should be replaced by 1, except when $-a-n_1 \geq \rho+q \in \mathbb{N}$ ($-b-n_2 \geq \rho+q \in \mathbb{N}$), in which case it should be replaced by $(1-z)^{\rho+q}$.*
- *(c) If $-a, -b \notin \mathbb{N}_0$ but $a-c \in \mathbb{N}_0$ and/or $b-c \in \mathbb{N}_0$, then the denominator should be replaced by $(1-z)^\rho$.*
- *(d) If $-a-n_1, -b-n_2 \notin \mathbb{N}_0$, but $a+n_1-c-m \in \mathbb{N}_0$ and/or $b+n_2-c-m \in \mathbb{N}_0$, then the numerator should be replaced by $(1-z)^{\rho+q}$.*

Proof. Suppose first that (10) is satisfied. Then, if $\rho = c-a-b \notin \mathbb{Z}$, according to [3] (15.8.4), we have

$${}_2F_1(a,b;c;1-z) = \frac{\Gamma(c)\Gamma(c-a-b)}{\Gamma(c-a)\Gamma(c-b)}{}_2F_1(a,b;1+\rho;z) + \frac{\Gamma(c)\Gamma(a+b-c)}{\Gamma(a)\Gamma(b)}z^\rho{}_2F_1(c-a,c-b;1-\rho;z).$$

If $\rho = c-a-b = s \in \mathbb{N}_0$, then according to [2] (2.10(12–13)) or [3] (15.8.10), we have

$$\begin{aligned} {}_2F_1(a,b;c;1-z) = \frac{\Gamma(c)\Gamma(c-a-b)}{\Gamma(c-a)\Gamma(c-b)}\sum_{n=0}^{s-1}\frac{(a)_n(b)_n}{(1-\rho)_n n!}z^n + \frac{(-1)^s\Gamma(c)}{\Gamma(a)\Gamma(b)s!}z^\rho\sum_{n=0}^{\infty}\frac{(c-a)_n(c-b)_n}{(1+\rho)_n n!}H_n z^n \\ - \frac{(-1)^s\Gamma(c)}{\Gamma(a)\Gamma(b)s!}z^\rho\log(z){}_2F_1(c-a,c-b;1+\rho;z), \end{aligned}$$

where the sum over the empty index set equals zero, and

$$H_n = \psi(n+1) + \psi(n+s+1) - \psi(a+n+s) - \psi(b+n+s), \quad \psi(z) = \Gamma'(z)/\Gamma(z).$$

If $\rho = c - a - b = -s$ for some $s \in \mathbb{N}_0$, according to [2] (2.10(14-15)), we have

$$
\begin{aligned}
{}_2F_1(a,b;c;1-z) &= \frac{\Gamma(c)\Gamma(a+b-c)z^{\rho}}{\Gamma(a)\Gamma(b)} \sum_{n=0}^{s-1} \frac{(c-a)_n(c-b)_n}{(1+\rho)_n n!} z^n \\
&+ \frac{(-1)^s\Gamma(c)}{\Gamma(c-a)\Gamma(c-b)s!} \sum_{n=0}^{\infty} \frac{(a)_n(b)_n}{(1-\rho)_n n!} \hat{H}_n z^n - \frac{(-1)^s\Gamma(c)}{\Gamma(c-a)\Gamma(c-b)s!} \log(z) {}_2F_1(a,b;1-\rho;z),
\end{aligned}
$$

and

$$\hat{H}_n = \psi(n+1) + \psi(n+s+1) - \psi(a+n) - \psi(b+n).$$

These formulae imply that

$$
{}_2F_1(a,b;c;1-z) = \begin{cases} A(1+\alpha_1 z + \alpha_2 z^2 + \cdots) + Bz^{\rho}(1+\beta_1 z + \beta_2 z^2 + \cdots), & \rho \notin \mathbb{Z}; \\ \hat{A}(1+\hat{\alpha}_1 z + \hat{\alpha}_2 z^2 + \cdots) + \hat{B}z^{\rho}\log(z)(1+\hat{\beta}_1 z + \hat{\beta}_2 z^2 + \cdots), & \rho \in \mathbb{N}_0; \\ \tilde{A}z^{\rho}(1+\tilde{\alpha}_1 z + \tilde{\alpha}_2 z^2 + \cdots) + \tilde{B}\log(z)(1+\tilde{\beta}_1 z + \tilde{\beta}_2 z^2 + \cdots), & -\rho \in \mathbb{N}, \end{cases}
$$

where the constants $A, \hat{A}, \tilde{A}, B, \hat{B}, \tilde{B}$ do not vanish due to condition (10). In a similar fashion,

$$
\begin{aligned}
&{}_2F_1(a+n_1, b+n_2; c+m; 1-z) \\
&= \begin{cases} C(1+\delta_1 z + \delta_2 z^2 + \cdots) + Dz^{\rho+q}(1+\gamma_1 z + \gamma_2 z^2 + \cdots), & \rho+q \notin \mathbb{Z}; \\ \hat{C}(1+\hat{\delta}_1 z + \hat{\delta}_2 z^2 + \cdots) + \hat{D}z^{\rho+q}\log(z)(1+\hat{\gamma}_1 z + \hat{\gamma}_2 z^2 + \cdots), & \rho+q \in \mathbb{N}_0; \\ \tilde{C}z^{\rho+q}(1+\tilde{\delta}_1 z + \tilde{\delta}_2 z^2 + \cdots) + \tilde{D}\log(z)(1+\tilde{\gamma}_1 z + \tilde{\gamma}_2 z^2 + \cdots), & -\rho-q \in \mathbb{N}, \end{cases}
\end{aligned}
$$

where the constants $C, \hat{C}, \tilde{C}, D, \hat{D}, \tilde{D}$ do not vanish due to condition (10). Substituting these formulae into definition (5) of the function $R_{n_1,n_2,m}(z)$ and analyzing the principal asymptotic term in each of the five possible cases (1) $\rho \notin \mathbb{Z}$; (2) $\rho \in \mathbb{N}_0$ and $\rho + q \in \mathbb{N}_0$; (3) $\rho \in \mathbb{N}_0$ and $-\rho - q \in \mathbb{N}$; (4) $-\rho \in \mathbb{N}$ and $\rho + q \in \mathbb{N}_0$; (5) $-\rho \in \mathbb{N}$ and $-\rho - q \in \mathbb{N}$, we arrive at Formula (11).

If condition (10) is violated, then claims (a)–(d) of the lemma follow from the following two facts: (1) If $-a \in \mathbb{N}_0$ and /or $-b \in \mathbb{N}_0$, then ${}_2F_1(a,b;c;z)$ reduces to a polynomial; (2) If $-a, -b \notin \mathbb{N}_0$, but $a - c \in \mathbb{N}_0$ and /or $b - c \in \mathbb{N}_0$, then Euler's transformation

$${}_2F_1(a,b;c;z) = (1-z)^{\rho} {}_2F_1(c-a, c-b; c; z)$$

implies that ${}_2F_1(a,b;c;z) = (1-z)^{\rho} \times$ polynomial. In view of a similar statement for ${}_2F_1(a+n_1, b+n_2; c+m; z)$, we arrive at the conclusions contained in claims (a)–(d) of the lemma on the basis of case-by-case analysis. □

We now turn our attention to the neighborhood of the point $z = \infty$. According to [23] (2.3.12) or [3] (15.8.2), as long as $a - b \notin \mathbb{Z}$, we have

$${}_2F_1(a,b;c;-z) = A(a,b,c)z^{-a}\left(1 + \sum\nolimits_{j=1}^{\infty} \hat{\alpha}_j z^{-j}\right) + A(b,a,c)z^{-b}\left(1 + \sum\nolimits_{j=1}^{\infty} \tilde{\alpha}_j z^{-j}\right) \quad (12)$$

for some finite numbers $\hat{\alpha}_j$, $\tilde{\alpha}_j$, where, in accord with (9),

$$A(x_1, x_2, x_3) = \frac{\Gamma(x_3)\Gamma(x_2 - x_1)}{\Gamma(x_2)\Gamma(x_3 - x_1)}.$$

Note that the situation $A(a,b,c) = A(b,a,c) = 0$ is not possible as long as we assume that $-c \notin \mathbb{N}_0$. With that, one of the numbers $A(a,b,c)$ or $A(b,a,c)$ vanishes when

$\{-a, -b, a-c, b-c\} \cap \mathbb{N}_0 \neq \emptyset$. This is precisely the degenerate case: ${}_2F_1(a,b;c;z)$ reduces to a polynomial, possibly times a power of $(1-z)$. A brief analysis shows that (12) remains valid in this degenerate case, despite the possibility that $a-b \in \mathbb{Z}$. In such a situation, one of the numbers $A(a,b,c)$ or $A(b,c,a)$ vanishes, while the other is well defined under the convention

$$\frac{\Gamma(-k)}{\Gamma(-n)} = (-1)^{n-k}\frac{n!}{k!},$$

which results from computing the limit of $\Gamma(-k+\varepsilon)/\Gamma(-n+\varepsilon)$ as $\varepsilon \to 0$. We will assume this extended definition of $A(x_1,x_2,x_3)$ in what follows. Define further for brevity

$$\begin{aligned} &A_1 = A(a+n_1, b+n_2, c+m), \quad A_2 = A(b+n_2, a+n_1, c+m), \\ &A_3 = A(a,b,c), \quad A_4 = A(b,a,c). \end{aligned} \tag{13}$$

Note that the condition $A_1A_2A_3A_4 \neq 0$ is equivalent to (10). The following quantities will play an important role for the sequel. Put $\alpha = \zeta(a+n_1, b+n_2, c+m)$ and $\gamma = \zeta(a,b,c)$ with ζ from (9). In detail,

$$\alpha = \begin{cases} -\min(a+n_1, b+n_2) \text{ if } A_1A_2 \neq 0 \\ -a-n_1 \text{ if } A_2 = 0 \\ -b-n_2 \text{ if } A_1 = 0 \end{cases}, \quad \gamma = \begin{cases} -\min(a,b) \text{ if } A_3A_4 \neq 0 \\ -a \text{ if } A_4 = 0 \\ -b \text{ if } A_3 = 0 \end{cases}. \tag{14}$$

Note that α is well defined since $A_1^2 + A_2^2 \neq 0$ as long as $-c-m \notin \mathbb{N}_0$, including the case when one of A_1, A_2 is infinite; similarly, γ is well defined since $A_3^2 + A_4^2 \neq 0$ as long as $-c \notin \mathbb{N}_0$, including the case when one of A_3, A_4 is infinite. Put further

$$A_\alpha = \begin{cases} A_1, \text{ if } \alpha = -a-n_1 \\ A_2, \text{ if } \alpha = -b-n_2 \end{cases}, \quad A_\gamma = \begin{cases} A_3, \text{ if } \gamma = -a \\ A_4, \text{ if } \gamma = -b \end{cases}. \tag{15}$$

The above definition implies that both A_α and A_γ do not vanish as long as $-c, -c-m \notin \mathbb{N}_0$. We will break the result in two sub-cases. The following lemma treats the case when no logarithmic terms appear in the asymptotics.

Lemma 2. *Suppose that the numbers A_1, A_2, A_3, A_4 defined in (13) are all finite. Then the principal asymptotics of $R_{n_1,n_2,m}(-z)$ have the form*

$$R_{n_1,n_2,m}(-z) \sim \frac{A_\alpha}{A_\gamma} z^{\alpha-\gamma}(1+o(1)) \text{ as } z \to \infty, \tag{16}$$

where α,γ are defined in (14) and A_α, A_γ are defined in (15). The term $o(1)$ is a (generally infinite) linear combination of negative powers of z.

Proof. In view of (12) and definitions (14) and (15), we have

$${}_2F_1(a,b;c;-z) = A_\gamma z^\gamma \Big(z^{-\delta} f(z) + g(z)\Big), \tag{17}$$

where $\delta = |a-b|$ in the non-degenerate case, or $\delta = 1$ in the degenerate case, while $f(z) = \sum_{j=0}^{\infty} \alpha'_j z^{-j}$ and $g(z) = 1 + \sum_{j=1}^{\infty} \tilde{\alpha}_j z^{-j}$ for some numbers α'_j, $\tilde{\alpha}_j$. Now, for $y \to 0$

$$\frac{1}{yf(z)+g(z)} = \frac{1/g(z)}{1-(-yf(z)/g(z))} = \sum_{k=0}^{\infty}(-y)^k \frac{f^k(z)}{g^{k+1}(z)}, \tag{18}$$

so the left-hand side is just a sum of the geometric series on the right-hand side. On plugging $y = z^{-\delta}$ into (18) and writing expansions of the ratios $f^k(z)/g^{k+1}(z)$ in powers of z^{-1}

through $f(z)$ and $g(z)$ using the standard recursion formulae (see also [24] (p. 141, notation on p. 6)), we arrive at

$$[{}_2F_1(a,b;c;-z)]^{-1} = (A_\gamma)^{-1}z^{-\gamma}\left(1+\sum_{k=1}^{\infty}\frac{\alpha_k}{z^{\hat{\sigma}_k}}\right) \tag{19}$$

for some positive numbers $\hat{\sigma}_k$. (In our case $f(z)$, $g(z)$ and, hence, $f^k(z)/g^{k+1}(z)$ actually converge to functions analytic near infinity; this makes the proof even simpler.) Analogous to (17),

$${}_2F_1(a+n_1,b+n_1;c+m;-z) = A_\alpha z^\alpha\left(1+\beta_1' z^{-\varepsilon}+\beta_2' z^{-\varepsilon-1}+\cdots+\bar{\beta}_1 z^{-1}+\bar{\beta}_2 z^{-2}+\cdots\right) \tag{20}$$

for some numbers β_j', $\bar{\beta}_j$ and $\varepsilon = |a+n_1-b-n_2|$ in the non-degenerate case or $\varepsilon = 1$ in the degenerate case. Multiplying (19) by (20), we arrive at (16). □

The condition $a-b \notin \mathbb{Z}$ in Lemma 2 ensures that no logarithms appear in the asymptotics. If, on the contrary, $a-b\in\mathbb{Z}$ such that also $a+n_1-b-n_2\in\mathbb{Z}$, the asymptotic expansions of the hypergeometric functions in both the numerator and denominator of $R_{n_1,n_2,m}(-z)$ will contain logarithmic terms if (10) holds true (i.e., $A_1A_2A_3A_4\neq 0$). We will treat this situation in the lemma below. If (10) is violated, however, then either the numerator (if $A_1A_2=0$) or denominator (if $A_3A_4=0$) or both will reduce to a polynomial possibly times a power of $(1-z)$ in which case the logarithmic terms are missing, and (12) holds. Note also that in the non-degenerate case when $a-b\in\mathbb{Z}\setminus\{0\}$, we have $0\neq|A_3|<\infty$, $|A_4|=\infty$ if $a<b$ and $0\neq|A_4|<\infty$, $|A_3|=\infty$ if $a>b$. This implies that $\gamma=-\min(a,b)$ in (14), and A_γ in (15) is well defined. Similar claims hold for α and A_α when $a+n_1-b-n_2\in\mathbb{Z}\setminus\{0\}$.

Lemma 3. *Suppose that $n_2-n_1\neq a-b\in\mathbb{Z}\setminus\{0\}$, $A_1A_2A_3A_4\neq 0$ ($\Leftrightarrow$ condition (10) holds) such that $\alpha=-\min(a+n_1,b+n_2)$ and $\gamma=-\min(a,b)$. Let A_α, A_γ be defined in (15). Then the asymptotic expansion of $R_{n_1,n_2,m}(-z)$ as $z\to\infty$ has the form*

$$R_{n_1,n_2,m}(-z)\sim\frac{A_\alpha}{A_\gamma}z^{\alpha-\gamma}\left(1+\sum_{k=1}^{\min(\delta,\varepsilon)-1}\frac{a_k}{z^k}+\sum_{k=\min(\delta,\varepsilon)}^{\infty}\frac{a_k}{z^k}\left[1+b_{1,k}\log(z)+\cdots+b_{k,k}\log^k(z)\right]\right), \tag{21}$$

where the sum over the empty index set is zero, a_k and $b_{j,k}$ are real numbers (possibly vanishing), $\varepsilon=|a+n_1-b-n_2|$ and $\delta=|a-b|$ are positive integers.

Proof. Indeed if $|a-b|\geq 1$, we apply [3] (15.8.8), which can be written in the form:

$${}_2F_1(a,b;c;-z)=A_\gamma z^\gamma\left(1+\sum_{j=1}^{\infty}\frac{f_j}{z^j}+\log(z)\sum_{k=\delta}^{\infty}\frac{e_k}{z^k}\right),$$

where as before $\gamma=-\min(a,b)$, $\delta=|a-b|\in\mathbb{N}$, and A_γ is defined in (15). Hence, letting $y=z^{-1}\log(z)$, $f(z)=\sum_{k=\delta}^{\infty}e_k/z^{k-1}$ and $g(z)=1+\sum_{j=1}^{\infty}f_j/z^j$ in (18) yields

$$[{}_2F_1(a,b;c;-z)]^{-1}=(A_\gamma)^{-1}z^{-\gamma}\left(1+\sum_{j=1}^{\infty}\frac{\hat{f}_j}{z^j}\left[1+\hat{e}_{j,1}\frac{\log(z)}{z^{\delta-1}}+\hat{e}_{j,2}\frac{\log^2(z)}{z^{2(\delta-1)}}+\cdots+\hat{e}_{j,j}\frac{\log^j(z)}{z^{j(\delta-1)}}\right]\right). \tag{22}$$

In a similar fashion,

$${}_2F_1(a+n_1,b+n_2;c+m;-z)=A_\alpha z^\alpha\left(1+\sum_{j=1}^{\infty}\frac{g_j}{z^j}+\log(z)\sum_{k=\epsilon}^{\infty}\frac{q_k}{z^k}\right), \tag{23}$$

where as before $\alpha=-\min(a+n_1,b+n_2)$, $\varepsilon=|a+n_1-b-n_2|\in\mathbb{N}$ and A_α is defined in (15). The multiplication of (22) and (23) yields (21). □

Note that in the above lemma, $\alpha - \gamma \in \mathbb{Z}$. The remaining cases not covered by Lemmas 2 and 3 are the following. If $a = b$, but $-a, a - c \notin \mathbb{N}_0$, according to [3] (15.8.8), we have

$$ {}_2F_1(a,a;c;-z) = \frac{\log(z)\Gamma(c)}{\Gamma(a)\Gamma(c-a)z^a}\left(1 + \frac{f_0}{\log(z)} + \sum_{k=1}^{\infty}\frac{e_k}{z^k}\left[1 + \frac{f_k}{\log(z)}\right]\right), $$

so that (18) with $y = 1/\log(z)$, $f(z) = f_0 + \sum_{k=1}^{\infty} e_k f_k / z^k$ and $g(z) = 1 + \sum_{k=1}^{\infty} e_k / z^k$ implies

$$ [{}_2F_1(a,a;c;-z)]^{-1} = \frac{\Gamma(a)\Gamma(c-a)z^a}{\Gamma(c)\log(z)}\left(1 + \sum_{k=1}^{\infty}\frac{f_0^k}{[\log(z)]^k} + \sum_{j=1}^{\infty}\frac{\hat{f}_j}{z^j}\left[1 + \frac{\hat{e}_{j,1}}{\log(z)} + \cdots + \frac{\hat{e}_{j,j}}{[\log(z)]^j}\right]\right). \tag{24} $$

In a similar fashion, if $a + n_1 = b + n_2$, but $-a - n_1, a + n_1 - c - m \notin \mathbb{N}_0$, we will have

$$ {}_2F_1(a+n_1, a+n_1; c+m; -z) = \frac{z^{-a-n_1}\log(z)\Gamma(c+m)}{\Gamma(a+n_1)\Gamma(c-a+m-n_1)}\left(1 + \frac{g_0}{\log(z)} + \sum_{k=1}^{\infty}\frac{q_k}{z^k}\left[1 + \frac{g_k}{\log(z)}\right]\right). \tag{25} $$

Hence, when both $a = b$ and $a + n_1 = b + n_2$, but there are no non-negative integers among the numbers $-a, a - c, -a - n_1, a + n_1 - c - m$, the asymptotic expansion of $R_{n_1,n_2,m}(-z)$ is obtained by the multiplication of (24) and (25). If $a = b$ but $a + n_1 \neq b + n_2$, we have to multiply (24) by (23) or, if $a + n_1 = b + n_2$ but $a \neq b$, then multiply (25) by (22). Finally, if the denominator is degenerate while the numerator is not, we multiply (19) by (23) when $a + n_1 \neq b + n_2$ or by (25) when $a + n_1 = b + n_2$. Similarly, if the numerator is degenerate while the denominator is not, we multiply (20) by (22) when $a \neq b$ or by (24) when $a = b$.

2.2. Boundary Values

For any integer r, define the Pochhammer symbol by $(z)_r = \Gamma(z+r)/\Gamma(z)$. Given three integers $n_1, n_2, m \in \mathbb{Z}$, define the following related quantities:

$$ \begin{gathered} \underline{n} = \min(n_1, n_2),\ \overline{n} = \max(n_1, n_2),\ p = (m - n_1 - n_2)_+,\ l = (n_1 + n_2 - m)_+ \\ r = l + (m)_+ - \underline{n} - 1 = \begin{cases} \max(m - \underline{n}, \overline{n}) - 1, & m \geq 0 \\ \max(-\underline{n}, \overline{n} - m) - 1, & m \leq 0. \end{cases} \end{gathered} \tag{26} $$

Note that $p - l = m - n_1 - n_2$ and r may only be negative when $n_1 = n_2 = m = 0$, in which case $r = -1$. In the following theorem, which forms the main result of this subsection, we give an explicit formula for the imaginary part of $R_{n_1,n_2,m}(z)$ on the banks of the branch cut $[1, \infty)$. Note that for $x > 1$, the function ${}_2F_1(a, b; c; x \pm i0)$ may vanish at finitely many points in the degenerate case $\{-a, -b, c - a, c - b\} \cap \mathbb{N}_0 \neq \varnothing$, but does not vanish otherwise, see, respectively, Theorem 4 and [8] (Lemma 2, p. 54).

Theorem 2. *Suppose that $n_1, n_2, m \in \mathbb{Z}$, $a, b, c \in \mathbb{R}$ and $c, c + m \notin -\mathbb{N}_0$. The following identity holds on the banks of the branch cut $x > 1$:*

$$ \operatorname{Im}[R_{n_1,n_2,m}(x \pm i0)] = \pm\pi B_{n_1,n_2,m}(a,b,c)\frac{x^{l-\underline{n}-c}(x-1)^{c-a-b-l}P_r(1/x)}{|{}_2F_1(a,b;c;x)|^2}, \tag{27a} $$

where

$$ B_{n_1,n_2,m}(a,b,c) = -\frac{\Gamma(c)\Gamma(c+m)}{\Gamma(a)\Gamma(b)\Gamma(c-a+m-n_1)\Gamma(c-b+m-n_2)} \tag{27b} $$

and $P_r(t)$ is a polynomial of degree r ($P_{-1} \equiv 0$) given by

$$ P_r(t) = (-1)^{\overline{n}}\sum_{k=0}^{r}(-t)^k \sum_{j=(k-p)_+ - \overline{n}}^{k-\overline{n}}(-1)^j\binom{p}{k-\overline{n}-j}K_j, \tag{28a} $$

where, with the convention $1/(-i)! = 0$ for $i \in \mathbb{N}$,

$$K_j = \frac{(1-a)_j(c-a)_{m+j}}{(b-a)_{n_2+j+1}(j+n_1)!}\,{}_4F_3\!\left(\begin{matrix}-j-n_1, a, 1+a-c, a-b-n_2-j\\ a-j, 1+a-c-m-j, 1+a-b\end{matrix}\middle|\,1\right)$$
$$+\frac{(1-b)_j(c-b)_{m+j}}{(a-b)_{n_1+j+1}(j+n_2)!}\,{}_4F_3\!\left(\begin{matrix}-j-n_2, b, 1+b-c, b-a-n_1-j\\ b-j, 1+b-c-m-j, 1+b-a\end{matrix}\middle|\,1\right). \quad (28b)$$

Remark 2. *Note that the coefficients of P_r depend on the parameters, so the whole expression (27a) may remain nonzero even when $B_{n_1,n_2,m}(a,b,c)$ vanishes. Furthermore, the polynomial $P_r(t) = P_r(t; n_1, n_2, m)$ depends on all three indices n_1, n_2, m and not only on the degree r. For example, rather, the straightforward calculation yields*

$$P_0(t;0;1;1) = -\frac{1}{b}, \quad P_0(t;1,1,1) = -\frac{1}{ab},$$
$$P_1(t;0,2,2) = -\frac{ct+b-a+1}{b(b+1)}, \quad P_1(t;0,0,2) = ct+a+b-2c-1.$$

The key fact that we will need for the proof of the above theorem is a more precise version of a particular case of [25] (Theorem 1), which (after some change of notation), reads:

Theorem 3. *Assume that $n_1, n_2, m \in \mathbb{Z}$. Then*

$$\frac{(\gamma-\alpha)_{-n_2}(\gamma-\beta)_{m-n_2}t^{n_1}}{(\gamma-1)_{n_1-n_2+1}}\,{}_2F_1\!\left(\begin{matrix}1-\gamma+\alpha, 1-\gamma+\beta\\ 2-\gamma\end{matrix}\middle|\,t\right){}_2F_1\!\left(\begin{matrix}\gamma-\alpha-n_2, \gamma-\beta+m-n_2\\ \gamma+n_1-n_2\end{matrix}\middle|\,t\right)+$$
$$\frac{(1-\alpha)_{-n_1}(1-\beta)_{m-n_1}t^{n_2}}{(1-\gamma)_{n_2-n_1+1}}\,{}_2F_1\!\left(\begin{matrix}\alpha,\beta\\ \gamma\end{matrix}\middle|\,t\right){}_2F_1\!\left(\begin{matrix}1-\alpha-n_1, 1-\beta+m-n_1\\ 2-\gamma+n_2-n_1\end{matrix}\middle|\,t\right) = \frac{t^{\underline{n}}P_r(t)}{(1-t)^p}, \quad (29)$$

where $P_r(t)$ is the polynomial (28) of degree r ($P_{-1} \equiv 0$) with parameters $a = \alpha$, $b = 1+\alpha-\gamma$, $c+\alpha-\beta$. This polynomial can also be computed by multiplying the left hand side of (29) by $t^{-\underline{n}}(1-t)^p$ and calculating the first $r+1$ Taylor coefficients on the left-hand side.

Remark 3. *The particular ${}_2F_1$ case of our general identity [25] (Theorem 1) given in (29) was essentially discovered by Ebisu in [26]. Namely, it can be derived by combining Theorem 3.7 with Proposition 3.4 from [26].*

Remark 4. *Our identity from [25] (Theorem 1) does not contain explicit expression (28) for the polynomial P_r. This expression is found in [27] (Lemma 6.1). It can also be computed by taking the limit $q \to 1$ in [28] (Theorem 2). For specific values of n_1, n_2, m, the second method of computing $P_r(t)$ indicated in the above theorem is more practical.*

Proof. The boundary values of the generalized hypergeometric function on the cut $[1, \infty)$ was found in [18] (Theorem 3). For the case of the Gauss function ${}_2F_1$, this theorem takes the form ($x > 1$):

$${}_2F_1(a,b;c;x \pm i0) = -\frac{\pi\Gamma(c)}{\Gamma(a)\Gamma(b)}G^{2,1}_{3,3}\!\left(\frac{1}{x}\,\middle|\,\begin{matrix}1, 3/2, c\\ a, b, 3/2\end{matrix}\right) \pm \pi i\frac{\Gamma(c)}{\Gamma(a)\Gamma(b)}G^{2,0}_{2,2}\!\left(\frac{1}{x}\,\middle|\,\begin{matrix}1, c\\ a, b\end{matrix}\right),$$

where $G^{m,n}_{p,q}$ denotes Meijer's G function defined by the Mellin–Barnes integral

$$G^{m,n}_{p,q}\!\left(z\,\middle|\,\begin{matrix}a_1,\ldots,a_p\\ b_1,\ldots,b_q\end{matrix}\right) := \frac{1}{2\pi i}\int_{\mathcal{L}}\frac{\Gamma(1-a_1-s)\cdots\Gamma(1-a_n-s)\Gamma(b_1+s)\cdots\Gamma(b_m+s)}{\Gamma(a_{n+1}+s)\cdots\Gamma(a_p+s)\Gamma(1-b_{m+1}-s)\cdots\Gamma(1-b_q-s)}z^{-s}ds, \quad (30)$$

where the contour $\mathcal{L}$ is a simple loop that starts and ends at infinity and separates the poles of $s \to \Gamma(b_j+s)$, $j = 1,\ldots,m$, leaving them on the left from those of $s \to \Gamma(1-a_j-s)$, $j = 1,\ldots,n$, leaving them on the right. Details regarding the choice of the contour $\mathcal{L}$ and the convergence of the above integral can be found, for instance, in [3] (Section 16.17), [27] (Formula (1.2)). As

$$\mathrm{Im}\left(\frac{\alpha+i\beta}{\gamma+i\delta}\right)=\frac{\beta\gamma-\alpha\delta}{|\gamma+i\delta|^2},$$

by writing $\phi_\pm(x)=\mathrm{Im}[R_{n_1,n_2,m}(x\pm i0)]$, we will get

$$\phi_\pm(x)=\mathrm{Im}\left[\frac{{}_2F_1(a+n_1,b+n_2;c+m;x\pm i0)}{{}_2F_1(a,b;c;x\pm i0)}\right]=\pm\frac{\pi^2\Gamma(c)\Gamma(c+m)}{|{}_2F_1(a,b;c;x)|^2\Gamma(a)\Gamma(b)\Gamma(a+n_1)\Gamma(b+n_2)}$$
$$\left\{G^{2,1}_{3,3}\left(\frac{1}{x}\middle|\begin{matrix}1,3/2,c+m\\a+n_1,b+n_2,3/2\end{matrix}\right)G^{2,0}_{2,2}\left(\frac{1}{x}\middle|\begin{matrix}1,c\\a,b\end{matrix}\right)-G^{2,1}_{3,3}\left(\frac{1}{x}\middle|\begin{matrix}1,3/2,c\\a,b,3/2\end{matrix}\right)G^{2,0}_{2,2}\left(\frac{1}{x}\middle|\begin{matrix}1,c+m\\a+n_1,b+n_2\end{matrix}\right)\right\}.$$

Meijer's G function here can be expanded as follows [18] (Proof of Theorem 3):

$$-G^{2,1}_{3,3}\left(t\middle|\begin{matrix}1,3/2,c\\a,b,3/2\end{matrix}\right)=\frac{\Gamma(b-a)\Gamma(a)t^a}{\pi\Gamma(c-a)}{}_2F_1\left(\begin{matrix}a,1-c+a\\1-b+a\end{matrix}\middle|t\right)\cos(\pi a)$$
$$+\frac{\Gamma(a-b)\Gamma(b)t^b}{\pi\Gamma(c-b)}{}_2F_1\left(\begin{matrix}b,1-c+b\\1-a+b\end{matrix}\middle|t\right)\cos(\pi b)$$

and

$$G^{2,0}_{2,2}\left(t\middle|\begin{matrix}1,c\\a,b\end{matrix}\right)=\frac{\Gamma(b-a)\Gamma(a)t^a}{\pi\Gamma(c-a)}{}_2F_1\left(\begin{matrix}a,1-c+a\\1-b+a\end{matrix}\middle|t\right)\sin(\pi a)$$
$$+\frac{\Gamma(a-b)\Gamma(b)t^b}{\pi\Gamma(c-b)}{}_2F_1\left(\begin{matrix}b,1-c+b\\1-a+b\end{matrix}\middle|t\right)\sin(\pi b).$$

Substituting these expansions into the above formula for $\phi_\pm(x)$ and collecting terms, the expression in the braces becomes

$$\frac{\Gamma(b-a)\Gamma(a+n_1-b-n_2)\Gamma(b+n_2)\Gamma(a)x^{-a-b-n_2}}{\pi^2\Gamma(c-a)\Gamma(c+m-b-n_2)}{}_2F_1\left(\begin{matrix}a,1-c+a\\1-b+a\end{matrix}\middle|\frac{1}{x}\right)$$
$$\times{}_2F_1\left(\begin{matrix}b+n_2,1-c-m+b+n_2\\1-a-n_1+b+n_2\end{matrix}\middle|\frac{1}{x}\right)\sin(\pi(b+n_2-a))$$
$$+\frac{\Gamma(a-b)\Gamma(b+n_2-a-n_1)\Gamma(a+n_1)\Gamma(b)x^{-b-a-n_1}}{\pi^2\Gamma(c-b)\Gamma(c+m-a-n_1)}{}_2F_1\left(\begin{matrix}b,1-c+b\\1-a+b\end{matrix}\middle|\frac{1}{x}\right)$$
$$\times{}_2F_1\left(\begin{matrix}a+n_1,1-c-m+a+n_1\\1-b-n_2+a+n_1\end{matrix}\middle|\frac{1}{x}\right)\sin(\pi(a+n_1-b)).$$

Then, writing $t=1/x$, applying Euler's transformation and the reflection formula $\Gamma(z)\Gamma(1-z)=\pi/\sin(\pi z)$, we obtain

$$
\begin{aligned}
&\frac{|{}_2F_1(a,b;c;1/t)|^2\Gamma(a)\Gamma(b)\Gamma(a+n_1)\Gamma(b+n_2)}{\Gamma(c)\Gamma(c+m)}\phi_+(1/t) = \\
&\qquad = \frac{\Gamma(a-b)\Gamma(b+n_2-a-n_1)\Gamma(a+n_1)\Gamma(b)t^{a+b+n_1}}{\Gamma(c-b)\Gamma(c+m-a-n_1)} \\
&\times {}_2F_1\left(\left.\begin{matrix} b, 1-c+b \\ 1-a+b \end{matrix}\right| t\right) {}_2F_1\left(\left.\begin{matrix} a+n_1, 1-c-m+a+n_1 \\ 1-b-n_2+a+n_1 \end{matrix}\right| t\right)\sin(\pi(a+n_1-b)) \\
&\qquad + \frac{\Gamma(b-a)\Gamma(a+n_1-b-n_2)\Gamma(b+n_2)\Gamma(a)t^{a+b+n_2}}{\Gamma(c-a)\Gamma(c+m-b-n_2)} \\
&\times {}_2F_1\left(\left.\begin{matrix} a, 1-c+a \\ 1-b+a \end{matrix}\right| t\right) {}_2F_1\left(\left.\begin{matrix} b+n_2, 1-c-m+b+n_2 \\ 1-a-n_1+b+n_2 \end{matrix}\right| t\right)\sin(\pi(b+n_2-a)) \\
&= \frac{\pi\Gamma(a-b)\Gamma(b-a+n_2-n_1)\Gamma(a+n_1)\Gamma(b)t^{a+b+n_1}(1-t)^{c-a-b+m-n_1-n_2}}{\Gamma(c-b)\Gamma(c-a+m-n_1)\Gamma(a-b+n_1)\Gamma(1+b-a-n_1)} \\
&\quad \times {}_2F_1\left(\left.\begin{matrix} b, 1-c+b \\ 1-a+b \end{matrix}\right| t\right) {}_2F_1\left(\left.\begin{matrix} 1-b-n_2, c-b+m-n_2 \\ 1+a-b+n_1-n_2 \end{matrix}\right| t\right) \\
&+ \frac{\pi\Gamma(b-a)\Gamma(a-b+n_1-n_2)\Gamma(b+n_2)\Gamma(a)t^{a+b+n_2}(1-t)^{c-a-b+m-n_1-n_2}}{\Gamma(c-a)\Gamma(c+m-b-n_2)\Gamma(b-a+n_2)\Gamma(1+a-b-n_2)} \\
&\qquad \times {}_2F_1\left(\left.\begin{matrix} a, 1-c+a \\ 1-b+a \end{matrix}\right| t\right) {}_2F_1\left(\left.\begin{matrix} 1-a-n_1, c-a+m-n_1 \\ 1+b-a+n_2-n_1 \end{matrix}\right| t\right).
\end{aligned}
$$

Further, writing $a = \alpha$, $b = 1-\gamma+\alpha$, $c = 1-\beta+\alpha$ after tedious but elementary transformations with the use of the relations

$$
(1-z)_{-k} = \frac{(-1)^k}{(z)_k} \text{ and } (z-r)_k = \frac{(z)_{k-r}}{(z)_{-r}} = (-1)^k\frac{(1-z)_r}{(1-z)_{r-k}},
$$

the above expression reduces to

$$
\begin{aligned}
&\frac{|{}_2F_1(a,b;c;1/t)|^2\Gamma(a)\Gamma(b)\Gamma(a+n_1)\Gamma(b+n_2)}{\Gamma(c)\Gamma(c+m)}\phi_+(1/t) \\
&\qquad = -\frac{\pi t^{2\alpha-\gamma+1}(1-t)^{\gamma-\alpha-\beta+m-n_1-n_2}\Gamma(\alpha+n_1)\Gamma(1+\alpha-\gamma+n_2)}{\Gamma(1-\beta+m-n_1)\Gamma(\gamma-\beta+m-n_2)}\times \\
&\left\{\frac{(\gamma-\alpha)_{-n_2}(\gamma-\beta)_{m-n_2}t^{n_1}}{(\gamma-1)_{n_1-n_2+1}}{}_2F_1\left(\left.\begin{matrix} 1-\gamma+\alpha, 1-\gamma+\beta \\ 2-\gamma \end{matrix}\right| t\right){}_2F_1\left(\left.\begin{matrix} \gamma-\alpha-n_2, \gamma-\beta+m-n_2 \\ \gamma+n_1-n_2 \end{matrix}\right| t\right)\right. \\
&\quad \left. + \frac{(1-\alpha)_{-n_1}(1-\beta)_{m-n_1}t^{n_2}}{(1-\gamma)_{n_2-n_1+1}}{}_2F_1\left(\left.\begin{matrix} \alpha, \beta \\ \gamma \end{matrix}\right| t\right){}_2F_1\left(\left.\begin{matrix} 1-\alpha-n_1, 1-\beta+m-n_1 \\ 2-\gamma+n_2-n_1 \end{matrix}\right| t\right)\right\} \\
&\qquad\qquad = -\frac{\pi t^{2\alpha-\gamma+1+\underline{n}}(1-t)^{\gamma-\alpha-\beta-l}\Gamma(\alpha+n_1)\Gamma(1+\alpha-\gamma+n_2)}{\Gamma(1-\beta+m-n_1)\Gamma(\gamma-\beta+m-n_2)}P_r(t),
\end{aligned}
$$

where the ultimate equality is an application of Theorem 3 with the notation introduced in (26).

Now substituting back $\alpha = a$, $\beta = 1-c+a$, $\gamma = 1-b+a$, we obtain

$$
|{}_2F_1(a,b;c;1/t)|^2\phi_+(1/t) = -\frac{\pi\Gamma(c)\Gamma(c+m)t^{a+b}(1-t)^{c-a-b}}{\Gamma(a)\Gamma(b)\Gamma(c-a+m-n_1)\Gamma(c-b+m-n_2)}\frac{t^{\underline{n}}P_r(t)}{(1-t)^l}.
$$

It remains to plug here $x = 1/t$ to arrive at (27a). □

2.3. Integral Representation

The goal of this subsection is to construct an explicit integral representation for $R_{n_1,n_2,m}(z)$—the central result of this paper. It will be based on a polynomial correction of the standard Schwarz formula expressing the analytic function in the upper half-plane via the boundary values of its real part. The Schwarz formula is a particular case of the Stieltjes–Perron inversion formula (the measure in the Stieltjes–Perron inversion formula is often assumed to be positive (see [7] (no. 39), [6] (p. 188) or [5] (p. 250)), although this requirement can be relaxed) applied for recovering the representing measure in (4). However, the integral representation of the form (4) may already be too restrictive for the Gauss ratio $G(z) = R_{0,1,1}(z)$, let alone $R_{n_1,n_2,m}(z)$. The two main reasons are that (1) the right-hand side of (4) is analytic in $\mathbb{C} \setminus \mathbb{R}$, while $R_{0,1,1}(z)$ may have complex poles for certain values of a, b, c, and (2) the representing measure may grow too fast for the integral in (4) to be convergent. We deal with the first problem in Theorem 4 below containing conditions ensuring that there are no poles in $\mathbb{C} \setminus [1, \infty)$ as well as on the banks of the branch cut. Under these conditions, the corresponding signed measure (or charge) is supported on $[1, +\infty)$ and has an analytic density. Thus, to obtain an integral representation we only need to deal with the asymptotic behavior of $R_{n_1,n_2,m}(z)$ near the points $z = 1$ and $z = \infty$ to handle the second problem. This was solved by our rational correction presented in [14] (Lemma 4). In this paper, we will only use a particular case of [14] (Lemma 4) containing a polynomial correction at infinity. Recall that an analytic function is called real if $f(\overline{z}) = \overline{f(z)}$ in the appropriate domain.

Lemma 4. *Let $f(z)$ be a real analytic function defined in the cut plane $\mathbb{C} \setminus [1, +\infty)$ and suppose that $u(x) := \frac{1}{\pi} \operatorname{Im} f(x + i0)$ is continuous on $(1, +\infty)$. Suppose that there exists $n \in \mathbb{N}_0$ such that*

$$\lim_{|z-1|\to 0} |f(z)(1-z)| = \lim_{|z|\to\infty} |f(z)z^{-n}| = 0 \tag{31}$$

and $u(x)x^{-n-1}$ is absolutely integrable over $(1, +\infty)$. Then

$$f(z) = \sum_{k=0}^{n-1} \frac{f^{(k)}(0)z^k}{k!} + z^n \int_1^{+\infty} \frac{u(x)\,dx}{(x-z)x^n}. \tag{32}$$

The above lemma assumes that the function f is analytic in $\mathbb{C} \setminus [1, +\infty)$. Hence, in order to apply it to $R_{n_1,n_2,m}(z)$, we need to make sure that the denominator ${}_2F_1(a, b; c; z)$ does not vanish in this domain. Such conditions will follow from an important theorem due to Runckel [8]. We will denote by $\lfloor \xi \rfloor$ the maximal integer number $\leq \xi$ for any $\xi \in \mathbb{R}$. Note that if ξ is non-integer, then $\lfloor -\xi \rfloor = -\lfloor \xi \rfloor - 1$.

Theorem 4. *The function ${}_2F_1(a, b; c; z)$ does not vanish for $z \in \mathbb{C} \setminus [1, +\infty)$, including on the banks of the branch cut if and only if $(a, b, c) \in V \subset \mathbf{R}^3$, where V is the set of points (a, b, c) with $c \neq 0$ satisfying any of the following conditions:*

(I) $-1 < \min(a, b) \leq c \leq \max(a, b) \leq 0$;
(II) $-1 < \min(a, b) \leq 0 \leq \max(a, b) \leq c$;
(III) $-1 < c \leq \min(a, b) \leq 0 \leq \max(a, b) < c + 1$;
(IV) $0 \leq \min(a, b) \leq c$ *and* $\max(a, b) < c + 1$;
(V) *$a, b, c, c-a, c-b$ are non-integer negative numbers, such that $\lfloor \xi_1 \rfloor + 1 = \lfloor \xi_4 \rfloor$ and $\lfloor \xi_2 \rfloor = \lfloor \xi_3 \rfloor$, where $\xi_1, \ldots, \xi_4$ are the numbers $a, b, c-a, c-b$ taken in non-decreasing order:*

$$\min(a, b, c-a, c-b) = \xi_1 \leq \xi_2 \leq \xi_3 \leq \xi_4 = \max(a, b, c-a, c-b);$$

(VI) $0 \in \{a, b, c-a, c-b\}$.

In this form, this theorem was formulated and proved by us in [14] (Corollary 2).

Remark 5. *Under condition (V), one necessarily has $c - \xi_4 = \xi_1 < \xi_2$ and $c - \xi_2 = \xi_3 < \xi_4$. Indeed, $\xi_1 + \xi_4 = c = \xi_2 + \xi_3$ in view of $a + (c-a) = c = b + (c-b)$. So, if we have one of* *the equalities $\xi_1 = \xi_2$ and $\xi_3 = \xi_4$, we automatically have the other, assuming that the last two equalities together will contradict to $\lfloor \xi_1 \rfloor + 1 = \lfloor \xi_4 \rfloor$ on account of $\lfloor \xi_2 \rfloor = \lfloor \xi_3 \rfloor$.*

In fact, (V) is generated by the following two basic cases,

$$-k-1 < a < \min(b, c-b) \le \max(b, c-b) < -k < c-a < -k+1, \quad k \in \mathbb{N}, \quad \text{and}$$
$$-k-1 < a < -k < \min(b, c-b) \le \max(b, c-b) < c-a < -k+1, \quad k \in \mathbb{N},$$

further extended through the symmetry $a \leftrightarrow b$ and Euler's transformation exchanging $(a,b) \leftrightarrow (c-a, c-b)$.

Another important fact established by Runckel is the following corollary of [8] (Lemma 2):

Lemma 5. *If $a, b, c-a, c-b \notin -\mathbb{N}_0$ and $x > 1$, then ${}_2F_1(a,b;c;x \pm i0) \neq 0$.*

Lemmas 2 and 3 and the subsequent remarks show that the asymptotic expansion of $R_{n_1,n_2,m}(z)$ at infinity is a combination of terms of the form $Az^{\mu}[\log(z)]^k$, where A and μ are real numbers, while k is an integer. Condition (34) in the theorem below requires each exponent μ satisfying $\mu \ge N$, $N \in \mathbb{N}_0$ to be an integer and the corresponding k to be zero (no logarithms at powers $\mu \ge N$). The following theorem is the main result of this section.

Theorem 5. *Suppose that $(a,b,c) \in V$, with V defined in Theorem 4, and $\eta(\cdot)$ given in (8) satisfies*

$$\eta(a+n_1, b+n_2, c+m) - \eta(a,b,c) > -1. \tag{33}$$

Assume further that there exists $N \in \mathbb{N}_0$ such that the asymptotics of $R_{n_1,n_2,m}(z)$ at infinity have the form

$$R_{n_1,n_2,m}(z) = Q_{a,b,c}(z) + o(z^N) \text{ as } z \to \infty, \tag{34}$$

where $Q_{a,b,c}(z)$ is a (possibly vanishing) polynomial with real coefficients and the lowest degree non-vanishing term $\sim z^N$. Then the following representation holds true:

$$R_{n_1,n_2,m}(z) = Q_{a,b,c}(z) + \sum_{k=0}^{N-1} \frac{R^{(k)}_{n_1,n_2,m}(0)}{k!} z^k + z^N B_{n_1,n_2,m}(a,b,c) \int_1^{\infty} \frac{x^{l-\underline{n}-c-N}(x-1)^{c-a-b-l} P_r(1/x)}{|{}_2F_1(a,b;c;x)|^2 (x-z)} dx, \tag{35}$$

where r, l and $B_{n_1,n_2,m}(a,b,c)$ retain their meanings from Theorem 2 and P_r is defined in (28). If (34) holds with $N = 0$, we obtain

$$R_{n_1,n_2,m}(z) = Q_{a,b,c}(z) + B_{n_1,n_2,m}(a,b,c) \int_1^{\infty} \frac{x^{l-\underline{n}-c}(x-1)^{c-a-b-l} P_r(1/x)}{|{}_2F_1(a,b;c;x)|^2 (x-z)} dx \tag{36}$$

In particular, (34) holds for $N = 0$, $Q_{a,b,c}(z)$ being a constant if $n_1, n_2 \ge 0$ and (10) is satisfied.

Remark 6. *Note that the choice of N and $Q_{a,b,c}(z)$ in (34) is not unique. In particular, it follows from Lemmas 2 and 3 that we can always take $Q_{a,b,c}(z) = 0$ by choosing a large enough N.*

Remark 7. *The first two terms of the Taylor expansion of $R_{n_1,n_2,m}(z)$ are given by*

$$R_{n_1,n_2,m}(z) = 1 + \frac{(an_2 + bn_1 + n_1 n_2)c - abm}{c(c+m)} z + O(z^2).$$

Remark 8. *Substitution $x = 1/t$ brings Formula (36) to the form (we write $B = B_{n_1,n_2,m}(a,b,c)$ for brevity):*

$$R_{n_1,n_2,m}(z) = Q_{a,b,c}(z) + \sum_{k=0}^{N-1} \frac{R^{(k)}_{n_1,n_2,m}(0)}{k!} z^k + z^N B \int_0^1 \frac{t^{a+b+\underline{n}+N-1}(1-t)^{c-a-b-l} P_r(t)}{|{}_2F_1(a,b;c;1/t)|^2 (1-zt)} dt. \quad (37)$$

This form turns out to be more convenient in most applications. Moreover, taking $z = 0$ or $z = 1$, we obtain the following curious integral evaluations:

$$\int_0^1 \frac{t^{a+b+\underline{n}+N-1}(1-t)^{c-a-b-l} P_r(t)}{|{}_2F_1(a,b;c;1/t)|^2} dt = \frac{R^{(N)}_{n_1,n_2,m}(0) - Q_N N!}{N! B}, \quad (38)$$

where Q_N denotes the coefficient at z^N in $Q_{a,b,c}(z)$, and

$$\int_0^1 \frac{t^{a+b+\underline{n}+N-1}(1-t)^{c-a-b-l-1} P_r(t)}{|{}_2F_1(a,b;c;1/t)|^2} dt = \frac{R_{n_1,n_2,m}(1) - Q_{a,b,c}(1)}{B} - \frac{1}{B} \sum_{k=0}^{N-1} \frac{R^{(k)}_{n_1,n_2,m}(0)}{k!}, \quad (39)$$

where, in view of the Gauss summation formula,

$$R_{n_1,n_2,m}(1) = \frac{(c)_m (c-a-b)_{m-n_1-n_2}}{(c-a)_{m-n_1} (c-b)_{m-n_2}}.$$

Multiplying the integrand in (39) by $(1-t)$, splitting the result in two summands, and using both formulae (38) and (39), we also obtain

$$\int_0^1 \frac{t^{a+b+\underline{n}+N}(1-t)^{c-a-b-l-1} P_r(t)}{|{}_2F_1(a,b;c;1/t)|^2} dt = \frac{R_{n_1,n_2,m}(1) - Q_{a,b,c}(1) + Q_N}{B} - \frac{1}{B} \sum_{k=0}^{N} \frac{R^{(k)}_{n_1,n_2,m}(0)}{k!}. \quad (40)$$

Remark 9. *The absolute value of ${}_2F_1$ on the branch cut in the integrands in (35) and (36) can be computed as follows ($x > 1$):*

$$\begin{aligned} |{}_2F_1(a,b;c;x)|^2 = \frac{\pi^2 \Gamma(c)^2}{\Gamma(a)^2 \Gamma(b)^2} \Bigg\{ & \frac{(x-1)^{2(c-a-b)}}{[\Gamma(c-a-b)]^2} \left[{}_2F_1\left(\begin{matrix} c-a, c-b \\ c-a-b \end{matrix} \middle| 1-x \right) \right]^2 \\ & + \left[\frac{\Gamma(b-a)\Gamma(a) x^{-a}}{\Gamma(c-a)\Gamma(1/2-a)\Gamma(1/2+a)} {}_2F_1\left(\begin{matrix} a, 1-c+a \\ 1-b+a \end{matrix} \middle| 1/x \right) \right. \\ & \left. + \frac{\Gamma(a-b)\Gamma(b) x^{-b}}{\Gamma(c-b)\Gamma(1/2-b)\Gamma(1/2+b)} {}_2F_1\left(\begin{matrix} b, 1-c+b \\ 1-a+b \end{matrix} \middle| 1/x \right) \right]^2 \Bigg\}. \end{aligned}$$

Proof of Theorem 5. Define $f(z) = R_{n_1,n_2,m}(z) - Q_{a,b,c}(z)$. As the lowest degree term in $Q_{a,b,c}(z)$ is $\sim z^N$, in view of the condition $(a,b,c) \in V$, Theorem 4 implies that the function

$$\hat{f}_N(z) = R_{n_1,n_2,m}(z) - Q_{a,b,c}(z) - \sum_{k=0}^{N-1} \frac{f^{(k)}(0)}{k!} z^k = R_{n_1,n_2,m}(z) - Q_{a,b,c}(z) - \sum_{k=0}^{N-1} \frac{R^{(k)}_{n_1,n_2,m}(0)}{k!} z^k$$

is holomorphic in $z \in \mathbb{C} \setminus [1,\infty)$ and has no singularities on the banks of the branch cut other than $z = 1$ and $z = \infty$. We aim at the application of Lemma 4 to the function $\hat{f}_N(z)$. Denote $u(x) = \mathrm{Im}(\hat{f}_N(x+i0))$. As $Q_{a,b,c}(z)$ has real coefficients, we conclude that $u(x) = \mathrm{Im}[R_{n_1,n_2,m}(x+i0)]$.

If condition (33) is satisfied, then Formula (6) from Theorem 1 guarantees that the first limit in (31) in Lemma 4 is indeed equal to zero for $R_{n_1,n_2,m}(z)$ and hence also for $\hat{f}_N(z)$. Moreover, for any $-1 < \theta < \eta(a+n_1, b+n_2, c+m) - \eta(a,b,c)$, we will have

$$|u(x) x^{-N-1}| \leq |R_{n_1,n_2,m}(x+i0)| \leq M|1-x|^{\theta} \quad (41)$$

for some $M > 0$ in certain neighborhood of $x = 1$. Hence, $u(x)x^{-N-1}$ is integrable in the neighborhood of $x = 1$.

Further, condition (34) leads to the second equality in (31) with $n = N$ for the function $\hat{f}_N(z)$. Indeed, the condition (34) gives precisely (31) for the function $f(z)$ by the definition of o symbol and the extra terms in $\hat{f}_N(z)$ go to zero as $z \to \infty$ after division by z^N. Then Lemmas 2 and 3 imply that the asymptotics at infinity must have one of the forms

$$z^{-N}\hat{f}_N(z) = \frac{C}{\log(z)}\left(1 + O\left([\log(z)]^{-1}\right)\right) \text{ as } z \to \infty$$

or

$$z^{-N}\hat{f}_N(z) = \frac{C}{z^{\tau}}(1 + o(1)) \text{ as } z \to \infty$$

for some $\tau > 0$. In view of

$$\left|\operatorname{Im}\frac{1}{\log(x + i0)}\right| \leq \frac{\pi}{\log^2|x| + \pi^2}$$

which leads to

$$\frac{u(x)}{x^{N+1}} = O\left(\frac{1}{x\log^2(x)}\right) \quad \text{or} \quad \frac{u(x)}{x^{N+1}} = O\left(\frac{1}{x^{1+\tau}}\right) \text{ as } x \to \infty.$$

This implies the absolute integrability of $x^{-N-1}u(x)$ on $(1, +\infty)$. Hence, we are in the position to apply Lemma 4 leading to formula (35) by an application of Theorem 2. The ultimate claim of the Theorem follows directly from Lemmas 2 and 3. □

3. Examples

In this section, we will apply Theorem 5 to 15 specific triples (n_1, n_2, m) to obtain integral representations of the ratio $R_{n_1,n_2,m}(z)$ defined in (5). These representations are only valid if $R_{n_1,n_2,m}(z)$ is well behaved near $z = 1$ and its denominator ${}_2F_1(a, b; c; z) \neq 0$ in the cut plane $\mathbb{C} \setminus [1, +\infty)$ and on the banks of the branch cut. Conditions for the latter are given in Theorem 4, while the former in ensured by the inequality (33). To relax these restrictions, one needs a kind of regularization near the point $z = 1$ as well as near all zeros of the denominator. Such regularizations were explored by us in [14]. We will further mention conditions for $R_{n_1,n_2,m}(z)$ to belong the Markov $\mathcal{M}$ and the Stieltjes $\mathcal{S}$ classes, whose definitions can be found below formula (4).

Example 1. *For the Gauss ratio $R_{0,1,1}(z)$ according to (26), we obtain $p = l = r = 0$. Theorem 3 and definition (27b) yield*

$$B_{0,1,1}P_0(t) \equiv \frac{\Gamma(c)\Gamma(c+1)}{\Gamma(a)\Gamma(b+1)\Gamma(c-a+1)\Gamma(c-b)}.$$

Next, using (16) and (21), or directly, it is easy to verify that

$$Q_{a,b,c} = \lim_{z\to\infty} R_{0,1,1}(z) = \begin{cases} 0, & b \leq a \\ [c(b-a)]/[b(c-a)], & b > a. \end{cases}$$

Then, Theorem 5 with $N = 0$ yields

$$R_{0,1,1}(z) = Q_{a,b,c} + \frac{\Gamma(c)\Gamma(c+1)}{\Gamma(a)\Gamma(b+1)\Gamma(c-b)\Gamma(c-a+1)}\int_0^1 \frac{t^{a+b-1}(1-t)^{c-a-b}dt}{(1-zt)|{}_2F_1(a, b; c; t^{-1})|^2}.$$

In order for this representation to hold, we need to assume that $(a, b, c) \in V$, that is to say (a, b, c) satisfies at least one of the conditions (I)–(VI) from Theorem 4. For $(a, b, c) \in V$ the condition (33) from Theorem 5 holds automatically since the parameter $q = m - n_1 - n_2$ in Lemma 1 vanishes such that $R_{0,1,1}(z)$ is integrable in the neighborhood of $z = 1$. We remark that the integrand is symmetric with respect to the interchange of a and b, and the asymmetry of $R_{0,1,1}(z)$ is only reflected in the constants $Q_{a,b,c}$ and $B_{0,1,1}$.

The above integral representation was first found by V. Belevitch in [11] (Formula (72)) under the restrictions $0 \le a, b \le c$, $c \ge 1$ (there is a small mistake in Belevitch's paper—a superfluous 2 in the denominator of the constant $Q_{a,b,c}$). Independently, using the Gauss continued fraction (2) and Wall's theorem, Küstner [10] (Theorem 1.5) proved that $R_{0,1,1}(z)$ is a Markov function (generating function of a Hausdorff moment sequence) if $0 < a \le c+1$, $0 < b \le c$. As we mentioned in introduction, the coefficients of the Gauss continued fraction (2) for $R_{0,1,1}(z)$ are all positive if (a) $-1 < a < 0$ and either $-1 < b < c < 0$ or $0 < c < b < c+1$ or (b) $0 < a < c+1$, $c > 0$ and $-1 < b < c$. If these conditions hold, while conditions of Runckel's Theorem 4 are violated, i.e., $(a, b, c) \notin V$, then representation (4) is true while the above integral representation is not. Hence, in this situation, $R_{0,1,1}(z)$ has pole(s) in the interval $(0, 1)$, which are reflected by the atoms of the representing measure in (4) at some real points $s_k > 1$. This is the case, for instance, if $0 < c < a < c+1$ and $-1 < b < 0$. In this situation $R_{0,1,1}(z)$ still belongs to the Stieltjes class $\mathcal{S}$.

Example 2. *For the ratio $R_{0,1,0}(z)$ according to (26), we obtain $l = 1$, $p = r = 0$. Theorem 3 and definition (27b) yield*

$$B_{0,1,0}P_0(t) \equiv \frac{[\Gamma(c)]^2}{\Gamma(a)\Gamma(b+1)\Gamma(c-a)\Gamma(c-b)}.$$

Next, using (16) and (21), or directly, we can verify that

$$Q_{a,b} = \lim_{z\to\infty} R_{0,1,0}(z) = \begin{cases} 0, & b \le a \\ (b-a)/b, & b > a. \end{cases}$$

Then Theorem 5 with $N = 0$ yields

$$R_{0,1,0}(z) = Q_{a,b} + \frac{[\Gamma(c)]^2}{\Gamma(a)\Gamma(b+1)\Gamma(c-a)\Gamma(c-b)} \int_0^1 \frac{t^{a+b-1}(1-t)^{c-a-b-1}dt}{(1-zt)|{}_2F_1(a,b;c;1/t)|^2}.$$

Note that similarly to Example 1, the integrand is symmetric with respect to the interchange of a and b, and the asymmetry of the left-hand side is only reflected in the constants. In order for this representation to hold, we need to assume that $(a, b, c) \in V$ in Theorem 4. Under this restriction and except for the degenerate cases $ab = 0$ and $(c-a)(c-b) = 0$, the condition (33) reads

$$(c-a-b-1)_- - (c-a-b)_- > -1,$$

which is easily seen to be equivalent to $c > a + b$. The above set of conditions holds, for example, if $-1 < a < 0$ and $0 < b < c$ or $a > 0$ and $-1 < b < c - a$. Note that the degenerate cases $ab = 0$ and $(c-a)(c-b) = 0$ yield the standard Euler's integral [23] (Theorem 2.2.4) in the above representation (although the integral may disappear when multiplied by zero). This remark is also true for all subsequent examples, so we will omit it in the sequel.

Using continued fractions, Küstner [10] (Theorem 1.5) proved that $R_{0,1,0}(z) \in \mathcal{M}$ (the Markov class) if $-1 \le b \le c$ and $0 < a \le c$. Askitis [29] (Lemma 6.2.2) found another proof for the this claim (without a use of continued fractions). We also remark that the continued fraction for $R_{0,1,0}$ was also found by Gauss; see [1] (Equation (26)) or [10] (Equation (2.7)), in the form

$$\cfrac{1}{1-\cfrac{\alpha_1 z}{1-\cfrac{\alpha_2 z}{1-\ddots}}},$$

where $\alpha_1 = a/c$, *and for* $k \geq 1$

$$\alpha_{2k} = \frac{(b+k)(c-a+k-1)}{(c+2k-2)(c+2k-1)}, \quad \alpha_{2k+1} = \frac{(a+k)(c-b+k-1)}{(c+2k-1)(c+2k)}.$$

From these formulae, it is also not difficult to formulate sufficient conditions for $\alpha_n \geq 0$ *ensuring that* $R_{0,1,0} \in \mathcal{S}$ *(the Stieltjes class).*

Example 3. *For the ratio* $R_{1,1,1}(z)$ *according to* (26), *we obtain* $l = 1$, $p = r = 0$. *Theorem* 3 *and definition* (27b) *yield*

$$B_{1,1,1}P_0(t) = \frac{\Gamma(c)\Gamma(c+1)}{\Gamma(a+1)\Gamma(b+1)\Gamma(c-a)\Gamma(c-b)}$$

Next, it is easy to verify using (16) *and* (21) *or directly that*

$$Q_{a,b,c} = \lim_{z\to\infty} R_{1,1,1}(z) = 0.$$

Then, according to the case $N = 0$ *of Theorem* 5, *we obtain*

$$R_{1,1,1}(z) = \frac{\Gamma(c)\Gamma(c+1)}{\Gamma(a+1)\Gamma(b+1)\Gamma(c-a)\Gamma(c-b)} \int_0^1 \frac{t^{a+b}(1-t)^{c-a-b-1}dt}{(1-zt)|{}_2F_1(a,b;c;1/t)|^2}.$$

In order for this representation to hold, we need to assume that $(a,b,c) \in V$ *in Theorem* 4. *Under this restriction and except for the degenerate cases* $ab = 0$ *and* $(c-a)(c-b) = 0$, *the condition* (33) *reads*

$$(c-a-b-1)_- - (c-a-b)_- > -1,$$

which is easily seen to be equivalent to $c > a+b$. *All these conditions are satisfied, for example, if (a)* $-1 < a < 0$ *and* $0 < b < c$ *or (b)* $0 < a < c$ *and* $-1 < b < c-a$. *The above integral representation obviously implies that* $R_{1,1,1} \in \mathcal{M}$ *if the constant in front of the integral is positive (or* $-R_{1,1,1} \in \mathcal{M}$ *otherwise).*

Example 4. *For the ratio* $R_{1,1,2}(z)$ *according to* (26), *we obtain* $l = p = r = 0$. *Theorem* 3 *and definition* (27b) *yield*

$$B_{1,1,2}P_0(t) = B_{1,1,2}P_0 = \frac{\Gamma(c+1)\Gamma(c+2)}{\Gamma(a+1)\Gamma(b+1)\Gamma(c-a+1)\Gamma(c-b+1)}.$$

Next, it is easy to verify using (16) *and* (21) *or directly that*

$$Q_{a,b,c} = \lim_{z\to\infty} R_{1,1,2}(z) = 0.$$

Then, according to the case $N = 0$ *of Theorem* 5, *we obtain*

$$R_{1,1,2}(z) = \frac{\Gamma(c+1)\Gamma(c+2)}{\Gamma(a+1)\Gamma(b+1)\Gamma(c-a+1)\Gamma(c-b+1)} \int_0^1 \frac{t^{a+b}(1-t)^{c-a-b}dt}{(1-zt)|{}_2F_1(a,b;c;1/t)|^2}.$$

In order for this representation to hold, we need to assume that $(a,b,c) \in V$ *in Theorem* 4. *Under this restriction and except for the degenerate cases* $ab = 0$ *and* $(c-a)(c-b) = 0$, *the condition* (33) *reads*

$$(c-a-b)_- - (c-a-b)_- > -1$$

and is trivially satisfied. If the above integral representation holds true, then $R_{1,1,2} \in \mathcal{M}$ *once the constant in front of the integral is positive, which is the case for parameters satisfying any of the conditions* (I)–(V) *of Theorem* 4.

Example 5. *For the ratio $R_{0,2,2}(z)$ according to (26), we obtain $l = p = 0$, $r = 1$. Theorem 3 and definition (27b) yield*

$$B_{0,2,2}P_1(t) = \frac{\Gamma(c)\Gamma(c+2)(ct+b-a+1)}{\Gamma(a)\Gamma(b+2)\Gamma(c-a+2)\Gamma(c-b)}.$$

Next, it is easy to verify using (16) and (21) or directly that

$$Q_{a,b,c} = \lim_{z\to\infty} R_{0,2,2}(z) = \begin{cases} 0, & b \le a \\ c(c+1)(b-a)(b-a+1)/[b(b+1)(c-a)(c-a+1)], & b > a. \end{cases}$$

Then, according to the case $N = 0$ of Theorem 5, we obtain

$$R_{0,2,2}(z) = Q_{a,b,c} + \frac{\Gamma(c)\Gamma(c+2)}{\Gamma(a)\Gamma(b+2)\Gamma(c-a+2)\Gamma(c-b)}\int_0^1 \frac{t^{a+b-1}(ct+b-a+1)(1-t)^{c-a-b}dt}{(1-zt)|{}_2F_1(a,b;c;1/t)|^2}.$$

In order for this representation to hold, we need to assume that $(a,b,c) \in V$ in Theorem 4. Under this restriction and except for the degenerate cases $ab = 0$ and $(c-a)(c-b) = 0$, the condition (33) reads

$$(c-a-b)_- - (c-a-b)_- > -1$$

and is trivially satisfied. Here, we need to require that the zero $t^* = (a-b-1)/c$ of the polynomial $ct+b-a+1$ lies outside the interval $(0,1)$ in order that $R_{0,2,2} \in \mathcal{M}$ or $-R_{0,2,2} \in \mathcal{M}$ (depending on the signs of the measure and the constant).

Example 6. *For the ratio $R_{0,2,0}(z)$ according to (26), we obtain $p = 0$, $l = 2$, $r = 1$. Theorem 3 and definition (27b) yield*

$$B_{0,2,0}P_1(t) = \frac{[\Gamma(c)]^2(t(c-2b-2)+b+1-a)}{\Gamma(a)\Gamma(b+2)\Gamma(c-a)\Gamma(c-b)}.$$

Next, it is easy to verify using (16) and (21) or directly that

$$Q_{a,b} = \lim_{z\to\infty} R_{0,2,0}(z) = \begin{cases} 0, & b \le a \\ (b-a)(b-a+1)/[b(b+1)], & b > a. \end{cases}$$

Then, according to the case $N = 0$ of Theorem 5, we obtain

$$R_{0,2,0}(z) = Q_{a,b} + \frac{[\Gamma(c)]^2}{\Gamma(a)\Gamma(b+2)\Gamma(c-a)\Gamma(c-b)}\int_0^1 \frac{t^{a+b-1}(b-a+1+t(c-2b-2))(1-t)^{c-a-b-2}dt}{(1-zt)|{}_2F_1(a,b;c;1/t)|^2}.$$

In order for this representation to hold, we need to assume that $(a,b,c) \in V$ in Theorem 4. Under this restriction and except for the degenerate cases $ab = 0$ and $(c-a)(c-b) = 0$, the condition (33) reads

$$(c-a-b-2)_- - (c-a-b)_- > -1$$

which is easily seen to be equivalent to $c > a+b+1$. Similar to the previous example, a necessary condition for $R_{0,2,0} \in \mathcal{M}$ or $-R_{0,2,0} \in \mathcal{M}$ is that the zero $t^* = (a-b-1)/(c-2b-2)$ of the polynomial $b-a+1+t(c-2b-2)$ lies outside the interval $(0,1)$.

Example 7. *For the ratio $R_{1,1,0}(z)$ according to (26), we obtain $p = 0$, $l = 2$, $r = 0$. Theorem 3 and definition (27b) yield*

$$B_{1,1,0}P_0(t) = -\frac{[\Gamma(c)]^2(c-a-b-1)}{\Gamma(a+1)\Gamma(b+1)\Gamma(c-a)\Gamma(c-b)}.$$

Next, it is easy to verify using (16) *and* (21) *or directly that*

$$Q_{a,b,c} = \lim_{z\to\infty} R_{1,1,0}(z) = 0.$$

Then, according to the case $N = 0$ *of Theorem* 5, *we obtain*

$$R_{1,1,0}(z) = -\frac{[\Gamma(c)]^2(c-a-b-1)}{\Gamma(a+1)\Gamma(b+1)\Gamma(c-a)\Gamma(c-b)}\int_0^1 \frac{t^{a+b}(1-t)^{c-a-b-2}dt}{(1-zt)|{}_2F_1(a,b;c;1/t)|^2}.$$

In order for this representation to hold, we need to assume that $(a,b,c) \in V$ *in Theorem* 4. *Under this restriction and except for the degenerate cases* $ab = 0$ *and* $(c-a)(c-b) = 0$, *the condition* (33) *reads*

$$(c-a-b-2)_- - (c-a-b)_- > -1$$

which is easily seen to be equivalent to $c > a+b+1$. *Now, if the above integral representation for* $R_{1,1,0}$ *holds true, then either* $-R_{1,1,0}$ *or* $R_{1,1,0}$ *belong to the class* $\mathcal{M}$ *(depending on the sign of the constant in front of the integral).*

Example 8. *For the ratio* $R_{0,0,1}(z)$ *according to* (26), *we obtain* $p = 1, l = r = 0$. *Theorem* 3 *and definition* (27b) *yield*

$$B_{0,0,1}P_0(t) = -\frac{\Gamma(c)\Gamma(c+1)}{\Gamma(a)\Gamma(b)\Gamma(c-a+1)\Gamma(c-b+1)}.$$

Next, it is easy to verify using (16) *and* (21) *or directly that*

$$Q_{a,b,c} = \lim_{z\to\infty} R_{0,0,1}(z) = \begin{cases} c/(c-b), & b \le a \\ c/(c-a), & b > a, \end{cases}$$

unless $c = \min(a,b)$. *Then, the case* $N = 0$ *of Theorem* 5 *leads to the representation*

$$R_{0,0,1}(z) = Q_{a,b,c} - \frac{\Gamma(c)\Gamma(c+1)}{\Gamma(a)\Gamma(b)\Gamma(c-a+1)\Gamma(c-b+1)}\int_0^1 \frac{t^{a+b-1}(1-t)^{c-a-b}dt}{(1-zt)|{}_2F_1(a,b;c;1/t)|^2}.$$

In order for this representation to hold, we need to assume that $(a,b,c) \in V$ *in Theorem* 4. *Under this restriction and except for the degenerate cases* $ab = 0$ *and* $(c-a)(c-b) = 0$, *the condition* (33) *reads*

$$(c-a-b+1)_- - (c-a-b)_- > -1$$

which is easily seen to be satisfied for all real a, b, c. *Here,* $R_{0,0,1}(z) - Q_{a,b,c}$ *or* $Q_{a,b,c} - R_{0,0,1}(z)$ *is a Markov function under conditions* (I)–(II) *or, respectively,* (III)–(V) *of Theorem* 4.

Example 9. *For the ratio* $R_{0,0,-1}(z)$ *according to* (26) *we obtain* $l = 1, p = r = 0$. *Theorem* 3 *and definition* (27b) *then yield*

$$B_{0,0,-1}P_0(t) = \frac{\Gamma(c)\Gamma(c-1)}{\Gamma(a)\Gamma(b)\Gamma(c-a)\Gamma(c-b)}.$$

Next, it is easy to verify using (16) *and* (21) *or directly that*

$$Q_{a,b,c} = \lim_{z\to\infty} R_{0,0,-1}(z) = \begin{cases} (c-b-1)/(c-1), & b \le a \\ (c-a-1)/(c-1), & b > a. \end{cases}$$

Then, the case $N = 0$ *of Theorem* 5 *leads to the representation*

$$R_{0,0,-1}(z) = Q_{a,b,c} + \frac{\Gamma(c)\Gamma(c-1)}{\Gamma(a)\Gamma(b)\Gamma(c-a)\Gamma(c-b)}\int_0^1 \frac{t^{a+b-1}(1-t)^{c-a-b-1}dt}{(1-zt)|{}_2F_1(a,b;c;1/t)|^2}.$$

In order for this representation to hold, we need to assume that $(a,b,c) \in V$ *in Theorem 4. Under this restriction and except for the degenerate cases* $ab = 0$ *and* $(c-a)(c-b) = 0$*, the condition (33) reads*

$$(c-a-b-1)_- - (c-a-b)_- > -1$$

which is easily seen to be equivalent to $c > a+b$*. All these conditions are satisfied, for example, if (a)* $-1 < a < 0$ *and* $0 < b < c-a$ *or (b)* $0 < a < c$ *and* $-1 < b < c-a$*. Here, the representing measure is again positive for all values of parameters so that* $R_{0,0,-1} \in \mathcal{M}$ *provided the above integral representation holds and the constants are positive.*

Example 10. *For the ratio* $R_{0,0,2}(z)$ *according to (26), we obtain* $p = 2$, $l = 0$, $r = 1$*. The application of Theorem 3 and definition (27b) yields*

$$B_{0,0,2}P_1(t) = \frac{\Gamma(c)\Gamma(c+2)[ct+a+b-2c-1]}{\Gamma(a)\Gamma(b)\Gamma(c-a+2)\Gamma(c-b+2)}.$$

Next, it is easy to verify using (16) and (21) or directly that

$$Q_{a,b,c} = \lim_{z\to\infty} R_{0,0,2}(z) = \begin{cases} c(c+1)/[(c-b)(c-b+1)], & b \le a \\ c(c+1)/[(c-a)(c-a+1)], & b > a. \end{cases}$$

Then, the case $N = 0$ *of Theorem 5 leads to the representation*

$$R_{0,0,2}(z) = Q_{a,b,c} + \frac{\Gamma(c)\Gamma(c+2)}{\Gamma(a)\Gamma(b)\Gamma(c-a+2)\Gamma(c-b+2)} \int_0^1 \frac{t^{a+b-1}(ct+a+b-2c-1)(1-t)^{c-a-b}dt}{(1-zt)|{}_2F_1(a,b;c;1/t)|^2}.$$

In order for this representation to hold, we need to assume that $(a,b,c) \in V$ *in Theorem 4. Under this restriction and except for the degenerate cases* $ab = 0$ *and* $(c-a)(c-b) = 0$*, the condition (33) reads*

$$(c-a-b+2)_- - (c-a-b)_- > -1$$

which is true for all real a, b, c*. The necessary condition for* $R_{0,0,2} \in \mathcal{M}$ *or* $-R_{0,0,2} \in \mathcal{M}$ *is that the zero* $t^* = (2c-a-b+1)/c$ *of the polynomial* $ct+a+b-2c-1$ *lies outside the interval* $(0,1)$*. Under this condition,* $R_{0,0,2} \in \mathcal{M}$ *for the values of parameters, making the constants positive.*

Example 11. *For the ratio* $R_{0,1,2}(z)$ *according to (26), we obtain* $p = 1$, $l = 0$, $r = 1$*. Theorem 3 and definition (27b) yield*

$$B_{0,1,2}P_1(t) = -\frac{\Gamma(c)\Gamma(c+2)(ct+b-c)}{\Gamma(a)\Gamma(b+1)\Gamma(c-a+2)\Gamma(c-b+1)}.$$

Next, it is easy to verify using (16) and (21) or directly that

$$Q_{a,b,c} = \lim_{z\to\infty} R_{0,1,2}(z) = \begin{cases} 0, & b \le a \\ c(c+1)(b-a)/[b(c-a)(c-a+1)], & b > a. \end{cases}$$

Then, the case $N = 0$ *of Theorem 5 leads to the representation*

$$R_{0,1,2}(z) = Q_{a,b,c} - \frac{\Gamma(c)\Gamma(c+2)}{\Gamma(a)\Gamma(b+1)\Gamma(c-a+2)\Gamma(c-b+1)} \int_0^1 \frac{t^{a+b-1}(ct+b-c)(1-t)^{c-a-b}dt}{(1-zt)|{}_2F_1(a,b;c;1/t)|^2}.$$

In order for this representation to hold, we need to assume that $(a,b,c) \in V$ *in Theorem 4. Under this restriction and except for the degenerate cases* $ab = 0$ *and* $(c-a)(c-b) = 0$*, the condition (33) reads*

$$(c-a-b+1)_- - (c-a-b)_- > -1$$

which is true for all real a, b, c. Similar to the previous example, the additional condition that $t^* = (c-b)/c \notin (0,1)$ yields $Q_{a,b,c} - R_{0,1,2} \in \mathcal{M}$ or $R_{0,1,2} - Q_{a,b,c} \in \mathcal{M}$ depending on whether the constant near the integral is positive or negative.

Example 12. *For the ratio $R_{0,-1,0}(z)$ according to (26) we obtain $l = 1$, $p = r = 0$. Theorem 3 and definition (27b) yield*

$$B_{0,-1,0}P_0(t) = -\frac{[\Gamma(c)]^2}{\Gamma(a)\Gamma(b)\Gamma(c-a)\Gamma(c-b+1)}.$$

Using Lemmas 2 and 3 or by direct, albeit tedious calculation, we obtain the following asymptotic approximations:

(1) *If $b+1 < a$, then $R_{0,-1,0}(z) = Az + B + o(1)$ as $z \to \infty$;*

(2) *If $b < a \le b+1$, then $R_{0,-1,0}(z) = Az + o(z)$ as $z \to \infty$;*

(3) *If $b-1 \le a \le b$, then $R_{0,-1,0}(z) = o(z)$ as $z \to \infty$;*

(4) *If $a < b-1$, then $R_{0,-1,0}(z) = C + o(1)$ as $z \to \infty$,*

where

$$A = \frac{b-a}{c-b}, \quad B = \frac{b(b+1) - 2ab + c(a-1)}{(c-b)(a-b-1)}, \quad C = \frac{b-1}{b-a-1}.$$

Hence, if $|a-b| > 1$, we have $R_{0,-1,0}(z) = \beta z + \alpha + o(1)$ as $z \to \infty$, with $(\beta, \alpha) = (A, B)$ if $a > b+1$ and $(\beta, \alpha) = (0, C)$ if $a < b-1$. Then for $|a-b| > 1$ we can choose $N = 0$ in Theorem 5 leading to the representation

$$R_{0,-1,0}(z) = \alpha + \beta z - \frac{[\Gamma(c)]^2}{\Gamma(a)\Gamma(b)\Gamma(c-a)\Gamma(c-b+1)} \int_0^1 \frac{t^{a+b-2}(1-t)^{c-a-b}}{(1-zt)|{}_2F_1(a,b;c;1/t)|^2} dt. \quad (42)$$

In addition to the condition $|a-b| > 1$, we need to assume that $(a,b,c) \in V$ in Theorem 4. Under these restrictions and except for the degenerate cases $ab = 0$ and $(c-a)(c-b) = 0$, the condition (33) reads

$$(c-a-b+1)_- - (c-a-b)_- > -1$$

which is true for all real a, b, c. If the above representation holds, we see that $\alpha + \beta z - R_{0,-1,0}(z) \in \mathcal{M}$ if the constant in front of the integral is positive.

For arbitrary a, b, we obtain $R_{0,-1,0}(z) = \beta z + o(z)$ as $z \to \infty$, with $\beta = A$ if $b < a$ and $\beta = 0$ if $a \le b$. Hence, we can remove the restriction $|a-b| > 1$ by taking $N = 1$ in Theorem 5, which leads to

$$R_{0,-1,0}(z) = 1 + \beta z - \frac{z[\Gamma(c)]^2}{\Gamma(a)\Gamma(b)\Gamma(c-a)\Gamma(c-b+1)} \int_0^1 \frac{t^{a+b-1}(1-t)^{c-a-b}}{(1-zt)|{}_2F_1(a,b;c;1/t)|^2} dt, \quad (43)$$

or, by taking $N = 2$, we obtain

$$R_{0,-1,0}(z) = 1 - \frac{ac}{c^2}z - \frac{z^2[\Gamma(c)]^2}{\Gamma(a)\Gamma(b)\Gamma(c-a)\Gamma(c-b+1)} \int_0^1 \frac{t^{a+b}(1-t)^{c-a-b}}{(1-zt)|{}_2F_1(a,b;c;1/t)|^2} dt. \quad (44)$$

Example 13. *For the ratio $R_{-1,-1,0}(z)$ according to (26), we obtain $p = 2$, $l = r = 0$. Theorem 3 and definition (27b) yields*

$$B_{-1,-1,0}P_0(t) = -\frac{[\Gamma(c)]^2(c-a-b+1)}{\Gamma(a)\Gamma(b)\Gamma(c-a+1)\Gamma(c-b+1)}.$$

Using Lemmas 2 and 3 or by direct, albeit tedious, calculation, we obtain the asymptotic approximations

(1) *If $a > b+1$, then $R_{-1,-1,0}(z) = B(a,b)z + A(a,b) + o(1)$ as $z \to \infty$;*

(2) *If $b \le a \le b+1$, then $R_{-1,-1,0}(z) = B(a,b)z + o(z)$ as $z \to \infty$;*

(3) *If $b-1 \le a \le b$, then $R_{-1,-1,0}(z) = B(b,a)z + o(z)$ as $z \to \infty$;*

(4) *If $a < b-1$, then $R_{1,-1,0}(z) = B(b,a)z + A(b,a) + o(1)$ as $z \to \infty$,*

where

$$B(a,b) = \frac{a-1}{b-c}, \quad A(a,b) = \frac{(a-1)(2b-c)}{(c-b)(1+b-a)}.$$

Hence, if $|a-b| > 1$, then $R_{1,-1,0}(z) = \beta z + \alpha + o(1)$ as $z \to \infty$, where $(\beta,\alpha) = (B(a,b), A(a,b))$ if $a > b+1$ and $(\beta,\alpha) = (B(b,a), A(b,a))$ if $a < b-1$. Hence, for $|a-b| > 1$, the $N = 1$ case of Theorem 5 leads to the representation

$$R_{-1,-1,0}(z) = \alpha + \beta z - \frac{[\Gamma(c)]^2(c-a-b+1)}{\Gamma(a)\Gamma(b)\Gamma(c-a+1)\Gamma(c-b+1)} \int_0^1 \frac{t^{a+b-2}(1-t)^{c-a-b}}{|{}_2F_1(a,b;c;1/t)|^2(1-zt)}dt. \tag{45}$$

In addition to the condition $|a-b| > 1$, we need to assume that $(a,b,c) \in V$ in Theorem 4. Under these restrictions and except for the degenerate cases $ab = 0$ and $(c-a)(c-b) = 0$ the condition (33) reads

$$(c-a-b+2)_- - (c-a-b)_- > -1,$$

which is true for all real a,b,c. The above representation implies that $\alpha + \beta z - R_{-1,-1,0}(z) \in \mathcal{M}$ if the constant in front of the integral is positive.

As $R_{-1,-1,0}(z) = \beta z + o(z)$ as $z \to \infty$, where $\beta = B(a,b)$ if $a \ge b$ and $\beta = B(b,a)$ if $a \ge b$, we can lift the restriction $|a-b| > 1$ by taking $N = 1$ in Theorem 5, which leads to

$$R_{-1,-1,0}(z) = 1 + \beta z - \frac{z[\Gamma(c)]^2(c-a-b+1)}{\Gamma(a)\Gamma(b)\Gamma(c-a+1)\Gamma(c-b+1)} \int_0^1 \frac{t^{a+b-1}(1-t)^{c-a-b}}{|{}_2F_1(a,b;c;1/t)|^2(1-zt)}dt, \tag{46}$$

or, by taking $N = 2$, we obtain

$$R_{-1,-1,0}(z) = 1 + \frac{(a+b-1)c}{c^2}z - \frac{z^2[\Gamma(c)]^2(c-a-b+1)}{\Gamma(a)\Gamma(b)\Gamma(c-a+1)\Gamma(c-b+1)} \int_0^1 \frac{t^{a+b}(1-t)^{c-a-b}}{|{}_2F_1(a,b;c;1/t)|^2(1-zt)}dt. \tag{47}$$

Example 14. *For the ratio $R_{-1,1,0}(z)$ according to (26), we obtain $p = l = r = 0$. Theorem 3 and definition (27b) yield:*

$$B_{-1,1,0}P_0 = \frac{[\Gamma(c)]^2(a-b-1)}{\Gamma(a)\Gamma(b+1)\Gamma(c-a+1)\Gamma(c-b)}.$$

The asymptotic behavior of $R_{-1,1,0}(z)$ as $z \to \infty$ is rather complicated and depends on the relation between a and b. The application of Lemmas 2 and 3 yields the following:

(1) *If $b+1 < a$, then $R_{-1,1,0}(z) = o(1)$ as $z \to \infty$;*

(2) *If $b \le a \le b+1$, then $R_{-1,1,0}(z) = o(z)$ as $z \to \infty$;*

(3) *If $b-1 \le a < b$, then $R_{-1,1,0}(z) = Bz + o(z)$ as $z \to \infty$;*

(4) *If $a < b-1$, then $R_{-1,1,0}(z) = Bz + C + o(1)$ as $z \to \infty$,*

where

$$B = \frac{(b-a)(b-a+1)}{b(a-c)}, \quad C = \frac{(b-a)(b-a+1)(c(a+b-1)-2ab)}{b(c-a)(a-b-1)(a-b+1)}.$$

Hence, if $|a-b| > 1$ we have $R_{-1,1,0}(z) = \beta z + \alpha + o(1)$ as $z \to \infty$, where $(\beta,\alpha) = (0,0)$ when $a > b+1$ and $(\beta,\alpha) = (B,C)$ when $a < b-1$. Then, for $|a-b| > 1$ the $N = 0$ case of Theorem 5 leads to the representation

$$R_{-1,1,0}(z) = \alpha + \beta z + \frac{[\Gamma(c)]^2(a-b-1)}{\Gamma(a)\Gamma(b+1)\Gamma(c-a+1)\Gamma(c-b)} \int_0^1 \frac{t^{a+b-2}(1-t)^{c-a-b}}{|{}_2F_1(a,b;c;1/t)|^2(1-zt)}dt. \tag{48}$$

In addition to the condition $|a-b|>1$, we need to assume that $(a,b,c)\in V$ in Theorem 4. Under these restrictions and except for the degenerate cases $ab=0$ and $(c-a)(c-b)=0$ the condition (33) reads

$$(c-a-b)_- - (c-a-b)_- > -1,$$

which is true for all real a,b,c. Here, $R_{-1,1,0}(z)-\alpha-\beta z\in\mathcal{M}$ provided that the above representation holds and the constant in front of the integral is positive.

For arbitrary values of a,b, we have $R_{-1,1,0}(z)=\beta z+o(z)$ as $z\to\infty$, where $\beta=0$ when $a\ge b$ and $\beta=B$ when $a<b$. Hence, we can use representation (35) with $N=1$ yielding

$$R_{-1,1,0}(z)=1+\beta z+\frac{z[\Gamma(c)]^2(a-b-1)}{\Gamma(a)\Gamma(b+1)\Gamma(c-a+1)\Gamma(c-b)}\int_0^1\frac{t^{a+b-1}(1-t)^{c-a-b}}{|{}_2F_1(a,b;c;1/t)|^2(1-zt)}dt \tag{49}$$

or with $N=2$ yielding

$$R_{-1,1,0}(z)=1+\frac{(a-b-1)c}{c^2}z+\frac{z^2[\Gamma(c)]^2(a-b-1)}{\Gamma(a)\Gamma(b+1)\Gamma(c-a+1)\Gamma(c-b)}\int_0^1\frac{t^{a+b}(1-t)^{c-a-b}}{|{}_2F_1(a,b;c;1/t)|^2(1-zt)}dt. \tag{50}$$

Example 15. For the ratio $R_{-2,-2,0}(z)$ according to (26), we obtain $p=4$, $l=0$, $r=1$. Theorem 3 and definition (27b) yield

$$B_{-2,-2,0}P_1(t)=-\frac{[\Gamma(c)]^2(c-a-b+2)(\rho_0+\rho_1 t)}{\Gamma(a)\Gamma(b)\Gamma(c-a+2)\Gamma(c-b+2)},$$

where $\rho_0=a^2+b^2-(c+2)(a+b)+3c+1$, $\rho_1=c(c-a-b+1)+2(ab-a-b+1)$. Using Lemmas 2 and 3 or by direct, albeit tedious, calculation, we obtain the following asymptotic approximations:

(1) If $a>b+2$, then $R_{-2,-2,0}(z)=\gamma_{a,b,c}z^2+\beta_{a,b,c}z+\alpha_{a,b,c}+o(1)$ as $z\to\infty$;

(2) If $b+1<a\le b+2$, then $R_{-2,-2,0}(z)=\gamma_{a,b,c}z^2+\beta_{a,b,c}z+o(z)$ as $z\to\infty$;

(3) If $b\le a\le b+1$, then $R_{-2,-2,0}(z)=\gamma_{a,b,c}z^2+o(z^2)$ as $z\to\infty$;

(4) If $b-1\le a\le b$, then $R_{-2,-2,0}(z)=\gamma_{b,a,c}z^2+o(z^2)$ as $z\to\infty$;

(5) If $b-2\le a<b-1$, then $R_{-2,-2,0}(z)=\gamma_{b,a,c}z^2+\beta_{b,a,c}z+o(z)$ as $z\to\infty$;

(6) If $a<b-2$, then $R_{-2,-2,0}(z)=\gamma_{b,a,c}z^2+\beta_{b,a,c}z+\alpha_{b,a,c}+o(1)$ as $z\to\infty$,

where

$$\gamma_{a,b,c}=\frac{(a-2)(a-1)}{(c-b)(c-b+1)},\quad \beta_{a,b,c}=\frac{2(a-2)(a-1)(c+1-2b)}{(c-b)(c-b+1)(b-a+1)},$$

$$\alpha_{a,b,c}=\gamma_{a,b,c}\frac{c(c+1)(a-1)+2b^2(a+4c-3b)-2ab(c+2)-b(3c^2-c-6)}{(a-b-2)(a-b-1)^2}.$$

Hence, for $|a-b|>2$, we have $R_{-2,-2,0}(z)=\gamma z^2+\beta z+\alpha+o(1)$ as $z\to\infty$, where $(\gamma,\beta,\alpha)=(\gamma_{a,b,c},\beta_{a,b,c},\alpha_{a,b,c})$ when $a>b+2$ and $(\gamma,\beta,\alpha)=(\gamma_{b,a,c},\beta_{b,a,c},\alpha_{b,a,c})$ when $a<b-2$. Then, for $|a-b|>2$, the case $N=0$ of Theorem 5 leads to the representation

$$R_{-2,-2,0}(z)=\gamma z^2+\beta z+\alpha-\frac{[\Gamma(c)]^2(c-a-b+2)}{\Gamma(a)\Gamma(b)\Gamma(c-a+2)\Gamma(c-b+2)}\int_0^1\frac{(\rho_0+\rho_1 t)t^{a+b-3}(1-t)^{c-a-b}}{|{}_2F_1(a,b;c;1/t)|^2(1-zt)}dt. \tag{51}$$

In addition to condition $|a-b|>2$, we need to assume that $(a,b,c)\in V$ in Theorem 4. Under these restrictions and except for the degenerate cases $ab=0$ and $(c-a)(c-b)=0$, the condition (33) reads

$$(c-a-b+4)_- - (c-a-b)_- > -1,$$

which is true for all real a,b,c. The above integral representation implies that either $\gamma z^2+\beta z+\alpha-R_{-2,-2,0}(z)\in\mathcal{M}$ or $R_{-2,-2,0}(z)-\gamma z^2-\beta z-\alpha\in\mathcal{M}$ if the zero $t^*=-\rho_0/\rho_1$ of the polynomial $\rho_0+\rho_1 t$ lies outside of the interval $(0,1)$.

If $1 < |a-b| \le 2$, we see that the asymptotics takes the form $R_{-2,-2,0}(z) = \gamma z^2 + \beta z + o(z)$ as $z \to \infty$, where $(\gamma, \beta) = (\gamma_{a,b,c}, \beta_{a,b,c})$ when $a > b+1$ and $(\gamma, \beta) = (\gamma_{b,a,c}, \beta_{b,a,c})$ when $a < b-1$. Hence, for $1 < |a-b|$ according to (35) with $N = 1$, we obtain

$$R_{-2,-2,0}(z) = \gamma z^2 + \beta z + 1 - \frac{z[\Gamma(c)]^2(c-a-b+2)}{\Gamma(a)\Gamma(b)\Gamma(c-a+2)\Gamma(c-b+2)} \int_0^1 \frac{(\rho_0+\rho_1 t)t^{a+b-2}(1-t)^{c-a-b}}{|{}_2F_1(a,b;c;1/t)|^2(1-zt)} dt. \tag{52}$$

Similarly, for $|a-b| \le 1$, the asymptotics takes the form $R_{-2,-2,0}(z) = \gamma z^2 + o(z^2)$, where $\gamma = \gamma_{a,b,c}$ when $a \ge b$ and $\gamma = \gamma_{b,a,c}$ when $a \le b$. Hence, without additional restrictions according to (35) with $N = 2$, we obtain

$$\begin{aligned} R_{-2,-2,0}(z) &= 1 + \frac{2(2-a-b)}{c^2} z + \gamma z^2 \\ &\quad - \frac{z^2[\Gamma(c)]^2(c-a-b+2)}{\Gamma(a)\Gamma(b)\Gamma(c-a+2)\Gamma(c-b+2)} \int_0^1 \frac{(\rho_0+\rho_1 t)t^{a+b-1}(1-t)^{c-a-b}}{|{}_2F_1(a,b;c;1/t)|^2(1-zt)} dt \end{aligned} \tag{53}$$

under the condition $(a,b,c) \in V$ from Theorem 4, but without any other restrictions.

4. Concluding Remarks

It turns out that our results may help in finding integral representations of elementary and special functions. For instance, Formulas (43) and (44) with $a = b = 1$ and $c = 2$ yield the following curious identity:

$$\frac{z}{\operatorname{Log}(1+z)} = 1 + z\int_1^\infty \frac{dx}{(\log^2(x-1)+\pi^2)(x+z)} = 1 + \frac{z}{2} - z^2 \int_1^\infty \frac{dx}{(\log^2(x-1)+\pi^2)(x+z)x}.$$

The first equality here after division by z corrects the representation [30] (Formula (34)). This identity may be easily generalized by applying (37) with arbitrary $N \in \mathbb{N}$, $a = b = 1$ and $c = 2$ to the results of Example 12:

$$\frac{z}{\operatorname{Log}(1+z)} = \sum_{k=0}^{N-1} \frac{C_k z^k}{k!} - (-z)^N \int_1^\infty \frac{dx}{(\log^2(x-1)+\pi^2)(x+z)x^{N-1}},$$

where $N = 1, 2, 3, \ldots$ and C_k is the kth Cauchy number [24] (p. 294).

Moreover, Theorem 5, in view of Remark 8, gives a way for calculating the "generalized beta integrals" of the form

$$I_{a,b}(j,k) := \int_0^1 \frac{t^{a+b+j}(1-t)^{c-a-b-k}}{|{}_2F_1(a,b;c;1/t)|^2} dt.$$

In particular, Examples 1–4, 7–9 and 12 lead immediately to explicit evaluations in terms of gamma functions of the integral $I_{a,b}(j,k)$ for the following pairs (j,k): $(-2,-1)$, $(-2,0)$, $(-1,-2)$, $(-1,-1)$, $(-1,0)$, $(0,-3)$, $(0,-2)$, $(0,-1)$, $(0,0)$, $(1,-3)$, $(1,-2)$, $(1,-1)$. This list can be extended by invoking Examples 6 and 15 with the following pairs: $(-3,-1)$, $(-3,0)$, $(-1,-3)$. For instance, for $j \in \{-1,0\}$ and $k \in \{0,1\}$ we get:

$$I_{a,b}(j,k) = \frac{\Gamma(a+1+j)\Gamma(b+1)\Gamma(c-a+1-k)\Gamma(c-b+n)}{\Gamma(c+n)\Gamma(c+2+j-k)}, \text{ where } n = \min(1+j, 1-k) \in \{0,1\},$$

provided that $a \ge b$; the case $a \le b$ follows by exchanging $a \leftrightarrow b$. Further examples are

$$I_{a,b}(0,2) = \frac{\Gamma(a+1)\Gamma(b+1)\Gamma(c-a)\Gamma(c-b)}{[\Gamma(c)]^2(a+b-c+1)}$$

and, if $a > b + 1$,

$$I_{a,b}(-2,0) = \frac{\Gamma(a)\Gamma(b+1)\Gamma(c-a+1)\Gamma(c-b)}{(a-b-1)\Gamma^2(c)}.$$

Note that the value of j in the above 15 pairs (j,k) may be increased by any positive integer (and hence made as large as desired) by choosing larger values of $N \in \mathbb{N}_0$ in (37). A natural limitation of the above integral evaluations is that the hypergeometric function in the denominator has to be non-vanishing in $\mathbb{C} \setminus [1,\infty)$ and on the branch cut, which can be verified via Theorem 4. For a general pair of integers (j,k), we can use formulae (26) to choose the corresponding shifts n_1, n_2, m and use Remark 8 to calculate the corresponding integral. The details of this algorithm will be elaborated in a separate publication.

Author Contributions: Conceptualization, A.D. and D.K.; Investigation, A.D. and D.K.; Methodology, A.D. and D.K. All authors contributed equally to this work. All authors have read and agreed to the published version of the manuscript.

Funding: This research received no external funding.

Data Availability Statement: Not applicable.

Conflicts of Interest: The authors declare no conflict of interest.

References

1. Gauss, C.F. Disquisitiones generales circa seriem infinitam. *Comment. Soc. Regiae Sci. Gottingensis Recent.* **1812**, *2*, 1–46; reprint in Gauß, C.F. *Werke, Band III*; Königliche Gesellschaft der Wissenschaften zu Göttingen: Göttingen, Germany, 1876; pp. 123–162.
2. Erdélyi, A. *Higher Transcendental Functions*; Volume I, Bateman Manuscript Project; Mc Graw-Hill Book Company, Inc.: New York, NY, USA, 1953.
3. Olver, F.W.J.; Olde Daalhuis, A.B.; Lozier, D.W.; Schneider, B.I.; Boisvert, R.F.; Clark, C.W.; Miller, B.R.; Saunders, B.V.; Cohl, H.S.; McClain, M.A.; et al. NIST Digital Library of Mathematical Functions. Release 1.1.6 of 2022-06-30. Available online: http://dlmf.nist.gov/ (accessed on 30 August 2022).
4. Ebisu, A.; Iwasaki, K. Three-term relations for ${}_3F_2(1)$. *J. Math. Anal. Appl.* **2018**, *463*, 593–610. [CrossRef]
5. Wall, H.S. *Analytic Theory of Continued Fractions*; Chelsea Publishing Company: New York, NY, USA, 1948.
6. Perron, O. *Die Lehre von den Kettenbrüchen*; Band II, Dritte, verbesserte und erweiterte Aufl., B.G. Teubner Verlagsgesellschaft: Stuttgart, Germany, 1957.
7. Stieltjes, T.J. Recherches sur les fractions continues. *Ann. Fac. Sci. Toulouse* **1894**, *8*, J1–J122. [CrossRef]
8. Runckel, H.-J. On the zeros of the hypergeometric function. *Math. Ann.* **1971**, *191*, 53–58. [CrossRef]
9. Pétréolle, M.; Sokal, A.D.; Zhu, B.-X. Lattice paths and branched continued fractions: An infinite sequence of generalizations of the Stieltjes–Rogers and Thron–Rogers polynomials, with coefficientwise Hankel-total positivity. *arXiv* **2018**, arXiv:1807.03271.
10. Küstner, R. Mapping properties of hypergeometric functions and convolutions of starlike or convex functions of order α. *Comput. Methods Funct. Theor.* **2002**, *2*, 597–610. [CrossRef]
11. Belevitch, V. The Gauss hypergeometric ratio as a positive real function. *SIAM J. Math. Anal.* **1982**, *13*, 1024–1040. [CrossRef]
12. Wimp, J. Explicit Formulas for the Associated Jacobi Polynomials and Some Applications. *Can. J. Math.* **1987**, *39*, 983–1000. [CrossRef]
13. Dyachenko, A.; Karp, D. Ratios of the Gauss hypergeometric functions with parameters shifted by integers: Part I, Preprint. *arXiv* **2021**, arXiv:2103.13312.
14. Dyachenko, A.; Karp, D. Ratios of the Gauss hypergeometric functions with parameters shifted by integers: More on integral representations. *Lobachevskii J. Math.* **2021**, *42*, 2764–2776. [CrossRef]
15. Ismail, M.E.H.; Kelker, D.H. Special Functions, Stieltjes Transfroms and Infinite Divisibility. *Sima J. Math. Anal.* **1979**, *10*, 5. [CrossRef]
16. Lima, H.; Loureiro, A. Multiple orthogonal polynomials with respect to Gauss' hypergeometric function. *Stud. Appl. Math.* **2021**, 1–32. [CrossRef]
17. Karp, D.B.; Prilepkina, E.G. Hypergeometric functions as generalized Stieltjes transforms. *J. Math. Anal. Appl.* **2012**, *393*, 348–359. [CrossRef]
18. Karp, D.B.; Prilepkina, E.G. Applications of the Stieltjes and Laplace transform representations of the hypergeometric functions. *Integral Transform. Spec. Funct.* **2017**, *28*, 710–731. [CrossRef]
19. Driver, K.; Jordaan, K.H.; Mbuyi, N. Interlacing of the zeros of Jacobi polynomials with different parameters. *Num. Alg.* **2008**, *49*, 143–152. [CrossRef]
20. Long, B.-Y.; Sugawa, T.; Wang, Q.-H. Completely monotone sequences and harmonic mappings. *Ann. Fenn. Math.* **2021** *47*, 237–250. [CrossRef]

21. Agrawal, S.; Sahoo, S.K. Geometric properties of basic hypergeometric functions. *J. Differ. Equ. Appl.* **2014**, *20*, 1502–1522. [CrossRef]
22. Baricz, Á.; Swaminathan, A. Mapping properties of basic hypergeometric functions. *J. Class. Anal.* **2014**, *5*, 115–128. [CrossRef]
23. Andrews, G.E.; Askey, R.; Roy, R. *Special Functions*; Cambridge University Press: Cambridge, UK, 1999.
24. Comtet, L. *Advanced Combinatorics*; D. Reidel Publishing Company: Dordrecht, The Netherlands; Boston, MA, USA, 1974.
25. Karp, D.; Kuznetsov, A. A new identity for a sum of products of the generalized hypergeometric functions. *Proc. Amer. Math. Soc.* **2021**, *149*, 2861–2870. [CrossRef]
26. Ebisu, A. Three Term Relations for the Hypergeometric Series. *Funkcial. Ekvac.* **2012**, *55*, 255–283. [CrossRef]
27. Çetinkaya, A.; Karp, D.; Prilepkina, E. Hypergeometric Functions at Unit Argument: Simple Derivation of Old and New Identities. *SIGMA* **2021**, *17*, 098. [CrossRef]
28. Yamaguchi, Y. Three-term relations for basic hypergeometric series. *J. Math. Anal. Appl.* **2018**, *464*, 662–678. [CrossRef]
29. Askitis, D. Geometric Function Theory, Completely Monotone Sequences and Applications in Special Functions. Master's Thesis, Copenhagen, Denmark, 2015.
30. Berg, C.; Pedersen, H.L. A one-parameter family of Pick functions defined by the gamma function and related to the volume of the unit ball in n-space. *Proc. Am. Math. Soc.* **2011**, *139*, 2121–2132. [CrossRef]

mathematics

MDPI

Article

Recovery of Inhomogeneity from Output Boundary Data

Vladislav V. Kravchenko [1,*], Kira V. Khmelnytskaya [2] and Fatma Ayça Çetinkaya [3]

[1] Department of Mathematics, Cinvestav, Campus Querétaro, Libramiento Norponiente #2000, Fracc. Real de Juriquilla, Querétaro 76230, Mexico
[2] Faculty of Engineering, Cerro de las Campanas s/n, col. Las Campanas Querétaro, Autonomous University of Queretaro, Querétaro 76010, Mexico
[3] Department of Mathematics, Faculty of Science, Mersin University, 33343 Mersin, Turkey
* Correspondence: vkravchenko@math.cinvestav.edu.mx

Abstract: We consider the Sturm–Liouville equation on a finite interval with a real-valued integrable potential and propose a method for solving the following general inverse problem. We recover the potential from a given set of the output boundary values of a solution satisfying some known initial conditions for a set of values of the spectral parameter. Special cases of this problem include the recovery of the potential from the Weyl function, the inverse two-spectra Sturm–Liouville problem, as well as the recovery of the potential from the output boundary values of a plane wave that interacted with the potential. The method is based on the special Neumann series of Bessel functions representations for solutions of Sturm–Liouville equations. With their aid, the problem is reduced to the classical inverse Sturm–Liouville problem of recovering the potential from two spectra, which is solved again with the help of the same representations. The overall approach leads to an efficient numerical algorithm for solving the inverse problem. Its numerical efficiency is illustrated by several examples.

Keywords: Sturm–Liouville equation; inverse problem; Weyl function; Neumann series of Bessel functions; numerical solution of inverse problem

MSC: 34A55; 34B24; 34A25; 42C10; 65L09

Citation: Kravchenko, V.V.; Khmelnytskaya, K.V.; Çetinkaya, F.A. Recovery of Inhomogeneity from Output Boundary Data. *Mathematics* **2022**, *10*, 4349. https://doi.org/10.3390/math10224349

Academic Editors: Vasily Novozhilov, Yury Shestopalov and Viktor N. Orlov

Received: 25 September 2022
Accepted: 17 November 2022
Published: 19 November 2022

Publisher's Note: MDPI stays neutral with regard to jurisdictional claims in published maps and institutional affiliations.

Copyright: © 2022 by the authors. Licensee MDPI, Basel, Switzerland. This article is an open access article distributed under the terms and conditions of the Creative Commons Attribution (CC BY) license (https://creativecommons.org/licenses/by/4.0/).

1. Introduction

Let $q \in \mathcal{L}_1(0,L)$ be real valued. Consider the one-dimensional Schrödinger equation

$$-y'' + q(x)y = \rho^2 y, \quad x \in (0,L), \tag{1}$$

where $\rho \in \mathbb{C}$ is a spectral parameter, and $L > 0$ is finite. Let $u(\rho,x)$ be a solution of (1), satisfying some prescribed initial conditions at the origin

$$u(\rho,0) = a(\rho),\ u'(\rho,0) = b(\rho),$$

where $a(\rho)$ and $b(\rho)$ are some known functions that are not identical zeros.

In the present work, we propose a method for solving the following inverse problem.

Problem 1. *Given*

$$a(\rho_k),\ b(\rho_k) \quad and \quad l_k := u(\rho_k, L) \tag{2}$$

for a number of values of $\rho_k \in \mathbb{C}$, find $q(x)$.

This problem is of practical importance. For example, consider the following model. A plane wave $g(\rho,x) = e^{-i\rho x}$, $x < 0$, incoming from $-\infty$, interacts with the potential $q(x)$ (i.e., $g(\rho,x)$ solves (1) for $x \in (0,L)$) and is measured at the output, i.e., at the point $x = L$

for a number of frequencies $\rho_k, k = 1, \cdots, m$. The potential $q(x)$ is to be recovered from these output boundary data. Thus, we have

$$a(\rho_k) = 1,\ b(\rho_k) = -i\rho_k \quad \text{and} \quad l_k = g(\rho_k, L),\ k = 1, \cdots, m, \tag{3}$$

and we need to recover $q(x)$, of course, approximately.

Note that $g(\rho, x)$ is a Jost solution for the potential $q(x)$ extended by zero from the segment $[0, L]$ onto the whole axis. Therefore, the problem consists in recovering the potential $q(x)$ from its Jost solution measured at the interface point $x = L$ at several frequencies ρ_k.

As another example, consider the problem of the recovery of the potential $q(x)$ from the Weyl function given at a number of points. By $\Phi(\rho, x)$ we denote the Weyl solution of (1), which satisfies (1) as well as the boundary conditions

$$\Phi'(\rho, 0) = 1 \quad \text{and} \quad \Phi(\rho, L) = 0.$$

If ρ^2 is not a Neumann–Dirichlet eigenvalue of (1), the solution $\Phi(\rho, x)$ exists and is unique. By $M(\rho)$, we denote the Weyl function $M(\rho) := \Phi(\rho, 0)$. Then, one of the frequently studied inverse Sturm–Liouville problems (see, e.g., [1–5]) consists in recovering $q(x)$ from the Weyl function $M(\rho)$ (given at a number of points). In other words, we have

$$a(\rho_k) = M(\rho_k),\ b(\rho_k) = 1 \quad \text{and} \quad l_k = 0,\ k = 1, 2, \cdots. \tag{4}$$

From these data, the potential $q(x)$ needs to be recovered.

Moreover, the classical two-spectra inverse problem (see, for example, [6–9]) is also a special case of Problem 1. Indeed, let μ_j^2 be the eigenvalues of the Sturm–Liouville problem for (1) with the boundary conditions

$$y'(0) - h_1 y(0) = 0 \quad \text{and} \quad y(L) = 0, \tag{5}$$

while ν_j^2 are the eigenvalues of the Sturm–Liouville problem for (1) with the conditions

$$y'(0) - h_2 y(0) = 0 \quad \text{and} \quad y(L) = 0, \tag{6}$$

$h_{1,2} \in \mathbb{R}, h_1 \neq h_2$. Consider a solution $u(\rho, x)$ of (1) such that

$$u(\mu_j, 0) = u(\nu_j, 0) = 1 \quad \text{for all} \quad j = 0, 1, \cdots,$$

and

$$u'(\mu_j, 0) = h_1,\ u'(\nu_j, 0) = h_2 \quad \text{for all} \quad j = 0, 1, \cdots.$$

That is, $u(\rho, x)$ is an eigenfunction of the problem (1) and (5) when $\rho = \mu_j$ and of the problem (1) and (6) when $\rho = \nu_j$. The set of ρ_k can be chosen in the form of $\{\mu_0, \nu_0, \mu_1, \nu_1, \cdots\}$ (here, in fact, the order does not matter). The set of data is

$$a(\rho_k) = 1 \quad \text{for all } k = 1, 2, \cdots,\ b(\rho_k) = \begin{cases} h_1, & \text{when } \rho_k = \mu_j, \\ h_2, & \text{when } \rho_k = \nu_j, \end{cases} \quad \text{and} \quad l_k = 0 \tag{7}$$

for all $k = 1, 2, \cdots$, because for all ρ_k, the solution $u(\rho_k, x)$ being an eigenfunction of (1) and (5) or (1) and (6) satisfies the homogeneous Dirichlet condition at $x = L$. Thus, the inverse two-spectra problem is a special case of Problem 1.

The Problem 1 of recovering $q(x)$ from the data

$$\{a(\rho_k), b(\rho_k), l_k\} \tag{8}$$

is generally not uniquely solvable even when the set of points ρ_k is infinite. For example, when all ρ_k are such that ρ_k^2 belongs to the Dirichlet–Dirichlet spectrum of (1), the knowledge of $M(\rho_k)$ is not sufficient for recovering $q(x)$. In general, the characterization of such infinite sets of ρ_k and of the rest of the data, for which the stated inverse problem is uniquely solvable, is a subtle matter (we refer to [5] for some results in this direction). In the present work, we restrict ourselves to the assumption that for a given infinite set of data of the form (8), the inverse problem is uniquely solvable, and we develop a method for its approximate solution. The overall approach is based on several recent results and ideas.

First of all, we use the Neumann series of Bessel functions (NSBF) representations for solutions of (1) obtained in [10]. They possess important properties, which make them especially convenient for dealing with problems, both direct and inverse, which require considering the spectral parameter ρ admitting a large range of values. In particular, the remainders of the partial sums of the NSBF representations admit estimates independent of $\Re(\rho)$. Roughly speaking, the partial sums approximate the exact solutions equally well for small and for large values of $\rho \in \mathbb{R}$. Moreover, the whole information on the potential $q(x)$ is contained already in the first coefficient of the NSBF representation; so, for recovering $q(x)$, it is sufficient to compute the first coefficient alone. Behind these and some other remarkable features of the NSBF representations there stands the fact that they are obtained by expanding into a Fourier–Legendre series the integral kernel of the transmutation (transformation) operator. For the theory of transmutation operators, we refer to [11–13].

Second, we develop further the idea proposed in [14,15], which can be formulated as follows. An inverse problem can be efficiently solved by converting the input data into the computed values of the coefficients from the NSBF representations at the endpoint of the interval. This leads to the possibility of computing two different spectra for (1). The knowledge of two spectra and of the NSBF coefficients at the endpoint gives us the possibility of computing the first NSBF coefficient on the whole segment $[0, L]$, which is sufficient for recovering $q(x)$.

The input data of the inverse problem can be of different nature. For example, in [14] they were the spectral data of the spectral problem on a quantum graph, while in [15] the input data were several first eigenvalues from two spectra for (1). In the present work, we show how the endpoint values of a solution of (1), which satisfies some given initial conditions, serve for recovering the potential $q(x)$, following the scheme described above.

In Section 2, we introduce the NSBF representations together with their basic properties. In Section 3, we develop the method for solving Problem 1. In Section 4, we summarize it in the form of an algorithm ready for implementation. In Section 5, we give several illustrations of its numerical performance. Finally, Section 6 contains some concluding remarks.

2. Preliminaries

By $\varphi(\rho, x)$ and $S(\rho, x)$ we denote the solutions of the equation

$$-y''(x) + q(x)y(x) = \rho^2 y(x), \quad x \in (0, L) \tag{9}$$

satisfying the initial conditions

$$\varphi(\rho, 0) = 1, \ \varphi'(\rho, 0) = 0,$$

$$S(\rho, 0) = 0, \ S'(\rho, 0) = 1.$$

The main tool used in the present work is the series representations obtained in [10] for the solutions $\varphi(\rho, x)$ and $S(\rho, x)$ of (9).

Theorem 1 ([10])**.** *The solutions $\varphi(\rho, x)$ and $S(\rho, x)$ admit the following series representations*

$$\varphi(\rho,x) = \cos(\rho x) + \sum_{n=0}^{\infty}(-1)^n g_n(x)\mathbf{j}_{2n}(\rho x), \tag{10}$$

$$S(\rho,x) = \frac{\sin(\rho x)}{\rho} + \frac{1}{\rho}\sum_{n=0}^{\infty}(-1)^n s_n(x)\mathbf{j}_{2n+1}(\rho x), \tag{11}$$

where $\mathbf{j}_k(z)$ *stands for the spherical Bessel function of order* k *(see, e.g., [16]). The coefficients* $g_n(x)$ *and* $s_n(x)$ *can be calculated following a simple recurrent integration procedure (see [10]), starting with*

$$g_0(x) = \varphi(0,x) - 1 \quad and \quad s_0(x) = 3\left(\frac{S(0,x)}{x} - 1\right). \tag{12}$$

For every $\rho \in \mathbb{C}$*, the series converges pointwise. For every* $x \in [0,L]$*, the series converges uniformly on any compact set of the complex plane of the variable* ρ*, and the remainders of their partial sums admit estimates independent of* $\Re(\rho)$*.*

This last feature of the series representations (the independence of the bounds for the remainders of $\Re(\rho)$) is a direct consequence of the fact that the representations are obtained by expanding the integral kernels of the transmutation operators (for their theory, we refer to [11–13]) into Fourier–Legendre series (see [10]). It is of crucial importance for what follows. In particular, it means that for

$$\varphi_N(\rho,x) := \cos(\rho x) + \sum_{n=0}^{N}(-1)^n g_n(x)\mathbf{j}_{2n}(\rho x)$$

and

$$S_N(\rho,x) := \frac{\sin(\rho x)}{\rho} + \frac{1}{\rho}\sum_{n=0}^{N}(-1)^n s_n(x)\mathbf{j}_{2n+1}(\rho x)$$

the estimates hold

$$|\varphi(\rho,x) - \varphi_N(\rho,x)| < \varepsilon_N(x) \quad \text{and} \quad |S(\rho,x) - S_N(\rho,x)| < \varepsilon_N(x) \tag{13}$$

for all $\rho \in \mathbb{R}$, where $\varepsilon_N(x)$ is a positive function tending to zero when $N \to \infty$. That is, roughly speaking, the approximate solutions $\varphi_N(\rho,x)$ and $S_N(\rho,x)$ approximate the exact ones equally well for small and for large values of ρ. This is especially convenient when considering direct and inverse spectral problems. Moreover, for a fixed z, the numbers $\mathbf{j}_k(z)$ rapidly decrease as $k \to \infty$, (see, e.g., [16] [(9.1.62)]). Hence, the convergence rate of the series for any fixed ρ is, in fact, exponential. More detailed estimates for the series remainders depending on the regularity of the potential can be found in [10].

Note that formulas (12) indicate that the potential $q(x)$ can be recovered from the first coefficients of the series (10) or (11). We have

$$q(x) = \frac{g_0''(x)}{g_0(x)+1} \tag{14}$$

and

$$q(x) = \frac{(xs_0(x))''}{xs_0(x)+3x}. \tag{15}$$

Note that the square roots of the Dirichlet–Dirichlet eigenvalues coincide with the zeros of the function $S(\rho,L)$:

$$S(\mu_n,L) = 0,\ n = 1,2,\cdots,$$

while the square roots of the Neumann–Dirichlet eigenvalues coincide with zeros of the function $\varphi(\rho, L)$:

$$\varphi(\rho_n, L) = 0, \ n = 0, 1, \cdots.$$

3. Solution of Problem 1

From the very beginning, we assume that the set of the numbers ρ_k, for which we dispose of the data (8), is finite. Thus, the problem consists in recovering approximately the potential $q(x)$ from the data

$$\{a(\rho_k), \ b(\rho_k), \ l_k\}_{k=1}^{m}, \tag{16}$$

where in general ρ_k and the other data are complex numbers.

3.1. Computation of Coefficients $g_n(L)$ and $s_n(L)$

In the first step, we use the data (16) to compute a number of the coefficients $\{g_n(L)\}_{n=0}^{N}$ and $\{s_n(L)\}_{n=0}^{N}$ from (10) and (11) evaluated at the endpoint $x = L$. For this, let us substitute (10) and (11) into (2). We have

$$\begin{aligned} a(\rho_k) \sum_{n=0}^{\infty} (-1)^n g_n(L) \mathbf{j}_{2n}(\rho_k L) \ &+ \tfrac{b(\rho_k)}{\rho_k} \sum_{n=0}^{\infty} (-1)^n s_n(L) \mathbf{j}_{2n+1}(\rho_k L) \\ &= l_k - a(\rho_k)\cos(\rho_k L) - \tfrac{b(\rho_k)}{\rho_k} \sin(\rho_k L), \end{aligned} \tag{17}$$

for all $k = 1, \cdots, m$. Note that if $\rho_k = 0$, from (10) and (11), we have $\varphi(0, x) = 1 + g_0(x)$ and $S(0, x) = x + x s_0(x)/3$, and (17) takes the form

$$a(0) g_0(L) + \frac{b(0)L}{3} s_0(L) = l_k - a(0) - b(0)L.$$

Choosing $N \in \mathbb{N}$ such that $2(N+1) \leq m$, we consider the system of linear algebraic equations obtained from (17) by truncating the infinite sums,

$$\begin{aligned} a(\rho_k) \sum_{n=0}^{N} (-1)^n g_n(L) \mathbf{j}_{2n}(\rho_k L) \ &+ \tfrac{b(\rho_k)}{\rho_k} \sum_{n=0}^{N} (-1)^n s_n(L) \mathbf{j}_{2n+1}(\rho_k L) \\ &= l_k - a(\rho_k)\cos(\rho_k L) - \tfrac{b(\rho_k)}{\rho_k} \sin(\rho_k L), \end{aligned} \tag{18}$$

for $k = 1, \cdots, m$. Note that here and below we do not look to deal with square systems of equations. In computations, a least-squares solution of an overdetermined system (provided by Matlab, which we used for computations in this work) gives very satisfactory results and allows one to make use of all available data, while keeping the number of coefficients relatively small (in practice, $N = 4$ or 5 may be sufficient).

Solving (18) gives us approximate values of the coefficients $\{g_n(L)\}_{n=0}^{N}$ and $\{s_n(L)\}_{n=0}^{N}$. Here, we come to the problem of converting the knowledge of the coefficients from (10) and (11) evaluated at the endpoint of the interval into the information on $q(x)$ on the whole interval.

The knowledge of the coefficients $\{g_n(L)\}_{n=0}^{N}$ and $\{s_n(L)\}_{n=0}^{N}$ allows us to compute the functions $\varphi_N(\rho, L)$ and $S_N(\rho, L)$ for any value of ρ. Due to the estimates in (13), we know that the accuracy of the approximation of the exact solutions $\varphi(\rho, L)$ and $S(\rho, L)$ by these approximate ones does not deteriorate for large values of $\rho \in \mathbb{R}$. So, in fact, we deal with the problem of converting the knowledge of the solutions or more generally of characteristic functions of two Sturm–Liouville problems for (9) at the endpoint into the information on $q(x)$ on the whole interval. This problem naturally arises in the framework of different methods for solving inverse Sturm–Liouville problems. For example, in [17] (see also [18]), this problem was approached via an iterative algorithm based on the use of properties of the corresponding transmutation operator. In the present work, we apply another approach, which extends the one proposed in [14,15], and consists in converting the knowledge of $\{g_n(L)\}_{n=0}^{N}$ and $\{s_n(L)\}_{n=0}^{N}$ into an auxiliary inverse problem for (9) consisting in the recovery of $q(x)$ from one spectrum and a sequence of corresponding multiplier constants. We formulate this problem in the next subsection and show how the knowledge of $\{g_n(L)\}_{n=0}^N$ and $\{s_n(L)\}_{n=0}^N$ allows us to reduce the inverse problem to that auxiliary inverse problem.

3.2. One Spectrum and Multiplier Constants Inverse Problem

Let $\left\{\alpha_j^2\right\}_{j=0}^\infty$ be the eigenvalues of (9) with the Neumann-Dirichlet boundary conditions

$$y'(0) = 0 \quad \text{and} \quad y(L) = 0. \tag{19}$$

Obviously, the solution $\varphi(\alpha_j, x)$ is an eigenfunction of the problem (9) and (19). Denote by $\psi(\rho, x)$ a solution of (9) satisfying the initial conditions at $x = L$:

$$\psi(\rho, L) = 0 \quad \text{and} \quad \psi'(\rho, L) = 1$$

for all ρ. Hence, for $\rho = \alpha_j$, the solution $\psi(\alpha_j, x)$ is also an eigenfunction of (9) and (19). Hence, there exist the multiplier constants $\beta_j \neq 0$, $j = 0, 1, \cdots$, such that

$$\varphi(\alpha_j, x) = \beta_j \psi(\alpha_j, x), \quad x \in [0, L]. \tag{20}$$

The auxiliary inverse problem can be formulated as follows.

Problem 2. *Given the Neumann–Dirichlet spectrum* $\left\{\alpha_j^2\right\}_{j=0}^\infty$ *of (9) and the multiplier constants* $\{\beta_j\}_{j=0}^\infty$*, find* $q(x)$.

A method for solving the problems of this type was proposed in [19]. Here, we develop the approach proposed in [14,15], where it was applied to slightly different situations. However, first, we show that the knowledge of the coefficients $\{g_n(L)\}_{n=0}^N$ and $\{s_n(L)\}_{n=0}^N$ can be used to reduce the original inverse Problem 1 to Problem 2.

As pointed out above, the knowledge of the coefficients $\{g_n(L)\}_{n=0}^N$ and $\{s_n(L)\}_{n=0}^N$ allows us to compute the approximate solutions $\varphi_N(\rho, L)$ and $S_N(\rho, L)$ for any value of ρ. This means that, in particular, we can compute zeros of these two functions. The following result establishes their proximity to zeros of the exact solutions $\varphi(\rho, L)$ and $S(\rho, L)$.

Theorem 2. *For any* $\varepsilon > 0$*, there exists such* $N \in \mathbb{N}$ *that all zeros of the functions* $\varphi(\rho, L)$ *and* $S(\rho, L)$ *are approximated by corresponding zeros of the functions* $\varphi_N(\rho, L)$ *and* $S_N(\rho, L)$*, respectively, with errors uniformly bounded by* ε*, and* $\varphi_N(\rho, L)$*,* $S_N(\rho, L)$ *have no other zeros.*

Proof. The proof of this statement is completely analogous to the proof of Proposition 7.1 in [20] and consists in the use of (13), properties of characteristic functions of regular Sturm–Liouville problems, and Rouché's theorem from complex analysis. □

Since the zeros of $\varphi(\rho, L)$ and $S(\rho, L)$ coincide with the square roots of the Neumann–Dirichlet and Dirichlet–Dirichlet eigenvalues of (9), the zeros of $\varphi_N(\rho, L)$ and $S_N(\rho, L)$ for a sufficiently large N give us the approximate values of these singular numbers. We denote the Dirichlet–Dirichlet eigenvalues of (9) as $\left\{\gamma_j^2\right\}_{j=1}^\infty$. Thus, computing the zeros of $\varphi_N(\rho, L)$ and $S_N(\rho, L)$, we obtain the approximate numbers $\{\alpha_j\}_{j=0}^\infty$ and $\{\gamma_j\}_{j=1}^\infty$. So, we reduce Problem 1 to a two-spectra inverse problem.

Analogously to solution (11), the solution $\psi(\rho, x)$ admits the series representation

$$\psi(\rho, x) = \frac{\sin(\rho(x - L))}{\rho} + \frac{1}{\rho} \sum_{n=0}^\infty (-1)^n t_n(x) \mathbf{j}_{2n+1}(\rho(x - L)), \tag{21}$$

where $t_n(x)$ are corresponding coefficients, analogous to $s_n(x)$ from (11). The multiplier constants can be easily calculated by recalling that $\varphi(\alpha_j, 0) = 1$. Thus,

$$\begin{aligned} \frac{1}{\beta_j} = \psi(\alpha_j, 0) &\approx \psi_N(\alpha_j, 0) \\ &= -\frac{\sin(\alpha_j L)}{\alpha_j} - \frac{1}{\alpha_j} \sum_{n=0}^{N} (-1)^n t_n(0) \mathbf{j}_{2n+1}(\alpha_j L), \end{aligned} \tag{22}$$

where we take into account that the spherical Bessel functions of odd order are odd functions. The coefficients $\{t_n(0)\}_{n=0}^{N}$ are computed with the aid of the singular numbers $\{\gamma_j\}$ as follows. Since the functions $\psi(\gamma_j, x)$, $j = 1, 2, \cdots$ are the Dirichlet–Dirichlet eigenfunctions of (9), we have that $\psi(\gamma_j, 0) = 0$; hence,

$$\sum_{n=0}^{\infty} (-1)^n t_n(0) \mathbf{j}_{2n+1}(\gamma_j L) = -\sin(\gamma_j L), \quad j = 1, 2, \cdots.$$

This leads to a system of linear algebraic equations for computing the coefficients $\{t_n(0)\}_{n=0}^{N}$, which has the form

$$\sum_{n=0}^{N} (-1)^n t_n(0) \mathbf{j}_{2n+1}(\gamma_j L) = -\sin(\gamma_j L), \quad j = 1, \cdots, N_D, \tag{23}$$

where N_D is the number of computed singular numbers γ_j, $N_D \geq N + 1$. Now, having computed $\{t_n(0)\}_{n=0}^{N}$, we compute the multiplier constants $\{\beta_j\}_{j=0}^{N_N}$ from (22), where N_N is the number of the computed singular numbers $\{\alpha_j\}_{j=0}^{N_N}$.

Next, we use Equation (20) to construct a system of linear algebraic equations for the coefficients $g_n(x)$ and $t_n(x)$. Indeed, Equation (20) can be written in the form

$$\begin{aligned} \sum_{n=0}^{\infty} (-1)^n g_n(x) \mathbf{j}_{2n}(\alpha_j x) - \frac{\beta_j}{\alpha_j} \sum_{n=0}^{\infty} (-1)^n t_{i,n}(x) \mathbf{j}_{2n+1}(\alpha_j (x - L)) \\ = \frac{\beta_j}{\alpha_j} \sin(\alpha_j (x - L)) - \cos(\alpha_j x). \end{aligned}$$

We have as many of these equations as the Neumann–Dirichlet singular numbers α_j computed. For computational purposes, we choose some natural number N_c—the number of the coefficients $g_n(x)$ and $t_n(x)$ to be computed. More precisely, we choose a sufficiently dense set of points $x_m \in (0, L)$, and at every x_m, we consider the equations

$$\begin{aligned} \sum_{n=0}^{N_c} (-1)^n g_n(x_m) \mathbf{j}_{2n}(\alpha_j x_m) &- \frac{\beta_j}{\alpha_j} \sum_{n=0}^{N_c} (-1)^n t_n(x_m) \mathbf{j}_{2n+1}(\alpha_j (x_m - L)) \\ &= \frac{\beta_j}{\alpha_j} \sin(\alpha_j (x_m - L)) - \cos(\alpha_j x_m), \quad j = 0, \cdots, N_N. \end{aligned} \tag{24}$$

Solving this system of equations, we find $g_0(x_m)$ and consequently $g_0(x)$ at a sufficiently dense set of points of the interval $(0, L)$. Finally, with the aid of (14), we compute $q(x)$.

4. Algorithm

Given the data (8), the algorithm of the solution of Problem 1 consists of the following steps.

1. Choose $N \in \mathbb{N}$, such that $2(N + 1) \leq m$, and compute the sets of coefficients $\{g_n(L)\}_{n=0}^{N}$ and $\{s_n(L)\}_{n=0}^{N}$ from (18).

2. Compute a number $N_N \geq N$ of zeros $\{\alpha_j\}_{j=0}^{N_N}$ of the function $\varphi_N(\rho, L)$, which approximate the Neumann–Dirichlet singular numbers, and a number $N_D \geq N+1$ of zeros $\{\gamma_j\}_{j=1}^{N_D}$ of the function $S_N(\rho, L)$, which approximate the Dirichlet–Dirichlet singular numbers of $q(x)$.
3. Compute the coefficients $\{t_n(0)\}_{n=0}^{N}$ from (23).
4. Compute the constants $\{\beta_j\}_{j=0}^{N_N}$ from (22).
5. Choose $N_c \in \mathbb{N}$, such that $2(N_c+1) \leq N_N + 1$, and a number of points $x_m \in (0, L)$. For each x_m, solve (24) to find $g_0(x_m)$.
6. Compute $q(x)$ from (14).

In the last step, we used the spline approximation for $g_0(x)$ and differentiated it twice.

5. Numerical Examples

The proposed method can be implemented directly using an available numeric computing environment. All the computations were performed in Matlab 2017 on an Intel i7-7600U (Intel, Santa Clara, CA, USA) equipped laptop computer. We start with the simplest example of a constant potential, which is convenient for illustrating the performance of the algorithm in each step by comparing the results with the exact ones.

Example 1. *Consider the potential $q_1(x) = c^2$, $x \in [0, \pi]$, where $c > 0$ is a constant. Let us consider the problem of recovering $q(x)$ from the Weyl function, that is, from the data of the form (4). For the constant potential, we have*

$$M(\rho) = -\frac{\tan\left(\sqrt{\rho^2 - c^2}L\right)}{\sqrt{\rho^2 - c^2}}.$$

We chose 15 points ρ_k distributed uniformly on $[0.1, 10]$ and computed $M(\rho_k)$. That gave us the data (4). For numerical implementation of the algorithm we chose $c = 1$ and $N = 4$, and with the coefficients $\{g_n(L)\}_{n=0}^{4}$ and $\{s_n(L)\}_{n=0}^{4}$ computed in the first step, we computed 40 Neumann–Dirichlet singular numbers α_j and 39 Dirichlet–Dirichlet singular numbers γ_j.

In Table 1, some of the exact and computed (marked by tilde) singular numbers α_j are provided together with the absolute error. Similar results were obtained for the Dirichlet–Dirichlet singular numbers, see Table 2.

Table 1. Neumann–Dirichlet singular numbers of q from Example 1.

j	α_j	$\tilde{\alpha}_j$	$\lvert\alpha_j - \tilde{\alpha}_j\rvert$
0	1.11803398	1.11803296	$1.02 \cdot 10^{-6}$
10	10.54751155	10.54751173	$1.8 \cdot 10^{-7}$
20	20.52437575	20.52437601	$2.6 \cdot 10^{-7}$
39	39.51265620	39.51265636	$1.6 \cdot 10^{-7}$

Table 2. Dirichlet–Dirichlet singular numbers of q from Example 1.

j	γ_j	$\tilde{\gamma}_j$	$\lvert\gamma_j - \tilde{\gamma}_j\rvert$
1	1.41421356	1.41421215	$1.41 \cdot 10^{-6}$
11	11.04536101	11.04536156	$5.43 \cdot 10^{-7}$
21	21.02379604	21.02379651	$4.74 \cdot 10^{-7}$
39	39.01281840	39.01281869	$2.90 \cdot 10^{-7}$

Thus, the partial sums $\varphi_4(\rho, L)$ and $S_4(\rho, L)$ with the corresponding coefficients computed from (18) allow us to compute both spectra with a remarkable accuracy. We emphasize that many more of the higher indices eigenvalues can be computed with a non-deteriorating accuracy, though usually several dozens are sufficient for recovering the potential.

Next, following the algorithm, we computed the coefficients $\{t_n(0)\}_{n=0}^{4}$ from (23) and $\{\beta_j\}_{j=0}^{39}$ from (22). In step 5, we chose $N_c = 10$, though the results were similar for an N_c chosen between $N_c = 4$ and $N_c = 20$. In Figure 1, the recovered potential is depicted; the maximum absolute error was equal to 0.0012.

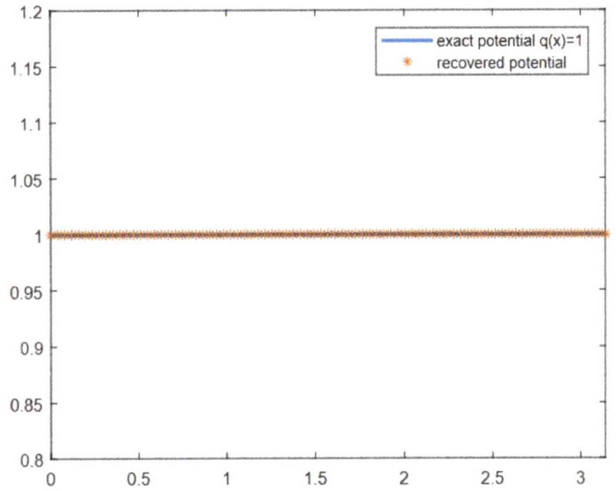

Figure 1. Potential from Example 1 recovered from the Weyl function given at 15 points and with $N = 4$.

Choosing more points ρ_k and a larger number N leads to more accurate results. For example, with 25 points ρ_k distributed uniformly on the same interval $[0.1, 10]$ and $N = 9$, the maximum absolute error of the recovered potential was $1.09 \cdot 10^{-5}$. Remarkably, the maximum absolute error of the first 40 Neumann–Dirichlet singular numbers computed was $8.6 \cdot 10^{-14}$ and $5.5 \cdot 10^{-14}$ for the Dirichlet–Dirichlet singular numbers. The numerical solution of the inverse incident plane wave problem of recovering the potential from the data (3) with the same choice of the points ρ_k and N led to similarly accurate results: the maximum absolute error of the recovered potential was $1.16 \cdot 10^{-5}$.

For the same constant potential, we considered the inverse problem with the data corresponding to two spectra (7) with $h_1 = -0.5$ and $h_2 = 0$. For the first ten eigenpairs given and $N = 9$, the potential was recovered with the maximum absolute error $1.34 \cdot 10^{-5}$, while for five eigenpairs given and $N = 4$, the maximum absolute error was 0.0035.

Example 2. *Consider the inverse incident plane wave problem for the non-smooth and continuous potential*

$$q_2(x) = |x - 1| + 1, \quad x \in [0, \pi].$$

We chose 25 points ρ_k distributed uniformly on the segment in the complex plane $[-1.5 + 0.1i, 1.5 + 0.1i]$ and the corresponding data of the type (3). In Figure 2, the result of the solution of the inverse problem is presented. The number of the coefficients was chosen as ten (i.e., $N = 9$). The maximum absolute error (attained at $x = 1$) was 0.04.

For the same potential and points ρ_k, we generated the data corresponding to $a(\rho) = \sin \rho$ and $b(\rho) = \cos \rho$, which led to similar results (Figure 3).

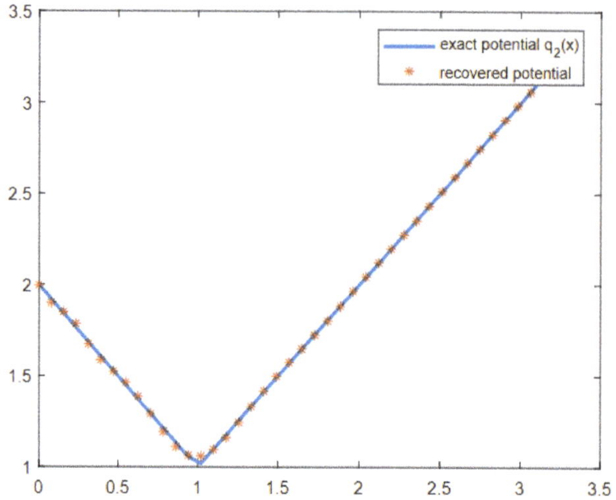

Figure 2. Potential $q_2(x)$ recovered from the data of type (3) with 25 points ρ_k distributed uniformly on the segment in the complex plane $[-1.5 + 0.1i, 1.5 + 0.1i]$ and $N = 9$.

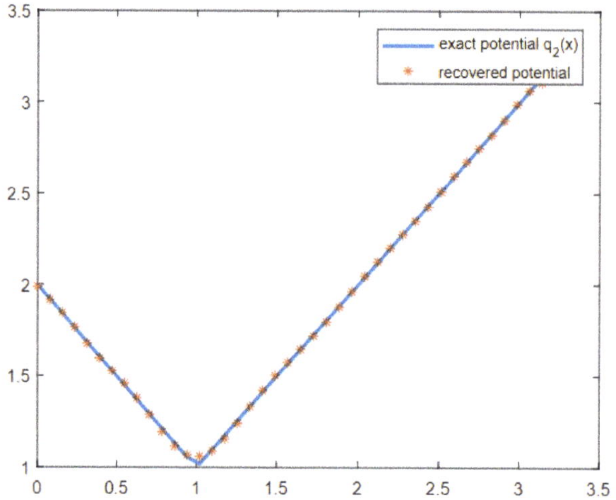

Figure 3. Potential $q_2(x)$ recovered from the data (8) with 25 points ρ_k distributed uniformly on the segment in the complex plane $[-1.5 + 0.1i, 1.5 + 0.1i]$, $a(k) = \sin \rho_k$ and $b(k) = \cos \rho_k$, corresponding to l_k, and $N = 9$.

Example 3. *Consider the following potential* [17,19]

$$q_3(x) = \begin{cases} -35.2x^2 + 17.6x, & 0 \le x < 0.25, \\ 35.2x^2 - 35.2x + 8.8, & 0.25 \le x < 0.75, \\ -35.2x^2 + 52.8x - 17.6, & 0.75 \le x \le 1. \end{cases}$$

In Figure 4, the result of the recovery of this potential from the data of type (3) given at 60 points ρ_k distributed uniformly on the segment $[0.1 + 0.1i, 15 + 0.1i]$ and $N = 24$ is shown. The maximum absolute error was approximately 0.07.

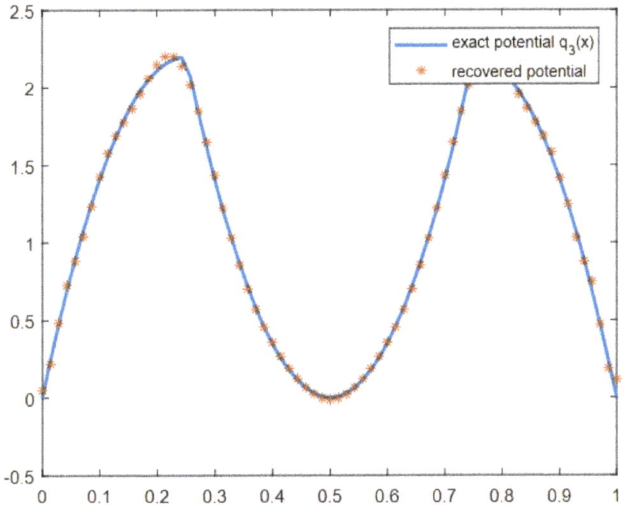

Figure 4. Potential $q_3(x)$ recovered from the data of type (3) given at 60 points ρ_k distributed uniformly on the segment $[0.1+0.1i, 15+0.1i]$ and $N = 24$.

6. Conclusions

A simple method for solving a general inverse problem for the Sturm–Liouville equation, consisting in recovering the potential from the output boundary values of a solution satisfying certain prescribed initial conditions, was developed. The data of the problem were converted into the knowledge of the coefficients of the Neumann series of Bessel functions, representations of two linearly independent solutions evaluated at the endpoint, which allowed us to reduce the problem to a two-spectra inverse Sturm–Liouville problem. This problem was solved by reducing it to a system of linear algebraic equations from which the first coefficient of the Neumann series of Bessel functions representation was found, which led to the recovery of the potential.

The method is simple, direct, accurate, and applicable to a large variety of inverse problems. Its performance was illustrated by numerical examples.

Author Contributions: Conceptualization, V.V.K.; Methodology, V.V.K.; Software, V.V.K. and K.V.K.; Formal analysis, V.V.K.; Investigation, V.V.K., K.V.K. and F.A.Ç.; Writing—original draft, V.V.K.; Writing—review and editing, K.V.K. and F.A.Ç.; Supervision, V.V.K.; Project administration, V.V.K.; Funding acquisition, V.V.K. All authors have read and agreed to the published version of the manuscript.

Funding: The research was supported by CONACYT, Mexico, via the project 284470 and partially performed at the Regional Mathematical Center of the Southern Federal University with the support of the Ministry of Science and Higher Education of Russia, agreement 075-02-2022-893.

Institutional Review Board Statement: Not applicable.

Informed Consent Statement: Not applicable.

Data Availability Statement: The data that support the findings of this study are available upon reasonable request.

Conflicts of Interest: The authors declare no competing interests.

References

1. Bondarenko, N.P. Inverse Sturm—Liouville problem with analytical functions in the boundary condition. *Open Math.* **2020**, *18*, 512–528. [CrossRef]
2. Bondarenko, N.P. Solvability and stability of the inverse Sturm–Liouville problem with analytical functions in the boundary condition. *Math. Methods Appl. Sci.* **2020**, *43*, 7009–7021. [CrossRef]
3. Gesztesy, F.; del Rio, R.; Simon, B. Inverse spectral analysis with partial information on the potential, III. Updating boundary conditions. *Int. Math. Res. Notices* **1997**, *15*, 751–758.
4. Horváth, M. Inverse spectral problems and closed exponential systems. *Ann. Math.* **2005**, *162*, 885–918. [CrossRef]
5. Yurko, V.A. *Introduction to the Theory of Inverse Spectral Problems*; Fizmatlit: Moscow, Russia, 2007.
6. Gao, Q.; Cheng, X.; Huang, Z. On a boundary value method for computing Sturm–Liouville potentials from two spectra. *Int. J. Comput. Math.* **2014**, *91*, 490–513. [CrossRef]
7. Guliyev, N.J. On two-spectra inverse problems. *Proc. Am. Math. Soc.* **2020**, *148*, 4491–4502. [CrossRef]
8. Kammanee, A.; Böckmann, C. Boundary value method for inverse Sturm–Liouville problems. *Appl. Math. Comput.* **2009**, *214*, 342–352. [CrossRef]
9. Savchuk, A.M.; Shkalikov, A.A. Inverse problem for Sturm–Liouville operators with distribution potentials: Reconstruction from two spectra. *Russ. J. Math. Phys.* **2005**, *12*, 507–514.
10. Kravchenko, V.V.; Navarro, L.J.; Torba, S.M. Representation of solutions to the one-dimensional Schrödinger equation in terms of Neumann series of Bessel functions. *Appl. Math. Comput.* **2017**, *314*, 173–192. [CrossRef]
11. Levitan, B.M. *Inverse Sturm–Liouville Problems*; VSP: Zeist, The Netherlands, 1987.
12. Marchenko, V.A. *Sturm–Liouville Operators and Applications: Revised Edition*; AMS Chelsea Publishing: New York, NY, USA, 2011.
13. Shishkina, E.L.; Sitnik, S.M. *Transmutations, Singular and Fractional Differential Equations with Applications to Mathematical Physics*; Elsevier: Amsterdam, The Netherlands, 2020.
14. Avdonin, S.; Kravchenko, V.V. Method for solving inverse spectral problems on quantum star graphs. *J. Inverse-Ill-Pose P.* 2022, *in press*.
15. Kravchenko, V.V. Spectrum completion and inverse Sturm-Liouville problems. *Math. Method Appl. Sci.* 2022, *in press*. [CrossRef]
16. Abramovitz, M.; Stegun, I.A. *Handbook of Mathematical Functions*; Unites States Department of Commerce: New York, NY, USA, 1972.
17. Rundell, W.; Sacks, P.E. Reconstruction techniques for classical inverse Sturm–Liouville problems. *Math. Comput.* **1992**, *58*, 161–183. [CrossRef]
18. Chadan, K.; Colton, D.; Päivxaxrinta, L.; Rundell, W. *An Introduction to Inverse Scattering and Inverse Spectral Problems*; SIAM: Philadelphia, PA, USA, 1997.
19. Brown, B.M.; Samko, V.S.; Knowles, I.W.; Marletta, M. Inverse spectral problem for the Sturm—Liouville equation. *Inverse Probl.* **2003**, *19*, 235–252. [CrossRef]
20. Kravchenko, V.V.; Torba, S.M. Analytic approximation of transmutation operators and applications to highly accurate solution of spectral problems. *J. Comput. Appl. Math.* **2015**, *275*, 1–26. [CrossRef]

mathematics

Article

Several Types of q-Differential Equations of Higher Order and Properties of Their Solutions

Cheon-Seoung Ryoo [1] and Jung-Yoog Kang [2,*]

1 Department of Mathematics, Hannam University, Daejeon 34430, Republic of Korea
2 Department of Mathematics Education, Silla University, Busan 46958, Republic of Korea
* Correspondence: jykang@silla.ac.kr

Abstract: The purpose of this paper is to organize various types of higher order q-differential equations that are connected to q-sigmoid polynomials and obtain certain properties regarding their solutions. Using the properties of q-sigmoid polynomials, we show the symmetric properties of q-differential equations of higher order. Moreover, we derive special properties for the approximate roots of q-sigmoid polynomials which are solutions of higher order q-differential equations.

Keywords: q-derivative; q-numbers; q-sigmoid numbers and polynomials; q-differential equations of higher order; q-sigmoid polynomials; symmetric property

MSC: 05A19, 11B83, 34A30, 65L99

Citation: Ryoo, C.-S.; Kang, J.-Y. Several Types of q-Differential Equations of Higher Order and Properties of Their Solutions. *Mathematics* **2022**, *10*, 4469. https://doi.org/10.3390/math10234469

Academic Editor: Sumit Chandok

Received: 1 November 2022
Accepted: 23 November 2022
Published: 26 November 2022

Publisher's Note: MDPI stays neutral with regard to jurisdictional claims in published maps and institutional affiliations.

Copyright: © 2022 by the authors. Licensee MDPI, Basel, Switzerland. This article is an open access article distributed under the terms and conditions of the Creative Commons Attribution (CC BY) license (https://creativecommons.org/licenses/by/4.0/).

1. Preliminaries and Introduction

In this section, we introduce q-numbers and the theorems involved. Moreover, the present paper contains an introduction to sigmoid numbers and polynomials and their importance to the aim of this paper. The theorems and definitions used here provide important context related to this paper.

Let $n, q \in \mathbb{R}$ with $q \neq 1$. The first q-number, discovered by Jackson, is

$$[n]_q = \frac{1-q^n}{1-q},$$

and note here that $\lim_{q\to 1}[n]_q = n$. Specifically, for $k \in \mathbb{Z}$, $[k]_q$ is called the q-integer; see [1,2]. Following the introduction of q-numbers, many mathematicians have attempted and published various studies working on q-numbers in various fields, such as q-discrete distribution, q-differential equations, q-series, q-calculus, and more; see [2–10].

The following equation

$$\begin{bmatrix} m \\ r \end{bmatrix}_q = \frac{[m]_q!}{[m-r]_q![r]_q!},$$

represents the q-Gaussian binomial coefficients, where m and r are non-negative integers; see [2,4,7]. Here, note that if $m < r$, then the value of the q-Gaussian binomials coefficients is 0 Moreover, note that $[n]_q! = [n]_q[n-1]_q \cdots [2]_q[1]_q$ and $[0]_q! = 1$. Thus, for $r = 0$, the value is 1.

Definition 1. *q-exponential functions are defined by*

$$(i) \quad e_q(z) = \sum_{n=0}^{\infty} \frac{z^n}{[n]_q!}, \quad 0 < |q| < 1, \quad |z| < \frac{1}{|1-q|},$$

$$(ii) \quad E_q(z) = \sum_{n=0}^{\infty} q^{\binom{n}{2}} \frac{z^n}{[n]_q!}, \quad 0 < |q| < 1, \quad z \in \mathbb{C}.$$

Note that $\lim_{q\to1} e_q(z) = e^z$. The above two kinds of q-exponential functions have different properties from general exponential functions. The following theorem is a representative property of the q-exponential function; see [2,6,11].

Theorem 1. *From Definition 1, note that*

$$\begin{aligned} &(i) \quad e_q(x)e_q(y) = e_q(x+y), \quad \text{if} \quad yx = qxy. \\ &(ii) \quad e_q(x)E_q(-x) = 1. \\ &(iii) \quad e_{q^{-1}}(x) = E_q(x). \end{aligned}$$

Definition 2. *The q-derivative of a function f regarding x is defined as*

$$D_{q,x}f(x) := D_qf(x) = \frac{f(x) - f(qx)}{(1-q)x}, \qquad \text{for} \quad x \neq 0,$$

and $D_qf(0) = f'(0)$.

It is clear that $D_qx^n = [n]_qx^{n-1}$, and it is easy to prove that f is differentiable at zero. We can find several formulas for q-derivatives from Definition 2.

Theorem 2. *From Definition 2, we have the following formulae:*

$$\begin{aligned} &(i) \quad D_q(f(x)g(x)) = q(x)D_qf(x) + f(qx)D_qg(x) = f(x)D_qg(x) + g(qx)D_qf(x). \\ &(ii) \quad D_q\left(\frac{f(x)}{g(x)}\right) = \frac{g(qx)D_qf(x) - f(qx)D_qg(x)}{g(x)g(qx)} = \frac{g(x)D_qf(x) - f(x)D_qg(x)}{g(x)g(qx)}. \\ &(iii) \quad \text{For arbitrary constants } a \text{ and } b, \quad D_q(af(x) + bg(x)) = aD_qf(x) + bD_qg(x). \\ &(iv) \quad \text{Where } u = u(x) = \alpha x^\beta \text{ with } \alpha, \beta \text{ bring constants,} \\ &\qquad D_qf(u(x)) = (D_{q^\beta}f)(u(x))D_qu(x). \end{aligned}$$

Based on the above concept, we now introduce the motivation behind this paper. When expanding the well-known Bernoulli differential equation as a q-Bernoulli differential equation, it is necessary to determine the form that the q-Bernoulli differential equation appears in as well as its solution. The Bernoulli differential equation is a particular differential equation that converts nonlinear equations into linear equations. A Bernoulli differential equation has the form

$$\frac{dy}{dx} + p(x)y - g(x)y^m = 0, \tag{1}$$

where m is any real number and $p(x)$ and $g(x)$ are continuous functions on the interval. The above equation is clear if $m = 0$ or $m = 1$; if not, it is unclear. By substituting $u = y^{1-m}$, the Bernoulli differential equation can be reduced to a linear differential equation. It is possible to organize a linear equation $\frac{du}{dx} + (1-m)p(x)u = (1-m)g(x)$ with respect to u. This Bernoulli differential equation can be applied to various problems based on nonlinear differential equations, equations concerning populations presented as logistic equations or Verhulst equations, physics, and more; see [12].

If $m = 0$ in (1), then the generating function of the sigmoid polynomials becomes the solution of the Bernoulli differential equation. The equation is as follows.

$$\frac{d}{dx}\mathcal{S}_{n-1}(x) + \frac{\mathcal{S}_0(-1) + x}{\mathcal{S}_1(-1)}\mathcal{S}_{n-1}(x) - \frac{1}{\mathcal{S}_1(-1)}\mathcal{S}_n(x) = 0, \tag{2}$$

where $\mathcal{S}_n(x)$ represents the sigmoid polynomials.

Definition 3. *The sigmiod polynomials are defined as*

$$\sum_{n=0}^{\infty} \mathcal{S}_n(x)\frac{t^n}{n!} = \frac{1}{1+e^{-t}}e^{tx}.$$

For $x = 0$ in Definition 3, we call $\mathcal{S}_n$ the sigmoid numbers or sigmoid function; see [13–17].

Extending the above concept, we consider the Bernoulli differential equation of the first order combined with q-numbers. Then, we consider $D_q y + p(x)y - g(x)y^m = 0$. For $m = 0$, the generating function of the sigmoid polynomials becomes the solution of the Bernoulli differential equation of the first order, which is as follows.

$$D_{q,x}^{(1)}\mathcal{S}_{n-1,q}(x) + \left(\frac{q\mathcal{S}_{0,q}(-1)}{\mathcal{S}_{1,q}(-1)} + \frac{q^2 x}{\mathcal{S}_{1,q}(-1)}\right)\mathcal{S}_{n-1,q}(x) - \frac{q^{-n+2}}{\mathcal{S}_{1,q}(-1)}\mathcal{S}_{n,q}(qx) = 0,$$

where $\mathcal{S}_{n,q}(x)$ represents the q-sigmoid polynomials.

Definition 4. *Let* $0 < q < 1$. *Then, we define the q-sigmiod polynomials as*

$$\sum_{n=0}^{\infty} \mathcal{S}_{n,q}(x)\frac{t^n}{[n]_q!} = \frac{1}{e_q(-t)+1}e_q(tx).$$

From Definition 4, we have

$$\sum_{n=0}^{\infty} \mathcal{S}_{n,q}(0)\frac{t^n}{[n]_q!} = \frac{1}{e_q(-t)+1} = \sum_{n=0}^{\infty} \mathcal{S}_{n,q}\frac{t^n}{[n]_q!},$$

where we call $\mathcal{S}_{n,q}$ the q-sigmoid numbers. We note that the q-sigmoid numbers are the same as the sigmoid function when q approaches 1; see [9,18].

Sigmoid polynomials are used as an activation function in deep learning, and are being studied in various forms; see [9,13–20]. The sigmoid function has the form of an Apell polynomial, and the related Apell polynomials have been a research topic for a long time; see [21–24].

The following theorem describes several basic properties of q-sigmoid polynomials.

Theorem 3. *Let* $x \in \mathbb{C}$. *Then, the following hold:*

(i) $\displaystyle\sum_{k=0}^{n} \begin{bmatrix} n \\ k \end{bmatrix}_q (-1)^{n-k}\mathcal{S}_{k,q}(x) + \mathcal{S}_{n,q}(x) = x^n.$

(ii) $\displaystyle\sum_{k=0}^{n} \begin{bmatrix} n \\ k \end{bmatrix}_q (-1)^k q^{\binom{k}{2}+\binom{n-k}{2}}\mathcal{S}_{n-k,q^{-1}}(x) + q^{\binom{n}{2}}\mathcal{S}_{n,q^{-1}}(x) = q^{\binom{n}{2}}x^n.$

(iii) $D_q\mathcal{S}_{n,q}(x) = [n]_q\mathcal{S}_{n-1,q}(x).$

(iv) $\displaystyle\mathcal{S}_{n,q}(x) = \sum_{k=0}^{n} \begin{bmatrix} n \\ k \end{bmatrix}_q q^{\binom{k}{2}}\mathcal{S}_{k,q^{-1}}(-1)x^{n-k}.$

Finding the properties of q-differential equations of higher order combined with q-sigmoid polynomials in various ways is the main topic of this paper. In Section 2, we find the forms of several q-differential equations of higher order which are related to q-sigmoid polynomials and obtain their symmetric properties, as well as relations of q-differential equations of higher order, differential equations, etc. In Section 3, we observe several properties based on the structure of the approximation roots of the q-sigmoid polynomials.

2. Various q-Differential Equations of Higher Order Forms Related to q-Sigmoid Polynomials

This section shows that the solution of a q-differential equation of higher order is the q-sigmoid polynomials. These q-differential equations of higher order have various forms. In addition, we confirm the form of the q-differential equation of higher order with symmetric properties.

Theorem 4. *For $0 < q < 1$, the q-sigmoid polynomials represent a solution of the q-differential equation of higher order shown below:*

$$\begin{aligned}&\frac{(-1)^n}{[n]_q!}D_{q,x}^{(n)}\mathcal{S}_{n,q}(x)+\frac{(-1)^{n-1}}{[n-1]_q!}D_{q,x}^{(n-1)}\mathcal{S}_{n,q}(x)+\frac{(-1)^{n-2}}{[n-2]_q!}D_{q,x}^{(n-2)}\mathcal{S}_{n,q}(x)+\cdots\\&-\frac{1}{[3]_q!}D_{q,x}^{(3)}\mathcal{S}_{n,q}(x)+\frac{1}{[2]_q!}D_{q,x}^{(2)}\mathcal{S}_{n,q}(x)-D_{q,x}^{(1)}\mathcal{S}_{n,q}(x)+x^n=0.\end{aligned}$$

Proof. For $e_q(-t) \neq 1$, the generating function of q-sigmoid polynomials can be transformed as

$$\sum_{n=0}^{\infty}\mathcal{S}_{n,q}(x)\frac{t^n}{[n]_q!}\left(1+\sum_{n=0}^{\infty}(-1)^n\frac{t^n}{[n]_q!}\right)=\sum_{n=0}^{\infty}x^n\frac{t^n}{[n]_q!}. \tag{3}$$

Using the Cauchy product in the left-hand side of Equation (3), we have

$$\begin{aligned}&\sum_{n=0}^{\infty}\mathcal{S}_{n,q}(x)\frac{t^n}{[n]_q!}\left(1+\sum_{n=0}^{\infty}(-1)^n\frac{t^n}{[n]_q!}\right)\\&=\sum_{n=0}^{\infty}\left(\mathcal{S}_{n,q}(x)-\sum_{k=0}^{n}\begin{bmatrix}n\\k\end{bmatrix}_q(-1)^k\mathcal{S}_{n-k,q}(x)\right)\frac{t^n}{[n]_q!}.\end{aligned} \tag{4}$$

From Equations (3) and (4), we obtain

$$\mathcal{S}_{n,q}(x)-\sum_{k=0}^{n}\begin{bmatrix}n\\k\end{bmatrix}_q(-1)^k\mathcal{S}_{n-k,q}(x)=x^n. \tag{5}$$

By applying the q-derivative in the generating function of the q-sigmoid polynomials, we derive

$$\mathcal{S}_{n-k,q}(x)=\frac{[n-k]_q!}{[n]_q!}D_{q,x}^{(k)}\mathcal{S}_{n,q}(x). \tag{6}$$

Substituting $D_{q,x}^{(k)}\mathcal{S}_{n,q}(x)$ of (6) in the left-hand side of (5), we have

$$\mathcal{S}_{n,q}(x)-x^n=\sum_{k=0}^{n}\frac{(-1)^k}{[k]_q!}D_{q,x}(k)\mathcal{S}_{n,q}(x). \tag{7}$$

From Equation (7), we find the required result. □

Corollary 1. *Setting $q \to 1$ in Theorem 4, it holds that*

$$\begin{aligned}&\frac{(-1)^n}{n!}\frac{d^n}{dx^n}\mathcal{S}_n(x)+\frac{(-1)^{n-1}}{(n-1)!}\frac{d^{n-1}}{dx^{n-1}}\mathcal{S}_n(x)+\frac{(-1)^{n-2}}{(n-2)!}\frac{d^{n-2}}{dx^{n-2}}\mathcal{S}_n(x)+\cdots\\&-\frac{1}{3!}\frac{d^3}{dx^3}\mathcal{S}_n(x)+\frac{1}{2!}\frac{d^2}{dx^2}\mathcal{S}_n(x)-\frac{d}{dx}\mathcal{S}_n(x)+x^n=0.\end{aligned}$$

where $\mathcal{S}_n(x)$ represents the sigmoid polynomials.

Theorem 5. *For $0 < q < 1$, the q-sigmoid polynomials $\mathcal{S}_{n,q}(x)$ satisfy the q-differential equation of higher order presented below:*

$$\begin{aligned}&\frac{\mathcal{S}_{n-1,q}(-1)}{q^n[n-1]_q!}D_{q,x}^{(n-1)}\mathcal{S}_{n-1,q}(x)+\frac{\mathcal{S}_{n-2,q}(-1)}{q^{n-1}[n-2]_q!}D_{q,x}^{(n-2)}\mathcal{S}_{n-1,q}(x)\\&+\frac{\mathcal{S}_{n-3,q}(-1)}{q^{n-2}[n-3]_q!}D_{q,x}^{(n-3)}\mathcal{S}_{n-1,q}(x)+\cdots+\frac{\mathcal{S}_{2,q}(-1)}{q^3[2]_q!}D_{q,x}^{(2)}\mathcal{S}_{n-1,q}(x)+\frac{\mathcal{S}_{1,q}(-1)}{q^2}D_{q,x}^{(1)}\mathcal{S}_{n-1,q}(x)\\&+\left(\frac{\mathcal{S}_{0,q}(-1)}{q}+x\right)\mathcal{S}_{n-1,q}(x)-q^{-n}\mathcal{S}_{n,q}(qx)=0.\end{aligned}$$

Proof. By substituting qx instead of x, we can consider the q-derivative in q-sigmoid polynomials. Then, we have the following equation:

$$\begin{aligned}&D_{q,t}\sum_{n=0}^{\infty}\mathcal{S}_{n,q}(qx)\frac{t^n}{[n]_q!}\\&=e_q(qtx)\left(\frac{e_q(-t)}{(1+e_q(-t))(1+e_q(-qt))}\right)+\frac{qx}{1+e_q(-qt)}e_q(qtx)\\&=\sum_{n=0}^{\infty}q^n\mathcal{S}_{n,q}(x)\frac{t^n}{[n]_q!}\left(\frac{e_q(-t)}{1+e_q(-t)}+qx\right).\end{aligned}\tag{8}$$

Using q-sigmoid polynomials in Equation (8), we obtain

$$\begin{aligned}&D_{q,t}\sum_{n=0}^{\infty}\mathcal{S}_{n,q}(qx)\frac{t^n}{[n]_q!}\\&=\sum_{n=0}^{\infty}\left(\sum_{k=0}^{n}\begin{bmatrix}n\\k\end{bmatrix}_q q^{n-k}\mathcal{S}_{k,q}(-1)\mathcal{S}_{n-k,q}(x)+q^{n+1}x\mathcal{S}_{n,q}(x)\right)\frac{t^n}{[n]_q!}.\end{aligned}\tag{9}$$

To simplify the calculations, we multiply t in the above Equation (9) as

$$\begin{aligned}&tD_{q,t}\sum_{n=0}^{\infty}\mathcal{S}_{n,q}(qx)\frac{t^n}{[n]_q!}\\&=\sum_{n=0}^{\infty}[n]_q\left(\sum_{k=0}^{n-1}\begin{bmatrix}n-1\\k\end{bmatrix}_q q^{n-k-1}\mathcal{S}_{k,q}(-1)\mathcal{S}_{n-k-1,q}(x)+q^nx\mathcal{S}_{n-1,q}(x)\right)\frac{t^n}{[n]_q!}.\end{aligned}\tag{10}$$

On the other hand, we can find the below equation using the generating function of the q-sigmoid polynomials.

$$tD_{q,t}\sum_{n=0}^{\infty}\mathcal{S}_{n,q}(qx)\frac{t^n}{[n]_q!}=\sum_{n=0}^{\infty}[n]_q\mathcal{S}_{n,q}(qx)\frac{t^n}{[n]_q!}.\tag{11}$$

By comparing Equations (10) and (11), we derive

$$\sum_{k=0}^{n-1}\begin{bmatrix}n-1\\k\end{bmatrix}_q q^{-(k+1)}\mathcal{S}_{k,q}(-1)\mathcal{S}_{n-k-1,q}(x)=q^{-n}\mathcal{S}_{n,q}(qx)-x\mathcal{S}_{n-1,q}(x).\tag{12}$$

Applying Equation (6) in the left-hand side of (12), we have

$$\sum_{k=0}^{n-1}\begin{bmatrix}n-1\\k\end{bmatrix}_q q^{-(k+1)}\mathcal{S}_{k,q}(-1)\mathcal{S}_{n-k-1,q}(x)=\sum_{k=0}^{n-1}\frac{\mathcal{S}_{k,q}(-1)}{q^{k+1}[k]_q!}D_{q,x}^{(k)}\mathcal{S}_{n-1,q}(x).\tag{13}$$

Substituting the right-hand side of Equation (13) into the left-hand side of Equation (12), we have

$$\sum_{k=0}^{n-1}\frac{\mathcal{S}_{k,q}(-1)}{q^{k+1}[k]_q!}D_{q,x}^{(k)}\mathcal{S}_{n-1,q}(x)=q^{-n}\mathcal{S}_{n,q}(qx)-x\mathcal{S}_{n-1,q}(x), \tag{14}$$

which provides the result of Theorem 5. □

Corollary 2. *Setting $q\to 1$ in Theorem 5, the following holds:*

$$\begin{aligned}&\frac{\mathcal{S}_{n-1}(-1)}{(n-1)!}\frac{d^{n-1}}{dx^{n-1}}\mathcal{S}_{n-1}(x)+\frac{\mathcal{S}_{n-2}(-1)}{(n-2)!}\frac{d^{n-2}}{dx^{n-2}}\mathcal{S}_{n-1}(x)\\&+\frac{\mathcal{S}_{n-3}(-1)}{(n-3)!}\frac{d^{n-3}}{dx^{n-3}}\mathcal{S}_{n-1}(x)+\cdots+\frac{\mathcal{S}_{2}(-1)}{2!}\frac{d^{2}}{dx^{2}}\mathcal{S}_{n-1}(x)+\mathcal{S}_1(-1)\frac{d}{dx}\mathcal{S}_{n-1}(x)\\&+(\mathcal{S}_0(-1)+x)\mathcal{S}_{n-1}(x)-\mathcal{S}_n(x)=0,\end{aligned}$$

where $\mathcal{S}_n(x)$ represents the sigmoid polynomials.

Corollary 3. *In Theorem 5, we have*

$$\frac{d}{dt}\mathcal{S}_n(x)=\sum_{k=0}^{n}\binom{n}{k}\mathcal{S}_k(-1)\mathcal{S}_{n-k}(x)+x\mathcal{S}_n(x),$$

where $\mathcal{S}_n(x)$ is the sigmoid polynomials.

Theorem 6. *For $0<q<1$, the q-sigmoid polynomials $\mathcal{S}_{n,q}(x)$ satisfy the following q-differential equation of higher order:*

$$\begin{aligned}&\sum_{l=0}^{n-1}\begin{bmatrix}n-1\\ l\end{bmatrix}_q\frac{(-1)^{n-l-1}\mathcal{S}_{l,q}}{q^n[n-1]_q!}D_{q,x}^{(n-1)}\mathcal{S}_{n-1,q}(x)+\sum_{l=0}^{n-2}\begin{bmatrix}n-2\\ l\end{bmatrix}_q\frac{(-1)^{n-l-2}\mathcal{S}_{l,q}}{q^{n-1}[n-2]_q!}D_{q,x}^{(n-2)}\mathcal{S}_{n-1,q}(x)\\&+\cdots+\sum_{l=0}^{2}\begin{bmatrix}2\\ l\end{bmatrix}_q\frac{(-1)^{2-l}\mathcal{S}_{l,q}}{q^3[2]_q!}D_{q,x}^{(2)}\mathcal{S}_{n-1,q}(x)+\sum_{l=0}^{1}\begin{bmatrix}1\\ l\end{bmatrix}_q\frac{(-1)^{1-l}\mathcal{S}_{l,q}}{q^2}D_{q,x}^{(1)}\mathcal{S}_{n-1,q}(x)\\&+(q^{-1}\mathcal{S}_{0,q}-x)\mathcal{S}_{n-1,q}(x)+q^{-n}\mathcal{S}_{n,q}(qx)=0.\end{aligned}$$

Proof. We can find an expression in which the coefficients of a q-differential equation of higher order consist of q-sigmoid numbers. From Equation (8), we obtain the other form as

$$\begin{aligned}&tD_{q,t}\mathcal{S}_{n,q}(qx)\\&=[n]_q q^n x\mathcal{S}_{n-1,q}(x)+[n]_q\sum_{k=0}^{n-1}\sum_{l=0}^{k}\begin{bmatrix}n-1\\ k\end{bmatrix}_q\begin{bmatrix}k\\ l\end{bmatrix}_q(-1)^{k-l}q^{n-k-1}\mathcal{S}_{l,q}\mathcal{S}_{n-k-1,q}(x).\end{aligned} \tag{15}$$

Combining the right-hand side of Equation (15) with the right-hand side of Equation (12), we obtain the following equation:

$$\sum_{k=0}^{n-1}\sum_{l=0}^{k}\begin{bmatrix}n-1\\ k\end{bmatrix}_q\begin{bmatrix}k\\ l\end{bmatrix}_q(-1)^{k-l}q^{-(k+1)}\mathcal{S}_{l,q}\mathcal{S}_{n-k-1,q}(x)=x\mathcal{S}_{n-1,q}(x)-q^{-n}\mathcal{S}_{n,q}(qx). \tag{16}$$

Applying Equation (6) to Equation (16), the right-hand side of (17) can be obtained as follows:

$$\begin{aligned}&\sum_{k=0}^{n-1}\sum_{l=0}^{k}\begin{bmatrix}n-1\\ k\end{bmatrix}_q\begin{bmatrix}k\\ l\end{bmatrix}_q(-1)^{k-l}q^{-(k+1)}\mathcal{S}_{l,q}\mathcal{S}_{n-k-1,q}(x)\\&=\sum_{k=0}^{n-1}\sum_{l=0}^{k}\begin{bmatrix}k\\ l\end{bmatrix}_q\frac{(-1)^{k-l}\mathcal{S}_{l,q}}{q^{k+1}[k]_q!}D_{q,x}^{(k)}\mathcal{S}_{n-1,q}(x).\end{aligned} \tag{17}$$

From Equation (17), we conclude the proof for Theorem 6. □

Corollary 4. *Let $q \to 1$ in Theorem 6. Then, it holds that*

$$\sum_{l=0}^{n-1}\binom{n-1}{l}\frac{(-1)^{n-l-1}\mathcal{S}_l}{(n-1)!}\frac{d^{n-1}}{dx^{n-1}}\mathcal{S}_{n-1}(x)+\sum_{l=0}^{n-2}\binom{n-2}{l}\frac{(-1)^{n-l-2}\mathcal{S}_l}{(n-2)!}\frac{d^{n-2}}{dx^{n-2}}\mathcal{S}_{n-1}(x)$$
$$+\cdots+\sum_{l=0}^{2}\binom{2}{l}\frac{(-1)^{2-l}\mathcal{S}_l}{2!}\frac{d^2}{dx^2}\mathcal{S}_{n-1}(x)+\sum_{l=0}^{1}\binom{1}{l}(-1)^{1-l}\mathcal{S}_l\frac{d}{dx}\mathcal{S}_{n-1}(x)$$
$$+(q^{-1}\mathcal{S}_0-x)\mathcal{S}_{n-1}(x)+\mathcal{S}_n(x)=0,$$

where $\mathcal{S}_n$ represents the q-sigmoid numbers and $\mathcal{S}_n(x)$ the q-sigmoid polynomials.

Theorem 7. *For $0<q<1$, the q-sigmoid polynomials represent a solution of the q-differential equation of higher order shown below:*

$$\frac{q^{n-1}\mathcal{S}_{n-1,q}(-1)}{[n-1]_q!}D_{q,x}^{(n-1)}\mathcal{S}_{n-1,q}(q^{-1}x)+\frac{q^{n-1}\mathcal{S}_{n-2,q}(-1)}{[n-2]_q!}D_{q,x}^{(n-2)}\mathcal{S}_{n-1,q}(q^{-1}x)$$
$$+\cdots+\frac{q^{n-1}\mathcal{S}_{2,q}(-1)}{[2]_q!}D_{q,x}^{(2)}\mathcal{S}_{n-1,q}(q^{-1}x)+q^{n-1}\mathcal{S}_{1,q}(-1)D_{q,x}^{(1)}\mathcal{S}_{n-1,q}(q^{-1}x)$$
$$+(x+\mathcal{S}_{0,q}(-1))q^{n-1}\mathcal{S}_{n-1,q}(q^{-1}x)-\mathcal{S}_{n,q}(x)=0.$$

Proof. To find the other q-differential equation of higher order, we can substitute qt instead of t into the q-sigmoid polynomials. From the generating function of thr q-sigmoid polynomials,
we have

$$tD_{q,t}\sum_{n=0}^{\infty}q^n\mathcal{S}_{n,q}(x)\frac{t^n}{[n]_q!}=\sum_{n=0}^{\infty}[n]_q q^n\mathcal{S}_{n,q}(x)\frac{t^n}{[n]_q!},\tag{18}$$

and

$$\begin{aligned}&tD_{q,t}\sum_{n=0}^{\infty}q^n\mathcal{S}_{n,q}(x)\frac{t^n}{[n]_q!}\\&=\sum_{n=0}^{\infty}[n]_q\left(\sum_{k=0}^{n-1}\begin{bmatrix}n-1\\k\end{bmatrix}_q q^{2n-k-1}\mathcal{S}_{k,q}(-1)\mathcal{S}_{n-k-1,q}(q^{-1}x)+q^{2n-1}x\mathcal{S}_{n-1,q}(q^{-1}x)\right)\frac{t^n}{[n]_q!}.\end{aligned}\tag{19}$$

From Equations (18) and (19), we obtain

$$\sum_{k=0}^{n-1}\begin{bmatrix}n-1\\k\end{bmatrix}_q q^{n-k-1}\mathcal{S}_{k,q}(-1)\mathcal{S}_{n-k-1,q}(q^{-1}x)=\mathcal{S}_{n,q}(x)-q^{n-1}x\mathcal{S}_{n-1,q}(q^{-1}x).\tag{20}$$

By using the q-derivative, we can find a relation between $\mathcal{S}_{n-k,q}(q^{-1}x)$ and $D_{q,x}^{(k)}\mathcal{S}_{n,q}(q^{-1}x)$, such as

$$\mathcal{S}_{n-k-1,q}(q^{-1}x)=\frac{q^k[n-k-1]_q!}{[n-1]_q!}D_{q,x}^{(k)}\mathcal{S}_{n-1,q}(q^{-1}x).\tag{21}$$

Substituting Equation (21) into Equation (20), we obtain the following:

$$\sum_{k=0}^{n-1}\frac{q^{n-1}\mathcal{S}_{k,q}(-1)}{[k]_q!}D_{q,x}^{(k)}\mathcal{S}_{n-1,q}(q^{-1}x)=\mathcal{S}_{n,q}(x)-q^{n-1}x\mathcal{S}_{n-1,q}(q^{-1}x),\tag{22}$$

and Equation (22) completes the proof of the theorem. □

Corollary 5. *Let $q \to 1$ in Theorem 7. Then, it holds that*

$$\frac{\mathcal{S}_{n-1}(-1)}{(n-1)!}\frac{d^{n-1}}{dx^{n-1}}\mathcal{S}_{n-1}(x)+\frac{\mathcal{S}_{n-2}(-1)}{(n-2)!}\frac{d^{n-2}}{dx^{n-2}}\mathcal{S}_{n-1}(x)+\cdots+\frac{\mathcal{S}_{2}(-1)}{2!}\frac{d^{2}}{dx^{2}}\mathcal{S}_{n-1}(x)$$
$$+\mathcal{S}_1(-1)\frac{d}{dx}\mathcal{S}_{n-1}(x)+(\mathcal{S}_0(-1)+x)\mathcal{S}_{n-1}(x)+\mathcal{S}_n(x)=0,$$

where $\mathcal{S}_n(x)$ represents the q-sigmoid polynomials.

Theorem 8. *For $0<q<1$, a solution of the following q-differential equation of higher order*

$$\sum_{k=0}^{n-1}\begin{bmatrix} n-1 \\ k\end{bmatrix}_q \frac{(-1)^k q^{n-1}\mathcal{S}_{n-k-1,q}}{[n-1]_q!}D_{q,x}^{(n-1)}\mathcal{S}_{n-1,q}(q^{-1}x)$$
$$+\sum_{k=0}^{n-2}\begin{bmatrix} n-2 \\ k\end{bmatrix}_q \frac{(-1)^k q^{n-2}\mathcal{S}_{n-k-2,q}}{[n-2]_q!}D_{q,x}^{(n-2)}\mathcal{S}_{n-1,q}(q^{-1}x)+\cdots$$
$$+\sum_{k=0}^{2}\begin{bmatrix} 2 \\ k\end{bmatrix}_q \frac{(-1)^k q^{2}\mathcal{S}_{2-k,q}}{[2]_q!}D_{q,x}^{(2)}\mathcal{S}_{n-1,q}(q^{-1}x)+\sum_{k=0}^{1}\begin{bmatrix} 1 \\ k\end{bmatrix}_q (-1)^k q\mathcal{S}_{1-k,q}D_{q,x}^{(1)}\mathcal{S}_{n-1,q}(q^{-1}x)$$
$$+(x+\mathcal{S}_{0,q})\mathcal{S}_{n-1,q}(q^{-1}x)-\mathcal{S}_{n,q}(x)=0$$

is represented by the q-sigmoid polynomials.

Proof. From the generating function of the q-sigmoid polynomials, we obtain

$$\begin{aligned}
&D_{q,t}\sum_{n=0}^{\infty}q^n\mathcal{S}_{n,q}(x)\frac{t^n}{[n]_q!}\\
&=e_q(qtx)\left(\frac{qe_q(-qt)-q(1-qt)e_q(-qt)}{(1-qt)(1-q^2t)}\right)+\frac{qxe_q(-q^2t)}{1-q^2t}e_q(qtx)\\
&=\sum_{n=0}^{\infty}q^{2n+1}\mathcal{S}_{n,q}(q^{-1}x)\frac{t^n}{[n]_q!}\left(E_q(q^2t)\sum_{n=0}^{\infty}q^n\mathcal{S}_{n,q}\frac{t^n}{[n]_q!}-E_q(q^2t)e_q(-qt)+qx\right)\\
&=\sum_{n=0}^{\infty}\left(\sum_{l=0}^{n}\sum_{k=0}^{l}\begin{bmatrix} n \\ l\end{bmatrix}_q\begin{bmatrix} l \\ k\end{bmatrix}_q\left((-1)^{k+1}q^{\binom{l-k}{2}+l-k}+q^{\binom{k}{2}+k}\mathcal{S}_{l-k,q}\right)q^{2n-l+1}\mathcal{S}_{n-l,q}(q^{-1}x)\right)\frac{t^n}{[n]_q!}\\
&+\sum_{n=0}^{\infty}q^{2n+1}x\mathcal{S}_{n,q}(q^{-1}x)\frac{t^n}{[n]_q!}.
\end{aligned}\tag{23}$$

In Equation (23), we can obtain the desired result by following a procedure similar to the process used for the proof of Theorem 8. □

Corollary 6. *Let $q \to 1$ in Theorem 8. Then, it holds that*

$$\sum_{k=0}^{n-1}\binom{n-1}{k}\frac{(-1)^k\mathcal{S}_{n-k-1}}{(n-1)!}\frac{d^{n-1}}{dx^{n-1}}\mathcal{S}_{n-1}(x)+\sum_{k=0}^{n-2}\binom{n-2}{k}\frac{(-1)^k\mathcal{S}_{n-k-2}}{(n-2)!}\frac{d^{n-2}}{dx^{n-2}}\mathcal{S}_{n-1}(x)$$
$$+\cdots+\sum_{k=0}^{2}\binom{2}{k}\frac{(-1)^k\mathcal{S}_{2-k}}{2!}\frac{d^{2}}{dx^{2}}\mathcal{S}_{n-1}(x)+\sum_{k=0}^{1}\binom{1}{k}(-1)^k\mathcal{S}_{1-k}\frac{d}{dx}\mathcal{S}_{n-1,q}(q^{-1}x)$$
$$+(x+\mathcal{S}_0)\mathcal{S}_{n-1}(x)-\mathcal{S}_{n,q}(x)=0,$$

where $\mathcal{S}_n$ represents the q-sigmoid numbers and $\mathcal{S}_n(x)$ the q-sigmoid polynomials.

Theorem 9. *For $a \neq 0$, $b \neq 0$, and $0 < q < 1$, we obtain*

$$\frac{b^n a^n \mathcal{S}_{n,q}}{[n]_q!} D_{q,x}^{(n)} \mathcal{S}_{n,q}(b^{-1}x) + \frac{b^n a^{n-1} \mathcal{S}_{n-1,q}}{[n-1]_q!} D_{q,x}^{(n-1)} \mathcal{S}_{n,q}(b^{-1}x) + \cdots$$
$$+ \frac{b^n a^2 \mathcal{S}_{2,q}}{[2]_q!} D_{q,x}^{(2)} \mathcal{S}_{n,q}(b^{-1}x) + b^n a \mathcal{S}_{1,q} D_{q,x}^{(1)} \mathcal{S}_{n,q}(b^{-1}x) + b^n \mathcal{S}_{0,q} \mathcal{S}_{n,q}(b^{-1}x)$$
$$= \frac{a^n b^n \mathcal{S}_{n,q}}{[n]_q!} D_{q,x}^{(n)} \mathcal{S}_{n,q}(a^{-1}x) + \frac{a^n b^{n-1} \mathcal{S}_{n-1,q}}{[n-1]_q!} D_{q,x}^{(n-1)} \mathcal{S}_{n,q}(a^{-1}x) + \cdots$$
$$+ \frac{a^n b^2 \mathcal{S}_{2,q}}{[2]_q!} D_{q,x}^{(2)} \mathcal{S}_{n,q}(a^{-1}x) + a^n b \mathcal{S}_{1,q} D_{q,x}^{(1)} \mathcal{S}_{n,q}(a^{-1}x) + a^n \mathcal{S}_{0,q} \mathcal{S}_{n,q}(a^{-1}x).$$

Proof. In order to find a symmetric property of the q-differential equation of higher order for the q-sigmoid polynomials, we consider form A as follows:

$$A := \frac{e_q(tx)}{(1+e_q(-at))(1+e_q(-bt))}.$$

Using form A, we can have

$$A = \sum_{n=0}^{\infty} \left(\sum_{k=0}^{n} \begin{bmatrix} n \\ k \end{bmatrix}_q a^k b^{n-k} \mathcal{S}_{k,q} \mathcal{S}_{n-k,q}(b^{-1}x) \right) \frac{t^n}{[n]_q!}, \tag{24}$$

and

$$A = \sum_{n=0}^{\infty} \left(\sum_{k=0}^{n} \begin{bmatrix} n \\ k \end{bmatrix}_q b^k a^{n-k} \mathcal{S}_{k,q} \mathcal{S}_{n-k,q}(a^{-1}x) \right) \frac{t^n}{[n]_q!}. \tag{25}$$

Comparing the coefficients of both sides in Equations (24) and (25), we have

$$\sum_{k=0}^{n} \begin{bmatrix} n \\ k \end{bmatrix}_q a^k b^{n-k} \mathcal{S}_{k,q} \mathcal{D}_{n-k,q}(b^{-1}x) = \sum_{k=0}^{n} \begin{bmatrix} n \\ k \end{bmatrix}_q b^k a^{n-k} \mathcal{S}_{k,q} \mathcal{D}_{n-k,q}(a^{-1}x). \tag{26}$$

Replacing Equation (21) with Equation (26), we find

$$b^n \sum_{k=0}^{n} \frac{a^k \mathcal{S}_{k,q}}{[k]_q!} D_{q,x}^{(k)} \mathcal{S}_{n-k,q}(b^{-1}x) = a^n \sum_{k=0}^{n} \frac{b^k \mathcal{S}_{k,q}}{[k]_q!} D_{q,x}^{(k)} \mathcal{S}_{n-k,q}(a^{-1}x). \tag{27}$$

From (27), we finish the proof of Theorem 9. □

Corollary 7. *Setting $a = 1$ in Theorem 9, we have*

$$\frac{b^n \mathcal{S}_{n,q}}{[n]_q!} D_{q,x}^{(n)} \mathcal{S}_{n,q}(b^{-1}x) + \frac{b^n \mathcal{S}_{n-1,q}}{[n-1]_q!} D_{q,x}^{(n-1)} \mathcal{S}_{n,q}(b^{-1}x) + \cdots$$
$$+ \frac{b^n \mathcal{S}_{2,q}}{[2]_q!} D_{q,x}^{(2)} \mathcal{S}_{n,q}(b^{-1}x) + b^n \mathcal{S}_{1,q} D_{q,x}^{(1)} \mathcal{S}_{n,q}(b^{-1}x) + b^n \mathcal{S}_{0,q} \mathcal{S}_{n,q}(b^{-1}x)$$
$$= \frac{b^n \mathcal{S}_{n,q}}{[n]_q!} D_{q,x}^{(n)} \mathcal{S}_{n,q}(x) + \frac{b^{n-1} \mathcal{S}_{n-1,q}}{[n-1]_q!} D_{q,x}^{(n-1)} \mathcal{S}_{n,q}(x) + \cdots$$
$$+ \frac{b^2 \mathcal{S}_{2,q}}{[2]_q!} D_{q,x}^{(2)} \mathcal{D}_{n,q}(x) + b \mathcal{S}_{1,q} D_{q,x}^{(1)} \mathcal{S}_{n,q}(x) + \mathcal{S}_{0,q} \mathcal{S}_{n,q}(x).$$

Corollary 8. *Consider $q \to 1$ in Theorem 9. Then, the following holds:*

$$\frac{b^n a^n \mathcal{S}_n}{n!}\frac{d^n}{dx^n}\mathcal{S}_n(b^{-1}x) + \frac{b^n a^{n-1}\mathcal{S}_{n-1}}{(n-1)!}\frac{d^{n-1}}{dx^{n-1}}\mathcal{S}_n(b^{-1}x) + \cdots$$
$$+ \frac{b^n a^2 \mathcal{S}_2}{2!}\frac{d^2}{dx^2}\mathcal{S}_n(b^{-1}x) + b^n a\mathcal{S}_1\frac{d}{dx}\mathcal{S}_n(b^{-1}x) + b^n\mathcal{S}_0\mathcal{S}_n(b^{-1}x)$$
$$= \frac{a^n b^n \mathcal{S}_n}{n!}\frac{d^n}{dx^n}\mathcal{S}_n(a^{-1}x) + \frac{a^n b^{n-1}\mathcal{S}_{n-1}}{(n-1)!}\frac{d^{n-1}}{dx^{n-1}}\mathcal{S}_n(a^{-1}x) + \cdots$$
$$+ \frac{a^n b^2 \mathcal{S}_2}{2!}\frac{d^2}{dx^2}\mathcal{S}_n(a^{-1}x) + a^n b\mathcal{S}_1\frac{d}{dx}\mathcal{S}_n(a^{-1}x) + a^n\mathcal{S}_0\mathcal{S}_n(a^{-1}x).$$

Theorem 10. *For $a \neq 0$, $b \neq 0$, and $0 < q < 1$, we investigate*

$$\frac{b^n a^n \mathcal{S}_{n,q}(a^{-1}x)}{[n]_q!}D_{q,y}^{(n)}\mathcal{S}_{n,q}(b^{-1}y) + \frac{b^n a^{n-1}\mathcal{S}_{n-1,q}(a^{-1}x)}{[n-1]_q!}D_{q,y}^{(n-1)}\mathcal{S}_{n,q}(b^{-1}y) + \cdots$$
$$+ b^n a\mathcal{S}_{1,q}(a^{-1}x)D_{q,y}^{(1)}\mathcal{S}_{n,q}(b^{-1}y) + b^n\mathcal{S}_{0,q}(a^{-1}x)\mathcal{S}_{n,q}(b^{-1}y)$$
$$= \frac{a^n b^n \mathcal{S}_{n,q}(b^{-1}x)}{[n]_q!}D_{q,y}^{(n)}\mathcal{S}_{n,q}(a^{-1}y) + \frac{a^n b^{n-1}\mathcal{S}_{n-1,q}(b^{-1}x)}{[n-1]_q!}D_{q,y}^{(n-1)}\mathcal{S}_{n,q}(a^{-1}y) + \cdots$$
$$+ a^n b\mathcal{S}_{1,q}(b^{-1}x)D_{q,y}^{(1)}\mathcal{S}_{n,q}(a^{-1}y) + a^n\mathcal{S}_{0,q}(b^{-1}x)\mathcal{S}_{n,q}(a^{-1}y).$$

Proof. In order to find a symmetric property of q-differential equations of higher order for the q-sigmoid polynomials, we suppose that form B is

$$B := \frac{e_q(tx)e_q(ty)}{(1+e_q(-at))(1+e_q(-bt))}.$$

Using form B in the same way as the proof of Theorem 9 we can finish the proof of the theorem. □

Corollary 9. *Setting $a = 1$ in Theorem 10, we have*

$$\frac{b^n \mathcal{S}_{n,q}(x)}{[n]_q!}D_{q,y}^{(n)}\mathcal{S}_{n,q}(b^{-1}y) + \frac{b^n\mathcal{S}_{n-1,q}(x)}{[n-1]_q!}D_{q,y}^{(n-1)}\mathcal{S}_{n,q}(b^{-1}y) + \cdots$$
$$+ b^n\mathcal{S}_{1,q}(x)D_{q,y}^{(1)}\mathcal{S}_{n,q}(b^{-1}y) + b^n\mathcal{S}_{0,q}(x)\mathcal{S}_{n,q}(b^{-1}y)$$
$$= \frac{b^n \mathcal{S}_{n,q}(b^{-1}x)}{[n]_q!}D_{q,y}^{(n)}\mathcal{S}_{n,q}(y) + \frac{b^{n-1}\mathcal{S}_{n-1,q}(b^{-1}x)}{[n-1]_q!}D_{q,y}^{(n-1)}\mathcal{S}_{n,q}(y) + \cdots$$
$$+ b\mathcal{S}_{1,q}(b^{-1}x)D_{q,y}^{(1)}\mathcal{S}_{n,q}(y) + \mathcal{S}_{0,q}(b^{-1}x)\mathcal{S}_{n,q}(y).$$

Corollary 10. *Consider $q \to 1$ in Theorem 10. Then, the following holds:*

$$\frac{b^n a^n \mathcal{S}_n(a^{-1}x)}{n!}\frac{d^n}{dy^n}\mathcal{S}_n(b^{-1}y) + \frac{b^n a^{n-1}\mathcal{S}_{n-1}(a^{-1}x)}{(n-1)!}\frac{d^{n-1}}{dy^{n-1}}\mathcal{S}_n(b^{-1}y) + \cdots$$
$$+ b^n a\mathcal{S}_1(a^{-1}x)\frac{d}{dy}\mathcal{S}_n(b^{-1}y) + b^n\mathcal{S}_0(a^{-1}x)\mathcal{S}_n(b^{-1}y)$$
$$= \frac{a^n b^n \mathcal{S}_n(b^{-1}x)}{n!}\frac{d^n}{dy^n}\mathcal{S}_n(a^{-1}y) + \frac{a^n b^{n-1}\mathcal{S}_{n-1}(b^{-1}x)}{(n-1)!}\frac{d^{n-1}}{dy^{n-1}}\mathcal{S}_n(a^{-1}y) + \cdots$$
$$+ a^n b\mathcal{S}_1(b^{-1}x)\frac{d}{dy}\mathcal{S}_n(a^{-1}y) + a^n\mathcal{S}_0(b^{-1}x)\mathcal{S}_n(a^{-1}y).$$

3. Properties and Structures of Approximation Roots of q-Sigmoid Polynomials

In this section, we try to confirm the approximate roots for the q-sigmoid polynomials mentioned for q-differential equations of higher order. By substituting various values for the q-number, we can check the properties of q-sigmoid polynomials.

Several q-sigmoid polynomials are provided below; see [18]:

$$\begin{aligned}
\mathcal{S}_{0,q}(x) &= \frac{1}{2}, \\
\mathcal{S}_{1,q}(x) &= \frac{1}{4}(1+2x), \\
\mathcal{S}_{2,q}(x) &= \frac{1}{8}(-1+q+2(1+q)x+4x^2), \\
\mathcal{S}_{3,q}(x) &= \frac{1}{16}(1+q(-2+(-2+q)q)-2x+2q^3x+4(1+q+q^2)x^2+8x^3), \\
\mathcal{S}_{4,q}(x) &= \frac{1}{32}(-1+3q+3q^2-3q^4-3q^5+q^6+2(1+q)^2(1+(-3+q)q)(1+q^2)x \\
&\quad +4(-1+q^2(-1+q+q^3))x^2+8(1+q)(1+q^2)x^3+16x^4), \\
&\cdots .
\end{aligned}$$

Figure 1 shows the structures of the approximate roots of the q-sigmoid polynomials. The graph in Figure 1a shows the condition of $q = 0.1$, while Figure 1b shows the condition of $q = 0.0001$. Under the condition of $0 < n \leq 50$, we can observe Figure 1, which is a figure that appears when viewed from above in 3D. The blue dots are the positions of the approximate roots that appear when the value of n is small, and the red dots are the positions of the approximate roots that appear when $n = 50$. Here, as the value of q is smaller, we can assume that most points have a certain circular shape, with the exception of only a few points.

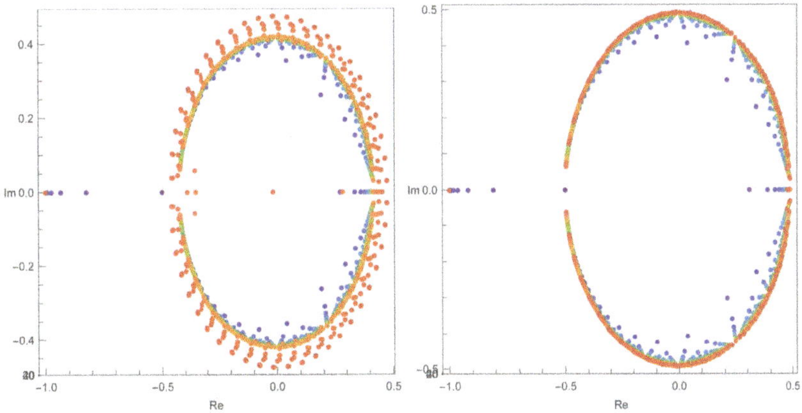

(a) (b)

Figure 1. Positions of the approximate roots of $\mathcal{S}_{n,q}(x)$ with $0 \leq n \leq 50$: (**a**) $q = 0.1$, (**b**) $q = 0.0001$.

Figure 2 shows the details of the guess made by looking at Figure 1. We fix $n = 50$ and change the values of q to 0.01, 0.001, and 0.0001, respectively. Figure 2a show the results with the value of q set to 0.01, Figure 2b shows the results with $q = 0.001$, and Figure 2c shows the results with $q = 0.0001$. In Figure 2, the red dots indicate only imaginary roots except for the real roots, and the blue lines indicate the closest circle to the approximate roots. The blue dot represents the center of the approximated circle. Figure 2 shows that the approximated root positions lie on a circle.

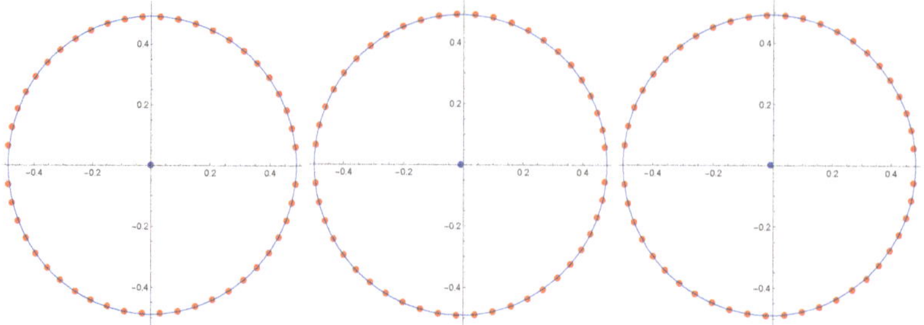

(**a**) (**b**) (**c**)

Figure 2. Approximate roots and approximated circles of $\mathcal{S}_{50,q}(x)$: (**a**) $q = 0.01$, (**b**) $q = 0.001$, (**c**) $q = 0.0001$.

Table 1 below is the result of accurately calculating Figure 2 using a computer. In Table 1, it can be seen that the center of the approximated circle is slightly shifted to the left when the value of q is smaller. Furthermore, it can be seen that the radius is closer to 0.4905 when the value of q is smaller. It can be observed in Table 1 that when the value of q is smaller, the error ranges of the approximated circle and the approximate roots are smaller as well; in other words, the positions of the approximate roots are located on the approximated circle. Here, we can make the following assumptions.

Table 1. The center and radius of the approximated circles of $\mathcal{S}_{50,q}(x)$.

	The Center (x, y)	The Radius	The Error Range
$q = 0.01$	$(-0.0013679,\ 4.21363 \times 10^{-13})$	0.489466	0.00013278
$q = 0.001$	$(-0.00911017,\ -8.92717 \times 10^{-12})$	0.490576	0.0000920933
$q = 0.0001$	$(-0.00890715,\ 1.6445 \times 10^{-12})$	0.490528	0.0000711247

Conjecture 11. *The locations of the approximation roots of q-sigmoid polynomials lie on the approximated circle under the condition in which* $n = 50$ *and* $q = 0.001$.

In Figure 1, it can be seen that, in addition to the circle, there are red dots, blue dots, etc., on the left side. Table 2 shows the real zeros of these approximation roots.

Based on Table 2, we can consider q-sigmoid polynomials by dividing n into even and odd. When n is an even number, it can be assumed that the q-sigmoid polynomials have two real roots regardless of the value of q-number. On the other hand, it can be assumed that the q-sigmoid polynomials will always have one real root regardless of the q-number when n is odd.

Figure 3 below shows another property of the approximate roots of q-sigmoid polynomials. In Figure 3, we can see that the approximate roots of this polynomial are stacked in two shapes. When $0 \leq n \leq 50$, one shape is a circular shape and the other shape is a straight shape. Because the shape of the circle is confirmed in Figure 2 and Table 1, we consider the straight shape.

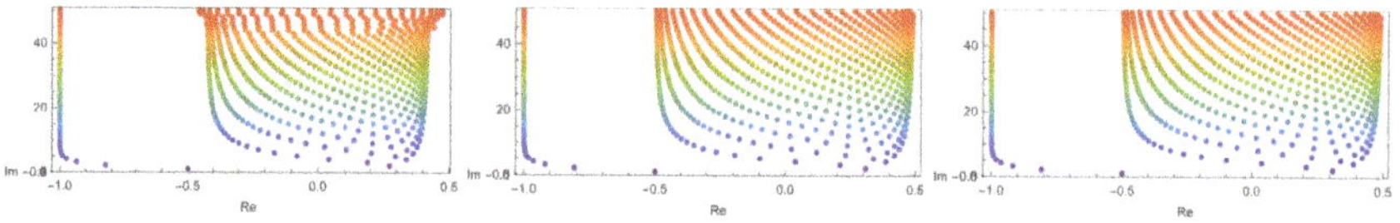

(**a**) (**b**) (**c**)

Figure 3. Approximate roots of $\mathcal{S}_{n,q}(x)$ with $0 \leq n \leq 50$: (**a**) $q = 0.01$, (**b**) $q = 0.001$, (**c**) $q = 0.0001$.

Table 2. Approximate real roots of $\mathcal{S}_{n,q}(x)$.

n \ q	0.01	0.001	0.0001
⋮	⋮	⋮	⋮
5	−0.983547	−0.983031	−0.98298
6	−0.992142, 0.415504	−0.991826, 0.419697	−0.991795, 0.420109
7	−0.99619	−0.996003	−0.995984
8	−0.998137, 0.433359	−0.998028, 0.437674	−0.998017, 0.438096
9	−0.999084	−0.999022	−0.999015
10	−0.999548, 0.444653	−0.999513, 0.449039	−0.99951, 0.449468
⋮	⋮	⋮	⋮
19	−0.999999	−0.999999	−0.999999
20	−1, 0.46868	−1, 0.473205	−1, 0.473645
⋮	⋮	⋮	⋮
29	−1	−1	−1
30	−1, 0.47715	−1, 0.481719	−1, 0.482163
⋮	⋮	⋮	⋮
39	−1	−1	−1
40	−1, 0.481477	−1, 0.486068	−1, 0.486516
⋮	⋮	⋮	⋮

Based on Table 2 and Figure 3, we can make the following assumptions.

Conjecture 12. *(i) Assume that the value of q is very small, while the value od n is even and increasing. Then, the q-sigmoid polynomial has two real approximations.*
(ii) Suppose that the value of q is very small, while the value of n is odd and increasing. Then, the q-sigmoid polynomial has only one real approximation.

4. Conclusions

In this paper, we find several types of q-differential equations of higher order and confirm that their solutions become q-sigmoid polynomials. In order to confirm the properties of the q-sigmoid polynomials which are the solutions of these differential equations of higher order, we conducted many different types of experiments based on varying assumptions. To solve these conjectures, it is necessary to study various approaches to special polynomials. In addition, we think that useful results can be obtained by conducting new research based on the defined function in [11].

Author Contributions: Conceptualization, C.-S.R. and J.-Y.K.; methodology, C.-S.R.; software, J.-Y.K.; writing—original draft preparation, J.-Y.K. All authors have read and agreed to the published version of the manuscript.

Funding: This research received no external funding.

Data Availability Statement: The data presented in this study are available on request from the corresponding author.

Conflicts of Interest: The authors declare no conflict of interest.

References

1. Jackson, H.F. q-Difference equations. *Am. J. Math* **1910**, *32*, 305–314. [CrossRef]
2. Kac, V.; Cheung, P. *Quantum Calculus*; Springer: Berlin/Heidelberg, Germany, 2002; ISBN 0-387-95341-8.
3. Bangerezako, G. *An Introduction to q-Difference Equations*; University of Burundi: Bujumbura, Burundi, 2008; preprint.
4. Comtet, L. *Advanced Combinatorics*; Reidel: Dordrecht, The Netherlands, 1974.
5. Carmichael, R.D. The general theory of linear q-qifference equations. *Am. J. Math* **1912**, *34*, 147–168. [CrossRef]

6. Jackson, H.F. On q-functions and a certain difference operator. *Trans. R. Soc. Edinb.* **1950**, *46*, 253–281. [CrossRef]
7. Konvalina, J. A unified interpretation of the binomial coefficients, the Stirling numbers, and the Gaussian coefficients. *Amer. Math. Mon.* **2000**, *107*, 10. [CrossRef]
8. Mason, T.E. On properties of the solution of linear q-difference equations with entire function coefficients. *Am. J. Math* **1915**, *37*, 439–444. [CrossRef]
9. Rodrigues, P.S.; Wachs-Lopes, G.; Santos, R.M.; Coltri, E.; Giraldi, G.A. A q-extension of sigmoid functions and the application for enhancement of ultrasound images. *Entropy* **2019**, *21*, 430. [CrossRef] [PubMed]
10. Trjitzinsky, W.J. Analytic theory of linear q-difference equations. *Acta Math.* **1933**, *61*, 1–38. [CrossRef]
11. Silindir, B.; Yantir, A. Generalized quantum exponential function and its applications. *Filomat* **2019**, *33*, 15. [CrossRef]
12. Zil, D.G. *A First Course in Differential Equations: With Modeling Applications*, 9th ed.; Brooks/Cole; Cengage Learning, Inc.: Boston, MA, USA; ISBN-13: 978-04951082452009.
13. Han, J.; Wilson, R.S.; Leurgans, S.E. Sigmoidal mixed models for longitudinal data, *Stat. Methods Med. Res.* 2018, 27, 863–875. [CrossRef]
14. Ito, Y. Representation of functions by superpositions of a step or sigmoid function and their applications to neural network theory. *Neural Netw.* **1991**, *4*, 385–394. [CrossRef]
15. Kim, M.; Song, Y.; Wang, S.; Xia, Y.; Jiang, X. Secure Logistic Regression Based on Homomorphic Encryption: Design and Evaluation. *JMIR Med. Inform.* **2018**, *6*, e19. [CrossRef] [PubMed]
16. Kang, J.Y. Some relationships between sigmoid polynomials and other polynomials. *J. Appl. Pure Math.* **2019**, *1*, 1–2.
17. Han, J.; Moraga, C. The influence of the sigmoid function parameters on the speed of backpropagation learning. In Proceedings of the International Workshop on Artificial Neural Networks, Malaga-Torremolinos, Spain, 7–9 June 1995. [CrossRef]
18. Kang, J.Y. Some properties and distribution of the zeros of the q-sigmoid polynomials. *Discret. Dyn. Nat. Soc.* **2020**, *2020*, 4169840. [CrossRef]
19. Kwan, H.K. Simple sigmoid-like activation function suitable for digital hardware implementation. *Electron. Lett.* **1992**, *28*, 1379–1380. [CrossRef]
20. Ryoo, C.S.; Kang, J.Y. Phenomenon of scattering of zeros of the (p,q)-cosine sigmoid polynomials and (p,q)-sine sigmoid polynomials. *Fractal Fract.* **2021**, *5*, 245. [CrossRef]
21. Andrews, G.E.; Askey, R.; Roy, R. *Special Functions*; Cambridge Press: Cambridge, UK, 1999.
22. Gi-Sang, C. A note on the Bernoulli and Euler polynomials. *Appl. Math. Lett.* **2003**, *16*, 3.
23. Endre, S.; David, M. *An Introduction to Numerical Analysis*; Cambridge University Press: Cambridge, UK, 2003; ISBN 0-521-00794-1.
24. Ryoo, C.S. Some identities involving the generalized polynomials of derangements arising from differential equation. *J. Appl. Math. Inform.* **2020**, *38*, 159–173.

Σ mathematics

MDPI

Article

Degenerate Multi-Term Equations with Gerasimov–Caputo Derivatives in the Sectorial Case

Vladimir E. Fedorov * and Kseniya V. Boyko

Department of Mathematical Analysis, Mathematics Faculty, Chelyabinsk State University, Kashirin Brothers St. 129, 454001 Chelyabinsk, Russia
* Correspondence: kar@csu.ru

Abstract: The unique solvability for the Cauchy problem in a class of degenerate multi-term linear equations with Gerasimov–Caputo derivatives in a Banach space is investigated. To this aim, we use the condition of sectoriality for the pair of operators at the oldest derivatives from the equation and the general conditions of the other operators' coordination with invariant subspaces, which exist due to the sectoriality. An abstract result is applied to the research of unique solvability issues for the systems of the dynamics and of the thermoconvection for some viscoelastic media.

Keywords: Gerasimov–Caputo derivative; fractional differential equation; analytic resolving family of operators; degenerate evolution equation; multi-term fractional equation; initial value problem; initial boundary value problem

MSC: 34G10; 34K37; 35R11

Citation: Fedorov, V.E.; Boyko, K.V. Degenerate Multi-Term Equations with Gerasimov–Caputo Derivatives in the Sectorial Case. *Mathematics* **2022**, *10*, 4699. https://doi.org/10.3390/math10244699

Academic Editor: Vasily E. Tarasov

Received: 23 November 2022
Accepted: 8 December 2022
Published: 11 December 2022

Publisher's Note: MDPI stays neutral with regard to jurisdictional claims in published maps and institutional affiliations.

Copyright: © 2022 by the authors. Licensee MDPI, Basel, Switzerland. This article is an open access article distributed under the terms and conditions of the Creative Commons Attribution (CC BY) license (https://creativecommons.org/licenses/by/4.0/).

1. Introduction

Fractional integro-differential calculus provides effective tools for the study of applied mathematical problems in various fields of science, such as physics, mathematical biology, theory of financial markets and many others. A large number of mathematical models of various real processes have appeared in the scientific literature, described in terms of equations with fractional derivatives and integrals [1–9]. At the same time, such equations are also of theoretical interest for the theory of differential equations and, therefore, have been the objects of research in a multitude of papers over the past few decades (see monographs [10–15] and the bibliographies therein).

In the theory of differential equations, a separate class consists of degenerate evolution equations, the special properties of which are entailed by the presence of a degenerate operator at the highest-order derivative. Various classes of degenerate evolution equations of an integer order have been studied by many authors [16–22]. Degenerate evolution equations with Gerasimov–Caputo, Riemann–Liouville and Dzhrbashyan–Nersesyan fractional derivatives were studied in [23–29].

In the present work, we study the unique solvability of a special initial value problem in the degenerate multi-term linear equation

$$D^{\alpha}Lx(t) = \sum_{l=1}^{n} D^{\alpha_l} M_l x(t) + g(t), \quad (1)$$

with the Gerasimov–Caputo derivatives D^{β}, $\beta \geq 0$, the Riemann–Liouville integrals D^{β}, $\beta < 0$ and the linear operators $L, M_1, M_2, \dots, M_n$, which act from a Banach space $\mathcal{X}$ into a Banach space $\mathcal{Y}$, $\ker L \neq \{0\}$. Here, $\alpha_1 < \alpha_2 < \cdots < \alpha_n < \alpha$, where some of α_l may be negative, $m-1 < \alpha \leq m$, $m_n - 1 < \alpha_n \leq m_n$, $T > 0$ and $g : [0, T] \to \mathcal{Z}$. The unique solvability of the Cauchy problem in such an equation with bounded operators $M_1, M_2, \dots, M_n$ in the nondegenerate case ($\mathcal{X} = \mathcal{Y}$, $L = I$) was proven in [30]. In [31], the Cauchy problem was researched for nondegenerate Equation (1) under the more general condition $(M_1, M_2, \dots, M_n) \in \mathcal{A}^n_{\alpha,G}$ on linear, closed, densely defined operators $M_1, M_2, \dots, M_n$.

In the study of degenerate equations of the form $D^\alpha Lx(t) = Mx(t)$ and $\ker L \neq \{0\}$, the conditions for the pair of operators (L, M) are often used, entailing the existence of the so-called pairs of invariant subspaces. We are talking about the representation of two Banach spaces in the form of the direct sums of the subspaces $\mathcal{X} = \mathcal{X}^0 \oplus \mathcal{X}^1$ and $\mathcal{Y} = \mathcal{Y}^0 \oplus \mathcal{Y}^1$, for which $L, M : \mathcal{X}^r \to \mathcal{Y}^r$ and there exist operators M_0^{-1} and L_1^{-1}, where $L_r = L|_{D_L \cap \mathcal{X}^r}$, $M_r = M|_{D_M \cap \mathcal{X}^r}$ and $r = 0, 1$. The direct sums correspond to the projectors P along $\mathcal{X}^0$ on $\mathcal{X}^1$ and Q along $\mathcal{Y}^0$ on $\mathcal{Y}^1$. Such an approach was used in [21] with the condition of an (L, p)-bounded operator and $p \in \mathbb{N}_0 := \mathbb{N} \cup \{0\}$ and in [25] with the condition $(L, M) \in \mathcal{H}_\alpha(\theta_0, a_0)$ for some $\theta_0 \in (\pi/2, \pi)$, $a_0 \geq 0$. This makes it possible to reduce the degenerate equation to a system of two simpler equations on two subspaces. A generalization of this approach to the case of three or more operators $L, M_1, M_2, \dots, M_n$ for degenerate equations is not evident, since in this case, we need to work with a pencil of operators $\mu^\alpha L - \mu^{\alpha_1} N_1 - \mu^{\alpha_2} N_2 - \dots$, and the standard technique does not look applicable due to the presence of several fractional powers of the parameter μ. However, the same conditions can be used for a pair of operators (L, M_n) if the action of the remaining operators $M_1, M_2, \dots, M_{n-1}$ is coordinated with the subspaces $\mathcal{X}^0$, $\mathcal{X}^1$, $\mathcal{Y}^0$ and $\mathcal{Y}^1$. The simplest variant of such a coordination is the equality $M_l P = Q M_l$, implying that $M_l : \mathcal{X}^r \to \mathcal{Y}^r$, $r = 0, 1$ and $l = 1, 2, \dots, n-1$. This is how multi-term degenerate Equation (1) with bounded operators $L, M_1, M_2, \dots, M_n$ was investigated in [30], namely by reducing to the system of two simpler equations on two subspaces under the condition of $(L, 0)$-boundedness of the operator M_n. In this paper, when studying Equation (1) with unbounded operators L, M_n, a condition $(L, M_n) \in \mathcal{H}_\alpha(\theta_0, a_0)$ [25] is used that allows us to obtain pairs of invariant subspaces. At the same time, the coordination of the other operators $M_1, M_2, \dots, M_{n-1}$ has a general form $M_l P = Q M_l + (I - Q) N_l P$ with some bounded operators N_l, where $l = 1, 2, \dots, n-1$.

In the second section, the preliminaries are given, including theorems on unique solvability of the Cauchy problem for two classes of nondegenerate ($\mathcal{X} = \mathcal{Y}$, $L = I$) multi-term equations (Equation (1)) with the Gerasimov–Caputo derivatives, where one of them has bounded operators $M_1, M_2, \dots, M_n$ [30], and for the other one, the condition $(M_1, M_2, \dots, M_n) \in \mathcal{A}^n_{\alpha,G}(\theta_0, a_0)$ is satisfied, which implies the existence of analytic resolving families of the operators [31]. In the third section, the theorem on the existence of a unique solution to the problem

$$D^k x(0) = x_k, \quad k = 0, 1, \dots, m_n - 1, \quad D^k P x(0) = x_k, \quad k = m_n, m_n + 1, \dots, m - 1,$$

for the degenerate multi-term Equation (1) is proven under conditions $(L, M_n) \in \mathcal{H}_\alpha(\theta_0, a_0)$ and $M_l P = Q M_l + (I - Q) N_l P$ with some bounded operators N_l, where $l = 1, 2, \dots, n-1$. To this aim, Equation (1) is reduced to a system of two nondegenerate multi-term equations on the subspaces of two classes, which are described in the second section. Abstract results are applied to the study of unique solvability issues for the initial boundary value problems of some systems of the dynamics of viscoelastic fluids in the framework of the abstract, non-degenerate multi-term equation and for the system of the thermoconvection for the Kelvin–Voigt fluid as a degenerate, multi-term equation in a Banach space.

2. Preliminaries

We define the Riemann–Liouville fractional integral of the order $\beta > 0$ [12,14] as follows:

$$J^\beta h(t) := \frac{1}{\Gamma(\beta)} \int_0^t (t - s)^{\beta - 1} h(s) ds, \ t > 0.$$

Let $m-1<\alpha\leq m\in\mathbb{N}$, D^m be the derivative of the order $m\in\mathbb{N}$ and D^α be the fractional Gerasimov–Caputo derivative of the order α [14,32]:

$$D^\alpha h(t):=D^m J^{m-\alpha}\left(h(t)-\sum_{k=0}^{m-1}D^k h(0)\frac{t^k}{k!}\right).$$

For $\beta<0$, by defintion, we will mean $D^\beta h(t):=J^{-\beta}h(t)$. Hereafter, with $D^\beta h(0)$ for $\beta\in\mathbb{R}$, we denote the limit $\lim\limits_{t\to 0+}D^\beta h(t)$.

Let $\mathcal{X}$ and $\mathcal{Y}$ be Banach spaces, denoting with $\mathcal{L}(\mathcal{X};\mathcal{Y})$ the Banach space of all linear bounded operators acting from $\mathcal{X}$ into $\mathcal{Y}$ and with $\mathcal{C}l(\mathcal{X};\mathcal{Y})$ the set of all linear closed operators acting on $\mathcal{Y}$ with a dense domain in $\mathcal{X}$. We also denote $\mathcal{L}(\mathcal{X};\mathcal{X}):=\mathcal{L}(\mathcal{X})$ and $\mathcal{C}l(\mathcal{X};\mathcal{X}):=\mathcal{C}l(\mathcal{X})$, for $A\in\mathcal{C}l(\mathcal{X})$ $R_\mu(A):=(\mu I-A)^{-1}$ and for $L,M\in\mathcal{C}l(\mathcal{X};\mathcal{Y})$ $R^L_\mu(M):=(\mu L-M)^{-1}L$, while $L^L_\mu(M):=L(\mu L-M)^{-1}$, $\rho^L(M)$ is the set of $\mu\in\mathbb{C}$ such that $\mu L-M:D_L\cap D_M\to\mathcal{Y}$ is injective mapping and $R^L_\mu(M)\in\mathcal{L}(\mathcal{X})$, $L^L_\mu(M)\in\mathcal{L}(\mathcal{Y})$. We will assume that $\ker L\neq\{0\}$.

2.1. Theorem on Pairs of Invariant Subspaces

Definition 1. [32]. *An operator $A\in\mathcal{C}l(\mathcal{X})$ belongs to the class $\mathcal{A}_\alpha(\theta_0,a_0)$ if*

(1) there exist $\theta_0\in(\pi/2,\pi)$ and $a_0\geq 0$ such that for all $\lambda\in S_{\theta_0,a_0}:=\{\mu\in\mathbb{C}:|\arg(\mu-a_0)|<\theta_0,\ \mu\neq a_0\}$, we have $\lambda^\alpha\in\rho(A):=\{\mu\in\mathbb{C}:(\mu I-A)^{-1}\in\mathcal{L}(\mathcal{X})\}$ and

(2) for every $\theta\in(\pi/2,\theta_0)$, $a>a_0$, there exists a constant $K=K(\theta,a)>0$ such that, for all $\lambda\in S_{\theta,a}$, we have

$$\|R_{\lambda^\alpha}(A)\|_{\mathcal{L}(\mathcal{X})}\leq\frac{K(\theta,a)}{|\lambda^{\alpha-1}(\lambda-a)|}.$$

Definition 2. [25]. *Let $L,M\in\mathcal{C}l(\mathcal{X};\mathcal{Y})$. A pair (L,M) belongs to the class $\mathcal{H}_\alpha(\theta_0,a_0)$ if*

(1) there exist $\theta_0\in(\pi/2,\pi)$ and $a_0\geq 0$ such that, for all $\lambda\in S_{\theta_0,a_0}$, we have $\lambda^\alpha\in\rho^L(M)$, and

(2) for every $\theta\in(\pi/2,\theta_0)$, $a>a_0$, there exists a constant $K=K(\theta,a)>0$ such that, for all $\lambda\in S_{\theta,a}$, we have

$$\max\{\|R^L_{\lambda^\alpha}(M)\|_{\mathcal{L}(\mathcal{X})},\|L^L_{\lambda^\alpha}(M)\|_{\mathcal{L}(\mathcal{Y})}\}\leq\frac{K(\theta,a)}{|\lambda^{\alpha-1}(\lambda-a)|}.$$

Remark 1. *In the case of the inverse operator $L^{-1}\in\mathcal{L}(\mathcal{X})$ existing, we have $(L,M)\in\mathcal{H}_\alpha(\theta_0,a_0)$ if and only if $L^{-1}M\in\mathcal{A}_\alpha(\theta_0,a_0)$ and $ML^{-1}\in\mathcal{A}_\alpha(\theta_0,a_0)$.*

From the pseudo-resolvent identity, which is valid for $R^L_\mu(M)$ and for $L^L_\mu(M)$ separately, it follows that the subspaces $\ker R^L_\mu(M)=\ker L$, $\operatorname{im}R^L_\mu(M)$ and $\ker L^L_\mu(M)$, $\operatorname{im}L^L_\mu(M)$ do not depend on $\mu\in\rho^L(M)$. We introduce the denotations $\ker R^L_\mu(M):=\mathcal{X}^0$ and $\ker L^L_\mu(M):=\mathcal{Y}^0$. With $\mathcal{X}^1$ ($\mathcal{Y}^1$), we denote the closure of the image $\operatorname{im}R^L_\mu(M)$ ($\operatorname{im}L^L_\mu(M)$) in the norm of the space $\mathcal{X}$ ($\mathcal{Y}$). With L_r (M_r), the restriction of the operator L (M) on $D_{L_r}:=D_L\cap\mathcal{X}^r$ ($D_{M_r}:=D_M\cap\mathcal{X}^r$) will be denoted, where $r=0,1$.

Theorem 1. [25]. *Let the Banach spaces $\mathcal{X}$ and $\mathcal{Y}$ be reflexive, where $(L,M)\in\mathcal{H}_\alpha(\theta_0,a_0)$. Then, the following are true:*

(1) $\mathcal{X}=\mathcal{X}^0\oplus\mathcal{X}^1$ *and* $\mathcal{Y}=\mathcal{Y}^0\oplus\mathcal{Y}^1$.
(2) *The projection P (Q) on the subspace $\mathcal{X}^1$ ($\mathcal{Y}^1$) along $\mathcal{X}^0$ ($\mathcal{Y}^0$) has the form $P:=s\text{-}\lim\limits_{n\to\infty}nR^L_n(M)$ ($Q:=s\text{-}\lim\limits_{n\to\infty}nL^L_n(M)$).*
(3) $L_0=0$, $M_0\in\mathcal{C}l(\mathcal{X}^0;\mathcal{Y}^0)$ *and* $L_1,M_1\in\mathcal{C}l(\mathcal{X}^1;\mathcal{Y}^1)$.
(4) *There exist inverse operators $L_1^{-1}\in\mathcal{C}l(\mathcal{Y}^1;\mathcal{X}^1)$ and $M_0^{-1}\in\mathcal{L}(\mathcal{Y}^0;\mathcal{X}^0)$.*
(5) $\forall x\in D_L$ $Px\in D_L$ *and* $LPx=QLx$.

(6) $\forall x \in D_M$ $Px \in D_M$ *and* $MPx = QMx$.
(7) *Let* $S := L_1^{-1}M_1 : D_S \to \mathcal{X}^1$. *Then,* $D_S := \{x \in D_{M_1} : M_1x \in \mathrm{im}L_1\}$ *is dense in* $\mathcal{X}$.
(8) *Let* $T := M_1L_1^{-1} : D_T \to \mathcal{Y}^1$. *Then,* $D_T := \{y \in \mathrm{im}L_1 : L_1^{-1}y \in D_{M_1}\}$ *is dense in* $\mathcal{Y}$.
(9) *If* $L_1 \in \mathcal{L}(\mathcal{X}^1;\mathcal{Y}^1)$ *or* $M_1 \in \mathcal{L}(\mathcal{X}^1;\mathcal{Y}^1)$, *then* $S \in \mathcal{C}l(\mathcal{X}^1)$, *and moreover,* $S \in \mathcal{A}_\alpha(\theta_0, a_0)$.
(10) *If* $L_1^{-1} \in \mathcal{L}(\mathcal{Y}^1;\mathcal{X}^1)$ *or* $M_1^{-1} \in \mathcal{L}(\mathcal{Y}^1;\mathcal{X}^1)$, *then* $T \in \mathcal{C}l(\mathcal{Y}^1)$, *and aside from that,* $T \in \mathcal{A}_\alpha(\theta_0, a_0)$.

2.2. Nondegenerate Multi-Term Equation

Let $m-1 < \alpha \leq m \in \mathbb{N}$, $\alpha_1 < \alpha_2 < \cdots < \alpha_n < \alpha$, $m_l - 1 < \alpha_l \leq m_l \in \mathbb{N}$, $l = 1,2,\ldots,n$. Some of α_l may be negative. Consider the Cauchy problem

$$D^k z(0) = z_k, \quad k = 0,1,\ldots,m-1, \tag{2}$$

for a linear multi-term fractional differential equation

$$D^\alpha z(t) = \sum_{l=1}^{n} D^{\alpha_l} A_l z(t) + f(t), \quad t \in (0,T], \tag{3}$$

where the operators $A_l \in \mathcal{C}l(\mathcal{X})$ have domains D_{A_l}, $l = 1,2,\ldots,n$ and $f \in C([0,T];\mathcal{X})$. A solution to problem (2), (3) is a function $z \in C^{m-1}([0,T];\mathcal{X})$, for which $D^\alpha z, D^{\alpha_l}A_l z_l \in C((0,T];\mathcal{X})$, $l = 1,2,\ldots,n$, and conditions (2) and equality (3) for all $t \in (0,T]$ hold.

We denote $D := \bigcap_{l=1}^n D_{A_l}$, $R_\lambda := \left(\lambda^\alpha I - \sum\limits_{l=1}^{n} \lambda^{\alpha_l} A_l\right)^{-1} : \mathcal{X} \to D$ and endow the set D with the norm $\|\cdot\|_D = \|\cdot\|_\mathcal{X} + \sum\limits_{l=1}^{n} \|A_l \cdot\|_\mathcal{X}$, with respect to which D is a Banach space, since it is the intersection of the Banach spaces $D_{A_1}, D_{A_2}, \ldots, D_{A_n}$ with the corresponding graph norms.

We also denote $n_k := \min\{l \in \{1,2,\ldots,n\} : k \leq m_l - 1\}$ for $k = 0,1,\ldots,m-1$. If the set $\{l \in \{1,2,\ldots,n\} : k \leq m_l - 1\}$ is empty for some $k \in \{0,1,\ldots,m-1\}$ (it is valid if and only if $\alpha_n \leq k$), then we apply $n_k := n+1$:

Definition 3. *A tuple of operators* $(A_1, A_2, \ldots, A_n)$ *belongs to the class* $\mathcal{A}^n_{\alpha,G}(\theta_0, a_0)$ *at some* $\theta_0 \in (\pi/2, \pi)$, $a_0 \geq 0$ *if the following are true:*
(1) D *is dense in* $\mathcal{X}$.
(2) *For all* $\lambda \in S_{\theta_0,a_0}$, $k = 0,1,\ldots,m-1$, *there exist operators* $R_\lambda \cdot \left(I - \sum\limits_{l=n_k}^{n} \lambda^{\alpha_l - \alpha} A_l\right) \in \mathcal{L}(\mathcal{X})$.
(3) *For any* $\theta \in (\pi/2, \theta_0)$, $a > a_0$, *there exists such a* $K(\theta, a) > 0$ *that for all* $\lambda \in S_{\theta,a}$, $k = 0,1,\ldots,m-1$,

$$\|R_\lambda\|_{\mathcal{L}(\mathcal{X})} \leq \frac{K(\theta,a)}{|\lambda - a||\lambda|^{\alpha-1}}, \quad \left\|R_\lambda\left(I - \sum_{l=n_k}^{n} \lambda^{\alpha_l - \alpha} A_l\right)\right\|_{\mathcal{L}(\mathcal{X})} \leq \frac{K(\theta,a)}{|\lambda - a||\lambda|^{\alpha-1}}.$$

Remark 2. *If* $n_k = n+1$, *then by the definition,* $\sum\limits_{l=n_k}^{n} \lambda^{\alpha_l - \alpha} A_l := 0$.

Remark 3. *In [31], the same class* $\mathcal{A}^n_{\alpha,G}(\theta_0, a_0)$ *of tuples of operators is denoted by* $\mathcal{A}^{n,r}_{\alpha,G}(\theta_0, a_0)$, *since in that case,* r *operators at a negative* α_l *value were grouped separately.*

Remark 4. *It is easy to show that in the case* $\alpha_l = 0$ *for some* $l \in \{0,1,\ldots,n\}$ *the condition* $(0,\ldots,0,A_l,0,\ldots,0) \in \mathcal{A}^n_{\alpha,G}(\theta_0, a_0)$ *is satisfied if and only if* $A_l \in \mathcal{A}_\alpha(\theta_0, a_0)$.

We denote at $t > 0$ that

$$Z_k(t) = \frac{1}{2\pi i}\int_\Gamma R_\lambda\left(\lambda^{\alpha-k-1}I - \sum_{l=n_k}^{n}\lambda^{\alpha_l-k-1}A_l\right)e^{\lambda t}d\lambda,\ k = 1,2,\ldots,m-1,$$

$$Z(t) := \frac{1}{2\pi i}\int_\Gamma R_\lambda e^{\lambda t}d\lambda,$$

where $\Gamma := \Gamma^+ \cup \Gamma^- \cup \Gamma^0, \Gamma^0 := \{\lambda \in \mathbb{C} : |\lambda - a| = r_0 > 0, \arg\lambda \in (-\theta,\theta)\}, \Gamma^\pm := \{\lambda \in \mathbb{C} : \arg(\lambda - a) = \pm\theta, |\lambda - a| \in [r_0,\infty)\}, \theta \in (\pi/2,\theta_0), a > a_0$ and $r_0 > 0$.

In [31], it is shown that there exist resolving families of operators $\{Z_k \in \mathcal{L}(\mathcal{X}) : t \geq 0\}$, $k = 0,1,\ldots,m-1$ of the homogeneous Equation (3) ($f \equiv 0$) if and only if $(A_1, A_2,\ldots,A_n) \in \mathcal{A}^n_{\alpha,G}(\theta_0,a_0)$. Therein, the following unique solvability theorem was proved for the Cauchy problem in the inhomogeneous equation:

Theorem 2. [31]. *Let $m-1 < \alpha \leq m \in \mathbb{N}$, $\alpha_1 < \alpha_2 < \cdots < \alpha_n < \alpha$, $m_l - 1 < \alpha_l \leq m_l \in \mathbb{N}$, $l = 1,2,\ldots,n$, $(A_1, A_2,\ldots,A_n) \in \mathcal{A}^n_{\alpha,G}(\theta_0,a_0)$, $z_k \in D$, $k = 0,1,\ldots,m-1$ and $f \in C([0,T];D)$. Then, there exists a unique solution to problem (2), (3), and it has the form*

$$z(t) = \sum_{k=0}^{m-1} Z_k(t)z_k + \int_0^t Z(t-s)f(s)ds. \quad (4)$$

In the case of bounded operators $A_1, A_2,\ldots,A_n$, an analogous result was obtained in [30]:

Theorem 3. [30]. *Let $m-1 < \alpha \leq m \in \mathbb{N}$, $\alpha_1 < \alpha_2 < \cdots < \alpha_n < \alpha$, $m_l - 1 < \alpha_l \leq m_l \in \mathbb{N}$, $l = 1,2,\ldots,n$, $A_1, A_2,\ldots,A_n \in \mathcal{L}(\mathcal{X})$, $z_k \in \mathcal{X}$, $k = 0,1,\ldots,m-1$ and $f \in C([0,T];\mathcal{X})$. Then, there exists a unique solution to problem (2), (3), and it has form (4).*

3. An Initial Value Problem for a Degenerate Equation

Suppose that $n \in \mathbb{N}$, $M_1, M_2,\ldots,M_{n-1} \in \mathcal{L}(\mathcal{X};\mathcal{Y})$ and $M_n, L \in \mathcal{C}l(\mathcal{X};\mathcal{Y})$ and that D_{M_n} and D_L are domains of the operators M_n, L, respectively, with the respective graph norms $\ker L \neq \{0\}$.

Let Banach spaces $\mathcal{X}$ and $\mathcal{Y}$ be reflexive, $(L, M_n) \in \mathcal{H}_\alpha(\theta_0,a_0)$, $\alpha_1 < \alpha_2 < \ldots < \alpha_n < \alpha$, $m-1 < \alpha \leq m$, $m_l - 1 < \alpha_l \leq m_l$, $l = 1,2,\ldots,n$ and $g \in C([0,T];\mathcal{Y})$. Some of α_l may be negative. Consider the initial value problem

$$D^k x(0) = x_k,\ k = 0,1,\ldots,m_n-1, \quad D^k Px(0) = x_k,\ k = m_n, m_n+1,\ldots,m-1, \quad (5)$$

for a multi-term fractional linear inhomogeneous equation

$$D^\alpha Lx(t) = \sum_{l=1}^{n} D^{\alpha_l}M_l x(t) + g(t), \quad (6)$$

which is called degenerate in the case where $\ker L \neq \{0\}$. The projector P is defined in Theorem 1.

A solution to problem (5), (6) is a function $x : [0,T] \to D_L \cap D_{M_n}$ such that $x \in C^{m_n-1}([0,T];\mathcal{X})$, $Px \in C^{m-1}([0,T];\mathcal{X})$, $D^\alpha Lx, D^{\alpha_l}M_l x \in C((0,T];\mathcal{Y})$, $l = 1,2,\ldots,n$, equality (6) for all $t \in (0,T]$ and conditions (5) are valid.

Lemma 1. *Let $(L, M_n) \in \mathcal{H}_\alpha(\theta_0, a_0)$ for some $\theta_0 \in (\pi/2, \pi)$, where $a_0 \geq 0$ and $\alpha > \alpha_n \geq 0$. Then, for every $\theta \in (\pi/2, \theta_0)$, $a > \max\{1, a_0^{\alpha/(\alpha-\alpha_n)}\}$, there exists $K_1(\theta, a) > 0$ such that*

$$\max\{\|(\mu^\alpha L - \mu^{\alpha_n} M_n)^{-1} L\|_{\mathcal{L}(\mathcal{X})}, \|L(\mu^\alpha L - \mu^{\alpha_n} M_n)^{-1}\|_{\mathcal{L}(\mathcal{Y})}\} \leq \frac{K_1(\theta, a)}{|\mu - a||\mu|^{\alpha-1}}.$$

Proof. Take $\theta \in (\pi/2, \theta_0)$, $a > \max\{1, a_0^{\alpha/(\alpha-\alpha_n)}\}$, $\mu \in S_{\theta,a}$ and $\lambda = \mu^{1-\alpha_n/\alpha}$ in the sense of the principal branch of the power function. Then, $\lambda \in S_{\theta_0,a_0}$, since $1 - \alpha_n/\alpha \in (0, 1)$. Hence, we have

$$\|(\mu^\alpha L - \mu^{\alpha_n} M_n)^{-1} L\|_{\mathcal{L}(\mathcal{X})} = |\mu|^{-\alpha_n} \|R^L_{\mu^{\alpha-\alpha_n}}(M_n)\|_{\mathcal{L}(\mathcal{X})} = |\mu|^{-\alpha_n} \|R^L_{\lambda^\alpha}(M_n)\|_{\mathcal{L}(\mathcal{X})} \leq$$

$$\leq \frac{K(\theta, a)}{|\lambda - a||\lambda|^{\alpha-1}|\mu|^{\alpha_n}} = \frac{K(\theta, a)}{|\mu^{1-\alpha_n/\alpha} - a||\mu|^{(1-\alpha_n/\alpha)(\alpha-1)}|\mu|^{\alpha_n}} \leq \frac{K_1(\theta, a)}{|\mu - a||\mu|^{\alpha-1}}.$$

Analogously, we can obtain a similar inequality for $\|L(\mu^\alpha L - \mu^{\alpha_n} M_n)^{-1}\|_{\mathcal{L}(\mathcal{Y})}$. □

For a negative α_n, we can obtain a similar result:

Lemma 2. *Let $(L, M_n) \in \mathcal{H}_\alpha(\theta_0, a_0)$ for some $\theta_0 \in (\pi/2, \pi)$, where $a_0 \geq 0$ and $\alpha > 0 > \alpha_n > \alpha(1 - 2\theta_0/\pi)$. Then, for every $\theta \in (\pi/2, \alpha\theta_0/(\alpha - \alpha_n))$, where $a > \max\{1, a_0\}$, there exists $K_1(\theta, a) > 0$ such that*

$$\max\{\|(\mu^\alpha L - \mu^{\alpha_n} M_n)^{-1} L\|_{\mathcal{L}(\mathcal{X})}, \|L(\mu^\alpha L - \mu^{\alpha_n} M_n)^{-1}\|_{\mathcal{L}(\mathcal{Y})}\} \leq \frac{K_1(\theta, a)}{|\mu - a||\mu|^{\alpha-1}}.$$

Proof. Since $1 - \alpha_n/\alpha > 1$, for $\theta \in (\pi/2, \alpha\theta_0/(\alpha - \alpha_n))$, $a > \max\{1, a_0\}$ and $\mu \in S_{\theta,a}$, we have $\lambda = \mu^{1-\alpha_n/\alpha} \in S_{\theta_0,a_0}$. The remaining part of the proof is the same as for the previous lemma. □

We denote for brevity that $P_0 := I - P$, $Q_0 := I - Q$, L_r ($M_{l,r}$) is the restriction of L (M_l) on $D_{L_r} := D_L \cap \mathcal{X}^r$ (on $D_{M_{l,r}} := D_{M_l} \cap \mathcal{X}^r$ for $l = 1, 2, \ldots, n$), where $r = 0, 1$. Due to Theorem 1 $LP = QL$ for $x \in D_L$, $M_n P x = Q M_n x$ for $x \in D_{M_n}$, and hence $M_{n,r} \in \mathcal{Cl}(\mathcal{X}^r; \mathcal{Y}^r)$ and $L_r \in \mathcal{L}(\mathcal{X}^r; \mathcal{Y}^r)$, where $r = 0, 1$. That aside, there exist $M_{n,0}^{-1} \in \mathcal{L}(\mathcal{Y}^0; \mathcal{X}^0)$ and $L_1^{-1} \in \mathcal{Cl}(\mathcal{Y}^1; \mathcal{X}^1)$.

Theorem 4. *Let $\mathcal{X}$ and $\mathcal{Y}$ be reflexive Banach spaces, $(L, M_n) \in \mathcal{H}_\alpha(\theta_0, a_0)$, $M_l \in \mathcal{L}(\mathcal{X}; \mathcal{Y})$, $l = 1, \ldots, n-1$, $L_1^{-1} \in \mathcal{L}(\mathcal{Y}^1; \mathcal{X}^1)$, $\alpha_1 < \alpha_2 < \cdots < \alpha_n < \alpha$ and $\alpha_n > \alpha(1 - 2\theta_0/\pi)$. Then, $(M_{1,1}L_1^{-1}, M_{2,1}L_1^{-1}, \ldots, M_{n,1}L_1^{-1}) \in \mathcal{A}^n_{\alpha,G}(\theta_1, a_1)$ for some $\theta_1 \in (\pi/2, \theta_0]$, $a_1 \geq a_0$.*

Proof. Since $L_1^{-1} \in \mathcal{L}(\mathcal{Y}^1; \mathcal{X}^1)$, by Theorem 1 (10), we have $M_{l,1}L_1^{-1} \in \mathcal{L}(\mathcal{Y}^1)$, where $l = 1, 2, \ldots, n-1$. Due to Lemma 1 for $\alpha_n \geq 0$ or Lemma 2 in the case where $\alpha_n \in (\alpha(1 - 2\theta_0/\pi), 0)$ for some $\theta_1 \in (\pi/2, \theta_0]$, $a_1 \geq a_0$ and $\mu \in S_{\theta,a}$, we have

$$\left(\mu^\alpha I - \sum_{l=1}^{n} \mu^{\alpha_l} M_{l,1} L_1^{-1}\right)^{-1} =$$

$$= (\mu^\alpha I - \mu^{\alpha_n} M_{n,1} L_1^{-1})^{-1} \left(I - \sum_{l=1}^{n-1} \mu^{\alpha_l} M_{l,1} L_1^{-1} (\mu^\alpha I - \mu^{\alpha_n} M_{n,1} L_1^{-1})^{-1}\right)^{-1},$$

$$\left\|\sum_{l=1}^{n-1} \mu^{\alpha_l} M_{l,1} L_1^{-1} (\mu^\alpha I - \mu^{\alpha_n} M_{n,1} L_1^{-1})^{-1}\right\|_{\mathcal{L}(\mathcal{Y}^1)} \leq$$

$$\leq \sum_{l=1}^{n-1} |\mu|^{\alpha_l} \|M_{l,1} L_1^{-1}\|_{\mathcal{L}(\mathcal{Y}^1)} \left\|L(\mu^\alpha L - \mu^{\alpha_n} M_n)^{-1}\right\|_{\mathcal{L}(\mathcal{Y})} \leq$$

$$\leq \frac{\sum\limits_{l=1}^{n-1} |\mu|^{\alpha_l-\alpha+1}\|M_{l,1}L_1^{-1}\|_{\mathcal{L}(\mathcal{Y})}K_1(\theta,a)}{|\mu-a|} < q < 1$$

for some $q \in (0,1)$, and hence

$$\left\| \left(\mu^{\alpha} I - \sum_{l=1}^{n} \mu^{\alpha_l} M_{l,1}L_1^{-1}\right)^{-1} \right\|_{\mathcal{L}(\mathcal{Y}^1)} \leq \frac{K_2(\theta,a)}{(1-q)|\mu-a||\mu|^{\alpha-1}}.$$

Finally, we have

$$\left(\mu^{\alpha} I - \sum_{l=1}^{n} \mu^{\alpha_l} M_{l,1}L_1^{-1}\right)^{-1}\left(I - \sum_{l=n_k}^{n} \mu^{\alpha_l-\alpha} M_{l,1}L_1^{-1}\right) =$$

$$= \mu^{-\alpha}\left(I + \left(\mu^{\alpha} I - \sum_{l=1}^{n} \mu^{\alpha_l} M_{l,1}L_1^{-1}\right)^{-1} \sum_{l=1}^{n_k-1} \mu^{\alpha_l} M_{l,1}L_1^{-1}\right),$$

$$\left\|\left(\mu^{\alpha} I - \sum_{l=1}^{n} \mu^{\alpha_l} M_{l,1}L_1^{-1}\right)^{-1}\left(I - \sum_{l=n_k}^{n} \mu^{\alpha_l-\alpha} M_{l,1}L_1^{-1}\right)\right\|_{\mathcal{L}(\mathcal{Y}^1)} \leq$$

$$\leq |\mu|^{-\alpha}\left(1 + \frac{K_2(\theta,a)}{(1-q)|\mu-a||\mu|^{\alpha-1}} \cdot \sum_{l=1}^{n_k-1} |\mu|^{\alpha_l}\|M_{l,1}L_1^{-1}\|_{\mathcal{L}(\mathcal{Y}^1)}\right) \leq \frac{K_3(\theta,a)}{|\mu-a||\mu|^{\alpha-1}}.$$

□

Theorem 5. *Let $\mathcal{X}$ and $\mathcal{Y}$ be reflexive Banach spaces, $(L, M_n) \in \mathcal{H}_{\alpha}(\theta_0, a_0)$, $M_l \in \mathcal{L}(\mathcal{X};\mathcal{Y})$, $M_l P = QM_l + Q_0 N_l P$ for some $N_l \in \mathcal{L}(\mathcal{X}^1;\mathcal{Y})$, $l = 1,2,\ldots,n-1$, $L_1^{-1} \in \mathcal{L}(\mathcal{Y}^1;\mathcal{X}^1)$, $\alpha_1 < \alpha_2 < \cdots < \alpha_n < \alpha$, $\alpha_n > \alpha(1-2\theta_0/\pi)$, $g \in C([0,T];\mathcal{Y})$, $Qg \in C([0,T]; D_{M_{n,1}L_1^{-1}})$, $x_k \in D_{M_{n,1}} \dot{+} \mathcal{X}^0$ for $k = 0,1,\ldots,m_n-1$ and $x_k \in D_{M_{n,1}}$ for $k = m_n, m_n+1,\ldots,m-1$. Then, there exists a unique solution to problem (5), (6).*

Proof. Note that $M_l P_0 = M_l(I-P) = M_l - QM_l - Q_0 N_l P = Q_0(M_l - N_l P)$ for $l = 1,2,\ldots,n-1$. Establish that $P_0 x(t) := w(t)$, $y(t) := Lx(t) = L_1 Px(t) + L_0 w(t) = L_1 Px(t)$, and then $x(t) = Px(t) + w(t) = L_1^{-1}y(t) + w(t)$. Thus, for $l = 1,2,\ldots,n-1$, we have $M_l x = M_l(L_1^{-1}y(t) + w(t)) = (QM_l + Q_0 N_l P)L_1^{-1}y(t) + Q_0(M_l - N_l P)w(t) = (QM_l + Q_0 N_l)L_1^{-1}y(t) + Q_0 M_l w(t)$.

Using the operator $M_{n,0}^{-1}Q_0 \in \mathcal{L}(\mathcal{Y}^0;\mathcal{X}^0)$, problem (5), (6) can be written as the system

$$D^{\alpha}y(t) = \sum_{l=1}^{n} D^{\alpha_l} QM_{l,1}L_1^{-1}y(t) + Qg(t), \tag{7}$$

$$D^{\alpha_n}w(t) = -\sum_{l=1}^{n-1} D^{\alpha_l} M_{n,0}^{-1}Q_0 M_{l,0}w(t) - \sum_{l=1}^{n-1} D^{\alpha_l} M_{n,0}^{-1}Q_0 N_l L_1^{-1}y(t) - M_{n,0}^{-1}Q_0 g(t), \tag{8}$$

with the initial conditions

$$D^k y(0) = L_1 Px_k,\ k = 0,1,\ldots,m-1, \tag{9}$$

$$D^k w(0) = P_0 x_k,\ k = 0,1,\ldots,m_n-1. \tag{10}$$

In the considered case $D := \bigcap\limits_{l=1}^{n} D_{M_{l,1}L_1^{-1}} = D_{M_{n,1}L_1^{-1}}$ with the graph norm of the operator $D_{M_{n,1}L_1^{-1}}$, since $x_k \in D_{M_{n,1}} \dot{+} \mathcal{X}^0$, then $L_1 Px_k \in D_{M_{n,1}L_1^{-1}}$ for $k = 0,1,\ldots,m_n-1$. Hence, through Theorem 2, there exists a unique solution to problem (7), (9). Problem (8), (10) have a unique solution due to Theorem 3, since the operators $M_{n,0}^{-1}Q_0M_{l,0}$, $l = 1, 2, \ldots, n-1$ are bounded and $\sum_{l=1}^{n-1} D^{\alpha_l} M_{n,0}^{-1}Q_0N_lL_1^{-1}y + M_{n,0}^{-1}Q_0g \in C([0,T];\mathcal{X}^0)$ is a known function. □

Remark 5. *The proof of Theorem 5 implies that the Cauchy problem $x^{(l)}(0) = x_l$, $l = 0, \ldots, m-1$ for Equation (6) has a unique solution under the additional conditions $P_0x_l = D^l w(0)$, $l = m_n, m_n+1, \ldots, m-1$ only. Here, w is a unique solution to problem (8), (10).*

4. Some Initial Value Problems for Viscoelastic Media Systems

Consider the initial boundary value problem

$$D_t^k v(s,0) = v_k(s), \quad s \in \Omega, \quad k = 0, 1, \ldots, m-1, \tag{11}$$

$$v(s,t) = 0, \quad (s,t) \in \partial\Omega \times (0,T], \tag{12}$$

$$D_t^\alpha v(s,t) = \chi D_t^\beta \Delta v(s,t) + \nu D_t^\gamma \Delta v(s,t) + \kappa D_t^\delta \Delta v(s,t) - r(s,t) + h(s,t), \ (s,t) \in \Omega \times (0,T], \tag{13}$$

$$\nabla \cdot v(s,t) = 0, \quad (s,t) \in \Omega \times (0,T], \tag{14}$$

in a bounded region $\Omega \subset \mathbb{R}^d$ with a smooth boundary $\partial\Omega$, $\chi, \nu, \kappa \in \mathbb{R}$, $m-1 < \alpha \leq m \in \mathbb{N}$, $\alpha > \beta > \gamma > \delta$, where some of numbers $\alpha, \beta, \gamma, \delta$ may be negative. Here, D_t^ε is a fractional Gerasimov–Caputo derivative of the order $\varepsilon \geq 0$ (or fractional Riemann–Liouville integral of the order $-\varepsilon > 0$ in the case where $\varepsilon < 0$) with respect to t, the velocity $v = (v_1, v_2, \ldots, v_d)$ and the pressure gradient $r = (r_1, r_2, \ldots, r_d) = \nabla p$ are unknown, and $h : \Omega \times [0,T] \to \mathbb{R}^d$ is a given function.

If $\alpha = \beta = 1$, $\gamma = 0$ and $\delta < 0$, then the system of Equations (13) and (14) is the linearization for the generalized Oskolkov system of the viscoelastic fluid dynamics with the kernel $h(s,t) = \kappa(t-s)^{-\delta-1}/\Gamma(-\delta)$ in the integral operator (see system (2.1.1), (2.1.2) in [33]). With $\alpha = 1$, $\beta > 0$, $\gamma = 0$ and $\kappa = 0$, it will be the linearized Kelvin–Voigt fluid system [34,35]. If, moreover, $\nu = 0$, then (13), (14) is the linearized system of the Scott-Blair fluid dynamics.

With $\mathbb{L}_2 := (L_2(\Omega))^n$, $\mathbb{H}^1 := (H^1(\Omega))^n$, $\mathbb{H}^2 := (H^2(\Omega))^n$, the closure of the subspace $\mathcal{L} := \{z \in (C_0^\infty(\Omega))^n : \nabla \cdot z = 0\}$ in the norm of the space $\mathbb{L}_2$ will be denoted by $\mathbb{H}_\sigma$, and in the norm of $\mathbb{H}^1$, it will be denoted by $\mathbb{H}_\sigma^1$. We denote $\mathbb{H}_\sigma^2 := \mathbb{H}_\sigma^1 \cap \mathbb{H}^2$, where $\mathbb{H}_\pi$ is the orthogonal complement for $\mathbb{H}_\sigma$ in $\mathbb{L}_2$ and $\Sigma : \mathbb{L}_2 \to \mathbb{H}_\sigma$, $\Pi = I - \Sigma$ are the corresponding orthoprojectors.

The operator $B := \Sigma\Delta$, extended to a closed operator in $\mathbb{H}_\sigma$ with the domain $\mathbb{H}_\sigma^2$, has a real negative discrete spectrum with finite multiplicities, which is condensed only at $-\infty$ [36].

The system of Equations (13) and (14) is equivalent to the equation

$$D_t^\alpha v(s,t) = \chi D_t^\beta Bv(s,t) + \nu D_t^\gamma Bv(s,t) + \kappa D_t^\delta Bv(s,t) + \Sigma h(s,t), \ (s,t) \in \Omega \times (0,T], \tag{15}$$

since

$$r(s,t) = \chi D_t^\beta \Pi\Delta v(s,t) + \nu D_t^\gamma \Pi\Delta v(s,t) + \kappa D_t^\delta \Pi\Delta v(s,t) + \Pi h(s,t), \quad (s,t) \in \Omega \times (0,T].$$

Therefore, we need to study problem (11), (12), (15). If $\alpha > \beta > \gamma > \delta$, $m-1 < \alpha \leq m \in \{1,2\}$, $\beta > -\alpha$, $\chi > 0$ and $\nu, \kappa \in \mathbb{R}$. Due to incompressibility Equation (14) take $\mathcal{X} = \mathbb{H}_\sigma$, $A_1 = \kappa B$, $A_2 = \nu B$ and $A_3 = \chi B$ are closed, densely defined operators. Then, by Lemma 3 from [31], $(A_1, A_2, A_3) \in \mathcal{A}^3_{\alpha,G}$, and by Theorem 2, for any $v_0, v_1 \in D = \mathbb{H}_\sigma^2$, $\Sigma h \in C([0,T];\mathbb{H}_\sigma^2)$, there exist a unique solution to problem (11), (12), (15). Therefore, problem (11)–(14) also have a unique solution.

If $\beta > \alpha > \gamma > \delta$, $m-1 < \alpha \leq m \in \mathbb{N}$ and $\chi, \nu, \kappa \in \mathbb{R}$, we rewrite Equation (15) into the form

$$D_t^{\beta} v(s,t) = \chi^{-1} D_t^{\alpha} B^{-1} v(s,t) - \chi^{-1} \nu D_t^{\gamma} v(s,t) - \chi^{-1} \kappa D_t^{\delta} v(s,t) - B^{-1} \Sigma h(s,t)$$

for $(s,t) \in \Omega \times (0,T]$. By setting $\mathcal{X} = \mathbb{H}_{\sigma}$, $A_1 = \chi^{-1} D_t^{\alpha} B^{-1}$, $A_2 = -\chi^{-1} \nu I$ and $A_3 = -\chi^{-1} \kappa I$, and by Theorem 3, since A_1, A_2, A_3 are bounded operators, for any $v_0, v_1 \in \mathbb{H}_{\sigma}$, $B^{-1} \Sigma h \in C([0,T]; \mathbb{H}_{\sigma})$, there exist a unique solution to problem (11)–(14).

Now, consider the initial boundary value problem

$$v(s,0) = v_0(s), \quad (m-1) D_t^1 v(s,0) = (m-1) v_1(s), \quad s \in \Omega, \tag{16}$$

$$\tau(s,0) = \tau_0(s), \quad (m-1) D_t^1 \tau(s,0) = (m-1) \tau_1(s), \quad s \in \Omega, \tag{17}$$

$$v(s,t) = 0, \quad \tau(s,t) = 0, \quad (s,t) \in \partial\Omega \times (0,T], \tag{18}$$

for the linearized system of the thermoconvection in the same medium

$$D_t^{\alpha} v(s,t) = \chi D_t^{\alpha} \Delta v(s,t) + \nu \Delta v(s,t) + \kappa D_t^{\delta} \Delta v(s,t) - r(s,t) + h(s,t), \quad (s,t) \in \Omega \times (0,T], \tag{19}$$

$$\nabla \cdot v(s,t) = 0, \quad (s,t) \in \Omega \times (0,T], \tag{20}$$

$$D_t^{\alpha} \tau(s,t) = \varrho \Delta \tau(s,t) + \varsigma v_n(s,t) + f(s,t), \quad (s,t) \in \Omega \times (0,T]. \tag{21}$$

where $m-1 < \alpha \leq m \in \{1,2\}$, $\delta < 0$, $\chi, \nu, \kappa, \varrho, \varsigma \in \mathbb{R}$ and $\triangle$ is the Laplace operator with the domain $H_0^2(\Omega) := \{w \in H^2(\Omega) : w(x) = 0, \, x \in \partial\Omega\}$, which is dense in $L_2(\Omega)$.

Remark 6. *If $\chi = 0$, then system of Equations (19)–(21) is the linear approximation of the thermoconvection in viscous media and not in viscoelastic media. In part, for $\chi = 0$, $\alpha = 1$ and $\kappa = 0$, we have the linearization of the Boussinesq system, which models the thermoconvection in viscous media. Operator methods close to the methods of this work are used for studying an initial boundary value problem and some control problems of the linearized Boussinesq system in [37].*

Set

$$\mathcal{X} = \mathbb{H}_{\sigma}^2 \times \mathbb{H}_{\pi} \times L_2(\Omega), \quad \mathcal{Y} = \mathbb{L}_2 \times L_2(\Omega) = \mathbb{H}_{\sigma} \times \mathbb{H}_{\pi} \times L_2(\Omega), \tag{22}$$

$$L = \begin{pmatrix} I - \chi B & \mathbb{O} & \mathbb{O} \\ -\chi \Pi \Delta & \mathbb{O} & \mathbb{O} \\ \mathbb{O} & \mathbb{O} & I \end{pmatrix}, \quad M_1 = \begin{pmatrix} \kappa B & \mathbb{O} & \mathbb{O} \\ \kappa \Pi \Delta & \mathbb{O} & \mathbb{O} \\ \mathbb{O} & \mathbb{O} & \mathbb{O} \end{pmatrix}, \quad M_2 = \begin{pmatrix} \nu B & \mathbb{O} & \mathbb{O} \\ \nu \Pi \Delta & -I & \mathbb{O} \\ \varsigma P_n & \mathbb{O} & \varrho \Delta \end{pmatrix}, \tag{23}$$

$$g(t) = \begin{pmatrix} \Sigma h(\cdot,t) \\ \Pi h(\cdot,t) \\ f(\cdot,t) \end{pmatrix}, \quad t \in [0,T].$$

Here, P_n is the projector $(v_1, v_2, \ldots, v_n) \to v_n$. Then, $L, M_1 \in \mathcal{L}(\mathcal{X}; \mathcal{Y})$, $M_2 \in \mathcal{C}l(\mathcal{X}; \mathcal{Y})$ and $D_{M_2} = \mathbb{H}_{\sigma}^2 \times \mathbb{H}_{\pi} \times H_0^2(\Omega)$. We have $x(t) \in \mathcal{X}$, where $x(t) = (v(\cdot,t), r(\cdot,t), \tau(\cdot,t))$.

Lemma 3. *Let $\alpha \in (0,2)$, $\chi, \nu, \varsigma \in \mathbb{R}$, $\chi \neq 0$, $\chi^{-1} \notin \sigma(B)$, $\varrho > 0$, spaces $\mathcal{X}$ and $\mathcal{Y}$ have form (22), and operators L and M_2 be defined by (23). Then, $(L, M_2) \in \mathcal{H}_{\alpha}(\theta_0, a_0)$ for some $a_0 \geq 0$, $\theta_0 \in (\pi/2, \pi)$, and in this case, we have*

$$P = \begin{pmatrix} I & \mathbb{O} & \mathbb{O} \\ \nu \Pi \Delta (I - \chi B)^{-1} & \mathbb{O} & \mathbb{O} \\ \mathbb{O} & \mathbb{O} & I \end{pmatrix}, \quad Q = \begin{pmatrix} I & \mathbb{O} & \mathbb{O} \\ -\chi \Pi \Delta (I - \chi B)^{-1} & \mathbb{O} & \mathbb{O} \\ \mathbb{O} & \mathbb{O} & I \end{pmatrix},$$

where $\mathcal{X}^0 = \{0\} \times \mathbb{H}_{\pi} \times \{0\}$, $\mathcal{X}^1 = \{(z, \nu \Pi \Delta (I - \chi B)^{-1} z, w) : z \in \mathbb{H}_{\sigma}^2, \, w \in L_2(\Omega)\}$, $\mathcal{Y}^0 = \{0\} \times \mathbb{H}_{\pi} \times \{0\}$ and $\mathcal{Y}^1 = \{(z, -\chi \Pi \Delta (I - \chi B)^{-1} z, w) : z \in \mathbb{H}_{\sigma}, \, w \in L_2(\Omega)\}$.

Proof. The Banach spaces $\mathcal{X}$ and $\mathcal{Y}$ are reflexive since they are Hilbert spaces. The operators $(I-\chi B)^{-1}:\mathbb{H}_\sigma\to\mathbb{H}^2_\sigma$, $(I-\chi B)^{-1}B=B(I-\chi B)^{-1}:\mathbb{H}_\sigma\to\mathbb{H}_\sigma$ and $(I-\chi B)^{-1}B=B(I-\chi B)^{-1}:\mathbb{H}^2_\sigma\to\mathbb{H}^2_\sigma$ are bounded. Therefore, we can choose $\theta_1\in(\pi/2,\pi)$, $a_0>0$ such that the disc $\{\mu\in\mathbb{C}:|\mu|\le 2^{-1/\alpha}|\nu|^{1/\alpha}\max\{\|(I-\chi B)^{-1}B\|^{1/\alpha}_{\mathbb{H}_\sigma},\|(I-\chi B)^{-1}B\|^{1/\alpha}_{\mathbb{H}^2_\sigma}\}\}$ is situated outside the sector S_{θ_1,a_0}. Then, for $\mu\in S_{\theta_1,a_0}$, using the Neumann series, we obtain

$$\|(\mu^\alpha I-\nu(I-\chi B)^{-1}B)^{-1}\|_{\mathbb{H}_\sigma}\le\frac{1}{|\mu|^\alpha-|\nu|\|(I-\chi B)^{-1}B\|_{\mathbb{H}_\sigma}}\le\frac{2}{|\mu|^\alpha}. \tag{24}$$

$$\|(\mu^\alpha I-\nu(I-\chi B)^{-1}B)^{-1}\|_{\mathbb{H}^2_\sigma}\le\frac{1}{|\mu|^\alpha-|\nu|\|(I-\chi B)^{-1}B\|_{\mathbb{H}^2_\sigma}}\le\frac{2}{|\mu|^\alpha}. \tag{25}$$

Now, we take $\alpha\in[1,2)$, $\delta\in(0,\pi(1/\alpha-1/2))$ and $\theta_0=\min\{\theta_1,\pi/2+\delta\}$. Then, $(\mu^\alpha I-\varrho\triangle)^{-1}\in\mathcal{L}(\mathbb{H}_\sigma)$ for all $\mu\in S_{\theta_0,a_0}$, since $|\arg\mu^\alpha|\in(\pi/2,\pi)$ and the spectrum of the operator $\varrho\triangle$ is real and negative. Moreover, for $w\in L_2(\Omega)$, we have

$$\|(\mu^\alpha I-\varrho\triangle)^{-1}w\|^2_{L_2(\Omega)}=\sum_{k=0}^{\infty}\frac{|\langle w,\varphi_k\rangle|^2}{|\mu^\alpha-\varrho\lambda_k|^2}\le\frac{\|w\|^2_{L_2(\Omega)}}{\sin^2\theta_0|\mu|^{2\alpha}}, \tag{26}$$

where $\langle\cdot,\cdot\rangle$ is the inner product in $L_2(\Omega)$, $\{\lambda_k\}$ is the eigenvalues of $\triangle$ and $\{\varphi_k\}$ is the orthonormal system of the corresponding eigenfunctions.

Thus, for $\mu\in S_{\theta_0,a_0}$, we have

$$\mu^\alpha L-M_2=\begin{pmatrix}\mu^\alpha(I-\chi B)-\nu B & \mathbb{O} & \mathbb{O}\\ -\mu^\alpha\chi\Pi\Delta-\nu\Pi\Delta & I & \mathbb{O}\\ -\varsigma P_n & \mathbb{O} & \mu^\alpha I-\varrho\triangle\end{pmatrix},$$

$$(\mu^\alpha L-M)^{-1}=$$

$$=\begin{pmatrix}(\mu^\alpha I-\nu(I-\chi B)^{-1}B)^{-1}(I-\chi B)^{-1} & \mathbb{O} & \mathbb{O}\\ (\mu^\alpha\chi\Pi\Delta+\nu\Pi\Delta)(\mu^\alpha I-\nu(I-\chi B)^{-1}B)^{-1}(I-\chi B)^{-1} & I & \mathbb{O}\\ \varsigma(\mu^\alpha I-\varrho\triangle)^{-1}P_n(\mu^\alpha I-\nu(I-\chi B)^{-1}B)^{-1}(I-\chi B)^{-1} & \mathbb{O} & (\mu^\alpha I-\varrho\triangle)^{-1}\end{pmatrix},$$

$$R^L_{\mu^\alpha}(M)=\begin{pmatrix}(\mu^\alpha I-\nu(I-\chi B)^{-1}B)^{-1} & \mathbb{O} & \mathbb{O}\\ (\mu^\alpha\chi\Pi\Delta+\nu\Pi\Delta)(\mu^\alpha I-\nu(I-\chi B)^{-1}B)^{-1}-\chi\Pi\Delta & \mathbb{O} & \mathbb{O}\\ \varsigma(\mu^\alpha I-\varrho\triangle)^{-1}P_n(\mu^\alpha I-\nu(I-\chi B)^{-1}B)^{-1} & \mathbb{O} & (\mu^\alpha I-\varrho\triangle)^{-1}\end{pmatrix}=$$

$$=\begin{pmatrix}(\mu^\alpha I-\nu(I-\chi B)^{-1}B)^{-1} & \mathbb{O} & \mathbb{O}\\ \nu\Pi\Delta(I-\chi B)^{-1}(\mu^\alpha I-\nu(I-\chi B)^{-1}B)^{-1} & \mathbb{O} & \mathbb{O}\\ \varsigma(\mu^\alpha I-\varrho\triangle)^{-1}P_n(\mu^\alpha I-\nu(I-\chi B)^{-1}B)^{-1} & \mathbb{O} & (\mu^\alpha I-\varrho\triangle)^{-1}\end{pmatrix},$$

$$L^L_{\mu^\alpha}(M)=\begin{pmatrix}(\mu^\alpha I-\nu B(I-\chi B)^{-1})^{-1} & \mathbb{O} & \mathbb{O}\\ -\chi\Pi\Delta(I-\chi B)^{-1}(\mu^\alpha I-\nu B(I-\chi B)^{-1})^{-1} & \mathbb{O} & \mathbb{O}\\ \varsigma(\mu^\alpha I-\varrho\triangle)^{-1}P_n(I-\chi B)^{-1}(\mu^\alpha I-\nu B(I-\chi B)^{-1})^{-1} & \mathbb{O} & (\mu^\alpha I-\varrho\triangle)^{-1}\end{pmatrix}.$$

Thus, $R^L_{\mu^\alpha}(M)\in\mathcal{L}(\mathcal{X})$ and $L^L_{\mu^\alpha}(M)\in\mathcal{L}(\mathcal{Y})$. Using inequalities (24)–(26), we obtain that $(L,M)\in\mathcal{H}_\alpha(a_0,\theta_0)$.

For $\alpha\in(0,1)$, the proof is similar..

The projectors P and Q and subspaces $\mathcal{X}^0=\ker P$, $\mathcal{X}^1=\mathrm{im}P$, $\mathcal{Y}^0=\ker Q$ and $\mathcal{Y}^1=\mathrm{im}Q$ can be calculated using Theorem 1 (2): □

Remark 7. *It is evident that in this case, $L_1^{-1}\in\mathcal{L}(\mathcal{Y}^1;\mathcal{X}^1)$.*

Theorem 6. *Let $\alpha\in(0,2)$, $\delta<0$, $\chi,\nu,\kappa,\varsigma\in\mathbb{R}$, $\chi\ne0$, $\chi^{-1}\notin\sigma(B)$, $\varrho>0$, $v_0\in\mathbb{H}_\sigma$ and $\tau_0\in H^2(\Omega)$ for $\alpha\in(0,1]$, and $v_0,v_1\in\mathbb{H}_\sigma$, $\tau_0,\tau_1\in H^2(\Omega)$ for $\alpha\in(1,2)$; $h\in C([0,T];\mathbb{L}_2)$, $\Sigma h\in C([0,T];\mathbb{H}^2_\sigma)$ and $f\in C([0,T];H^2(\Omega))$. Then, there exist a unique solution to problem (16)–(21).*

Proof. We reduce problem (16)–(21) to problem (5), (6) with $n = 2$, using operators (23) in spaces (22). Note that in this case, $\alpha_1 = \delta < 0$, $\alpha_2 = 0$ and $m_2 = 0$. Hence, conditions (5) have the form $Px(0) = x_0$ for $\alpha \in (0,1]$, $Px(0) = x_0$ and $D^1Px(0) = x_1$ for $\alpha \in (1,2)$, which are equivalent to conditions (16) and (17) due to the form of the projector P (see Lemma 3). Here, $m = 1$ for $\alpha \in (0,1]$ and $m = 2$ for $\alpha \in (1,2)$. Therefore, for $m = 1$, the second condition in (16) and in (17) is absent.

According to Remark 7, $L_1^{-1} \in \mathcal{L}(\mathcal{Y}^1;\mathcal{X}^1)$, and moreover, $D_{M_{n,1}L_1^{-1}} = L[D_{M_n}] = \mathbb{H}_\sigma \times \mathbb{H}_\pi \times H_0^2(\Omega)$. Hence, $(v_0, \nu\Pi\Delta(I-\chi B)^{-1}v_0, \tau_0), (v_1, \nu\Pi\Delta(I-\chi B)^{-1}v_1, \tau_1) \in D_{M_{n,1}L_1^{-1}}$ under the conditions of the present theorem. We also have $Qg(t) = (\Sigma h(\cdot,t), -\chi\Pi\Delta(I-\chi B)^{-1}\Sigma h(\cdot,t), f(\cdot,t)) \in C([0,T]; D_{M_{n,1}L_1^{-1}})$. Finally, we have

$$M_1P - QM_1 = \begin{pmatrix} \mathbb{O} & \mathbb{O} & \mathbb{O} \\ \kappa\Pi\Delta(I-\chi B)^{-1} & \mathbb{O} & \mathbb{O} \\ \mathbb{O} & \mathbb{O} & \mathbb{O} \end{pmatrix} := N_1 \in \mathcal{L}(\mathcal{X};\mathcal{Y}).$$

It is obvious that $N_1 = Q_0 N_1 P$. Under Theorem 5, we obtain the required statement. □

5. Conclusions

An initial value problem for a class of degenerate multi-term linear equations in Banach spaces with Gerasimov–Caputo derivatives was studied by the methods of pairs of invariant subspaces. Under the conditions of the operators at the two oldest derivatives, by implying the existence of pairs of invariant subspaces and analytic resolving families of operators for the linear homogeneous equation with these two operators, we reduced the degenerate equation to a system of two nondegenerate equations in the subspaces. This allowed us to prove the existence of a unique solution. The obtained abstract unique solvability theorem was used for the research of the initial boundary value problems for the systems of the dynamics and of the thermoconvection of the Kelvin–Voigt-type media.

As for the development of the results obtained and their significance, we note that the results for the solvability of initial problem (5), (6) will further allow us to consider other problems for Equation (6) (boundary value problems on a segment, nonlocal problems, etc.). Aside from that, the proof of the solvability theorem (Theorem 5), coupled with solution formula (4) for the nondegenerate equation, gives the form of a solution to the degenerate equation, which can become a starting point for finding new methods for the numerical solutions of initial boundary value problem (16)–(21).

Author Contributions: Conceptualization, V.E.F.; methodology, V.E.F.; software, K.V.B.; validation, K.V.B.; formal analysis, K.V.B.; investigation, V.E.F.; resources, K.V.B.; data curation, K.V.B.; writing—original draft preparation, K.V.B.; writing—review and editing, V.E.F.; visualization, K.V.B.; supervision, V.E.F.; project administration, V.E.F.; funding acquisition, V.E.F. All authors have read and agreed to the published version of the manuscript.

Funding: The reported study was funded by the Russian Science Foundation, project number 22-21-20095.

Institutional Review Board Statement: Not applicable.

Informed Consent Statement: Not applicable.

Data Availability Statement: Not applicable.

Conflicts of Interest: The authors declare no conflict of interest.

References

1. Oldham, K.B.; Spanier, J. *The Fractional Calculus*; Academic Press: Boston, MA, USA, 1974.
2. Samko, S.G.; Kilbas, A.A.; Marichev, O.I. *Fractional Integrals and Derivatives. Theory and Applications*; Gordon and Breach Science Publishers: Philadelphia, PA, USA, 1993.
3. Hilfer, R. *Applications of Fractional Calculus in Physics*; WSPC: Singapore, 2000.
4. Nakhushev, A.M. *Fractional Calculus ant Its Applications*; Fizmatlit: Moscow, Russia, 2003. (In Russian)

5. Tarasov, V.E. *Fractional Dynamics: Applications of Fractional Calculus to Dynamics of Particles, Fields and Media*; Springer: New York, NY, USA, 2011.
6. Uchaikin, V.V. *Fractional Derivatives for Physicists and Engineers, Volume I Background and Theory, Volume II Applications*; Springer: Berlin/Heidelberg, Germany, 2013.
7. Sibatov, R.T.; Uchaikin, V.V. Fractional kinetics of charge carriers in supercapacitors. In *Handbook of Fractional Calculus with Applications*; Tenreiro Machado, J.A., Ed.; De Gruyter: Berlin, Germany; Boston, MA, USA, 2019.
8. Thach, T.N.; Tuan, N.H. Stochastic pseudo-parabolic equations with fractional derivative and fractional Brownian motion. *Stoch. Anal. Appl.* **2021**, *40*, 1906274. [CrossRef]
9. Tuan, N.H.; Phuong, N.D.; Thach, T.N. New well-posedness results for stochastic delay Rayleigh—Stokes equations. *Discret. Contin. Dyn. Syst. Ser. B* **2022**, *28*, 347–358. [CrossRef]
10. Nishimoto, K. *Fractional Calculus and Its Applications*; Nihon University: Koriyama, Japan, 1990.
11. Miller, K.S.; Ross, B. *An Introduction to the Fractional Calculus and Fractional Differential Equations*; John Wiley & Sons: Hoboken, NJ, USA, 1993.
12. Podlubny, I. *Fractional Differential Equations*; Academic Press: Boston, MA, USA, 1999.
13. Pskhu, A.V. *Partial Differential Equations of Fractional Order*; Nauka: Moscow, Russia, 2005. (In Russian)
14. Kilbas, A.A.; Srivastava H.M.; Trujillo, J.J. *Theory and Applications of Fractional Differential Equations*; Elsevier: Amsterdam, The Netherlands, 2006.
15. Diethelm, K. *The Analysis of Fractional Differential Equations. An Application-Oriented Exposition Using Differential Operators of Caputo Type*; Springer: Berlin/Heidelberg, Germany, 2010.
16. Caroll, R.W.; Showalter, R.E. *Singular and Degenerate Cauchy Problems*; Academic Press: New York, NY, USA; San Francisco, CA, USA, 1976.
17. Favini, A.; Yagi, A. *Degenerate Differential Equations in Banach Spaces*; Marcel Dekker Inc.: New York, NY, USA, 1999.
18. Pyatkov, S.G. *Operator Theory: Nonclassical Problems*; VSP: Utrecht, The Netherlands, 2002.
19. Sidorov, N.; Loginov, B.; Sinitsyn, A.; Falaleev, M. *Lyapunov—Schmidt Method in Nonlinear Analysis and Applications*; Kluwer Academic Publishers: Dordrecht, Germany, 2002.
20. Demidenko, G.V.; Uspenskii, S.V. *Partial Differential Equations and Systems Not Solvable with Respect to the Highest-Order Derivative*; CRC Press: Boca Raton, FL, USA, 2003.
21. Sviridyuk, G.A.; Fedorov, V.E. *Linear Sobolev Type Equations and Degenerate Semigroups of Operators*; VSP: Utrecht, The Netherlands, 2003.
22. Kostić, M. *Abstract Volterra Integro-Differential Equations*; CRC Press: Boca Raton, FL, USA, 2015.
23. Plekhanova, M.V. Strong solutions of quasilinear equations in Banach spaces not solvable with respect to the highest-order derivative. *Discret. Contin. Dyn. Syst. Ser.* **2016**, *9*, 833–847. [CrossRef]
24. Plekhanova, M.V. Distributed control problems for a class of degenerate semilinear evolution equations. *J. Comput. Appl. Math.* **2017**, *312*, 39–46. [CrossRef]
25. Fedorov, V.E.; Romanova, E.A.; Debbouche, A. Analytic in a sector resolving families of operators for degenerate evolution fractional equations. *J. Math. Sci.* **2018**, *228*, 380–394. [CrossRef]
26. Fedorov, V.E.; Avilovich, A.S. A Cauchy type problem for a degenerate equation with the Riemann—Liouville derivative in the sectorial case. *Sib. Math. J.* **2019**, *60*, 359–372. [CrossRef]
27. Debbouche, A.; Fedorov, V.E. A class of fractional degenerate evolution equations with delay. *Mathematics* **2020**, *8*, 1700. [CrossRef]
28. Fedorov, V.E.; Plekhanova, M.V.; Izhberdeeva, E.M. Initial value problems of linear equations with the Dzhrbashyan—Nersesyan derivative in Banach spaces. *Symmetry* **2021**, *13*, 1058. [CrossRef]
29. Fedorov, V.E.; Turov, M.M. The defect of a Cauchy type problem for linear equations with several Riemann—Liouville derivatives. *Sib. Math. J.* **2021**, *62*, 925–942. [CrossRef]
30. Fedorov, V.E.; Boyko, K.V.; Phuong, T.D. Initial value problems for some classes of linear evolution equations with several fractional derivatives. *Math. Notes Nefu* **2021**, *28*, 85–104.
31. Boyko, K.V.; Fedorov, V.E. The Cauchy problem for a class of multi-term equations with Gerasimov—Caputo derivatives. *Lobachevskii J. Math.* **2022**, *43*, 1293–1302. [CrossRef]
32. Bajlekova, E.G. Fractional Evolution Equations in Banach Spaces. Ph.D. Thesis, Eindhoven University of Technology, Eindhoven, The Netherlands, 2001.
33. Zvyagin V.G., Turbin M.V. The study of initial-boundary value problems for mathematical models of the motion of Kelvin — Voigt fluids. *J. Math. Sci.* **2010**, *168*, 157–308. [CrossRef]
34. Oskolkov, A.P. Initial-boundary value problems for equations of motion of Kelvin—Voight fluids and Oldroyd fluids. *Proc. Steklov Inst. Math.* **1989**, *179*, 137–182.
35. Mainardi, F.; Spada, G. Creep, relaxation and viscosity properties for basic fractional models in rheology. *Eur. Phys. J. Spec. Top.* **2011**, *193*, 133–160. [CrossRef]
36. Ladyzhenskaya, O.A. *The Mathematical Theory of Viscous Incompressible Flow*; Gordon and Breach Science Publishers: New York, NY, USA, 1963.
37. Plekhanova, M.V.; Islamova, A.F. Problems with a robust mixed control for the linearized Boussinesq equation. *Differ. Equ.* **2012**, *48*, 574–585. [CrossRef]

mathematics MDPI

Article

Initial Problem for Two-Dimensional Hyperbolic Equation with a Nonlocal Term

Vladimir Vasilyev [1,*] and Natalya Zaitseva [2]

1 Center of Applied Mathematics, Belgorod State National Research University, Pobedy Street 85, Belgorod 308015, Russia
2 Faculty of Computational Mathematics and Cybernetics, Lomonosov Moscow State University, Moscow 119991, Russia
* Correspondence: vladimir.b.vasilyev@gmail.com; Tel.: +7-4722301300; Fax: +7-4722301012

Abstract: In this paper, we study the Cauchy problem in a strip for a two-dimensional hyperbolic equation containing the sum of a differential operator and a shift operator acting on a spatial variable that varies over the real axis. An operating scheme is used to construct the solutions of the equation. The solution of the problem is obtained in the form of a convolution of the function found using the operating scheme and the function from the initial conditions of the problem. It is proved that classical solutions of the considered initial problem exist if the real part of the symbol of the differential-difference operator in the equation is positive.

Keywords: hyperbolic equation; differential-difference equation; initial problem; Fourier transform; operational scheme

MSC: 5L15; 42A38

Citation: Vasilyev, V.; Zaitseva, N. Initial Problem for Two-Dimensional Hyperbolic Equation with a Nonlocal Term. *Mathematics* **2023**, *11*, 130. https://doi.org/10.3390/math11010130

Academic Editor: Sitnik Sergey

Received: 17 November 2022
Revised: 20 December 2022
Accepted: 22 December 2022
Published: 27 December 2022

Copyright: © 2022 by the authors. Licensee MDPI, Basel, Switzerland. This article is an open access article distributed under the terms and conditions of the Creative Commons Attribution (CC BY) license (https://creativecommons.org/licenses/by/4.0/).

1. Introduction

In recent years, functional-differential equations, or, their special case, differential equations with a deviating argument, have become widespread in applications of mathematics. The systematic study of equations with a deviating argument began in the 1940s in connection with applications to automatic control theory and it was associated with the research by Pinney [1], Bellman and Cooke [2], Hale [3], and other authors.

Interest in problems for differential-difference equations is due to their numerous applications: in the mechanics of a deformable solid body; in relativistic electrodynamics; when studying the processes of vortex formation and the formation of complex coherent spots; when solving some problems related to plasma; in simulation of vibrations of the crystal lattice; in problems of nonlinear optics; in the study of neural networks; when studying models of population dynamics in mathematical biology; in the study of environmental and economic processes; in a wide range of tasks in the theory of automatic control; when solving problems of optimizing the treatment of oncological diseases (see, for example, works [4–6]); etc.

Differential-difference equations form a special class of functional-differential equations for which the theory of boundary value problems is currently developed. Problems for elliptic differential-difference equations in bounded domains have been studied quite comprehensively by now; the theory for such equations was created and developed by Skubachevskii [7,8].

Problems for parabolic and hyperbolic differential-difference equations have been studied to a much lesser extent [9–11].

As far as the authors know, at present, there are few papers dealing with hyperbolic differential-difference equations containing shifts with respect to the spatial variable. In [12–14], the families of classical solutions are constructed for two-dimensional hyperbolic equations with shifts in the only space variable x ranging over the real line; the shifts occur either in the potentials or in the highest derivative. Some similar problems for elliptic equations were studied in [15,16].

In this paper, we study the solvability of the Cauchy problem in a strip for a two-dimensional hyperbolic equation with a nonlocal potential.

Let $D = \{(x,t) : x \in \mathbf{R}, 0 < t < T\}$ be the coordinate plane area Oxt, where $T > 0$ is the given real number, $\overline{D} = \{(x,t) : x \in \mathbf{R}, 0 \leq t \leq T\}$. Let us consider in the domain D the hyperbolic differential-difference equation, which contains the sum of the differential operator and the shift operator with respect of the spatial variable x:

$$Lu \stackrel{\text{def}}{=} \frac{\partial^2 u(x,t)}{\partial t^2} - a^2 \frac{\partial^2 u(x,t)}{\partial x^2} + b\,u(x-h,t) = 0, \tag{1}$$

where $a, b > 0$, $h \neq 0$ are given real numbers.

Suppose that for all $\xi \in \mathbf{R}$ the inequality

$$a^2\xi^2 + b\cos(h\xi) > 0, \tag{2}$$

holds.

Inequality (2) means that the real part of the symbol of the differential-difference operator in Equation (1) is positive.

Consider the function $a^2\xi^2 + b\cos(h\xi)$, $\xi \in [0, +\infty)$. The derivative of this function is

$$2a^2\xi - bh\sin(h\xi) = 2a^2\xi\left(1 - \frac{bh^2}{2a^2}\frac{\sin(h\xi)}{h\xi}\right).$$

Since $\sin(h\xi)/h\xi \longrightarrow 1$ at $\xi \longrightarrow 0$, and $\sin(h\xi)/h\xi \longrightarrow 0$ at $\xi \to +\infty$, then the derivative is non-negative on the interval $\xi \in [0, +\infty)$ if

$$0 < b \leq \frac{2a^2}{h^2}. \tag{3}$$

In this case, the function $a^2\xi^2 + b\cos(h\xi)$ at $\xi \in [0, +\infty)$ is non-decreasing and its smallest value is equal to $b > 0$; hence,

$$a^2\xi^2 + b\cos(h\xi) \geq b > 0, \tag{4}$$

for all $\xi \in [0, +\infty)$.

Since the function $a^2\xi^2 + b\cos(h\xi)$ is even, this value b is the smallest for all real $\xi \in (-\infty, +\infty)$. Thus, the condition (2) is satisfied if the coefficients a, b and the shift h of the equality (1) satisfy the inequalities (3).

Formulation of the problem. Find a function $u(x,t)$ that satisfies the conditions

$$u(x,t) \in C^1(\overline{D}) \cap C^2(D); \tag{5}$$

$$Lu(x,t) \equiv 0, \quad (x,t) \in D; \tag{6}$$

$$u(x,0) = u_0(x), \quad u_t(x,0) = 0, \quad x \in \mathbf{R}, \tag{7}$$

where the initial function satisfies the conditions $u_0(x) \in L_1(\mathbf{R})$, and $u_0(x) \in C^1(\mathbf{R})$.

Definition 1. *A function $u(x,t)$ is called a classical solution of the problem (5)–(7), if*

- *It is continuous and continuously differentiable with respect to the variables x and t in the set $\overline{D}$;*
- *It has continuous derivatives u_{xx} and u_{tt} in the domain D;*
- *It satisfies at each point $(x,t) \in D$ Equation (1);*
- *For each point $x_0 \in (-\infty, +\infty)$, the limits of the functions $u(x_0,t) - u_0(x_0)$ and $u_t(x_0,t)$ at $t \longrightarrow 0+$ exists and are equal to zero.*

This paper studies the initial problem (5)–(7) for two-dimensional hyperbolic equation with a nonlocal term. The solution of the problem is obtained in the form of a convolution of the function found by using the operating scheme and the initial conditions (7).

2. Construction of Solutions of the Equation

The fundamental solution of a linear differential operator L with constant coefficients is a generalized function $\mathcal{E}(x,t)$, that satisfies the equation

$$L\mathcal{E}(x,t) \equiv \frac{\partial^2\mathcal{E}(x,t)}{\partial t^2} - a^2\frac{\partial^2\mathcal{E}(x,t)}{\partial x^2} + b\,\mathcal{E}(x-h,t) = \delta(x,t), \tag{8}$$

where $\delta(x,t)$ is the Dirac δ-function.

We formally apply the Fourier transform with respect to the variable x to Equation (1), and passes to the dual variable ξ. For the function $\widehat{\mathcal{E}}(\xi,t) := F_x[\mathcal{E}](\xi,t)$, we obtain the equation

$$\frac{\partial^2\widehat{\mathcal{E}}(x,t)}{\partial t^2} + \left(a^2\xi^2 + b\,e^{ih\xi}\right)\widehat{\mathcal{E}}(x,t) = 1(\xi)\delta(t). \tag{9}$$

The solution of Equation (9) has the form

$$\widehat{\mathcal{E}}(\xi,t) = \theta(t)Z(t), \tag{10}$$

where $\theta(t)$ is the Heaviside step function and the function $Z(t)$ satisfies the equation

$$Z''(t) + \left(a^2\xi^2 + b\,e^{ih\xi}\right)Z(t) = 0, \tag{11}$$

with the initial conditions

$$Z(0) = 0, \quad Z'(0) = 1. \tag{12}$$

The characteristic equation for Equation (11) has the roots

$$k_{1,2} = \pm\sqrt{-(a^2\xi^2 + b\,e^{ih\xi})} = \pm i\sqrt{a^2\xi^2 + b\,e^{ih\xi}} = \pm i\rho(\xi)e^{i\,\varphi(\xi)},$$

where the functions $\rho(\xi)$ and $\varphi(\xi)$ are denoted by

$$\rho(\xi) := \left[\left(a^2\xi^2 + b\cos(h\xi)\right)^2 + b^2\sin^2(h\xi)\right]^{1/4}, \tag{13}$$

$$\varphi(\xi) := \frac{1}{2}\mathrm{arctg}\frac{b\sin(h\xi)}{a^2\xi^2 + b\cos(h\xi)}. \tag{14}$$

Note that, whenever the condition (2) is satisfied, Functions (13) and (14) are defined correctly.

The general solution of Equation (11) is determined by the formula

$$Z(t) = C_1(\xi)\cos(\rho(\xi)[\cos\varphi(\xi) + i\sin\varphi(\xi)]t) + C_2(\xi)\sin(\rho(\xi)[\cos\varphi(\xi) + i\sin\varphi(\xi)]t),$$

where $C_1(\xi)$ and $C_2(\xi)$ are arbitrary constants depending on the parameter ξ. To find these constants, substitute we substitute the last expression to the conditions (12):

$$C_1(\xi) = 0, \quad C_2(\xi) = \frac{1}{\rho(\xi)[\cos\varphi(\xi) + i\sin\varphi(\xi)]}.$$

As a result, the solution to the problem (11), (12) has the form

$$Z(t) = \frac{\sin(\rho(\xi)[\cos\varphi(\xi) + i\sin\varphi(\xi)]t)}{\rho(\xi)[\cos\varphi(\xi) + i\sin\varphi(\xi)]}.$$

Taking into account Equation (10), the solution of Equation (9) is determined by the formula

$$\widehat{\mathcal{E}}(\xi,t)=\theta(t)\frac{\sin\left(\rho(\xi)[\cos\varphi(\xi)+i\sin\varphi(\xi)]t\right)}{\rho(\xi)[\cos\varphi(\xi)+i\sin\varphi(\xi)]}.$$

Applying the inverse Fourier transform F_{ξ}^{-1} to the last expression, we obtain

$$\begin{aligned}\mathcal{E}(x,t)&=\theta(t)F_{\xi}^{-1}\left[\frac{\sin\left(\rho(\xi)[\cos\varphi(\xi)+i\sin\varphi(\xi)]t\right)}{\rho(\xi)[\cos\varphi(\xi)+i\sin\varphi(\xi)]}\right]\\&=\frac{1}{2\pi}\int_{-\infty}^{+\infty}\frac{\sin\left(\rho(\xi)[\cos\varphi(\xi)+i\sin\varphi(\xi)]t\right)}{\rho(\xi)[\cos\varphi(\xi)+i\sin\varphi(\xi)]}e^{-ix\xi}d\xi\\&=\frac{1}{2\pi}\int_{-\infty}^{+\infty}\frac{\sin\left(\rho(\xi)[\cos\varphi(\xi)+i\sin\varphi(\xi)]t\right)}{\rho(\xi)}e^{-i(\varphi(\xi)+x\xi)}d\xi.\end{aligned}$$

Transform this expression using the equalities $\rho(-\xi)=\rho(\xi)$ and $\varphi(-\xi)=\varphi(\xi)$:

$$\begin{aligned}\mathcal{E}(x,t)&=\frac{1}{2\pi}\int_{-\infty}^{0}\frac{\sin\left(\rho(\xi)[\cos\varphi(\xi)+i\sin\varphi(\xi)]t\right)}{\rho(\xi)}e^{-i(\varphi(\xi)+x\xi)}d\xi\\&\quad+\frac{1}{2\pi}\int_{0}^{+\infty}\frac{\sin\left(\rho(\xi)[\cos\varphi(\xi)+i\sin\varphi(\xi)]t\right)}{\rho(\xi)}e^{-i(\varphi(\xi)+x\xi)}d\xi\\&=\frac{1}{2\pi}\int_{0}^{+\infty}\frac{\sin\left(\rho(\xi)[\cos\varphi(\xi)-i\sin\varphi(\xi)]t\right)}{\rho(\xi)}e^{i(\varphi(\xi)+x\xi)}d\xi\\&\quad+\frac{1}{2\pi}\int_{0}^{+\infty}\frac{\sin\left(\rho(\xi)[\cos\varphi(\xi)+i\sin\varphi(\xi)]t\right)}{\rho(\xi)}e^{-i(\varphi(\xi)+x\xi)}d\xi\\&=\frac{1}{\pi}\int_{0}^{+\infty}\frac{1}{\rho(\xi)}[\sin\left(t\rho(\xi)\cos\varphi(\xi)\right)\cos\left(\varphi(\xi)+x\xi\right)\cos\left(it\rho(\xi)\sin\varphi(\xi)\right)\\&\qquad-i\cos\left(t\rho(\xi)\cos\varphi(\xi)\right)\sin\left(\varphi(\xi)+x\xi\right)\sin\left(it\rho(\xi)\sin\varphi(\xi)\right)]d\xi.\end{aligned}$$

Define the functions

$$G_1(\xi):=\rho(\xi)\sin\varphi(\xi),\quad G_2(\xi):=\rho(\xi)\cos\varphi(\xi).\tag{15}$$

Since $\cos(ix)=\mathrm{ch}x$ and $-i\sin(ix)=\mathrm{sh}x$, we can write $\mathcal{E}(x,t)$ in the form

$$\begin{aligned}\mathcal{E}(x,t)&=\frac{1}{\pi}\int_{0}^{+\infty}\frac{1}{\rho(\xi)}[\sin\left(tG_2(\xi)\right)\cos\left(\varphi(\xi)+x\xi\right)\mathrm{ch}(tG_1(\xi))\\&\qquad+\cos\left(tG_2(\xi)\right)\sin\left(\varphi(\xi)+x\xi\right)\mathrm{sh}(tG_1(\xi))]d\xi\\&=\frac{1}{2\pi}\int_{0}^{+\infty}\frac{1}{\rho(\xi)}\Big[[\sin\left(tG_2(\xi)\right)\cos\left(\varphi(\xi)+x\xi\right)+\cos\left(tG_2(\xi)\right)\sin\left(\varphi(\xi)+x\xi\right)]e^{tG_1(\xi)}\\&\qquad+[\sin\left(tG_2(\xi)\right)\cos\left(\varphi(\xi)+x\xi\right)-\cos\left(tG_2(\xi)\right)\sin\left(\varphi(\xi)+x\xi\right)]e^{-tG_1(\xi)}\Big]d\xi\\&=\frac{1}{2\pi}\int_{0}^{+\infty}\frac{1}{\rho(\xi)}\Big[\sin\left(tG_2(\xi)+\varphi(\xi)+x\xi\right)e^{tG_1(\xi)}+\sin\left(tG_2(\xi)-\varphi(\xi)-x\xi\right)e^{-tG_1(\xi)}\Big]d\xi.\end{aligned}$$

We will use the resulting integral to construct a solution to the system (5)–(7).

We introduce a weight function $A(\xi)$ (according to [15]), that is continuous, non-negative for each $\xi \in [0, +\infty)$, and satisfies the conditions:

(1) For any arbitrarily small number $\alpha > 0$:

$$\lim_{\xi \to +\infty} A(\xi) e^{t\,G_1(\xi)} \xi^{1+\alpha} = 0, \quad \lim_{\xi \to +\infty} A(\xi) e^{-t\,G_1(\xi)} \xi^{1+\alpha} = 0; \tag{16}$$

(2) Improper integrals

$$\int_0^{+\infty} \frac{A(\xi)\,\xi}{e^{-t\,G_1(\xi)}} d\xi, \quad \int_0^{+\infty} \frac{A(\xi)\,\xi}{e^{t\,G_1(\xi)}} d\xi, \quad \int_0^{+\infty} \frac{A(\xi)\,\xi^2}{e^{-t\,G_1(\xi)}} d\xi, \quad \int_0^{+\infty} \frac{A(\xi)\,\xi^2}{e^{t\,G_1(\xi)}} d\xi, \tag{17}$$

converge for each $t \in (0, T]$;

(3) Improper integrals

$$\int_0^{+\infty} \frac{A(\xi)}{e^{-t\,G_1(\xi)}} d\xi, \quad \int_0^{+\infty} \frac{A(\xi)}{e^{t\,G_1(\xi)}} d\xi \tag{18}$$

converge for each $t \in [0, T]$.

As an example of such weight function $A(\xi)$, which is continuous and non-negative for any value of $\xi \in [0, +\infty)$, and satisfies conditions (16)–(18), one can take any function $\xi^\beta e^{-TC\xi}$ where $\beta \geq 0$ and $C > a > 0$ are any real constants.

Indeed, Function (13) is represented in the following form:

$$\rho(\xi) = \left[\left(a^2\xi^2 + b\cos(h\xi) \right)^2 + b^2 \sin^2(h\xi) \right]^{1/4} =$$

$$= \left[a^4\xi^4 + 2a^2 b\xi^2 \cos(h\xi) + b^2 \right]^{1/4} = a|\xi| \left[1 + \frac{2b\cos(h\xi)}{a^2\xi^2} + \frac{b^2}{a^4\xi^4} \right]^{1/4},$$

that is, for $\xi \longrightarrow +\infty$, the function $\rho(\xi)$ is equivalent to the function $a\xi(1+\varepsilon)$, where $\varepsilon > 0$ is any arbitrarily small number.

From Formula (14), it follows that $|\varphi(\xi)| < \pi/4$, which means that $|\sin\varphi(\xi)| < \sqrt{2}/2$. Thus, for Function (15) for $\xi \longrightarrow +\infty$ we have the estimate

$$|G_1(\xi)| = |\rho(\xi)\sin\varphi(\xi)| < \frac{\sqrt{2}}{2} a(1+\varepsilon)\xi.$$

Since the inequalities

$$-a\xi < -\frac{\sqrt{2}}{2} a(1+\varepsilon)\xi < G_1(\xi) < \frac{\sqrt{2}}{2} a(1+\varepsilon)\xi < a\xi,$$

hold for any arbitrarily small number $\varepsilon > 0$ and $\xi \to +\infty$, we obtain the conditions

$$TC\xi - tG_1(\xi) > (TC - ta)\xi > 0, \quad TC\xi + tG_1(\xi) > (TC - ta)\xi > 0. \tag{19}$$

Using the inequalities

$$0 \leq \frac{\xi^\beta}{e^{TC\xi - t\,G_1(\xi)}} \xi^{1+\alpha} < \frac{\xi^{1+\alpha+\beta}}{e^{(TC-ta)\xi}}$$

and Lopital's rule, one can show that

$$\lim_{\xi \to +\infty} \frac{\xi^{1+\alpha+\beta}}{e^{(TC-ta)\xi}} = 0,$$

therefore,

$$\lim_{\xi\to+\infty}\frac{\xi^{1+\alpha+\beta}}{e^{TC\xi-t\,G_1(\xi)}}=0.$$

Thus, for the function $A(\xi)=\xi^{\beta}e^{-TC\xi}$, the first condition from (16) is satisfied.

Similarly, taking into account the second inequality from (19), we can check that the second condition from (16) for the function $A(\xi)=\xi^{\beta}e^{-TC\xi}$ is also satisfied.

To prove the convergence of the integrals (17) and (18), we use the criterion for the convergence of improper integrals: if there is a finite limit $\lim\limits_{x\to+\infty}|f(x)|\cdot x^{p}$ at $p>1$, then the integral $\int\limits_{a}^{+\infty} f(x)dx$ converges. The existence of finite limits

$$\lim_{\xi\to+\infty}\frac{\xi^{1+\alpha+\beta}}{e^{TC\xi-t\,G_1(\xi)}}=0,\quad \lim_{\xi\to+\infty}\frac{\xi^{1+\alpha+\beta}}{e^{TC\xi+t\,G_1(\xi)}}=0$$

implies the convergence of the integrals (18) for the function $A(\xi)=\xi^{\beta}e^{-TC\xi}$ for any fixed values $t\in[0,T]$, $\beta\geq 0$ and $C>a>0$.

Using the inequalities (19) and Lopital's rule, one can check that all four limits

$$\lim_{\xi\to+\infty}\frac{\xi^{1+\beta}}{e^{TC\xi-t\,G_1(\xi)}}\xi^{1+\alpha},\quad \lim_{\xi\to+\infty}\frac{\xi^{1+\beta}}{e^{TC\xi+t\,G_1(\xi)}}\xi^{1+\alpha};$$

$$\lim_{\xi\to+\infty}\frac{\xi^{2+\beta}}{e^{TC\xi-t\,G_1(\xi)}}\xi^{1+\alpha},\quad \lim_{\xi\to+\infty}\frac{\xi^{2+\beta}}{e^{TC\xi+t\,G_1(\xi)}}\xi^{1+\alpha}$$

are equal to zero for any arbitrarily small number $\alpha>0$. This means that the integrals (17) converge for the function $A(\xi)=\xi^{\beta}e^{-TC\xi}$ ($\beta\geq 0, C>a>0$) and each $t\in[0,T]$.

Let us prove the following assertion.

Lemma 1. *Under condition (2), the function*

$$G(x,t):=\int\limits_{0}^{+\infty}\frac{A(\xi)}{\rho(\xi)}\Big[\sin\left(t\,G_2(\xi)+\varphi(\xi)+x\xi\right)e^{t\,G_1(\xi)}+\sin\left(t\,G_2(\xi)-\varphi(\xi)-x\xi\right)e^{-t\,G_1(\xi)}\Big]d\xi \tag{20}$$

satisfies the equality (1) in the classical sense. Here, $A(\xi)$ is a definite and non-negative for any value $\xi\in[0,+\infty)$ function, which satisfies the conditions (16)–(18); functions $G_1(\xi)$ and $G_2(\xi)$ are determined by Equation (15).

Proof. As noted above, if the condition (2) is satisfied, the functions $\rho(\xi)$ and $\varphi(\xi)$ are defined correctly for all values of the parameters a, b, h, and ξ. Moreover, the function $\rho(\xi)$ is non-zero. That is, the integrand in (20) is continuous at every point $\xi\in[0,+\infty)$ as a composition of continuous functions.

Let us first investigate the convergence of the integral:

$$\int\limits_{0}^{+\infty}F(x,t;\xi)d\xi:=\int\limits_{0}^{+\infty}\frac{A(\xi)\,\sin\left(t\,G_2(\xi)+\varphi(\xi)+x\xi\right)}{\rho(\xi)e^{-t\,G_1(\xi)}}d\xi. \tag{21}$$

It follows from Formulas (4) and (13) that for the function $\rho(\xi)$ satisfies the estimate

$$\rho(\xi)=\left[\left(a^2\xi^2+b\cos\left(h\xi\right)\right)^2+b^2\sin^2\left(h\xi\right)\right]^{1/4}\geq\left[b^2+b^2\sin^2\left(h\xi\right)\right]^{1/4}\geq\sqrt{b} \tag{22}$$

Consider the expression

$$\left|\frac{A(\xi)\sin\left(t\,G_2(\xi)+\varphi(\xi)+x\xi\right)}{\rho(\xi)e^{-t\,G_1(\xi)}}\xi^{1+\alpha}\right|,$$

where $\alpha > 0$ is any arbitrarily small number. Taking into account (22), we have

$$0 \le \left|\frac{A(\xi)\sin\left(t\,G_2(\xi)+\varphi(\xi)+x\xi\right)}{\rho(\xi)e^{-t\,G_1(\xi)}}\xi^{1+\alpha}\right| \le \frac{A(\xi)\,|\sin\left(t\,G_2(\xi)+\varphi(\xi)+x\xi\right)|}{\sqrt{b}\,e^{-t\,G_1(\xi)}}\xi^{1+\alpha} \le \frac{1}{\sqrt{b}}\frac{A(\xi)}{e^{-t\,G_1(\xi)}}\xi^{1+\alpha}.$$

Using the first condition from (16) we obtain

$$\lim_{\xi\to+\infty}\left|\frac{A(\xi)\sin\left(t\,G_2(\xi)+\varphi(\xi)+x\xi\right)}{\rho(\xi)e^{-t\,G_1(\xi)}}\xi^{1+\alpha}\right| = 0,$$

that is, the integral $\int\limits_0^{+\infty} F(x,t;\xi)d\xi$ converges.

Similarly, it can be shown that when the second condition in (16) is satisfied, the integral

$$\int\limits_0^{+\infty} H(x,t;\xi)d\xi := \int\limits_0^{+\infty} \frac{A(\xi)\sin\left(t\,G_2(\xi)-\varphi(\xi)-x\xi\right)}{\rho(\xi)e^{t\,G_1(\xi)}}d\xi \tag{23}$$

converges.

Let us now check that Function (21) satisfies Equation (1). To do this, we formally differentiate Function (21) with respect to the variables x and t up to the second order under the integral sign.

$$\int\limits_0^{+\infty} F_x(x,t;\xi)d\xi = \int\limits_0^{+\infty} \frac{A(\xi)\,\xi\,\cos\left(t\,G_2(\xi)+\varphi(\xi)+x\xi\right)}{\rho(\xi)e^{-t\,G_1(\xi)}}d\xi; \tag{24}$$

$$\int\limits_0^{+\infty} F_{xx}(x,t;\xi)d\xi = -\int\limits_0^{+\infty} \frac{A(\xi)\,\xi^2\sin\left(t\,G_2(\xi)+\varphi(\xi)+x\xi\right)}{\rho(\xi)e^{-t\,G_1(\xi)}}d\xi; \tag{25}$$

$$\int\limits_0^{+\infty} F_t(x,t;\xi)d\xi = \int\limits_0^{+\infty} \frac{A(\xi)}{\rho(\xi)e^{-t\,G_1(\xi)}}[G_2(\xi)\cos\left(t\,G_2(\xi)+\varphi(\xi)+x\xi\right) + G_1(\xi)\sin\left(t\,G_2(\xi)+\varphi(\xi)+x\xi\right)]d\xi; \tag{26}$$

$$\int\limits_0^{+\infty} F_{tt}(x,t;\xi)d\xi = \int\limits_0^{+\infty} \frac{A(\xi)}{\rho(\xi)e^{-t\,G_1(\xi)}}\Big[\left(G_1^2(\xi)-G_2^2(\xi)\right)\sin\left(t\,G_2(\xi)+\varphi(\xi)+x\xi\right) +2G_1(\xi)G_2(\xi)\cos\left(t\,G_2(\xi)+\varphi(\xi)+x\xi\right)]d\xi. \tag{27}$$

Taking into account Equation (15), we obtain $2G_1(\xi)G_2(\xi) = \rho^2(\xi)\sin 2\varphi(\xi)$. Since $\varphi(\xi)$ is determined by Equation (14), the inequality $|2\varphi(\xi)| < \pi/2$ is satisfied, and therefore, $\cos 2\varphi(\xi) > 0$. Therefore,

$$\begin{aligned}\sin 2\varphi(\xi) &= \frac{\operatorname{tg} 2\varphi(\xi)}{\sqrt{1+\operatorname{tg}^2 2\varphi(\xi)}}\\ &= \operatorname{tg}\left(\operatorname{arctg}\frac{b\sin(h\xi)}{a^2\xi^2+b\cos(h\xi)}\right)\left[1+\operatorname{tg}^2\left(\operatorname{arctg}\frac{b\sin(h\xi)}{a^2\xi^2+b\cos(h\xi)}\right)\right]^{-1/2}\\ &= \frac{b\sin(h\xi)}{a^2\xi^2+b\cos(h\xi)}\left[1+\frac{b^2\sin^2(h\xi)}{(a^2\xi^2+b\cos(h\xi))^2}\right]^{-1/2}\\ &= \frac{b\sin(h\xi)}{a^2\xi^2+b\cos(h\xi)}\left[\frac{(a^2\xi^2+b\cos(h\xi))^2}{(a^2\xi^2+b\cos(h\xi))^2+b^2\sin^2(h\xi)}\right]^{1/2}\end{aligned}$$

is true.

Taking into account the inequality (2) and Equation (13), we deduce that $\sin 2\varphi(\xi) = b\sin(h\xi)/\rho^2(\xi)$, whence, $2G_1(\xi)G_2(\xi) = b\sin(h\xi)$.

If the inequality $\cos 2\varphi(\xi) > 0$ and the condition (2) are satisfied, we can calculate

$$\begin{aligned}G_1^2(\xi) - G_2^2(\xi) &= \rho^2(\xi)\left[\sin^2\varphi(\xi) - \cos^2\varphi(\xi)\right]\\ &= -\rho^2(\xi)\cos 2\varphi(\xi) = -\frac{\rho^2(\xi)}{\sqrt{1+\operatorname{tg}^2 2\varphi(\xi)}}\\ &= -\rho^2(\xi)\left[\frac{(a^2\xi^2+b\cos(h\xi))^2}{(a^2\xi^2+b\cos(h\xi))^2+b^2\sin^2(h\xi)}\right]^{1/2} = -a^2\xi^2 - b\cos(h\xi).\end{aligned}$$

Using the obtained expressions for $G_1^2(\xi) - G_2^2(\xi)$ and $2G_1(\xi)G_2(\xi)$, from equality (27) we obtain

$$\begin{aligned}\int_0^{+\infty} F_{tt}(x,t;\xi)d\xi = \int_0^{+\infty} \frac{A(\xi)}{\rho(\xi)e^{-tG_1(\xi)}}\Big[-\left(a^2\xi^2+b\cos(h\xi)\right)\sin(t\,G_2(\xi)+\varphi(\xi)+x\xi)\\ +b\sin(h\xi)\cos(t\,G_2(\xi)+\varphi(\xi)+x\xi)\Big]d\xi. \quad (28)\end{aligned}$$

Substitute the obtained expressions of the derivatives $\int_0^{+\infty} F_{tt}(x,t;\xi)d\xi$ and $\int_0^{+\infty} F_{xx}(x,t;\xi)d\xi$ to Equation (1):

$$\begin{aligned}&\int_0^{+\infty} F_{tt}(x,t;\xi)d\xi - a^2\int_0^{+\infty} F_{xx}(x,t;\xi)d\xi\\ &= -b\int_0^{+\infty} A(\xi)\frac{\sin(t\,G_2(\xi)+\varphi(\xi)+x\xi)\cdot\cos(h\xi) - \cos(t\,G_2(\xi)+\varphi(\xi)+x\xi)\cdot\sin(h\xi)}{\rho(\xi)e^{-tG_1(\xi)}}d\xi\\ &= -b\int_0^{+\infty}\frac{A(\xi)\sin(t\,G_2(\xi)+\varphi(\xi)+(x-h)\xi)}{\rho(\xi)e^{-tG_1(\xi)}}d\xi = -b\int_0^{+\infty} F(x-h,t;\xi)d\xi.\end{aligned}$$

Thus, Function (21) satisfies Equation (1) in the classical sense.

Now let us prove the uniform convergence of the integrals (24) and (25) with respect to the variable x on any segment $[x_1, x_2] \subset (-\infty, +\infty)$, and the uniform convergence of the integrals (26) and (28) with respect to the variable t on any segment $[t_1, t_2] \subset (0, T]$. Note that the integrands of all these integrals have no singularities at the point $\xi = 0$.

Let us investigate the integral (24) for the uniform convergence, taking into account the estimate (22) and using the Weierstrass criterion:

$$\int_0^{+\infty} |F_x(x,t;\xi)|d\xi = \int_0^{+\infty} \left| \frac{A(\xi)\,\xi\,\cos\,(t\,G_2(\xi) + \varphi(\xi) + x\xi)}{\rho(\xi)e^{-t\,G_1(\xi)}} \right| d\xi \leq \frac{1}{\sqrt{b}} \int_0^{+\infty} \frac{A(\xi)\,\xi}{e^{-t\,G_1(\xi)}} d\xi.$$

According to the convergence of the integrals (17), the integral on the right-hand side of the latter inequality converges and the integrand does not depend on the variable x; hence, the integral (24) converges uniformly with respect to the variable x on any finite segment $[x_1, x_2] \subset (-\infty, +\infty)$.

Let us investigate the uniform convergence of the integral (25) with respect to the variable x on any finite segment $[x_1, x_2] \subset (-\infty, +\infty)$. Using the inequality (22), we calculate

$$\int_0^{+\infty} |F_{xx}(x,t;\xi)|d\xi = \int_0^{+\infty} \left| \frac{A(\xi)\,\xi^2\,\sin\,(t\,G_2(\xi) + \varphi(\xi) + x\xi)}{\rho(\xi)e^{-t\,G_1(\xi)}} \right| d\xi \leq \frac{1}{\sqrt{b}} \int_0^{+\infty} \frac{A(\xi)\,\xi^2}{e^{-t\,G_1(\xi)}} d\xi.$$

By virtue of the convergence of the integrals (17), the integral on the right-hand side of the latter inequality converges, and the integrand does not depend on the variable x. Thus, the integral (25) converges uniformly, which means that differentiation under the integral sign of Function (21) with respect to the variable x up to the second order including was legal.

It remains to check the uniform convergence of the integral (26) with respect to the variable t on any finite segment $[t_1, t_2] \subset [0, T]$, and the integral (28) with respect to the variable t on any finite segment $[t_1, t_2] \subset (0, T]$. Using the definition (15), we can write Function (26) as

$$\int_0^{+\infty} F_t(x,t;\xi)d\xi = \int_0^{+\infty} \frac{A(\xi)}{e^{-t\,G_1(\xi)}} [\cos\varphi(\xi)\cos\,(t\,G_2(\xi) + \varphi(\xi) + x\xi)$$

$$+ \sin\varphi(\xi)\sin\,(t\,G_2(\xi) + \varphi(\xi) + x\xi)]d\xi = \int_0^{+\infty} \frac{A(\xi)}{e^{-t\,G_1(\xi)}} \cos\,(t\,G_2(\xi) + x\xi)\,d\xi.$$

Hence,

$$\int_0^{+\infty} |F_t(x,t;\xi)|d\xi \leq \int_0^{+\infty} \frac{A(\xi)}{e^{-t\,G_1(\xi)}} d\xi \leq \begin{cases} \int_0^{+\infty} \frac{A(\xi)}{e^{-t_2\,G_1(\xi)}} d\xi, & G_1(\xi) \geq 0, \\ \int_0^{+\infty} \frac{A(\xi)}{e^{-t_1\,G_1(\xi)}} d\xi, & G_1(\xi) < 0. \end{cases}$$

Since the integral (18) converges, the integrals on the right side of the latter inequality converge and not depend on the variable t. Therefore, the integral (26) converges uniformly for any value of $t \in [0, T]$.

Let us now estimate the integral (28):

$$\int_0^{+\infty} |F_{tt}(x,t;\xi)|d\xi = \int_0^{+\infty} \left| \frac{A(\xi)}{\rho(\xi)e^{-t\,G_1(\xi)}} \right| \left| - \left(a^2\xi^2 + b\cos\,(h\xi)\right) \sin\,(t\,G_2(\xi) + \varphi(\xi) + x\xi) \right.$$

$$+ b\sin(h\xi)\cos(t\,G_2(\xi) + \varphi(\xi) + x\xi)|d\xi$$

$$\leq \frac{1}{\sqrt{b}} \int\limits_0^{+\infty} \frac{A(\xi)\,(a^2\xi^2 + 2b)}{e^{-t\,G_1(\xi)}} d\xi \leq \begin{cases} \frac{1}{\sqrt{b}} \int\limits_0^{+\infty} \frac{A(\xi)\,(a^2\xi^2+2b)}{e^{-t_2\,G_1(\xi)}} d\xi, & G_1(\xi) \geq 0, \\ \frac{1}{\sqrt{b}} \int\limits_0^{+\infty} \frac{A(\xi)\,(a^2\xi^2+2b)}{e^{-t_1\,G_1(\xi)}} d\xi, & G_1(\xi) < 0. \end{cases}$$

Since the integrand in the latter integral does not depend on t, then, according to the Weierstrass test, the integral (28) converges uniformly in the variable t on any finite segment $[t_1, t_2] \subset (0, T]$. This means that differentiation under the integral sign in (21) with respect to the variable t up to the second order including was legal if the integral

$$\int\limits_0^{+\infty} \frac{A(\xi)\,(a^2\xi^2 + 2b)}{e^{-t\,G_1(\xi)}} d\xi = a^2 \int\limits_0^{+\infty} \frac{A(\xi)\,\xi^2}{e^{-t\,G_1(\xi)}} d\xi + 2b \int\limits_0^{+\infty} \frac{A(\xi)}{e^{-t\,G_1(\xi)}} d\xi$$

converges for any value $t \in (0, T]$. And this is true, since the integrals (17) and (18) converge.

It can be shown similarly that the improper integrals obtained after the formal differentiation under the sign of the integral over the variables x and t up to the second order including of the integrand in (23) converge uniformly if the integrals

$$\int\limits_0^{+\infty} \frac{A(\xi)}{e^{t\,G_1(\xi)}} d\xi, \quad \int\limits_0^{+\infty} \frac{A(\xi)\,\xi}{e^{t\,G_1(\xi)}} d\xi, \quad \int\limits_0^{+\infty} \frac{A(\xi)\,\xi^2}{e^{t\,G_1(\xi)}} d\xi$$

converge. Their convergence was considered above, see (17) and (18).

Thus, we have proved that the function $G(x,t)$, defined by Equation (20), exists at every point of the area D and satisfies the equality (1) in the classical sense. Hence, the lemma is proved.

□

Theorem 1. *Under conditions* (2) *and* $u_0(x) \in L_1(\mathbf{R})$, *the function*

$$u(x,t) = \frac{1}{2\pi} \int\limits_{-\infty}^{+\infty} G(x - \eta, t) u_0(\eta) d\eta, \tag{29}$$

where $G(x,t)$ *is defined by the equality* (20), *satisfies the equality* (1) *in the classical sense.*

Proof. Function (29) has the following form

$$u(x,t) = \frac{1}{2\pi} \int\limits_{-\infty}^{+\infty} G(x - \eta, t) u_0(\eta) d\eta$$

$$= \frac{1}{2\pi} \int\limits_{-\infty}^{+\infty} u_0(\eta) \int\limits_0^{+\infty} \left[\frac{A(\xi)\,\sin(t\,G_2(\xi) + \varphi(\xi) + x\xi - \eta\xi)}{\rho(\xi) e^{-t\,G_1(\xi)}} \right.$$

$$\left. + \frac{A(\xi)\,\sin(t\,G_2(\xi) - \varphi(\xi) - x\xi + \eta\xi)}{\rho(\xi) e^{t\,G_1(\xi)}} \right] d\xi d\eta.$$

Function (29) exists in the region D if the condition

$$\int\limits_{-\infty}^{+\infty} |u_0(\eta)| d\eta \int\limits_{-\infty}^{+\infty} |G(\eta, t)| d\eta < +\infty$$

holds.

Since $u_0(x)$ is an integrable function for all $x \in \mathbf{R}$, we are to check the fulfillment of condition $G(x,t) \in L_1(\mathbf{R})$ for any $t \in (0,T]$.

Let us find the majorant of Function (20). From the equality (13), we obtain the estimate

$$\rho(\xi) = \left[a^4\xi^4 + 2a^2\xi^2 b\cos(h\xi) + b^2\right]^{1/4} \le \left[a^4\xi^4 + 2a^2\xi^2 b + b^2\right]^{1/4} = \sqrt{a^2\xi^2 + b}. \quad (30)$$

The equality (14) implies that $|\varphi(\xi)| < \pi/4$, hence; $\sqrt{2}/2 < \cos\varphi(\xi) \le 1$. Then, from (15) and (30), we have

$$|G_2(\xi)| = \rho(\xi)|\cos\varphi(\xi)| \le \frac{\sqrt{2}}{2}\sqrt{a^2\xi^2 + b}. \quad (31)$$

Taking into account the inequalities (22), (31) and $|\sin\alpha/\alpha| < 1$, we can estimate the function

$$|G(x,t)| \le \int_0^{+\infty} \left| \frac{A(\xi)\sin(t\,G_2(\xi) + \varphi(\xi) + x\xi)}{\rho(\xi)e^{-tG_1(\xi)}} + \frac{A(\xi)\sin(t\,G_2(\xi) - \varphi(\xi) - x\xi)}{\rho(\xi)e^{tG_1(\xi)}} \right| d\xi$$

$$\le \int_0^{+\infty} \left(\frac{A(\xi)\,|\sin(t\,G_2(\xi) + \varphi(\xi) + x\xi)|}{\rho(\xi)e^{-tG_1(\xi)}} + \frac{A(\xi)\,|\sin(t\,G_2(\xi) - \varphi(\xi) - x\xi)|}{\rho(\xi)e^{tG_1(\xi)}} \right) d\xi$$

$$\le \frac{1}{\sqrt{b}} \int_0^{+\infty} \left(\frac{A(\xi)\,|\sin(t\,G_2(\xi) + \varphi(\xi) + x\xi)|}{e^{-tG_1(\xi)}} + \frac{A(\xi)\,|\sin(t\,G_2(\xi) - \varphi(\xi) - x\xi)|}{e^{tG_1(\xi)}} \right) d\xi$$

$$< \frac{1}{\sqrt{b}} \int_0^{+\infty} \left(\frac{A(\xi)\,|t\,G_2(\xi) + \varphi(\xi) + x\xi|}{e^{-tG_1(\xi)}} + \frac{A(\xi)\,|t\,G_2(\xi) - \varphi(\xi) - x\xi|}{e^{tG_1(\xi)}} \right) d\xi$$

$$\le \frac{1}{\sqrt{b}} \int_0^{+\infty} \left(\frac{t|G_2(\xi)| + |\varphi(\xi)| + |x|\xi}{e^{-tG_1(\xi)}} + \frac{t|G_2(\xi)| + |\varphi(\xi)| + |x|\xi}{e^{tG_1(\xi)}} \right) A(\xi)d\xi$$

$$\le \frac{1}{\sqrt{b}} \int_0^{+\infty} \left(\frac{\frac{\sqrt{2}}{2}\sqrt{a^2\xi^2 + b}\,t + \pi/4 + |x|\xi}{e^{-tG_1(\xi)}} + \frac{\frac{\sqrt{2}}{2}\sqrt{a^2\xi^2 + b}\,t + \pi/4 + |x|\xi}{e^{tG_1(\xi)}} \right) A(\xi)d\xi.$$

Replace the integration variable in the latter integral according to the formula $|x|\xi = \tau$ for $x \ne 0$:

$$|G(x,t)| <$$

$$< \frac{1}{\sqrt{b}\,|x|} \int_0^{+\infty} \left(\frac{\frac{\sqrt{2}}{2}\sqrt{a^2\tau^2/x^2 + b}\,t + \pi/4 + \tau}{e^{-tG_1(\tau/|x|)}} + \frac{\frac{\sqrt{2}}{2}\sqrt{a^2\tau^2/x^2 + b}\,t + \pi/4 + \tau}{e^{tG_1(\tau/|x|)}} \right) A(\tau/|x|)d\tau$$

$$= \frac{t}{\sqrt{b}\,x^2} \int_0^{+\infty} \left(\frac{\frac{\sqrt{2}}{2}\sqrt{a^2\tau^2 + bx^2} + \frac{\pi|x|}{4t} + \frac{|x|}{t}\tau}{e^{-tG_1(\tau/|x|)}} + \frac{\frac{\sqrt{2}}{2}\sqrt{a^2\tau^2 + bx^2} + \frac{\pi|x|}{4t} + \frac{|x|}{t}\tau}{e^{tG_1(\tau/|x|)}} \right) A(\tau/|x|)d\tau. \quad (32)$$

The integrals on the right-hand side of (32), due to conditions (17) and (3), converge for any $t \in (0,T]$ and any $x \in \mathbf{R}\backslash\{0\}$. Thus, we have shown that the function $|G(x,t)|$ is majorized by the function $\widetilde{C}t/x^2$, where $t \in (0,T]$, $x \ne 0$, where $\widetilde{C}$ is an absolute constant. This implies the convergence of the integral $\int_{-\infty}^{+\infty} G(\eta,t)d\eta$, that is $G(x,t) \in L_1(\mathbf{R})$ for any $t \in (0,T]$. This means that Function (20) exists in the domain D and, by virtue of the proved Lemma, it is a classical solution of Equation (1).

Note also that, by virtue of the same Lemma, Function (29) belongs to the class $C^1(\overline{D}) \cap C^2(D)$ (the integrand in (29) is continuous, the integrals $u_x(x,t)$ and $u_{xx}(x,t)$ converge uniformly in the variable x on any finite segment $[x_1, x_2] \subset (-\infty, +\infty)$, the integrals $u_t(x,t)$ and $u_{tt}(x,t)$ converge uniformly in the variable t on any finite segment $[t_1, t_2] \subset (0, T]$, and the integral $u_t(x,t)$ converges at the border $t = 0$). Thus, the theorem is proved.

□

3. Fulfillment of the Initial Conditions of the Problem

Theorem 2. *Under conditions* (2), $u_0(x) \in L_1(\mathbf{R})$ *and* $u_0(x) \in C^1(\mathbf{R})$ *the limit relations*

$$\lim_{t\to 0+} u(x_0,t) = u_0(x_0), \quad \lim_{t\to 0+} u_t(x_0,t) = 0 \tag{33}$$

are valid for any $x_0 \in (-\infty, +\infty)$.

Proof. 1. Let $x_0 \in (-\infty, +\infty)$. In the equality (29), make the change of variable $(x_0 - \eta)/t = \tau$, and consider the difference

$$\begin{aligned} u(x_0,t) - u_0(x_0) &= \frac{t}{2\pi}\int_{-\infty}^{+\infty} G(t\tau,t)u_0(x_0 - t\tau)d\tau - \frac{1}{\pi}\int_{-\infty}^{+\infty}\frac{u_0(x_0)}{1+\tau^2}d\tau \\ &= \frac{1}{2\pi}\int_{-\infty}^{+\infty}\left[tG(t\tau,t)u_0(x_0 - t\tau) - \frac{2u_0(x_0)}{1+\tau^2}\right]d\tau \\ &= \frac{1}{2\pi}\left[\int_{-\infty}^{-A} + \int_{-A}^{A} + \int_{A}^{+\infty}\right] \stackrel{\text{def}}{=} I_{1,A} + I_{2,A} + I_{3,A}. \end{aligned} \tag{34}$$

Using the inequality (2) and the equality $\operatorname{arctg} x = \arccos(1/\sqrt{1+x^2})$, we write the functions (15) as follows:

$$\begin{aligned} G_1(\xi) &= \rho(\xi)\sin\varphi(\xi) = \rho(\xi)\sqrt{\frac{1-\cos 2\varphi(\xi)}{2}} \\ &= \frac{\rho(\xi)}{\sqrt{2}}\left[1 - \cos\left(\operatorname{arctg}\frac{b\sin(h\xi)}{a^2\xi^2 + b\cos(h\xi)}\right)\right]^{1/2} \\ &= \frac{\rho(\xi)}{\sqrt{2}}\left[1 - \frac{|a^2\xi^2 + b\cos(h\xi)|}{\sqrt{(a^2\xi^2 + b\cos(h\xi))^2 + b^2\sin^2(h\xi)}}\right]^{1/2} \\ &= \frac{\rho(\xi)}{\sqrt{2}}\left[\frac{\rho^2(\xi) - a^2\xi^2 - b\cos(h\xi)}{\rho^2(\xi)}\right]^{1/2} = \frac{1}{\sqrt{2}}\left[\rho^2(\xi) - a^2\xi^2 - b\cos(h\xi)\right]^{1/2} \\ &= \frac{1}{\sqrt{2}}\left[\sqrt{a^4\xi^4 + 2a^2b\xi^2\cos(h\xi) + b^2} - a^2\xi^2 - b\cos(h\xi)\right]^{1/2}, \end{aligned} \tag{35}$$

and

$$G_2(\xi) = \rho(\xi)\cos\varphi(\xi) = \rho(\xi)\sqrt{\frac{1+\cos 2\varphi(\xi)}{2}}$$

$$= \frac{\rho(\xi)}{\sqrt{2}}\left[1 + \frac{|a^2\xi^2 + b\cos(h\xi)|}{\sqrt{(a^2\xi^2 + b\cos(h\xi))^2 + b^2\sin^2(h\xi)}}\right]^{1/2} = \frac{\rho(\xi)}{\sqrt{2}}\left[\frac{\rho^2(\xi) + a^2\xi^2 + b\cos(h\xi)}{\rho^2(\xi)}\right]^{1/2}$$

$$= \frac{1}{\sqrt{2}}\left[\sqrt{a^4\xi^4 + 2a^2b\xi^2\cos(h\xi) + b^2} + a^2\xi^2 + b\cos(h\xi)\right]^{1/2}. \quad (36)$$

Obviously, the resulting radical expressions in (35) and (36) are always non-negative. Then,

$$t\,G_1(\xi) = \frac{1}{\sqrt{2}}\left[\sqrt{a^4t^4\xi^4 + 2a^2bt^4\xi^2\cos(h\xi) + b^2t^4} - a^2t^2\xi^2 - bt^2\cos(h\xi)\right]^{1/2},$$

$$t\,G_2(\xi) = \frac{1}{\sqrt{2}}\left[\sqrt{a^4t^4\xi^4 + 2a^2bt^4\xi^2\cos(h\xi) + b^2t^4} + a^2t^2\xi^2 + bt^2\cos(h\xi)\right]^{1/2},$$

and the function $t\,G(t\tau, t)$ can be written as

$$t\,G(t\tau,t) = t\int_0^{+\infty}\left[\frac{A(\xi)\,\sin\left(t\,G_2(\xi) + \varphi(\xi) + t\tau\xi\right)}{\rho(\xi)e^{-t\,G_1(\xi)}} + \frac{A(\xi)\,\sin\left(t\,G_2(\xi) - \varphi(\xi) - t\tau\xi\right)}{\rho(\xi)e^{t\,G_1(\xi)}}\right]d\xi$$

$$= t\int_0^{+\infty}\left[\frac{A(\xi)\,\sin\left(\frac{1}{\sqrt{2}}\left[\sqrt{a^4t^4\xi^4 + 2a^2bt^4\xi^2\cos(h\xi) + b^2t^4} + a^2t^2\xi^2 + bt^2\cos(h\xi)\right]^{1/2} + \varphi(\xi) + t\tau\xi\right)}{\rho(\xi)e^{-\frac{1}{\sqrt{2}}\left[\sqrt{a^4t^4\xi^4+2a^2bt^4\xi^2\cos(h\xi)+b^2t^4} - a^2t^2\xi^2 - bt^2\cos(h\xi)\right]^{1/2}}}\right.$$

$$\left.+ \frac{A(\xi)\,\sin\left(\frac{1}{\sqrt{2}}\left[\sqrt{a^4t^4\xi^4 + 2a^2bt^4\xi^2\cos(h\xi) + b^2t^4} + a^2t^2\xi^2 + bt^2\cos(h\xi)\right]^{1/2} - \varphi(\xi) - t\tau\xi\right)}{\rho(\xi)e^{\frac{1}{\sqrt{2}}\left[\sqrt{a^4t^4\xi^4+2a^2bt^4\xi^2\cos(h\xi)+b^2t^4} - a^2t^2\xi^2 - bt^2\cos(h\xi)\right]^{1/2}}}\right]d\xi.$$

After the substitution $t\xi = z$, from the latter equality we obtain

$$t\,G(t\tau,t) = \int_0^{+\infty}\left[\frac{A(z/t)}{\rho(z/t)e^{-\frac{1}{\sqrt{2}}\left[\sqrt{a^4z^4+2a^2bt^2z^2\cos(hz/t)+b^2t^4} - a^2z^2 - bt^2\cos(hz/t)\right]^{1/2}}}\right.$$

$$\times\sin\left(\frac{1}{\sqrt{2}}\left[\sqrt{a^4z^4 + 2a^2bt^2z^2\cos(hz/t) + b^2t^4} + a^2z^2 + bt^2\cos(hz/t)\right]^{1/2} + \varphi(z/t) + \tau z\right)$$

$$+ \frac{A(z/t)}{\rho(z/t)e^{\frac{1}{\sqrt{2}}\left[\sqrt{a^4z^4+2a^2bt^2z^2\cos(hz/t)+b^2t^4} - a^2z^2 - bt^2\cos(hz/t)\right]^{1/2}}}$$

$$\left.\sin\left(\frac{1}{\sqrt{2}}\left[\sqrt{a^4z^4 + 2a^2bt^2z^2\cos(hz/t) + b^2t^4} + a^2z^2 + bt^2\cos(hz/t)\right]^{1/2} - \varphi(z/t) - \tau z\right)\right]dz.$$

Denote the functions

$$g_1(z,t) := \frac{1}{\sqrt{2}}\left[\sqrt{a^4z^4 + 2a^2bt^2z^2\cos(hz/t) + b^2t^4} - a^2z^2 - bt^2\cos(hz/t)\right]^{1/2}, \quad (37)$$

and

$$g_2(z,t) := \frac{1}{\sqrt{2}}\left[\sqrt{a^4z^4 + 2a^2bt^2z^2\cos(hz/t) + b^2t^4} + a^2z^2 + bt^2\cos(hz/t)\right]^{1/2}. \quad (38)$$

Using this notation, we can write

$$t\,G(t\tau,t) = \int\limits_0^{+\infty}\left[\frac{A(z/t)\sin(g_2(z,t)+\varphi(z/t)+\tau z)}{\rho(z/t)e^{-g_1(z,t)}} + \frac{A(z/t)\sin(g_2(z,t)-\varphi(z/t)-\tau z)}{\rho(z/t)e^{g_1(z,t)}}\right]dz. \quad (39)$$

2. Let us now prove that the limit relation

$$\lim_{t\to 0+} t\,G(t\tau,t) = \frac{2}{1+\tau^2} \quad (40)$$

is satisfied uniformly with respect to $\tau \in (-\infty,+\infty)$. To do this, it suffices to show that for any arbitrarily small number $\varepsilon > 0$ there is a number $0 < \delta \le T$ such that for any $t \in (0,\delta)$ and $\tau \in (-\infty,+\infty)$ holds the inequality

$$\left|t\,G(t\tau,t) - \frac{2}{1+\tau^2}\right| < \varepsilon. \quad (41)$$

Represent the function in the form $2/(1+\tau^2) = 2\int\limits_0^{+\infty} e^{-z}\cos(\tau z)dz$ and consider the difference

$$\begin{aligned}
&t\,G(t\tau,t) - \frac{2}{1+\tau^2} \\
&= \int\limits_0^{+\infty}\left[\frac{A(z/t)\sin(g_2(z,t)+\varphi(z/t)+\tau z)}{\rho(z/t)e^{-g_1(z,t)}} + \frac{A(z/t)\sin(g_2(z,t)-\varphi(z/t)-\tau z)}{\rho(z/t)e^{g_1(z,t)}}\right]dz \\
&\qquad - 2\int\limits_0^{+\infty} e^{-z}\cos(\tau z)dz \\
&= \int\limits_0^{+\infty}\left[\frac{A(z/t)e^{g_1(z,t)}}{\rho(z/t)}\sin(g_2(z,t)+\varphi(z/t)+\tau z) - e^{-z}\cos(\tau z)\right]dz \\
&+ \int\limits_0^{+\infty}\left[\frac{A(z/t)e^{-g_1(z,t)}}{\rho(z/t)}\sin(g_2(z,t)-\varphi(z/t)-\tau z) - e^{-z}\cos(\tau z)\right]dz \\
&= \int\limits_0^{+\infty} e^{-z}\left[\frac{A(z/t)e^{z+g_1(z,t)}}{\rho(z/t)}\sin(g_2(z,t)+\varphi(z/t)) - 1\right]\cos(\tau z)dz \\
&\qquad + \int\limits_0^{+\infty}\frac{A(z/t)e^{g_1(z,t)}}{\rho(z/t)}\cos(g_2(z,t)+\varphi(z/t))\sin(\tau z)dz
\end{aligned}$$

$$+\int_0^{+\infty} e^{-z}\left[\frac{A(z/t)e^{z-g_1(z,t)}}{\rho(z/t)}\sin\left(g_2(z,t)-\varphi(z/t)\right)-1\right]\cos(\tau z)dz$$
$$-\int_0^{+\infty}\frac{A(z/t)e^{-g_1(z,t)}}{\rho(z/t)}\cos\left(g_2(z,t)-\varphi(z/t)\right)\sin(\tau z)dz$$
$$=\int_0^{+\infty} e^{-z}\left[\frac{A(z/t)e^{z+g_1(z,t)}}{\rho(z/t)}\sin\left(g_2(z,t)+\varphi(z/t)\right)-1\right]\cos(\tau z)dz$$
$$+\int_0^{+\infty} e^{-z}\left[\frac{A(z/t)e^{z-g_1(z,t)}}{\rho(z/t)}\sin\left(g_2(z,t)-\varphi(z/t)\right)-1\right]\cos(\tau z)dz$$
$$+\int_0^{+\infty}\frac{A(z/t)e^{g_1(z,t)}}{\rho(z/t)}\left(1-2\sin^2\frac{g_2(z,t)+\varphi(z/t)}{2}\right)\sin(\tau z)dz$$
$$-\int_0^{+\infty}\frac{A(z/t)e^{-g_1(z,t)}}{\rho(z/t)}\left(1-2\sin^2\frac{g_2(z,t)-\varphi(z/t)}{2}\right)\sin(\tau z)dz$$
$$=\int_0^{+\infty} e^{-z}\left[\frac{A(z/t)e^{z+g_1(z,t)}}{\rho(z/t)}\sin\left(g_2(z,t)+\varphi(z/t)\right)-1\right]\cos(\tau z)dz$$
$$+\int_0^{+\infty} e^{-z}\left[\frac{A(z/t)e^{z-g_1(z,t)}}{\rho(z/t)}\sin\left(g_2(z,t)-\varphi(z/t)\right)-1\right]\cos(\tau z)dz$$
$$-2\int_0^{+\infty}\frac{A(z/t)e^{g_1(z,t)}}{\rho(z/t)}\sin^2\frac{g_2(z,t)+\varphi(z/t)}{2}\sin(\tau z)dz$$
$$+2\int_0^{+\infty}\frac{A(z/t)e^{-g_1(z,t)}}{\rho(z/t)}\sin^2\frac{g_2(z,t)-\varphi(z/t)}{2}\sin(\tau z)dz$$
$$+\int_0^{+\infty}\frac{A(z/t)e^{-g_1(z,t)}}{\rho(z/t)}\left(e^{2g_1(z,t)}-1\right)\sin(\tau z)dz.$$

We use the formulas for the sine of the sum and difference in the third and fourth integrals in the last expression. Taking into account their squaring and the formula for the sine of a double angle, we obtain

$$tG(t\tau,t)-\frac{2}{1+\tau^2}=\int_0^{+\infty} e^{-z}\left[\frac{A(z/t)e^{z+g_1(z,t)}}{\rho(z/t)}\sin\left(g_2(z,t)+\varphi(z/t)\right)-1\right]\cos(\tau z)dz$$
$$+\int_0^{+\infty} e^{-z}\left[\frac{A(z/t)e^{z-g_1(z,t)}}{\rho(z/t)}\sin\left(g_2(z,t)-\varphi(z/t)\right)-1\right]\cos(\tau z)dz$$

$$-2\int_0^{+\infty}\frac{A(z/t)e^{g_1(z,t)}}{\rho(z/t)}\left(\sin^2\frac{g_2(z,t)}{2}\cos^2\frac{\varphi(z/t)}{2}+\cos^2\frac{g_2(z,t)}{2}\sin^2\frac{\varphi(z/t)}{2}\right.$$
$$\left.+\frac{1}{2}\sin g_2(z,t)\sin\varphi(z/t)\right)\sin(\tau z)dz$$
$$+2\int_0^{+\infty}\frac{A(z/t)e^{-g_1(z,t)}}{\rho(z/t)}\left(\sin^2\frac{g_2(z,t)}{2}\cos^2\frac{\varphi(z/t)}{2}+\cos^2\frac{g_2(z,t)}{2}\sin^2\frac{\varphi(z/t)}{2}\right.$$
$$\left.-\frac{1}{2}\sin g_2(z,t)\sin\varphi(z/t)\right)\sin(\tau z)dz$$
$$+\int_0^{+\infty}\frac{A(z/t)e^{-g_1(z,t)}}{\rho(z/t)}\left(e^{2g_1(z,t)}-1\right)\sin(\tau z)dz$$
$$=\int_0^{+\infty}e^{-z}\left[\frac{A(z/t)e^{z+g_1(z,t)}}{\rho(z/t)}\sin\left(g_2(z,t)+\varphi(z/t)\right)-1\right]\cos(\tau z)dz$$
$$+\int_0^{+\infty}e^{-z}\left[\frac{A(z/t)e^{z-g_1(z,t)}}{\rho(z/t)}\sin\left(g_2(z,t)-\varphi(z/t)\right)-1\right]\cos(\tau z)dz$$
$$-\int_0^{+\infty}\frac{A(z/t)e^{g_1(z,t)}}{\rho(z/t)}\sin g_2(z,t)\sin\varphi(z/t)\sin(\tau z)dz$$
$$-\int_0^{+\infty}\frac{A(z/t)e^{-g_1(z,t)}}{\rho(z/t)}\sin g_2(z,t)\sin\varphi(z/t)\sin(\tau z)dz$$
$$-2\int_0^{+\infty}\frac{A(z/t)e^{-g_1(z,t)}\left(e^{2g_1(z,t)}-1\right)}{\rho(z/t)}\sin^2\frac{g_2(z,t)}{2}\cos^2\frac{\varphi(z/t)}{2}\sin(\tau z)dz$$
$$-2\int_0^{+\infty}\frac{A(z/t)e^{-g_1(z,t)}\left(e^{2g_1(z,t)}-1\right)}{\rho(z/t)}\cos^2\frac{g_2(z,t)}{2}\sin^2\frac{\varphi(z/t)}{2}\sin(\tau z)dz$$
$$+\int_0^{+\infty}\frac{A(z/t)e^{-g_1(z,t)}}{\rho(z/t)}\left(e^{2g_1(z,t)}-1\right)\sin(\tau z)dz.$$

In the resulting expression, we expand the sine of the sum in the integrand in the first integral, which we then group with the third integral, and write the sine of the difference in the second integral and group it with the fourth integral as follows:

$$\int_0^{+\infty}e^{-z}\left[\frac{A(z/t)e^{z+g_1(z,t)}}{\rho(z/t)}\sin g_2(z,t)\cos\varphi(z/t)-1\right]\cos(\tau z)dz$$

$$+\int_0^{+\infty}\frac{A(z/t)e^{g_1(z,t)}}{\rho(z/t)}[\cos g_2(z,t)\cos(\tau z)-\sin g_2(z,t)\sin(\tau z)]\sin\varphi(z/t)dz$$
$$+\int_0^{+\infty}e^{-z}\left[\frac{A(z/t)e^{z-g_1(z,t)}}{\rho(z/t)}\sin g_2(z,t)\cos\varphi(z/t)-1\right]\cos(\tau z)dz$$
$$-\int_0^{+\infty}\frac{A(z/t)e^{-g_1(z,t)}}{\rho(z/t)}[\cos g_2(z,t)\cos(\tau z)+\sin g_2(z,t)\sin(\tau z)]\sin\varphi(z/t)dz$$
$$-2\int_0^{+\infty}\frac{A(z/t)e^{-g_1(z,t)}\left(e^{2g_1(z,t)}-1\right)}{\rho(z/t)}\sin^2\frac{g_2(z,t)}{2}\cos^2\frac{\varphi(z/t)}{2}\sin(\tau z)dz$$
$$-2\int_0^{+\infty}\frac{A(z/t)e^{-g_1(z,t)}\left(e^{2g_1(z,t)}-1\right)}{\rho(z/t)}\cos^2\frac{g_2(z,t)}{2}\sin^2\frac{\varphi(z/t)}{2}\sin(\tau z)dz$$
$$+\int_0^{+\infty}\frac{A(z/t)e^{-g_1(z,t)}}{\rho(z/t)}\left(e^{2g_1(z,t)}-1\right)\sin(\tau z)dz$$
$$=\int_0^{+\infty}e^{-z}\left[\frac{A(z/t)e^{z+g_1(z,t)}}{\rho(z/t)}\sin g_2(z,t)\cos\varphi(z/t)-1\right]\cos(\tau z)dz$$
$$+\int_0^{+\infty}e^{-z}\left[\frac{A(z/t)e^{z-g_1(z,t)}}{\rho(z/t)}\sin g_2(z,t)\cos\varphi(z/t)-1\right]\cos(\tau z)dz$$
$$+\int_0^{+\infty}\frac{A(z/t)e^{g_1(z,t)}}{\rho(z/t)}\cos(g_2(z,t)+\tau z)\sin\varphi(z/t)dz$$
$$-\int_0^{+\infty}\frac{A(z/t)e^{-g_1(z,t)}}{\rho(z/t)}\cos(g_2(z,t)-\tau z)\sin\varphi(z/t)dz$$
$$-2\int_0^{+\infty}\frac{A(z/t)e^{-g_1(z,t)}\left(e^{2g_1(z,t)}-1\right)}{\rho(z/t)}\sin^2\frac{g_2(z,t)}{2}\cos^2\frac{\varphi(z/t)}{2}\sin(\tau z)dz$$
$$-2\int_0^{+\infty}\frac{A(z/t)e^{-g_1(z,t)}\left(e^{2g_1(z,t)}-1\right)}{\rho(z/t)}\cos^2\frac{g_2(z,t)}{2}\sin^2\frac{\varphi(z/t)}{2}\sin(\tau z)dz$$
$$+\int_0^{+\infty}\frac{A(z/t)e^{-g_1(z,t)}}{\rho(z/t)}\left(e^{2g_1(z,t)}-1\right)\sin(\tau z)dz$$
$$=\int_0^{+\infty}e^{-z}\left[\frac{A(z/t)e^{z+g_1(z,t)}}{\rho(z/t)}\sin g_2(z,t)\cos\varphi(z/t)-1\right]\cos(\tau z)dz$$

$$+\int_0^{+\infty} e^{-z}\left[\frac{A(z/t)e^{z-g_1(z,t)}}{\rho(z/t)}\sin g_2(z,t)\cos\varphi(z/t)-1\right]\cos(\tau z)dz$$
$$+\int_0^{+\infty}\frac{A(z/t)e^{g_1(z,t)}\cos(g_2(z,t)+\tau z)-A(z/t)e^{-g_1(z,t)}\cos(g_2(z,t)-\tau z)}{\rho(z/t)}\sin\varphi(z/t)dz$$
$$-2\int_0^{+\infty}\frac{A(z/t)e^{-g_1(z,t)}\left(e^{2g_1(z,t)}-1\right)}{\rho(z/t)}\sin^2\frac{g_2(z,t)}{2}\cos^2\frac{\varphi(z/t)}{2}\sin(\tau z)dz$$
$$-2\int_0^{+\infty}\frac{A(z/t)e^{-g_1(z,t)}\left(e^{2g_1(z,t)}-1\right)}{\rho(z/t)}\cos^2\frac{g_2(z,t)}{2}\sin^2\frac{\varphi(z/t)}{2}\sin(\tau z)dz$$
$$+\int_0^{+\infty}\frac{A(z/t)e^{-g_1(z,t)}}{\rho(z/t)}\left(e^{2g_1(z,t)}-1\right)\sin(\tau z)dz$$
$$\stackrel{\text{def}}{=} I_1(\tau,t)+I_2(\tau,t)+I_3(\tau,t)-2I_4(\tau,t)-2I_5(\tau,t)+I_6(\tau,t).$$

3. Consider first the integral $I_6(\tau,t)$. Using the definition (37) and inequality (4), transform the expression

$$2g_1^2(z,t)=\sqrt{a^4z^4+2a^2b\,t^2z^2\cos(hz/t)+b^2t^4}-a^2z^2-bt^2\cos(hz/t)$$
$$=\frac{b^2t^4-b^2t^4\cos^2(hz/t)}{\sqrt{a^4z^4+2a^2b\,t^2z^2\cos(hz/t)+b^2t^4}+a^2z^2+bt^2\cos(hz/t)}$$
$$=\frac{b^2t^4\sin^2(hz/t)}{\sqrt{a^4z^4+2a^2b\,t^2z^2\cos(hz/t)+b^2t^4}+t^2\left(a^2\frac{z^2}{t^2}+b\cos(hz/t)\right)}.$$

Taking into account that $\sqrt{a^4z^4+2a^2b\,t^2z^2\cos(hz/t)+b^2t^4}\geq 0$ and the inequality (4), from the last expression, we obtain

$$\frac{b^2t^4\sin^2(hz/t)}{\sqrt{a^4z^4+2a^2b\,t^2z^2\cos(hz/t)+b^2t^4}+t^2\left(a^2\frac{z^2}{t^2}+b\cos(hz/t)\right)}\leq\frac{b^2t^4\sin^2(hz/t)}{bt^2}\leq\frac{b^2t^4}{bt^2}=bt^2,$$

whence,

$$0\leq g_1(z,t)\leq\sqrt{\frac{b}{2}}t. \tag{42}$$

Using the inequalities (22) and (42), we estimate the integral $I_6(\tau,t)$:

$$|I_6(\tau,t)|\leq\int_0^{+\infty}\left|\frac{A(z/t)e^{-g_1(z,t)}}{\rho(z/t)}\left(e^{2g_1(z,t)}-1\right)\sin(\tau z)\right|dz$$
$$=\int_0^{+\infty}\frac{A(z/t)\left(e^{2g_1(z,t)}-1\right)}{\rho(z/t)e^{g_1(z,t)}}|\sin(\tau z)|dz\leq\frac{1}{\sqrt{b}}\int_0^{+\infty}\frac{A(z/t)\left(e^{\sqrt{2b}\,t}-1\right)}{e^{g_1(z,t)}}dz.$$

Since the asymptotic representation of the function $e^{\sqrt{2b}t}=1+\sqrt{2b}\,t+o(t)$ is valid for $t\longrightarrow 0+$, the latter integral for $t\longrightarrow 0+$ can be bounded as

$$\frac{1}{\sqrt{b}}\int\limits_0^{+\infty}\frac{A(z/t)(\sqrt{2b}t+o(t))}{e^{g_1(z,t)}}dz=\sqrt{2}t\int\limits_0^{+\infty}\frac{A(z/t)(1+o(1))}{e^{g_1(z,t)}}dz\le \mathrm{const}\cdot\sqrt{2}t\int\limits_0^{+\infty}\frac{A(z/t)}{e^{g_1(z,t)}}dz.$$

After the reverse change of the variable according to the formula $t\xi=z$, we finally obtain

$$|I_6(\tau,t)|\le \mathrm{const}\cdot\sqrt{2}t\int\limits_0^{+\infty}\frac{A(z/t)}{e^{g_1(z,t)}}dz=\mathrm{const}\cdot\sqrt{2}t^2\int\limits_0^{+\infty}\frac{A(\xi)}{e^{t\,G_1(\xi)}}d\xi.$$

Since the resulting integral on the right-hand side is a convergent integral from the series (18), the last inequality for $t\longrightarrow 0+$ implies the estimate

$$|I_6(\tau,t)|<\frac{\varepsilon}{6}. \tag{43}$$

4. Similarly, we estimate the integrals $I_4(\tau,t)$ and $I_5(\tau,t)$ for $t\longrightarrow 0+$.

$$|I_4(\tau,t)|\le\int\limits_0^{+\infty}\left|\frac{A(z/t)e^{-g_1(z,t)}\left(e^{2g_1(z,t)}-1\right)}{\rho(z/t)}\sin^2\frac{g_2(z,t)}{2}\cos^2\frac{\varphi(z/t)}{2}\sin(\tau z)\right|dz$$
$$\le\frac{1}{\sqrt{b}}\int\limits_0^{+\infty}\frac{A(z/t)\left(e^{\sqrt{2b}t}-1\right)}{e^{g_1(z,t)}}dz=\sqrt{2}t\int\limits_0^{+\infty}\frac{A(z/t)(1+o(1))}{e^{g_1(z,t)}}dz\le\mathrm{const}\cdot\sqrt{2}t^2\int\limits_0^{+\infty}\frac{A(\xi)}{e^{t\,G_1(\xi)}}d\xi;$$

and

$$|I_5(\tau,t)|\le\int\limits_0^{+\infty}\left|\frac{A(z/t)e^{-g_1(z,t)}\left(e^{2g_1(z,t)}-1\right)}{\rho(z/t)}\cos^2\frac{g_2(z,t)}{2}\sin^2\frac{\varphi(z/t)}{2}\sin(\tau z)\right|dz$$
$$\le\frac{1}{\sqrt{b}}\int\limits_0^{+\infty}\frac{A(z/t)\left(e^{\sqrt{2b}t}-1\right)}{e^{g_1(z,t)}}dz=\sqrt{2}t\int\limits_0^{+\infty}\frac{A(z/t)(1+o(1))}{e^{g_1(z,t)}}dz\le\mathrm{const}\cdot\sqrt{2}t^2\int\limits_0^{+\infty}\frac{A(\xi)}{e^{t\,G_1(\xi)}}d\xi.$$

From the last two expressions for $t\longrightarrow 0+$, we can deduce

$$|I_4(\tau,t)|<\frac{\varepsilon}{12},\quad |I_5(\tau,t)|<\frac{\varepsilon}{12}, \tag{44}$$

for any arbitrarily small fixed number $\varepsilon>0$.

5. Let us now estimate the integral $I_3(\tau,t)$. Taking into account the inequalities (22) and (42), we obtain

$$|I_3(\tau,t)|\le\int\limits_0^{+\infty}\left|\frac{A(z/t)e^{g_1(z,t)}\cos(g_2(z,t)+\tau z)-A(z/t)e^{-g_1(z,t)}\cos(g_2(z,t)-\tau z)}{\rho(z/t)}\right||\sin\varphi(z/t)|dz$$

$$\le\int\limits_0^{+\infty}A(z/t)\frac{e^{g_1(z,t)}+e^{-g_1(z,t)}}{\rho(z/t)}dz=\int\limits_0^{+\infty}A(z/t)\frac{e^{-g_1(z,t)}\left(e^{2g_1(z,t)}+1\right)}{\rho(z/t)}dz$$
$$\le\int\limits_0^{+\infty}A(z/t)\frac{e^{-g_1(z,t)}\left(e^{\sqrt{2b}\,t}+1\right)}{\rho(z/t)}dz\le\frac{e^{\sqrt{2b}\,T}+1}{\sqrt{b}}\int\limits_0^{+\infty}\frac{A(z/t)}{e^{g_1(z,t)}}dz=\frac{e^{\sqrt{2b}\,T}+1}{\sqrt{b}}t\int\limits_0^{+\infty}\frac{A(\xi)}{e^{t\,G_1(\xi)}}d\xi.$$

Since the resulting integral converges as the partial case of (18), the latter chain of inequalities for $t \longrightarrow 0+$ implies the estimate

$$|I_3(\tau,t)| < \frac{\varepsilon}{6} \tag{45}$$

for any arbitrarily small number $\varepsilon > 0$.

6. Consider now the integral $I_2(\tau,t)$. Let the function $A(z/t)$ be such that for $z \in [1,+\infty)$ the integrand in the integral $I_2(\tau,t)$ is majorized (in absolute value) by the function $|\mathrm{Const}+1|e^{-z}$, where Const > 0 is a real constant. Therefore, you can choose such a large enough number $B > 0$ such that the inequality

$$\left| \int\limits_{B}^{+\infty} e^{-z} \left[\frac{A(z/t)e^{z-g_1(z,t)}}{\rho(z/t)} \sin g_2(z,t) \cos \varphi(z/t) - 1 \right] \cos(\tau z) dz \right| < \frac{\varepsilon}{12}$$

will be satisfied.

Fix the number $B > 0$ and evaluate for $0 \le z \le B$ the expression

$$\frac{A(z/t)e^{z-g_1(z,t)}}{\rho(z/t)} \sin g_2(z,t) \cos \varphi(z/t).$$

Let at $t = 0$ the value of the function

$$\tilde{g}_1(z,t) := \frac{A(z/t)e^{z-g_1(z,t)}}{\rho(z/t)} \sin g_2(z,t) \cos \varphi(z/t) \tag{46}$$

be equal to one for any z. Let us show that the function defined in this way tends to unity at $t \longrightarrow 0+$ uniformly with respect to $z \in [0,B]$.

Suppose the contrary, that is, there is such a number $\varepsilon_0 > 0$ that for any positive number δ there are $t(\delta) \in (0,\delta)$ and $z(\delta) \in [0,B]$ such that the inequality

$$\frac{A(z/t)e^{z-g_1(z,t)}}{\rho(z/t)} \sin g_2(z,t) \cos \varphi(z/t) > 1 + \varepsilon_0$$

is satisfied.

Consider the sequence $\delta_n = 1/n$, $n = 1,2,\ldots$. There exist the sequences $\{t_n\} \subset (0,1/n)$ and $\{z_n\} \subset [0,B]$ for which the inequality

$$|\tilde{g}_1(z_n,t_n)| > 1 + \varepsilon_0$$

holds for any $n \in \mathbf{N}$. Without loss of generality, we can assume that the sequence $\{(z_n,t_n)\}$ of elements $(z_n,t_n) \in \mathbf{R}^2$ converges, and we denote its limit as (z_0,t_0). Obviously, $z_0 \in [0,B]$ and $t_0 = 0$; hence, $|\tilde{g}_1(z_0,0)| > 1 + \varepsilon_0$, which contradicts the definition of the function $\tilde{g}_1(z,t)$ on the axis $t = 0$. Thus, we have proved the inequality

$$\left| \int\limits_{0}^{B} e^{-z} \left[\frac{A(z/t)e^{z-g_1(z,t)}}{\rho(z/t)} \sin g_2(z,t) \cos \varphi(z/t) - 1 \right] \cos(\tau z) dz \right| < \frac{\varepsilon}{12}.$$

So, we have proved the estimate

$$|I_2(\tau,t)| \le \left| \int_0^B e^{-z} \left[\frac{A(z/t)e^{z-g_1(z,t)}}{\rho(z/t)} \sin g_2(z,t) \cos\varphi(z/t) - 1 \right] \cos(\tau z) dz \right|$$

$$+ \left| \int_B^{+} e^{-z} \left[\frac{A(z/t)e^{z-g_1(z,t)}}{\rho(z/t)} \sin g_2(z,t) \cos\varphi(z/t) - 1 \right] \cos(\tau z) dz \right| < \frac{\varepsilon}{24} + \frac{\varepsilon}{24} = \frac{\varepsilon}{6}. \quad (47)$$

7. Similarly, it can be shown that if, for $t = 0$, the value of the function

$$\tilde{g}_2(z,t) := \frac{A(z/t)e^{z+g_1(z,t)}}{\rho(z/t)} \sin g_2(z,t) \cos\varphi(z/t) \quad (48)$$

is equal to one for any z, then the following inequality holds:

$$|I_1(\tau,t)| \le \left| \int_0^B e^{-z} \left[\frac{A(z/t)e^{z+g_1(z,t)}}{\rho(z/t)} \sin g_2(z,t) \cos\varphi(z/t) - 1 \right] \cos(\tau z) dz \right|$$

$$+ \left| \int_B^{+\infty} e^{-z} \left[\frac{A(z/t)e^{z+g_1(z,t)}}{\rho(z/t)} \sin g_2(z,t) \cos\varphi(z/t) - 1 \right] \cos(\tau z) dz \right| < \frac{\varepsilon}{12} + \frac{\varepsilon}{12} = \frac{\varepsilon}{6}. \quad (49)$$

Estimates (43)–(45), (47), and (49) prove the fulfillment of inequality (41), which implies the validity of relation (40).

8. Let us now estimate the expression (34). From the inequality (32), it follows that for $x \neq 0$ and $t \in (0,T]$ the inequality

$$|G(x,t)| \le \frac{\tilde{C}t}{x^2}$$

is satisfied, where $\tilde{C} > 0$ is a constant. Hence, for $\tau \neq 0$ and $t \in (0,T]$, the estimate

$$|t\,G(t\tau,t)| \le \frac{\tilde{C}}{\tau^2}$$

holds. This means that the integrand in the integral $I_{3,A}$ is majorized by the function $2\tilde{C}\sup|u_0|/\tau^2$, that is, for any $A > 0$, the inequality

$$|I_{3,A}| \le \frac{\tilde{C}\sup|u_0|}{\pi A}$$

is satisfied. Choose the number $A > 0$ sufficiently large so that we obtain the estimate

$$|I_{3,A}| < \varepsilon/3,$$

for any arbitrarily small number $\varepsilon > 0$.

The integral $I_{1,A}$ is estimated in a similar way:

$$|I_{1,A}| < \varepsilon/3.$$

Write the integrand in the integral $I_{2,A}$ in the following form:

$$t\,G(t\tau,t)u_0(x_0-t\tau)-t\,G(t\tau,t)u_0(x_0)+t\,G(t\tau,t)u_0(x_0)-\frac{2u_0(x_0)}{1+\tau^2}$$
$$=t\,G(t\tau,t)[u_0(x_0-t\tau)-u_0(x_0)]+u_0(x_0)\left[t\,G(t\tau,t)-\frac{2}{1+\tau^2}\right].$$

Let us write down $|I_{2,A}|=\left|\int\limits_{-A}^{0}+\int\limits_{0}^{A}\right|\leq 2\left|\int\limits_{0}^{A}\right|$. Given Equation (40), there is such $t_1\in(0,T]$ that the inequality

$$\left|t\,G(t\tau,t)-\frac{2}{1+\tau^2}\right|<\frac{\varepsilon}{12A\sup|u_0|}$$

is satisfied for any $t\in(0,t_1)$ and $\tau\in\mathbf{R}$, and for a chosen sufficiently large number $A>0$. Let $\varepsilon<12A\sup|u_0|$, then for any $t\in(0,t_1)$ we obtain the inequalities

$$\frac{2}{1+\tau^2}-1<t\,G(t\tau,t)<\frac{2}{1+\tau^2}+1,$$

that is, $|t\,G(t\tau,t)|\leq 3$.

Since the function $u_0(x)$ is continuous over the real line (together with its first derivative), there exists $t_0\in(0,t_1)$, such that the inequality

$$|u_0(x_0-t\tau)-u_0(x_0)|<\frac{\varepsilon}{36A\sup|u_0|}$$

is satisfied for any $t\in(0,t_0)$ and $\tau\in[-A,A]$. Thus, it is proved that for $0<t<t_0\leq T$ the following estimate holds:

$$|I_{2,A}|<\varepsilon/3.$$

The resulting estimates $|I_{1,A}|<\varepsilon/3$, $|I_{2,A}|<\varepsilon/3$ and $|I_{3,A}|<\varepsilon/3$, by virtue of an arbitrary choice of $\varepsilon>0$ and $x_0\in(-\infty,+\infty)$, prove that the first relation in (33) holds.

9. Let us now prove the second relation in (33). Using the definition (15), we first calculate

$$G_t(x,t)=\int\limits_{0}^{+\infty}\frac{A(\xi)}{\rho(\xi)}\Big[G_2(\xi)\cos\left(t\,G_2(\xi)+\varphi(\xi)+x\xi\right)e^{t\,G_1(\xi)}$$
$$+G_1(\xi)\sin\left(t\,G_2(\xi)+\varphi(\xi)+x\xi\right)e^{t\,G_1(\xi)}+G_2(\xi)\cos\left(t\,G_2(\xi)-\varphi(\xi)-x\xi\right)e^{-t\,G_1(\xi)}$$
$$-G_1(\xi)\sin\left(t\,G_2(\xi)-\varphi(\xi)-x\xi\right)e^{-t\,G_1(\xi)}\Big]d\xi$$
$$=\int\limits_{0}^{+\infty}A(\xi)\Big[[\cos\varphi(\xi)\cos\left(t\,G_2(\xi)+\varphi(\xi)+x\xi\right)+\sin\varphi(\xi)\sin\left(t\,G_2(\xi)+\varphi(\xi)+x\xi\right)]e^{t\,G_1(\xi)}$$
$$+[\cos\varphi(\xi)\cos\left(t\,G_2(\xi)-\varphi(\xi)-x\xi\right)-\sin\varphi(\xi)\sin\left(t\,G_2(\xi)-\varphi(\xi)-x\xi\right)]e^{-t\,G_1(\xi)}\Big]d\xi$$
$$=\int\limits_{0}^{+\infty}A(\xi)\Big[\cos\left(t\,G_2(\xi)+x\xi\right)e^{t\,G_1(\xi)}+\cos\left(t\,G_2(\xi)-x\xi\right)e^{-t\,G_1(\xi)}\Big]d\xi.$$

Let $x_0\in(-\infty,+\infty)$ be an arbitrary value. Consider the function

$$u_t(x_0,t) = \frac{1}{2\pi}\int_{-\infty}^{+\infty} G_t(x_0-\eta,t)u_0(\eta)d\eta$$
$$= \frac{1}{2\pi}\int_{-\infty}^{+\infty} u_0(\eta)\int_0^{+\infty}\left(\frac{A(\xi)\,\cos\left(t\,G_2(\xi)+x_0\xi-\eta\xi\right)}{e^{-t\,G_1(\xi)}}+\frac{A(\xi)\,\cos\left(t\,G_2(\xi)-x_0\xi+\eta\xi\right)}{e^{t\,G_1(\xi)}}\right)d\xi\,d\eta.$$

In the last expression, make the change of variable $(x_0-\eta)/t=\tau$ and obtain

$$u_t(\eta+t\tau,t) = \frac{t}{2\pi}\int_{-\infty}^{+\infty} G_t(t\tau,t)u_0(x_0-t\tau)d\tau.$$

Since the condition

$$\int_{-\infty}^{+\infty} |u_0(\eta)|d\eta \int_{-\infty}^{+\infty} |G_t(\eta,t)|d\eta < +\infty$$

is satisfied, the function $\int_{-\infty}^{+\infty} G_t(t\tau,t)u_0(x_0-t\tau)d\tau$ exists in the region $\overline{D}$.

Since, according to the condition of the theorem, the function $u_0(x)$ is integrable over the real line, it is enough to check the condition $G_t(x,t)\in L_1(\mathbf{R})$. To do this, taking into account inequalities (30), we estimate the function

$$|G_t(x,t)| \le \int_0^{+\infty}\left(\left|\frac{A(\xi)\,\cos\left(t\,G_2(\xi)+x\xi\right)}{e^{-t\,G_1(\xi)}}\right|+\left|\frac{A(\xi)\,\cos\left(t\,G_2(\xi)-x\xi\right)}{e^{t\,G_1(\xi)}}\right|\right)d\xi$$
$$\le \int_0^{+\infty}\frac{A(\xi)}{e^{-t\,G_1(\xi)}}d\xi+\int_0^{+\infty}\frac{A(\xi)}{e^{t\,G_1(\xi)}}d\xi.$$

The integrals on the right-hand side in the latter expression converge as the partial case of the integrals (18) for any $t\in[0,T]$. Thus, we have shown that $G_t(x,t)\in L_1(\mathbf{R})$ for any $t\in[0,T]$, which means that the function $\int_{-\infty}^{+\infty} G_t(t\tau,t)u_0(x_0-t\tau)d\tau$ exists in the area $\overline{D}$.

Thus, for $t\longrightarrow 0+$, the estimate

$$|u_t(x_0,t)| = \left|\frac{t}{2\pi}\int_{-\infty}^{+\infty} G_t(t\tau,t)u_0(x_0-t\tau)d\tau\right| < \varepsilon$$

is satisfied for any arbitrarily small number $\varepsilon>0$. This implies the fulfillment of the second relation in (33). Thus, the theorem is proved.

□

Author Contributions: Conceptualization, V.V. and N.Z.; methodology, V.V. and N.Z.; validation, V.V. and N.Z.; formal analysis, V.V. and N.Z.; investigation, V.V. and N.Z.; data curation, V.V. and N.Z.; writing and original draft preparation, N.Z.; writing and review and editing, V.V. and N.Z. All authors have read and agreed to the published version of the manuscript.

Funding: The second author was financially supported by the Ministry of of Science and Higher Education of the Russian Federation within the program of the Moscow Center for Fundamental and Applied Mathematics under the agreement No 075-15-2022-284.

Institutional Review Board Statement: Not applicable.

Informed Consent Statement: Not applicable.

Data Availability Statement: Not applicable.

Conflicts of Interest: The authors declare no conflict of interest.

References

1. Pinney, E. *Ordinary Difference-Differential Equations*; University of California Press: Berkeley, CA, USA; Los Angeles, CA, USA, 1958.
2. Bellman, R.; Cooke, K.L. *Differential-Difference Equations*; Academic Press: New York, NY, USA, 1963.
3. Hale, J. *Theory of Functional-Differential Equations*; Springer: New York, NY, USA, 1977.
4. Kuang, Y. *Delay Differential Equations with Applications in Population Dinamics*; Academic Press: Boston, MA, USA, 1993.
5. Schulman, L.S. Some difference-differential equations containing both advance and retardiation. *J. Math. Phys.* **1974**, *15*, 295–298. [CrossRef]
6. Wheeler, J.A.; Feynman, R.P. Classical electrodynamics in terms of direct interparticle actions. *Rev. Mod. Phys.* **1949**, *21*, 425–433. [CrossRef]
7. Skubachevskii, A.L. *Elliptic Functional-Differential Equations and Applications*; Birkhäuser: Basel, Switzerland; Boston, MA, USA; Berlin, Germany, 1997.
8. Skubachevskii, A.L. Boundary-value problems for elliptic functional-differential equations and their applications. *Rus. Math. Surv.* **2016**, *71*, 801–906. [CrossRef]
9. Shamin, R.V.; Skubachevskii, A.L. The mixed boundary value problem for parabolic differential-difference equation. *Func. Diff. Equ.* **2001**, *8*, 407–424.
10. Muravnik, A.B. Functional-differential parabolic equations: Integral transformations and qualitative properties of solutions of the Cauchy problem. *J. Math. Sci.* **2016**, *216*, 345–496. [CrossRef]
11. Vlasov, V.V.; Medvedev, D.A. Functional-differential equations in Sobolev spaces and related problems of spectral theory. *J. Math. Sci.* **2010**, *164*, 659–841. [CrossRef]
12. Zaitseva, N.V. Global classical solutions of some two-dimensional hyperbolic differential-difference equations. *Diff. Equ.* **2020**, *56*, 734–739. [CrossRef]
13. Zaitseva, N.V. Classical solutions of hyperbolic equations with nonlocal potentials. *Dokl. Math.* **2021**, *103*, 127–129. [CrossRef]
14. Zaitseva, N.V. Classical solutions of hyperbolic differential-difference equations in a half-space. *Diff. Equ.* **2021**, *57*, 1629–1639. [CrossRef]
15. Vasil'ev, V.B. *Wave Factorization of Elliptic Stmbols: Theory and Applications: Introduction to the Theory of Boundary Value Problems in Non-Smooth Domains*; Kluwer Academic Publishers: Dordrecht, The Netherlands; Boston, MA, USA; London, UK, 2000.
16. Vasilyev, A.V.; Vasilyev, V.B. Difference equations in a multidimensional space. *Math. Model. Anal.* **2016**, *21*, 336–349. [CrossRef]

Disclaimer/Publisher's Note: The statements, opinions and data contained in all publications are solely those of the individual author(s) and contributor(s) and not of MDPI and/or the editor(s). MDPI and/or the editor(s) disclaim responsibility for any injury to people or property resulting from any ideas, methods, instructions or products referred to in the content.

mathematics

MDPI

Article

Analytical Description of the Diffusion in a Cellular Automaton with the Margolus Neighbourhood in Terms of the Two-Dimensional Markov Chain

Anton E. Kulagin [1,*,†] and Alexander V. Shapovalov [2,3,*,†]

[1] Division for Electronic Engineering, Tomsk Polytechnic University, 30 Lenina av., 634050 Tomsk, Russia
[2] Department of Theoretical Physics, Tomsk State University, 1 Novosobornaya Sq., 634050 Tomsk, Russia
[3] Laboratory for Theoretical Cosmology, International Centre of Gravity and Cosmos, Tomsk State University of Control Systems and Radioelectronics, 40 Lenina av., 634050 Tomsk, Russia
* Correspondence: aek8@tpu.ru (A.E.K.); shpv@phys.tsu.ru (A.V.S.)
† These authors contributed equally to this work.

Abstract: The one-parameter two-dimensional cellular automaton with the Margolus neighbourhood is analyzed based on considering the projection of the stochastic movements of a single particle. Introducing the auxiliary random variable associated with the direction of the movement, we reduce the problem under consideration to the study of a two-dimensional Markov chain. The master equation for the probability distribution is derived and solved exactly using the probability-generating function method. The probability distribution is expressed analytically in terms of Jacobi polynomials. The moments of the obtained solution allowed us to derive the exact analytical formula for the parametric dependence of the diffusion coefficient in the two-dimensional cellular automaton with the Margolus neighbourhood. Our analytic results agree with earlier empirical results of other authors and refine them. The results are of interest for the modelling two-dimensional diffusion using cellular automata especially for the multicomponent problem.

Keywords: two-dimensional Markov chain; cellular automata; Margolus neighbourhood; diffusion; probability distribution

MSC: 37B15; 60J10; 60J20; 60J60

Citation: Kulagin, A.E.; Shapovalov, A.V. Analytical Description of the Diffusion in a Cellular Automaton with the Margolus Neighbourhood in Terms of the Two-Dimensional Markov Chain. *Mathematics* **2023**, *11*, 584. https://doi.org/10.3390/math11030584

Academic Editor: Sitnik Sergey

Received: 30 December 2022
Revised: 19 January 2023
Accepted: 19 January 2023
Published: 22 January 2023

Copyright: © 2023 by the authors. Licensee MDPI, Basel, Switzerland. This article is an open access article distributed under the terms and conditions of the Creative Commons Attribution (CC BY) license (https://creativecommons.org/licenses/by/4.0/).

1. Introduction

Cellular automata (CA) are a powerful tool for modelling matter transport [1]. The attractive feature of CA is that contemporary algorithms of parallel computing can be naturally embedded in them. Various cellular algorithms were successfully implemented on field-programmable gate arrays (FPGA) [2,3] and on graphic cards [4,5].

In the study of diffusion phenomena in physics, chemistry, and biology, CA are positioned as one of the effective tools for modelling systems of many particles. The simplest CA with boolean alphabet modelling the diffusion are the asynchronous CA with naive diffusion and the synchronous CA with Margolus neighbourhood [6] or briefly Margolus CA (MCA). The last one is the object of our study. Exactly this type of the CA attracted our attention since synchronous CA are more advantageous in terms of the computing speed (see, e.g., comparison in [7]). Note that the MCA is representative of partitioning CA.

The most common macroscopic characteristics of the diffusion transfer is the diffusion coefficient $\mathcal{D}_c$ that is defined as the proportionality factor in Fick's law [8,9]. The diffusion coefficient is usually invariant when the movements of particles are caused just by random fluctuations rather than by any fields. Nevertheless, the processes with the time-dependent diffusion coefficient are also of interest, e.g., in the ambipolar diffusion phenomena [10–12].

The most popular model of the diffusion is the kinetic model, which is based on a differential equations that can be solved, for example, using difference schemes [13–15]. In such approach, the diffusion coefficient is an explicit parameter of the model. For cellular automata, the diffusion coefficient is not presented in the model explicitly. Calculating the diffusion coefficient for the CA with naive diffusion is a trivial task since it directly models the random walk of particles that is well-studied. However, it is not trivial for partitioning CA including MCA. We show here that the diffusion in the two-dimensional MCA can be described in terms of one two-dimensional Markov chain as opposed to the one-dimensional random walk. In our paper, we study the exact solution of this two-dimensional Markov chain whose characteristics are crucial for the mathematical description of the diffusion in MCA.

While multidimensional Markov chains arise in a number of applications in service theory [16], genetic networks [17], Gibbs sampling [18], and other areas [19], there are very few exactly solvable multidimensional Markov chains that do not degenerate to the one-dimensional one. Therefore, the exact solutions to the two-dimensional Markov chain under consideration can be of interest for specialists in applied mathematics and useful for applications other than cellular automaton theory.

The paper is organized as follows. In Section 2, we describe the diffusion model within the framework of the two-dimensional cellular automata with Margolus neighbourhood. Furthermore, we explain the way of obtaining the diffusion coefficient for this model based on the considering one-dimensional movement of a single particle. In Section 3, the stochastic process describing the one-dimensional movement of a single particle is given. The idea of introducing the auxiliary random variable associated with the direction of movement is proposed. This approach allows us to consider the process under consideration as the two-dimensional Markov chain. In Section 4, the formal mathematical definition of this chain and basic notations are given. In Section 5, we solve the master equation for the probability distribution of the particle coordinate using the probability generating function method. The moments of this distribution are derived. In Section 6, the obtained results are discussed within the framework of the diffusion model. The exact analytical formula for the diffusion coefficient is derived, and properties of the cellular automaton with the Margolus neighbourhood are discussed. In Section 7, we conclude with some remarks.

2. Diffusion in the Margolus Cellular Automaton

In the two-dimensional cellular automata with Margolus neighbourhood, the diffusion is described based on the following algorithm [6]:

(1) The plane is divided into identical square cells forming a cell grid. One cell contains a boolean variable that takes the value 0 or 1 corresponding to the absence or presence of a *particle* in the cell, respectively.

(2) The cell grid is divided into blocks of 2×2 cells. Such partition can be even or odd (see Figure 1). The even partition corresponds to the case when the left lower cell of each block has even vertical and horizontal numbers. The odd partition corresponds to the case when the left lower cell of each block has odd vertical and horizontal numbers.

(3) Beginning from an initial state, on each discrete time step the following *rule* is applied to each block independently. We rotate the block 90° clockwise or counterclockwise with the probability of $0 < p \leq 0.5$ for each outcome. The *rule* is applied to blocks of the even partition on even time steps and it is applied to blocks of the odd partition on odd time steps. If each time step corresponds to the same time interval Δt and $p = \text{const}$, then such MCA simulates the diffusion with the time independent diffusion coefficient $\mathcal{D}_c$.

The classic MCA uses $p = 0.5$, i.e., blocks always rotate. In such approach, the diffusion rate is controlled with the length of the time interval corresponding to one discrete time step and with the size of a cell. However, this model can be applied to the multicomponent diffusion problem. In this case, the cell contains few bits that correspond to *particles* of different substances. It can be treated as few layers of the cell grid. Then, we can not directly apply the described *rule* with $p = 0.5$ for every layer of *particles* if the diffusion rates for these substances are not equal. The difference in diffusion rates can be realized using different p for different substances. The only drawback of such approach is that the diffusion coefficient $\mathcal{D}_c = \mathcal{D}_c(p)$ nonlinearly depends on p. The other way is using the same $p = 0.5$ for each layer but skip two consecutive time steps for one or few layers with a probability equal to p_s (the rotation *rule* is not applied to any blocks of the respective layer on the skipped time step). In this approach, the diffusion coefficient linearly depends on p_s. The differences between these two approaches will be discussed in Section 6.

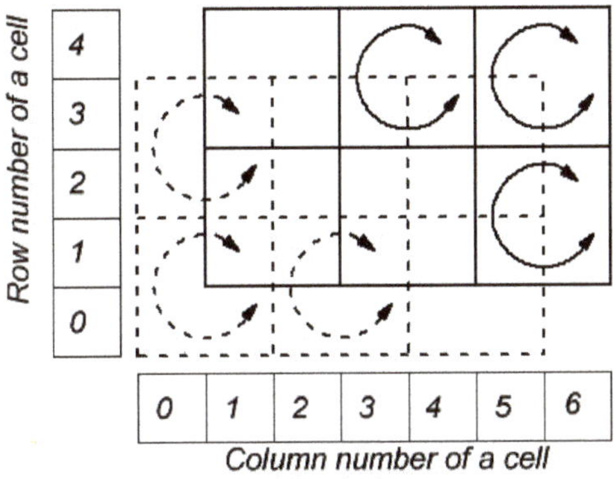

Figure 1. Odd and even partitions of the cell grid. Solid lines divide the cell grid into blocks of the odd partition and dashed lines divide the cell grid into blocks of the even partition. Arrows demonstrate the rotation *rule*.

In order to model the diffusion using the MCA, the diffusion coefficient corresponding to the particular MCA must be determined. It can be shown (see, e.g., [20]) that

$$\mathcal{D}_c(p) = k(p)\frac{\Delta x^2}{\Delta t}, \tag{1}$$

where $\mathcal{D}_c(p)$ is the diffusion coefficient, Δx is the side length of the cell, Δt is the time interval corresponding to the discrete time step, and $k(p)$ is the proportionality factor. However, relation (1) does not help to obtain the exact value of the multiplier k. Moreover, k nonlinearly depends on p as it was mentioned earlier. One way is to determine k is to compute the specific diffusion problem using the numerical realization of the MCA and to compare the result with the analytical or numerical solutions of the respective diffusion equation. Such approach allows one to find k approximately. However, it is hard to estimate the error of the obtained value. Moreover, this error depends on the choice of the specific diffusion problem. The other way is to obtain the distribution of the *particle* position in the MCA. Assuming that the correlation of these distributions for two *particles* tends to zero with the growth of time steps number, the distribution of the position of the single *particle* is equal to the Green function of the diffusion equation that is given by

$$G(\vec{r}, \tau) \sim \exp\left(-\frac{\vec{r}^{\,2}}{4\mathcal{D}_c\tau}\right), \tag{2}$$

where $\vec{r}$ is the radius vector of the particle position at time $t = \tau$ relative to the initial position at time $t_0 = 0$, $\mathcal{D}_c$ is the diffusion coefficient. For the isotropic and homogeneous problem, one can consider the projection of the *particle* position on one axis (let it be x). As $t \to \infty$, the distribution of the *particle* position tends to the normal distribution with the probability density function given by

$$P_{X_n}(x) \sim \exp\left(-\frac{(x - M_{X_n})^2}{2D_{X_n}}\right), \qquad t = n\Delta t, \qquad n \in \mathbb{N}, \tag{3}$$

where X_n is the random position of the *particle* at the n-th time step, M_{X_n} is the expectation of X_n, and D_{X_n} is the dispersion of X_n. Then, for $\Delta x = 1$, $\Delta t = 1$, we have

$$\begin{aligned} &M_{X_n} \to 0, \qquad n \to \infty, \\ &\frac{D_{X_n}}{2n} \to \mathcal{D}_c, \qquad n \to \infty. \end{aligned} \tag{4}$$

Hereinafter, $\mathcal{D}_c$ will be given for $\Delta x = 1$, $\Delta t = 1$ unless otherwise stated. The trick is to find the distribution $P_{X_n}(x)$ or its moments analytically. In [21], the authors tried to obtain the diffusion coefficient using this approach for $p = 0.5$. However, they assumed that X_n is the one-dimensional Markov chain, i.e., the simplest random walk. Later on, using the software realization of MCA with higher number of cells and time steps, it was shown that this assumption led to the diffusion coefficient obtained in [21] for 2D MCA is approximately three times higher than the real one (see, e.g., [20,22,23]). However, the exact distribution of X_n and the diffusion coefficient of MCA were not obtained since then. In this work, we present the exact distribution of X_n in MCA and obtain the exact analytical formula of $\mathcal{D}_c(p)$ for an arbitrary p including the special case $p = 0.5$.

3. One-Dimensional Movement of a Single Particle

In this Section, we will describe the rules of the stochastic movement of a single *particle* in MCA. As it was mentioned in the previous Section, we consider the movement along the x-axis that is directed along the side of a cell. Notice that if a *particle* is in an odd column at an odd time step, then its x-coordinate can either increase by 1 or does not change according to the rotation *rule* of the MCA (see Figure 2). The same rule works for a *particle* in a even column at an even time step. Let the variable d show the direction of possible movement of the *particle* along the x-axis. If $d = 1$, then x can either increase by one or does not change. If $d = -1$, then x can either decrease by one or does not change. It is easy to see that $d = -1$ corresponds to a *particle* in an even column at an odd time step and to a *particle* in an odd column at an even time step.

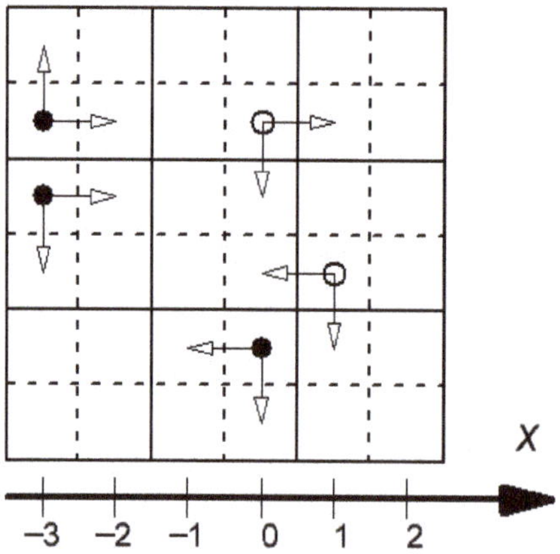

Figure 2. Examples of possible movements of a particle in the MCA. The black dot is for the particle movement at an odd time step (the rotation *rule* applies for blocks of the odd partition) and the white dot is for the particle movement at an even time step (the rotation *rule* applies for block of the even partition).

Notice that the direction d does not change when the x-coordinate changes and the direction d reverts its sign when the coordinate x does not change. The first outcome is realized with the probability of p at every time step while the second outcome is realized with the probability $(1 - p)$. Note that the sequence of the x-coordinates of the single *particle* has a memory, i.e., the current x-coordinate of the *particle* depends the history of its movements. It the main issue in the analytical description of partitioning cellular automata.

4. Master Equation

Next, we give the formal definition of the two-dimensional Markov chain described in Section 3.

Let $X_t : \Omega \to \mathbb{Z}$ and $\Delta_t : \Omega \to \{-1, +1\}$ be sequences of random variables where $t \in \mathbb{Z}_+$ and Ω is a set of outcomes. We associate the values of X_t with the discrete x-coordinate of the *particle* on a discrete time step t, and Δ_t is associated with its direction. The probability of transitions for the chain under consideration, which were described in Section 3, are given by

$$\begin{aligned} \mathrm{Prob}(X_{t+1} = X_t + \Delta_t; \Delta_{t+1} = \Delta_t) &= p, \\ \mathrm{Prob}(X_{t+1} = X_t; \Delta_{t+1} = -\Delta_t) &= 1 - p. \end{aligned} \tag{5}$$

The semicolon in (5) implies the logical conjunction.

Let us denote

$$P_t(x, d) = \mathrm{Prob}(X_t = x; \Delta_t = d). \tag{6}$$

The transition rules (5) in notations (6) yield the following master equation:

$$P_{t+1}(x, d) = pP_t(x - d, d) + (1 - p)P_t(x, -d). \tag{7}$$

Hereinafter, $x \in \mathbb{Z}$, $d \in \{-1, +1\}$, and $t \in \mathbb{Z}_+$. We consider the problem with the deterministic initial position of the *particle*, i.e., $\mathrm{Prob}(X_0 = 0) = 1$. Then, the initial condition for (7) reads

$$P_0(x, +1) = \varepsilon \cdot \delta_{x,0}, \qquad P_0(0, -1) = (1 - \varepsilon) \cdot \delta_{x,0}, \tag{8}$$

where $\delta_{i,j}$ is the Kronecker delta.

Within the framework of the diffusion problem, it is natural to consider the symmetric case $P_0(0, +1) = P_0(0, -1)$. Thus, the following initial condition will be considered:

$$P_0(x, +1) = \frac{\delta_{x,0}}{2}, \qquad P_0(x, -1) = \frac{\delta_{x,0}}{2}. \tag{9}$$

Since the distribution over x is of primary interest to us, we will study the marginal distribution given by

$$P_t(x) = P_t(x, +1) + P_t(x, -1). \tag{10}$$

In order to construct the analytical description of the two-dimensional Markov chain under consideration, we will solve the master Equation (7) with the initial condition (9) in the next Section.

5. Probability Generating Function

The exact solution of (7), (9) can be derived using the method of the probability generating function [24] for the marginal distribution (10). Such probability-generating function reads

$$G_t(z) = \sum_{x=-\infty}^{\infty} P_t(x) z^x. \tag{11}$$

Let us also introduce the following probability-generating functions:

$$G_t^+(z) = \sum_{x=-\infty}^{\infty} P_t(x, +1) z^x, \qquad G_t^-(z) = \sum_{x=-\infty}^{\infty} P_t(x, -1) z^x. \tag{12}$$

In view of (10), one readily gets

$$G_t(z) = G_t^+(z) + G_t^-(z). \tag{13}$$

The master Equation (7) can be written as

$$\begin{cases} P_{t+1}(x,+1) = pP_t(x-1,+1) + (1-p)P_t(x,-1), \\ P_{t+1}(x,-1) = pP_t(x+1,-1) + (1-p)P_t(x,+1). \end{cases} \tag{14}$$

Multiplying the system (14) by z^x and summing over $x \in \mathbb{Z}$, we derive the following equation for the probability generating functions (12):

$$\begin{aligned} g_{t+1}(z) &= b(z)g_t(z), & g_0(z) &= \frac{1}{2}\begin{pmatrix}1\\1\end{pmatrix}, \\ g_t(z) &= \begin{pmatrix}G_t^+(z)\\G_t^-(z)\end{pmatrix}, & b(z) &= \begin{pmatrix} pz & 1-p \\ 1-p & pz^{-1}\end{pmatrix}, \end{aligned} \tag{15}$$

where $g_0(z)$ is obtained from (9), (12).

The solution of the system (15) has the following form:

$$g_t(z) = u(z)\begin{pmatrix}\lambda_1^t(z) & 0 \\ 0 & \lambda_2^t(z)\end{pmatrix}u^{-1}(z)g_0(z), \qquad u(z)u^\top(z) = u^\top(z)u(z) = 1, \tag{16}$$

where the solution of the associated matrix eigenvalue problem yields

$$\begin{aligned} &\lambda_1(z) = \frac{p}{2}\left(z+\frac{1}{z}\right) + \frac{m(z)}{2}, \qquad \lambda_2(z) = \frac{p}{2}\left(z+\frac{1}{z}\right) - \frac{m(z)}{2}, \\ &u(z) = \begin{pmatrix} c_1(z)(1-p) & c_2(z)(1-p) \\ \frac{c_1(z)}{2}(m(z)-r(z)) & -\frac{c_2(z)}{2}(m(z)+r(z)) \end{pmatrix}, \qquad m(z) = \sqrt{p^2\left(z+\frac{1}{z}\right)^2 - 8p + 4}, \\ &r(z) = p\left(z-\frac{1}{z}\right), \qquad c_1(z) = \sqrt{\frac{m(z)+r(z)}{2(1-p)^2 m(z)}}, \qquad c_2(z) = \sqrt{\frac{m(z)-r(z)}{2(1-p)^2 m(z)}}. \end{aligned} \tag{17}$$

The solution (16), (17) can be rewritten as

$$\begin{aligned} G_t^+(z) &= \frac{1}{2m(z)}\left[-\lambda_1^t(z)\lambda_2(z) + \lambda_1(z)\lambda_2^t(z) + (1-p+pz)(\lambda_1^t(z) - \lambda_2^t(z))\right], \\ G_t^-(z) &= \frac{1}{2m(z)}\left[\lambda_1^{t+1}(z) - \lambda_2^{t+1}(z) + (1-p-pz)(\lambda_1^t(z) - \lambda_2^t(z))\right]. \end{aligned} \tag{18}$$

Raw moments of X_t for the given Δ_t read

$$\mu_t^{(n)\pm} = \sum_{x\in\mathbb{Z}} x^n P_t(x,\pm 1). \tag{19}$$

The moments (19) can be obtained from

$$\mu_t^{(n)\pm} = \left.\frac{d^n G_t^\pm(z)}{dz^n}\right|_{z=1}. \tag{20}$$

Using (20), (18), one readily gets

$$\begin{aligned} \mu_t^{(1)+} = -\mu_t^{(1)-} &= \frac{p}{4-4p}(1-(2p-1)^t), \\ \mu_t^{(2)+} = \mu_t^{(2)-} &= \frac{p^2}{4(1-p)^2}\left(-1 + \frac{2(1-p)}{p}t + (2p-1)^t\right). \end{aligned} \tag{21}$$

Then, the expectation M_{X_t} and the dispersion D_{X_t} of the marginal distribution (10), which are given by

$$M_{X_t} = \sum_{x \in \mathbb{Z}} x P_t(x), \qquad D_{X_t} = \sum_{x \in \mathbb{Z}} (x - M_{X_t})^2 P_t(x), \tag{22}$$

read

$$M_{X_t} = 0, \qquad D_{X_t} = \frac{p^2}{2(1-p)^2}\left(-1 + \frac{2(1-p)}{p}t + (2p-1)^t\right), \qquad t = \overline{0, \infty}. \tag{23}$$

While the Formula (18) is convenient for the derivation of moments, it does not allow one to directly obtain the distribution (10). The explicit representation of the probability generating function as the power series in z is a bit tricky. The analytical form for the marginal distribution (10) is given by the following theorem.

Theorem 1. *The marginal distribution $P_t(x)$ reads*

$$P_{2n+1}(2j) = (1-p)p^{2j}(1-2p)^{n-j} P_{n-j}^{(2j,0)}\left[\frac{2p^2}{1-2p} + 1\right], \qquad j = \overline{0, n}; \tag{24}$$

$$P_{2n}(2j) = (1-p)^2 p^{2j}(1-2p)^{n-j-1} \frac{n}{n-j} P_{n-j-1}^{(2j,1)}\left[\frac{2p^2}{1-2p} + 1\right], \qquad j = \overline{0, n-1}; \tag{25}$$

$$P_{2n}(2j+1) = (1-p)p^{2j+1}(1-2p)^{n-j-1} P_{n-j-1}^{(2j+1,0)}\left[\frac{2p^2}{1-2p} + 1\right], \qquad j = \overline{0, n-1}; \tag{26}$$

$$P_{2n+1}(2j+1) = (1-p)^2 p^{2j+1}(1-2p)^{n-j-1} \frac{n+\frac{1}{2}}{n-j} P_{n-j-1}^{(2j+1,1)}\left[\frac{2p^2}{1-2p} + 1\right], \quad j = \overline{0, n-1}; \tag{27}$$

$$\begin{aligned} P_n(n) &= \frac{1}{2}p^n; \\ P_t(-x) &= P_t(x), \qquad n \in \mathbb{N}. \end{aligned} \tag{28}$$

where $P_n^{\alpha,\beta}[x]$ are the Jacobi polynomials, and $C_n^k = \dfrac{n!}{k!(n-k)!}$ are the binomial coefficients.

For $p = \dfrac{1}{2}$, the Formulae (24)–(27) yield

$$\begin{aligned} P_{2n+1}(2j) &= 2^{-2n} C_{2n}^{j+n}, \qquad j = \overline{0, n}; \\ P_{2n}(2j) &= 2^{-2n} C_{2n}^{j+n}, \qquad j = \overline{0, n-1} \\ P_{2n}(2j+1) &= 2^{-2n+1} C_{2n-1}^{j+n}, \qquad j = \overline{0, n-1} \\ P_{2n+1}(2j+1) &= 2^{-2n-1} C_{2n+1}^{j+n+1}, \qquad j = \overline{0, n-1}. \end{aligned} \tag{29}$$

The proof of this theorem is given in Appendix A.

6. Discussion of the Results

Now, from (4) and (23), we can obtain the diffusion coefficient $\mathcal{D}_c(p)$:

$$\mathcal{D}_c(p) = \lim_{t \to \infty} \frac{D_{X_t}}{2t} = \frac{1}{2}\frac{p}{1-p}. \tag{30}$$

In Figure 3–5, the probability distribution from (24)–(27) (or (29) for $p = \frac{1}{2}$), and (28) is plotted along with the following normal probability distribution:

$$f_t(x) = \sqrt{\frac{1-p}{2t\pi p}} \exp\left(-\frac{(1-p)x^2}{2tp}\right). \tag{31}$$

Note that in view of (3), (4) the distribution $P_t(x)$ tends to $f_t(x)$ as $t \to \infty$ at least for $p \in [0; \frac{1}{2}]$. The moments of the normal distribution (31) are given by (30), (23).

From Figures 3 and 4, it is clear that the distribution is very close the normal one even for small t.

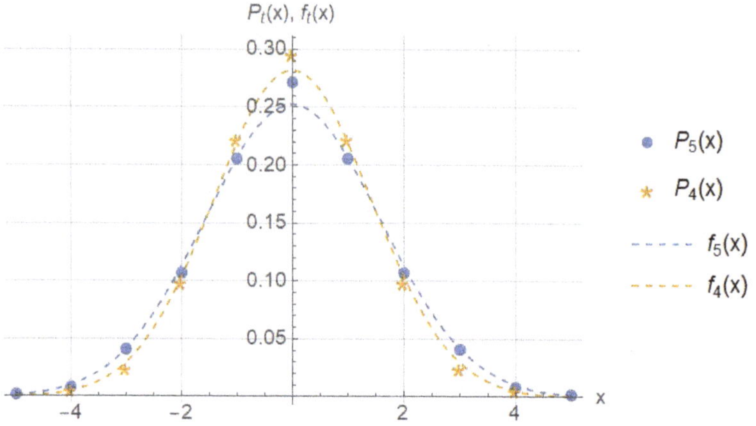

(**a**) For $t = 5$ and $t = 4$

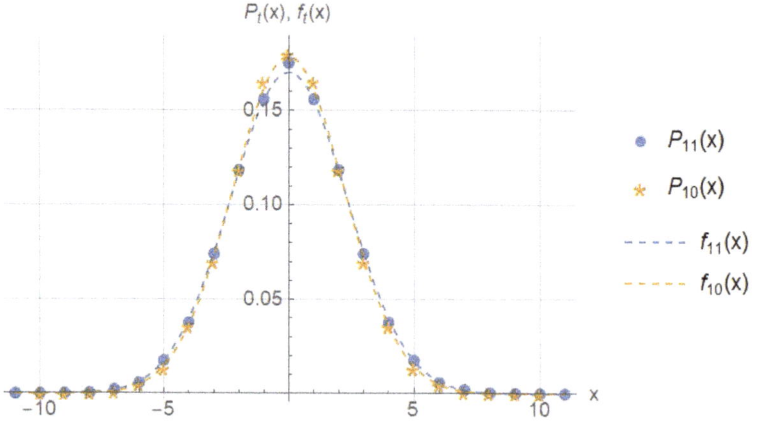

(**b**) For $t = 11$ and $t = 10$

Figure 3. The plot of the probability distribution $P_t(x)$ along with the plot of the normal probability distribution function $f_t(x)$ for $p = \dfrac{1}{3}$.

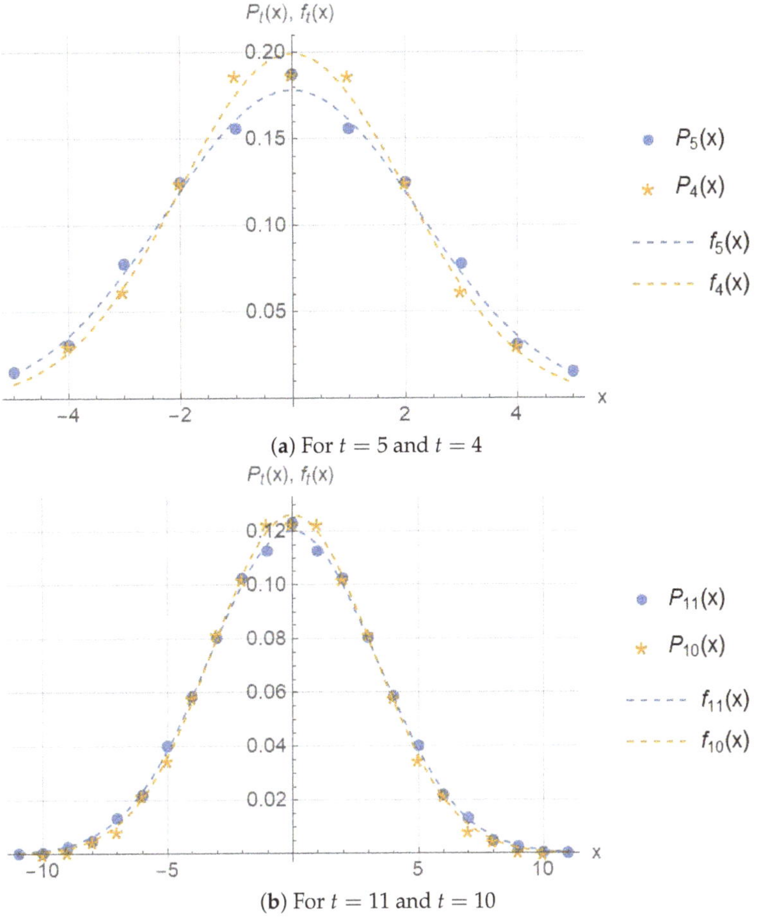

Figure 4. The plot of the probability distribution $P_t(x)$ along with the plot of the normal probability distribution $f_t(x)$ for $p = \frac{1}{2}$.

Note that the probability $p > \frac{1}{2}$ does not make sense for MCA. However, the definition (5) of the two-dimensional Markov chain under consideration admits $p \in (0;1)$ ($p = 0$ and $p = 1$ are trivial cases), and Theorem 1 holds for $p \in (0;1)$. For completeness, we have shown the probability distribution for $p > \frac{1}{2}$ in Figure 5. Apart from the fact that $p > \frac{1}{2}$ has no physical meaning regarding the diffusion, we can note that the probability distribution $P_t(x)$ is a nonmonotonic function with respect to $x \geq 0$ for $p > \frac{1}{2}$.

Next, we will discuss the differences between the two types of MCA mentioned in Section 2. Let the MCA parameterized by p be termed the first type MCA. The second type MCA corresponds to the $p = \frac{1}{2}$ but it is parameterized by p_s. The parameter p_s determines the probability that the rotation *rule* does not applies to any block of the odd and even partition at the next two time steps. In Section 2, we described it as the probability of skipping two consecutive time steps. We will limit ourselves to the simple case when the probability p_s is checked only at odd time steps. Note that p_s corresponds to the global rule while the probability p corresponds to the local *rule* since it is checked for each individual block independently.

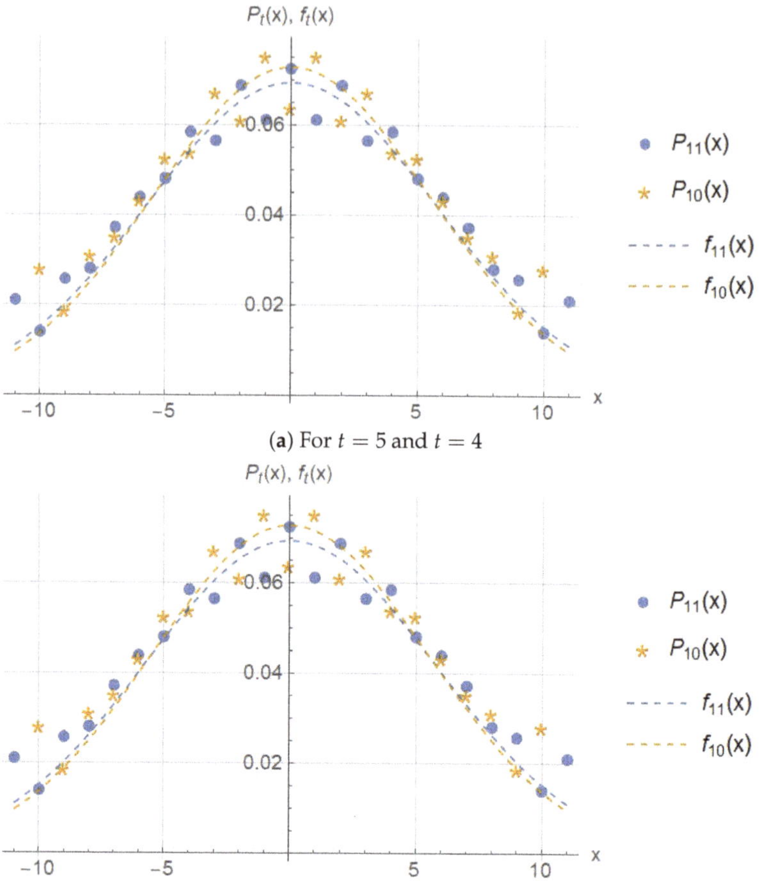

(**a**) For $t = 5$ and $t = 4$

(**b**) For $t = 11$ and $t = 10$

Figure 5. The plot of the probability distribution $P_t(x)$ along with the plot of the normal probability distribution $f_t(x)$ for $p = \frac{3}{4}$.

We have shown that the diffusion coefficient $\mathcal{D}_c(p)$ (30) in the first type MCA nonlinearly depends on p. On the other hand, the diffusion coefficient $\tilde{\mathcal{D}}_c(p_s)$ in the second type MCA linearly depends on p_s and is given as follows:

$$\tilde{\mathcal{D}}_c(p_s) = (1 - p_s)\mathcal{D}_c(0.5). \tag{32}$$

Both of these MCA can be adjusted to the same diffusion coefficient by the appropriate choice of p and p_s, i.e., they have the same macroscopic behaviour at large times. However, they behave differently at small times t. Since the first and the third moments of the distribution given by (24)–(28) equal to zero, the core information about the process behaviour is carried by the dispersion. The behaviour of the first type MCA corresponds to the dispersion $D_{X_t}(p)$ given by (23) while the behaviour of the second type MCA corresponds to the dispersion $\tilde{D}_{X_t}(p_s)$ given by

$$\tilde{D}_{X_t}(p_s) = (1 - p_s) \cdot D_{X_t}(0.5). \tag{33}$$

In Figure 6, the time dependence of $D_{X_t}(p)$ and $\tilde{D}_{X_t}(p_s)$ are shown.

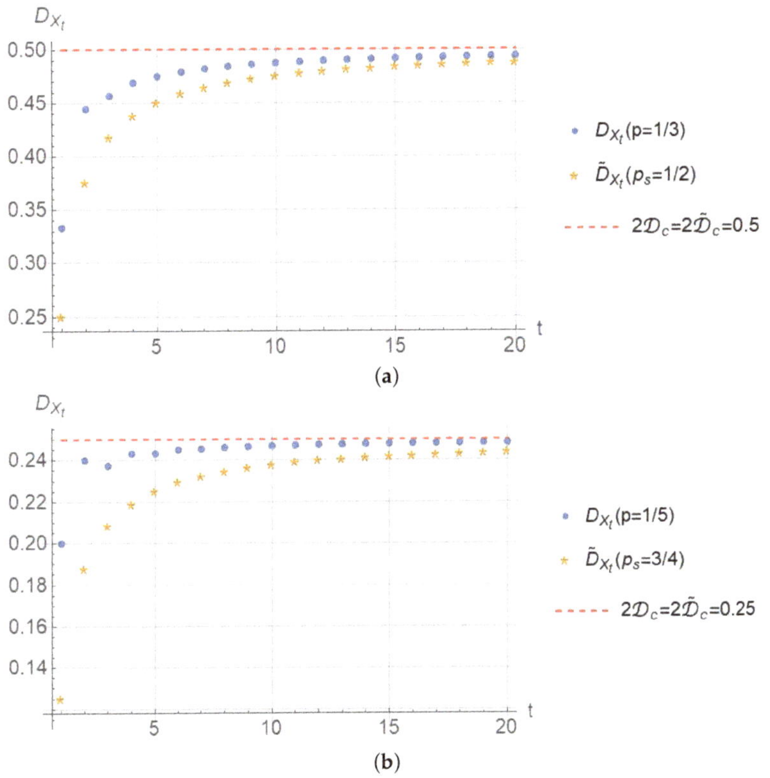

Figure 6. The time plot of the dispersion of the X_t for two types of the MCA. It illustrates the macroscopic behaviour of these MCA at small times. The parameters in (**a**) correspond to MCA with the diffusion coefficient of 0.25, and the parameters in (**b**) correspond to MCA with the diffusion coefficient of 0.125.

We see that the dispersion $D_{X_t}(p)$ tends to its large time asymptotic value faster than $\tilde{D}_{X_t}(p_s)$. Moreover, for small t, it is also much closer to this value that determines the diffusion coefficient in MCA especially for $p < \frac{1}{2}$. It means that the first type MCA shows its macroscopic diffusion behaviour at smaller t. That can be treated as a better time resolution of such MCA. Note that the comparison of the dispersions yields a lower estimate for the time resolution since we do not take into account correlation between the movement of different particles in MCA. However, there is a reason to believe that this correlation is even higher for the second type MCA with $p_s \neq 1$ since the skipping of the two consecutive time steps is performed for the whole cellular grid as opposite to the first type MCA, where it is checked for the every block whether it rotates or not on the current time step. Hence, the difference mentioned above may be even greater than one obtained from our estimates.

Let us compare our analytical results with some empirical results of other authors.

In [20], the author has compared the results of modelling with MCA and solutions of PDE numerically. The diffusion coefficient $\mathcal{D}_c(0.5) = 0.512$ was obtained. The error of 5% was declared in [20]. Their numerical results agrees with the exact value of 0.5 obtained in this work.

In [23], the authors have empirically obtained the dependence of $\mathcal{D}_c(p)$ (in relative units) on p. They constructed the following regression model for this dependence:

$$p = -0.35\left(\frac{\mathcal{D}_c(p)}{\mathcal{D}_c(0.5)}\right)^2 + 0.86\frac{\mathcal{D}_c(p)}{\mathcal{D}_c(0.5)}. \tag{34}$$

Their experimental values for (34) fit well to the curve (30) taking into account the inaccuracy of their method of matching the solutions of MCA and PDE. Hence, they could obtain the regression model that is close to the exact formula if they would use the rational function approximation, which is widely used in many applications [25], instead of the polynomial model.

Note that along with the MCA with the Boolean alphabet the one with the integer alphabet is also used [7,26]. Such approach allows one to lower the concentration noise [27] when modelling reaction–diffusion systems. In order to control the diffusion coefficient independently of reaction rates in such MCA, the rotation *rule* applies not to the whole integer value but to its percentage. Applying the rotation *rule* to the percentage of *particles* is equivalent to the changing the block rotation probability p by the same factor in terms of the diffusion coefficient. Thus, the dependence of the diffusion coefficient on the percentage ξ of *particles* that are involved in the rotation has the same form as the dependence (30) up to changing $\xi = 2p$.

We should note that, in some works related to the multicomponent MCA, reseachers falsely suppose that the dependence $\mathcal{D}_c(p)$ should be linear for a wide range of p. This assumption originates from the work [28], where the authors claimed that $\mathcal{D}_c(p)$ is linear on p even when the rotation probability is independent for each block. Our exact analytical Formula (30) shows that the linear approximation is inaccurate when p is substantially lower than $\frac{1}{2}$. Note that it also agrees with the cited numerical results [23].

7. Conclusions

We have considered the one-parameter stochastic process describing the one-dimensional movement (projection on the x-axis) of a single particle in two-dimensional MCA. In order to find the distribution of the x-coordinate of the particle at every discrete time step (the probability distribution of the random variable X_t), we have introduced the additional random variable Δ_t associated with the direction of the movement of the particle. Using our approach, we have reduced this process to the two-dimensional Markov chain of X_t and Δ_t and have obtained the desired distribution by the probability generating function method. In particular, we have derived the analytic formula for the probability distribution (Theorem 1) and for two first moments (23) of X_t. The probability distribution is expressed in compact form in terms of Jacobi polynomials.

The primary results of this work are the Theorem 1 and Formula (30). The Formula (30) gives the diffusion coefficient of the one-parameter two-dimensional MCA. It establishes the correspondence between the cellular automaton model of the diffusion and the kinetic theory. Note that in our formalist diffusion coefficient is given by the asymptotic behaviour of the dispersion of X_t for the distribution under consideration. It is shown that the Formula (30) agrees with earlier empirical results of other authors in the specified cases. Since the diffusion rate of real substances is usually given by their diffusion coefficient, the Formula (30) is an important mathematical result for modelling the diffusion using MCA. Theorem 1 gives the probability distribution of a single particle in MCA that is given by the exact solutions to the two-dimensional Markov chain (7), (8), while (30) is of main applied interest, Theorem 1 is a more general fundamental result. It allows us to study specific features of various realizations of MCA discussed in Section 6. Moreover, the exactly solvable two-dimensional Markov chain are also valuable for the fundamental mathematics. In view of Theorem 1, the empirically proven fact that MCA describes the diffusion can be presented as a specific property of Jacobi polynomials (see Figures 3 and 4).

Due to the potential interest of Theorem 1 for other applications, it is worth studying other properties of the process under consideration. Note that the formulae derived in this work are valid for the range $p \in (0;1)$ while only $p \in (0;\frac{1}{2})$ have a physical meaning in MCA. Therefore, the more detailed study of this process for the parameter $p \in (\frac{1}{2};1)$ is planned in a separate future work. Furthermore, it is of interest to generalize our approach for the three-dimensional MCA, especially the Formula (30).

Author Contributions: Conceptualization, A.E.K. and A.V.S.; methodology, A.E.K. and A.V.S.; validation, A.E.K. and A.V.S.; formal analysis, A.E.K. and A.V.S.; investigation, A.E.K. and A.V.S.; writing—original draft preparation, A.E.K. and A.V.S.; writing—review and editing, A.E.K. and A.V.S.; visualization, A.E.K. All authors have read and agreed to the published version of the manuscript.

Funding: This research received no external funding.

Institutional Review Board Statement: Not applicable.

Informed Consent Statement: Not applicable.

Data Availability Statement: Not applicable.

Acknowledgments: We are thankful to M.L. Gromov and N.A. Shalyapina for stimulating discussions.

Conflicts of Interest: The authors declare no conflict of interest.

Appendix A. Proof of Theorem 1

Let us write the probability generating function (18) as

$$\begin{aligned} G_t^+(z,t) &= \frac{1}{2^{t+1}m(z)}\Big[-\lambda\big[(q(z)+m(z))^{t-1}-(q(z)-m(z))^{t-1}\big]+ \\ &\quad +2(1-p+pz)\Big((q(z)+m(z))^t-(q(z)-m(z))^t\Big)\Big], \\ G_t^-(z,t) &= \frac{1}{2^{t+1}m(z)}\Big[(q(z)+m(z))^{t+1}-(q(z)-m(z))^{t+1}+ \\ &\quad +2(1-p-pz)\Big((q(z)+m(z))^t-(q(z)-m(z))^t\Big)\Big], \end{aligned} \tag{A1}$$

where $q(z) = p\left(z+\frac{1}{z}\right)$, $\lambda = 4(2p-1)$, and $m(z)$ is defined in (17). Next, we use the following properties:

$$\begin{aligned} (q+m)^t+(q-m)^t &= \begin{cases} 2\sum\limits_{k=0}^{n} C_{2n}^{2k} q^{2k} m^{2n-2k}, & t=2n, \\ 2\sum\limits_{k=0}^{n} C_{2n+1}^{2k+1} q^{2k+1} m^{2n-2k}, & t=2n+1, \end{cases} \\ \frac{(q+m)^t-(q-m)^t}{m} &= \begin{cases} 2\sum\limits_{k=0}^{n-1} C_{2n}^{2k+1} q^{2k+1} m^{2n-2k-2}, & t=2n, \\ 2\sum\limits_{k=0}^{n} C_{2n+1}^{2k} q^{2k} m^{2n-2k}, & t=2n+1, \end{cases} \end{aligned} \tag{A2}$$

and arrive at the following formulae:

$$
\begin{aligned}
G^{+}_{2n+1}(z) &= \frac{1}{2^{2n+1}}\Big\{-\lambda\sum_{j=0}^{n-1} q(z)^{2(n-j)-1} m(z)^{2j} C^{2j+1}_{2n} + \\
&+2(1-p+pz)\sum_{j=0}^{n} q(z)^{2(n-j)} m(z)^{2j} C^{2j+1}_{2n+1}\Big\},\\
G^{+}_{2n}(z) &= \frac{1}{2^{2n}}\Big\{-\lambda\sum_{j=0}^{n-1} q(z)^{2j} m(z)^{2(n-1-j)} C^{2j}_{2n-1} + \\
&+2(1-p+pz)\sum_{j=0}^{n-1} q(z)^{2j+1} m(z)^{2(n-j)-2} C^{2j+1}_{2n}\Big\},\\
G^{-}_{2n+1}(z) &= \frac{1}{2^{2n+1}}\Big\{\sum_{j=0}^{n} q(z)^{2(n-j)+1} m(z)^{2j} C^{2j+1}_{2n+2} + \\
&+2(1-p-pz)\sum_{j=0}^{n} q(z)^{2(n-j)} m(z)^{2j} C^{2j+1}_{2n+1}\Big\},\\
G^{-}_{2n}(z) &= \frac{1}{2^{2n}}\Big\{\sum_{j=0}^{n} q(z)^{2j} m(z)^{2(n-j)} C^{2j}_{2n+1} + \\
&+2(1-p-pz)\sum_{j=0}^{n-1} q(z)^{2j+1} m(z)^{2(n-j)-2} C^{2j+1}_{2n}\Big\}.
\end{aligned}
\tag{A3}
$$

Using the relation $m^2(z) = q^2(z) - \lambda$, the binomial theorem, and changing the order of summation, we transform (A3) to the power series in $q(z)$:

$$
\begin{aligned}
G^{+}_{2n+1}(z) &= \frac{1}{2^{2n+1}}\Big\{\sum_{k=0}^{n-1} q(z)^{2(n-k)-1}(-1)^{k+1}\lambda^{k+1}R(n-1,k) + \\
&+2(1-p+pz)\sum_{k=0}^{n} q(z)^{2(n-k)}(-1)^{k}\lambda^{k}Q(n,k)\Big\},\\
G^{+}_{2n}(z) &= \frac{1}{2^{2n}}\Big\{\sum_{k=0}^{n-1} q(z)^{2(n-k-1)}(-1)^{k+1}\lambda^{k+1}Q(n-1,k) + \\
&+2(1-p+pz)\sum_{k=0}^{n-1} q(z)^{2(n-k)-1}(-1)^{k}\lambda^{k}R(n-1,k)\Big\},\\
G^{-}_{2n+1}(z) &= \frac{1}{2^{2n+1}}\Big\{\sum_{k=0}^{n} q(z)^{2(n-k)+1}(-1)^{k}\lambda^{k}R(n,k) + \\
&+2(1-p-pz)\sum_{k=0}^{n} q(z)^{2(n-k)}(-1)^{k}\lambda^{k}Q(n,k)\Big\},\\
G^{-}_{2n}(z) &= \frac{1}{2^{2n}}\Big\{\sum_{k=0}^{n} q(z)^{2(n-k)}(-1)^{k}\lambda^{k}Q(n,k) + \\
&+2(1-p-pz)\sum_{k=0}^{n-1} q(z)^{2(n-k)-1}(-1)^{k}\lambda^{k}R(n-1,k)\Big\},
\end{aligned}
\tag{A4}
$$

where the numbers Q, R are given by

$$
\begin{gathered}
R(n,k) = \sum_{j=0}^{n-k} C^{2j+1}_{2n+2} C^{k}_{n-j}, \qquad Q(n,k) = \sum_{j=0}^{n-k} C^{2j}_{2n+1} C^{k}_{n-j},\\
R(n,-1) = Q(n,-1) \equiv 0.
\end{gathered}
\tag{A5}
$$

Using the binomial theorem for the power of $q(z)$, changing the order of summation, in view of (13), we obtain the following identities:

$$\begin{aligned} G_{2n+1}(z) &= \frac{1}{2^{2n+2}}\Big\{ \sum_{j=0}^{n} \Big(\sum_{l=j}^{n} p^{2l+1} a_{n,l} C_{2l+1}^{l-j} \Big) z^{2j+1} + \\ &+ \sum_{j=-n-1}^{-1} \Big(\sum_{l=-j-1}^{n} p^{2l+1} a_{n,l} C_{2l+1}^{l-j} \Big) z^{2j+1} + \\ &+ 4(1-p) \sum_{j=-n}^{n} \Big(\sum_{l=|j|}^{n} p^{2l} b_{n,l} C_{2l}^{l-j} \Big) z^{2j} \Big\}, \\ G_{2n}(z) &= \frac{1}{2^{2n+1}}\Big\{ \sum_{j=-n}^{n} \Big(\sum_{l=|j|}^{n} p^{2l} r_{n,l} C_{2l}^{l-j} \Big) z^{2j} + \\ &+ 4(1-p) \sum_{j=0}^{n-1} \Big(\sum_{l=j}^{n-1} p^{2l+1} d_{n-1,l} C_{2l+1}^{l-j} \Big) z^{2j+1} + \\ &+ 4(1-p) \sum_{j=-n}^{-1} \Big(\sum_{l=-j-1}^{n-1} p^{2l+1} d_{n-1,l} C_{2l+1}^{l-j} \Big) z^{2j+1} \Big\}, \end{aligned} \tag{A6}$$

where

$$\begin{aligned} a_{n,l} &= (-1)^{n-l} \lambda^{n-l} \big[R(n-1, n-1-l) + R(n, n-l) \big], \\ b_{n,l} &= (-1)^{n-l} \lambda^{n-l} Q(n, n-l), \\ r_{n,l} &= (-1)^{n-l} \lambda^{n-l} \big[Q(n-1, n-1-l) + Q(n, n-l) \big], \\ d_{n,l} &= (-1)^{n-l} \lambda^{n-l} R(n, n-l). \end{aligned} \tag{A7}$$

In view of (11), we have

$$\begin{aligned} P_{2n}(2j) &= \frac{1}{2^{2n+1}} \sum_{l=j}^{n} p^{2l} r_{n,l} C_{2l}^{l-j}, \qquad j = \overline{0,n}; \\ P_{2n}(2j+1) &= \frac{1-p}{2^{2n-1}} \sum_{l=j}^{n-1} p^{2l+1} d_{n-1,l} C_{2l+1}^{l-j}, \qquad j = \overline{0,n-1}; \\ P_{2n+1}(2j) &= \frac{1-p}{2^{2n}} \sum_{l=j}^{n} p^{2l} b_{n,l} C_{2l}^{l-j}, \qquad j = \overline{0,n}; \\ P_{2n+1}(2j+1) &= \frac{1}{2^{2n+2}} \sum_{l=j}^{n} p^{2l+1} a_{n,l} C_{2l+1}^{l-j}, \qquad j = \overline{0,n}. \end{aligned} \tag{A8}$$

In order to simplify (A8), let us prove the lemma below.

Lemma A1. *The following relation holds true:*

$$\sum_{j=0}^{n-k} C_{2n+1}^{2j} C_{n-j}^{k} = 2^{2(n-k)} C_{2n-k}^{k}. \tag{A9}$$

Proof. Let us define

$$T(n,k,j) = C_{2n+2}^{2j+1} C_{n-j}^{k} = \frac{(2n+1)!}{(2j)!(2n-2j+1)!} \frac{(n-j)!}{k!(n-j-k)!}. \tag{A10}$$

Using the relation [29]

$$(2n)! = 1^{\overline{2n}} = 4^n \left(\frac{1}{2}\right)^{\overline{n}} 1^{\overline{j}}, \tag{A11}$$

where $x^{\overline{n}}$ is the Pochhammer function (upper factorial), one readily gets

$$T(n,k,j) = (-1)^j \frac{\left(-n - \frac{1}{2}\right)^{\overline{j}} n!}{\left(\frac{1}{2}\right)^{\overline{j}} j!k!(n-j-k)!}. \tag{A12}$$

Then, we have

$$Q(n,k) = \sum_{j=0}^{n-k} T(n,k,j) = C_n^k \cdot {}_2F_1\left[k-n, -n-\frac{1}{2}, \frac{1}{2}, 1\right]. \tag{A13}$$

Here, we have used the formula

$$\sum_{j=0}^{n} C_n^k (-1)^j \frac{a^{\overline{j}}}{b^{\overline{j}}} z^n = {}_2F_1[-n, a, b, z], \tag{A14}$$

where ${}_2F_1[m,a,b,z]$ is the hypergeometric function [30,31].
The Gauss summation theorem yields

$${}_2F_1\left[k-n, -n-\frac{1}{2}, \frac{1}{2}, 1\right] = \frac{\Gamma\left[\frac{1}{2}\right]\Gamma[1+2n-k]}{\Gamma\left[\frac{1}{2}+n-k\right]\Gamma[1+n]} = 2^{2(n-k)} \frac{(2n-k)!(n-k)!}{(2n-2k)!n!}, \tag{A15}$$

where $\Gamma[x]$ is the gamma function. Then, (A13) and (A15) yield (A9). □

Corollary A1. *The numbers $Q(n,k)$ and $R(n,k)$ given by (A5) can be generalized to the functions of a half-integer n that are related as follows:*

$$R(n,k) = Q(n+\frac{1}{2}, k). \tag{A16}$$

Proof. From (A5) and Lemma A1, we have

$$Q(n,k) = 2^{2(n-k)} C_{2n-k}^k. \tag{A17}$$

In a similar way, one can derive the formula

$$R(n,k) = 2^{2(n-k)+1} C_{2n-k+1}^k, \tag{A18}$$

Assuming n to be a half-integer number, one readily gets (A16) from (A17) and (A18). □

Let us consider $P_{2n+1}(2j)$ from (A8). In view of (A9), (A16), and (A7), substituting $l = n-k$, we obtain

$$P_{2n+1}(2j) = (1-p)p^{2j}(1-2p)^{j-n} \sum_{k=0}^{n-j} (-1)^k \left(\frac{p^2}{2p-1}\right)^k \frac{(n+k+j)!}{k!(2j+k)!(n-j-k)!}. \tag{A19}$$

Using (A14), we arrive at

$$P_{2n+1}(2j) = (1-p)p^{2j}(1-2p)^{n-j}C_{j+n}^{2j} \cdot {}_2F_1\left[j-n, 1+j+n, 1+2j, \tfrac{p^2}{2p-1}\right], \quad j = \overline{0,n}. \tag{A20}$$

In a similar way, one readily gets

$$P_{2n}(2j) = \frac{1}{2}p^{2j}(1-2p)^{n-j}\left(C_{j+n}^{2j} \cdot {}_2F_1\left[j-n, 1+j+n, 1+2j, \frac{p^2}{2p-1}\right] + \right.$$
$$\left. + C_{n+j-1}^{2j} \cdot {}_2F_1\left[j-n+1, j+n, 1+2j, \tfrac{p^2}{2p-1}\right]\right), \qquad j = \overline{0, n-1};$$

$$P_{2n}(2j+1) = (1-p)p^{2j+1}(1-2p)^{n-j-1}C_{j+n}^{2j+1} \times$$
$$\times {}_2F_1\left[j-n+1, 1+j+n, 2+2j, \tfrac{p^2}{2p-1}\right], \qquad j = \overline{0, n-1}; \tag{A21}$$

$$P_{2n+1}(2j+1) = \frac{1}{2}p^{2j+1}(1-2p)^{n-j} \times$$
$$\times \left(C_{j+n}^{2j+1} \cdot {}_2F_1\left[j-n+1, 1+j+n, 2+2j, \tfrac{p^2}{2p-1}\right] + \right.$$
$$\left. + C_{j+n+1}^{2j+1} \cdot {}_2F_1\left[j-n, 2+j+n, 2+2j, \tfrac{p^2}{2p-1}\right]\right), \qquad j = \overline{0, n-1}.$$

Finally, using the identities [32]

$$P_n^{(\alpha,\beta)}(z) = \frac{(\alpha+1)^{\overline{n}}}{n!} \cdot {}_2F_1\left[-n, 1+\alpha+\beta+n, \alpha+1, \frac{1}{2}(1-z)\right],$$
$$\frac{n+\frac{1}{2}\alpha+1}{n+1}(1+x)P_n^{(\alpha,1)}(x) = P_{n+1}^{(\alpha,0)}(x) + P_n^{(\alpha,0)}(x), \tag{A22}$$

we arrive at the formulae (24), (25), (26), (27).

The probability $P_n(n)$ (28) can be readily obtained if one notice that the special case $X_t = t$ for the given $t > 0$ is equivalent to $\Delta_t = +1 \; \forall t \in \mathbb{N}$.

For $p = \frac{1}{2}$, (18) and (13) yield

$$G_t(z) = 2^{-t}\left(\frac{1}{z} + 2 + z\right)\sum_{k=0}^{t-1} C_{t-1}^k s^{2k-t+1}, \qquad t \in \mathbb{N}. \tag{A23}$$

From (A23) and (11), we have (29).

References

1. Wolfram, S. *A New Kind of Science*; Wolfram Media: Champaign, IL, USA, 2002.
2. Palchaudhuri, A.; Anand, D.; Dhar, A. FPGA fabric conscious architecture design and automation of speed-area efficient Margolus neighborhood based cellular automata with variegated scan path insertion. *J. Parallel Distrib. Comput.* **2022**, *167*, 50–63. [CrossRef]
3. Cicuttin, A.; De Micco, L.; Crespo, M.; Antonelli, M.; Garcia, L.; Florian, W. Physical implementation of asynchronous cellular automata networks: mathematical models and preliminary experimental results. *Nonlinear Dyn.* **2021**, *105*, 2431–2452. [CrossRef]
4. Cagigas-Muñiz, D.; Diaz-del Rio, F.; Sevillano-Ramos, J.; Guisado-Lizar, J.L. Efficient simulation execution of cellular automata on GPU. *Simul. Model. Pract. Theory* **2022**, *118*, 102519. [CrossRef]
5. Matolygin, A.; Shalyapina, N.; Gromov, M.; Torgaev, S. Tensor approach to software implementation of cellular automata model of diffusion. *J. Phys.: Conf. Ser.* **2020**, *1680*, 012035. [CrossRef]
6. Toffoli, T.; Margolus, N. *Cellular Automata Machines: A New Environment for Modeling*; MIT Press: Cambridge, MA, USA, 1987; p. 276.

7. Kireeva, A.; Sabelfeld, K.K.; Kireev, S. Synchronous multi-particle cellular automaton model of diffusion with self-annihilation. In *Parallel Computing Technologies*; Lecture Notes in Computer Science (Including Subseries Lecture Notes in Artificial Intelligence and Lecture Notes in Bioinformatics); Springer: Cham, Switzerland, 2019; Volume 11657, pp. 345–359. [CrossRef]
8. Fick, A. On liquid diffusion. J Membr Sci. *J. Membr. Sci.* **1995**, *100*, 33–38. [CrossRef]
9. Paul, A.; Laurila, T.; Vuorinen, V.; Divinski, S. Fick's Laws of Diffusion. In *Thermodynamics, Diffusion and the Kirkendall Effect in Solids*; Springer: Cham, Switzerland, 2014; pp. 115–139. [CrossRef]
10. Shapovalov, A.; Kulagin, A. Semiclassical approach to the nonlocal kinetic model of metal vapor active media. *Mathematics* **2021**, *9*, 2995. [CrossRef]
11. Shapovalov, A.; Kulagin, A.; Siniukov, S. Family of Asymptotic Solutions to the Two-Dimensional Kinetic Equation with a Nonlocal Cubic Nonlinearity. *Symmetry* **2022**, *14*, 577. [CrossRef]
12. Odintsov, S. Editorial for Feature Papers 2021–2022. *Symmetry* **2022**, *15*, 32. [CrossRef]
13. Mickens, R. Nonstandard finite difference schemes for reaction–diffusion equations having linear advection. *Numer. Methods Partial Differ. Equations* **2000**, *16*, 361–364. [CrossRef]
14. Pankov, P.; Zheentaeva, Z.; Shirinov, T. Asymptotic reduction of solution space dimension for dynamic systems. *TWMS J. Pure Appl. Math.* **2021**, *12*, 243–253.
15. Shokri, A. The multistep multiderivative methods for the numerical solution of first order initial value problems. *TWMS J. Pure Appl. Math.* **2016**, *7*, 88–97.
16. Rachinskaya, M.; Fedotkin, M. Research of a multidimensional Markov Chain as a model for the class of queueing systems controlled by a threshold priority algorithm. *Reliab. Theory Appl.* **2018**, *13*, 47–58.
17. Ching, W.K.; Fung, E.S.; Ng, M.K. Higher-order Markov chain models for categorical data sequences. *Nav. Res. Logist.* **2004**, *51*, 557–574. [CrossRef]
18. Morzfeldi, M.; Tong, X.T.; Marzouk, Y.M. Localization for MCMC: Sampling high-dimensional posterior distributions with local structure. *J. Comput. Phys.* **2019**, *380*, 1–28. [CrossRef]
19. Ching, W.K.; Ng, M.K.; Fung, E.S. Higher-order multivariate Markov chains and their applications. *Linear Algebra Its Appl.* **2008**, *428*, 492–507. [CrossRef]
20. Bandman, O.L. Comparative study of cellular-automata diffusion models. *Parallel Comput. Technol.* **1999**, *1662*, 395–409. [CrossRef]
21. Malinetskii, G.G.; Stepantsov, M.E. Modeling of diffusion processes by cellular automata with Margolus neighborhood. *Comput. Math. Math. Phys.* **1998**, *38*, 973–975.
22. Bandman, O.L. Invariants of cellular automata models for reaction-diffusion processes. *Appl. Discret. Math.* **2012**, *3*, 108–120. (In Russian) [CrossRef]
23. Shalyapina, N.; Gromov, M.; Matolygin, A.; Torgaev, S. Empirical dependence of the probability of blocks rotations on the diffusion coefficient in a cellular automaton with a Margolus neighbourhood. *J. Phys. Conf. Ser.* **2021**, *2140*, 012031. [CrossRef]
24. Nelson, R. *Probability, Stochastic Processes, and Queueing Theory*; Springer: New York, NY, USA, 1995. [CrossRef]
25. Gluzman, S. Padé and Post-Padé Approximations for Critical Phenomena. *Symmetry* **2020**, *12*, 1600. [CrossRef]
26. Medvedev, Y. Multi-particle cellular-automata models for diffusion simulation. In *Methods and Tools of Parallel Programming Multicomputers*; Lecture Notes in Computer Science; Springer: Berlin/Heidelberg, Germany, 2010, Volume 6083, pp. 204–211. [CrossRef]
27. Bandman, O.L. Computation properties of spatial dynamics simulation by probabilistic cellular automata. *Future Gener. Comput. Syst.* **2005**, *21*, 633–643. [CrossRef]
28. Chopard, B.; Frachebourg, L.; Droz, M. Multiparticle lattice gas automata for reaction diffusion systems. *Int. J. Mod. Phys. C* **1994**, *5*, 47–63. [CrossRef]
29. Bateman, H.; Erdélyi, A. *Higher Transcendental Functions*; McGraw-Hill: New York, NY, USA, 1953; Volume 1.
30. Srivastava, H.M. A Survey of Some Recent Developments on Higher Transcendental Functions of Analytic Number Theory and Applied Mathematics. *Symmetry* **2021**, *13*, 2294. [CrossRef]
31. Srivastava, H.M. Some Families of Generating Functions Associated with Orthogonal Polynomials and Other Higher Transcendental Functions. *Mathematics* **2022**, *10*, 3730. [CrossRef]
32. Bateman, H.; Erdélyi, A. *Higher Transcendental Functions*; McGraw-Hill: New York, NY, USA, 1953; Volume 2.

Disclaimer/Publisher's Note: The statements, opinions and data contained in all publications are solely those of the individual author(s) and contributor(s) and not of MDPI and/or the editor(s). MDPI and/or the editor(s) disclaim responsibility for any injury to people or property resulting from any ideas, methods, instructions or products referred to in the content.

mathematics

MDPI

Article

Highly Accurate and Efficient Time Integration Methods with Unconditional Stability and Flexible Numerical Dissipation

Yi Ji [1,*] and Yufeng Xing [2,*]

1 MOE Key Laboratory of Dynamics and Control of Flight Vehicle, School of Aerospace Engineering, Beijing Institute of Technology, Beijing 100081, China
2 Institute of Solid Mechanics, Beihang University, Beijing 100083, China
* Correspondence: jiyi0319@outlook.com (Y.J.); xingyf@buaa.edu.cn (Y.X.)

Abstract: This paper constructs highly accurate and efficient time integration methods for the solution of transient problems. The motion equations of transient problems can be described by the first-order ordinary differential equations, in which the right-hand side is decomposed into two parts, a linear part and a nonlinear part. In the proposed methods of different orders, the responses of the linear part at the previous step are transferred by the generalized Padé approximations, and the nonlinear part's responses of the previous step are approximated by the Gauss–Legendre quadrature together with the explicit Runge–Kutta method, where the explicit Runge–Kutta method is used to calculate function values at quadrature points. For reducing computations and rounding errors, the 2^m algorithm and the method of storing an incremental matrix are employed in the calculation of the generalized Padé approximations. The proposed methods can achieve higher-order accuracy, unconditional stability, flexible dissipation, and zero-order overshoots. For linear transient problems, the accuracy of the proposed methods can reach 10^{-16} (computer precision), and they enjoy advantages both in accuracy and efficiency compared with some well-known explicit Runge–Kutta methods, linear multi-step methods, and composite methods in solving nonlinear problems.

Keywords: transient problems; generalized Padé approximations; Gauss–Legendre quadrature; high accuracy and efficiency

MSC: 37M05; 37M10; 70E55; 37M15

Citation: Ji, Y.; Xing, Y. Highly Accurate and Efficient Time Integration Methods with Unconditional Stability and Flexible Numerical Dissipation. *Mathematics* **2023**, *11*, 593. https://doi.org/10.3390/math11030593

Academic Editor: Sitnik Sergey

Received: 5 January 2023
Revised: 18 January 2023
Accepted: 20 January 2023
Published: 23 January 2023

Copyright: © 2023 by the authors. Licensee MDPI, Basel, Switzerland. This article is an open access article distributed under the terms and conditions of the Creative Commons Attribution (CC BY) license (https://creativecommons.org/licenses/by/4.0/).

1. Introduction

Owing to the complexity of practical problems, analytical solutions are generally not available for transient analyses, and thus numerical methods are pre-dominantly used to approximate the transient response. In finite element analyses (FEA) of transient problems, time integration methods [1] are widely used. A large number of time integration methods [1–3] have been developed over the last decades, and novel ones are continuously proposed. In commercial finite element software and also in scientific applications that are directed at studying transient problems, the Newmark method [1] and the HHT-α method [1] are popular.

In general, conventional time integration methods can be described as either implicit or explicit methods [1]. Explicit methods are conditionally stable in terms of the algorithm structure, causing an allowable time step size to be severely limited by stability in the simulations of dynamic systems. Implicit methods can achieve unconditional stability for linear systems, but considering that an iteration method is necessary for implicit methods, their computations are more expensive compared with explicit methods in the simulations of nonlinear systems.

For improving the accuracy of traditional single-step implicit methods, such as the Newmark [1], WBZ-α [1], and generalized-α methods [1], composite methods based on the multi-sub-step concept are developed. The composite methods first appeared in the research of Bank and his co-workers [4], wherein they proposed a two-sub-step method consisting of the trapezoidal rule (TR) and the backward difference formula (BDF), and used it to analyze the transient behavior of silicon devices and circuits. Later, the two-sub-step based on TR and BDF was employed to solve structural dynamics by Bathe [5] in 2005, and the composite method was conceptualized. Motived by Bathe's work, composite methods that collect the advantage of the sub-step method attract wide attention and rapid development. The three-sub-step [6,7], four-sub-step [8,9], and five-sub-step [8,9] composite methods based on TR and BDF were constructed to obtain a higher low-frequency accuracy. Due to the use of BDF, the composite methods adopting the combinations of TR and BDF are L-stable (or asymptotically annihilating), meaning that the high-frequency modes are quickly eliminated. For flexibly controlling the amount of high-frequency numerical dissipation, composite methods including TR and backward interpolation formula (BIF) [10–13] have been proposed, such as the ρ_∞-Bathe method [10], the Kim method [11], and the TR-TR-BIF [12]. Among these methods, the TR-TR-BIF [12] proposed by the present authors has been generalized to the dynamic analysis of multibody systems [14] and structures under seismic response [15,16], further showing its superiority in the analysis of transient problems. Recently, composite methods with higher-order accuracy have been constructed [17–19], and they show a considerable advantage in phase accuracy compared with the second-order accurate composite methods.

Some time integration methods that are unconditionally stable for linear systems, such as the trapezoidal rule, may be unstable when applied to nonlinear systems [20,21], promoting the development of energy-conserving methods based on the energy constraint principle [22]. Therefore, different from most time integration methods, the equilibrium equations of motion at discrete time points cannot be satisfied for energy-conserving methods. The designs of most energy-conserving methods [23–25] are for nonlinear geometric systems, and energy-conserving methods can provide stable predictions for such types of transient problems. For dynamic systems, including nonlinear geometric and nonlinear damping terms, few energy-conserving methods, such as the ECM [26], have been constructed. The superiority of energy-conserving methods is that they can strictly keep energy for conservative systems, but they are not suitable for dynamic problems wherein some high-frequency information should be damped out. Additionally, the required modification of energy functions reduces the computational efficiency of this type of method.

To simultaneously improve the efficiency and stability of time integration methods, structure-dependent (or model-based) methods [27–32] were developed. In 2002, Chang proposed an unconditionally stable single-step method (noted as Chang2002) [27] for pseudo-dynamic systems, in which algorithmic parameters closely depend on dynamics characteristics at the initial moment and the selected size of the time step. The Chang2002 method achieves unconditional stability for linearity and stiffness softening systems. Based on the Chang2002 method, some more desirable structure-dependent methods [28–32] were constructed, such as the CR [28], KR [29], and Fu–Zhang methods [32]. Taking into account the properties of the model and the evolution of the computed fields, the locally adaptive time integration methods [33,34] proposed by Soares can reduce the contradiction of accuracy and efficiency. At present, this type of method has been applied in the analysis of wave propagation [35] and thermo-mechanical systems [36].

The emergence of exponential methods by making use of matrix theory reduces the contradiction of time integration methods in accuracy, efficiency, and stability. The so-called precise time integration method (PIM) for linear ordinarily differential equations (ODEs) proposed by Zhong and Williams [37] is a representative work wherein the Taylor series expansion is utilized to obtain the homogeneous solution, and the external excitations are assumed to be piecewise linear, and their contributions are obtained with the convolution integral. Due to the algorithmic structure, the PIM can converge to computer precision for homogeneous equations, and it is conditionally stable. Following the research of Zhong and Williams [37], some improved precise time integrators [38–42] were developed in the past decades, such as the PEC/DMn [41] and the Song method [42]. The PEC/DMn proposed by the present authors possesses the advantages of the PIM in accuracy and efficiency, and it can achieve unconditional stability and exactly controllable dissipation. In addition to using existing time integration methods to approximate the amplification matrix, Song et al. [42] constructed higher-order precise integrators for linear wave propagation problems, in which the responses of the previous time step are transferred by the classical Padé expansion with L-stability, and the external force vectors are calculated based on a least-squares fit of the polynomial functions. An important feature of the higher scheme [42] is that no direct inversion of the mass matrix is required, further reducing its computational costs. At present, some exponential integrators [43–46] for nonlinear initial value problems have been constructed. In the type of methods, the responses of nonlinear terms at the present moment are replaced by the ones of the previous moment [45] or are approximated by the Euler method [43,44,46]. In comparison with traditional methods based on dynamics equilibrium equations, numerical experiments validate that exponential integrators [43–46] show improvements both in accuracy and efficiency in solving nonlinear transient problems.

From the above review, one can find that, in the past decades, various time integration methods have been developed for quickly, accurately, and/or stably solving transient problems. Among these methods, the exponential methods seem to be a superior candidate to fill the gap that stability, accuracy, and efficiency are hard to be simultaneously enhanced. Some exponential methods that are suitable both for linear and nonlinear problems have been applied in the analysis of elastodynamics [44], multibody dynamics [45], and so on, but these methods do not have the order of magnitude improvements in accuracy and/or efficiency compared with those of representative methods, such as the Newmark method and the Runge–Kutta method. In this context, focusing on the first-order linear and nonlinear initial value problems [47], this paper develops a new solution strategy. The combination of the generalized Padé expansion with A-stability [48], the 2^m algorithm, and the technology of storing incremental matrices is used in the calculation of responses of linear parts. The responses of nonlinear parts are approximated by the combination of the Gauss–Legendre quadrature formula and the explicit Runge–Kutta method. The two combinations can ensure that the proposed methods can accurately and quickly compute the responses of transient problems. Numerical experiments validate that when the proposed methods have the same computation as other methods, the accuracy of the proposed methods is greater than or equal to three orders of magnitude. The theoretical analysis finds that the time integration methods can obtain higher-order accuracy, unconditional stability, controllable dissipation, and zero-order overshoots. Therefore, the proposed methods are suitable both for conservative and non-conservative systems due to flexibly controllable numerical properties.

The rest of this work is organized as follows. The procedure of the new strategy is presented in Section 2. The numerical properties of the present methods, including stability, dissipation, accuracy, and overshoot characteristics, are analyzed in Section 3. Numerical experiments are implemented in Section 4. Finally, the conclusions are drawn in Section 5.

2. Basic Idea of the New Strategy

This paper focuses on the physically stable dynamic problems governed by the following first-order ordinary differential equation:

$$\dot{\boldsymbol{y}}(t) = \boldsymbol{H}\boldsymbol{y}(t) + \boldsymbol{f}(\boldsymbol{y}, t), \boldsymbol{y}(t_0) = \boldsymbol{y}_0, \tag{1}$$

where $\boldsymbol{H}$ is a matrix that includes eigenvalues with large negative real parts or with purely imaginary eigenvalues of large modulus [47], and the nonlinear term $\boldsymbol{f}$ is supposed to be a non-stiff satisfying the Lipschitz condition. If the term $\boldsymbol{f}$ only relates to time t, the nonlinear Equation (1) reduces to the linear one. The discretized dynamic system (1) arises in many applications [37–47,49–51], such as structural dynamics [39–41], multibody dynamics [45], molecular dynamics [49], and so on. It is well-known that the general solution [47] of Equation (1) has the form of

$$\boldsymbol{y}_{t+\Delta t} = \mathrm{e}^{\Delta t\boldsymbol{H}}\boldsymbol{y}_t + \int_t^{t+\Delta t} \mathrm{e}^{\Delta t\boldsymbol{H}}\boldsymbol{f}(\boldsymbol{y},\tau)\mathrm{d}\tau := \boldsymbol{A}_{\mathrm{ana}}\boldsymbol{y}_t + \boldsymbol{L}_{\mathrm{ana}}, \tag{2}$$

where the analytical amplification matrix $\boldsymbol{A}_{\mathrm{ana}} = \mathrm{e}^{\Delta t\boldsymbol{H}}$ can transfer the free responses of the previous step, and the forced responses of the current step are computed by the analytical vector $\boldsymbol{L}_{\mathrm{ana}} = \int_t^{t+\Delta t} e^{\Delta t\boldsymbol{H}}\boldsymbol{f}(\boldsymbol{y},\tau)d\tau$. For practical systems, especially for large-scale problems, the computations of the matrix $\boldsymbol{A}_{\mathrm{ana}}$ and the vector $\boldsymbol{L}_{\mathrm{ana}}$ are expensive. The task of this strategy is to quickly construct highly accurate substitutes for $\boldsymbol{A}_{\mathrm{ana}}$ and $\boldsymbol{L}_{\mathrm{ana}}$.

In our work, the generalized Padé approximation [48] that is regarded as the most accurate rational approximation of exp($\Delta t\boldsymbol{H}$) is used to approximate $\boldsymbol{A}_{\mathrm{ana}}$, and the corresponding numerical matrix $\boldsymbol{A}_{\mathrm{num}}$ can be formulated as

$$\boldsymbol{A}_{\mathrm{num}}(\Delta t\boldsymbol{H}) = \bar{\boldsymbol{Q}}^{-1}(\Delta t\boldsymbol{H})\bar{\boldsymbol{P}}(\Delta t\boldsymbol{H}), \tag{3}$$

where

$$\bar{\boldsymbol{Q}}(\Delta t\boldsymbol{H}) = (1-\rho_\infty)\boldsymbol{Q}_{n-1,n}(\Delta t\boldsymbol{H}) + 2\rho_\infty\boldsymbol{Q}_{n,n}(\Delta t\boldsymbol{H}), \bar{\boldsymbol{P}}(\Delta t\boldsymbol{H}) = (1-\rho_\infty)\boldsymbol{P}_{n-1,n}(\Delta t\boldsymbol{H}) + 2\rho_\infty\boldsymbol{P}_{n,n}(\Delta t\boldsymbol{H}), \text{ and} \tag{4}$$

$$\boldsymbol{P}_{i,j}(\Delta t\boldsymbol{H}) = \sum_{p=0}^{i} \frac{i!(j+i-p)!}{(i-p)!(j+i)!p!}(\Delta t\boldsymbol{H})^p, \boldsymbol{Q}_{i,j}(\Delta t\boldsymbol{H}) = \sum_{p=0}^{j} (-1)^p \frac{j!(j+i-p)!}{(j-p)!(j+i)!p!}(\Delta t\boldsymbol{H})^p, (i,j=0,1,2,\ldots). \tag{5}$$

From Equations (3)–(5), one can observe that the generalized Padé approximations are the rational functions with polynomials of degree n in both the numerator and denominator. The generalized Padé approximation has A-stability; in addition, for the case of $0 \le \rho_\infty < 1$, it has $(2n-1)$th-order accuracy and $(2n)$th-order accuracy if $\rho_\infty = 1$. To further improve the accuracy of $\boldsymbol{A}_{\mathrm{num}}(\Delta t\boldsymbol{H})$ given in Equation (3), the 2^m algorithm and storage of incremental matrix technology are used in the preparation of $\boldsymbol{A}_{\mathrm{num}}(\Delta t\boldsymbol{H})$, which is shown below. Applying Equation (5) to Equation (3) can yield

$$\bar{\boldsymbol{Q}}(\Delta t\boldsymbol{H}) = \alpha_0\boldsymbol{I} + \boldsymbol{S}_1(\Delta t\boldsymbol{H}), \bar{\boldsymbol{P}}(\Delta t\boldsymbol{H}) = \beta_0\boldsymbol{I} + \boldsymbol{S}_2(\Delta t\boldsymbol{H}), \text{ and} \tag{6}$$

$$\boldsymbol{S}_1(\Delta t\boldsymbol{H}) = \alpha_1(\Delta t\boldsymbol{H}) + \alpha_2(\Delta t\boldsymbol{H})^2 + \cdots + \alpha_n(\Delta t\boldsymbol{H})^n, \boldsymbol{S}_2(\Delta t\boldsymbol{H}) = \beta_1(\Delta t\boldsymbol{H}) + \beta_2(\Delta t\boldsymbol{H})^2 + \cdots + \beta_n(\Delta t\boldsymbol{H})^n. \tag{7}$$

Then, the matrix $\boldsymbol{A}_{\mathrm{num}}(\Delta t\boldsymbol{H}) = \bar{\boldsymbol{Q}}(\Delta t\boldsymbol{H})^{-1}\bar{\boldsymbol{P}}(\Delta t\boldsymbol{H})$ that is equivalent to $\bar{\boldsymbol{Q}}(\Delta t\boldsymbol{H})\boldsymbol{A}_{\mathrm{num}}(\Delta t\boldsymbol{H}) = \bar{\boldsymbol{P}}(\Delta t\boldsymbol{H})$ can be reformulated as

$$\begin{aligned}
\left[\boldsymbol{I} + \tfrac{1}{\alpha_0}\boldsymbol{S}_1(\Delta t\boldsymbol{H})\right]\boldsymbol{A}_{\mathrm{num}}(\Delta t\boldsymbol{H}) &= \tfrac{\beta_0}{\alpha_0}\left[\boldsymbol{I} + \tfrac{1}{\alpha_0}\boldsymbol{S}_1(\Delta t\boldsymbol{H}) + \tfrac{1}{\beta_0}\boldsymbol{S}_2(\Delta t\boldsymbol{H}) - \tfrac{1}{\alpha_0}\boldsymbol{S}_1(\Delta t\boldsymbol{H})\right] \to \\
\boldsymbol{A}_{\mathrm{num}}(\Delta t\boldsymbol{H}) &= \tfrac{\beta_0}{\alpha_0}\left[\boldsymbol{I} + \left(\boldsymbol{I} + \tfrac{1}{\alpha_0}\boldsymbol{S}_1(\Delta t\boldsymbol{H})\right)^{-1}\left(\tfrac{1}{\beta_0}\boldsymbol{S}_2(\Delta t\boldsymbol{H}) - \tfrac{1}{\alpha_0}\boldsymbol{S}_1(\Delta t\boldsymbol{H})\right)\right] \\
&= \tfrac{\beta_0}{\alpha_0}\left[\boldsymbol{I} + \left(\boldsymbol{I} + \alpha_0\boldsymbol{S}_1(\Delta t\boldsymbol{H})^{-1}\right)^{-1}\boldsymbol{S}_1(\Delta t\boldsymbol{H})^{-1}\left(\tfrac{\alpha_0}{\beta_0}\boldsymbol{S}_2(\Delta t\boldsymbol{H}) - \boldsymbol{S}_1(\Delta t\boldsymbol{H})\right)\right]
\end{aligned}, \tag{8}$$

where the incremental matrix relative to the identity matrix $\boldsymbol{I}$ is defined as $\Delta\boldsymbol{S}(\Delta t\boldsymbol{H})$, as follows:

$$\Delta\boldsymbol{S}(\Delta t\boldsymbol{H}) = \left[\boldsymbol{I} + \alpha_0\boldsymbol{S}_1(\Delta t\boldsymbol{H})^{-1}\right]^{-1}\boldsymbol{S}_1(\Delta t\boldsymbol{H})^{-1}\left[\frac{\alpha_0}{\beta_0}\boldsymbol{S}_2(\Delta t\boldsymbol{H}) - \boldsymbol{S}_1(\Delta t\boldsymbol{H})\right]. \tag{9}$$

The multi-sub-step notion is used to obtain a more accurate $\boldsymbol{A}_{\text{num}}(\Delta t\boldsymbol{H})$. Here, a time step size Δt is divided into $N = 2^m$ parts, leading to

$$\boldsymbol{A}_{\text{num}}(\Delta t\boldsymbol{H}) = \underbrace{\boldsymbol{A}_{\text{num}}(\Delta t_N\boldsymbol{H}) \quad \cdots \quad \boldsymbol{A}_{\text{num}}(\Delta t_N\boldsymbol{H})}_{N} = \boldsymbol{A}_{\text{num}}^N(\Delta t_N\boldsymbol{H}). \tag{10}$$

With the increase of m, the incremental matrix $\Delta\boldsymbol{S}(\Delta t_N\boldsymbol{H})$ is very small compared with the identity matrix $\boldsymbol{I}$, so during the calculation of Equation (10), the $\Delta\boldsymbol{S}(\Delta t_N\boldsymbol{H})$ is stored instead of $\boldsymbol{A}_{\text{num}}(\Delta t_N\boldsymbol{H})$ to reduce rounding errors. It is well-known that

$$(\boldsymbol{I} + \Delta\boldsymbol{S}(\Delta t_N)) \times (\boldsymbol{I} + \Delta\boldsymbol{S}(\Delta t_N)) = \boldsymbol{I} + 2\Delta\boldsymbol{S}(\Delta t_N) + \Delta\boldsymbol{S}(\Delta t_N) \times \Delta\boldsymbol{S}(\Delta t_N). \tag{11}$$

For calculating the matrix $\boldsymbol{A}_{\text{num}}(\Delta t\boldsymbol{H})$, Equation (11) should be iterated m times. Then, the calculation in Equation (10) is equivalent to executing the following statement

$$\begin{array}{c} \text{for } i = 1:1:m \\ \Delta\boldsymbol{S}(\Delta t_N) = 2\Delta\boldsymbol{S}(\Delta t_N) + \Delta\boldsymbol{S}(\Delta t_N) \times \Delta\boldsymbol{S}(\Delta t_N) \\ \text{end} \\ \boldsymbol{A}_{\text{num}}(\Delta t\boldsymbol{H}) = \left(\frac{\beta_0}{\alpha_0}\right)^{2^m}(\boldsymbol{I} + \Delta\boldsymbol{S}(\Delta t_N)) \end{array}. \tag{12}$$

After m times multiplication, the matrix $\Delta\boldsymbol{S}(\Delta t_N\boldsymbol{H})$ is no longer a very small matrix, and the above addition will have no serious numerical round-off error again. To show the accuracy advantage of the method of storing incremental matrix, a simple model is considered here, in which $\boldsymbol{H} = 1$ and $\Delta t = 0.1$. Table 1 provides absolute errors of the method of storing the total matrix and the method of storing the incremental matrix, and one can see that with the increase of m, (a) the former's accuracy firstly increases and then continuously decreases; (b) the errors of the latter trend to zero.

Table 1. Absolute errors of the method of storing total matrix and the method of storing incremental matrix.

	$m = 1$	$m = 10$	$m = 100$	$m = 1000$
Total	0.00267091807564768	$5.39597800242042 \times 10^{-6}$	0.105170918075648	0.105170918075648
increment	0.00267091807564768	$5.39597790183422 \times 10^{-6}$	0	0

Considering that the multi-sub-step notion is employed in the calculation of $\boldsymbol{A}_{\text{num}}(\Delta t\boldsymbol{H})$ for exactly controlling the amount of numerical dissipation via ρ_∞, the matrix $\boldsymbol{A}_{\text{num}}(\Delta t\boldsymbol{H})$ shown in Equation (3) for the case of $N \geq 1$ is reformulated as

$$\boldsymbol{A}_{\text{num}}(\Delta t\boldsymbol{H}) = \left[(1 - \sqrt[N]{\rho_\infty})\boldsymbol{Q}_{n-1,n}(\Delta t\boldsymbol{H}) + 2\sqrt[N]{\rho_\infty}\boldsymbol{Q}_{n,n}(\Delta t\boldsymbol{H})\right]^{-1}\left[(1 - \sqrt[N]{\rho_\infty})\boldsymbol{P}_{n-1,n}(\Delta t\boldsymbol{H}) + 2\sqrt[N]{\rho_\infty}\boldsymbol{P}_{n,n}(\Delta t\boldsymbol{H})\right] := \bar{\boldsymbol{Q}}^{-1}(\Delta t\boldsymbol{H})\bar{\boldsymbol{P}}(\Delta t\boldsymbol{H}). \tag{13}$$

Then, the incremental matrix $\Delta\boldsymbol{S}(\Delta t\boldsymbol{H})$ in Equation (9) becomes the function of $\sqrt[N]{\rho_\infty}$.

The calculation of the convolution integral $\boldsymbol{L}_{\text{ana}}$ in Equation (2) is relatively expensive. Hence, in our work, the vector $\boldsymbol{L}_{\text{ana}}$ is approximated by r-node Gauss–Legendre quadrature method ($r = 1, 2, \ldots$), and its expression has the form as

$$\boldsymbol{L}_{\text{num}}(\Delta t) = \frac{\Delta t}{2}\sum_{l=1}^{r} w_l \boldsymbol{A}_{\text{num}}\left[\frac{\Delta t}{2}(1 - \xi_l)\right]\boldsymbol{f}\left[\boldsymbol{y}_{t+\frac{\Delta t}{2}(1+\xi_l)}, t + \frac{\Delta t}{2}(1 + \xi_l)\right]. \tag{14}$$

The explicit expression of which is known for linear systems; hence, together with Equations (12) and (14), the numerical results at discretized time points can be obtained. For nonlinear systems, the values of the state vector $\boldsymbol{y}$ at the quadrature points of $t + (1 + \xi_l)\Delta t/2$ ($l = 1, 2, \ldots, r$), which are used in Equation (14), are calculated by the explicit Runge–Kutta methods [3], as follows

$$\begin{cases} y_{t+\Delta t_l} = y_t + \Delta t_l \sum_{i=1}^{s} b_i k_i \\ k_i = H\left(y_t + \Delta t_l \sum_{j=1}^{s} a_{ij} k_j\right) + f\left(y_t + \Delta t_l \sum_{j=1}^{s} a_{ij} k_j, t + c_i \Delta t_l\right) \end{cases}, \Delta t_l = \frac{\Delta t}{2}(1+\xi_l),\ l = 1,2,\ldots r, \tag{15}$$

where

$$\begin{array}{c|c} c & A \\ \hline & b^{\mathrm{T}} \end{array} \rightarrow \begin{array}{c|cccc} 0 & 0 & & & \\ c_2 & a_{21} & \ddots & & \\ \vdots & \vdots & \ddots & \ddots & \\ c_s & a_{s1} & \cdots & a_{s,s-1} & 0 \\ \hline & b_1 & \cdots & \cdots & b_s \end{array}. \tag{16}$$

For linear systems, the time integration methods of different orders (or different n) based on the above strategy have unconditional stability, controllable dissipation, and higher-order accuracy, refer to Section 3. Additionally, for the force-free case, the constructed methods can reach computer precision with the increase of m.

For nonlinear systems, the time integration methods produced by the proposed strategy have advantages both in accuracy and efficiency because the responses are arrived at by highly accurate $A_{\mathrm{num}}(\Delta t H)$ and $L_{\mathrm{num}}(\Delta t H)$, and the Newton iteration method can be avoided.

In the simulations of practical dynamics, the second-order accurate time integration methods, such as the central difference method (CDM) and the TR, are widely utilized. In addition, the fourth-stage fourth-order Runge–Kutta method is also popular. Therefore, in the following, second- and fourth-order accurate schemes based on the present strategy are formulated, and their properties are deliberately discussed in Section 3.

2.1. Second-Order Accurate Scheme

In this case, the generalized Padé approximation with n = 1 [48] and the second-order accurate Runge–Kutta method (or named modified Euler method) [3] are employed. Then, from Equation (5), we can read that

$$P_{0,1}(\Delta t H) = I, P_{1,1}(\Delta t H) = I + \frac{1}{2}(\Delta t H) \tag{17}$$

$$\text{and } Q_{0,1}(\Delta t H) = I - (\Delta t H), Q_{1,1}(\Delta t H) = I - \frac{1}{2}(\Delta t H). \tag{18}$$

Substituting Equations (17) and (18) into Equation (4) can lead to

$$\bar{P}(\Delta t H) = (1+\rho_\infty) I + \rho_\infty(\Delta t H) \tag{19}$$

$$\text{and } \bar{Q}(\Delta t H) = (1+\rho_\infty) I - (\Delta t H). \tag{20}$$

With the comparison between Equation (6) and Equations (19) and (20), we can see that

$$\alpha_0 = (1+\rho_\infty), S_1(\Delta t H) = -(\Delta t H) \tag{21}$$

$$\text{and } \beta_0 = (1+\rho_\infty), S_2(\Delta t H) = \rho_\infty(\Delta t H). \tag{22}$$

Then, applying Equations (21) and (22) to Equation (9) can yield the expression of the incremental matrix $\Delta S(\Delta t H)$ as follows

$$\Delta S(\Delta t H) = -(1+\rho_\infty)\left[I - (1+\rho_\infty)(\Delta t H)^{-1}\right]^{-1}. \tag{23}$$

$\Delta S(\Delta t H)$, the highly accurate matrix $A_{\mathrm{num}}(\Delta t H)$, can be obtained from Equations (10)–(13). Together with Equation (23) and the Gauss–Legendre quadrature method, the transient response can be solved for linear systems. For nonlinear systems, here we adopt the modified Euler method to explicitly calculate the values of nonlinear terms $f(y, t)$ at Gauss–Legendre quadrature points. The tableau of the modified Euler method has the form as

$$\begin{array}{c|c} c & A \\ \hline & b^{\mathrm{T}} \end{array} \rightarrow \begin{array}{c|cc} 0 & 0 & 0 \\ 1 & 1 & 0 \\ \hline & 1/2 & 1/2 \end{array}. \tag{24}$$

2.2. Fourth-Order Accurate Scheme

In this scheme, the generalized Padé approximation with $n = 2$ [48] and the classical four-order Runge–Kutta method [3] are employed. It can be obtained from Equation (5) that

$$\boldsymbol{P}_{1,2}(\Delta t\boldsymbol{H}) = \boldsymbol{I} + \frac{1}{3}(\Delta t\boldsymbol{H}), \boldsymbol{P}_{2,2}(\Delta t\boldsymbol{H}) = \boldsymbol{I} + \frac{1}{2}(\Delta t\boldsymbol{H}) + \frac{1}{12}(\Delta t\boldsymbol{H})^2 \tag{25}$$

$$\text{and } \boldsymbol{Q}_{1,2}(\Delta t\boldsymbol{H}) = \boldsymbol{I} - \frac{2}{3}(\Delta t\boldsymbol{H}) + \frac{1}{6}(\Delta t\boldsymbol{H})^2, \boldsymbol{Q}_{2,2}(\Delta t\boldsymbol{H}) = \boldsymbol{I} - \frac{1}{2}(\Delta t\boldsymbol{H}) + \frac{1}{12}(\Delta t\boldsymbol{H})^2. \tag{26}$$

Substituting Equations (25) and (26) into Equation (4) leads to

$$\bar{\boldsymbol{P}}(\Delta t\boldsymbol{H}) = (1+\rho_\infty)\boldsymbol{I} + \frac{1}{3}(1+2\rho_\infty)(\Delta t\boldsymbol{H}) + \frac{1}{6}\rho_\infty(\Delta t\boldsymbol{H})^2 \tag{27}$$

$$\text{and } \bar{\boldsymbol{Q}}(\Delta t\boldsymbol{H}) = (1+\rho_\infty)\boldsymbol{I} - \frac{1}{3}(2+\rho_\infty)(\Delta t\boldsymbol{H}) + \frac{1}{6}(\Delta t\boldsymbol{H})^2. \tag{28}$$

From this, we can read that

$$\alpha_0 = (1+\rho_\infty), \boldsymbol{S}_1(\Delta t\boldsymbol{H}) = -\frac{1}{3}(2+\rho_\infty)(\Delta t\boldsymbol{H}) + \frac{1}{6}(\Delta t\boldsymbol{H})^2 \tag{29}$$

$$\text{and } \beta_0 = (1+\rho_\infty), \boldsymbol{S}_2(\Delta t\boldsymbol{H}) = \frac{1}{3}(1+2\rho_\infty)(\Delta t\boldsymbol{H}) + \frac{1}{6}\rho_\infty(\Delta t\boldsymbol{H})^2. \tag{30}$$

Then, inserting Equations (29) and (30) into Equation (9) yields the expression of the incremental matrix $\Delta\boldsymbol{S}(\Delta t\boldsymbol{H})$ of the fourth-order scheme, as follows:

$$\Delta\boldsymbol{S}(\Delta t\boldsymbol{H}) = \left\{\boldsymbol{I} + (1+\rho_\infty)\left[-\frac{1}{3}(2+\rho_\infty)\boldsymbol{I} + \frac{1}{6}(\Delta t\boldsymbol{H})\right]^{-1}(\Delta t\boldsymbol{H})^{-1}\right\}^{-1}\left[-\frac{1}{3}(2+\rho_\infty)\boldsymbol{I} + \frac{1}{6}(\Delta t\boldsymbol{H})\right]^{-1}\left[(1+\rho_\infty)\boldsymbol{I} + \frac{1}{6}(\rho_\infty - 1)(\Delta t\boldsymbol{H})\right]. \tag{31}$$

One can find that, for the case of $\rho_\infty = 1$, Equation (31) turns into

$$\Delta\boldsymbol{S}(\Delta t\boldsymbol{H}) = 2\left\{\boldsymbol{I} + 2\left[-\boldsymbol{I} + \frac{1}{6}(\Delta t\boldsymbol{H})\right]^{-1}(\Delta t\boldsymbol{H})^{-1}\right\}^{-1}\left[-\boldsymbol{I} + \frac{1}{6}(\Delta t\boldsymbol{H})\right]^{-1}, \tag{32}$$

and for the case of $\rho_\infty = 0$, Equation (31) becomes

$$\Delta\boldsymbol{S}(\Delta t\boldsymbol{H}) = \left\{\boldsymbol{I} + \left[-\frac{2}{3}\boldsymbol{I} + \frac{1}{6}(\Delta t\boldsymbol{H})\right]^{-1}(\Delta t\boldsymbol{H})^{-1}\right\}^{-1}\left[-\frac{2}{3}\boldsymbol{I} + \frac{1}{6}(\Delta t\boldsymbol{H})\right]^{-1}\left[\boldsymbol{I} - \frac{1}{6}(\Delta t\boldsymbol{H})\right]. \tag{33}$$

It can be concluded from Equations (31)–(33) that the computations of the fourth-order scheme with $\rho_\infty = 1$ are the lowest. The classical fourth-order Runge–Kutta method [3] is utilized in the present scheme to compute nonlinear function $f(y, t)$ at Gauss–Legendre quadrature points to avoid the loss-of-accuracy order and the tableau of the Runge–Kutta method is

$$\begin{array}{c|c} c & A \\ \hline & b^{\mathrm{T}} \end{array} \rightarrow \begin{array}{c|cccc} 0 & & & & \\ 1/2 & 1/2 & & & \\ 1/2 & 0 & 1/2 & & \\ 1 & 0 & 0 & 1 & \\ \hline & 1/6 & 1/3 & 1/3 & 1/6 \end{array}. \tag{34}$$

3. Numerical Properties Analysis

The basic idea of the proposed strategy has been described in the last section, and two schemes are formulated, which are second-order accurate and fourth-order accurate. In this section, the spectral characteristics, convergence rates, and overshoot characteristics for both undamped and damped systems are investigated. Additionally, the critical value of m is noted as m_{cr}, and ensures that the constructed matrix $\boldsymbol{A}_{\mathrm{num}}(\Delta t\boldsymbol{H})$ can be calculated with up to computer precision, which is also discussed below.

Spectral analysis has been widely employed in the evaluation of the stability, accuracy, and dissipation characteristics of time integration methods. In spectral analysis, owing to the mode superposition principle, it is common and enough to consider a single degree-of-freedom Equation [1]

$$\ddot{x} + 2\xi\omega\dot{x} + \omega^2 x = f(t), \tag{35}$$

where ξ is the damping ratio, and ω is the natural frequency. The equivalent first-order differential equation for the free-force case [52] has the following form as

$$\dot{y} = \begin{bmatrix} 0 & 1 \\ -\omega^2 & -2\xi\omega \end{bmatrix} y,\ y = \begin{bmatrix} x \\ \dot{x} \end{bmatrix}, \tag{36}$$

from which we can find that

$$\boldsymbol{H} = \begin{bmatrix} 0 & 1 \\ -\omega^2 & -2\xi\omega \end{bmatrix}. \tag{37}$$

Applying Equations (3)–(5) to Equation (36) generates

$$\begin{bmatrix} x_{t+\Delta t} \\ \dot{x}_{t+\Delta t} \end{bmatrix} = \bar{\boldsymbol{Q}}^{-1}(\Delta t\boldsymbol{H})\bar{\boldsymbol{P}}(\Delta t\boldsymbol{H}) \begin{bmatrix} x_t \\ \dot{x}_t \end{bmatrix} := \boldsymbol{A}_{\mathrm{num}}(\Delta t\boldsymbol{H}) \begin{bmatrix} x_t \\ \dot{x}_t \end{bmatrix}. \tag{38}$$

The characteristic polynomial [1] of the transfer matrix $\boldsymbol{A}_{\mathrm{num}}$ is

$$\lambda^2 - A_1\lambda + A_2 = 0, \tag{39}$$

where $A_1 = \mathrm{tr}(\boldsymbol{A}_{\mathrm{num}})$ and $A_2 = \det(\boldsymbol{A}_{\mathrm{num}})$, and the two eigenvalues can be written as the form of $\lambda_{1,2} = a \pm \mathrm{i}b$, in which $\mathrm{i} = \sqrt{-1}$. The definition of the spectral radius [1] is

$$\rho = \max\{|\lambda_1|, |\lambda_2|\}, \tag{40}$$

which can be used to analyze the stability and dissipation characteristics of time integration methods. Numerical damping ratio $\bar{\xi}$ [1] and period elongation (PE) [1] can evaluate the amplitude and phase accuracy of time integration methods in the low-frequency range, and their definitions are

$$\bar{\xi} = -\frac{\ln(\rho)}{2\bar{\tau}} \text{ and PE} = \frac{\tau}{\bar{\tau}} - 1, \tag{41}$$

where $\tau = \omega\Delta t$ and $\bar{\tau} = \arctan(b/a)$. In the following, the above theory given in Equations (35)–(41) is used to analyze the fundamental numerical properties of the two schemes provided in Section 2. In this work, the time integration methods based on the proposed strategy are named Accurate-Efficient-Conservative/Dissipative-Method-n (AEC/DMn), in which n stands for polynomials of degree in the numerator or denominator of the generalized Padé approximation. The non-dissipative AECMn ($\rho_\infty = 1$) can keep all information of a dynamic system, while the dissipative AEDM*n* ($0 \leq \rho_\infty < 1$) can filter out the high-frequency modes.

3.1. Stability, Dissipation, and Accuracy of the Second-Order Scheme

3.1.1. Spectral Characteristics

The spectral radius of AEC/DM1 versus τ for the undamped case ($\xi = 0$) is plotted in Figure 1, in which one can see that (a) for linear systems, the AEC/DM1 is unconditionally stable, satisfying $0 \leq \rho_\infty \leq 1$, and the amount of its high-frequency dissipation can be exactly controlled via ρ_∞. (b) Additionally, with the increase of m, the low-frequency range, where the spectral radius trends to 1, becomes wider and preserves more low-frequency modes.

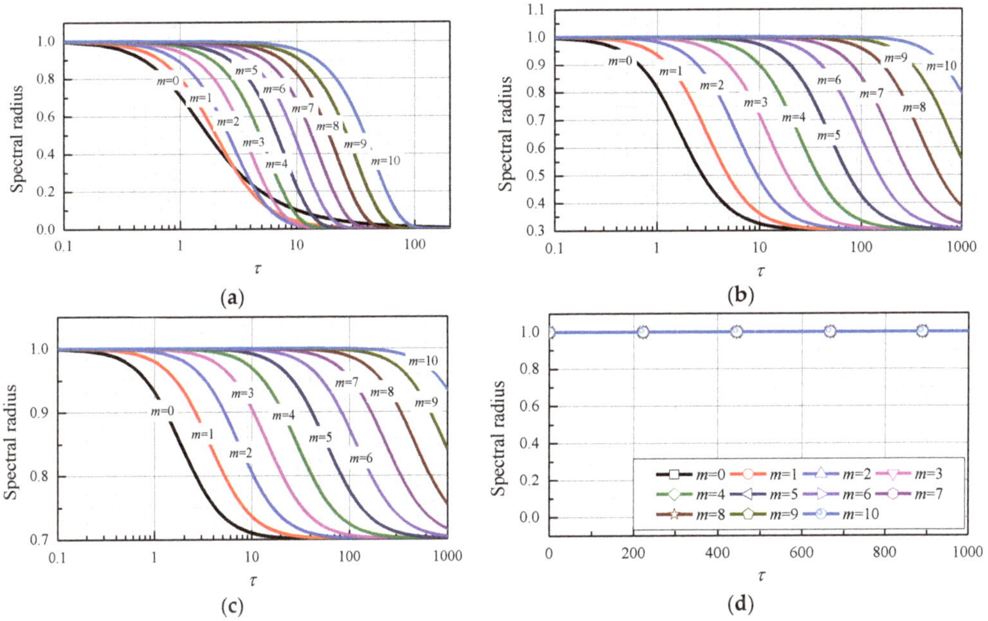

Figure 1. Spectral radius of the AEC/DM1 versus τ for the undamped case: (**a**) AEDM1, $\rho_\infty = 0$; (**b**) AEDM1, $\rho_\infty = 0.3$; (**c**) AEDM1, $\rho_\infty = 0.7$; and (**d**) AECM1, $\rho_\infty = 1$.

The AEDM1 ($\rho_\infty = 0$) and AECM1 ($\rho_\infty = 1$), which are the representative schemes, are considered below for analyzing the amplitude and phase accuracy of the present scheme. Amplitude and period errors of the AEDM1 ($\rho_\infty = 0$) and AECM1 ($\rho_\infty = 1$) versus τ for the undamped case are shown in Figures 2 and 3, respectively, in which it can be seen that (a) with the increase in m, both the amplitude and period errors can be simultaneously decreased; (b) for the same m, the non-dissipative scheme and the dissipative schemes almost have the same phase accuracy, implying that the numerical dissipation mainly affects the amplitude accuracy of the AEC/DM1.

The spectral radii ρ and absolute values of (ρ-ρ_{exact}) of the AEC/DM1 for the damped case ($\xi = 0.5$) are shown in Figures 4–6, in which $\rho_{exact} = \exp(-\xi\tau)$ [52]. It follows that: (a) With the increase of m, the numerical spectral radius approaches the analytical one; (b) Among the low-frequency range, the accuracy of the AECM1 is higher than that of the AEDM1; (c) For smaller m, because the AECM1 cannot provide numerical dissipation, their spectral radii do not agree well with analytical one in the high-frequency range ($\tau > 10$).

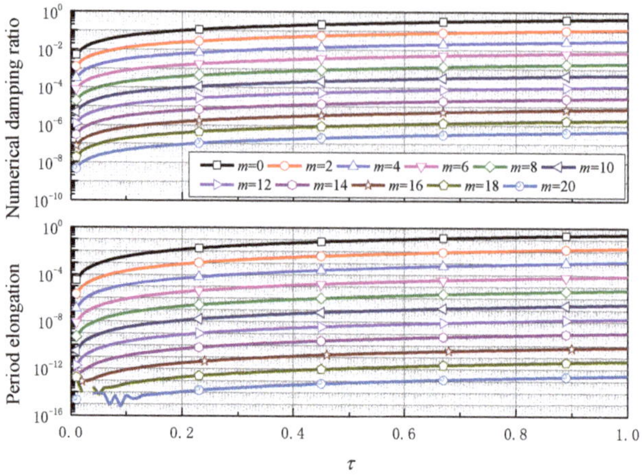

Figure 2. Numerical damping ratio and period elongation of the AEDM1 ($\rho_\infty = 0$) versus τ for the undamped case.

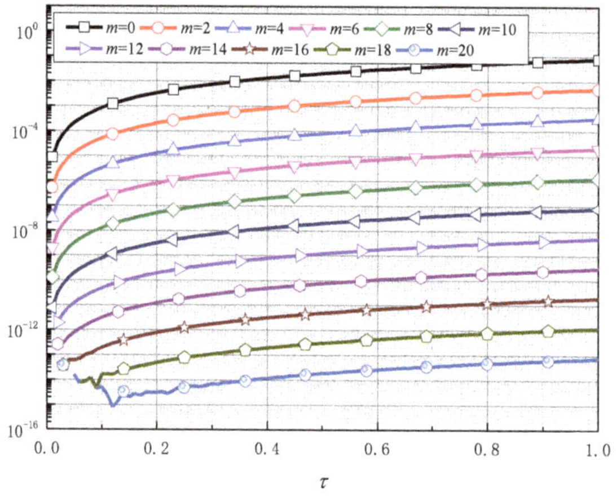

Figure 3. Period elongation of the AECM1 ($\rho_\infty = 1$) versus τ for the undamped case.

3.1.2. Rounding Errors

As well known, the accuracy of numerical results depends on the truncation error, which can be reduced by decreasing step size or increasing m. However, when m is large enough, all significant digits of the incremental matrix reserved by the computer are completely accurate. At this time, the truncation error does not exist, and the rounding error of the computer dominates, where further increasing m cannot further improve accuracy. That is to say, there exists a critical value of m, denoted as m_{cr}. When $m < m_{cr}$, the truncation error dominates, and increasing m can improve accuracy, but when $m \geq m_{cr}$, the rounding error dominates, and increasing m cannot improve accuracy further. From the phase accuracy analysis shown in Figures 2 and 3, one can find that the value of ρ_∞ has a slight influence on the phase accuracy of the proposed methods; therefore, we only determine m_{cr} for the AECM1.

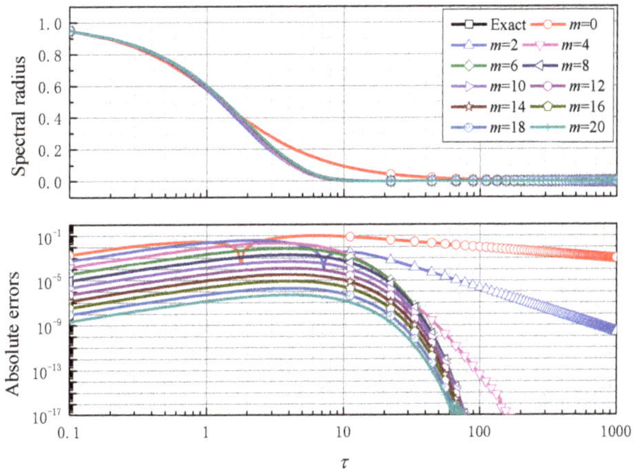

Figure 4. Spectral radius of the AEDM1 ($\rho_\infty = 0$) versus τ for the damped case ($\xi = 0.5$).

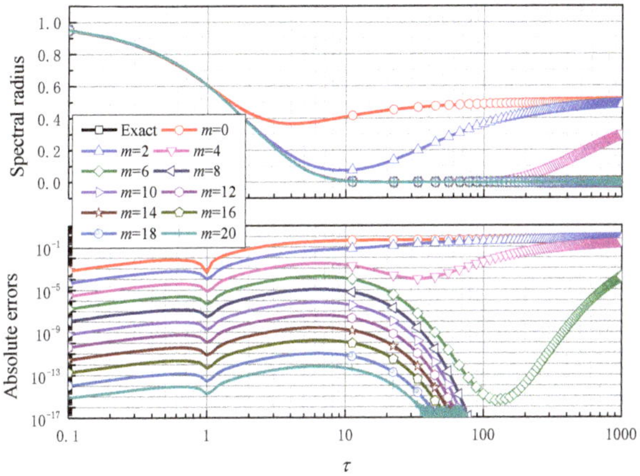

Figure 5. Spectral radius of the AEDM1 ($\rho_\infty = 0.5$) versus τ for the damped case ($\xi = 0.5$).

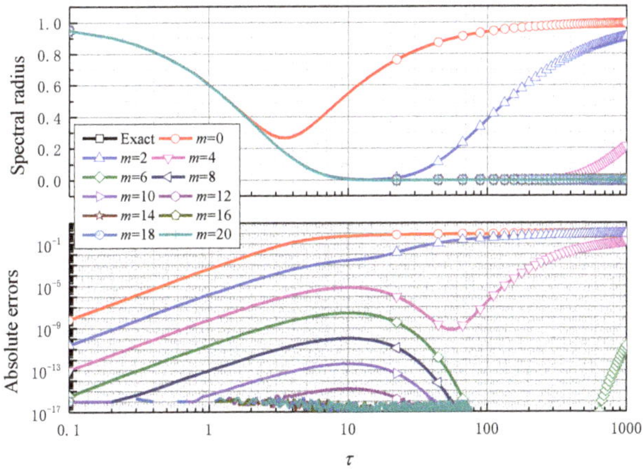

Figure 6. Spectral radius of the AECM1 versus τ for the damped case ($\xi = 0.5$).

The transfer matrix of the AEC/DM1 has the form as

$$\boldsymbol{A}_{\text{num}}(\Delta t\boldsymbol{H}) = \begin{bmatrix} A_{11} & A_{12} \\ A_{21} & A_{22} \end{bmatrix}, \tag{42}$$

which elements for the case of $\rho_\infty = 1$ have the forms as

$$A_{\text{num},11} = 1 - \frac{\Delta t_N^2\omega^2}{2} + \frac{\xi\Delta t_N^3\omega^3}{2} + \frac{\Delta t_N^4\omega^4}{8} - \frac{\xi^2\Delta t_N^4\omega^4}{2} - \frac{\xi\Delta t_N^5\omega^5}{4} + \frac{\xi^3\Delta t_N^5\omega^5}{2}, \tag{43}$$

$$A_{\text{num},12} = \Delta t_N - \xi\Delta t_N^2\omega - \frac{\Delta t_N^3\omega^2}{4} + \xi^2\Delta t_N^3\omega^2 + \frac{\xi\Delta t_N^4\omega^3}{2} - \xi^3\Delta t_N^4\omega^3 + \frac{\Delta t_N^5\omega^4}{16} - \frac{3\xi^2\Delta t_N^5\omega^4}{4} + \xi^4\Delta t_N^5\omega^4, \tag{44}$$

$$A_{\text{num},21} = -\Delta t_N\omega^2\left(1 - \xi\Delta t_N\omega - \frac{1}{4}\Delta t_N^2\omega^2 + \xi^2\Delta t_N^2\omega^2 + \frac{1}{2}\xi\Delta t_N^3\omega^3 - \xi^3\Delta t_N^3\omega^3 + \frac{1}{16}\Delta t_N^4\omega^4 - \frac{3}{4}\xi^2\Delta t_N^4\omega^4 + \xi^4\Delta t_N^4\omega^4\right), \tag{45}$$

$$\text{and } \begin{array}{l} A_{\text{num},22} = 1 - 2\xi\Delta t_N\omega - \frac{\Delta t_N^2\omega^2}{2} + 2\xi^2\Delta t_N^2\omega^2 + \xi\Delta t_N^3\omega^3 - 2\xi^3\Delta t_N^3\omega^3 + \frac{\Delta t_N^4\omega^4}{8} \\ -\frac{3\xi^2\Delta t_N^4\omega^4}{2} + 2\xi^4\Delta t_N^4\omega^4 - \frac{3\xi\Delta t_N^5\omega^5}{8} + 2\xi^3\Delta t_N^5\omega^5 - 2\xi^5\Delta t_N^5\omega^5 \end{array}. \tag{46}$$

Then, the corresponding elements of the incremental matrix are

$$S_{\text{num},11} = A_{\text{num},11} - 1, \tag{47}$$

$$S_{\text{num},12} = A_{\text{num},12}, \tag{48}$$

$$S_{\text{num},21} = A_{\text{num},21}, \tag{49}$$

$$\text{and } S_{\text{num},22} = A_{\text{num},22} - 1. \tag{50}$$

The analytical sub-step transfer matrix based on Taylor series expansion has the same form as that of the numerical one shown in Equation (42), but its elements turn into

$$A_{\text{ana},11} = \begin{array}{c} 1 - \frac{\Delta t_N^2\omega^2}{2} + \frac{\xi\Delta t_N^3\omega^3}{3} + \frac{\Delta t_N^4\omega^4}{24} - \frac{\xi^2\Delta t_N^4\omega^4}{6} - \frac{\xi\Delta t_N^5\omega^5}{30} + \frac{\xi^3\Delta t_N^5\omega^5}{15} - \\ \frac{\Delta t_N^6\omega^6}{720} + \frac{\xi^2\Delta t_N^6\omega^6}{60} - \frac{\xi^4\Delta t_N^6\omega^6}{45} + \frac{\xi\Delta t_N^7\omega^7}{840} - \frac{2\xi^3\Delta t_N^7\omega^7}{315} + \frac{2\xi^5\Delta t_N^7\omega^7}{315} + \frac{\Delta t_N^8\omega^8}{40320} - \cdots \end{array}, \tag{51}$$

$$A_{\text{ana},12} = \Delta t_N\left(\begin{array}{l} 1 - \xi\Delta t_N\omega - \frac{1}{6}\Delta t_N^2\omega^2 + \frac{2}{3}\xi^2\Delta t_N^2\omega^2 + \frac{1}{6}\xi\Delta t_N^3\omega^3 - \frac{1}{3}\xi^3\Delta t_N^3\omega^3 + \frac{1}{120}\Delta t_N^4\omega^4 - \frac{1}{10}\xi^2\Delta t_N^4\omega^4 + \frac{2}{15}\xi^4\Delta t_N^4\omega^4 - \\ \frac{1}{120}\xi\Delta t_N^5\omega^5 + \frac{2}{45}\xi^3\Delta t_N^5\omega^5 - \frac{2}{45}\xi^5\Delta t_N^5\omega^5 - \frac{1}{5040}\Delta t_N^6\omega^6 + \frac{1}{210}\xi^2\Delta t_N^6\omega^6 - \frac{1}{63}\xi^4\Delta t_N^6\omega^6 + \frac{4}{315}\xi^6\Delta t_N^6\omega^6 - \cdots \end{array}\right), \tag{52}$$

$$A_{\text{ana},21} = -\Delta t_N\omega^2\left(\begin{array}{l} 1 - \xi\Delta t_N\omega - \frac{1}{6}\Delta t_N^2\omega^2 + \frac{2}{3}\xi^2\Delta t_N^2\omega^2 + \frac{1}{6}\xi\Delta t_N^3\omega^3 - \frac{1}{3}\xi^3\Delta t_N^3\omega^3 + \frac{1}{120}\Delta t_N^4\omega^4 - \frac{1}{10}\xi^2\Delta t_N^4\omega^4 + \frac{2}{15}\xi^4\Delta t_N^4\omega^4 - \\ \frac{1}{120}\xi\Delta t_N^5\omega^5 + \frac{2}{45}\xi^3\Delta t_N^5\omega^5 - \frac{2}{45}\xi^5\Delta t_N^5\omega^5 - \frac{1}{5040}\Delta t_N^6\omega^6 + \frac{1}{210}\xi^2\Delta t_N^6\omega^6 - \frac{1}{63}\xi^4\Delta t_N^6\omega^6 + \frac{4}{315}\xi^6\Delta t_N^6\omega^6 - \cdots \end{array}\right), \tag{53}$$

$$\text{and } \begin{array}{l} A_{\text{ana},22} = 1 - 2\xi\Delta t_N\omega - \frac{\Delta t_N^2\omega^2}{2} + 2\xi^2\Delta t_N^2\omega^2 + \frac{2\xi\Delta t_N^3\omega^3}{3} - \frac{4\xi^3\Delta t_N^3\omega^3}{3} + \frac{\Delta t_N^4\omega^4}{24} - \frac{\xi^2\Delta t_N^4\omega^4}{2} + \\ \frac{2\xi^4\Delta t_N^4\omega^4}{3} - \frac{\xi\Delta t_N^5\omega^5}{20} + \frac{4\xi^3\Delta t_N^5\omega^5}{15} - \frac{4\xi^5\Delta t_N^5\omega^5}{15} - \frac{\Delta t_N^6\omega^6}{720} + \frac{\xi^2\Delta t_N^6\omega^6}{30} - \frac{\xi^4\Delta t_N^6\omega^6}{9} + \frac{4\xi^6\Delta t_N^6\omega^6}{45} + \cdots \end{array}. \tag{54}$$

The undamped case ($\xi = 0$) is investigated first. By comparing Equations (43)–(46) with Equations (51)–(54), we have the relative sizes between four truncation terms and four main terms in $\boldsymbol{S}(\Delta t_N)$ as

$$\begin{cases} \left|\frac{\chi_{\text{truncation}}(A_{\text{num},11} - A_{\text{ana},11})}{\chi_{\text{main}}(S_{\text{num},11})}\right| = \left|\frac{\Delta t_N^2\omega^2/8 - \Delta t_N^2\omega^2/24}{\Delta t_N^2\omega^2/2}\right| = \left|\frac{\Delta t_N^2\omega^2}{6}\right| \\ \left|\frac{\chi_{\text{truncation}}(A_{\text{num},12} - A_{\text{ana},12})}{\chi_{\text{main}}(S_{\text{num},12})}\right| = \left|\frac{\Delta t_N^3\omega^2/6 - \Delta t_N^3\omega^2/4}{\Delta t_N}\right| = \left|\frac{\Delta t_N^2\omega^2}{12}\right| \\ \left|\frac{\chi_{\text{truncation}}(A_{\text{num},21} - A_{\text{ana},21})}{\chi_{\text{main}}(S_{\text{num},21})}\right| = \left|\frac{\Delta t_N^3\omega^4/6 - \Delta t_N^3\omega^4/4}{\Delta t_N\omega^2}\right| = \left|\frac{\Delta t_N^2\omega^2}{12}\right| \\ \left|\frac{\chi_{\text{truncation}}(A_{\text{num},22} - A_{\text{ana},22})}{\chi_{\text{main}}(S_{\text{num},22})}\right| = \left|\frac{\Delta t_N^2\omega^2/8 - \Delta t_N^2\omega^2/24}{\Delta t_N^2\omega^2/2}\right| = \left|\frac{\Delta t_N^2\omega^2}{6}\right| \end{cases}. \tag{55}$$

Then, the truncation errors can be eliminated if

$$\max\left\{\left|\frac{\Delta t_N^2\omega^2}{6}\right|, \left|\frac{\Delta t_N^2\omega^2}{12}\right|, \left|\frac{\Delta t_N^2\omega^2}{12}\right|, \left|\frac{\Delta t_N^2\omega^2}{6}\right|\right\} = \frac{\Delta t^2\omega^2}{6 \times 2^{2m}} \le \varepsilon,\ \varepsilon = 10^{-16}. \tag{56}$$

From this, the critical value of m for the undamped case can be obtained as

$$m_{cr} = \frac{\log(\Delta t^2 \omega^2 / 6\varepsilon)}{2\log(2)},\ \varepsilon = 10^{-16}. \quad (57)$$

In the following, the performances of the AEC/DM1 in dealing with rounding errors are discussed. The undamped case of Equation (35) is considered first, in which $\xi = 0$, $\omega = \pi$, $x_0 = 1$, and $\dot{x}_0 = 1$; $\Delta t = 1$ and $\Delta t_N = 1/N$ are used in the AEC/DM1 and TR, respectively. The absolute errors in displacement, velocity, and acceleration of the AECM1 and TR are drawn in Figure 7, and one can see that: (a) When $m > m_{cr} = 27$ is achieved from Equation (57), the absolute errors of the AECM1 trends with computer precision; (b) With the increase of m, the accuracy of TR increases for the case of $m < 20$, and then its accuracy begins to decline when $m > 20$ due to the rounding errors. Figure 8 plots the relative errors of the two methods for the damped case, in which $\xi = 0.5$, $\omega = 2\pi$, $x_0 = 1$, and $\dot{x}_0 = 0$, and it follows that the accuracy of the AECM1 has no considerable variation when $m > m_{cr} = 27$. Therefore, one can conclude that the selection of m_{cr} can only consider the undamped case. The m_{cr} corresponding to different $\omega\Delta t$ is given in Table 2, in which one can find that with the increase of $\omega\Delta t$, the m_{cr} becomes larger.

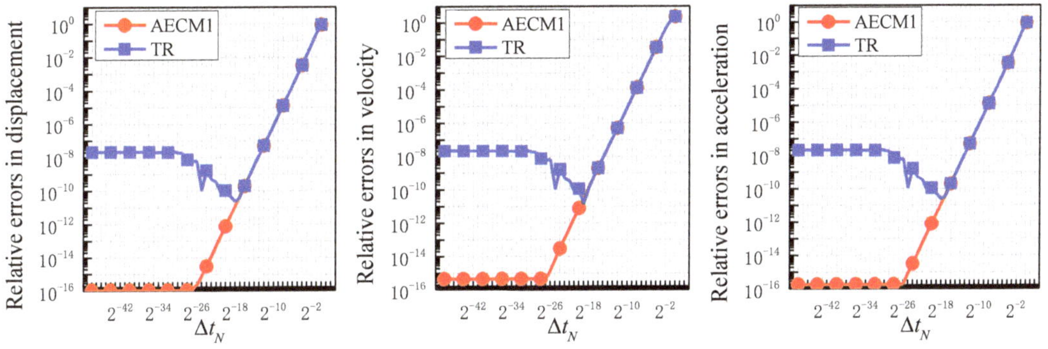

Figure 7. Relative errors in displacement, velocity, and acceleration of the AECM1 for the case of $\xi = 0$ and $f(t) = 0$.

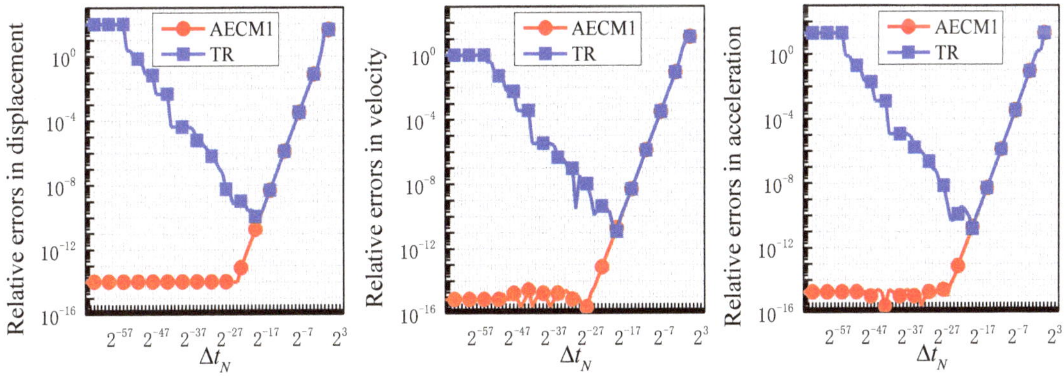

Figure 8. Relative errors in displacement, velocity, and acceleration of the AECM1 for the case of $\xi = 0.5$ and $f(t) = 0$.

Table 2. The critical value of m of the AECM1 for different $\omega\Delta t$.

$\omega\Delta t$	0.01	0.1	1	10	20	50	100	1000	10,000
m_{cr}	19	22	26	29	30	31	32	36	39

At last, the selections of Gauss–Legendre points are discussed below. The standard SDOF test equation given in Equation (35) is considered here, and the $\xi = 2/\sqrt{5}$, $\omega = \sqrt{5}$, $x_0 = 57/65$, $\dot{x}_0 = 2/65$, and $f(t) = \sin(2t)$ are used. The absolute errors of the AECM1 and the TR are compared in Figure 9, in which one can see that: (a) The AECM1 has the same convergence rates with the second-order-accurate TR before $m < 22$; (b) Due to the rounding errors, the accuracy of the TR begins to decrease after $m \geq 23$; (c) The accuracy of the AECM1 trends to constants with the decrease in time-step size, and the accuracy of the AECM1 with four Gauss–Legendre nodes is close to computer precision after $m > m_{cr} = 23$ is achieved from Equation (57). Therefore, four Gauss–Legendre nodes are suggested for the AEC/DM1.

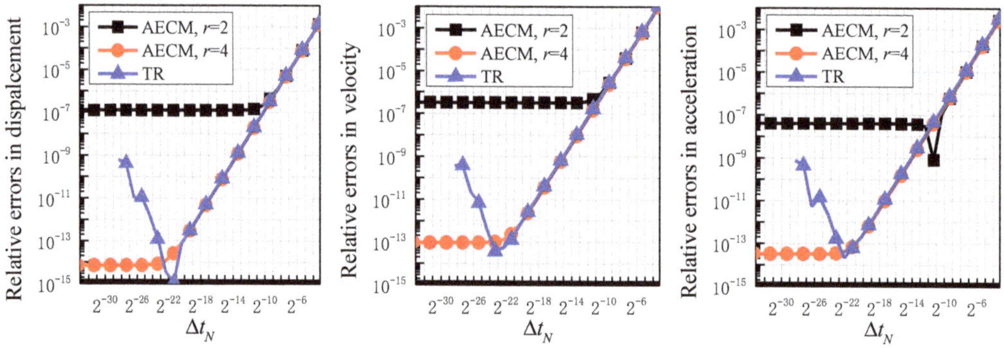

Figure 9. Relative errors in displacement, velocity, and acceleration of the AECM1 for the case of $\xi = 2/\sqrt{5}$) and $f(t) = \sin(2t)$ (r represents number of Gauss–Legendre nodes).

3.2. *Stability, Dissipation, and Accuracy of the Fourth-Order Scheme*

3.2.1. Spectral Characteristics

Figure 10 plots the spectral radius of AEC/DM2 versus τ for the undamped case, in which one can see that: (a) Compared with the second-order AEC/DM1, the range wherein spectral radius trending to one can rapidly widen with the increase of m (or increasing accuracy order can keep more low-frequency information); (b) Such as in the AEC/DM1, the amount of numerical dissipation of the AEC/DM2 can be exactly adjusted by ρ_∞.

Amplitude and period accuracy of the AEDM2 ($\rho_\infty = 0$) and AECM2 versus τ for the undamped case are shown in Figures 11 and 12, respectively. It can be seen that: (a) With the increase in m, the amplitude and period errors can be simultaneously decreased; (b) From the comparison between Figures 2 and 11, one can find that the accuracy, including amplitude and phase of the AEDM2, is far higher than that of the AEDM1 ($\rho_\infty = 0$); (c) One can observe by comparing Figures 3 and 12 that the AECM2 has a considerable phase advantage compared with the AECM1; (d) For the same m, the phase accuracy of the non-dissipative scheme and the dissipative schemes are nearly the same, implying that m mainly affect the amplitude accuracy of the AEC/DM2.

The spectral radii of the AEC/DM2 for the damped case are discussed here, and from Figures 13–15, the conclusions for the AEC/DM1 hold for the AEC/DM2. However, with the same m, the absolute errors of the AEC/DM2 are smaller than those of AEC/DM1 for the damped case.

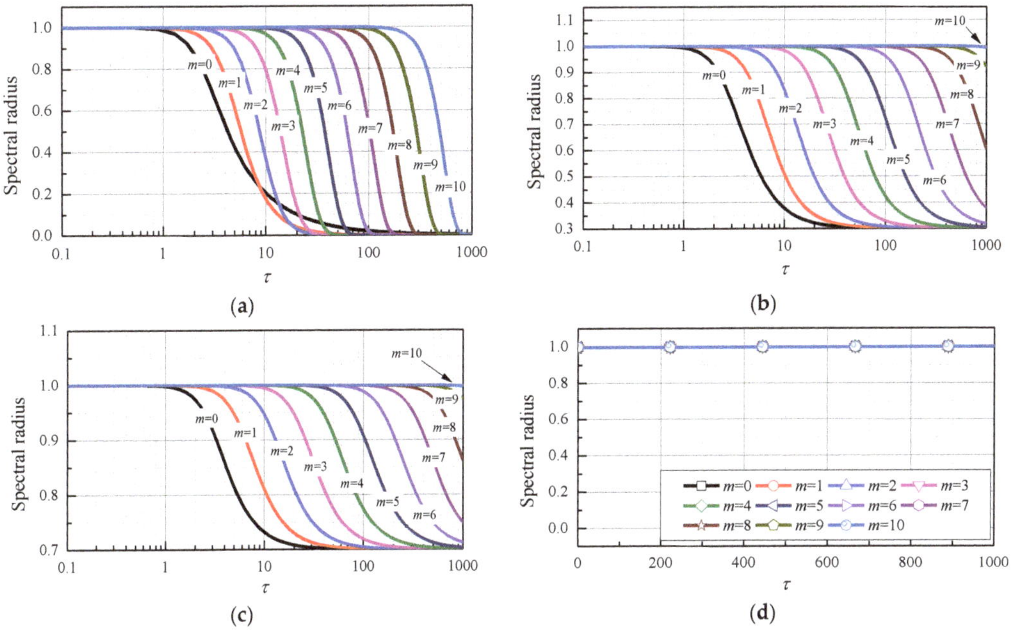

Figure 10. Spectral radius of the AEC/DM2 versus τ for the undamped case: (**a**) AEDM2, $\rho_\infty = 0$; (**b**) AEDM2, $\rho_\infty = 0.3$; (**c**) AEDM2, $\rho_\infty = 0.7$; and (**d**) AECM2, $\rho_\infty = 1$.

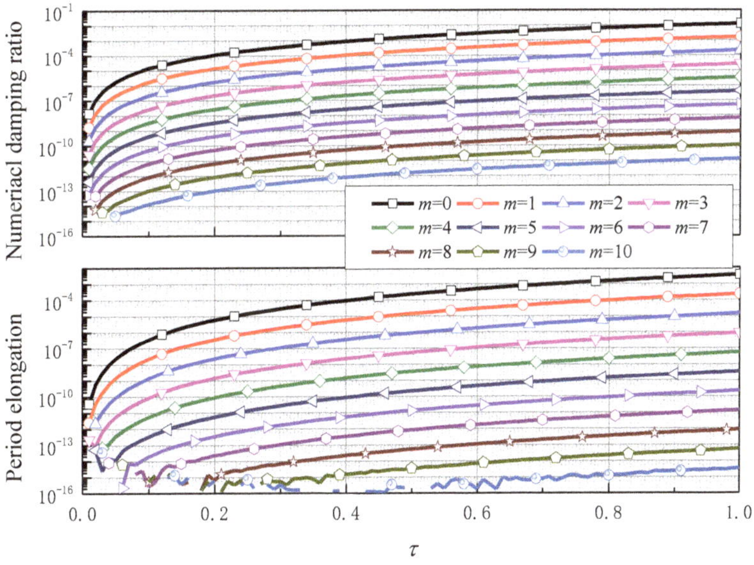

Figure 11. Numerical damping ratio and period elongation of the AEC/DM2 ($\rho_\infty = 0$) versus τ for the undamped case.

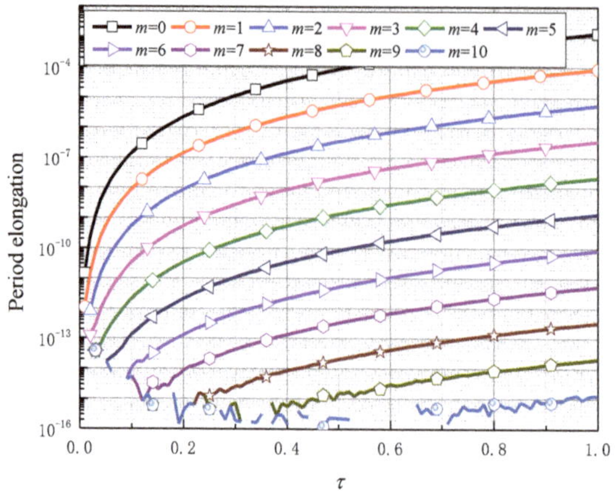

Figure 12. Period elongation of the AEC/DM2 ($\rho_\infty = 1$) versus τ for the undamped case.

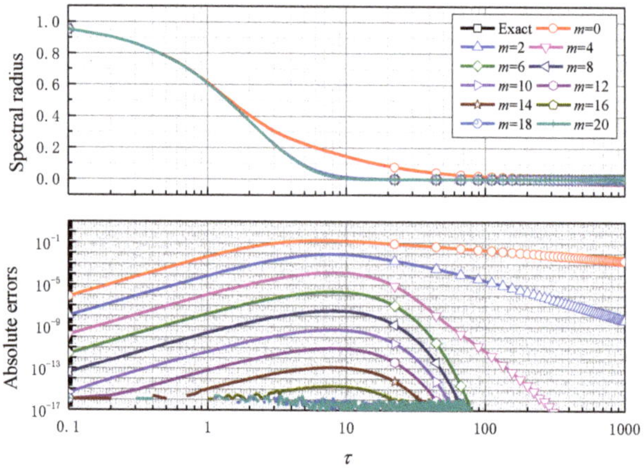

Figure 13. Spectral radius of the AEC/DM2 ($\rho_\infty = 0$) versus τ for the damped case.

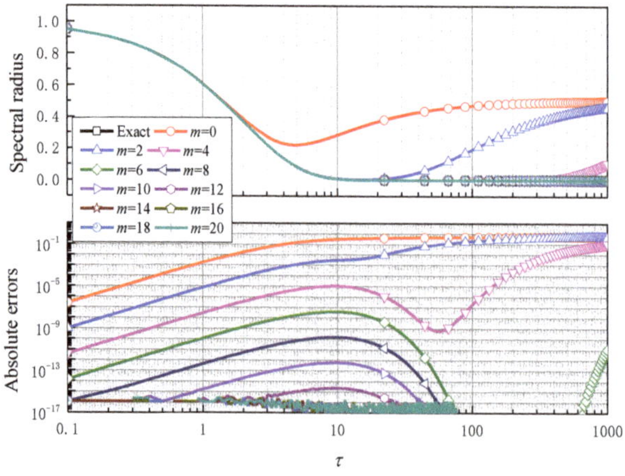

Figure 14. Spectral radius of the AEC/DM2 ($\rho_\infty = 0.5$) versus τ for the damped case.

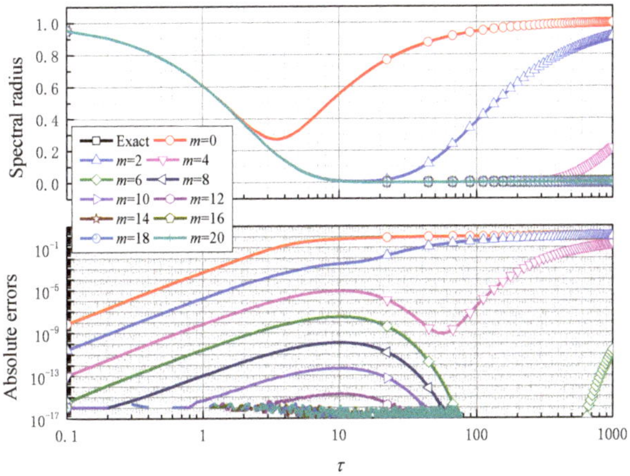

Figure 15. Spectral radius of the AEC/DM2 ($\rho_\infty = 1$) versus τ for the damped case.

3.2.2. Rounding Errors

It can be found from Figures 11 and 12 that, for the AEC/DM2, the effect of numerical dissipation on phase accuracy can be omitted. Thus, in the following, only the critical m of the AECM2 is investigated. The elements of the numerical transfer matrix of the AECM2 have the forms as

$$\begin{array}{rl} A_{\text{num},11} = & 1 - \frac{\Delta t_N^2 \omega^2}{2} + \frac{\xi \Delta t_N^3 \omega^3}{3} + \frac{\Delta t_N^4 \omega^4}{24} - \frac{\xi^2 \Delta t_N^4 \omega^4}{6} - \frac{\xi \Delta t_N^5 \omega^5}{36} + \frac{\xi^3 \Delta t_N^5 \omega^5}{18} - \\ & \frac{\xi \Delta t_N^7 \omega^7}{288} + \frac{\xi^3 \Delta t_N^7 \omega^7}{54} - \frac{\xi^5 \Delta t_N^7 \omega^7}{54} - \frac{\Delta t_N^8 \omega^8}{3456} - \cdots \end{array}, \quad (58)$$

$$A_{\text{num},12} = \Delta t_N \left(\begin{array}{c} 1 - \xi \Delta t_N \omega - \frac{1}{6} \Delta t_N^2 \omega^2 + \frac{2}{3} \xi^2 \Delta t_N^2 \omega^2 + \frac{1}{6} \xi \Delta t_N^3 \omega^3 - \frac{1}{3} \xi^3 \Delta t_N^3 \omega^3 + \frac{1}{144} \Delta t_N^4 \omega^4 - \frac{1}{12} \xi^2 \Delta t_N^4 \omega^4 + \\ \frac{1}{9} \xi^4 \Delta t_N^4 \omega^4 + \frac{1}{1728} \Delta t_N^6 \omega^6 - \frac{1}{72} \xi^2 \Delta t_N^6 \omega^6 + \frac{5}{108} \xi^4 \Delta t_N^6 \omega^6 - \frac{1}{27} \xi^6 \Delta t_N^6 \omega^6 - \frac{1}{432} \xi \Delta t_N^7 \omega^7 \end{array} \right), \quad (59)$$

$$A_{\text{num},21} = -\Delta t_N \omega^2 \left(\begin{array}{c} 1 - \xi \Delta t_N \omega - \frac{1}{6} \Delta t_N^2 \omega^2 + \frac{2}{3} \xi^2 \Delta t_N^2 \omega^2 + \frac{1}{6} \xi \Delta t_N^3 \omega^3 - \frac{1}{3} \xi^3 \Delta t_N^3 \omega^3 + \frac{1}{144} \Delta t_N^4 \omega^4 - \frac{1}{12} \xi^2 \Delta t_N^4 \omega^4 + \\ \frac{1}{9} \xi^4 \Delta t_N^4 \omega^4 + \frac{1}{1728} \Delta t_N^6 \omega^6 - \frac{1}{72} \xi^2 \Delta t_N^6 \omega^6 + \frac{5}{108} \xi^4 \Delta t_N^6 \omega^6 - \frac{1}{27} \xi^6 \Delta t_N^6 \omega^6 - \frac{1}{432} \xi \Delta t_N^7 \omega^7 \end{array} \right), \text{ and} \quad (60)$$

$$\begin{array}{rl} A_{\text{num},22} = & 1 - 2\xi \Delta t_N \omega - \frac{\Delta t_N^2 \omega^2}{2} + 2\xi^2 \Delta t_N^2 \omega^2 + \frac{2\xi \Delta t_N^3 \omega^3}{3} - \frac{4\xi^3 \Delta t_N^3 \omega^3}{3} + \frac{\Delta t_N^4 \omega^4}{24} - \frac{\xi^2 \Delta t_N^4 \omega^4}{2} + \frac{2\xi^4 \Delta t_N^4 \omega^4}{3} - \frac{\xi \Delta t_N^5 \omega^5}{24} + \\ & \frac{2\xi^3 \Delta t_N^5 \omega^5}{9} - \frac{2\xi^5 \Delta t_N^5 \omega^5}{9} - \frac{\xi \Delta t_N^7 \omega^7}{216} + \frac{5\xi^3 \Delta t_N^7 \omega^7}{108} - \frac{\xi^5 \Delta t_N^7 \omega^7}{9} + \frac{2\xi^7 \Delta t_N^7 \omega^7}{27} - \frac{\Delta t_N^8 \omega^8}{3456} \end{array}. \quad (61)$$

It can be concluded from Section 3.1 that the physical damping has slight effects on the values of m_{cr}; thus, only the undamped case ($\xi = 0$) is considered for the present scheme. By comparing Equation (58)–(61) with Equation (51)–(54), we have the relative sizes between four truncation terms and four main terms in $S(\Delta t_N)$ by

$$\left\{ \begin{array}{l} \left| \frac{\chi_{\text{truncation}}(A_{\text{num},11} - A_{\text{ana},11})}{\chi_{\text{main}}(S_{\text{num},11})} \right| = \left| \frac{\Delta t_N^6 \omega^6 / 720}{\Delta t_N^2 \omega^2 / 2} \right| = \left| \frac{\Delta t_N^4 \omega^4}{360} \right| \\ \left| \frac{\chi_{\text{truncation}}(A_{\text{num},12} - A_{\text{ana},12})}{\chi_{\text{main}}(S_{\text{num},12})} \right| = \left| \frac{\Delta t_N^3 \omega^4 / 144 - \Delta t_N^5 \omega^4 / 120}{\Delta t_N} \right| = \left| \frac{\Delta t_N^4 \omega^4}{720} \right| \\ \left| \frac{\chi_{\text{truncation}}(A_{\text{num},21} - A_{\text{ana},21})}{\chi_{\text{main}}(S_{\text{num},21})} \right| = \left| \frac{\Delta t_N^3 \omega^6 / 144 - \Delta t_N^5 \omega^6 / 120}{\Delta t_N \omega^2} \right| = \left| \frac{\Delta t_N^4 \omega^4}{720} \right| \\ \left| \frac{\chi_{\text{truncation}}(A_{\text{num},22} - A_{\text{ana},22})}{\chi_{\text{main}}(S_{\text{num},22})} \right| = \left| \frac{\Delta t_N^6 \omega^6 / 720}{\Delta t_N^2 \omega^2 / 2} \right| = \left| \frac{\Delta t_N^4 \omega^4}{360} \right| \end{array} \right. . \quad (62)$$

Then, the truncation error can be eliminated if

$$\max \left\{ \left| \frac{\Delta t_N^4 \omega^4}{360} \right|, \left| \frac{\Delta t_N^4 \omega^4}{720} \right|, \left| \frac{\Delta t_N^4 \omega^4}{720} \right|, \left| \frac{\Delta t_N^4 \omega^4}{360} \right| \right\} = \frac{\Delta t^4 \omega^4}{360 \times 2^{4m}} \le \varepsilon, \ \varepsilon = 10^{-16}. \quad (63)$$

From this, the critical value of m can be solved as

$$m_{\rm cr} = \frac{\log\left(\Delta t^4 \omega^4 / 360\varepsilon\right)}{4\log(2)}. \tag{64}$$

In the following, the performances of the AECM2 in dealing with rounding errors are discussed. The undamped case is firstly considered, in which $\xi = 0$, $\omega = \pi$, $x_0 = 1$, and $\dot{x}_0 = 1$. The absolute errors in displacement, velocity, and acceleration of the AECM2 and the Fox–Goodwin method are drawn in Figure 16, in which $\Delta t = 1$ and $\Delta t_N = 1/N$ are used in the AEC/DM2 and Fox–Goodwin method, respectively. The well-known Fox–Goodwin method is fourth-order accurate for the undamped system, whereas it is third-order accurate for the damped case. One can see from Figure 16 that the AECM2 and the Fox–Goodwin method have the same slope before $m < 13$, meaning that the AECM2 is strictly fourth-order accurate. Additionally, one can find that: (a) When $m > m_{\rm cr} = 13$, the absolute errors of the AECM2 trend to constants; (b) With the increase of m, the accuracy of the Fox–Goodwin method increases when $m < 13$, and then its accuracy begins to decline when $m \geq 13$.

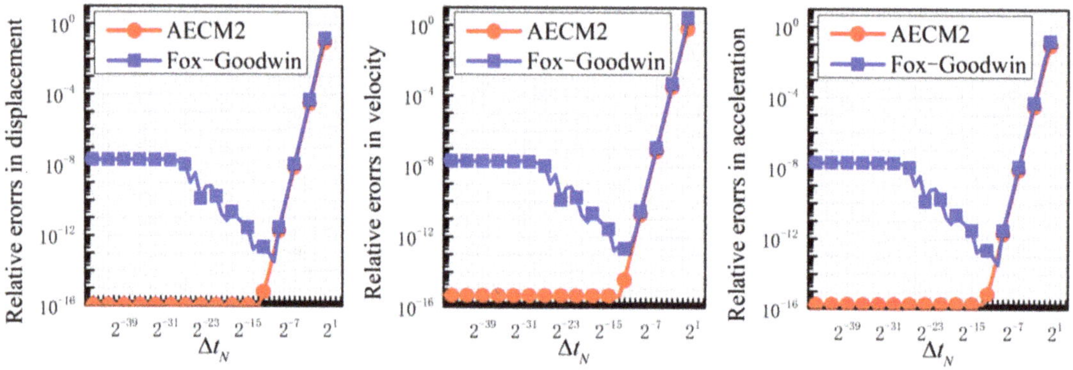

Figure 16. Relative errors in displacement, velocity, and acceleration of the AECM2 for the case of $\xi = 0$ and $f(t) = 0$.

Figure 17 plots the absolute errors of the two methods for the damped case, in which $\xi = 0.5$, $\omega = 2\pi$, $x_0 = 1$, and $\dot{x}_0 = 0$. One can see from Figure 17 that the AECM2 is fourth-order accurate, but the Fox–Goodwin method turns out to be third-order accurate due to the presence of physical damping. In addition, it follows that the accuracy of the AECM2 has no observable variation when $m > m_{\rm cr} = 13$; thus, $m_{\rm cr}$ given in Equation (64) is suitable for the analysis of damped dynamic systems. The critical values of m of the AECM2 are provided in Table 3, wherein one can find that compared with the second-order AECM1, the AECM2 has a smaller $m_{\rm cr}$ for the same $\omega\Delta t$. As shown in Figure 18, when $\omega\Delta t < 1$, the $m_{\rm cr}$ of the AECM2 is about 1/2~1/4 that of the AECM1, implying that the AECM2 enjoys an advantage in efficiency when applied to dynamic systems wherein the low-frequency modes dominate.

Table 3. The critical value of m of the AECM2 for different $\omega\Delta t$.

$\omega\Delta t$	0.01	0.1	1	10	20	50	100	1000	10,000
$m_{\rm cr}$	5	8	12	15	16	17	18	22	25

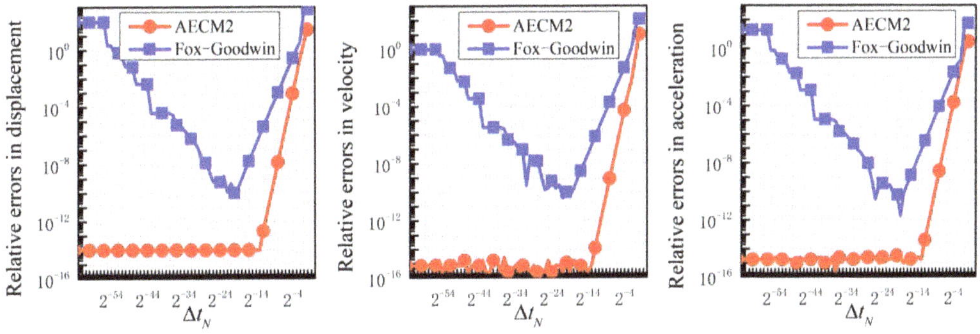

Figure 17. Relative errors in displacement, velocity, and acceleration of the AECM2 for the case of ξ = 0.5 and $f(t) = 0$.

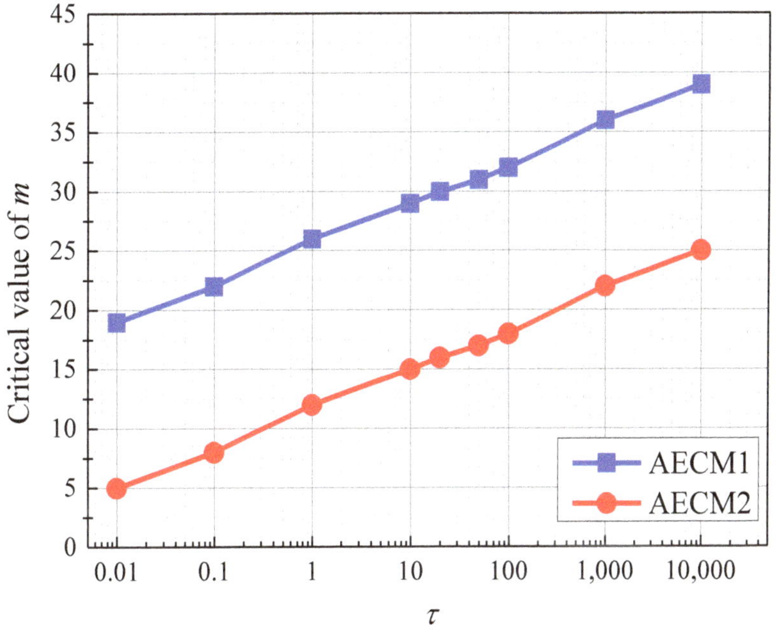

Figure 18. Critical values of m of the AECM1 and AECM2.

At last, the selection of the Gauss–Legendre nodes is discussed here. The standard SDOF test equation (35) is considered again, wherein $\xi = 2/\sqrt{5}$, $\omega = \sqrt{5}$, $x_0 = 57/65$, $\dot{x}_0 = 2/65$, and $f(t) = \sin(2t)$ are adopted. The absolute errors of the AECM2 and the Fox–Goodwin method are compared in Figure 19. It can be seen that: (a) The AECM2 is fourth-order accurate for the dynamic systems including external excitation; (b) Due to the rounding errors, the accuracy of the Fox–Goodwin method begins to decrease after $m > 24$; (c) The accuracy of the AECM2 trend to constants with the decrease in time-step size, and together with four Gauss–Legendre nodes, the accuracy of AECM2 is close to computer precision after $m > m_{cr} = 10$ is achieved from Equation (64). Then, four Gauss–Legendre nodes are employed in the AEC/DM2.

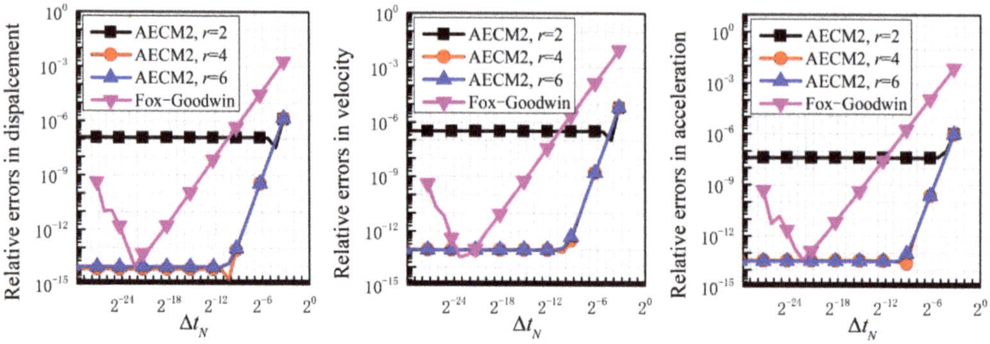

Figure 19. Relative errors in displacement, velocity, and acceleration of the AECM2 for the case of $\xi = 2/\sqrt{5}$ and $f(t) = \sin(2t)$ (r represents number of Gauss–Legendre nodes).

3.3. Overshoot Characteristics

The overshooting phenomenon may occur in the first several time steps. For a convergent method, there is no overshoot as $\tau \to 0$, so only the case of $\tau \to \infty$ needs to be considered. The analysis of overshooting should take into account the effect of physical damping. With physical damping, first-order overshooting components enter into several well-known time integration methods [53], which were previously thought to exhibit zero-order overshooting. The recursive schemes at the first step of the AEC/DM1 and AEC/DM2 are the same for the case of $\tau \to \infty$, which have the forms of

$$x_{t+\Delta t} \approx -\rho_\infty x_t \tag{65}$$

$$\text{and } \Delta t \dot{x}_{t+\Delta t} \approx \rho_\infty \Delta t \dot{x}_t. \tag{66}$$

Through the observation of Equations (65) and (66), one can find that the AEC/DM1 and AEC/DM2 are both zero-order overshoots. The SDOF system given in Equation (35) with $x_0 = 1$ and $\dot{x}_0 = 0$ is considered for testing overshooting behavior. Figures 20 and 21 draw the displacement and velocity of the AEC/DM1 and the AEC/DM2, respectively, at the first step versus $\Delta t/T$, and numerical results validate that our methods have no overshoots both in displacement and velocity.

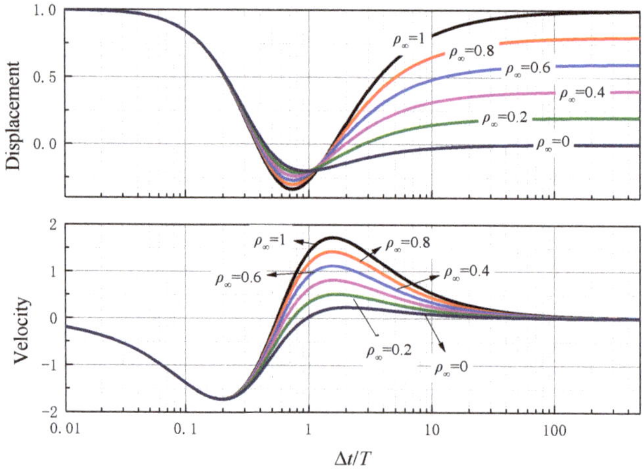

Figure 20. Displacement and velocity at the end of the first time step versus $\Delta t/T$ of the AEC/DM1.

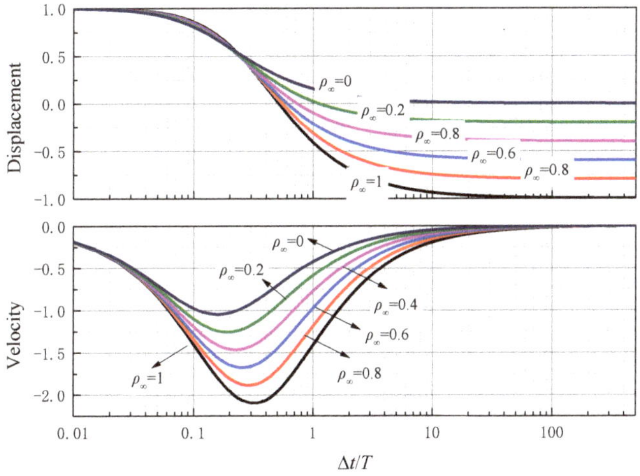

Figure 21. Displacement and velocity at the end of the first time step versus $\Delta t/T$ of the AEC/DM2.

4. Numerical Experiments

The theoretical analysis presented in Section 3 has shown that the time integrators, including the AEC/DM1 and the AEC/DM2 based on the proposed strategy, are unconditionally stable, controllably dissipative, higher-order accurate, and have zero-order overshoots. For linear systems, including the undamped and damped cases, the newly constructed time integrators can converge to computer precision with the increase of m. In this section, some representative linear and nonlinear dynamic systems are simulated to validate the advantages of the proposed methods in stability, accuracy, efficiency, and dissipation compared with some widely-used time integration methods.

4.1. Linear Systems

Two linear numerical experiments are conducted here to validate the conclusions given in Section 3, which can compare the accuracy and efficiency of the proposed methods and the well-known implicit methods, including the TR and Fox–Goodwin methods.

4.1.1. Stiff System

A subclass of the initial value problems [54] involving rapidly decaying transient solutions might arise in a wide variety of engineering applications, such as problems in chemical kinetics, the study of spring and damping systems, and the analysis of control systems. This type of problem is known as a stiff problem. Thus, to test the accuracy and efficiency of the proposed methods in dealing with stiff systems, the following mathematical model is considered as

$$\begin{bmatrix} \dot{y}_1 \\ \dot{y}_2 \end{bmatrix} = \begin{bmatrix} 0 & 1 \\ -10000 & -10001 \end{bmatrix} \begin{bmatrix} y_1 \\ y_2 \end{bmatrix}. \tag{67}$$

The initial conditions are taken to be $y_1(0) = 5$, $y_2(0) = -5$, and the theoretical solutions are

$$y_1(t) = 5\mathrm{e}^{-t}, y_2(t) = -5\mathrm{e}^{-t}. \tag{68}$$

From the governing equations, the natural frequency $\omega = 100$ and numerical damping ratio $\xi = 50.0050$. In this example, the time step sizes of these compared methods are assumed to be: Δt(AECM1) = 0.1, Δt(AECM2) = 0.2, Δt(TR) = 0.1, 0.01, and Δt(Fox–Goodwin) = 0.1, 0.01.

The results in y_1 of all methods are shown in Figure 22, in which one can find that: (a) Among these single-step methods, the higher-order accurate Fox–Goodwin method is unstable for the larger time step size $\Delta t = 0.1$ due to intrinsic conditional stability, while other methods are convergent; (b) With the increase of m, the proposed methods' accuracy can be noticeably improved; (c) The AECM1 ($m > 25$) and AECM2 ($m > 15$) converge to computer precision 10^{-16}, validating that the m_{cr} given in Section 3 is reliable; (d) With the decrease of step size, the TR and Fox–Goodwin methods can both obtain higher accuracy, but their accuracy is far lower than that of the proposed methods.

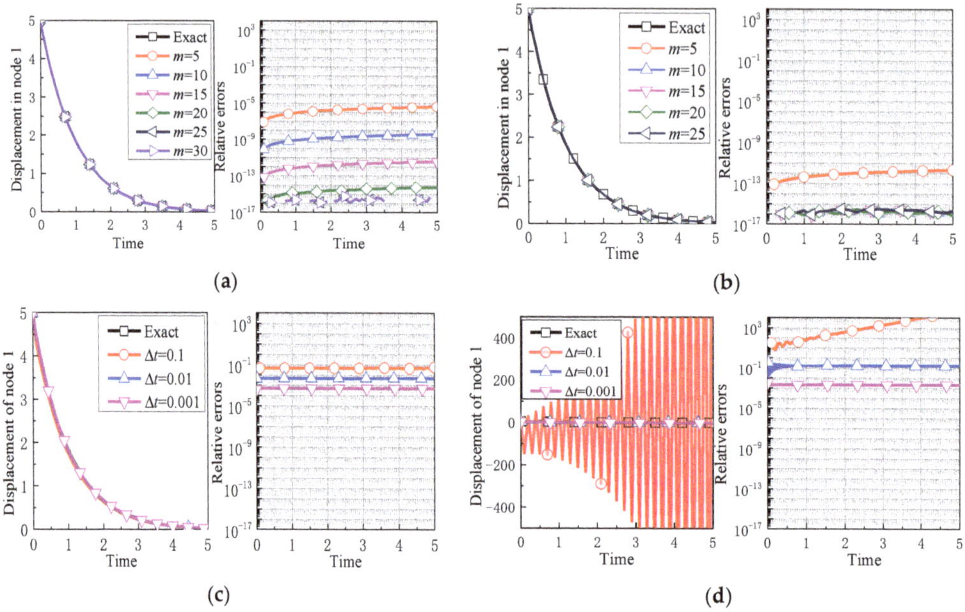

Figure 22. Displacement at the first node and absolute errors versus time: (**a**) AECM1; (**b**) AECM2; (**c**) TR; and (**d**) Fox–Goodwin.

The results in y_2 of these methods are drawn in Figure 23, and some new phenomena can be found. With physical damping, the first-order overshooting components enter into TR, meaning that they induce obvious oscillations for the larger time step size. Since the proposed methods have no overshoots both for undamped and damped systems, they can accurately simulate dynamic problems, including stiff modes.

Additionally, the CPUs of these methods are compared in Table 4. For the proposed methods, the CPU contains 'Preparations' and 'Recursions' in which 'Preparations' is the CPU time for the calculation of $A_{\mathrm{num}}(\Delta t\boldsymbol{H})$, and 'Recursions' represents recursive computations of all time steps. Considering that the DOFs of this example are only two, we only discuss the effect of the value of m and the size of the time step on computational costs. From Table 3, we can find that: (a) The value of m has little effect on the computations for the proposed methods, meaning that the proposed methods' can accuracy be enhanced without efficiency loss; (b) With the decrease of time step size, the accuracy of the TR and Fox–Goodwin methods can be slowly improved, and they need considerable computational costs.

It can be concluded from this example that: (a) Compared with the fourth-order Fox–Goodwin method with conditional stability, the higher-order accurate methods based on our strategy enjoy stability advantage; (b) The proposed methods can obtain computer precision without the extra cost of computations, but the methods based on the difference concept needs heavy burdens to obtain slightly accuracy improvement.

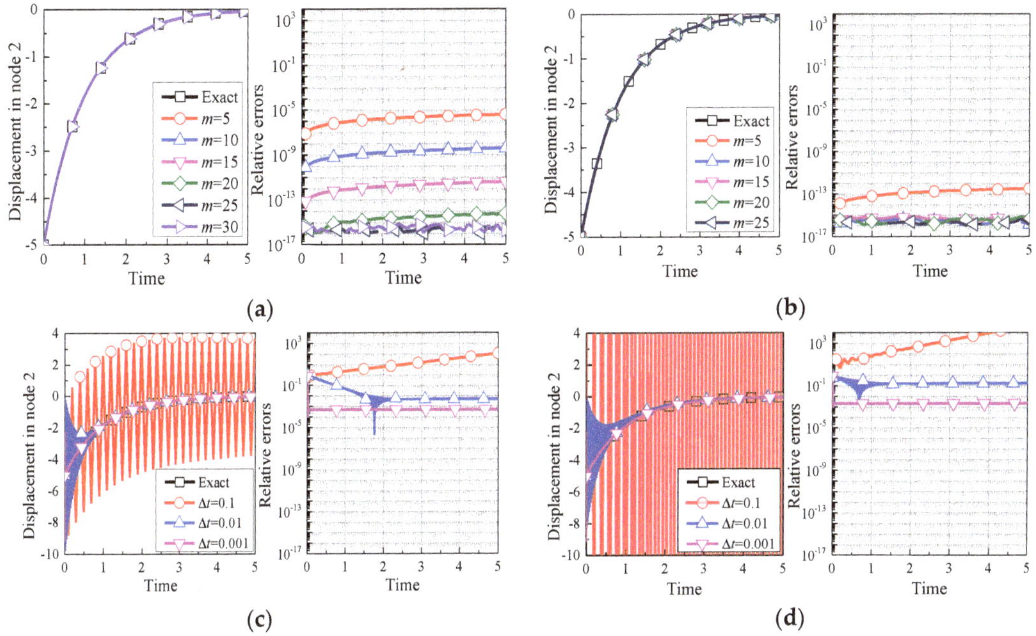

Figure 23. Displacement at the second node and absolute errors versus time: (**a**) AECM1; (**b**) AECM2; (**c**) TR; and (**d**) Fox–Goodwin.

Table 4. CPUs of the AECM1, AECM2, TR, and Fox–Goodwin in the interval [0, 500]s.

	AECM1				**AECM2**			
	$m = 5$	$m = 10$	$m = 20$	$m = 25$	$m = 5$	$m = 10$	$m = 20$	$m = 25$
Preparation	5.7800×10^{-5}	6.2700×10^{-5}	6.3500×10^{-5}	6.6700×10^{-5}	0.0016	0.0017	0.0018	0.0016
Recursion	0.0177	0.0135	0.0139	0.0138	0.0144	0.0125	0.0125	0.0109
Total	0.0178	0.0136	0.0140	0.0139	0.0160	0.0142	0.0143	0.0125
	TR				**Fox–Goodwin**			
	$\Delta t = 0.1$	$\Delta t = 0.01$	$\Delta t = 0.001$		$\Delta t = 0.1$	$\Delta t = 0.01$	$\Delta t = 0.001$	
Preparation	-	-	-		-	-	-	
Recursion	0.0100	0.1251	1.8498		0.0122	0.1063	1.3964	
Total	0.0100	0.1251	1.8498		0.0122	0.1063	1.3964	

4.1.2. Cantilever Plane Truss

The second example forces the accuracy and efficiency performance of the AECM1 and AECM2 in solving linear systems under external excitations. Figure 24 shows the material and geometry properties of the cantilever plane truss [55], which contains 25 repeated structures. In the vertical direction of nodes 42 and 52, two harmonic loads are applied, which have the forms of

$$f_1(t) = -2\sin(1000t)\text{MN} \tag{69}$$

$$\text{and } f_2(t) = -2\sin(10000t)\text{MN}. \tag{70}$$

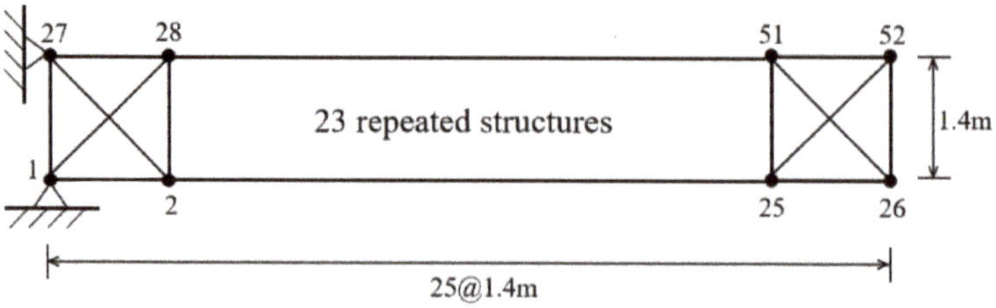

Figure 24. Cantilever plane truss.

The structure has 52 nodes, 226 elements, and 100 DOFs. The modulus of elasticity, density, and sectional areas are $E = 2.5 \times 10^{11}$ N/m^2, $\rho = 1.78 \times 10^3$ kg/m^3, and $A = 1.96 \times 10^{-3}$ m^2, respectively. In this example, $\Delta t = 10^{-5}$ is used in the proposed methods, and $\Delta t = 10^{-5}$, $\Delta t = 10^{-6}$, and $\Delta t = 10^{-7}$ are employed in the TR and Fox–Goodwin methods. The maximum natural frequency of the cantilever plane truss is 24,378, and then the m_{cr} for the AECM1 and the AECM2 can be determined from Section 3, which are 22 and 8, respectively.

The numerical results of these methods are compared in Figures 25–27, from which one can conclude that: (a) The accuracy of the AECM1 no longer improves after $m > 20$, and if $m > 5$, the accuracy of the AECM2 is the same, validating that the reliability of theoretical analysis about m_{cr}; (b) The accuracy improvement of the proposed methods can be achieved by increasing m, while other methods can increase accuracy by decreasing the step size; (c) Among them, the second-order accuracy TR exhibits observable numerical errors in the simulations of velocities and accelerations.

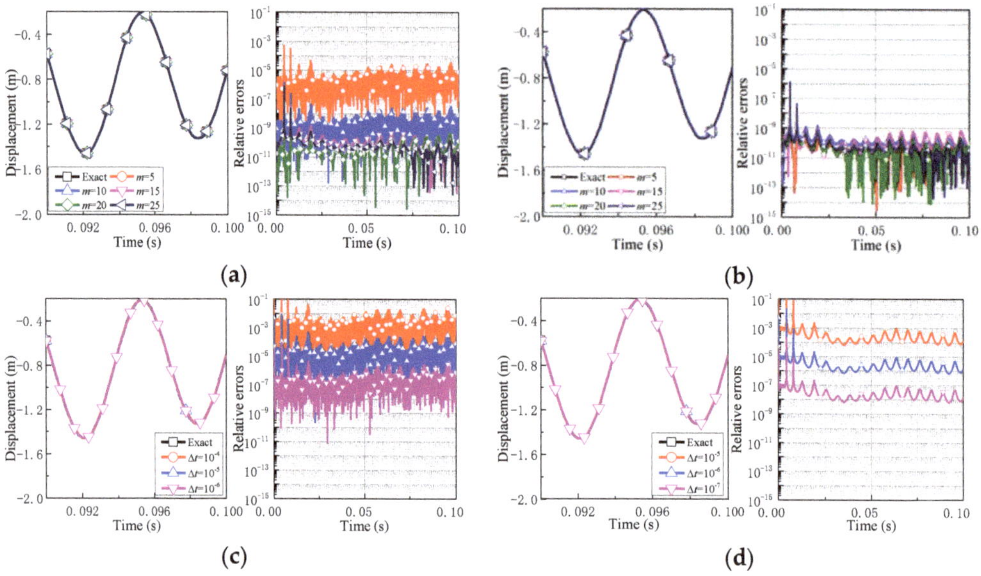

Figure 25. Displacement of node 52 in vertical direction and absolute errors: (**a**) AECM1; (**b**) AECM2; (**c**) TR; and (**d**) Fox–Goodwin.

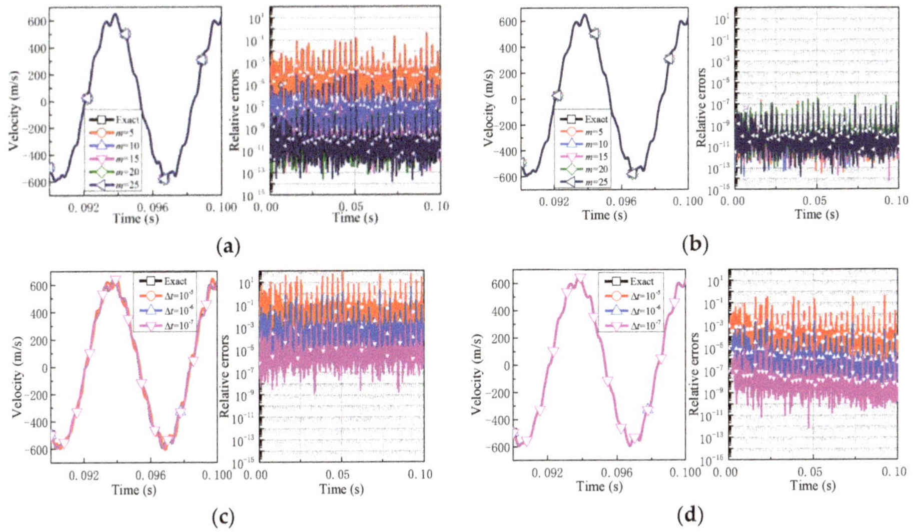

Figure 26. Velocity of node 52 in a vertical direction and absolute errors: (**a**) AECM1; (**b**) AECM2; (**c**) TR; and (**d**) Fox–Goodwin.

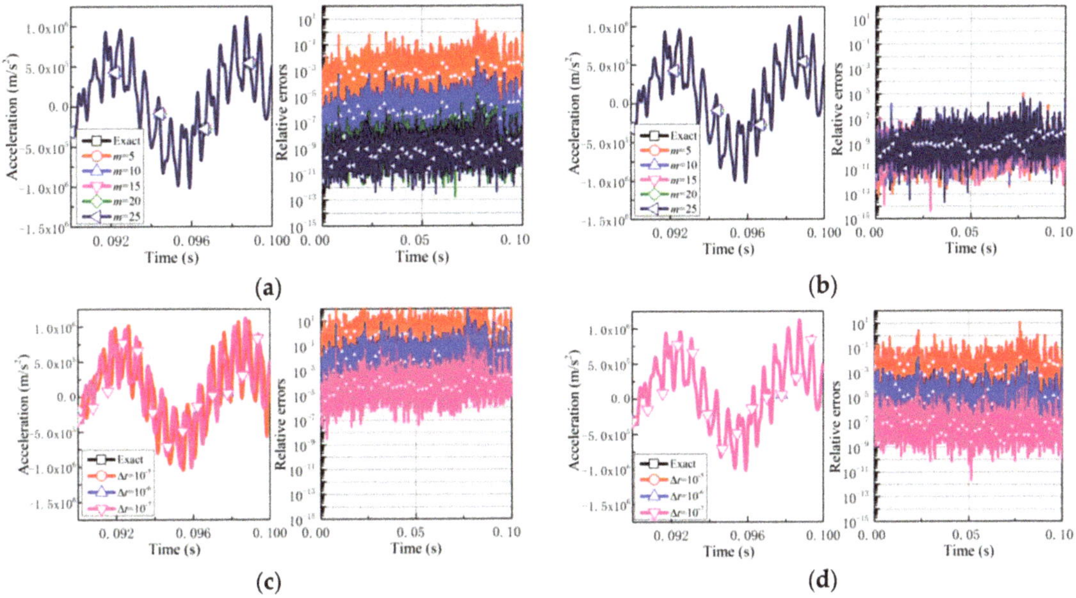

Figure 27. Acceleration of node 52 in a vertical direction and absolute errors: (**a**) AECM1; (**b**) AECM2; (**c**) TR; and (**d**) Fox–Goodwin.

Additionally, the CPUs of these methods are compared in Table 5. It can be seen that: (a) With the increase of m, the proposed methods almost do not produce extra computations; (b) The computational efficiency of the TR and Fox–Goodwin methods dramatically drop with the decrease of the time step size; (c) The TR and Fox–Goodwin methods with $\Delta t = 10^{-6}$ have the same costs with those of the proposed methods, but our methods perform with higher accuracy.

Table 5. CPUs of the AECM1, AECM2, TR, and Fox–Goodwin in the interval [0, 0.1]s.

	AECM1				AECM2			
	$m = 5$	$m = 10$	$m = 20$	$m = 25$	$m = 5$	$m = 10$	$m = 20$	$m = 25$
Preparation	0.0183	0.0254	0.0353	0.0385	0.0209	0.0286	0.0383	0.0459
Recursion	2.2373	2.4461	2.8605	2.8807	2.7853	2.6430	2.9451	2.9320
Total	2.2556	2.4715	2.8958	2.9192	2.8062	2.6716	2.9834	2.9779
	TR				**Fox–Goodwin**			
	$\Delta t = 10^{-5}$	$\Delta t = 10^{-6}$	$\Delta t = 10^{-7}$		$\Delta t = 10^{-5}$	$\Delta t = 10^{-6}$	$\Delta t = 10^{-7}$	
Preparation	-	-	-		-	-	-	
Recursion	0.1629	1.8562	26.8233		0.1306	1.8313	21.9914	
Total	0.1629	1.8562	26.8233		0.1306	1.8313	21.9914	

4.2. Nonlinear Systems

Some representative nonlinear numerical examples are considered in this section. As applied to nonlinear dynamic systems, the proposed methods do not need the Newton iteration method; thus, they are compared with some well-known explicit methods, including the second-order modified Euler method and the classical fourth-order Runge–Kutta method (noted as RK4). Additionally, some advanced multi-step methods and composite methods are considered for comparison.

4.2.1. Averaged System in Wind-Induced Oscillation

The first nonlinear example considers an average system [43] in wind-induced oscillation, and its motion of equation has the form of

$$\begin{cases} \dot{x}_1 = -\zeta x_1 - \lambda x_2 + x_1 x_2 \\ \dot{x}_2 = \lambda x_1 - \zeta x_2 + 0.5\left(x_1^2 - x_2^2\right) \end{cases}, \tag{71}$$

where $\zeta \geq 0$ is a damping factor and λ is a detuning parameter with ζ = rcos(θ), λ = rsin(θ), and $\zeta \geq 0$, $0 \leq \theta \leq \pi/2$. The case of $\theta = \pi/2$ is considered here to analyze the energy-conservation ability of the proposed methods, and the corresponding energy function of this system is

$$E = 0.5r\left(x_1^2 + x_2^2\right) - 0.5\sin\theta\left(x_1^2 x_2 - 1/3x_2^3\right) + 0.5\cos\theta\left(1/3x_2^3 - x_1^2 x_2\right). \tag{72}$$

Consider the initial conditions $x_1(0) = 0$ and $x_2(0) = 1$, and $r = 200$. To improve the stability of these proposed methods in solving dynamic systems, including geometric nonlinearity, $\rho_\infty = 0$ is utilized. The AEDM1 and AEDM2 adopt $\Delta t = 1/(2r)$ and $\Delta t = 1/r$, respectively; $\Delta t = 1/(8r)$, $\Delta t = 1/(15r)$ and $\Delta t = 1/(20r)$ are used in the modified Euler method; $\Delta t = 1/(4r)$, $\Delta t = 1/(10r)$ and $\Delta t = 1/(15r)$ are used in the RK4 method. The relative values of energy errors of these methods are plotted in Figure 28, and Table 6 provides their computations. One can find that: (a) With the increase of the m, the accuracy of the AEDM1 and AEDM2 can be obviously enhanced without additional burdens; (b) The accuracy of the modified Euler method and the RK4 method can be improved by decreasing the size of time step; (c) When the computations of these methods are the roughly same, the AEDM2 is four orders of magnitude more accurate than the modified Euler method and the RK method.

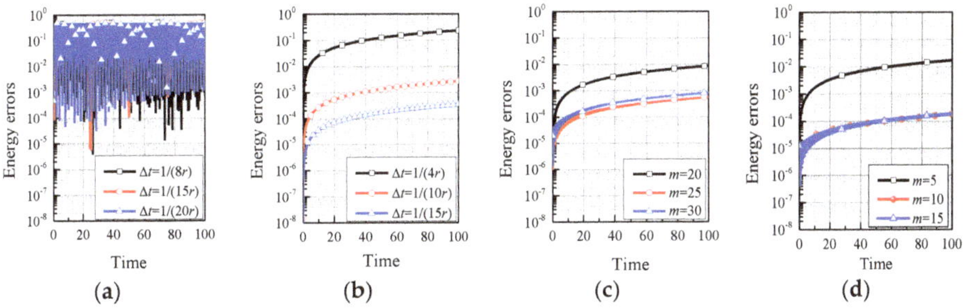

Figure 28. Energy errors of these methods versus time: (**a**) Euler; (**b**) RK4; (**c**) AEDM1; and (**d**) AEDM2.

Table 6. CPUs of the AEDM1, AEDM2, Euler, and RK4 in the simulations of the interval [0, 1000]s.

	AEDM1			**AEDM2**		
	m = 20	m = 25	m = 30	m = 5	m = 10	m = 15
Preparation	0.000169	0.000140	0.000396	0.002044	0.001902	0.002686
Recursion	4.006249	4.395022	4.950563	4.867872	5.423115	6.616388
Total	4.006418	4.395162	4.950959	4.869916	5.425017	6.619074
	Euler			**RK4**		
	Δ*t* = 1/(8*r*)	**Δ*t* = 1/(15 *r*)**	**Δ*t* = 1/(20 *r*)**	**Δ*t* = 1/(4 *r*)**	**Δ*t* = 1/(10 *r*)**	**Δ*t* = 1/(15 *r*)**
Preparation	-	-	-	-	-	-
Recursion	4.054805	6.3309	10.699817	7.299833	16.232617	26.404818
Total	4.054805	6.3309	10.699817	7.299833	16.232617	26.404818

In terms of the initial conditions, we can find the suggested m of the proposed methods as when applied to nonlinear systems. From Equation (71), one can read that the Jacobin matrix of this system at the initial moment has the form of

$$J = \begin{bmatrix} -\zeta + x_2(0) & -\lambda \\ \lambda + x_1(0) & -\zeta - x_2(0) \end{bmatrix} = \begin{bmatrix} 1 & -200 \\ 200 & -1 \end{bmatrix}. \quad (73)$$

Then, the norms of two eigenvalues can be solved, which are equal to 199.9975. In this example, if the time step sizes of the AEDM1 and AEDM2 are 0.0025 and 0.005, respectively, then the $\omega\Delta t$ of them are 0.5 and 1, respectively. Therefore, the m_{cr} can be obtained from Tables 2 and 3, and m_{cr} = 22~26 for AEDM1 and m_{cr} = 12 for AEDM2. From Figure 28, one can observe that the AEDM1 with $m > 25$ and the AEDM2 with $m > 10$ have no observable accuracy improvements. In a way, as applied to nonlinear systems, the proposed methods can select appropriate values of m in terms of the initial dynamic characteristic of nonlinear problems.

4.2.2. Seven-Story Shear Building with Bouc–Wen Hysteresis Model

For analyzing the accuracy and efficiency of the AECM*n* in solving nonlinear systems with physical damping, the second nonlinear example considers a seven-story shear building containing the Bouc–Wen hysteresis model [56–58]. The system is idealized as a simple shear model with seven DOFs, as shown in Figure 29, and it is subjected to sinusoidal excitation.

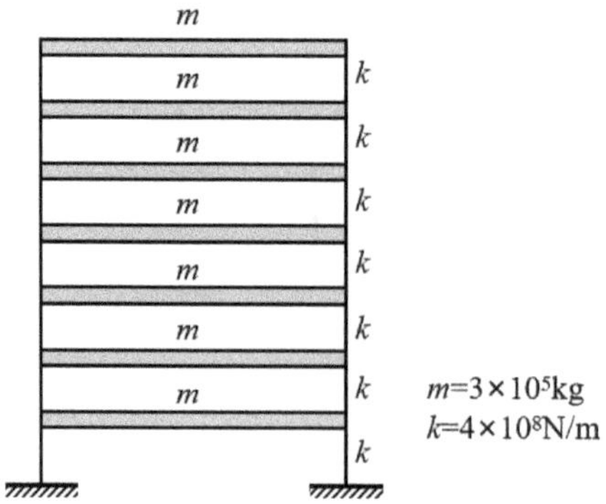

Figure 29. Seven-story shear building.

The governing equation of the system with viscous damping and a hysteretic restoring force given by the Bouc–Wen hysteresis model has the form of

$$\boldsymbol{M}\ddot{\boldsymbol{x}} + \boldsymbol{C}\dot{\boldsymbol{x}} + \mu\boldsymbol{K}\boldsymbol{x} + (1-\mu)\boldsymbol{K}\boldsymbol{z} = -\boldsymbol{M}\ddot{\boldsymbol{x}}_g, \tag{74}$$

where μ is the rigidity ratio that separates the restoring force into a linear component and a hysteretic component; $\boldsymbol{z}$ represents the hysteretic displacement vector related to the displacement $\boldsymbol{x}$; $\ddot{\boldsymbol{x}}_g$ is the vector of ground motion acceleration which has the form of $\ddot{\boldsymbol{x}}_g = [\boldsymbol{0}^{\mathrm{T}} \sin(t)]^{\mathrm{T}}$. In this model, the damping matrix $\boldsymbol{C}$ is defined as

$$\boldsymbol{C} = \alpha\boldsymbol{M} + \beta\boldsymbol{K},\ \alpha = 2\frac{\xi_1\omega_1\omega_2^2 - \xi_2\omega_2\omega_1^2}{\omega_2^2 - \omega_1^2},\ \beta = 2\frac{\xi_2\omega_2 - \xi_1\omega_1}{\omega_2^2 - \omega_1^2}, \tag{75}$$

where ξ_1 and ξ_2 are the viscous damping ratios, which are assumed to be 3% and 5%, respectively, and ω_1 and ω_2 are the first two frequencies. The hysteretic displacement vector $\boldsymbol{z}$ is formulated as

$$\dot{z}_l(t) = h(z_l)\frac{A\dot{x}_l(t) - v_z(t)\left(\beta_z|\dot{x}_l(t)||z_l(t)|^{n_z-1}z_l(t) + \gamma_z\dot{x}_l(t)|z_l(t)|^{n_z}\right)}{\eta_z(t)}, \tag{76}$$

where l is the number of elements; A determines the tangent stiffness; β_z, γ_z, and n_z stand for the hysteretic shape parameters; $h(z_l)$ stands for the pinching function; $v_z(t)$ and $\eta_z(t)$ are the strength and stiffness degradation functions, respectively. The $v_z(t)$ and $\eta_z(t)$ can be obtained by setting

$$v_z(t) = 1 + \delta_v\varepsilon(t),\ \eta_z(t) = 1 + \delta_\eta\varepsilon(t), \tag{77}$$

where δ_v and δ_η represent the strength and stiffness degradation ratios, respectively; the hysteretic energy function $\varepsilon(t)$ has the form of

$$\varepsilon(t) = \int_0^t f_{z,l}(t)\dot{x}(t)\mathrm{d}t, \tag{78}$$

where $f_{z,l}(t)$ represents the associated internal hysteretic force variables collected in the hysteretic restoring force vector $(1-\mu)\boldsymbol{K}\boldsymbol{z}(t)$. The pinching function $h(z_l)$ is formulated as

$$h(z_l) = 1 - \zeta_1(t)\exp\left(-\left(z_l(t)\mathrm{sgn}(\dot{x}_l(t)) - q_z z_{u,l}\right)^2/\zeta_2^2(t)\right), \tag{79}$$

where sgn(.) is the signum function; q_z represents a constant that sets the pinching level as a fraction of $z_{\max}$; $z_{u,l}$ is the ultimate value of $z_l(t)$, which is obtained by

$$z_{u,l} = \left(\frac{1}{v_z(\beta_z + \gamma_z)}\right)^{1/n_z}. \tag{80}$$

The ζ_1(t) controls the magnitude of the initial drop in slope, which is given by

$$\zeta_1(t) = \zeta_s(1 - \exp(-p_z\varepsilon(t))), \tag{81}$$

where p_z is a constant that contributes to the rate of the initial drop in slope and ζ_s is the measure of total slip. The ζ_2(t) causes the pinching region to spread, and its expression is

$$\zeta_2(t) = (\psi + \delta_\psi)(\lambda + \zeta_1(t)), \tag{82}$$

where ψ and δ_ψ represent the pinching magnitude and rate, respectively; λ is a parameter that controls the variation rate of ζ_2(t) with a change of ζ_1(t). The hysteretic model is controlled by the above-mentioned 13 parameters, which are {A, μ, β_z, γ_z, n_z, δ_v, δ_η, ζ_s, p_z, q_z, ψ, δ_ψ, λ} wherein {μ, β_z, γ_z, n_z} determine the shape of the hysteretic model; {δ_v, δ_η} control the system degradation; {ζ_s, p_z, q_z, ψ, δ_ψ, λ} control the pinching phenomenon. In this example, these parameters are assumed to be A = 1, μ = 0.02, β_z = 100, γ_z = 100, n_z = 1.1, δ_v = 0.02, δ_η = 0.1, p_z = 0.02, q_z = 0.3, ζ_s = 0.9, ψ = 0.1, δ_ψ = 0.11, and λ = 0.1.

The displacement and velocity of the bottom story are shown in Figures 30–33, in which the AECM1 and AECM2 adopt Δt = 0.004 and Δt = 0.008, respectively; Δt = 0.001, Δt = 0.0002, and Δt = 0.0001 are used in the modified Euler method; Δt = 0.002, Δt = 0.0004, and Δt = 0.0002 are used in the RK4 method. The reference solution is obtained by the AECM2 with m = 20 using a smaller time step size. The CPUs of these methods are provided in Table 7. It can be found that: (a) With the decrease of time step size, both the modified Euler method and the RK4 method are closer to the reference solution, and the accuracy of the proposed methods can be enhanced by increasing m; (b) Under the same computations, the accuracy of the proposed methods is far higher than that of other methods. To further compare the accuracy of the AECM1 and AECM2, Figure 34 plots their relative errors in displacement, wherein one can see that the accuracy of the AECM2 is higher than that of the AECM1.

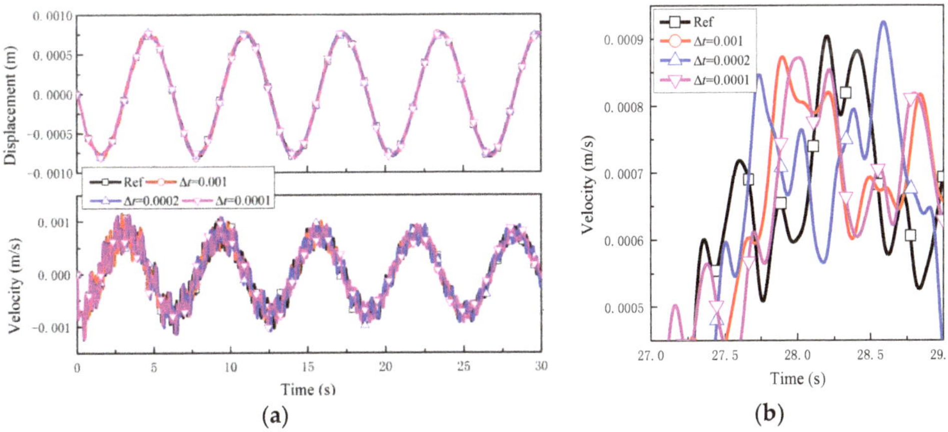

Figure 30. Numerical results of the modified Euler method at the bottom story: (**a**) Numerical results of the bottom story in the [0, 30]s; (**b**) Velocity of the bottom story in the [27, 29]s.

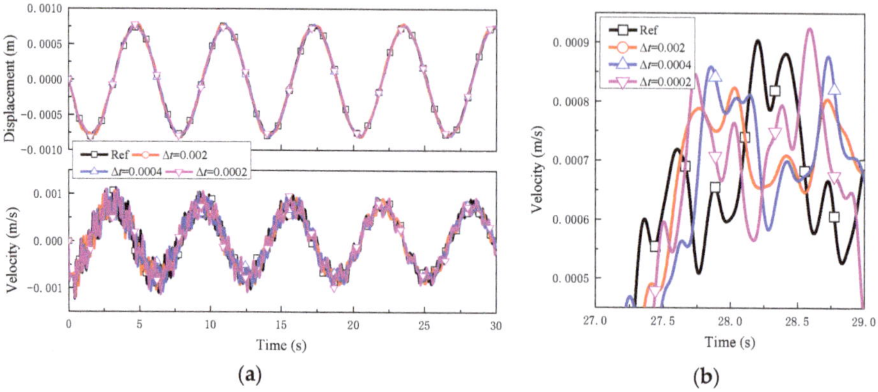

Figure 31. Numerical results of the RK4 method at the bottom story: (**a**) Numerical results of the bottom story in the [0, 30]s; (**b**) Velocity of the bottom story in the [27, 29]s.

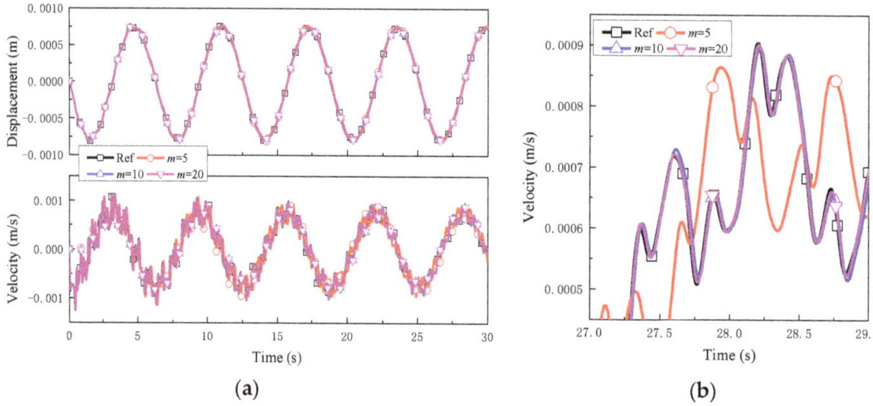

Figure 32. Numerical results of the AECM1 at the bottom story: (**a**) Numerical results of the bottom story in the [0, 30]s; (**b**) Velocity of the bottom story in the [27, 29]s.

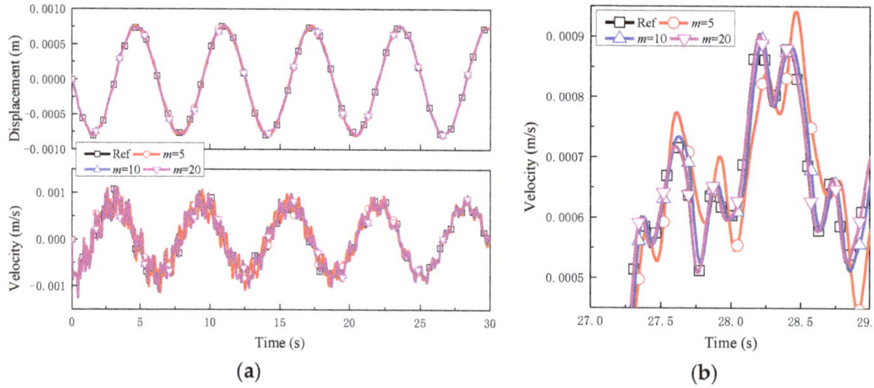

Figure 33. Numerical results of the AECM2 at the bottom story: (**a**) Numerical results of the bottom story in the [0, 30]s; (**b**) Velocity of the bottom story in the [27, 29]s.

Table 7. CPUs of the AECM1, AECM2, Euler, and RK4 in the simulations of the interval [0, 30]s.

	AECM1			**AECM2**		
	m = 5	m = 10	m = 20	m = 5	m = 10	m = 20
Preparation	7.2980×10^{-4}	5.4800×10^{-4}	7.3120×10^{-4}	0.0027	0.0029	0.0029
Recursion	25.7393	26.2247	27.3551	23.0725	23.5911	25.9989
Total	25.7400	26.2252	27.3558	23.0752	23.5940	26.0018
	Euler			**RK4**		
	Δt = 0.001	**Δt = 0.0002**	**Δt = 0.0001**	**Δt = 0.002**	**Δt = 0.0004**	**Δt = 0.0002**
Preparation	-	-	-	-	-	-
Recursion	16.3542	75.2145	155.6917	14.6172	58.4983	139.2688
Total	16.3542	75.2145	155.6917	14.6172	58.4983	139.2688

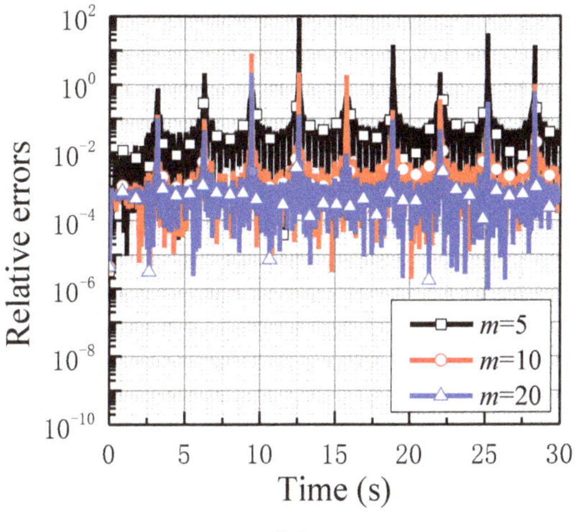

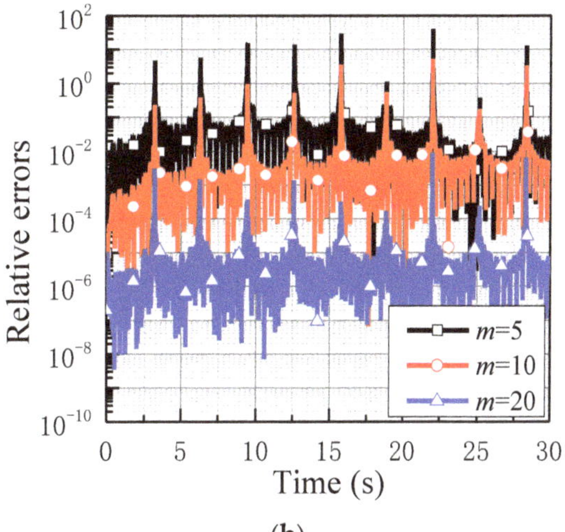

Figure 34. Relative errors of the AECM1 and AECM2 in displacement at the bottom story: (**a**) AECM1; and (**b**) AECM2.

4.2.3. N-Degree-of-Freedom Mass-Spring System

The last example considers an N-degree-of-freedom mass-spring system [59], as shown in Figure 35, to investigate the efficiency performances of the proposed methods in solving large-scale nonlinear problems. The system parameters are as follows:

$$m_i = 1 \quad i = 1, \ldots, N \tag{83}$$

$$\text{and } k_i = \begin{cases} k & i = 1 \\ k\left[1 + \alpha(x_i - x_{i-1})^2\right] & 2 \le i \le N' \end{cases} \tag{84}$$

where $k = 10^5$ N/m and $\alpha = -2$. Additionally, all masses are subjected to the external forces of $f_i(t) = m_i \sin(t)$ ($i = 1, \ldots, N$). In this example, two advanced time integration methods, the LMS2 [60] and the ρ_∞-Bathe method [10], are considered for comparison. The two-step LMS2 is especially effective for stiff systems, and the two-sub-step ρ_∞-Bathe method has been integrated with ADINA due to its superior properties. With zero initial conditions, two cases of N = 100 and 1000 are simulated.

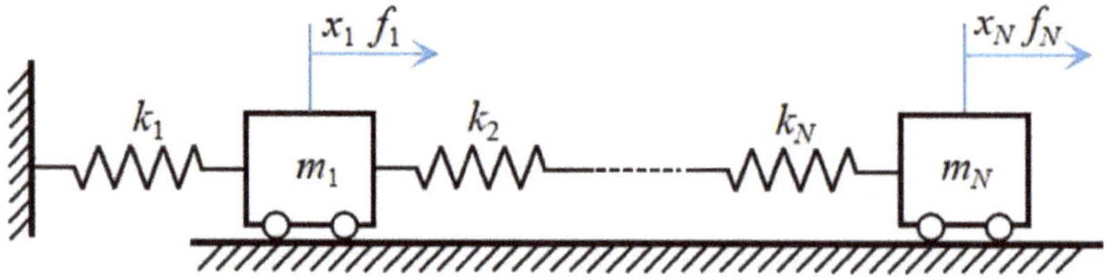

Figure 35. Mass-spring system.

The results of the AECM1 (m = 3, Δt = 0.01 s), the AECM2 (m = 3, Δt = 0.015 s), the LMS2 (Δt = 0.001 s), and the ρ_∞-Bathe method (Δt = 0.002 s) are drawn in Figures 36 and 37, and their computations are provided in Tables 8 and 9. It can be concluded that under the same accuracy performances and compared with the LMS2 and the ρ_∞-Bathe method, the AECM1 and the AECM2 perform considerable advantages in computational efficiency, especially for dynamic problems containing large degree-of-freedoms.

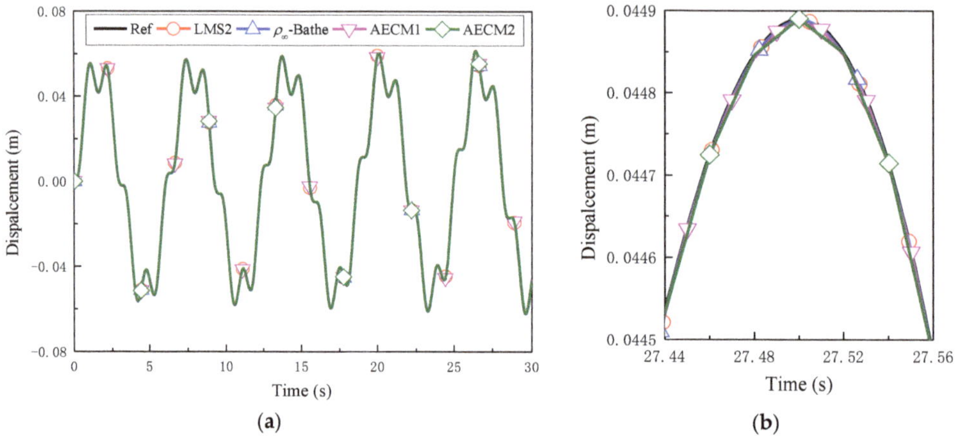

Figure 36. Displacement of the Nth mass (N = 100): (**a**) Simulations in the interval [0, 30]s; (**b**) Simulations in the interval [27.44, 27.56]s.

Table 8. CPUs of the AECM1, AECM2, LMS2, and ρ_∞-Bathe method (N = 100, Total = 30 s).

	AECM1	**AECM2**	**LMS2**	**ρ_∞-Bathe**
Preparation	0.0197	0.0184	-	-
Recursion	3.7715	2.4026	19.8547	19.5784
Total	3.7912	2.4210	19.8547	19.5784

Table 9. CPUs of the AECM1, AECM2, LMS2, and ρ_∞-Bathe method (N = 1000, Total = 30 s).

	AECM1	**AECM2**	**LMS2**	**ρ_∞-Bathe**
Preparation	13.6961	22.8801	-	-
Recursion	339.4413	248.7944	820.9083	686.0195
Total	353.1374	271.6745	820.9083	686.0195

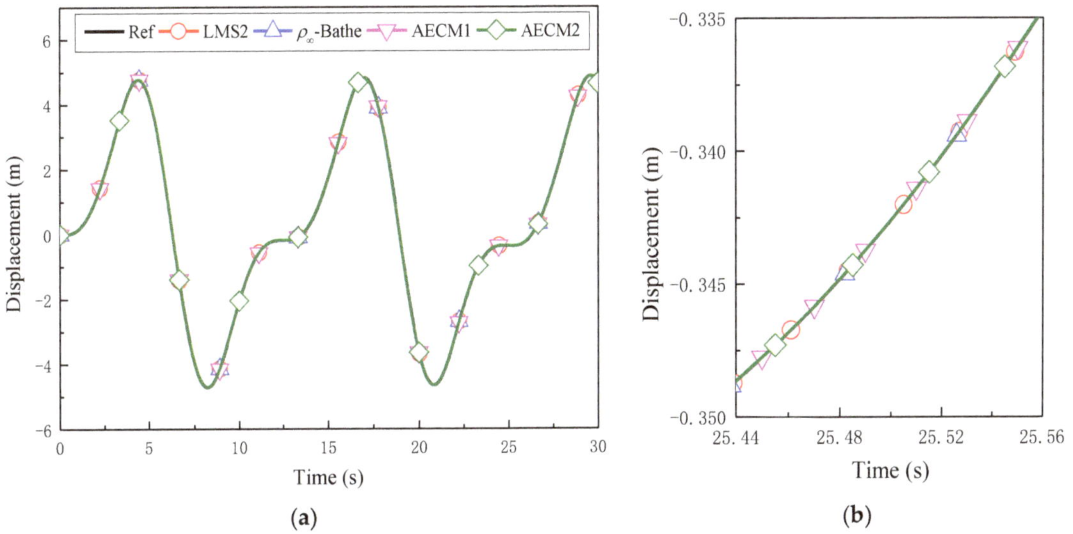

Figure 37. Displacement of the Nth mass (N = 1000): (**a**) Simulations in the interval [0, 30]s; (**b**) Simulations in the interval [25.44, 25.56]s.

5. Conclusions

For the analysis of dynamic systems, this work proposed a family of highly accurate and efficient time integration methods, named the AEC/DMn, based on the generalized Padé approximation, Gauss–Legendre quadrature, and explicit Runge–Kutta method, which was used to calculate function values at Gauss–Legendre quadrature points. The proposed methods can achieve higher-order accuracy, controllable dissipation, and unconditional stability. The 2^m algorithm and the storage of an incremental matrix method were adopted in the proposed methods to quickly and accurately transfer the response of the linear responses, and the nonlinear responses are approximated by the Gauss–Legendre quadrature and explicit Runge–Kutta method. For linear-free vibration problems, the proposed methods can converge to computer precision, and for linear-forced vibration problems and nonlinear problems, the proposed methods enjoy considerable advantages both in accuracy and efficiency compared with the widely-used time integration methods.

The second-order method (AEC/DM1) and the fourth-order method (AEC/DM2) were deeply studied. Their numerical properties, including the spectral characteristics, the rounding errors, and the overshoot characteristics, are deliberately investigated. Additionally, through the analysis of rounding errors, the critical values of sub-steps m that make numerical results converge to computer precision were found. Numerical experiments validated that the two methods have obvious accuracy and efficiency advantages compared with some widely-used methods, and the critical values of m given in this work are reliable. It was concluded from the theoretical analysis and numerical experiments that the speed of the fourth-order AEC/DM2 in accuracy improvement is quicker than that of the second-order AEC/DM1. In a way, this work has provided good candidates for the analysis of transient problems that widely exist in structural dynamics, multibody dynamics, heat conduction, and so on.

Author Contributions: Conceptualization, Y.J.; data curation, Y.J.; funding acquisition, Y.J. and Y.X.; software, Y.J.; supervision, Y.X.; validation, Y.J.; writing—original draft, Y.J.; writing—review and editing, Y.X. All authors have read and agreed to the published version of the manuscript.

Funding: This work was supported by the National Natural Science Foundation of China (12202058, 12172023, and 11872090), the China Postdoctoral Science Foundation (2022M710386), and the Outstanding Research Project of Shen Yuan Honors College BUAA (230121104).

Data Availability Statement: Not applicable.

Conflicts of Interest: The authors declare that they have no conflict of interest.

References

1. Hughes, T.J.R. *The Finite Element Method: Linear Static and Dynamic Finite Element Analysis*; Prentice-Hall: Englewood Cliffs, NJ, USA, 1987.
2. Saleh, M.; Kovacs, E.; Barna, I.F.; Matyas, L. New analytical results and comparison of 14 numerical schemes for the diffusion equation with space-dependent diffusion coefficient. *Mathematics* **2022**, *10*, 2813. [CrossRef]
3. Butcher, J.C. *Numerical Methods for Ordinary Differential Equations*; John Wiley & Sons, Ltd.: Chichester, UK, 2016.
4. Bank, R.E.; Coughran, W.M.; Fichtner, W.; Grosse, E.H.; Rose, D.J.; Smith, R.K. Transient simulation of silicon devise and circuits. *IEEE Trans. Comput.-Aided Des. Integr. Circuits Syst.* **1985**, *32*, 1992–2007.
5. Bathe, K.J.; Baig, M.M.I. On a composite implicit time integration procedure for nonlinear dynamics. *Comput. Struct.* **2005**, *83*, 2513–2524. [CrossRef]
6. Chandra, Y.; Zhou, Y.; Stanciulescu, I.; Eason, T.; Spottswood, S. A robust composite time integration scheme for snap-through problems. *Comput. Mech.* **2015**, *55*, 1041–1056. [CrossRef]
7. Wen, W.B.; Wei, K.; Lei, H.S.; Duan, S.Y.; Fang, D.N. A novel sub-step composite implicit time integration scheme for structural dynamics. *Comput. Struct.* **2017**, *182*, 176–186. [CrossRef]
8. Zhang, H.M.; Xing, Y.F. Optimization of a class of composite method for structural dynamics. *Comput. Struct.* **2018**, *202*, 60–73. [CrossRef]
9. Xing, Y.F.; Ji, Y.; Zhang, H.M. On the construction of a type of composite time integration methods. *Comput. Struct.* **2019**, *221*, 157–178. [CrossRef]
10. Noh, G.; Bathe, K.J. The Bathe time integration method with controllable spectral radius: The ρ_∞-Bathe method. *Comput. Struct.* **2019**, *212*, 299–310. [CrossRef]
11. Kim, W.; Choi, S.Y. An improved implicit time integration algorithm: The generalized composite time integration algorithm. *Comput. Struct.* **2018**, *196*, 341–354. [CrossRef]
12. Ji, Y.; Xing, Y.F. An optimized three-sub-step composite time integration method with controllable numerical dissipation. *Comput. Struct.* **2020**, *231*, 106210. [CrossRef]
13. Li, J.Z.; Yu, K.P.; Li, X.Y. A novel family of controllably dissipative composite integration algorithms for structural dynamic analysis. *Nonlinear Dyn.* **2019**, *96*, 2475–2507. [CrossRef]
14. Ji, Y.; Zhang, H.; Xing, Y.F. New insights into a three-sub-step composite method and its performance on multibody systems. *Mathematics* **2022**, *10*, 2375. [CrossRef]
15. Liu, T.H.; Huang, F.L.; Wen, W.B.; He, X.H.; Duan, S.Y.; Fang, D.N. Further insights of a composite implicit time integration scheme and its performance on linear seismic response analysis. *Eng. Struct.* **2021**, *241*, 112490. [CrossRef]
16. Zhang, J.Y.; Shi, L.; Liu, T.H.; Zhou, D.; Wen, W.B. Performance of a three-substep time integration method on structural nonlinear seismic analysis. *Math. Probl. Eng.* **2021**, *2021*, 6442260. [CrossRef]
17. Li, J.Z.; Zhao, R.; Yu, K.P.; Li, X.Y. Directly self-starting higher-order implicit integration algorithms with flexible dissipation control for structural dynamics. *Comput. Method Appl. Mech. Eng.* **2022**, *389*, 114274. [CrossRef]
18. Zhang, H.M.; Zhang, R.S.; Xing, Y.F.; Masarati, P. On the optimization of n-sub-step composite time integration methods. *Nonlinear Dyn.* **2021**, *21*, 2150073. [CrossRef]
19. Rezaiee-Pajand, M.; Sarafrazi, S.R. A mixed and multi-step higher-order implicit time integration family. *Proc. Inst. Mech. Eng. Part C J. Mech. Eng. Sci.* **2010**, *224*, 2097–2108. [CrossRef]
20. Kuhl, D.; Crisfield, M.A. Energy-conserving and decaying algorithms in non-linear structural dynamics. *Int. J. Numer. Methods Eng.* **1999**, *45*, 569–599. [CrossRef]
21. Park, K.C. Improved stiffly stable method for direct integration of nonlinear structural dynamics. *J. Appl. Mech. ASME* **1975**, *42*, 464–470. [CrossRef]
22. Belytschko, T.; Schoeberle, D.F. On the unconditional stability of an implicit algorithm for nonlinear structural dynamics. *J. Appl. Mech. ASME* **1975**, *42*, 865–869. [CrossRef]
23. Lavrencic, M.; Brank, B. Comparison of numerically dissipative schemes for structural dynamics: Generalized-alpha versus energy-decaying methods. *Thin-Wall. Struct.* **2020**, *157*, 107075. [CrossRef]
24. Xue, T.; Wang, Y.Z.; Aanjaneya, M.; Tamma, K.K.; Qin, G.L. On a generalized energy conservation/dissipation time finite element method for Hamiltonian mechanics. *Comput. Method Appl. Mech. Eng.* **2021**, *373*, 113509. [CrossRef]
25. Luo, J.H.; Feng, X.G.; Xu, X.M.; Peng, H.J.; Wu, Z.G. A parameter-preadjusted energy-conserving integration for rigid body dynamics in terms of convected base vectors. *Int. J. Numer. Methods Eng.* **2020**, *121*, 4921–4943. [CrossRef]
26. Zhang, H.M.; Xing, Y.F.; Ji, Y. An energy-conserving and decaying time integration method for general nonlinear dynamics. *Int. J. Numer. Methods Eng.* **2020**, *121*, 925–944. [CrossRef]

27. Chang, S.Y. Explicit pseudodynamic algorithm with unconditional stability. *J. Eng. Mech.* **2002**, *128*, 935–947. [CrossRef]
28. Chen, C.; Ricles, J.M. Development of direct integration algorithms for structural dynamics using discrete control theory. *J. Eng. Mech.* **2008**, *134*, 676–683. [CrossRef]
29. Kolay, C.; Ricles, J.M. Improved explicit integration algorithms for structural dynamic analysis with unconditional stability and controllable numerical dissipation. *J. Earthq. Eng.* **2019**, *23*, 771–792. [CrossRef]
30. Li, J.Z.; Yu, K.P.; Li, X.Y. A generalized structure-dependent semi-explicit method for structural dynamics. *J. Comput. Nonlinear Dyn.* **2018**, *13*, 111008. [CrossRef]
31. Namadchi, A.H.; Jandaghi, E.; Alamatian, J. A new model-dependent time integration scheme with effective numerical damping for dynamic analysis. *Eng. Comput.* **2021**, *37*, 2543–2558. [CrossRef]
32. Fu, B.; Zhang, F.T. A dual-explicit model-based integration algorithm with higher-order accuracy for structural dynamics. *Appl. Math. Model.* **2022**, *110*, 513–541. [CrossRef]
33. Soares, D. A simple and effective single-step time marching technique based on adaptive time integrators. *Int. J. Numer. Methods Eng.* **2017**, *109*, 1344–1368. [CrossRef]
34. Soares, D. Nonlinear dynamic analysis considering explicit and implicit time marching techniques with adaptive time integration parameters. *Acta Mech.* **2018**, *229*, 2097–2116. [CrossRef]
35. Soares, D. An improved adaptive formulation for explicit analyses of wave propagation models considering locally-defined self-adjustable time-integration parameters. *Comput. Method Appl. Mech. Eng.* **2022**, *399*, 115324. [CrossRef]
36. Soares, D. A locally stabilized explicit approach for coupled thermo-mechanical analysis. *Adv. Eng. Softw.* **2020**, *149*, 102883. [CrossRef]
37. Zhong, W.X.; Williams, F.W. A precise time step integration method. *Proc. Inst. Mech. Eng. Part C J. Mech. Eng. Sci.* **1994**, *208*, 427–430. [CrossRef]
38. Gao, Q.; Nie, C.B. An accurate and efficient Chebyshev expansion method for large-scale transient heat conduction problems. *Comput. Struct.* **2021**, *249*, 106513. [CrossRef]
39. Ding, Z.; Li, L.; Hu, Y.J. A modified precise integration method for transient dynamic analysis in structural systems with multiple damping models. *Mech. Syst. Signal Process.* **2018**, *98*, 613–633. [CrossRef]
40. Tian, W.; Yang, Z.C.; Gu, Y.S. Dynamic analysis of an aeroelastic airfoil with freeplay nonlinearity by precise integration method based on Padé approximation. *Nonlinear Dyn.* **2017**, *89*, 2173–2194. [CrossRef]
41. Ji, Y.; Xing, Y.F. Highly precise and efficient solution strategy for linear heat conduction and structural dynamics. *Int. J. Numer. Methods Eng.* **2022**, *123*, 366–395. [CrossRef]
42. Song, C.M.; Eisentrager, S.; Zhang, X.R. High-order implicit time integration scheme based on Padé expansions. *Comput. Method Appl. Mech. Eng.* **2022**, *390*, 114436. [CrossRef]
43. Li, L. A new symmetric linearly implicit exponential integrator preserving polynomial invariants or Lyapunov functions for conservative or dissipative systems. *J. Comput. Phys.* **2022**, *449*, 110800. [CrossRef]
44. Michels, D.L.; Luan, V.T.; Tokman, M. A stiffly accurate integrator for ealstodynamic problems. *ACM Trans. Graph.* **2017**, *36*, 116. [CrossRef]
45. Hammoud, B.; Olivieri, L.; Righetti, L.; Carpentier, J.; Prete, A. Exponential integration for efficient and accurate multibody simulation with stiff viscoelastic contacts. *Multibody Syst. Dyn.* **2022**, *54*, 443–460. [CrossRef]
46. Chen, Y.J.; Ascher, U.M.; Pai, D.K. Exponential rosenbrock-euler integrators for elastodynamic simulation. *IEEE Trans. Vis. Comput. Graph.* **2018**, *24*, 2702. [CrossRef]
47. Hochbruck, M.; Ostermann, A. Exponential integrators. *Acta Numer.* **2010**, *19*, 209–286. [CrossRef]
48. Fung, T.C. Construction of higher-order accurate time-step integration algorithms by equal-order polynomial projection. *J. Vib. Control* **2005**, *11*, 19–49. [CrossRef]
49. Nettesheim, P.; Bornemann, F.A.; Schmidt, B.; Schutte, C. An explicit and symplectic integrator for quantum-classical molecular dynamics. *Chem. Phys. Lett.* **1996**, *256*, 581–588. [CrossRef]
50. Rambeerich, N.; Tangman, D.Y.; Gopaul, A.; Bhuruth, M. Exponential time integration for fast finite element solutions of some financial engineering problems. *J. Comput. Appl. Math.* **2009**, *224*, 668–678. [CrossRef]
51. Matute, J.; Pardo, D.; Demkowicz, L. Equivalence between the DPG method and the exponential integrators for linear parabolic problems. *J. Comput. Phys.* **2021**, *429*, 110016. [CrossRef]
52. Zhang, J.; Liu, Y.L.; Liu, D.H. Accuracy of a composite implicit time integration scheme for structural dynamics. *Int. J. Numer. Methods Eng.* **2017**, *109*, 368–406. [CrossRef]
53. Maxam, D.J.; Tamma, K.K. A re-evaluation of overshooting in time integration schemes: The neglected effect of physical damping in the starting procedure. *Int. J. Numer. Methods Eng.* **2022**, *123*, 2683–2704. [CrossRef]
54. Chang, S.Y. A novel series of solution methods for solving nonlinear stiff dynamic problems. *Nonlinear Dyn.* **2022**, *107*, 2539–2562. [CrossRef]
55. Rezaiee-Pajand, M.; Alamatian, J. Implicit higher-order accuracy method for numerical integration in dynamic analysis. *J. Struct. Eng.* **2008**, *134*, 973–985. [CrossRef]
56. Loh, C.H.; Mao, C.H.; Huang, J.R.; Pan, T.C. System identification and damage evaluation of degrading hysteresis of reinforced concrete frames. *Earthq. Eng. Struct. Dyn.* **2011**, *40*, 623–640. [CrossRef]
57. Yang, Y.; Ma, F. Constrained Kalman filter for nonlinear structural identification. *J. Vib. Control* **2003**, *9*, 1343–1357. [CrossRef]

58. Sengupta, P.; Li, B. Modified Bouc-Wen model for hysteresis behavior of RC beam -column joints with limited transverse reinforcement. *Eng. Struct.* **2013**, *46*, 392–406. [CrossRef]
59. Ji, Y.; Xing, Y.F.; Wiercigroch, M. An unconditionally stable time integration method with controllable dissipation for second-order nonlinear dynamics. *Nonlinear Dyn.* **2021**, *105*, 3341–3358. [CrossRef]
60. Zhang, H.M.; Zhang, R.S.; Masarati, P. Improved second-order unconditionally stable schemes of linear multi-step and equivalent single-step integration methods. *Comput. Mech.* **2021**, *67*, 289–313. [CrossRef]

Disclaimer/Publisher's Note: The statements, opinions and data contained in all publications are solely those of the individual author(s) and contributor(s) and not of MDPI and/or the editor(s). MDPI and/or the editor(s) disclaim responsibility for any injury to people or property resulting from any ideas, methods, instructions or products referred to in the content.

mathematics

MDPI

Article

Solution of the Goursat Problem for a Fourth-Order Hyperbolic Equation with Singular Coefficients by the Method of Transmutation Operators

Sergei M. Sitnik [1,*] and Shakhobiddin T. Karimov [2]

[1] Department of Applied Mathematics and Computer Modeling, Belgorod State National Research University (BelGU), Pobedy Street, 85, 308015 Belgorod, Russia

[2] Department of Applied Mathematics and Informatics, Fergana State University (FSU), Murabbiylar Street, 3A, Fergana 150100, Uzbekistan

* Correspondence: sitnik@bsu.edu.ru

Abstract: In this paper, the method of transmutation operators is used to construct an exact solution of the Goursat problem for a fourth-order hyperbolic equation with a singular Bessel operator. We emphasise that in many other papers and monographs the fractional Erdélyi-Kober operators are used as integral operators, but our approach used them as transmutation operators with additional new properties and important applications. Specifically, it extends its properties and applications to singular differential equations, especially with Bessel-type operators. Using this operator, the problem under consideration is reduced to a similar problem without the Bessel operator. The resulting auxiliary problem is solved by the Riemann method. On this basis, an exact solution of the original problem is constructed and analyzed.

Keywords: Goursat problem; Bessel operator; transmutation operator; Erdélyi-Kober operator; Riemann method; fourth-order equation

MSC: 26D07; 26D10; 26D15; 26A33

Citation: Sitnik, S.M.; Karimov, S.T. Solution of the Goursat Problem for a Fourth-Order Hyperbolic Equation with Singular Coefficients by the Method of Transmutation Operators. *Mathematics* **2023**, *11*, 951. https://doi.org/10.3390/math11040951

Academic Editor: Hongyu Liu

Received: 6 January 2023
Revised: 3 February 2023
Accepted: 5 February 2023
Published: 13 February 2023

Copyright: © 2023 by the authors. Licensee MDPI, Basel, Switzerland. This article is an open access article distributed under the terms and conditions of the Creative Commons Attribution (CC BY) license (https://creativecommons.org/licenses/by/4.0/).

1. Introduction: Formulation of the Problem

The study of more complex higher-order equations with singular coefficients is a natural next step on the path of theoretical generalizations. The value of the theoretical results obtained in this way increases substantially in connection with the fact that such equations or their special cases occur in applications.

We especially note the class of partial differential equations with singularities in the coefficients, typical representatives of which are equations with Bessel operators of the form

$$B_\eta^x = x^{-2\eta-1}\frac{d}{dx}x^{2\eta+1}\frac{d}{dx} = \frac{d^2}{dx^2} + \frac{2\eta+1}{x}\frac{d}{dx} \tag{1}$$

For equations of elliptic, hyperbolic, and parabolic types with the Bessel operator in single or several variables, I.A. Kipriyanov [1] introduced the terminology B-elliptic, B-hyperbolic, and B-parabolic equations, respectively. The importance of equations from these classes is also determined by their use in applications to problems of generalized axially symmetric potential theory (GASPT) [2,3], Euler-Poisson-Darboux (EPD) equations [4,5], Radon transform and tomography [6–8], gas dynamics and acoustics [9], the theory of jets in hydrodynamics [10], the linearized Maxwell-Einstein equations [11,12], mechanics, the theory of elasticity and plasticity [13], and many others.

In a certain approximation, we can say that these three classes of differential equations according to the terminology of I.A. Kipriyanov were once considered in three well-known monographs: B-elliptic equations in the monograph by I.A. Kipriyanov [1], B-hyperbolic equations in the monograph by R. Carroll and R. Showalter [14], and B-parabolic equations in the monograph by M.I. Matiichuk [15]. Of course, many other problems are covered in these books.

The entire range of questions for equations with Bessel operators was most fully studied by the Voronezh mathematician I.A. Kipriyanov and his students. Note also that the 2023rd year is a centennial jubilee of Professor Ivan Alexandrovich Kipriyanov. More detailed information about this direction can be found in the monographs of V.V. Katrakhov and S.M. Sitnik [16], S.M. Sitnik, and E.L. Shishkina [17,18]. These types of equations is also deeply connected with fractional type operators, via Riemann–Liouville, Gerasimov, Erdélyi-Kober and other classes of operators, different classical integral transforms, and integral transforms with special function kernels, cf. [17–22].

The theory of equations with singular coefficients is closely related to the theory of equations degenerating on the boundary of a domain. By means of a change of variables, one can reduce a rather wide class of degenerate equations to equations with singular coefficients.

The difficulty to solve problems in the theory of partial differential equations with singular coefficients, as well as the resulting equations that degenerate at the boundary of the domain under consideration, has been extremely stimulating and continues to stimulate intensive research in this area. This is confirmed by numerous scientific publications over the past fifty years, noted the monographs of M.S. Salakhitdinov and A.K. Urinov [20], T.D. Dzhuraev and A. Sapuev [23], V.I. Zhegalov, A.N. Mironov, E.A. Utkina [24], A.M. Nakhushev [25], M.S. Salakhitdinov and M. Mirsaburov [26], V. V. Katrakhov and S. M. Sitnik [16], S. M. Sitnik and E. L. Shishkina [17,18], M.S. Salakhitdinov and B. Islamov [27], O.A. Marichev, A.A. Kilbas and O.A. Repin [28], A.K. Urinov [29,30], A. K. Urinov and Sh.T. Karimov [21], and others.

Note that in this paper, we consider only mathematical problems of differential equations and transmutations, and do not consider computational aspects of related problems or applications to physics, mechanics, etc.

In this paper in the domain $\Omega = \{(x,y) : 0 < x < l,\ 0 < y < h\}$, we consider the equation

$$L_{a,b}^{c}(u) \equiv \frac{\partial^4 u}{\partial x^2 \partial y^2} + \frac{a}{x}\frac{\partial^3 u}{\partial x \partial y^2} + \frac{b}{y}\frac{\partial^3 u}{\partial y \partial x^2} + \frac{ab}{xy}\frac{\partial^2 u}{\partial x \partial y} + cu = 0, \tag{2}$$

where $l, h, a, b, c \in R$, and $l, h > 0, 0 < a, b < 1$.

Equation (2) for $a = b = 0$ was studied in [23] and, according to the classification of this work, it belongs to the hyperbolic type. The straight lines $x = const,\ \ y = const$ are real double characteristics of Equation (2).

In [23], the problems were considered in the characteristic quadrangle, and the coefficients of the equation were smooth enough to ensure the existence of the Riemann function, in terms of which, ultimately, the solutions of the problems were written. However, the problems for Equation (2), whose coefficients have singularities, are almost not studied. The coefficients of Equation (2) have a singularity on the lines $x = 0,\ \ y = 0$; such equations are called equations with singular coefficients. In addition, the singularity lines are simultaneously the characteristics of this equation.

A systematic study of two-dimensional equations of the fourth order was considered in the works of M.S. Salakhitdinov [31], T.D. Dzhuraev and A. Sopuev [23], V.I. Zhegalov, A.N. Mironov, E.A. Utkina [24], M.M. Smirnov [32], M.M. Meredov [33], A.K. Urinov [29] and their students. In the works of T.D. Dzhuraev and A. Sopuev [23], the questions of complete classification and reduction to the canonical form of a general linear fourth-order equation with two independent variables were studied. It is known that degenerate and singular equations of the second order have the peculiarity that the well-posedness of classical problems does not always hold for them. The formulation of the problem is significantly affected by lower coefficients. Such questions for high-order equations with singular coefficients have hardly been studied. In this paper, in domain Ω, we study an analogue of the Goursat problem for Equation (2).

Problem G. It is required to find a function $u(x,y) \in C(\bar{\Omega})$ satisfying Equation (1) and boundary conditions

$$u(0,y) = \varphi_1(y), \ \lim_{x\to 0} x^a u_x(x,y) = \varphi_2(y), \ 0 \leqslant y \leqslant h \tag{3}$$

$$u(x,0) = \psi_1(x), \ \lim_{y\to 0} y^b u_y(x,y) = \psi_2(x), \ 0 \leqslant x \leqslant l. \tag{4}$$

where $\varphi_k(y)$, $\psi_k(x)$, $(k = 1,2)$ are given smooth functions, such that $\varphi_1(0) = \psi_1(0)$, $\varphi_2(0) = \psi_2(0) = 0$. In this paper, in contrast to the cited sources, we use a different approach to solve the problem. Namely, taking into account the specifics of equations with singular coefficients, we use the Erdélyi-Kober transmutation operator.

Definition 1 ([16,17,34–36]). *Let a pair of operators (A,B) be given. A non-zero operator T is called a transmutation operator if the relation holds*

$$TA = BT. \tag{5}$$

In order for (5) to be a rigorous definition, it is necessary to specify spaces or sets of functions on which the operators A, B, and, consequently, T, act; various transmutation operators' issues are also considered in [17,36].

The Erdélyi-Kober operators for a certain choice of parameters are a generalization of the classical Sonin and Poisson transmutation operators [16,17,21,34–36]. We emphasise that in many of the above mentioned papers and monographs, the fractional Erdélyi-Kober operators are used as integral operators, but our approach uses them as transmutation operators with additional new properties and important applications. To be specific, it extends its properties and applications to singular differential equations, especially with Bessel-type operators.

Therefore, we first consider some properties of this operator.

2. Erdélyi—Kober Transmutation Operator

To construct a solution to the problem posed, we apply the multidimensional Erdélyi-Kober operator. This is for Erdélyi-Kober operators cf. [16–19,21,22] and namely for multidimensional ones and its generalizations cf. [37–39].

Let us emphasise the role of *multidimensional* Erdélyi-Kober operators with Bessel functions as kernels. They provide an instrument to transform more complex *multidimensional* singular differential equations with a spectral parameter into more simple ones. As a consequence, in this way we receive connection formulas for solutions to more complex *multidimensional* singular differential equations via solutions to more simple equations. As an example, this property of generalized Erdélyi-Kober operators was successfully applied to particular types of *multidimensional* singular differential equations in [37–39].

Therefore, we first consider some properties of this operator. Exactly, let us introduce the multidimensional generalized Erdélyi-Kober operator

$$J_\lambda \begin{pmatrix} \alpha \\ p \end{pmatrix} f(x) = J_{\lambda_1,\dots,\lambda_n} \begin{pmatrix} \alpha_1, \ \dots, \ \alpha_n \\ p_1, \ \dots, \ p_n \end{pmatrix} f(x_1, x_2, \dots, x_n) = \prod_{k=1}^{n} \left[\frac{2x_k^{-2(\alpha_k+p_k)}}{\Gamma(\alpha_k)} \right]$$

$$\int_0^{x_1}\int_0^{x_2}\dots\int_0^{x_n} \prod_{k=1}^{n} \left[\frac{\bar{J}_{\alpha_k-1}\left(\lambda_k\sqrt{x_k^2-t_k^2}\right)}{\left(x_k^2-t_k^2\right)^{1-\alpha_k}} t_k^{2p_k+1} \right] f(t_1, \dots, t_n)dt_1\dots dt_n \tag{6}$$

its properties and their application to multidimensional equations of hyperbolic and parabolic types with singular coefficients, where $\alpha_k > 0$, $p_k \geqslant -1/2$, $k = \overline{1,n}$, $\bar{J}_\nu(z)$ is the Bessel-Clifford function [22], which is expressed in terms of the Bessel functions

$J_\nu(z)$ according to the formula $\bar{J}_\nu(z) = \Gamma(\nu+1)(z/2)^{-\nu}J_\nu(z)$, $\Gamma(\nu)$ is the gamma function, parameters λ_k, $k \geq 1$ are all real or purely imaginary.

Note that in this paper, we use the term "Bessel-Clifford function", which is introduced by A.A.Kilbas in [22]. Often, another term is used for this function—"normalized" or "small" Bessel function, cf. [1,16–18].

Integral (6) is a multidimensional analogue of the one-dimensional generalized Erdélyi-Kober operator with the Bessel function in the kernel [22], ch. 7, §37.2, pp. 737–741. The integral (6) satisfies the following theorem [21], ch.2–3; [19], ch. 3; [37,38].

Theorem 1. *Let* $\alpha_k > 0$, $p_k \geqslant -1/2$, $k = \overline{1,n}$, $f(x) \in C^{2n}(\Omega_n)$, $x_k^{2p_k+1} B_{p_k}^{x_k} f(x)$ *are integrable in a neighborhood of* $x_k = 0$ *and* $\lim\limits_{x_k \to 0} x_k^{2p_k+1} f_{x_k}(x) = 0$, $k = \overline{1,n}$.

Then, the next equality is valid

$$\prod_{k=1}^{n} (B_{p_k+\alpha_k}^{x_k} + \lambda_k^2) J_\lambda \begin{pmatrix} \alpha \\ p \end{pmatrix} f(x) = J_\lambda \begin{pmatrix} \alpha \\ p \end{pmatrix} \prod_{k=1}^{n} B_{p_k}^{x_k} f(x),$$

where $\Omega_n = \prod\limits_{k=1}^{n} (0, a_k)$ *is the Cartesian product,* $a_k > 0$, $k = \overline{1,n}$ *is the Bessel operator with respect to* x_k*, parameters, and* $\lambda_k, k \geq 1$ *are all real or purely imaginary.*

Note that the theorem is also true for some or all of

$$\lambda_k = 0, \; k = \overline{1,m}, \; m \leqslant n.$$

3. Application of the Erdélyi-Kober Operator to the Solution of the Problem

Theorem 1 allows us to apply operator (6) as a transmutation operator that allows one to transform equations of high even order with singular coefficients into equations without singular coefficients. This fact is applicable to the study of problem G for Equation (2).

Due to the linearity of Equation (2), we first consider the following auxiliary problem.

Problem G₀. It is required to find a function $u_1(x,y) \in C(\bar{\Omega})$ satisfying Equation (2) and boundary conditions

$$u_1(0,y) = \varphi_1(y), \; u_{1x}(0,y) = 0, \; 0 \leqslant y \leqslant h, \tag{7}$$

$$u_1(x,0) = \psi_1(x), \; u_{1y}(x,0) = 0, \; 0 \leqslant x \leqslant l, \tag{8}$$

where $\varphi_1(y)$, $\psi_1(x)$ are given smooth functions, and $\varphi_1(0) = \psi_1(0)$. Assume that a solution to problem (2), (7) and (8) exists. This solution is sought in the form

$$u_1(x,y) = J_{0,0} \begin{pmatrix} \alpha, & \beta \\ -\frac{1}{2}, & -\frac{1}{2} \end{pmatrix} U(x,y), \tag{9}$$

where $U(x,y)$ is an unknown differentiable function, $\alpha = a/2$, $\beta = b/2$.

Substituting (9) into Equation (2) and boundary conditions (7) and (8), and then, using Theorem 1 for $n = 2, \lambda_1 = 0, \lambda_2 = 0$, $p_1 = p_2 = -1/2$, we obtain the problem of finding a solution $U(x,y)$ of the equation

$$U_{xxyy} + cU = 0, \; (x,y) \in \Omega \tag{10}$$

satisfying the boundary conditions

$$U(0,y) = \Phi_1(y), \; U_x(0,y) = 0, \; 0 \leqslant y \leqslant h, \tag{11}$$

$$U(x,0) = \Psi_1(x), \; U_y(x,0) = 0, \; 0 \leqslant x \leqslant l, \tag{12}$$

where

$$\Phi_1(y) = A_0 \frac{d}{dy} \int_0^y \left(y^2 - s^2\right)^{-\alpha} s^{2\alpha} \varphi_1(s) ds, \ \ A_0 = \Gamma(\alpha + 1/2)/[\sqrt{\pi}\Gamma(1-\beta)], \tag{13}$$

$$\Psi_1(x) = B_0 \frac{d}{dx} \int_0^x \left(x^2 - s^2\right)^{-\alpha} s^{2\alpha} \psi_1(s) ds, \ \ B_0 = \Gamma(\beta + 1/2)/[\sqrt{\pi}\Gamma(1-\alpha)]. \tag{14}$$

To construct a solution to problem (10)–(12), we apply the Riemann method. The Riemann function $R(x, y; \xi, \eta)$ is the solution—the adjoint Equation [23]

$$L^*(R) = R_{\eta\eta\xi\xi} + cR = 0, \tag{15}$$

satisfying the conditions

$$R(x, y; \xi, \eta)|_{\xi=x} = 0, \ \ R_\xi(x, y; \xi, \eta)\big|_{\xi=x} = \eta - y,$$

$$R(x, y; \xi, \eta)|_{\eta=y} = 0, \ \ R_\eta(x, y; \xi, \eta)\big|_{\eta=y} = \xi - x.$$

If the Riemann function is known, then the solution of the problem G_0 can be represented as [23]

$$u(x, y) = R_{\eta\xi}(x, y; 0, y)\varphi_1(y) - \int_0^y R_{\xi\eta\eta}(x, y; 0, \eta)\varphi_1(\eta) d\eta - \int_0^x R_\eta(x, y; \xi, 0)\psi''_1(\xi) d\xi. \tag{16}$$

We are looking for the Riemann function in the form

$$R(x, y; \xi, \eta) = pw(\sigma), \tag{17}$$

where $p = (\xi - x)(\eta - y), \sigma = \lambda(\xi - x)^2(\eta - y)^2, \ \ \lambda = -c/16, w(\sigma)$ is an unknown function.

Calculating the derivatives of the expression (17) and substituting into the conjugate Equation (15), we find the equation

$$\sigma^3 w''''(\sigma) + 7\sigma^2 w'''(\sigma) + \frac{41}{4}\sigma w''(\sigma) + \frac{9}{4} w'(\sigma) - w(\sigma) = 0. \tag{18}$$

Generalized hypergeometric function [40]

$${}_0F_3(a, b, c; z) = \sum_{n=0}^{\infty} \frac{z^n}{(a)_n (b)_n (c)_n n!},$$

satisfies the equation

$$z^3 w''''(z) + (3 + a + b + c) z^2 w'''(z) + (1 + a + b + c + ab + ac + bc) z w''(z)$$
$$+ abcw'(z) - w(z) = 0. \tag{19}$$

Comparing (18) and (19) with respect to the parameters, we obtain the system of equations

$$\begin{cases} 3 + a + b + c = 7, \\ 1 + a + b + c + ab + ac + bc = 41/4, \\ abc = 9/4, \end{cases}$$

Solving this system by Vieta formulas for a cubic equation, we find the solution of Equation (18) in the form

$$w(\sigma) = {}_0F_3(3/2, \ 3/2, \ 1; \ \sigma)$$

and substituting this solution into representation (17), we determine the Riemann function for problem G:

$$R(x,y;\ \xi,\eta) = {}_0F_3(3/2,\ 3/2,\ 1;\ \sigma). \quad (20)$$

By virtue of the equalities $(3/2)_n = 2^{-2n}\frac{(2n+1)!}{n!}$ and $(1)_n = n!$, function (20) coincides with the Riemann function from [23], constructed as a series

$$R(x,y;\ \xi,\eta) = \sum_{m=0}^{\infty} \frac{(-1)^m c^m (\xi - x)^{2m+1} (\eta - y)^{2m+1}}{[(2m+1)!]^2}.$$

Calculating the corresponding derivatives of function (20) and substituting them into equality (16), we obtain the solution of problem (10)–(12) in the form

$$\begin{aligned} U(x,y) &= \Phi_1(y) + \Psi_1(x) - \Psi_1(0)\,{}_0F_3(1/2,\ 1/2,\ 1; \lambda x^2 y^2) \\ &+ \frac{cx^2}{2} \int_0^y [(t-y)\,{}_0F_3(3/2,\ 3/2,\ 2; \sigma_0)]\Phi_1(t)dt + \\ &+ \frac{cy^2}{2} \int_0^x [(s-x)\,{}_0F_3(3/2,\ 3/2,\ 2; \omega_0)]\Psi_1(s)ds, \end{aligned} \quad (21)$$

where $\sigma_0 = \lambda x^2 (t-y)^2$, $\omega_0 = \lambda y^2 (s-x)^2$, $\lambda = -c/16$.

Substituting (21) into (9) and taking into account (13) and (14), we change the order of integration, and then, after calculating the internal integrals, we obtain

$$\begin{aligned} u_1(x,y) &= \psi_1(x) + \varphi_1(y) - \varphi_1(0)\,{}_0F_3(\alpha + 1/2,\ \beta + 1/2, 2;\ \lambda x^2 y^2\,) - \\ &- \gamma_1 y^2 \int_0^x K_1(x,y,s;\alpha,\beta)\psi_1(s)ds - \gamma_2 x^2 \int_0^y K_2(x,y,s;\alpha,\beta)\varphi_1(s)ds, \end{aligned} \quad (22)$$

where $\gamma_1 = c2^{2\alpha-2}/(1+2\beta)$, $\gamma_2 = c2^{2\beta-2}/(1+2\alpha)$,

$$K_1(x,y,s;\alpha,\beta) = \frac{s^{2\alpha}(x-s)}{(x+s)^{2\alpha}} F^{1;0;1}_{1;3;0}\left[\begin{matrix} 1/2+\alpha;\ -;\ \alpha; \\ 3/2;\ 3/2+\beta,\ 1/2+\alpha, 2;\ -; \end{matrix}\ \sigma_1,\ \omega_1 \right],$$

$$K_2(x,y,s;\alpha,\beta) = \frac{s^{2\beta}(y-s)}{(y+s)^{2\beta}} F^{1;0;1}_{1;3;0}\left[\begin{matrix} 1/2+\beta;\ -;\ \beta; \\ 3/2;\ 3/2+\alpha,\ 1/2+\beta, 2;\ -; \end{matrix}\ \sigma_2,\ \omega_2 \right],$$

$\sigma_1 = \lambda y^2 (x-s)^2$, $\omega_1 = (x-s)^2/(x+s)^2$, $\sigma_2 = \lambda x^2 (y-s)^2$, $\omega_2 = (y-s)^2/(y+s)^2$, and $0 \le \omega_k \le 1$, $k = 1,2$; $F^{p;q;k}_{l;m;n}$ is the hypergeometric function of Kampé de Fériet, which has the form

$$F^{p;q;k}_{l;m;n}\left[\begin{matrix} (a_p); & (b_q); & (c_k); \\ (\alpha_l); & (\beta_m); & (\gamma_n); \end{matrix}\ x, y \right] =$$

$$= \sum_{r,s=0}^{\infty} \frac{\prod_{j=1}^{p} (a_j)_{r+s} \prod_{j=1}^{q} (b_j)_r \prod_{j=1}^{k} (c_j)_s}{\prod_{j=1}^{l} (\alpha_j)_{r+s} \prod_{j=1}^{m} (\beta_j)_r \prod_{j=1}^{n} (\gamma_j)_s} \frac{x^r}{r!} \frac{y^s}{s!},$$

here, $(a_p) = a_1, a_2, \ldots, a_p$.

This series converges at

1. $p+q < l+m+1$, $p+k < l+n+1$, $|x| < \infty$, $|y| < \infty$ or
2. $p+q = l+m+1$, $p+k = l+n+1$ and

$$\begin{cases} |x|^{1/(p-l)} + |y|^{1/(p-l)} < 1, \ \text{at} p > l, \\ \max\{|x|, |y|\} < 1, \ \text{at} p \le l, \end{cases}$$ and besides that $\alpha_j \neq 0, -1, -2, \ldots, \ j = \overline{1, l}$; $\beta_j \neq 0, -1, -2, \ldots, \ j = \overline{1, m}; \ \gamma_j \neq 0, -1, -2, \ldots, j = \overline{1, n}$.

To construct a solution to Equation (20) that satisfies the conditions

$$u(0,y) = 0, \ \lim_{x \to 0} x^{2\alpha} u_x(x,y) = \varphi_2(y), \ 0 < y < h,$$

$$u(x,0) = 0, \ \lim_{y \to 0} y^{2\beta} u_y(x,y) = \psi_2(x), \ 0 < x < l,$$

we use the following, easily proven property of the solution to Equation (20): if $u_1(x, y; 1-\alpha, 1-\beta)$ is a solution to the equation $L^c_{1-\alpha,1-\beta}(u_1) = 0$, satisfying conditions (7) and (8), then the function $u_2(x, y; \alpha, \beta) = x^{1-2\alpha} y^{1-2\beta} u_1(x, y; 1-\alpha, \ 1-\beta)$ for $0 < \alpha, \beta < 1/2$ will be a solution of the equation $L^c_{\alpha,\beta}(u_2) = 0$ satisfying the conditions

$$u_2(0,y) = 0, \ \lim_{x \to 0} x^{2\alpha} u_{2x}(x,y) = (1-2\alpha)\varphi_1(y), \ 0 < y < h;$$

$$u_2(x,0) = 0, \ \lim_{y \to 0} y^{2\beta} u_{2y}(x,y) = (1-2\beta)\psi_1(x), \ 0 < x < l.$$

Taking into account this property and replacing $(1-2\alpha)\varphi_1(y)$ and $(1-2\beta)\psi_1(x)$, respectively, by $\varphi_2(y)$ and $\psi_2(x)$, from equality (22), we obtain

$$\begin{aligned} u_2(x,y) = {} & \frac{y^{1-2\beta}}{1-2\beta}\psi_2(x) + \frac{x^{1-2\alpha}}{1-2\alpha}\varphi_2(y) - \\ & -\tilde{\gamma}_1 y^{3-2\beta} \int_0^x K_1(x, y, s; \alpha, 1-\beta)\psi_2(s)ds - \\ & - \tilde{\gamma}_2 x^{3-2\alpha} \int_0^y K_2(x, y, s; 1-\alpha, \beta)\varphi_2(s)ds, \end{aligned} \tag{23}$$

where $\tilde{\gamma}_1 = c2^{2\alpha-2}/(3-2\beta)(1-2\beta)$, $\tilde{\gamma}_2 = c2^{2\beta-2}/(3-2\alpha)(1-2\alpha)$.

By virtue of the principle of the linear superposition, the solution of Problem G can be represented as $u(x,y) = u_1(x,y) + u_2(x,y)$.

Note that problem G is equivalent to a Volterra integral equation of the second kind of the form

$$u(x,y) + c \int_0^x \int_0^y K(x, y; s, t) u(s,t) ds dt = F(x,y) \tag{24}$$

where

$$K(x,y;s,t) = \frac{s^a t^b}{(1-a)(1-b)} [x^{1-a} - s^{1-a}][y^{1-b} - t^{1-b}],$$

$$F(x,y) = \frac{x^{1-a}}{1-a}[\varphi_2(y) - \varphi_2(0)] + \frac{y^{1-b}}{1-b}[\psi_2(y) - \psi_2(0)] + \psi_1(x) + \varphi_1(y) - \varphi_1(0).$$

By virtue of the general theory of Volterra integral equations of the second kind [41], the integral Equation (24) has a unique solution. At the same time, it is fair

Theorem 2. *If* $0 < a, b < 1$ *and* $\varphi_k(y) \in C[0,h] \cap C^2(0,h)$, $\psi_k(x) \in C[0,l] \cap C^2(0,l)$, $k = 1, 2$, *where* $\varphi_2'(y)$ *and* $\psi_2'(x)$*, respectively, can have order singularities less than b at* $y \to 0$ *and less than a at* $x \to 0$*, then there exists a unique classical solution to Problem G.*

For other values of the parameters a and b, the problem is solved by the method of analytic continuation of the operator (6) with respect to these parameters for $a = 2\alpha$ and $b = 2\beta$.

This method can also be applied to solving the boundary value problems for a multidimensional equation, a high-order equation of the (2) type, and a nonclassical Sobolev-type equation with many singular coefficients.

4. Conclusions

Using the Erdélyi-Kober transmutation operator, an exact solution of the problem is constructed. Despite the development of modern computer technology, the construction of exact solutions to boundary value problems for partial differential equations is still an important and urgent task. These solutions allow a deeper understanding of the qualitative features of the described processes and phenomena, the properties of mathematical models, and can also be used as test cases for asymptotic, approximate and numerical methods.

Author Contributions: Writing—original draft, S.M.S. and S.T.K. All authors have read and agreed to the published version of the manuscript.

Funding: This research received no external funding.

Data Availability Statement: Not applicable.

Conflicts of Interest: The author declares no conflict of interest.

References

1. Kipriyanov, I. *Singular Elliptic Boundary Value Problems;* Nauka-Fizmatlit: Moscow, Russia, 1997.
2. Weinstein, A. Discontinuous integrals and generaliztheory of potential. *Trans. Am. Math. Soc.* **1948**, *63*, 342–354. [CrossRef]
3. Weinstein, A. Generalized axially symmetric potential theory. *Bull. Am. Math. Soc.* **1953**, *59*, 20–38. [CrossRef]
4. Volkodavov, V.; Nikolaev, N. *Boundary Value Problems for the Euler-Pausson-Darboux Equation*; Kuibyshev. State Ped. Institut: Kuibyshev, Russia, 1984.
5. Jayani, G. *Euler-Pausson-Darboux Equation;* Tbilisi Publishing House: Tbilisi, Georgia, 1984.
6. Natterer, F. *Mathematical Aspects of Computed Tomography;* Mir: Moscow, Russia, 1990.
7. Estrada, R.; Rubin, B. Null spaces Of Radon transforms. *arXiv* **2015**, arXiv:1504.03766.
8. Ludwig, D. The Radon transform on Euclidean space. *Math. Methods Appl. Sci.* **1966**, *XIX*, 49–81. [CrossRef]
9. Bers, L. On a class of differential equations in mechanics of continua. *Quart. Appl. Math.* **1943**, *1*, 168–188. [CrossRef]
10. Gurevich, M. *The Theory of Jets of an Ideal Fluid;* Nauka: Moscow, Russia, 1979.
11. Bitsadze, A.; Pashkovsky, V. On the theory of Maxwell–Einstein equations. *Dokl. Acad. Sci. USSR* **1974**, *216*, 249–250.
12. Bitsadze, A.; Pashkovsky, V. On some classes of solutions of the Maxwell–Einstein equation. *Trudy MIAN USSR* **1975**, *134*, 26–30.
13. Jayani, G. *Solution of Some Problems for a Degenerate Elliptic Equation and Their Applications to Prismatic Shells;* Tbilisi Publishing House: Tbilisi, Georgia, 1982.
14. Carroll, R.; Showalter, R.E. *Singular and Degenerate Cauchy Problems;* Academic Press: New York, NY, USA, 1976.
15. Matiychuk, M. *Parabolic Singular Boundary Value Problems*; Institute of Mathematics of the National Academy of Sciences of Ukraine: Kiev, Ukraine, 1999.
16. Katrakhov, V.V.; Sitnik, S.M. *Method of Transmutation Operators and Boundary Value Problems for Singular Elliptic Equations. Modern Mathematics;* English Translation: arXiv:2210.02246, 2022; Fundamental Directions: Moscow, Russia, 2018; Volume 64, pp. 211–426. (In Russian)
17. Shishkina, E.; Sitnik, S. *Singular and Fractional Differential Equations with Applications to Mathematical Physics;* Series: Mathematics in Science and Engineering; Academic Press: Cambridge, MA, USA, 2020.
18. Sitnik, S.M.; Shishkina, E.L. *The Transmutation Operators Method for Differential Equations with Bessel Operators;* Fizmatlit: Moscow, Russia, 2019.
19. Urinov, A.; Sitnik, S.; Shishkina, E.; Karimov, S. *Fractional Integrals and Derivatives (Generalizations and Applications);* Fargona Publishing: Fergana, Uzbekistan, 2020.
20. Salakhitdinov, M.; Urinov, A. *Boundary Value Problems for Equations of Mixed Type with a Spectral Parameter;* Fan: Tashkent, Uzbekistan, 1997.
21. Urinov, A.; Karimov, S. *Erdélyi—Kober Operators and Their Applications to Partial Differential Equations. Monograph;* Fargona: Fergana, Uzbekistan, 2021.
22. Samko, S.; Kilbas, A.; Marichev, O. *Fractional Integrals and Derivatives. Theory and Applications;* Gordon and Breach Science Publishers: Philadelphia, PA, USA, 1993.

23. Dzhuraev, T.; Sopuev, A. *On the Theory of Differential Equations in Partial Derivatives of the Fourth Order*; FAN: Tashkent, Uzbekistan, 2000.
24. Zhegalov, V.I.; Mironov, A.; Utkina, E. *Equations with Dominant Partial Derivative*; Kazan Publishing House: Kazan, Russia, 2014.
25. Nakhushev, A. *Problems with Displacement for Partial Differential Equations*; Nauka: Moscow, Russia, 2007.
26. Salakhitdinov, M.; Mirsaburov, M. *Nonlocal Problems for Mixed Type Equations with Singular Coefficients*; National University of Uzbekistan: Tashkent, Uzbekistan, 2005.
27. Salakhitdinov, M.; Islomov, B. *Equations of Mixed Type with Two Lines of Degeneracy*; Mumtoz so'z: Tashkent, Uzbekistan, 2010.
28. Marichev, O.; Kilbas, A.; Repin, O. *Boundary Value Problems for Partial Differential Equations with Discontinuous Coefficients*; Samara State University: Samara, Russia, 2008.
29. Urinov, A. *On the Theory of Euler-Pousson-Darboux Equations*; Forgona: Fergana, Uzbekistan, 2015.
30. Urinov, A.; Ismoilov, A.; Mamanazarov, A. Darboux problem for the generalized Euler–Poisson–Darboux equation. *Ukr. Math. J.* **2017**, *69*, 52–70.
31. Salakhitdinov, M. *Equations of Mixed-Composite Type*; Fan: Tashkent, Uzbekistan, 1974.
32. Smirnov, M. *Model Equation of the Mixed Type of the Fourth Order*; Publishing House of Leningrad State University: Leningrad, Russia, 1972.
33. Meredov, M. On the uniqueness of the solution of boundary value problems for a fourth-order mixed-type equation. *Izvestiya AN Turkm. SSR. Ser. Phys. Tech. Chem. Geol. Sci.* **1967**, *4*, S11–S16.
34. Carroll, R. *Transmutation and Operator Differential Equations*; North Holland: Amsterdam, The Netherlands, 1979.
35. Carroll, R. *Transmutation Theory and Applications*; North Holland: Amsterdam, The Netherlands, 1986.
36. Kiryakova, V. *Generalized Fractional Calculus and Applications*; Longman Scitific and Technical: Essex, UK; J. Wiley & Sons: New York, NY, USA, 1994.
37. Karimov, S. Multidimensional generalized Erdélyi-Kober operator and its application to solving Cauchy problems for differential equations with singular coefficients. *Fract. Calc. Appl. Anal.* **2015**, *18*, 845–861. [CrossRef]
38. Karimov, S. An Analog of the Cauchy Problem for the Inhomogeneous Multidimensional Polycaloric Equation Containing the Bessel Operator. *J. Math. Sci.* **2021**, *254*, 703–717. [CrossRef]
39. Karimov, S.; Sitnik, S. On some generalizations of the properties of the multidimensional generalized Erdélyi-Kober operator and their applications. In *Transmutation Operators and Applications*; Kravchenko, V., Sitnik, S.M., Eds.; Trends in Mathematics; Springer: Berlin/Heidelberg, Germany, 2020; pp. 85–115.
40. Bateman, G.; Erdéyi, A. *Higher Transcendental Functions*; Nauka: Moscow, Russia, 1973.
41. Manzhirov, A.; Polyanin, A. *Handbook of Integral Equations. Solution Methods*; Publishing House "Factorial Press": Moscow, Russia, 2000.

Disclaimer/Publisher's Note: The statements, opinions and data contained in all publications are solely those of the individual author(s) and contributor(s) and not of MDPI and/or the editor(s). MDPI and/or the editor(s) disclaim responsibility for any injury to people or property resulting from any ideas, methods, instructions or products referred to in the content.

mathematics

Article

Qualitative Properties of Solutions of Equations and Inequalities with KPZ-Type Nonlinearities

Andrey B. Muravnik

Nikol'skii Mathematical Institute, Peoples Friendship University of Russia, Miklukho-Maklaya ul. 6, Moscow 117198, Russia; amuravnik@mail.ru

Abstract: For quasilinear partial differential and integrodifferential equations and inequalities containing nonlinearities of the Kardar–Parisi–Zhang type, various (old and recent) results on qualitative properties of solutions (such as the stabilization of solutions, blow-up phenomena, long-time decay of solutions, and others) are presented. Descriptive examples demonstrating the Bitsadze approach (the technique of monotone maps) applied in this research area are provided.

Keywords: quasilinear equations and inequalities; KPZ-nonlinearities; qualitative properties of solutions; methods of monotonous maps; blow-up; stabilization

MSC: 35R45; 35K55; 35B40

1. Introduction

1.1. History and Motivation

The unfailing worldwide interest to quasilinear differential operators with the so-called KPZ-type nonlinearities (i.e., operators containing the second power of the first derivative) is mainly caused by the following two circumstances. The first one is purely theoretical: it is known (see, e.g., [1–3]) that the second power is the greatest one such that Bernstein-type conditions for the corresponding boundary-value problem guarantee the validity of a priori L_∞-estimates of first-order derivatives of the solution via the L_∞-estimate of the solution itself. On the other hand, such operators arise in applications to various areas not covered by classical linear differential equations: multidimensional interface dynamics (see [4–6]), directed polymer growth (see [5,7–9]), fractional diffusion models (see [10,11]), game-addiction models with unsustainable control (see [12]), models of finite-temperature free fermions (see [13]), stochastic heat propagation under subcritical regimes (see [14]), etc. For the first time, this phenomenon is seemingly noted in the famous paper [4] (and the used abbreviation goes from the names of its authors). Nowadays, the number of publications of those applications cannot be estimated; it suffices to provide several most recent remarkable examples: [6,9–29].

It is worth to note that an efficient tool to investigate such nonlinearities is proposed in [30]: one has to construct monotonous maps taking solutions of quasilinear equations (this Bitsadze approach is easily extended to inequalities as well) to solutions of linear ones. A clear example of the constructing of such a map is provided in the next section. The remaining part of the present paper is devoted to various results on qualitative properties of nonlinear problems, obtained by means of this tool.

Results of Section 5 deserve a special attention: up to the knowledge of the author, KPZ-nonlinearities in the functional-differential case were not considered earlier. Taking into account that the variety of functional-differential operators is much broader than differential-convolutional operators considered in the specified section (e.g., differential-difference operators, operators with contractions and extensions of independent variables, and general-kind integrodifferential operators are quite important for the theory and

Citation: Muravnik, A.B. Qualitative Properties of Solutions of Equations and Inequalities with KPZ-Type Nonlinearities. *Mathematics* **2023**, *11*, 990. https://10.3390/math11040990

Academic Editor: Sitnik Sergey

Received: 16 January 2023
Revised: 11 February 2023
Accepted: 13 February 2023
Published: 15 February 2023

Copyright: © 2023 by the author. Licensee MDPI, Basel, Switzerland. This article is an open access article distributed under the terms and conditions of the Creative Commons Attribution (CC BY) license (https://creativecommons.org/licenses/by/4.0/).

applications), one can reasonably treat functional-differential inequalities (equations) with KPZ-nonlinearities as a very significant and promising area of further investigations.

1.2. Illustrative Example: Gidas–Spruck Theorem and Its Generalizations

The main idea of the Bitsadze approach can be clearly explained on the following simple example.

It is known from [31] that the *semilinear equation* $-\Delta u = u^q$ has no global positive solutions provided that $1 < q < \frac{n+2}{n-2}$.

Applying advanced nonlinear capacity methods, one can extend this pioneering result to the case of the following *quasilinear inequality*:

$$-\sum_{i,j=1}^{n} \frac{\partial^2}{\partial x_i \partial x_j} a_{i,j}(x,u) \geq b(x)|u|^q, \tag{1}$$

where $a_{i,j}$ are Caratheodory functions of $n+1$ variables such that

$$|a_{i,j}(x,s)| \leq a(x)|s|^p, \; x \in \mathbb{R}^n, \; s \in (-\infty, +\infty), \; i,j = 1,2,\ldots,n, \tag{2}$$

with a positive p and nonnegative $a(x)$ (see [32]).

Note that this is a very substantial generalization: apart from the passage from the semilinear case to the quasilinear one, we pass from equations to nonstrict inequalities. Such results are always stronger: if an inequality has no solutions, then the corresponding equation has no solutions a fortiori.

However, the question whether Condition (2) is essential or it is just a technical restriction remains open. Let us show how to resolve it, using the Bitsadze approach.

In $\mathbb{R}^n$, consider the inequality

$$\Delta u + \alpha |\nabla u|^2 + e^{\gamma u} \leq 0, \tag{3}$$

where $\frac{\gamma}{\alpha} > 0$. To prove that no global solutions of that inequality exist, assume, to the contrary, that a function $u(x)$ satisfies inequality (3) in $\mathbb{R}^n$. Then introduce the following function in $\mathbb{R}^n$:

$$v(x) \stackrel{\text{def}}{=} \frac{1}{\alpha} e^{\alpha u(x) - 1}. \tag{4}$$

Then, for each j,

$$\frac{\partial v}{\partial x_j} = e^{\alpha u - 1} \frac{\partial u}{\partial x_j}, \; \frac{\partial^2 v}{\partial x_j^2} = \frac{\partial^2 u}{\partial x_j^2} e^{\alpha u - 1} + \frac{\partial u}{\partial x_j} \alpha \frac{\partial u}{\partial x_j} e^{\alpha u - 1} = e^{\alpha u - 1} \left[\frac{\partial^2 u}{\partial x_j^2} + \alpha \left(\frac{\partial u}{\partial x_j} \right)^2 \right],$$

and, therefore,

$$\Delta v = e^{\alpha u - 1} \left[\Delta u + \alpha |\nabla u|^2 \right].$$

Hence,

$$-e^{1-\alpha u} \Delta v \geq e^{\gamma u} \Rightarrow -\Delta v \geq e^{(\alpha+\gamma)u - 1}.$$

From (4), it follows that $\alpha v(x)$ is always positive, i.e., $v(x)$ is a constant-sign function, $\operatorname{sgn}[v(x)] = \operatorname{sgn}(\alpha)$, and $\alpha e v = e^{\alpha u} > 0$. Then

$$e^{\gamma u} = (e^{\alpha u})^{\frac{\gamma}{\alpha}} = (\alpha e v)^{\frac{\gamma}{\alpha}}$$

and, therefore,

$$e^{(\alpha+\gamma)u - 1} = (\alpha e v)^{\frac{\gamma}{\alpha}+1} e^{-1} = (\alpha v)^{\frac{\gamma}{\alpha}+1} e^{\frac{\gamma}{\alpha}} = (|\alpha||v|)^{\frac{\gamma}{\alpha}+1} e^{\frac{\gamma}{\alpha}}$$

because α and v always have a same sign. The last expression is equal to $|\alpha|^{\frac{\gamma}{\alpha}+1}e^{\frac{\gamma}{\alpha}}|v|^{\frac{\gamma}{\alpha}+1}$, which means that the introduced function $v(x)$ satisfies the inequality

$$-\Delta v \geq |\alpha|^{\frac{\gamma}{\alpha}+1}e^{\frac{\gamma}{\alpha}}|v|^{\frac{\gamma}{\alpha}+1}, \tag{5}$$

which is inequality (1) with $q = \frac{\gamma}{\alpha} + 1$ and $a_{i,j}(x,s) = \delta_i^j s$. Thus, Condition (2) is satisfied. Then, due to the above Mitidieri–Pohozaev generalization, inequality (5) has no global solutions, which yields a contradiction.

Now, represent inequality (3) in the form

$$-\sum_{i,j=1}^{n} \frac{\partial^2 u}{\partial x_i \partial x_j}\left(\delta_i^j \frac{1}{\alpha} e^{\alpha u}\right) \geq e^{(\alpha+\gamma)u}.$$

The left-hand part of the last inequality is a special case of the left-hand part of inequality (1), but Condition (2) is satisfied for no p. This confirms that the above Mitidieri–Pohozaev generalization (as well as the corresponding general theory) are actually restricted neither by the growth speed of coefficients nor by the power-like shape of nonlinearities.

2. Parabolic Stabilization

Full proofs of the results of this section are provided in [33].

2.1. Regular Case

Let a bounded function $u(x,t)$ satisfy the equation

$$\frac{\partial u}{\partial t} = \Delta u + g(u)|\nabla u|^2, \quad x \in \mathbb{R}^n,\ t > 0, \tag{6}$$

where g is continuous.

Define the function $f(s)$ as follows:

$$f(s) = \int_0^s e^{\int_0^x g(\tau)d\tau} dx. \tag{7}$$

Then $f'(s) = e^{\int_0^s g(\tau)d\tau} > 0$ and $f''(s) = g(s)e^{\int_0^s g(\tau)d\tau}$ so $g(s) = \frac{f''(s)}{f'(s)}$, where f is strictly monotone.

Denoting $f(u)$ by $v(x,t)$, we see that

$$\frac{\partial v}{\partial t} = f'(u)\frac{\partial u}{\partial t},\ \frac{\partial v}{\partial x_j} = f'(u)\frac{\partial u}{\partial x_j} \text{ and } \frac{\partial^2 v}{\partial x_j^2} = f''(u)\left(\frac{\partial u}{\partial x_j}\right)^2 + f'(u)\frac{\partial^2 u}{\partial x_j^2}.$$

Then $\frac{\partial v}{\partial t} = \Delta v$. On the other hand, from the continuity of f and boundedness of u, it follows that the function $v(x,t)$ is bounded as well (as a continuous function f on the segment $[\inf u, \sup u]$). Thus, $v(x,t)$ is a bounded solution of the heat equation. Hence, the following stabilization criterion is valid (see [34]):

for any $x \in \mathbb{R}^n$, $\lim_{t\to\infty} v(x,t)$ exists if and only if $\lim_{t\to\infty} \frac{n\Gamma(\frac{n}{2})}{2\pi^{\frac{n}{2}}t^n} \int_{|x|<t} v(x,0)dx$ exists; if those limits exist, then they are equal to each other.

Taking into account that f is invertible due its strong monotonicity and f^{-1} is continuous due the smoothness of f, we obtain the following assertion:

Theorem 1. *Let g be continuous and $u(x,t)$ be a bounded solution of the Cauchy problem for Equation (6) with a continuous and bounded initial-value function $u_0(x)$. Then for any $x \in \mathbb{R}^n$, $\lim_{t\to\infty} u(x,t)$ exists if and only if $\lim_{t\to\infty} \frac{n\Gamma(\frac{n}{2})}{2\pi^{\frac{n}{2}} t^n} \int_{|x|<t} f[u_0(x)]dx$ exists, where f is defined by (7); if those limits exist, then the latter limit is equal to $f\left[\lim_{t\to\infty} u(x,t)\right]$.*

Remark 1. *It is not necessary to assume that g is continuous on the whole real axis; it suffices to assume that it is continuous (and even defined) only in the closure of the range of $u_0(x)$. However, any function continuous in $[\inf u_0, \sup u_0]$ can be extended, preserving the continuity, to the whole axis. Thus, the initial approach does not restrict the generality.*

2.2. Singular Case

In Equation (6), assume that $g(s) = \alpha s^\beta$, where $\beta \in (-1,0)$. Then ansatz (7) is still applicable, but, to guarantee the monotonicity, we have to add the restriction of the positivity of the solution. This yields the following result for the Cauchy problem

$$\frac{\partial u}{\partial t} = \Delta u + \alpha u^\beta |\nabla u|^2, \quad x \in \mathbb{R}^n,\ t > 0, \tag{8}$$

$$u\Big|_{t=0} = u_0(x), \quad x \in \mathbb{R}^n. \tag{9}$$

Theorem 2. *Let $\alpha \in \mathbb{R}^1, \beta \in (-1,0)$, and u_0 be continuous, bounded, nonnegative, and nontrivial in $\mathbb{R}^n$. Then there exists a unique positive bounded solution of problem (8) and (9) and the assertion of Theorem 1 holds for it.*

If $\beta = -1$, i.e., the equation takes the form

$$\frac{\partial u}{\partial t} = \Delta u + \frac{\alpha}{u}|\nabla u|^2, \tag{10}$$

then we cannot use ansatz (7), but we can define $f(s)$ as $s^{\alpha+1}$.

This yields the following result.

Theorem 3. *Let $\alpha > -1$ and $u_0(x)$ be bounded and nonnegative. Then there exists a unique positive bounded solution of problem (10), (9) and the following criterion is valid: for any $x \in \mathbb{R}^n$, $\lim_{t\to\infty} u(x,t)$ exists if and only if $\lim_{t\to\infty} \frac{1}{t^n} \int_{|x|<t} u_0^{\alpha+1}(x)dx$ exists. If those limits exist, then*

$$\lim_{t\to\infty} u(x,t) = \left[\frac{n\Gamma(\frac{n}{2})}{2\pi^{\frac{n}{2}}} \lim_{t\to\infty} \frac{1}{t^n} \int_{|x|<t} u_0^{\alpha+1}(x)dx\right]^{\frac{1}{\alpha+1}}.$$

Remark 2. *If we change the condition of the nonnegativity of the initial-value function by the stronger condition of its positive definiteness, i.e., assume that there exists a positive a such that $u_0(x) \geq a$ for each x, then the assertion of Theorem 3 is valid for $\alpha < -1$ as well. However, it is not valid for $\alpha = -1$.*

3. Elliptic Stabilization

The nonclassical nature of the half-space Dirichlet problem for elliptic equations is known for a long time (see, e.g., [35,36]): the independent variable varying within a half-line possesses the so-called *timelike* properties, which means, e.g., that the resolving operator possesses the semigroup property with respect to that special variable (though all independent variables remain to be spatial). Thus, the question about the stabilization of the solution with respect to the timelike variable becomes reasonable. The said phenomenon is explained in this section; full proofs are provided in [37,38].

Denoting $x = (x_1, \dots, x_n, x_{n+1})$ by (x', x_{n+1}), consider the problem

$$\Delta u + g(u)|\nabla u|^2 = 0, \quad x' \in \mathbb{R}^n,\ x_{n+1} > 0, \tag{11}$$

$$u\Big|_{x_{n+1}=0} = \varphi(x), \quad x' \in \mathbb{R}^n, \tag{12}$$

where φ is continuous and bounded in $\mathbb{R}^n$.

The following assertions are valid.

Theorem 4. *Let g be continuous in $(-\infty, +\infty)$. Then there exists a unique bounded solution $u(x,t)$ of problem (11) and (12) and the following equivalence takes place for each $x' \in \mathbb{R}^n$ and each $l \in (-\infty, +\infty)$:*

$$\lim_{x_{n+1}\to+\infty} u(x) = l \text{ if and only if } \lim_{R\to+\infty} \frac{n\Gamma(\frac{n}{2})}{2\pi^{\frac{n}{2}} R^n} \int\limits_{|y|<R} f[\varphi(y)]dy = f(l).$$

Theorem 5. *Let $g = \alpha u^\beta$, where $-1 < \beta < 0$, and $0 \le \varphi \not\equiv 0$. Then there exists a unique bounded positive solution $u(x,t)$ of problem (11) and (12) and the following equivalence takes place for each $x' \in \mathbb{R}^n$ and each nonnegative l:*

$$\lim_{x_{n+1}\to+\infty} u(x) = l \text{ if and only if } \lim_{R\to+\infty} \frac{n\Gamma(\frac{n}{2})}{2\pi^{\frac{n}{2}} R^n} \int\limits_{|y|<R} \tilde{f}[\varphi(y)]dy = \tilde{f}(l),$$

where

$$\tilde{f}(s) = \int\limits_0^s e^{\frac{\alpha}{1-\beta}\tau^{1-\beta}} d\tau.$$

Theorem 6. *Let $g = \frac{\alpha}{u}$, where $\alpha > -1$, and $0 \le \varphi \not\equiv 0$. Then there exists a unique bounded positive solution $u(x,t)$ of problem (11) and (12) and the following equivalence takes place for each $x' \in \mathbb{R}^n$ and any nonnegative l:*

$$\lim_{x_{n+1}\to+\infty} u(x) = l \text{ if and only if } \lim_{R\to+\infty} \frac{n\Gamma(\frac{n}{2})}{2\pi^{\frac{n}{2}} R^n} \int\limits_{|y|<R} \varphi^{\alpha+1}(y)dy = l^{\alpha+1}.$$

Remark 3. *The stabilization phenomenon takes place for parabolic and elliptic equations with the singular Bessel operator*

$$B_{k,y} := \frac{\partial^2}{\partial y^2} + \frac{k}{y}\frac{\partial}{\partial y} = \frac{1}{y^k}\frac{d}{dy}\Big(y^k \frac{d}{dy}\Big), k > 0,$$

acting with respect to spatial variables, as well. Pertinent results can be found in [39–42].

4. Blow-Up for Partial Differential Inequalities

This section is devoted to the blow-up phenomenon both for stationary and nonstationary problems with KPZ-type nonlinearities. In this section (as well as in the next one), we follow the Pokhozhaev paradigm (see, e.g., [32]): *blow-up phenomena are equivalent to the absence of global solutions*. Note that all presented results refer to differential inequalities instead of differential equations, i.e., the maximal generality is guaranteed. Full proofs of the results of this section as well as local (instantaneous) results for inequalities with KPZ-type nonlinearities are provided in [43–46].

4.1. Elliptic Case

Theorem 7. *Let g be continuous on $(-\infty, +\infty)$ and β be measurable and a. e. positive in $\mathbb{R}^n$. Let there exist $q > 1$ such that $\beta^{\frac{1}{1-q}}(x)$ is locally summable in $\mathbb{R}^n$, excluding, perhaps, a bounded set, and $\omega(s) \geq \left|\int_0^s e^{\int_0^\tau g(t)dt} d\tau\right|^q e^{-\int_0^s g(\tau)d\tau}$ on $(-\infty, +\infty)$. Then the inequality*

$$\Delta u + \sum_{j=1}^{n} g_j(u) \left(\frac{\partial u}{\partial x_j}\right)^2 + \beta(x)\omega(u) \leq 0 \tag{13}$$

has no classical global solutions provided that $g_j(x) \geq g(x)$, $j = 1, 2, \ldots, n$.

Example 1. *Suppose that $\beta > 0$ and $0 < \frac{\gamma}{\alpha} \leq \frac{2}{n-2}$. Then the inequality $\Delta u + \alpha|\nabla u|^2 + \beta e^{\gamma u} \leq 0$ has no global solutions. The critical value $\frac{2}{n-2}$ is exact.*

Note that inequality (13) is a particular case of inequality (3) considered in Section 1.2. Consider the inequality

$$\Delta u - \sum_{j=1}^{n} \alpha_j(x, u) \left(\frac{\partial u}{\partial x_j}\right)^2 \geq \omega(x, u), \ x \in \mathbb{R}^n, \tag{14}$$

under the assumption that $\alpha_j(x, s) \geq \frac{1}{s}$, $j = 1, 2, \ldots, n$.

The following assertions are valid.

Theorem 8. *Let there exist a nonnegative function $k(x)$, a positive constant R_0, and a positive function θ defined on $[R_0, +\infty)$ such that $\lim\limits_{t\to\infty} \theta(t) = \infty$, $\frac{\theta(t)}{t^2}$ is a nonincreasing function, and $k(x) \geq \frac{\theta(|x|)}{|x|^2}$ provided that $|x| \geq R_0$. Suppose that there exists a constant p from the interval $(1, +\infty)$ such that $\omega(x, s) \geq k(x)s^p$. Then inequality (14) has no positive solutions.*

Theorem 9. *Let there exist a nonnegative function $k(x)$ and constants R_0 from $[1, +\infty)$, C_1 from $(0, +\infty)$, and C_0, b, and d from $\mathbb{R}$ such that $k(x) \geq 0$ provided that $|x| \leq R_0$ and $\frac{C_1}{|x|^b} \leq k(x) \leq C_0|x|^d$ provided that $|x| > R_0$. Suppose that there exists a constant p from the interval $(-\infty, 1)$ such that $\omega(x, s) \geq k(x)s^p$. Then, for any real C_2 and any a from the interval $\left(-\infty, \frac{2-b}{1-p}\right)$, inequality (14) has no positive solutions satisfying the inequality $u(x) \leq C_2|x|^a$ outside the ball $|x| < R_0$.*

4.2. Parabolic Case

Consider the inequality

$$\frac{\partial u}{\partial t} \geq \Delta u + \sum_{j=1}^{n} g_j(u) \left(\frac{\partial u}{\partial x_j}\right)^2 + \beta(x, t)\omega(u), \ x \in \mathbb{R}^n, t > 0, \tag{15}$$

where $g_1, \ldots, g_n$ are continuous on $\mathbb{R}^1$, $\beta(x, t)$ is a measurable and a. e. positive function, there exists $q > 1$ such that $\beta^{\frac{1}{1-q}}(x, t)$ is locally summable in $\mathbb{R}^n \times (0, \infty)$, excluding, perhaps, a bounded set, and $\omega(s) \geq \left| \int_0^s e^{\int_0^\tau g_0(\theta)d\theta} d\tau \right|^q e^{-\int_0^s g_0(\tau)d\tau}$ on $\mathbb{R}^1$, where $g_0(s) = \min_{j=1,2,\ldots,n} g_j(s)$. Assume that u_0 is continuous and nonnegative on $\mathbb{R}^1$ and define on $(0,\infty)$ the following function depending on parameters $\varkappa$ and μ:

$$C_{\varkappa,\mu}(R) \overset{\text{def}}{=} R^{n+\frac{\mu}{\varkappa}} \left[R^{\frac{2q}{1-q}} + R^{\frac{\mu q}{\varkappa(1-q)}} \right] \int_{1<\tau^\varkappa+|\xi|^\mu<2} \beta^{\frac{1}{1-q}}\left(R\xi, R^{\frac{\mu}{\varkappa}}\tau\right) d\xi d\tau. \tag{16}$$

The following assertion is valid:

Theorem 10. *If there exist $\varkappa \geq 1$ and $\mu \geq 2$ such that $\liminf_{R\to\infty} C_{\varkappa,\mu}(R)$ is finite, then problem (15), (9) has no classical nontrivial solutions.*

Remark 4. *The last assertion remains to be valid if the nonnegativity assumption for $u_0(x)$ is replaced by the following weaker assumption:*

$$\liminf_{R\to\infty} \int_{|x|<R} \int_0^{u_0(x)} e^{\int_0^\tau g_0(\theta)d\theta} d\tau dx \geq 0.$$

Consider the inequality

$$\frac{\partial u}{\partial t} \geq \Delta u + \frac{\alpha}{u^\gamma} |\nabla u|^2 + \beta(x,t)\omega(u), \quad x \in \mathbb{R}^n,\ t > 0, \tag{17}$$

where β is as above, $\alpha \neq 0, 0 < \gamma \neq 1$, ω satisfies the inequality $\omega(s) \geq \left(\int_0^s e^{\frac{\alpha}{1-\gamma}\tau^{1-\gamma}} d\tau \right)^q e^{\frac{\alpha}{\gamma-1}s^{1-\gamma}}$ in $(0,+\infty)$, and $0 \not\equiv u_0 \in C(\mathbb{R}^n)$. Then problem (17), (9) has no classical positive solutions under the assumptions of Theorem 10.

For the inequality

$$\frac{\partial u}{\partial t} \geq \Delta u + \frac{\alpha}{u} |\nabla u|^2 + \beta(x,t)\omega(u), \quad x \in \mathbb{R}^n,\ t > 0, \tag{18}$$

the following assumptions are imposed: $\alpha > -1$ and there exists $\rho > 1$ such that $\omega(s) \geq s^\rho$ on $(0,+\infty)$ and $\beta^{\frac{1+\alpha}{1-\rho}}(x,t)$ is locally summable in $\mathbb{R}^n \times (0,\infty)$, excluding, perhaps, a bounded set. Then, for continuous and different from the identical zero initial-value functions, the nonexistence of classical positive solutions for the Cauchy problem is guaranteed by the following condition: *there exist $\varkappa \geq 1$ and $\mu \geq 2$ such that*

$$\liminf_{R\to\infty} R^{n+\frac{\mu}{\varkappa}} \left[R^{\frac{2(\alpha+\rho)}{1-\rho}} + R^{\frac{(\alpha+\rho)\mu}{(1-\rho)\varkappa}} \right] \int_{1<\tau^\varkappa+|\xi|^\mu<2} \beta^{\frac{1+\alpha}{1-\rho}}\left(R\xi, R^{\frac{\mu}{\varkappa}}\tau\right) d\xi d\tau < \infty.$$

The inequality

$$\frac{\partial u}{\partial t} \geq \Delta u - \frac{|\nabla u|^2}{u} + \omega(x,t,u), \quad x \in \mathbb{R}^n,\ t > 0, \tag{19}$$

can be considered under the following assumptions: there exist $q > 1$, $\sigma > 0$, and a measurable and a.e. positive function $\beta(x,t)$ such that $\beta^{\frac{1}{1-q}}(x,t)$ is locally summable in $\mathbb{R}^n \times (0,\infty)$, excluding, perhaps, a bounded set, $\omega(x,t,s) \geq \beta(x,t)s\left|\ln\frac{s}{\sigma}\right|^q$ on $\mathbb{R}^n \times (0,+\infty) \times (0,+\infty)$, and there exist $\varkappa \geq 1$ and $\mu \geq 2$ such that $\liminf_{R\to\infty} C_{\varkappa,\mu}(R)$ is finite, where $C_{\varkappa,\mu}(R)$ is defined by (16).

Then, for continuous initial-value functions, problem (19), (9) has no solutions such that $\sigma \leq u(x,t) \not\equiv \sigma$.

Remark 5. *If we additionally restrict the behavior of the initial-value function by the inequality* $\liminf\limits_{R\to\infty} \int\limits_{|x|<R} \ln u_0(x)dx \geq 0$ *and assume that* $\omega(x,t,s) \geq \beta(x,t)s|\ln s|^q$ *in* $\mathbb{R}^n \times (0,+\infty) \times (0,+\infty)$, *then problem* (19), (9) *has no positive solutions at all.*

Example 2. *For* $\alpha > -1$, $\rho > 1$, *and nontrivial initial-value functions, the Cauchy problem for the inequality*

$$\frac{\partial u}{\partial t} \geq \Delta u + \frac{\alpha}{u}|\nabla u|^2 + u^\rho$$

has no positive solutions if $\dfrac{\alpha+1}{\rho-1} \geq \dfrac{n}{2}$, *and this critical value is exact.*

5. Integrodifferential Blow-Up

In this section, the investigation gets out the framework of *differential* inequalities: we deal with *functional-differential* ones, i.e., with inequalities containing other operators (apart from differential ones) acting on the desired functions. In our case, the operators different from differential ones, are convolution ones.

Full proofs of the results of this section are provided in [47].

5.1. Stationary Case

The following assertions are valid.

Proposition 1. *Let there exist from* $(-1,\infty)$ *such that* $a_j(x,s) \geq \frac{}{s}$, $j = 1,2,\ldots,n$, *and* $b(x,s) \geq \dfrac{1}{(+1)s}$. *Assume that* $K(x)$ *is bounded from below by the function* $|x|^{\beta-n}$, $\beta \in (0,n)$, *and* $\gamma > +1$. *For* $\beta < n-2$, *assume (additionally) that* $\gamma \leq \dfrac{(+1)n}{n-2-\beta}$. *Then the inequality*

$$\Delta u + \sum_{j=1}^{n} a_j(x,u)\left(\frac{\partial u}{\partial x_j}\right)^2 + b(x,u)\,K{*}u^\gamma \leq 0$$

has no global positive solutions.

Proposition 2. *Assume that* $K(x)$ *is bounded from above by the function* $|x|^{\beta-n}$, $\beta \in (0,n)$, *and* $\gamma < +1$. *For* $\beta < n-2$, *assume (additionally) that* $\gamma \geq \dfrac{(+1)n}{n-2-\beta}$. *Let there exist from* $(-\infty,-1)$ *such that* $a_j(x,s) \leq \frac{}{s}$, $j = 1,2,\ldots,n$, *and* $b(x,s) \leq \dfrac{1}{(+1)s}$. *Then the inequality*

$$\Delta u + \sum_{j=1}^{n} a_j(x,u)\left(\frac{\partial u}{\partial x_j}\right)^2 + b(x,u)\,K{*}u^\gamma \geq 0$$

has no global positive solutions.

Proposition 3. *Let real numbers* q *and* β *and a positive integer* n *satisfy the inequalities*

$$0 < \beta < n,\ q > 1,\ \text{and}\ q(n-2-\beta) \leq n$$

and there exist a function g continuous on the real line and such that the inequalities

$$a_j(x,s) \geq g(s),\ b(x,s) \geq e^{-\int_0^s g(\tau)d\tau},\ \text{and}\ K(s) \geq \left| \int_0^s e^{\int_0^t g(\tau)d\tau} dt \right|^q$$

are satisfied for $j = 1,2,\ldots,n$, $s \in \mathbb{R}^1$, *and* $x \in \mathbb{R}^n$. *Then the inequality*

$$\Delta u + \sum_{j=1}^{n} a_j(x,u) \left(\frac{\partial u}{\partial x_j} \right)^2 + b(x,u)\, K[u(x)] * |x|^{\beta-n} \leq 0$$

has no classical solutions in $\mathbb{R}^n$.

5.2. Nonstationary Case

The following assertions are valid.

Proposition 4. *Let* $\varkappa > -1$, $0 < \beta < n$, $u_0^{\varkappa+1} \in L_{1,loc}(\mathbb{R}^n)$, *and there exist positive constants C and* R_0 *and a nonnegative constant* γ *such that inequality*

$$\int_{|x|<R} u_0^{\varkappa+1}(x)dx \geq CR^{\gamma}$$

holds for each R from $(R_0, +\infty)$. *Let* $a_j(x,t,s) \geq \frac{\varkappa}{s}$, $j = 1,2,\ldots,n$, $b(x,t,s) \geq \frac{1}{(\varkappa+1)s^{\varkappa}}$, *and the function* $K(x)$ *be bounded from below by the Riesz kernel* $|x|^{\beta-n}$. *Then, for* $\gamma \geq n$, *the Cauchy problem for the inequality*

$$\frac{\partial u}{\partial t} \geq \Delta u + \sum_{j=1}^{n} a_j(x,t,u) \left(\frac{\partial u}{\partial x_j} \right)^2 + b(x,t,u)\, K * u^{\omega}$$

has no classical positive solutions provided that ω *satisfies the inequality* $\omega > \varkappa + 1$, *while, for* $\gamma < n$, *it has no classical positive solutions provided that* ω *satisfies the inequality* $1 < \frac{\omega}{\varkappa+1} < 1 + \frac{\beta+2}{n - \max\{\gamma,\beta\}}$.

Proposition 5. *Let real numbers q and* β *and a positive integer n satisfy the inequalities*

$$0 < \beta < n,\ q > 1,\ \text{and}\ 1 < q \leq \frac{n+2}{n-\beta}.$$

Let there exist a function g continuous on the real line and such that the inequalities

$$a_j(x,t,s) \geq g(s),\ b(x,t,s) \geq e^{-\int_0^s g(\tau)d\tau},\ \text{and}\ K(s) \geq \left| \int_0^s e^{\int_0^t g(\tau)d\tau} dt \right|^q$$

are satisfied for $j = 1,2,\ldots,n$, $s \in \mathbb{R}^1$, $x \in \mathbb{R}^n$, *and* $t > 0$, *while the function* $u_0(x)$ *satisfies the conditions*

$$\int_0^{u_0(x)} e^{\int_0^s g(\tau)d\tau} ds \in L_{1,loc}(\mathbb{R}^n)\ \text{and}\ \varliminf_{R\to\infty} \frac{1}{R^{\beta}} \int_{|x|<R} \int_0^{u_0(x)} e^{\int_0^s g(\tau)d\tau} dsdx \geq 0.$$

Then the Cauchy problem for the inequality

$$\frac{\partial u}{\partial t} \geq \Delta u + \sum_{j=1}^{n} a_j(x,t,u)\left(\frac{\partial u}{\partial x_j}\right)^2 + b(x,t,u)\, K(u) * |x|^{\beta-n}$$

has no nontrivial classical solutions.

6. Qualitative Properties of Solutions

6.1. Parabolic Equations Admitting Degenerations at Infinity

Full proofs of the results of this section are provided in [48].

Consider the equation

$$\rho(x)\frac{\partial u}{\partial t} = \Delta u + g(u)|\nabla u|^2,\ x \in \mathbb{R}^n,\ t \in (0,+\infty), \tag{20}$$

under the assumption that the equation $\Delta w + \rho(x) = 0$ has a solution bounded in $\mathbb{R}^n$.

The following assertions are valid.

Theorem 11. *Let $u(x,t)$ be a bounded solution of the Cauchy problem for Equation (20), where g is continuous and there exists a constant , $0 < \ < 1$, such that $\rho \in C^{+1}_{\text{loc}}(\mathbb{R}^n)$ and $f(u_0) \in C_{\text{loc}}(\mathbb{R}^n)$, where f is defined by relation (7). Then there exists a Lipschitz on $[0,+\infty)$ function A such that the relation*

$$\lim_{R\to\infty} \frac{1}{R^{n-1}} \int\limits_{|x|=R} \int\limits_0^t f[u(x,\tau)]d\tau d\sigma_x = \frac{2\pi^{\frac{n}{2}}}{\Gamma(\frac{n}{2})} A(t)$$

is satisfied for any positive t and the relation

$$\lim_{R\to\infty} \frac{1}{R^{n-1}} \int\limits_{|x|=R} \left(\int\limits_0^t f[u(x,\tau)]d\tau - A(t)\right) d\sigma_x = 0$$

is satisfied uniformly with respect to t from $[0,T]$ for any positive T.

Theorem 12. *Let $u(x,t)$ be a bounded positive solution of the Cauchy problem for Equation (20), where $g(s) = \alpha s^{\beta}$, $\beta \in (-1,0)$, $\alpha \in \mathbb{R}^1$, and the coefficient $\rho(x)$ and the initial-value function $u_0(x)$ satisfy the assumptions of Theorem 11. Then the assertion of Theorem 11 holds.*

Theorem 13. *Let $u(x,t)$ be a bounded positive solution of the Cauchy problem for the equation*

$$\rho(x)\frac{\partial u}{\partial t} = \Delta u + \frac{\alpha}{u}|\nabla u|^2,\ x \in \mathbb{R}^n,\ t \in (0,+\infty), \tag{21}$$

where $\alpha > -1$, the coefficient $\rho(x)$ satisfies the assumptions of Theorem 11, and the initial-value function $u_0(x)$ is such that $u_0^{\alpha+1} \in C_{\text{loc}}(\mathbb{R}^n)$. Then there exists a Lipschitz on $[0,+\infty)$ function A such that the relation

$$\lim_{R\to\infty} \frac{1}{R^{n-1}} \int\limits_{|x|=R} U_{\alpha+1}(x,t)dx = \frac{n\pi^{\frac{n}{2}}}{\Gamma(\frac{n}{2}+1)} A(t)$$

is satisfied for any positive t and the relation

$$\lim_{R\to\infty} \frac{1}{R^{n-1}} \int\limits_{|x|=R} [U_{\alpha+1}(x,t) - A(t)]dx = 0$$

is satisfied uniformly with respect to t from $[0,T]$ *for any positive* T, *where*

$$U_s(x,t) = \int_0^t u^s(x,\tau)d\tau,\ s>0.$$

Proposition 6. *Let* $u(x,t)$ *be a bounded solution of the Cauchy problem for Equation* (21), *where* $\alpha \neq -1$, $\inf u \geq B > 0$, *the coefficient* $\rho(x)$ *satisfies the assumptions of Theorem* 11, *and the initial-value function* $u_0(x)$ *is such that* $u_0^{\alpha+1} \in C_{\text{loc}}(\mathbb{R}^n)$. *Then the assertion of Theorem* 13 *holds.*

Proposition 7. *Let* $u(x,t)$ *be a bounded solution of the Cauchy problem for the equation*

$$\rho(x)\frac{\partial u}{\partial t} = \Delta u - \frac{1}{u}|\nabla u|^2,$$

where $\inf u \geq B > 0$, *the coefficient* $\rho(x)$ *satisfies the assumptions of Theorem* 11, *and the initial-value function* $u_0(x)$ *is such that* $\ln u_0 \in C_{\text{loc}}(\mathbb{R}^n)$. *Then there exists a Lipschitz on* $[0,+\infty)$ *function* A *such that the relation*

$$\lim_{R\to\infty} \frac{1}{R^{n-1}} \int_{|x|=R} \int_0^t \ln u(x,\tau)d\tau d\sigma_x = \frac{2\pi^{\frac{n}{2}}}{\Gamma(\frac{n}{2})}A(t)$$

is satisfied for any positive t and the relation

$$\lim_{R\to\infty} \frac{1}{R^{n-1}} \int_{|x|=R} \left(\int_0^t \ln u(x,\tau)d\tau - A(t) \right) d\sigma_x = 0$$

is satisfied uniformly with respect to t from $[0,T]$ *for any positive* T.

6.2. Extinction Phenomena

6.2.1. Parabolic Inequalities

Full proofs of the results of this section are provided in [49].

The Cauchy problem for the inequality

$$\Delta u + \sum_{j=1}^{n} a_j(x,u)\left(\frac{\partial u}{\partial x_j}\right)^2 - \frac{\partial u}{\partial t} \geq f(u), \tag{22}$$

where $u_0(x)$ is continuous, bounded, and nonnegative in $\mathbb{R}^n$ and $\lim\limits_{|x|\to\infty} u_0(x) = 0$, is considered. The following functions are introduced:

$$F(s) \overset{\text{def}}{=} \int_0^s e^{\int_0^x g(\tau)d\tau} dx \text{ and } \beta(s) \overset{\text{def}}{=} e^{\int_0^{F^{-1}(s)} g(\tau)d\tau} f\left[F^{-1}(s)\right].$$

Under the above assumptions, the following assertions are valid.

Theorem 14. *Let there exist a continuous function* $g(s)$ *such that* $a_j(x,s) \leq g(s)$, $j = 1,2,\ldots,n$, *in* $[0,+\infty)$. *Let* $f(0) = 0$, $f(s) > 0$ *in* $(0,+\infty)$, β *is a nonincreasing function on* $(0,+\infty)$, *and* $\int_0^1 \frac{ds}{\sqrt{s\beta(s)}} < \infty$. *Then any nonnegative solution of the above Cauchy problem for Equation* (22) *possesses the following properties:*

(i) $\operatorname{supp} u(x,t)$ is bounded for any positive t;

(ii) $\lim_{|x|\to\infty} u(x,t) = 0$ uniformly with respect to t from $[0, +\infty)$;

(iii) there exists a positive T such that $u(x,t) \equiv 0$ in the half-space $\mathbb{R}^n \times [T, +\infty)$.

Theorem 15. *Let there exist a from $(-1, +\infty)$ such that $a_j(x,s) \leq \frac{a}{s}$ in $\mathbb{R}^n \times (0, +\infty)$, $j = 1, 2, \ldots, n$, b from $(0, +\infty)$, and p from $(-a, 1)$ such that $f(s) \geq bs^p$ in $(0, +\infty)$. Then the above Cauchy problem for Equation (22) has no positive solutions.*

6.2.2. Parabolic Equations with Potentials

Full proofs of the results of this section are provided in [50].

The Cauchy problem for the equation

$$\frac{\partial u}{\partial t} = \Delta u + \frac{\beta}{u}|\nabla u|^2 + C(x,t)u, \tag{23}$$

where $n \geq 3$ and $u_0(x)$ is continuous and bounded in $\mathbb{R}^n$, is considered.

Under the above assumptions, the following assertions are valid.

Theorem 16. *If $\beta < -1$ and*

$$C(x,t) \geq \alpha \min\left(1, \frac{1}{|x|^2}\right),$$

then the above Cauchy problem for Equation (23) has no positively definite solutions.

Theorem 17. *If $\beta > -1$, then*

(i) *there exists at most one classical bounded nonnegative solution of the Cauchy problem for Equation (23);*

(ii) *if*

$$C(x,t) \leq -\alpha \min\left(1, \frac{1}{|x|^2}\right), \tag{24}$$

then $u \overset{t\to\infty}{\longrightarrow} 0$ uniformly with respect to x in each compactum of the space $\mathbb{R}^n$ provided that $u(x,t)$ exists;

(iii) *if $C(x,t) \leq -\alpha$ (this inequality is stronger), then there exists a positive constant a such that the inequality*

$$u(x,t) \leq \sup_{x\in\mathbb{R}^n} u_0(x)\, e^{-at}$$

holds in $\mathbb{R}^n \times (0, \infty)$ provided that $u(x,t)$ exists.

Theorem 18. *If $\beta > -1$, $u(x,t)$ is a classical bounded nonnegative solution of the Cauchy problem for Equation (23), and there exists α such that $\frac{\alpha}{\beta+1} > n-1$ and $C(x,t)$ satisfies Condition (24). Then for each compactum K of the space $\mathbb{R}^n$ there exist constants M and T such that*

$$u(x,t) \leq \frac{M}{t}, \quad = \frac{2-n+\sqrt{(2-n)^2+4\alpha}}{6(\beta+1)},$$

for each (x,t) from $K \times (T, +\infty)$.

6.3. Singular Equations with Nonclassical Neumann Conditions

Full proofs of the results of this section are provided in [51].

6.3.1. Stationary Case

The problem

$$\begin{gathered}\Delta u+\frac{\alpha}{u}|\nabla u|^2-a(x')u^p=0,\ x':=(x_1,\ldots,x_n)\in\Omega,\ x_{n+1}\geq 0,\\ u^\alpha\frac{\partial u}{\partial n}=0,\ x'\in\partial\Omega,\ x_{n+1}\geq 0,\end{gathered}\tag{25}$$

where Ω is a bounded domain with a Lipschitz boundary in $\mathbb{R}^n$ and a is a bounded measurable function, is considered.

Under the above assumptions, the following assertion is valid.

Theorem 19. *Let a positive function $u(x)$ satisfy problem (25) and the condition*

$$\lim_{x_{n+1}\to\infty}\frac{1}{x_{n+1}}\int_\Omega u^{\alpha+1}(x')dx'=0.$$

Let one of the systems of inequalities

$$\begin{cases}\alpha>-1,\\ p>1,\\ \int_\Omega a(y)dy>0,\\ a(y)\geq 0 \text{ in } \Omega\end{cases}\quad or\quad\begin{cases}\alpha<-1,\\ p<1,\\ \int_\Omega a(y)dy<0,\\ a(y)\leq 0 \text{ in } \Omega\end{cases}$$

be satisfied. Then $\lim_{x_{n+1}\to\infty} x_{n+1}^{\frac{2(\alpha+1)}{p-1}}u^{\alpha+1}(x)$ *exists for each x' from Ω, this limit is uniform with respect to x' from $\overline{\Omega}$, and it is equal either to zero or to*

$$\left(\frac{2(2\alpha+p+1)\text{mes}\Omega}{(\alpha+1)^2\int_\Omega a(y)dy\left[(\alpha+1)a(x')-1\right]^2}\right)^{\frac{\alpha+1}{p-1}}.$$

6.3.2. Nonstationary Case: Blow-Up

The problem

$$\begin{gathered}\frac{\partial u}{\partial t}=\Delta u+\frac{\alpha}{u}|\nabla u|^2-a(x)u^p,\ x\in\Omega,\ 0<t<T,\\ u^\alpha\frac{\partial u}{\partial n}=0,\ x\in\partial\Omega,\ 0<t<T,\end{gathered}\tag{26}$$

where T is a positive constant, Ω is a bounded domain with a Lipschitz boundary in $\mathbb{R}^n$, the function a is bounded and measurable, and the constant α is different from -1, is considered.

Under the above assumptions, the following assertions are valid.

Theorem 20. *For each (arbitrarily small) positive T, problem (26) has no positive solutions if one of the following two collections of conditions is satisfied:*

(*i*) $\int_\Omega a(x)dx<0,\ \alpha>-1$, *and* $p>1$;

(*ii*) $\int_\Omega a(x)dx>0,\ \alpha<-1$, *and* $p<1$.

Theorem 21. *Problem* (26) *in the cylinder* $\Omega \times (0, \infty)$ *has no positive bounded solutions if* $\int_\Omega a(x)dx = 0$*, the function* $a(x)$ *is different from the identical zero,* $\alpha > -1$*, and* $p > 1$.

Theorem 22. *Problem* (26) *in the cylinder* $\Omega \times (0, \infty)$ *has no positively definite bounded solutions provided that* $\int_\Omega a(x)dx = 0$*, the function* $a(x)$ *is different from the identical zero,* $\alpha < -1$*, and* $p < 1$.

6.3.3. Nonstationary Case: Large-Time Behavior

Under the above assumptions of Section 6.3.2, the following assertion is valid.

Theorem 23. *If a positive function* $u(x,t)$ *satisfies problem* (17) *in the cylinder* $\Omega \times (0, \infty)$ *and one of the systems of inequalities*

$$\begin{cases} a(x) \geq 0 \ in\ \Omega, \\ \int_\Omega a(x)dx > 0, \\ p > 1 \end{cases} \quad or \quad \begin{cases} a(x) \leq 0 \ in\ \Omega, \\ \int_\Omega a(x)dx < 0, \\ p < 1 \end{cases}$$

is satisfied, then $\lim_{t\to\infty} t^{\frac{\alpha+1}{p-1}} u^{\alpha+1}(x,t)$ *exists, this limit is uniform in* $\overline{\Omega}$*, and it is equal either to zero or to the constant* $\left[\frac{p-1}{\operatorname{mes}\Omega}\int_\Omega a(y)dy\right]^{\frac{1+\alpha}{1-p}}$.

7. Conclusions

In this paper, we provide various results on qualitative properties of solutions of inequalities with KPZ-nonlinearities. Since they are nonstrict, the corresponding equations can be treated as particular cases of inequalities and, therefore, the provided results are valid for those equations as well. The provided results (obtained by methods based on properties of monotonic maps) refer to the global nonexistence, stabilization and extinction phenomena, compactification of solution supports, and other significant properties. The considered inequalities and equations contain not only partial differential operators; a number of results is obtained for integrodifferential (more exactly, convolutional-differential) inequalities and equations as well.

Funding: This research received no external funding.

Data Availability Statement: Not applicable.

Acknowledgments: The author acknowledges useful discussions with participants of the 7th International Conference on Nonlinear Analysis and Extremal Problems (Irkutsk, July 2022), encouraging a better understanding of the obtained results and improving of their presentation.

Conflicts of Interest: The author declares no conflict of interest.

References

1. Amann, H.; Crandall, M.G. On some existence theorems for semi-linear elliptic equations. *Ind. Univ. Math. J.* **1978**, *27*, 779–790. [CrossRef]
2. Kazdan, I.L.; Kramer, R.I. Invariant criteria for existence of solutions to second-order quasilinear elliptic equations. *Commun. Pure Appl. Math.* **1978**, *31*, 619–645. [CrossRef]
3. Pohožaev, S. Equations of the type $\Delta u = f(x, u, Du)$. *Mat. Sb.* **1980**, *113*, 324–338.
4. Kardar, M.; Parisi, G.; Zhang, Y.-C. Dynamic scaling of growing interfaces. *Phys. Rev. Lett.* **1986**, *56*, 889–892. [CrossRef]
5. Medina, E.; Hwa, T.; Kardar, M.; Zhang, Y.-C. Burgers equation with correlated noise: Renormalization group analysis and applications to directed polymers and interface growth. *Phys. Rev.* **1989**, *A39*, 3053–3075. [CrossRef]

6. Toninelli, P. $(2+1)$-dimensional interface dynamics: Mixing time, hydrodynamic limit and anisotropic KPZ growth. In *Proceedings of ICM 2018. Volume III. Invited Lectures*; World Scientific Publishing: Hackensack, NJ, USA, 2018; pp. 2733–2758.
7. Schehr, G. Extremes of N vicious walkers for large N: Application to the directed polymer and KPZ interfaces. *J. Stat. Phys.* **2012**, *149*, 385–410. [CrossRef]
8. Spohn, H. KPZ scaling theory and the semidiscrete directed polymer model. *Math. Sci. Res. Inst. Publ.* **2014**, *65*, 483–493.
9. Chatterjee, S. Local KPZ behavior under arbitrary scaling limits. *Commun. Math. Phys.* **2022**, *396*, 1277–1304. [CrossRef]
10. Abdellaoui, B.; Peral, I. Towards a deterministic KPZ equation with fractional diffusion: The stationary problem. *Nonlinearity* **2018**, *31*, 1260–1298. [CrossRef]
11. Abdellaoui, B.; Peral, I.; Primo, A.; Soria, F. On the KPZ equation with fractional diffusion: Global regularity and existence results. *J. Differ. Equ.* **2022**, *312*, 1260–1298. [CrossRef]
12. Zhao, K. Global stability of a novel nonlinear diffusion online game addiction model with unsustainable control. *AIMS Math.* **2022**, *7*, 20752–20766. [CrossRef]
13. Charlier, C.; Claeys, T.; Ruzza, G. Uniform tail asymptotics for Airy kernel determinant solutions to KdV and for the narrow wedge solution to KPZ. *J. Funct. Anal.* **2022**, *283*, 109608. [CrossRef]
14. S. Nakajima, M. Nakashima, Fluctuations of two-dimensional stochastic heat equation and KPZ equation in subcritical regime for general initial conditions. *Electron. J. Probab.* **2023**, *28*, 1. [CrossRef]
15. Funaki, T.; Hoshino, M. A coupled KPZ equation, its two types of approximations, and existence of global solutions. *J. Funct. Anal.* **2017**, *273*, 1165–1204. [CrossRef]
16. Labbé, C. Weakly asymmetric bridges and the KPZ equation. *Commun. Math. Phys.* **2017**, *353*, 1261–1298. [CrossRef]
17. Parekh, S. The KPZ limit of ASEP with boundary. *Commun. Math. Phys.* **2019**, *365*, 569–649. [CrossRef]
18. Chhita, S.; Toninelli, F.L. A (2+1)-dimensional anisotropic KPZ growth model with a smooth phase. *Commun. Math. Phys.* **2019**, *367*, 483–516. [CrossRef]
19. Legras, M.; Toninelli, P. Hydrodynamic limit and viscosity solutions for a two-dimensional growth process in the anisotropic KPZ class. *Commun. Pure Appl. Math.* **2019**, *72*, 620–666. [CrossRef]
20. Corwin, I.; Ghosal, P. Lower tail of the KPZ equation. *Duke Math. J.* **2020**, *169*, 1329–1395. [CrossRef]
21. Wio, H.S.; Rodriguez, M.A.; Gallego, R. Variational approach to KPZ: Fluctuation theorems and large deviation function for entropy production. *Chaos* **2020**, *30*, 073107. [CrossRef]
22. Abdellaoui, B.; Peral, I.; Primo, A.; Soria, F. Fractional KPZ equations with critical growth in the gradient respect to Hardy potential. *Nonlinear Anal. Theory Methods Appl. Ser. A Theory Methods* **2020**, *201*, 111942. [CrossRef]
23. Lin, Y. KPZ equation limit of stochastic higher spin six vertex model. *Math. Phys. Anal. Geom.* **2020**, *23*, 1. [CrossRef]
24. Lin, Y.; Tsai, L.-C. Short time large deviations of the KPZ equation. *Commun. Math. Phys.* **2021**, *386*, 359–393. [CrossRef]
25. Matetski, K.; Quastel, J.; Remenik, D. The KPZ fixed point. *Acta Math.* **2021**, *227*, 115–203. [CrossRef]
26. Liechty, K.; Nguyen, G.B.; Remenik, D. Airy process with wanderers, KPZ fluctuations, and a deformation of the Tracy–Widom GOE distribution. *Ann. Inst. H. Poincaré Probab. Statist.* **2022**, *58*, 2250–2283. [CrossRef]
27. Tsai, L.-C. Exact lower-tail large deviations of the KPZ equation. *Duke Math. J.* **2022**, *171*, 1879–1922. [CrossRef]
28. Corwin, I.; Hammond, A.; Hegde, M.; Matetski, K. Exceptional times when the KPZ fixed point violates Johansson's conjecture on maximizer uniqueness. *Electron. J. Probab.* **2023**, *28*, 11. [CrossRef]
29. Quastel, J.; Sarkar, S. Convergence of exclusion processes and the KPZ equation to the KPZ fixed point. *J. Am. Math. Soc.* **2023**, *36*, 251–289. [CrossRef]
30. Bitsadze, A.V. On the theory of a class of nonlinear partial differential equations. *Differ. Equ.* **1977**, *13*, 1993–2008.
31. Gidas, B.; Spruck, J. Global and local behavior of positive solutions of nonlinear elliptic equations. *Commun. Pure Appl. Math.* **1981**, *34*, 525–598. [CrossRef]
32. Mitidieri, È.; Pokhozhaev, S.I. A priori estimates and the absence of solutions of nonlinear partial differential equations and inequalities. *Proc. Steklov Inst. Math.* **2001**, *234*, 1–362.
33. Denisov, V.N.; Muravnik, A.B. On stabilization of the solution of the Cauchy problem for quasilinear parabolic equations. *Differ. Equ.* **2002**, *38*, 369–374. [CrossRef]
34. Repnikov, V. D.; Eidel'man, S. D. Necessary and sufficient conditions for the establishment of a solution of the Cauchy problem. *Sov. Math. Dokl.* **1966**, *7*, 388–391.
35. Stein, E.M.; Weiss, G. On the theory of harmonic functions of several variables. I: The theory of H^p spaces. *Acta Math.* **1960**, *103*, 25–62. [CrossRef]
36. Stein, E.M.; Weiss, G. On the theory of harmonic functions of several variables. II: Behavior near the boundary. *Acta Math.* **1961**, *106*, 137–174. [CrossRef]
37. Denisov, V.N.; Muravnik, A.B. On asymptotic behavior of solutions of the Dirichlet problem in half-space for linear and quasi-linear elliptic equations. *Electron. Res. Announc. Amer. Math. Soc.* **2003**, *9*, 88–93. [CrossRef]
38. Denisov, V.N.; Muravnik, A.B. On the asymptotic behavior of the solution of the Dirichlet problem for an elliptic equation in a half-space. In *Nonlinear Analysis and Nonlinear Differential Equations*; FizMatLit: Moscow, Russia, 2003; pp. 397–417. (In Russian)
39. Muravnik, A.B. On stabilisation of solutions of singular quasi-linear parabolic equations with singular potentials. *Fluid Mech. Appl.* **2002**, *71*, 335–340.

40. Muravnik, A.B. Stabilization of solutions of certain singular quasilinear parabolic equations. *Math. Notes.* **2003**, *74*, 812–818. [CrossRef]
41. Muravnik, A.B. On stabilization of solutions of elliptic equations containing Bessel operators. In *Integral Methods in Science and Engineering. Analytic and Numerical Techniques*; Birkhäuser: Boston, MA, USA, 2004; pp. 157–162.
42. Muravnik, A.B. On stabilization of solutions of singular elliptic equations. *J. Math. Sci.* **2008**, *150*, 2408–2421. [CrossRef]
43. Muravnik, A.B. On a quasilinear analog of Gidas–Spruck theorem. *Nonlinear Bound. Value Probl.* **2004**, *14*, 105–111.
44. Muravnik, A.B. On local blow-up of solutions of quasilinear elliptic and parabolic inequalities. *Nonlinear Bound. Value Probl.* **2006**, *16*, 86–95.
45. Muravnik, A.B. On nonexistence of global solutions of the Cauchy problem for quasilinear parabolic inequalities. In *Analytic Methods of Analysis and Differential Equations: AMADE 2003*; Cambridge Scientific Publishers: Cambridge, UK, 2006; pp. 183–197.
46. Muravnik, A.B. On absence of global positive solutions of elliptic inequalities with KPZ-nonlinearities. *Complex Var. Elliptic Equ.* **2019**, *64*, 736–740. [CrossRef]
47. Muravnik, A.B. On absence of global solutions of quasilinear differential-convolutional inequalities. *Complex Var. Elliptic Equ.* **2020**, *65*, 977–985. [CrossRef]
48. Muravnik, A.B. On qualitative properties of solutions to quasilinear parabolic equations admitting degenerations at infinity. *Ufa Math. J.* **2018**, *10*, 77–84. [CrossRef]
49. Muravnik, A.B. On the qualitative properties of sign-constant solutions of some quasilinear parabolic problems. *J. Math. Sci.* **2021**, *257*, 85–94. [CrossRef]
50. Muravnik, A.B. Decay of nonnegative solutions of singular parabolic equations with KPZ-nonlinearities. *Comput. Math. Math. Phys.* **2020**, *60*, 1375–1380. [CrossRef]
51. Muravnik, A.B. Nonclassical stationary and nonstationary problems with weight Neumann conditions for singular equations with KPZ-nonlinearities. *Complex Var. Elliptic Equ.* **2021**, *66*, 1774–1781. [CrossRef]

Disclaimer/Publisher's Note: The statements, opinions and data contained in all publications are solely those of the individual author(s) and contributor(s) and not of MDPI and/or the editor(s). MDPI and/or the editor(s) disclaim responsibility for any injury to people or property resulting from any ideas, methods, instructions or products referred to in the content.

mathematics

MDPI

Article

The General Fractional Integrals and Derivatives on a Finite Interval

Mohammed Al-Refai [1] and Yuri Luchko [2,*]

1 Department of Mathematics, Yarmouk University, Irbid 21163, Jordan
2 Department of Mathematics, Physics, and Chemistry, Berlin University of Applied Sciences and Technology, 13353 Berlin, Germany
* Correspondence: luchko@bht-berlin.de

Abstract: The general fractional integrals and derivatives considered so far in the Fractional Calculus literature have been defined for the functions on the real positive semi-axis. The main contribution of this paper is in introducing the general fractional integrals and derivatives of the functions on a finite interval. As in the case of the Riemann–Liouville fractional integrals and derivatives on a finite interval, we define both the left- and the right-sided operators and investigate their interconnections. The main results presented in the paper are the 1st and the 2nd fundamental theorems of Fractional Calculus formulated for the general fractional integrals and derivatives of the functions on a finite interval as well as the formulas for integration by parts that involve the general fractional integrals and derivatives.

Keywords: Sonin kernels; Sonin condition; general fractional integral; general fractional derivative; fundamental theorems of fractional calculus

MSC: 26A33; 26A24; 45E10

Citation: Al-Refai, M.; Luchko, Y. The General Fractional Integrals and Derivatives on a Finite Interval. *Mathematics* **2023**, *11*, 1031. https://doi.org/10.3390/math11041031

Academic Editor: Sergey Sitnik

Received: 28 January 2023
Revised: 12 February 2023
Accepted: 15 February 2023
Published: 17 February 2023

Copyright: © 2023 by the authors. Licensee MDPI, Basel, Switzerland. This article is an open access article distributed under the terms and conditions of the Creative Commons Attribution (CC BY) license (https://creativecommons.org/licenses/by/4.0/).

1. Introduction

The so-called general fractional integrals (GFIs) and the general fractional derivatives (GFDs) in their nowadays form appeared for the first time in the paper [1] by Sonin published in 1884. In this famous paper, the Sonin condition and the Sonin kernels that satisfy this condition were defined and an important class of such kernels in form of products of the power law functions and analytical functions was introduced. However, Sonin did not mention any connection of his operators to Fractional Calculus (FC). Moreover, his derivations were mostly formal and without providing exact conditions for their validity, including the spaces of functions.

The first publication devoted to the GFIs and the GFDs embedded in the framework of FC was the paper [2] by Kochubei published in 2011. In this paper, Kochubei first introduced a very important class of the Sonin kernels in terms of their Laplace transforms. He also established a connection of these kernels to the complete Bernstein functions and the Stieltjes functions and introduced a regularized form of the general fractional derivatives with these kernels, nowadays referred to as the Kochubei kernels. Moreover, Kochubei initiated a new line of FC research devoted to the ordinary and partial differential equations with the GFDs. In particular, he deduced some important results for the fractional relaxation equation and the Cauchy problem for the time-fractional diffusion equations with the GFDs with the Kochubei kernels; see the paper [3] for a survey of the recent results regarding these fractional differential equations.

The next publication devoted to the GFIs, the GFDs, and the fractional differential equations with the GFDs was the paper [4] by Luchko and Yamamoto published in 2018. In Ref. [4], some important estimates for the GFDs of the functions at their maximum points were first derived. Then these estimates were applied to prove a weak maximum principle for solutions to the initial-boundary-value problems for the general time-fractional diffusion equations with the GFDs. It is worth mentioning that in Ref. [4], the GFIs and the GFDs with the Sonin kernels from a different class of kernels compared to the Kochubei set were considered.

Very recently, a series of papers [5–11] devoted to the GFIs and the GFDs with the kernels from several different sets was published by Luchko. In Refs. [5,7,8], the general FC operators with the Sonin kernels that are continuous of the positive real semi-axis and can possess an integrable singularity of a power function type at the origin were defined and investigated. In Ref. [6], the Sonin condition was extended in the manner that allows introducing the GFIs and the GFDs of arbitrary order (please note that in the previous publications only the case of the order less than or equal to one has been treated). In Ref. [11], another extension of the Sonin condition to the case of three kernels has been suggested and the so-called 1st level GFDs with these kernels were defined for the first time. The 1st level GFDs contain the GFDs and the regularized GFDs introduced so far as their particular cases just in the same manner as the Hilfer fractional derivative covers both the Riemann–Liouville and the Caputo fractional derivatives. It is worth mentioning that the GFIs and the GFDs with the Luchko kernels have already been applied in FC literature both for mathematical and applied problems. In particular, in Ref. [9], they were employed for derivation of two different forms of a generalized convolution Taylor formula that provides a representation of a function as a convolution polynomial with a remainder in form of a composition of the n-fold GFIs and the n-fold sequential GFDs or the regularized GFDs. In Refs. [12–18], Tarasov used these operators for formulation of a general fractional dynamics, a general non-Markovian quantum dynamics, a general fractional vector calculus, a general non-local continuum mechanics, a non-local probability theory, a non-local statistical mechanics, and a non-local gravity theory, respectively.

The framework of the GFIs and the GFDs introduced by Sonin in Ref. [1] is very general. For developing a reasonable theory of these general FC operators, both the special sets of the kernels (such as, e.g., the Kochubei set, the Luchko set, etc.) and the suitable spaces of functions are needed. In this sense, there exists not only one but several different theories of the GFIs and the GFDs.

Another aspect of the GFIs and the GFDs that was not yet taken into consideration in the FC literature concerns their domains. It is well-known that the properties and even the definitions of the classical Riemann–Liouville fractional integrals and derivatives are very different in the case of the functions defined on a final interval, on the semi-axes, or on the real axes, respectively (see, e.g., Ref. [19]). The GFIs and the GFDs considered so far were introduced for the functions defined on the real positive semi-axes. In this paper, we suggest the definitions of the GFIs and the GFDs for the functions defined on a finite interval and study their basic properties for the first time in the FC literature.

It is worth mentioning that there exist some other concepts of the general FC operators defined in a completely different form compared to those mentioned above. In particular, we refer to Refs. [20,21], and Ref. [22] devoted to this topic. However, in this paper, we restrict ourselves to the general FC operators generated by the modified Sonin kernels and do not consider the approaches suggested in Refs. [20–22], and in other publications of this type.

The rest of this paper is organized as follows: In Section 2, we define the spaces of functions that we use in the further discussions, formulate a suitably modified Sonin condition, and introduce the GFIs with the kernels from a certain set in the case of the functions defined on a finite interval. In contrast to the GFIs defined for the functions on the real positive semi-axes, we define both the left- and the right-sided operators and then investigate their interconnections. Section 3 is devoted to the GFDs and their properties. The main results presented here are the 1st and the 2nd fundamental theorems of FC formulated for the GFIs and the GFDs for the functions defined on a finite interval as well as the formulas for integration by parts that involve the GFDs. In Section 4, some conclusions and directions for further research are formulated.

2. The General Fractional Integrals on a Finite Interval

We start this section by specifying the spaces of functions suitable for our constructions of the GFIs and the GFDs. The spaces of this type were introduced by Dimovski in Ref. [23] in connection with his operational calculus for the hyper-Bessel differential operators. Then these spaces were extensively employed in the publications by Luchko devoted to the operational calculus for different fractional derivatives (see Ref. [24] for a survey of these results) and in his recent papers dealing with the general fractional integrals and derivatives for the functions on the real positive semi-axis ([5–11]).

Definition 1. *For $\alpha \geq -1$ and $n \in \mathbb{N}$, we define the spaces of functions*

$$C^n_\alpha(a,b] = \{f \in C_\alpha(a,b] : f^{(n)} \in C_\alpha(a,b]\},$$

$$C^n_\alpha[a,b) = \{f \in C_\alpha[a,b) : f^{(n)} \in C_\alpha[a,b)\},$$

where

$$C_\alpha(a,b] = \{f : (a,b] \to \mathbb{R} : f(t) = (t-a)^p f_1(t),\ p > \alpha,\ f_1 \in C[a,b]\},$$

$$C_\alpha[a,b) = \{f : [a,b) \to \mathbb{R} : f(t) = (b-t)^p f_1(t),\ p > \alpha,\ f_1 \in C[a,b]\},$$

and the spaces $C_\alpha(a,b]$ and $C_\alpha(a,b]$ are interpreted as $C^0_\alpha(a,b]$ and $C^0_\alpha(a,b]$, respectively.

Because the kernels of the fractional derivatives defined on a finite or infinite interval should be singular at one of the ends of the interval (see, e.g., Ref. [25]), the spaces of functions introduced in Definition 1 are very natural in the context of FC. As already mentioned, in Ref. [5–11], similar spaces were successfully employed for the development of the general FC on the semi-axis.

Another important remark is that the families of the spaces $C^n_\alpha(a,b]$ and $C^n_\alpha[a,b)$, $n = 0,1,2,\ldots$ are ordered with respect to the parameter α, i.e., for $\alpha_1 > \alpha_2 \geq -1$, the inclusions

$$C^n_{\alpha_1}(a,b] \subset C^n_{\alpha_2}(a,b] \text{ and } C^n_{\alpha_1}[a,b) \subset C^n_{\alpha_2}[a,b)$$

hold valid. This means that the spaces $C^n_{-1}(a,b]$ and $C^n_{-1}[a,b)$ are the largest in their families and contain all other spaces $C^n_\alpha(a,b]$ or $C^n_\alpha[a,b)$, respectively, as their sub-spaces. Thus, in what follows, we mainly employ the spaces $C^n_{-1}(a,b]$ and $C^n_{-1}[a,b)$. Evidently, all results derived for these spaces are also valid for the spaces $C^n_\alpha(a,b]$ and $C^n_\alpha[a,b)$ with any $\alpha \geq -1$.

In this paper, we introduce and investigate the GFIs and the GFDs on a finite interval $(a,\ b)$ with the kernels from the space $C_{-1}(0,b-a]$. Moreover, we often suppose that the kernels $\kappa \in C_{-1}(0,b-a]$ of the GFIs and the kernels $k \in C_{-1}(0,b-a]$ of the GFDs are the Sonin kernels that satisfy the Sonin condition [1]

$$(\kappa * k)(t) = \int_0^t \kappa(t-\tau)k(\tau)d\tau = \{1\},\ 0 < t \leq b-a, \tag{1}$$

where $\{1\}$ stands for the function identically equal to one for $t \in (0,\ b-a]$. The set of such kernels will be denoted by $\mathcal{S}_f$.

In the literature, several pairs of the Sonine kernels from $\mathcal{S}_f$ were derived in terms of the elementary and special functions (see, e.g., Refs. [2,5,7,26,27] and the references therein). The most prominent example known already to Abel (see Refs. [28,29]) is a pair of the power law kernels

$$\kappa(t) = h_\alpha(t),\ k(t) = h_{1-\alpha}(t),\ 0 < \alpha < 1, \tag{2}$$

where the function h_α is given by

$$h_\alpha(t) = \frac{t^{\alpha-1}}{\Gamma(\alpha)},\ \alpha > 0. \tag{3}$$

Another important example of the Sonin kernels was derived in Ref. [26]:

$$\kappa(t) = h_{1-\beta+\alpha}(t) + h_{1-\beta}(t),\ k(t) = t^{\beta-1}E_{\alpha,\beta}(-t^{\alpha}),\ 0 < \alpha < \beta < 1, \tag{4}$$

where

$$E_{\alpha,\beta}(z) = \sum_{n=0}^{\infty} \frac{z^n}{\Gamma(\alpha n + \beta)},\ \alpha > 0, \beta, z \in \mathbb{C}$$

is the two-parameters Mittag-Leffler function and h_α is defined by (3).

We also mention the following pair of the Sonin kernels that was first deduced by Sonin in Ref. [1]:

$$\kappa(t) = (\sqrt{t})^{-\alpha} I_{-\alpha}(2\sqrt{t}),\ k(t) = (\sqrt{t})^{\alpha-1} J_{\alpha-1}(2\sqrt{t}),\ 0 < \alpha < 1, \tag{5}$$

where

$$J_\mu(t) = \sum_{n=0}^{\infty} \frac{(-1)^n (t/2)^{2n+\mu}}{n!\Gamma(n+\mu+1)},\ I_\nu(t) = \sum_{n=0}^{\infty} \frac{(t/2)^{2n+\nu}}{n!\Gamma(n+\nu)}$$

are the Bessel and the modified Bessel functions, respectively.

Definition 2. *Let a kernel κ belong to the space $C_{-1}(0, b-a]$.*

The left-sided general fractional integral (LGFI) and the right-sided general fractional integral (RGFI) are defined by the following formulas, respectively:

$$({}_l\mathbb{I}_{(\kappa)}\, f)(t) = (\kappa * f)(t) = \int_a^t \kappa(t-\tau) f(\tau) d\tau,\ a < t \le b, \tag{6}$$

$$({}_r\mathbb{I}_{(\kappa)}\, f)(t) = \int_t^b \kappa(\tau - t) f(\tau) d\tau,\ a \le t < b. \tag{7}$$

In the rest of this section, we discuss the properties of the LGFIs (6) and the RGFIs (7) that are valid any kernel κ from the space $C_{-1}(0, b-a]$. However, in the next section, where the GFDs are introduced and investigated, we suppose that κ is a Sonin kernel from the set $\mathcal{S}_f$. In particular, the power law kernel $\kappa(t) = h_\alpha(t)$ generates the well-known left- and right-sided Riemann–Liouville fractional integrals that have been extensively studied in the FC literature (see, e.g., Ref. [19] for their properties). The kernel $\kappa(t) = h_{1-\beta+\alpha}(t) + h_{1-\beta}(t),\ 0 < \alpha < \beta < 1$ from (4) leads to a sum of two left- and right-sided Riemann–Liouville fractional integrals of the orders $1-\beta+\alpha$ and $1-\beta$, respectively. Finally, the kernel $\kappa(t) = (\sqrt{t})^{-\alpha} I_{-\alpha}(2\sqrt{t}),\ 0 < \alpha < 1$ from (5) generates the following pair of the left- and right-sided GFIs:

$$({}_l\mathbb{I}_{(\kappa)}\, f)(t) = \int_a^t (\sqrt{(t-\tau)})^{-\alpha} I_{-\alpha}(2\sqrt{(t-\tau)}) f(\tau) d\tau,\ a < t \le b, \tag{8}$$

$$({}_r\mathbb{I}_{(\kappa)}\, f)(t) = \int_t^b (\sqrt{(\tau-t)})^{-\alpha} I_{-\alpha}(2\sqrt{(\tau-t)}) f(\tau) d\tau,\ a \le t < b. \tag{9}$$

The LGFI and the RGFI introduced in Definition 2 can be studied on different spaces of functions, see e.g., Ref. [19] for the theory of the left- and right-sided Riemann–Liouville fractional integrals and derivatives on the finite intervals. In this paper, we focus on the properties of the LGFI and the RGFI on the spaces introduced in Definition 1.

Proposition 1. *Let a kernel κ belong to the space $C_{-1}(0, b-a]$.*

The LGFI (6) maps the space $C_{-1}(a, b]$ into itself:

$${}_l\mathbb{I}_{(\kappa)} : C_{-1}(a, b] \longrightarrow C_{-1}(a, b] \tag{10}$$

and the RGFI (7) maps the space $C_{-1}[a,b)$ into itself:

$$ {}_r\mathbb{I}_{(\kappa)} : C_{-1}[a,b) \longrightarrow C_{-1}[a,b). \tag{11} $$

Proof. First we prove the mapping property (10). Since $f \in C_{-1}(a,b]$, then $f(t) = (t-a)^p f_1(t), p > -1, f_1 \in C[a,b]$. Because the kernel κ belongs to the space $C_{-1}(0,b-a]$, the representation $\kappa(t) = t^q \kappa_1(t)$ with $q > -1$ and $\kappa_1(t) \in C[0,b-a]$ holds true. Then we get the relation

$$ ({}_l\mathbb{I}_{(\kappa)} f)(t) = \int_a^t (t-\tau)^q (\tau - a)^p \kappa_1(t-\tau) f_1(\tau) d\tau,\ a < t \le b. \tag{12} $$

Using the variables substitution $z = \frac{t-\tau}{t-a}$, we arrive at the formula

$$ ({}_l\mathbb{I}_{(\kappa)} f)(t) = (t-a)^{q+p+1} \int_0^1 z^q (1-z)^p \kappa_1\big(z(t-a)\big) f_1\big(t - z(t-a)\big) dz,\ a < t \le b. \tag{13} $$

Denoting the product $\kappa_1\big(z(t-a)\big) f_1\big(t-z(t-a)\big)$ by $g(t,z)$, the inclusions $\kappa_1 \in C[0,\,b-a]$, $f_1 \in C[a,b]$ mean that the function g is continuous for $0 \le z \le 1$ and $a \le t \le b$. Because the function $z^q(1-z)^p \ge 0$ is integrable, the mean value theorem for integrals yields the representation

$$ \begin{aligned} ({}_l\mathbb{I}_{(\kappa)} f)(t) &= (t-a)^{q+p+1} g(\hat{t}, z_0) \int_0^1 z^q (1-z)^p dz \\ &= (t-a)^{q+p+1} g(\hat{t}, z_0) B(q+1, p+1),\ \text{ for some } 0 < z_0 < 1,\ \hat{t} > a, \end{aligned} \tag{14} $$

which proves the Formula (10).

The proof of the mapping property (11) is completely analogous and we omit it here. □

Now we proceed with formulations and proofs of other important properties of the LGFIs and the RGFIs on the spaces $C_{-1}(a,b]$ and $C_{-1}[a,b)$, respectively.

Proposition 2. *Let a kernel κ belong to the space $C_{-1}(0,b-a]$.*

For any functions $f \in C_{-1}[a,b)$ and $g \in C_{-1}(a,b]$, the formula for fractional integration by parts

$$ \int_a^b f(t)\,({}_l\mathbb{I}_{(\kappa)} g)(t) dt = \int_a^b ({}_r\mathbb{I}_{(\kappa)} f)(t)\, g(t) dt $$

holds true.

Proof. We start with the representation

$$ \begin{aligned} \int_a^b f(t)\,({}_l\mathbb{I}_{(\kappa)} g)(t) dt &= \int_a^b f(t) \int_a^t \kappa(t-\tau) g(\tau) d\tau dt \\ &= \int_a^b \int_a^t f(t) \kappa(t-\tau) g(\tau) d\tau dt. \end{aligned} \tag{15} $$

Because the integrals in the last formula are absolutely convergent, we can interchange the order of integration by Fubini's theorem and get the formula

$$ \begin{aligned} \int_a^b f(t)\,({}_l\mathbb{I}_{(\kappa)} g)(t) dt &= \int_a^b \int_\tau^b f(t) \kappa(t-\tau) g(\tau) dt d\tau \\ &= \int_a^b g(\tau) \int_\tau^b f(t) \kappa(t-\tau) dt d\tau = \int_a^b g(\tau)\,({}_r\mathbb{I}_{(\kappa)} f)(\tau) d\tau, \end{aligned} \tag{16} $$

which completes the proof of the theorem. □

Proposition 3. *Let κ_1 and κ_2 be two kernels from the space $C_{-1}(0,\,b-a]$.*

The LGFI (6) and the RGFI (7) possess the semi-group properties in the form

$$(_l\mathbb{I}_{(\kappa_1)}\, _l\mathbb{I}_{(\kappa_2)} f)(t) \;=\; (_l\mathbb{I}_{(\kappa_1\,*\,\kappa_2)}\, f)(t),\;\; f\in C_{-1}(a,b], \tag{17}$$
$$(_r\mathbb{I}_{(\kappa_1)}\, _r\mathbb{I}_{(\kappa_2)} f)(t) \;=\; (_r\mathbb{I}_{(\kappa_1\,*\,\kappa_2)}\, f)(t),\;\; f\in C_{-1}[a,b). \tag{18}$$

As a consequence, the following commutative laws are valid:

$$(_l\mathbb{I}_{(\kappa_1)}\, _l\mathbb{I}_{(\kappa_2)} f)(t) \;=\; (_l\mathbb{I}_{(\kappa_2)}\, _l\mathbb{I}_{(\kappa_1)}\, f)(t),\;\; f\in C_{-1}(a,b], \tag{19}$$
$$(_r\mathbb{I}_{(\kappa_1)}\, _r\mathbb{I}_{(\kappa_2)} f)(t) \;=\; (_r\mathbb{I}_{(\kappa_2)}\, _r\mathbb{I}_{(\kappa_1)}\, f)(t),\;\; f\in C_{-1}[a,b). \tag{20}$$

Proof. We start with a proof of the relation (18) and first represent its left-hand side as follows:

$$\begin{aligned}(_r\mathbb{I}_{(\kappa_1)}\, _r\mathbb{I}_{(\kappa_2)} f)(t) &= \int_t^b \kappa_1(\tau-t)(_r\mathbb{I}_{(\kappa_2)}\, f)(\tau)d\tau \\ &= \int_t^b \kappa_1(\tau-t)\int_\tau^b \kappa_2(y-\tau)f(y)dyd\tau \\ &= \int_t^b\int_\tau^b \kappa_1(\tau-t)\kappa_2(y-\tau)f(y)dyd\tau.\end{aligned}$$

Interchanging the order of integration in the last double integral yields the relation

$$\begin{aligned}(_r\mathbb{I}_{(\kappa_1)}\, _r\mathbb{I}_{(\kappa_2)} f)(t) &= \int_t^b\int_t^y \kappa_1(\tau-t)\kappa_2(y-\tau)f(y)d\tau dy \\ &= \int_t^b f(y)\int_t^y \kappa_1(\tau-t)\kappa_2(y-\tau)d\tau dy.\end{aligned} \tag{21}$$

By employing the variables substitution $\tau_1 = y-\tau$, the inner integral of the last formula can be represented in the form

$$\int_t^y \kappa_1(\tau-t)\kappa_2(y-\tau)d\tau = \int_0^{y-t} \kappa_1(y-t-\tau_1)\kappa_2(\tau_1)d\tau_1 = (\kappa_1\,*\,\kappa_2)(y-t)$$

which leads to the Formula (18):

$$(_r\mathbb{I}_{(\kappa_1)}\, _r\mathbb{I}_{(\kappa_2)} f)(t) \;=\; \int_t^b f(y)(\kappa_1\,*\,\kappa_2)(y-t)dy \;=\; (_r\mathbb{I}_{(\kappa_1\,*\,\kappa_2)}\, f)(t).$$

For $\kappa_1,\ \kappa_2 \in C_{-1}(0,\, b-a]$, the inclusion $\kappa_1\,*\,\kappa_2 \in C_{-1}(0,\, b-a]$ is ensured by the Formula (10) from Proposition 1.

The Formula (17) is a simple consequence from the known properties of the Laplace convolution:

$$\begin{aligned}(_l\mathbb{I}_{(\kappa_1)}\, _l\mathbb{I}_{(\kappa_2)} f)(t) &= (\kappa_1\,*\,(\kappa_2\,*\,f))(t) \\ &= ((\kappa_1\,*\,\kappa_2)\,*\,f)(t) = (_l\mathbb{I}_{(\kappa_1\,*\,\kappa_2)}\, f)(t).\end{aligned}$$

In its turn, the Formulas (19) and (20) immediately follow from the Formulas (17) and (18), respectively, because of the well-known fact that the Laplace convolution is commutative. □

It is worth mentioning that, in general, the semi-group properties presented in Proposition 3 are not valid for the GFIs with the Sonin kernels from the set $\mathcal{S}_f$ because the convolution of the two kernels from $\mathcal{S}_f$ does not always belong to $\mathcal{S}_f$. The reason is that the generalized order of the LGFI (6) and the RGFI (7) with the kernels from $\mathcal{S}_f$ is restricted to the interval $(0,\, 1)$. This is a direct consequence from the Sonin condition (1) because the constant function $\{1\}$ at its right-hand side corresponds to the definite integral of order one.

However, it is possible to extend the Sonin condition (1) and to define the GFIs of arbitrary order that fulfill the semi-group property (see Ref. [6] for the case of the GFIs of arbitrary order on a positive real semi-axes). This will be done elsewhere.

3. The General Fractional Derivatives on a Finite Interval

In this section, we introduce several different kinds of the GFDs on a finite interval and study their basic properties including the 1st and the 2nd fundamental theorems of FC. As in the case of the Riemann–Liouville and the Caputo fractional derivatives with the power law kernels, we define the GFD (of the Riemann–Liouville type) and the regularized GFD (of the Caputo type). Moreover, both the left- and the right-sided GFDs will be introduced and studied.

In what follows, we suppose that the kernels of the GFIs and the GFDs are the Sonin kernels from the set $\mathcal{S}_f$.

Definition 3. *Let a pair of the kernels* $(\kappa,\, k)$ *belong to the set* $\mathcal{S}_f$.

The left-sided general fractional derivative (LGFD) and the right-sided general fractional derivative (RGFD) are defined by the following formulas, respectively:

$$({}_{l}\mathbb{D}_{(k)}\, f)(t) = \frac{d}{dt}\int_a^t k(t-\tau)f(\tau)\,d\tau,\ a < t \le b, \tag{22}$$

$$({}_{r}\mathbb{D}_{(k)}\, f)(t) = -\frac{d}{dt}\int_t^b k(\tau-t)f(\tau)\,d\tau,\ a \le t < b. \tag{23}$$

The regularized left-sided general fractional derivative (RLGFD) and the regularized right-sided general fractional derivative (RRGFD) are defined as follows:

$$({}_{l_*}\mathbb{D}_{(k)}\, f)(t) = \int_a^t k(t-\tau)f'(\tau)\,d\tau,\ a < t \le b, \tag{24}$$

$$({}_{r_*}\mathbb{D}_{(k)}\, f)(t) = -\int_t^b k(\tau-t)f'(\tau)\,d\tau,\ a \le t < b. \tag{25}$$

A well-known example of the left- and right-sided GFDs introduced above are the Riemann–Liouville and the Caputo left- and right-sided fractional derivatives with the power law kernel $k(t) = h_{1-\alpha}(t),\ 0 < \alpha < 1$ from the Sonin pair of the kernels defined by (2).

Another important example is generated by the kernel $k(t) = t^{\beta-1}E_{\alpha,\beta}(-t^{\alpha}),\ 0 < \alpha < \beta < 1$ from the Sonin pair (4). For this kernel, the left-sided GFD and the left-sided regularized GFD on the positive real semi-axes have been already defined and investigated (see, e.g., Refs. [5,30]). However, to the best of our knowledge, the right-sided GFDs on a finite interval are introduced here for the first time in the FC literature:

$$\begin{aligned}
({}_{r}\mathbb{D}_{(k)}\, f)(t) &= -\frac{d}{dt}\int_t^b (\tau-t)^{\beta-1}E_{\alpha,\beta}(-(\tau-t)^{\alpha})f(\tau)d\tau,\ a \le t < b,\\
({}_{r_*}\mathbb{D}_{(k)}\, f)(t) &= -\int_t^b (\tau-t)^{\beta-1}E_{\alpha,\beta}(-(\tau-t)^{\alpha})f'(\tau)d\tau,\ a \le t < b.
\end{aligned}$$

Finally, we mention the right-sided GFDs on a finite interval with the Sonin kernel $k(t) = (\sqrt{t})^{-\alpha}I_{-\alpha}(2\sqrt{t}), 0 < \alpha < 1$ from the Sonin pair (5):

$$\begin{aligned}
({}_{r}\mathbb{D}_{(k)}\, f)(t) &= -\frac{d}{dt}\int_t^b (\sqrt{\tau-t})^{-\alpha}I_{-\alpha}(2\sqrt{\tau-t})f(\tau)d\tau,\ a \le t < b,\\
({}_{r_*}\mathbb{D}_{(k)}\, f)(t) &= -\int_t^b (\sqrt{\tau-t})^{-\alpha}I_{-\alpha}(2\sqrt{\tau-t})f'(\tau)d\tau,\ a \le t < b.
\end{aligned}$$

In what follows, we consider the left- and right-sided GFDs introduced above on the spaces $C_{-1}^1(a,b]$ and $C_{-1}^1[a,b)$, respectively (see Definition 1). First, a connection between the GFDs and the regularized GFDs on a finite interval is established.

Proposition 4. *For any functions $f \in C_{-1}^1(a,b]$ and $g \in C_{-1}^1[a,b)$, the relations*

$$({}_l\mathbb{D}_{(k)}\, f)(t) \;=\; f(a)k(t-a) + ({}_{l_*}\mathbb{D}_{(k)}\, f)(t),\;\; a < t \le b \tag{26}$$

and

$$({}_r\mathbb{D}_{(k)}\, g)(t) \;=\; g(b)k(b-t) + ({}_{r_*}\mathbb{D}_{(k)}\, g)(t),\;\; a \le t < b, \tag{27}$$

hold true, respectively.

Proof. To prove the Formula (27), let us introduce an auxiliary function $\hat{k}(t) = \int_0^t k(s)ds$. Then we have the relations

$$\hat{k}(0) = 0 \text{ and } \frac{d}{dt}\hat{k} = k(t), t > 0.$$

Integration by parts yields

$$\begin{aligned}
({}_r\mathbb{D}_{(k)}\, g)(t) &= -\frac{d}{dt}\int_t^b k(\tau - t)g(\tau)d\tau \\
&= -\frac{d}{dt}\left(\Big[g(\tau)\hat{k}(\tau - t)\Big]_t^b\right) + \frac{d}{dt}\int_t^b \hat{k}(\tau - t)g'(\tau)d\tau \\
&= -\frac{d}{dt}(g(b)\hat{k}(b-t)) - \int_t^b k(\tau - t)g'(\tau)d\tau \\
&= g(b)k(b-t) + ({}_{r_*}\mathbb{D}_{(k)}\, g)(t),
\end{aligned}$$

which completes the proof of the Formula (27). The Formula (26) can be derived using analogous steps and we omit its proof here. □

The next result concerns different kinds of integration by parts formulas for the GFDs introduced above. It is well known that such formulas play a very important role, say, in the fractional calculus of variations involving the functionals that depend on the fractional derivatives.

Proposition 5. *The following integration by parts formulas hold true*

$$\begin{aligned}
\int_a^b f(t)({}_l\mathbb{D}_{(k)}\, g)(t)dt &= \int_a^b g(t)({}_{r_*}\mathbb{D}_{(k)}\, f)(t)dt + \Big[f(t)({}_l\mathbb{I}_{(k)} g)(t)\Big]_a^b, \\
&\quad f \in C_{-1}^1[a,b), g \in C_{-1}^1(a,b], \qquad (28) \\
\int_a^b f(t)({}_r\mathbb{D}_{(k)}\, g)(t)dt &= \int_a^b g(t)({}_{l_*}\mathbb{D}_{(k)}\, f)(t)dt - \Big[f(t)({}_r\mathbb{I}_{(k)} g)(t)\Big]_a^b, \\
&\quad f \in C_{-1}^1(a,b], g \in C_{-1}^1[a,b), \qquad (29) \\
\int_a^b f(t)({}_{l_*}\mathbb{D}_{(k)}\, g)(t)dt &= \int_a^b g(t)({}_r\mathbb{D}_{(k)}\, f)(t)dt + \Big[g(t)({}_r\mathbb{I}_{(k)} f)(t)\Big]_a^b, \\
&\quad f \in C_{-1}^1[a,b), g \in C_{-1}^1(a,b], \qquad (30) \\
\int_a^b f(t)({}_{r_*}\mathbb{D}_{(k)}\, g)(t)dt &= \int_a^b g(t)({}_l\mathbb{D}_{(k)}\, f)(t)dt - \Big[g(t)({}_l\mathbb{I}_{(k)} f)(t)\Big]_a^b, \\
&\quad f \in C_{-1}^1(a,b], g \in C_{-1}^1[a,b). \qquad (31)
\end{aligned}$$

Proof. We start with a proof of the Formula (28) and first represent its left-hand side in the form

$$\int_a^b f(t)({}_l\mathbb{D}_{(k)}\, g)(t)dt = \int_a^b f(t)\left(\frac{d}{dt}\int_a^t k(t-\tau)g(\tau)d\tau\right)dt.$$

Integration by parts in the last integral yields a chain of the relations

$$\begin{aligned}\int_a^b f(t)({}_l\mathbb{D}_{(k)}\, g)(t)dt &= \left[f(t)\int_a^t k(t-\tau)g(\tau)d\tau\right]_a^b - \int_a^b f'(t)\int_a^t k(t-\tau)g(\tau)d\tau dt \\ &= \left[f(t)({}_l\mathbb{I}_{(k)}g)(t)\right]_a^b - \int_a^b\int_a^t f'(t)k(t-\tau)g(\tau)d\tau dt \\ &= \left[f(t)({}_l\mathbb{I}_{(k)}g)(t)\right]_a^b - \int_a^b g(\tau)\int_\tau^b f'(t)k(t-\tau)dtd\tau \\ &= \left[f(t)({}_l\mathbb{I}_{(k)}g)(t)\right]_a^b + \int_a^b g(\tau)({}_{r_*}\mathbb{D}_{(k)}\, f)(\tau)d\tau,\end{aligned}$$

which completes the proof the Formula (28). The Formula (29) is proved by following the exact same lines, whereas the Formula (30) immediately follows from (29) and the Formula (31) is a direct consequence from the Formula (28). □

In the rest of this section, we formulate and prove the 1st and the 2nd fundamental theorems of FC for the GFIs and the GFDs introduced above.

Theorem 1. *(1st Fundamental Theorem of FC)*
Let a pair of the kernels (κ, k) belong to the set $\mathcal{S}_f$.
The left- and the right-sided GFDs are the left-inverse operators to the corresponding GFIs:

$$({}_l\mathbb{D}_{(k)}\, {}_l\mathbb{I}_{(\kappa)}f)(t) = f(t),\ f \in C^1_{-1}(a,b],\ a < t \le b, \tag{32}$$
$$({}_{l_*}\mathbb{D}_{(k)}\, {}_l\mathbb{I}_{(\kappa)}f)(t) = f(t),\ f \in C^1_{-1}(a,b],\ a < t \le b, \tag{33}$$
$$({}_r\mathbb{D}_{(k)}\, {}_r\mathbb{I}_{(\kappa)}f)(t) = f(t),\ f \in C^1_{-1}[a,b),\ a \le t < b, \tag{34}$$
$$({}_{r_*}\mathbb{D}_{(k)}\, {}_r\mathbb{I}_{(\kappa)}f)(t) = f(t),\ f \in C^1_{-1}[a,b),\ a \le t < b. \tag{35}$$

Proof. We start with a proof of the Formula (32). By definition, the left-hand side of (32) takes the form

$$\begin{aligned}({}_l\mathbb{D}_{(k)}\, L\mathbb{I}_{(\kappa)}f)(t) &= \frac{d}{dt}\int_a^t k(t-\tau)({}_l\mathbb{I}_{(\kappa)}f)(\tau)d\tau \\ &= \frac{d}{dt}\int_a^t k(t-\tau)\int_a^\tau \kappa(\tau-y)f(y)dyd\tau.\end{aligned}$$

Interchanging the order of integration in the last integral yields

$$({}_l\mathbb{D}_{(k)}\, {}_l\mathbb{I}_{(\kappa)}f)(t) = \frac{d}{dt}\int_a^t f(y)\int_y^t k(t-\tau)\kappa(\tau-y)d\tau dy. \tag{36}$$

Due to the relation

$$\int_y^t k(t-\tau)\kappa(\tau-y)d\tau = \int_0^{t-y} k(\tau)\kappa(t-y-\tau)d\tau = (k*\kappa)(t-y) = 1,\ 0 < t-y \le b-a, \tag{37}$$

the representation (36) immediately leads to the formula

$$({}_l\mathbb{D}_{(k)}\, {}_l\mathbb{I}_{(\kappa)}f)(t) = \frac{d}{dt}\int_a^t f(y)dy = f(t),\ t > a,$$

which completes the proof of (32).

Now we verify the relation (33) and first show that

$$({}_l\mathbb{I}_{(\kappa)}f)(a) = 0 \tag{38}$$

for any $f \in C^1_{-1}(a,b]$.

Indeed, the inclusion $\kappa \in C_{-1}(0, b-a]$ leads to the representation $\kappa(t) = t^{p-1}h(t)$, $p > 0, h \in C[0, b-a]$. Since $f \in C^1_{-1}(a,b]$, the same arguments that were employed in [31] for the space $C^1_{-1}(0, +\infty)$ lead to the inclusion $f \in C[a,b]$ and it holds that

$$({}_l\mathbb{I}_{(\kappa)}f)(t) = \int_a^t (t-\tau)^{p-1}h(t-\tau)f(\tau)d\tau.$$

Using the substitution $z = \frac{t-\tau}{t-a}$ in the last integral, we arrive at the representation

$$({}_l\mathbb{I}_{(\kappa)}f)(t) = (t-a)^p \int_0^1 z^{p-1}h(z(t-a))f(t-z(t-a))dz. \tag{39}$$

Now let us introduce an auxiliary function as follows: $g(t,z) = h(z(t-a))f(t-z(t-a))$. Because the functions f and h are continuous, the function g is continuous in z on the interval $[0,1]$. Then we can apply the mean value theorem (the function $z^{p-1} \geq 0$ is integrable) to the integral at the right-hand side of the Formula (39) and thus obtain the representation

$$\begin{aligned} ({}_l\mathbb{I}_{(\kappa)}f)(t) &= (t-a)^p g(\hat{t}, z_0) \int_0^1 z^{p-1}dz \\ &= (t-a)^p g(\hat{t}, z_0)\frac{1}{p},\ 0 < z_0 < 1,\ \hat{t} > a,\ p > 0, \end{aligned}$$

which completes the proof of the Formula (38).

Because $({}_l\mathbb{I}_{(\kappa)}f)(a) = 0$, the formula (33) follows by combining the results provided in the Equations (26), (32), and (38).

The proof of the Formula (34) is completely analogous to the proof of (32) and the proof of (35) follows the lines of the proof of (33). □

Remark 1. *Applying the methods used in Ref. [5] for the GFI and the GFDs on the real positive semi-axis, the relations (32)–(35) can be proved on the following spaces of functions that are larger than $C^1_{-1}(a,b]$ and $C^1_{-1}[a,b)$, respectively (see Ref. [5] for details):*

$$C_{-1,(\kappa)}(a,b] = \{f : {}_l\mathbb{I}_{(\kappa)}f \in C^1_{-1}(a,b],\ ({}_l\mathbb{I}_{(\kappa)}f)(a) = 0\},$$

$$C_{-1,(\kappa)}[a,b) = \{f : {}_r\mathbb{I}_{(\kappa)}f \in C^1_{-1}[a,b),\ ({}_r\mathbb{I}_{(\kappa)}f)(b) = 0\}.$$

Now we formulate and prove the 2nd fundamental theorem of FC for the left- and right-sided GFIs and GFDs.

Theorem 2. *(2nd Fundamental Theorem of FC)*

Let a pair of the kernels (κ, k) belong to the set $\mathcal{S}_f$.

The compositions of the left- and the right-sided GFIs and the corresponding GFDs take the following form:

$$({}_l\mathbb{I}_{(\kappa)}\ {}_{l_*}\mathbb{D}_{(k)}f)(t) = f(t) - f(a),\ f \in C^1_{-1}(a,b], \tag{40}$$

$$({}_l\mathbb{I}_{(\kappa)}\ {}_l\mathbb{D}_{(k)}f)(t) = f(t),\ f \in C^1_{-1}(a,b], \tag{41}$$

$$({}_r\mathbb{I}_{(\kappa)}\ {}_{r_*}\mathbb{D}_{(k)}f)(t) = f(b) - f(t),\ f \in C^1_{-1}[a,b), \tag{42}$$

$$({}_r\mathbb{I}_{(\kappa)}\ {}_{r_*}\mathbb{D}_{(k)}f)(t) = f(t),\ f \in C^1_{-1}[a,b). \tag{43}$$

Proof. We start with a proof of the Formula (40). By definition, its left-hand side can be represented as follows:

$$\begin{aligned}({}_l\mathbb{I}_{(\kappa)}\, {}_{l_*}\mathbb{D}_{(k)} f)(t) &= \int_a^t \kappa(t-\tau)({}_{l_*}\mathbb{D}_{(k)} f)(\tau)d\tau \\ &= \int_a^t \kappa(t-\tau)\int_a^\tau k(\tau-y) f'(y)dyd\tau.\end{aligned}$$

Interchanging the order of integration in the last integral and using the Formula (37) yields

$$\begin{aligned}({}_l\mathbb{I}_{(\kappa)}\, {}_{l_*}\mathbb{D}_{(k)} f)(t) &= \int_a^t f'(y)\int_y^t \kappa(t-\tau)k(\tau-y)d\tau dy \\ &= \int_a^t f'(y)dy = f(t)-f(a), \end{aligned} \tag{44}$$

which proves the Formula (40).

To prove the Formula (41), we first show that

$$\big({}_l\mathbb{I}_{(\kappa)}\, k(\tau-a)\big)(t) = \{1\},\ a < t \le b. \tag{45}$$

Indeed, we have the following chain of relations:

$$\begin{aligned}\big({}_l\mathbb{I}_{(\kappa)}\, k(\tau-a)\big)(t) &= \int_a^t \kappa(t-\tau)k(\tau-a)d\tau = \int_0^{t-a}\kappa(t-a-\tau)k(\tau)d\tau \\ &= (\kappa * k)(t-a) = \{1\},\ a<t\le b.\end{aligned}$$

Because of the inclusion $f \in C^1_{-1}(a,b]$, the function f' is from the space $C_{-1}(a,b]$. Now we can employ the representation (26) and get the following relations:

$$\begin{aligned}({}_l\mathbb{I}_{(\kappa)}\, {}_l\mathbb{D}_{(k)} f)(t) &= \big({}_l\mathbb{I}_{(\kappa)}\,({}_{l_*}\mathbb{D}_{(k)} f)(\tau) + f(a)k(\tau-a)\big)(t) \\ &= \big({}_l\mathbb{I}_{(\kappa)}\, {}_{l_*}\mathbb{D}_{(k)} f\big)(t) + f(a)\big({}_l\mathbb{I}_{(\kappa)} k(\tau-a)\big)(t) \\ &= f(t)-f(a)+f(a) = f(t),\end{aligned}$$

which completes the proof of the Formula (41).

The proof of the Formula (42) follows the lines of the proof of (40) and the proof of (43) is completely analogous to the proof of (41). □

4. Conclusions and Directions for Further Research

In this paper, to the best of authors' knowledge, the left- and right-sided GFIs and GFDs on a finite interval have been introduced for the first time in the FC literature. We also provided some of their basic properties on the spaces of functions that are continuous of the finite open intervals, but can have an integrable singularity of a power function type at one of its end points and on their suitable sub-spaces.

In particular, we derived the formulas that connect the GFDs (of the Riemann–Liuville type) and the regularized GFDs (of the Caputo type) as well as several integration by parts formulas for the right- and left-sided GFIs and GFDs. The formulas of this type are especially important while dealing with the fractional variation calculus for the functionals that involve the left- and right-sided fractional derivatives.

The main results presented in the paper are the 1st and the 2nd fundamental theorems of FC formulated for the left- and right-sided GFIs and GFDs on a finite interval. These theorems allow for an interpretation of the operators introduced in the paper as some FC operators. In particular, we showed that the GFDs are the left-inverse operators to the corresponding GFIs. In fact, this property can be interpreted as a definition of the fractional derivatives as soon as the notion of the fractional integrals is fixed (see Ref. [32] for a discussion of properties of the FC operators).

The research line initiated in this paper can be extended in several directions. The first important topic for further research would be to develop a theory of the left- and right-sided GFIs and GFDs on a finite interval on other classical spaces of functions, say, on the Hölder spaces or the weighted L_p-spaces (see Ref. [19] for a theory of the Riemann–Liouville fractional integrals and derivatives on a finite interval on these spaces of functions).

In this paper, we dealt only with the GFIs and the GFDs on a finite interval of the "generalized order" less or equal to one (see the Sonin condition (1)). However, in Ref. [6], the Sonin condition has been extended in a manner that allows defining GFIs and the GFDs of arbitrary order on the positive real semi-axis. It would be worth to develop similar constructions for the case of the GFIs and the GFDs on a finite interval.

In a recent paper [11], the so-called 1st level GFDs on the positive real semi-axis were introduced and investigated. These derivatives contain the GFDs (of the Riemann–Liouville type) and the regularized GFDs (of the Caputo type) as their particular cases. Thus, any result that concerns the 1st level GFDs covers the corresponding results for the GFDs and for the regularized GFDs. Similarly to the case of the positive real semi-axis, a general construction of the GFDs on a finite interval that covers both the GFDs (of the Riemann–Liouville type) and the regularized GFDs (of the Caputo type) introduced in this paper would be useful.

Finally, we mention here the open problems related to the ordinary and partial fractional differential equations with the GFDs. In Ref. [2], this line of research was initiated by Kochubei for the GFDs on the positive real semi-axis with the Sonin kernels from the Kochubei set. In the meantime, many other papers devoted to this topic have been published, see, e.g., Refs. [33–41] and the recent survey in Ref. [3]. The fractional differential equations with the left- and right-sided GFDs on a finite interval introduced in this paper would be another important topic for further research.

Author Contributions: Conceptualization, M.A.-R. and Y.L.; methodology, M.A.-R. and Y.L.; validation, M.A.-R. and Y.L.; formal analysis, M.A.-R.; investigation, Y.L.; writing—original draft preparation, M.A.-R.; writing—review and editing, Y.L.; visualization, M.A.-R. and Y.L. All authors have read and agreed to the published version of the manuscript.

Funding: There are no external funding resources of this research.

Data Availability Statement: Not Applicable.

Acknowledgments: The first author would like to express his sincere appreciation to the Research Affairs at Yarmouk University for their support.

Conflicts of Interest: The authors have no conflict of interest to disclose.

References

1. Sonine, N. Sur la généralisation d'une formule d'Abel. *Acta Math.* **1884**, *4*, 171–176. [CrossRef]
2. Kochubei, A.N. General fractional calculus, evolution equations, and renewal processes. *Integr. Equa. Oper. Theory* **2011**, *71*, 583–600. [CrossRef]
3. Luchko, Y.; Yamamoto, M. The general fractional derivative and related fractional differential equations. *Mathematics* **2020**, *8*, 2115. [CrossRef]
4. Luchko, Y.; Yamamoto, M. General time-fractional diffusion equation: Some uniqueness and existence results for the initial-boundary-value problems. *Fract. Calc. Appl. Anal.* **2018**, *19*, 676–695. [CrossRef]
5. Luchko, Y. General fractional integrals and derivatives with the Sonine kernels. *Mathematics* **2021**, *9*, 594. [CrossRef]
6. Luchko, Y. General fractional integrals and derivatives of arbitrary order. *Symmetry* **2021**, *13*, 755. [CrossRef]
7. Luchko, Y. Operational calculus for the general fractional derivative and its applications. *Fract. Calc. Appl. Anal.* **2021**, *24*, 338–375. [CrossRef]
8. Luchko, Y. Special functions of fractional calculus in the form of convolution series and their applications. *Mathematics* **2021**, *9*, 2132. [CrossRef]
9. Luchko, Y. Convolution series and the generalized convolution Taylor formula. *Fract. Calc. Appl. Anal.* **2022**, *25*, 207–228. [CrossRef]
10. Luchko, Y. Fractional differential equations with the general fractional derivatives of arbitrary order in the Riemann-Liouville sense. *Mathematics* **2022**, *10*, 849. [CrossRef]
11. Luchko, Y. The 1st level general fractional derivatives and some of their properties. *J. Math. Sci.* **2022**, *268*, 1–14. [CrossRef]

12. Tarasov, V.E. General fractional dynamics. *Mathematics* **2021**, *9*, 1464. [CrossRef]
13. Tarasov, V.E. General non-Markovian quantum dynamics. *Entropy* **2021**, *23*, 1006. [CrossRef]
14. Tarasov, V.E. General fractional vector calculus. *Mathematics* **2021**, *9*, 2816. [CrossRef]
15. Tarasov, V.E. General non-local continuum mechanics: Derivation of balance equations. *Mathematics* **2022**, *10*, 1427. [CrossRef]
16. Tarasov, V.E. Nonlocal probability theory: General fractional calculus approach. *Mathematics* **2022**, *10*, 3848. [CrossRef]
17. Tarasov, V.E. Nonlocal statistical mechanics: General fractional Liouville equations and their solutions. *Phys. A Stat. Mech. Its Appl.* **2023**, *609*, 128366. [CrossRef]
18. Tarasov, V.E. Nonlocal classical theory of gravity: Massiveness of nonlocality and mass shielding by nonlocality. *Eur. Phys. J. Plus.* **2022**, *137*, 1336. [CrossRef]
19. Samko, S.G.; Kilbas, A.A.; Marichev, O.I. *Fractional Integrals and Derivatives. Theory and Applications*; Gordon and Breach: New York, NY, USA, 1993.
20. Agrawal, O.P. Generalized variational problems and Euler–Lagrange equations. *Comput. Math. Appl.* **2010**, *59*, 1852–1864. [CrossRef]
21. Agrawal, O.P. Some generalized fractional calculus operators and their applications in integral equations. *Fract. Calc. Appl. Anal.* **2012**, *15*, 700–711. [CrossRef]
22. Fernandez, A.; Fahad, H.M. Weighted fractional calculus: A general class of operators. *Fractal Fract.* **2022**, *6*, 208. [CrossRef]
23. Dimovski, I.H. Operational calculus for a class of differential operators. *Compt. Rend. Acad. Bulg. Sci.* **1966**, *19*, 1111–1114.
24. Luchko, Y. Operational method for fractional ordinary differential equations. In *Handbook of Fractional Calculus with Applications*; Volume 2: Fractional Differential Equations; Kochubei, A., Luchko, Y., Eds.; Walter de Gruyter: Berlin, Germany; Boston, MA, USA, 2019; pp. 91–118.
25. Diethelm, K.; Garrappa, R.; Giusti, A.; Stynes, M. Why fractiona derivatives with nonsingular kernels should not be used. *Fract. Calc. Appl. Anal.* **2020**, *23*, 610–634. [CrossRef]
26. Hanyga, A. A comment on a controversial issue: A generalized fractional derivative cannot have a regular kernel. *Fract. Calc. Anal. Appl.* **2020**, *23*, 211–223. [CrossRef]
27. Samko, S.G.; Cardoso, R.P. Integral equations of the first kind of Sonine type. *Intern. J. Math. Sci.* **2003**, *57*, 3609–3632. [CrossRef]
28. Abel, N.H. Auflösung einer mechanischen Aufgabe. *Die Reine Angew. Math.* **1826**, *1*, 153–157.
29. Abel, N.H. Oplösning af et par opgaver ved hjelp af bestemte integraler. *Mag. Naturvidenskaberne* **1823**, *2*, 2.
30. Al-Refai, M. Maximum principles and applications for fractional differential equations with operators involving Mittag-Leffler function. *Fract. Calc. Appl. Anal.* **2021**, *24*, 1220–1230. [CrossRef]
31. Luchko, Y.; Gorenflo, R. An operational method for solving fractional differential equations. *Acta Math. Vietnam.* **1999** *24*, 207–234.
32. Hilfer, R.; Luchko, Y. Desiderata for Fractional Derivatives and Integrals. *Mathematics* **2019**, *7*, 149. [CrossRef]
33. Kinash, N.; Janno, J. An Inverse Problem for a Generalized Fractional Derivative with an Application in Reconstruction of Time- and Space-Dependent Sources in Fractional Diffusion and Wave Equations. *Mathematics* **2019**, *7*, 1138. [CrossRef]
34. Al-Refai, M.; Luchko, Y. Comparison principles for solutions to the fractional differential inequalities with the general fractional derivatives and their applications. *J. Differ. Equ.* **2022**, *319*, 312–324. [CrossRef]
35. Janno, J.; Kasemets, K. Identification of a kernel in an evolutionary integral equation occurring in subdiffusion. *J. Inverse Ill-Posed Probl.* **2017**, *25*, 777–798. [CrossRef]
36. Kinash, N.; Janno, J. Inverse problems for a generalized subdiffusion equation with final overdetermination. *Math. Model. Anal.* **2019**, *24*, 236–262.
37. Kochubei, A.N. General fractional calculus. In *Handbook of Fractional Calculus with Applications*; Volume 1: Basic Theory; Kochubei, A., Luchko, Y., Eds.; Walter de Gruyter: Berlin, Germany; Boston, MA, USA, 2019; pp. 111–126.
38. Kochubei, A.N. Equations with general fractional time derivatives. Cauchy problem. In *Handbook of Fractional Calculus with Applications*; Volume 2: Fractional Differential Equations; Kochubei, A., Luchko, Y., Eds.; Walter de Gruyter: Berlin, Germany; Boston, MA, USA, 2019; pp. 223–234.
39. Kochubei, A.N.; Kondratiev, Y. Growth Equation of the General Fractional Calculus. *Mathematics* **2019**, *7*, 615. [CrossRef]
40. Sin, C.-S. Well-posedness of general Caputo-type fractional differential equations. *Fract. Calc. Appl. Anal.* **2018**, *21*, 819–832. [CrossRef]
41. Sin, C.-S. Cauchy problem for general time fractional diffusion equation. *Fract. Calc. Appl. Anal.* **2020**, *23*, 1545–1559. [CrossRef]

Disclaimer/Publisher's Note: The statements, opinions and data contained in all publications are solely those of the individual author(s) and contributor(s) and not of MDPI and/or the editor(s). MDPI and/or the editor(s) disclaim responsibility for any injury to people or property resulting from any ideas, methods, instructions or products referred to in the content.

mathematics

MDPI

Article

Inverse Sturm–Liouville Problem with Spectral Parameter in the Boundary Conditions

Natalia P. Bondarenko [1,2,3,*] and **Egor E. Chitorkin** [2,4]

1. Department of Applied Mathematics and Physics, Samara National Research University, Moskovskoye Shosse 34, 443086 Samara, Russia
2. Department of Mechanics and Mathematics, Saratov State University, Astrakhanskaya 83, 410012 Saratov, Russia
3. S.M. Nikolskii Mathematical Institute, Peoples' Friendship University of Russia (RUDN University), Miklukho-Maklaya Street 6, 117198 Moscow, Russia
3. Institute of IT and Cybernetics, Samara National Research University, Moskovskoye Shosse 34, 443086 Samara, Russia

* Correspondence: bondarenkonp@info.sgu.ru

Abstract: In this paper, for the first time, we study the inverse Sturm–Liouville problem with polynomials of the spectral parameter in the first boundary condition and with entire analytic functions in the second one. For the investigation of this new inverse problem, we develop an approach based on the construction of a special vector functional sequence in a suitable Hilbert space. The uniqueness of recovering the potential and the polynomials of the boundary condition from a part of the spectrum is proved. Furthermore, our main results are applied to the Hochstadt–Lieberman-type problems with polynomial dependence on the spectral parameter not only in the boundary conditions but also in discontinuity (transmission) conditions inside the interval. We prove novel uniqueness theorems, which generalize and improve the previous results in this direction. Note that all the spectral problems in this paper are investigated in the general non-self-adjoint form, and our method does not require the simplicity of the spectrum. Moreover, our method is constructive and can be developed in the future for numerical solution and for the study of solvability and stability of inverse spectral problems.

Keywords: inverse spectral problems; Sturm–Liouville operator; polynomials in the boundary conditions; entire functions in the boundary conditions; uniqueness theorems; half-inverse problems; discontinuity inside the interval

MSC: 34A55; 34B07; 34B09; 34B24; 34L40

Citation: Bondarenko, N.P.; Chitorkin, E.E. Inverse Sturm–Liouville Problem with Spectral Parameter in the Boundary Conditions. *Mathematics* **2023**, *11*, 1138. https://doi.org/10.3390/math11051138

Academic Editor: Sitnik Sergey

Received: 20 January 2023
Revised: 21 February 2023
Accepted: 22 February 2023
Published: 24 February 2023

Copyright: © 2023 by the authors. Licensee MDPI, Basel, Switzerland. This article is an open access article distributed under the terms and conditions of the Creative Commons Attribution (CC BY) license (https://creativecommons.org/licenses/by/4.0/).

1. Introduction

In this paper, we consider the following boundary value problem $L = L(q, p_1, p_2, f_1, f_2)$:

$$-y''(x) + q(x)y(x) = \lambda y(x), \quad x \in (0, \pi), \tag{1}$$

$$p_1(\lambda)y'(0) + p_2(\lambda)y(0) = 0, \quad f_1(\lambda)y'(\pi) + f_2(\lambda)y(\pi) = 0, \tag{2}$$

where (1) is the Sturm–Liouville equation with the complex-valued potential $q \in L_2(0, \pi)$, λ is the spectral parameter, the boundary condition (BC) (2) at $x = 0$ contains relatively prime polynomials $p_j(\lambda)$, $j = 1, 2$, and the BC at $x = \pi$, arbitrary functions $f_j(\lambda)$, $j = 1, 2$, which are analytical in the whole λ-plane.

This paper aims to study the inverse spectral problem that consists in the recovery of the potential $q(x)$ and the polynomials $p_1(\lambda)$ and $p_2(\lambda)$ from some part of the problem L's spectrum. Inverse spectral theory for the Sturm–Liouville operators with *constant* coefficients in the boundary conditions has been developed fairly completely (see the monographs [1–4]). There is also a number of studies concerning eigenvalue problems with *polynomial* dependence on the spectral parameter in the BCs. Such problems arise in various physical applications, e.g., in mechanical engineering [5], in flow dust acoustics [6], in heat conduction, diffusion, and electric circuit problems (see [7,8] and references therein). The theory of *direct* spectral problems for general classes of differential operators depending nonlinearly on the spectral parameter can be found in [9–11].

Inverse Sturm–Liouville problems with polynomials in the BCs have been studied in [12–25], and other papers. We mention that there is a large number of research works on the Sturm–Liouville problems with linear or quadratic dependence on the spectral parameter (see, e.g., [26–28]). However, in this paper, we mostly focus on the bibliography concerning the inverse Sturm–Liouville problems with polynomials of arbitrary degrees in the BCs. The majority of the studies in this direction deal with self-adjoint problems containing rational Herglotz–Nevanlinna functions of the spectral parameter in the BCs (see, e.g., [13,14,21,23–25,29]). It is easy to check that the BCs of that type can be reduced to the form with polynomial dependence on the spectral parameter. A constructive solution of the inverse Sturm–Liouville problem on a finite interval with the polynomial BCs in the general non-self-adjoint form has been obtained by Freiling and Yurko [17] by using the method of spectral mappings. The case of the half-line was considered in [18]. In recent years, significant progress for the self-adjoint Sturm–Liouville inverse problems with Herglotz–Nevanlinna functions of λ in the BCs has been achieved by Guliyev (see [23–25,29]), who obtained the spectral data characterization for regular potentials of class $L_2(0,\pi)$, as well as for singular potentials of class $W_2^{-1}(0,\pi)$.

Recently, a new class of the inverse Sturm–Liouville problems with entire analytic functions in one of the BCs has started to be investigated (see [30–34]). Such problems cause interest in connection with the so-called *partial* inverse problems, which consist in the recovery of the differential expression coefficients (e.g., of the Sturm–Liouville potentials) on a part of an interval or a geometrical graph from the spectral data, while the coefficients on the remaining part are known a priori. Naturally, partial inverse problems require less spectral data than the complete ones. In particular, Hochstadt and Lieberman [35] have proved that, if the potential $q(x)$ is known on the half of the interval $(0,\pi)$, then $q(x)$ on the other half is uniquely specified by one spectrum. In general, due to the classical result by Borg [36], two spectra are required for the unique reconstruction of the potential. The Hochstadt–Lieberman-type problems for the Sturm–Liouville operators with polynomial BCs also attract the attention of scholars. For some special cases, such problems were considered in [19,22,24].

In the mentioned papers [30–34], a unified approach has been developed for a variety of partial inverse problems. That approach consists in the reduction in a partial inverse problem to the Sturm–Liouville inverse problem with entire functions in the BC. The idea of that method appeared from the investigation of partial inverse problems on metric graphs [37] and of the inverse transmission eigenvalue problem [38]. Later on, that approach was transferred to the discrete Jacobi systems (see [39]). We also mention that the Sturm–Liouville inverse problems with entire functions in the BC considered in [30–32] are closely related to the problem of the recovery of the potential from the values of the Weyl function at a countable set of points (see [40,41]).

This paper is concerned with the development of the inverse spectral theory for the Sturm–Liouville problem L of form (1)-(2), with polynomial dependence on λ in one of the BCs, and with analytical dependence in the other one. To the best of the authors' knowledge, inverse problems for L have not been considered before. For the investigation of this new inverse problem, we develop an approach based on the construction of a special vector functional sequence $\{v_n\}_{n=1}^{\infty}$ in a suitable Hilbert space. We prove that the completeness of $\{v_n\}_{n=1}^{\infty}$ is sufficient for the uniqueness of the inverse problem solution. Our approach relies on the ideas of [30] and on some results of [16,17] for the inverse problems with only polynomial BCs. Note that we consider the problem L in the general non-self-adjoint form, and our method does not require the simplicity of the spectrum. Moreover, our method is constructive and can be developed in the future for numerical solution and for the study of solvability and stability of inverse spectral problems.

Furthermore, we apply our main results to the Hochstadt–Lieberman-type problems, with polynomial dependence on the spectral parameter not only in BCs but also in discontinuity (transmission) conditions inside the interval. The developed approach allows us to investigate various cases in the same way. We prove the uniqueness theorems which generalize and improve the results of [19,22,24] for the case of polynomials contained only in BCs. In particular, we show that, in some cases, a part of the eigenvalues can be excluded, and the remaining subspectrum is still sufficient for the uniqueness. For the case of polynomials in the discontinuity conditions, our problem statement is novel, and the obtained results are the first ones in this direction.

It is worth mentioning that eigenvalue problems with discontinuity conditions depending on the spectral parameter have attracted the interest of mathematicians in recent years. Bartels et al. [42,43] obtained the Hilbert space formulation and the eigenvalue asymptotics for the Sturm–Liouville problems with Herglotz–Nevanlinna functions of λ in the discontinuity conditions arising in microelectronics. Some issues of inverse spectral theory for differential operators with linear dependence on the spectral parameter in the discontinuity conditions were considered in [44,45]. Polynomials of higher degree in the discontinuity conditions appear in the study of the inverse Sturm–Liouville problems on time scales (see [46,47]). However, there are only fragmentary results for boundary value problems with polynomials of λ in the discontinuity conditions, and the general inverse spectral theory of such problems has not been created yet. The methods of this paper may be useful for future research in this direction. In addition, we point out that spectral problems with differential expression coefficients depending on the eigenparameter also arise in applications. In particular, a problem of this kind appeared in the recent study [48] of the full-waveform inversion with frequency-dependent offset-preconditioning, having applications in exploration geophysics. From the inverse spectral theory viewpoint, boundary value problems' eigenparameter dependence in equation coefficients are different from the ones considered in this paper and so require a separate investigation.

The paper is organized as follows. In Section 2, the inverse problem statements and the main results are formulated. In Section 3, we prove the uniqueness theorem and provide a constructive algorithm for solving the inverse problem for L. In Section 4, we obtain the sufficient conditions of uniqueness, which are convenient for applications. In Section 5, the main results are applied to the Hochstadt–Lieberman-type problems.

2. Main Results

Consider the boundary value problem $L = L(q, p_1, p_2, f_1, f_2)$ of form (1)-(2). The spectrum of the problem L consists of the eigenvalues being the zeros of some analytic entire function which depends on $f_1(\lambda)$ and $f_2(\lambda)$. Therefore, we cannot say anything specific about the behavior of the spectrum. However, we can consider the reconstruction of the potential from some countable subset of the spectrum $\{\lambda_n\}_{n=1}^{\infty}$ and obtain sufficient conditions on the subspectrum $\{\lambda_n\}_{n=1}^{\infty}$ for the unique solvability of the inverse problem.

The polynomials $p_1(\lambda)$ and $p_2(\lambda)$ can be represented in the form

$$p_1(\lambda) = \sum_{n=0}^{N_1} a_n \lambda^n, \quad p_2(\lambda) = \sum_{n=0}^{N_2} b_n \lambda^n, \quad a_{N_1} \neq 0, \quad b_{N_2} \neq 0, \quad N_1, N_2 \geq 0. \tag{3}$$

Here, we exclude the case of the Dirichlet BC $y(0) = 0$, that is, $p_1(\lambda) \equiv 0$, $p_2(\lambda) \equiv 1$, since this case has been studied in [30]. Without loss of generality, we assume that $a_{N_1} = 1$ if $N_1 \geq N_2$ and $b_{N_2} = 1$ if $N_2 > N_1$. Introduce the notations

$$\omega = \frac{1}{2}\int_0^{\pi} q(t)\, dt, \quad \varpi = \begin{cases} \omega - b_{N_1}, & N_1 = N_2 \\ \omega + a_{N_1}, & N_1 = N_2 - 1 \\ \omega, & \text{otherwise}. \end{cases} \tag{4}$$

In this paper, we consider the following inverse problem.

Problem 1. *Suppose that the degrees N_1, N_2 of the polynomials and functions $f_1(\lambda)$, $f_2(\lambda)$ are known a priori. Given a subspectrum $\{\lambda_n\}_{n=1}^{\infty}$ of the problem L and the number ω, find the potential $q(x)$ and the polynomials $p_1(\lambda)$, $p_2(\lambda)$.*

The subspectrum $\{\lambda_n\}_{n=1}^{\infty}$ can contain multiple eigenvalues of finite multiplicities. Note that, in the applications to the Hochstadt–Lieberman-type problems, the constant ω usually can be found from the eigenvalue asymptotics.

For investigating Problem 1, we construct the special sequence of vector functions $\{v_n\}_{n=1}^{\infty}$ in the Hilbert space

$$\mathcal{H}_K = L_2(0,\pi) \oplus L_2(0,\pi) \oplus \underbrace{\mathbb{C} \oplus \mathbb{C} \oplus \cdots \oplus \mathbb{C}}_{K},$$

where $K = \max\{2N_1, 2N_2 - 1\}$. The construction of the sequence $\{v_n\}_{n=1}^{\infty}$ is different for $N_1 \geq N_2$ and $N_1 < N_2$ and, moreover, is technically complicated (see Formulas (22), (26), and (29)), so we do not provide it here. It is important to note that $\{v_n\}_{n=1}^{\infty}$ are constructed by using only the given data of Problem 1, that is, N_j, $f_j(\lambda)$, $j = 1,2$, $\{\lambda_n\}_{n=1}^{\infty}$, and ω.

Along with $L = L(q, p_1, p_2, f_1, f_2)$, we consider the problem $\tilde{L} = L(\tilde{q}, \tilde{p}_1, \tilde{p}_2, \tilde{f}_1, \tilde{f}_2)$ of the same form (1)-(2) but with different coefficients. We agree that, if a symbol γ denotes an object related to L, then the symbol $\tilde{\gamma}$ with tilde denotes the analogous object related to $\tilde{L}$. One of the main results of this paper is the following uniqueness theorem for Problem 1.

Theorem 1. *Let $\{\lambda_n\}_{n=1}^{\infty}$ and $\{\tilde{\lambda}_n\}_{n=1}^{\infty}$ be subspectra of the problems L and $\tilde{L}$, respectively. Suppose that the sequence $\{v_n\}_{n=1}^{\infty}$ constructed for the problem L and its subspectrum $\{\lambda_n\}_{n=1}^{\infty}$ by formulas (22), (26), and (29) is complete in $L_2(0,\pi)$, and let $N_j = \tilde{N}_j$, $f_j(\lambda) \equiv \tilde{f}_j(\lambda)$, $j = 1,2$, $\lambda_n = \tilde{\lambda}_n$, $n \geq 1$, $\omega = \tilde{\omega}$. Then $q = \tilde{q}$ in $L_2(0,\pi)$ and $p_j(\lambda) \equiv \tilde{p}_j(\lambda)$, $j = 1,2$.*

For the case when the sequence $\{v_n\}_{n=1}^{\infty}$ is a Riesz basis in $\mathcal{H}_K$, we provide a constructive algorithm for solving Problem 1 (see Algorithm 1).

Since the sequence $\{v_n\}_{n=1}^{\infty}$ has a complex structure, it is important to find such sufficient conditions of its completeness that are (i) easy for checking and (ii) natural for applications. Such conditions are provided in the next theorem. For clarity, here, we formulate the result for the case of simple eigenvalues $\{\lambda_n\}_{n=1}^{\infty}$. For multiple eigenvalues, the analogous theorem is provided in Section 4.

Theorem 2. *Suppose that the eigenvalues of the subspectrum $\{\lambda_n\}_{n=1}^{\infty}$ are simple, $f_1(\lambda_n) \neq 0$ or $f_2(\lambda_n) \neq 0$ for every $n \geq 1$, and the system $\{\cos\sqrt{\lambda_n}t\}_{n=\max\{2N_1+1, 2N_2\}}^{\infty}$ is complete in $L_2(0,2\pi)$. Then, the system $\{v_n\}_{n=1}^{\infty}$ is complete in $\mathcal{H}_K$.*

Our next goal is to study the uniqueness of solution for the Hochstadt–Lieberman-type problems with polynomials of λ in the BCs. Consider the following boundary value problem $\mathscr{L} = \mathscr{L}(q, p_1, p_2, r_1, r_2)$:

$$-y''(x) + q(x)y(x) = \lambda y(x), \quad x \in (0, 2\pi), \tag{5}$$

$$p_1(\lambda)y'(0) + p_2(\lambda)y(0) = 0, \quad r_1(\lambda)y'(2\pi) + r_2(\lambda)y(2\pi) = 0, \tag{6}$$

where $q(x)$ is the complex-valued potential of class $L_2(0,2\pi)$, the BC at $x = 0$ contains relatively prime polynomials $p_j(\lambda)$, $j = 1,2$, and the BC at $x = 2\pi$ contains relatively prime polynomials $r_j(\lambda)$, $j = 1, 2$. The polynomials $p_1(\lambda)$, $p_2(\lambda)$ can be represented in the form (3) and the polynomials $r_1(\lambda)$, $r_2(\lambda)$, in the following analogous form:

$$r_1(\lambda) = \sum_{n=0}^{M_1} c_n \lambda^n, \quad r_2(\lambda) = \sum_{n=0}^{M_2} d_n \lambda^n, \quad c_{M_1} \neq 0, \quad d_{M_2} \neq 0, \quad M_1, M_2 \geq 0, \tag{7}$$

Without loss of generality, we assume that $a_{N_1} = 1$ if $N_1 \geq N_2$, $b_{N_2} = 1$ if $N_1 < N_2$, $c_{M_1} = 1$ if $M_1 \geq M_2$, $d_{M_2} = 1$ if $M_1 < M_2$.

The spectrum of $\mathscr{L}$ is a countable set of eigenvalues, which are asymptotically simple (see [17]), but a finite number of eigenvalues can be multiple. Let us denote the eigenvalues of $\mathscr{L}$ by $\{\mu_n\}_{n=1}^{\infty}$ (counting with multiplicities), and formulate the Hochstadt–Lieberman-type problem.

Problem 2. *Suppose that the degrees N_1, N_2 of the polynomials $p_j(\lambda)$, $j = 1, 2$, the polynomials $r_j(\lambda)$, $j = 1, 2$, and the potential $q(x)$ for $x \in (\pi, 2\pi)$ are known a priori. Given a subspectrum $\{\mu_n\}$ of the problem $\mathscr{L}$, find the potential $q(x)$ for $x \in (0, \pi)$ and the polynomials $p_1(\lambda)$, $p_2(\lambda)$.*

By reducing Problem 2 to Problem 1, we prove the following uniqueness theorem.

Theorem 3. *Let $\{\mu_n\}_{n=1}^{\infty}$ and $\{\tilde{\mu}_n\}_{n=1}^{\infty}$ be the spectra of the problems $\mathscr{L} = \mathscr{L}(q, p_1, p_2, r_1, r_2)$ and $\tilde{\mathscr{L}} = \mathscr{L}(\tilde{q}, \tilde{p}_1, \tilde{p}_2, \tilde{r}_1, \tilde{r}_2)$, respectively. Assume that $N_j = \tilde{N}_j$, $r_j(\lambda) \equiv \tilde{r}_j(\lambda)$, $j = 1, 2$, and $q(x) = \tilde{q}(x)$ a.e. on $(\pi, 2\pi)$. Additionally, impose the following assumptions.*

- *In the case $N_1 \geq N_2$, $M_1 \geq M_2$, suppose that $M_1 \geq N_1$ and $\mu_n = \tilde{\mu}_n$ for all $n \geq M_1 - N_1 + 1$.*
- *In the case $N_1 < N_2$, $M_1 \geq M_2$, suppose that $M_1 \geq N_2 - 1$ and $\mu_n = \tilde{\mu}_n$ for all $n \geq M_1 - N_2 + 2$.*
- *In the case $N_1 \geq N_2$, $M_1 < M_2$, suppose that $M_2 \geq N_1$ and $\mu_n = \tilde{\mu}_n$ for all $n \geq M_2 - N_1 + 1$.*
- *In the case $N_1 < N_2$, $M_1 < M_2$, suppose that $M_2 \geq N_2$ and $\mu_n = \tilde{\mu}_n$ for all $n \geq M_2 - N_2 + 1$.*

Then, $q(x) = \tilde{q}(x)$ a.e. on $(0, \pi)$ and $p_j(\lambda) \equiv \tilde{p}_j(\lambda)$, $j = 1, 2$.

Theorem 3 provides sufficient conditions for the uniqueness of solution of Problem 2. For instance, in the first case $N_1 \geq N_2$, $M_1 \geq M_2$, the potential $q(x)$ on $(0, \pi)$ and the polynomials $p_1(\lambda)$, $p_2(\lambda)$ are uniquely specified by the subspectrum $\{\mu_n\}_{n \geq M_1 - N_1 + 1}$ if $M_1 \geq N_1$. The numbering of the eigenvalues $\{\mu_n\}_{n=1}^{\infty}$ is not uniquely fixed, so if $M_1 > N_1$, then any $(M_1 - N_1)$ eigenvalues can be excluded (taking the multiplicities into account).

In order to prove Theorem 3, we analyze the asymptotics of the eigenvalues $\{\mu_n\}$ and conclude that, for the chosen subspectrum in each case, the conditions of Theorem 2 are fulfilled. Applying Theorem 4 and then Theorem 1, we arrive at the assertion of Theorem 3.

Theorem 3 generalizes the previously known results of [19,24] on the Hochstadt–Lieberman-type problems with polynomial BCs. Namely, in [19], the uniqueness theorem has been proved for the case $N_1 = N_2$, $M_1 = M_2$ and, in [24], for the case $N_2 = N_1 + 1$, $M_2 = M_1 + 1$ under an additional restriction of the self-adjointness. Moreover, the authors of [19,24] use the whole spectrum for the reconstruction, even if $M_1 > N_1$ and $M_2 > N_2$, respectively, while our Theorem 3 shows that a finite number of eigenvalues can be removed.

Furthermore, we show that our approach can be applied to the following boundary value problem $\mathcal{L} = \mathcal{L}(q, p_1, p_2, r_1, r_2, p_{ij})$, which contains polynomials of λ not only in the BCs but also in the discontinuity conditions inside the interval:

$$-y''(x) + q(x)y(x) = \lambda y(x), \quad x \in (0, \pi) \cup (\pi, 2\pi), \tag{8}$$

$$p_1(\lambda)y'(0)+p_2(\lambda)y(0)=0, \quad r_1(\lambda)y'(2\pi)+r_2(\lambda)y(2\pi)=0, \tag{9}$$

$$p_{1j}(\lambda)y^{(j)}(\pi-0)=p_{2j}(\lambda)y(\pi+0)+p_{3j}(\lambda)y'(\pi+0), \quad j=0,1. \tag{10}$$

Obviously, the problem $\mathscr{L}(q,p_1,p_2,r_1,r_2)$ is the special case of the problem $\mathcal{L}$ with $p_{10}(\lambda)\equiv p_{20}(\lambda)\equiv p_{11}(\lambda)\equiv p_{31}(\lambda)\equiv 1$, $p_{30}(\lambda)\equiv p_{21}(\lambda)\equiv 0$. So, we similarly denote the eigenvalues of $\mathcal{L}$ by $\{\mu_n\}_{n=1}^{\infty}$ (counting with multiplicities) and study the following Hochstadt–Lieberman-type problem.

Problem 3. *Suppose that the degrees N_1, N_2 of the polynomials $p_j(\lambda)$, the polynomials $r_j(\lambda)$, $j=1,2$, the polynomials $p_{ij}(\lambda)$, $i=\overline{1,3}$, $j=0,1$, and the potential $q(x)$ for $x\in(\pi,2\pi)$ are known a priori. Given a subspectrum $\{\mu_n\}$ of the problem $\mathcal{L}$, find the potential $q(x)$ for $x\in(0,\pi)$ and the polynomials $p_1(\lambda)$, $p_2(\lambda)$.*

In Section 5, we prove the uniqueness theorem (Theorem 5) for the solution of Problem 3. Throughout the paper, we use the following **notations**:

1. $\lambda=\rho^2$, $\tau:=\operatorname{Im}\rho$, $\rho_n=\sqrt{\lambda_n}$, $\arg\rho_n\in\left[-\frac{\pi}{2},\frac{\pi}{2}\right)$.
2. Denote by B_a^+ the class of entire functions $F(\rho)$ satisfying the conditions $F(\rho)=O(\exp(|\tau|a))$ in $\mathbb{C}$, $F\in L_2(\mathbb{R})$, and $F(\rho)=F(-\rho)$. Thus, B_a^+ is the class of even Paley–Wiener functions, which can be represented as $F(\rho)=\int\limits_0^a f(t)\cos\rho t\,dt$, $f\in L_2(0,a)$.

3. Proof of the Main Theorem

The goal of this section is to prove Theorem 1 on the uniqueness of solution for Problem 1. We begin with some preliminaries.

Let us define the functions $S(x,\lambda)$ and $C(x,\lambda)$ as the solutions of Equation (1) satisfying the initial conditions: $S(0,\lambda)=0$, $S'(0,\lambda)=1$, $C(0,\lambda)=1$, $C'(0,\lambda)=0$. It can be easily seen that the eigenvalues of the problem L coincide with the zeros of the entire characteristic function

$$\Delta(\lambda)=f_1(\lambda)\Delta_1(\lambda)+f_2(\lambda)\Delta_0(\lambda), \tag{11}$$

where

$$\Delta_j(\lambda)=p_1(\lambda)C^{(j)}(\pi,\lambda)-p_2(\lambda)S^{(j)}(\pi,\lambda), \quad j=0,1. \tag{12}$$

It is worth noting that, for $j=0,1$, the zeros of the function $\Delta_j(\lambda)$ coincide with the eigenvalues of the corresponding boundary value problem L_j for Equation (1) with the BCs

$$p_1(\lambda)y'(0)+p_2(\lambda)y(0)=0, \quad y^{(j)}(\pi)=0.$$

In order to prove the main result, we need the following technical lemma.

Lemma 1. *The functions $\Delta_0(\lambda)$ and $\Delta_1(\lambda)$ can be represented as follows.*

In the first case $N_1\ge N_2$:

$$\Delta_1(\lambda)=-\rho^{2N_1+1}\sin\rho\pi+\omega\rho^{2N_1}\cos\rho\pi+\rho^{2N_1}\int_0^{\pi}\mathcal{G}(t)\cos\rho t\,dt+\sum_{j=1}^{N_1}C_j\rho^{2j-2}, \tag{13}$$

$$\Delta_0(\lambda)=\rho^{2N_1}\cos\rho\pi+\omega\rho^{2N_1-1}\sin\rho\pi+\rho^{2N_1-1}\int_0^{\pi}\mathcal{Q}(t)\sin\rho t\,dt+\sum_{j=1}^{N_1}D_j\rho^{2j-2}. \tag{14}$$

In the second case $N_2>N_1$:

$$\Delta_1(\lambda) = -\rho^{2N_2}\cos\rho\pi - \varpi\rho^{2N_2-1}\sin\rho\pi + \rho^{2N_2-1}\int_0^\pi \mathcal{G}(t)\sin\rho t\,dt + \sum_{j=1}^{N_2} C_j\rho^{2j-2}, \tag{15}$$

$$\Delta_0(\lambda) = -\rho^{2N_2-1}\sin\rho\pi + \varpi\rho^{2N_2-2}\cos\rho\pi + +\rho^{2N_2-2}\int_0^\pi \mathcal{Q}(t)\cos\rho t\,dt + \sum_{j=1}^{N_2-1} D_j\rho^{2j-2}. \tag{16}$$

In both cases, $\mathcal{G}$ and $\mathcal{Q}$ are some functions of $L_2(0,\pi)$, and C_j, D_j are constants.

Proof. The solutions $S(x,\lambda)$ and $C(x,\lambda)$ admit the following representations in terms of transformation operators (see, e.g., [1]):

$$S(x,\lambda) = \frac{\sin\rho x}{\rho} + \int_0^x K(x,t)\frac{\sin\rho t}{\rho}\,dt,$$
$$C(x,\lambda) = \cos\rho x + \int_0^x P(x,t)\cos\rho t\,dt,$$

where $K(x,x) = P(x,x) = \frac{1}{2}\int_0^x q(\xi)\,d\xi$. Using these representations, we obtain the following standard relations for $S(\pi,\lambda)$, $S'(\pi,\lambda)$, $C(\pi,\lambda)$, and $C'(\pi,\lambda)$:

$$\begin{cases} S(\pi,\lambda) = \dfrac{\sin\rho\pi}{\rho} - \dfrac{\omega\cos\rho\pi}{\lambda} + \dfrac{1}{\lambda}\displaystyle\int_0^\pi \mathcal{K}(t)\cos\rho t\,dt, \\ S'(\pi,\lambda) = \cos\rho\pi + \dfrac{\omega\sin\rho\pi}{\rho} + \dfrac{1}{\rho}\displaystyle\int_0^\pi \mathcal{N}(t)\sin\rho t\,dt, \\ C(\pi,\lambda) = \cos\rho\pi + \dfrac{\omega\sin\rho\pi}{\rho} + \dfrac{1}{\rho}\displaystyle\int_0^\pi \mathcal{M}(t)\sin\rho t\,dt, \\ C'(\pi,\lambda) = -\rho\sin\rho\pi + \omega\cos\rho\pi + \displaystyle\int_0^\pi \mathcal{P}(t)\cos\rho t\,dt, \end{cases} \tag{17}$$

where $\mathcal{K}(t), \mathcal{N}(t), \mathcal{M}(t), \mathcal{P}(t) \in L_2(0,\pi)$.

The relations (13)–(16) are obtained by substitution of (3) and (17) into (12). For definiteness, let us derive the relation (13) for $\Delta_1(\lambda)$ in the case $N_1 \ge N_2$. Substituting (3) and (17) into (12) for $j = 1$, we obtain

$$\Delta_1(\lambda) = \sum_{n=0}^{N_1} a_n\lambda^n\left(-\rho\sin\rho\pi + \omega\cos\rho\pi + \int_0^\pi \mathcal{P}(t)\cos\rho t\,dt\right) -$$
$$- \sum_{n=0}^{N_2} b_n\lambda^n\left(\cos\rho\pi + \frac{\omega\sin\rho\pi}{\rho} + \frac{1}{\rho}\int_0^\pi \mathcal{N}(t)\sin\rho t\,dt\right).$$

This expression can be easily converted to the form

$$\Delta_1(\lambda) = -\rho^{2N_1+1}\sin\rho\pi + \varpi\rho^{2N_1}\cos\rho\pi + \rho^{2N_1}\left(\int_0^\pi \mathcal{P}(t)\cos\rho t\,dt + F_1(\rho)\right), \tag{18}$$

where

$$F_1(\rho) = \sum_{n=0}^{N_1-1} a_n\rho^{-2(N_1-n)}\left(-\rho\sin\rho\pi + \omega\cos\rho\pi + \int_0^\pi \mathcal{P}(t)\cos\rho t\,dt\right)$$
$$- \sum_{n=0}^{N_2} b_n\rho^{-2(N_1-n)}\left(\cos\rho\pi + \frac{\omega\sin\rho\pi}{\rho} + \frac{1}{\rho}\int_0^\pi \mathcal{N}(t)\sin\rho t\,dt\right) + (\omega - \varpi)\cos\rho\pi.$$

Obviously, the function $F_1(\rho)$ is even and fulfills the estimate

$$|F_1(\rho)| \le \frac{C\exp(|\tau|\pi)}{|\rho|}, \quad |\rho| \ge \rho^*. \tag{19}$$

Furthermore, $F(\rho)$ has a pole of order of at most $2N_1$ at $\rho = 0$, so the Laurent series has the form

$$F_1(\rho) = \frac{C_1}{\rho^{2N_1}} + \frac{C_2}{\rho^{2N_1-2}} + \ldots + \frac{C_{N_1-1}}{\rho^4} + \frac{C_{N_1}}{\rho^2} + F_2(\rho), \tag{20}$$

where $F_2(\rho)$ is an even entire function. It follows from (19) and (20) that $F_2(\rho)$ satisfies the same estimate as (19). Hence, $F_2(\rho) \in L_2(-\infty, +\infty)$, so $F_2(\rho) \in B_\pi^+$ and can be represented in the form $F_2(\rho) = \int_0^\pi \mathcal{S}(t) \cos \rho t \, dt$, where $\mathcal{S}(t) \in L_2(0, \pi)$. Substituting this equality into (20) and (18), we arrive at the relation (13) with $\mathcal{G}(t) = \mathcal{S}(t) + \mathcal{P}(t)$. $\square$

Consider the Hilbert space

$$\mathcal{H}_K = L_2(0,\pi) \oplus L_2(0,\pi) \oplus \underbrace{\mathbb{C} \oplus \mathbb{C} \oplus \cdots \oplus \mathbb{C}}_{K}$$

of elements

$$h = [H_1, H_2, h_1, ..., h_K], \quad H_1, H_2 \in L_2(0,\pi), \quad h_j \in \mathbb{C}, \; j = \overline{1,K}.$$

The scalar product and the norm in $\mathcal{H}_K$ are defined as follows:

$$(g,h) = \int_0^\pi (\overline{G_1(t)} H_1(t) + \overline{G_2(t)} H_2(t))\, dt + \sum_{j=1}^K \overline{g_j} h_j, \quad \|h\| = \sqrt{(h,h)},$$

where

$$g = [G_1, G_2, g_1, ..., g_K], \quad h = [H_1, H_2, h_1, ..., h_K].$$

Consider some countable set of eigenvalues $\{\lambda_n\}_{n=1}^\infty$ of the problem L. Suppose that the sequence $\{\lambda_n\}_{n=1}^\infty$ may contain multiple values of finite multiplicities. Introduce the set $I = \{n \geq 1 : \lambda_n \neq \lambda_k, k = \overline{1,n}\}$ and the number $m_k = \#\{l \geq 1 : \lambda_l = \lambda_k\}$. Thus, I is the index set of all the distinct numbers in the sequence $\{\lambda_n\}_{n=1}^\infty$, and m_k is the multiplicity of λ_k in this sequence. Due to these notations, λ_k is the zero of the characteristic function $\Delta(\lambda)$ of multiplicity at least m_k.

Our next goal is to define the sequence $\{v_n\}_{n=1}^\infty$ by using N_j, $f_j(\lambda)$, $j = 1, 2$, $\{\lambda_n\}_{n=1}^\infty$, and ϖ. Consider the two cases.

The first case: $N_1 \geq N_2$.

In this case, put $K = 2N_1$. Define the vector functions

$$u(t) = [\overline{\mathcal{G}(t)}, \overline{\mathcal{Q}(t)}, \overline{C}_{N_1}, \ldots, \overline{C}_1, \overline{D}_{N_1}, ..., \overline{D}_1], \tag{21}$$

$$v(t,\lambda) = [f_1(\lambda)\rho^{2N_1} \cos \rho t, f_2(\lambda)\rho^{2N_1-1} \sin \rho t, f_1(\lambda)\rho^{2N_1-2}, \ldots, f_1(\lambda), f_2(\lambda)\rho^{2N_1-2}, \ldots, f_2(\lambda)], \tag{22}$$

and find their scalar product in $\mathcal{H}_K$:

$$\begin{aligned}(u(t), v(t,\lambda)) = f_1(\lambda)\rho^{2N_1} \textstyle\int_0^\pi \mathcal{G}(t) \cos \rho t \, dt + f_2(\lambda)\rho^{2N_1-1} \int_0^\pi \mathcal{Q}(t) \sin \rho t \, dt + \\ + C_{N_1} f_1(\lambda) \rho^{2N_1-2} + \cdots + C_1 f_1(\lambda) + D_{N_1} f_2(\lambda)\rho^{2N_1-2} + \cdots + D_1 f_2(\lambda).\end{aligned}$$

According to (11), (13), and (14), we can conclude that

$$(u(t), v(t,\lambda)) = \Delta(\lambda) + w(\lambda), \tag{23}$$

where

$$w(\lambda) = \frac{f_1(\lambda)\lambda^{N_1+1} \sin \rho\pi}{\rho} - f_1(\lambda)\lambda^{N_1} \varpi \cos \rho\pi - f_2(\lambda)\lambda^{N_1} \cos \rho\pi - \frac{f_2(\lambda)\lambda^{N_1} \varpi \sin \rho\pi}{\rho}. \tag{24}$$

The second case: $N_2 > N_1$.

In this case, put $K = 2N_2 - 1$. Define the vector functions

$$u(t) = [\overline{\mathcal{G}(t)}, \overline{\mathcal{Q}(t)}, \overline{C}_{N_2}, \ldots, \overline{C}_1, \overline{D}_{N_2-1}, \ldots, \overline{D}_1], \tag{25}$$

$$v(t,\lambda) = [f_1(\lambda)\rho^{2N_2-1}\sin\rho t, f_2(\lambda)\rho^{2N_2-2}\cos\rho t, f_1(\lambda)\rho^{2N_2-2}, \ldots, f_1(\lambda), f_2(\lambda)\rho^{2N_2-4}, \ldots, f_2(\lambda)], \tag{26}$$

Finding their scalar product in $\mathcal{H}_K$ and using (11), (15), (16), we conclude that

$$(u(t), v(t,\lambda)) = \Delta(\lambda) + w(\lambda), \tag{27}$$

where

$$w(\lambda) = f_1(\lambda)\lambda^{N_2}\cos\rho\pi + \frac{f_1(\lambda)\lambda^{N_2}\omega\sin\rho\pi}{\rho} + \frac{f_2(\lambda)\lambda^{N_2}\sin\rho\pi}{\rho} - f_2(\lambda)\lambda^{N_2-1}\omega\cos\rho\pi. \tag{28}$$

Introduce the notation

$$f^{<n>}(\lambda) = \frac{d^n f}{d\lambda^n}, \quad n \geq 0.$$

Since λ_k is the zero of $\Delta(\lambda)$ of multiplicity at least m_k, we have

$$\Delta^{<n>}(\lambda_k) = 0, \quad k \in I, \quad n = \overline{0, m_k - 1}.$$

Consequently, it follows from (23) and (27) that

$$(u(t), v^{<n>}(t,\lambda_k))_{\mathcal{H}} = w^{<n>}(\lambda_k), \quad k \in I, \quad n = \overline{0, m_k - 1},$$

in the both cases.

Put

$$v_{k+n}(t) = v^{<n>}(t,\lambda_k), \quad w_{k+n}(t) = w^{<n>}(t,\lambda_k), \quad k \in I, \quad n = \overline{0, m_k - 1}. \tag{29}$$

Thus, we defined the sequence $\{v_n\}_{n=1}^{\infty}$ in $\mathcal{H}_K$ and the sequence of complex numbers $\{w_n\}_{n=1}^{\infty}$. Using (23) and (27), we arrive at the relation

$$(u, v_n) = w_n, \quad n \geq 1, \tag{30}$$

which plays a crucial role in the investigation of the inverse problem. Here, $\{v_n\}_{n=1}^{\infty}$ and $\{w_n\}_{n=1}^{\infty}$ are constructed by using the known data of Problem 1, while $u \in \mathcal{H}_K$ is related to the unknown potential $q(x)$ and the polynomials $p_1(\lambda)$, $p_2(\lambda)$.

In order to prove Theorem 1, we use the relation (30) to reduce Problem 1 to the problem studied in [16]. Define the Weyl function $M(\lambda) := \dfrac{\Delta_0(\lambda)}{\Delta_1(\lambda)}$ of the boundary value problem L_1 and consider the following auxiliary inverse problem.

Problem 4. *Given the Weyl function $M(\lambda)$, find $q(x)$, $p_1(\lambda)$, and $p_2(\lambda)$.*

The uniqueness of solution for Problem 4 has been proved by Chernozhukova and Freiling [16]. We formulate the uniqueness result in the following proposition.

Proposition 1. *If $M(\lambda) \equiv \tilde{M}(\lambda)$, then $q(x) \equiv \tilde{q}(x)$ a.e. on $(0,\pi)$ and $p_j(\lambda) \equiv \tilde{p}_j(\lambda)$, $j = 1, 2$.*

Now, we are ready to prove the uniqueness theorem for Problem 1.

Proof of Theorem 1. Suppose that two boundary value problems L and $\tilde{L}$ of form (1)-(2) and their subspectra $\{\lambda_n\}_{n=1}^{\infty}$ and $\{\tilde{\lambda}_n\}_{n=1}^{\infty}$ fulfill the conditions of Theorem 1. By construction, we have $v_n = \tilde{v}_n$ in the Hilbert space $\mathcal{H}_K$ and $w_n = \tilde{w}_n$ for all $n \geq 1$. Then, for the problem $\tilde{L}$, we obtain $(\tilde{u}, v_n) = w_n$, $n \geq 1$. Therefore, $(u - \tilde{u}, v_n)_{\mathcal{H}} = 0$, $n \geq 1$. Due to the completeness of the sequence $\{v_n\}_{n=1}^{\infty}$ in $\mathcal{H}_K$, this implies $u = \tilde{u}$ in $\mathcal{H}_K$. Hence, $\mathcal{G}(t) = \tilde{\mathcal{G}}(t)$, $\mathcal{Q}(t) = \tilde{\mathcal{Q}}(t)$ in $L_2(0,\pi)$, and

$$C_i = \tilde{C}_i, \quad i = \overline{1, \max\{N_1, N_2\}}, \qquad D_i = \tilde{D}_i, \quad i = \overline{1, \max\{N_1, N_2 - 1\}},$$

so it follows from (13)-(16) and $\omega = \tilde{\omega}$ that $\Delta_j(\lambda) \equiv \tilde{\Delta}_j(\lambda)$, $j = 0, 1$. Consequently, $M(\lambda) \equiv \tilde{M}(\lambda)$. According to Proposition 1, we conclude that $q = \tilde{q}$ in $L_2(0,\pi)$ and $p_j(\lambda) \equiv \tilde{p}_j(\lambda)$, $j = 1, 2$. □

If the sequence $\{v_n\}_{n=1}^{\infty}$ is a Riesz basis in $\mathcal{H}_K$, one can solve Problem 1 by Algorithm 1.

Algorithm 1: Solution of the inverse problem

Suppose that the integers N_1 and N_2, the entire functions $f_1(\lambda)$ and $f_2(\lambda)$, the subspectrum $\{\lambda_n\}_{n=1}^{\infty}$, and the number ω are given. We have to find $q(x)$, $p_1(\lambda)$, and $p_2(\lambda)$.

1. Put $K := \max\{2N_1, 2N_2 - 1\}$ and, depending on the case $N_1 \ge N_2$ or $N_1 < N_2$, construct the functions $v(t,\lambda)$ and $w(\lambda)$ by either (22), (24) or (26), (28).
2. Construct the sequences $\{v_n\}_{n=1}^{\infty}$ and $\{w_n\}_{n=1}^{\infty}$ by (29).
3. Find the biorthonormal sequence $\{v_n^*\}_{n=1}^{\infty}$ to $\{v_n\}_{n=1}^{\infty}$ in $\mathcal{H}_K$, that is,

$$(v_n, v_k^*) = \begin{cases} 1, & n = k, \\ 0, & n \ne k. \end{cases}$$

4. Find the element $u \in \mathcal{H}_K$ satisfying (30) by the formula

$$u = \sum_{n=1}^{\infty} \overline{w_n} v_n^*.$$

5. Using the entries of u (see (21) and (25)), find $\Delta_0(\lambda)$ and $\Delta_1(\lambda)$ by the formulas of Lemma 1, and then find $M(\lambda) = \frac{\Delta_0(\lambda)}{\Delta_1(\lambda)}$.
6. Use the method of [17] to recover the potential $q(x)$ and the polynomials $p_1(\lambda)$, $p_2(\lambda)$ from the Weyl function $M(\lambda)$.

Algorithm 1 is theoretical. In this paper, we do not aim to elaborate in detail the algorithm's numerical implementation. This issue requires a separate work. Here, we only outline the main idea of the inverse problem solution.

4. Sufficient Conditions

In this section, we prove Theorem 2 and then generalize it to the case of multiple eigenvalues. First, we need the following proposition, which is analogous to Lemma 1 in [17].

Proposition 2. *If θ is a zero of $\Delta_1(\lambda)$, then $\Delta_0(\theta) \ne 0$.*

Proof of Theorem 2. Consider the problem $L = L(q, p_1, p_2, f_1, f_2)$ of form (1)-(2) and its simple subspectrum $\{\lambda_n\}_{n=1}^{\infty}$. This means $\lambda_n \ne \lambda_k$ for $n \ne k$.

In ***the first case*** $N_1 \ge N_2$, we have

$$v(t,\lambda) = [f_1(\lambda)\rho^{2N_1}\cos\rho t, f_2(\lambda)\rho^{2N_1-1}\sin\rho t, \rho^{2N_1-2}f_1(\lambda), \dots, f_1(\lambda), \rho^{2N_1-2}f_2(\lambda), \dots, f_2(\lambda)].$$

Consider an element

$$h = [H_1, H_2, h_1^1, \dots, h_1^{N_1}, h_2^1, \dots, h_2^{N_1}] \in \mathcal{H}_K \tag{31}$$

such that

$$(h, v_n) = 0, \quad n \geq 1, \tag{32}$$

where $v_n = v(t, \lambda_n)$, $n \geq 1$.

Let us find the scalar product

$$\begin{aligned}(h, v_n) = \lambda_n^{N_1} \int_0^{\pi} \Big(H_1(t) f_1(\lambda_n) \cos \rho_n t + H_2(t) f_2(\lambda_n) \tfrac{\sin \rho_n t}{\rho_n} \Big) \, dt \\ + \sum_{m=1}^{N_1} \lambda^{N_1 - m} (h_1^m f_1(\lambda_n) + h_2^m f_2(\lambda_n)).\end{aligned} \tag{33}$$

From (11) and the relation $\Delta(\lambda_n) = 0$, we can obtain that

$$\begin{aligned} f_2(\lambda_n) &= -\frac{\Delta_1(\lambda_n)}{\Delta_0(\lambda_n)} f_1(\lambda_n), f_1(\lambda_n) \neq 0 \\ f_1(\lambda_n) &= -\frac{\Delta_0(\lambda_n)}{\Delta_1(\lambda_n)} f_2(\lambda_n), f_2(\lambda_n) \neq 0 \end{aligned} \tag{34}$$

In both expressions of system (34), the denominator is nonzero. Let us show this fact for the expression for $f_1(\lambda_n)$. Indeed, if $\Delta_1(\lambda_n) = 0$, then from (11), we obtain that $f_2(\lambda_n)\Delta_0(\lambda_n) = 0$. Using Proposition 2, we conclude that $f_2(\lambda_n) = 0$. However, $f_2(\lambda_n) \neq 0$ in this case. From this contradiction, we obtain that $\Delta_1(\lambda_n) \neq 0$.

Consider the case $f_1(\lambda_n) \neq 0$. The other case is similar. Using (32), (33), and (34), we obtain

$$\lambda_n^{N_1} \int_0^{\pi} \Big(H_1(t) \cos \rho_n t - H_2(t) \frac{\Delta_1(\lambda_n)}{\Delta_0(\lambda_n)} \frac{\sin \rho_n t}{\rho_n} \Big) \, dt + \sum_{m=1}^{N_1} \lambda^{N_1 - m} \Big(h_1^m - \frac{\Delta_1(\lambda_n)}{\Delta_0(\lambda_n)} h_2^m \Big) = 0, \quad n \geq 1. \tag{35}$$

Define the function

$$\begin{aligned} G(\lambda) := \lambda^{N_1} \int_0^{\pi} \Big(H_1(t) \Delta_0(\lambda) \cos \rho t - H_2(t) \Delta_1(\lambda) \frac{\sin \rho t}{\rho} \Big) \, dt \\ + \sum_{n=1}^{N_1} \lambda^{N_1 - n} (h_1^n \Delta_0(\lambda) - h_2^n \Delta_1(\lambda)).\end{aligned} \tag{36}$$

It follows from (35) and $\Delta_0(\lambda_n) \neq 0$ that $G(\lambda_n) = 0$, $n \geq 1$.

Using Lemma 1, we can obtain the asymptotic formulas

$$\Delta_0(\lambda) = \rho^{2N_1} \cos \rho\pi + O(|\rho|^{2N_1 - 1} e^{\pi|\tau|}), \tag{37}$$

$$\Delta_1(\lambda) = -\rho^{2N_1 + 1} \sin \rho\pi + O(|\rho|^{2N_1} e^{\pi|\tau|}). \tag{38}$$

Substituting (37) and (38) into (36), we obtain

$$\begin{aligned} G(\lambda) &= \lambda^{2N_1} (G_1(\lambda) + O(|\rho|^{-1} e^{2\pi|\tau|})), \\ G_1(\lambda) &= \int_0^{\pi} (H_1(t) \cos \rho t \cos \rho\pi + H_2(t) \sin \rho\pi \sin \rho t) \, dt. \end{aligned} \tag{39}$$

Clearly, $G_1(\rho^2) \in B_{2\pi}^+$, so

$$G(\lambda) = \lambda^{2N_1} \Big(\int_0^{2\pi} g(t) \cos \rho t \, dt + O(|\rho|^{-1} e^{2\pi|\tau|}) \Big), \quad g \in L_2(0, 2\pi). \tag{40}$$

Let us exclude the zeros $\{\lambda_n\}_{n=1}^{2N_1}$ of $G(\lambda)$ and define the function

$$R(\lambda) := \frac{G(\lambda)}{\prod_{n=1}^{2N_1} (\lambda - \lambda_n)}. \tag{41}$$

It can be easily shown that $R(\rho^2) \in L_2(0, 2\pi)$, so $R(\lambda) = \int_0^{2\pi} r(t) \cos \rho t \, dt$, where $r(t) \in L_2(0, 2\pi)$. From (41), we conclude that

$$R(\lambda_n) = \int_0^{2\pi} r(t) \cos \rho_n t \, d = 0, \quad n \geq 2N_1 + 1.$$

Hence, if the system $\{\cos \rho_n t\}_{n=2N_1+1}^{\infty}$ is complete in $L_2(0, 2\pi)$, then $r(t) \equiv 0$, $R(\lambda) \equiv 0$, and so $G(\lambda) \equiv 0$.

Let $\{\theta_n\}_{n=1}^{\infty}$ be the zeros of $\Delta_1(\lambda)$, so $\{\theta_n\}_{n=1}^{\infty}$ are the eigenvalues of the boundary value problem L_1. Then, we obtain from (36) that

$$G(\theta_n) = \theta_n^{N_1} \int_0^{\pi} H_1(t) \Delta_0(\theta_n) \cos \sqrt{\theta_n} t dt + \sum_{n=1}^{N_1} \theta_n^{N_1 - n} h_1^n \Delta_0(\theta_n) = 0, \quad n \geq 1. \tag{42}$$

Consider the function

$$H(\lambda) = \lambda^{N_1} \int_0^{\pi} H_1(t) \cos \rho t \, dt + \sum_{n=1}^{N_1} \lambda^{N_1 - n} h_1^n.$$

The relation (42) implies that $H_1(\theta_n) = 0$, $n \geq 1$. Let us obtain the first N_1 values from $\{\theta_n\}_{n=1}^{\infty}$. Define function

$$F(\lambda) := \frac{H(\lambda)}{\prod_{n=1}^{N_1} (\lambda - \theta_n)}.$$

Obviously, $F(\rho^2) \in B_{\pi}^{+}$, so it can be represented in the form $F(\lambda) = \int_0^{\pi} f(t) \cos \rho t \, dt$, where $f(t) \in L_2(0, \pi)$. Clearly, we have

$$\int_0^{\pi} f(t) \cos \sqrt{\theta_n} t \, dt = 0, \quad n \geq N_1 + 1. \tag{43}$$

Using the methods of [17], one can obtain the asymptotic formula

$$\sqrt{\theta_n} = n - N_1 - 1 + O(n^{-1}), \quad n \geq 1. \tag{44}$$

For simplicity, assume that the values $\{\theta_n\}_{n=N_1+1}$ are distinct. The opposite case requires minor changes. Then, it follows from (44) the the sequence $\{\cos \sqrt{\theta_n} t\}_{n=N_1+1}^{\infty}$ is complete in $L_2(0, \pi)$. Hence, (43) implies $f(t) = 0$ a.e. on $(0, \pi)$ and so and $H_1 = 0$ in $L_2(0, \pi)$, $h_1^j = 0$, $j = \overline{1, N_1}$. Taking (36) and $G(\lambda) \equiv 0$ into account, we conclude that $H_2 = 0$ in $L_2(0, \pi)$, $h_2^j = 0$, $j = \overline{1, N_1}$. Thus, we proved that, if $h \in \mathcal{H}_K$ fulfills (32), then $h = 0$. Consequently, the system $\{v_n\}_{n=1}^{\infty}$ is complete in $\mathcal{H}_K$.

The second case $N_2 > N_1$ is similar to the first one. In this case, it can be shown that the completeness of the system $\{\cos \rho_n t\}_{n=2N_2}^{\infty}$ in $L_2(0, 2\pi)$ is sufficient for the completeness of $\{v_n\}_{n=1}^{\infty}$ in $\mathcal{H}_K$.

We have

$$v(t, \lambda) = [f_1(\lambda) \rho^{2N_2 - 1} \sin \rho t, f_2(\lambda) \rho^{2N_2 - 2} \cos \rho t, \rho^{2N_2 - 2} f_1(\lambda), \ldots, f_1(\lambda), \rho^{2N_1 - 4} f_2(\lambda), \ldots, f_2(\lambda)].$$

Consider an element

$$h = [H_1, H_2, h_1^1, \ldots, h_1^{N_2}, h_2^1, \ldots, h_2^{N_2 - 1}] \in \mathcal{H}_K$$

that $(h, v_n) = 0$, $n \geq 1$, where $v_n = v(t, \lambda_n)$.

Analogously to the first case, we obtain that $G(\lambda_n) = 0$, $n \geq 0$, for the function

$$G(\lambda) := \lambda^{N_2-1} \int_0^{\pi} \Big(H_1(t)\Delta_0(\lambda)\rho \sin \rho t - H_2(t)\Delta_1(\lambda) \cos \rho t \Big)\, dt \\ + \lambda^{N_2-1} h_1^{N_2-1} \Delta_0(\lambda) + \sum_{n=2}^{N_2} \lambda^{N_2-n} (h_1^n \Delta_0(\lambda) - h_2^{n-1} \Delta_1(\lambda)), \tag{45}$$

Then, using the asymptotics for $\Delta_0(\lambda)$ and $\Delta_1(\lambda)$ and (45), we obtain

$$G(\lambda) = \lambda^{2N_2-1} \bigg(\int_0^{2\pi} g(t) \cos \rho t \, dt + O(|\rho|^{-1} e^{2\pi|\tau|}) \bigg), \quad g \in L_2(0, 2\pi). \tag{46}$$

Excluding the first $(2N_2 - 1)$ zeros of $G(\lambda)$, we obtain the function

$$R(\lambda) := \frac{G(\lambda)}{\prod\limits_{n=1}^{2N_2-1} (\lambda - \lambda_n)}. \tag{47}$$

We have $R(\rho^2) \in B^+_{2\pi}$, and so $R(\lambda) = \int_0^{2\pi} r(t) \cos \rho t \, dt$, where $r(t) \in L_2(0, 2\pi)$. From (41), we can conclude that

$$R(\lambda_n) = \int_0^{2\pi} r(t) \cos \rho_n t \, dt = 0, \quad n \geq 2N_2.$$

Therefore, if system $\{\cos \rho_n t\}_{n=2N_2}^{\infty}$ is complete in $L_2(0, 2\pi)$, then $r(t) \equiv 0$, $R(\lambda) \equiv 0$ and $G(\lambda) \equiv 0$. Consequently, one can show that $h = 0$ in $\mathcal{H}_K$, which concludes the proof. □

Now, we consider the general situation when the subspectrum $\{\lambda_n\}_{n=1}^{\infty}$ may contain multiple eigenvalues of finite multiplicities. Put $N := \max\{2N_1 + 1, 2N_2\}$. Denote by $\mathcal{A}$ any subset of indices $\mathbb{N}$ such that $|\mathcal{A}| = N$ and put $\mathcal{B} := \mathbb{N} \setminus \mathcal{A}$. Consider the subset $\{\lambda_n\}_{n \in \mathcal{B}}$. Thus, we have excluded arbitrary N values (counting with multiplicities) from the sequence $\{\lambda_n\}_{n=1}^{\infty}$. Denote by $\mathcal{I}$ the set of indices of distinct eigenvalues among $\{\lambda_n\}_{n \in \mathcal{B}}$ and by $\{\nu_k\}_{k \in \mathcal{I}}$ the multiplicities of the corresponding values $\{\lambda_k\}_{k \in \mathcal{I}}$:

$$\mathcal{I} := \{k \in \mathcal{B} \colon \lambda_k \neq \lambda_n,\, n \in \mathcal{B},\, n < k\}, \quad \nu_k := \#\{\lambda_n = \lambda_k \colon n \in \mathcal{B}\},\ k \in \mathcal{I}.$$

Define the functions

$$c(x, \lambda) := \cos \sqrt{\lambda} x, \quad c_{k,j}(x) = c^{<j>}(x, \lambda_k), \quad k \in \mathcal{I},\ j = \overline{0, \nu_k - 1}.$$

Then, by using the technique of [30], we obtain the following generalization of Theorem 2 to the case of multiple eigenvalues.

Theorem 4. *Suppose that $f_1(\lambda_n) \neq 0$ or $f_2(\lambda_n) \neq 0$ for every $n \geq 1$, and the system $\{c_{k,j}(x)\}_{k \in \mathcal{I},\, j=\overline{0,\nu_k-1}}$ is complete in $L_2(0, 2\pi)$. Then, the system $\{v_n\}_{n=1}^{\infty}$ is complete in $\mathcal{H}_K$.*

5. Hochstadt–Lieberman-Type Problems

In this section, we prove the uniqueness theorems for the Hochstadt–Lieberman-type inverse problems, namely, for Problems 2 and 3. The method of the proofs is based on the reduction in the Hochstadt–Lieberman-type problems to Problem 1, with entire functions in the right-hand side BC. Then, we successively apply Theorems 2 and 1.

Consider the boundary value problem $\mathscr{L} = \mathscr{L}(q, p_1, p_2, r_1, r_2)$ of form (5)-(6). Define the functions $\varphi(x, \lambda)$ and $\psi(x, \lambda)$ as the solutions of Equation (5) satisfying the initial conditions

$$\varphi(0, \lambda) = p_1(\lambda), \quad \varphi'(0, \lambda) = -p_2(\lambda), \quad \psi(2\pi, \lambda) = r_1(\lambda), \quad \psi'(2\pi, \lambda) = -r_2(\lambda). \tag{48}$$

It can be easily seen that the eigenvalues $\{\mu_n\}_{n=1}^{\infty}$ of the problem $\mathscr{L}$ coincide with the zeros of the characteristic function

$$\Delta(\lambda) = \varphi(\pi,\lambda)\psi'(\pi,\lambda) - \varphi'(\pi,\lambda)\psi(\pi,\lambda). \tag{49}$$

The function $\varphi(x,\lambda)$ can be represented in the form

$$\varphi(x,\lambda) = p_1(\lambda)C(x,\lambda) - p_2(\lambda)S(x,\lambda). \tag{50}$$

Substituting (50) into (49), we obtain

$$\Delta(\lambda) = \sum_{j=0}^{1}(-1)^j\psi^{(1-j)}(\pi,\lambda)(p_1(\lambda)C^{(j)}(\pi,\lambda) - p_2(\lambda)S^{(j)}(\pi,\lambda)). \tag{51}$$

Comparing (51) with (11), we conclude that the eigenvalues of the boundary value problem $\mathscr{L} = \mathscr{L}(q,p_1,p_2,r_1,r_2)$ coincide with the eigenvalues of the problem $L = L(q,p_1,p_2,f_1,f_2)$ with $f_1(\lambda) = -\psi(\pi,\lambda)$ and $f_2(\lambda) = \psi'(\pi,\lambda)$.

Proof of Theorem 3. Consider the case $N_1 \geq N_2, M_1 \geq M_2$. The other cases can be treated similarly. Introduce the notations

$$\Omega = \frac{1}{2}\int_0^{2\pi} q(t)\,dt, \quad \Theta = \begin{cases} \Omega + d_{M_2} - b_{N_2}, & N_1 = N_2, M_1 = M_2 \\ \Omega - b_{N_2}, & N_1 = N_2, M_1 \neq M_2 \\ \Omega + d_{M_2}, & N_1 > N_2, M_1 = M_2 \\ \Omega, & \textit{otherwise} \end{cases} \tag{52}$$

Instead of (51), it is more convenient to use another representation of the characteristic function:

$$\Delta(\lambda) = \sum_{j=0}^{1}(-1)^j r_{2-j}(\lambda)(p_1(\lambda)C^{(j)}(2\pi,\lambda) - p_2(\lambda)S^{(j)}(2\pi,\lambda)). \tag{53}$$

Using (53), we obtain the following asymptotics for $\Delta(\lambda)$:

$$\Delta(\lambda) = \rho^{2(N_1+M_1)+1}\sin 2\rho\pi + O(|\rho|^{2(N_1+M_1)}e^{2\pi|\tau|})$$

and for the eigenvalues

$$\sqrt{\mu_n} = \frac{n-1}{2} - (N_1+M_1) + \frac{\Theta}{\pi n} + \frac{\chi_n}{n}, \quad n \geq 1, \quad \{\chi_n\} \in l_2. \tag{54}$$

For simplicity, assume that the eigenvalues $\{\mu_n\}_{n=N_1+M_1+1}^{\infty}$ are simple. The general case requires technical changes. Then, the asymptotics (54) imply that the system $\{\cos\sqrt{\mu_n}t\}_{n=N_1+M_1+1}^{\infty}$ is complete in $L_2(0,2\pi)$.

Let us pass from the problem $\mathscr{L}(q,p_1,p_2,r_1,r_2)$ to the corresponding problem $L(q,p_1,p_2,f_1,f_2)$ with $f_1(\lambda) = -\psi(\pi,\lambda)$ and $f_2(\lambda) = \psi'(\pi,\lambda)$. It follows from Proposition 2 that $f_1(\lambda)$ and $f_2(\lambda)$ do not have common zeros. Suppose that $M_1 \geq N_1$ and consider the subspectrum $\{\lambda_n\}_{n=1}^{\infty} := \{\mu_n\}_{n=M_1-N_1+1}^{\infty}$ of the problem L. Thus, in the case $N_1 = M_1$, we consider the whole spectrum of $\mathscr{L}$ and, in the case $N_1 < M_1$, we exclude $(M_1 - N_1)$ eigenvalues. The excluded eigenvalues can be chosen arbitrarily. According to the above arguments, we have that the system $\{\cos\sqrt{\lambda_n}t\}_{n=2N_1+1}^{\infty}$ is complete in $L_2(0,2\pi)$. Hence, the conditions of Theorem 2 are fulfilled for the sequence $\{v_n\}_{n=1}^{\infty}$ constructed by L and $\{\lambda_n\}_{n=1}^{\infty}$.

Now, consider two boundary value problems $\mathscr{L} = \mathscr{L}(q,p_1,p_2,r_1,r_2)$ and $\tilde{\mathscr{L}} = \mathscr{L}(\tilde{q},\tilde{p}_1,\tilde{p}_2,\tilde{r}_1,\tilde{r}_2)$ satisfying the conditions of the theorem, that is, $N_1 = \tilde{N}_1$, $N_2 = \tilde{N}_2$,

$r_j(\lambda) = \tilde{r}_j(\lambda)$, $j = 1,2$, $q(x) = \tilde{q}(x)$ a.e. on $(\pi, 2\pi)$, and $\mu_n = \tilde{\mu}_n$ for $n \geq M_1 - N_1 + 1$. Then, it follows from (54) that $\Theta = \tilde{\Theta}$. Observe that

$$\varpi = \Theta - d_{M_2} - \int_{\pi}^{2\pi} q(t)\, dt,$$

where ϖ and Θ are defined by (4) and (52), respectively. Moreover, since $q(t) = \tilde{q}(t)$ a.e. on $(\pi, 2\pi)$, then $\int_{\pi}^{2\pi} q(t)\, dt = \int_{\pi}^{2\pi} \tilde{q}(t)\, dt$. Hence, $\varpi = \tilde{\varpi}$. Furthermore, the solution $\psi(x,\lambda)$ on $[\pi, 2\pi]$ is uniquely specified by the polynomials $r_j(\lambda)$, $j = 1,2$, and the potential $q(x)$ on $(\pi, 2\pi)$. Consequently, $\psi(x,\lambda) \equiv \tilde{\psi}(x,\lambda)$, $x \in [\pi, 2\pi]$. Consider the equivalent problems $L = L(q, p_1, p_2, f_1, f_2)$ and $\tilde{L} = L(\tilde{q}, \tilde{p}_1, \tilde{p}_2, \tilde{f}_1, \tilde{f}_2)$ for the problems $\mathscr{L}$ and $\tilde{\mathscr{L}}$, respectively. By the above arguments, we have $f_j(\lambda) \equiv \tilde{f}_j(\lambda)$, $j = 1,2$. Consider the subspectra $\{\lambda_n\}_{n=1}^{\infty} := \{\mu_n\}_{n=M_1-N_1+1}^{\infty}$ and $\{\tilde{\lambda}_n\}_{n=1}^{\infty} := \{\tilde{\mu}_n\}_{n=M_1-N_1+1}^{\infty}$ of the problems L and $\tilde{L}$, respectively. By virtue of Theorem 2, the sequence $\{v_n\}_{n=1}^{\infty}$ constructed by L and $\{\lambda_n\}_{n=1}^{\infty}$ is complete in $\mathcal{H}_K$. Thus, the conditions of Theorem 1 hold. Applying Theorem 1, we conclude that $q(x) = \tilde{q}(x)$ a.e. on $(0, \pi)$ and $p_j(\lambda) \equiv \tilde{p}_j(\lambda)$, $j = 1,2$. □

Proceed to the second boundary value problem $\mathcal{L} = \mathcal{L}(q, p_1, p_2, r_1, r_2, p_{ij})$ for the Sturm–Liouville Equation (8) with the complex-valued potential $q \in L_2(0, 2\pi)$, the BC at $x = 0$ containing the relatively prime polynomials $p_j(\lambda)$, $j = 1,2$, the BC at $x = 2\pi$, the relatively prime polynomials $r_j(\lambda)$, $j = 1,2$, and the discontinuity conditions (10), the polynomials $p_{ij}(\lambda)$, $i = \overline{1,3}$, $j = \overline{0,1}$. Suppose that the polynomials $p_1(\lambda)$, $p_2(\lambda)$ have the form (3), the polynomials $r_1(\lambda)$, $r_2(\lambda)$, the form (7), and the polynomials $p_{ij}(\lambda)$, $i = \overline{1,3}$, $j = 0,1$, the form

$$p_{ij}(\lambda) = \sum_{n=0}^{K_{ij}} g_n^{ij} \lambda^n, \quad g_{K_{ij}}^{ij} \neq 0, \quad K_{ij} \geq 0, \quad i = \overline{1,3}, \quad j = 0,1. \tag{55}$$

For definiteness, we confine ourselves to the case $N_1 > N_2$, $M_1 > M_2$, $K_{20} > K_{30}$, $K_{21} > K_{31}$, $K_{10} + K_{21} > K_{11} + K_{20}$. Without loss of generality, we assume that $a_{N_1} = 1$, $c_{M_1} = 1$, $g_{K_{10}}^{10} = g_{K_{11}}^{11} = 1$.

Consider the solutions $\varphi(x,\lambda)$ and $\psi(x,\lambda)$ of Equation (5) satisfying the initial conditions (48) on the segments $[0, \pi]$ and $[\pi, 2\pi]$, respectively. It can be easily seen that the eigenvalues of the problem $\mathcal{L}$ coincide with the zeros of the characteristic function

$$\Delta(\lambda) = \sum_{j=0}^{1} (-1)^{1-j} \varphi^{(j)}(\pi,\lambda) p_{1,j}(\lambda) (p_{2,1-j}(\lambda)\psi(\pi,\lambda) + p_{3,1-j}(\lambda)\psi'(\pi,\lambda)). \tag{56}$$

The function $\varphi(x,\lambda)$ can be represented in the form (50). So, substituting (50) into (56), we obtain

$$\begin{aligned} \Delta(\lambda) = \sum_{j=0}^{1} (-1)^{1-j} &(p_1(\lambda) C^{(j)}(\pi,\lambda) - p_2(\lambda) S^{(j)}(\pi,\lambda)) \\ &\times p_{1,j}(\lambda)(p_{2,1-j}(\lambda)\psi(\pi,\lambda) + p_{3,1-j}(\lambda)\psi'(\pi,\lambda)). \end{aligned} \tag{57}$$

Comparing (57) with (11), we conclude that the eigenvalues of the boundary value problem $\mathcal{L} = \mathcal{L}(q, p_1, p_2, r_1, r_2, p_{ij})$ coincide with the eigenvalues of the problem $L = L(q, p_1, p_2, f_1, f_2)$ with

$$f_1(\lambda) = p_{11}(\lambda)(p_{20}(\lambda)\psi(\pi,\lambda) + p_{30}(\lambda)\psi'(\pi,\lambda)), \tag{58}$$

$$f_2(\lambda) = -p_{10}(\lambda)(p_{21}(\lambda)\psi(\pi,\lambda) + p_{31}(\lambda)\psi'(\pi,\lambda)). \tag{59}$$

The following theorem implies the uniqueness of solution for Problem 3.

Theorem 5. *Let $\{\mu_n\}_{n=1}^{\infty}$ and $\{\tilde{\mu}_n\}_{n=1}^{\infty}$ be the spectra of the problems $\mathcal{L} = \mathcal{L}(q, p_1, p_2, r_1, r_2, p_{ij})$ and $\tilde{\mathcal{L}} = \mathcal{L}(\tilde{q}, \tilde{p}_1, \tilde{p}_2, \tilde{r}_1, \tilde{r}_2, \tilde{p}_{ij})$, respectively. Suppose that $N_j = \tilde{N}_j$, $r_j(\lambda) \equiv \tilde{r}_j(\lambda)$, $j = 1, 2$, $p_{ij}(\lambda) \equiv \tilde{p}_{ij}(\lambda)$, $i = \overline{1,3}$, $j = 0, 1$, $q(x) = \tilde{q}(x)$ a.e. on $(\pi, 2\pi)$, $N_1 \le M_1 + K_{10} + K_{21}$, and $\mu_n = \tilde{\mu}_n$ for all $n \ge n_1$, $n_1 := -N_1 + M_1 + K_{10} + K_{21} + 1$. In addition, assume that $f_1(\mu_n) \ne 0$ or $f_2(\mu_n) \ne 0$ for each $n \ge n_1$, where the functions $f_1(\lambda)$ and $f_2(\lambda)$ are defined by (58)–(59). Then, $q(x) = \tilde{q}(x)$ a.e. on $(0, \pi)$ and $p_j(\lambda) \equiv \tilde{p}_j(\lambda)$, $j = 1, 2$.*

Proof. The idea of the proof is based on the reduction in Problem 3 to Problem 1.

Using (57), we obtain the following asymptotics for the characteristic function

$$\Delta(\lambda) = \rho^{2n_0}\left(g^{21}_{K_{21}} \cos^2 \rho\pi + \frac{g^{21}_{K_{21}}\Omega}{2\rho} \cos \rho\pi \sin \rho\pi + o(\rho^{-1} e^{2|\tau|\pi})\right), \tag{60}$$

and for the eigenvalues

$$\sqrt{\mu_n} = n - \frac{1}{2} - n_0 + O(n^{-\frac{1}{2}}), \quad n \ge 1, \tag{61}$$

where $\Omega = \frac{1}{2}\int_0^{2\pi} q(t)\,dt$ and $n_0 := N_1 + M_1 + K_{10} + K_{21}$.

Define the function

$$\Delta^1(\lambda) = \frac{\Delta(\lambda)}{\prod\limits_{n=1}^{n_0} (\lambda - \mu_n)}. \tag{62}$$

It has only zeros $\{\mu_n\}_{n=n_0+1}^{\infty}$. Suppose that the eigenvalues $\{\mu_n\}_{n>n_0}$ are simple. The general case requires minor technical changes. Let us prove that the sequence $\{\cos \sqrt{\mu_n} t\}_{n=n_0+1}^{\infty}$ is complete in $L_2(0, 2\pi)$. Let $h \in L_2(0, 2\pi)$ be such a function that

$$\int_0^{2\pi} h(t) \cos \sqrt{\mu_n} t\,dt = 0, \quad n > n_0.$$

We have to show that $h \equiv 0$. Consider the function $H(\lambda) := \int\limits_0^{2\pi} h(t) \cos \rho t\,dt$. Clearly, $\frac{H(\lambda)}{\Delta^1(\lambda)}$ is an entire function and $H(\lambda) = o(e^{2|\tau|\pi})$, $|\lambda| \to \infty$. It can be shown that $|\Delta^1(\lambda)| \ge C_\delta e^{2|\tau|\pi}$ in the region

$$G_\delta = \{\rho \in \mathbb{C}\colon |\rho - (n - \frac{1}{2})| \ge \delta, n \in \mathbb{Z}\}, \quad |\rho| \ge \rho^*,$$

for some positive constants δ, ρ^*, and C_δ. So, we can conclude that $\dfrac{H(\lambda)}{\Delta^1(\lambda)} \to 0$ as $|\lambda| \to \infty$, $\lambda = \rho^2$, $\rho \in G_\delta$. By Liouville's theorem, we conclude that $\dfrac{H(\lambda)}{\Delta^1(\lambda)} \equiv 0$, then $H(\lambda) \equiv 0$ and $h(t) = 0$ a.e. on $(0, 2\pi)$. Hence, the system $\{\cos \sqrt{\mu_n} t\}_{n \ge n_0+1}$ is complete in $L_2(0, 2\pi)$.

Let us pass from the problem $\mathcal{L}(q, p_1, p_2, r_1, r_2, p_{ij})$ to the corresponding problem $L(q, p_1, p_2, f_1, f_2)$, with the functions $f_1(\lambda)$ and $f_2(\lambda)$ defined by (58) and (59), respectively. Suppose that $N_1 \le M_1 + K_{10} + K_{21}$ and consider the subspectrum $\{\lambda_n\}_{n=1}^{\infty} := \{\mu_n\}_{n=n_1}^{\infty}$ of the problem L. Thus, in the case $N_1 = M_1 + K_{10} + K_{21}$, we consider the whole spectrum of $\mathcal{L}$ and, in the case $N_1 < M_1 + K_{10} + K_{21}$, we exclude $(M_1 + K_{10} + K_{21} - N_1)$ eigenvalues. The excluded eigenvalues can be chosen arbitrarily. According to the above arguments, we have that the system $\{\cos \sqrt{\lambda_n} t\}_{n=2N_1+1}^{\infty}$ is complete in $L_2(0, 2\pi)$. Hence, the conditions of Theorem 2 are fulfilled for the sequence $\{v_n\}_{n=1}^{\infty}$ constructed by L and $\{\lambda_n\}_{n=1}^{\infty}$.

Let us show that the value ω is uniquely specified by the subspectrum $\{\mu_n\}_{n=n_0+1}^{\infty}$ and the potential $q(x)$ on $(\pi, 2\pi)$. By using Hadamard's factorization theorem, one can reconstruct the function $\Delta^1(\lambda)$ from its zeros $\{\mu_n\}_{n=n_0+1}^{\infty}$ uniquely up to a multiplicative constant:

$$P(\lambda) := \prod_{n=n_0+1}^{\infty}\left(1-\frac{\lambda}{\mu_n}\right), \quad P(\lambda) = c_1\Delta^1(\lambda), \quad c_1 \neq 0.$$

From (60) and (62), we obtain

$$P(\lambda) = c_1\left(g_1\cos^2\rho\pi + g_2\rho^{-1}\sin\rho\pi\cos\rho\pi + o(\rho^{-1}e^{2|\tau|\pi})\right), \tag{63}$$

where $g_1 = g_{K_{21}}^{21}$, $g_2 = g_{K_{21}}^{21}\frac{\Omega}{2}$.

Taking $\rho = i\tau$ in (63), we derive

$$c_1 g_1 = 2\lim_{\tau\to+\infty} P(-\tau^2)e^{-2\tau\pi} =: \kappa_1,$$

$$c_1 g_2 = 2\lim_{\tau\to+\infty} \tau(2P(-\tau^2)e^{-2\tau\pi} - \kappa_1) =: \kappa_2.$$

Then, we can find $\Omega = \dfrac{2\kappa_2}{\kappa_1}$. Observe that

$$\omega = \Omega - \int_{\pi}^{2\pi} q(t)\,dt.$$

Now, consider two boundary value problems $\mathcal{L} = \mathcal{L}(q, p_1, p_2, r_1, r_2, p_{ij})$ and $\tilde{\mathcal{L}} = \mathcal{L}(\tilde{q}, \tilde{p}_1, \tilde{p}_2, \tilde{r}_1, \tilde{r}_2, \tilde{p}_{ij})$ and their subspectra $\{\mu_n\}_{n\geq n_1}$ and $\{\tilde{\mu}_n\}_{n\geq n_1}$ satisfying the conditions of the theorem. Since $\mu_n = \tilde{\mu}_n$, $n \geq n_1$, then $\Delta^1(\lambda) = \tilde{\Delta}^1(\lambda)$. Hence, $\kappa_j = \tilde{\kappa}_j$, $j = 1,2$, and, consequently, $\Omega = \tilde{\Omega}$. Moreover, since $q(t) = \tilde{q}(t)$ a.e. on $(\pi, 2\pi)$, then $\int_\pi^{2\pi} q(t)\,dt = \int_\pi^{2\pi}\tilde{q}(t)\,dt$. Hence, $\omega = \tilde{\omega}$. Furthermore, the solution $\psi(x,\lambda)$ on $(\pi, 2\pi)$ is uniquely specified by the polynomials $r_j(\lambda)$, $j = 1,2$, and the potential $q(x)$ on $(\pi, 2\pi)$. Consequently, $\psi(x,\lambda) \equiv \tilde{\psi}(x,\lambda)$, $x \in (\pi, 2\pi)$. Consider the equivalent problems $L = L(q, p_1, p_2, f_1, f_2)$ and $\tilde{L} = L(\tilde{q}, \tilde{p}_1, \tilde{p}_2, \tilde{f}_1, \tilde{f}_2)$ for the problems $\mathcal{L}$ and $\tilde{\mathcal{L}}$, respectively. By the above arguments, we have $f_j(\lambda) \equiv \tilde{f}_j(\lambda)$, $j = 1,2$. Consider the subspectra $\{\lambda_n\}_{n=1}^{\infty} := \{\mu_n\}_{n=n_1}^{\infty}$ and $\{\tilde{\lambda}_n\}_{n=1}^{\infty} := \{\tilde{\mu}_n\}_{n=n_1}^{\infty}$ of the problems L and $\tilde{L}$, respectively. By virtue of Theorem 2, the sequence $\{v_n\}_{n=1}^{\infty}$ constructed by L and $\{\lambda_n\}_{n=1}^{\infty}$ is complete in $\mathcal{H}_K$. Thus, the conditions of Theorem 1 hold. Applying Theorem 1, we conclude that $q(x) = \tilde{q}(x)$ a.e. on $(0, \pi)$ and $p_j(\lambda) \equiv \tilde{p}_j(\lambda)$, $j = 1,2$. □

Author Contributions: Conceptualization, N.P.B.; Methodology, N.P.B.; Validation, N.P.B.; Investigation, E.E.C.; Writing—original draft, E.E.C.; Writing—review & editing, N.P.B.; Supervision, N.P.B. All authors have read and agreed to the published version of the manuscript.

Funding: This work was supported by Grant 21-71-10001 of the Russian Science Foundation, https://rscf.ru/en/project/21-71-10001/ (access date: 18 January 2023).

Data Availability Statement: Not applicable.

Conflicts of Interest: The authors declare no conflict of interest.

References

1. Marchenko, V.A. *Sturm–Liouville Operators and Their Applications*; Birkhäuser: Basel, Switzerland, 1986.
2. Levitan, B.M. *Inverse Sturm–Liouville Problems*; VNU Sci. Press: Utrecht, The Netherlands, 1987.
3. Pöschel, J.; Trubowitz, E. *Inverse Spectral Theory*; Academic Press: New York, NY, USA, 1987.
4. Freiling, G.; Yurko, V. *Inverse Sturm–Liouville Problems and Their Applications*; Nova Science Publishers: Huntington, NY, USA, 2001.
5. Collatz, L. *Eigenwertaufgaben mit technischen Anwendungen, Akad*; Verlagsgesellschaft Geest & Portig: Leipzig, Germany, 1963.
6. Kraft, R.E.; Wells, W.R. Adjointness properties for differential systems with eigenvalue-dependent boundary conditions, with application to flow-duct acoustics. *J. Acoust. Soc. Am.* **1977**, *61*, 913–922. [CrossRef]

7. Fulton, C.T. Two-point boundary value problems with eigenvalue parameter contained in the boundary conditions. *Proc. R. Soc. Edinb. Sect. A* **1977**, *77*, 293–308. [CrossRef]
8. Fulton, C.T. Singular eigenvalue problems with eigenvalue parameter contained in the boundary conditions. *Proc. R. Soc. Edinb. Sect. A* **1980**, *87*, 1–34. [CrossRef]
9. Mennicken, R.; Möller, M. *Non-Self-Adjoint Boundary Eigenvalue Problems*; North-Holland Mathematic Studies Series; Elsevier: Amsterdam, The Netherlands, 2003; Volume 192.
10. Shkalikov, A.A. Boundary problems for ordinary problems for differential equations with parameter in the boundary conditions. *J. Sov. Math.* **1986**, *33*, 1311–1342. [CrossRef]
11. Tretter, C. Boundary eigenvalue problems with differential equations $N\eta = \lambda P\eta$ with λ-polynomial boundary conditions. *J. Diff. Eqns.* **2001**, *170*, 408–471. [CrossRef]
12. Chugunova, M.V. Inverse spectral problem for the Sturm–Liouville operator with eigenvalue parameter dependent boundary conditions. *Oper. Theory Advan. Appl.* **2001**, *123*, 187–194.
13. Binding, P.A.; Browne P.J.; Watson, B.A. Sturm–Liouville problems with boundary conditions rationally dependent on the eigenparameter. I. *Proc. Edinb. Math. Soc.* **2002**, *45*, 631–645. [CrossRef]
14. Binding, P.A.; Browne, P.J.; Watson, B.A. Sturm–Liouville problems with boundary conditions rationally dependent on the eigenparameter. II. *J. Comput. Appl. Math.* **2002**, *148*, 147–168. [CrossRef]
15. Binding, P.A.; Browne, P.J.; Watson, B.A. Equivalence of inverse Sturm–Liouville problems with boundary conditions rationally dependent on the eigenparameter. *J. Math. Anal. Appl.* **2004**, *291*, 246–261. [CrossRef]
16. Chernozhukova, A.; Freiling, G. A uniqueness theorem for the boundary value problems with non-linear dependence on the spectral parameter in the boundary conditions. *Inv. Probl. Sci. Eng.* **2009**, *17*, 777–785. [CrossRef]
17. Freiling, G.; Yurko V. Inverse problems for Sturm–Liouville equations with boundary conditions polynomially dependent on the spectral parameter. *Inverse Probl.* **2010**, *26*, 055003. [CrossRef]
18. Freiling, G.; Yurko, V. Determination of singular differential pencils from the Weyl function. *Adv. Dynam. Syst. Appl.* **2012**, *7*, 171–193.
19. Wang, Y.P. Uniqueness theorems for Sturm–Liouville operators with boundary conditions polynomially dependent on the eigenparameter from spectral data. *Results Math.* **2013**, *63*, 1131–1144. [CrossRef]
20. Yang, C.-F.; Xu, X.-C. Ambarzumyan-type theorem with polynomially dependent eigenparameter. *Math. Meth. Appl. Sci.* **2015**, *38*, 4411–4415. [CrossRef]
21. Yang, Y.; Wei, G. Inverse scattering problems for Sturm–Liouville operators with spectral parameter dependent on boundary conditions. *Math. Notes* **2018**, *103*, 59–66. [CrossRef]
22. Mosazadeh S.; Akbarfam A. On Hochstadt-Lieberman theorem for impulsive Sturm–Liouville problems with boundary conditions polynomially dependent on the spectral parameter. *Turk. J. Math.* **2018**, *42*, 3002–3009. [CrossRef]
23. Guliyev, N.J. Schrödinger operators with distributional potentials and boundary conditions dependent on the eigenvalue parameter. *J. Math. Phys.* **2019**, *60*, 063501. [CrossRef]
24. Guliyev, N.J. Essentially isospectral transformations and their applications. *Ann. Di Mat. Pura Ed Appl.* **2020**, *199*, 1621–1648. [CrossRef]
25. Guliyev, N.J. On two-spectra inverse problems. *Proc. AMS* **2020**, *148*, 4491–4502. [CrossRef]
26. Browne, P.J.; Sleeman, B.D. A uniqueness theorem for inverse eigenparameter dependent Sturm–Liouville problems. *Inverse Probl.* **1997**, *13*, 1453–1462. [CrossRef]
27. Guliyev, N.J. Inverse eigenvalue problems for Sturm–Liouville equations with spectral parameter linearly contained in one of the boundary condition. *Inverse Probl.* **2005**, *21*, 1315–1330. [CrossRef]
28. Buterin, S.A. On half inverse problem for differential pencils with the spectral parameter in boundary conditions. *Tamkang J. Math.* **2011**, *42*, 355–364. [CrossRef]
29. Guliyev, N.J. Inverse square singularities and eigenparameter dependent boundary conditions are two sides of the same coin. *arXiv* **2001**, arXiv:2001.00061.
30. Bondarenko, N.P. Inverse Sturm–Liouville problem with analytical functions in the boundary condition. *Open Math.* **2020**, *18*, 512–528. [CrossRef]
31. Bondarenko, N.P. Solvability and stability of the inverse Sturm–Liouville problem with analytical functions in the boundary condition. *Math. Meth. Appl. Sci.* **2020**, *43*, 7009–7021. [CrossRef]
32. Yang, C.-F.; Bondarenko, N.P.; Xu, X.-C. An inverse problem for the Sturm–Liouville pencil with arbitrary entire functions in the boundary condition. *Inverse Probl. Imag.* **2020**, *14*, 153–169. [CrossRef]
33. Bondarenko, N.P. A partial inverse Sturm–Liouville problem on an arbitrary graph. *Math. Meth. Appl. Sci.* **2021**, *44*, 6896–6910. [CrossRef]
34. Kuznetsova, M.A. On recovering quadratic pencils with singular coefficients and entire functions in the boundary conditions. *Math. Meth. Appl. Sci.* **2022**. [CrossRef]
35. Hochstadt, H.; Lieberman, B. An inverse Sturm–Liouville problem with mixed given data. *SIAM J. Appl. Math.* **1978**, *34*, 676–680. [CrossRef]
36. Borg, G. Eine Umkehrung der Sturm–Liouvilleschen Eigenwertaufgabe: Bestimmung der Differentialgleichung durch die Eigenwerte. *Acta Math.* **1946**, *78*, 1–96. [CrossRef]

37. Bondarenko, N.P. A partial inverse problem for the Sturm–Liouville operator on a star-shaped graph. *Anal. Math. Phys.* **2018**, *8*, 155–168. [CrossRef]
38. Bondarenko N.; Buterin S. On a local solvability and stability of the inverse transmission eigenvalue problem. *Inverse Probl.* **2017**, *33*, 115010. [CrossRef]
39. Bondarenko, N.P.; Yurko, V.A. A new approach to the inverse discrete transmission eigenvalue problem. *Inverse Probl. Imag.* **2022**, *16*, 739–751. [CrossRef]
40. Horváth, M. Inverse spectral problems and closed exponential systems. *Ann. Math.* **2005**, *162*, 885–918. [CrossRef]
41. Kravchenko, V.V.; Torba, S.M. A practical method for recovering Sturm–Liouville problems from the Weyl function. *Inverse Probl.* **2021**, *37*, 065011. [CrossRef]
42. Bartels, C.; Currie, S.; Nowaczyk, M.; Watson, B.A. Sturm–Liouville problems with transfer condition Herglotz dependent on the eigenparameter: Hilbert space formulation. *Integr. Equ. Oper. Theory* **2018**, *90*, 34. [CrossRef]
43. Bartels, C.; Currie, S.; Watson, B.A. Sturm–Liouville Problems with transfer condition Herglotz dependent on the eigenparameter: eigenvalue asymptotics. *Complex Anal. Oper. Theory* **2021**, *15*, 71. [CrossRef]
44. Ozkan, A.S.; Keskin, B. Spectral problems for Sturm–Liouville operator with boundary and jump conditions linearly dependent on the eigenparameter. *Inv. Probl. Sci. Engin.* **2012**, *20*, 799–808. [CrossRef]
45. Wei, Z.; Wei, G. Inverse spectral problem for non selfadjoint Dirac operator with boundary and jump conditions dependent on the spectral parameter. *J. Comput. Appl. Math.* **2016**, *308*, 199–214. [CrossRef]
46. Kuznetsova, M.A. A uniqueness theorem on inverse spectral problems for the Sturm–Liouville differential operators on time scales. *Results Math.* **2020**, *75*, 44. [CrossRef]
47. Kuznetsova, M.A. On recovering the Sturm–Liouville differential operators on time scales. *Math. Notes* **2021**, *109*, 74–88. [CrossRef]
48. da Silva, S.L.E.F; Carvalho, P.T.C.; da Costa, C.A.N; de Araujo, J.M; Corso, G. An objective function for full-waveform inversion based on -dependent offset-preconditioning. *PLoS ONE* **2020**, *15*, e0240999. [CrossRef] [PubMed]

Disclaimer/Publisher's Note: The statements, opinions and data contained in all publications are solely those of the individual author(s) and contributor(s) and not of MDPI and/or the editor(s). MDPI and/or the editor(s) disclaim responsibility for any injury to people or property resulting from any ideas, methods, instructions or products referred to in the content.

mathematics

MDPI

Article

General Fractional Calculus in Multi-Dimensional Space: Riesz Form

Vasily E. Tarasov

Department of Physics, 915, Moscow Aviation Institute, National Research University, 125993 Moscow, Russia; tarasov@theory.sinp.msu.ru

Abstract: An extension of the general fractional calculus (GFC) is proposed as a generalization of the Riesz fractional calculus, which was suggested by Marsel Riesz in 1949. The proposed Riesz form of GFC can be considered as an extension GFC from the positive real line and the Laplace convolution to the m-dimensional Euclidean space and the Fourier convolution. To formulate the general fractional calculus in the Riesz form, the Luchko approach to construction of the GFC, which was suggested by Yuri Luchko in 2021, is used. The general fractional integrals and derivatives are defined as convolution-type operators. In these definitions the Fourier convolution on m-dimensional Euclidean space is used instead of the Laplace convolution on positive semi-axis. Some properties of these general fractional operators are described. The general fractional analogs of first and second fundamental theorems of fractional calculus are proved. The fractional calculus of the Riesz potential and the fractional Laplacian of the Riesz form are special cases of proposed general fractional calculus of the Riesz form.

Keywords: general fractional calculus; fractional derivatives; fractional integrals; Riesz potential; nonlocality

MSC: 26A33

1. Introduction

Fractional calculus of integrals and derivatives of arbitrary order is an analogous to standard mathematical calculus of integer-order integrals and derivatives [1–8]. Fractional calculus is used to describe systems and processes with non-locality in space and time (for example see books [9–18]), in which one can see the application of fractional calculus in various fields of sciences from mechanics to economics. Handbooks [19,20] contain descriptions of the application of fractional calculus in 25 different areas of physics.

The operators of fractional calculus have different interpretations [21–30], which include the following: (GI) Interpretations in terms of geometry [31–38], (PhI) Interpretations in terms of physics [25–30,35–38], (EcI) Interpretations in terms of economics [39,40], (PrI) Interpretations in terms of probability theory [41–45], and (InI) Interpretations in terms of information theory [46,47].

The fractional calculus is usually used to describe systems and processes with non-locality of the power-law type. To describe different forms of nonlocalities, a general fractional calculus should be formulated. Note that in order for some general operators to form a general fractional calculus, they must satisfy some fractional analogues of the first and second fundamental theorems of standard calculus [48]. These theorems allow us to interpret general fractional operators as some analogues of integrals and derivatives of integer order [49]. It should be noted that these theorems lead to the fact that at least one of the two operator kernels, which describe the respectively a general integral and a general derivative, should be singular [50,51].

The general fractional calculus actually arose in Sonin's work published in 1884 [52] (see also [53,54]). However, the name "general fractional calculus" began to be used

Citation: Tarasov, V.E. General Fractional Calculus in Multi-Dimensional Space: Riesz Form. *Mathematics* **2023**, *11*, 1651. https://doi.org/10.3390/math11071651

Academic Editor: Sitnik Sergey

Received: 2 March2023
Revised: 26 March 2023
Accepted: 27 March 2023
Published: 29 March 2023

Copyright: © 2023 by the author. Licensee MDPI, Basel, Switzerland. This article is an open access article distributed under the terms and conditions of the Creative Commons Attribution (CC BY) license (https://creativecommons.org/licenses/by/4.0/).

starting from the work of Kochubei in 2011 [55]. In the last decade, the general fractional calculus has been actively developed and applied in various fields of science [56–75]. The important form of the general fractional calculus was proposed by Luchko in works of 2021–2022 [76–85]. Different applications of the Luchko general fractional calculus has been considered in works [86–94].

Problems and trends in the development and application of the general fractional calculus were described in work [95]. One of the problems is the extension of the general fractional calculus to the entire real axis and the entire m-dimensional Euclidean space. An extension of Luchko type of GFC on multi-dimensional case is proposed in [87], where a general fractional vector calculus is considered. However, this GFC was proposed for the regions from the set $\mathbb{R}^m_+ = \{(x_1, \ldots, x_m) : x_j \geq 0 \text{ for all } j = 1 \ldots m\}$. The entire m-dimensional Euclidean space is not considered in [87].

One of the important types of fractional calculus in multi-dimensional Euclidean spaces is the theory proposed by Marcel Riesz. The Riesz fractional derivatives and potentials were first suggested in works [96,97] (see also [1,98]). Note that important interpretation of the Riesz fractional Laplacianis noted in paper [98]. These operators also are considered in different works (see [1,4,99–118]). Note that the Riesz fractional derivative are connected with the Liouville fractional derivatives (for example, see Section 12 in [1] for $\mathbb{R}$). The Riesz derivative is also related to Grünwald–Letnikov fractional derivatives (Section 20 in [1]), and the Marchaud fractional derivative (Section 5.4 in [1]). The Riesz fractional derivative can be connected with the Caputo fractional derivatives (see Equations 2.4.6 and 2.4.7 of [4]). The Grünwald–Letnikov–Riesz derivative of this type is considered and applied in [119–122].

This article proposes the construction of an extension of the Riesz fractional calculus to a wide class of operator kernels. In this extension GFC, the m-dimensional Euclidean space and the Fourier convolution are used instead of the positive real line and the Laplace convolution. In the formulation of the GFC in the Riesz form, the Luchko approach to construction of the GFC, which was proposed in [76–85], is used. Therefore this extension can be considered as an extension of the Luchko's general fractional calculus for m-dimensional Euclidean spaces. The sets of pairs of operator kernels for general fractional operators in the Riesz form are defined. The spaces of functions, for which the proposed operators exist, are also defined. Some basic properties of the proposed Riesz general fractional integrals and the Riesz general fractional operators are described. The first and second fundamental theorems of general fractional calculus in the Riesz form are proved. The well-known fractional calculus of the Riesz potential and the fractional Laplacian of the Riesz form are special cases of proposed general fractional calculus of the Riesz form.

It should be note that there are many different definitions of fractional Laplacian [123–125]. In this case, the fractional derivatives of the Riesz form are usually interpreted as a fractional Laplacian. The fractional integrals of the Riesz form are usually interpreted as a fractional Riesz potential. In the framework of these interpretations, the general fractional derivatives and integrals of the Riesz form can be interpreted as a general fractional Laplacian and general fractional Riesz potential.

The content of the article is following. In Section 2, the Fourier convolution and its properties are described as preliminaries. In Section 3, sets of functions and kernel pairs are defined. In Section 4, general fractional integrals, general fractional derivatives of the Caputo type and Riemann–Liouville types are defined in the framework of the GFC in the Riesz form. In Section 5, semi-group properties of GF integration of the Riesz form are proved. In Section 6, action of the Laplacian on GF integrals of the Riesz form is described. In Section 7, first amd second fundamental theorems of GFC in Riesz form are proved. A brief conclusion is given in Section 8.

2. Preliminaries: Fourier Convolution and Its Properties

For m-dimensional Euclidean space $\mathbb{R}^m$, the distance between points $P(x_1,\ldots,x_m)$ and $Q(y_1,\ldots,y_m)$ is described by the equation

$$r_{PQ} = r_{QP} = |\mathbf{x} - \mathbf{y}| = \sqrt{\sum_{j=1}^{m} (x_j - y_j)^2} \tag{1}$$

that can be considered as the length of the vector

$$\mathbf{r}_{QP} = -\mathbf{r}_{PQ} = \mathbf{x} - \mathbf{y}, \tag{2}$$

where $\mathbf{x}(x_1,\ldots,x_m)$ and $\mathbf{y}(y_1,\ldots,y_m)$.

The Riesz fractional integrals (the Riesz potential) and its generalization can be defined by using the Fourier convolution (see Section 25.3 in [1], pp. 494–495). Therefore, definition of this convolution and some well-known properties will be given below.

Let $f(\mathbf{x})$ and $g(\mathbf{x})$ belong to the space $L_1(\mathbb{R}^m)$. The Fourier convolution is defined by the equation

$$(f * g)(\mathbf{x}) = \int_{\mathbb{R}^m} g(\mathbf{x} - \mathbf{y})\, f(\mathbf{y})\, d^m\mathbf{y} = \int_{\mathbb{R}^m} f(\mathbf{x} - \mathbf{y})\, g(\mathbf{y})\, d^m\mathbf{y}. \tag{3}$$

The Fourier convolution exists only if functions $f(\mathbf{x})$ and $g(\mathbf{x})$ decay sufficiently rapidly at infinity. Conditions for the existence of the convolution can include different conditions on the functions, since a blow-up in $g(\mathbf{x})$ at infinity can be compensated by sufficiently rapid decay in $f(\mathbf{x})$ at infinity.

For example, convolution (3) of $f(\mathbf{x})$ and $g(\mathbf{x})$ exists, if $f(\mathbf{x})$ and $g(\mathbf{x})$ are Lebesgue integrable in $L_1(\mathbb{R}^m)$. TIn this case, the Fourier convolution $(f * g)(\mathbf{x})$ is also integrable (for example, see Theorem 1.3 in [126], p. 3).

As another example, one can consider $f(\mathbf{x}) \in L_1(\mathbb{R}^m)$ and $g(\mathbf{x}) \in L_p(\mathbb{R}^m)$, where $1 \leq p \leq \infty$. In this case, $(f * g)(\mathbf{x}) \in L_p(\mathbb{R}^m)$ and the following inequality is satisfied

$$\|(f * g)(\mathbf{x})\|_p \leq \|f(\mathbf{x})\|_1 \, \|g(\mathbf{x})\|_p. \tag{4}$$

For the case $p = 1$, inequality (4) gives that the space $L_1(\mathbb{R}^m)$ is a Banach algebra under the convolution.

In the general case, the Young's inequality for convolution [127] states the following property of the Fourier convolution. If $f(\mathbf{x}) \in L_p(\mathbb{R}^m)$ and $g(\mathbf{x}) \in L_q(\mathbb{R}^m)$, where $1 \leq p, q, r \leq \infty$, then $(f * g)(\mathbf{x}) \in L_r(\mathbb{R}^m)$ and the following inequality is satisfied

$$\|(f * g)(\mathbf{x})\|_r \leq \|f(\mathbf{x})\|_p \, \|g(\mathbf{x})\|_q, \tag{5}$$

where

$$\frac{1}{p} + \frac{1}{q} = \frac{1}{r} + 1. \tag{6}$$

The Fourier convolution can be defined such that the associativity property is satisfied

$$(f * (g * h))(\mathbf{x}) = ((f * g) * h)(\mathbf{x}). \tag{7}$$

Note that one can to define the Fourier convolution of a function with a generalized function (distribution). The Fourier convolution of two generalized functions (distributions) can also be defined. Let $f(\mathbf{x})$ be a function with compact support and $g(\mathbf{x})$ a generalized function (distribution). Then $(f * g)(\mathbf{x})$ is a smooth function defined by equation analogous to Equation (3), [1]. For a wide class of functions, for which the Fourier convolution is performed, one can consider convolution of these functions with the Dirac delta function $\delta(\mathbf{x})$ in the form

$$(f * \delta)(\mathbf{x}) = f(\mathbf{x}). \tag{8}$$

For distributions $f(\mathbf{x})$ and $g(\mathbf{x})$ the convolution is defined by the equation

$$(f * g) = (f(\mathbf{x}) \times g(\mathbf{y}), \varphi(\mathbf{x} + \mathbf{y}), \tag{9}$$

where $\times$ is direct product, φ is a function that belongs to the space of infinitely differentiable finite functions. Equation (9) is valid if at least one of $f(\mathbf{x})$ and $g(\mathbf{x})$ has compact support.

3. Sets of Functions and Kernel Pairs

Let us first define sets of functions on the Euclidean space $\mathbb{R}^m$.

Definition 1. *Let a function $f(\mathbf{x})$ on the space $\mathbb{R}^m$ can be represented in the form*

$$f(\mathbf{x}) = |\mathbf{x}|^a A(\mathbf{x}), \tag{10}$$

where $a > -m$ and $A(\mathbf{x}) \in C(\mathbb{R}^m)$.

Then the set of such functions will be denoted by the symbol $C_{-m}(\mathbb{R}^m)$.

The set $C_{-m}(\mathbb{R}^m)$ is an analog (m-dimensional analog) of the set $C_{-1}(0, \infty)$ that is used in the general fractional calculus in the Luchko form [76,77,80,81], which was formulated for the positive semi-axis.

Definition 2. *Let $p \in \mathbb{N}_0$ and let a function $f(\mathbf{x})$ on the space $\mathbb{R}^m$ satisfy the condition*

$$(-\Delta)^p f(\mathbf{x}) \in C_{-m}(\mathbb{R}^m), \tag{11}$$

where Δ is the Laplace operator

$$\Delta = \sum_{j=1}^{m} \frac{\partial^2}{\partial x_j^2}. \tag{12}$$

Then, the set of such functions is denoted as $C^{2p}_{-m}(\mathbb{R}^m)$.

Definition 3. *Let $p \in \mathbb{N}_0$ and let a function $f(\mathbf{x})$ satisfy the conditions:*

(1) $(-\Delta)^p f(\mathbf{x}) \in L_1(\mathbb{R}^m)$,

(2) $(-\Delta)^p f(\mathbf{x}) \in C_{-m}(\mathbb{R}^m)$.

Then, the set of such functions is denoted as $\mathfrak{C}^{2p}_{-m}(\mathbb{R}^m)$.

Let us now define sets of pairs of operator kernels for operators on the Euclidean space $\mathbb{R}^m$.

Definition 4. *Let pair of two functions $M(\mathbf{x}) = M(|\mathbf{x}|) \in L_1(\mathbb{R}^m)$, and $K(\mathbf{x}) = K(|\mathbf{x}|) \in L_1(\mathbb{R}^m)$ satisfy the following conditions.*

(1) The functions $M(|\mathbf{x}|)$ and $K(|\mathbf{x}|)$ belong to the set $C_{-m}(\mathbb{R}^m)$.

(2) The Fourier convolution of these functions has the form

$$(M * K)(|\mathbf{x}|) = M_{2-m}(|\mathbf{x}|), \tag{13}$$

where for $m \neq 2$,

$$M_{2-m}(|\mathbf{x}|) = \frac{|\mathbf{x}|^{2-m}}{H_m(2)} = \frac{1}{4\,\pi^{m/2}} \Gamma\left(\frac{m-2}{2}\right) |\mathbf{x}|^{2-m}. \tag{14}$$

Then, the set of such pairs is denoted as $\mathfrak{R}^m$.

As an example of kernel pair $(M,\ K)$ that belongs to the set $\mathcal{R}^m$, one can consider the functions

$$M(|\mathbf{x}|) = M_{\alpha-m}(|\mathbf{x}|) = \frac{|\mathbf{x}|^{\alpha-m}}{H_m(\alpha)}, \tag{15}$$

$$K(|\mathbf{x}|) = M_{2-\alpha-m}(|\mathbf{x}|) = \frac{|\mathbf{x}|^{2-\alpha-m}}{H_m(2-\alpha)}, \tag{16}$$

where

$$H_m(\alpha) = \frac{\pi^{m/2}\, 2^\alpha\, \Gamma\left(\frac{\alpha}{2}\right)}{\Gamma\left(\frac{m-\alpha}{2}\right)} \tag{17}$$

with $0 < \alpha < m$ and $0 < 2 - \alpha < m$.

Definition 5. *Let a pair of functions $M(\mathbf{x}) = M(|\mathbf{x}|) \in L_1(\mathbb{R}^m)$, and $K(\mathbf{x}) = K(|\mathbf{x}|) \in L_1(\mathbb{R}^m)$ satisfy the following conditions.*

(1) The functions $M(|\mathbf{x}|)$ and $K(|\mathbf{x}|)$ belong to the set $C_{-m}(\mathbb{R}^m)$.

(2) The Fourier convolution of these functions has the form

$$(M * K)(|\mathbf{x}|) = M_{2p-m}(|\mathbf{x}|). \tag{18}$$

Then, the set of such functions is denoted as $\mathcal{R}^m_{2p}$.

The set $\mathcal{R}^m_{2p}$ can be interpreted as an analog of the Luchko set $\mathcal{L}_n$ that is proposed in works [76,77,80,81] for the GFC on $(0,\infty)$.

As an example of kernel pair $(M,\ K)$ that belongs to the set $\mathcal{R}^m_{2p}$, one can consider the functions

$$M(|\mathbf{x}|) = M_{\alpha-m}(|\mathbf{x}|) = \frac{|\mathbf{x}|^{\alpha-m}}{H_m(\alpha)}, \tag{19}$$

$$K(|\mathbf{x}|) = M_{2p-\alpha-m}(|\mathbf{x}|) = \frac{|\mathbf{x}|^{2p-\alpha-m}}{H_m(2p-\alpha)}, \tag{20}$$

where $0 < \alpha < m$ and $0 < 2p - \alpha < m$, the function $H_m(\alpha)$ is defined by Equation (17). The convolution of kernels (19) and (20) is proved in [97] by the following transformations

$$(M * K)(|\mathbf{x}|) = (M_{\alpha-m} * M_{2p-\alpha-m})(|\mathbf{x}|) = M_{\alpha+(2p-\alpha)-m}(|\mathbf{x}|) = M_{2p-m}(|\mathbf{x}|). \tag{21}$$

As another example of a kernel pair $(M,\ K)$ one can consider the following

$$M(|\mathbf{x}|) = (M_{2p-m} * M_G)(|\mathbf{x}|), \tag{22}$$

$$K(|\mathbf{x}|) = K_G(|\mathbf{x}|), \tag{23}$$

where

$$(M_G * K_G)(|\mathbf{x}|) = \delta^m(|\mathbf{x}|) \tag{24}$$

with m-dimensional Dirac delta function δ^m. Condition (24) means that $M_G = S$ and $K_G = S^{-1}$, where S is a distributions (generalized function), which has have an inverse element S^{-1} for the Fourier convolution. It is known that some generalized functions (distributions) S have an inverse S^{-1} with respect to the convolution, for which the equation

$$(S * S^{-1})(|\mathbf{x}|) = \delta^m(|\mathbf{x}|) \tag{25}$$

is satisfied in the generalized sense. For distributions $M_G(|\mathbf{x}|)$ and $K_G(|\mathbf{x}|)$ the convolution is defined by the equation

$$(M_G * K_G) = (M_G(|\mathbf{x}|) \times K_G(|\mathbf{y}|), \varphi(\mathbf{x} + \mathbf{y})), \tag{26}$$

where $\times$ is direct product, φ is a function belonging to the space of infinitely differentiable finite functions. Equation (26) is valid if at least one of $M_G(|\mathbf{x}|)$ and $K_G(|\mathbf{x}|)$ has compact support. Note that the set of invertible generalized functions (distributions) is an abelian group the Fourier convolution.

4. General Fractional Operators of Riesz Form

Let us now define general fractional operators of Riesz form that are interpreted as general fractional integrals (GFIs) and general fractional derivatives (GFDs).

Below are the definitions are generalizations of the well-known Riesz operators [97] (the Riesz fractional integral and the Riesz fractional derivatives) from the case of operator kernels of the power-law types to operator kernels of general type (belonging to the set $\mathcal{R}^m_{2p}$). The definitions of the general fractional operators proposed below in a sense can be considered as the expansion of the definitions of the general fractional integral and the general fractional derivatives, which are proposed by Luchko for the $[0, \infty)$ in [76], for the m-dimensional Euclidean space $\mathbb{R}^m$. In this consideration, the first-order derivative in the GFD of the Luchko form of GFC is replaced by standard Laplace operator.

Definition 6. *Let kernel pair (M, K) belong to the set $\mathcal{R}^m_{2p}$.*
Then the general fractional integral of the Riesz form is defined by the equation

$$(I_{(M)} f)(\mathbf{x}) = (M * f)(\mathbf{x}) = \int_{\mathbb{R}^m} M(|\mathbf{x} - \mathbf{y}|) f(\mathbf{y})\, d^m\mathbf{y}, \tag{27}$$

where $f(\mathbf{x}) \in \mathcal{C}^0_{-m}(\mathbb{R}^m)$, i.e., $f(\mathbf{x}) \in L_1(\mathbb{R}^m)$ such that $f(\mathbf{x}) \in C_{-m}(\mathbb{R}^m)$.

Definition 7. *Let kernel pair (M, K) belong to the set $\mathcal{R}^m_{2p}$.*
Then the Riesz general fractional derivative of the Caputo (C) type is defined by the equation

$$(D^*_{(K)} f)(\mathbf{x}) = (K * (-\Delta)^p f)(\mathbf{x}) = \int_{\mathbb{R}^m} K(|\mathbf{x} - \mathbf{y}|)\, (-\Delta)^p f(\mathbf{y})\, d^m\mathbf{y}, \tag{28}$$

where $f(\mathbf{x}) \in \mathcal{C}^{2p}_{-m}(\mathbb{R}^m)$, i.e., $(-\Delta)^p f(\mathbf{x}) \in L_1(\mathbb{R}^m)$ such that $(-\Delta)^p f(\mathbf{x}) \in C_{-m}(\mathbb{R}^m)$.

Definition 8. *Let kernel pair (M, K) belong to the set $\mathcal{R}^m_{2p}$.*
Then the Riesz general fractional derivative of the Riemann–Liouville (RL) type (R-GFD-RL) is defined by the equation

$$(D_{(K)} f)(\mathbf{x}) = (-\Delta)^p\, (K * f)(\mathbf{x}) = (-\Delta)^p \int_{\mathbb{R}^m} K(|\mathbf{x} - \mathbf{y}|) f(\mathbf{y})\, d^m\mathbf{y}, \tag{29}$$

where $f(\mathbf{x}) \in \mathcal{C}^0_{-m}(\mathbb{R}^m)$, i.e., $f(\mathbf{x}) \in L_1(\mathbb{R}^m)$ such that $f(\mathbf{x}) \in C_{-m}(\mathbb{R}^m)$.

The Riesz GF derivative of the Caputo type can be written as

$$(D^*_{(K)} f)(\mathbf{x}) = (I_{(K)}\, (-\Delta)^p f)(\mathbf{x}). \tag{30}$$

The Riesz GF derivative of the RL type can be written as

$$(D_{(K)} f)(\mathbf{x}) = (-\Delta)^p\, (I_{(K)} f)(\mathbf{x}). \tag{31}$$

Example 1. *As an example of the Riesz GFI, one can consider the Riesz potential (Riesz fractional integral) that is defined in [97] by the equation*

$$(I^{\alpha} f)(\mathbf{x}) = \int_{\mathbb{R}^m} M_{\alpha-m}(|\mathbf{x} - \mathbf{y}|) \, f(\mathbf{y}) \, d^m\mathbf{y}, \tag{32}$$

where $0 < \alpha < m$, *and the kernel* $M_{\alpha-m}(|\mathbf{x}|)$ *can be written in the form*

$$M_{\alpha-m}(|\mathbf{x}|) = \frac{|\mathbf{x}|^{\alpha-m}}{H_m(\alpha)} = \frac{\Gamma\left(\frac{m-\alpha}{2}\right)}{\pi^{m/2} \, 2^{\alpha} \, \Gamma\left(\frac{\alpha}{2}\right)} |\mathbf{x}|^{\alpha-m}. \tag{33}$$

The parameter α *is called the order of the fractional integral. The Riesz general fractional integral with kernel (33) describes the well-known Riesz potential [1,4,97].*

As an example of the Riesz GFD, one can consider the operator

$$(D^{*}_{(K)} f)(\mathbf{x}) = \int_{\mathbb{R}^m} M_{2p-\alpha-m}(|\mathbf{x} - \mathbf{y}|) \, (-\Delta)^p \, f(\mathbf{y}) \, d^m\mathbf{y}, \tag{34}$$

where $0 < \alpha < m$, $0 < 2p - \alpha < m$, *and the kernel* $K(|\mathbf{x}|) = M_{2p-\alpha-m}(|\mathbf{x}|)$ *is defined by Equation (20).*

Remark 1. *In order for some general operators to form a general fractional calculus, they must satisfy some fractional analogues of the first and second fundamental theorems of standard calculus [48]. These theorems allow us to interpret general fractional operators as some analogues of integrals and derivatives of integer order [49]. Note that these fundamental theorems of GFC lead to the fact that at least one of the two operator kernels, which describe the respectively a general integral and a general derivative, should be singular [50,51]. It should be noted that standard Riesz fractional derivative is called the fractional Laplacian of the Riesz form and it is defined by the hyper-singular integral [1].*

If an equation with some integral and differential operators can be presented as a differential equation with a finite number of integer-order derivatives, then these operators cannot describe nonlocality. This statement is based on the fact that integer-order derivatives are determined by properties of differentiable functions only in an infinitely small neighborhood of the considered point. For example, the GF derivatives of the Riesz form are local derivatives, if the kernel pair is defined by Equations (19) and (20).

5. Semi-Group Properties of Riesz GF Integration

Let us describe semi-group property of the Riesz general fractional integrals.

Property 1 (Semi-group property of Riesz GFI). *Let kernels* $M_1 = M_1(|\mathbf{x}|)$ *and* $M_2 = M_2(|\mathbf{x}|)$ *belong to the space* $L_1(\mathbb{R}^m)$ *and to the set* $C_{-m}(\mathbb{R}^m)$ *such that the following condition is satisfied*

$$(M_1 * M_2)(\mathbf{x}) \in C_{-m}(\mathbb{R}^m). \tag{35}$$

Then, the semi-group property is satisfied for the Riesz general fractional integrals in the form

$$(I_{(M_1)} \, I_{(M_2)} \, f)(\mathbf{x}) = (I_{(M_1 * M_2)} \, f)(\mathbf{x}) \tag{36}$$

for all $\mathbf{x} \in \mathbb{R}^m$, *if the function* $f(\mathbf{x})$ *belongs to the space* $L_q(\mathbb{R}^m)$ *with* $1 \leq q \leq \infty$.

Proof. It is well known that the convolution of the kernels $M_1 = M_1(|\mathbf{x}|)$ and $M_2 = M_2(|\mathbf{x}|)$ belongs to the space $L_1(\mathbb{R}^m)$, i.e.,

$$(M_1 * M_2)(\mathbf{x}) \in L_1(\mathbb{R}^m), \tag{37}$$

if functions $M_1 = M_1(|\mathbf{x}|)$ and $M_2 = M_2(|\mathbf{x}|)$ belong to the space $L_1(\mathbb{R}^m)$.

The semi-group property (36) follows directly from the associativity property of the Fourier convolution and definition of Riesz GFI

$$(I_{(M_1)}\, I_{M_2} f)(\mathbf{x}) = (I_{(M_1)}(M_2 * f))(\mathbf{x}) = (M_1 * (M_2 * f))(\mathbf{x}) =$$

$$((M_1 * M_2) * f)(\mathbf{x}) = (I_{(M_1 * M_2)} f)(\mathbf{x}). \tag{38}$$

Condition (35) means that the Riesz GF integral $(I_{(M_1 * M_2)} f)(\mathbf{x})$ exists, if, for example, $f(\mathbf{x})$ belongs to the space $L_q(\mathbb{R}^m)$ with $1 \leq q \leq \infty$. □

As an example of the semi-group property (36), one can consider the semi-group property for the Riesz potentials. In this case, the kernels has the form

$$M_1 = M_1(|\mathbf{x}|) = M_{\alpha-m}(|\mathbf{x}|), \quad M_2 = M_2(|\mathbf{x}|) = M_{\beta-m}(|\mathbf{x}|) \tag{39}$$

and, property (36) is presented by the equation

$$(I^{\alpha}\, I^{\beta} f)(\mathbf{x}) = (I^{\alpha+\beta} f)(\mathbf{x}) \tag{40}$$

with $0 < \alpha < m$, and $0 < \beta < m$, where the condition (35), is satisfied if the inequality

$$0 < \alpha + \beta < m, \tag{41}$$

holds (see [97], p. 20).

6. Action of Laplacian on Riesz GF Integrals

Let us consider an action of the Laplacian on the Riesz GF integrals. First consider the action of the Laplacian on the Newtonian potential, which can be considered as the Riesz GFI with the kernel $M = M_{2-m}(|\mathbf{x}|)$.

It is well-known that the Newtonian potential

$$\varphi(\mathbf{x}) = (I^2 f)(\mathbf{x}) = \int_{\mathbb{R}^m} \frac{|\mathbf{x} - \mathbf{y}|^{2-m}}{H_m(2)} f(\mathbf{y})\, d^m\mathbf{y}. \tag{42}$$

is the solution of the equation

$$\Delta\, \varphi(\mathbf{x}) = -f(\mathbf{x}). \tag{43}$$

As a result, the substitution of function (42) into Equation (43) gives that the following property

$$\Delta\, (I^2 f)(\mathbf{x}) = -f(\mathbf{x}) \tag{44}$$

is satisfied for all $\mathbf{x} \in \mathbb{R}^m$. Using the notations of Riesz GFI, Equation (44) can be presented in the form

$$\Delta\, (I_{M_{2-m}} f)(\mathbf{x}) = -f(\mathbf{x}). \tag{45}$$

Using the semi-group property of the Riesz GFI in the form

$$I_{M_{2p-m}} = I^{2p} = (I^2)^p = (I_{M_{2-m}})^p, \tag{46}$$

one can see that Equation (45) gives

$$(-\Delta)^p\, (I_{M_{2p-m}} f)(\mathbf{x}) = f(\mathbf{x}), \tag{47}$$

where $p \in \mathbb{N}_0$ and $2p < m$.

Remark 2. *Note that Equation (45) means that the operator $I^2 = I_{(M_{2-m})}$ is the inverse of the operator $(-\Delta)$ (see [97], p. 21), where for $m \neq 2$ the integral $I^2 = I_{(M_{2-m})}$ is described by the equation*

$$(I^2 f)(\mathbf{x}) = \int_{\mathbb{R}^m} \frac{|\mathbf{x} - \mathbf{y}|^{2-m}}{H_m(2)} f(\mathbf{y})\, d^m \mathbf{y}, \tag{48}$$

where

$$H_m(2) = \frac{4\,\pi^{m/2}}{\Gamma\left(\frac{m-2}{2}\right)}. \tag{49}$$

Let us prove the following property that describes the action of the Laplacians on the Riesz GFIs.

Property 2 (Action of Laplacian on Riesz GFI). *Let kernel $M_{2p-m}(|\mathbf{x}|)$ and $M(|\mathbf{x}|)$ belong to the space $L_1(\mathbb{R}^m)$ and to the set $C_{-m}(\mathbb{R}^m)$ such that the following condition is satisfied*

$$(M_{2p-m} * M)(\mathbf{x}) \in C_{-m}(\mathbb{R}^m). \tag{50}$$

Then, the action of the Laplacian (Laplace operator) on the Riesz general fractional integral is described by the equation

$$(-\Delta)^p \,(I_{(M_{2p-m} * M)} f)(\mathbf{x}) = (I_{(M)} f)(\mathbf{x}). \tag{51}$$

As a special case $p = 1$, Equation (51) has the form

$$\Delta\,(I_{(M_{2-m} * M)} f)(\mathbf{x}) = -\,(I_{(M)} f)(\mathbf{x}). \tag{52}$$

Proof. The proof of property (52) follows directly from the semi-group property of the Riesz general fractional integrals (36) in the form

$$\Delta\,(I_{(M_{2-m} * M)} f)(\mathbf{x}) = \Delta\,(I_{(M_{2-m})}\, I_{(M)} f)(\mathbf{x}) =$$

$$(\Delta\, I_{(M_{2-m})}\,(I_{(M)} f))(\mathbf{x}) = \Delta\,(I^2\,(I_{(M)} f))(\mathbf{x}) = \Delta\,(I^2 g)(\mathbf{x}) \tag{53}$$

with $g(\mathbf{x}) = (I_{(M)} f)(\mathbf{x})$. Using property (44), Equation (53) gives equality (52).

Using the semi-group property of the Riesz GFI in the form

$$I_{(M_{2p-m})*M)} = I^{2p}\, I_{(M)} = (I^2)^p\, I_{(M)}, \tag{54}$$

the successive repetitions of applying Equation (53) gives equality (51). □

As an example of Equation (52) of Property 2, one can consider the action of the Laplacian on the Riesz potential that is described by the equation

$$\Delta\,(I^{\alpha+2} f)(\mathbf{x}) = -\,(I^{\alpha} f)(\mathbf{x}). \tag{55}$$

In paper [97], it was proved that the Riesz potential

$$\varphi(\mathbf{x}) = (I^{\alpha} f)(\mathbf{x}) = (I_{(M_{\alpha-m})} f)(\mathbf{x}) = \int_{\mathbb{R}^m} \frac{|\mathbf{x} - \mathbf{y}|^{\alpha-m}}{H_m(\alpha)} f(\mathbf{y})\, d^m \mathbf{y} \tag{56}$$

is the solution of the equation

$$(D_{(K)}\,\varphi)(\mathbf{x}) = -\,f(\mathbf{x}), \tag{57}$$

where $K(\mathbf{x}) = M_{2p-\alpha-m}(\mathbf{x})$ and $p \in \mathbb{N}_0, 0 \leq p < m$.

Remark 3. *The limiting case of a zero-order Riesz fractional integral (the Riesz potential) is described by the equation (see Equation (16) in [97], p. 23) in the form*

$$(I^0 f)(\mathbf{x}) = \lim_{\alpha \to 0+} (I^\alpha f)(\mathbf{x}) = f(\mathbf{x}). \tag{58}$$

Using Equation (58), one can see that

$$\lim_{\alpha \to 0+} \Delta (I^{\alpha+2} f)(\mathbf{x}) = - \lim_{\alpha \to 0+} (I^\alpha f)(\mathbf{x}), \tag{59}$$

gives

$$\Delta (I^2 f)(\mathbf{x}) = - (I^0 f)(\mathbf{x}) = - f(\mathbf{x}). \tag{60}$$

7. Fundamental Theorems of GFC in Riesz Form

Let us define a set of functions that is used in the first fundamental theorem of the GFC in the Riesz form.

Definition 9. *Let a function $K = K(|\mathbf{x}|)$ belong to the set $C_{-m}(\mathbb{R}^m)$, and let a function $f(x)$ can be represented in the form*

$$f(\mathbf{x}) = (I_{(K)} \varphi)(\mathbf{x}) \tag{61}$$

for all $\mathbf{x} \in \mathbb{R}$, where $\varphi(\mathbf{x}) \in C_{-m}(\mathbb{R}^m)$.

Then, the set of such functions $f(x)$ is denoted as $C_{-m,(K)}(\mathbb{R}^m)$.

Theorem 1 (First Fundamental Theorem for Riesz GFD of RLtype)**.** *Let (M, K) be a pair of the kernels from the set $\mathcal{R}_{2p}$.*

The Riesz GFD of the Riemann–Liouville type is a left inverse operator to the Riesz GFI and the equation

$$(D_{(K)} I_{(M)} f)(\mathbf{x}) = f(\mathbf{x}) \tag{62}$$

holds for all $\mathbf{x} \in \mathbb{R}$, if the function $f(\mathbf{x})$ belongs to the space $C_{-m}(\mathbb{R}^m)$.

Proof. To prove Equation (62), the definition of the Riesz GFD of the Riemann–Liouville type can be written in the form

$$(D_{(K)} g)(\mathbf{x}) = ((-\Delta)^p I_{(K)} g)(\mathbf{x}), \tag{63}$$

where one can use $g(\mathbf{x}) = (I_{(M)} f)(\mathbf{x})$. Then, the left side of Equation (62) takes the form

$$(D_{(K)} I_{(M)} f)(\mathbf{x}) = ((-\Delta)^p I_{(K)} I_{(M)} f)(\mathbf{x}) = f(\mathbf{x}). \tag{64}$$

Using that the Riesz GFI can be represented through the Fourier convolution and the fact that the pair (M, K) belongs to the set $\mathcal{R}_{2p}$, one can get

$$(D_{(K)} I_{(M)} f)(\mathbf{x}) = (-\Delta)^p (K * M * f)(\mathbf{x}) = (-\Delta)^p (M_{2p-m} * f)(\mathbf{x}) =$$

$$(-\Delta)^p (I_{(M_{2p-m})} f)(\mathbf{x}) = ((-\Delta)^p I^{2p} f)(\mathbf{x}) = f(\mathbf{x}), \tag{65}$$

where the equality

$$(\Delta I^2 h)(\mathbf{x}) = -h(\mathbf{x})$$

is used p times. □

Theorem 2 (First Fundamental Theorem for Riesz GFD of Caputo type)**.** *Let (M, K) be a pair of the kernels from the set $\mathcal{R}_{2p}$.*

The Riesz GFD of the Caputo type is a left inverse operator to the Riesz GFI and the equation

$$(D^{*}_{(K)}\, I_{(M)}\, f)(\mathbf{x}) \;=\; f(\mathbf{x}) \tag{66}$$

holds for all $\mathbf{x} \in \mathbb{R}$*, if the function* $f(\mathbf{x})$ *belongs to the set* $C_{-m,(K)}(\mathbb{R}^m)$.

Proof. To prove Equation (66), the definition of the Riesz GFD of the Caputo type can be written in the form

$$(D^{*}_{(K)}\, g)(\mathbf{x}) \;=\; (I_{(K)}\, (-\Delta)^p\, g)(\mathbf{x}), \tag{67}$$

where one can use $g(\mathbf{x}) = (I_{(M)}\, f)(\mathbf{x})$. Using the fact that $f(\mathbf{x})$ belongs to the set $C_{-m,(K)}(\mathbb{R}^m)$, where

$$f(\mathbf{x}) \;=\; (I_{(K)}\, \varphi)(\mathbf{x}), \tag{68}$$

one can represent the function $g(\mathbf{x})$ in the form

$$g(\mathbf{x}) \;=\; (I_{(M)}\, f)(\mathbf{x}) \;=\; (I_{(M)}\, I_{(K)}\, \varphi)(\mathbf{x}) \;=\; (M * K * \varphi)(\mathbf{x}). \tag{69}$$

Using the fact that the pair (M, K) belongs to the set $\mathcal{R}_{2p}$, i.e., $(M * K) = M_{2p-m}$ one can get

$$g(\mathbf{x}) \;=\; (M_{2p-m} * \varphi)(\mathbf{x}) \;=\; (I_{(M_{2p-m})}\, \varphi)(\mathbf{x}) \;=\; (I^{2p}\, \varphi)(\mathbf{x}). \tag{70}$$

Then, using Equation (70), Equation (67) takes the form

$$(D^{*}_{(K)}\, g)(\mathbf{x}) \;=\; (I_{(K)}\, (-\Delta)^p\, I^{2p}\, \varphi)(\mathbf{x}) \;=\; (I_{(K)}\, \varphi)(\mathbf{x}) \;=\; f(\mathbf{x}), \tag{71}$$

where the equality$(\Delta\, I^2\, h)(\mathbf{x}) = -h(\mathbf{x})$ is used p times and Equation (68) is taken into account. □

Theorem 3 (Second Fundamental Theorem for Riesz GFD of RL type). *Let* (M, K) *be a pair of the kernels from the set* $\mathcal{R}_{2p}$.

The Riesz GFD of the Riemann–Liouville type is a right inverse operator to the Riesz GFI and the equation

$$(I_{(M)}\, D_{(K)}\, f)(\mathbf{x}) \;=\; f(\mathbf{x}) \tag{72}$$

holds for all $\mathbf{x} \in \mathbb{R}$*, if the function* $f(\mathbf{x})$ *belongs to the space* $C_{-m,(M)}(\mathbb{R}^m)$.

Proof. To prove Equation (72), the definition of the Riesz GFD of the Riemann–Liouville type can be written in the form

$$(D_{(K)}\, f)(\mathbf{x}) \;=\; (-\Delta)^p\, (I_{(K)}\, f)(\mathbf{x}). \tag{73}$$

Using the fact that $f(\mathbf{x})$ belongs to the set $C_{-m,(M)}(\mathbb{R}^m)$, where

$$f(\mathbf{x}) \;=\; (I_{(M)}\, \varphi)(\mathbf{x}), \tag{74}$$

and the representation of the Riesz GFI as the Fourier convolution, the Riesz GFD (73) can be represented in the form

$$(D_{(K)}\, f)(\mathbf{x}) \;=\; (-\Delta)^p\, (I_{(K)}\, I_{(M)}\, \varphi)(\mathbf{x}) \;=\; (-\Delta)^p\, (K * M * \varphi)(\mathbf{x}). \tag{75}$$

Then, using the fact that the pair (M, K) belongs to the set $\mathcal{R}_{2p}$, Equation (75) gives

$$(D_{(K)}\, f)(\mathbf{x}) \;=\; (-\Delta)^p\, (K * M * \varphi)(\mathbf{x}) \;=\; (-\Delta)^p\, (M_{2p-m} * \varphi)(\mathbf{x}) \;=$$

$$(-\Delta)^p\, (I_{(M_{2p-m})}\, \varphi)(\mathbf{x}) \;=\; (-\Delta)^p\, (I^{2p}\, \varphi)(\mathbf{x}) \;=\; \varphi(\mathbf{x}), \tag{76}$$

where the equality $(\Delta\, I^2\, h)(\mathbf{x}) \;=\; -\, h(\mathbf{x})$ is used p times for $h_k \;=\; (I^{2(p-k)}\varphi),\, k \;=\; 1,\ldots,p$. Using Equation (76), the left side of Equation (72) takes the form

$$(I_{(M)}\, D_{(K)}\, f)(\mathbf{x}) \;=\; (I_{(M)}\, \varphi)(\mathbf{x}) \;=\; f(\mathbf{x}), \tag{77}$$

where Equation (74) is taken into account. □

Remark 4. *Using Equation (12) in [97], p. 21, in the form*

$$\Delta \frac{|\mathbf{x}|^{\alpha+2-m}}{H_m(\alpha+2)} \;=\; -\, \frac{|\mathbf{x}|^{\alpha-m}}{H_m(\alpha)}, \tag{78}$$

which can be written as

$$\Delta\, M_{\alpha+2-m}(\mathbf{x}) \;=\; -\, M_{\alpha-m}(\mathbf{x}), \tag{79}$$

and applying p times the Green's equation (see [97], p. 23) in the form

$$\int_{\mathbb{R}^m} f(\mathbf{y})\, \Delta\, g(\mathbf{y})\, d^m\mathbf{y} \;=\; \int_{\mathbb{R}^m} g(\mathbf{y})\, \Delta\, f(\mathbf{y})\, d^m\mathbf{y}, \tag{80}$$

the following equation is proved in [97] one can get

$$(I^\alpha\, f)(\mathbf{x}) \;=\; (-1)^p\, (I^{\alpha+2p}\, (-\Delta)^p\, f)(\mathbf{x}), \tag{81}$$

where $p \in \mathbb{N}$. Here it is assumed the following conditions: (A) the function $f(\mathbf{x})$ has continuous derivatives of any order $k \leq 2p$; (B) the function $f(\mathbf{x})$ and its derivatives behave at infinity in such a way that the integrals are absolutely convergent and that the integrations by parts are satisfied.

Using Equation (81), one can have the analytic extension of the operator $(I^\alpha\, f)(\mathbf{x})$ for any value of $\alpha \,>\, -2p$.

Let us give a formulation of the second fundamental theorem of the Riesz GF calculus.

Theorem 4 (Second Fundamental Theorem for Riesz GFD of C type). *Let $(M,\, K)$ be a pair of the kernels from the set $\mathcal{R}_{2p}$.*

The Riesz GFD of the Caputo type is a right inverse operator to the Riesz GFI and the equation

$$(I_{(M)}\, D^*_{(K)}\, f)(\mathbf{x}) \;=\; f(\mathbf{x}) \tag{82}$$

holds for all $\mathbf{x} \in \mathbb{R}$, if the function $f(\mathbf{x})$ belongs to the set $C^{2p}_{-m,(K)}(\mathbb{R}^m)$ and conditions of Remark 4 are satisfied for $f(\mathbf{x})$.

Proof. To prove Equation (82), one should use the definition of the Riesz GFD of the Caputo type has the form

$$(D^*_{(K)}\, f)(\mathbf{x}) \;=\; (I_{(K)}\, (-\Delta)^p\, f)(\mathbf{x}). \tag{83}$$

Then, using Equation (83) and the representation of the Riesz GFI as the Fourier convolution, the left side of Equation (82) takes the form

$$(I_{(M)}\, D^*_{(K)}\, f)(\mathbf{x}) \;=\; (I_{(M)}\, I_{(K)}\, (-\Delta)^p\, f)(\mathbf{x}) \;=\; (M * K * ((-\Delta)^p\, f))(\mathbf{x}). \tag{84}$$

Then, using the fact that the pair (M, K) belongs to the set $\mathcal{R}_{2p}$, Equation (84) gives

$$(I_{(M)} D^*_{(K)} f)(\mathbf{x}) = (M_{2p-m} * ((-\Delta)^p f))(\mathbf{x}) = (I_{(M_{2p-m})} (-\Delta)^p f)(\mathbf{x}) = (I^{2p} (-\Delta)^p f)(\mathbf{x}). \quad (85)$$

Using Equation (17) in [97], p. 23, with $\alpha = 0+$ in the form

$$(I^{\alpha+2p} (-\Delta)^p f)(\mathbf{x}) = (I^{\alpha} f)(\mathbf{x}) \quad (\alpha \to 0+) \quad (86)$$

for functions $f(\mathbf{x})$ that satisfy the conditions of Remark 4. As a result, Equation (85) gives Equation (82). □

Remark 5. *The assumptions about the properties of functions $f(\mathbf{x})$ and its derivatives, which are used in Remark 4, were put forward for the entire space $\mathbb{R}^m$. Equations become more complicated, if one can admit certain $(m-1)$-surfaces of discontinuity (see [97], p. 24). Let us restrict ourselves to the case where $f(\mathbf{x})$ is identically zero outside a closed surface S, sufficiently regular, while the function $f(\mathbf{x})$ and the derivatives thereof intervene are continuous in the closed domain bounded by this surface, without canceling out on the surface, in general.*

Using the Riesz fractional integral that is defined as

$$(I^{\alpha} f)(\mathbf{x}) = \int_{\Omega} \frac{|\mathbf{x} - \mathbf{y}|^{\alpha - m}}{H_m(\alpha)} f(\mathbf{y})\, d^m\mathbf{y}, \quad (87)$$

and the Green's equation, one can get (see Equation (20) in [97], p. 24) the equation

$$(I^{\alpha} f)(\mathbf{x}) = (I^{\alpha+2p} (-\Delta)^p f)(\mathbf{x}) +$$

$$\sum_{k=1}^{p} \int_S \left(\left((-\Delta)^{k-2} f\right)(\mathbf{y}) \frac{dM_{\alpha+2k-m}(|\mathbf{x}-\mathbf{y}|)}{dn} - \frac{d(-\Delta)^{k-1} f(\mathbf{y})}{dn} M_{\alpha+2k-m}(|\mathbf{x}-\mathbf{y}|) \right) dS, \quad (88)$$

where

$$M_{\alpha+2k-m}(|\mathbf{x}|) = \frac{|\mathbf{x}|^{\alpha+2k-m}}{H_m(\alpha+2k)}, \quad (89)$$

and n is the normal to the point $\mathbf{y}(y_1, \dots y_m)$ of S directed towards the interior of this surface, and dS the surface element around the point $Q(y_1, \dots y_m)$.

As a special case of Equation (88) one can consider the limit $\alpha \to 0+$, to get

$$(I^{2p} (-\Delta)^p f)(\mathbf{x}) = f(\mathbf{x}) -$$

$$\sum_{k=1}^{p} \int_S \left(\left((-\Delta)^{k-2} f\right)(\mathbf{y}) \frac{dM_{2k-m}(|\mathbf{x}-\mathbf{y}|)}{dn} - \frac{d(-\Delta)^{k-1} f(\mathbf{y})}{dn} M_{2k-m}(|\mathbf{x}-\mathbf{y}|) \right) dS. \quad (90)$$

Taking into account Remark 5, the second fundamental theorem for Riesz GFD of Caputo type can be formulated in the following more general form.

Theorem 5 (Second Fundamental Theorem for Riesz GFD of C type in general form). *Let (M, K) be a pair of the kernels from the set $\mathcal{R}_{2p}$.*

Let function $f(\mathbf{x})$ belongs to the space $C^{2p}_{-m,(K)}(\mathbb{R}^m)$ and let $f(\mathbf{x})$ be identically zero outside a closed surface S, sufficiently regular, while the function $f(\mathbf{x})$ and the derivatives thereof intervene are continuous in the closed domain bounded by this surface.

Then, the action of the Riesz GFD of the Caputo type on the Riesz GFI is described by the equation

$$(I_{(M)}\, D^{*}_{(K)}\, f)(\mathbf{x}) \; = $$

$$f(\mathbf{x}) - \sum_{k=1}^{p} \int_{S} \Big(\big((-\Delta)^{k-2} f \big)(\mathbf{y}) \, \frac{d M_{2k-m}(|\mathbf{x} - \mathbf{y}|)}{dn} \; - \; \frac{d (-\Delta)^{k-1} f(\mathbf{y})}{dn} \, M_{2k-m}(|\mathbf{x} - \mathbf{y}|) \Big)\, dS \quad (91)$$

holds for all $\mathbf{x} \in \mathbb{R}$.

Proof. To prove Equation (91), one can use the proof of Theorem 4 and repeat the transformation from Equation (83) to Equation (85). Then, using Equation (85) in the form

$$(I_{(M)}\, D^{*}_{(K)}\, f)(\mathbf{x}) \; = \; (I^{2p}\, (-\Delta)^{p}\, f)(\mathbf{x}), \quad (92)$$

where one should be used Equation (90) of Remark 5 to get equality (91). □

8. Conclusions

An extension of the general fractional calculus in Luchko's form to the multi-dimensional case was first proposed in [87]. Then, this calculus was applied to construct nonlocal physical models in [90–92,94] and nonlocal probability theory [93]. However, this extension did not use the entire multi-dimensional Euclidean space $\mathbb{R}^m$.

In this paper, an extension of the general fractional calculus, which takes into account the entire multi-dimensional Euclidean space $\mathbb{R}^m$, is proposed. The suggested extension of the GFC is in fact a generalization of the well-known fractional Riesz calculus [1,97,98] from power-type operator kernels to a wider class of operator kernels. The proposed multi-dimensional form of GFC can also be considered as an extension GFC from positive real line, which is used in [76–85], and the Laplace convolution to the entire m-dimensional Euclidean space and the Fourier convolution.

Let us briefly list the main results of this work.

(a) The general fractional integrals and derivatives are defined as convolution type operators. In these definitions the Fourier convolution on m-dimensional Euclidean space is used instead of the Laplace convolution on positive semi-axis. These operators are called the Riesz general fractional operators.

(b) The sets of operator kernels for general fractional operators in the Riesz form are described. The spaces of functions, for which the proposed operators exist, are also described.

(c) Some basic properties of the proposed Riesz general fractional integrals and the Riesz general fractional operators are considered.

(d) The general fractional analogs of first and second fundamental theorems of calculus are proved for the general fractional operators.

(e) The fractional calculus of the Riesz potential and the Riesz fractional Laplacian are special cases of proposed general fractional calculus in the Riesz form.

Let us describe some possibility of future research in the framework of the proposed approach to building a general fractional calculus of the Riesz type and possible generalizations of the proposed multi-dimensional general fractional calculus.

(M1) It is important, the derive the series representations of kernels that belongs to the set, which will be analogous of the Sonin representations proposed in [52,53] and described by Equations (21)–(23) in Luchko papers [76,77].

(M2) It is important to get various examples of the operator pairs that belongs to the set $\mathcal{R}^m_{2p}$, which can be considered as analogs of the examples of the operator kernels that are given in Table 1 in [90], page 6 and [91], p.15. (see also [93], pp. 22–23, [92], p. 6, [94], p. 11).

(M3) It should be noted that Riesz proposed a fractional calculus not only for the Euclidean space, but also for the Minkowski space, which is actively used in relativistic physics. Therefore it is important to extend the proposed general fractional operators of the Riesz form from the Euclidean space, but also for the Minkowski space by using results of the Riesz paper [97] and the propose work.

(M4) The proposed GF derivatives of the Riesz form can be interpreted as GF Laplacians of the Riesz form. The GF integrals of the Riesz form can be interpreted as GF Riesz potentials. It is interesting to derive an exact discretization of the general fractional Laplacian of the Riesz form by using the approach, which is is proposed in [128]. This exact discrete GF Laplacian can be considered as an extension of the exact discretization of the Riesz fractional Laplacian proposed in [129]. Note that exact finite differences of integer and fractional orders are proposed in [128–130] are a generalization in some sense of the Mickens non-standard finite differences (see papers [131–133] and bookd [134–136]). Note that exact finite differences of integer order satisfy the same characteristic algebraic identities and properties as derivatives of integer order. Note that non-standard finite difference are used for fractional-order differential equations [137]. The exact fractional differences can be considered as an exact discrete analog of the fractional-order operators of the Riesz type, which are connected by the transform operation preserving algebraic structure. Note the exact discretization of the Riesz fractional Laplacian in proposed in [129]. One can assume that exact general fractional differences can also defined as discrete analogs of the proposed general fractional operators of the Riesz form.

(M5) A lattice analog of fractional calculus in the Riesz form is proposed in papers [113–115]. This lattice fractional calculus can also be generalized from power-type operator kernels to a wider class of operator kernels by used the proposed multi-dimensional general fractional calculus. This lattice GFC calculus can be important in application to physical lattice models with long-range interactions, including the lattice models in quantum field theory [120].

Let us describe briefly some important elements for future research in applications of the proposed approach to formulate nonlocal physical models by using general fractional calculus of the Riesz type. Note that the proposed GF derivatives of the Riesz form can be interpreted as GF Laplacians of the Riesz form. The GF integrals of the Riesz form can be interpreted as GF Riesz potentials. These interpretations of the proposed GF operators largely dictate their possible applications in physics and mechanics.

(P1) The proposed GF derivatives of the Riesz form (the GF Laplacians of the Riesz form) can be used to generalize results proposed in papers for fractional gravity theory [117,138,139] and general nonlocal gravity theory [92].

(P2) The proposed GF derivatives of the Riesz form (the GF Laplacians of the Riesz form) can be used to generalize results proposed in papers [140–142], to describe electrodynamics of plasma-like media [143–145] and spatial dispersion in crystal optics [146–148]. Nonlocal models of such media can be considered as a special form of general nonlocal electrodynamics [91].

(P3) The GF Laplacians of the Riesz form (GF derivatives of the Riesz form) can be used to describe wide class of nonlocality in the framework of fractional gradient elasticity models of media with spatial dispersion. The models with GF Laplacian will be generalizations of the fractional gradient elasticity models that are the first time proposed proposed in [149,150] (see aalso [151,152]. These models an also be considered in the framework of the general nonlocal comtinuum mechan that is proposed in [90].

(P4) The GF Laplacians of the Riesz form can be useful to describe chaotic systems with long-range interaction [153,154].

(P5) The proposed general fractional derivatives (GF Laplacians) of the Riesz form can be used to generalized the fractional Schrodinger equation, which are described by Laskin in [155,156] (see also important comments in [157–159]). The general form of operator kenlals can be also important in nonlocal quantum field theory [120].

Funding: This research received no external funding.

Institutional Review Board Statement: Not applicable.

Informed Consent Statement: Not applicable.

Data Availability Statement: Not applicable.

Conflicts of Interest: The authors declare no conflict of interest.

References

1. Samko, S.G.; Kilbas, A.A.; Marichev, O.I. *Fractional Integrals and Derivatives: Theory and Applications*; Gordon and Breach: New York, NY, USA, 1993.
2. Kiryakova, V. *Generalized Fractional Calculus and Applications*; Longman and J. Wiley: New York, NY, USA, 1994; ISBN 9780582219779.
3. Podlubny, I. *Fractional Differential Equations*; Academic Press: San Diego, CA, USA, 1998; ISBN 978-0-12-558840-9.
4. Kilbas, A.A.; Srivastava, H.M.; Trujillo, J.J. *Theory and Applications of Fractional Differential Equations*; Elsevier: Amsterdam, The Netherlands, 2006; ISBN 9780444518323.
5. Diethelm, F. *The Analysis of Fractional Differential Equations. An Application-Oriented Exposition Using Differential Operators of Caputo Type*; Springer: Berlin/Heidelberg, Germany, 2010. [CrossRef]
6. Kochubei, A.; Yu, L. (Eds.) *Handbook of Fractional Calculus with Applications*; Basic Theory Series; Walter de Gruyter GmbH: Berlin, Germany; Boston, MA, USA, 2019; Volume 1, 481p. [CrossRef]
7. Kochubei, A.; Yu, L. (Eds.) *Handbook of Fractional Calculus with Applications*; Fractional Differential Equations Series; Walter de Gruyter GmbH: Berlin, Germany; Boston, MA, USA, 2019; Volume 2. [CrossRef]
8. Beghin, L.; Mainardi, F.; Garrappa, R. *Nonlocal and Fractional Operators*; Springer: Cham, Switzerland, 2021; 308p. [CrossRef]
9. Tarasov, V.E. *Fractional Dynamics: Applications of Fractional Calculus to Dynamics of Particles, Fields and Media*; Springer: New York, NY, USA, 2010. [CrossRef]
10. Klafter, J.; Lim, S.C.; Metzler, R. (Eds.) *Fractional Dynamics. Recent Advances*; World Scientific: Singapore, 2011. [CrossRef]
11. Mainardi, F. *Fractional Calculus and Waves in Linear Viscoelasticity: An Introduction to Mathematical Models*; World Scientific: Singapore, 2010. [CrossRef]
12. Uchaikin, V.; Sibatov, R. *Fractional Kinetics in Solids: Anomalous Probability Transport in Semiconductors, Dielectrics and Nanosystems*; World Scientific: Singapore, 2013. [CrossRef]
13. Atanackovic, T.; Pilipovic, S.; Stankovic, B.; Zorica, D. *Fractional Calculus with Applications in Mechanics: Vibrations and Diffusion Processes*; Wiley-ISTE: London, UK, 2014.
14. Atanackovic, T.; Pilipovic, S.; Stankovic, B.; Zorica, D. *Fractional Calculus with Applications in Mechanics: Wave Propagation, Impact and Variational Principles*; Wiley-ISTE: London, UK, 2014.
15. Povstenko, Y. *Fractional Thermoelasticity*; Springer International Publishing: Cham, Switzerland; Heidelberg, Germanny; New York, NY, USA; Dordrecht, The Netherland; London, UK, 2015. [CrossRef]
16. Uchaikin, V.; Sibatov, R. *Fractional Kinetics in Space. Anomalous Transport Models*; Worls Scientific: Singapore, 2018. [CrossRef]
17. MDPI. *Mathematical Economics: Application of Fractional Calculus*; MDPI: Basel, Switzerland, 2020. . [CrossRef]
18. Tarasov, V.E.; Tarasova, V.V. *Economic Dynamics with Memory: Fractional Calculus Approach*; De Gruyter: Berlin, Germany, 2021; 602p. [CrossRef]
19. Tarasov, V.E. *Handbook of Fractional Calculus with Applications. Volume 4. Application in Physics. Part A*; Walter de Gruyter GmbH: Berlin, Germany, 2019. [CrossRef]
20. Tarasov, V.E. *Handbook of Fractional Calculus with Applications. Volume 5. Application in Physics. Part B*; Walter de Gruyter GmbH: Berlin, Germany, 2019. [CrossRef]
21. Mainardi, F. Considerations on fractional calculus: Interpretations and applications. In *Transform Methods and Special Functions*; Rusev, P., Dimovski, I., Kiryakova, V., Eds.; Bulgarian Academy of Sciences: Sofia, Bulgaria, 1998; pp. 594–597, ISBN 954-8986-05-1.
22. Gorenflo, R. Afterthoughts on interpretation of fractional derivatives and integrals. In *Transform Methods and Special Functions*; Rusev, P., Dimovski, I., Kiryakova, V., Eds.; Bulgarian Academy of Sciences: Sofia, Bulgaria, 1998; pp. 589–591, ISBN 954-8986-05-1.
23. Kiryakova, V. A long standing conjecture failes? In *Transform Methods and Special Functions*; Rusev, P.; Dimovski, I.; Kiryakova, V., Eds.; Bulgarian Academy of Sciences: Sofia, Bulgaria, 1998; pp. 579–588.
24. Butkovskii, A.G.; Postnov, S.S.; Postnova, E.A. Fractional integro-differential calculus and its control-theoretical applications. I. Mathematical fundamentals and the problem of interpretation. *Autom. Remote Control* **2013**, *74*, 543–574. [CrossRef]
25. Nigmatullin, R.R. A fractional integral and its physical interpretation. *Theor. Math. Phys.* **1992**, *90*, 242–251. [CrossRef]
26. Rutman, R.S. A fractional integral and its physical interpretation. *Theor. Math. Phys.* **1994**, *100*, 1154–1156. [CrossRef]
27. Rutman, R.S. On physical interpretations of fractional integration and differentiation. *Theor. Math. Phys.* **1995**, *105*, 1509–1519. [CrossRef]
28. Mainardi, F. Fractional relaxation-oscillation and fractional diffusion-wave phenomena. *Chaos Solitons Fractals* **1996**, *7*, 1461–1477. [CrossRef]
29. Heymans, N.; Podlubny, I. Physical interpretation of initial conditions for fractional differential equations with Riemann-Liouville fractional derivatives. *Rheol. Acta* **2006**, 45, 765–772. [CrossRef]
30. Molz, F.J.; Fix, G.J.; Lu, S. A physical interpretation for the fractional derivatives in Levy diffusion. *Appl. Math. Lett.* **2002**, *15*, 907–911. [CrossRef]
31. Podlubny, I.; Despotovic, V.; Skovranek, T.; McNaughton, B.H. Shadows on the walls: Geometric interpretation of fractional integration. *J. Online Math. Its Appl.* **2007**, *7*, 1664.
32. Herrmann, R. Towards a geometric interpretation of generalized fractional integrals—Erdelyi-Kober type integrals on R^N, as an example. *Fract. Calc. Appl. Anal.* **2014**, *17*, 361–370. [CrossRef]
33. Tarasov, V.E. Geometric interpretation of fractional-order derivative. *Fract. Calc. Appl. Anal.* **2016**, *19*, 1200–1221. [CrossRef]

34. Husain, H.S.; Sultana, M. Principal parts of a vector bundle on projective line and the fractional derivative. *Turk. J. Math.* **2019**, *43*, 3. [CrossRef]
35. Podlubny, I. Geometrical and physical interpretation of fractional integration and fractional differentiation. *Fract. Calc. Appl. Anal.* **2002**, *5*, 367–386.
36. Moshrefi-Torbati, M.; Hammond, J.K. Physical and geometrical interpretation of fractional operators. *J. Frankl. Inst.* **1998**, *335*, 1077–1086. [CrossRef]
37. Tavassoli, M.H.; Tavassoli, A.; Ostad Rahimi, M.R. The geometric and physical interpretation of fractional order derivatives of polynomial functions. *Differ. Geom.-Dyn. Syst.* **2013**, *15*, 93–104.
38. Cioc, R. Physical and geometrical interpretation of Grünwald-Letnikov differintegrals: Measurement of path and acceleration. *Fract. Calc. Appl. Anal.* **2016**, *19*, 161–172. [CrossRef]
39. Tarasova, V.V.; Tarasov, V.E. Economic interpretation of fractional derivatives. *Prog. Fract. Differ. Appl.* **2017**, *3*, 1–7. [CrossRef]
40. Rehman, H.U.; Darus, M.; Salah, J. A note on Caputo's derivative operator interpretation in economy. *J. Appl. Math.* **2018**, *2018*, 1260240. [CrossRef]
41. Stanislavsky, A.A. Probability interpretation of the integral of fractional order. *Theor. Math. Phys.* **2004**, *138*, 418–431. [CrossRef]
42. Tenreiro Machado, J.A. A probabilistic interpretation of the fractional-order differentiation. *Fract. Calc. Appl. Anal.* **2009**, *6*, 73–80.
43. Tenreiro Machado, J.A. Fractional derivatives: Probability interpretation and frequency response of rational approximations. *Commun. Nonlinear Sci. Numer. Simul.* **2009**, *14*, 3492–3497. [CrossRef]
44. Tarasov, V.E.; Tarasova, S.S. Probabilistic interpretation of Kober fractional integral of non-integer order. *Prog. Fract. Differ. Appl.* **2019**, *5*, 1–5. [CrossRef]
45. Tarasov, V.E.; Tarasova, S.S. Fractional and integer derivatives with continuously distributed lag. *Commun. Nonlinear Sci. Numer. Simul.* **2019**, *70*, 125–169. [CrossRef]
46. Tarasov, V.E. Interpretation of fractional derivatives as reconstruction from sequence of integer derivatives. *Fundam. Informaticae* **2017**, *151*, 431–442. [CrossRef]
47. Tarasov, V.E. Entropy interpretation of Hadamard type fractional operators: Fractional cumulative entropy. *Entropy* **2022**, *24*, 1852. [CrossRef] [PubMed]
48. Luchko, Y. Fractional derivatives and the fundamental theorem of fractional calculus. *Fract. Calc. Appl. Anal.* **2020**, 23, 939–966. [CrossRef]
49. Hilfer, R.; Luchko, Y. Desiderata for fractional derivatives and integrals. *Mathematics* **2019**, *7*, 149, . [CrossRef]
50. Diethelm, K.; Garrappa, R.; Giusti, A.; Stynes, M. Why fractional derivatives with nonsingular kernels should not be used. *Factional Calc. Appl. Anal.* **2020**, *23*, 610–634. [CrossRef]
51. Hanyga, A. A comment on a controversial issue: A generalized fractional derivative cannot have a regular kernel. *Fract. Calc. Appl. Anal.* **2020**, *23*, 211–223. [CrossRef]
52. Sonine, N. On the generalization of an Abel formula. (Sur la generalisation d'une formule d'Abel). *Acta Math.* **1884**, 4, 171–176. (In French) [CrossRef]
53. Sonin, N.Y. On the generalization of an Abel formula. In *Investigations of Cylinder Functions and Special Polynomials*; GTTI: Moscow, Russia, 1954; pp. 148–154. Available online: https://ur.zlibcdn2.com/book/2157173/2a8410 (accessed on 22 February 2023).
54. Rogosin, S.; Dubatovskaya, M. Fractional calculus in Russia at the end of XIX century. *Mathematics* **2021**, *9*, 1736. [CrossRef]
55. Kochubei, A.N. General fractional calculus, evolution equations and renewal processes. *Integral Equations Oper. Theory* **2011**, *71*, 583–600. [CrossRef]
56. Samko, S.G.; Cardoso, R.P. Integral equations of the first kind of Sonine type. *Int. J. Math. Math. Sci.* **2003**, *57*, 3609–3632. [CrossRef]
57. Samko, S.G.; Cardoso, R.P. Sonine integral equations of the first kind in $L_y(0;b)$. *Fract. Calc. Appl. Anal.* **2003**, *6*, 235–258.
58. Toaldo, B. Convolution-type derivatives, hitting times of subordinators and time-changed C_0-semigroups. *Potential Anal.* **2015**, *42*, 115–140. [CrossRef]
59. Luchko, Y.; Yamamoto, M. General time-fractional diffusion equation: Some uniqueness and existence results for the initial-boundary-value problems. *Fract. Calc. Appl. Anal.* **2016**, *19*, 675–695. [CrossRef]
60. Luchko, Y.; Yamamoto, M. The general fractional derivative and related fractional differential equations. *Mathematics* **2020**, *8*, 2115. [CrossRef]
61. Kochubei, A.N.; Kondratiev, Y.G. Fractional kinetic hierarchies and intermittency. Kinetic and related models. *Am. Inst. Math. Sci.* **2017**, *10*, 725–740. [CrossRef]
62. Kochubei A.N.; Kondratiev, Y.G. Growth equation of the general fractional calculus. *Mathematics* **2019**, *7*, 615. [CrossRef]
63. Kondratiev, Y.; da Silva, J. Cesaro limits for fractional dynamics. *Fractal Fract.* **2021**, 5, 133, . [CrossRef]
64. Sin, C.-S. Well-posedness of general Caputo-type fractional differential equations. *Fract. Calc. Appl. Anal.* **2018**, *21*, 819–832. [CrossRef]
65. Kochubei, A.N. General fractional calculus. Chapter 5. In *Handbook of Fractional Calculus with Applications. Volume 1. Basic Theory*; Kochubei, A., Luchko, Y., Machado, J.A.T., Eds.; De Gruyter: Berlin, Germany, 2019; pp. 111–126. [CrossRef]
66. Kochubei, A.N. Equations with general fractional time derivatives. Cauchy problem. Chapter 11. In *Handbook of Fractional Calculus with Applications. Volume 2. Fractional Differential Equations*; Machado, J.A.T., Ed.; De Gruyter: Berlin, Germany, 2019; pp. 223–234. [CrossRef]

67. Kinash, N.; Janno, J. Inverse problems for a generalized subdiffusion equation with final overdetermination. *Math. Model. Anal.* **2019**, *24*, 236–262. [CrossRef]
68. Kinash, N.; Janno, J. An inverse problem for a generalized fractional derivative with an application in reconstruction of time- and space- dependent sources in fractional diffusion and wave equations. *Mathematics* **2019**, *7*, 1138. [CrossRef]
69. Ascione, G. Abstract Cauchy problems for the generalized fractional calculus. *Nonlinear Anal.* **2021**, 209, 112339. [CrossRef]
70. Giusti, A. General fractional calculus and Prabhakar's theory. *Commun. Nonlinear Sci. Numer. Simul.* **2020**, 83, 105114. [CrossRef]
71. Bazhlekova, E. Estimates for a general fractional relaxation equation and application to an inverse source problem. *Math. Methods Appl. Sci.* **2018**, *41*, 9018–9026. [CrossRef]
72. Bazhlekova, E.; Bazhlekov, I. Identification of a space-dependent source term in a nonlocal problem for the general time-fractional diffusion equation. *J. Comput. Appl. Math.* **2021**, *386*, 113213. [CrossRef]
73. Atanackovic, T.M.; Pilipovic, S. Zener model with deneral fractional calculus: Thermodynamical restrictions. *Fractal Fract.* **2022**, *6*, 617. [CrossRef]
74. Miskovic-Stankovic, V.; Janev, M.; Atanackovic, T.M., Two compartmental fractional derivative model with general fractional derivative. *J. Pharmacokinet. Pharmacodyn.* **2022**, 1–9. [CrossRef] [PubMed]
75. Al-Refai, M.; Fernandez, A. Generalising the fractional calculus with Sonine kernels via conjugations. *J. Comput. Appl. Math.* **2023**, *427*, 115159. [CrossRef]
76. Luchko, Y. General fractional integrals and derivatives with the Sonine kernels. *Mathematics* **2021**, *9*, 594. [CrossRef]
77. Luchko, Y. General fractional integrals and derivatives of arbitrary order. *Symmetry* **2021**, *13*, 755, . [CrossRef]
78. Luchko, Y. Operational calculus for the general fractional derivatives with the Sonine kernels. *Fract. Calc. Appl. Anal.* **2021**, *24*, 338–375. [CrossRef]
79. Luchko, Y. Special functions of fractional calculus in the form of convolution series and their applications. *Mathematics* **2021**, *9*, 2132. [CrossRef]
80. Luchko, Y. Convolution series and the generalized convolution Taylor formula. *Fract. Calc. Appl. Anal.* **2022**, *25*, 207–228. [CrossRef]
81. Luchko, Y. Fractional differential equations with the general fractional derivatives of arbitrary order in the Riemann-Liouville sense. *Mathematics* **2022**, *10*, 849. [CrossRef]
82. Luchko, Y. The 1st level general fractional derivatives and some of their properties. *J. Math. Sci.* **2022**. [CrossRef]
83. Al-Kandari, M.; Hanna, L.A.M.; Luchko, Y., Operational calculus for the general fractional derivatives of arbitrary order. *Mathematics* **2022**, *10*, 1590. [CrossRef]
84. Al-Refai, M.; Luchko, Y. Comparison principles for solutions to the fractional differential inequalities with the general fractional derivatives and their applications. *J. Differ. Equations* **2022**, *319*, 312–324. [CrossRef]
85. Al-Refai, M.; Luchko, Y. The general fractional integrals and derivatives on a finite interval. *Mathematics* **2023**, *11*, 1031. [CrossRef]
86. Tarasov, V.E. General fractional calculus: Multi-kernel approach. *Mathematics* **2021**, *9*, 1501. [CrossRef]
87. Tarasov, V.E. General fractional vector calculus. *Mathematics* **2021**, *9*, 2816. [CrossRef]
88. Tarasov, V.E. General fractional dynamics. *Mathematics* **2021**, *9*, 1464. [CrossRef]
89. Tarasov, V.E. General non-Markovian quantum dynamics. *Entropy* **2021**, *23*, 1006. [CrossRef]
90. Tarasov, V.E. General non-local continuum mechanics: Derivation of balance Equations. *Mathematics* **2022**, *10*, 1427. [CrossRef]
91. Tarasov, V.E. General non-local electrodynamics: Equations and non-local effects. *Ann. Phys.* **2022**, *445*, 169082. [CrossRef]
92. Tarasov, V.E. Nonlocal classical theory of gravity: Massiveness of nonlocality and mass shielding by nonlocality. *Eur. Phys. J. Plus* **2022**, *137*, 1336. [CrossRef]
93. Tarasov, V.E. Nonlocal probability theory: General fractional calculus approach. *Mathematics* **2022**, *10*, 848. [CrossRef]
94. Tarasov, V.E. Nonlocal statistical mechanics: General fractional Liouville equations and their solutions. *Phys. A Stat. Mech. Its Appl.* **2023**, *609*, 128366. [CrossRef]
95. Diethelm, K.; Kiryakova, V.; Luchko, Y.; Tenreiro Machado, J.A.; Tarasov, V.E. Trends, directions for further research, and some open problems of fractional calculus. *Nonlinear Dyn.* **2022**, *107*, 3245–3270. [CrossRef]
96. Riesz, M. L'integrale de Riemann-Liouville et le probleme de Cauchy pour l'equation des ondes. *Bull. Soc. Math. Fr.* **1939**, *67*, 153–170. Available online: https://eudml.org/doc/86724 (accessed on 22 February 2023). [CrossRef]
97. Riesz, M. L'intégrale de Riemann-Liouville et le probléme de Cauchy. *Acta Math.* **1949**, *81*, 1–222. (In French) [CrossRef]
98. Prado, H.; Rivero, M.; Trujillo, J.J.; Velasco, M.P. New results from old investigation: A note on fractional m-dimensional differential operators. The fractional Laplacian. *Fract. Calc. Appl. Anal.* **2015**, *18*, 290–306. [CrossRef]
99. Lizorkin, P.I. Characterization of the spaces $L^r_p(\mathbb{R}^n)$ in terms of difference singular integrals. *Mat. Sb.* **1970**, *81*, 79–91. (In Russian)
100. Feller, W. On a generalization of Marcel Riesz potentials and the semi-groups generated by them. In *Meddelanden Lunds Universitetes Matematiska Seminarium (Comm. Sem. Mathem. Universite de Lund)*; Tome Suppl. dedie a M. Riesz; C. W. K. Gleerup: Lund, Sweden, 1952; pp. 73–81.
101. Samko, S. Convolution and potential type operators in $L^{p(x)}$. *Integral Transform. Spec. Funct.* **1998**, *7*, 261–284. [CrossRef]
102. Samko, S. Convolution type operators in $L^{p(x)}$. *Integral Transform. Spec. Funct.* **1998**, *7*, 123–144. [CrossRef]
103. Samko, S. On local summability of Riesz potentials in the case $Re\alpha > 0$. *Anal. Math.* **1999**, *25*, 205–210. [CrossRef]
104. Samko, S. On a progress in the theory of Lebesgue spaces with variable exponent: Maximal and singular operators. *Integral Transform. Spec. Funct.* **2005**, *16*, 461–482. [CrossRef]
105. Samko, S. A new approach to the inversion of the Riesz potential operator. *Fract. Calc. Appl. Anal.* **1998**, *1*, 225–245.

106. Rafeiro, H.; Samko, S. Approximative method for the inversion of the Riesz potential operator in variable Lebesgue spaces. *Fract. Calc. Appl. Anal.* **2008**, *11*, 269–280.
107. Rafeiro, H.; Samko, S. On multidimensional analogue of Marchaud formula for fractional Riesz-type derivatives in domains in R^n. *Fract. Calc. Appl. Anal.* **2005**, *8*, 393–401.
108. Almeida, A.; Samko, S. Characterization of Riesz and Bessel potentials on variable Lebesgue spaces. *J. Funct. Spaces Appl.* **2006**, *4*, 113–144. [CrossRef]
109. Samko, S.G. On spaces of Riesz potentials. *Math. USSR-Izv.* **1976**, *10*, 1089–1117. . [CrossRef]
110. Ortigueira, M.D.; Laleg-Kirati, T.-M.; Tenreiro Machado, J.A. Riesz potential versus fractional Laplacian. *J. Stat. Mech. Theory Exp.* **2014**, *2014*, 09032. [CrossRef]
111. Cerutti, R.A.; Trione, S.E. The inversion of Marcel Riesz ultrahyperbolic causal operators. *Appl. Math. Lett.* **1999**, *12*, 25–30. [CrossRef]
112. Cerutti, R.A.; Trione, S.E. Some properties of the generalized causal and anticausal Riesz potentials. *Appl. Math. Lett.* **2000**, *13*, 129–136. [CrossRef]
113. Tarasov, V.E. Toward lattice fractional vector calculus. *J. Phys. A* **2014**, *47*, 355204. [CrossRef]
114. Tarasov, V.E. Lattice fractional calculus. *Appl. Math. Comput.* **2015**, *257*, 12–33. [CrossRef]
115. Tarasov, V.E. United lattice fractional integro-differentiation. *Fract. Calc. Appl. Anal.* **2016**, *19*, 625–664. [CrossRef]
116. Darve, E.; D'Elia, M.; Garrappa, R.; Giusti, A.; Rubio, N.L., On the fractional Laplacian of variable order. *Fract. Calc. Appl. Anal.* **2022**, *25*, 15–28. [CrossRef]
117. Giusti, A.; Garrappa, R.; Vachon, G. On the Kuzmin model in fractional Newtonian gravity. *Eur. Phys. J. Plus* **2020**, *135*, 1–12. [CrossRef]
118. Sitnik, S.M.; Fedorov, V.E.; Polovinkina, M.V.; Polovinkin, I.P. On recovery of the singular differential Laplace-Bessel operator from the Fourier-Bessel transform. *Mathematics* **2023**, *11*, 1103. [CrossRef]
119. Tarasov, V.E. Lattice model of fractional gradient and integral elasticity: Long-range interaction of Grunwald-Letnikov-Riesz type. *Mech. Mater.* **2014**, *70*, 106–114. [CrossRef]
120. Tarasov, V.E. Fractional quantum field theory: From lattice to continuum. *Adv. High Energy Phys.* **2014**, *2014*, 957863, . [CrossRef]
121. Tarasov, V.E. Fractional-order difference equations for physical lattices and some applications. *J. Math. Phys.* **2015**, *56*, 103506. [CrossRef]
122. Tarasov, V.E. Three-dimensional lattice models with long-range interactions of Grunwald-Letnikov type for fractional generalization of gradient elasticity. *Meccanica* **2016**, *51*, 125–138. . [CrossRef]
123. Lischke, A.; Pang, G.; Gulian, M.; Song, F.; Glusa, C.; Zheng, X.; Mao, Z.; Cai, W.; Meerschaert, M.M.; Ainsworth, M.; et al. What is the fractional Laplacian? A comparative review with new results. *J. Comput. Phys.* **2020**, *404*, 109009. [CrossRef]
124. Stinga, P.R. User's guide to the fractional Laplacian and the method of semigroups. In *Handbook of Fractional Calculus with Applications. Volume 2. Fractional Differential Equations*; Kochubei, A., Luchko, Y., Eds.; Walter de Gruyter GmbH: Berlin, Germany, 2019; pp. 235–265. [CrossRef]
125. Kwasnicki, M. Ten equivalent definitions of the fractional Laplace operator. *Fract. Calc. Appl. Anal.* **2017**, *20*, 7–51. [CrossRef]
126. Stein, E.M.; Weiss, G. *Introduction to Fourier Analysis on Euclidean Spaces*; Princeton University Press: Princeton, NJ, USA, 1971; ISBN 069108078X.
127. Young, W.H. On the multiplication of successions of Fourier constants. *Proc. R. Soc. A* **1912**, *87*, 331–339. [CrossRef]
128. Tarasov, V.E. Exact discretization by Fourier transforms. *Commun. Nonlinear Sci. Numer. Simul.* **2016**, *37*, 31–61. [CrossRef]
129. Tarasov, V.E. Exact discretization of fractional Laplacian. *Comput. Math. Appl.* **2017**, *73*, 855–863. [CrossRef]
130. Tarasov, V.E. Exact discrete analogs of derivatives of integer orders: Differences as infinite series. *J. Math.* **2015**, *2015*, 134842. [CrossRef]
131. Mickens, R.E. Difference equation models of differential equations. *Math. Comput. Model.* **1988**, *11*, 528–530. [CrossRef]
132. Mickens, R.E. Discretizations of nonlinear differential equations using explicit nonstandard methods. *J. Comput. Appl. Math.* **1999**, *110*, 181–185. [CrossRef]
133. Mickens, R.E. Nonstandard finite difference schemes for differential equations. *J. Differ. Equations Appl.* **2002**, *8*, 823–847. [CrossRef]
134. Mickens, R.E. *Nonstandard Finite Difference Models of Differential Equations*; World Scientific: Singapore, 1994. [CrossRef]
135. Mickens, R.E. (Ed.) *Applications of Nonstandard Finite Difference Schemes*; World Scientific: Singapore, 2000. [CrossRef]
136. Mickens, R.E. (Ed.) *Advances in the Applications of Nonstandard Finite Difference Schemes*; World Scientific: Singapore, 2005. [CrossRef]
137. Ongun, M.Y.; Arslan, D.; Garrappa, R. Nonstandard finite difference schemes for a fractional-order Brusselator system. *Adv. Differ. Equations* **2013**, *2013*, 102. [CrossRef]
138. Giusti, A. MOND-like fractional Laplacian theory. *Phys. Rev. D.* **2020**, *101*, 124029. [CrossRef]
139. Calcagni. G. Classical and quantum gravity with fractional operators. *Class. Quantum Gravity* **2021**, *38*, 165005. [CrossRef]
140. Tarasov, V.E.; Trujillo, J.J. Fractional power-law spatial dispersion in electrodynamics. *Ann. Phys.* **2014**, *334*, 1–23. [CrossRef]
141. Tarasov, V.E. Power-law spatial dispersion from fractional Liouville equation. *Phys. Plasmas* **2013**, *20*, 102110. [CrossRef]
142. Tarasov, V.E. Fractional electrodynamics with spatial dispersion. In *Handbook of Fractional Calculus with Applications. Volume 5. Application in Physics. Part B* ; Walter de Gruyter GmbH: Berlin, Germany, 2019; pp. 25–52. [CrossRef]
143. Rukhadze, A.A.; Silin, V.P. Electrodynamics of media with spatial dispersion. *Sov. Phys. Uspekhi* **1961**, *4*, 459–484. [CrossRef]

144. Alexandrov, A.F.; Rukhadze, A.A. *Lectures on Electrodynamics of Plasma-Like Media, 2. Nonequilibrium Environment*; Moscow State University Press: Moscow, Russia, 2002.
145. Kuzelev, M.V.; Rukhadze, A.A. *Methods of Waves Theory in Dispersive Media*; World Scientific: Singapore, 2009;
146. Agranovich, V.M.; Ginzburg, V.L. *Crystal Optics with Spatial Dispersion and Excitons: An Account of Spatial Dispersion*; Springer: Berlin, Germany, 1984; 441p.
147. Agranovich, V.M.; Ginzburg, V.L. *Spatial Dispersion in Crystal Optics and the Theory of Excitons*; John Wiley and Sons: Hoboken, NJ, USA, 1966.
148. Agranovich, V.M.; Ginzburg, V.L. *Crystal Optics with Spatial Dispersion and Theory of Exciton*, 1st ed.; Nauka: Moscow, Russia, 1965.
149. Tarasov, V.E. Lattice model with power-law spatial dispersion for fractional elasticity. *Cent. Eur. J. Phys. (Open Phys.)* **2013**, *11*, 1580–1588. [CrossRef]
150. Tarasov, V.E. Fractional gradient elasticity from spatial dispersion law. *ISRN Condens. Matter Phys.* **2013**, *2014*, 794097. [CrossRef]
151. Tarasov, V.E.; Aifantis, E.C. Non-standard extensions of gradient elasticity: Fractional non-locality, memory and fractality. *Commun. Nonlinear Sci. Numer. Simul.* **2015**, *22*, 197–227. [CrossRef]
152. Tarasov, V.E.; Aifantis, E.C. On fractional and fractal formulations of gradient linear and nonlinear elasticity. *Acta Mech.* **2019**, *230*, 2043–2070. [CrossRef]
153. Tarasov, V.E.; Zaslavsky, G.M. Fractional dynamics of coupled oscillators with long-range interaction. *Chaos Interdiscip. J. Nonlinear Sci.* **2006**, *16*, 023110. [CrossRef]
154. Tarasov, V.E.; Zaslavsky, G.M. Fractional dynamics of systems with long-range interaction. *Commun. Nonlinear Sci. Numer. Simul.* **2006**, *11*, 885–898. [CrossRef]
155. Laskin, N. Fractional Schrodinger equation. *Phys. Rev. E* **2002**, *66*, 056108. [CrossRef] [PubMed]
156. Laskin, N. *Fractional Quantum Mechanics*; World Scientific: Singapore, 2018; 360p. [CrossRef]
157. Luchko, Y. Fractional Schrodinger equation for a particle moving in a potential well. *J. Math. Phys.* **2013**, *54*, 012111. [CrossRef]
158. Al-Saqabi, B.; Boyadjiev, L.; Luchko, Y. Comments on employing the Riesz-Feller derivative in the Schrodinger equation. *Eur. Phys. J. Spec. Top.* **2013**, *222*, 1779–1794. [CrossRef]
159. Jeng, M.; Xu, S.-L.-Y.; Hawkins, E.; Schwarz, J.M. On the nonlocality of the fractional Schrodinger equation. *J. Math. Phys.* **2010**, *51*, 062102. [CrossRef]

Disclaimer/Publisher's Note: The statements, opinions and data contained in all publications are solely those of the individual author(s) and contributor(s) and not of MDPI and/or the editor(s). MDPI and/or the editor(s) disclaim responsibility for any injury to people or property resulting from any ideas, methods, instructions or products referred to in the content.

mathematics

MDPI

Article

On Mathieu-Type Series with (p,ν)-Extended Hypergeometric Terms: Integral Representations and Upper Bounds

Rakesh K. Parmar [1], Tibor K. Pogány [2,3,*] and S. Saravanan [1]

1 Department of Mathematics, Ramanujan School of Mathematical Sciences, Pondicherry University, Puducherry 605014, India
2 Institute of Applied Mathematics, John von Neumann Faculty of Informatics, Óbuda University, Bécsi út 96/b, 1034 Budapest, Hungary
3 Faculty of Maritime Studies, University of Rijeka, Studentska 2, 51000 Rijeka, Croatia
* Correspondence: tibor.poganj@uniri.hr

Abstract: Integral form expressions are obtained for the Mathieu-type series and for their associated alternating versions, the terms of which contain a (p,ν)-extended Gauss hypergeometric function. Contiguous recurrence relations are found for the Mathieu-type series with respect to two parameters, and finally, particular cases and related bounding inequalities are established.

Keywords: (p,ν)-extended Beta function; (p,ν)-extended Gauss hypergeometric function; (p,ν)-extended confluent hypergeometric function; (p,ν)-extended Mathieu-type series; modified Bessel function of the second kind; bounding inequalities for (p,ν)-extended Mathieu-type series

MSC: Primary 26D15; 33B15; Secondary 33C20; 33E20

Citation: Parmar, R.K.; Pogány, T.K.; Saravanan, S. On Mathieu-Type Series with (p,ν)-Extended Hypergeometric Terms: Integral Representations and Upper Bounds. *Mathematics* **2023**, *11*, 1710. https://doi.org/10.3390/math11071710

Academic Editor: Sitnik Sergey

Received: 27 February 2023
Revised: 26 March 2023
Accepted: 31 March 2023
Published: 3 April 2023

Copyright: © 2023 by the authors. Licensee MDPI, Basel, Switzerland. This article is an open access article distributed under the terms and conditions of the Creative Commons Attribution (CC BY) license (https://creativecommons.org/licenses/by/4.0/).

1. Introduction and Preliminaries

The series

$$S(x)=\sum_{n\geq 0}\frac{2n}{(n^2+x^2)^2},\qquad x>0,$$

occurring in the classical literature in mathematical physics [1–4] and nowadays called the Mathieu series, was firstly considered by Émile Leonard Mathieu in his study of the clamped plate and membrane vibration models described by the fourth-order homogeneous and non-homogeneous differential equation $\Delta^2 U=g(x,y)$ associated with the Neumann boundary condition. He also studied the same-type Neumann problem for 3D prisms and other applied mathematical models, which occur in elasticity problems of rigid body motion, see, e.g., ([5], Section 8.3), Meleshko [6,7], and Meleshko and Gomilko [8]. The Mathieu-type series built with the help of a Gauss hypergeometric function was introduced by Pogány in ([9], pp. 309–310) in the following form:

$$S(x,\mu,\nu,\boldsymbol{a})=\sum_{n\geq 0}\frac{{}_2F_1(\frac{\nu-\mu+1}{2},\frac{\nu-\mu}{2}+1;\nu+1;-\frac{x^2}{a_n^2})}{a_n^{\nu-\mu+1}(a_n^2+x^2)^{\mu-\frac{1}{2}}},\qquad x>0,\tag{1}$$

where $(x,\mu-\frac{1}{2})\in\mathbb{R}_+^2;\ \nu<\mu-1$, whilst the positive sequence $\boldsymbol{a}=(a_n)$ monotonely increases and tends toward infinity. The Gauss hypergeometric function ([10], §15.2)

$$ {}_2F_1(a,b;c;z)=\sum_{n\geq 0}\frac{(a)_n\,(b)_n}{(c)_n}\frac{z^n}{n!},\tag{2}$$

completes the Mathieu-type series definition (1).

Later, Pogány [9], both alone and as a co-author, published a series of articles on more general Mathieu-type series and alternating Mathieu-type series, the terms of which include other higher transcendental functions, such as the generalized hypergeometric function ${}_rF_s$ [11], the Fox–Wright generalized ${}_r\Psi_s$ function, Meijer's G-function [12,13], the Fox H-function [14], the (p,q)-extended τ-hypergeometric function [15], V. P. Saxena's I-function, and the $\aleph$-function [12]; see also [16,17].

For any $b, c \in \mathbb{C}$, $\Re(c) > \Re(b) > 0$, we can transform the ratio of Pochhammer symbols' as follows:

$$\frac{(b)_n}{(c)_n} = \frac{\mathrm{B}(b+n, c-b)}{\mathrm{B}(b, c-b)}, \qquad \Re(c-b) > 0,\ n \in \mathbb{N}_0,$$

which implies

$$ {}_2F_1(a,b;c;z) = \sum_{n\geq 0} (a)_n \frac{\mathrm{B}(b+n, c-b)}{\mathrm{B}(b, c-b)} \frac{z^n}{n!}. \tag{3}$$

The same stands for Kummer's confluent hypergeometric function:

$$\Phi(b;c;z) = \sum_{n\geq 0} \frac{(b)_n}{(c)_n} \frac{z^n}{n!} = \sum_{n\geq 0} \frac{\mathrm{B}(b+n, c-b)}{\mathrm{B}(b, c-b)} \frac{z^n}{n!}, \tag{4}$$

where in both series, $-c \notin \mathbb{N}_0$ and $|z| < 1$.

The next main generalization direction concerns Euler's Beta integral:

$$\mathrm{B}(s,t) = \int_0^1 x^{s-1}(1-x)^{t-1}\,\mathrm{d}x, \qquad \min\{s,t\} > 0\,.$$

The Beta integral transform of some suitable input function h *viz.*

$$\mathrm{B}[h](s,t) = \int_0^1 x^{s-1}(1-x)^{t-1} h(x)\,\mathrm{d}x\,,$$

was considered by Krattenthaler and Srinivasa Rao [18,19], assuming that this integral converges in a certain sense. When $h_1(x) = \exp\{-\frac{p}{x(1-x)}\}$; $\Re(p) \geq 0$, we arrive at the p-extended Beta function introduced by Chaudhry *et al.* ([20], p. 20, Equation (1.7))

$$\mathrm{B}_p(x,y) := \mathrm{B}[h_1](x,y) = \int_0^1 t^{x-1}(1-t)^{y-1}\mathrm{e}^{-\frac{p}{t(1-t)}}\,\mathrm{d}t\,, \qquad \Re(p) \geq 0;\ \min\{\Re(x), \Re(y)\} > 0. \tag{5}$$

When we replace $B(x,y)$ with $\mathrm{B}_p(x,y)$ in both (3) and (4), we obtain the p-variant of related p-Gauss hypergeometric and p-Kummer confluent hypergeometric functions (see below).

Recently, Parmar *et al.* [21] introduced the (p,ν)-extended Beta function by choosing

$$h_2(x) = \sqrt{\frac{2p}{\pi x(1-x)}}\, K_{\nu+\frac{1}{2}}\left(\frac{p}{x(1-x)}\right),$$

where $\Re(p) \geq 0$; $\min\{\Re(x), \Re(y)\} > 0$, $\sqrt{p}$ takes its principal value, and $K_\mu(z)$ stands for the modified Bessel function of the second kind of the order μ ([10], p. 251, Equation (10.27.4))

$$K_\mu(x) = \frac{\pi}{2}\frac{I_{-\mu}(x) - I_\mu(x)}{\sin(\pi\mu)}\,.$$

If μ is not an integer, then $\lim_{\mu\to n}$, $n \in \mathbb{Z}$. Consequently, the related (p,ν)-extended Beta function reads as follows ([21], p. 93, Equation (13)):

$$\mathrm{B}_{p,\nu}(x,y) := \mathrm{B}[h_2](x,y) = \sqrt{\frac{2p}{\pi}} \int_0^1 t^{x-\frac{3}{2}}(1-t)^{y-\frac{3}{2}} K_{\nu+\frac{1}{2}}\left(\frac{p}{t(1-t)}\right) \mathrm{d}t. \tag{6}$$

The mentioned extensions of Euler's Beta functions have recently been studied by a number of authors (see [20,22,23]).

In view of the above, the (p, ν)-extended Gauss hypergeometric and (p, ν)-extended Kummer confluent hypergeometric functions are, respectively ([21], p. 98, Equations (40) and (41))

$$F_{p,\nu}(a, b; c; z) = \sum_{n\geq 0} (a)_n \frac{\mathrm{B}_{p,\nu}(b+n,\, c-b)}{\mathrm{B}(b,\, c-b)} \frac{z^n}{n!}, \qquad p \geq 0;\ \Re(c) > \Re(b) > 0\,; |z| < 1, \tag{7}$$

$$\Phi_{p,\nu}(b; c; z) = \sum_{n\geq 0} \frac{\mathrm{B}_{p,\nu}(b+n,\, c-b)}{\mathrm{B}(b,\, c-b)} \frac{z^n}{n!}, \qquad p \geq 0;\ \Re(c) > \Re(b) > 0, \tag{8}$$

when $\nu = 0$ and ([10], p. 254, Eq. 10.39.2)

$$K_{\frac{1}{2}}(z) = \sqrt{\frac{\pi}{2z}}\, \mathrm{e}^{-z}. \tag{9}$$

The Bessel $K_{\frac{1}{2}}$ needs to be convoluted with the integrand of Euler's Beta function to obtain (5), from (7) and (8) and their special cases, the p-extended Gauss hypergeometric and the p-extended Kummer confluent hypergeometric functions ([22], pp. 591–592, Equaions (2.2)–(2.3))

$$F_p(a, b; c; z) = \sum_{n\geq 0}^{\infty} (a)_n \frac{\mathrm{B}_p(b+n,\, c-b)}{\mathrm{B}(b,\, c-b)} \frac{z^n}{n!}, \qquad p \geq 0;\ \Re(c) > \Re(b) > 0\,; |z| < 1,$$

$$\Phi_p(b; c; z) = \sum_{n\geq 0} \frac{\mathrm{B}_p(b+n,\, c-b)}{\mathrm{B}(b,\, c-b)} \frac{z^n}{n!}, \qquad p \geq 0;\ \Re(c) > \Re(b) > 0.$$

Now, extending the Mathieu-type series studied in [9] by imposing the $F_{p,\nu}(a, b; c; z)$ building block function instead of the originally used ${}_2F_1$ in the summands, we define the Mathieu-type $\boldsymbol{a}$-series $\mathcal{R}_{\mu,\zeta}$ and its alternating variant $\widetilde{\mathcal{R}}_{\mu,\zeta}$ in the power series definition:

$$\mathcal{R}_{\mu,\zeta}(F_{p,\nu}; \boldsymbol{a}; r) := \sum_{n\geq 1} \frac{F_{p,\nu}\left(\mu,\, b;\, c;\, -\frac{r^2}{a_n}\right)}{a_n^{\mu}(a_n + r^2)^{\zeta}} \qquad (p \geq 0;\ \mu, \zeta, r \in \mathbb{R}^+\,), \tag{10}$$

and

$$\widetilde{\mathcal{R}}_{\mu,\zeta}(F_{p,\nu}; \boldsymbol{a}; r) := \sum_{n\geq 1} \frac{(-1)^{n-1} F_{p,\nu}\left(\mu,\, b;\, c;\, -\frac{r^2}{a_n}\right)}{a_n^{\mu}(a_n + r^2)^{\zeta}} \qquad (p \geq 0;\ \mu, \zeta, r \in \mathbb{R}^+). \tag{11}$$

In this article, we provide integral representations for the Mathieu–type series and its alternating versions, the terms of which are constructed from the (p, ν)-extended Gauss hypergeometric function. The main achievements of the manuscript are the contiguous recurrence relations obtained for (p, ν)-extended Mathieu-type series with respect to both of their constituting parameters in Theorem 1 and Corollary 1. An upper bound is derived in Lemma 1. for the (p, ν)-extended Beta function $\mathrm{B}_{p,\nu}$, which further implies the bounds for the moduli of the (p, ν)-extended hypergeometric function $F_{p,\nu}$ and the (p, ν)-extended Kummer's function $\Phi_{p,\nu}$ in Theorem 2. Finally, related bounding inequalities are given for the (p, ν)-extended Mathieu-type series $\mathcal{R}_{\mu,\zeta}(F_{p,\nu}; \boldsymbol{a}; r)$ and for its alternating variant $\widetilde{\mathcal{R}}_{\mu,\zeta}(F_{p,\nu}; \boldsymbol{a}; r)$ in Theorem 3.

2. Contiguous Recurrence Integral Representations of $\mathcal{R}_{\mu,\zeta}(F_{p,\nu}; \boldsymbol{a}; r)$ and $\widetilde{\mathcal{R}}_{\mu,\zeta}(F_{p,\nu}; \boldsymbol{a}; r)$

This section deals with integral expressions for the series $\mathcal{R}_{\mu,\zeta}(F_{p,\nu}; \boldsymbol{a}; r)$ and $\widetilde{\mathcal{R}}_{\mu,\zeta}(F_{p,\nu}; \boldsymbol{a}; r)$. Now, we prove that there are first-order contiguous recurrence relations for both series with respect to the parameters μ and ζ. Some particular cases of our first main result are also considered.

Theorem 1. Let $\mu > 0$, $\zeta > 0$, $r > 0$, and the real positive sequence $\mathbf{a} = (a_n)_{n \geq 1}$ monotonely increases to ∞. Then, for $\Re(p) > 0$, we have

$$\mathcal{R}_{\mu,\zeta}(F_{p,\nu}; \mathbf{a}; r) = \mu \, \mathscr{I}_{p,\nu}(\mu+1, \zeta) + \zeta \, \mathscr{I}_{p,\nu}(\mu, \zeta+1) \tag{12}$$

$$\widetilde{\mathcal{R}}_{\mu,\zeta}(F_{p,\nu}; \mathbf{a}; r) = \mu \, \widetilde{\mathscr{I}}_{p,\nu}(\mu+1, \zeta) + \zeta \, \widetilde{\mathscr{I}}_{p,\nu}(\mu, \zeta+1), \tag{13}$$

where

$$\mathscr{I}_{p,\nu}(\mu, \zeta) = \int_{a_1}^{\infty} \frac{F_{p,\nu}\left(\mu, b; c; -\frac{r^2}{x}\right)[a^{-1}(x)]}{x^{\mu}(x+r^2)^{\zeta}} \, dx \tag{14}$$

$$\widetilde{\mathscr{I}}_{p,\nu}(\mu, \zeta) = \int_{a_1}^{\infty} \frac{F_{p,\nu}\left(\mu, b; c; -\frac{r^2}{x}\right) \sin^2\left(\frac{\pi}{2}[a^{-1}(x)]\right)}{x^{\mu}(x+r^2)^{\zeta}} \, dx \tag{15}$$

and $a : \mathbb{R}^+ \mapsto \mathbb{R}^+$ is an arbitrary increasing function restriction of which $a(x)|_{x \in \mathbb{N}} = \mathbf{a}$ and $[w]$ stands for the integer part of the quantity w.

Proof. Consider the Laplace transform formula of $t^{\mu-1} \, \Phi_{p,\nu}(b;c;z)$ by using the definition (7). For a real ω,

$$F_{p,\nu}\left(\mu, b; c; \frac{\omega}{z}\right) = \frac{z^{\mu}}{\Gamma(\mu)} \int_0^{\infty} e^{-zt} t^{\mu-1} \, \Phi_{p,\nu}(b; c; \omega t) \, dt. \tag{16}$$

Inserting $\xi = a_n + r^2$ into the Gamma function formula

$$\Gamma(\eta)\xi^{-\eta} = \int_0^{\infty} e^{-\xi t} t^{\eta-1} \, dt, \qquad \Re(\xi) > 0, \, \Re(\eta) > 0,$$

and, after rearrangement, by specifying $\omega = -r^2$, $z = a_n$, in (16), the auxiliary function in (14) becomes

$$\mathscr{I}_{p,\nu}(\mu, \zeta) = \frac{1}{\Gamma(\mu)\Gamma(\zeta)} \int_0^{\infty} \int_0^{\infty} e^{-r^2 s} t^{\mu-1} s^{\zeta-1} \left(\sum_{n \geq 1} e^{-a_n(t+s)} \right) \Phi_{p,\nu}(b; c; -r^2 t) \, dt \, ds.$$

Using the Cahen formula [24] for summing up the Dirichlet series with the method developed in ([9], p. 310, Equations (5) and (6)), we conclude

$$\mathcal{D}_a(t+s) = \sum_{n \geq 1} e^{-a_n(s+t)} = (s+t) \int_{a_1}^{\infty} e^{-(t+s)x} [a^{-1}(x)] \, dx.$$

This gives

$$\mathscr{I}_{p,\nu}(\mu, \zeta) = \frac{1}{\Gamma(\mu)\Gamma(\zeta)} \int_0^{\infty} \int_0^{\infty} \int_{a_1}^{\infty} e^{-(r^2+x)s - tx}(t+s) t^{\mu-1} s^{\zeta-1} [a^{-1}(x)]$$
$$\cdot \Phi_{p,\nu}(b; c; -r^2 t) \, dt \, ds \, dx =: \mathcal{J}_t + \mathcal{J}_s, \tag{17}$$

where

$$\mathcal{J}_t = \frac{1}{\Gamma(\zeta)} \int_0^{\infty} \left(\int_{a_1}^{\infty} \left(\int_0^{\infty} \frac{e^{-xt} t^{\mu}}{\Gamma(\mu)} \Phi_{p,\nu}(b; c; -r^2 t) \, dt \right) e^{-xs} [a^{-1}(x)] \, dx \right) e^{-r^2 s} s^{\zeta-1} \, ds$$

$$= \frac{\mu}{\Gamma(\zeta)} \int_{a_1}^{\infty} \left(\int_0^{\infty} e^{-(x+r^2)s} s^{\zeta-1} \, ds \right) \frac{[a^{-1}(x)]}{x^{\mu+1}} F_{p,\nu}\left(\mu+1, b; c; -\frac{r^2}{x}\right) dx$$

$$= \mu \int_{a_1}^{\infty} \frac{[a^{-1}(x)]}{x^{\mu+1}(x+r^2)^{\zeta}} F_{p,\nu}\left(\mu+1, b; c; -\frac{r^2}{x}\right) dx = \mu \, \mathscr{I}(\mu+1, \zeta). \tag{18}$$

In a similar way, we obtain

$$\mathcal{J}_s = \int_{a_1}^{\infty} \left(\int_0^{\infty} \left(\int_0^{\infty} \frac{s^{\zeta}}{\Gamma(\zeta)} e^{-(x+r^2)s} \, ds \right) \frac{e^{-xt} t^{\mu-1}}{\Gamma(\mu)} \Phi_{p,\nu}(b;c;-r^2 t) \, dt \right) [a^{-1}(x)] \, dx$$

$$= \zeta \int_{a_1}^{\infty} \frac{[a^{-1}(x)]}{(x+r^2)^{\zeta+1}} \left(\int_0^{\infty} \frac{e^{-xt} t^{\mu-1}}{\Gamma(\mu)} \Phi_{p,\nu}(b;c;-r^2 t) \, dt \right) dx$$

$$= \zeta \int_{a_1}^{\infty} \frac{[a^{-1}(x)]}{x^{\mu}(x+r^2)^{\zeta+1}} F_{p,\nu}\left(\mu, b; c; -\frac{r^2}{x}\right) dx = \zeta \, \mathscr{I}(\mu, \zeta+1). \tag{19}$$

By applying (18) and (19) to (17), we obtain the expression (12).

The derivation of (14) is similar to the exposed proving procedure. Having in mind again the Cahen formula, since the counting function equals

$$\widetilde{A}(t) = \sum_{n:\, a_n \leq t} (-1)^{n-1} = \frac{1-(-1)^{[a^{-1}(t)]}}{2} = \sin^2\left(\frac{\pi}{2} [a^{-1}(t)]\right),$$

the integral form of the alternating Dirichlet series $\mathcal{D}_a(x)$ becomes ([25], p. 79)

$$\widetilde{\mathcal{D}}_a(x) = \sum_{n \geq 1} (-1)^{n-1} e^{-a_n x} = x \int_{a_1}^{\infty} e^{-xt} \widetilde{A}(t) \, dt,$$

and

$$\widetilde{\mathcal{D}}_a(x) = x \int_{a_1}^{\infty} e^{-xt} \sin^2\left(\frac{\pi}{2} [a^{-1}(t)]\right) dt.$$

Because

$$\widetilde{\mathcal{D}}_a(t+s) = (t+s) \int_{a_1}^{\infty} e^{-(t+s)x} \sin^2\left(\frac{\pi}{2} [a^{-1}(x)]\right) dx,$$

we conclude (15), and *a fortiori* (13) by obvious steps. □

When $\nu = 0$ and by using (9), the results of Theorem 1 are simplified.

Corollary 1. *Let $\mu > 0$, $\zeta > 0$, $r > 0$, and the real sequence a monotonely increases and tends to ∞. Then, for $\Re(p) \geq 0$, we have*

$$\mathcal{R}_{\mu,\zeta}(F_p; a; r) = \mu \, \mathscr{I}_p(\mu+1, \zeta) + \zeta \, \mathscr{I}_p(\mu, \zeta+1)$$
$$\widetilde{\mathcal{R}}_{\mu,\zeta}(F_p; a; r) = \mu \, \widetilde{\mathscr{I}}_p(\mu+1, \zeta) + \zeta \, \widetilde{\mathscr{I}}_p(\mu, \zeta+1),$$

where

$$\mathscr{I}_p(\mu, \zeta) = \int_{a_1}^{\infty} \frac{F_p\left(\mu, b; c; -\frac{r^2}{x}\right)[a^{-1}(x)]}{x^{\mu}(x+r^2)^{\zeta}} \, dx,$$

$$\widetilde{\mathscr{I}}_p(\mu, \zeta) = \int_{a_1}^{\infty} \frac{F_p\left(\mu, b; c; -\frac{r^2}{x}\right) \sin^2\left(\frac{\pi}{2}[a^{-1}(x)]\right)}{x^{\mu}(x+r^2)^{\zeta}} \, dx.$$

Remark 1. *The special case $\nu = p = 0$ immediately reduces the claim of Theorem 1 to the Gauss $_2F_1$ hypergeometric function's case studied in [9].*

3. Bounding Inequalities for the (p, ν)-Extended Mathieu-Type Series

In this section, our main goal is to derive an upper bound for the (p, ν)-extended Beta function $B_{p,\nu}(x, y)$ in (6). By making use of this upper bound, we obtain bounds for the (p, ν)-extended Gauss hypergeometric $F_{p,\nu}$ and the (p, ν)-extended Kummer's confluent hypergeometric $\Phi_{p,\nu}$ via series representations (7) and (8). Finally, we obtain bounding inequalities for the (p, ν)-extended Mathieu-type series (10) and (11).

3.1. *Upper Bound for* (p,ν)*-Extended Beta Function*

Firstly, we establish the upper bound for the (p,ν)-extended hypergeometric function $F_{p,\nu}$ by applying the following result ([26], p. 17, Equation (5.3)):

$$\left|K_{\nu+\frac{1}{2}}(z)\right| < \frac{\sqrt{\pi}\left(\frac{1}{2}|z|\right)^{\nu+\frac{1}{2}}}{\Gamma(\nu+1)} \frac{\Gamma(2\nu+1,\Re(z))}{(\Re(z))^{2\nu+1}}, \qquad \Re(z) > 0, \tag{20}$$

where the upper incomplete Gamma function is

$$\Gamma(a,x) = \int_x^\infty t^{a-1}\mathrm{e}^{-t}\,\mathrm{d}t, \qquad \Re(a),\Re(x) > 0.$$

Consequently, since $\Gamma(a,x) < \Gamma(a)$, there holds ([26], p. 17)

$$\left|K_{\nu+\frac{1}{2}}\left(\frac{p}{t(1-t)}\right)\right| < \frac{1}{2}\left(\frac{2|p|\,t(1-t)}{\Re^2(p)}\right)^{\nu+\frac{1}{2}}\Gamma(\nu+\tfrac{1}{2}), \qquad \Re(p) > 0,\, t \in (0,1). \tag{21}$$

The immediate implication of (21) follows by means of (6).

Lemma 1. *For all* $\Re(p) > 0$, $\nu > 0$, $\min\{\Re(x),\Re(y)\} > 0$ *and* $t \in (0,1)$, *we have*

$$\left|\mathrm{B}_{p,\nu}(x,y)\right| \le \frac{2^\nu |p|^{\nu+1}\Gamma(\nu+\frac{1}{2})}{\sqrt{\pi}(\Re(p))^{2\nu+1}}\,\mathrm{B}(x+\nu,y+\nu). \tag{22}$$

This upper bound plays an important role in the whole section (indirectly) applied either for the sum or integral representations of the families of (p,ν)-extended special functions.

3.2. *Bounds Obtained* via *Series Representations*

The functional bound (21) will be used in proving our first set of the main bounding inequalities. More precisely, by applying (22) to all the series representations of the (p,ν)-extended special functions, which contain $\mathrm{B}_{p,\nu}(x,y)$, such as the (p,ν)-extended Gauss hypergeometric $F_{p,\nu}$ and (p,ν)-extended Kummer's confluent hypergeometric $\Phi_{p,\nu}$, described in (7) and (8), we arrive at the results below.

Theorem 2. *For all* $\Re(p) > 0$, $\nu > 0$; $\Re(c) > \Re(b) > 0$ *and for all* $|z| < 1$, *we have*

$$\left|F_{p,\nu}(a,b;c;z)\right| \le \frac{2^\nu |p|^{\nu+1}\Gamma(\nu+\frac{1}{2})}{\sqrt{\pi}(\Re(p))^{2\nu+1}} \frac{\mathrm{B}(b+\nu,\,c-b+\nu)}{\mathrm{B}(b,\,c-b)}\,{}_2F_1(a,b+\nu;c+2\nu;|z|), \tag{23}$$

$$\left|\Phi_{p,\nu}(b;c;z)\right| \le \frac{2^\nu |p|^{\nu+1}\Gamma(\nu+\frac{1}{2})}{\sqrt{\pi}(\Re(p))^{2\nu+1}} \frac{\mathrm{B}(b+\nu,\,c-b+\nu)}{\mathrm{B}(b,\,c-b)}\,\Phi(b+\nu;c+2\nu;|z|).$$

Proof. Regarding assertion (23), because all parameters and expressions involved are positive, by means of the series representation of the (p,ν)-extended Gauss hypergeometric function (7), and by Lemma 1, we conclude

$$\begin{aligned}
F_{p,\nu}(a,b;c;z) &\le \frac{2^\nu |p|^{\nu+1}\Gamma(\nu+\frac{1}{2})}{\sqrt{\pi}(\Re(p))^{2\nu+1}\mathrm{B}(b,c-b)} \sum_{n\ge 0}(a)_n\mathrm{B}(b+\nu+n,c-b+\nu)\,\frac{|z|^n}{n!} \\
&= \frac{2^\nu |p|^{\nu+1}\Gamma(\nu+\frac{1}{2})}{\sqrt{\pi}(\Re(p))^{2\nu+1}\mathrm{B}(b,c-b)} \sum_{n\ge 0}\frac{(a)_n\Gamma(b+\nu+n)\Gamma(c-b+\nu)}{\Gamma(c+2\nu+n)}\,\frac{|z|^n}{n!} \\
&= \frac{2^\nu |p|^{\nu+1}\Gamma(\nu+\frac{1}{2})\Gamma(c-b+\nu)\Gamma(b+\nu)}{\sqrt{\pi}(\Re(p))^{2\nu+1}\mathrm{B}(b,c-b)\Gamma(c+2\nu)} \sum_{n\ge 0}\frac{(a)_n(b+\nu)_n}{(c+2\nu)_n}\,\frac{|z|^n}{n!}.
\end{aligned}$$

The rest is obvious. Moreover, by applying similar transformations *per definitionem*, we prove the second statement for the (p,ν)-extended confluent hypergeometric function (8). $\square$

Furthermore, we need a certain Luke's upper bound for the Gauss hypergeometric function. Precisely, for all $b \in (0,1]$, $c \geq a > 0$ and $z > 0$, there holds ([27], p. 52, Equation (4.7))

$$ {}_2F_1(a,b;c;-z) < 1 - \frac{2ab(c+1)}{c(a+1)(b+1)}\left(1 - \frac{2(c+1)}{2(c+1)+(a+1)(b+1)\,z}\right). \tag{24} $$

Theorem 3. *Let $\mu \in (0,1]$, $\zeta > 0, \nu > 0$, and the positive real sequence $\boldsymbol{a} = (a_n)_{n\geq 1}$ monotonely increases and tends to ∞. Then, for all $r \in (0, \sqrt{a_1}\,)$, $\Re(p) > 0$ and $\Re(c) > \Re(b) > 0$, we have*

$$ \begin{aligned} \mathcal{R}_{\mu,\zeta}(F_{p,\nu};\boldsymbol{a};r) \leq \mu\, \mathcal{Y}_{p,\nu} \Bigg\{ &\left(1 - \frac{2(\mu+1)(b+\nu)(c+2\nu+1)}{c(\mu+2)(b+\nu+1)}\right) \mathscr{X}_a(\mu+1,\zeta) \\ &+ \frac{4(\mu+1)(b+\nu)(c+2\nu+1)^2\, \mathscr{X}_a(\mu,\zeta)}{(c+2\nu)(\mu+2)(b+\nu+1)\,[(\mu+2)(b+\nu+1)r^2 + 2(c+2\nu+1)a_1]} \Bigg\} \\ + \zeta\, \mathcal{Y}_{p,\nu} \Bigg\{ &\left(1 - \frac{2\mu(b+\nu)(c+2\nu+1)}{(c+2\nu)(\mu+1)(b+\nu+1)}\right) \mathscr{X}_a(\mu,\zeta+1) \\ &+ \frac{4\mu(b+\nu)(c+2\nu+1)^2\, \mathscr{X}_a(\mu-1,\zeta+1)}{(c+2\nu)(\mu+1)(b+\nu+1)\,[(\mu+1)(b+\nu+1)r^2 + 2(c+2\nu+1)a_1]} \Bigg\}. \end{aligned} \tag{25} $$

Moreover, for all $\mu + \zeta > 1, \nu > 0$; $r \in (0, \sqrt{a_1}\,)$, $\Re(p) > 0$ and $\Re(c) > \Re(b) > 0$, we have

$$ \begin{aligned} \widetilde{\mathcal{R}}_{\mu,\zeta}(F_{p,\nu};\boldsymbol{a};r) \leq \mu\, \mathcal{Y}_{p,\nu} \Bigg\{ &\left(1 - \frac{2(\mu+1)(b+\nu)(c+2\nu+1)}{(c+2\nu)(\mu+2)(b+\nu+1)}\right) \frac{a_1^{-\mu-\zeta}}{\mu+\zeta}\, {}_2F_1\left(\zeta, \mu+\zeta; \zeta+1; -\frac{r^2}{a_1}\right) \\ &+ \frac{4(\mu+1)(b+\nu)(c+2\nu+1)^2}{(c+2\nu)(\mu+2)(b+\nu+1)} \frac{a_1^{1-\mu-\zeta}\, {}_2F_1\left(\zeta, \mu+\zeta-1; \zeta+1; -\frac{r^2}{a_1}\right)}{(\mu+\zeta-1)((\mu+2)(b+\nu+1)r^2 + 2(c+2\nu+1)a_1)} \Bigg\} \\ + \zeta\, \mathcal{Y}_{p,\nu} \Bigg\{ &\left(1 - \frac{2\mu(b+\nu)(c+2\nu+1)}{(c+2\nu)(\mu+1)(b+\nu+1)}\right) \frac{a_1^{-\mu-\zeta}}{\mu+\zeta}\, {}_2F_1\left(\zeta+1, \mu+\zeta; \zeta+2; -\frac{r^2}{a_1}\right) \\ &+ \frac{4\mu(b+\nu)(c+2\nu+1)^2}{(c+2\nu)(\mu+1)(b+\nu+1)} \frac{a_1^{1-\mu-\zeta}\, {}_2F_1\left(\zeta+1, \mu+\zeta-1; \zeta+2; -\frac{r^2}{a_1}\right)}{(\mu+\zeta-1)((\mu+1)(b+\nu+1)r^2 + 2(c+2\nu+1)a_1)} \Bigg\}, \end{aligned} \tag{26} $$

where the integral's shorthand reads

$$ \mathscr{X}_a(\mu,\zeta) := \int_{a_1}^{\infty} \frac{[a^{-1}(x)]}{x^{\mu}(x+r^2)^{\zeta}}\, \mathrm{d}x; \quad \textit{and} \quad \mathcal{Y}_{p,\nu} := \frac{2^{\nu}|p|^{\nu+1}\,\Gamma(\nu+\frac{1}{2})}{\sqrt{\pi}(\Re(p))^{2\nu+1}} \frac{\mathrm{B}(b+\nu,\, c-b+\nu)}{\mathrm{B}(b,\, c-b)}. $$

Proof. Firstly, consider the relation (10)

$$ \mathcal{R}_{\mu,\zeta}(F_{p,\nu};\boldsymbol{a};r) = \mu\, \mathscr{I}_{p,\nu}(\mu+1,\zeta) + \zeta\, \mathscr{I}_{p,\nu}(\mu,\zeta+1), $$

in which we bound from above the auxiliary integral $\mathscr{I}_{p,\nu}$ described in (14). To do this, we quote that $F_{p,\nu}(a,b;c;z) > 0$ for all $a,b,c > 0$ and all non-positive values of z. Indeed, it is enough to consider the integral expression ([21], p. 99, Equation (42))

$$ F_{p,\nu}(a,b;c;z) = \sqrt{\frac{2p}{\pi}} \frac{1}{\mathrm{B}(b,c-b)} \int_0^1 t^{b-\frac{3}{2}}(1-t)^{c-b-\frac{3}{2}}(1-zt)^{-a}\, K_{\nu+\frac{1}{2}}\left(\frac{p}{t(1-t)}\right) \mathrm{d}t, $$

where $p > 0$; $\Re(c) > \Re(b) > 0$; $|z| < 1$. Therefore, by virtue of (14) and (23),

$$\mathscr{I}_{p,\nu}(\mu,\zeta) = \int_{a_1}^{\infty} \frac{F_{p,\nu}(\mu, b; c; -\frac{r^2}{x})[a^{-1}(x)]}{x^\mu (x+r^2)^\zeta}\, dx \le \mathcal{Y}_{p,\nu} \int_{a_1}^{\infty} \frac{{}_2F_1(\mu, b+\nu; c+2\nu; -\frac{r^2}{x})[a^{-1}(x)]}{x^\mu (x+r^2)^\zeta}\, dx$$

$$\le \mathcal{Y}_{p,\nu}\left\{\left(1 - \frac{2\mu(b+\nu)(c+2\nu+1)}{(c+2\nu)(\mu+1)(b+\nu+1)}\right) \int_{a_1}^{\infty} \frac{[a^{-1}(x)]}{x^\mu (x+r^2)^\zeta}\, dx\right.$$

$$\left. + \frac{4\mu(b+\nu)(c+2\nu+1)^2}{(c+2\nu)(\mu+1)(b+\nu+1)} \int_{a_1}^{\infty} \frac{x^{1-\mu}(x+r^2)^{-\zeta}[a^{-1}(x)]\,dx}{(\mu+1)(b+\nu+1)r^2 + 2(c+2\nu+1)x}\right\}$$

$$\le \mathcal{Y}_{p,\nu}\left\{\left(1 - \frac{2\mu(b+\nu)(c+2\nu+1)}{(c+2\nu)(\mu+1)(b+\nu+1)}\right)\mathscr{X}_a(\mu,\epsilon)\right.$$

$$\left. + \frac{4\mu(b+\nu)(c+2\nu+1)^2\,\mathscr{X}_a(\mu-1,\epsilon)}{(c+2\nu)(\mu+1)(b+\nu+1)\left((\mu+1)(b+\nu+1)r^2 + 2(c+2\nu+1)a_1\right)}\right\}.$$

The rest in deriving (25) is straightforward.

Secondly, we recall (13), which reads as follows:

$$\widetilde{\mathcal{R}}_{\mu,\zeta}(F_{p,\nu}; a; r) = \mu\,\widetilde{\mathscr{I}}_{p,\nu}(\mu+1,\zeta) + \zeta\,\widetilde{\mathscr{I}}_{p,\nu}(\mu,\zeta+1).$$

By the positivity of the integrand of (15), since (23), we conclude

$$\widetilde{\mathscr{I}}_{p,\nu}(\mu,\zeta) \le \int_{a_1}^{\infty} \frac{F_{p,\nu}(\mu, b; c; -\frac{r^2}{x})}{x^\mu (x+r^2)^\zeta}\, dx \le \mathcal{Y}_{p,\nu} \int_{a_1}^{\infty} \frac{{}_2F_1(\mu, b+\nu; c+2\nu; -\frac{r^2}{x})}{x^\mu (x+r^2)^\zeta}\, dx.$$

In turn, with the aid of (24), we deduce that

$$\widetilde{\mathscr{I}}_{p,\nu}(\mu,\zeta) \le \mathcal{Y}_{p,\nu}\left\{\left(1 - \frac{2\mu(b+\nu)(c+2\nu+1)}{(c+2\nu)(\mu+1)(b+\nu+1)}\right) \int_{a_1}^{\infty} \frac{dx}{x^\mu (x+r^2)^\zeta}\right.$$

$$\left. + \frac{4\mu(b+\nu)(c+2\nu+1)^2}{(c+2\nu)(\mu+1)(b+\nu+1)} \int_{a_1}^{\infty} \frac{x^{1-\mu}(x+r^2)^{-\zeta}\,dx}{(\mu+1)(b+\nu+1)r^2 + 2(c+2\nu+1)x}\right\}.$$

If $\mu + \zeta > 2$, then ([28], p. 313, Equation (**3.194** 1)).

$$\int_{a_1}^{\infty} \frac{dx}{x^\mu (x+r^2)^\zeta} = \int_0^{\frac{1}{a_1}} \frac{t^{\mu+\zeta-2}}{(1+r^2 t)^\zeta}\, dt = \frac{a_1^{1-\mu-\zeta}}{\mu+\zeta-1}\,{}_2F_1\left(\zeta, \mu+\zeta-1; \zeta+1; -\frac{r^2}{a_1}\right),$$

which implies

$$\int_{a_1}^{\infty} \frac{dx}{x^{\mu-1}(x+r^2)^\zeta\left((\mu+1)r^2 + 2\frac{c+2\nu+1}{b+\nu+1}x\right)} \le \frac{a_1^{2-\mu-\zeta}\,{}_2F_1\left(\zeta, \mu+\zeta-2; \zeta+1; -\frac{r^2}{a_1}\right)}{(\mu+\zeta-2)\left((\mu+1)r^2 + 2\frac{c+2\nu+1}{b+\nu+1}a_1\right)}.$$

Collecting these formulae, we infer

$$\widetilde{\mathscr{I}}_{p,\nu}(\mu,\zeta) \le \mathcal{Y}_{p,\nu}\left\{\left(1 - \frac{2\mu(b+\nu)(c+2\nu+1)}{(c+2\nu)(\mu+1)(b+\nu+1)}\right)\frac{a_1^{1-\mu-\zeta}}{\mu+\zeta-1}\,{}_2F_1\left(\zeta, \mu+\zeta-1; \zeta+1; -\frac{r^2}{a_1}\right)\right.$$

$$\left. + \frac{4\mu(b+\nu)(c+2\nu+1)^2}{(c+2\nu)(\mu+1)(b+\nu+1)}\frac{a_1^{2-\mu-\zeta}\,{}_2F_1\left(\zeta, \mu+\zeta-2; \zeta+1; -\frac{r^2}{a_1}\right)}{(\mu+\zeta-2)[(\mu+1)(b+\nu+1)r^2 + 2(c+2\nu+1)a_1]}\right\}.$$

Now, obvious steps lead to the asserted upper bound (26). □

4. Concluding Remarks

A The cited references for the Mathieu-type series are given concerning the integral representations, which are mainly obtained by virtue of Cahen's formula for the sum of Dirichlet series in the form of a Laplace integral. The contiguous recurrence relations exist for almost all already considered cases, together with the bounding inequalities for the studied general Mathieu-type series up to the related multiplicative constants.

B It is worth mentioning that there is also another type of extended Beta function, which was introduced in [29], where the extended Beta function consists of the Beta integral transform of the Kummer confluent hypergeometric function, *viz.* ([29], p. 631, Definition 1.1.)

$$\mathrm{B}_{p;\kappa,\lambda}^{(\alpha,\beta)}(x,y) = \int_0^1 t^{x-1}(1-t)^{y-1}\,{}_1F_1\Big(\alpha;\beta;-\frac{p}{t^\kappa(1-t)^\lambda}\Big)\,\mathrm{d}t\,, \tag{27}$$

where the parameters $\kappa, \lambda \geq 0$; $\min\{\Re(\alpha), \Re(\beta)\} > 0$; $\Re(x) > -\Re(\kappa\alpha)$, $\Re(y) > -\Re(\lambda\alpha)$. The special case $\mathrm{B}_{p;1,1}^{(\alpha,\alpha)}(x,y) = \mathrm{B}_p(x,y)$ coincides with the p-extended Beta function (5) introduced by Chaudhry *et al.* in [20].

C The results for the extended hypergeometric functions $F_p^{(\alpha,\beta;\kappa,\mu)}$ relative to $\mathrm{B}_{p;\kappa,\lambda}^{(\alpha,\beta)}(x,y)$ are published in ([30], pp. 140–143, Theorem 1 *et seq.*), together with the integral representations for the extended Mathieu-type series ([30], p. 140, Equations (1.3) and (1.4)).

$$\mathfrak{F}_{\lambda,\eta}(F_p^{(\alpha,\beta;\kappa,\mu)};\boldsymbol{a};r) = \sum_{n\geq 1} \frac{F_p^{(\alpha,\beta;\kappa,\mu)}(\lambda,\, b;\, c;\, -\frac{r^2}{a_n})}{a_n^\lambda(a_n+r^2)^\eta}$$

$$\widetilde{\mathfrak{F}}_{\lambda,\eta}(F_p^{(\alpha,\beta;\kappa,\mu)};\boldsymbol{a};r) = \sum_{n\geq 1} \frac{(-1)^{n-1}F_p^{(\alpha,\beta;\kappa,\mu)}(\lambda,\, b;\, c;\, -\frac{r^2}{a_n})}{a_n^\lambda(a_n+r^2)^\eta},$$

where $\lambda, \eta, r > 0$; $\Re(c) > \Re(b) > 0$.

D Further research directions may include the asymptotic expansion of generalized Mathieu series [31,32], connections with the Riemann zeta and Dirichlet Beta functions [33], Mathieu series associated with the Mittag–Leffler function, harmonic Mathieu series, Fourier–Mathieu series and connections with the Butzer–Flocke–Hauss Omega function, the multiparameter variants of Mathieu–type series with reference to the recent monograph [34], and article [5]. Moreover, the probability distributions and allied topics defined in terms of Mathieu-type series are also studied, for instance in [35,36] and the appropriate references therein. These publications suggested some ideas for generalizing the Mathieu-type series studied here, e.g., new generalizations of the Beta functions related to (27), that can result in novel forms of the associated hypergeometric functions and the related Mathieu series.

Author Contributions: All authors participated in the conceptualization, methodology, and writing—review and editing. All authors have read and agreed to the published version of the manuscript.

Funding: This research received no external funding.

Data Availability Statement: Not applicable.

Acknowledgments: The authors highly appreciate the corrections and constructive suggestions made by the editors and all three referees, which strongly improved the completeness of the exposition, and the readability and clear recognition of the presented ideas and results of this article.

Conflicts of Interest: The authors declare no conflict of interest.

References

1. Mathieu, É. Mémoire sur des intégrations relatives a l'équilibre d'élasticité. *J. Ecole Polytéch.* **1880**, *29*, 163–206.
2. Mathieu, É. Mémoire sur l'équilibre d'élasticité d'un prisme rectangle. *J. Ecole Polytéch.* **1881**, *30*, 173–196.
3. Mathieu, É. Sur léquilibre d'élasticité d'un prisme rectangle. *C. R. Acad. Sci. Paris* **1890**, *90*, 1272–1274.
4. Mathieu, É.L. *Traité de Physique Mathématique, VI-VII: Théorie de l'élasticité des Corps Solides*; Gauthier–Villars: Paris, France, 1890.
5. Parmar, R.K.; Milovanović, V.G.; Pogány, T.K. Multi-parameter Mathieu, and alternating Mathieu series. *Appl. Math. Comput.* **2021**, *400*, 126099. [CrossRef]
6. Meleshko, V.V. Equilibrium of elastic rectangle: Mathieu–Inglis–Pickett solution revisited. *J. Elast.* **1995**, *40*, 207–238. [CrossRef]
7. Meleshko, V.V. Selected topics in the history of the two-dimensional biharmonic problem. *Appl. Mech. Rev.* **2003**, *56*, 33–85. [CrossRef]
8. Meleshko, V.V.; Gomilko, A.M. On the bending of clamped rectangular plates. *Mech. Res. Commun.* **1994**, *21*, 19–24. [CrossRef]
9. Pogány, T.K. Integral representation of a series which includes the Mathieu $\boldsymbol{a}$-series. *J. Math. Anal. Appl.* **2004**, *296*, 309–313. [CrossRef]
10. Olver, F.W.J.; Lozier, D.W.; Boisvert, R.F.; Clark, C.W. (Eds.) *NIST Handbook of Mathematical Functions*; University Press: Cambridge, UK, 2010.
11. Pogány, T.K.; Srivastava, H.M. Some Mathieu-type series associated with the Fox–Wright function. *Comput. Math. Appl.* **2009**, *57*, 127–140. [CrossRef]
12. Saxena, R.K.; Pogány, T.K. Mathieu-type series for the $\aleph$-function occurring in Fokker-Planck equation. *Eur. J. Pure Appl. Math.* **2010**, *3*, 980–988.
13. Pogány, T.K.; Tomovski, Ž. On Mathieu–type series which terms contain generalized hypergeometric function ${}_pF_q$ and Meijer's G-function. *Math. Comput. Model.* **2008**, *47*, 952–969. [CrossRef]
14. Pogány, T.K. Integral expressions of Mathieu-type series whose terms contain Fox's H-function. *Appl. Math. Lett.* **2007**, *20*, 764–769. [CrossRef]
15. Parmar, R.K.; Saxena, R.K.; Pogány, T.K. On properties and applications of (p,q)–extended τ–hypergeometric functions. *C. R. Acad. Sci. Paris Ser. I* **2018**, *356*, 278–282. [CrossRef]
16. Choi, J.; Parmar, R.K.; Pogány, T.K. Mathieu–type series built by (p,q)–extended Gaussian hypergeometric function. *Bull. Korean Math. Soc.* **2017**, *54*, 789–797. [CrossRef]
17. Pogány, T.K.; Parmar, R.K. On p–extended Mathieu series. *Rad Hrvat. Akad. Znan. Umjet. Mat. Znan.* **2018**, *22*, 107–117. [CrossRef]
18. Krattenthaler, C.; Srinivasa Rao, K. Automatic generation of hypergeometric identities by the beta integral method. *J. Comput. Appl. Math.* **2003**, *160*, 159–173. [CrossRef]
19. Ismail, M.E.H.; Pitman, J. Algebraic evaluations of some Euler integrals, duplication formulae for Appell's hypergeometric function F_1, and Brownian variations. *Canad. J. Math.* **2000**, *52*, 961–981. [CrossRef]
20. Chaudhry, M.A.; Qadir, A.; Rafique, M.; Zubair, S.M. Extension of Euler's Beta function. *J. Comput. Appl. Math.* **1997**, *78*, 19–32. [CrossRef]
21. Parmar, R.K.; Paris, R.B.; Chopra, P. On an extension of extended beta and hypergeometric functions. *J. Classical Anal.* **2017**, *11*, 91–106. [CrossRef]
22. Chaudhry, M.A.; Qadir, A.; Srivastava, H.M.; Paris, R.B. Extended hypergeometric and confluent hypergeometric functions. *Appl. Math. Comput.* **2004**, *159*, 589–602. [CrossRef]
23. Choi, J.; Rathie, A.K.; Parmar, R.K. Extension of extended beta, hypergeometric and confluent hypergeometric functions. *Honam Math. J.* **2014**, *36*, 339–367. [CrossRef]
24. Cahen, E. Sur la fonction $\zeta(s)$ de Riemann et sur des fontions analogues. *Ann. Sci. l'École Norm. Sup. Sér. Math.* **1894**, *11*, 75–164. [CrossRef]
25. Pogány, T.K.; Srivastava, H.M.; Tomovski, Ž. Some families of Mathieu $\boldsymbol{a}$-series and alternating Mathieu $\boldsymbol{a}$-series. *Appl. Math. Comput.* **2006**, *173*, 69–108. [CrossRef]
26. Dar, S.A.; Paris, R.B. A (p,ν)–extension of the Appell function $F_1(\cdot)$ and its properties. *J. Comput. Appl. Math.* **2019**, *358*, 12–19. [CrossRef]
27. Luke, Y.L. Inequalities for generalized hypergeometric functions. *J. Approx. Theory* **1974**, *5*, 41–65. [CrossRef]
28. Gradshteyn, I.S.; Ryzhik, I.M. *Table of Integrals, Series, and Products*, 6th ed.; Jeffrey, A., Zwillinger, D., Eds.; Academic Press, Inc.: San Diego, CA, USA, 2000.
29. Luo, M.-J.; Milovanović, G.V.; Agarwal, P. Some results on the extended beta and extended hypergeometric functions. *Appl. Math. Comput.* **2014**, *248*, 631–651. [CrossRef]
30. Parmar, R.K.; Pogány, T.K. On Mathieu–type series for the unified Gaussian hypergeometric functions. *Appl. Anal. Discrete Math.* **2020**, *14*, 138–149. [CrossRef]
31. Paris, R.B. The asymptotic expansion of a generalised Mathieu series. *Appl. Math. Sci. (Ruse)* **2013**, *7*, 6209–6216. [CrossRef]
32. Gerhold, S.; Hubalek, F.; Tomovski, Ž. Asymptotics of some generalized Mathieu series. *Math. Scand.* **2020**, *126*, 424–450. [CrossRef]
33. Cerone, P. On zeta and Dirichlet beta function families as generators of generalized Mathieu series, providing approximation and Bounds. *Facta Univ. Ser. Math. Inform.* **2022**, *37*, 251–282. [CrossRef]
34. Tomovski, Ž.; Leškovski, D.; Gerhold, S. *Generalized Mathieu Series*; Springer: Cham, Switzerland, 2021.

35. Srivastava, H.M.; Tomovski, Ž.; Leškovski, D. Some families of Mathieu type series and Hurwitz–Lerch zeta functions and associated probability distributions. *Appl. Comput. Math.* **2015**, *14*, 349–380.
36. Tomovski, Ž.; Mehrez, K. Some families of generalized Mathieu-type power series, associated probability distributions and related inequalities involving complete monotonicity and log-convexity. *Math. Inequal. Appl.* **2017**, *20*, 973–986. [CrossRef]

Disclaimer/Publisher's Note: The statements, opinions and data contained in all publications are solely those of the individual author(s) and contributor(s) and not of MDPI and/or the editor(s). MDPI and/or the editor(s) disclaim responsibility for any injury to people or property resulting from any ideas, methods, instructions or products referred to in the content.

Σ mathematics

MDPI

Article

Sums Involving the Digamma Function Connected to the Incomplete Beta Function and the Bessel Functions

Juan Luis González-Santander † and Fernando Sánchez Lasheras *,†

Department of Mathematics, Universidad de Oviedo, 33007 Oviedo, Asturias, Spain; gonzalezmarjuan@uniovi.es
* Correspondence: sanchezfernando@uniovi.es
† These authors contributed equally to this work.

Abstract: We calculate some infinite sums containing the digamma function in closed form. These sums are related either to the incomplete beta function or to the Bessel functions. The calculations yield interesting new results as by-products, such as parameter differentiation formulas for the beta incomplete function, reduction formulas of ${}_3F_2$ hypergeometric functions, or a definite integral which does not seem to be tabulated in the most common literature. As an application of certain sums involving the digamma function, we calculated some reduction formulas for the parameter differentiation of the Mittag–Leffler function and the Wright function.

Keywords: digamma function; Bessel functions; incomplete beta function; Wright function; Mittag–Leffler function; differentiation with respect to parameters

MSC: 33B15; 33C20; 33E12; 33C10

Citation: González-Santander, J.L.; Sánchez Lasheras, F. Sums Involving the Digamma Function Connected to the Incomplete Beta Function and the Bessel Functions. *Mathematics* **2023**, *11*, 1937. https://doi.org/10.3390/math11081937

Academic Editor: Sitnik Sergey

Received: 24 March 2023
Revised: 13 April 2023
Accepted: 17 April 2023
Published: 20 April 2023

Copyright: © 2023 by the authors. Licensee MDPI, Basel, Switzerland. This article is an open access article distributed under the terms and conditions of the Creative Commons Attribution (CC BY) license (https://creativecommons.org/licenses/by/4.0/).

1. Introduction

In the existing literature [1,2], we found some compilations of series and finite sums involving the digamma function. Some authors contributed to these compilations, such as Doelder [3], Miller [4], and Cvijović [5]. More recently, the authors published some novel results in this regard [6].

Sums involving the digamma function occur in the expressions of the derivatives of the Mittag–Leffler function and the Wright function with respect to parameters [7,8]. In addition, they occur in the derivation of asymptotic expansions for Mellin–Barnes integrals [9,10]. Further, Doelder [3] calculate sums involving the digamma function in connection to the dilogarithm function [11]. As an application in physics, this type of sums arises in the evaluation of Feynman amplitudes in quantum field theory [12].

The aim of this paper is the derivation of some new sums involving the digamma function by using the derivative of the Pochhammer symbol and some reduction formulas of the generalized hypergeometric function. As a consistency test, for many particular values of the results obtained, we recover expressions given in the existing literature. In addition, we developed a MATHEMATICA program to numerically check all the new expressions derived in the paper. This program is available at https://bit.ly/3LG2gej (accessed on 19 April 2023).

This paper is organized as follows. In Section 2, we present some basic properties of the Pochhammer symbol, the beta and the digamma functions, as well as the definitions of the generalized hypergeometric function and the Meijer-G function. In Section 3, we derive some sums connected to the parameter differentiation of the incomplete beta function. In Section 4, we calculate, in a similar way, some other sums connected to the order derivatives of the Bessel and the modified Bessel functions. Section 5 is devoted to the application of some sums involving the digamma function to reduction formulas for the parameter differentiation of the Wright and Mittag–Leffler functions. Finally, we compile our conclusions in Section 6.

2. Preliminaries

The Pochhamer symbol is defined as [13], Equation 18:12:1

$$(x)_n = \frac{\Gamma(x+n)}{\Gamma(x)}, \tag{1}$$

where $\Gamma(x)$ denotes the gamma function with the following basic properties [13] (Ch. 43):

$$\Gamma(z+1) = z\Gamma(z), \tag{2}$$

$$2^{2z-1}\Gamma(z)\Gamma\left(z+\frac{1}{2}\right) = \sqrt{\pi}\,\Gamma(2z). \tag{3}$$

In addition, the beta function, defined as [14] (Equation 1.5.3)

$$\mathrm{B}(x,y) = \int_0^1 t^{x-1}(1-t)^{y-1}dt,$$
$$\operatorname{Re} x,\ \operatorname{Re} y > 0,$$

satisfies the property [14] (Equation 1.5.5)

$$\mathrm{B}(x,y) = \frac{\Gamma(x)\Gamma(y)}{\Gamma(x+y)}. \tag{4}$$

Further, the incomplete beta function is defined as [15] (Equation 8.17.1):

$$\mathrm{B}_z(x,y) = \int_0^z t^{x-1}(1-t)^{y-1}dt, \tag{5}$$

which satisfies the property [13] (Equation 58:5:1),

$$\mathrm{B}_z(a,b) + \mathrm{B}_{1-z}(b,a) = \mathrm{B}(a,b). \tag{6}$$

A function related to the incomplete beta function is the Lerch function, defined as

$$\Phi(z,a,b) = \sum_{k=0}^{\infty} \frac{z^k}{(k+b)^a}. \tag{7}$$

According to (1), we have

$$\frac{d}{dx}[(x)_n] = (x)_n[\psi(x+n) - \psi(x)], \tag{8}$$

and

$$\frac{d}{dx}\left[\frac{1}{(x)_n}\right] = \frac{1}{(x)_n}[\psi(x) - \psi(x+n)], \tag{9}$$

where $\psi(x)$ denotes the digamma function [13] (Ch. 44)

$$\psi(x) = \frac{\Gamma'(x)}{\Gamma(x)}, \tag{10}$$

with the following properties [14] (Equations 1.3.3-4&8)

$$\psi\left(\frac{1}{2}\right) = -\gamma - 2\ln 2, \tag{11}$$

$$\psi(z+1) = \frac{1}{z} + \psi(z), \tag{12}$$

$$\psi(1-z) - \psi(z) = \pi\cot(\pi z), \tag{13}$$

with γ being the Euler–Mascheroni constant.

Finally, ${}_pF_q(z)$ denotes the generalized hypergeometric function, usually defined by means of the hypergeometric series [15] (Section 16.2):

$$ {}_pF_q\left(\begin{array}{c} a_1,\ldots,a_p \\ b_1,\ldots b_q \end{array} \middle| z \right) = \sum_{k=0}^{\infty} \frac{(a_1)_k \cdots (a_p)_k}{(b_1)_k \cdots (b_q)_k} \frac{z^k}{k!}, \tag{14} $$

whenever this series converges and elsewhere by analytic continuation.

In addition, the Meijer-G function is defined via the Mellin–Barnes integral representation [15] (Equation 16.17.1):

$$ \begin{aligned} & G_{p,q}^{m,n}\left(z \middle| \begin{array}{c} a_1,\ldots,a_p \\ b_1,\ldots b_q \end{array} \right) \\ = & \frac{1}{2\pi i} \int_L \frac{\prod_{\ell=1}^{m}\Gamma(b_\ell - s)\prod_{\ell=1}^{m}\Gamma(1-a_\ell+s)}{\prod_{\ell=m}^{q-1}\Gamma(1-b_{\ell+1}+s)\prod_{\ell=n}^{p-1}\Gamma(a_{\ell+1}-s)} z^s ds, \end{aligned} $$

where the integration path L separates the poles of the factors $\Gamma(b_\ell - s)$ from those of the factors $\Gamma(1-a_\ell+s)$.

3. Sums Connected to the Incomplete Beta Function

3.1. Derivatives of the Incomplete Beta Function with Respect to the Parameters

Theorem 1. *The following parameter derivative holds true:*

$$ \frac{\partial}{\partial a} \mathrm{B}_z(a,b) = \ln z\, \mathrm{B}_z(a,b) - \frac{z^a}{a^2}\, {}_3F_2\left(\begin{array}{c} 1-b,a,a \\ a+1,a+1 \end{array} \middle| z \right). \tag{15} $$

Proof. According to the definition of the incomplete beta function (5), we have

$$ \frac{\partial}{\partial a} \mathrm{B}_z(a,b) = \int_0^z t^{a-1}(1-t)^{b-1} \ln t\, dt. \tag{16} $$

Now, apply the formulas [13] (Equation 18:3:4),

$$ \frac{1}{(1-t)^{\nu}} = \sum_{k=0}^{\infty} (\nu)_k \frac{t^k}{k!}, \tag{17} $$

and [16] (Equation 1.6.1(18))

$$ \int x^p \ln x\, dx = x^{p+1}\left[\frac{\ln x}{p+1} - \frac{1}{(p+1)^2} \right], \tag{18} $$

in order to rewrite (16) as

$$ \frac{\partial}{\partial a} \mathrm{B}_z(a,b) = z^a \left\{ \ln z \sum_{k=0}^{\infty} \frac{(1-b)_k z^k}{k!(a+k)} - \sum_{k=0}^{\infty} \frac{(1-b)_k z^k}{k!(a+k)^2} \right\}. \tag{19} $$

Taking into account the property

$$ \frac{1}{\alpha+k} = \frac{(\alpha)_k}{\alpha(\alpha+1)_k}, $$

and the definition of the generalized hypergeometric function (14), we may recast the the sums given in (19) as

$$ \frac{\partial}{\partial a} \mathrm{B}_z(a,b) = z^a \left\{ \frac{\ln z}{a}\, {}_2F_1\left(\begin{array}{c} 1-b,a \\ a+1 \end{array} \middle| z \right) - \frac{1}{a^2}\, {}_3F_2\left(\begin{array}{c} 1-b,a,a \\ a+1,a+1 \end{array} \middle| z \right) \right\}. \tag{20} $$

Finally, apply to (20) the reduction formula [17] (Equation 7.3.1(28))

$$ {}_2F_1\left(\begin{array}{c} \alpha, \beta \\ \beta+1 \end{array} \middle| z \right) = \beta\, z^{-\beta}\, \mathrm{B}_z(\beta, 1-\alpha), \tag{21} $$

in order to arrive at (15), as we wanted to prove. □

As a consequence of the last theorem, we calculate the next integral, which does not seem to be tabulated in the most common literature.

Theorem 2. *For* $\mathrm{Re}\,\alpha > -1$ *and* $\mathrm{Re}\,z > 0$, *the following integral holds true:*

$$ \int_0^z \frac{u^\alpha}{1-u^2} \ln u\, du = \frac{1}{2} \ln z\, \mathrm{B}_{z^2}\left(\frac{1+\alpha}{2}, 0 \right) - \frac{z^{\alpha+1}}{4}\, \Phi\left(z^2, 2, \frac{1+\alpha}{2} \right). \tag{22} $$

Proof. According to [13] (Equation 58:14:7), we have

$$ \mathrm{B}_{\tanh^2(x)}(\lambda, 0) = 2 \int_0^x \tanh^{2\lambda-1} t\, dt. $$

Performing the substitutions $z = \tanh x$ and $u = \tanh t$, we obtain

$$ \mathrm{B}_{z^2}(\lambda, 0) = 2 \int_0^z \frac{u^{2\lambda-1}}{1-u^2}\, du. \tag{23} $$

On the one hand, calculate the derivative of the LHS of (23) with respect to the parameter λ, taking into account (15),

$$ \frac{\partial}{\partial \lambda} \mathrm{B}_{z^2}(\lambda, 0) = 2 \ln z\, \mathrm{B}_{z^2}(\lambda, 0) - \frac{z^{2\lambda}}{\lambda^2}\, {}_3F_2\left(\begin{array}{c} 1, \lambda, \lambda \\ \lambda+1, \lambda+1 \end{array} \middle| z^2 \right). \tag{24} $$

In order to calculate the ${}_3F_2$ function given in (24), we apply the reduction formula [17] (Equation 7.4.1(5))

$$ {}_3F_2\left(\begin{array}{c} a, b, c \\ a+1, b+1 \end{array} \middle| x \right) = \frac{1}{b-a} \left[b\, {}_2F_1\left(\begin{array}{c} a, c \\ a+1 \end{array} \middle| x \right) - a\, {}_2F_1\left(\begin{array}{c} b, c \\ b+1 \end{array} \middle| x \right) \right]. $$

Thus, taking $c = 1$ and applying the reduction formula [17] (Equation 7.3.1(122))

$$ {}_2F_1\left(\begin{array}{c} 1, b \\ b+1 \end{array} \middle| x \right) = b\, \Phi(x, 1, b), $$

as well as the definition of the Lerch function (7), we have

$$ \begin{aligned} {}_3F_2\left(\begin{array}{c} 1, a, b \\ a+1, b+1 \end{array} \middle| x \right) &= \frac{ab}{b-a} [\Phi(x, 1, a) - \Phi(x, 1, b)] \\ &= \frac{ab}{b-a} \sum_{k=0}^{\infty} x^k \left(\frac{1}{k+a} - \frac{1}{k+b} \right) \\ &= ab \sum_{k=0}^{\infty} \frac{x^k}{(k+a)(k+b)}. \end{aligned} $$

Therefore, taking $a = \lambda$, $b = \lambda + \epsilon$, we have

$$ \begin{aligned} {}_3F_2\left(\begin{array}{c} 1, \lambda, \lambda \\ \lambda+1, \lambda+1 \end{array} \middle| z^2 \right) &= \lim_{\epsilon \to 0} \lambda(\lambda+\epsilon) \sum_{k=0}^{\infty} \frac{z^{2k}}{(k+\lambda)(k+\lambda+\epsilon)} \\ &= \lambda^2\, \Phi\left(z^2, 2, \lambda \right). \end{aligned} \tag{25} $$

Insert (25) in (24) to obtain

$$\frac{\partial}{\partial\lambda}\mathrm{B}_{z^2}(\lambda,0) = 2\ln z\,\mathrm{B}_{z^2}(\lambda,0) - z^{2\lambda}\,\Phi\left(z^2,2,\lambda\right). \tag{26}$$

On the other hand, calculate the derivative of the RHS of (23) as

$$2\frac{\partial}{\partial\lambda}\int_0^z \frac{u^{2\lambda-1}}{1-u^2}\,du = 4\int_0^z \frac{u^{2\lambda-1}}{1-u^2}\ln u\,du. \tag{27}$$

Finally, equate (26) to (27) and perform the substitution $\alpha = 2\lambda - 1$ to complete the proof. □

Lemma 1. *For* $\alpha \neq 1$, $\mathrm{Re}\,\alpha < 2$, *the following reduction formula holds true:*

$${}_3F_2\left(\begin{array}{c}\alpha,\beta,\beta\\ \beta+1,\beta+1\end{array}\middle|1\right) = \beta^2\,\mathrm{B}(1-\alpha,b)[\psi(1+\beta-\alpha)-\psi(\beta)]. \tag{28}$$

Proof. Take $a=\beta+\epsilon, b=\beta, c=\alpha$ and calculate the limit $\epsilon\to 0$ in the following reduction formula [17] (Equation 7.4.4(16))

$${}_3F_2\left(\begin{array}{c}a,b,c\\ a+1,b+1\end{array}\middle|1\right) = \frac{a\,b}{a-b}\Gamma(1-c)\left\{\frac{\Gamma(b)}{\Gamma(1+b-c)}-\frac{\Gamma(a)}{\Gamma(1+a-c)}\right\},$$
$$a\neq b,\ c\neq 1,\ \mathrm{Re}\,c<2,$$

to obtain:

$$\begin{aligned}&{}_3F_2\left(\begin{array}{c}\alpha,\beta,\beta\\ \beta+1,\beta+1\end{array}\middle|1\right) \\ =\ &\lim_{\epsilon\to 0}\beta(\beta+\epsilon)\,\Gamma(1-\alpha)\,\frac{\Gamma(\beta)\,\Gamma(1+\beta-\alpha+\epsilon)-\Gamma(1+\beta-\alpha)\,\Gamma(\beta+\epsilon)}{\epsilon\,\Gamma(1+\beta-\alpha)\,\Gamma(1+\beta-\alpha+\epsilon)}.\end{aligned} \tag{29}$$

Apply the Taylor series expansion

$$\Gamma(x+\epsilon) = \Gamma(x)+\Gamma(x)\,\psi(x)\,\epsilon + O\left(\epsilon^2\right),$$

to calculate (29). After simplification, we arrive at (28), as we wanted to prove. □

Theorem 3. *The following parameter derivative holds true:*

$$\begin{aligned}\frac{\partial}{\partial b}\mathrm{B}_z(a,b) &= \frac{(1-z)^b}{b^2}\,{}_3F_2\left(\begin{array}{c}1-a,b,b\\ b+1,b+1\end{array}\middle|1-z\right) \\ &\quad -\ln(1-z)\,\mathrm{B}_{1-z}(b,a) - \mathrm{B}(a,b)[\psi(a+b)-\psi(b)].\end{aligned} \tag{30}$$

Proof. According to the definition of the incomplete beta function (5), we have

$$\frac{\partial}{\partial b}\mathrm{B}_z(a,b) = \int_0^z t^{a-1}(1-t)^{b-1}\ln(1-t)dt.$$

Perform the substitution $\tau = 1 - t$ and apply the Formulas (17) and (18) to obtain

$$\begin{aligned}&\frac{\partial}{\partial b}\mathrm{B}_z(a,b) \\ =\;& (1-z)^b\left\{\sum_{k=0}^{\infty}\frac{(1-a)_k(1-z)^k}{k!(b+k)^2} - \ln(1-z)\sum_{k=0}^{\infty}\frac{(1-a)_k(1-z)^k}{k!(b+k)}\right\} \\ &-\sum_{k=0}^{\infty}\frac{(1-a)_k}{k!(b+k)^2}.\end{aligned} \tag{31}$$

Finally, write the sums given in (31) as hypergeometric functions and apply the results given in (21) and (28) to arrive at (30), as we wanted to prove. □

Proof. (Alternative). Consider (15) perform the substitutions $a \leftrightarrow b$ and $z \to 1-z$ to obtain

$$\frac{\partial}{\partial b}\mathrm{B}_{1-z}(b,a) = \ln(1-z)\,\mathrm{B}_{1-z}(b,a) - \frac{(1-z)^b}{b^2}\,{}_3F_2\left(\left.\begin{array}{c}1-a,b,b\\ b+1,b+1\end{array}\right|1-z\right). \tag{32}$$

Take into account (6) in order to rewrite (32) as

$$\begin{aligned}&\frac{\partial}{\partial b}\mathrm{B}_z(a,b) \\ =\;& \frac{(1-z)^b}{b^2}\,{}_3F_2\left(\left.\begin{array}{c}1-a,b,b\\ b+1,b+1\end{array}\right|1-z\right) - \ln(1-z)\,\mathrm{B}_{1-z}(b,a) - \frac{\partial}{\partial b}\mathrm{B}(a,b).\end{aligned} \tag{33}$$

According to (4) and (10), note that

$$\begin{aligned}\frac{\partial}{\partial b}\mathrm{B}(a,b) &= \frac{\partial}{\partial b}\left(\frac{\Gamma(a)\,\Gamma(b)}{\Gamma(a+b)}\right) \\ &= \mathrm{B}(a,b)[\psi(b)-\psi(a+b)].\end{aligned} \tag{34}$$

Insert (34) in (33) to complete the proof. □

3.2. *Calculation of Sums Involving the Digamma Function*

Theorem 4. *For $b \neq c+1$ and $z \in \mathbb{C}$, $|z| < 1$ the following sum holds true:*

$$\begin{aligned}&\sum_{k=0}^{\infty}\frac{(b)_k}{(c)_k}\psi(b+k)\,z^k \\ =\;& (c-1)z^{1-c}\left\{\frac{1}{(b-c+1)^2}\,{}_3F_2\left(\left.\begin{array}{c}2-c,b-c+1,b-c+1\\ b-c+2,b-c+2\end{array}\right|1-z\right)\right. \\ &\left.+(1-z)^{c-b-1}[(\psi(b-c+1)-\ln(1-z))\,\mathrm{B}(b-c+1,c-1)+\psi(b)\,\mathrm{B}_{1-z}(b-c+1,c-1)]\right\}\end{aligned} \tag{35}$$

Proof. On the one hand, applying the ratio test, we see that the sum given in (35) converges for $|z| < 1$ and diverges for $|z| > 1$. Indeed, taking

$$a_k = \frac{(b)_k}{(c)_k}\psi(b+k)z^k,$$

and taking into account (12), we have

$$\begin{aligned}\lim_{k\to\infty}\left|\frac{a_{k+1}}{a_k}\right| &= \lim_{k\to\infty}\left|\frac{(b+k)\psi(b+k+1)}{(c+k)\psi(b+k)}z\right| \\ &= \lim_{k\to\infty}\left|\frac{b+k}{c+k}\left(\frac{1}{(b+k)\psi(b+k)}+1\right)z\right| = |z|.\end{aligned}$$

On the other hand, let us differentiate both sides of the reduction formula [17] (Equation 7.3.1(119)) with respect to parameter b:

$$\begin{aligned} \sum_{k=0}^{\infty} \frac{(b)_k}{(c)_k} z^k &= {}_2F_1\left(\begin{array}{c} 1, b \\ c \end{array} \middle| z \right) \\ &= z^{1-c}(1-z)^{c-b-1}(c-1)\, \mathrm{B}_z(c-1, b-c+1). \end{aligned} \tag{36}$$

Apply (8) and (36) to the LHS of (36), to obtain:

$$\begin{aligned} \frac{\partial}{\partial b} \sum_{k=0}^{\infty} \frac{(b)_k}{(c)_k} z^k &= \sum_{k=0}^{\infty} \frac{(b)_k}{(c)_k} [\psi(b+k) - \psi(b)] z^k \\ = \sum_{k=0}^{\infty} \frac{(b)_k}{(c)_k} [\psi(b+k)] z^k &- \psi(b)\, z^{1-c}(1-z)^{c-b-1}(c-1)\, \mathrm{B}_z(c-1, b-c+1). \end{aligned} \tag{37}$$

On the RHS of (36), we obtain

$$\begin{aligned} & (c-1) z^{1-c} \frac{\partial}{\partial b} \left[(1-z)^{c-b-1}\, \mathrm{B}_z(c-1, b-c+1) \right] \\ = \; & (c-1) z^{1-c} (1-z)^{c-b-1} \left[-\ln(1-z) \mathrm{B}_z(c-1, b-c+1) + \frac{\partial}{\partial b} \mathrm{B}_z(c-1, b-c+1) \right]. \end{aligned} \tag{38}$$

According to (30), we have

$$\begin{aligned} & \frac{\partial}{\partial b} \mathrm{B}_z(c-1, b-c+1) \\ = \; & \frac{(1-z)^{b-c+1}}{(b-c+1)^2}\, {}_3F_2\left(\begin{array}{c} 2-c, b-c+1, b-c+1 \\ b-c+2, b-c+2 \end{array} \middle| 1-z \right) \\ & - \ln(1-z)\, \mathrm{B}_{1-z}(b-c+1, c-1) + \mathrm{B}(c-1, b-c+1)[\psi(1+b-c) - \psi(b)]. \end{aligned} \tag{39}$$

Now, insert (39) in (38) and apply the Formula (6) to arrive at

$$\begin{aligned} & (c-1) z^{1-c} \frac{\partial}{\partial b} \left[(1-z)^{c-b-1}\, \mathrm{B}_z(c-1, b-c+1) \right] \\ = \; & (c-1) z^{1-c} \Big\{ (1-z)^{c-b+1} \mathrm{B}(c-1, b-c+1)[\psi(1+b-c) - \psi(b) - \ln(1-z)] \\ & + \frac{1}{(b-c+1)^2}\, {}_3F_2\left(\begin{array}{c} 2-c, b-c+1, b-c+1 \\ b-c+2, b-c+2 \end{array} \middle| 1-z \right) \Big\}. \end{aligned} \tag{40}$$

Finally, equate the results given in (37) and (40) and apply (6) again to complete the proof. □

Remark 1. *It is worth noting that for $z = 1$, the sum given in (35) can be calculated taking $a = 1$ in [6] (Equation (23)):*

$$\begin{aligned} & \sum_{k=0}^{\infty} \frac{(a)_k (b)_k}{k!(c)_k} \psi(b+k) \\ = \; & \frac{\Gamma(c)\Gamma(c-a-b)}{\Gamma(c-b)\Gamma(c-a)} [\psi(c-b) - \psi(c-a-b) + \psi(b)], \\ & \mathrm{Re}(c-a-b) > 0, \end{aligned} \tag{41}$$

thus

$$\begin{aligned} & \sum_{k=0}^{\infty} \frac{(b)_k}{(c)_k} \psi(b+k) = \frac{c-1}{c-b-1} \left[\frac{1}{c-b-1} + \psi(b) \right], \\ & \mathrm{Re}(c-b) > 1. \end{aligned}$$

Corollary 1. *For $z \in \mathbb{C}$ and $|z| < 1$ the following formula holds true:*

$$\begin{aligned} &\sum_{k=1}^{\infty} \psi(b+k) z^k \\ = \;& (b-1) z^{1-b} {}_3F_2\left(\begin{array}{c} 1,1,2-b \\ 2,2 \end{array} \middle| 1-z \right) + \frac{z^{1-b}}{z-1}[\gamma + \ln(1-z)] + \frac{z^{1-b}}{z-1}\psi(b). \end{aligned} \tag{42}$$

Proof. Put apart the term for $k = 0$ in (35) and take $b = c$. □

Corollary 2. *For $z \in \mathbb{C}$, and $a \neq 1$, the following reduction formula holds true:*

$$ {}_3F_2\left(\begin{array}{c} 1,1,a \\ 2,2 \end{array} \middle| z \right) = \frac{\psi(2-a) + \gamma + \ln z + \mathrm{B}_{1-z}(2-a,0)}{(1-a)z}. \tag{43}$$

Proof. Taking into account (36) for $c = b+1$, compare (42) to the result found in the existing literature [4] (Equation (1.2)):

$$\begin{aligned} \sum_{k=1}^{\infty} \psi(b+k) z^k &= \frac{z}{1-z}\left[\psi(b) + \frac{1}{b}\, {}_2F_1\left(\begin{array}{c} 1,b \\ b+1 \end{array} \middle| z \right)\right] \\ &= \frac{z}{1-z}\left[\psi(b) + \frac{\mathrm{B}_z(b,0)}{z^b}\right], \end{aligned}$$

and solve for the ${}_3F_2$ function with $a = 2 - b$ to obtain the desired result. □

Remark 2. *It is worth noting that for $(2-a) \in \mathbb{Q} - \{-1,-2,\ldots\}$, the incomplete beta function $\mathrm{B}_{1-z}(2-a,0)$ given in (43) can be expressed in terms of elementary functions [18]. For instance, taking $a = 3/2$ in (43) and considering (11) and the formula for $n = 0,1,\ldots$ [18]*

$$\mathrm{B}_z\left(n+\frac{1}{2},0\right) = 2\left(\tanh^{-1}\sqrt{z} - \sum_{k=0}^{n-1} \frac{z^{k+1/2}}{2k+1}\right),$$

we arrive at

$$ {}_3F_2\left(\begin{array}{c} 1,1,\frac{3}{2} \\ 2,2 \end{array} \middle| z \right) = \frac{4}{z}\ln\left(\frac{2(1-\sqrt{1-z})}{z}\right),$$

which is given in the existing literature [17] (Equation 7.4.2(365)).

Remark 3. *As a consistency test, we can recover a known formula by taking the limit $a \to 1$ in (43). Indeed,*

$$ {}_3F_2\left(\begin{array}{c} 1,1,1 \\ 2,2 \end{array} \middle| z \right) = \lim_{a\to 1} \frac{\psi(2-a) + \gamma + \ln z + \mathrm{B}_{1-z}(2-a,0)}{(1-a)z}.$$

Perform the substitution $b = 1 - a$, take into account (5) and the Formula [15] (Equation 5.9.16):

$$\psi(z) + \gamma = \int_0^1 \frac{1-t^{z-1}}{1-t}dt,$$

to obtain

$$\begin{aligned} {}_3F_2\left(\begin{array}{c} 1,1,1 \\ 2,2 \end{array} \middle| z \right) &= \lim_{b\to 0} \frac{\psi(1+b) + \gamma + \ln z + \mathrm{B}_{1-z}(1+b,0)}{b\,z} \\ &= \lim_{b\to 0} \frac{1}{b\,z}\left[\ln z + \int_0^1 \frac{1-t^b}{1-t}dt + \int_0^{1-z} \frac{t^b}{1-t}dt\right]. \end{aligned}$$

Now, perform the susbstitution $\tau = 1 - t$, and apply the Taylor series:

$$(1-\tau)^b = \sum_{n=0}^{\infty} \frac{\ln^n(1-\tau)}{n!} b^n,$$

to arrive at

$$\begin{aligned}
&{}_3F_2\left(\begin{array}{c} 1,1,1 \\ 2,2 \end{array} \middle| z \right) \\
=& \lim_{b\to 0} \frac{1}{b\,z} \left[\ln z - \int_0^1 \frac{1-(1-\tau)^b}{\tau} d\tau + \int_1^z \frac{(1-\tau)^b}{\tau} dt \right] \\
=& \lim_{b\to 0} \frac{1}{b\,z} \left[\ln z - \int_0^1 \frac{\ln(1-\tau)}{\tau} b\, d\tau - \int_1^z \left(\frac{1}{\tau} + \frac{\ln(1-\tau)}{\tau} b \right) dt \right] \\
=& -\frac{1}{z} \int_0^z \frac{\ln(1-\tau)}{\tau} d\tau.
\end{aligned}$$

From the following formula of the dilogarithm function [15] (Equation 25.12.2)

$$\mathrm{Li}_2(z) = -\int_0^z \frac{\ln(1-\tau)}{\tau} d\tau,$$

we recover the following result found in the existing literature [17] (Equation 7.4.2(355)):

$${}_3F_2\left(\begin{array}{c} 1,1,1 \\ 2,2 \end{array} \middle| z \right) = \frac{\mathrm{Li}_2(z)}{z}.$$

Theorem 5. *For $a \neq 1$ and $z \in \mathbb{C}$, $|z| < 1$, the following sum holds true:*

$$\begin{aligned}
&\sum_{k=0}^{\infty} \frac{(a)_k (b)_k}{k!(b+1)_k} \psi(a+k) z^k \qquad (44) \\
=& \; b\,z^{-b} \{ [\ln(1-z) - \psi(a)]\, \mathrm{B}_{1-z}(1-a,b) + [\psi(1+b-a) - \pi\cot(\pi a)]\, \mathrm{B}(b,1-a) \\
&- \frac{(1-z)^{1-a}}{(1-a)^2} {}_3F_2\left(\begin{array}{c} 1-b, 1-a, 1-a \\ 2-a, 2-a \end{array} \middle| 1-z \right) \right\}.
\end{aligned}$$

Proof. On the one hand, applying the ratio test, we see that the sum given in (44) converges for $|z| < 1$ and diverges for $|z| > 1$. Indeed, taking

$$c_k = \frac{(a)_k (b)_k}{k!(b+1)_k} \psi(a+k) z^k$$

and taking into account (12), we have

$$\begin{aligned}
\lim_{k\to\infty} \left| \frac{c_{k+1}}{c_k} \right| &= \lim_{k\to\infty} \left| \frac{(a+k)(b+k)\psi(a+k+1)}{(k+1)(b+1+k)\psi(a+k)} z \right| \\
&= \lim_{k\to\infty} \left| \frac{(a+k)(b+k)}{(k+1)(b+1+k)} \left(\frac{1}{(a+k)\psi(a+k)} + 1 \right) z \right| = |z|.
\end{aligned}$$

On the other hand, taking into account (8), differentiate the reduction Formula (21), i.e.,

$${}_2F_1\left(\begin{array}{c} a,b \\ b+1 \end{array} \middle| z \right) = \sum_{k=0}^{\infty} \frac{(a)_k (b)_k}{k!(b+1)_k} z^k = b\,z^{-b}\, \mathrm{B}_z(b,1-a),$$

with respect to the parameter a to obtain

$$\sum_{k=0}^{\infty} \frac{(a)_k (b)_k}{k!(b+1)_k} [\psi(a+k) - \psi(a)] z^k = b\, z^{-b} \frac{\partial}{\partial a} \mathrm{B}_z(b, 1-a). \tag{45}$$

Apply (21) on the LHS of (45) and (30) on the RHS of (45) to arrive at

$$\begin{aligned} &\sum_{k=0}^{\infty} \frac{(a)_k (b)_k}{k!(b+1)_k} \psi(a+k) z^k \\ = \; & b\, z^{-b} \{ \ln(1-z)\, \mathrm{B}_{1-z}(1-a, b) + \mathrm{B}(b, 1-a)[\psi(1+b-a) - \psi(1-a)] \\ & + \psi(a)\, \mathrm{B}_z(b, 1-a) - \frac{(1-z)^{1-a}}{(1-a)^2}\, {}_3F_2\left(\begin{array}{c} 1-b, 1-a, 1-a \\ 2-a, 2-a \end{array} \middle| 1-z \right) \right\}. \end{aligned} \tag{46}$$

Finally, apply (6) and (13) in order to reduce (46) to (44), as we wanted to prove. □

Remark 4. *It is worth noting that for $z = 1$, the sum given in (44) can be calculated taking $c = b+1$ in (41) and applying (2), (4) and (13), to obtain:*

$$\sum_{k=0}^{\infty} \frac{(a)_k (b)_k}{k!(b+1)_k} \psi(b+k) = b\, \mathrm{B}(b, 1-a) [\psi(1+b-a) - \pi \cot(\pi a)],$$
$$\mathrm{Re}\, a < 1.$$

Corollary 3. *For $a \neq 1$, and $z \in \mathbb{C}$, $|z| < 1$ the following formula holds true:*

$$\begin{aligned} &\sum_{k=0}^{\infty} \frac{(a)_k}{(k+1)!} \psi(a+k) z^k = \frac{1}{(1-a)z} \\ &\left\{ (1-z)^{1-a} \left[\ln(1-z) - \psi(a) + \frac{1}{a-1} \right] + \psi(2-a) - \pi \cot(\pi a) \right\}. \end{aligned} \tag{47}$$

Proof. Take $b = 1$ in (44) and consider that for $a \neq 1$ we have

$$\begin{aligned} \mathrm{B}_{1-z}(1-a, 1) &= \frac{(1-z)^{1-a}}{1-a}, \\ \mathrm{B}(1, 1-a) &= \frac{1}{1-a}. \end{aligned}$$

□

4. Sums Connected to Bessel Functions

If we differentiate the following sum formulas [17] (Equation 7.13.1(1)):

$${}_0F_1\left(\begin{array}{c} - \\ b \end{array} \middle| -z \right) = \sum_{k=0}^{\infty} \frac{(-z)^k}{k!(b)_k} = \Gamma(b)\, z^{(1-b)/2} J_{b-1}(2\sqrt{z}),$$

and

$${}_0F_1\left(\begin{array}{c} - \\ b \end{array} \middle| z \right) = \sum_{k=0}^{\infty} \frac{z^k}{k!(b)_k} = \Gamma(b)\, z^{(1-b)/2} I_{b-1}(2\sqrt{z}),$$

with respect to parameter b, taking into account (9), we obtain:

$$\begin{aligned} &\sum_{k=0}^{\infty} \frac{(-z)^k \psi(k+b)}{k!(b)_k} \\ = \; & z^{(1-b)/2} \Gamma(b) \left[J_{b-1}(2\sqrt{z}) \ln \sqrt{z} - \frac{\partial J_{b-1}(2\sqrt{z})}{\partial b} \right], \end{aligned} \tag{48}$$

and

$$\sum_{k=0}^{\infty} \frac{z^k \psi(k+b)}{k!(b)_k} \tag{49}$$
$$= z^{(1-b)/2}\Gamma(b) \left[I_{b-1}(2\sqrt{z}) \ln \sqrt{z} - \frac{\partial I_{b-1}(2\sqrt{z})}{\partial b} \right],$$

which are found in an equivalent form in [1] (Equations 55.7.11-12). For $b = n \in \mathbb{N}$, we found a closed-form expression for (49) in [4] (Equation (5.11)). We can obtain closed-form expressions for other values of b using the following formulas [19] (Equations (93) and (99)) for $\nu \geq 0$, $\mathrm{Re}\, z > 0$:

$$\frac{\partial J_\nu(z)}{\partial \nu} = \frac{\pi}{2} \left[\frac{Y_\nu(z)(z/2)^{2\nu}}{\Gamma^2(\nu+1)}\, {}_2F_3\left(\begin{array}{c} \nu, \nu+\frac{1}{2} \\ 2\nu+1, \nu+1, \nu+1 \end{array} \middle| -z^2 \right) - \frac{\nu J_\nu(z)}{\sqrt{\pi}} G^{3,0}_{2,4}\left(z^2 \middle| \begin{array}{c} \frac{1}{2}, 1 \\ 0, 0, \nu, -\nu \end{array} \right) \right], \tag{50}$$

and

$$\frac{\partial I_\nu(z)}{\partial \nu} = \frac{-\nu I_\nu(z)}{2\sqrt{\pi}} G^{3,1}_{2,4}\left(z^2 \middle| \begin{array}{c} \frac{1}{2}, 1 \\ 0, 0, \nu, -\nu \end{array} \right) - \frac{K_\nu(z)(z/2)^{2\nu}}{\Gamma^2(\nu+1)}\, {}_2F_3\left(\begin{array}{c} \nu, \nu+\frac{1}{2} \\ 2\nu+1, \nu+1, \nu+1 \end{array} \middle| z^2 \right). \tag{51}$$

Theorem 6. *For $b \geq 1$ and $\mathrm{Re}\, z > 0$, the following sum holds true:*

$$\sum_{k=0}^{\infty} \frac{(-z)^k \psi(k+b)}{k!(b)_k} \tag{52}$$
$$= \frac{z^{-(1+b)/2}}{8\,\Gamma(b)} \left\{ \Gamma^2(b) J_{b-1}(2\sqrt{z}) \left[\sqrt{\pi}(b-1) G^{3,0}_{2,4}\left(4z \middle| \begin{array}{c} \frac{3}{2}, 2 \\ 1, 1, b, 2-b \end{array} \right) + 4z \ln z \right] - 4\pi\, z^b Y_{b-1}(2\sqrt{z})\, {}_2F_3\left(\begin{array}{c} b-1, b-\frac{1}{2} \\ b, b, 2b-1 \end{array} \middle| -4z \right) \right\}.$$

Proof. Calculate (48) taking into account (50) to arrive at the desired result. □

Theorem 7. *For $b \geq 1$ and $\mathrm{Re}\, z > 0$, the following sum holds true:*

$$\sum_{k=0}^{\infty} \frac{z^k \psi(k+b)}{k!(b)_k} \tag{53}$$
$$= \frac{z^{-(1+b)/2}}{8\sqrt{\pi}\Gamma(b)} \left\{ \Gamma^2(b) I_{b-1}(2\sqrt{z}) \left[(b-1) G^{3,1}_{2,4}\left(4z \middle| \begin{array}{c} \frac{3}{2}, 2 \\ 1, 1, b, 2-b \end{array} \right) + 4\sqrt{\pi} z \ln z \right] + 8\sqrt{\pi}\, z^b K_{b-1}(2\sqrt{z})\, {}_2F_3\left(\begin{array}{c} b-1, b-\frac{1}{2} \\ b, b, 2b-1 \end{array} \middle| 4z \right) \right\}.$$

Proof. Calculate (49) taking into account (51) to arrive at the desired result. □

Theorem 8. *For $b \geq 1$ and $\mathrm{Re}\, z > 0$, the following sum holds true:*

$$\sum_{k=0}^{\infty} \frac{z^k \psi(2k+b)}{k!\left(\frac{1}{2}\right)_k \left(\frac{b}{2}\right)_k \left(\frac{b+1}{2}\right)_k} \tag{54}$$
$$= \frac{\Gamma(b)}{2^b z^{(b-1)/4}}$$
$$\left\{ \ln\left(2\,z^{1/4}\right)\left[J_{b-1}\left(4\,z^{1/4}\right) + I_{b-1}\left(4\,z^{1/4}\right)\right] - \frac{\partial J_{b-1}\left(4\,z^{1/4}\right)}{\partial b} - \frac{\partial I_{b-1}\left(4\,z^{1/4}\right)}{\partial b} \right\},$$

where the order derivatives of the Bessel functions are calculated using (50) and (51).

Proof. Sum up (48) and (49) using the duplication formula of the gamma function (3) to arrive at the desired result. □

Theorem 9. *For $b \geq 1$ and $\operatorname{Re} z > 0$, the following sum holds true:*

$$\sum_{k=0}^{\infty} \frac{z^k \psi(2k+b)}{k!\left(\frac{3}{2}\right)_k \left(\frac{b}{2}\right)_k \left(\frac{b+1}{2}\right)_k} \tag{55}$$
$$= \frac{\Gamma(b)}{2^{b+1} z^{b/4}}$$
$$\left\{ \ln\left(2\,z^{1/4}\right)\left[I_{b-2}\left(4\,z^{1/4}\right) - J_{b-2}\left(4\,z^{1/4}\right)\right] - \frac{\partial I_{b-2}\left(4\,z^{1/4}\right)}{\partial b} + \frac{\partial J_{b-2}\left(4\,z^{1/4}\right)}{\partial b} \right\},$$

where the order derivatives of the Bessel functions are calculated using (50) and (51).

Proof. Substract (49) from (48) and apply (3) again to arrrive at the desired result. □

5. Application to the Parameter Derivative of Some Special Functions

5.1. Application to the Derivative of the Wright Function with Respect to the Parameters

The Wright function is defined as [15] (Equation 10.46.1):

$$\mathrm{W}_{\alpha,\beta}(z) = \sum_{k=0}^{\infty} \frac{z^k}{k!\,\Gamma(\alpha k+\beta)}, \quad \alpha > -1,$$

thus,

$$\frac{\partial \mathrm{W}_{\alpha,\beta}(z)}{\partial \alpha} = -\sum_{k=1}^{\infty} \frac{k\,z^k \psi(\alpha k+\beta)}{k!\,\Gamma(\alpha k+\beta)}, \tag{56}$$
$$\frac{\partial \mathrm{W}_{\alpha,\beta}(z)}{\partial \beta} = -\sum_{k=0}^{\infty} \frac{z^k \psi(\alpha k+\beta)}{k!\,\Gamma(\alpha k+\beta)}, \tag{57}$$

and the following equation is satisfied:

$$\frac{\partial \mathrm{W}_{\alpha,\beta}(z)}{\partial \alpha} = z\frac{\partial}{\partial z}\left(\frac{\partial \mathrm{W}_{\alpha,\beta}(z)}{\partial \beta}\right). \tag{58}$$

In reference [20], we found some reduction formulas for the first derivative of the Wright function with respect to the parameters for particular values of α and β. Next, we extend these reduction formulas. For this purpose, apply (53) to arrive at the following result:

Theorem 10. *For $\beta \geq 1$ and $\operatorname{Re} z > 0$, we have*

$$\left.\frac{\partial W_{\alpha,\beta}(z)}{\partial \beta}\right|_{\alpha=1} \tag{59}$$
$$= z^{-(1+\beta)/2}\left\{ I_{\beta-1}(2\sqrt{z})\left[\frac{1-\beta}{8\sqrt{\pi}} G^{3,1}_{2,4}\left(4z \left| \begin{array}{c} 3/2, 2 \\ 1, 1, \beta, 2-\beta \end{array}\right.\right) - \frac{z}{2}\ln z\right] - \frac{z^{\beta}}{\Gamma^2(\beta)} K_{\beta-1}(2\sqrt{z})\, {}_2F_3\left(\begin{array}{c} \beta-1, \beta-\frac{1}{2} \\ \beta, \beta, 2\beta-1 \end{array} \middle| 4z\right)\right\}.$$

Remark 5. *It is worth noting that for $\beta = 1$, Equation (59) is reduced to*

$$\left.\frac{\partial W_{\alpha,\beta}(z)}{\partial \beta}\right|_{\alpha=\beta=1} = -\frac{1}{2}\ln z\, I_0(2\sqrt{z}) - K_0(2\sqrt{z}),$$

which is found in [20] (Equation (6.8)).

Further, from (58) and (59) and with the aid of the MATHEMATICA program, we arrive at the following result:

Theorem 11. *For $\beta \geq 1$ and $\operatorname{Re} z > 0$, we have*

$$\left.\frac{\partial W_{\alpha,\beta}(z)}{\partial \alpha}\right|_{\alpha=1} = \frac{z^{-(\beta+1)/2}}{2} \tag{60}$$
$$\left\{\frac{\beta-1}{8\sqrt{\pi}}\{(\beta-1)I_{\beta-1}(2\sqrt{z}) - \sqrt{z}[I_{\beta-2}(2\sqrt{z}) + I_{\beta}(2\sqrt{z})]\} G^{3,1}_{2,4}\left(4z \left| \begin{array}{c} 3/2, 2 \\ 1, 1, \beta, 2-\beta \end{array}\right.\right)\right.$$
$$+\frac{z^{\beta}}{\Gamma^2(\beta)}\{(\beta-1)K_{\beta-1}(2\sqrt{z}) + \sqrt{z}[K_{\beta-2}(2\sqrt{z}) + K_{\beta}(2\sqrt{z})]\}\, {}_2F_3\left(\begin{array}{c} \beta-1, \beta-\frac{1}{2} \\ \beta, \beta, 2\beta-1 \end{array} \middle| 4z\right)$$
$$+\frac{I_{\beta-1}(2\sqrt{z})}{4\sqrt{\pi}}\left[2\sqrt{\pi}z[(\beta-1)\ln z - 2] + (\beta-1)G^{2,1}_{1,3}\left(4z \left| \begin{array}{c} 3/2 \\ 1, \beta, 2-\beta \end{array}\right.\right)\right]$$
$$\left. -\frac{z^{3/2}\ln z}{2}[I_{\beta-2}(2\sqrt{z}) + I_{\beta}(2\sqrt{z})] + \frac{2(1-\beta)z^{\beta}}{\Gamma^2(\beta)} K_{\beta-1}(2\sqrt{z})\, {}_1F_2\left(\begin{array}{c} \beta-\frac{1}{2} \\ \beta, 2\beta-1 \end{array} \middle| 4z\right)\right\}.$$

Remark 6. *It is worth noting that for $\beta = 1$, Equation (60) is reduced to*

$$\left.\frac{\partial W_{\alpha,\beta}(z)}{\partial \alpha}\right|_{\alpha=\beta=1} = \frac{\sqrt{z}[K_1(2\sqrt{z}) - \ln z\, I_1(2\sqrt{z})] - I_0(2\sqrt{z})}{2},$$

which is also found in [20] (Equation (6.14)).

5.2. Application to the Derivative of the Mittag–Leffler Function with Respect to the Parameters

The two-parameter Mittag–Leffler function is defined as [15] (Equation 10.46.3):

$$E_{\alpha,\beta}(z) = \sum_{k=0}^{\infty} \frac{z^k}{\Gamma(\alpha k + \beta)}, \quad \alpha > 0, \tag{61}$$

thus,

$$\frac{\partial E_{\alpha,\beta}(z)}{\partial \alpha} = -\sum_{k=0}^{\infty} \frac{k\, z^k \psi(\alpha k + \beta)}{\Gamma(\alpha k + \beta)}, \tag{62}$$
$$\frac{\partial E_{\alpha,\beta}(z)}{\partial \beta} = -\sum_{k=0}^{\infty} \frac{z^k \psi(\alpha k + \beta)}{\Gamma(\alpha k + \beta)}, \tag{63}$$

and

$$\frac{\partial \mathrm{E}_{\alpha,\beta}(z)}{\partial \alpha} = z \frac{\partial}{\partial z}\left(\frac{\partial \mathrm{E}_{\alpha,\beta}(z)}{\partial \beta}\right). \tag{64}$$

For this purpose, consider the following functions:

Definition 1. *According to [2] (Equation 6.2.1(63)), define*

$$\begin{aligned} Q(a,t) &= \sum_{k=0}^{\infty} \frac{t^k}{(a)_k} \psi(k+a) \\ &= \psi(a) + e^t \left[t^{1-a} \psi(a) \gamma(a,t) + \frac{t}{a^2} \, {}_2F_2\left(\begin{array}{c} a,a \\ a+1,a+1 \end{array} \middle| -t \right) \right], \end{aligned} \tag{65}$$

thus

$$\begin{aligned} P(a,t) &= \frac{\partial Q(a,t)}{\partial t} \\ &= \psi(a) + e^t \\ & \left\{ \frac{t-a+1}{a^2} \, {}_2F_2\left(\begin{array}{c} a,a \\ a+1,a+1 \end{array} \middle| -t \right) + t^{-a} \gamma(a,t) [1 + (t-a+1)\psi(a)] \right\}. \end{aligned} \tag{66}$$

In reference [20], we found some reduction formulas of the first derivative of the Mittag–Leffler function with respect to the parameters for particular values of α and β. In particular, we found for $q = 1, 2, \ldots$ that

$$\begin{aligned} & \left.\frac{\partial \mathrm{E}_{\alpha,\beta}(z)}{\partial \alpha}\right|_{\alpha=1/q} \\ &= -\sum_{h=0}^{q-1} \frac{h\left[\psi\left(\frac{h}{q}+\beta\right) + \tilde{Q}\left(\frac{h}{q}+\beta, z^q\right) + q\, z^q \, P\left(\frac{h}{q}+\beta, z^q\right)\right]}{\Gamma\left(\frac{h}{q}+\beta\right)} z^h, \end{aligned} \tag{67}$$

and

$$\left.\frac{\partial \mathrm{E}_{\alpha,\beta}(z)}{\partial \beta}\right|_{\alpha=1/q} = -\sum_{h=0}^{q-1} \frac{\psi\left(\frac{h}{q}+\beta\right) + \tilde{Q}\left(\frac{h}{q}+\beta, z^q\right)}{\Gamma\left(\frac{h}{q}+\beta\right)} z^h, \tag{68}$$

where

$$\tilde{Q}(a,t) = Q(a,t) - \psi(a).$$

Next, we extend these reduction formulas to other values of the parameters. For this purpose, consider the following lemma.

Lemma 2. *For $n = 1, 2, \ldots$, the following sum identity holds true:*

$$\sum_{k=0}^{\infty} a_{nk} = \sum_{k=0}^{\infty} \theta_{n,k} \, a_k, \tag{69}$$

where

$$\theta_{n,k} = \frac{1}{n} \sum_{m=1}^{n} \exp\left(\frac{2\pi\, i\, m\, k}{n}\right). \tag{70}$$

Theorem 12. *For $n = 1, 2, \ldots$, the following reduction formula holds true:*

$$\left.\frac{\partial \mathrm{E}_{\alpha,\beta}(z)}{\partial \beta}\right|_{\alpha=n} = -\frac{1}{n\,\Gamma(\beta)} \sum_{m=1}^{n} Q\left(\beta, z^{1/n} e^{i2\pi m/n}\right). \tag{71}$$

Proof. According to (63) and Lemma 2, we have

$$\begin{aligned}\left.\frac{\partial \mathrm{E}_{\alpha,\beta}(z)}{\partial \beta}\right|_{\alpha=n} &= -\sum_{k=0}^{\infty} \frac{z^k \psi(nk+\beta)}{\Gamma(nk+\beta)} \\ &= -\sum_{k=0}^{\infty} \theta_{n,k} \frac{z^{k/n}\psi(k+\beta)}{\Gamma(k+\beta)} \\ &= -\frac{1}{n\,\Gamma(\beta)} \sum_{m=1}^{n} \exp\left(\frac{2\pi\, i\, m\, k}{n}\right) \sum_{k=0}^{\infty} \frac{z^{k/n}\psi(k+\beta)}{(\beta)_k}.\end{aligned}$$

Finally, take into account (65) to arrive at the desired result. □

Theorem 13. *For $n = 1, 2, \ldots$, the following reduction formula holds true:*

$$\left.\frac{\partial \mathrm{E}_{\alpha,\beta}(z)}{\partial \alpha}\right|_{\alpha=n} = -\frac{z^{1/n}}{n^2\,\Gamma(\beta)} \sum_{m=1}^{n} e^{i2\pi m/n} P\left(\beta, z^{1/n} e^{i2\pi m/n}\right). \tag{72}$$

Proof. Apply (64) to (71) and take into account the definition given in (66). □

Remark 7. *It is worth noting that for $\alpha = 1$, (72) is equivalent to (67) and (71) is equivalent to (68).*

For particular values of α and β, the first derivative of the Mittag–Leffler function with respect to the parameters are shown in Tables 1 and 2, using the results given in (71) and (72) with the aid of the MATHEMATICA program.

Table 1. First derivative of the Mittag–Leffler function with respect to α.

α	β	$\frac{\partial \mathrm{E}_{\alpha,\beta}(z)}{\partial \alpha}$
1	1	$1 - e^z\{z[\ln z + \Gamma(0,z)] + 1\}$
1	2	$\frac{1}{z}\{1 + \gamma - e^z[1 + (z-1)(\ln z + \Gamma(0,z))]\}$
2	1	$\frac{1}{8}e^{-\sqrt{z}}\left\{\sqrt{z}\left[\ln z - 2\,\mathrm{Ei}(\sqrt{z}) - e^{2\sqrt{z}}\left(2\,\mathrm{E}_1(\sqrt{z}) + \ln z\right)\right] - 2\left(e^{\sqrt{z}} - 1\right)^2\right\}$
2	2	$\frac{1}{8\sqrt{z}}e^{-\sqrt{z}}\left\{e^{2\sqrt{z}}\left[(1-\sqrt{z})\left(2\,\mathrm{E}_1(\sqrt{z}) + \ln z\right) - 2\right] + (1+\sqrt{z})\left[2\,\mathrm{Ei}(\sqrt{z}) - \ln z\right] + 2\right\}$

Table 2. First derivative of the Mittag–Leffler function with respect to β.

α	β	$\frac{\partial \mathrm{E}_{\alpha,\beta}(z)}{\partial \beta}$
1	1	$-e^z[\ln z + \Gamma(0,z)]$
1	2	$-\frac{1}{z}\{e^z[\ln z + \Gamma(0,z)] + \gamma\}$
2	1	$\frac{1}{4}e^{-\sqrt{z}}\left\{2\,\mathrm{Ei}(\sqrt{z}) - \ln z - e^{2\sqrt{z}}\left[\ln z + 2\,\Gamma(0,\sqrt{z})\right]\right\}$
2	2	$\frac{1}{4\sqrt{z}}e^{-\sqrt{z}}\left\{\ln z - 2\,\mathrm{Ei}(\sqrt{z}) - e^{2\sqrt{z}}\left[\ln z + 2\,\Gamma(0,\sqrt{z})\right]\right\}$

6. Conclusions

We calculated some new infinite sums involving the digamma function. On the one hand, some of these new sums are connected to the incomplete beta function, i.e., Equations (35) and (44). For this purpose, we derived a new ${}_3F_2$ hypergeometric sum at argument unity in (28). We also calculated new expressions for the derivatives of the incomplete beta function $\mathrm{B}_z(a,b)$ with respect to the parameters a and b in (15) and (30). As a consequence of the latter, we obtained a definite integral in (22) that does not seem to be tabulated in the most common literature. In addition, in (43) we derived a new reduction formula for a ${}_3F_2$ hypergeometric function.

On the other hand, we calculated sums involving the digamma function which are connected to the Bessel functions, i.e., Equations (52)–(55). For this purpose, we used the derivative of the Pochhammer symbol given in (9), as well as some expressions found in the existing literature for the order derivatives of $J_\nu(z)$ and $I_\nu(z)$, given in (50) and (51) respectively.

Finally, we calculated some reduction formulas for the derivatives of some special functions with respect to the parameters as an application of the sums involving the digamma function. In particular, we applied the sum presented in (53) to the calculation of the reduction Formulas (59) and (60) for the derivatives of the Wright function with respect to the parameters. Similarly, applying the sum given in (65), we calculated the reduction Formulas (71) and (72) for the derivatives of the Mittag–Leffler function with respect to the parameters.

Author Contributions: Conceptualization, J.L.G.-S. and F.S.L.; Methodology, J.L.G.-S. and F.S.L.; Writing—original draft, J.L.G.-S. and F.S.L.; Writing—review & editing, J.L.G.-S. and F.S.L. All authors have read and agreed to the published version of the manuscript.

Funding: This research received no external funding.

Data Availability Statement: Not applicable.

Conflicts of Interest: The authors declare no conflict of interest.

References

1. Hansen, E. *A Table of Series and Products*; Prentice-Hall: Hoboken, NJ, USA, 1975.
2. Brychkov, Y. *Handbook of Special Functions: Derivatives, Integrals, Series and Other Formulas*; Chapman and Hall/CRC: Boca Raton, FL, USA, 2008.
3. De Doelder, P. On some series containing $\psi(x) - \psi(y)$ and $(\psi(x) - \psi(y))^2$ for certain values of x and y. *J. Comput. Appl. Math.* **1991**, *37*, 125–141. [CrossRef]
4. Miller, A. Summations for certain series containing the digamma function. *J. Phys. A Math. Gen.* **2006**, *39*, 3011. [CrossRef]
5. Cvijović, D. Closed-form summations of certain hypergeometric-type series containing the digamma function. *J. Phys. A Math. Theor.* **2008**, *41*, 455205. [CrossRef]
6. González-Santander, J.; Sánchez Lasheras, F. Finite and infinite hypergeometric sums involving the digamma function. *Mathematics* **2022**, *10*, 2990. [CrossRef]
7. Apelblat, A. Differentiation of the Mittag-Leffler functions with respect to parameters in the Laplace transform approach. *Mathematics* **2020**, *8*, 657. [CrossRef]
8. Apelblat, A.; González-Santander, J. The Integral Mittag-Leffler, Whittaker and Wright Functions. *Mathematics* **2021**, *9*, 3255. [CrossRef]
9. Paris, R.; Kaminski, D. *Asymptotics and Mellin-Barnes Integrals*; Cambridge University Press: Cambridge, UK, 2001; Volume 85.
10. Olver, F. *Introduction to Asymptotic Analysis*; Academic Press Inc.: Cambridge, MA, USA, 1974.
11. Lewin, L. *Polylogarithms and Associated Functions*; North Holland: Amsterdam, The Netherlands, 1981.
12. Coffey, M. On one-dimensional digamma and polygamma series related to the evaluation of Feynman diagrams. *J. Comput. Appl. Math.* **2005**, *183*, 84–100. [CrossRef]
13. Oldham, K.; Myland, J.; Spanier, J. *An Atlas of Functions: With Equator, the Atlas Function Calculator*; Springer: Berlin/Heidelberg, Germany, 2009.
14. Lebedev, N. *Special Functions and Their Applications*; Prentice-Hall Inc.: Hoboken, NJ, USA, 1965.
15. Olver, F.W.; Lozier, D.W.; Boisvert, R.; Clark, C. *NIST Handbook of Mathematical Functions*; Cambridge University Press: Cambridge, UK, 2010.
16. Prudnikov, A.; Brychkov, Y.; Marichev, O. *Integrals and Series: More Special Functions*; CRC Press: Boca Raton, FL, USA, 1986; Volume 1.
17. Prudnikov, A.; Brychkov, Y.; Marichev, O. *Integrals and Series: More Special Functions*; CRC Press: Boca Raton, FL, USA, 1986; Volume 3.
18. González-Santander, J. A note on some reduction formulas for the incomplete beta function and the Lerch transcendent. *Mathematics* **2021**, *9*, 1486. [CrossRef]
19. González-Santander, J. Closed-form expressions for derivatives of Bessel functions with respect to the order. *J. Math. Anal. Appl.* **2018**, *466*, 1060–1081. [CrossRef]
20. Apelblat, A.; González-Santander, J. Differentiation of integral Mittag-Leffler and integral Wright functions with respect to parameters. *Fract. Calc. Appl. Anal.* **2023**, *26*, 567–598. [CrossRef]

Disclaimer/Publisher's Note: The statements, opinions and data contained in all publications are solely those of the individual author(s) and contributor(s) and not of MDPI and/or the editor(s). MDPI and/or the editor(s) disclaim responsibility for any injury to people or property resulting from any ideas, methods, instructions or products referred to in the content.

mathematics

MDPI

Article

Explicit Properties of Apostol-Type Frobenius–Euler Polynomials Involving q-Trigonometric Functions with Applications in Computer Modeling

Yongsheng Rao [1], Waseem Ahmad Khan [2,*], Serkan Araci [3,*] and Cheon Seoung Ryoo [4]

1 Institute of Computing Science and Technology, Guangzhou University, Guangzhou 510006, China; rysheng@gzhu.edu.cn
2 Department of Mathematics and Natural Sciences, Prince Mohammad Bin Fahd University, P.O. Box 1664, Al Khobar 31952, Saudi Arabia
3 Department of Basic Sciences, Faculty of Engineering, Hasan Kalyoncu University, TR-27010 Gaziantep, Turkey
4 Department of Mathematics, Hannam University, Daejeon 34430, Republic of Korea; ryoocs@hnu.kr
* Correspondence: wkhan1@pmu.edu.sa (W.A.K.); serkan.araci@hku.edu.tr (S.A.)

Abstract: In this article, we define q-cosine and q-sine Apostol-type Frobenius–Euler polynomials and derive interesting relations. We also obtain new properties by making use of power series expansions of q-trigonometric functions, properties of q-exponential functions, and q-analogues of the binomial theorem. By using the Mathematica program, the computational formulae and graphical representation for the aforementioned polynomials are obtained. By making use of a partial derivative operator, we derived some interesting finite combinatorial sums. Finally, we detail some special cases for these results.

Keywords: q-trigonometric functions; q-exponential functions; Frobenius–Euler polynomials; Apostol Frobenius–Euler polynomials; generating functions; combinatorial sums

MSC: 11B68; 11B73; 05A15; 05A19

Citation: Rao, Y.; Khan, W.A.; Araci, S.; Ryoo, C.S. Explicit Properties of Apostol-Type Frobenius–Euler Polynomials Involving q-Trigonometric Functions with Applications in Computer Modeling. *Mathematics* **2023**, *11*, 2386. https://doi.org/10.3390/math11102386

Academic Editor: Sitnik Sergey

Received: 4 May 2023
Revised: 17 May 2023
Accepted: 18 May 2023
Published: 20 May 2023

Copyright: © 2023 by the authors. Licensee MDPI, Basel, Switzerland. This article is an open access article distributed under the terms and conditions of the Creative Commons Attribution (CC BY) license (https://creativecommons.org/licenses/by/4.0/).

1. Introduction

Recently, many authors have considered and applied the generating functions techniques to new families of special polynomials, including two parametric kinds of polynomials, such as Bernoulli, Euler, Genocchi, etc. (see [1–10]). They have firstly derived the basic identities of these polynomials. Additionally, they have established more identities and relations among trigonometric functions, using two parametric kinds of polynomials by using generating functions. By applying the partial derivative operator to these generating functions, derivative formulae, and finite combinatorial sums involving the special polynomials and numbers are obtained. We would like to note that these special polynomials facilitate the derivation of various helpful properties in a fairly straightforward way and lead to introducing new families of special polynomials. The Apostol-type polynomials appear in combinatorial mathematics and play an important role in theory, generalization, applications and modeling; thus, many number theorists and combinatorics experts have extensively investigated their properties and obtained a series of interesting results (see [5,8,9,11–13]). Inspired by the above polynomials, in this study, we are in a position to state the parametric kinds of Apostol-type Frobenius–type Euler polynomials by introducing the two specific q-analogues of exponential generating functions. Additionally, we prove many formulas and relations for these polynomials, including some implicit summation formulas, differentiation rules and correlations with the earlier polynomials by utilizing some series manipulation methods. Additionally, as an application, we show the zero values of q-Apostol-type Frobenius–type Euler polynomials using tables and draw some graphical representations.

We begin by stating the following definitions and notations of q-calculus reviewed here, which are taken from (see [14]):
A q-analogue of the shifted factorial $(a)_n$ is given by

$$(a;q)_0 = 1, (a;q)_n = \prod_{m=0}^{n-1}(1-q^m a), n \in \mathbb{N}.$$

A q-analogue of a complex number a and of the factorial function are given by

$$[a]_q = \frac{1-q^a}{1-q}, (q \in \mathbb{C} \setminus \{1\}; a \in \mathbb{C}),$$

$$[n]_q! = \prod_{m=1}^{n}[m]_q = [1]_q[2]_q \cdots [n]_q = \frac{(q;q)_n}{(1-q)^n}, q \neq 1; n \in \mathbb{N},$$

$$[0]_q! = 1, q \in \mathbb{C}; 0 <\mid q \mid< 1.$$

The Gauss q-binomial coefficient $\left(\begin{array}{c} n \\ k \end{array}\right)_q$ is given by

$$\left(\begin{array}{c} n \\ k \end{array}\right)_q = \frac{[n]_q!}{[k]_q![n-k]_q!} = \frac{(q;q)_n}{(q;q)_k(q;q)_{n-k}}, k = 0, 1, \cdots, n.$$

The q-analogue of the function $(x+y)_q^n$ is given by

$$(x+y)_q^n = \sum_{k=0}^{n}\left(\begin{array}{c} n \\ k \end{array}\right)_q q^{k(k-1)/2}x^{n-k}y^k, n \in \mathbb{N}_0. \tag{1}$$

The q-analogues of exponential functions are given by

$$e_q(x) = \sum_{n=0}^{\infty}\frac{x^n}{[n]_q!} = \frac{1}{((1-q)x;q)_\infty}, 0 <\mid q \mid< 1; \mid x \mid<\mid 1-q \mid^{-1}, \tag{2}$$

$$E_q(x) = \sum_{n=0}^{\infty}\frac{q^{\binom{n}{2}}}{[n]_q!}x^n = (-(1-q)x;q)_\infty, 0 <\mid q \mid< 1; x \in \mathbb{C}. \tag{3}$$

These two functions are related by the equation (see [14])

$$e_q(x)E_q(-x) = 1.$$

A q-derivative operator of a function is defined by

$$D_{q,z}f(z) := D_q f(z) = \frac{f(qz) - f(z)}{qz - z}, 0 <\mid q \mid< 1,$$

and $D_q f(0) = f'(0)$ provided that f is differentiable at $x = 0$.

A q-derivative fulfills the following product and quotient rules

$$D_{q,z}(f(z)g(z)) = f(z)D_{q,z}g(z) + g(qz)D_{q,z}f(z), \tag{4}$$

$$D_{q,z}\left(\frac{f(z)}{g(z)}\right) = \frac{g(qz)D_{q,z}f(z) - f(qz)D_{q,z}g(z)}{g(z)g(qz)}. \tag{5}$$

The Apostol-type q-Bernoulli polynomials $\mathbb{B}_{n,q}^{(\alpha)}(x;\lambda)$ of order α, the Apostol-type q-Euler polynomials $\mathbb{E}_{n,q}^{(\alpha)}(x;\lambda)$ of order α and the Apostol-type q-Genocchi polynomials $\mathbb{G}_{n,q}^{(\alpha)}(x;\lambda)$ of order α are defined by (see [15,16]):

$$\left(\frac{t}{\lambda e_q(t)-1}\right)^{\alpha} e^{xt} = \sum_{n=0}^{\infty} \mathbb{B}_{n,q}^{(\alpha)}(x;\lambda)\frac{t^n}{[n]_q!}, \tag{6}$$

$$\left(\frac{2}{\lambda e_q(t)+1}\right)^{\alpha} e^{xt} = \sum_{n=0}^{\infty} \mathbb{E}_{n,q}^{(\alpha)}(x;\lambda)\frac{t^n}{[n]_q!}, \tag{7}$$

$$\left(\frac{2t}{\lambda e_q(t)+1}\right)^{\alpha} e^{xt} = \sum_{n=0}^{\infty} \mathbb{G}_{n,q}^{(\alpha)}(x;\lambda)\frac{t^n}{[n]_q!}, \tag{8}$$

respectively.

Clearly, we can obtain

$$\mathbb{B}_{n,q}^{(\alpha)}(\lambda) = \mathbb{B}_{n,q}^{(\alpha)}(0;\lambda), \mathbb{E}_{n,q}^{(\alpha)}(\lambda) = \mathbb{E}_{n,q}^{(\alpha)}(0;\lambda), \mathbb{G}_{n,q}^{(\alpha)}(\lambda) = \mathbb{G}_{n,q}^{(\alpha)}(0;\lambda),$$

and

$$\mathbb{B}_{n,q}^{(1)}(x;\lambda) = \mathbb{B}_{n,q}(x;\lambda), \mathbb{E}_{n,q}^{(1)}(x;\lambda) = \mathbb{E}_{n,q}(x;\lambda), \mathbb{G}_{n,q}^{(1)}(x;\lambda) = \mathbb{G}_{n,q}(x;\lambda).$$

Let $u \in \mathbb{C}$ with $u \neq 1$ and $\xi \in \mathbb{R}$. The Apostol-type q-Frobenius–Euler polynomials $\mathbb{H}_{n,q}^{(\alpha)}(x,y;u;\lambda)$ of order $\alpha \in \mathbb{C}$ are defined by (see [11,12]):

$$\left(\frac{1-u}{\lambda e_q(t)-u}\right)^{\alpha} e_q(xt)E_q(yt) = \sum_{n=0}^{\infty} \mathbb{H}_{n,q}^{(\alpha)}(x,y;u;\lambda)\frac{t^n}{[n]_q!}, \quad |z| < \left|\ln\left(\frac{\lambda}{u}\right)\right|. \tag{9}$$

It is obvious that

$$\mathbb{H}_{n,q}^{(\alpha)}(u;\lambda) = \mathbb{H}_{n,q}^{(\alpha)}(0,0;u;\lambda) \quad \lim_{q\to 1^-} \mathbb{H}_{n,q}^{(\alpha)}(x,y;u;\lambda) = \mathbb{H}_{n}^{(\alpha)}(x+y;u;\lambda).$$

Kang et al. [2,4] introduced the q-Bernoulli and q-Euler polynomials defined by

$$\frac{z}{e_q(z)-1}e_q(\xi z)COS_q(\eta z) = \sum_{j=0}^{\infty} \frac{\mathbb{B}_{j,q}((\xi+i\eta)_q)+\mathbb{B}_j((\xi-i\eta)_q)}{2}\frac{z^j}{[j]_q!} = \sum_{j=0}^{\infty}\mathbb{B}_{j,q}^{(C)}(\xi,\eta)\frac{z^j}{[j]_q!}, \tag{10}$$

$$\frac{z}{e_q(z)-1}e_q(\xi z)SIN_q(\eta z) = \sum_{j=0}^{\infty} \frac{\mathbb{B}_{j,q}((\xi+i\eta)_q)-\mathbb{B}_{j,q}((\xi-i\eta)_q)}{2i}\frac{z^j}{[j]_q!} = \sum_{j=0}^{\infty}\mathbb{B}_{j,q}^{(S)}(\xi,\eta)\frac{z^j}{[j]_q!}, \tag{11}$$

and

$$\frac{2}{e_q(z)+1}e_q(\xi z)COS_q(\eta z) = \sum_{j=0}^{\infty} \frac{\mathbb{E}_{j,q}((\xi+i\eta)_q)+\mathbb{E}_{j,q}((\xi-i\eta)_q)}{2}\frac{z^j}{[j]_q!} = \sum_{j=0}^{\infty}\mathbb{E}_{j,q}^{(C)}(\xi,\eta)\frac{z^j}{[j]_q!}, \tag{12}$$

$$\frac{2}{e_q(z)+1}e_q(\xi z)SIN_q(\eta z) = \sum_{j=0}^{\infty} \frac{\mathbb{E}_{j}((\xi+i\eta)_q)-\mathbb{E}_{j}((\xi-i\eta))_q}{2i}\frac{z^j}{[j]_q!} = \sum_{j=0}^{\infty}\mathbb{E}_{j,q}^{(S)}(\xi,\eta)\frac{z^j}{[j]_q!}, \tag{13}$$

respectively.

Additionally, they have proved that (see [2,4]):

$$e_q(\xi z)COS_q(\eta z) = \sum_{r=0}^{\infty} C_{r,q}(\xi,\eta)\frac{z^r}{[r]_q!}, \tag{14}$$

and

$$e_q(\xi z)SIN_q(\eta z)=\sum_{r=0}^{\infty}S_{r,q}(\xi,\eta)\frac{z^r}{[r]_q!},\tag{15}$$

where

$$C_{r,q}(\xi,\eta)=\sum_{j=0}^{[\frac{r}{2}]}\left(\begin{array}{c}r\\2j\end{array}\right)_q(-1)^jq^{2j-1}\xi^{r-2j}\eta^{2j},\tag{16}$$

and

$$S_{r,q}(\xi,\eta)=\sum_{j=0}^{[\frac{r-1}{2}]}\left(\begin{array}{c}r\\2j+1\end{array}\right)_q(-1)^jq^{(2j+1)j}\xi^{r-2j-1}\eta^{2j+1}.\tag{17}$$

2. q-Apostol-Type Frobenius–Euler Polynomials of Complex Variable

In this section, we consider the q-Cosine and q-Sine Apostol-type Frobenius–Euler polynomials of a complex variable and deduce some identities of these polynomials. First, we present the following definition.

$$\left(\frac{1-u}{\lambda e_q(t)-u}\right)^{\alpha}e_q(xt)E_q(ity)=\sum_{n=0}^{\infty}\mathbb{H}_{n,q}^{(\alpha)}((\xi+iy)_q;u;\lambda)\frac{t^n}{[n]_q!}.\tag{18}$$

It is well-known from ([4] Definition 5) that

$$e_q(xt)E_q(ity)=e_q(xt)(COS_q(yt)+iSIN_q(yt)).\tag{19}$$

Thus, by (18) and (19), we have

$$\begin{aligned}\sum_{n=0}^{\infty}\mathbb{H}_{n,q}^{(\alpha)}((x+iy)_q;u;\lambda)\frac{t^n}{n!}&=\left(\frac{1-u}{\lambda e_q(t)-u}\right)^{\alpha}e_q(xt)E_q(ity)\\&=\left(\frac{1-u}{\lambda e_q(t)-u}\right)^{\alpha}e_q(xt)(COS_q(yz)+iSIN_q(yz)),\end{aligned}\tag{20}$$

and

$$\begin{aligned}\sum_{n=0}^{\infty}\mathbb{H}_{n,q}^{(\alpha)}((x-iy)_q;u;\lambda)\frac{t^n}{[n]_q!}&=\left(\frac{1-u}{\lambda e_q(t)-u}\right)^{\alpha}e_q(xt)E_q(-ity)\\&=\left(\frac{1-u}{\lambda e_q(t)-u}\right)^{\alpha}e_q(xt)(COS_q(yt)-iSIN_q(yt)).\end{aligned}\tag{21}$$

From (20) and (21), we get

$$\left(\frac{1-u}{\lambda e_q(t)-u}\right)^{\alpha}e_q(xt)COS_q(yt)=\sum_{n=0}^{\infty}\left(\frac{\mathbb{H}_{n,q}^{(\alpha)}((x+iy)_q;u;\lambda)+\mathbb{H}_{n,q}^{(\alpha)}((x-iy)_q;u;\lambda)}{2}\right)\frac{t^n}{[n]_q!},\tag{22}$$

and

$$\left(\frac{1-u}{\lambda e_q(t)-u}\right)^{\alpha}e_q(xt)SIN_q(yt)=\sum_{n=0}^{\infty}\left(\frac{\mathbb{H}_{n,q}^{(\alpha)}((x+iy)_q;u;\lambda)-\mathbb{H}_{n,q}^{(\alpha)}((x-iy)_q;u;\lambda)}{2}\right)\frac{t^n}{[n]_q!}.\tag{23}$$

Definition 1. *Let $j\geq 0$. We define two parametric kinds of q-Cosine Apostol-type Frobenius–Euler polynomials $\mathbb{H}_{n,q}^{(\alpha,c)}(x,y;u;\lambda)$ and q-Sine Apostol-type Frobenius–Euler polynomials $\mathbb{H}_{n,q}^{(\alpha,s)}(x,y;u;\lambda)$, for a non negative integer n, by*

$$\left(\frac{1-u}{\lambda e_q(t)-u}\right)^{\alpha}e_q(xt)COS_q(yt)=\sum_{n=0}^{\infty}\mathbb{H}_{j,q}^{(\alpha,c)}(x,y;u;\lambda)\frac{t^n}{[n]_q!},\tag{24}$$

and

$$\left(\frac{1-u}{\lambda e_q(t)-u}\right)^{\alpha} e_q(xt)SIN_q(yt) = \sum_{n=0}^{\infty} \mathbb{H}_{n,q}^{(\alpha,s)}(x,y;u;\lambda)\frac{t^n}{[n]_q!}, \tag{25}$$

respectively.

Note that $\mathbb{H}_{n,q}^{(\alpha,c)}(0,0;u;\lambda) = \mathbb{H}_{n,q}(u;\lambda)$, $\mathbb{H}_{n,q}^{(\alpha,s)}(0,0;u;\lambda) = 0, (n \geq 0)$.
From (22)–(25), we have

$$\mathbb{H}_{n,q}^{(\alpha,c)}(x,y;u;\lambda) = \frac{\mathbb{H}_{n,q}((x+iy)_q;u;\lambda) + \mathbb{H}_{n,q}((x-iy)_q;u;\lambda)}{2}, \tag{26}$$

$$\mathbb{H}_{n,q}^{(\alpha,s)}(x,y;u;\lambda) = \frac{\mathbb{H}_{n,q}((x+iy)_q;u;\lambda) - \mathbb{H}_{n,q}((x-iy)_q;u;\lambda)}{2i}. \tag{27}$$

Remark 1. *For $x = 0$ in (24) and (25), we obtain*

$$\left(\frac{1-u}{\lambda e^t-u}\right)^{\alpha} COS_q(yt) = \sum_{j=0}^{\infty} \mathbb{H}_{n,q}^{(\alpha,c)}(y;u;\lambda)\frac{t^n}{[n]_q!}, \tag{28}$$

and

$$\left(\frac{1-u}{\lambda e^t-u}\right)^{\alpha} SIN_q(yt) = \sum_{n=0}^{\infty} \mathbb{H}_{n,q}^{(\alpha,s)}(y;u;\lambda)\frac{t^n}{[n]_q!}, \tag{29}$$

respectively.

It is clear that

$$\mathbb{H}_{n,q}^{(\alpha,c)}(0;u;\lambda) = \mathbb{H}_{n,q}(u;\lambda), \ \mathbb{H}_{n,q}^{(\alpha,s)}(0;u;\lambda) = 0, (n \geq 0).$$

Now, we provide some basic properties of these polynomials.

Theorem 1. *Let $n \geq 0$. Then,*

$$\mathbb{H}_{n,q}^{(\alpha,c)}(y;u;\lambda) = \sum_{v=0}^{[\frac{n}{2}]} \binom{n+v}{2v}_q (-1)^v q^{(2v-1)v} y^{2v} \mathbb{H}_{n-2v,q}(u;\lambda), \tag{30}$$

and

$$\mathbb{H}_{j,q}^{(\alpha,s)}(u;\lambda) = \sum_{v=0}^{[\frac{n-1}{2}]} \binom{n+v}{2v+1}_q (-1)^v q^{(2v+1)v} y^{2v+1} \mathbb{H}_{n-2v-1,q}(u;\lambda). \tag{31}$$

Proof. By (28) and (29), we can derive the following equations

$$\sum_{n=0}^{\infty} \mathbb{H}_{n,q}^{(\alpha,c)}(y;u;\lambda)\frac{t^n}{[n]_q!} = \left(\frac{1-u}{\lambda e_q(t)-u}\right)^{\alpha} COS_q(yt)$$

$$= \sum_{n=0}^{\infty} \mathbb{H}_{n,q}^{(\alpha)}(u;\lambda)\frac{t^n}{[n]_q!} \sum_{v=0}^{\infty} (-1)^v q^{(2v-1)v} y^{2v} \frac{t^v}{[2v]_q!}.$$

$$= \sum_{n=0}^{\infty} \left(\sum_{v=0}^{[\frac{n}{2}]} \binom{n+v}{2v}_q (-1)^v q^{(2v-1)v} y^{2v} \mathbb{H}_{n-2v,q}(u;\lambda) \right) \frac{t^n}{[n]_q!}, \tag{32}$$

and

$$\sum_{n=0}^{\infty} \mathbb{H}_{n,q}^{(\alpha,s)}(y;u;\lambda)\frac{t^n}{n!} = \left(\frac{1-u}{\lambda e_q(t)-u}\right)^{\alpha} SIN_q(yt)$$

$$= \sum_{n=0}^{\infty} \left(\sum_{v=0}^{[\frac{n-1}{2}]} \binom{n}{2v+1}_q (-1)^v q^{(2v+1)v} y^{2v+1} \mathbb{H}_{j-2v-1,q}(u;\lambda) \right) \frac{t^n}{[n]_q!}. \tag{33}$$

Therefore, with (32) and (33), we get (30) and (31). □

Theorem 2. *Let $n \geq 0$. Then,*

$$\mathbb{H}_{n,q}^{(\alpha)}((x+iy)_q;u;\lambda) = \sum_{k=0}^{n} \binom{n}{k}_q (x+iy)_q^k \mathbb{H}_{n-k,q}^{(\alpha)}(u;\lambda)$$

$$= \sum_{k=0}^{n} \binom{n}{k}_q (iy)^k \mathbb{H}_{j-k,q}^{(\alpha)}(x;u;\lambda), \tag{34}$$

and

$$\mathbb{H}_{n,q}^{(\alpha)}((x-iy)_q;u;\lambda) = \sum_{k0}^{n} \binom{n}{k}_q (x-iy)_q^k \mathbb{H}_{n-k,q}^{(\alpha)}(u;\lambda)$$

$$= \sum_{k=0}^{n} \binom{n}{k}_q (-1)^k (iy)^k \mathbb{H}_{n-k,q}(x;u;\lambda). \tag{35}$$

Proof. By using (20) and (21), we obtain (34) and (35). So, we omit the proof. □

Theorem 3. *Let $n \geq 0$. Then,*

$$\mathbb{H}_{n,q}^{(\alpha,c)}(x,y;u;\lambda) = \sum_{k=0}^{n} \binom{n}{k}_q \mathbb{H}_{k,q}^{(\alpha)}(u;\lambda) C_{n-k,q}(x,y), \tag{36}$$

and

$$\mathbb{H}_{n,q}^{(\alpha,s)}(x,y;u;\lambda) = \sum_{k=0}^{n} \binom{n}{k}_q \mathbb{H}_{k,q}(u;\lambda) S_{n-k,q}(x,y). \tag{37}$$

Proof. Consider

$$\left(\sum_{n=0}^{\infty} a_n \frac{t^n}{n!}\right)\left(\sum_{k=0}^{\infty} b_k \frac{t^k}{k!}\right) = \sum_{n=0}^{\infty}\left(\sum_{k=0}^{j} a_{n-k} b_k\right)\frac{t^n}{n!}.$$

Now,

$$\sum_{n=0}^{\infty} \mathbb{H}_{j,q}^{(\alpha,c)}(x,y;u;\lambda)\frac{t^n}{[n]_q!} = \left(\frac{1-u}{\lambda e_q(t)-u}\right)^{\alpha} e_q(xt) COS_q(yt)$$

$$= \left(\sum_{k=0}^{\infty} \mathbb{H}_{k,q}^{(\alpha)}(u;\lambda)\frac{t^k}{k!}\right)\left(\sum_{n=0}^{\infty} C_{n,q}(x,y)\frac{t^n}{[n]_q!}\right)$$

$$= \sum_{n=0}^{\infty}\left(\sum_{k=0}^{n} \binom{n}{k}_q \mathbb{H}_{k,q}^{(\alpha)}(u;\lambda) C_{n-k,q}(x,y)\right)\frac{t^n}{[n]_q!},$$

which proves (36). The proof of (37) is similar.
□

By using Definition 1, we can easily obtain the following Theorems. So, we omit the proofs.

Theorem 4. *Let $j \geq 0$. Then,*

$$\mathbb{H}_{j,q}^{(\alpha,c)}(x+s,y;u;\lambda) = \sum_{k=0}^{n} \binom{n}{k}_q \mathbb{H}_{k,q}^{(\alpha,c)}(x,y;u;\lambda) r^{n-k}, \tag{38}$$

and

$$\mathbb{H}_{n,q}^{(\alpha,s)}(x,y;u;\lambda) = \sum_{k=0}^{n} \left(\begin{array}{c} n \\ k \end{array} \right)_q \mathbb{H}_{k,q}^{(\alpha,s)}(x,y;u;\lambda) r^{n-k}. \tag{39}$$

Theorem 5. *Let $j \geq 1$. Then,*

$$\frac{\partial}{\partial x} \mathbb{H}_{n,q}^{(\alpha,c)}(x,y;u;\lambda) = [n]_q \mathbb{H}_{n-1,q}^{(\alpha,c)}(x,y;u;\lambda), \tag{40}$$

$$\frac{\partial}{\partial y} \mathbb{H}_{n,q}^{(\alpha,c)}(x,y;u;\lambda) = -[n]_q \mathbb{H}_{n-1,q}^{(\alpha,s)}(x,qy;u;\lambda), \tag{41}$$

and

$$\frac{\partial}{\partial x} \mathbb{H}_{n,q}^{(\alpha,s)}(x,y;u;\lambda) = [n]_q \mathbb{H}_{n-1,q}^{(\alpha,s)}(x,y;u;\lambda), \tag{42}$$

$$\frac{\partial}{\partial y} \mathbb{H}_{n,q}^{(\alpha,s)}(x,y;u;\lambda) = [n]_q \mathbb{H}_{n-1,q}^{(\alpha,c)}(x,qy;u;\lambda). \tag{43}$$

Theorem 6. *Let n be a nonnegative integer, the following formulas hold true.*

$$\begin{aligned} &\lambda \mathbb{H}_{n,q}^{(\alpha,c)}(1,y;u;\lambda) - u \mathbb{H}_{n,q}^{(\alpha,c)}(0,y;u;\lambda) \\ &= (1-u) \mathbb{H}_{n,q}^{(\alpha-1,c)}(0;y;u;\lambda), \end{aligned} \tag{44}$$

$$\begin{aligned} &\lambda \mathbb{H}_{n,q}^{(\alpha,s)}(1,y;u;\lambda) - u \mathbb{H}_{n,q}^{(\alpha,s)}(0,y;u;\lambda) \\ &= (1-u) \mathbb{H}_{n,q}^{(\alpha-1,s)}(0;y;u;\lambda), \end{aligned} \tag{45}$$

Theorem 7. *The following relations hold true.*

$$\mathbb{H}_{n,q}^{(\alpha+\beta,c)}(x,y;u;\lambda) = \sum_{m=0}^{n} \binom{n}{m}_q \mathbb{H}_{n-m,q}^{(\alpha,c)}(x,y;u;\lambda) \mathbb{H}_{m,q}^{(\beta)}(u;\lambda), \tag{46}$$

$$\mathbb{H}_{n,q}^{(\alpha+\beta,s)}(x,y;u;\lambda) = \sum_{m=0}^{n} \binom{n}{m}_q \mathbb{H}_{n-m,q}^{(\alpha,s)}(x,y;u;\lambda) \mathbb{H}_{m,q}^{(\beta)}(u;\lambda), \tag{47}$$

$$\mathbb{H}_{n,q}^{(\alpha-\beta,c)}(x,y;u;\lambda) = \sum_{m=0}^{n} \binom{n}{m}_q \mathbb{H}_{n-m,q}^{(\alpha,c)}(x,y;u;\lambda) \mathbb{H}_{m,q}^{(-\beta)}(u;\lambda), \tag{48}$$

$$\mathbb{H}_{n,q}^{(\alpha-\beta,s)}(x,y;u;\lambda) = \sum_{m=0}^{n} \binom{n}{m}_q \mathbb{H}_{n-m,q}^{(\alpha,s)}(x,y;u;\lambda) \mathbb{H}_{m,q}^{(-\beta)}(u;\lambda), \tag{49}$$

Theorem 8. *Let x, y, and r be any real numbers. Then, we have*

(i)

$$\begin{aligned} &\mathbb{H}_{n,q}^{(\alpha,c)}((x+r)_q, y;u;\lambda) + \mathbb{H}_{n,q}^{(\alpha,s)}((x-r)_q, y;u;\lambda) \\ &= \sum_{k=0}^{n} \binom{n}{l}_q q^{\binom{n-l}{2}} r^{n-l} \Big(\mathbb{H}_{n,q}^{(\alpha,c)}(x,y;u;\lambda) + (-1)^{n-k} \mathbb{H}_{n,q}^{(\alpha,s)}(x,y;u;\lambda) \Big), \end{aligned} \tag{50}$$

(ii)

$$\begin{aligned} &\mathbb{H}_{n,q}^{(\alpha,s)}((x+r)_q, y;u;\lambda) + \mathbb{H}_{n,q}^{(\alpha,c)}((x-r)_q, y;u;\lambda) \\ &= \sum_{k=0}^{n} \binom{n}{l}_q q^{\binom{n-l}{2}} r^{n-l} \Big(\mathbb{H}_{n,q}^{(\alpha,s)}(x,y;u;\lambda) + (-1)^{n-k} \mathbb{H}_{n,q}^{(\alpha,c)}(x,y;u;\lambda) \Big). \end{aligned} \tag{51}$$

Corollary 1. *Let $j \geq 0$. Then,*

$$\mathbb{H}^{(c)}_{n,q}((x+r)_q, y; u; \lambda) + \mathbb{H}^{(c)}_{n,q}((x-r)_q, y; u; \lambda)$$

$$= \sum_{k=0}^{n} \binom{n}{k}_q q^{\binom{k}{2}} r^k \left(\mathbb{H}^{(c)}_{n-k,q}(x, y; u; \lambda) + (-1)^k \mathbb{H}^{(c)}_{n-k,q}(x, y; u; \lambda) \right), \tag{52}$$

and

$$\mathbb{H}^{(s)}_{n,q}((x+r)_q, y; u; \lambda) + \mathbb{H}^{(s)}_{n,q}((x-r)_q, y; u; \lambda)$$

$$= \sum_{k=0}^{n} \binom{n}{k}_q q^{\binom{k}{2}} r^k \left(\mathbb{H}^{(s)}_{n-k,q}(x, y; u; \lambda) + (-1)^k \mathbb{H}^{(s)}_{n-k,q}(x, y; u; \lambda) \right). \tag{53}$$

Corollary 2. *For $r = 1$ in Theorem 8, we obtain*

$$\mathbb{H}^{(c)}_{n,q}((x+1)_q, y; u; \lambda) + \mathbb{H}^{(s)}_{n,q}((x-1)_q, y; u; \lambda)$$

$$= \sum_{k=0}^{n} \binom{n}{k}_q q^{\binom{k}{2}} r^k \left(\mathbb{H}^{(c)}_{n-k,q}(x, y; u; \lambda) + (-1)^k \mathbb{H}^{(s)}_{n-k,q}(x, y; u; \lambda) \right), \tag{54}$$

and

$$\mathbb{H}^{(s)}_{n,q}((x+1)_q, y; u; \lambda) + \mathbb{H}^{(c)}_{n,q}((x-1)_q, y; u; \lambda)$$

$$= \sum_{k=0}^{n} \binom{n}{k}_q q^{\binom{n-k}{2}} r^{n-k} \left(\mathbb{H}^{(s)}_{k,q}(x, y; u; \lambda) + (-1)^{n-k} \mathbb{H}^{(c)}_{k,q}(x, y; u; \lambda) \right). \tag{55}$$

3. Summation Formulas for q-Cosine and q-Sine Apostol-Type Frobenius–Euler Polynomials

In this section, we derive some correlations for the q-cosine and q-sine Apostol-type Frobenius–Euler polynomials of order α associated with the q-Bernoulli, Euler, and Genocchi polynomials and the q-Stirling numbers of the second kind. We first provide the following theorems.

Theorem 9. *The following results hold true:*

$$(2u-1) \sum_{k=0}^{n} \binom{n}{k}_q \mathbb{H}_{k,q}(x, 0; u; \lambda) \mathbb{H}^{(c)}_{n-k,q}(0, y; 1-u; \lambda)$$

$$= u\mathbb{H}^{(c)}_{n,q}(x, y; u; \lambda) - (1-u)\mathbb{H}^{(c)}_{n,q}(x, y; 1-u; \lambda), \tag{56}$$

and

$$(2u-1) \sum_{k=0}^{n} \binom{n}{k}_q \mathbb{H}_{k,q}(x, 0; u; \lambda) \mathbb{H}^{(s)}_{n-k,q}(0, y; 1-u; \lambda)$$

$$= u\mathbb{H}^{(s)}_{n,q}(x, y; u; \lambda) - (1-u)\mathbb{H}^{(s)}_{n,q}(x, y; 1-u; \lambda). \tag{57}$$

Proof. We set

$$\frac{(2u-1)}{(\lambda e_q(t) - u)(\lambda e_q(t) - (1-u))} = \frac{1}{\lambda e_q(t) - u} - \frac{1}{\lambda e_q(t) - (1-u)}.$$

From the above equation, we see that

$$(2u-1) \frac{(1-u)e_q(xt)(1-(1-u))COS_q(yt)}{(\lambda e_q(t) - u)(\lambda e_q(t) - (1-u))}$$

$$= \frac{(1-u)e_q(xt)uCOS_q(yt)}{\lambda e_q(t) - u} - \frac{(1-u)e_q(xt)COS_q(yt)(1-(1-u))}{\lambda e_q(t) - (1-u)},$$

which when using Equations (9) and (24) on both sides, we can obtain

$$(2u-1)\left(\sum_{k=0}^{\infty}\mathbb{H}_{k,q}(x,0;u;\lambda)\frac{t^k}{[k]_q!}\right)\left(\sum_{n=0}^{\infty}\mathbb{H}_{n,q}^{(c)}(0,y;1-u;\lambda)\frac{t^n}{[n]_q!}\right)$$
$$=u\sum_{n=0}^{\infty}\mathbb{H}_{n,q}^{(c)}(x,y;u;\lambda)\frac{t^n}{[n]_q!}-(1-u)\sum_{n=0}^{\infty}\mathbb{H}_{n,q}^{(c)}(x,y;1-u;\lambda)\frac{t^n}{[n]_q!}.$$

By applying the Cauchy product rule in the above equation and then equating the coefficients of like powers of t on both sides of the resultant equation, assertion (56) follows. Similarly, we obtain (57). □

Theorem 10. *The following relations hold true:*

$$u\mathbb{H}_{n,q}^{(c)}(x,y;u;\lambda)=\sum_{k=0}^{n}\binom{n}{k}_q\mathbb{H}_{n,q}^{(c)}(x,y;u;\lambda)-(1-u)\,C_{n,q}(x,y), \tag{58}$$

and

$$u\mathbb{H}_{n,q}^{(s)}(x,y;u;\lambda)=\sum_{k=0}^{n}\binom{n}{k}_q\mathbb{H}_{n,q}^{(s)}(x,y;u;\lambda)-(1-u)\,S_{n,q}(x,y). \tag{59}$$

Proof. Consider the following identity

$$\frac{u}{\lambda(\lambda e_q(t)-u)e_q(t)}=\frac{1}{(\lambda e_q(t)-u)}-\frac{1}{\lambda e_q(t)}.$$

Evaluating the following fraction using the above identity, we find

$$\frac{u(1-u)e_q(xt)COS_q(yt)}{\lambda(\lambda e_q(t)-u)e_q(t)}=\frac{(1-u)e_q(xt)COS_q(yt)}{\lambda e_q(t)-u}-\frac{(1-u)e_q(xt)COS_q(yt)}{\lambda e_q(t)}$$

$$u\sum_{n=0}^{\infty}\mathbb{H}_{n,q}^{(c)}(x,y;u;\lambda)\frac{t^n}{[n]_q!}=\lambda\sum_{n=0}^{\infty}\mathbb{H}_{n,q}^{(c)}(x,y;u;\lambda)\frac{t^n}{[n]_q!}\sum_{k=0}^{\infty}\frac{t^k}{[k]_q!}-(1-u)\sum_{n=0}^{\infty}C_{n,q}(x,y)\frac{t^n}{[n]_q!}.$$

By applying the Cauchy product rule in the above equation and then equating the coefficients of like powers of t on both sides of the resultant equation, assertion (58) follows. Similarly, we obtain (59). □

The following Theorems can be easily derived by making use of the definitions of used polynomials and series manipulations. So, we omit the proofs.

Theorem 11. *The following relation holds true:*

$$\mathbb{H}_{n,q}^{(\alpha,c)}(x,y;u;\lambda)$$
$$=\frac{1}{1-u}\sum_{k=0}^{n}\binom{n}{k}_q\Big[\lambda\mathbb{H}_{n-k,q}(u;\lambda)\mathbb{H}_{k,q}^{(\alpha,c)}(x,y;u;\lambda)$$
$$-u\mathbb{H}_{n-k,q}(u;\lambda)\mathbb{H}_{k,q}^{(\alpha,c)}(x,y;u;\lambda)\Big]. \tag{60}$$

and

$$\mathbb{H}_{n,q}^{(\alpha,s)}(x,y;u;\lambda)$$
$$=\frac{1}{1-u}\sum_{k=0}^{n}\binom{n}{k}_q\Big[\lambda\mathbb{H}_{n-k,q}(u;\lambda)\mathbb{H}_{k,q}^{(\alpha,s)}(x,y;u;\lambda)$$
$$-u\mathbb{H}_{n-k,q}(u;\lambda)\mathbb{H}_{k,q}^{(\alpha,s)}(x,y;u;\lambda)\Big]. \tag{61}$$

Theorem 12. *The following relations hold true:*

$$\mathbb{H}_{n,q}^{(\alpha,c)}(x,y;u;\lambda)=\sum_{k=0}^{n+1}\binom{n+1}{k}_q\left(\lambda\sum_{r=0}^{k}\binom{k}{r}_q\mathbb{B}_{k-r,q}(x;\lambda)-\mathbb{B}_{k,q}(x;\lambda)\right)$$
$$\times\mathbb{H}_{n-k+1,q}^{(\alpha,c)}(0,y;u;\lambda). \tag{62}$$

and

$$\mathbb{H}_{n,q}^{(\alpha,s)}(x,y;u;\lambda)=\sum_{k=0}^{n+1}\binom{n+1}{k}_q\left(\lambda\sum_{r=0}^{k}\binom{k}{r}_q\mathbb{B}_{k-r,q}(x;\lambda)-\mathbb{B}_{k,q}(x;\lambda)\right)$$
$$\times\mathbb{H}_{n-k+1,q}^{(\alpha,s)}(0,y;u;\lambda). \tag{63}$$

Theorem 13. *The following relations hold true:*

$$\mathbb{H}_{n,q}^{(\alpha,c)}(x,y;u;\lambda)=\frac{1}{2}\sum_{k=0}^{n}\binom{n}{k}_q\left(\lambda\sum_{r=0}^{k}\binom{k}{r}_q\mathbb{E}_{k-r,q}(\lambda)+\mathbb{E}_{k,q}(\lambda)\right)$$
$$\times\mathbb{H}_{n-k,q}^{(\alpha,c)}(x,y;u;\lambda). \tag{64}$$

and

$$\mathbb{H}_{n,q}^{(\alpha,s)}(x,y;u;\lambda)=\frac{1}{2}\sum_{k=0}^{n}\binom{n}{k}_q\left(\lambda\sum_{r=0}^{k}\binom{k}{r}_q\mathbb{E}_{k-r,q}(\lambda)+\mathbb{E}_{k,q}(\lambda)\right)$$
$$\times\mathbb{H}_{n-k,q}^{(\alpha,s)}(x,y;u;\lambda). \tag{65}$$

Theorem 14. *The following relations hold true:*

$$\mathbb{H}_{n,q}^{(\alpha,c)}(x,y;u;\lambda)=\frac{1}{2}\sum_{k=0}^{n+1}\binom{n+1}{k}_q\left(\lambda\sum_{r=0}^{k}\binom{k}{r}_q\mathbb{G}_{k-r,q}(\lambda)+\mathbb{G}_{k,q}(\lambda)\right)$$
$$\times\mathbb{H}_{n-k+1,q}^{(\alpha,c)}(x,y;u;\lambda). \tag{66}$$

and

$$\mathbb{H}_{n,q}^{(\alpha,s)}(x,y;u;\lambda)=\frac{1}{2}\sum_{k=0}^{n+1}\binom{n+1}{k}_q\left(\lambda\sum_{r=0}^{k}\binom{k}{r}_q\mathbb{G}_{k-r,q}(\lambda)+\mathbb{G}_{k,q}(\lambda)\right)$$
$$\times\mathbb{H}_{n-k+1,q}^{(\alpha,s)}(x,y;u;\lambda). \tag{67}$$

Theorem 15. *Let α and γ be nonnegative integers. The following relations hold true:*

$$\left(\frac{1-u}{u}\right)^{\alpha}C_{n,q}(x,y)=\alpha!\sum_{l=0}^{n}\binom{n}{l}_q\mathbb{H}_{n-l,q}^{(\alpha,c)}(x,y;u;\lambda)S\left(l,\alpha,\frac{\lambda}{u}:q\right), \tag{68}$$

$$\left(\frac{1-u}{u}\right)^{\alpha}S_{n,q}(x,y)=\alpha!\sum_{l=0}^{n}\binom{n}{l}_q\mathbb{H}_{n-l,q}^{(\alpha,s)}(x,y;u;\lambda)S\left(l,\alpha,\frac{\lambda}{u}:q\right), \tag{69}$$

$$\mathbb{H}_{n,q}^{(\alpha-\gamma,c)}(x,y;u;\lambda)$$
$$=\gamma!\left(\frac{u}{1-u}\right)^{\gamma}\alpha!\sum_{l=0}^{n}\binom{n}{l}_q\mathbb{H}_{n-l,q}^{(\alpha,c)}(x,y;u;\lambda)S\left(l,\alpha,\frac{\lambda}{u}:q\right), \tag{70}$$

and

$$\mathbb{H}_{n,q}^{(\alpha-\gamma,s)}(x,y;u;\lambda)$$

$$= \gamma!\left(\frac{u}{1-u}\right)^{\gamma}\alpha!\sum_{l=0}^{n}\binom{n}{l}_{q}\mathbb{H}_{n-l,q}^{(\alpha,s)}(x,y;u;\lambda)S\left(l,\alpha,\frac{\lambda}{u}:q\right). \quad (71)$$

Theorem 16. *The following relations hold true:*

$$\mathbb{H}_{n,q}^{(\alpha,c)}(x,y;u;\lambda)$$

$$= \sum_{j=0}^{n}\sum_{l=j}^{n}\binom{\alpha+j-1}{j}_{q}j!\binom{n}{l}_{q}(1-u)^{-j}S(l,j;\lambda:q)(\lambda-1)^{l-j}C_{n-l,q}(x,y). \quad (72)$$

and

$$\mathbb{H}_{n,q}^{(\alpha,s)}(x,y;u;\lambda)$$

$$= \sum_{j=0}^{n}\sum_{l=j}^{n}\binom{\alpha+j-1}{j}_{q}j!\binom{n}{l}_{q}(1-u)^{-j}S(l,j;\lambda:q)(\lambda-1)^{l-j}S_{n-l,q}(x,y). \quad (73)$$

Theorem 17. *The following relationships hold true:*

$$\mathbb{H}_{n,q}^{(\alpha,c)}(x,y;u;\lambda) = \sum_{k=0}^{n}(\alpha)_k(u-1)^{-k}S_{n,q}^{(k,c)}(x,y;\lambda) \quad (74)$$

and

$$\mathbb{H}_{n,q}^{(\alpha,s)}(x,y;u;\lambda) = \sum_{k=0}^{n}(\alpha)_k(u-1)^{-k}S_{n,q}^{(k,s)}(x,y;\lambda), \quad (75)$$

where

$$e_q(xt)COS_q(yt)\frac{(\lambda e_q(t)-1)^k}{[k]_q!} = \sum_{n=k}^{\infty}S_{n,q}^{(k,c)}(x,y;\lambda)\frac{t^n}{[n]_q!}$$

and

$$e_q(xt)SIN_q(yt)\frac{(\lambda e_q(t)-1)^k}{[k]_q!} = \sum_{n=k}^{\infty}S_{n,q}^{(k,s)}(x,y;\lambda)\frac{t^n}{[n]_q!}.$$

4. Symmetry Identities for q-Cosine and q-Sine Apostol-Type Frobenius–Euler Polynomials

In this section, we describe the general symmetry identities for the q-cosine and q-sine Apostol-type Frobenius–Euler polynomials and generalized Apostol-type Frobenius–Euler polynomials by applying the generating functions (9), (24) and (25). We begin with the following theorem.

Theorem 18. *Let $a, b, > 0$ with $a \neq b$ and $j \geq 0$. Then,*

(i)

$$\sum_{k=0}^{n}\binom{n}{k}_{q}b^k a^{n-k}\mathbb{H}_{n-k,q}^{(\alpha,c)}(bx,by;u;\lambda)\mathbb{H}_{k,q}^{(\alpha,c)}(ax,ay;u;\lambda)$$

$$= \sum_{k=0}^{n}\binom{n}{k}_{q}a^k b^{n-k}\mathbb{H}_{n-k,q}^{(\alpha,c)}(ax,ay;u;\lambda)\mathbb{H}_{k,q}^{(\alpha,c)}(bx,by;u;\lambda), \quad (76)$$

(ii)

$$\sum_{k=0}^{n}\binom{n}{k}_{q}b^k a^{n-k}\mathbb{H}_{n-k,q}^{(\alpha,s)}(bx,by;u;\lambda)\mathbb{H}_{k,q}^{(\alpha,s)}(ax,ay;u;\lambda)$$

$$= \sum_{k=0}^{n}\binom{n}{k}_{q}a^k b^{n-k}\mathbb{H}_{n-k,q}^{(\alpha,s)}(ax,ay;u;\lambda)\mathbb{H}_{k,q}^{(\alpha,s)}(bx,by;u;\lambda). \quad (77)$$

Proof. Let

$$A(z)=\left(\frac{(1-u)^2(e_q(abxt)COS_q(abyt))^2}{(\lambda e_q(az)-u)(\lambda e_q(bz)-u)}\right)^{2\alpha}. \tag{78}$$

Then, the expression for $A(z)$ is symmetric in a and b, and we obtain

$$A(z)=\sum_{n=0}^{\infty}\mathbb{H}_{n,q}^{(\alpha,c)}(bx,by;u;\lambda)\frac{(at)^n}{[n]_q!}\sum_{k=0}^{\infty}H_{k,q}^{(\alpha,c)}(ax,ay;u;\lambda)\frac{(bt)^k}{[k]_q!}$$

$$=\sum_{n=0}^{\infty}\left(\sum_{k=0}^{n}\binom{j}{k}_q b^k a^{j-k}\mathbb{H}_{n-k,q}^{(\alpha,c)}(bx,by;u;\lambda)\mathbb{H}_{k,q}^{(\alpha,c)}(ax,ay;u;\lambda)\right)\frac{t^n}{[n]_q!}.$$

Similarly, we can show that

$$A(z)=\sum_{n=0}^{\infty}\mathbb{H}_{n,q}^{(\alpha,c)}(ax,ay;u;\lambda)\frac{(bt)^n}{[n]_q!}\sum_{k=0}^{\infty}\mathbb{H}_{k,q}^{(\alpha,c)}(bx,by;u;\lambda)\frac{(at)^k}{k!}$$

$$=\sum_{n=0}^{\infty}\left(\sum_{k=0}^{n}\binom{n}{k}_q a^k b^{n-k}\mathbb{H}_{n-k,q}^{(\alpha,c)}(ax,ay;u;\lambda)\mathbb{H}_{k,q}^{(\alpha,c)}(bx,by;u;\lambda)\right)\frac{t^n}{[n]_q!}.$$

On comparing the coefficients of t^n on the right hand sides of the last two equations, we arrive at the desired result (76). Similarly, we obtain (77). □

Remark 2. *For $\alpha=1$ in Theorem 18, the result reduces to*

(i)

$$\sum_{k=0}^{n}\binom{n}{k}_q b^k a^{n-k}\mathbb{H}_{n-k,q}^{(c)}(bx,by;u;\lambda)\mathbb{H}_{k,q}^{(c)}(ax,ay;u;\lambda)$$

$$=\sum_{k=0}^{n}\binom{n}{k}_q a^k b^{n-k}\mathbb{H}_{n-k,q}^{(c)}(ax,ay;u;\lambda)\mathbb{H}_{k,q}^{(c)}(bx,by;u;\lambda), \tag{79}$$

(ii)

$$\sum_{k=0}^{n}\binom{n}{k}_q b^k a^{n-k}\mathbb{H}_{n-k,q}^{(s)}(bx,by;u;\lambda)\mathbb{H}_{k,q}^{(s)}(ax,ay;u;\lambda)$$

$$=\sum_{k=0}^{n}\binom{n}{k}_q a^k b^{n-k}\mathbb{H}_{n-k,q}^{(s)}(ax,ay;u;\lambda)\mathbb{H}_{k,q}^{(s)}(bx,by;u;\lambda). \tag{80}$$

Remark 3. *Assume $q\to 1$ in Theorem 18, the result reduces to*

(i)

$$\sum_{k=0}^{n}\binom{n}{k} b^k a^{n-k}\mathbb{H}_{n-k}^{(\alpha,c)}(bx,by;u;\lambda)\mathbb{H}_{k}^{(\alpha,c)}(ax,ay;u;\lambda)$$

$$=\sum_{k=0}^{n}\binom{n}{k} a^k b^{n-k}\mathbb{H}_{n-k}^{(\alpha,c)}(ax,ay;u;\lambda)\mathbb{H}_{k}^{(\alpha,c)}(bx,by;u;\lambda), \tag{81}$$

(ii)

$$\sum_{k=0}^{n}\binom{n}{k} b^k a^{n-k}\mathbb{H}_{n-k}^{(\alpha,s)}(bx,by;u;\lambda)\mathbb{H}_{k}^{(\alpha,s)}(ax,ay;u;\lambda)$$

$$=\sum_{k=0}^{n}\binom{n}{k} a^k b^{n-k}\mathbb{H}_{n-k}^{(\alpha,s)}(ax,ay;u;\lambda)\mathbb{H}_{k}^{(\alpha,s)}(bx,by;u;\lambda). \tag{82}$$

Theorem 19. *Let $a,b,>0$ with $a\neq b$ and $n\geq 0$. Then,*

(i)

$$\sum_{k=0}^{n}\binom{n}{k}_q\sum_{i=0}^{a-1}\sum_{j=0}^{b-1}(-\lambda)^{i+j}a^{n-k}b^k\mathbb{H}_{n-k,q}^{(\alpha,c)}\left(bx+\frac{b}{a}i+j,by;u;\lambda\right)\mathbb{H}_{k,q}^{(\alpha,c)}(ax,ay;u;\lambda)$$

$$=\sum_{k=0}^{n}\binom{n}{k}_q\sum_{i=0}^{b-1}\sum_{j=0}^{a-1}(-\lambda)^{i+j}b^{n-k}a^k\mathbb{H}_{n-k,q}^{(\alpha,c)}\left(ax+\frac{a}{b}i+j,ay;u;\lambda\right)\mathbb{H}_{k,q}^{(\alpha,c)}(bx,by;u;\lambda). \tag{83}$$

(ii)

$$\sum_{k=0}^{n}\binom{n}{k}_q\sum_{i=0}^{a-1}\sum_{j=0}^{b-1}(-\lambda)^{i+j}a^{n-k}b^k\mathbb{H}_{n-k,q}^{(\alpha,s)}\left(bx+\frac{b}{a}i+j,by;u;\lambda\right)\mathbb{H}_{k,q}^{(\alpha,s)}(ax,ay;u;\lambda)$$

$$=\sum_{k=0}^{n}\binom{n}{k}_q\sum_{i=0}^{b-1}\sum_{j=0}^{a-1}(-\lambda)^{i+j}b^{n-k}a^k\mathbb{H}_{n-k,q}^{(\alpha,s)}\left(ax+\frac{a}{b}i+j,ay;u;\lambda\right)\mathbb{H}_{k,q}^{(\alpha,s)}(bx,by;u;\lambda). \tag{84}$$

Proof. Consider the identity

$$B(t)=\left(\frac{(1-u)^2}{(\lambda e_q(at)-u)(\lambda e_q(bt)-u)}\right)^{2\alpha}\frac{1+\lambda(-1)^{a+1}e^{abz}}{(\lambda e^{at}+1)(\lambda e^{bz}+1)}(e_q(abxt)COS_q(abyt))^2. \tag{85}$$

$$B(t)=\left(\frac{1-u}{\lambda e_q(az)-u}\right)^{\alpha}e_q(abxt)COS_q(abyt)\left(\frac{1-\lambda(-e_q(-bt))^a}{\lambda e_q(bt)+1}\right)\left(\frac{1-u}{\lambda e_q(bz)-u}\right)^{\alpha}$$
$$\times\left(\frac{1-\lambda(-e_q(-az))^b}{\lambda e_q(az)+1}\right)e_q(abxt)COS_q(abyt)$$
$$=\left(\frac{1-u}{\lambda e_q(az)-u}\right)^{\alpha}e_q(abxt)COS_q(abyt)\sum_{i=0}^{a-1}(-\lambda)^i e_q(bzi)\left(\frac{1-u}{\lambda e_q(bt)-u}\right)^{\alpha}e_q(abxt)COS_q(abyt)\sum_{j=0}^{b-1}(-\lambda)^j e_q(azj)$$
$$=\left(\frac{1-u}{\lambda e_q(az)-u}\right)^{\alpha}Cos_q(abyt)\sum_{i=0}^{a-1}\sum_{j=0}^{b-1}(-\lambda)^{i+j}e_q\left((bx+\frac{b}{a}i+j)at\right)\sum_{k=0}^{\infty}\mathbb{H}_{k,q}^{(\alpha,c)}(ax,ay;u;\lambda)\frac{(bt)^k}{[k]_q!}$$
$$=\sum_{n=0}^{\infty}\sum_{i=0}^{a-1}\sum_{j=0}^{b-1}(-\lambda)^{i+j}\mathbb{H}_{n,q}^{(\alpha,c)}\left(bx+\frac{b}{a}i+j,by;u;\lambda\right)\frac{(at)^n}{[n]_q!}\sum_{k=0}^{\infty}\mathbb{H}_{k,q}^{(\alpha,c)}(ax,ay;u;\lambda)\frac{(bt)^k}{[k]_q!}$$
$$=\sum_{n=0}^{\infty}\sum_{k=0}^{n}\binom{n}{k}_q\sum_{i=0}^{a-1}\sum_{j=0}^{b-1}(-\lambda)^{i+j}a^{s-k}b^k\mathbb{H}_{n-k,q}^{(\alpha,c)}\left(byx+\frac{b}{a}i+j,b\eta;u;\lambda\right)$$
$$\times\mathbb{H}_{k,q}^{(\alpha,c)}(ax,ay;u;\lambda)\frac{t^n}{[n]_q!}. \tag{86}$$

On the other hand, we obtain

$$B(t)=\sum_{n=0}^{\infty}\sum_{k=0}^{n}\binom{n}{k}_q\sum_{i=0}^{b-1}\sum_{j=0}^{a-1}(-\lambda)^{i+j}b^{n-k}a^k\mathbb{H}_{n-k}^{(\alpha,c)}\left(ax+\frac{a}{b}i+j,ay;u;\lambda\right)$$
$$\times\mathbb{H}_{k,q}^{(\alpha,c)}(bx,by;u;\lambda)\frac{t^n}{[n]_q!}. \tag{87}$$

By using (86) and (87), we arrive at the desired result (82). Similarly, we obtain (83). □

Theorem 20. *Let $a, b, > 0$ with $a \neq b$ and $j \geq 0$. Then,*

$$\sum_{k=0}^{n} \binom{n}{k}_q b^k a^{n-k} \mathbb{H}_{n-k,q}^{(\alpha,c)}(bx, by; u; \lambda) \mathbb{H}_{k,q}^{(\alpha,s)}(ax, ay; u; \lambda)$$

$$= \sum_{k=0}^{n} \binom{n}{k}_q a^k b^{n-k} \mathbb{H}_{n-k,q}^{(\alpha,s)}(ax, ay; u; \lambda) \mathbb{H}_{k,q}^{(\alpha,c)}(bx, by; u; \lambda). \quad (88)$$

Proof. Suppose that

$$A(t) = \left(\frac{(1-u)^2 (e_q(abxt))^2 COS_q(abyt) SIN_q(abyt)}{(\lambda e^{az} - u)(\lambda e^{bz} - u)} \right)^{2\alpha}. \quad (89)$$

Then, the expression for $A(t)$ is symmetric in a and b, and we obtain

$$C(t) = \sum_{n=0}^{\infty} \mathbb{H}_{n,q}^{(\alpha,c)}(bx, by; u; \lambda) \frac{(at)^n}{[n]_q!} \sum_{k=0}^{\infty} \mathbb{H}_{k,q}^{(\alpha,s)}(ax, ay; u; \lambda) \frac{(bt)^k}{[k]_q!}$$

$$= \sum_{n=0}^{\infty} \left(\sum_{k=0}^{n} \binom{j}{k}_q b^k a^{j-k} \mathbb{H}_{n-k,q}^{(\alpha,c)}(bx, by; u; \lambda) \mathbb{H}_{k,q}^{(\alpha,s)}(ax, ay; u; \lambda) \right) \frac{t^n}{[n]_q!}.$$

Similarly, we can show that

$$A(z) = \sum_{n=0}^{\infty} \mathbb{H}_{n,q}^{(\alpha,s)}(ax, ay; u; \lambda) \frac{(bt)^n}{n!} \sum_{k=0}^{\infty} \mathbb{H}_{k,q}^{(\alpha,c)}(bx, by; u; \lambda) \frac{(at)^k}{k!}$$

$$= \sum_{n=0}^{\infty} \left(\sum_{k=0}^{n} \binom{n}{k}_q a^k b^{n-k} \mathbb{H}_{n-k,q}^{(\alpha,s)}(ax, ay; u; \lambda) \mathbb{H}_{k,q}^{(\alpha,c)}(bx, by; u; \lambda) \right) \frac{t^n}{n!}.$$

On comparing the coefficients of t^n on the right hand sides of the last two equations, we arrive at the desired result (88). □

Remark 4. *Assume that $q \to 1$ in Theorem 18, for which the result reduces to*

$$\sum_{k=0}^{n} \binom{n}{k} b^k a^{n-k} \mathbb{H}_{n-k}^{(\alpha,c)}(bx, by; u; \lambda) \mathbb{H}_{k}^{(\alpha,s)}(ax, ay; u; \lambda)$$

$$= \sum_{k=0}^{n} \binom{n}{k} a^k b^{n-k} \mathbb{H}_{n-k}^{(\alpha,s)}(ax, ay; u; \lambda) \mathbb{H}_{k}^{(\alpha,c)}(bx, by; u; \lambda). \quad (90)$$

5. Symmetric Structure of Approximate Roots for q-Cosine Apostol-Type Frobenius–Euler Polynomials and Their Application

In this section, certain zeros of the q-Cosine Apostol-type Frobenius–Euler polynomials $\mathbb{H}_{n,q}^{(\alpha,c)}(x, y; u; \lambda)$ and graphical representations are shown.

A few of them are as follows:

$$\mathbb{H}_{0,q}^{(\alpha,c)}(x,y;u;\lambda) = \left(\frac{-1+u}{u-\lambda}\right)^{\alpha},$$

$$\mathbb{H}_{1,q}^{(\alpha,c)}(x,y;u;\lambda) = -\frac{ux\left(\frac{-1+u}{u-\lambda}\right)^{\alpha}}{-u+\lambda} + \frac{x\left(\frac{-1+u}{u-\lambda}\right)^{\alpha}\lambda}{-u+\lambda} - \frac{\alpha\left(\frac{-1+u}{u-\lambda}\right)^{\alpha}\lambda}{-u+\lambda},$$

$$\begin{aligned}\mathbb{H}_{2,q}^{(\alpha,c)}(x,y;u;\lambda) = {} & \frac{x^2\left(\frac{-1+u}{u-\lambda}\right)^{\alpha}}{(1-q)(1+q)} - \frac{q^2x^2\left(\frac{-1+u}{u-\lambda}\right)^{\alpha}}{(1-q)(1+q)} - \frac{y^2\left(\frac{-1+u}{u-\lambda}\right)^{\alpha}}{(1-q)(1+q)} + \frac{q^2y^2\left(\frac{-1+u}{u-\lambda}\right)^{\alpha}}{(1-q)(1+q)} \\ & + \frac{u\alpha\left(\frac{-1+u}{u-\lambda}\right)^{\alpha}\lambda}{(1-q)(1+q)(-u+\lambda)^2} - \frac{q^2u\alpha\left(\frac{-1+u}{u-\lambda}\right)^{\alpha}\lambda}{(1-q)(1+q)(-u+\lambda)^2} - \frac{\alpha\left(\frac{-1+u}{u-\lambda}\right)^{\alpha}\lambda^2}{2(1-q)(1+q)(-u+\lambda)^2} \\ & + \frac{q\alpha\left(\frac{-1+u}{u-\lambda}\right)^{\alpha}\lambda^2}{2(1-q)(1+q)(-u+\lambda)^2} + \frac{q^2\alpha\left(\frac{-1+u}{u-\lambda}\right)^{\alpha}\lambda^2}{2(1-q)(1+q)(-u+\lambda)^2} - \frac{q^3\alpha\left(\frac{-1+u}{u-\lambda}\right)^{\alpha}\lambda^2}{2(1-q)(1+q)(-u+\lambda)^2} \\ & + \frac{\alpha^2\left(\frac{-1+u}{u-\lambda}\right)^{\alpha}\lambda^2}{2(1-q)(1+q)(-u+\lambda)^2} + \frac{q\alpha^2\left(\frac{-1+u}{u-\lambda}\right)^{\alpha}\lambda^2}{2(1-q)(1+q)(-u+\lambda)^2} - \frac{q^2\alpha^2\left(\frac{-1+u}{u-\lambda}\right)^{\alpha}\lambda^2}{2(1-q)(1+q)(-u+\lambda)^2} \\ & - \frac{q^3\alpha^2\left(\frac{-1+u}{u-\lambda}\right)^{\alpha}\lambda^2}{2(1-q)(1+q)(-u+\lambda)^2} - \frac{x\alpha\left(\frac{-1+u}{u-\lambda}\right)^{\alpha}\lambda}{(1-q)(-u+\lambda)} + \frac{q^2x\alpha\left(\frac{-1+u}{u-\lambda}\right)^{\alpha}\lambda}{(1-q)(-u+\lambda)}.\end{aligned}$$

We investigate the zeros of the q-Cosine Apostol-type Frobenius–Euler polynomials $\mathbb{H}_{n,q}^{(\alpha,c)}(x,y;u;\lambda)$ by using a computer. We plot the zeros of the q-Cosine Apostol-type Frobenius–Euler polynomials $\mathbb{H}_{n,q}^{(\alpha,c)}(x,y;u;\lambda) = 0$ for $n = 20$ (Figure 1).

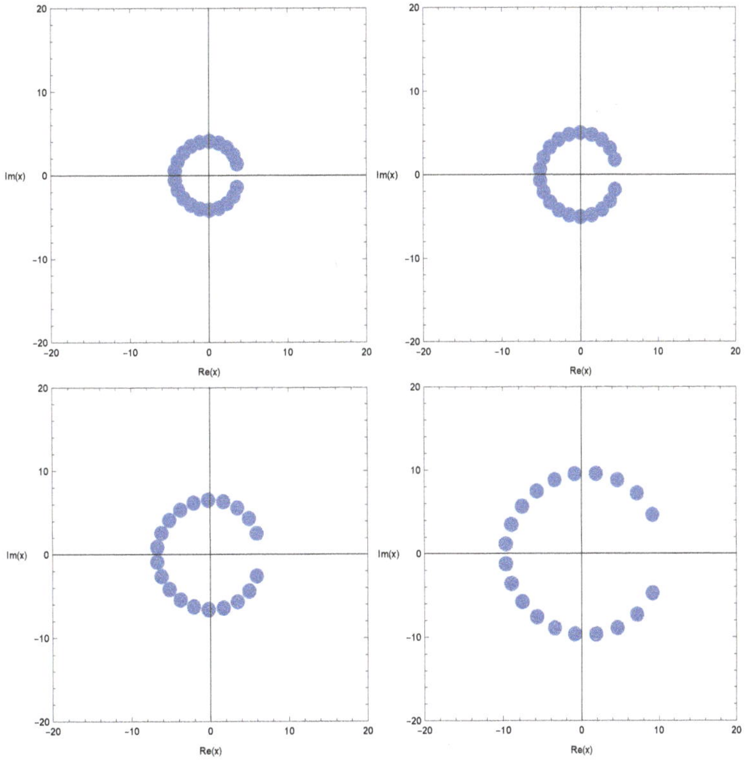

Figure 1. Zeros of $\mathbb{H}_{n,q}^{(\alpha,c)}(x,y;u;\lambda)$.

In Figure 1 (top-left), we choose $\alpha = 4, \lambda = 2, u = 3$, and $q = \frac{1}{10}, y = 3$. In Figure 1 (top-right), we choose $\alpha = 4, \lambda = 2, u = 3$, and $q = \frac{3}{10}, y = 3$. In Figure 1 (bottom-left), we choose $\alpha = 4, \lambda = 2, u = 3$, and $q = \frac{5}{10}, y = 3$. In Figure 1 (bottom-right), we choose $\alpha = 4, \lambda = 2, u = 3$, and $q = \frac{7}{10}, y = 3$.

Stacks of zeros of the q-Cosine Apostol-type Frobenius–Euler polynomials $\mathbb{H}_{n,q}^{(\alpha,c)}(x, y; u; \lambda) = 0$ for $1 \leq n \leq 20$, forming a 3D structure, are presented (Figure 2).

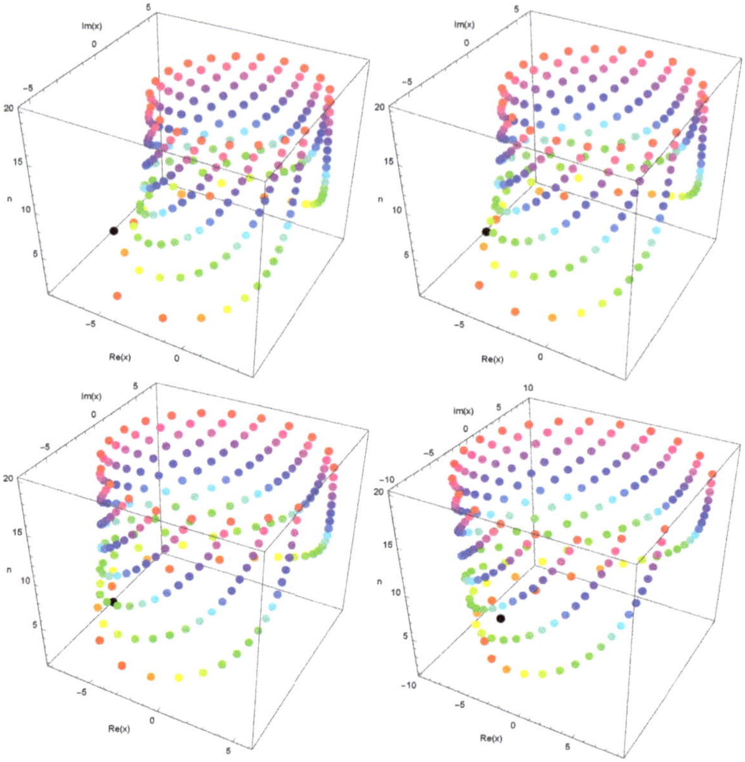

Figure 2. Zeros of $\mathbb{H}_{n,q}^{(\alpha,c)}(x, y; u; \lambda)$.

In Figure 2 (top-left), we choose $\alpha = 4, \lambda = 2, u = 3$, and $q = \frac{1}{10}, y = 3$. In Figure 2 (top-right), we choose $\alpha = 4, \lambda = 2, u = 3$, and $q = \frac{3}{10}, y = 3$. In Figure 2 (bottom-left), we choose $\alpha = 4, \lambda = 2, u = 3$, and $q = \frac{5}{10}, y = 3$. In Figure 2 (bottom-right), we choose $\alpha = 4, \lambda = 2, u = 3$, and $q = \frac{7}{10}, y = 3$.

Next, we calculated an approximate solution satisfying the q-Cosine Apostol-type Frobenius–Euler polynomials $\mathbb{H}_{n,q}^{(\alpha,c)}(x, y; u; \lambda) = 0$ for $q = \frac{1}{10}$. The results are provided in Table 1.

Table 1. Approximate solutions of $\mathbb{H}_{n,q}^{(4,c)}(x,3;3;2)=0$.

Degree n	x
1	−8.0000
2	−4.4000 − 4.8621 i, −4.4000 + 4.8621 i
3	−6.5429, −1.1686 − 5.5743 i, −1.1686 + 5.5743 i
4	−5.1586 − 2.9339 i, −5.1586 + 2.9339 i, 0.7146 − 5.2176 i, 0.7146 + 5.2176 i
5	−5.8344, −3.3214 − 4.2756 i, −3.3214 + 4.2756 i, 1.7942 − 4.6626 i, 1.7942 + 4.6626 i
6	−5.1069 − 2.0266 i, −5.1069 + 2.0266 i, −1.7739 − 4.7670 i, −1.7739 + 4.7670 i, 2.4363 − 4.1334 i, 2.4363 + 4.1334 i
7	−5.4063, −3.9859 − 3.2720 i, −3.9859 + 3.2720 i, −0.5893 − 4.8378 i, −0.5893 + 4.8378 i, 2.8338 − 3.6774 i, 2.8338 + 3.6774 i
8	−4.9566 − 1.5254 i, −4.9566 + 1.5254 i, −2.8747 − 3.9790 i, −2.8747 + 3.9790 i, 0.2982 − 4.7116 i, 0.2982 + 4.7116 i, 3.0887 − 3.2950 i, 3.0887 + 3.2950 i
9	−5.1150, −4.2106 − 2.6028 i, −4.2106 + 2.6028 i, −1.8968 − 4.3377 i, −1.8968 + 4.3377 i, 0.9638 − 4.5004 i, 0.9638 + 4.5004 i, 3.2566 − 2.9754 i, 3.2566 + 2.9754 i

6. Symmetric Structure of Approximate Roots for q-Sine Apostol-Type Frobenius–Euler Polynomials and Their Application

In this section, certain zeros of the q-Sine Apostol-type Frobenius–Euler polynomials $\mathbb{H}_{n,q}^{(\alpha,s)}(x,y;u;\lambda)$ and beautiful graphical representations are shown.

A few of them are as follows:

$$\mathbb{H}_{0,q}^{(\alpha,s)}(x,y;u;\lambda)=0,$$

$$\mathbb{H}_{1,q}^{(\alpha,s)}(x,y;u;\lambda)=y\left(\frac{-1+u}{u-\lambda}\right)^{\alpha},$$

$$\begin{aligned}\mathbb{H}_{2,q}^{(\alpha,s)}(x,y;u;\lambda)=&-\frac{uxy\left(\frac{-1+u}{u-\lambda}\right)^{\alpha}}{(1-q)(-u+\lambda)}+\frac{q^2uxy\left(\frac{-1+u}{u-\lambda}\right)^{\alpha}}{(1-q)(-u+\lambda)}+\frac{xy\left(\frac{-1+u}{u-\lambda}\right)^{\alpha}\lambda}{(1-q)(-u+\lambda)}\\&-\frac{q^2xy\left(\frac{-1+u}{u-\lambda}\right)^{\alpha}\lambda}{(1-q)(-u+\lambda)}-\frac{y\alpha\left(\frac{-1+u}{u-\lambda}\right)^{\alpha}\lambda}{(1-q)(-u+\lambda)}+\frac{q^2y\alpha\left(\frac{-1+u}{u-\lambda}\right)^{\alpha}\lambda}{(1-q)(-u+\lambda)},\end{aligned}$$

$$\begin{aligned}\mathbb{H}_{3,q}^{(\alpha,s)}(x,y;u;\lambda)=&\frac{x^2y\left(\frac{-1+u}{u-\lambda}\right)^{\alpha}}{(1-q)^2(1+q)}-\frac{q^2x^2y\left(\frac{-1+u}{u-\lambda}\right)^{\alpha}}{(1-q)^2(1+q)}-\frac{q^3x^2y\left(\frac{-1+u}{u-\lambda}\right)^{\alpha}}{(1-q)^2(1+q)}\\&+\frac{q^5x^2y\left(\frac{-1+u}{u-\lambda}\right)^{\alpha}}{(1-q)^2(1+q)}-\frac{q^3y^3\left(\frac{-1+u}{u-\lambda}\right)^{\alpha}}{(1-q)^2(1+q)(1+q+q^2)}+\frac{q^5y^3\left(\frac{-1+u}{u-\lambda}\right)^{\alpha}}{(1-q)^2(1+q)(1+q+q^2)}\\&+\frac{q^6y^3\left(\frac{-1+u}{u-\lambda}\right)^{\alpha}}{(1-q)^2(1+q)(1+q+q^2)}-\frac{q^8y^3\left(\frac{-1+u}{u-\lambda}\right)^{\alpha}}{(1-q)^2(1+q)(1+q+q^2)}+\frac{uy\alpha\left(\frac{-1+u}{u-\lambda}\right)^{\alpha}\lambda}{(1-q)^2(1+q)(-u+\lambda)^2}\\&-\frac{q^2uy\alpha\left(\frac{-1+u}{u-\lambda}\right)^{\alpha}\lambda}{(1-q)^2(1+q)(-u+\lambda)^2}-\frac{q^3uy\alpha\left(\frac{-1+u}{u-\lambda}\right)^{\alpha}\lambda}{(1-q)^2(1+q)(-u+\lambda)^2}+\frac{q^5uy\alpha\left(\frac{-1+u}{u-\lambda}\right)^{\alpha}\lambda}{(1-q)^2(1+q)(-u+\lambda)^2}\\&-\frac{y\alpha\left(\frac{-1+u}{u-\lambda}\right)^{\alpha}\lambda^2}{2(1-q)^2(1+q)(-u+\lambda)^2}+\frac{qy\alpha\left(\frac{-1+u}{u-\lambda}\right)^{\alpha}\lambda^2}{2(1-q)^2(1+q)(-u+\lambda)^2}+\frac{q^2y\alpha\left(\frac{-1+u}{u-\lambda}\right)^{\alpha}\lambda^2}{2(1-q)^2(1+q)(-u+\lambda)^2}\end{aligned}$$

$$
\begin{aligned}
&-\frac{q^4 y\alpha\left(\frac{-1+u}{u-\lambda}\right)^{\alpha}\lambda^2}{2(1-q)^2(1+q)(-u+\lambda)^2}-\frac{q^5 y\alpha\left(\frac{-1+u}{u-\lambda}\right)^{\alpha}\lambda^2}{2(1-q)^2(1+q)(-u+\lambda)^2}+\frac{q^6 y\alpha\left(\frac{-1+u}{u-\lambda}\right)^{\alpha}\lambda^2}{2(1-q)^2(1+q)(-u+\lambda)^2}\\
&+\frac{y\alpha^2\left(\frac{-1+u}{u-\lambda}\right)^{\alpha}\lambda^2}{2(1-q)^2(1+q)(-u+\lambda)^2}+\frac{qy\alpha^2\left(\frac{-1+u}{u-\lambda}\right)^{\alpha}\lambda^2}{2(1-q)^2(1+q)(-u+\lambda)^2}-\frac{q^2 y\alpha^2\left(\frac{-1+u}{u-\lambda}\right)^{\alpha}\lambda^2}{2(1-q)^2(1+q)(-u+\lambda)^2}\\
&-\frac{q^3 y\alpha^2\left(\frac{-1+u}{u-\lambda}\right)^{\alpha}\lambda^2}{(1-q)^2(1+q)(-u+\lambda)^2}-\frac{q^4 y\alpha^2\left(\frac{-1+u}{u-\lambda}\right)^{\alpha}\lambda^2}{2(1-q)^2(1+q)(-u+\lambda)^2}+\frac{q^5 y\alpha^2\left(\frac{-1+u}{u-\lambda}\right)^{\alpha}\lambda^2}{2(1-q)^2(1+q)(-u+\lambda)^2}\\
&+\frac{q^6 y\alpha^2\left(\frac{-1+u}{u-\lambda}\right)^{\alpha}\lambda^2}{2(1-q)^2(1+q)(-u+\lambda)^2}-\frac{xy\alpha\left(\frac{-1+u}{u-\lambda}\right)^{\alpha}\lambda}{(1-q)^2(-u+\lambda)}+\frac{q^2 xy\alpha\left(\frac{-1+u}{u-\lambda}\right)^{\alpha}\lambda}{(1-q)^2(-u+\lambda)}\\
&+\frac{q^3 xy\alpha\left(\frac{-1+u}{u-\lambda}\right)^{\alpha}\lambda}{(1-q)^2(-u+\lambda)}-\frac{q^5 xy\alpha\left(\frac{-1+u}{u-\lambda}\right)^{\alpha}\lambda}{(1-q)^2(-u+\lambda)}
\end{aligned}
$$

In Figure 3 (top-left), we choose $\alpha = 4, \lambda = 2, u = 3$, and $q = \frac{2}{10}, y = 3$. In Figure 3 (top-right), we choose $\alpha = 4, \lambda = 2, u = 3$, and $q = \frac{4}{10}, y = 3$. In Figure 3 (bottom-left), we choose $\alpha = 4, \lambda = 2, u = 3$, and $q = \frac{6}{10}, y = 3$. In Figure 3 (bottom-right), we choose $\alpha = 4, \lambda = 2, u = 3$, and $q = \frac{8}{10}, y = 3$.

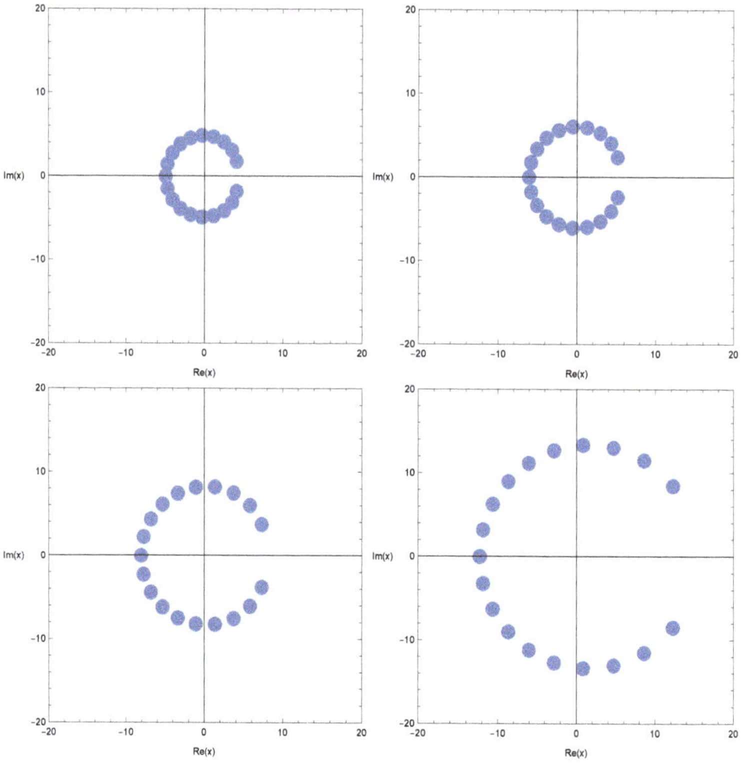

Figure 3. Zeros of $\mathbb{H}_{n,q}^{(\alpha,s)}(x,y;u;\lambda)$.

Stacks of zeros of the q-Sine Apostol-type Frobenius–Euler polynomials $\mathbb{H}_{n,q}^{(\alpha,s)}(x,y;u;\lambda) = 0$ for $2 \leq n \leq 20$, forming a 3D structure, are presented (Figure 4).

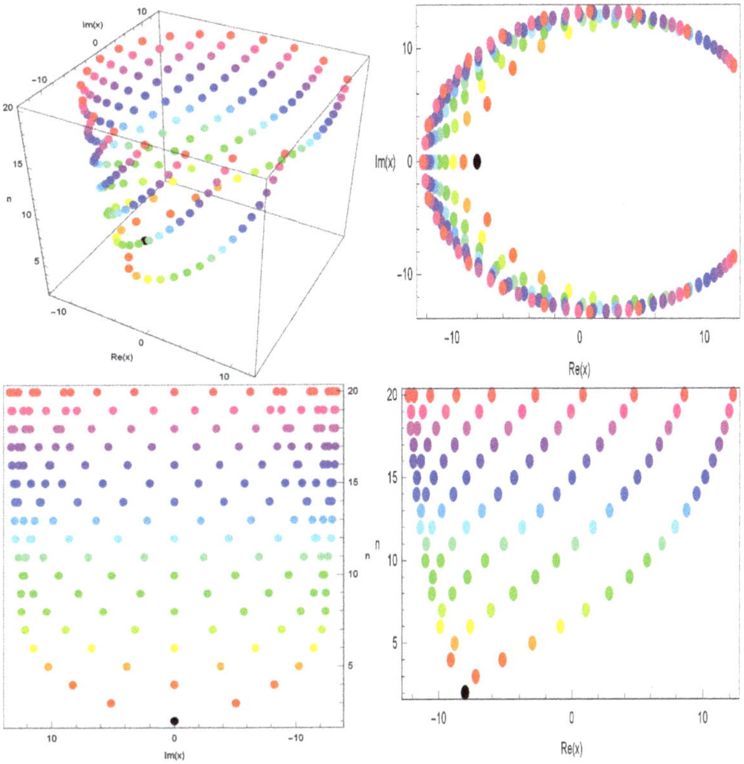

Figure 4. Zeros of $\mathbb{H}_{n,q}^{(\alpha,s)}(x,y;u;\lambda)$.

In Figure 4 (top-left), we plot stacks of zeros of $\mathbb{H}_{n,q}^{(\alpha,s)}(x,y;u;\lambda) = 0$ for $2 \leq n \leq 30$, $q = \frac{8}{10}, \alpha = 4, \lambda = 2, u = 3, y = 3$. In Figure 4 (top-right), we draw x and y axes but no z axis in three dimensions. In Figure 4 (bottom-left), we draw y and z axes but no x axis in three dimensions. In Figure 4 (bottom-right), we draw x and z axes but no y axis in three dimensions.

Next, we calculated an approximate solution satisfying the q-Sine Apostol-type Frobenius–Euler polynomials $\mathbb{H}_{n,q}^{(\alpha,s)}(x,y;u;\lambda) = 0$ for $q = \dfrac{8}{10}$. The results are given in Table 2.

Table 2. Approximate solutions of $\mathbb{H}_{n,q}^{(4,s)}(x,3;3;2)=0$.

Degree n	x
2	−8.0000
3	−7.2000 − 5.1256 i, −7.2000 + 5.1256 i
4	−9.0707, −5.2247 − 8.2772 i, −5.2247 + 8.2772 i
5	−8.7853 − 3.8486 i, −8.7853 + 3.8486 i, −3.0227 − 10.2577 i, −3.0227 + 10.2577 i
6	−9.8793, −7.6190 − 6.7293 i, −7.6190 + 6.7293 i, −0.8878 − 11.4618 i, −0.8878 + 11.4618 i
7	−9.7452 − 3.1858 i, −9.7452 + 3.1858 i, −6.0868 − 8.8578 i, −6.0868 + 8.8578 i, 1.0748 − 12.1326 i, 1.0748 + 12.1326 i
8	−10.501, −8.9527 − 5.7661 i, −8.9527 + 5.7661i, −4.4346 − 10.3981 i, −4.4346 + 10.3981 i, 2.8319 − 12.4327 i, 2.8319 + 12.4327 i
9	−10.4252 − 2.7531 i, −10.4252 + 2.7531 i, −7.8126 − 7.8189 i, −7.8126 + 7.8189 i, −2.7879 − 11.4801 i, −2.7879 + 11.4801 i, 4.3811 − 12.4748 i, 4.3811 + 12.4748 i
10	−10.985, −9.8411 − 5.0793 i, −9.8411 + 5.0793 i, −6.5042 − 9.4234 i, −6.5042 + 9.4234 i, −1.2119 − 12.2069 i, −1.2119 + 12.2069 i, 5.7340 − 12.3389 i, 5.7340 + 12.3389 i
11	−10.9347 − 2.4373 i, −10.9347 + 2.4373 i, −8.9518 − 7.0112 i, −8.9518 + 7.0112 i, −5.1343 − 10.6536 i, −5.1343 + 10.6536 i, 0.2605 − 12.6598 i, 0.2605 + 12.6598 i, 6.9078 − 12.0821 i, 6.9078 + 12.0821 i

7. Conclusions

By making use of q-numbers and q-concepts, Jang et al. [2,4] defined q-Bernoulli polynomials and numbers, q-Genocchi polynomials and numbers and q-Euler polynomials and numbers and provided some new and interesting identities and formulae. With this viewpoint, several authors have introduced q-analogues of special numbers and polynomials and have investigated their properties. In this paper, by making use of the q-cosine polynomials and q-sine polynomials, we have considered a new class of q-analogues of Apostol-type Frobenius–Euler polynomials and have obtained new properties and identities. In addition, we have analysed the behaviour of q-integral and q-derivative representations. Additionally, we have checked the roots and graphical representations of these polynomials by making use of Mathematica software. This approach led us to consider different methods, and special cases of used variables of newly defined polynomial in the paper. In this viewpoint, we will try to continue working on newly considered polynomials in this line.

Author Contributions: All authors contributed equally to the manuscript and written, read, and approved the final manuscript. All authors have read and agreed to the published version of the manuscript.

Funding: This work was supported by the National Natural Science Foundation of China (No. 62172116) and the Basic Research Programs of Guizhou Province (No. QianKeHe ZK[2023]279).

Data Availability Statement: Not applicable.

Acknowledgments: The authors would like to thank the reviewers who have improved the presentation of the paper substantially.

Conflicts of Interest: The authors declare no conflict of interest.

References

1. Alam, N.; Khan, W.A.; Ryoo, C.S. A note on Bell-based Apostol-type Frobenius-Euler polynomials of complex variable with its certain applications. *Mathematics* **2022**, *10*, 2109. [CrossRef]
2. Kang, J.Y.; Ryoo, C.S. Various structures of the roots and explicit properties of q-cosine Bernoulli polynomials and q-sine Bernoulli polynomials. *Mathematics* **2020**, *8*, 463. [CrossRef]
3. Muhiuddin, G.; Khan, W.A.; Al-Kadi, D. Construction on the degenerate poly-Frobenius-Euler polynomials of complex variable. *J. Funct. Spaces* **2021**, *2021*, 3115424. [CrossRef]
4. Ryoo, C.S.; Kang, J.Y. Explicit properties of q-Cosine and q-Sine Euler polynomials containing symmetric structures. *Symmetry* **2020**, *12*, 1247. [CrossRef]
5. Kim, D.S.; Kim, T.; Lee, H. A Note on Degenerate Euler and Bernoulli Polynomials of Complex Variable. *Symmetry* **2019**, *11*, 1168. [CrossRef]
6. Kim, T.; Ryoo, C.S. Some Identities for Euler and Bernoulli Polynomials and Their Zeros. *Axioms* **2018**, *7*, 56. 10.3390/axioms7030056. [CrossRef]
7. Masjed-Jamei, M.; Beyki, M.R.; Koepf, W. A New Type of Euler Polynomials and Numbers. *Mediterr. J. Math.* **2018**, *15*, 138. [CrossRef]
8. Srivastava, H.M.; Masjed-Jamei, M.; Beyki, M.R. A Parametric Type of the Apostol-Bernoulli, Apostol-Euler and Apostol-Genocchi Polynomials. *Appl. Math. Inf. Sci.* **2018**, *12*, 907–916. [CrossRef]
9. Arjika, S. On q^2-Trigonometric functions and their q^2-Fourier transform. *J. Math. Syst. Sci.* **2019**, *9*, 130–135. [CrossRef]
10. Koekoek, R.; Lesky, P.A.; Swarttouw, R.F. *Hypergeometric Orthogonal Polynomials and Their q-Analogues*; Springer: Berlin, Germany, 2010.
11. Kurt, B. A note on the Apostol type q-Frobenius-Euler polynomials and generalizations of the Srivastava-Pinter addition theorems. *Filomat* **2016**, *30*, 65–72. [CrossRef]
12. Kang, J.Y.; Khan, W.A. A new class of q-Hermite based Apostol type Frobenius Genocchi polynomials. *Commun. Korean Math. Soc.* **2020**, *35*, 759–771.
13. Kim, T.; Kim, D.S.; Jang, L.C.; Kim, H.-Y. On type 2 degenerate Bernoulli and Euler polynomials of complex variable. *Adv. Differ. Equ.* **2019**, *2019*, 490. [CrossRef]
14. Kac, V.; Cheung, P. *Quantum Calculus*; Springer: New York, NY, USA, 2001.
15. Mahmudov, N.I. q-analogues of the Bernoulli and Genocchi polynomials and the Srivastava-Pinter addition theorems. *Discrete Dyn. Nat. Soc.* **2012**, *2012*, 169348. [CrossRef]
16. Mahmudov, N.I. On a class of q-Bernoulli and q-Euler polynomials. *Adv. Differ. Equ.* **2013**, *2013*, 108. [CrossRef]

Disclaimer/Publisher's Note: The statements, opinions and data contained in all publications are solely those of the individual author(s) and contributor(s) and not of MDPI and/or the editor(s). MDPI and/or the editor(s) disclaim responsibility for any injury to people or property resulting from any ideas, methods, instructions or products referred to in the content.

mathematics

MDPI

Article

Differential-Difference Elliptic Equations with Nonlocal Potentials in Half-Spaces

Andrey B. Muravnik

Nikol'skii Mathematical Institute, Peoples Friendship University of Russia, Miklukho–Maklaya ul. 6, 117198 Moscow, Russia; amuravnik@mail.ru

Abstract: We investigate the half-space Dirichlet problem with summable boundary-value functions for an elliptic equation with an arbitrary amount of potentials undergoing translations in arbitrary directions. In the classical case of partial *differential* equations, the half-space Dirichlet problem for *elliptic* equations attracts great interest from researchers due to the following phenomenon: the solutions acquire qualitative properties specific for *nonstationary* (more exactly, parabolic) equations. In this paper, such a phenomenon is studied for nonlocal generalizations of elliptic differential equations, more exactly, for elliptic differential-difference equations with nonlocal potentials arising in various applications not covered by the classical theory. We find a Poisson-like kernel such that its convolution with the boundary-value function satisfies the investigated problem, prove that the constructed solution is infinitely smooth outside the boundary hyperplane, and prove its uniform power-like decay as the timelike independent variable tends to infinity.

Keywords: differential-difference equations; nonlocal potential elliptic equations; half-space Dirichlet problem; summable boundary-value functions

MSC: 35R10; 35J25

Citation: Muravnik, A.B. Differential-Difference Elliptic Equations with Nonlocal Potentials in Half-Spaces. *Mathematics* **2023**, *11*, 2698. https://doi.org/10.3390/math11122698

Academic Editor: Sitnik Sergey

Received: 29 May 2023
Revised: 11 June 2023
Accepted: 12 June 2023
Published: 14 June 2023

Copyright: © 2023 by the author. Licensee MDPI, Basel, Switzerland. This article is an open access article distributed under the terms and conditions of the Creative Commons Attribution (CC BY) license (https://creativecommons.org/licenses/by/4.0/).

1. Introduction

1.1. Elliptic Equations in Half-Spaces

It is well-known that for classical partial differential equations, the half-space problem with a single boundary-value condition is well posed both for the parabolic and elliptic cases (see, e.g., [1,2]). This is the Cauchy problem in the former case and the Dirichlet problem in the latter one. Though all independent variables are spatial in the elliptic case, the only independent variable varying on a semiaxis (unlike the other ones varying on whole real lines) acquires the so-called *timelike properties* (and the said variable itself is called the *timelike variable*): the resolving operator of the problem possesses the semigroup property with respect to that variable, and the behavior of the solutions for large values of that variable are similar to the large-time behavior of the solutions of the Cauchy problem for parabolic equations (see, e.g., [3]).

It turns out that in both cases (the parabolic one and the elliptic one), those qualitative properties of solutions substantially depend on the class of the boundary-value functions of the problem. If the boundary-value function belongs to $L_\infty(\mathbb{R}^n)$, then the well-known Repnikov–Ei'delman stabilization condition is valid (see [4]): depending on the limit properties of means of the boundary-value function, the solution either has a limit or does not have it. If the boundary-value function belongs to $L_1(\mathbb{R}^n)$, then the case qualitatively changes: the solution always has a limit, it is always equal to zero, and this decay is uniform.

1.2. Differential-Difference Equations

The phenomenon described in the previous section is quite far from being a specific property of two prototype equations (the Laplace one and the heat one). In particular, it occurs for differential-difference equations, i.e., equations where translation operators (apart from differential ones) act on the desired function. The unfailing worldwide interest in this generalization of classical differential equations started (within the contemporary mathematical approach) from the pioneering paper [5]) and is mainly caused by the following two reasons. The first one is purely theoretical: due to the *nonlocal nature* of differential-difference (and, more broadly, functional-differential) operators, not all research tools, methods, and approaches developed for differential equations can be helpful for functional-differential ones. For instance, no technique based on the maximum principle works in the differential-difference case. Thus, for functional-differential equations, one has to invent new research methods. Another reason is the existence of various applications of functional-differential equations in areas not covered by classical differential equations.

For the general theory, both aspects are comprehensively covered in [6–9] (also see references therein). It should be noted that non-differential operators contained in the studied equations might be quite diverse. For instance, they might be integrodifferential operators (see, e.g., [10–16] and references therein), operators of contractions and extensions of the independent variables (see, e.g., [17–21] and references therein), or others (see, e.g., [22,23] and references therein). In general, those operators are bounded (unlike differential ones), but due to their *nonlocal nature*, they cannot be treated as subordinate terms or small perturbations: their presence cause qualitatively new properties of the solutions.

The present paper is devoted to the timelike properties of elliptic differential-difference problems, as described in Section 1.1. The specified problem with essentially bounded boundary-value functions has already been studied for a relatively long time (see, e.g., [24] and references therein); the most-general result obtained up to now can be found in [25]. The investigation of this problem with summable boundary-value functions (i.e., the problem with finite-energy boundary data) started quite recently (see [26]). For differential-difference equations (regardless of their types), it is reasonable and natural to consider the following two cases separately: the case where differential and translation operators form *superpositions* and the case where they form *sums*. At the moment, the most general result for the former case is obtained in [27]. The present paper is devoted to the latter case. Its investigation started from [28], where a prototype equation is considered: the nonlocal term is single and the translation acts with respect to a coordinate direction. In [29], this result is generalized as follows: the translation operator acts in an *arbitrary* direction, but the nonlocal term is still *single*. Here, we present the most general result in this direction: the equation contains several nonlocal terms, and no restrictions for the directions of the translations are imposed.

Thus, in the half-space $\mathbb{R}^n \times (0,\infty)$, we consider the equation

$$\sum_{j=1}^{n} \frac{\partial^2 u}{\partial x_j^2}(x,y) - \sum_{k=1}^{m} a_k u(x+h_k,y) + \frac{\partial^2 u}{\partial y^2}(x,y) = 0, \tag{1}$$

where m and n are positive integers, $a_1,\dots,a_m$ are nonnegative constants, and $h_k := (h_{k1},\dots,h_{kn})$, $k \in \overline{1,m}$ are vectors from $\mathbb{R}^n$ with real coordinates.
We introduce the nonnegative constants $a_0 := \sum\limits_{k=1}^{m} a_k$ and $h_0 := \max\limits_{k\in\overline{1,m}} |h_k|$. Note that both constants are strictly positive because we deal with classical differential equations (instead of differential-difference once); otherwise: if $a_0 = 0$, then Equation (1) is just the Laplace equation, while if $h_0 = 0$, then Equation (1) is the Laplace equation with a constant positive potential.

We impose the following restriction on the parameters a_0 and h_0:

$$h_0 \max\{a_0, \sqrt{a_0}\} < \frac{\pi}{2}. \tag{2}$$

Apart from Equation (1), we consider the boundary-value condition

$$u\Big|_{y=0} = u_0(x), x \in \mathbb{R}^n, \tag{3}$$

where $u_0 \in L_1(\mathbb{R}^n)$.

2. Integral Representations of Solutions

The following assertion is valid.

Theorem 1. *The function*

$$u(x, y) = \int_{\mathbb{R}^n} \mathcal{E}(x - \xi, y)u(\xi)d\xi, \tag{4}$$

where

$$\mathcal{E}(x, y) = \frac{1}{(2\pi)^n} \int_{\mathbb{R}^n} e^{-yG_1(\xi)} \cos[x \cdot \xi - yG_2(\xi)]d\xi, \tag{5}$$

$$G_{\left\{ {1 \atop 2} \right\}}(\xi) = \rho(\xi) \left\{ {\cos \atop \sin} \right\} \theta(\xi), \tag{6}$$

$$\rho(\xi) = \left(\left[|\xi|^2 + a(\xi)\right]^2 + b^2(\xi) \right)^{\frac{1}{4}}, \tag{7}$$

$$\theta(\xi) = \frac{1}{2} \arctan \frac{b(\xi)}{|\xi|^2 + a(\xi)}, \tag{8}$$

and

$$\left\{ {a \atop b} \right\}(\xi) = \sum_{k=1}^{m} a_k \left\{ {\cos \atop \sin} \right\} h_k \cdot \xi,$$

satisfies Equation (1) in the half-space $\mathbb{R}^n \times (0, \infty)$.

Proof. First, let us prove that all the introduced functions are well-defined.

We investigate the sign of the function $|\xi|^2 + a(\xi)$ in dependence on the relations between the vector $(a_1, \ldots, a_m)$ of the coefficients and the translation vectors $h_1, \ldots, h_m$ from $\mathbb{R}^n$.

If $|h_k \cdot \xi| < \frac{\pi}{2}$, then $\cos h_k \cdot \xi > 0$, and therefore, $\xi_k^2 + a_k \cos h_k \cdot \xi > 0$.

If $|h_k \cdot \xi| \geq \frac{\pi}{2}$, then $|h_k||\xi||\cos(\widehat{h_k, \xi})| \geq \frac{\pi}{2}$, which means that $|h_k||\xi| \geq \frac{\pi}{2}$, i.e., $|\xi| \geq \frac{\pi}{2|h_k|}$, and therefore,

$$|\xi|^2 + a(\xi) \geq \frac{\pi^2}{4|h_k|^2} + \sum_{l=1}^{m} a_l \cos h_l \cdot \xi.$$

The right-hand side of the last inequality is positive due to Condition (2). Hence, the function $|\xi|^2 + a(\xi)$ is positive everywhere.

Thus, the denominator in (8) is positive everywhere, which means that function (8) and, therefore, functions (6) are well-defined.

Now, to prove the well-definiteness of function (5), we estimate the function $G_1(\xi)$ from below. Since

$$2\theta(\xi) = \arctan \frac{b(\xi)}{|\xi|^2 + a(\xi)},$$

it follows that $-\frac{\pi}{2} < 2\theta(\xi) < \frac{\pi}{2}$ and $-\frac{\pi}{4} < \theta(\xi) < \frac{\pi}{4}$. Therefore, $\cos 2\theta(\xi) > 0$ and $\cos \theta(\xi) > \frac{\sqrt{2}}{2}$. Then

$$\cos 2\theta(\xi) = \frac{1}{\sqrt{1 + \tan^2 2\theta(\xi)}} = \left(1 + \frac{b^2(\xi)}{\left[|\xi|^2 + a(\xi)\right]^2}\right)^{-\frac{1}{2}} = \sqrt{\frac{\left[|\xi|^2 + a(\xi)\right]^2}{\left[|\xi|^2 + a(\xi)\right]^2 + b^2(\xi)}}.$$

Since the denominator of the last fraction is equal to $\rho^4(\xi)$ and the positivity of the function $|\xi|^2 + a(\xi)$ is guaranteed by Condition (2), it follows that $\cos 2\theta(\xi) = \frac{|\xi|^2 + a(\xi)}{\rho^2(\xi)}$. Further, since $\cos\theta(\xi) > 0$, it follows that $\cos\theta(\xi) = \sqrt{\frac{1+\cos 2\theta(\xi)}{2}}$. Therefore,

$$G_1(\xi) = \rho(\xi)\frac{1}{\sqrt{2}}\sqrt{1 + \frac{|\xi|^2 + a(\xi)}{\rho^2(\xi)}} = \sqrt{\frac{\rho^2(\xi) + |\xi|^2 + a(\xi)}{2}}. \tag{9}$$

Now, we take into account that

$$\rho^4(\xi) = \left[|\xi|^2 + a(\xi)\right]^2 + b^2(\xi) = |\xi|^4 + 2a(\xi)|\xi|^2 + a^2(\xi) + b^2(\xi) \geq |\xi|^4 - 2|a(\xi)||\xi|^2 + a^2(\xi) = \left[|\xi|^2 - |a(\xi)|\right]^2.$$

Since $|a(\xi)| \leq \sum_{k=1}^{m} = a_0 > 0$, it follows that the inequality $\rho^2(\xi) \geq |\xi|^2 - |a(\xi)|$ is valid outside the ball $\{|\xi| < a_0\}$. Hence, the inequality $G_1(\xi) \geq \sqrt{|\xi|^2 - |a(\xi)|} \geq \sqrt{|\xi|^2 - a_0}$ is valid outside the same ball.

Thus, for each positive y, the absolute value of the integrand function in (5) is majorized by the function $e^{-y\sqrt{|\xi|^2 - a_0}}$ in $\mathbb{R}^n \setminus \{|\xi| < 2a_0\}$ and by the identical unit in $\{|\xi| < 2a_0\}$, which proves the well-definiteness of the function $\mathcal{E}(x,y)$ in the half-space $\mathbb{R}^n \times (0,\infty)$. The formal differentiating of function (5) inside the integral (with respect to each of its independent variables) causes the appearance of integrand factors that do not grow faster than the power functions of ξ. Hence, all derivatives of function (5) are well-defined in $\mathbb{R}^n \times (0,\infty)$.

Now, we have to prove that the function $\mathcal{E}(x,y)$ satisfies Equation (1). Taking into account that

$$(2\pi)^n \mathcal{E}_y(x,y) = -\int_{\mathbb{R}^n} G_1(\xi)e^{-yG_1(\xi)}\cos[x\cdot\xi - yG_2(\xi)]d\xi + \int_{\mathbb{R}^n} G_2(\xi)e^{-yG_1(\xi)}\sin[x\cdot\xi - yG_2(\xi)]d\xi$$

and, therefore,

$$\begin{aligned}(2\pi)^n \mathcal{E}_{yy}(x,y) = &\int_{\mathbb{R}^n} G_1^2(\xi)e^{-yG_1(\xi)}\cos[x\cdot\xi - yG_2(\xi)]d\xi - \int_{\mathbb{R}^n} G_1(\xi)G_2(\xi)e^{-yG_1(\xi)}\sin[x\cdot\xi - yG_2(\xi)]d\xi \\ &- \int_{\mathbb{R}^n} G_1(\xi)G_2(\xi)e^{-yG_1(\xi)}\sin[x\cdot\xi - yG_2(\xi)]d\xi - \int_{\mathbb{R}^n} G_2^2(\xi)e^{-yG_1(\xi)}\cos[x\cdot\xi - yG_2(\xi)]d\xi \\ = &\int_{\mathbb{R}^n}\left[G_1^2(\xi) - G_2^2(\xi)\right]e^{-yG_1(\xi)}\cos[x\cdot\xi - yG_2(\xi)]d\xi - 2\int_{\mathbb{R}^n} G_1(\xi)G_2(\xi)e^{-yG_1(\xi)}\sin[x\cdot\xi - yG_2(\xi)]d\xi,\end{aligned}$$

we compute

$$G_1^2(\xi) - G_2^2(\xi) = \rho^2(\xi)\cos 2\theta(\xi) = |\xi|^2 + a(\xi)$$

and

$$2G_1(\xi)G_2(\xi) = \rho^2(\xi)\cos 2\theta(\xi)\tan 2\theta(\xi) = \left[|\xi|^2 + a(\xi)\right]\frac{b(\xi)}{\left[|\xi|^2 + a(\xi)\right]} = b(\xi).$$

Then, we can substitute the function $\mathcal{E}(x,y)$ in Equation (1):

$$(2\pi)^n\left[\sum_{j=1}^{n}\frac{\partial^2 u}{\partial x_j^2}(x,y) + \frac{\partial^2 u}{\partial y^2}(x,y)\right] = \int_{\mathbb{R}^n}\left(-\sum_{j=1}^{n}\xi^2 + |\xi|^2\right)e^{-yG_1(\xi)}\cos[x\cdot\xi - yG_2(\xi)]d\xi$$

$$+\int\limits_{\mathbb{R}^n} e^{-yG_1(\xi)}\Big(a(\xi)\cos[x\cdot\xi - yG_2(\xi)] - b(\xi)\sin[x\cdot\xi - yG_2(\xi)]\Big)d\xi$$

$$=\int\limits_{\mathbb{R}^n} e^{-yG_1(\xi)}\sum_{k=1}^{m} a_k\Big(\cos h_k\cdot\xi\cos[x\cdot\xi - yG_2(\xi)] - \sin h_k\cdot\xi\sin[x\cdot\xi - yG_2(\xi)]\Big)d\xi$$

$$=\int\limits_{\mathbb{R}^n} e^{-yG_1(\xi)}\sum_{k=1}^{m} a_k\cos\Big[\cos(x+h_k)\cdot\xi - yG_2(\xi)\Big]d\xi = \sum_{k=1}^{m} a_k\int\limits_{\mathbb{R}^n} e^{-yG_1(\xi)}\cos\Big[\cos(x+h_k)\cdot\xi - yG_2(\xi)\Big]d\xi$$

$$= 2\pi\sum_{k=1}^{m} a_k\mathcal{E}(x+h_k, y).$$

Thus, function (5) satisfies Equation (1) in the half-space $\mathbb{R}^n \times (0,\infty)$.

Now, we have to prove that function (4) satisfies Equation (1) in the same half-space and that it can be differentiated inside the integral. To do that, we estimate the function $\mathcal{E}$ and its derivatives as follows.

First, we estimate the function $|\xi|^2 + a(\xi) = |\xi|^2 + a_1\cos h_1\cdot\xi + \cdots + a_m\cos h_m\cdot\xi$ from below.

If $h_k\cdot\xi \in \left(-\frac{\pi}{2}, \frac{\pi}{2}\right)$, $k\in\overline{1,m}$, then $h_k\cdot\xi > 0$. Hence, $|\xi|^2 + a(\xi) \geq |\xi|^2$ provided that $|h_k||\xi| < \frac{\pi}{2}$ for each $k\in\overline{1,m}$.

Thus, in the ball $\left\{|\xi| < \frac{\pi}{2\max\limits_{k\in\overline{1,m}}|h_k|} = \frac{\pi}{2h_0}\right\}$, the function $|\xi|^2 + a(\xi)$ is bounded from below by the function $|\xi|^2$.

Outside this ball, the following estimate holds:

$$|\xi|^2 + a(\xi) \geq \frac{\pi^2}{4h_0^2} - \sum_{k=1}^{m} a_k = \frac{\pi^2}{4h_0^2} - a_0 > 0$$

by virtue of Condition (2).

Therefore, the function $|\xi|^2 + a(\xi)$ is nonnegative, which means that function (9) is estimated from below by the function $\frac{1}{\sqrt{2}}\sqrt{|\xi|^2 + a(\xi)}$. We use the estimate $G_1(\xi) \geq \frac{|\xi|}{\sqrt{2}}$ inside the ball $\left\{|\xi| < \frac{\pi}{2h_0}\right\}$ and the estimate $G_1(\xi) \geq \sqrt{|\xi|^2 - a_0}$ outside the ball $\{|\xi| < a_0\}$. By virtue of Condition (2), $a_0 < \frac{\pi}{2h_0}$, and therefore, function (5) satisfies the estimate

$$(2\pi)^n|\mathcal{E}(x,y)| \leq \int\limits_{\left\{|\xi|<\frac{\pi}{2h_0}\right\}} e^{-\frac{y}{\sqrt{2}}|\xi|}d\xi + \int\limits_{\left\{|\xi|>\frac{\pi}{2h_0}\right\}} e^{-y\sqrt{|\xi|^2-a_0}}d\xi = \int\limits_0^{\frac{\pi}{2h_0}} r^{n-1}e^{-\frac{y}{\sqrt{2}}r}dr + \int\limits_{\frac{\pi}{2h_0}}^{\infty} r^{n-1}e^{-y\sqrt{r^2-a_0}}dr.$$

The first term of the last sum is estimated from above by the following expression:

$$\int\limits_0^{\infty} r^{n-1}e^{-\frac{y}{\sqrt{2}}r}dr = \frac{2^{\frac{n}{2}}}{y^n}\int\limits_0^{\infty}\rho^{n-1}e^{-\rho}d\rho = \frac{2^{\frac{n}{2}}(n-1)!}{y^n}.$$

The second one is equal to

$$\frac{1}{2}\int\limits_{\frac{\pi^2}{4h_0^2}-a_0}^{\infty}(\tau+a_0)^{\frac{n}{2}-1}e^{-y\sqrt{\tau}}d\tau \leq \frac{1}{2}\int\limits_{\frac{\pi^2}{4h_0^2}-a_0}^{\infty}\left(\tau+\frac{\tau}{C}\right)^{\frac{n}{2}-1}e^{-y\sqrt{\tau}}d\tau = \frac{C+1}{2C}\int\limits_{\frac{\pi^2}{4h_0^2}-a_0}^{\infty}\tau^{\frac{n}{2}-1}e^{-y\sqrt{\tau}}d\tau,$$

where $C = \dfrac{\frac{\pi^2}{4h_0^2} - a_0}{a_0}$.

The last integral is estimated from above by the integral

$$\int\limits_0^{\infty}\tau^{\frac{n}{2}-1}e^{-y\sqrt{\tau}}d\tau = \frac{2}{y^2}\int\limits_0^{\infty}\left(\frac{\rho^2}{y^2}\right)^{\frac{n}{2}-1}e^{-\rho}\rho d\rho = \frac{2}{y^n}\int\limits_0^{\infty}\rho^{n-1}e^{-\rho}d\rho = \frac{2(n-1)!}{y^n}.$$

Thus, $|\mathcal{E}(x,y)|$ is estimated from above by the function $\frac{\text{const}}{y^n}$, which means that integral (4) absolutely converges for each positive y and that the function u defined by it satisfies the following estimate in $\mathbb{R}^n \times (0,\infty)$:

$$|u(x,y)| \leq \frac{\text{const}\|u_0\|_1}{y^n}. \tag{10}$$

Differentiating the function $\mathcal{E}(x,y)$ with respect to each its independent variable, we add one more regular integrand factor that does not increase faster than $|\xi|$. No finite amount of such factors affect the convergence of the integral, while the right-hand side of estimate (10) is affected as follows:

$$|D^l u(x,y)| \leq \frac{\text{const}\|u_0\|_1}{y^{n+l}}, \tag{11}$$

where l is an arbitrary positive integer and the left-hand side denotes an arbitrary partial derivative of order l of the function $u(x,y)$.

Therefore, the integral obtained after the formal differentiating of integral (4) with respect to each variable absolutely converges in $\mathbb{R}^n \times (0,\infty)$. Combining this fact with the fact that the function $\mathcal{E}(x,y)$ satisfies Equation (1) in $\mathbb{R}^n \times (0,\infty)$, we obtain that (4) is an infinitely smooth solution of Equation (1) in $\mathbb{R}^n \times (0,\infty)$. □

3. Operational Scheme

In this section, we show the way to find the Poisson-like kernel $\mathcal{E}(x,y)$. We apply the well-known Gel'fand–Shilov operational scheme (see, e.g., [30] (Sec. 10)), using the fact that translation operators are Fourier multipliers.

Thus, we (formally) apply the Fourier transformation with respect to the (n-dimensional) variable x to problem (1),(3). This operation takes the boundary-value problem for a *partial functional-differential* equation to an initial-value problem for an *ordinary differential* equation, i.e., to the problem:

$$\frac{d^2\widehat{u}}{dy^2} = \left(|\xi|^2 + \sum_{k=1}^{m} a_k \cos h_k\cdot\xi + i\sum_{k=1}^{m} a_k \sin h_k\cdot\xi\right)\widehat{u},\ y \in (0,+\infty), \tag{12}$$

$$\widehat{u}(0;\xi) = \widehat{u_0}(\xi). \tag{13}$$

The characteristic equation of Equation (12), which is a linear ordinary second-order differential equation with constant coefficients depending on the n-dimensional parameter ξ, is equal to $\pm\rho(\xi)[\cos\theta(\xi) + i\sin\theta(\xi)]$, where $\rho(\xi)$ and $\theta(\xi)$ are defined by relations (7) and (8), respectively. We solve problem (12) and (13), suitably select the value of the "free" arbitrary constant (it exists because the amount of boundary-value conditions is less than the order of the equation), and (formally) apply the inverse Fourier transformation to the obtained solution. This yields:

$$\frac{1}{(2\pi)^n}\int\limits_{\mathbb{R}^n} e^{ix\cdot\xi - y\rho(\xi)[\cos\theta(\xi)+i\sin\theta(\xi)]}\int\limits_{\mathbb{R}^n} u_0(z)e^{iz\cdot\xi}dzd\xi = \frac{1}{(2\pi)^n}\int\limits_{\mathbb{R}^n} u_0(z)\int\limits_{\mathbb{R}^n} e^{i(x-z)\cdot\xi - y\rho(\xi)[\cos\theta(\xi)+i\sin\theta(\xi)]}d\xi dz$$

$$= \frac{1}{(2\pi)^n}\int\limits_{\mathbb{R}^n} u_0(z)\int\limits_{\mathbb{R}^n} e^{i[(x-z)\cdot\xi - y\rho(\xi)\sin\theta(\xi)]}e^{-y\rho(\xi)\cos\theta(\xi)}d\xi dz$$

$$= \frac{1}{(2\pi)^n}\int\limits_{\mathbb{R}^n} u_0(z)\int\limits_{\mathbb{R}^n} \cos[(x-z)\cdot\xi - y\rho(\xi)\sin\theta(\xi)]e^{-y\rho(\xi)\cos\theta(\xi)}d\xi dz$$

$$+\frac{i}{(2\pi)^n}\int\limits_{\mathbb{R}^n} u_0(z)\int\limits_{\mathbb{R}^n} \sin[(x-z)\cdot\xi - y\rho(\xi)\sin\theta(\xi)]e^{-y\rho(\xi)\cos\theta(\xi)}d\xi dz.$$

Taking into account the oddness of the function $b(\xi)$ with respect to each variable ξ_j, we obtain function (4).

Note that all actions undertaken in this section do not constitute a proof: we change the order of the integrating, apply the direct and inverse Fourier transformations, and nullify integrals of odd functions over symmetric regions, but we do not care about the convergence of the corresponding integrals. Thus, the function $u(x, y)$ obtained at this step is obtained *heuristically* (in the total correspondence of the specified Gel'fand–Shilov scheme). Once this function is obtained, we have to prove that it is well-defined, can be differentiated inside the integral, and satisfies the investigated equation. This strict proof is provided in Section 2 (see Theorem 1).

Remark 1. *By construction, the obtained solution of Equation (1) satisfies Condition (3) in the sense of generalized functions (according to the Gel'fand–Shilov definition, i.e.,* $u(\cdot, y) \to u_0(\cdot)$ *in the topology of generalized functions of the* n*-dimensional variable* x *as the real parameter* y *tends the zero from the right). The proof is totally the same as in [31] (Remark 2).*

Combining this remark with estimate (11), we obtain the following main assertion of the paper.

Theorem 2. *If* $u_0 \in L_1(\mathbb{R}^n)$ *and Condition (2) is satisfied, then function (4) satisfies problem (1),(3) in the sense of generalized functions. This solution is infinitely smooth in the open half-space* $\mathbb{R}^n \times (0, \infty)$ *and satisfies (together with all its derivatives) estimate (11) in the specified half-space, where* l *is an arbitrary positive integer and the constant depends only on* n, l, a_0, *and* h_0.

4. Conclusions

In this paper, we continue the investigation of half-space boundary-value problems for differential-difference elliptic equations with nonlocal potentials, extending the consideration to the most general case of the equation: the amount of the nonlocal potentials is arbitrary, no commensurability requirements are imposed on the coefficients at the potentials, and the directions of the translations of the potentials (and, therefore, the angles between them) are arbitrary. We construct a solution, express it by a Poisson-like integral representation, prove its infinite smoothness outside the boundary hyperplane, and show that the following general phenomenon (common for a quite broad class of half-space elliptic and parabolic problems) takes place in the considered case as well: if the boundary-value function is summable, then the constructed solution uniformly decays (with all its partial derivatives with respect to all independent variables) as the timelike independent variable tends to infinity. The rate of this decay is estimated by the power function of the timelike variable.

Funding: This work is supported by the Ministry of Science and Higher Education of the Russian Federation (project number FSSF-2023-0016).

Acknowledgments: The author expresses his profound gratitude to A.L. Skubachevskii for his valuable considerations and his permanent attention to this work.

Conflicts of Interest: The author declares no conflict of interest.

References

1. Stein, E.M.; Weiss, G. On the theory of harmonic functions of several variables. I: The theory of H^p spaces. *Acta Math.* **1960**, *103*, 25–62. [CrossRef]
2. Stein, E.M.; Weiss, G. On the theory of harmonic functions of several variables. II: Behavior near the boundary. *Acta Math.* **1961**, *106*, 137–174. [CrossRef]
3. Denisov, V.N.; Muravnik, A.B. On asymptotic behavior of solutions of the Dirichlet problem in half-space for linear and quasi-linear elliptic equations. *Electron. Res. Announc. Am. Math. Soc.* **2003**, *9*, 88–93. [CrossRef]
4. Repnikov, V.D.; Eidelman, S.D. Necessary and sufficient conditions for the establishment of a solution of the Cauchy problem. *Sov. Math. Dokl.* **1966**, *7*, 388–391.
5. Hartman, P.; Stampacchia, G. On some nonlinear elliptic differential functional equations. *Acta Math.* **1966**, *115*, 271–310. [CrossRef]
6. Skubachevskii, A.L. *Elliptic Functional Differential Equations and Applications*; Birkhäuser: Basel, Switzerland; Boston, MA, USA; Berlin, Germany, 1997.
7. Skubachevskii, A.L. Nonclassical boundary-value problems. I. *J. Math. Sci.* **2008**, *155*, 199–334. [CrossRef]
8. Skubachevskii, A.L. Nonclassical boundary-value problems. II. *J. Math. Sci.* **2010**, *166*, 377–561. [CrossRef]
9. Skubachevskii, A.L. Boundary-value problems for elliptic functional-differential equations and their applications. *Russ. Math. Surv.* **2016**, *71*, 801–906. [CrossRef]
10. Vlasov, V.V. On some classes of integro-differential equations on the half-line and related operator functions. *Trans. Mosc. Math. Soc.* **2012**, *2012*, 121–138. [CrossRef]
11. Vlasov, V.V.; Rautian, N.A. Spectral analysis and correct solvability of abstract integrodifferential equations that arise in thermophysics and acoustics. *J. Math. Sci.* **2013**, *190*, 34–65. [CrossRef]
12. Vlasov, V.V.; Rautian, N.A. Properties of solutions of integro-differential equations arising in heat and mass transfer theory. *Trans. Mosc. Math. Soc.* **2014**, *2014*, 185–204. [CrossRef]
13. Vlasov, V.V.; Rautian, N.A. Spectral analysis of linear models of viscoelasticity. *J. Math. Sci.* **2018**, *230*, 668–672. [CrossRef]
14. Vlasov, V.V.; Rautian, N.A. Well-posedness and spectral analysis of integrodifferential equations arising in viscoelasticity theory. *J. Math. Sci.* **2018**, *233*, 555–577. [CrossRef]
15. Vlasov, V.V.; Rautian, N.A. Spectral analysis and representation of solutions of integro-differential equations with fractional exponential kernels. *Trans. Mosc. Math. Soc.* **2019**, *80*, 169–188. [CrossRef]
16. Vlasov, V.V.; Rautian, N.A. Well-posedness and spectral analysis of integrodifferential equations of hereditary mechanics. *Comput. Math. Math. Phys.* **2020**, *60*, 1322–1330. [CrossRef]
17. Rossovskii, L.E. Boundary value problems for elliptic functional-differential equations with dilatations and compressions of the arguments. *Trans. Mosc. Math. Soc.* **2001**, *2001*, 185–212.
18. Rossovskii, L.E. Elliptic functional differential equations with contractions and extensions of independent variables of the unknown function. *J. Math. Sci.* **2017**, *223*, 351–493. [CrossRef]
19. Rossovskii, L.E. Elliptic functional differential equations with incommensurable contractions. *Math. Model. Nat. Phenom.* **2017**, *12*, 226–239. [CrossRef]
20. Rossovskii, L.E.; Tasevich, A.L. Unique solvability of a functional-differential equation with orthotropic contractions in weighted spaces. *Differ. Equ.* **2017**, *53*, 1631–1644. [CrossRef]
21. Tasevich, A.L. Analysis of functional-differential equation with orthotropic contractions. *Math. Model. Nat. Phenom.* **2017**, *12*, 240–248. [CrossRef]
22. Cooke, K.; Rossovskii, L.E.; Skubachevskii, A.L. A boundary value problem for a functional-differential equation with a linearly transformed argument. *Differ. Equ.* **1995**, *31*, 1294–1299.
23. Rossovskii, L.E.; Tovsultanov, A.A. Elliptic functional differential equation with affine transformations. *J. Math. Anal. Appl.* **2019**, *480*, 123403. [CrossRef]
24. Muravnik, A.B. Nonlocal problems and functional-differential equations: Theoretical aspects and applications to mathematical modelling. *Math. Model. Nat. Phenom.* **2019**, *14*, 601. [CrossRef]
25. Muravnik, A.B. Half-plane differential-difference elliptic problems with general-kind nonlocal potentials. *Complex Var. Elliptic Equ.* **2022**, *67*, 1101–1120. [CrossRef]
26. Muravnik, A.B. Elliptic differential-difference equations in the half-space. *Math. Notes* **2020**, *67*, 727–732. [CrossRef]
27. Liiko, V.V.; Muravnik, A.B. Elliptic equations with arbitrarily directed translations in half-spaces. *Bull. Irkutsk. State Univ. Ser. Math.* **2023**, *43*, 64–77. [CrossRef]

28. Muravnik, A.B. Elliptic differential-difference equations with nonlocal potentials in a half-space. *Comput. Math. Math. Phys.* **2022**, *62*, 955–961. [CrossRef]
29. Muravnik, A.B. Elliptic equations with general-kind nonlocal potentials in half-spaces. *Lobachevskii J. Math.* **2022**, *43*, 2725–2730. [CrossRef]
30. Gel'fand, I.M.; Šhilov, G.E. Fourier transforms of rapidly increasing functions and questions of uniqueness of the solution of Cauchy problem. *Uspekhi Matem. Nauk.* **1953**, *8*, 3–54. (In Russian)
31. Šhilov, G.E. *Generalized Functions and Partial Differential Equations*; Gordon and Breach Science Publishers: New York, NY, USA, 1968.

Disclaimer/Publisher's Note: The statements, opinions and data contained in all publications are solely those of the individual author(s) and contributor(s) and not of MDPI and/or the editor(s). MDPI and/or the editor(s) disclaim responsibility for any injury to people or property resulting from any ideas, methods, instructions or products referred to in the content.

MDPI
St. Alban-Anlage 66
4052 Basel
Switzerland
www.mdpi.com

Mathematics Editorial Office
E-mail: mathematics@mdpi.com
www.mdpi.com/journal/mathematics

Disclaimer/Publisher's Note: The statements, opinions and data contained in all publications are solely those of the individual author(s) and contributor(s) and not of MDPI and/or the editor(s). MDPI and/or the editor(s) disclaim responsibility for any injury to people or property resulting from any ideas, methods, instructions or products referred to in the content.

www.ingramcontent.com/pod-product-compliance
Lightning Source LLC
LaVergne TN
LVHW070053120526
838202LV00102B/2233
9783036586267